THE PRESIDENCY

THE PRESIDENCY

Edited by AARON WILDAVSKY

University of California, Berkeley

 Little, Brown and Company BOSTON

LIBRARY OF CONGRESS CATALOG CARD NO. 71-75397

FIFTH PRINTING

Published simultaneously in Canada
by Little, Brown & Company (Canada) Limited

PRINTED IN THE UNITED STATES OF AMERICA

CONTENTS

PUBLICS

THE PRESIDENCY AND THE PEOPLE

THE PRESIDENCY AND THE PRESS

THE PRESIDENCY AND THE PARTIES

THE PRESIDENCY
AND CONGRESS

THE PRESIDENCY AND
THE EXECUTIVE BRANCH

THE PRESIDENCY
AND THE COURTS

INTRODUCTION

The presidency is the most important political institution in American life. It makes a larger number of important decisions over the broadest range of policy questions than any competitor. As decision-maker, symbol of the nation, and repository of legitimacy the presidency is unrivaled. The eminence of the institution, however, is matched only by the extraordinary neglect shown to it by political scientists. Compared to the hordes of researchers who regularly descend on Congress, local communities, and the most remote foreign principalities, there is an extraordinary dearth of students of the presidency, although scholars ritually swear that the presidency is where the action is before they go somewhere else to do their research.

One result of this neglect of the presidency is the evident lack of a textbook for advanced students. The beginning student is fortunate in having Clinton Rossiter's lively and sensitive *The American Presidency* (New York: Mentor Books, rev. ed., 1960). The student may then consider Richard Neustadt's fascinating view of presidential action guided by the desire to protect the man in office. But Neustadt's *Presidential Power* (New York: Mentor Books, 1964) covers only part of a large institution. This collection of readings is intended to provide a substitute for an advanced text on the presidency.

In selecting material, part of which is original, I have been guided by the desire to make the presidency a subject of social science analysis. Historical studies of individual Presidents remain indispensable, and psychoanalytic biographies of these men have much to offer. Examples of both genre are offered here; but my intention is to focus on the office, not the man, on the role rather than the individual occupants. Analysis of the presidential office tells us that there is considerable room for individual variation. It does matter that one man rather than another is President. No one is contesting this elementary conclusion. It is also true, however, that all modern Presidents must respond to environmental factors. Certain forces impose themselves on the occupant of the presidency, no matter who he is. To concentrate on individual Presidents is to be limited to a discussion of their term of office. To place emphasis on the presidency as an institution, a pattern of action, is to give hope of securing knowledge that may be applicable to many cases. The first part of this volume is organized around three basic concepts necessary for a study of the presidency: role, personality, and power.

The presidential role is largely defined by the expectations that others have developed about the man and the office. We are fortunate to have an analysis of role conflict by Andrew McFarland that is explicitly devoted to exploring the consequences of conflicts in expectations of political actors. He takes many examples from presidential behavior. Lester Seligman and Michael Baer, Louis Brownlow, and Clinton Rossiter write about what Americans, especially party and governmental elites, expect from Presidents. Brownlow and Rossiter want Presidents to move men and affairs. These scholars favor the expansion of presidential powers. Hence they look kindly upon presidential attempts to meet expectations for aggressive leadership. Alfred de Grazia questions almost everything others take for granted. His slashing attack has the good effect of revealing many fundamental assumptions that usually are not examined. Since his expectations of desirable presidential behavior differ markedly from most modern views, his evaluation is correspondingly more harsh. Though the subject is important, I have not been able to locate a suitable article on the expectations of the presidency held by foreign governments and their citizens.

A discussion of expectations surrounding the presidency naturally leads to the question of how individual occupants of the office fit into the role that has been defined for them. How much can a man mold the office and how much is he shaped by it? What can one man, even if he is President, cause to happen? Every serious discussion of the presidency must include the problem of "the hero in history." Most of these discussions founder because the problem is posed so badly as to prohibit intelligent inquiry. Fred Greenstein's article is included because it is the clearest statement of how to study the impact of individuals on large events. It also unravels the knotty problems involved in assessing the importance of personality variables in an explanation of individual action.

Since there is now no general study of presidential personality, we cannot present a comparative analysis of differences in the styles of presidential activity. Nor can we explain how the experiences of men who become President affect the decisions they make while in office. Precisely this kind of study of two Presidents has been undertaken by James D. Barber, however, and we are fortunate to have his discussion of the presidential styles of Calvin Coolidge and Herbert Hoover. David Donald's fine account discusses the uncanny sensitivity and psychic strength necessary for Abraham Lincoln to carry through the political juggling act that enabled him to maintain his position and the Union with it. Arthur Schlesinger, Jr., is more explicitly psychological as he considers the apparently contradictory impulses that lay behind Franklin Roosevelt's administrative style. None of the Presidents examined had an easy time meeting the demands of their office.

Whether we lament the torment of the presidency, celebrate its noblest accomplishments, or condemn it for usurpation, we cannot avoid talking about power. The language of the Constitution is the language of power. "The executive Power shall be vested in a President. . . . The President shall be Commander in Chief of the Army and Navy. . . . He shall have Power, by and with the Advice and Consent of the Senate, to make Treaties." The President "shall have Power to Grant Reprieves and Pardons." "He may require the Opinion in writing of the principal Officer in each of the executive Departments." "He shall take Care that the Laws be faithfully executed." The President of the United States shall recommend to Congress "such Measures as he shall judge necessary and expedient." To meet the constitutional duties of the office as well as the strong expectations of others, Presidents must persuade, bargain, or coerce; Presidents are required to exercise power.

For our purposes power shall be taken to mean cause. A full statement of power relationships is equivalent to an explanation of why human actions cause men to act as they do rather than in some other way. Similarly, a leader is a man who causes people to do what they otherwise would not do. Power, cause, and leadership are nearly equivalent words. When we say that Presidents exercise power or exert leadership we mean that they are causal agents.[1] Our exploration of presidential relationships with strategic publics begins with Robert Dahl's formulation of the concept of power.

There is a regrettable lack of analytical material on the ability of Presidents to exercise power by controlling governmental decisions. The most significant work on decision making is Richard Neustadt's *Presidential Power*. Although — or because — it is read by Presidents and college freshmen alike and has become a modern classic, *Presidential Power* has received little scholarly discussion. Yet neither its arguments nor the implications to be drawn from them are always clear. Fortunately, Peter Sperlich has explained the central propositions found in *Presidential Power* and has shown their relationships to one another. Richard Neustadt himself is represented by a wide-ranging review of the difficulties facing Presidents at mid-twentieth century. My article attempts to explain why the resources available to modern Presidents enable them to exert greater control over foreign than domestic policies.

It is difficult to find clear examples of the successful exercise of power by Presidents. Eugene Rosi's analysis of poll data about the treaty banning tests of atomic weapons reveals the ability of one President to change public opinion. The difficulties that Presidents have had with recalcitrant congressmen are notorious. William Riker's empirical study of presidential attempts to prevent unfriendly legislators of their own party from being nominated shows the pitfalls of these attempts but also suggests that the record has not been as bleak as most writers have supposed. It would be desirable to analyze the effectiveness with which Presidents have used their resources to get what they want. We shall have to be content with Stanley Kelley's original exploration of the presidential use of patronage in order to further legislative programs.

[1] This usage is based on my reading of Andrew McFarland's *Power and Leadership in Pluralist Systems* (Stanford, Calif.: Stanford University Press, 1968) and Robert Dahl's article in this volume.

Someone has written that if you know more about how a third base-man behaves in a baseball game by knowing his personality instead of the rules and relationships of the game, then that player is sick. If we know more about what a President will do by knowing who he is than by a general understanding of the American political system, something is wrong with our political life. An institution is defined by its most important relationships. Most of what we call the presidency is the product of the mutual interaction between Presidents and their most vital publics. I have therefore organized the readings in the second part of this volume around the relationships between the presidency and its publics.

What Presidents can do is both limited and enhanced by the place they have in the lives of citizens. The central position that the presidency occupies with the general public is illustrated by Fred Greenstein's articles on children and adults and Roberta Sigel's study of popular feelings about the exercise of presidential power.

The relationships between the presidency and its publics are mediated through the instruments of mass communication. The growing importance of the presidency in the news is vividly portrayed in Elmer Cornwell's study. Presidents are rarely satisfied with their portrayal in newspapers, however, and reporters constantly complain about attempts to mislead or control them. They never seem to find a President who loves public criticism. It would be highly desirable to include a chapter on the ways in which modern Presidents deal with newspapermen, but no such study exists. Leo Rosten's account of disillusionment with Franklin Roosevelt is still the classic statement of reporters' disappointment in finding that a President could not live up to their ideal as a cross between a tough but tender Hemingway hero and a political magician. Though it is concerned only with Franklin Roosevelt's relationship with reporters, "The Washington Correspondents" establishes a model that is relevant today. Fauneil Rinn evaluates the importance of the presidential press conference as she considers alternative practices. Underneath the rules and procedures of the press conference lies a struggle for advantage. We are greatly in need of a study of presidential use of television but that has not yet been done.

The necessity to compete for the presidential office has certainly helped create broad national party organization. Although nomination and election are the most critical links between Presidents and their parties, nearly everything the chief executive does affects his party relationships. We begin our consideration of the presidency and the parties with Daniel Elazar's study of the career lines leading to the presidency. Since Nelson Polsby and I have tried to systematize the literature on national conventions in *Presidential Elections* (New York: Scribner's, 2d ed., 1968), there is no point in repeating that here. I would like to suggest, however, that no one now knows whether conventions will resume their place as arenas for decision, or whether they will even maintain their more recent position as legitimizers of choices made elsewhere. Much of the best work on the presidency, using the broad view of that institution suggested here, has been done in the field of voting behavior. Since *The American Voter* by Angus Campbell *et al.* (New York: John Wiley and Sons, 1964) is now available in paperback and since there are many excellent short studies available, I have limited coverage here to a piece by Donald Stokes that concentrates on voters' responses to candidates. Unfortunately, there is virtually no analytic material on presidential campaigns. It is not possible to say what an increment of this or that type of campaigning would do to the outcome of an election. So far as I know, the only recent attempt to order the literature on presidential campaigns is found in chapter 3 of Nelson Polsby and Aaron Wildavsky's *Presidential Elections* (New York: Charles Scribner's Sons, 2nd ed., 1968). In order to capture the contemporary trauma over the 1968 election, as well as to point to critical issues for the survival of the two-party system, I have included an article of my own. The reader can judge how well my predictions turned out through Walter Dean Burnham's analysis of the results. The current sense of crisis surrounding the party system is evident in both papers. We can guess what party leadership is like without the assistance of the man in the White House by reading Ralph Goldman's account of the plight of the titular head of the party.

Nothing is more important for a knowledge of American politics and the presidency than an understanding of executive-legislative relationships. Rather than attempt to define a modal pattern, I have chosen to present a variety of patterns of relationships between Presidents and congressmen. James S. Young, Henry Jones Ford, Lawrence H. Chamberlain, and David B. Truman take the subject from the earliest days of the Republic through the 1950's. The contrast between early Presidents, who except for Jefferson lived in a nightmare of unstructured and weak relationships with party and Congress, and the post-Civil War leaders, who had something to work with, is striking testimony to the development of national institutions. Forthcoming studies on the recent growth of presidential liaison with Congress will add to that impression. A television interview with Larry O'Brien, who was President Kennedy's liaison, gives us a participant's observations. Future work will show that the apparatus was also remarkably well developed in Eisenhower's administration.

David Truman and Richard Neustadt forcefully express the perpetual problem of who will control the executive departments. There is no reason to believe that the dilemmas made evident by Richard Fenno's account of modern cabinets have changed much in recent years. What is new, as reported by Laurin Henry, is the greater presidential interest in staffing the federal bureaucracy. Ideally, these introductory pieces should be followed by studies of presidential action with the large federal departments. Despite several case studies, the part played by a President in departmental actions still is rather vague. No works examine a series of events involving Presidents with one or more departments, although no insuperable difficulties in gaining sufficient access to studying some of the departments and their interactions with the presidential office are evident.

We are fortunate to have a wide range of literature on the executive office of the president, from Richard Neustadt's study of the Bureau of the Budget, Lester Seligman's and Edward Flash's discussions of the Council of Economic Advisers, Stanley Falk's and Ernest May's articles on the National Security Council, to my own brief discussion of proposals for helping Presidents by giving them more staff. Despite the apparent abundance of material, however, the most important work on the executive branch still remains to be done. We are in great need of a comprehensive analysis of the presidential office that studies the relationships between the chief actors under different Presidents, explores their division of labor, shows how participants maintain or lose access to their boss, and otherwise views the president's advisory and information apparatus as a subsystem of presidential politics. The article by Ernest May is valuable because he shows how the National Security Council has evolved to meet needs recognized by many Presidents.

At one time the relationship between the presidency and the Supreme Court was considered the most significant topic that could be studied. It is manifestly not now so important. Why? John Roche and Glendon Schubert show how difficult it is to limit a determined President. The articles by Robert Goostree and Harry Kranz demonstrate, as only detailed examinations of a specific dilemma can, the problems involved in determining whether a constitutional provision applies to a particular circumstance in such a way as to circumscribe presidential discretion. Applying the Constitution to a specific problem is more than a matter of being clear; it involves an assessment of how political men will respond to future action. The advantages and limitations of amending the Constitution to deal with a complex problem are discussed in my policy analysis of presidential succession and disability.

Just as our beliefs about the presidency influence what we study, so does our understanding of what the presidency has been affect our hopes for what it might become. If an institution is important enough to be studied by many men, it is manifestly worth improving. Thus several papers in this collection focus on the desirability of changes in the presidency. The paucity of information of presidential decision-making, however, makes it difficult to suggest viable reforms.

It may appear that lack of access to Presidents is the crucial stumbling block to research. No doubt the inability to observe Presidents directly deters many students. Nevertheless, I believe that the basic problem is the lack of a unit of analysis. The use of "decisions" will not quite do because we have not achieved understanding on how to recognize them and, equally important, where one stops and another begins. What looks like 86 decision units to one man looks like 24 or 246 or just 1 to others. Possibilities such as "initiatives" or "communications" or "interactions" suffer from an almost total lack of conceptualization and operational definition. How can we study presidential action if we cannot define the unit of that action or compare one such action to others? One way is to study relationships between the presidency and other institutions. James Young's book, *The Washington Community 1800–1828* (New York: Columbia University Press, 1966), is a brilliant example of this approach. Another way is to make better use of data we do have, such as the presidential "batting averages" with Congress. Yet these efforts, however laudatory, are not a substitute for the direct study of presidential action. That is the challenge of the future.

If this collection of readings is to serve its purpose as a substitute for a textbook, it should be revised frequently to include new research or old work that I have missed. I hope that readers who know about analytical material on the presidency will call it to my attention.

I am grateful to the authors and publishers of the various papers for permission to reprint them here. I owe a special debt to those who wrote original papers. Russel Edgerton and Robert Jervis deserve thanks for telling me about the excellent articles by Ernest May and David Donald. I would also like to thank Mary Ellen Anderson, June Black, Pat O'Donnell, and Sheila Saxby for their assistance in preparing the manuscript for publication.

THE PRESIDENCY

CONCEPTS

ROLE

Role and Role Conflict

Andrew S. McFarland

A fruitful method for studying leaders' response to conflict and socio-political innovation is the examination of models of role conflict. Unfortunately, although the concept "role" is central in the social sciences, "role," like "power" and "culture," has been used in many somewhat different ways.[1] But the following statement expresses the central idea that most scholars have in mind. A "role" is a regularly recurring pattern of social interaction that can be described by (1) who expects (2) whom (3) to do what (4) in which situation. Rewards for conformity and punishments for deviance might play a part in such a description.[2] Yinger describes the concept similarly: "We can say that a role is the list of what most members of a social group believe a position occupant should and should not, may and may not, do. It is *not* a list of what most occupants of a position *in fact do*."[3] [Emphasis added.] Here we see a disagreement in the definition of "role" — the definition may stress expectations (norms) or it may stress behavior. Though one can aptly stress behavior, I prefer to focus on expectations. Only research can show which is the better usage; however, anyone using the term should state precisely which way he is using it. Gross, Mason, and McEachern, in their brilliant *Explorations in Role Analysis,* conclude their survey of definitions of "role" with this observation: "Although their formulations have some fundamental differences, most of the authors whose definitions have been presented are concerned with the same phenomenon. Three basic ideas which appear in most of the conceptualizations considered,

Reprinted by permission of the author and publishers from *Power and Leadership in Pluralist Systems,* by Andrew S. McFarland (Stanford: Stanford University Press, 1969), pp. 202–219. The author would like to thank Fred DuBow and Anne Murray for helpful suggestions.

[1] Neal Gross, Ward S. Mason, and Alexander W. McEachern, *Explorations in Role Analysis* (New York, Wiley, 1958), pp. 11–20; J. Milton Yinger, *Towards a Field Theory of Behavior* (New York, McGraw-Hill, 1965), Ch. 6.

[2] My description of "role" is nearly equivalent to Harry M. Johnson's description of "norm"; Harry M. Johnson, *Sociology: A Systematic Introduction* (New York, Harcourt, Brace, 1960), p. 9.

[3] Yinger, *op. cit.,* p. 100.

if not in the definitions of role themselves, are that individuals: (1) in *social locations* (2) *behave* (3) with reference to *expectations.*" [4] . . . I am interested in how *leaders* (individuals in social location or position) *behave with reference to conflicting expectations.* Hence, I am interested in the theory of role conflict.

First, however, let us note one ambiguity in the theory of role conflict. A person's social location is variously termed "position," "role," or "status," depending on the author. (Moreover, authors may use each of the three terms to mean something other than social location.) For example, the social locations of occupation or family (e.g., father) are called positions, roles, or statuses by various authors (e.g., the role of professor, the status of professor, the position of professor). Following Yinger, I use the term "position" (instead of "status" or "role") to denote social location.[5] For a position, there are counterpositions, which taken together form a self-other combination. Counterpositions for the position of professor include student in course A, student in course B, department chairman, dean of the college, etc. We can call the set of position-counterpositions a "position-set." (Merton calls it a "role-set.")[6] Hence we see that there are two different types of role conflict: conflicting expectations among the others *within* a position-set and conflicting expectations *among* position-sets. An example of the latter is the professor's conflict between professional expectations and family expectations, such as the allocation of his time. When I consider conflicting expectations involving politicians, I am most interested in conflicting expectations among the others within the position-set of his political role, e.g., as legislator. At times, however, we may be interested in conflicting expectations among the politician's position-sets, such as the conflict between political activity and attention to family.[7] This sort of conflict must have a lot to do with the entry and exit of persons into politics. Certain personality types may tend to be screened in or out of leadership positions, a process that may have some impact on the character of the political process and policy outcomes.[8]

What happens when there are conflicting expectations among others about the person's behavior in a position? What are the types of response to such multilateral conflict? Robert Merton outlines six such responses of the position holder and the others in the position-set, which he terms a "role-set." [9] Two of these "social mechanisms articulating role-sets" are among the basic stuff of politics: "differences of power of those in the

[4] Gross *et al., op. cit.,* p. 17.

[5] Yinger, *op. cit.,* p. 99.

[6] Robert K. Merton, "The Role-Set: Problems in Sociological Theory," *British Journal of Sociology,* 8 (June 1957), pp. 106–120; Merton, *Social Theory and Social Structure* (New York, The Free Press, 1957, rev. ed.), pp. 368–384.

[7] Charles L. Clapp, *The Congressman: His Work as He Sees It* (Garden City, N.Y., Anchor Books, 1964), pp. 444–493.

[8] See James David Barber, *The Lawmakers* (New Haven, Conn., Yale University Press, 1965).

[9] Merton, "The Role-Set," pp. 113–117.

role-set"; "insulation of role-activities from observability by members of the role-set." [10] Obviously, when faced with conflicting demands, the politician may respond to the demands of the most powerful, or he may carry out both demands but attempt to hide the fact. (Such deception is difficult in a polity with organized interest groups that disseminate information to their members.)

The other four of Merton's "social mechanisms articulating role-sets" are also important to the student of leadership: "observability of conflicting demands by members of a role-set"; "mutual support among status-occupants"; "relative importance of various statuses"; "abridging the role-set." [11] In the first, the members of a position-set may become conscious of their own conflicting expectations and subsequently resolve them, attaining such agreement either through a power struggle or through compromise. In such cases, the constituents (i.e., those in the counter-position), not the politician, resolve their conflicting expectations. Perhaps insufficient attention has been paid by scholars to such resolution of conflicts. This mechanism may be found in administrative organization; Eisenhower, for example, preferred to force others to resolve their conflicting expectations, but evidently went too far. Roosevelt and Kennedy, on the other hand, preferred to let others bring their conflicting expectations to the President, thereby providing the leader with more information and more policy alternatives.[12]

"Mutual support among status-occupants" is a familiar theme in the literature of legislatures. Partly because of the conflicting demands thrust on the legislator, holders of this position often have a considerable degree of feeling for fellow legislators, and thereby form a self-conscious status group, valuing a distinctive way of life. Such solidarity has mitigated conflict over redistricting at the state level; loyalty to the legislative status group may override loyalty to party platform, leading to the protection of seats of minority-party incumbents in the event of redistricting.[13] The socially stipulated relative importance of various positions (statuses) limits the conflicting expectations of others. I shall deal with the political relevance of such phenomena in my subsequent discussion of hierarchies of role obligations. Likewise, I shall treat the sixth of Merton's categories, abridging the role-set, in my subsequent discussion of "escape" and "repudiation."

In general we can see that, by reducing conflicting expectations, Merton's six "social mechanisms articulating role-sets" refer to political phenomena. There is, then, some relevance of the literature on role

[10] *Ibid.*, pp. 113 f.

[11] *Ibid.*, pp. 113, 116 f.

[12] Richard E. Neustadt, *Presidential Power* (New York, Wiley, 1960).

[13] Malcolm E. Jewell, *The Politics of Reapportionment* (New York, Atherton, 1962), pp. 13, 26–28; Donald Matthews, *U.S. Senators and Their World* (Chapel Hill, N.C., University of North Carolina Press, 1960), pp. 68–117; Nelson W. Polsby, "Two Strategies of Influence: Choosing a Majority Leader, 1962," in Robert L. Peabody and Nelson W. Polsby, eds., *New Perspectives on the House of Representatives* (Chicago, Rand McNally, 1963), pp. 237–270.

conflict to the understanding of the relationships between leadership, conflict, and sociopolitical innovation.

Although less known than Merton's article on the theory of role-sets, Jackson Toby's article "Some Variables in Role Conflict Analysis" [14] provides a useful framework for the study of leadership, conflict, and innovation. In his introduction, Toby aligns himself with those who point to the relationship between social conflict and social change: "It is obvious that an individual in a role conflict situation is uncomfortable. For him, the cross-fire of competing claims is an obnoxious problem to be solved as quickly as possible. From society's point of view, however, role conflicts may be useful; they often give a social system flexibility by providing an entering wedge for social change." [15] This observation can be applied to our interest in politics and politicians. We may say that the politician, having conflicting constituent expectations, is uncomfortable if these conflicting demands are subjectively experienced by him. "For him, the cross-fire of competing claims is an obnoxious problem to be solved as quickly as possible," although a solution might be the strategy of detachment from the conflict situation and subsequent waiting until a clear preponderance of forces emerges.

Toby notes that to deal with contradictory demands of others on the self, social mores provide hierarchies of role obligations, which can be applied to some situations. Consequently, we can observe such socially approved strategies of noncompliance as the excuse, the accident, systems of etiquette, and tact. [16] All of these are relevant to political situations characterized by conflicting demands. In specific situations, they may be linked to policy innovations.

Toby notes that "the 'excuse' is a highly important sociological category. It is an approved technique for avoiding sanctions by asserting that an equally high or higher claim prevented the individual from fulfilling his obligations." [17] For example, when California's Governor Brown was challenged by the Delano grape strikers to meet them on the Easter Sunday conclusion of their 250-mile march to Sacramento, the Governor stated that he had promised to spend the day with his family, and that he could not break this promise. While this excuse infuriated the strikers, it provided a persuasive "out" for the Governor, who probably wished to avoid being put on the spot in a widely publicized, dramatic confrontation.

Another such socially justified solution is the strategy of commitment to conscience. For example, Senator Wayne Morse was in 1965 the most outspoken Senatorial critic of the American position in Vietnam, even though the majority of his Oregon constituents did not support his position; nevertheless, Morse's political popularity did not immediately drop

---

[14] Jackson W. Toby, "Some Variables in Role Conflict Analysis," *Social Forces*, 30 (March 1952), pp. 323–327.

[15] *Ibid.*, p. 324.

[16] *Ibid.*, pp. 324–326.

[17] *Ibid.*, p. 324. [Original emphasis omitted.]

in Oregon, evidently because he was able to convince a large number of his constituents that he is a political conscientious objector. In other words, many Oregon voters, disagreeing with Morse's stand on Vietnam, excused his actions because he was seen as a man who must act according to the dictates of his conscience.[18] Such political conscientious objectors within a democracy provide opportunities for sociopolitical changes. Such leaders operate beyond the normal limits imposed by social controls (in this case the sanctions of voting), and thus have greater leeway for imposing their personal preferences on policy making, i.e., they exercise more power, defined in terms of causality.[19]

The second of Toby's socially legitimated solutions to conflicting demands is the "accident," which is similar to Thomas Schelling's concept of "commitment." [20] "Another kind of legitimate non-compliance, a cousin of the 'excuse,' is the claim of the actor that his failure to fulfill his obligations is involuntary. No higher claims are invoked, but the actor escapes sanctions by demonstrating that circumstances beyond his control prevented him from carrying out his good intentions." [21] For example, Franklin Roosevelt argued that economic events beyond his control prevented him from reducing the federal budget, as he had promised in his 1932 campaign. Supporters of Lyndon Johnson have argued that he, indeed, was a peace candidate in the 1964 election, but that circumstances beyond his control prevented him from carrying out his good intentions in Vietnam.

Toby's third category of role-conflict resolution is etiquette, which he describes as "rituals for reducing social friction." He notes that "Emily Post is sometimes ridiculed by people who pride themselves on being rational. They naively suppose that etiquette consists of meaningless ceremonials, for they do not realize the importance of prescribed rituals in solving the dilemmas [conflicts] of daily life." [22] This conclusion is familiar to those students of international diplomacy who have perceived the conflict-reducing and stabilizing functions of diplomatic etiquette.[23] The etiquette of systems of political bargaining among top leaders of a nation's politics is also worth noting. For example, Brazilian political leaders, even though they use threats of force in national crises, have had an

---

[18] A. Robert Smith, *The Tiger in the Senate: The Biography of Wayne Morse* (Garden City, N.Y., Doubleday, 1962), pp. 19–21 and *passim; Newsweek,* "Oregon: The Morse Code," March 21, 1966, p. 29: "A recent state poll [in Oregon] revealed public sentiment running about 4 to 1 in support of the Administration's handling of the war. At the same time, political observers report no important loss of popularity by Wayne Morse as a result of his persistent attack on Administration policy."

[19] However, we must note that the activities of such conscientious objectors may be highly controversial, as in the case of Morse's stand on Vietnam, although his electoral defeat in November 1968 evidently did not result primarily from the Vietnam issue.

[20] Thomas C. Schelling, *The Strategy of Conflict* (Cambridge, Mass., Harvard University Press, 1960), pp. 24–28, 121–123, 184–186.

[21] Toby, *op. cit.,* p. 325.

[22] *Ibid.*

[23] Robert L. Jervis, in a forthcoming book, as yet untitled, to be published by Princeton University Press.

etiquette of retreat, when it is clear to one person that he is weaker than his opponent. Such systems of etiquette among the political leaders of a country are an important part of an "elite political ethos," the aggregate of elite political culture (attitudes) and their overt behavior, which differentiates the political style of various nations.[24]

Etiquette, defined as prescribed rituals for mitigating the severity of conflict, is an important phenomenon in legislatures of democratic systems. The American Senate and the British Parliament are especially noted in this respect. Thus, it is not surprising that the next lines of Toby's discussion of etiquette are also an important conclusion of students of legislative behavior:

> Consider the chaos of competing demands for social recognition which would ensue if etiquette did not exist. Etiquette formalizes the rank order of claims for deference, thus avoiding in most cases the problem of deciding between one individual's right to attention and another's. The very arbitrariness of the ritual takes the problem out of the realm of idiosyncratic judgment; precedence is automatically evaluated according to the institutionalized criteria. Less specific than etiquette but analogous in function are rules of social intercourse like "first come, first served." [25]

We have, for example, an etiquette of seniority in our national Congress; seniority is the institutionalization of the everyday first-come-first-served rule, and hence "formalizes the rank order of claims for deference." Matthews and Huitt, among others, have delineated the Senatorial etiquette involved in "one individual's right to attention and another's" on the Senate floor by observing the informal folkways restricting the junior Senator's speechmaking.[26] Fenno, Manley, and others have observed similar patterns in some House committees, and even in House subcommittees.[27] They have concluded that such systems of etiquette (e.g., seniority, committee norms of minimal partisanship) are "rituals for reducing social friction" in Toby's terms. Nevertheless, integrative norms, which hold

[24] The study of elite political etiquette within particular countries will provide a way to link the study of international relations, bargaining, and diplomacy and the study of comparative politics. Application of symbolic-interaction sociology, as represented by the work of Herbert Blumer and Erving Goffman, may provide a common conceptual framework for the study of *intra*national elite ethos and *inter*national diplomacy. See Herbert Blumer, "Society as Symbolic Interaction," in Arnold M. Rose, ed., *Human Behavior and Social Processes* (Boston, Houghton Mifflin, 1962), pp. 179–192; Erving Goffman, *The Presentation of Self in Everyday Life* (Garden City, N.Y., Doubleday, 1959); Jervis, *op. cit.*

[25] Toby, *op. cit.*, p. 325.

[26] See, for example, Matthews, *op. cit.*, pp. 92–94; Ralph K. Huitt, "The Outsider in the Senate: An Alternative Role," *American Political Science Review*, 55 (Sept. 1961), 566–575.

[27] Richard F. Fenno, Jr., "The House Appropriations Committee as a Political System: The Problem of Integration," *American Political Science Review*, 56 (June 1962), pp. 310–324; John F. Manley, "The House Committee on Ways and Means: Conflict Management in a Congressional Committee," *American Political Science Review*, 59 (December 1965), pp. 927–939.

the group together by reducing conflict, can contradict the social function of goal attainment, however it is partisanly defined. Thus we may wish to restrict legislative minuets for the sake of achieving our policy preferences, even at the expense of increasing conflict within the legislature. For example, an observer such as the liberal Congressman Richard Bolling, while accepting the ritualized first-come-first-served rule of seniority, will also ask: "All right; it's first-come, first-served, but how much should the first-comer get?" [28]

Thus, we see that political etiquette is an institutionalized mechanism for reducing social friction. As such, it is a socio-political innovation of leaders responding to conflict. However, we must distinguish a system of etiquette itself, such as the congressional seniority system, from its policy consequences, which often are not innovative, if we use the latter term in any kind of useful sense. Thus, in recent years, congressional political etiquette has usually helped stand-pat conservatives. Yet, as Wolfinger has pointed out, liberals in the Congress are increasingly profiting from the seniority system, which therefore may become a conflict-reducing mechanism that aids the cause of sociopolitical innovation.[29]

Toby's fourth social mechanism for legitimating conflict resolution is tact, or legitimate deception: "This solicitude for the feelings of others is the circumstance that makes the white lie socially 'right.' The ordinary lie is unreservedly disapproved because it lacks precisely this quality. It is a selfish attempt to manipulate other people by controlling their access to information. Tact, on the other hand, is institutionalized deception for the primary purpose of sparing the feelings of others." [30] Actually, we may view such legitimate deception in terms of a continuum from the white lie (an actual untruth) through various forms of tact (not telling the whole truth, partial lying). A cynical or sardonic attitude toward the statements of political leaders is a part of folk wisdom throughout the world. However, I think that scholars have paid insufficient attention to analyzing political lying and political tact. For instance, few American politicians are outright liars, but, on the other hand, few will tell the whole truth. Most politicians must be tactful and avoid the whole truth, for "this solicitude for the feelings of others" gains votes. Tact, like lying, can help you get ahead.

Because tact gains votes, avoiding the whole truth is an inherent part of democratic elections. But we should note that, in Toby's words, tact "is institutionalized deception for the primary purpose of sparing the feelings of others." To realize the function of tact in democratic campaigning, imagine an electoral campaign in which two politicians tell the whole truth as they see it. Candidate Conservative viciously attacks the squalor and crime of Negro slums, and states that while some of the finest men he knows are Negroes, in general colored people are inferior

---

28 Richard Bolling, *House Out of Order* (New York, Dutton, 1965), pp. 237–244.
29 See Raymond E. Wolfinger and Joan Heifetz, "Safe Seats, Seniority, and Power in Congress," *American Political Science Review*, 59 (June 1965), pp. 337–349.
30 Toby, *op. cit.*, p. 325.

to other Americans. Candidate Conservative states that he believes that Negro squalor and crime are the fault of the Negroes themselves, because in our individualistic society, all men have an equal chance to get ahead and it is the person's own fault if he lives in a slum, as the Chinese and Japanese have proven. Candidate Liberal, on the other hand, states that although some of the finest men he knows are real-estate salesmen, morticians, and loan-company executives, in general men in these trades are bloodsucking leeches on society. Thus, such telling of the truth, the whole truth, and nothing but the truth (as seen by each person) in political oratory could increase viciousness and hatred throughout society. One man's meat is another man's poison. Thus, we see the importance of tact, or sugarcoated deception, as a response to conflict.

Toby writes: "Institutionalized techniques exist for preventing role conflicts from arising. These are not perfect, however, and role conflicts arise. But there are only a limited number of possible solutions to these dilemmas. The problem for research is the conditions under which one solution is chosen over another." [31] Toby lists seven alternatives open to persons who "find themselves in situations where two or more groups make incompatible demands upon them," a statement that applies to political behavior. These seven alternatives are: repudiation of one group, playing off one group against the other, stalling until the pressures subside, redefinition of the role, leading a double life, escaping from the field, and illness. All these behavior patterns are important for understanding political leaders. Some of them are equivalent to Merton's categories of "social mechanisms articulating role-sets." Thus, "playing off one group against the other" (Toby) is seen by Merton as one instance of relying on differences of power of those in the role-set. "Leading a double life" is subsumed under Merton's "observability of conflicting demands by members of a role-set." "Repudiation of one group" and "escaping from the field" are equivalent to Merton's "abridging the role-set." [32]

Repudiation of one group making an incompatible demand is certainly a common course of action. However, the competitive, economic-model electoral system, with its competing elites pursuing public office,[33] restricts such repudiation as a mechanism for reducing conflict. For example, Barry Goldwater's beliefs about the nature of the federal system and the United States Constitution forced him to vote against the Civil Rights Bill of 1964, a de facto repudiation of the Negro vote, which was cast 28 per cent for Nixon in 1960, but only 6 per cent for Goldwater in

---

31 *Ibid.*, p. 327.

32 Merton, "The Role-Set," pp. 113–117; Toby, *op. cit.*, pp. 326–327.

33 Anthony Downs, *An Economic Theory of Democracy* (New York, Harper, 1957); Joseph A. Schumpeter, *Capitalism, Socialism, and Democracy* (New York, Harper, 1950, 3d ed.), pp. 269–302; E. E. Schattschneider, *The Semisovereign People* (New York, Holt, Rinehart & Winston, 1960), pp. 129–142; Aaron B. Wildavsky, "The Goldwater Phenomenon: Purists, Politicians, and the Two-Party System," *The Review of Politics*, 27 (July 1965), pp. 386–413.

1964. If Goldwater had voted for the Civil Rights Bill, thereby avoiding the repudiation of the Negro vote, he not only would have faced incompatible demands from Negroes, Southern segregationists, and ultra-conservative Goldwater activists, but also would have complicated his own conservative conscience. On the other hand, Lyndon Johnson, the master politician, repudiated nobody but Communists and Klansmen, and accordingly suffered the complexities of finding himself "in situations where two or more groups make incompatible demands" upon him. Parenthetically, it is interesting to note that by March 1966 Johnson was reportedly on reasonably civil terms with Wayne Morse, whereas he was reacting almost savagely to the milder, sporadic, and more institutionally expressed criticism of Senator Vance Hartke of Indiana, whom Johnson regarded as a double-crossing protegé.[34] We see that if a politician repudiates a group or a person whose demands contradict those of another group or person, the politician's life becomes simpler, except that he loses political support. If the politician repudiates nobody, his life is full of complicated situations, yet he may retain massive political support.

(We have all known at least one attractive girl who has followed this political pattern: for one reason or another, our subject will not choose one male admirer and repudiate the rest. If she were to do this, her life would become simpler, yet her band of admirers would become smaller. However, our femme fatale cannot repudiate any man she likes, and thus she has a large band of admirers/supporters but finds herself constantly in complicated situations, when two or more admirers make incompatible demands on her. Our lovable female might be an egoist, or she might be very kind. More likely, she is a very kind egoist, like Abraham Lincoln and Franklin Delano Roosevelt.)

Illness or resigning from politics are leaders' responses to conflict that deserve more attention by scholars. However, political conflicts may or may not produce extreme psychological and physical stress in the leader who is subjectively aware of incompatible demands. My impression is that Theodore Roosevelt, Franklin Roosevelt, Truman, Kennedy, and Johnson often regarded political conflicts, even those involving incompatible demands, as psychologically and physically invigorating up to a certain point. On the other hand, Taft, Wilson, Harding, Coolidge, Hoover, and Eisenhower seem to have had a lower tolerance for conflict; they found incompatible demands psychologically and physically depressing. Taft was a first-class judge and administrator but a poor manager of political conflict; Wilson had great political talent yet he propelled himself into tragically needless dilemmas, rendered insolvable by his own peculiar combination of principled moralism and stubbornness.[35]

The failure of Wilson in the Versailles Treaty controversy, and the tragic promotion of Warren Harding to a post beyond his abilities and thus to his early death, bring to mind one of Chester Barnard's observa-

[34] *Newsweek*, "Congress: One-Way Street," March 28, 1966, pp. 34–36.
[35] See Alexander L. George and Juliette L. George, *Woodrow Wilson and Colonel House: A Personality Study* (New York, John Day, 1956).

tions about "the executive function." Barnard states that "the higher the grade [of executive responsibility] the more complex the *moralities* involved, and the more necessary higher abilities to discharge the responsibilities, that is, to resolve the moral conflicts implicit in the positions." [36] The situations of role conflict, or "situations where two or more groups make incompatible demands" on the politician are situations of complex moral conflict. Thus, Barnard is concerned with the same questions that I am dealing with here, using the role-conflict model. Barnard continues: "It is apparent that executives frequently fail. This failure may be ascribed in most cases, I believe, to inadequate abilities as a first cause, usually resulting in the destruction of responsibility. But in many cases it may be inferred that the conditions impose a moral complexity and a moral conflict presumably not soluble. Some actions which may within reason appear to be dictated by the good of the organization as a whole will obviously be counter to nearly all other codes, personal or official." [37] Woodrow Wilson, for example, was a man of tremendous abilities, but among the least of these was a reliable capacity to deal with "moral complexity." He was morally incapable of compromising his principles, as embodied in the League of Nations Covenant, to meet the demands of Senator Lodge and his supporters. Wilson's conduct and subsequent collapse were instrumental in the complete defeat of the Versailles Treaty in the Senate. Wilson seems to have had a significant impact on history by his sagacious management of America's entry into World War I and his personal influence on the peace settlement and on the League Covenant. But Wilson's personal influence was also an important factor in the American nonparticipation in the League. In this case, too, if Wilson had acted differently, the course of human events (at least in the short run) would have been significantly different. Wilson's inability to deal with moral complexity was the cause of his defeat in the League controversy, but it is interesting to note that he handled the extraordinarily complex morality of American diplomacy in the August 1914–March 1917 period with impressive judiciousness. As Alexander and Juliette George note in their biography and psychological interpretation of Wilson, this unusual man seems to have asked for trouble by assuming needlessly moralistic positions at certain times, although he was quite capable of engaging in adroit maneuvering of a complex moral nature at other times.[38] Thus, Wilson seemed capable of dealing with situations of great moral complexity, but at times he just refused to do so. Harding, on the other hand, was promoted to a position beyond his abilities. In particular, he was destroyed by the moral complexity of having to punish his corrupt, boorish friends of the Ohio gang. (More specifically, perhaps Harding was unable to deal

36 C. I. Barnard, *The Functions of the Executive* (Cambridge, Mass., Harvard University Press, 1938), p. 276.

37 *Ibid.*, pp. 277–278.

38 For an example of Wilson's adroit political maneuvering, see George and George, *op. cit.*, pp. 47–74.

with the moral complexity of refusing prestigious jobs to friends who were technically and morally incapable of filling them.)

Coolidge escaped from conflict and complexity by sleeping twelve hours a day.[39] Hoover, on the other hand, was a most energetic man but an ideologue. We could term Hoover a "Christian technocratic individualist" (individualism in the sense of Adam Smith and laissez faire liberalism). He was not a politician — someone who specialized in authoritatively allocating scarce values and hence dealing with political conflict. Nor was he ideologically flexible or pragmatic; thus he was a magnificent organizer of resources toward agreed ends, but he was unable to deal with situations or people that contradicted his belief in laissez faire liberalism, Smithian economics, the preeminence of business, and the subordination of government. He too was a man of tremendous ability who could not deal with certain situations of moral complexity — i.e., when economic events contradicted his personal ideology. Lenin could institute a New Economic Policy, but not Hoover! Hoover had much in common with Wilson, as Hoover himself perhaps realized.[40] Hoover could not deal with certain situations because of his personal ideology, which was no doubt inextricably linked with his personality structure. Similarly, Wilson, with his Calvinist psychological structure, sometimes could not deal with complex situations, in which it became necessary to compromise the specific content of particular policies.

Neustadt writes: "everything suggests that with his motivations as with methods, Eisenhower has been a sort of [Franklin] Roosevelt in reverse," [41] for, whereas Roosevelt delighted in sorting out conflicting information and policy alternatives presented by conflicting personalities in his administrative organization, Eisenhower evidently was annoyed by disagreement, especially intense disagreement, about "the one best way" of achieving a goal. Hence, Franklin Roosevelt had an informally organized ad hoc staffing system; Eisenhower established a formally organized system under the guidance of the assistant president, Sherman Adams. According to Neustadt, Eisenhower thought of himself as a great conciliator.

> He [Eisenhower] genuinely thought himself the hero others thought him. . . . And he genuinely thought the Presidency was, or ought to be, the source of unifying, moderating influence above the struggle on the model of George Washington — the Washington, that is to say, of legend, not of life. . . . What drew him to the Presidency and held him there, it seems, was a conception of the good man above politics, emulating the Father of his Country. . . . With this to guide him he could not dispute the arguments of all his friends that his "place in the world was unique," that he had "a God-given ability for reconciling differ-

[39] Arthur M. Schlesinger, Jr., *The Crisis of the Old Order* (Boston, Houghton Mifflin, 1964, paperback ed.), p. 57.

[40] Hoover certainly admired Wilson and even wrote a book about him — *The Ordeal of Woodrow Wilson* — in which the preface is especially interesting.

[41] Neustadt, *op. cit.*, p. 163.

ences among . . . nations," and for "healing divisions among
the American people." . . . But the reverse side of the coin was
a diminished confidence when he dealt with the hard, divisive
issues forced upon a President by dates and by events.[42]

On illness and death as a response to complex conflict, this quotation
from Neustadt is very intriguing. "Robert Donovan supplies us Eisenhower's answer when it was suggested to him a few weeks before his
heart attack that Congress might be called back for a special session in
the fall of 1955: 'He slowly twisted his head around to [Arthur] Burns
and told him painfully that the cost of a special session might be the
sanity and possibly the life of one Dwight D. Eisenhower.' Such comments simply strengthen the suggestion . . . that this man neither liked
the game he was engaged in nor had gained much understanding of its
rules." [43] Thus, in the solution of role conflicts, escape from the field and
illness are important responses of politicians to "situations where two or
more groups make incompatible demands."

The sixth of Toby's seven behavioral patterns aimed at reducing
conflict "in situations where two or more groups make incompatible demands" is "stalling until the pressures subside." Toby describes this pattern as follows: "If the cross-pressures are of a temporary nature, it may
be possible for the individual to postpone making a decision until one
or both of the groups relax their demands. Stalling is, however, not
passive waiting; it is an art. It involves placating and promising while
the competing obligations are not being fulfilled." [44] Stalling alleviates
political conflict while the leader waits until the conflicting interests subside or the conflicting groups resolve their differences. Stalling thus is
linked to the strategies of relying on differences of power among the
others in the position-set (role-set) and playing off one group against the
other. On the other hand, stalling is another word for *immobilisme* —
inaction — the term descriptive of a serious weakness of some representative governments. During the Fourth Republic, the French National
Assembly followed a policy of stalling on the major issues of the Algerian
War, for example.

Stalling, and observing the balance of forces in the group environment,
is the central political strategy pursued by Chicago politicians, as observed by Banfield in the six case studies described in his *Political Influence*. Banfield writes:

> The political heads are slow to take up an issue presented to
> them by the "civic leaders." *They know from experience that
> what one organization wants is almost certain to be opposed by
> others.* Chicago is much too big a city, and the interests in it far
> too diverse, to allow of quick and easy agreement on anything.

42 *Ibid.*, pp. 165, 166.
43 *Ibid.*, p. 165. Neustadt cites Robert J. Donovan, *Eisenhower: The Inside Story*
(New York, Harper, 1956), p. 357.
44 Toby, *op. cit.*, p. 327.

By approaching an issue slowly, the political head gives opposing interests time to emerge, to formulate their positions, and to present their arguments. Before he commits himself he wants to see what the alignment on each side is likely to be and what is at stake politically. The longer the evil hour of decision can be postponed, the better he likes it; he has nothing to lose as long as the argument continues, and *any settlement he imposes will make him enemies.* What the public housing leader said of Mayor Kennelly — that his idea of a beautiful world was to sit around a table and have the opposing parties come to an agreement for which he would then take the credit without ever having opened his mouth — can be said of the other politicians as well.[45] [Emphasis added.]

The political strategy of stalling maintains the politician's popularity, since in most situations those annoyed at the leader's indecision have more diffused emotions than the (probably) smaller group that would be intensely angry, no matter which decision the leader makes. The political behavior of stalling until a clear balance of forces emerges is a response of leadership to conflict, but it is seldom an innovative response, for the political leader merely rubber-stamps a coalescence of group influence. In such a case, group forces are the *independent* variable, while the politician is the *dependent* variable.

The last of Toby's seven behavior patterns for reconciling conflicting demands is "redefinition of the role or roles." He defines this pattern as follows: "The individual reacts upon the situation and changes it so that the role expectations are no longer incompatible." [46] In other words, the person (leader), in redefining the situation, acts as an independent variable, exercises causal impact on events, or exerts power, as he changes the situation to mitigate the conflicting demands and thus realizes his will. Furthermore, in redefining the situation, he exercises creativity — i.e., he innovates — a new situation. In situations of extreme value heterogeneity and confusion, such a redefinition of the situation denotes extraordinary leadership, defined as influence, of the great man of history. . . . In situations of value homogeneity, general agreement, and conflict over only limited changes in political policy, the redefinition of the situation is an important case of pluralist leaders' changing the course of events in a significant way (albeit less significant than that of a hero of history or revolution). By redefining a conflict situation in order to resolve incompatible demands, the politician acts as an independent force, exercises influence, and introduces sociopolitical innovation. Hence, the concept of redefinition of the situation, as a means of reducing role conflict, helps the analyst link leadership, political conflict, and sociopolitical innovation.

Ernst Haas' concept of "upgrading the common interest" is a type of redefinition of the situation by leaders responding to multilateral conflict,

[45] Edward C. Banfield, *Political Influence* (New York, The Free Press, 1961), p. 270.
[46] Toby, *op. cit.*, p. 327.

which leads to sociopolitical innovation (in this case international integration). Haas categorizes the outcomes of international bargaining among leaders into three types: (1) "accommodation on the basis of the minimum common denominator"; (2) "accommodation by 'splitting the difference'"; (3) "accommodation on the basis of deliberately or inadvertently upgrading the common interests of the parties." [47] Haas comments that upgrading the common interests may mean

> that the parties succeeded in redefining their conflict so as to work out a solution at a higher level, which almost invariably implies the expansion of the initial mandate or task. In terms of results, this mode of accommodation maximizes what I have elsewhere called the "spill-over" effect of international decisions: policies made in carrying out an initial task and grant of power can be made real only if the task itself is expanded, as reflected in the compromises among the states interested in the task. In terms of method, the upgrading of the parties' common interests relies heavily on the services of an *institutionalized mediator,* whether a single person or a board of experts, *with an autonomous range of powers.*[48] [Emphasis added.]

In a pluralist society, the "institutionalized mediator" "with an autonomous range of power" can be a certain type of politician who is sensitive to multilateral conflict and accordingly redefines particular, limited situations to resolve conflict, satisfy the majority of conflicting interests involved, and enhance his own popularity. A case of such redefinition of a multilateral conflict situation, involving the upgrading of common interests of Democratic senators, is described in Huitt's analysis of Lyndon Johnson's leadership in the Senate.[49] In 1954, Democratic senators were split into a pro-labor Northern group, and an anti-labor predominantly Southern group, over the nomination of a certain Albert Beeson to the National Labor Relations Board. Pro-labor senators wanted to reject Beeson's nomination because he retained connections with a California corporation; anti-labor senators saw no reason why an NLRB appointee should be friendly to unions. As minority leader, Johnson unified the Democrats on this issue by redefining the situation in terms of the honor of the Senate itself. Johnson, finding that Beeson had contradicted himself in testimony between hearings, succeeded in persuading Senator Walter George that Beeson should be rejected for flouting the dignity of the Senate. George, highly influential with conservative Southern Democrats, convinced them to accept Johnson's new

47 Ernst B. Haas, *Beyond the Nation-State* (Stanford, Calif., Stanford University Press, 1964), p. 111. See also his "International Integration," *International Organization,* 15 (Summer 1961), pp. 367–392. In this connection, see also Henry C. Metcalf and L. Urwick, eds., *Dynamic Administration: The Collected Papers of Mary Parker Follett* (London, Pitman, 1941), pp. 30–49 and *passim.*
48 Haas, *Beyond the Nation-State,* p. 111.
49 Ralph K. Huitt, "Democratic Party Leadership in the Senate," *American Political Science Review,* 55 (June 1961), pp. 339–340.

definition of the situation, and consequently the Democratic minority (of 1954) "stood solidly together on the kind of issue which usually divided them." [50] Accordingly, Lyndon Johnson, serving as a mediating leader, redefined a situation by deliberately "upgrading the common interests of the parties" involved.

Another case, more directly involving task expansion and political innovation, is that of the outstanding urban renewal program of New Haven's Mayor Richard Lee. Dahl reports that Lee's unusual political success has been based to a great extent on his creation of an urban renewal program that unified otherwise conflicting interests. Lee's response to multilateral political conflict led to a partial redefinition of the political situation, an upgrading of the common interest, dynamic political mediation satisfying the majority of otherwise contending interests, and an increase in the popularity of a political leader. The person's innovative response resulted in the exercise of power — the Mayor caused substantial changes in others' behavior according to his intentions (support for urban renewal, getting reelected).[51]

Haas' concept of upgrading common interests evidently has much in common with Mannheim's concept of dynamic intellectual (or political) mediation. Thus Mannheim shows that an awareness of conflicting perspectives (goals, interests) is crucial for redefining a situation in terms of dynamic political mediation.[52] In many cases, a pluralist political system, having multilateral conflict, may force its political leadership to gain such an awareness of conflicting perspectives. Such leaders may exhibit an innovative response — a creative, if limited, redefinition of the situation in terms of upgrading common interests.

[50] *Ibid.*, p. 340.
[51] Robert A. Dahl, *Who Governs?* (New Haven, Conn., Yale University Press, 1961), pp. 115–140.
[52] Karl Mannheim, *Ideology and Utopia* (New York, Harcourt, Brace, Harvest paperback edition, 1961, first published 1936), Ch. 3.

Expectations of Presidential Leadership in Decision-Making

Lester G. Seligman and Michael A. Baer

I. THE PUBLIC AND THE PRESIDENT

A major political trend of our time is the growth in public expectations of the presidency and the expanding scope of presidential action.[1] This trend has contributed to make the presidency central in our political system. The various roles of the President — architect of legislative programs, chief executive, director of foreign policy, leader of his political party — are interdependent and have grown cumulatively. These result from continuous role differentiation and a new institutionalization of presidential leadership.[2] An important contributor to these developments is the closer and more intensive relationship between the public and the President. The President has invited and encouraged the public to identify with him, and the public, in turn, has responded by focusing its demands and expectations on the President.[3] This paper is an exploratory study of the types of public expectations of presidential action and their variability with decision situations.

There are three principal variables in our study: (1) expectations; (2) decision situations; and (3) the occupant of the presidential office. We shall discuss each of these variables, and then the hypotheses that relate these variables. Then we will explain the methodology of our investigation and report the findings and conclusions.

The expectations that citizens have of political leadership may be divided into two types: (1) specific and (2) diffuse. David Easton defined these two types of support in the following words: "Specific support flows from the favorable attitudes and predispositions stimulated by outputs that are perceived by members to meet their demands as they arise or in

Printed by permission of the authors.

1 Richard Neustadt, *Presidential Leadership* (New York: Wiley, 1960); Donald B. Johnson and Jack L. Walker, *The Dynamics of the American Presidency* (New York: Wiley, 1964); David E. Haight and Larry D. Johnston, *The President: Roles and Powers* (Chicago: Rand, McNally, 1965); E. Hargrove, *Presidential Leadership: Personality and Political Style* (New York: Macmillan, 1966).

2 Lester G. Seligman, "Developments in the Presidency and the Conception of Political Leadership," *American Sociological Review*, XX, No. 6 (December 1955), p. 711; Lester G. Seligman, "Presidential Leadership: The Inner Circle and Institutionalization," *Journal of Politics*, XVIII, No. 3 (August 1956), pp. 410–26; James M. Burns, *Presidential Government* (Boston: Houghton Mifflin, 1966).

3 Fillmore H. Sanford, "Public Orientation to Roosevelt," *Public Opinion Quarterly*, XV (Summer 1951), pp. 189–216; Roberta S. Sigel, "Image of the American Presidency — Part II of an Exploration into Popular Views of Presidential Power," *Midwest Journal of Politics*, X, No. 1 (February 1966), pp. 123–36.

anticipation." In contrast, diffuse support is ". . . an attachment to a political object for its own sake, it constitutes a store of political good will. As such it taps deep political sentiments and is not easily depleted through disappointments without outputs." [4] The same criteria may be applied to expectations. Thus, specific expectations are focused on particular decisions, and diffuse expectations are directed toward the decision-makers as symbolic or consensual leaders. The different types of expectations are related to functional distinctions in leadership.

Leadership has been differentiated into its instrumental functions and its expressive functions.[5] Both are regarded as necessary to the maintenance of a system. The instrumental functions include decision-making activities that contribute to the fulfillment of specific system goals. Expressive functions include leadership activities that enhance common sentiments and solidarity feelings that contribute to system maintenance.

More attention has been given to the expressive aspects of presidential leadership than to the instrumental aspects.[6] Public opinion survey organizations regularly monitor the degree of diffuse public approval or disapproval of presidential action. The mass media devote much attention to the activities of the President that symbolize national values. Election data are interpreted as generalized presidential mandates to carry out certain broad directives of public policy. More commonly, under the heading of "charisma," attempts are made to identify the psychological relationship between the President and the public. The strong personal identifications with the President especially have been subject to analysis. But it is reasonable to suggest that public attitudes toward the President are more complex. Analyses of public expectations toward instrumental functions of the President have been neglected. The study presented here is an exploratory attempt to determine whether expectations of presidential decision-making — an instrumental function — in a set of hypothetical decision situations are specific or diffuse.

A. *The Content of Expectations.* Observers of the American political ethos have discovered a peculiar dualism of values.[7] On the one hand, political life and political activity are expected to conform to high moral standards. On the other hand, equally high value and esteem are attached to political effectiveness and expedient political success. This dual regard for rectitude and expediency, it is alleged, explains the peculiar cycles of agitation for reform and the tolerance of corruption so

[4] David Easton, *A Systems Analysis of Political Life* (New York: Wiley, 1965), pp. 273–74.

[5] Dorwin Cartwright and Alvin Zander, *Group Dynamics* (Evanston, Ill.: Row, Peterson and Co., 1960, 2nd ed.); Robert F. Bales and Philip E. Slater, "Role Differentiation in Small Decision-Making Groups," in Talcott Parsons and Robert F. Bales, *Family, Socialization and Interaction Process* (Glencoe, Ill.: Free Press, 1955), pp. 259–306.

[6] Fred I. Greenstein, "Popular Images of the President," *American Journal of Psychiatry*, CXXII (November 1965), pp. 523–29.

[7] Daniel Bell, *The End of Ideology* (New York: Free Press, 1960), pp. 115–136; Abraham Kaplan, "American Ethics and Public Policy," in *The American Style* (New York: Harper, 1958), pp. 3–110.

typical in our political history. Further, these contradictory expectations have made public attitudes especially ambivalent toward politicians.[8]

For these reasons, the polarities of morality and expediency were used in this study as qualitative distinctions of expectations about presidential actions. Thus we were concerned with learning whether a respondent's expectations in various decision-making situations were consistently moralistic or expedient, or whether his or her expectations varied with the particular situation that the President faced.

B. *The Content of Decisions.* The President must make complex decisions because of the many expectations and demands that are made upon him. The numerous competing roles and obligations that the President incurs entail choices of priorities.[9] Alternative courses of action are choices among benefits and costs, advantages and disadvantages. The President, then, is in a situation where what ever course of action he chooses results in losses or gains of support from Congress, his political party, the opposing political party, significant interest groups, and public opinion. Presidential decisions are based on estimates of costs and benefits to a President's objectives.

C. *Institutionalized Office and the Person.* The focus on public expectations leads us to examine the object of these expectations, the office of the President. Any institutionalized office may be meaningfully analyzed by dividing it into two components: the office and the person who holds the office. By "office" we mean the rules and constraints that prescribe an institutionalized position. By "person" we mean the particular behavior of the office holder that derives from his personality, style, and the special talents that he imparts to the office.[10] The presidency is a continuous political office whose boundaries are an inheritance that must be and is respected by all Presidents. Yet, individual Presidents have stretched or contracted these limits and have given the office their special stamp and style. In this sense, the presidency is a blend of individual styles and the historical legacy of legal boundaries, tradition, and innovation. Therefore, when we analyze public expectations, we must keep the components of office and person in mind, and ask whether expectations concern the *man* who happens to be the President or the presidential *office,* regardless of the occupant.

II. THE HYPOTHESES

Four hypotheses about expectations were formulated. The first two centered on the moralistic-expediential dimension of expectations. The third was suggested by Almond and Verba's chapter "Patterns of Partisanship"

8 William C. Mitchell, "Ambivalent Social Status of the American Politician," *Western Political Science Quarterly,* XII (December 1959), pp. 683–98.

9 Lester G. Seligman, "The Presidential Office and the President as Party Leader," *Law and Contemporary Problems,* XXI (Autumn 1956), pp. 724–34.

10 Everett Hughes, "Institutional Office and the Person," *American Journal of Sociology,* XLIII (November 1937), pp. 404–13.

in *Civic Culture*.[11] The fourth hypothesis was the most significant because it stated the probability that the *situation* would effect expectations more than the particular occupant of the presidential office.

Hypothesis 1. In presidential decision situations, a higher percentage of respondents will expect the President to choose a moral course of action rather than an expedient one.

Hypothesis 2. In presidential decision situations, a higher percentage of respondents will expect the President to act in accordance with moral ends than in accordance with moral means.

Hypothesis 3. Although both Democrats and Republicans perceive a President of the opposing party as more moralistic than expedient, Republicans will expect moralistic decisions more frequently from a Democratic President than Democrats will expect from a Republican President.

Hypothesis 4. Differences in decision situations will have greater effect upon respondents' expectations than differences in the occupants of the office of the President.

These hypotheses are summarized in the following table:

Independent Variables	*Intervening Variables*	*Dependent Variables* *Expectations*	
		Means	*Ends*
1. Liberals-Conservatives	Decision situations	Moralistic	Moralistic
2. Republicans-Democrats	The person (Eisenhower-Kennedy) or presidential office	Expedient	Expedient

III. METHODOLOGY

Our questionnaire included twelve presidential decision dilemmas, derived and generalized from the experience of recent Presidents. (See appendix.) The decision situations were not selected by any particular criteria other than that they were common. Some of them dealt with domestic politics, others concerned international problems. Some dilemmas involved the President's relations with the opposing party, others involved relations with his party. Under each decision dilemma, four specific alternative courses of action were listed. Each course of action was a combination of expediency and morality, with regard to both means and ends, as Figure 1 illustrates. An independent panel of judges evaluated and classified each alternative as expedient or moral with regard to both means and ends. The judges' consensus determined for the researchers the final classification of a course of action.

The two independent variables were (1) party affiliation and (2) the conservatism or liberalism of the respondents. Our sample consisted of

11 Gabriel A. Almond and Sidney Verba, *The Civic Culture* (Boston: Little, Brown, 1965), pp. 85–116.

FIGURE 1

Types of Expectations

MEANS		ENDS	MORALITY	EXPEDIENCY
	1		*Means*	*Ends*
Moral		Moral		
	2 ╳ 3		1. Moral-Moral (MM)	
Expedient	4	Expedient	2. Moral-Expedient (ME)	
			3. Expedient-Moral (EM)	
			4. Expedient-Expedient (EE)	

fifty-six Republican and Democratic precinct committeemen and women, randomly selected in the Eugene-Springfield, Oregon, metropolitan area. Thirty-five were Republicans and twenty-one were Democrats. Precinct committeemen were selected because the politically active were expected to respond more easily to a questionnaire that presupposed a fair amount of political information. The seven items of the conservatism-liberalism scale of the Michigan Survey Research Center were included in the questionnaire. The sample scores on the seven items were cumulated and the sample was divided into two groups. Democrats proved preponderantly liberal and Republicans were preponderantly conservative. The interviews were conducted in 1962 and 1963.

Each respondent was asked to respond twice. The first time the respondent was presented with each situation and was asked how he expected the modern presidential office to act without reference to a particular President. The second time half of the respondents were presented with each dilemma and were asked their expectations if Eisenhower were President, while the other half were asked to respond as if John Kennedy were President. In this way we hoped to determine whether respondents had (1) rigid expectations that did not vary with the situation and the occupant of the office, or (2) flexible expectations that did vary with the situation and the occupant of the office.

Table 1 lists the groups and subgroups that were examined in testing these hypotheses.

IV. THE FINDINGS

Hypothesis 1. A higher percentage of respondents will expect the President to choose a moral course of action rather than an expedient one.

Data related to the first hypothesis was examined in three ways. First, the responses were collapsed into categories of moral ends and moral means. To do this we added the percentage of MM and EM answers for each dilemma and then averaged these sums for each subgroup. We followed the same procedure in collapsing the MM and ME responses. This

TABLE 1

Sample Groups

Group/Subgroup	Responding To:	N:
Total Sample	Modern Presidency	56
Kennedy's Sample	Modern Presidency	25
Eisenhower's Sample	Modern Presidency	27
Eisenhower's Sample	Eisenhower	27
Kennedy's Sample	Kennedy	25
Liberals	Modern Presidency	27
Liberals	Kennedy	14
Liberals	Eisenhower	13
Conservatives	Modern President	29
Conservatives	Kennedy	11
Conservatives	Eisenhower	14
Republicans	Modern President	35
Republicans	Kennedy	15
Republicans	Eisenhower	16
Democrats	Modern President	21
Democrats	Kennedy	10
Democrats	Eisenhower	11

resulted in two figures for each subgroup: the average percentage of expectations of moral ends, and the average percentage of expectations of moral means. (See Table 2.) For all seventeen subgroups every percentage, both for means and ends, was above 50 per cent. In seventeen of the possible thirty-four cases this percentage exceeded 60 per cent.

The second method of viewing the data was more qualitative than quantitative. We drew graphs for each of the 204 possible subgroup-expectation combinations. These graphs showed in each of the four possible ways the percentage of responses within a subgroup. The graph was constructed as illustrated in Figure 2.

If a large proportion of the sample responded with the same expectations in a decision situation the result was a unimodal or bimodal graph. For our first hypothesis — that more respondents will expect the President to choose a moral course of action rather than an expedient one — we counted the number of modal peaks at the MM and EM points to determine the number of cases where moral ends were expected by respondents. In a similar manner we counted the peaks at the MM and ME positions to determine the number of those who expected moral means. Of the possible 204 cases, 44 did not peak, and only 160 were left to judge. Modal peaks of 126 cases occurred at moral ends and modal peaks of 102 cases occurred at moral means. The number was substantial in both cases.

TABLE 2

Percentage Expecting Moral Ends and
Moral Means for Each Subgroup

	All	Sample with Eisenhower as President	Sample with Kennedy as President	Lib.	Con.	Dem.	Rep.
Responding to Modern Presidency:							
Avg. percentage Moral ends	65	67	60	65	64	63	67
Avg. percentage Moral means	68	61	53	56	57	56	58
Responding to Eisenhower:							
Avg. percentage Moral ends	—	60	—	60	61	55	64
Avg. percentage Moral means	—	57	—	57	66	52	65
Responding to Kennedy:							
Avg. percentage Moral ends	—	—	60	65	54	67	56+
Avg. percentage Moral means	—	—	55	53	57	55	56

FIGURE 2

Axes of Graph for Measuring Distribution of
Answers Plotted Against Type of Expectations

```
100%
 75%
 50%
 25%
  0%        MM              ME              EM              EE
                    Types of Expectations
```

MM – moral ends, moral means   ME – moral ends, expedient means
EM – expedient ends, moral means   EE – expedient ends, expedient means

The third way of measuring the number of moral and expedient expectations was similar to the second method, but more quantitative. We constructed a chart of those subgroup combinations in which one answer received greater than 50 per cent of the respondents' choices. This method identified a minimal consensus among respondents. There were 109 out of a possible 204 such cases. Of these 109 answers where minimal consensus was reached, 93 expected moral ends, 84 expected moral means.

The findings that resulted from these three methods were identical. In an overwhelming number of cases respondents expected Presidents to choose moral means and ends (MM). Using the method of modal responses or peaks this was true in 75 cases, and using the minimal consensus criterion this was true in 67 cases. This finding substantiates our first hypothesis that a higher percentage of the people expect the President to choose a moral course of action rather than an expedient one.

Hypothesis 2. A higher percentage of respondents will expect the President to act in accordance with moral ends than in accordance with moral means.

Much of the same data that we used to test hypothesis 1 was used in testing this hypothesis. The mean averages for expectations about means were compared with the mean averages for expectations about ends found for the twelve dilemmas in each of the seventeen subgroups. (See Table 2.) This comparison showed that in thirteen of the seventeen cases the average for moral ends exceeded the average for moral means. This significantly supports the second hypothesis. The exceptions where expectations of moral means exceeded those of ends included answers by two conservative samples and a Republican subgroup with such expectations of both Eisenhower and Kennedy. This is consistent with the popular conception of conservatism as a style as well as attitudes toward issues.

The results for the second hypothesis using modal, or peak, analysis indicated that moral ends were expected 126 times as compared with 102 expectations of moral means. When the test of consensus was used, greater consensus appeared about expectations of moral ends than moral means. These three tests sustained the second hypothesis.

Hypothesis 3. Although both Democrats and Republicans perceive a President of the opposing party as more moralistic than expedient, Republicans will expect moralistic decisions more frequently from a Democratic President than Democrats will expect from a Republican President.

We derived the third hypothesis from Gabriel Almond and Sidney Verba's chapter on "Patterns of Partisanship" in *Civic Culture*.[12] Their measurements indicated that the left was generally more tolerant of the right than the reverse, except in the United States, where Republicans were slightly more tolerant than Democrats. The hypothesis may be tested by expecting that the American people will prefer the moral decision over the expedient one. However there are some reasons to be cautious about such an equation. Though we have shown that Americans seem to expect the moral choice, this does not mean they consider it the wisest choice or the best one in *all* situations. By examining those issues where a minimal consensus was reached we can see the number of dilemmas in which the expectations of moral ends and means by various subgroups with Kennedy and Eisenhower as President are apparent.

12 *Ibid.*

Table 3 shows a clear correspondence of moralistic expectations when the party of the respondent coincides with the party of the President. Therefore we can accept for this study the equation between "the moral" and "the best." There are four relationships we can examine for both means and ends: the Republicans' attitude toward Kennedy and the Democrats' attitude toward Eisenhower. In three of the four cases the third hypothesis is supported by a small margin and bears out the relationship that Almond and Verba found between Democrats and Republicans in the United States. They indicated that "American responses show least antagonism or polarization between major parties. The Republicans appear to be somewhat more favorably disposed toward the Democrats than vice-versa."

TABLE 3

Minimal Consensus on MM Expectations by Subgroup with Eisenhower and Kennedy as President

President		Subgroups		
	Dem.	Rep.	Lib.	Con.
Eisenhower	2	6	2	6
Kennedy	6	3	5	2

Hypothesis 4. Differences in decision situations will have greater effect upon respondents' expectations than differences in the occupants of the office of the President.

The data indicated considerable variation of expectations with situational differences. To examine the affect of the occupant of the office, we constructed tables like the one in Figure 3 for each situation and held constant the independent variables, party and liberalism or conservatism. In many cases the expectations by each subgroup of the decisions of any occupant of the office in the same situation were similar. Even though there were five basic types of graphs, the same type of graph resulted regardless of the occupant of the office or the group of respondents. Although we found that *both* situation and particular President influence expectations, the situation affected expectations more than the particular occupant of the presidential office. The respondents, however, may not have perceived great differences between Kennedy and Eisenhower and therefore had similar expectations of both. Perhaps if we had questioned the same respondents about more Presidents, their expectations might have varied as much with particular Presidents as with situation. Nevertheless, the modest evidence of this study yields the conclusion that expectations are influenced by both situation and the occupant of the presidential office, but the decision situation has greater influence.

FIGURE 3

Decision Situations

		Office	Eisenhower	Kennedy
Responses	MM			
	ME			
	EM			
	EE			

Although the decision situations were not constructed to fit a typology of situations, nevertheless, respondents' expectations reflected consistencies *as if* they perceived some patterns in the situations. In order to discern what these patterns might be, we grouped the decision situations into four categories: (1) those with a similar context; (2) those with crisis situations; (3) those with domestic situations only and international situations only; and (4) those with bargaining, morality, legitimacy, and security problem situations.

When the situations were grouped according to similarity of contexts, such as the foreign leader involved, the minority group problem, or the amount of federal control, we obtained fourteen groupings with similar responses. When we grouped the decision situations into crisis and non-crisis situations, three of the four crisis situations had matching graphs that clustered at expedient means and moral ends. The crisis response that did not fit this cluster referred to an anticipated crisis, not one described as a present one. (See Appendix, situation I.)

V. CONCLUSIONS

This brief discussion of an exploratory study was designed to test certain hypotheses about activists' expectations. Several limitations of the study qualified its conclusions. One basic limitation was that efforts were made to ensure that respondents expressed their expectations and not their wishes at all times. The term expectation, however, has both probabilistic and evaluational meaning. An expectation of a presidential decision might express what the President should do, as well as what he is likely to do. That the respondents were party activists increased the likelihood that they would express their wishes.

Our sample of Republican and Democratic precinct committeemen expected moral ends and means from their Presidents in the decision situations we presented. The public does expect presidential decisions to conform to established public norms, as defined constitutionally, by statute, or by tradition. A preponderant number of respondents expected the President to choose both moral ends and means although respondents expected the President to choose moral ends more frequently than moral means. Republicans expected Democratic Presidents to be more moralistic than Democrats expected Republican Presidents to be, and liberals had moralistic expectations more often than conservatives.

Expectations varied primarily with the President and with the situation, but the situation influenced expectations more than the occupant of the presidency. The differences in expectations between crisis and non-crisis situations indicate that there are distinct expectations for crisis situations that allow changes in political structure. These structural changes include sharply increased concentrations of presidential authority, a heightened degree of public awareness, and a diminished participation of Congress and interest groups in the decision-making process. Our findings about crisis expectations suggest the need for more extensive research on situational variations in public attitudes toward the President.

An interesting finding is that in some situations the various subgroups did not differ greatly in their expectations. Is this lack of difference one of the reasons for political stability? If so, how do people, regardless of their political party identification or the President in office, acquire expectations of similar actions from our presidential leaders? Is the absence of difference another expression of shared assumptions in American political beliefs and behavior? Does it indicate that citizens feel sure that the President will act in certain predictable ways, regardless of who he is, or who they are?

The evidence that the expectations of political activists tend to be specific to particular decision situations gives rise to more general questions about public attitudes toward leadership. Is the public divided into more sophisticated activists whose orientations toward leadership are specific and instrumental and less active citizens who have more diffuse and expressive orientations? Perhaps these two orientations are not opposites but complement each other. There may be times when expectations are specific — when the issues or decisions involve interests that are close to the individual — and other times when expectations are more diffuse because the issues are more remote.

Further and more refined research about public expectations of presidential leadership, simulated or real, should prove fruitful. More sophisticated investigations might probe expectations and demands in decision situations selected because they fit a typology of situations. It would be useful to employ a sample of respondents chosen in a stratified way according to their degree of political participation or their political roles. This line of research might contribute toward an understanding of leadership because we need to know more about the interaction between followers' expectations and demands upon political leaders in particular situations. We suspect that specific and diffuse expectations of leadership at any given time are meaningful indicators of political stratification in the perceptions of leadership.[13]

13 On the diffuse character of public evaluations, see Donald E. Stokes and Warren Miller, "Party Government and the Saliency of Congress," *Public Opinion Quarterly,* XXVI (Winter, 1962), pp. 531–46.

APPENDIX: PRESIDENTIAL DECISION SITUATIONS

I

The President is now completing his second term and the Vice President has announced that he will run in the coming election for President. But the President regards the Vice President as not competent to lead the country in critical times. The Vice President appears to have a great deal of support in his party. What would you expect the President to do?

Alternatives

A. The President states that he does not have confidence in the Vice President's leadership ability and will not support his candidacy. (MM)
B. The President asks the Vice President to undertake a special mission abroad, knowing that while the Vice President is overseas, the President can quietly but actively throw his support to another candidate. (EE)
C. The President says he is leaving public life and therefore does not feel that he should play an active role in the selection of his successor. (ME)
D. The President appoints the Vice President to the Supreme Court. The following day he announces that he will back another leader. (EM)

II

The President receives a special communication from Khrushchev that provides for a very realistic settlement of the Berlin situation, but the solution proposed will entail a long period of time for its implementation. Mr. Khrushchev emphatically states that the agreement, if signed, must be kept top secret because of the present political situation in the Soviet Union. The President realizes that this is the opportunity to settle a problem that has plagued the world for fifteen years; but to sign this agreement in secret is contrary to constitutional law. What would you expect the President to do?

Alternatives

A. The President will sign the agreement, regardless of the Constitution, feeling that he has eliminated one of the major potential causes of World War III. (EM)
B. The President will not sign the agreement, choosing to use the incident as a means of pressuring Congress to gain more treaty-making powers for the President. (ME)
C. The President will sign the agreement, keeping the agreement secret and timing the announcement with his campaign for reelection. (EE)

D. The President refuses to sign the agreement because to do so would be contrary to the Constitution. (MM)

III

A bill sponsored by the President for medical aid includes setting the salaries of doctors. The bill appears likely to pass in Congress. The American Medical Association declares a national strike as protest against the bill. The President realizes the importance of getting the doctors back to work immediately for the national welfare. There is also tremendous pressure from labor unions and old-age groups in support of this program. These groups are threatening sanctions against the President if he gives in to the doctors. What would you expect the President to do?

Alternatives

A. The President confers with labor leaders and old-age groups, promises them support in their other programs, and vetoes the bill to maintain the national welfare. (EM)
B. In a nationwide television address, the President denounces the doctors, but he privately offers to soften the provisions of the bill that doctors object to. (ME)
C. The President states that in the public interest, regardless of the present oppositon of the doctors, he will sign the bill. (EE)
D. The President intimates that if the doctors will give him support during his election campaign he will reverse his judgment. (MM)

IV

An esteemed neutral leader personally asks the President to designate foreign aid funds to his overpopulated nation for personnel and devices for a national birth control campaign. Religious groups, whose support the President has just gained by the terms of an educational aid bill, attack the proposal while other religious and secular groups support it. If the request is granted, the President will lose support from major religious elements in his own party as well as receive world-wide criticism. At the same time, the President is told by his advisors that foreign aid to emerging nations is not succeeding because of overpopulation. Assistance in birth control represents needed progress in foreign aid at the price of the loss of needed political support. What would you expect the President to do?

Alternatives

A. The President refuses the request in exchange for commitments from the groups opposing the assistance to support him in the next election. (EM)

B. The President grants the request in the name of international cooperation. (ME)
C. The President turns down the request but offers support for a plan in which UNESCO will provide the birth control assistance. (MM)
D. The President tells the opposing groups that he will support the educational assistance they are seeking from the Congress if they will drop their opposition so as to preserve the stability of this vital, overpopulated country. (EE)

V

The President submits a budget to Congress calling for a large increase in spending in all programs, especially the welfare items. This increase in welfare spending is in accord with his campaign promises. The next day the Secretary of the Treasury makes it known at a press conference that he is against such a large increase in welfare spending because it will add to inflation. What would you expect the President to do?

Alternatives

A. The President would appeal to the Secretary to not criticize an item that is needed to take care of an ever increasing part of the population. (MM)
B. The President publicly calls upon the Secretary to reappraise the situation and sends him a private memo that emphasizes that the welfare recipients could be a critical force in the next election. (ME)
C. The President negotiates with the Secretary in order to make the welfare program economically sound. (EM)
D. The President avoids taking public issue with the Secretary while mobilizing his congressional support against the Secretary. (EE)

VI

The President has a new foreign policy program in mind with regard to Latin American states. He doesn't want to entrust its administration to the State Department bureaus, because he believes they are incompetent to handle it. He creates a special position outside the State Department to handle its administration. The Secretary of State is angry and threatens resignation. What would you expect the President to do?

Alternatives

A. The President says that this program is a must and that he will risk the resignation of the Secretary of State. (MM)
B. The President creates the new agency but makes it accountable to the Secretary of State. (EM)
C. The President says that the program has to be independent of the State Department. At the same time, he makes a private agreement

with the Secretary of State allowing him a voice in the agency and policies. (ME)

D. The President assigns the program to the State Department and, in return, the Secretary takes steps to improve the department's administration. (EE)

VII

It has always been a tradition for the President to place a wreath on the Tomb of the Unknown Soldier on Memorial Day. But this is the campaign season, and the President has been invited to speak before a large national convention in California on Memorial Day. There is a good chance that at this convention the President can raise a considerable amount of money to support him in his reelection campaign. What would you expect the President to do?

Alternatives

A. The President attends the national convention in California to promote party unity. (EE)
B. The President stays in Washington and carries out the traditional duties of placing a wreath on the tomb. (MM)
C. The President stays in Washington for the wreath laying ceremony and at a later date throws an elaborate White House dinner for the convention leaders. (ME)
D. The President attends the national convention, issues a proclamation, and asks the Vice President to place the wreath on the tomb. (EM)

VIII

Congress passes a measure that states that labor unions may not use dues money for contributions to political campaigns. The President was elected mainly through the support of organized labor. The legislative program of the President has not been acted upon. It is a fear of the President that Congress will be very hostile to him in the future if he vetoes the measure. He also fears that he may lose labor's support if he does not veto it. What would you expect the President to do?

Alternatives

A. The President vetoes the measure arguing that all groups should be free to make political contributions. (MM)
B. He publicly denounces the sponsors of the bill and, several weeks later, quietly permits the bill to become law. (ME)
C. He accepts the bill promising labor strong support on one of their favorite measures. (EE)
D. The President exchanges patronage with Congress in order to prevent legal discrimination against labor groups. (EM)

IX

During the campaign, the President promised that on his next vacancy he would appoint a Negro to a federal judgeship. The chairman of the Senate Judiciary Committee, a Southerner and a member of the President's party, says that he will "fight the appointment tooth and nail." Southern support is vital to the President's party's control of Congress. The President fears that if he does not appoint the Negro he will lose prestige in Congress and in the country, and, probably, a lot of Negro support, but, on the other hand, that he will lose Southern support if he does appoint him. What would you expect the President to do?

Alternatives

A. The President says he will stand by his appointment because he regards the Negro as without question the most qualified. (MM)
B. He denounces bigotry in Congress and says he will stand by the appointment at all costs, and he does nothing else, giving in to the Senator. (ME)
C. The President promises an appointment of the Senator's own choosing in turn for fulfilling his promise. (EM)
D. He appoints the Negro to an administrative position not requiring Senate confirmation, promising his elevation to a judgeship at the earliest opportunity. (EE)

X

The Secretary of Labor has been hailed as one of the most competent leaders in the history of that department. However, he has made a few enemies in Congress. The President had to clear the Secretary of charges that he had been a Communist prior to his appointment. Months later, the President receives conclusive proof that the Secretary had belonged to the Communist Party in the 1930's. The President feels that the Secretary is almost irreplaceable. Yet, the President fears the political costs to his administration in the event of the Secretary's exposure. What would you expect the President to do?

Alternatives

A. The President exposes the Secretary and dismisses him. (MM)
B. The President finds the Secretary a non-governmental position, and the matter is dropped. (EE)
C. The President institutes an administration security investigation of the executive branch to reassure the public about the past charges. The only result of the investigation is the exposure and departure from office of the Secretary of Labor. (ME)
D. The President explains the situation and asks for the Secretary's resignation in order to maintain public confidence in the government.

The President promises firm and continued support for all the programs the Secretary has previously worked for. (EM)

XI

Telephone operators have been on strike for six months demanding higher wages, shorter hours, and better working conditions. A month after the strike began, the President invoked the Taft-Hartley Law, which provided an eighty-day "cooling off period." This eighty-day period has passed and the operators are still on strike. The disruption in communication has slowed business almost to a standstill. Factories are being shut down and employees are out of work. The President will stand for election in two months. A serious crisis with Russia is developing and defense needs are paramount. What would you expect the President to do?

Alternatives

A. The President pronounces the threat of war and calls for the settlement of the strike for the safety of the American people. (MM)
B. The President calls the union leaders into his office and tells them if they send their workers back to the switchboards, he will give his support to their legislative demands. (EE)
C. The President promises a subsidy to the industry in order to settle the strike in the face of the impending crisis. (EM)
D. The President points out the imminence of the threat to national security and convinces both labor and management to return to work for the duration of the crisis, anticipating this action will bolster his prestige in the coming election. (ME)

XII

For years Laos has received huge financial grants from the United States. A congressional investigation found that most of this money was simply going to line the pockets of the Laotian ruling clique, and the President ordered the grants sharply reduced. The Laotians did not like this move. One week later, reports began reaching the United States that foreign Communist troops had invaded Laos. Responding to appeals from several Asian nations, the President ordered American troops and urgently needed defense materials airlifted to Laos. Two days later, news reports state that no signs of an invasion are evident. What would you expect the President to do?

Alternatives

A. The President states that the Communists in small numbers had indeed infiltrated Laos, but that American military might had scared them off. (ME)

B. The President tells the Laotian elite that our troops will remain until their administration adopts policies in conformity with our foreign aid objectives. (EM)
C. The President claims that had the United States not cut the Laotian assistance program the current crisis would never have occurred. Despite the cost and consequences to us, the country in need of help can count on America. (MM)
D. The President restores financial assistance to Laos, and in return, the Laotian ruler group warmly praises the efficacy of the American action. (EE)

What We Expect the President to Do

Louis Brownlow

Whatever else a President newly come to the White House may look forward to, he will, if he be wise, realize from the first moment that he is certain to disappoint the hopes of many of the members of his constituency who collectively compose the nation. There are at least two reasons in support of this expectation. In the first place, as the President exercises the duties of his high office he will be compelled to make choices, and every choice he makes, whether in respect of measures or of men, will displease or disillusion those who do not agree with him. In the second place — and in the number of citizens affected this is the more important category — the nation expects more of the President than he can possibly do; more than we give him either the authority or the means to do. Thus, expecting from him the impossible, inevitably we shall be disappointed in his performance.

That is merely another way of saying that by custom and tradition as well as by statute and Constitution, we have endowed the Presidency with such lofty attributes that any man chosen by us to be the President, while he is charged with the obligation to aspire, may never quite achieve the full splendor of its lofty heights. That these things are true flows from the fact that we expect the President to symbolize the nation in his office and in his person. It follows, then, that each of us identifies the President with his own private and particular notion of what this nation is and what Americans are. Each person expects the President to mirror that image, and as no two of us have precisely the same idea of

Reprinted by permission of the publisher from Louis Brownlow, *The President and the Presidency* (Chicago: University of Chicago Press, 1949), pp. 52–56, 62–72.

our national being and destiny, we are inevitably disturbed when the man who symbolizes them does not conform to our ideals.

It is precisely because we do so differ that we organize into groups in which these differences of outlook, opinion, and hopes seem smaller, and then by processes of political alchemy organize ourselves into two political parties. One of these parties — sometimes it is the one that puts forward the better candidate, sometimes it is the one with the better platform of promises or the better platform of protests — sees its choice for President become the nation's choice at the polls. The candidate becomes President. Just after he takes the oath of office, many of us — I am inclined to think most of us, perhaps indeed all of us except the few who are professional politicians — tend to forget that he was first a party choice and a party leader. More than that, we seem at this particular stage to regret the necessity for party machinery, and exhibit displeasure at any sign of partisan activity by the President.

At this stage we insist — and in deference to public opinion many Presidents at the commencement of their term of office have publicly proclaimed — that the President is not the President of a party but the President of all the people, as of course he is. Thus is created that phenomenon we call "the Presidential honeymoon." At first, everybody seems to be with the President; he seems to be the man we may count on to continue to do all the things that his predecessor did of which we approved, and upon whom we may rely to correct and redress all the errors made by his predecessor. Even the members of the opposition party (with the exception, perhaps, of the professionals) who proclaimed during the campaign his unfitness for the office, at this stage seem to say: "Well, after all, he's a good fellow Let's back him up and give him a chance." His partisans, of course, hail him as one who will solve all problems.

As the honeymoon draws to its inevitable end, we no longer expect the President completely to fulfill our notions of what the symbol of the nation should be, but by the same token we tend to emphasize and insist upon our expectations that he will do for us certain things. We expect the President to be, first, a competent manager of the machinery of government; second, a skilled engineer of the economy of the nation; and, third, a faithful representative of the opinion of the people. These three expectations I have set down in the inverse order of their importance in popular esteem, but perhaps in their correct order with respect to the choices and decisions the President must make if he is to fulfill to the maximum what the citizens expect of him. Yet it must not be imagined for an instant that because we accept the new President as President of all the people and make manifest our distaste when he too patently shows that he is also party leader, that he can afford to abandon his party role. What is required of him if he is to be successful is that — he become not only the leader of the political party but the political leader of the country as well.

Woodrow Wilson stated this problem in a lecture he gave at Columbia

University in 1907. This was four years before he became Governor of New Jersey and six years before he became President; at a time when he was regarded primarily as a professor and the president of Princeton; at a time when his political powers were for the most part unrecognized; and at a time when he was not *en rapport* with the leadership of his own party — for he was then writing to Mr. Adrian H. Joline the famous letter in which he expressed the wish that he might knock Mr. Bryan into a cocked hat. Speaking of the President of the United States as a political leader, Mr. Wilson said: [1]

> He cannot escape being the leader of his party except by in-capacity and lack of personal force, because he is at once the choice of the party and of the nation. He is the party nominee, and the only party nominee for whom the whole nation votes. Members of the House and Senate are representatives of locali-ties, are voted for only by sections of voters, or by local bodies of electors like the members of the state legislatures. There is no national party choice except that of President. No one else represents the people as a whole, exercising a national choice; and inasmuch as his strictly executive duties are in fact subordi-nated, so far at any rate as all detail is concerned, the President represents not so much the party's governing efficiency as its con-trolling ideals and principles. He is not so much part of its or-ganization as its vital link of connection with the thinking nation. He can dominate his party by being spokesman for the real sentiment and purpose of the country, by giving direction to opinion, by giving the country at once the information and the statements of policy which will enable it to form its judg-ments alike of parties and of men.
>
> For he is also the political leader of the nation, or has it in his choice to be. The nation as a whole has chosen him, and is con-scious that it has no other political spokesman. His is the only national voice in affairs. Let him once win the admiration and confidence of the country, and no other single force can with-stand him, no combination of forces will easily overpower him. His position takes the imagination of the country. He is the representative of no constituency, but of the whole people. When he speaks in his true character, he speaks for no special interest. If he rightly interpret the national thought and boldly insist upon it, he is irresistible; and the country never feels the zest of action so much as when its President is of such insight and calibre. Its instinct is for unified action, and it craves a single leader. It is for this reason that it will often prefer to choose a man rather than a party. A President whom it trusts can not only lead it, but form it to his own views.
>
> It is the extraordinary isolation imposed upon the President by our system that makes the character and opportunity of his office so extraordinary. In him are centred both opinion and party. He

may stand, if he will, a little outside party and insist as if it were upon the general opinion. It is with the instinctive feeling that it is upon occasion such a man that the country wants that nominating conventions will often nominate men who are not their acknowledged leaders, but only such men as the country would like to see lead both its parties. The President may also, if he will, stand within the party counsels and use the advantage of his power and personal force to control its actual programs. He may be both the leader of his party and the leader of the nation, or he may be one or the other. If he lead the nation, his party can hardly resist him. His office is anything he has the sagacity and force to make it.

Thus Mr. Wilson, before he was President, saw that the potentialities of the office were bounded only by the ability of the President for the time being to live up to the nation's expectations. It was in the same series of lectures, published as *Constitutional Government in the United States,* that Mr. Wilson repeated what he had said in 1900 in the Preface to the 15th edition of his *Congressional Government* namely, that the Presidency itself had changed in character because of the Spanish War and the consequent entry of the American Republic into the arena of world affairs, in which the initiative of the President would inevitably enhance the prestige as well as the power of the office. . . .

The expectancy is that the President will be the general manager of the entire machinery of government. It is true that if he undertakes this larger task with vigor and strength of will, he must needs assert himself in his capacity as Chief Legislator, he will have to recommend to the Congress measures that he deems expedient, he will have to report to the Congress on the state of the Union, and sometimes he will have to use or threaten to use his veto. At such times those of us who are opposed to his politics are apt to denounce him for attempting to reduce the Congress to the status of a rubber stamp, and will call him a dictator, and so on. But at the same time, if he does not get his policies adopted by the Congress, we say of him: "He has failed to get along with Congress."

Not only do we expect him to do more than administer the departments and win the assent of the Congress; we expect him also to manage in one way or another those great independent commissions which regulate certain aspects of our economic life, and which have been set up as quasi-legislative or quasi-judicial bodies with the express purpose of keeping them from being dominated by the President. If he attempts to meet this expectation of ours, and — even if successful — does it by the use of any public means or gesture, then with charming inconsistency we complain that he has overstepped the bounds of his office. Thus the President is compelled, in his efforts to meet this general expectation that he be the over-all general manager of the whole federal government, to consider the political expediency of each step he takes and to appraise the political implications of each act in terms not only of party, but also of popular and Congressional politics. As Pendleton Herring has said in his book, *Presidential Leadership:* [2]

> We have created a position of great power but have made the full realization of that power dependent upon influence rather than legal authority. Hence if our president is to be effective, he must be a politician as well as a statesman. He must consider the political expedience of contemplated actions as well as their consistency with his concept of the public interest.
>
> The element of contingency in our system is inherent in the uncertainty of party programs and party discipline. We are apparently willing to give popular support to a president while at the same time rejecting some of his most cherished measures. The president is titular head of the nation, chief legislator, and chief representative, as well as chief executive; we do not necessarily support him in all roles at the same time.

With respect to the narrower range of management, we expect him to coordinate the administrative policies of the far-flung, intricate, and complex maze of federal activities. But he knows that in his attempt to meet our expectations in this field he will encounter opposition, now from this pressure group and now from that; that he will encounter difficulties, now in this geographical section, now in that; that he will run into trouble, now with his own party, now with the opposition. He knows that to the extent that he succeeds he will be denounced by some of us as an autocrat unwilling to delegate authority and to trust his own chosen subordinates. And equally well he knows that if he fails, practically all of us will say: "He was too weak for his job."

In this task of management of the machinery of government what we really expect and require of the President is, then, what has come to be known as top management. A top manager is one who exploits his position by whatever means he can devise to evoke the prime loyalty of divers parts of the great governmental machine, each part being also animated by a loyalty to its particular purpose. Thus the President must have, for example, at the head of the Departments of Agriculture, Commerce, and Labor men who are loyal to the principal purposes of the work entrusted to their departments, and who inevitably will express that departmental loyalty in conflicts of opinion among themselves, thus reflecting pressures from their particular supporters. But at the same time the President must resolve these particularistic differences and evoke the prime loyalty of these department heads to himself and the policies of his administration. Details of execution of these policies will be left to the lieutenants at lower echelons, but the President must be on top: he cannot delegate any part of that supreme task to another. He himself must be able to admonish and restrain his subordinates within his orbit and also be willing to protect and defend them from outside attack; and

2 *Presidential Leadership*, by Pendleton Herring. New York: Farrar and Rinehart, Inc. (copyright now held by Rinehart & Co., Inc.), 1940, p. 2 ff.

on occasion when particularistic loyalties overcome loyalty to the President, he must not hesitate to dismiss a lieutenant and choose another.

We have not put the President into this job as a top manager for the sake of giving him power over the largest and most complex machine in the world, or for the sake of giving someone we like and admire an opportunity to exhibit his skill of manipulation. But we have decided in the Constitution and the laws, in our customs and traditions, that one man and one alone may be top manager (just as we have decided that in war one man and one alone may be top commander) because that is the only way we think we can get results. We may not yet be willing to equip him properly for this job; we may not yet be willing to give him authority commensurate with his responsibilities for this task; but nevertheless we expect him to accomplish it.

Leaving aside for the moment the question of his authority and equipment, we see that here again what we expect of the President is leadership. Top management is not accomplished, even in small organizations, by requiring instant and implicit obedience to precise and particular commands. It is not accomplished by slavish adherence to rigid rules and precise procedures. Top management must, of course, employ the skills of scientific method, but in its expression it is the art of leadership. In a position of supreme responsibility such as that which rests on the President, this art will express itself in persuasiveness, in pervasive persuasiveness. In some Presidents this quality has been described as "charm" (in the case of Franklin D. Roosevelt), as a "winning way" (in the case of Woodrow Wilson), as "strenuosity" (in the case of Theodore Roosevelt). There was, too, the "whimsy" of Calvin Coolidge, but he did not choose to manage.

The second of the great things that we expect of our President is that he be a skilled engineer of the economy of the nation. Couched in the crudest form of political expression, the dictum runs that if the country is prosperous the President gets the credit, if it is not prosperous the President gets the blame. In its more subtle expression, our expectation of the President takes this form: We demand that he so manage the governmental machinery that we have good times and not hard times, and that the diverse sections of the economy be kept in reasonable balance; that in this part of his job the President act as the representative of all the people in the capacity of an impartial umpire rather than as Chief of State; and that he bring about this balanced prosperity through the exercise of his art of persuasion rather than through the exercise of his executive power. . . .

The President is expected to keep management and labor at peace and at the same time to keep industry in balance with agriculture and commerce. The struggle between the mercantile and the agrarian interests was not new when Washington took the oath as the first President; it was the small landowners who, banded together with the mechanics in the towns, overthrew the Federalists and brought Jefferson into the White House; it was the combination of small farmers and day laborers in the cities that ushered in Jackson and the Democratic revolution in 1828; the labor question, slave labor or free labor, divided the Republic almost from its beginning and all but destroyed it in the 1860's. The bankers, manufacturers, and merchants were hard pushed to elect McKinley over the crusading Bryan with his following of discontented farmers and laborers in 1896. Struggles of this kind are not new and they will not soon be ended.

Nevertheless, I think I am on safe ground in saying that not until the time of Theodore Roosevelt did the people of the country consciously expect the President to take the leadership in minimizing the detrimental effects on the public welfare of such conflicts. There had been occasional demands for Presidential action and occasional compliance with those demands, but they seem to have been exceptional.

It was in Theodore Roosevelt's administration that the people turned to the President to act not in his official capacity but as their representative to settle the great anthracite coal strike in Pennsylvania, to alleviate the effects of the banking crisis of 1907, and to prevent the threatened railroad strikes. To bring about a balance, a more equitable relationship among these varying groups, was the avowed purpose of the Square Deal of Theodore Roosevelt, of the New Freedom of Woodrow Wilson, of the New Deal of Franklin D. Roosevelt. It was also the avowed purpose of the other Presidents of this period, although they chose other methods. Only one of them, Herbert Hoover, gave his plan a name — the New Era.

After the first World War there was boom and there was bust. After the recovery from the bust there was inequality. The industrial regions prospered while the agricultural regions lagged. There was boom again and bust again, and then the great depression from '29 to '34, the recovery, the recession of '37, recovery again, and then World War II. Through all this, we have strengthened the emphasis we place on our expectations that the President engineer the national economy and maintain it in balance. And by gradual degrees we have formalized what we expect of the President in the realm of economic activity. In the administration of Herbert Hoover there was legislative sanction for the establishment of the Employment Stabilization Board. Later, the powers of this board were turned over to the National Resources Planning Board, which was set up in the Executive Office of the President during Franklin D. Roosevelt's administration. However, the Congress later abolished it because it was doing something that was deemed sinful: it had undertaken economic planning among other things. Now, under Truman, there has been set up in the Executive Office of the President the Council of Economic Advisers with which the President is expected to collaborate to present to the country and the Congress a continuing program for full employment, a continuing scheme for prosperity, a continuing guarantee against boom and bust. The powers now vested in the new Council of Economic Advisers, it should be mentioned, are practically the same as those of its predecessor, the National Resources Planning Board.

The third great thing that we expect of the President is that he be a faithful representative of the opinion of the people. The people are neither so naive nor so doctrinaire that they imagine the existence of one general opinion that reflects the views of the whole country. Rather they are insistent in their diverse groups that each group has the right opinion; that contrary opinions held by other groups are wrong; that the opinion of their group is right and should prevail as the national opinion; and that the way to bring about that desirable end is to persuade the President to go along with them. Here the processes of persuasion are reversed; they flow not outward from the White House but inward toward it. It is a centripetal, not a centrifugal, force.

Whether they meet as three people in a room or as 3,000 in a convention, the groups pass resolutions telling the President what to do; if they publish a journal, they publicly advise the President how to conduct himself; if they fear a rival group in a particular field, they hasten to claim from the President sole recognition as the representatives of their bailiwick.

One measure of the extent of this persuasive process of the people upon the President is provided by the size of the Presidential mailbag during various administrations. Just recently Mr. Ira Smith, who for fifty years, since McKinley, has been in charge of the mail room at the White House, was interviewed on the fiftieth anniversary of his service. He said that he, and he alone, took care of all mail that came to the President from McKinley's time until the end of the Hoover administration. During that time there had been two peaks. One was in the administration of Theodore Roosevelt, when during the anthracite coal strike the letters for a short time got up to a thousand a day. People did not write very much to Mr. Taft, and during his administration the volume dropped to about 200 a week. Then Wilson came in and the letters went up to an average of a thousand a day during periods of crisis, dropping off after he became ill. They dropped again under Mr. Hoover, and Mr. Smith, having no aid at all, took care of all the letters.

Then F.D.R. came in. One sentence at the conclusion of his inaugural address — "We have nothing to fear but fear itself" — so electrified the nation, recreating its hopes, that it alone brought into the White House 460,000 letters. The Presidential mailbag grew to such proportions that Mr. Smith had to get two additional rooms in the State Department building and accumulate a staff of 50 persons to help him. Throughout the entire twelve years of Franklin D. Roosevelt's administration, the average was more than 5,000 letters a day. It rose at times on the March of Dimes birthday celebration to as high as 150,000 to 175,000 a day. In times of great crises, it would frequently run as much as 25,000 a day for a week. The average of 5,000 over the twelve years of Franklin Roosevelt's administration includes a great falling off in the war years, when sometimes there would be a week or two with only 2,000 or 3,000 letters a day.

The mail under the Truman administration is continuing at about the rate that it was toward the end of the Roosevelt administration, something around 4,000 letters a day. In this huge body of correspondence that flows to the White House all kinds of views and desires find expression. Not all of the letters are written in praise. Many of them are full of denunciation or admonition; some again are appeals for assistance or special consideration.

It must not be imagined, however, that in this category of expectations the people expect the President to represent them only in political matters or economic matters. They press upon him all sorts of things. They extract from him proclamations for Mother's Day, and for Be Kind to Animals Week. They expect him to express their opinion with respect to the necessity of contributing to the Community Chest and see to it that a properly formulated letter is submitted to the White House for his signature. He is sore beset by these importunities. He knows that he must in a measure meet this expectation, but he knows also that at any moment in one of these seemingly minor matters he may stub his toe. Yet the President must always be aware of this third great expectation — that he reflect public opinion. It is addressed not to the party chieftain, not to the head of the government, but to the Chief of State, the man who is the symbol of the nation.

These three expectations I have been examining are great indeed, but they represent simply the methodological aspects of accredited and acknowledged leadership. If the President fails as a leader or if, as he sometimes does, he rejects the role of leader and insists upon keeping himself confined to his strictly legal, strictly constitutional, strictly official duties, then the pressure of the public will be withdrawn, but at the cost of a sense of loss. In that sense of loss the people turn to the future and to the successor of the President, as they did turn from Taft and from Hoover, neither of whom so much failed to lead as refused to lead.

In the endowment of leadership by Constitution and custom, there remains, however, the greatest expectation of all. It is the expectation that the President, with his unquestioned responsibility for maintaining the initiative in foreign affairs, shall keep us at peace; but that if war does come, he shall as Commander-in-Chief lead us to victory. Here again we fail to give him authority commensurate with his responsibility, but despite this failure to provide him with the means of accomplishing what we ask him to do, we still expect the President to give effect to the national purpose.

Reluctantly, tardily, we have apparently come to the conclusion that peace is not a thing apart, but that it must be achieved in a concert of nations. The United States is now a member of the United Nations. And as a consequence of that new relationship the people of the United States now expect their President to do even more. Whether out of pride or out of trepidation, we believe our country to be the greatest nation in the world; we expect our President to lead the nation; we expect him to assume the leadership of the world.

The Presidency — Focus of Leadership

Clinton Rossiter

No American can contemplate the Presidency [today] without a feeling of solemnity and humility — solemnity in the face of a historically unique concentration of power and prestige, humility in the thought that he has had a part in the choice of a man to wield the power and enjoy the prestige.

Perhaps the most rewarding way to grasp the significance of this great office is to consider it as a focus of democratic leadership. Freemen, too, have need of leaders. Indeed, it may well be argued that one of the decisive forces in the shaping of American democracy has been the extraordinary capacity of the Presidency for strong, able, popular leadership. If this has been true of our past, it will certainly be true of our future, and we should therefore do our best to grasp the quality of this leadership. Let us do this by answering the essential question: For what men and groups does the President provide leadership?

First, the President is *leader of the Executive Branch.* To the extent that our Federal civil servants have need of common guidance, he alone is in a position to provide it. We cannot savor the fullness of the President's duties unless we recall that he is held primarily accountable for the ethics, loyalty, efficiency, frugality and responsiveness to the public's wishes of the two and one-third million Americans in the national administration.

Both the Constitution and Congress have recognized his power to guide the day-to-day activities of the Executive Branch, strained and restrained though his leadership may often be in practice. From the Constitution, explicitly or implicitly, he receives the twin powers of appointment and removal, as well as the primary duty, which no law or plan or circumstances can ever take away from him, to "take care that the laws be faithfully executed."

From Congress, through such legislative mandates as the Budget and Accounting Act of 1921 and the succession of Reorganization Acts, the President has received further acknowledgment of his administrative leadership. Although independent agencies such as the Interstate Commerce Commission and the National Labor Relations Board operate by design outside his immediate area of responsibility, most of the Government's administrative tasks are still carried on within the fuzzy-edged pyramid that has the President as its lonely peak; the laws that are executed daily in his name and under his general supervision are numbered in the hundreds.

Many observers, to be sure, have argued strenuously that we should not ask too much of the President as administrative leader, lest we burden him with impossible detail, or give too much to him, lest we inject political considerations too forcefully into the steady business of the civil service. Still, he cannot ignore the blunt mandate of the Constitution, and we should not forget the wisdom that lies behind it. The President has no more important tasks than to set a high personal example of integrity and industry for all who serve the nation, and to transmit a clear lead downward through his chief lieutenants to all who help shape the policies by which we live.

Next, the President is *leader of the forces of peace and war.* Although authority in the field of foreign relations is shared constitutionally among three organs — President, Congress, and, for two special purposes, the Senate — his position is paramount, if not indeed dominant. Constitution, laws, customs, the practice of other nations and the logic of history have combined to place the President in a dominant position. Secrecy, dispatch, unity, continuity and access to information — the ingredients of successful diplomacy — are properties of his office, and Congress, needless to add, possesses none of them. Leadership in foreign affairs flows today from the President — or it does not flow at all.

The Constitution designates him specifically as "Commander in Chief of the Army and Navy of the United States." In peace and war he is the supreme commander of the armed forces, the living guarantee of the American belief in "the supremacy of the civil over military authority."

In time of peace he raises, trains, supervises and deploys the forces that Congress is willing to maintain. With the aid of the Secretary of Defense, the Joint Chiefs of Staff and the National Security Council — all of whom are his personal choices — he looks constantly to the state of the nation's defenses. He is never for one day allowed to forget that he will be held accountable by the people, Congress and history for the nation's readiness to meet an enemy assault.

In time of war his power to command the forces swells out of all proportion to his other powers. All major decisions of strategy, and many of tactics as well, are his alone to make or approve. Lincoln and Franklin Roosevelt, each in his own way and time, showed how far the power of military command can be driven by a President anxious to have his generals and admirals get on with the war.

But this, the power of command, is only a fraction of the vast responsibility the modern President draws from the Commander-in-Chief clause. We need only think back to three of Franklin D. Roosevelt's actions in World War II — the creation and staffing of a whole array of emergency boards and offices, the seizure and operation of more than sixty strike-bound or strike-threatened plants and industries, and the forced evacuation of 70,000 American citizens of Japanese descent from the West

Coast — to understand how deeply the President's authority can cut into the lives and liberties of the American people in time of war. We may well tremble in contemplation of the kind of leadership he would be forced to exert in a total war with the absolute weapon.

The President's duties are not all purely executive in nature. He is also intimately associated, by Constitution and custom, with the legislative process, and we may therefore consider him as *leader of Congress*. Congress has its full share of strong men, but the complexity of the problems it is asked to solve by a people who still assume that all problems are solvable has made external leadership a requisite of effective operation.

The President alone is in a political, constitutional and practical position to provide such leadership, and he is therefore expected, within the limits of propriety, to guide Congress in much of its lawmaking activity. Indeed, since Congress is no longer minded or organized to guide itself, the refusal or inability of the President to serve as a kind of prime minister results in weak and disorganized government. His tasks as leader of Congress are difficult and delicate, yet he must bend to them steadily or be judged a failure. The President who will not give his best thoughts to leading Congress, more so the President who is temperamentally or politically unfitted to "get along with Congress," is now rightly considered a national liability.

The lives of Jackson, Lincoln, Wilson and the two Roosevelts should be enough to remind us that the President draws much of his real power from his position as *leader of his party*. By playing the grand politician with unashamed zest, the first of these men gave his epic administration a unique sense of cohesion, the second rallied doubting Republican leaders and their followings to the cause of the Union, and the other three achieved genuine triumphs as catalysts of Congressional action. That gifted amateur, Dwight D. Eisenhower, has also played the role for every drop of drama and power in it. He has demonstrated repeatedly what close observers of the Presidency know well: that its incumbent must devote an hour or two of every working day to the profession of Chief Democrat or Chief Republican.

It troubles many good people, not entirely without reason, to watch the President dabbling in politics, distributing loaves and fishes, smiling on party hacks, and endorsing candidates he knows to be unfit for anything but immediate delivery to the county jail. Yet if he is to persuade Congress, if he is to achieve a loyal and cohesive administration, if he is to be elected in the first place (and re-elected in the second), he must put his hand firmly to the plow of politics. The President is inevitably the nation's No. 1 political boss.

Yet he is, at the same time if not in the same breath, *leader of public opinion*. While he acts as political chieftain of some, he serves as moral spokesman for all. It took the line of Presidents some time to sense the nation's need of a clear voice, but since the day when Andrew Jackson thundered against the Nullifiers of South Carolina, no effective President has doubted his prerogative to speak the people's mind on the great issues of his time, to serve, in Wilson's words, as "the spokesman for the real sentiment and purpose of the country."

Sometimes, of course, it is no easy thing, even for the most sensitive and large-minded of Presidents, to know the real sentiment of the people or to be bold enough to state it in defiance of loudly voiced contrary opinion. Yet the President who senses the popular mood and spots new tides even before they start to run, who practices shrewd economy in his appearances as spokesman for the nation, who is conscious of his unique power to compel discussion on his own terms and who talks the language of Christian morality and the American tradition, can shout down any other voice or chorus of voices in the land. The President is the American people's one authentic trumpet, and he has no higher duty than to give a clear and certain sound.

The President is easily the most influential leader of opinion in this country principally because he is, among all his other jobs, our Chief of State. He is, that is to say, the ceremonial head of the Government of the United States, the *leader of the rituals of American democracy*. The long catalogue of public duties that the Queen discharges in England and the Governor General in Canada is the President's responsibility in this country, and the catalogue is even longer because he is not a king, or even the agent of one, and is therefore expected to go through some rather undignified paces by a people who think of him as a combination of scoutmaster, Delphic oracle, hero of the silver screen and father of the multitudes.

The role of Chief of State may often seem trivial, yet it cannot be neglected by a President who proposes to stay in favor and, more to the point, in touch with the people, the ultimate support of all his claims to leadership. And whether or not he enjoys this role, no President can fail to realize that his many powers are invigorated, indeed are given a new dimension of authority, because he is the symbol of our sovereignty, continuity and grandeur as a people.

When he asks a Senator to lunch in order to enlist his support for a pet project, when he thumps his desk and reminds the antagonists in a labor dispute of the larger interests of the American people, when he orders a general to cease caviling or else be removed from his command, the Senator and the disputants and the general are well aware — especially if the scene is laid in the White House — that they are dealing with no ordinary head of government. The framers of the Constitution took a momentous step when they fused the dignity of a king and the power of a Prime Minister in one elective office — when they made the President a national leader in the mystical as well as the practical sense.

Finally, the President has been endowed — whether we or our friends abroad like it or not — with a global role as a *leader of the free nations*. His leadership in this area is not that of a dominant executive. The power he exercises is in a way comparable to that which he holds as a leader of Congress. Senators and Congressmen can, if they choose, ignore the President's leadership with relative impunity. So, too, can our friends abroad; the action of Britain and France in the Middle East is a case in point. But so long as the United States remains the richest and most powerful member of any coalition it may enter, then its President's words and deeds will have a direct bearing on the freedom and stability of a great many other countries.

Having engaged in this piecemeal analysis of the categories of Presidential leadership, we must now fit the pieces back together into a seamless unity. For that, after all, is what the Presidency is, and I hope this exercise in political taxonomy has not obscured the paramount fact that this focus of democratic leadership is a single office filled by a single man.

The President is not one kind of leader one part of the day, another kind in another part — leader of the bureaucracy in the morning, of the armed forces at lunch, of Congress in the afternoon, of the people in the evening. He exerts every kind of leadership every moment of the day, and every kind feeds upon and into all the others. He is a more exalted leader of ritual because he can guide opinion, a more forceful leader in diplomacy because he commands the armed forces personally, a more effective leader of Congress because he sits at the top of his party. The conflicting demands of these categories of leadership give him trouble at times, but in the end all unite to make him a leader without any equal in the history of democracy.

I think it important to note the qualification: "the history of democracy." For what I have been talking about here is not the Fuehrerprinzip of Hitler or the "cult of personality," but the leadership of free men. The Presidency, like every other instrument of power we have created for our use, operates within a grand and durable pattern of private liberty and public morality, which means that the President can lead successfully only when he honors the pattern — by working toward ends to which a "persistent and undoubted" majority of the people has given support, and by selecting means that are fair, dignified and familiar.

The President, that is to say, can lead us only in the direction we are accustomed to travel. He cannot lead the gentlemen of Congress to abdicate their functions; he cannot order our civil servants to be corrupt and slothful; he cannot even command our generals to bring off a coup d'état. And surely he cannot lead public opinion in a direction for which public opinion is not prepared — a truth to which our strongest Presidents would make the most convincing witnesses. The leadership of free men must honor their freedom. The power of the Presidency can move as a mighty host only with the grain of liberty and morality.

The President, then, must provide a steady focus of leadership — of administrators, Ambassadors, generals, Congressmen, party chieftains, people and men of good will everywhere. In a constitutional system compounded of diversity and antagonism, the Presidency looms up as the countervailing force of unity and harmony. In a society ridden by centrifugal forces, it is the only point of reference we all have in common. The relentless progress of this continental republic has made the Presidency our one truly national political institution.

There are those, to be sure, who would reserve this role to Congress, but, as the least aggressive of our Presidents, Calvin Coolidge, once testified, "It is because in their hours of timidity the Congress becomes subservient to the importunities of organized minorities that the President comes more and more to stand as the champion of the rights of the whole country." The more Congress becomes, in Burke's phrase, "a confused and scuffling bustle of local agency" the more the Presidency must become a clear beacon of national purpose.

It has been such a beacon at most great moments in our history. In this great moment, too, we may be confident it will burn brightly.

The Myth of the President

Alfred de Grazia

> *For you they call, the swaying mass,*
> *their eager faces turning,*
> *Here Captain! dear father!*   Walt Whitman

"Imagine, if you will, an official body provided for by the Constitution and set up in Washington. It is composed of several hundred men who come from all over the United States. They have large powers. Although they are disciplined by some leadership, particularly expressed in one man, and must direct themselves therefore at certain given national ideals, most of them have their own jobs to think about and are reaching for their own way in life. Though sometimes they act in unseemly haste, they usually take a long time to resolve an issue. They are not necessarily responsive to the 'popular will,' though they swear by it frequently. Individuals among them have often very little information of what others are up to; even the most powerful and best informed among them may be unaware of what is happening either in the group or in the government and outer world. Such is the presidency of the United States."

Such also is the Congress of the United States. The paragraph begins to make two important points about American government: the presi-

Reprinted by permission from Alfred de Grazia, *Republic in Crisis* (New York: Federal Legal Publications, 1965), Ch. 5.

dency is a collective organ of the government; the President is part man and part myth.

By myth is meant that a number of qualities are given to every President that are either quite fictitious or large exaggerations of the real man. The myth is not alone the property of the untutored mind, but of academicians, scientists, newspapermen, and even congressmen.

In fact, much of the difficulty with the institution of the presidency is the overlay of myth and magic on the President. The fatal need for personification of society, animation of ideals, and worship of heroes introduces continuous disorder into the matter-of-fact problems of running a country.

Be it as it may, the Constitution has provided a single chief of state who is both the ceremonial and expressive monarch and the active executive head; the democracy has provided that he be elected by direct popular vote; and it is up to each generation to contain him.

THE PRESIDENT AS EXECUTIVE

In some commonwealths where the legislative is not always in being, and the executive is vested in a single person who has also a share in the legislative, there that single person, in a very tolerable sense, may also be called supreme.

John Locke, *Of Civil Government* (1690)

In a hundred places the President-at-work is described. The description usually contains a listing of his duties and powers. The implication is that he takes care of these matters personally. Actually, the President does almost nothing by himself. He is surrounded by staff. The Executive Office numbers over 1500 persons, of which a third pertain to the White House, and another third to the Bureau of the Budget, the rest falling in various special agencies such as the Council of Economic Advisers, the National Security Council, and others.

The Central Intelligence Agency is usually included in the Executive Office of the President and numbers some thousands of employees. But then also the heads of agencies and just about anyone else in the executive establishment and a number of outside consultants are at the beck and call of the President. Thus the decision-making of the President can take on the aspects of crowd behavior, or, when organized, the conciliar decision-making of Congress.

On a normal issue that comes before the "President" some dozens of persons are involved. It might be presumptuous to say that more of a collectivity is engaged than when the same type of issue would come before the Congress; but it would be equally presumptuous to say that *fewer* persons were taken up with the matter. Stephen Horn shows, for instance, how dozens of executive officials became involved in the development of a White House position with respect to Senator Kefauver's bill to set up a question period in Congress. All the while, World War II was going on, but the President and cabinet officers became seriously involved too.

To take another example, despite the gross haste with which it was actually designed, the anti-poverty bill of 1964 was proudly described by Sargent Shriver, introducing it in congressional committee hearings, as the product of dozens of informed opinions in the executive agencies.

On the whole, probably *more* persons occupy themselves with the executive's policy than with the legislature's and for longer periods of time. But the character of their involvement differs greatly. The executives file politely aboard; the congressmen sometimes swamp the boat of policy in launching it.

It would perhaps be permitted to say that the President has a determinative voice on the normal issue that the presidency takes up whereas the top oligarchs of the Congress pay more courtesy to one another's determinativeness. (Yet President Truman *did* say: "One word from me, and everyone does as he pleases!")

It might also be permissible to say that the President is the step-up transformer for more initiatives than any one of the congressional oligarchs; that is, one can say a little more accurately "to get a new national policy, get the President's support" than "to get a new national policy, get the Speaker's support" or "to get a new national policy, get the support of the Speaker and the Majority Floor Leader." Still, no matter how carefully these ideas may be phrased, they are bound to appear incredible to the vast majority of people in America and the world outside. The President is an image of power to get things done, the Congress is not.

The President is a Congress with a skin thrown over him. Let us suppose that we have a gymnast executing various movements that end in a good round of applause. As he appears to the naked eye, he seems well-coordinated, graceful, smooth, tireless, and properly directed. But let the eye of the watcher perceive the true action of the muscles, the organs, and the mind beneath the skin, and he will observe all the near-misses, the strains, the compensated inadequacies, and the poisons formed, gathered, and discharged through the system under exercise. The hesitancies of muscle and mind that must accompany even the best performance will be visible. Should he be harsher in his judgment of the athlete exposed than the athlete covered? The President is the athlete covered; even the presidency, the collectivity, is the athlete covered because it operates under all the fictions of the single person. The Congress is of course the athlete exposed.

Presidents can come from private life, from Congress, and from governorships. If they are mediocre before they become President, they immediately lose that quality and become heroes. It is doubtful that the average President is of greater education, oratorical ability, IQ, experience in governmental affairs or physical beauty than the average Congressman. In fact, Lord Bryce, the well-known commentator upon

American institutions at the end of the last century, thought fit to write an answer to the question: why great men are not chosen Presidents. Perhaps he begged the question. It can be argued far into the night that Presidents are no less "able" than Prime Ministers of England, French Premiers, and Russian Czars and dictators. Since such arguments would be more than likely on a completely confused plane, it would be best to eschew them. The only point of consequence here is that the office makes the man, very much as in the slogan that "clothes make the man."

And the President plays to the office. His first term is filled with reelection politics: he is primarily creating a personal image that might dwarf any potential opponent in the reelection campaign to come. Congress responds with resentment, and the build-up of paranoia in the legislative branch commences, so that the business of government can never be conducted in a matter-of-fact way. Each branch must fortify itself and perceive in the other not the normally cooperative or conflicting humans, but a spiteful menace.

The President, one personalized being, has the advantage with the mass media and the general public. Under the tutelage of journalists and historians, they speak of him as the author of the years of government in which he serves — the Administration of Jefferson, of Jackson, of Buchanan, of F. D. Roosevelt. It would not only be psychologically more healthful, given republican premises, to reduce American national history to congressional periods rather than presidential ones, but it would be scientifically more accurate in that the more regular changing of Congress each two years produces greater effects typically, even given the same presidential incumbent, than the change of Presidents. That this is so little done, except precisely among those expert in government, is indicative of the connection between personification and reputation for power.

The myth of the President is thus wrapped up in the fictions of a single heroic leader, which defies the truth of the normalcy of the typical President and the collectivity of his behavior. Many more myths are related to the central one and derived from it, creating a veritable fairyland.

One myth begins with the Constitution. It has it that the President is responsible for seeing that the laws shall be faithfully executed. We do not speak here of the growth in the legislative power of the President. It is well known that every last opportunity for leverage in the constitutional powers of the President has been used to increase his powers. This is no myth; the Constitution has simply been stretched and interpreted to accommodate the development. We speak rather of the fiction that the President executes the laws. He cannot do so personally, of course. Once he might, today he cannot. The President in a real sense is no longer the President.

There is a grand irony. The more powers that are put to the President to swallow, the less of a constitutional President he can be in reality. But not in fiction. The law of agency is a marvelous and mysterious creation of the human mind over many centuries from its birth in the great

Roman legal system. By its operations, people are said to do things that they not only do *not* do but that are actually not known to them as having been done by anybody else. The trouble caused by this situation is not so much that it occurs, because indeed it must occur out of the plethora of business, but that it is believed *not* to occur and therefore people act in terms of its "truth" rather than in terms of its utility.

In part the President is an office, the presidency, whose head knows what is going on in government and has something to say about it. Secondly the President is an office whose head knows what is going on but has nothing to say about it. Thirdly, the President is an office whose head does not know what is going on and has nothing to say about it. There is a little of the first in the presidency, a good deal of the second, and a great amount of the third. It is well to understand this fact. The Constitution provided for the President; it did not provide explicitly for the presidency; nor could it provide for an all-seeing all-doing executive. The President should be seen as a person furnished with a license to capture as much as he can, and as Congress will let him, of the flora and fauna of a gigantic reservation. He should not be regarded as a highly efficient omniscient commander of a vast country.

Majority (Minority) Champion

The artistic ability of Thrasymachus seems to me to have gained him victory in the field of pathetic expressions on old age and poverty. Really, he has acquired ability to stir a whole crowd of people at one and the same time to frenzy and then to charm them out of it by magic, as he said. He has become very good, too, at attacking or answering allegations on almost any basis.

Plato, *Phaedrus*

Many feel regretful that the President cannot oversee and do everything. The President is the only true representative of the people, they believe. If he does not command the apparatus of the government and society, he should. So says for example, Theodore Roosevelt. Woodrow Wilson from whom the theory of the omnipotent President sprang full-blown puts the case appealingly:

> His is the only national voice in affairs. Let him once win the admiration and confidence of the country, and no other single force can withstand him, no combination of forces will easily overpower him. . . . If he rightly interpret the national thought and boldly insist upon it, he is irresistible; and the country never feels the zest of action so much as when its President is of such insight and calibre. Its instinct is for unified action, and it craves a single leader. . . . A President whom it trusts can not only lead it, but form it to his own views. . . . If he lead the nation, his party can hardly resist him. His office is anything he has the sagacity and force to make it. (*Constitutional Government in the United States*, 1907, pp. 67–9.)

Wilson rightly placed the President as potential popular idol, and declared that even the political party would bow before the people's anointed. Ordinary reasoning and logical behavior are useless before the rush of public emotions. The President represents by his personality and by a free choice of issues to place before the country. Unlike Congress, he can conceal his doubts in his inner office and behind seeming action. For so powerful is the amplification of the press behind the President that his expressions are taken for action itself and an expressed will to save the country from Disaster X is taken in the absence of vivid proof to the contrary to *actually* saving the country.

Despite all of this force, on many occasions the President cannot be said to represent the nation but is asserted to do so by those who command the written word. Such occurrences are common when the nation is well-off and the attention given politics is small or an issue is abstract or principled and discourages mass participation. Examples would be found in Truman's efforts to repeal the Taft-Hartley Act, and Roosevelt's attempt to increase the Supreme Court's membership. Strenuous presidential efforts could not raise a great favorable public. Yet since the President is "liberal" by the nature of his office and the character of his constituency, and since the writers about politics and government are largely liberal, the President is alleged to have a pipeline to the great people that he in fact does not have.

In a literal sense, in fact, no American President has been the proven choice of a majority of the people. Suffrage restrictions, indirect election of the President, apathy among potential voters are only several reasons why this is true. On a dozen occasions, among them Lincoln in 1860 and Wilson in 1912 and 1916, the winning presidential candidate received less than a majority of votes cast. But what begins non-logically cannot be destroyed by logic. Where a majority cannot be found, a plurality will do, or in the end just a bigger crowd.

If the President represents the whole people, he would not so often represent the minorities; yet the latter is the reputation that he also bears. The President does represent some minorities. He may have felt a majority pulse in going into the first World War, but he did not feel the pulse of the German-American minority who saw the war as a conflict of self-interested European powers, with America as a dupe of England. He may have supported the aspirations of Negro minorities a generation later in civil rights matters but could not be said to express the views of other urban minorities who wished to check the liberties of Negroes. All of this is said without need to mention the many sectional minorities that have been represented or not represented by the presidency in history, such as the South.

One must conclude that far from representing the majority or the minorities, or for that matter the "little people" who through the ages have always looked to remote ruling figures for succor, the President represents now one and now another and then again both at the same time. He is the champion of the minority when the minority is angry, critically positioned, and uses its votes (perhaps for lack of other weapons of social justice). He is the champion of the majority when the majority is alert and demanding. He is the representative of the "little people" in any case, and of the minority and majority in all cases except the above, too, whenever he engages in the thousands of acts and expressions of daily life that show the head of state to be not only ordinarily human but more so.

ADVOCATE OF THE PUBLIC INTEREST

Of the three forms of government, the democratic form, in the real meaning of the word, is necessarily a despotism, because it establishes an executive power; for the "all" which is not really all decides concerning, and sometimes against, the one who has not participated in the decision. The general will is a contradiction to itself and to freedom.   I. Kant

Stemming no doubt from his image as representative of the whole people is the prevalent myth that the President's views constitute the public interest or the national interest. We have already given grounds for believing that the idea of a national interest is approximately the same as that of the public interest with the national security element added, and that the public interest is whatever one asserts to be good for the country and is agreed with by others. The others, of course, can be few, many, or practically everybody. To say that the President is custodian of the public interest or of the national interest is presumptuous. The President is custodian of *a* public interest, his own, and that may be popular or not, shared by Congress or not. In short, he is no better off than any other citizen in supplying a public philosophy, except that he has more power to implement his views.

Actually, if anything is meant by the slippery expression, it is that, because of how he is chosen and because of his role in the system, the President will emphasize certain policies and propound certain ideas. It appears, for example, that it is very difficult for a federalist, "voluntarist," decentralizing, "isolationist" politician to be elected President, or if elected President to espouse such policies. Neither Robert Taft nor Dwight D. Eisenhower could move ahead at the presidential level with his original notions.

On the other hand, it is perfectly possible for a man to rise to eminence in Congress with such views. Robert Taft, Howard Smith, Styles Bridges, and William Knowland are several of many cases that could be offered in proof.

At the same time, opponents of such views may likewise lead Congress: one thinks of Rayburn, Humphrey, McCormack, or Lucas. Does that mean that Congress lacks the key to the public interest that the President has? Not at all. It means that congressional leadership may be coming up with an alternative conception of public interest, which may be accepted or rejected by citizens as they please. Was President Jackson acting in the public interest when he wrecked the United States Bank?

Should Grant have annexed Santo Domingo? The secret service policy of Theodore Roosevelt, the cabinet appointments of Hayes, the denial of access to public papers by Cleveland — in these and many other cases Congress and the President clashed vehemently.

Take the Cleveland incident. Congress must have a relatively unrestricted access to public agency information if it must legislate. Cleveland dismissed over 600 officials without cause and by denying Congress access to the papers on their dismissals prevented it from judging the adequacy or even the legality of the dismissals. The aware public apparently supported Cleveland. One might reasonably argue that the public interest was on the side of Congress.

All of which should be obvious, save that people (and scholars) are usually shortsighted and uninterested in indirect consequences. Few of the many dozens of books written about Congress and the President suggest that the Congress may be as amply expressive of the public interest as the President. This becomes indeed a great hurdle in achieving a permanent balance of power between the executive and legislative.

Professor Lawrence Chamberlain not so long ago prepared an analysis of leading legislation over a fifty-year period, in an endeavor to see what were the origins of the laws. They are listed [in Table 1] as they were found by him to have originated in the Congress, in the office of the President, in both equally, or through the efforts of lobbyists. We shall comment upon the origins of the laws later. The important conclusion to be suggested here is that only the most presumptuous of partisans would be able to see in the list of laws a correlation between the presidency (or the Congress for that matter) and laws in the public interest.

Two among various reasons for the continued adherence of the notion of public interest to the presidency may be suggested. One is that Congress passes a great number of private bills and bills affecting localities. It constantly rises, too, in support of individuals being abused. This gives the impression of localism, and partialism. The fact that the executive branch of government from day to day engages in hundreds of thousands of similar actions, as part of its obligation, does not reflect back upon the President. The congressman cannot turn down even some dubious cases and must fight for many an unromantic petitioner; the President can confine his special acts to giving medals to heroes, a hero by definition being a person already certified to be in the public interest.

At the other end of the spectrum of actions, the President derives identification with the public interest from the fact that he is concerned with foreign affairs and military security. Naturally, here in a vast area where there are no constituents, the national interest appears plain, and the President is its custodian. This image seeps back into the domestic areas of policy and lends a convincing quality to presidential pretenses in this area as well.

Furthermore, the government, the public, and the nation are tied up together semantically; as words they hang together and permit any one of five million federal employees to impress a private citizen with the

TABLE 1
Origin of Legislation [1]

PRESIDENTIAL INFLUENCE PREPONDERANT

Agriculture	1	Agricultural Adjustment Act of 1933.*
Banking	3	Silver Purchase Repeal Act of 1893; Emergency Banking Act of 1933; Gold Reserve Act of 1934.*
Business	3	Securities Act of 1933; * Securities and Exchange Act of 1934; * Public Utilities Holding Company Act of 1935.*
Credit	3	War Finance Corporation Act of 1918; Reconstruction Finance Corporation Act of 1932; Home Owners' Loan Corporation Act of 1933.*
Immigration	0	
Labor	1	Second Employers' Liability Act of 1908.*
National Defense	6	Militia Act of 1903; General Staff Act of 1903; Selective Service Act of 1917; Naval Construction Acts of 1901–1905; Naval Construction Act of 1916; Navy Act of 1938.*
Natural Resources	0	
Railroads	0	
Tariff	2	Underwood Act of 1913; * Reciprocal Trade Agreements Act of 1934.*

$\overline{19}$

CONGRESSIONAL INFLUENCE PREPONDERANT

Agriculture	2	Capper-Volstead Act of 1922; * McNary-Haugen bills, 1924–1928.*
Banking	6	Currency Acts of 1873; * 1878; * 1890; * 1900; * 1908; * Glass-Steagall Act of 1933.*
Business	1	Sherman Act of 1890.*
Credit	3	Federal Farm Loan Act of 1916; * War Finance Corporation Revival Act of 1921; * Agricultural Credits Act of 1923.*
Immigration	9	Chinese Exclusion Act of 1882; * Chinese Exclusion Act of 1892; * General Immigration Acts of 1882; * 1903; * 1907; * 1913; * 1917; * 1921; * 1924.*
Labor	3	Department of Labor Act of 1913; * Second Child Labor Act of 1919; * Norris-LaGuardia Act of 1932.*
National Defense	4	National Defense Act of 1916; * National Defense Act of 1920; Selective Service Act of 1940; * Naval Disarmament Act of 1920–21.*
Natural Resources	2	Carey Act of 1894; * Act of 1897.*
Railroads	3	Interstate Commerce Act of 1887; * Valuation Act of 1913; * Transportation Act of 1920.*
Tariff	2	Wilson Act of 1894; * Payne-Aldrich Act of 1909.*

$\overline{35}$

TABLE 1 (*Continued*)

JOINT PRESIDENTIAL-CONGRESSIONAL INFLUENCE

Agriculture	3	Agricultural Marketing Act of 1929; * Soil Conservation Act of 1936; Agricultural Adjustment Act of 1938.*
Banking	4	Federal Reserve Act of 1913; * Thomas Silver Amendment of 1933; * Silver Purchase Act of 1934; * Banking Act of 1935.*
Business	2	Clayton Act of 1914; * National Industrial Recovery Act of 1933.*
Credit	2	Federal Home Loan Bank Act of 1932; * Emergency Farm Mortgage Act of 1933.*
Labor	4	First Employers' Liability Act of 1906; * First Child Labor Act of 1916; * National Labor Relations Act of 1935; * Wages and Hours Acts of 1938. *
National Defense	3	Army Act of 1901; * Naval Construction Act of 1929; * Naval Construction Act of 1934.*
Natural Resources	7	General Revision Act of 1891; * Newlands Act of 1902; * Weeks Act of 1911; * Migratory Bird Act of 1913; * Migratory Bird Treaty Act of 1918; * Migratory Bird Refuge Act of 1929; * Taylor Grazing Act of 1934.*
Railroads	4	Hepburn Act of 1906; * Mann-Elkins Act of 1910; Emergency Railroad Transportation Act of 1933; Transportation Act of 1940.*
Tariff	0	
	29	

PRESSURE GROUP INFLUENCE PREPONDERANT

Labor	1	Railway Labor Disputes Act of 1926.*
Natural Resources	1	Clarke-McNary Act of 1924.*
Railroads	1	Elkins Act of 1903.
Tariff	4	McKinley Tariff Act of 1890; * Dingley Tariff Act of 1897; * Fordney-McCumber Tariff Act of 1922; * Hawley-Smoot Tariff Act of 1930.
	7	

---

[1] Of the ninety major laws studied, approximately twenty per cent fall to the credit of the President; roughly forty per cent were chiefly the product of Congress; about thirty per cent fall into the joint presidential-congressional category; and slightly less than ten per cent are identified as primarily the handiwork of external pressure groups.

* An asterisk indicates that one or more bills dealing with this subject had been introduced without administration support and had received substantial consideration of Congress before the administration took a definite position.

allegation that only the nation, that is, the national employee, can define what the national interest is, and only the public, that is, the public servant, may define the public interest. These distortions of meaning are none the less effective for being childish; the vast presidential constituency is not the best educated constituency to be found. It operates on a rather low level of political awareness, information, and skill.

RESPONSIBILITY AND INITIATIVE

Shell game. A sleight-of-hand swindling game in which a small pellet, the size of a pea, three walnut shells are used, and the victim bets as to which shell conceals the object; hence, any game in which the victim has no chance to win.
                    Webster's New International Dictionary

If the President lacks a monopoly of the national interest, may he not still be the center of responsible government? "The Buck Stops Here," said the little sign by President Truman's desk; no matter who may "pass the buck" to someone else in an evasion of responsibility, the President — luckily for the nation — cannot evade final responsibility.

This is another myth. What are election campaigns but at least large-scale efforts at claiming credit, that is responsibility, and disclaiming blame, that is "passing the buck"? And on a smaller scale, the campaigning goes on all the time. The President, it is true, is charged with signing certain documents, cutting various ribbons, and even with the giving of an indubitable (momentarily) order to fire a great missile volley upon an enemy. But only the veritable acts in themselves are inescapably his. Everything else about them may be passed off, concealed, distorted, parcelled off, and denied. An equally true little sign could read "If it's bad for us, kick it around until it gets lost."

In days of old, it was both a childlike belief and a formal myth of the law that "the king can do no wrong." All mistakes were ascribed to officials and outsiders. One must not imagine of course that the king always escaped political blame. The myth had its limits of acceptance, depending upon conditions, and so with the President. Indeed, the President, though better situated to receive the benefits of this myth than anyone in the country and far more its beneficiary than anyone likes to admit, is more readily blamed than many a chief officer of American business corporations such as the General Electric Company, or benevolent associations such as the Ford Foundation. Yet the blame is not lightly ascribed to the President: it is rare indeed that a public opinion poll of the nation will show a majority who will not say: "The President is doing a good job."

Devotees of the presidency are fond of the phrase "strengthening the responsibility of the President," by which they mean usually "making the President more powerful." If the idea is that of trying to gather together all of the mistakes that several million federal employees can make all over the world and laying them upon the presidential doorstep, it is mad. If the idea is one of making the presidency so strong that it can suppress and control the evidences of malfeasance and neglect from all over, the idea has possibilities.

If the idea is to make the President "who is responsible to the people by election" now "responsible in fact for all that the people elect him for," we must ask what in fact the people do make him responsible for. The "people's mandate" is a term that may satisfy newspaper editors and even many congressmen, but rarely a careful scholar or expert upon opinion. When the people's mandate is boiled down, what remains is "get in" or "get out." And in the case of Presidents, no matter what they have done in their first term, it usually says "stay in." Such general expressions are scarcely calculated to assist the President in being "responsible."

It is probable that the more sophisticated advocates of "placing greater responsibility" upon the President and "making the government responsible to the President" are actually urging a greater coordination and integration of government — in the departments, the separate independent commissions, the Congress, and the state governments. Again the President is to be given greater powers. He is pictured as the Great Coordinator and Integrator.

Yet the President is already charged with so many responsibilities that he has enlarged his staff by several hundred times in the last century. If he is to be given even more extensive powers of making determinations for the agencies, for the Congress, and for the country as a whole, it stands to reason that he will not make the determinations himself but will turn them over (if he ever receives them personally at all) to subordinates. These are not and would not really be "subordinates"; they make the final determinations in a great many important cases and only by fiction and by courtesy are called "subordinates."

If we are to confine our analysis only to the present, we do not see in the operations of the presidency a degree of coordination and integration of work that is higher than that to be observed in Congress. Nor do we discuss the larger executive establishment here. Confining oneself to the thousand-man Congress-cum-assistants body and the thousand-man President-cum-staff-and-associates, that is, the presidency — which body functions in a more integrated, coordinated, and efficient way? To answer such a question, it must be asked, what are the veritable measures of such performance? These are not impossible to devise.

Comparing Congress and the presidency:

1. Which body's members know more about what their co-members are doing?
2. Whose members know more about what the other body is doing?
3. Whose members know more about what the bureaucracy is doing?
4. Whose members know more about what is going on in the country?
5. In which body does an idea have the greatest chance of being born, and once born, of achieving some consideration?

6. In which body does an idea that is to be ultimately adopted pursue a path that a group of outside scientists and experts on logic, intelligence operations, and administrative procedure would say bring to bear the more powerful interests and instruments of intelligence?

7. In which group does an order by the top leadership obtain the quickest response throughout the group?

8. Which group's ordinances obtain the quickest response in the country and in the executive establishment at large?

9. In which group is a policy originated and processed into final form most quickly?

10. Which group can give the most ready and thorough response to problems arising out of the operations of the executive establishment?

Here are ten criteria of coordination, integration, and efficiency, three terms that are almost useless and certainly dangerous unless they are qualified. To every one of these ten questions, the general answer may very well be: "Congress." And if such is the answer, then a serious indictment may be read to the numerous contingents of experts upon government who over many years have played upon these supposedly neutral and scientific terms to transform the nature of American society and government from a republican form to an executive system.

It is untrue that congressional work is generally undertaken in confusion, without expert knowledge and planning, and without consideration of all points of view. Sometimes when this happens, as with the "War on Poverty" Bill of 1964, the faults lie with the President. It is a myth that the presidency embodies more discipline, foreknowledge and expertness.

The scientific planning, technocracy, and scientific management movements in America have in this century produced an image which, transferred to the presidency, has provoked this myth. Rational foresight, long-range planning, and full and deliberate consideration of alternatives are supposed to be features of the top executive. If they are not already, they would be, save for an obstructionist attitude on the part of old-fashioned congressmen. In a fat work which is good on details but short on general order and intelligence, Professor Holcombe has written, "The experience of the generations under the Constitution has taught that only Presidents, and candidates for the presidency, can conveniently produce plans for the effective use of the legislative powers of Congress."

Holcombe himself gives examples of the contrary and there is no firm basis for his conclusion. In fact, both the presidency and the Congress plan for the most part unscientifically. Their capacity to use applied social science — economics, sociology, and administration — is untutored and inadequate. Yet that Congress is worse in this regard is doubtful. Holcombe might more accurately have said that "the teachers of the constitution have lately taught that only Presidents . . . etc."

So far as sheer knowledge is concerned (and knowledge is after all *one* concern of good planning), Congress is superior to the presidency. So much is admitted by writers who may be in the course of appealing for more permanence in the high offices of the executive branch. As the Second Hoover Commission reported: ". . . Men of long experience just change places in the Congress in taking over the important committee posts. The Congress continues to have men of experience in its important positions, and a large pool from which to draw these people, while the executive branch tends to get a group of limited political experience in the highest political positions of secretary, under secretary, and assistant secretary." [2]

The President himself and his immediate staff may or may not have extensive governmental and political experience. Still there are and will always be a group of congressmen who know more about any single agency than does the Chief Executive. They are the only people, these congressmen, who know any considerable amount about the agency outside of the civil servants running the agency. Their potential great value must be admitted, even if their realization of it for the national good be doubted.

But is knowledge used for planning? Individual congressmen may be experts, but does the whole Congress have a program? The answer must be first a question: "What is a plan?" And what are the limits of planning? So that we have four questions from one. Congress has only a very limited notion of planning and programming. The noblest effort in that direction in recent history, and perhaps since the Radical Republicans of the reconstruction period, was that of Senator Robert Taft in the Eightieth Congress, 1946–48. He had several proposals, inter-related and consistent generally with his philosophy. But this was not treated too well by his colleagues and only part of it was enacted.

Holcombe records that "only two congresses, the Fifty-first (1889–1891), which was Republican, and the Fifty-third (1893–1895), which was Democratic, were able to execute comprehensive party programs. Both of these programs the voters promptly repudiated at the polls." (p. 210) It cannot be ventured that a certain way to political success is a program, even a successful one.

In consequence, it is not surprising that Presidents, too, lack comprehensive programs in the valid sense of the term. A program, or plan, is ordinarily defined as a group of proposals connected by a set of consistent underlying principles. If this is too strict a definition, it may at least be said that a program cannot be whatever the President may wish at any given moment. But that in fact is the way in which the word is used by the presidential party and to a large extent adopted by the press and Congress. The President's program is more a smorgasbord than a diet, but whatever he wants is called part of his program.

It is actually his calendar, that is, those matters that he hopes at any given moment to get congressional action on before the next time he revises the calendar. Thus in 1962–64, a strong Civil Rights bill was part

[2] Commission on Organization of the Executive Branch of the Government, *Personnel and Civil Service* (1955), p. 220.

of the President's "program"; it was accelerated or decelerated with changing conditions, and at times was bypassed by other bills such as agricultural support bills.

When the President, as has been the practice for the past several terms, presents to the country at the beginning of each year in his State of the Union message, a long list of goals, he again does not present a program and certainly not a plan, at least not by our terms. For his program is a stringing-together of a great many things that he would like to do for the country — a few of which are concrete enough to be legislative proposals and fewer still of which would be enacted into law. Therefore, one would not be doing the presidential system an injustice to say that the President's program is another myth of the presidency.

It is even doubtful whether the President should be conceded to have more initiative than the Congress, although the impressive sort of listing of goals that was just referred to would seem to clinch the title of the Great Legislator for him.

It has become the pattern in the last generation for Presidents to have rousing, if childish, slogans. "The New Deal," "The Fair Deal," "The Great Crusade," "The New Frontier," "The War Against Poverty" and "The Great Society" help create the impression that the President has creative ideas, energy, and a program. Sober reality testifies to the contrary. Becoming President is too much a merry-go-round to fix a program in mind. Staying President is too dizzying to remedy the lack.

Neither Congress nor the presidency produces programs in the logical long-range sense. Individual laws are another matter.

Lawrence Chamberlain's documented survey of the origins of major legislation shows, for example, that the Congress was the source of many more important laws over a period of half a century than the presidency. (See Table 1.) A large group of laws was, to be sure, attributed to the joint efforts of both congressmen and presidency. Perhaps the situation has changed to give the President more of the initiative in the past few years. This is doubtful, however, once the cobwebs of myth are wafted away from the hard facts.

Between 1953 and 1963 less than 50% of the legislation proposed by the President were enacted into law. Those enacted were only one-third of all laws enacted. These were the findings of a Congressional Quarterly survey. For instance, in 1959 Congress approved 93 of the 228 proposals submitted by President Eisenhower; in 1963 it passed 109 of the 401 proposals of President Kennedy. Still these are only surface indications: the President often proposes hopeless bills; further, his ideas often come from congressmen originally. The Peace Corps, for example, would be remembered by most people as President Kennedy's creation. Actually its creator might better be said to be Congressman Reuss of Wisconsin.

The story of Congress, though that of a marvellously organized machine from one perspective, is, from an equally valid perspective, a set of biographies of legislative heroes, men who have by themselves or with a couple of colleagues worked strenuously and brilliantly to originate, research, develop, and enact into law through the tortuous mazes and disheartening obstacles of the legislative and executive processes some vision of a better arrangement of human relations in society.

TIME, SPEED, AND CRISIS

Banded together as they are — working a system which, like all systems, necessarily proceeds in great measure by fixed rules — the official body are under the constant temptation of sinking into indolent routine, or, if they now and then desert that mill-horse round, of rushing into some half-examined crudity which has struck the fancy of some leading member of the corps.

J. S. Mill, *On Liberty*

It is also a myth that more time is wasted in Congress than in the presidency. The President's time is "wasted" in many ways, some of them impossible of reform, as the time he must spend with numerous minor potentates, and signing a great many letters and documents as Head of State. Other time he may choose to spend on petty matters, taking a day to name a boat, or three days to appoint a postmaster of Pittsfield, to use examples from the schedule of John Kennedy. Actually it may be offered for consideration that the President is so much needed for the petty ceremonials of government that he cannot possibly be an executive and should not be given the more serious tasks of running the great agencies and studying the processes of legislation on numerous substantive questions.

Since the President's time is so occupied, it is likely to be a myth also that "speed and dispatch are the characteristics of the presidency" in contrast to Congress. A new idea born in a bureau will normally take several years to grow to acceptable maturity in a budget message of the President. Another year for the test of the legislative process is required for final acceptance. If the Congress were eliminated from the process, the idea would simply move more slowly through the executive offices. An idea born in congressional circles often shortcuts or speeds through several bureaucratic echelons. What passes for "speed and dispatch" in the presidency is usually emergency action — referred to variously as "fire-fighting," "trouble-shooting," "crash programs," "disaster relief," etc. And of course there are the prompt responses to foreign aggression against American interests, which the presidency has the power to make, with or without simultaneous consultation with congressional leaders. This species of emergency action, civil and military, has produced an unwarranted reputation for speed and dispatch on affairs in general.

To expand the domain of the presidency further, the whole area of governmental powers has been opened up by the doctrine of the age of crisis. The "age of crisis," the "permanent crisis," the "cold war," the "critical times" — all demand mobilization of the country for decisiveness, speed and dispatch. Again occurs the premise that these abilities are incorporated in the presidency, which is quite doubtful. But the other premise is doubtful too. The problems of today are perhaps grave and critical, but none of them are likely to be solved by collapsing the decision-making process by some months to save time. The French had a decade to save the whole of Indochina from the Communists; the United States had another decade to save South Viet Nam. Never during this period could it be said that the executives of either government revealed some intrinsic advantage over the legislature, or were compelled to act urgently and without recourse to deliberative councils.

Almost invariably "time saved" is time wasted: important decisions are badly made, consequences are not foreseen, opposing views are not taken in account, and remedial measures are sooner called for. The attempt in 1961, directed by the presidency, to unseat the Cuban government of Fidel Castro resulted in the Bay of Pigs invasion, which one authority, T. Draper, wrote is generally considered to be "one of those rare politico-military events — a perfect failure."

Crisis is where one seeks it. It is everywhere, if one feels it. The age of anxiety is itself a potent cause of the age of crisis. The presidency is in this sense much more excitable than Congress. It is by the same token the focus of the anxious crowd of the age.

The story of how real crisis has in the past brought power to the presidency — power that was not to be relinquished thereafter — has been often told. The presidency rides tall in the saddle with every American military adventure. The bigger the war, the larger the shift of power from Congress to the presidency, and the longer the period required for partial recovery. Laws and practices of World War II inimical to the Republican Force still rule the country, even some that are poorly translated into civilian terms.

The largest reason why the presidency grows in wartime is psychological, not administrative. The conduct of war by the presidency is not impressively efficient by comparison with war conducted by Congress. History is biased as it is read on this point. The Continental Congress gave General Washington no more trouble than Lincoln and his cabinet gave his generals, or Truman and his advisors his. The confusion in the presidency during World War II was as astonishing as any in the history of the country; by contrast, except for its initial over-enthusiasm, the conduct of Congress was decorous, matter-of-fact, and effective.

Congress was too modest in fact. This has been a constant trouble in times of emergency. Congressmen, being only human, are themselves subject to the man-on-horseback hallucinations. The releasing of powers in generous and vague terms to President Johnson in 1965 to deal as he saw fit with the Viet Nam conflict was typical; congressmen were stuck between their feelings of patriotism and their rational role as initiator and critic of policy, and surrendered completely to the former. And they are pushed by many of their constituents. Any remedy for presidential aggrandizement during military emergencies has to circumvent the psychological paramountcy of the President; this cannot be challenged directly without further exciting popular demands for dictatorship. The procedure in wartime must be coolness and careful constitutionalism; when peace comes it must be prompt and complete reversion. When war and peace are undistinguishable, both procedures must be continuously undertaken.

In this age, which as well as being an age of anxiety and an age of crisis is an age of applied social science, it is a growing practice to create crises. And at creating crises the presidency has no peer. It has the instruments. It can stir up the press, call White House conferences, begin "crash programs," point with alarm to underprivileged people of different sorts, and altogether discover innumerable pockets of crisis in the world.

Each crisis can mean a new program and increased functions for the government, that is, the executive establishment. The crises of today are the programs of tomorrow. The presidency is almost always then a permanent beneficiary of crises that it may discover at home or abroad, for from them it achieves powers and personnel in abundance.

The crisis myth lends support and substantiation to the myth of the lonely and overworked President. A European writer, Roberto Michels, long ago pointed out that the complete picture of the "duce" required the alternation of periods of frenzied sociability with periods of equally intense loneliness. The American President is rarely alone but it is said that he is lonely, made so presumably by "the terrible weight of decisions only he can make."

Apart from the fact that the President *need* take no decision himself, there is the question of how many presidents have made up their minds alone how many times, and whether when such occurred a feeling of loneliness was imparted. One might submit that every man and woman, unless deficient in normal mental qualities, makes decisions of equal relative and subjective weight in life, and often feels misunderstood and afraid, which gives rise to a feeling of aloneness.

With a million-dollar income, in cash and kind, and a huge staff and retinue, the President need be neither lonely nor hardworking. If he wishes to drive himself into a state of fatigue and desperation from working, he may of course do so. But he has less excuse for so doing than, let us say, the small businessman, the writer, the newspaper editor, or the congressman, all of whom lack the bolstering environment the President inherits and the luxurious resources for easy decision-making that he has. Every busy person has to protect himself from pestering and self-pity. It is probable that in this recurring legend of the President lies an attempt to aggrandize the person and office; in it lies a risk of making him nervous at the thought of overwork and fearful of appearing indecisive to himself.

The latter would be bad, for, goes the myth, good Presidents are strong. Said Woodrow Wilson in 1898, "Other Executives lead; our Executive obeys." But he did his best to change this lamented condition. So the "good" Presidents manipulate Congress, bulldoze Congress, set the people upon Congress and achieve their ends. *Ipso facto* this is the public interest — and really the writings of Wilson, Binkley, Lippmann, and other authorities on the President say no more than this. On the other hand, when congressional groups overpower the President or frustrate his demands, Congress is said to be recalcitrant, obstructive, and incompetent.

Actually, can it not be said that a "weak" President is good when inaction, cooperation, etc., is desired, and a "strong" President is good under other circumstances? Presidents are of many types, and even if weak and strong were used objectively, they would be terms far too simple for the reality of presidential-congressional relations.

There are passive Presidents, such as Eisenhower, Coolidge and Hoover, who usually let Congress alone and hope for the best. There are positively principled Presidents such as Wilson and Truman, who believe and act on the idea that they should present a large legislative program to the Congress for enactment, but exert pressure from a fair distance. Some Presidents see Congress as a body to be dominated and exploited, as the two Roosevelts. Jefferson and Kennedy worked to win over Congress to their proposals by party intervention and continuous liaison. These categories and others can be distinguished. They are useful principally to underline how varied the sets of relations between Presidents and Congresses can be.

The background of Presidents is far from uniform and leaves little hope of generalities. No one type has a monopoly of "better relations" (a meaningless phrase in itself) with Congress. The presidency has sometimes been a means for outside forces to push through into the top policy levels of the federal government against the will of the professionalized, long-tenure congressional oligarchy. The cases of Eisenhower, Grant, and other generals, not to mention unsuccessful candidates such as John W. Davis and Wendell Willkie, come to mind. A military man is ideal for the spearhead of such a movement to reorganize a party against its regular congressional faction or to get a new contingent of managers at the top in Washington. Yet success does not necessarily attend such efforts. Congress usually finds that a general, perhaps because of his West Point education and his eternal concern over funds in his military experience, is deferential to it.

The development of the institution of state governor as the proving ground for presidential candidates in a way accomplishes the same purpose. In the last two generations, Wilson and Franklin Roosevelt exemplified the supposed trend, which, it must be admitted, is scarcely detectable since Roosevelt, except among potential and actual candidates for the President's office. Whether it be military men or governors under consideration, it is not at all sure that any dominating influence over Congress and congressional government must be met facing outward.

Congress itself has its own complement of men who would gladly "reform" it drastically.

REPUBLICANISM OF THE PRESIDENTS

I happen, temporarily, to occupy this White House.

Abraham Lincoln

Given the numerous types that occupy the presidency, is it not possible to have a long-term cyclical balance that will produce eternal equilibrium? A strong President and a complaisant Congress would be followed by a weak President and a domineering Congress, and so on indefinitely. And occasional lapses from this situation would be more than made up for by the untidiness of historical waves, so that the very uncertainty of events would prevent any stabilizing of a new order of executive supremacy or dictatorship.

This might be the case if it were not for the growth of the executive establishment. As in the Roman Empire and the French Republic, the bureaucracy provided all the background cushioning that was needed to accommodate the weak executive chiefs who happened along. We are getting ahead of our story here, but it is well to appreciate how dictatorial revolutions happen and what they signify.

It seems absurd to the average American to contemplate a presidential dictator. It seems absurd for three reasons. He thinks of the genial past incumbents. He has had a deficit of experience with a government that challenges his root ideas. And he dreams that a dictatorship is a government that is disliked by the people (and by himself who identifies with the people). When a foreign authority like Dennis Brogan calls the President "an elective emperor," the American smiles; he knows better.

Concerning the geniality of presidents, the "average American" can be logically refuted, though actually he cannot be changed. From a small schoolboy, he has been taught to respect the President, particularly the dead Presidents, and the text writers have taken to heart as nobody else the ancient injunction, *de mortuis nil nisi bonum.* The harsh, violent Jackson becomes a thoughtful liberal, at the hands of a liberal modern historian. So no matter how reviled the live politician, the dead President is revered.

As Professor Charles Beard pointed out once, the authors of the Constitution and most early Americans were not so sure of the automatic virtue of the President. Wrote Hamilton in Number 22 of *The Federalist,* "In republics, persons elevated from the mass of the community, by the suffrages of their fellow-citizens, to great stations of preeminence and power, may find compensations for betraying their trust. . . . Hence it is that history furnishes us with so many mortifying examples of the prevalency of foreign corruption in republican government."

Indeed, when it came time to explain why the President was not given complete power to make treaties with foreign powers, Hamilton wrote, in Number 75 of *The Federalist*, "The history of human conduct does not warrant that exalted opinion of human virtue which would make it wise in a nation to commit interests of so delicate and momentous a kind, as those which concern its intercourse with the rest of the world, to the sole disposal of a magistrate created and circumstanced as would be the President of the United States."

But we need not rest with theoretical writings, no matter how sound. Just before the Civil War, it might have occurred that a President was elected who had confederate sympathies and who might in a subsequent conflict have joined his interests with the seceding states against a presumed majority; who would have been the traitor, who the would-be dictator if the secession had been made unnecessary by his partisanship with the confederate cause?

Franklin D. Roosevelt would probably have gone on as President for so long as he lived, a kind of American Salazar as the ideas of the New Deal receded in originality and importance in the new America.

Under the peculiar circumstances of American foreign policy just after World War II, there were the circumstances of the candidacies of Henry Wallace, first for Vice-President whence he would have been President and later as candidate of the Progressive Party for President.

And then there was Aaron Burr. His name rings ominously in American ears. They must remember who he was. He was a man of "impeccable" background, intelligent, well-educated, son of a University President and minister, handsome, adroit in human relations, admired by men for his virility, courage and skill, and by women for his courtliness and sweetness of disposition.

He tied Jefferson in the vote for President of the United States, and was eliminated only after unprincipled bargaining that might have elected as well as defeated him. He thereafter seems to have engaged in a conspiracy to seize the western territories of the United States and to form a new nation with himself as President. Tried by the Supreme Court for treason he was acquitted for lack of two witnesses to the overt act. The founding fathers, in their anxiety to protect the rights of individuals at the bar made it difficult to accomplish full protection against treasonable officials, even though they may have perceived such possibilities.

Thus, the average American, thinking of past Presidents, exercises a selective memory. With historians to help him, he represses unfavorable experiences. Not so much the Southerner, who has had them in unerasable abundance. It is simple to educate a Southerner to the dangers of presidential tyranny because he believes that his ancestors were suppressed under Lincoln, and to a lesser degree under other Northern Presidents.

Most Northerners, of course, will dismiss this illustration as wrong. What they may ignore, in their haste to dismiss, is that dictatorship has to do with loss of freedoms and it is illogical to dismiss another man's view of freedom as inconsequential when seeking to determine whether a dictatorship exists. They further conceive that a "good" man cannot be a source of despotism. They finally forget, in their enthusiasm over Lincoln for having saved the Union, that a number of serious blows were directed at republican institutions during the course of the war. If they wish in fact to venerate Lincoln, they might most fittingly do so because, in Charles Beard's words "his violations of the Constitution, if such they were in fact, were trivial in comparison with his fidelity to the mandates imposed on him by the supreme law of the land." (*The Republic*, p. 62.)

"THE FREEDOM BOSS"

It is impossible to make great largesses to the people without great extortion: and to compass this, the state must be subverted. The greater the advantages they seem to derive from their liberty, the nearer they approach towards the critical moment of losing it. Petty tyrants arise who have all the vices of a single tyrant. The small remains of liberty soon becomes insupportable; a single tyrant starts up, and the people are stripped of everything, even of the profits of their corruption.
de Montesquieu, *Spirit of the Laws*, Bk. VIII, ch. 2

Again and again in discussions of dictatorship it appears that people reject its possibility because of their notion that despots must be evil men. They are quite wrong. The opposite is the case. Despots are usually well loved. And to say that the American people cannot love a despot shows little knowledge of American history, the American character, and the nature of despotism. The American states and cities have had a goodly number of bosses. Characters such as Huey Long of Louisiana, Stephenson the Ku Klux Klan Governor of Indiana, Boss Hague of Jersey City and Talmadge the Elder of Georgia.

Imagine, then, the "freedom boss," as he can be called. He becomes dictator by giving people freedom. He gives to 30,000,000 old people greater security by national welfare schemes, and "security is freedom." He champions Negro rights and ingratiates himself to 12,000,000 Americans to whom "rights are liberties." To the intelligentsia — writers, artists, architects, and performing artists — go grants and subsidies and understanding; another million people who believe this to be in support of "free expression" will admire him.

A million scientists too will pocket their subsidies, enjoy their new laboratories and approve, in the form of a quietly reasoned dogmatism, his "understanding of science" that enables the free world to grow great in knowledge. Large grants to educators from the federal treasury and cordial "acknowledgment of their important role in American life" through a multitude of well-financed conferences, fellowships, and research projects will bring applause and support from 5,000,000 more who need these "tools of freedom."

Such activities give ample scope to the ambitions of a great many bureaucrats; society will now award them greater respect, and to the bureaucrat "respect is freedom to do a useful job with dignity." To 2,000,000 civil servants are added three millions of the armed forces whose energies are needed (respect again) and freed for many missions throughout the world. There remains but one more necessary ingredient and here the presidential dictator must make a choice. He may decide on the one hand to give to unions "freedom of association" (the Peron formula). On the other hand he can give employers "freedom of management" and "every worker's right to a job" (the Mussolini formula). In the first case he will gain 30 millions and in the latter 20 million adherents.

Some 74 to 84 millions of adults are included in the previous calculations out of a total adult population in the United States of about 110,000,000 persons. Thus about two-thirds of the American people are caught in the net of "the Freedom Boss." A great many ideological opponents, cynics, sceptics, apathetics, and hostile interests can be eliminated from these larger groupings, and from the remainder of the population, and still there would be an ample basis for a popular dictatorship in the name of freedom. In a country of "nice guys" a dictator should be a "nice guy" too; but that quality is easy to find and, if not found, to create.

An advantage of our speculative analysis is that the interweaving of the executive establishment with the presidency is to be perceived. The problem of dictatorship in America is linked up with an administrative revolution. Unless we are treating of a "banana republic," it is the bureaucracy that finally creates the conditions of dictatorship in a land — not economic conditions, wars, corruption, "bad leadership," popular apathy, or lunatic fringes.

That is, there must be the essential conditions of centralization, integration, a monolithic concept of the public interest, a welfare or socialist state, and a prepared uniformity of opinion, if a President is to become dictator. The congressional and Republican Force will tend to resign and disintegrate under the steady wearing power of the great state. And there is a dictator only because the bureaucratic state must have a face. It wants a personality to supply blood and guts to the form of rule. It needs the President as the frozen pond needs a skater to make a winter scene perfectly human.

"TRUSTEE OF THE NATION"

This natural royal law is conceived under this natural formula of eternal usefulness: since in free commonwealths all look out for their own private interests, into the service of which they press their public arms at the risk of ruin to their nations. To preserve the latter from destruction a single man must arise, as did Augustus in Rome, and take all public concerns by force of arms

into his own hands, leaving his subjects free to look after their
private affairs, and after just so much public business and of just
such kinds, as the monarch may entrust to them.
            Giambattista Vico, *The New Science* (1725)

The last sticking point of the person who will not believe that we have a permanent problem of dictatorship by the Executive Force in America is in the precise imagining of the machinery of transition. That is because he personalizes the process excessively — vaguely but excessively. The transition is accomplished in a hundred guises that in the end amount to a complete set of transfers from old institutions to newer ones, from republican to bureaucratic ones. The personality element is minor; whether the Head is hated or loved is relatively unimportant. The institutional change is major. That institutional change is well on its way too; at least two-thirds of the necessary transformations have been accomplished. They need to be routinized and expanded.

As to the physical achievement of a permanent head of the Executive Force, along, say, Soviet lines, where indefinite tenure is the rule, this may come through an elected President, or in the line of succession to a resigned President (forced by a presidential-executive party in Congress allied with elements of the executive branch). The transition might even be accomplished by a person who has been called in or elevated in position to act as arbitrator of a deadlock between the President and Congress. A military man of courage and prestige, such as the late General MacArthur, would be the type sought out for such a role. He would then maintain his position as "Trustee of the Nation" afterwards, for the "duration of the crisis."

That the Constitution might not carry such a title and give it powers is not an insurmountable barrier. If only that which the Constitution prescribed were in being, half the apparatus of government would have to disappear. The President himself is mostly a non-Constitutional creation. If George Washington had decided to become Speaker of the House instead of President under the new Constitutional government, the whole history of the institution of the presidency and Congress would probably have been changed. In any event, amendments to the Constitution are no longer thought to be as difficult to bring about as they once were. They will be much easier for the presidential party after the reorganization of the state legislatures and Congress brought about by the Supreme Court in the decisions of *Baker* vs. *Carr* and *Wesberry* vs. *Sanders*. And finally, even if an amendment to repeal the 22nd Amendment and permit a President to succeed himself were desired rather than one creating the Trustee of the Nation, but were politically impossible to bring about, the law of the Constitution might not interfere with an incumbent President from remaining on and on in office.

For the Supreme Court as constituted and as it has laid down that law, has shown a capacity for admitting interpretations of the Constitution far at variance with the language of the document but in accord with the existing pattern of political power. If the President ran for reelection, only the Supreme Court could deny him the right under the Constitution, and the Court would have to take up the case in the first place, and then, if it did so, might well decide the question was too political to handle (for it *has* but it also *has not* denied itself that luxury in recent months) and the 22nd Amendment itself might be found in conflict with other powers granted the presidency under the Constitution and therefore declared invalid or strictly limited.

There is little use to further conjecture on how the Amendment might be repealed, cancelled, or ignored. It is not difficult to reason how, with or without the Constitution, a determined and powerful move to keep a President or Trustee in the highest position of power indefinitely can succeed. The more critical problem is how the Executive Force manages to triumph over the Republican Force. This is the salient question of sociological history, retrospective and prospective. The other, a minor sociological problem, descends into petty legalisms and personalities and neither protects a nation from disaster nor prepares it for glory.

PERSONALITY

The Impact of Personality on Politics:
An Attempt to Clear Away Underbrush

Fred I. Greenstein

There is a great deal of political activity which can be explained adequately only by taking account of the personal characteristics of the actors involved. The more intimate the vantage, the more detailed the perspective, the greater the likelihood that political actors will loom as full-blown individuals influenced by all of the peculiar strengths and weaknesses to which the species *homo sapiens* is subject, in addition to being role-players, creatures of situation, members of a culture, and possessors of social characteristics such as occupation, class, sex, and age.

To a non-social scientist the observation that individuals are important in politics would seem trite. Undergraduates, until they have been trained to think in terms of impersonal categories of explanation, readily make assertions about the psychology of political actors in their explanations of politics. So do journalists. Why is it that most political scientists are reluctant to deal explicitly with psychological matters (apart from using a variety of rather impersonal psychological constructs such as "party identification," "sense of political efficacy," and the like)? Why is political psychology not a systematically developed subdivision of political science, occupying the skill and energy of a substantial number of scholars?

A partial answer can be found in the formidably tangled and controversial status of the existing scholarly literature on the topic. I am referring to the disparate research that is commonly grouped under the heading "personality and politics": e.g., psychological biographies; questionnaire studies of "authoritarianism," "dogmatism," or "misanthropy"; discussions of "national character"; and attempts to explain international "tensions" by reference to individual insecurities. The interpretations made in psychological biographies often have seemed arbitrary and "subjective"; questionnaire studies have encountered formidable methodological difficulties; attempts to explain large-scale social processes in personality terms have been open to criticism on grounds of "reduction-

Reprinted by permission of the publisher and author from *The American Political Science Review*, LXI (1967), pp. 628–641.

ism." And beyond the specific shortcomings of the existing "personality and politics" research, a variety of arguments have been mounted suggesting that there are *inherent* shortcomings in research strategies that attempt to analyze the impact of "personality" on politics. It is not surprising that most political scientists choose to ignore this seeming mare's nest.

If progress is to be made toward developing a more systematic and solidly grounded body of knowledge about personality and politics, there will have to be considerable clarification of standards of evidence and inference in this area.[1] My present remarks are merely a prolegomenon to methodological clarification of "personality and politics" research. It will not be worthwhile to invest in explicating this gnarled literature with a view to laying out standards unless there is a basis for believing that the research itself is promising. Therefore I shall attempt to clear away what seem to be the main reasons for arguing that there are inherent objections — objections in principle — to the study of personality and politics.

Clearing away the formal objections to this *genre* can serve to liberate energy and channel debate into inquiry. More important, several of the objections may be rephrased in ways that are substantively interesting — ways that move us from the vague question "Does personality have an important impact on politics?" to conditional questions about the circumstances under which diverse psychological factors have varying political consequences. As will be evident, the several objections are based on a number of different implicit definitions of "personality." This is not surprising, since psychologists have never come close to arriving at a single, agreed-upon meaning of the term.[2]

I. OBJECTIONS TO THE STUDY OF PERSONALITY AND POLITICS

A bewildering variety of criticisms have been leveled at this heterogeneous literature. The criticism has been so profuse that there is considerable accuracy to the sardonic observation of David Riesman and Nathan Glazer that the field of culture-and-personality research (within

---

[1] In my own efforts to do this I find that much of the existing research can be considered under three broad headings: psychological studies of single political actors, such as political biographies; studies which classify political actors into types, such as the literature on authoritarianism; and aggregative accounts, in which the collective effects of personality are examined in institutional contexts — ranging from small aggregates such as face-to-face groups all the way through national and international political processes. Needless to say, it is one thing to suggest that clarification of such diverse endeavors is possible and another thing actually to make some progress along these lines.

[2] A standard discussion by Allport notes a full fifty *types* of definition of the term (apart from colloquial usages): Gordon Allport, *Personality* (New York: Holt, 1937), 24–54.

which many of the past accounts of personality and politics fall) has "more critics than practitioners." [3]

The more intellectually challenging of the various objections asserting that *in principle* personality and politics research is not promising (even if one avoids the methodological pitfalls) seem to fall under five headings. In each case the objection is one that can be generalized to the study of how personality relates to any social phenomenon. Listed rather elliptically the five objections are that:

1. Personality characteristics tend to be randomly distributed in institutional roles. Personality therefore "cancels out" and can be ignored by analysts of political and other social phenomena.

2. Personality characteristics of individuals are less important than their social characteristics in influencing behavior. This makes it unpromising to concentrate research energies on studying the impact of personality.

3. Personality is not of interest to political and other social analysts, because individual actors (personalities) are severely limited in the impact they can have on events.

4. Personality is not an important determinant of behavior because individuals with varying personal characteristics will tend to behave similarly when placed in common situations. And it is not useful to study personal variation, if the ways in which people vary do not affect their behavior.

5. Finally, there is a class of objections deprecating the relevance of personality to political analysis in which "personality" is equated with particular aspects of individual psychological functioning. We shall be concerned with one of the objections falling under this heading — *viz.*, the assertion that so-called "deep" psychological needs (of the sort that sometimes are summarized by the term "ego-defensive") do not have an important impact on behavior, and that therefore "personality" in this sense of the term need not be studied by the student of politics.

The first two objections seem to be based on fundamental misconceptions. Nevertheless they do point to interesting problems for the student of political psychology. The final three objections are partially well taken. These are the objections that need to be rephrased in conditional form as "Under what circumstances?" questions. Let me now expand upon these assertions.

[3] David Riesman and Nathan Glazer, "The Lonely Crowd: A Reconsideration in 1960," in Seymour M. Lipset and Leo Lowenthal (eds.), *Culture and Social Character* (New York: The Free Press of Glencoe, 1961), p. 437. For examples of discussions that are in varying degrees critical of personality and politics writings see the essays by Shils and Verba cited in note 17, Reinhard Bendix, "Compliant Behavior and Individual Personality," *American Journal of Sociology*, 58 (1952), 292–303, and David Spitz, "Power and Personality: The Appeal to the 'Right Man' in Democratic States," *American Political Science Review*, 52 (1958), 84–97.

II. Two Erroneous Objections

The Thesis That Personality "Cancels Out." The assumption underlying the first objection seems, as Alex Inkeles points out, to be that "in 'real' groups and situations, the accidents of life history and factors other than personality which are responsible for recruitment [into institutional roles] will 'randomize' personality distribution in the major social statuses sufficiently so that taking systematic account of the influence of personality composition is unnecessary." But, as Inkeles easily shows, this assumption is false on two grounds.

First, "even if the personality composition of any group is randomly determined, random assortment would not in fact guarantee the *same* personality composition in the membership of all institutions of a given type. On the contrary, the very fact of randomness implies that the outcome would approximate a normal distribution. Consequently, some of the groups would by chance have a personality composition profoundly different from others, with possibly marked effects on the functioning of the institutions involved." Secondly,

> there is no convincing evidence that randomness does consistently describe the assignment of personality types to major social statuses. On the contrary, there is a great deal of evidence to indicate that particular statuses often attract, or recruit preponderantly for, one or another personality characteristic and that fact has a substantial effect on individual adjustment to roles and the general quality of institutional functioning.[4]

The objection turns out therefore to be based on unwarranted empirical assumptions. It proves not to be an obstacle to research, but rather — once it is examined — an opening gambit for identifying a crucial topic of investigation for the political psychologist: How are personality types distributed in social roles and with what consequences?

The Thesis That Social Characteristics Are More Important Than Personality Characteristics. The second objection — asserting that individuals' social characteristics are "more important" than their personality characteristics — seems to result from a conceptual rather than empirical error. It appears to be an objection posing a pseudo-problem that needs to be dissolved conceptually rather than resolved empirically.

Let us consider what the referents are of "social characteristic" and "personality characteristic." By the latter we refer to some inner predisposition of the individual. The term "characteristic" applies to a state of the organism. And, using the familiar paradigm of "stimulus → organism → response," or "environment → predispositions → response," we operate on the assumption that the environmental stimuli (or "situa-

---

[4] Alex Inkeles, "Sociology and Psychology," in Sigmund Koch (ed.), *Psychology: A Study of A Science*, VI (New York: McGraw-Hill, 1963), p. 354.

tions") that elicit behavior are mediated through the individual's psychological predispositions.[5]

But we also, of course, presume that the individual's psychological predispositions are themselves to a considerable extent environmentally determined, largely by his prior social experiences. And it is these prior environmental states (which may occur at any stage of the life cycle and which may or may not persist into the present) that we commonly refer to when we speak of "social characteristics." Social "characteristics," then, are not states of the organism, but of its environment. (This is made particularly clear by the common usage "*objective* social characteristics.")

It follows that social and psychological characteristics are in no way mutually exclusive. They do not compete as candidates for explanation of social behavior, but rather are complementary. Social "characteristics" can cause psychological "characteristics"; they are not substitutes for psychological characteristics. The erroneous assumption that social characteristics could even in principle be more important than psychological characteristics probably arises in part from the misleading impression of identity fostered by the usage of "characteristics" in the two expressions.[6]

This confusion also very probably is contributed to by the standard techniques used by social scientists to eliminate spurious correlations, namely, controlling for "third factors" and calculating partial correlations. Control procedures, when used indiscriminately and without reference to the theoretical standing of the variables that are being analyzed, can lead to the failure to recognize what Herbert Hyman, in the heading of an important section of his *Survey Design and Analysis,* describes as "The Distinction Between Developmental Sequences or Configurations and Problems of Spuriousness." [7]

For an example of how this problem arises, we can consider the very interesting research report by Urie Bronfenbrenner entitled "Personality and Participation: The Case of the Vanishing Variables." [8] Bronfenbrenner reports a study in which it was found that measures of personality were associated with participation in community affairs. However,

---

5 It is a matter of convenience whether the terms "personality" and "psychological" are treated as synonymous (as in the present passage), or whether the first is defined as some subset of the second (as in my discussion of the fifth objection). Given the diversity of uses to which all of the terms in this area are put, the best one can do is to be clear about one's usage in specific contexts.

6 My criticism of the second objection would of course not stand in any instance where some acquired inner characteristic (such as a sense of class consciousness) was being defined as a social characteristic, and was being argued that this "social" characteristic was "more important" than a "personality" characteristic. In terms of my usage this would imply an empirical assertion about the relative influence of two types of psychological, or "personality" variables. My remarks in the text on the meaning of terms are simply short-hand approaches to clarifying the underlying issue. They are not canonical efforts to establish "correct" usage.

7 Herbert Hyman, *Survey Design and Analysis* (Glencoe, Ill.: The Free Press, 1955), 254–257.

8 Urie Bronfenbrenner, "Personality and Participation: The Case of the Vanishing Variables," *Journal of Social Issues,* 16 (1960), 54–63.

as he notes, "It is a well-established fact that extent of participation varies with social class, with the lower classes participating the least." Therefore, he proceeds to establish the relationship between personality and participation controlling for social class (and certain other factors). The result: "Most of the earlier . . . significant relationships between personality measures and participation now disappear, leaving only two significant correlations, both of them quite low."

One common interpretation of such a finding would be that Bronfenbrenner had shown the irrelevance of personality to participation. But his finding should not be so interpreted. Hyman's remarks, since they place the problem of relating social background data to psychological data in its more general context, are worth quoting at some length.

> . . . the concept of spuriousness cannot *logically* be intended to apply to antecedent conditions which are associated with the particular independent variable as part of a developmental sequence. Implicitly, the notion of an uncontrolled factor which was operating so as to produce a spurious finding involves the image of something *extrinsic* to the . . . apparent cause. Developmental sequences, by contrast, involve the image of a series of entities which are *intrinsically* united or substituted for one another. All of them constitute a unity and merely involve different ways of stating the same variable as it changes over time. . . . Consequently, to institute procedures of control is to remove so-to-speak some of the very cause one wishes to study. . . . How shall the analyst know what antecedent conditions are intrinsic parts of a developmental sequence? . . . One guide, for example, can be noted: instances where the "control" factor and the apparent explanation involve *levels of description from two different systems* are likely to be developmental sequences. For instance, an explanatory factor that was a personality trait and a control factor that was biological such as physique or glandular functions can be conceived as levels of description from different systems. Similarly, an explanatory factor that is *psychological* and a control factor that is *sociological* can be conceived as two different levels of description, i.e., one might regard an attitude as derivative of objective position or status or an objective position in society as leading to psychological processes such as attitudes. Thus, the concept of spuriousness would not be appropriate.[9]

In the Bronfenbrenner example, then, an individual's "objective" socio-economic background (as opposed to such subjective concomitants as his sense of class consciousness) needs to be analyzed as a possible social determinant of the psychological correlates of participation, taking account of the fact that, as Allport puts it, "background factors never directly cause behavior; they cause attitudes [and other mental sets]" and

[9] Herbert Hyman, *Survey Design and Analysis* (Glencoe, Ill.: The Free Press, 1955), 254–257. Italics in the original. Also see Hubert Blalock, "Controlling for Background Factors: Spuriousness Versus Developmental Sequences," *Sociological Inquiry*, Vol. 34 (1964), 28–39, for a discussion of the rather complex implications of this distinction for data analysis.

the latter "in turn determine behavior." [10] A more general lesson for the student of psychology and politics emerges from our examination of the second objection. We can see that investigators in this realm will often find it necessary to lay out schemes of explanation that are developmental — schemes that place social and psychological factors in the sequence in which they seem to have impinged upon one another.

III. THREE PARTIALLY CORRECT OBJECTIONS

The three remaining objections bear on (a) the question of how much impact individual actors can have on political outcomes, (b) the question of whether the situations political actors find themselves in impose uniform behavior on individuals of varying personal characteristics, making it unprofitable for the political analyst to study variations in the actors' personal characteristics, and (c) the numerous questions that can be raised about the impact on behavior of particular classes of personal characteristics — including the class of characteristics I shall be discussing, the so-called "ego-defensive" personality dispositions. In the remainder of this essay, I shall expand upon each of these three questions, rephrase them in conditional form, and lay out a number of general propositions stating the circumstances under which the objection is or is not likely to hold. As will be evident, the propositions are not hypotheses stated with sufficient precision to be testable. Rather, they are quite general indications of the circumstances under which political analysts are and are not likely to find it desirable to study "personality" in the several senses of the term implicit in the objections.

When Do Individual Actors Affect Events ("Action Dispensability")? The objection to studies of personality and politics that emphasizes the limited capacity of single actors to shape events does not differ in its essentials from the nineteenth and early twentieth century debates

[10] Gordon Allport, review of *The American Soldier, Journal of Abnormal and Social Psychology,* 45 (1950), p. 173. Nothing in this discussion is intended to gainsay the use of controls. "I am not, of course, arguing against the use of breakdowns or matched groups," Allport adds. "They should, however, be used to show where attitudes come from, and not to imply that social causation acts automatically apart from attitudes." Often a control, by suggesting the source of a psychological state, helps explain its dynamics and functions. A good example can be found in Hyman and Sheatsley's well-known critique of *The Authoritarian Personality.* The critique shows that certain attitudes and ways of viewing the world which the authors of *The Authoritarian Personality* explained in terms of a complex process of personal pathology are in fact typical of the thought processes and vocabulary of people of lower socio-economic status. Hyman and Sheatsley are therefore able to suggest that such attitudes may be a learned part of the respondents' *cognitions* rather than a psychodynamic manifestation serving ego-defensive functions. It should be clear from what I have said in the text, however, that Hyman and Sheatsley's thesis cannot legitimately be phrased as an argument that such attitudes are social (or cultural) rather than psychological: Herbert Hyman and Paul B. Sheatsley, "The Authoritarian Personality — A Methodological Critique," in Richard Christie and Marie Jahoda (eds.), *Studies in the Scope and Method of "The Authoritarian Personality"* (Glencoe, Ill.: The Free Press, 1954), 50–122.

over social determinism — that is, over the role of individual actors (Great Men or otherwise) in history. In statements of this objection emphasis is placed on the need for the times to be ripe in order for the historical actor to make his contribution. Questions are asked such as, "What impact could Napoleon have had on history if he had been born in the Middle Ages?" Possibly because of the parlor game aura of the issues that arise in connection with it, the problem of the impact of individuals on events has not had as much disciplined attention in recent decades as the two remaining issues I shall be dealing with. Nevertheless, at one time or another this question has received the attention of Tolstoy, Carlyle, Spencer, William James, Plekhanov, and Trotsky (in his *History of the Russian Revolution*). The main attempt at a balanced general discussion seems to be Sidney Hook's vigorous, but unsystematic, 1943 essay *The Hero in History*.[11]

Since the degree to which actions are likely to have significant impacts is clearly variable, I would propose to begin clarification by asking: What are the circumstances under which the actions of single individuals are likely to have a greater or lesser effect on the course of events? For shorthand purposes this might be called the question of *action dispensability*. We can conceive of arranging the actions performed in the political arena along a continuum, ranging from those which are indispensable for outcomes that concern us through those which are utterly dispensable. And we can make certain general observations about the circumstances which are likely to surround dispensable and indispensable action. In so reconstructing this particular objection to personality explanations of politics we make it clear that what is at stake is not a psychological issue, but rather one bearing on social processes on decision-making. The question is about the impact of action, not about its determinants.

It is difficult to be precise in stipulating circumstances under which an individual's actions are likely to be a link in further events, since a great deal depends upon the interests of the investigator and the specific context of investigation (the kinds of actions being studied; the kinds of effects that are of interest). Therefore, the following three propositions are necessarily quite abstract.

The impact of an individual's actions varies with (1) the degree to which the actions take place in an environment which admits of restructuring, (2) the location of the actor in that environment, and (3) the actor's peculiar strengths or weaknesses.

(1) *The likelihood of personal impact increases to the degree that the environment admits of restructuring.* Technically speaking we might describe situations or sequences of events in which modest interventions can produce disproportionately large results as "unstable." They are in a precarious equilibrium. The physical analogies are massive rock formations at the side of a mountain which can be dislodged by the motion of a single keystone, or highly explosive compounds such as nitroglycer-

11 Sidney Hook, *The Hero in History* (Boston: Beacon Press, 1943).

ine. Instability in this sense is by no means synonymous with what is loosely known as political instability, the phrase we typically employ to refer to a variety of "fluid" phenomena — political systems in which governments rise and fall with some frequency, systems in which violence is common, etc. Many of the situations commonly referred to as unstable do not at all admit of restructuring. In the politics of many of the "unstable" Latin American nations, for example, most conceivable substitutions of actors and actions would lead to little change in outcomes (or at least in "larger" outcomes). Thus, to continue the physical analogy, an avalanche in motion down a mountainside is for the moment in stable equilibrium, since it cannot be influenced by modest interventions.

The situation (or chain of events) which does not admit readily of restructuring usually is one in which a variety of factors conspire to produce the same outcome.[12] Hook, in *The Hero in History*, offers the outbreak of World War I and of the February Revolution as instances of historical sequences which, if not "inevitable," probably could not have been averted by the actions of any single individual. In the first case the vast admixture of multiple conflicting interests and inter-twined alliances and in the second the powerful groundswell of discontent were such as to make us feel that no intervention by any single individual (excluding the more far-fetched hypothetical instances that invariably can be imagined) would have averted the outcome. On the other hand, Hook attempts to show in detail that without the specific actions of Lenin the October Revolution might well not have occurred. By implication he suggests that Lenin was operating in an especially manipulable environment. A similar conclusion might be argued about the manipulability of the political environment of Europe prior to the outbreak of World War II, on the basis of the various accounts at our disposal of the sequence of events that culminated with the invasion of Poland in 1939.[13]

(2) *The likelihood of personal impact varies with the actor's location in the environment.* To shape events, an action must be performed not only in an unstable environment, but also by an actor who is strategically placed in that environment. It is, for example, a commonplace that actors in the middle and lower ranks of many bureaucracies are unable to accomplish much singly, since they are restrained or inhibited by other actors. Robert C. Tucker points out what may almost be a limiting

[12] Compare Wassily Leontief's interesting essay "When Should History be Written Backwards?" *The Economic History Review*, 16 (1963), 1–8.

[13] For an account of European politics in the 1930's that is consistent with this assertion see Alan Bullock, *Hitler: A Study in Tyranny* (New York: Harper, rev. ed., 1962). Needless to say, any attempt to seek operational indicators of environments that "admit of restructuring" in order to restate the present proposition in testable form could not take the circular route of simply showing that the environment *had* been manipulated by a single actor.

case on the other end of the continuum in an essay on the lack of restraint on Russian policy-makers, both under the Czars and since the Revolution. He quotes with approval Nikolai Turgenev's mid-nineteenth century statement that "In all countries ruled by an unlimited power there has always been and is some class, estate, some traditional institutions which in certain instances compel the sovereign to act in a certain way and set limits to his caprice; nothing of the sort exists in Russia." [14] Elsewhere, Tucker points to the tendency in totalitarian states for the political machinery to become "a conduit of the dictatorial psychology" [15] — that is for there to be a relatively unimpeded conversion of whims of the dictator into governmental action as a consequence of his authoritarian control of the bureaucratic apparatus.

(3) *The likelihood of personal impact varies with the personal strengths or weaknesses of the actor.* My two previous observations can be recapitulated with an analogy from the poolroom. In the game of pocket billiards the aim of the player is to clear as many balls as possible from the table. The initial distribution of balls parallels my first observation about the manipulability of the environment. With some arrays a good many shots are possible; perhaps the table can even be cleared. With other arrays no successful shots are likely. The analogy to point two — the strategic location of the actor — is, of course, the location of the cue ball. As a final point, we may note the political actor's peculiar strengths or weaknesses. In the poolroom these are paralleled by the player's skill or lack of skill. The greater the actor's skill, the less his initial need for a favorable position or a manipulable environment, and the greater the likelihood that he will himself subsequently contribute to making his position favorable and his environment manipulable.[16]

The variable of skill is emphasized in Hook's detailed examination of Lenin's contribution to the events leading up to the October Revolution. Hook concludes that Lenin's vigorous, persistent, imaginative participation in that sequence was a necessary (though certainly not sufficient) condition for the outcome. Hook's interest, of course, is in lending precision to the notion of the Great Man. Therefore he is concerned with the individual who, because of especially great talents, is able to alter the course of events. But for our purposes, the Great Failure is equally significant: an actor's capabilities may be relevant to an outcome in a negative as well as a positive sense.

14 Robert C. Tucker, *The Soviet Political Mind* (New York: Praeger, 1963), 145–65; quotation from Turgenev at p. 147.

15 Robert C. Tucker, "The Dictator and Totalitarianism," *World Politics*, Vol. 17 (1965), p. 583.

16 In other words, the skill of the actor may feed back into the environment, contributing to its instability or stability. To the degree that we take environmental conditions as given (i.e., considering them statically at a single point in time), we underestimate the impact of individuals on politics. For examples of political actors shaping their own roles and environments see Hans Gerth and C. Wright Mills, *Character and Social Structure* (London: Routledge and Kegan Paul, 1953), Chapter 14.

When Does Personal Variability Affect Behavior ("Actor Dispensability")? Often it may be acknowledged that a particular action of an individual is a crucial node in a process of decision-making, but it may be argued that this action is one that might have been performed by any actor placed in a comparable situation, or by anyone filling a comparable role. If actors with differing personal characteristics perform identically when exposed to common stimuli, we quite clearly can dispense with study of the actors' personal differences, since a variable cannot explain a uniformity. This objection to personality explanations of political behavior — and here "personality" means personal variability — is illustrated by Easton with the example of political party leaders who differ in their personality characteristics and who are "confronted with the existence of powerful groups making demands upon their parties." Their "decisions and actions," he suggests, will tend "to converge." [17]

The task of rephrasing this objection conditionally and advancing propositions about the circumstances under which it obtains is not overly burdensome, since the objection is rarely stated categorically. Exponents of the view that situational pressures eliminate or sharply reduce the effects of personality usually acknowledge that this is not always the case. Similarly, proponents of the view that personality *is* an important determinant of political behavior also often qualify their position and note circumstances that dampen the effects of personal variability. These qualifications point to an obvious reconstruction of the question. Under what circumstances, we may ask, do different actors (placed in common situations) vary in their behavior and under what circumstances is behavior uniform? We might call this the question of *actor dispensability*.[18]

The question of under what circumstances the variations in actors' personal characteristics are significant for their behavior has received a good bit of intermittent attention in recent years. The several propositions I shall set forth are assembled, and to some extent reorganized, from a variety of observations made by Herbert Goldhamer, Robert E. Lane, Daniel Levinson, Edward Shils, and Sidney Verba, among others.[19]

---

[17] David Easton, *The Political System* (New York: Knopf, 1953), p. 196.

[18] Strictly speaking, it is not the actor who is dispensable in this formulation, but rather his personal characteristics. In an earlier draft I referred to "actor substitutability," but the antonym, "non-substitutability," is less successful than "indispensability" as a way of indicating the circumstances under which an explanation of action demands an account of the actor. On the other hand, "substitutability" is a very handy criterion for rough and ready reasoning about the degree to which the contribution of any historical actor is uniquely personal, since one may easily perform the mental exercise of imagining how other available actors would have performed under comparable circumstances.

[19] Robert E. Lane, *Political Life* (Glencoe, Ill.: The Free Press, 1959), pp. 99–100; Edward A. Shils, "Authoritarianism: 'Right' and 'Left'," in Richard Christie and Marie Jahoda (eds.), *op. cit.*, pp. 24–49; Herbert Goldhamer, "Public Opinion and Personality," *American Journal of Sociology*, 55 (1950), 346–354; Daniel J. Levinson, "The Relevance of Personality for Political Participation," *Public Opinion Quarterly*, 22 (1958), 3–10; Sidney Verba, "Assumptions of Rationality and Non-Rationality in Models of the International System," *World Politics*, 14 (1961), 93–117.

But before proceeding to lay out these propositions, it will be instructive to consider a possible objection to the notion of actor dispensability.

The circumstances of actor dispensability are those in which, as Shils puts it, "persons of quite different dispositions" are found to "behave in a more or less uniform manner." [20] A personality-oriented social analyst might attempt to deny the premise that behavior *ever* is uniform (and indeed, Shils says "behave in a *more or less* uniform manner.") The objection is, of course, correct in the trivial, definitional sense: every different act is different. The objection is also empirically correct in that, if we inspect actions with sufficient care, we can always detect differences between them — even such heavily "situation-determined" actions as "the way in which a man, when crossing a street, dodges the cars which move on it" [21] vary from individual to individual. Nevertheless, the objection — if it is meant to invalidate Shils' assertion — is not well taken, since it denies the principle (necessary for analytic purposes) that we can classify disparate phenomena, treating them as uniform for certain purposes. Furthermore, a significant sociological proposition follows from Shils' point: "To a large extent, large enough indeed to enable great organizations to operate in a quite predictable manner, . . . [different individuals] will conform [i.e., behave uniformly] despite the conflicting urges of their personalities." [22]

Yet the objection leads to an important observation. What we mean by uniform behavior depends upon our principle of classification, which in turn depends upon the purposes of our investigation. If our interests are sufficiently microscopic, we are likely to find variability where others see uniformity. Nor, it should be added, is there anything intrinsically unworthy about being interested in microscopic phenomena — in nuances and "small" variations.

Even if one *is* interested in the macroscopic (major institutions, "important" events), the irrelevance of microscopic variations introduced by actors' personal characteristics cannot be assumed, since action dispensability and actor dispensability are independent of each other. Small actor variations may lead to actions with large consequences. Thus, for example, there might be relatively little room for personal variation in the ways that American Presidents would be likely to respond to the warning system that signals the advent of a missile attack, but the consequences of the President's action are so great that even the slightest variations between one or another incumbent in a comparable situation would be of profound interest.

---

20 Shils, *op. cit.,* p. 43.

21 This is a quotation from a well-known passage in Karl Popper's *The Open Society and Its Enemies* (New York: Harper Torchbook edition, 1963), II, p. 97, arguing that sociology is an "autonomous" discipline because psychological evidence is so often of limited relevance — compared with situational evidence — to explanations of behavior. For a critique of Popper's analysis see Richard Lichtman, "Karl Popper's Defense of the Autonomy of Sociology," *Social Research*, 32 (1965), 1–25.

22 Shils, *op. cit.,* p. 44.

In noting the conditions under which actors' personal characteristics tend to be dispensable and those under which they tend to be indispensable, we may examine conditions that arise from the *environmental situations* within which actions occur, from the *predispositions* of the actors themselves, and from the *kinds of acts* (responses) that are performed — that is, from all three elements of the familiar paradigm of $E \rightarrow P \rightarrow R$ (or $S \rightarrow O \rightarrow R$). The propositions I shall list under these headings are neither exhaustive nor fully exclusive of each other, but they do serve to pull together and organize crudely most of the diverse observations that have been made on the circumstances that foster the expression of personal variability.

1. *There is greater room for personal variability in the "peripheral" aspects of actions than in their "central" aspects.*

Examples of "peripheral" aspects of action include evidences of the personal *style* of an actor (for example, his mannerisms), the *zealousness* of his performance, and the *imagery* that accompanies his behavior at the preparatory and consummatory phases of action (for example, fantasies about alternative courses of action).

By "central" I refer to the gross aspects of the action — for example, the very fact that an individual votes, writes a letter to a Congressman, etc.

Lane suggests that "the idiosyncratic features of personality" are likely to be revealed in the "images" political actors hold "of other participants." There also is "scope for the expressions of personal differences," Lane points out, in "the grounds" one selects "for rationalizing a political act," and in one's style "of personal interaction in a political group." [23]

Shils, after arguing that "persons of quite different dispositions" often "will behave in a more or less uniform manner," then adds: "Naturally not all of them will be equally zealous or enthusiastic. . . ." [24]

Riesman and Glazer point out that although "different kinds of character" can "be used for the same kind of work within an institution," a "price" is paid by "the character types that [fit] badly, as against the release of energy provided by the congruence of character and task." [25]

2. *The more demanding the political act — the more it is not merely a conventionally expected performance — the greater the likelihood that it will vary with the personal characteristics of the actor.*

Lane suggests that there is little personal variation in "the more conventional items, such as voting, expressing patriotic opinions and accepting election results as final." On the other hand, his list of actions which "reveal . . . personality" includes "selecting types of political behavior over and above voting": [26] writing public officials, volunteering to work for a political party, seeking nomination for public office, etc.

23 Lane, *op. cit.*, p. 100.
24 Shils, *op. cit*, p. 43.
25 Riesman and Glazer, *op. cit.*, pp. 438–439.
26 Lane, *op. cit.*, p. 100.

3. *Variations in personal characteristics are more likely to be exhibited to the degree that behavior is spontaneous — that is, to the degree that it proceeds from personal impulse, without effort or premeditation.*

Goldhamer refers to "a person's . . . casual ruminations while walking along the street, sudden but perhaps transient convictions inspired by some immediate experience, speculations while reading the newspaper or listening to a broadcast, remarks struck off in the course of an argument. . . . If we have any theoretical reason for supposing that a person's opinions are influenced by his personality structure, it is surely in these forms of spontaneous behavior that we should expect to find the evidence of this relationship." [27]

We may now consider two propositions about actor dispensability that relate to the environment in which actions take place.

4. *Ambiguous situations leave room for personal variability to manifest itself.*

As Sherif puts it, "the contribution of internal factors increases as the external-stimulus situation becomes more unstructured." [28] (A classically unstructured environmental stimulus, leaving almost infinite room for personal variation in response, is the Rorschach ink blot.)

Budner [29] distinguishes three types of ambiguous situations. Each relates to instances which have been given by various writers of actor dispensability or indispensability. Budner's three types of situations include (a) a "completely new situation in which there are no familiar cues."

Shils comments that in new situations "no framework of action [has been] set for the newcomer by the expectations of those on the scene. A new political party, a newly formed religious sect will thus be more amenable to the expressive behavior of the personalities of those who make them up than an ongoing government or private business office or university department with its traditions of scientific work." [30]

Goldhamer argues that the public opinion process moves from unstructured conditions admitting of great personal variability to more structured conditions that restrain individual differences. Immediate reactions to public events, he argues, reflect personal idiosyncrasies. But gradually the individual is constrained by his awareness that the event has become a matter of public discussion. "There is reason to believe that, as the individual becomes aware of the range and intensity of group preoccupation with the object, his orientation to it becomes less individualized, less intimately bound to an individual perception and judgment of the object . . . [H]e is drawn imperceptibly to view this object anew, no longer now as an individual percipient, but as one who selects (unconsciously, perhaps) an 'appropriate' position in an imagined range of

27 Goldhamer, *op. cit.*, p. 349.
28 Muzafer Sherif, "The Concept of Reference Groups in Human Relations," in Muzafer Sherif and M. O. Wilson (eds.), *Group Relations at the Crossroads* (New York: Harper, 1953), p. 30.
29 Stanley Budner, "Intolerance of Ambiguity as a Personality Variable," *Journal of Personality*, 30 (1960), p. 30.
30 Shils, *op. cit.*, pp. 44–45.

public reactions . . . a limitation is thus placed on the degree to which the full uniqueness of the individual may be expected to influence his perceptions and opinions." [31]

The second type of ambiguity referred to by Budner is (b) "a complex situation in which there are a great number of cues to take into account."

Levinson suggests that the availability of "a wide range of . . . socially provided . . . alternatives" increases "the importance of intrapersonal determinants" of political participation. "The greater the number of opportunities for participation, the more the person can choose on the basis of personal congeniality. Or, in more general terms, the greater the richness and complexity of the stimulus field, the more will internal organizing forces determine individual adaptation. This condition obtains in a relatively unstructured social field, and, as well, in a pluralistic society that provides numerous structured alternatives." [32]

Finally, Budner refers to (c) "a contradictory situation in which different elements suggest different structures."

Several of Lane's examples fall under this heading: "Situations where reference groups have politically conflicting points of view . . . Situations at the focus of conflicting propaganda. . . . Current situations which for an individual are in conflict with previous experience." [33]

5. *The impact of personal differences on behavior is increased to the degree that sanctions are not attached to certain of the alternative possible courses of behavior.*

"The option of refusing to sign a loyalty oath," Levinson comments, "is in a sense 'available' to any member of an institution that requires such an oath, but the sanctions operating are usually so strong that nonsigning is an almost 'unavailable' option to many who would otherwise choose it." [34]

The foregoing environmental determinants of actor dispensability suggest several aspects of actors' predispositions which will affect the likelihood that any of the ways in which they differ from each other will manifest themselves in behavior.

6. *The opportunities for personal variation are increased to the degree that political actors lack mental sets which might lead them to structure their perceptions and resolve ambiguities.*

The sets they may use to help reduce ambiguity include cognitive capacities (intelligence, information) that provide a basis of organizing perceptions, and preconceptions that foster stereotyping.

Verba, in an essay on "Assumptions of Rationality and Non-Rationality in Models of the International System," comments that "the more information an individual has about international affairs, the less likely it is that his behavior will be based upon non-logical influences. In the

31 Goldhamer, *op. cit.*, pp. 346–347.
32 Levinson, *op. cit.*, p. 9.
33 Lane, *op. cit.*, p. 99.
34 Levinson, *op. cit.*, p. 10.

absence of information about an event, decisions have to be made on the basis of other criteria. A rich informational content, on the other hand, focuses attention on the international event itself. . . ." [35]

Wildavsky, in an account of adversary groups in the Dixon-Yates controversy, points to ways in which the preconceptions of members of factions lead them to respond in predictable fashions that are likely to be quite independent of their personal differences. "The public versus private power issue . . . has been fought out hundreds of times at the city, state, county, and national levels of our politics in the past sixty years. A fifty year old private or public power executive, or a political figure who has become identified with one or another position, may well be able to look back to twenty-five years of personal involvement in this controversy. . . . The participants on each side have long since developed a fairly complete set of attitudes on this issue which have crystallized through years of dispute. . . . They have in reserve a number of prepared responses ready to be activated in the direction indicated by their set of attitudes whenever the occasion demands. . . ." [36]

7. *If the degree to which certain of the alternative courses of action are sanctioned reduces the likelihood that personal characteristics will produce variation in behavior, then any intense dispositions on the part of actors in a contrary direction to the sanctions increase that likelihood.*

"Personality structure . . . will be more determinant of political activity when the impulses and the defenses of the actors are extremely intense" — for example, "when the compulsive elements are powerful and rigid or when the aggressiveness is very strong." [37]

8. *If, however, the disposition that is strong is to take one's cues from others, the effects of personal variation on behavior will be reduced.*

Personality may dispose some individuals to adopt uncritically the political views in their environment, but as a result, Goldhamer comments, the view adopted will "have a somewhat fortuitous character in relation to the personality and be dependent largely on attendant situational factors." [38] (Dispositions toward conformity are, of course, a key variable for students of political psychology. The point here is merely that these dispositions reduce the impact of the individual's other psychological characteristics on his behavior.)

9. *A situational factor working with individual tendencies to adopt the views of others to reduce personal variation is the degree to which the individual is placed in a group context in which "the individual's decision or attitude is visible to others."* [39]

---

[35] Verba, *op. cit.*, p. 100. By "non-logical" Verba means influences resulting from ego-defensive personality needs, but his point applies generally to personal variability.

[36] Aaron Wildavsky, "The Analysis of Issue-Contexts in the Study of Decision-Making," *Journal of Politics,* 24 (1962), 717–732.

[37] Shils, *op. cit.*, p. 45.

[38] Goldhamer, *op. cit.*, p. 353.

[39] Verba, *op. cit,* p. 103.

Another predispositional determinant:

10. *The more emotionally involved a person is in politics, the greater the likelihood that his personal characteristics will affect his political behavior.*

Goldhamer comments that "the bearing of personality on political opinion is conditioned and limited by the fact that for large masses of persons the objects of political life are insulated from the deeper concerns of the personality." [But, he adds to a footnote], "this should not be interpreted to mean that personality characteristics are irrelevant to an understanding of the opinions and acts of political personages. In such cases political roles are so central to the entire life organization that a close connection between personality structure and political action is to be expected." [40]

Levinson argues that "[t]he more politics 'matters,' the more likely it is that political behavior will express enduring inner values and dispositions. Conversely, the less salient the issues involved, the more likely is one to respond on the basis of immediate and external pressures. When a personally congenial mode of participation is not readily available, and the person cannot create one for himself, he may nominally accept an uncongenial role but without strong commitment or involvement. In this case, however, the person is likely . . . to have a strong potential for change toward a new and psychologically more functional role." [41]

The final proposition has reference to political roles and does not fit neatly into any of the three elements of the Environment→Predispositions→Response formula.

11. *Personality variations will be more evident to the degree that the individual occupies a position "free from elaborate expectations of fixed content."* [42]

Typically these are leadership positions. We have already seen that such positions figure in the conditions of action indispensability; their importance for the student of personality and politics is evident a fortiori when we note that the leader's characteristics also are likely to be reflected in his behavior, thus meeting the requirement of actor indispensability.

The military leader, it has been said, may have an especially great impact. "Even those who view history as fashioned by vast impersonal forces must recognize that in war personality plays a particularly crucial part. Substitute Gates for Washington, and what would have happened to the American cause? Substitute Marlborough or Wellington for Howe or Clinton, and what would have happened? These are perhaps idle ques-

---

[40] Goldhamer, *op. cit.*, p. 349.

[41] Levinson, *op. cit.*, p. 10.

[42] Shils, *op. cit.*, p. 45. The term "role" is commonly used so as to have both an environmental referent (the prevailing expectations about his duties in a role incumbent's environment) and a predispositional referent (the incumbent's own expectations). For a valuable discussion see Daniel Levinson, "Role, Personality, and Social Structure in the Organizational Setting," *Journal of Abnormal and Social Psychology,* 58 (1959), 170–180.

tions, but they illustrate the fact that the course of a war can depend as much upon the strengths and failings of a commander-in-chief as upon the interaction of geography and economics and social system." [43]

Under What Circumstances Are Ego-Defensive Needs Likely to Manifest Themselves in Political Behavior? The final objection to explanations of politics in terms of personality is one in which the term "personality" denotes not the impact of individuals on social processes (action dispensability), or the mere fact of individual variability (actor dispensability), but rather the specific ways in which "personalities" vary. Once we have found it necessary to explain political behavior by referring to the ways in which political actors vary, objections can be made to whatever specific personality variables we choose to employ. (Objections falling into this final category might be summarized under the heading "actor characteristics.")

Some choices of variables are particularly controversial, especially the variables based on "depth" psychology that have so commonly been drawn upon in such works as Lasswell's *Psychopathology and Politics,* Fromm's *Escape from Freedom,* and *The Authoritarian Personality.*[44] It is the deep motivational variables that many commentators have in mind when they argue that "personality" does not have an important impact on politics. It is sometimes said, for example, that such personality factors do not have much bearing on politics, because the psychic forces evident in the pathological behavior of disturbed individuals do not come into play in the daily behavior of normal people. Rephrasing this assertion conditionally, then, we arrive at the question: Under what circumstances are ego-defensive [45] needs likely to manifest themselves in behavior? It should be emphasized that my selection of this particular question about actor characteristics carries no implication that "personality" should be conceived of in psychodynamic terms, or that it should be equated with the unconscious, the irrational, and the emotional. It simply is convenient to consider this class of personality characteristics, because psychoanalytic notions have guided so much of the personality and politics literature and have antagonized so many of the literature's critics.

Much of what I have said about actor dispensability also applies to the present question. Wherever the circumstances of political behavior

[43] Henry Wilcox, *Portrait of a General* (New York: Knopf, 1964), ix–x.

[44] Harold D. Lasswell, *Psychopathology and Politics,* originally published in 1930, reprinted in *The Political Writings of Harold D. Lasswell* (Glencoe, Ill.: The Free Press, 1951); Erich Fromm, *Escape from Freedom* (New York: Rinehart, 1941); T. W. Adorno, et al., *The Authoritarian Personality* (New York: Harper, 1950).

[45] For the present purposes a detailed conceptual side-trip into the meaning of "ego-defensive needs" will not be necessary. In general, I am referring to the kind of seemingly inexplicable, "pathological" behavior that classical, pre-ego psychology psychoanalysis was preoccupied with. A rough synonym would be needs resulting from "internally induced anxieties," a phrase that appears in Daniel Katz's remarks on ego-defense. "The Functional Approach to the Study of Attitudes," *Public Opinion Quarterly,* 24 (1960), 163–204. Also see Fred I. Greenstein, "Personality and Political Socialization: The Theories of Authoritarian and Democratic Character," *Annals,* 361 (1965), 81–95.

leave room for individuality, the possibility exists for ego-defensive aspects of personality to assert themselves. These circumstances include "unstructured" political situations; settings in which sanctions are weak or conflicting, so that individuals of diverse inclinations are not coerced into acting uniformly; and the various other considerations discussed under the previous heading. These circumstances make it *possible* for ego-defensive personality needs to come to the fore. They do not, of course, make it necessary — or even highly likely — that behavior will have a significant basis in ego defense.

Given the foregoing circumstances, which make ego-defensive behavior possible, what, then, makes it likely (or at least adds to the likelihood) that deeper psychodynamic processes will be at work? We may briefly note these three classes of factors, locating them conveniently in terms of environment, predispositions, and response.

1. *Certain types of environmental stimuli undoubtedly have a greater "resonance" with the deeper layers of the personality than do others.* These are the stimuli which evoke "disproportionately" emotional responses — people seem to be "over-sensitive" to them. They are stimuli which politicians learn to be wary of — for example, such issues as capital punishment, cruelty to animals, and, in recent years, fluoridation of drinking water. Often their stimulus value may be to only a rather small segment of the electorate, but their capacity to arouse fervid response may be such that a Congressman would prefer to confront his constituents on such knotty matters as revision of the tariff affecting the district's principal industry than on, in the phrase of the authors of *Voting*, a "style issue" [46] such as humane slaughtering.

One element in these sensitive issues, Lane and Sears suggest, is that they touch upon "topics dealing with material commonly repressed by individuals. . . . Obvious examples are war or criminal punishment (both dealing with aggression) and birth control or obscenity legislation (both dealing with sexuality). Socially 'dangerous' topics, such as communism and religion, also draw a host of irrational defensive maneuvers. The social 'dangers' that they represent frequently parallel unconscious intra-psychic 'dangers.' For example, an individual with a strong unconscious hatred for all authority may see in Soviet communism a system which threatens intrusion of authoritarian demands into every area of his life. His anti-communism may thus stem more from a residual hatred for his father than for any rational assessment of its likely effects on his life."

Lane and Sears also suggest that, "Opinions dealing with people (such as political candidates) or social groups (such as 'bureaucrats,' 'blue bloods,' or the various ethnic groups) are more likely to invite irrational thought than opinions dealing with most domestic economic issues. Few people can give as clear an account of why they like a man as why they

[46] Bernard Berelson, et al., *Voting* (Chicago: University of Chicago Press, 1954), p. 184.

like an economic policy; the 'warm' — 'cold' dimension seems crucial in many 'person perception' studies, but the grounds for 'warm' or 'cold' feelings are usually obscure. Studies of ethnic prejudice and social distance reveal the inaccessibility of many such opinions to new evidence; they are often compartmentalized, and usually rationalized; that is, covered by plausible explanation which an impartial student of the opinion is inclined to discount." [47]

2. *The likelihood that ego-defensive needs will affect political behavior also is related to the degree to which actors "have" ego-defensive needs.* This assertion is not quite the truism it appears to be. We still have very little satisfactory evidence of various patterns of psychopathology in society [48] and even less evidence about the degree to which emotional disturbance tends to become channelled into political action.

Although it is not a truism, the proposition *is* excessively general. It needs to be expanded upon and elaborated into a series of more specific hypotheses about types of ego-defensive needs and their corresponding adaptations as they relate to political behavior. For example, one of the more convincing findings of the prejudice studies of a decade ago was an observation made not in the well-known *The Authoritarian Personality* but rather in the somewhat neglected *Anti-Semitism and Emotional Disorder* by Ackerman and Jahoda.[49] Personality disorders which manifested themselves in depressive behavior, it was noted, were not accompanied by anti-semitism. But anti-semitism was likely if the individual's typical means of protecting himself from intra-psychic conflict was extrapunitive — that is, if he was disposed to reduce internal tension by such mechanisms as projection. There is no reason to believe that this hypothesis is relevant only to the restricted sphere of anti-semitism.

3. *Finally, certain types of response undoubtedly provide greater occasion for deep personality needs to find outlet than do others* — for example, such responses as affirmations of loyalty in connection with the rallying activities of mass movements led by charismatic leaders and the various other types of response deliberately designed to channel affect into politics. Both in politics and in other spheres of life it should be possible to rank the various classes of typical action in terms of the degree

[47] The quotations are from Robert E. Lane and David O. Sears, *Public Opinion* (Englewood Cliffs, New Jersey: Prentice-Hall, 1964), p. 76. Also see Heinz Hartmann, "The Application of Psychoanalytic Concepts to Social Science," in his *Essays on Ego Psychology* (New York: International Universities Press, 1964), p. 90 f. Lane and Sears also suggest that "irrational" opinion formation is fostered where the "referents of an opinion" are "vague," where the issue is "remote" and it is "difficult to assess its action consequences," and where the "terms of debate" are "abstract." These are points which, in terms of the present discussion, apply generally to the possibility that personal variability will affect behavior (actor dispensability), as well as more specifically to the possibility that ego-defense will come to the fore.

[48] But see Leo Srole, et al., *Mental Health in the Metropolis* (New York: McGraw-Hill, 1962).

[49] Nathan W. Ackerman and Marie Jahoda, *Anti-Semitism and Emotional Disorder* (New York: Harper, 1950).

to which the participants take it as a norm that affective expression is appropriate.

IV. SUMMARY AND CONCLUSIONS

My purpose has been to reconsider a topic that too often has been dealt with in a rather off-hand (and sometimes polemical) fashion: "Is personality important as a determinant of political behavior?" Five of the more intellectually challenging assertions about the lack of relevance of "personality" to the endeavors of the student of politics have been considered. Two of these seem to be based on misconceptions, albeit interesting ones. The three additional objections can be rephrased so that they no longer are objections, but rather provide the occasion for advancing propositions about how and under what circumstances "personality" affects political behavior.

In rephrasing these objections we see three of the many ways in which the term "personality" has been used in statements about politics: to refer to the impact of individual political actions, to designate the fact that individual actors vary in their personal characteristics, and to indicate the specific content of individual variation (and, particularly, "deeper," ego-defensive, psychological processes). It therefore becomes clear that the general question "How important is personality?" is not susceptible to a general answer. It must be broken down into the variety of sub-questions implied in it, and these — when pursued — lead not to simple answers but rather to an extensive examination of the terrain of politics in terms of the diverse ways in which "the human element" comes into play.

Classifying and Predicting Presidential Styles: Two "Weak" Presidents

James D. Barber

In the United States, no one can be president but the President. If he withholds his energies or fritters them away ineffectively, we endure or enjoy a period of national stalemate. So we need to know as much about why some presidents fail to lead as about why others succeed. Indeed,

Reprinted by permission of the publisher and author from *Journal of Social Issues*, XXIV (1968), pp. 51–80.

it can be argued that our periods of political drift have been as fateful for the nation as our eras of New Freedom, New Deal and New Frontier.

But the dull presidents are a trial for the political analyst, particularly for the student of personality and political leadership. It is not just that they sap one's intellectual verve, but that their personality configurations are, on the surface, indistinct. They thus provide "hard-case" tests for the supposition that personality helps shape a president's politics. If a personality approach can work with Coolidge and Hoover, it can work with any chief executive. I mean to show here how these two men illustrate some recurrent dynamics of presidential style and how these dynamics can be caught in a theory with predictive possibilities.

The following pages take up these themes in order. First I shall set forth a scheme for classifying presidents according to the major dimensions of their political styles and demonstrate the applicability of the classification scheme to Coolidge and Hoover. The purpose of this section is to define and apply concepts potentially useful for classifying political leaders in terms of patterned regularities in political styles, not simply to describe each president as a unique case. The data I shall use are biographical; their presentation in small space requires radical summarization.

The second section poses a theory, focusing primarily on the president's first independent political success, of the development of a political style. In brief, I argue that a president's style is a reflection of the ways of performing which brought him success at the time, usually in late adolescence or early adulthood, when he emerged as a personality distinctive from his family heritage, in a role involving relatively intensive participation in a socially organized setting. It is at this point that the argument moves from classification to prediction, from an emphasis on naming to an emphasis on explaining. Biographical materials are then treated in a more dynamic fashion, in an effort to reveal the psychological functioning which sustains an integrated pattern of behavior, that is, a distinctive and consistent political style.

STYLE

"Style" in this context means a collection of habitual action patterns in meeting role demands. Viewed from outside, a man's style is the observed quality and character of his performance. Viewed from inside, it is his bundle of strategies for adapting, for protecting and enhancing self-esteem. The main outlines of a political style can be usefully delineated, I have argued, by the interaction of two main dimensions.[1] The first is *activity-passivity* in performing the role. Presidents have often been typed in this way. The question here is not one of effectiveness but of effort.

[1] See James David Barber, *The Lawmakers: Recruitment and Adaptation to Legislative Life* (1965) and "Leadership strategies for legislative party cohesion." David Shapiro's *Neurotic Styles* (1965) is helpful in understanding styles in general and several specific style patterns.

Political roles, including the presidency, allow for wide variation in the amount of energy the person invests in his work. Such investment has a large voluntary component and typically reflects to a high degree the man's personal habits as these interact with the demands of the situation. The second dimension is *positive-negative affect* toward his activity. Action *per se* tells us nothing of affect. The way one feels about his work — specifically, whether he goes about his tasks reasonably happily or with an air of discouragement and sadness — tells much about the fit between his needs and his duties. His affect toward his work represents the self's way of registering that fit. Like activity-passivity, the affect dimension links personality with political leadership.

Put together, these two crude and simple variables delineate four political types. Briefly, the active-positive shows a style oriented primarily toward productiveness; the active-negative toward personal ambition; the passive-positive toward affection; and the passive-negative toward (minimal) performance of duty. Within these general nuclear types, a series of personality dynamics relate the self-system, reactions to political experience, strategies of adaptation to political roles, types of vulnerability to political persuasion and effectiveness in performing political tasks. In psychological terms, activity and affect interact to give, respectively, generally adjusted, compulsive, compliant and withdrawn types. There is no one "political man," no universal pattern of leadership performance.

For the analysis of political behavior in collegial bodies such as legislatures, this classificatory scheme may capture the main comparisons. For the Presidency, an office of immense individual power, we need more precise characterizations. I propose here to deepen the analysis within each category by elaborating three subcategories. These subcategories emerge when we ask (extending the major dimensions of activity and affect) to what extent and with what adjustive purpose the president takes advantage of the main opportunities the role affords him. Specifically, how does he integrate his personal style with the role's opportunities for:

> *Rhetoric:* A leader may accentuate certain kinds of expressiveness to audiences, ranging from the world audience to his companions at dinner.
> *Business:* He may or may not concentrate on managing the endless flow of details that flood onto his desk, the studying and budget calculations, the reviewing of memoranda, the personnel problems, etc.
> *Personal Relations:* A president may concentrate in various ways on bargaining with, dominating, combatting and depending on the political elite close around him.

Obviously all presidents do all of these things. But equally obviously they vary in their devotion to each and in their style of performance in each. The first task in analyzing a presidential style, then, is to characterize, within the general framework of activity and affect, the way the man habitually meets the role's demands that he speak, that he manage ordinary business, and that he operate with others at close range. The examples presented — and they are only that — show how these style elements can be distinctive and habitual for the man and politically significant for the nation.

Once the styles are understood, we move to an even more difficult question: how might they have been predicted? How might we have supposed, on the basis of the man's known history, what he would do with the office?

THE COOLIDGE STYLE

Calvin Coolidge as president fits the passive-negative, or withdrawn, type. Of the three main dimensions of style he emphasized rhetoric. His rhetorical style was sharply compartmentalized according to the audience: witty banter with reporters, highminded addresses to the nation, silence at social occasions. He avoided detailed work on presidential business. His personal relations were cooly detached. These patterns are evident as the main themes of the Coolidge presidency.[2]

Rhetoric

Coolidge complained that "One of the most appalling trials which confront a President is the perpetual clamor for public utterances." But this "foster-child of silence" was anything but quiet in public. In office 67 months, he held 520 press conferences, an average of 7.8 per month, compared with Franklin Roosevelt's 6.9. He gave radio addresses about once a month. He got off to an excellent start with the reporters, cracking jokes at this first conference; their "hearty applause" on that occasion made it "one of my most pleasant memories." They were "the boys" who came along on his vacations. Clearly he enjoyed their enjoyment, particularly when he could surprise or titillate them with Yankee humor. He carefully stage-managed his "I do not choose to run for President in nineteen twenty-eight" statement, releasing the news at noon on the fourth anniversary of taking office, grinning broadly. His wife was as surprised as the reporters were. He let himself be photographed in full Indian headdress, cowboy chaps and hat, overalls and any number of other outfits; there is a picture of him presenting a sap bucket to Henry Ford. When a friend protested that his antics made people laugh, Coolidge said, "Well, it's good for people to laugh."

His formal addresses had a completely different tone. They were sermons from the church of New England idealism. "When the President speaks," he wrote, "it ought to be an event," by which he meant a serious and dignified and uplifting event. He spoke on "Education: the Corner-

2 On Coolidge, I have found most useful the biographies by Fuess and White, and Coolidge's *Autobiography*. McCoy's new biography, which appeared as I finished this piece, seems to confirm its interpretation. The short quotations, too numerous to attribute individually here, are from the above three books and from Cornwell's, on which I have relied for much material on presidential rhetoric. Lowry (1921) is also helpful.

stone of Self-Government," "The High Place of Labor," "Ordered Liberty and World Peace," "Authority and Religious Liberty," "Religion and the Republic," "The Genius of America," "Destiny is in you," "Do the day's work," "The things of the spirit come first," and "The chief ideal of the American people is idealism," — this was Coolidge in the presidential pulpit. And he was quite serious. When Will Rogers imitated his nasal twang and penchant for cliches, he was much offended and refused Rogers' apology.

Business

Coolidge sincerely believed in hard work. He felt busy, even rushed, but his constant routine included a daily nap and often eleven hours of sleep in twenty-four. Often tired and bored, he gradually abandoned all physical exercise except for brief walks and spent much time in silent contemplation, gazing out his office window. His strength was not effort but patience. "Let well enough alone," was his motto. He was the "provincial who refuses to become excited over events for which he has no direct responsibility." He kept Harding's cabinet, let Daugherty hang on for a long time, tried to delay his friends' efforts to boost him in 1924. Asked how he kept fit he said, "By avoiding the big problems." Most of the time Coolidge simply did not want to be bothered.

Underneath these tactics, supporting and justifying them, was a strain of mystical resignation. "I am only in the clutch of forces that are greater than I am," he wrote, despite being "the most powerful man in the world." He bore his young son's death with Roman stoicism: "The ways of Providence are beyond our understanding." The dedicated man, he wrote in his newspaper column, "finds that in time of need some power outside himself directs his course." Coolidge could wait, storing up his meager energies with a feeling of rightness in entrusting himself to fate. "Government is growth," he said, and added: " — slow growth." He and Providence presided while the rate slowed down.

Personal Relations

Coolidge got rid of much work by giving it to others, and he believed in doing just that. "One rule of action more important than all others consists in never doing anything that some one else can do for you." He appointed or retained "men of sufficient ability so that they can solve all the problems that arise under their jurisdiction." He rarely interfered and he resented others interfering with him. His loyal helper Frank Stearns got repeated rebuffs for his trouble. Coolidge seldom discussed political matters with his wife. He complained of Hoover as Secretary of Commerce (Coolidge called him "the wonder boy" or "the miracle worker"): "That man has offered me unsolicited advice for six years, all of it bad!"

Yet he was always surrounded by people. He and Grace entertained more than any previous family in the White House. Alone, he said, he got "a sort of naked feeling." His poker face, his long impenetrable silences at social affairs were known to all Washington and gave rise to scores of anecdotes as matron after matron tried to pry a few words from him. Occasionally he could be induced to talk about Vermont. More often, he simply sat. This was "a form of defense," his biographer says. "Can't hang you for what you don't say," said Coolidge. "In order to function at all," he warned his successors, the President "has to be surrounded by many safeguards. If these were removed for only a short time, he would be overwhelmed by the people who would surge in upon him." He learned not to smile, as smiling encouraged longer office visits. He had very little interest in women and was, his biographer says, "embarrassed when left for even a short period in the company of the other sex." Undoubtedly much of Coolidge's acerbity at dinner parties was a reaction to intensified shyness at having to cope with the matron to his left and right. When he did speak, it was some tart, pithy puckishness, mildly aggressive, disconcerting, with a quality of surprise in a conventional conversational setting. In a rare and revealing confession, he once told Frank Stearns why:

> Do you know, I've never really grown up? It's a hard thing for me to play this game. In politics, one must meet people, and that's not easy for me . . . When I was a little fellow, as long ago as I can remember, I would go into a panic if I heard strange voices in the kitchen. I felt I just couldn't meet the people and shake hands with them. Most of the visitors would sit with Father and Mother in the kitchen, and the hardest thing in the world was to have to go through the kitchen door and give them a greeting. I was almost ten before I realized I couldn't go on that way. And by fighting hard I used to manage to get through that door. I'm all right with old friends, but every time I meet a stranger, I've got to go through the old kitchen door, back home, and it's not easy. (Fuess, 1965, 25.)

Coolidge "tried deliberately to suppress 'aggressive wittiness'," but "it broke out repeatedly in quaint comments."

Even this brief account shows the main features of the Coolidge style. Clearly he belongs in the withdrawn type. Aside from his banter with reporters, he did not particularly enjoy being President, given all the demands that were made on him, and he conserved his energies stingily. Many of his characteristics — his rural Yankee background; his persistent turning back to his past, his father, his homeplace; his avoidance of controversy and patient faith in Providence: his penchant for reverie and retreat; his sense of strangeness in a cosmopolitan environment ("Puritan in Babylon") — concord with empirical findings on this type in a very different environment. His style within that type is also clear. Words for Coolidge were shaped heavily by his relations to different audiences. The "serious" audience was the nation, to which he addressed sermons on common virtue, purveying the illusion of specificity through epigram. In fact, his abstract pseudo-Hegelian fatalism had little clear connection with the political issues of the day. His humor at news conferences was badinage with the boys, a show with much audience participation, full of little surprises. There as in his dinner table silences and mild insults, the focus was on Coolidge as a clown, one who could touch the heart but leave the political brain and brawn of the nation relaxed.

His philosophy helped him rationalize his leisurely pace. His method was to concentrate on matters only the President had to decide, and to define that category as narrowly as possible. Most everything could wait. And Coolidge himself could wait, with utter, unflappable calm for longer than the last of his advisors. He also managed to rationalize his independence of others; clearly his style in close interpersonal relations cut him off effectively from much of the Washington conversational froth — but also from any effective political bargaining with administrative or legislative or party leaders. He was a loner who endured in order to serve, while the nation drifted.

THE HOOVER STYLE

Hoover belongs in the active-negative category, the compulsive type. He emphasized hard work on detail and endless conferences behind the scenes. He avoided and detested the rhetorical demands of the office. In personal relations, his was a stance of highly restrained aggression. Again, some illustrative evidence is necessary to make this pattern clear.[3]

Rhetoric

The rise of Herbert Hoover coincided with an immense expansion in the mass media, particularly newspapers and radio. Hoover was a genuine hero; his remarkable effectiveness in European relief activities cannot be seriously questioned. He was the subject, not the instigator, of a vast public relations build-up largely due to increased media demands for news and to the drama and success of his works. But Hoover in the presidency "transmuted all adventure into business," as Arthur Schlesinger (1957) complains. He detested the office's demands for dramatization. "The presidency is more than an executive's responsibility," he wrote; "it is an inspiring symbol of all that is highest in American purpose and ideals." Yet he could not bring himself to practice the pretense such inspiration requires. "This is not a showman's job," he said, "I will not step out of character," and "You can't make a Teddy Roosevelt out of me." He felt uncomfortable when forced to perform in public: "I have never liked the clamor of crowds. I intensely dislike superficial social contacts. I made no pretensions to oratory and I was terrorized at the opening of every speech." The "miracle worker" disdained "the crowd" which "only feels: it has no mind of its own which can plan. The crowd is credulous, it destroys, it hates and it dreams — but it never builds."

[3] On Hoover, the most useful sources are Irwin, Lyons and Hoover's *Memoirs*. Here again Cornwell's chapters have supplied much material. The short quotations are too numerous to attribute individually. They are taken from the above and from Liggett, 1932; Meyers, 1934; Warren, 1967; Wolfe, 1956; Wood, 1932; and Hinshaw, 1950.

Extremely sensitive to criticism, Hoover reacted to personal abuse with "hurt contempt." He was rarely aggressive, normally suffering in silence with only an occasional private complaint. He got off to a good start with the press, setting more liberal rules for the conference, but even before the stock market crash he began to restrict the reporters, became more secretive and admonished them for the error of their ways. Often he withdrew to his forest camp in Virginia without notice to the press; there he set up guards to keep the newsmen away. He began to play favorites among them and to go over their heads to editors and publishers. He cancelled conferences on short notice, ignored questions and took to reading prepared statements. Eventually, most of the White House reporters turned against him. He met them less and less frequently and virtually eliminated conferences near the end of his term.

Hoover's public addresses rarely discussed specific policies in detail. His twenty-one radio addresses were mainly "greetings" to specific groups, full of vague moral precepts. Speech-writing was as hard for him as speech-making. He drafted each one in longhand, went through a dozen or more drafts and heavily edited proofs to produce a labored and ordinary address. But perhaps the most peculiar feature of the tone of Hoover's presidential statements was their public optimism in the midst of social disaster. As the Depression deepened, again and again he found business fundamentally sound, the worst of the crisis over, employment gradually increasing, government efforts remarkably successful, no one actually starving — or so he said, giving rise to a 'credibility gap' of modern proportions. His pollyanna reassurances stand in stark relief against both the condition of the country and the character of the man. His secretary put it more kindly: "Figuratively, he was the father protecting his family against the troubles impending, shouldering their burdens for them, keeping the 'bad news' to himself, outwardly trying to be as smiling and cheerful as possible."

Business

Meanwhile, he slaved and suffered in silence. Long before the Depression Hoover was frequently discouraged. At the Paris Peace Conference in 1919, Colonel House found him "simply reveling in gloom"; Ike Hoover remembered that in the White House he "never laughed aloud" and "always had a frown on his face," and his secretary recalls that "he worried as have few Presidents in our history with discouragement at his lot most of the time." He was glad when it was all over: "All the money in the world could not induce me to live over the last nine months. The conditions we have experienced make this office a compound hell." He worked as hard as he worried. Even before the crash his routine was a rigorous one, beginning with an energetic medicine ball game first thing in the morning. After his inauguration he immediately set about a series of programs for change and reform. Then when the panic hit, "he began that grinding, brutal, self-lacerating labor, often eighteen or twenty hours a day or clear around the clock, which would continue unbroken until the blessed hour of release more than three years later. No galley slave of old was more firmly riveted to his drudgery, for he was chained by his surpassing sense of duty." "So tired that every bone in my body aches," Hoover trudged on. Near the close of his tenure he allowed himself one bitter outburst in public, significantly in reply to charges that he had "done nothing." In "the one harsh word that I have uttered in public office," he called such charges "deliberate, intolerable falsehoods."

And so they were. He had done plenty, but to little effect. Hoover was immersed in detail. As Bernard Baruch put it, "To Hoover's brain facts are as water to a sponge. They are absorbed into every tiny interstice." He had a "card index" mind which could grasp and retain details and figures without notes. He commissioned endless policy studies to produce the facts on which to base programs. His whole orientation, in other words, was away from the vagaries of opinion and toward the hard precision of fact.

Much of his energy went into an endless round of conferences. Hoover appeared to believe that if only he could bring the right people together and give them the right proposal, they would agree and march off to execute his plan. John Kenneth Galbraith called these "no-business meetings," designed to accomplish nothing, but there is little doubt Hoover had high hopes for this technique of "coordination." In almost all such encounters he had more pertinent information and had worried through a more thoroughly organized proposal than any other participant. And he was President of the United States. The others he expected to behave as had his subordinates in business, in the European relief organization, and in the Department of Commerce: as willing endorsers and enforcers. When cabinet members and congressmen failed to respond in this way, Hoover's gloom deepened. His personal discouragement proved contagious; to Henry L. Stimson, his Secretary of State, a private conversation with Hoover was "like sitting in a bath of ink."

Personal Relations

Hoover kept his aggressive feelings tightly controlled in close relations as in public ones. At a time when, as he complained, "My men are dropping around me," when H. G. Wells found him a "sickly, overworked and overwhelmed man," Hoover was often tempted to lash out. Deep inside he may have been, as his apologist Lyons believed, "a sensitive, soft-hearted person who craves affection, enjoys congenial company, and suffers under the slings of malice," but he could also feel intense anger. "I'll rattle his bones" was his typical expression when thwarted by some obstructionist. In 1932 he meant to "carry the fight right to Roosevelt . . . We have got to crack him every time he opens his mouth." But he would quickly rein in these feelings:

> He was almost always the master of his emotions, however provoked he might be. If something went wrong, if some individual

really aroused him he would, in common parlance, "blow off steam." But it was only for a moment. The next minute he would be pressing his buzzer. When the stenographer was seated beside his desk, instead of telling Mr. Blank cryptically what he thought, he dictated a most diplomatic communication. There was never a barb in it. Rather, it represented earnest and skillful effort to induce that individual to see eye to eye with him. (Joslin, 1934, 19)

With his immediate staff "there were no cross words if a subordinate made an error." Nor would he "let himself be baited into a controversy if he could possibly avoid it." Many a time it was tried out on him. His usual comment, made with supreme contempt, was: "A man should not become embroiled with his inferior." His expression was one of "pained disbelief" when other political and congressional leaders failed to keep their commitments.

Of course his demeanor affected his political relations. His inability to enter into genuinely cooperative relations with others, relations involving compromise, an appreciation for the irrational in politics, a sense for the other man's position, meant that his endeavors to induce an enthusiastic response were doomed to failure. He could lead an organization of committed subordinates, but he could not create that commitment among leaders with their own bases of power and their own overriding purposes.

Hoover did accept renomination in 1932, but reluctantly. He "had no overpowering desire to run again," expressed his indifference to the subject, anticipated defeat, and found the campaign a "miserable experience." But he "felt that he must follow through to the end of the struggle. Be that as it may, he had a desperate desire for vindication of himself and his policies." The purpose was defensive, not for any positive achievement. The expected defeat brought relief, not despair.

No brief account can do justice to a complex character, but it seems clear that Hoover belongs in the compulsive type of political leader, outlined by much activity and much unhappiness in the role. Many themes fit this pattern: his struggles with the 'exposure' element of the public figure role, resulting in the adoption of a propagandistic orientation; his history as a rapidly upward mobile young man whose links to politics developed out of his nonpolitical occupation; his feelings of frustration and powerlessness in the face of an unresponsive or hostile environment; his anxious, unremitting labor; his suffering and struggle to restrain his aggression. Deeper analysis, one would predict, would reveal a self dominated by the conflict between conscience and ambition, alternating between feelings of guilt and feelings of impotence.

The main distinctive elements in Hoover's style can also be readily summarized. Words were difficult for him; he resisted expression and fell back on a rhetoric of exaggeration when forced into the limelight. Work was his main strategy for success, intensely compulsive work on detail. And in his relations with others he stressed restraint of aggression, an anticipation that his plan would win and succeed in execution. These strategies failed. That Hoover sustained them in the face of repeated negative messages from the environment attests to their rootedness in his personality. The office no more made the man than it made his successor.

TOWARD A PREDICTIVE THEORY

Where did these styles come from? Our problem is not to discover why Coolidge and Hoover became presidents while others with similar background took different paths, but to find out why, being presidents, they acted as they did. Furthermore, we want an *economical* method for answering that question, a method amenable to *generalization* to other cases, and a method which produces *predictive* statements. That requires a theory. Let me set mine out as starkly as I can.

First Independent Political Success

In the lives of most political leaders there is a clearly discernible period, usually in late adolescence or early adulthood, in which a style is adopted. Typically that period can be identified (a) by marked infusions of confidence from relative success, (b) by a relatively new and special relationship to group life, and (c) by a relatively sudden emergence from obscurity to wider attention. The way in which the man finds words to relate himself to an expanded audience, the role of work in bringing him new success, and the mode of his more intimate links with others around him presage his style in the presidency. If we can discover how future presidents met and resolved these fundamental problems in their own critical periods, we should be able to predict how they are likely to attempt (not necessarily successfully) to solve similar problems as chief executives.[4]

    Motives. How can one understand this formative period? First one must view it against the background of compensatory needs inherited from childhood. It is important to highlight the significance of change in the person's life situation. We want the meanings his new development had for him, and that requires knowledge of what he was before. A style's staying power, its persistence and resurgence, depends on its rootedness in strong motives. Viewed retrospectively, a style offers important compensations; viewed prospectively, it promises the continuation and extension of rewards. There is a turning away from an unsatisfactory prior condition to a possibly more satisfactory condition for the future. These satisfactions, and the anticipation of them, are the motive forces which energize the new system.

    Resources. Second, the formative period can only be discerned in the light of the resources a man brings to it. The condition of one's body is a simple example of personal resource. The condition of one's mind

---

[4] On the significance of compensation in political leadership, see Lasswell, 1930 and 1945. . . .

is a subtler case, depending as it does on learning and on the collection of relevant experiences and perceptions a person brings to the formative period. These constitute a repertoire of potential style elements upon which he can draw when his time comes. His learning until then can be considered as a rehearsal, though rarely in any conscious sense, for a decisive commitment to a particular style. His experiments in self definition, real and vicarious, set out boundaries and pathways for his map of the future.

Opportunities. And last, a style is not formed in a vacuum but in a context of opportunities. Just as we do not expect a person who has always had all the affection he has wanted to seek an unending succession of affection in adulthood, and just as we do not expect an illiterate to adopt an identity as a writer, so not every environment available at the time offers the same chances for personal development. These constraints and stimuli in the immediate culture may have a great deal to do with the kinds of strategies one translates into part of his personal identity.[5]

As a beginning test, then, the following pages examine Coolidge and Hoover at the time of their first independent political success, introduced in each case by a radically summarized account of the needs and resources brought from childhood. A final section draws together these themes with the conclusions derived from the material on their presidential styles.

Coolidge: Needs from Childhood

John Calvin Coolidge, Jr., was born in Plymouth, Vermont, on the Fourth of July, 1872, the first child, after four years of marriage, of John Calvin Coolidge and Victoria Josephine Coolidge, nephew of Julius Caesar Coolidge, grandson of Calvin Galusha Coolidge, descendent of five generations of his family in a Vermont village. His mother was a quiet, delicately beautiful person, a chronic invalid since shortly after her marriage. Coolidge remembered "a touch of mysticism and poetry in her nature." His father was a big, stern-visaged man, a storekeeper and pillar of the community who had held many town offices and went to the state legislature. His son admired him for "qualities that were greater than any I possess," and accepted much paternal admonition without complaint.

Calvin's early hero was his grandfather "Galoosh," tall, spare and handsome, an expert horseman and practical joker, said to have a trace of Indian blood, who raised colts and puppies and peacocks and taught the boy to ride standing up behind him. His grandmother ("The Puritan severity of her convictions was tempered by the sweetness of womanly charity") read the Bible to him and when he misbehaved shut him up in the dark, windowless attic, "dusty with cobwebs."

Calvin's younger sister Abbie, his constant playmate, was "a lively affectionate girl, with flaming red hair, who was full of energy and impressed everybody by her personality," — almost the exact opposite of

---

[5] On the interactions of motivations, resources and opportunities in accounting for political action, see Barber (1965, 10–15, 217–240).

her shy brother. Calvin himself was small and frail, with his mother's features, punctual and methodical, only occasionally joining in the schoolyard teasing.

So much for the cast of characters. Life began its hammer blows at this shy boy when he was six. His hero Galusha died as Calvin read him the Bible. Six years later his invalid mother, "who used what strength she had to lavish care upon me and my sister," died as a result of an accident with a runaway horse. Her passing left an indelible mark on him:

> In an hour she was gone. It was her thirty-ninth birthday. I was
> twelve years old. We laid her away in the blustering snows of
> March. The greatest grief that can come to a boy came to me.
> Life was never to seem the same again. (Coolidge, 1929, 13)

Calvin was despondent too long. His family became concerned; but he kept up his school work "with no tardy marks and good deportment."

Later at the nearby Black River Academy, where his parents and grandmother had gone to school, he was unhappy and homesick, though his father brought him home nearly every weekend. In his third year Abbie joined him there; Calvin had written he hoped she could come. A year and a half later, at age fifteen, she was dead of appendicitis. Calvin came home to be with her in her last hours.

There was another unsettled time for Calvin, like that following his mother's death. He failed the entrance examinations for Amherst College. He had caught cold and stayed home "for a considerable time." In late winter he went back to Black River Academy to get "certified" for Amherst. There he worked hard, "made almost no acquaintances," and in two months was approved for Amherst. In September his father married a Plymouth neighbor, a spinster Calvin had known all his life. "For thirty years," Coolidge wrote much later, "she watched over and loved me." They corresponded regularly until her death in 1920.

Amherst was an all-male place where three-quarters or more of the students belonged to fraternities, "the most unique feature of Amherst life . . . strongly recommended by the members of the faculty," as the *Students' Handbook* said. Calvin needed no urging. He had written his father from school that he and a friend should visit the college "to see about getting me into a society there." But the scheme did not work. Calvin moved into a boardinghouse. The others there were quickly pledged. He remained an "Ouden," an outsider in a small community of clans. "I don't seem to get acquainted very fast," he wrote home in October. After Christmas he wrote that "Every time I get home I hate to go away worse than before and I don't feel so well here now as the first day I came here last fall but suppose I will be all right in a day or two." Two days later: "I feel quite reconciled to being here tonight but felt awful mean yesterday and the day before. I don't know why, I never was homesick any before." In his first two years at Amherst Coolidge was "to say the least, an inconspicuous member of the class." He faithfully attended class meetings, but did not join in the myriad activities, formal and informal, scholarly and athletic, religious and amorous, going on around him. He took long walks in the woods.

Nor was his social isolation balanced with scholarly achievement; his first term marks averaged 2 on a scale of 5. "The marks seem pretty low, don't they?" he wrote his father. He remembered much later that "It needed some encouragement from my father for me to continue." He had begun with the hope that he could do well in his courses with plenty of time to spare.

Thus at twenty-one Calvin Coolidge was an indistinct personality, in-articulate, ineffective, alone. Particularly in affection and achievement he stood on the threshold of adulthood much deprived.

Coolidge: Resources from Childhood. In his mind he had been gathering impressions and registering experiences which would later be useful. He had known his father and grandfather as political leaders in the community. He saw how his father made decisions — "painstaking, precise, and very accurate" — and came to understand government as "restraints which the people had imposed upon themselves in order to promote the common welfare." In the summer before he entered Amherst his father took him to a gathering in Bennington to hear President Benjamin Harrison; there he heard much high oratory about the "high consecration to liberty."

As a boy he had taken a minor part in speaking "pieces," acting in amateur plays, and was even an "end man" once in a local minstrel show. Cicero's orations stuck with him from Latin classes. At graduation from Black River Academy, in a class of five boys and four girls, he delivered an address on "Oratory in History," the newspaper called it "masterly" and his teacher said his speech was "the best one he had seen." After his freshman year at Amherst, at the Independence Day celebration in Plymouth — "Of course, the Fourth of July meant a good deal to me, because it was my birthday" — he delivered a speech on "Freedom," "burning with fervor, replete with denunciation of Proud Albion, and rich with the glorification of our Revolutionary heroes." Perhaps inspired by his freshman rhetoric teacher, this was his last experiment in the florid style of oratory.

Had Coolidge's life taken a different turn, other events, other impressions would have lasted into his autobiographical years. As it was, he had in his mind a number of important images: of small scale Yankee democracy, of his mother reading the romantic poets, of his father succeeding by being careful, of the familial legitimacy of politics, and of himself surviving before audiences. So far he had made nothing of these resources. But they were waiting.

Coolidge: First Independent Political Success. Of the events in his first two years at Amherst, Coolidge wrote:

> In the development of every boy who is going to amount to any-thing there comes a time when he emerges from his immature ways and by the greater precision of his thought and action realizes that he has begun to find himself. Such a transition

finally came to me. It was not accidental but the result of hard work. If I had permitted my failure, or what seemed to me at the time a lack of success to discourage me, I cannot see any way in which I would ever have made progress. If we keep our faith in ourselves, and what is even more important, keep our faith in regular and persistent application to hard work, we need not worry about the outcome. (Coolidge, 1929, 60)

As a matter of fact, what he calls his "transition" was triggered by events nearly "accidental"; his success did not result primarily from "hard work"; and he was, as we have seen, "discouraged" by his earlier lack of success. (Perhaps every autobiography is a mixture of real memories and new meanings, a last attempt to join together life and belief.) In any case, Coolidge did begin his junior year an isolated boy with no real achievements and left Amherst as a young man with a distinctive style of action. In between the whole intensity of his experience, its pace and significance were revolutionized.

Amherst upperclassmen could wear high derbies and carry canes. Each fall the members of the junior class raced from one end of the athletic field to the other, clad in "topper" and stick. The last seven across the line had to provide dinner and entertainment for the rest. Coolidge was not last, but was one of the losers. His assignment was a speech on "Why I Got Stuck." He began in silence by turning his pockets inside out to show that he had lost all his money on the race. Then: "You wouldn't expect a plow horse to make time on the race track or a follower of the plow to be a Mercury," he said. Pitching hay didn't fit one as a sprinter. And other such comments. Then, in conclusion: "Remember, boys, the Good Book says that the first shall be last and the last shall be first." The speech was a success — the whole class laughed and gave him an ovation. It was his first such appearance and it brought him more attention and notoriety than anything he had done at Amherst so far. He began to emerge as a character, although the incident is not mentioned in his *Autobiography*.

That same year he began to attract attention as a debater. Public speaking and debating were compulsory parts of the curriculum. One of his classmates wrote: "It was in his junior year that we discovered Coolidge. In that year we began debating, and in the debates we found that he could talk. It was as if a new and gifted man had joined the class." Coolidge now became more and more adept at brief and direct statement. He won frequently in debating, perhaps every time in the junior debates. In November of that year he wrote his father proudly: "In view of the fact that yesterday I put up a debate said to be the best heard on the floor of the chapel this term . . . can you send me $25?" In January he wrote home another glowing report of a successful debate. At the end of his junior year the students in the public speaking class voted to split the prize between Coolidge and another speaker. He continued debating in his senior year. In September he was elected to present the "Grove Oration" at the graduation exercises the following June. This was meant to be a humorous speech following the ponderousness of more formal addresses. In June, after a long series of indoor sermons and addresses, the students went to the College Grove, lit up their corncob pipes and settled back on the grass. Coolidge began this way: "The mantle of truth falls upon the Grove Orator on condition he wear it wrong side out," and went on through a series of in-house jokes, continually interrupted by hecklers and shouts of laughter. "The oration was packed with what today would be called 'wisecracks'," his biographer says, "many of them sarcastic observations on members of the faculty — remarks which, although good-natured in tone and intention, had nevertheless something of a bite." The speech was a smashing success.

In parallel with these oratorical victories, Coolidge achieved social ones. He was elected a member of Phi Gamma Delta on January 15th of his senior year. This began a life-long, active tie, his only fraternal connection. From the start he entered into the group's affairs; a classmate recalls that

> He took a deep interest in the chapter, was most faithful in attending "goat" and committee meetings, and while he did not live at the house, he passed considerable time there. We soon began to rely upon his counsel and judgment, and he was a distinct help to us in many serious problems we had to meet at that time. (Fuess, 1965, 54)

He wrote his father that "being in a society" would cost a little more money. From that time on, Coolidge was a faithful "Fiji," raising money, acting as the chapter's lawyer, returning to inspect the house carefully from cellar to garret, organizing (while he was President) the "Fiji Sires and Sons." His role in his brief membership as a student was that of the faithful attender and business helper; he skipped the dances and card games and "wild parties." At long last he had found a band of brothers. He was not a central figure in this group, but it is obvious that his membership meant a great deal to him after years of being left out. The moral he draws from this in the *Autobiography* is touching: "It has been my observation in life that, if one will only exercise the patience to wait, his wants are likely to be filled."

Garman's Influence. He had found a voice and developed a relationship to his audience; he had a club of friends. At the same time, Coolidge found a model, an idol with whom to identify and a set of philosophical beliefs to guide him. This was Charles E. Garman, professor of philosophy, whose course, as Coolidge took it, ran from the spring term of junior year through senior year, moving from psychology to philosophy to ethics. "It always seemed to me that all our other studies were in the nature of a preparation for the course in philosophy," Coolidge remembered. Garman, a tall, cadaverous man with piercing black eyes, was a dramatic character, "a middle-aged Hamlet," extremely popular among the students.

Garman was in reality "a devout and rather orthodox New England

Congregationalist" with a strong neo-Hegelian bent. Our interest is less in what he taught than in what Coolidge carried away from him and retained for thirty-five years. Garman did not carry his question-raising method to the point of not providing answers. Coolidge recalled his emphasis on rational judgment in ethical matters, the existence of a personal God and of "the complete dependence of all the universe on Him," man as set "off in a separate kingdom from all other creatures," the "spiritual appeal" of art as Divine revelation, the essential quality of men, the dignity of work and industry's right to work's rewards, "that might does not make right, that the end does not justify the means, and that expediency as a working principle is bound to fail." All of this Coolidge lays out in an unusually lengthy passage of his memoirs. Garman posted aphorisms on the walls of his classroom — "Carry all questions back to fundamental principles," "Weigh the evidence," "The question *how* answers the question *what*," "Process not product," and so forth. But perhaps the key lesson Coolidge retained is found later in the *Autobiography* in the context of his early steps in politics, when he was elected Mayor of Northampton, Massachusetts:

> Ever since I was in Amherst College I have remembered how Garman told his class in philosophy that if they would go along with events and hold to the main stream, without being washed ashore by the immaterial cross currents, they would some day be men of power. (Coolidge, 1929, 99–100)

Already the echoes of Coolidge as President are apparent.

Coolidge remembered that "We looked upon Garman as a man who walked with God," and that he was "one of the most remarkable men with whom I ever came in contact," a man who "was given a power which took his class up into a high mountain of spiritual life and left them alone with God," who had "no pride of opinion, no atom of self-ishness," "a follower of the truth, a disciple of the Cross, who bore the infirmities of us all." Coolidge did not try to defend Garman's position theoretically. But

> I knew that in experience it has worked. In time of crisis my be-lief that people can know the truth, that when it is presented to them they must accept it, has saved me from many of the coun-sels of expediency. (Coolidge, 1929, 67)

He had found a rule of life, and the words to express it with.

The Break with His Past. Coolidge had written a romantic story for the Amherst *Literary Monthly* in the summer between his junior and senior years. In his senior year, he tried his hand at a very different liter-ary task, undertaken in secret: an essay for a national contest on "The Principles Fought for in the War of the American Revolution." The Amherst History Department awarded his piece a silver medal; the fol-lowing December when he was working in a law office in Northampton, Coolidge learned he was also the national winner. One of the partners asked him, "Have you told your father?" To which he replied, "No, do you think I'd better?" In his *Autobiography* Coolidge recalled that

> I had a little vanity in wishing my father to learn about it first from the press, which he did. He had questioned some whether I was really making anything of my education, in pretense I now think, not because he doubted it but because he wished to impress me with the desirability of demonstrating it. (Coolidge, 1929, 74)

Coolidge had moved from an emotional psychology, a sentimental dramatism in his story ("Margaret's Mist") to the logic of principles, the metier of ethical philosophy which he would continue to emphasize all his life. But his "No, do you think I'd better?" also represented a change. Right after graduation he returned to the farm for a summer's work and then went to Northampton to learn law. As late as January of his senior year he had not yet decided whether the law or storekeeping would be his profession. He wrote his father then, "You will have to decide." He did know that he wanted "to live where I can be of some use to the world and not simply where I should get a few dollars together." By graduation he had decided that the law was "the highest of the professions." On his own, Coolidge sought a place and in September 1895 he went to work in a law office in Northampton. When he joined the law office Coolidge made a break with his past. The boy whose name had been recorded in various forms now discarded the "John" and became plain Calvin Coolidge. And "during these first years he worked so hard that for three years he did not find time to go back to Plymouth." The distance was about a hundred miles.

"That I was now engaged in a serious enterprise of life I so fully realized that I went to the barber shop and divested myself of the college fashion of long hair." He who had so often written home of his successes kept the largest one a secret. He found a job without his father's help. None of the Coolidges had been lawyers. Calvin had formed his style and begun his own life. He had found a way to be; he was not entirely certain where he was going.

As we have seen, Coolidge himself attributed to his experience in the last two years at Amherst a shaping influence on his mind and heart. His biographers agree. Fuess is convinced that "he was, during his first two years at Amherst, acutely conscious of his slow progress. His ambitions had been thwarted; he had failed to make a fraternity, he was unnoticed by those around him, his marks were only mediocre, and he had no compensating successes." Then "perhaps his entire political philosophy" was shaped by his junior and senior teachers as he combined a spurt of learning with social success. William Allen White goes farther: his "spirit awoke in Amherst," Garman "unlocked for him the philosophic mysteries of life," he was "baptized for life," "this reborn spirit whom Garman begot," and "Body and mind and spirit were cast into the iron mold of a fate which guided him through life."

Clearly Coolidge had found at Amherst the major features of the style that served him as President. The similarity in his rhetoric, business management, and personal relations habits in these widely separate periods of his life are striking.

Hoover: Needs from Childhood

Five generations of Coolidges lived in the confining culture of a small New England town; five generations of Hoovers lived in the confining culture of Quakerism, moving about from time to time but retaining their religion and its peculiar community practices. Gentle and free in ideology, Quakerism was often harsh and repressive in practice. Quaker meetings left Hoover with a sense of "the intense repression upon a ten-year-old who might not even count his toes."

Herbert Clark Hoover was born on August 10, 1874 in West Branch, Iowa, two and a half years after his brother Theodore and two years before his sister May, to Jesse Clark Hoover, a blacksmith and farm implement salesman of 27 and Huldah Minthorn Hoover, a seminary-educated lady of 26. An aunt present at his birth wrote that "Jesse and Huldah always made much of thee because thee represented the little girl they hoped soon to have." Hoover remembered his mother vaguely as "a sweet-faced woman." She was very religious, spoke often in meeting, an efficient and serious-minded person. His father had a teasing humor, but was capable of punishing Herbert severely.

A plump baby, Herbert nearly died of croup in his second winter and suffered many other illnesses and accidents. But as he grew stronger and older he became a healthy, outdoor-loving boy.

His father died suddenly in the summer of Herbert's sixth year. His mother became "less and less a creature of this world after her husband died," leaving the children for long periods while she travelled about preaching. Herbert was passed around from uncle to uncle, each of whom worked him hard but also let him play in the woods and fields. In the winter after his eighth birthday, his mother died of pneumonia. "Bereavement put a sudden end to his little-boyhood, as it had to his babyhood," Will Irwin writes.

Separated from his brother and sister and sent to an uncle's farm, Herbert "took it hard — but with his mouth shut and grief showing only in his eyes." At age ten, he was again uprooted and sent to Oregon to live with his mother's brother, Henry John Minthorn, whose only son had just died. "Thee is going to Oregon," he was told, and "his lips closed very tight." Minthorn put him to school and chores, for a time of "sober routine." His uncle was a severe taskmaster; once Herbert "stalked out in anger and boarded with other relatives." At fifteen he was taken with his uncle to open a "Quaker land-settlement business" in Salem. A visitor told him of opportunities for engineering education at the newly opening Stanford University. Over the family's objection — and this is the first report of Herbert arguing — he took the Stanford entrance examinations, failed them, but was admitted for special tutoring in the summer.

Hoover thus left home and childhood with understandable enthusiasm. The major deprivations are clear: he lost both his parents, suddenly and unexpectedly, by the age of eight, a severe loss of affection and stability, and he had been shuffled about, against his will, from one stern relative to another, separated from his brother and sister, powerless to shape any segment of his own life. He needed others, and he needed to get his own place in the world and hold it. All his work so far had brought him nothing but more work. Words were not yet part of his equipment; he had kept a tight-lipped sense of humiliation as person after person he relied on had agreed to abandon him to others.

Hoover: Resources from Childhood. Neither the political nor the rhetorical emphasis in Coolidge's upbringing were there for Hoover. His uncle Laban was an Indian agent and his Uncle Henry Minthorn had been one; Hoover vaguely remembered the Garfield campaign of 1880 and the lone (and drunken) Democrat in West Branch. That appears to have been the extent of his political exposure. Nor is there any record of early appearances before an audience. He did not like school: years later, asked to name his favorite study, he replied "None. They were something to race through — so I could get out of doors." He remembered some of his teachers with affection, but their lessons appear to have made no substantive impression on him. At home there were no novels, "save those with Total Abstinence as hero and Rum as villain." He and his brother read — surreptitiously — "Youth's Companion," a mild thriller of the day, and, with their cousin George acted out the parts. At first "Bertie" acted as lookout in case someone should discover this sinful behavior; then he was promoted to "super parts":

> When Tad commanded the Colonial army, Bertie was that army;
> he was also the white maiden bound to the stake, while George
> as the Indian Chief tortured her and Tad as the *Deerslayer* came
> to the rescue. (Irwin, 1928, 15)

Not even at play, then, did he take the lead.

But these indoor intellectual forays never compared in Hoover's experience or memory with the outdoors and the physical. The early pages of his *Memoirs* read like a nature book, full of owls and rabbits and fish. He and his cousins played with machinery and put an old thresher back together; in Oregon he and another office boy tried to repair sewing machines for sale. The heritage was much stronger from the males of his line — the farmers and blacksmith — than from his mother's religiousness. In the office he was efficient in detail, learned to run a typewriter, and spent as much time as he could in the hills. The focus was on things, not words. He recalls a kind teacher who got him started on *Ivanhoe*, an "opening of the door to a great imaginative world" which "led me promptly through much of Scott and Dickens, often at the cost of sleep," but "Oregon lives in my mind for its gleaming wheat fields, its abundant fruit, its luxuriant forest vegetation, and the fish in the mountain streams." On Sunday evening he was allowed to read "an improving book," but one wonders how much of that there was after the Sabbath routine:

> On Sunday mornings, when work of necessity was done, came Sabbath school; then the long meeting; then dinner; then a period of sluggish rest followed by a Band of Hope meeting, where the lecturer or teacher displayed colored prints of the drunkard's dreadful interior on each stage of his downward path, with corresponding illustrations of his demeanor and conduct. (Irwin, 1928, 30)

Unlike most men who have become President, Hoover had in his background virtually nothing of legitimating family example, identification with political figures, or practice in expressing ideas to audiences.

Hoover: First Independent Political Success. The same September that Coolidge entered Amherst, Hoover entered Stanford. At seventeen he was the youngest and, reportedly, the youngest-looking student in the first class at that new university. Will Irwin describes the effect the next four years had on Herbert Hoover:

> He had lived, so far as he was aware, a happy childhood. But after all, that sympathetic brooding which makes childhood supremely happy had been lacking to his life since he was nine (sic) years old; for the greater part of another seven years a repressed atmosphere, wherein his extraordinary intelligence had no proper soil for growth; and hard work at menial or mechanical tasks. The atmosphere of freedom, of high animal spirits, the intellectual stimulus of those original young professors who went adventuring to Stanford — these struck in. Here he knew his first joy of the intellect, here he felt the initial stirring of his higher powers, here he found his wife. Stanford became a kind of complex with Herbert Hoover. Within fifteen years his interests and his wanderings were to embrace the globe; but those golden hills above Palo Alto were always the pole to his compass. (Irwin, 1928, 33–34)

Hoover came to Stanford early in the summer of 1891 to be tutored. Still one subject short of the number required at the end of the summer, he studied a couple of physiology textbooks for two straight nights and passed an examination. He was admitted "conditioned in English" — the language came hard for him, "then and for many years he was impatient with words." He took English examinations twice a year for the next several years without success. In his senior year he failed German. The English "condition" was finally removed to allow him to graduate, when two of his engineering professors argued that his technical reports showed sufficient literary skill. In class and out of class he "said little and listened a lot; there was a wordless eagerness about him," as Lyons puts it. As a sophomore he was "shy to the point of timidity — rarely spoke unless spoken to," his classmate Lester Hinsdale recalled from their lunches together. Irwin remembers Hoover visiting him in the infirmary when Hoover was a senior.

> He did not say a word of sympathy for me — in pain and forever out of football — but I felt it nevertheless. Then, at the door he turned for an instant and jerked out: "I'm sorry." Just that; but it was as though another man had burst into maudlin tears. (Irwin, 1928, 60)

When he met his future wife in geological laboratory — he was a senior, she a freshman — he was tongue-tied and red-faced. No other girls were among his close friends at Stanford, nor were there any "frivolous flirtations." It is important to note, then, that verbal expressiveness had no part in Hoover's success at Stanford. He never found there a way to attract attention or to achieve his goals through speechmaking or even facile conversation. That mouth so tightly shut at critical moments in his childhood symbolized his verbal restraint at Stanford and as President (though not as Secretary of Commerce). Typically Hoover talked haltingly, rarely looking the other in the eye, with one foot thrust forward as he jingled the keys in his pocket.

Success Came from Systematic and Ordered Work. Hoover's success at Stanford came from work, not words, and from a way of relating to others. He began his extracurricular working career at college by hiring on as a clerk in the registration of the new class. The skill exercised was meticulous attention to detail. Later in his freshman year Professor Branner employed him to do typing, again a matter of careful mechanical work. Then he branched out; he and two partners established a newspaper route and a laundry service for the students. These were soon sublet to other students, providing a small but regular income for Hoover. His entrepreneurial talents were beginning to emerge. Later he sold out the laundry for $40 and he and a new friend started a cooperative residence for students in Palo Alto, a project he dropped soon because it kept him away from the campus.

In the summer after Hoover's freshman year, Professor Branner got him a job with the Geological Survey of Arkansas, of which Branner had been State Geologist, at $60 a month and expenses. In his two subsequent Stanford summers he worked for the United States Geological Survey in California and in Nevada. That first summer "I did my job on foot, mostly alone, stopping at nights at the nearest cabin" in the Ozarks, making systematic notes, gathering and filing away facts, observations. The mountaineers were suspicious of travelling inquirers: "I finally gave up trying to explain." In the subsequent summers Hoover was "far happier," he writes. He worked as a "cub assistant" to Dr. Waldemar Lindgren, riding a horse all day and camping out with the survey team at night. Hoover very much wanted this job. At the first of the post-sophomore summer he was not yet employed, so he and a friend canvassed San Francisco for contracts for putting up billboard advertising. They signed up "a few hundred dollars" worth of contracts and went to work. Then Hoover heard of the geological survey and that there was a place for him with it. He walked 80 miles in three days to take it on.

Hoover's exact role in these two latter summers needs specification. He was, "as the youngest member of the Geological party," the disbursing officer: "I had to buy supplies and keep the accounts according to an elaborate book of regulations which provided wondrous safeguards for the public treasury." Carefulness by the book again, combined with out-door energy and listening to the experts around the campfire.

Hoover returned to Stanford and extended his business enterprises. For a brief time he was a shortstop on the baseball team but soon became manager, "arranging games, collecting the gate money and otherwise finding cash for equipment and uniforms." He did so well at that he was advanced to manager of the football team. One game produced $30,018. Hoover was acquiring a reputation for management. Operating in a new and developing environment without precedents he was under demand as the man who could — and would — take care of a wide variety of chores and enterprises for his fellows. Branner knew him for his efficiency; when other students complained that Hoover seemed to have too much pull with the famous geologist, he replied "But I can tell Hoover to do a thing and never think of it again." These talents also gave him his start in campus politics.

His Start in Campus Politics. Like Coolidge, Hoover was a "Barbarian" at Stanford. Fraternities developed quickly among the richer students interested in social prominence. He was not one of those. Sam Collins, one of the oldest members of Hoover's class, had proposed the cooperative rooming house at the beginning of their sophomore year. Collins was impressed with Hoover's system and order in straightening out the finances. Under Collins' tutelage Hoover first got involved in college politics when he was brought in with a group of "Barbarians" that organized to overthrow fraternity control of the student offices and activities. A zealot named "Sosh" (for "socialist") Zion declared his candidacy for student body president; "Collins swung in behind him in this campaign, and Hoover followed." He was assigned to canvass the "camp," the students who lived in rough shacks left over by the workers constructing the new college. Still he was "rather inarticulate — this repressed boy of eighteen" but he did what he could and the Barbs won, in a close vote.

The next summer Hoover worked for Dr. Lindgren, but he also thought about ways of organizing the many student activities at Stanford some of which had been very sloppily run and one of which had had a scandal. Hoover returned in the fall with a draft of a new constitution in which student activities would be brought together under the control of the student body. In addition to a president and a football manager, a treasurer, bonded and double-audited, would handle the finances. Hoover's plan was modified in some detail in bull sessions with Collins and others; they decided to put off a move for it until electing, under the existing rules, a student government sympathetic to the plan the following spring.

In the spring term, this group gathered again and developed a ticket, with Lester Hinsdale as candidate for president, Herbert Hicks for football manager, and Herbert Hoover for treasurer. Hoover was reluctant. He thought the treasurer, who would collect a salary, should be a graduate student.

> "But there's the salary," they said: "you can drop your work for Doc Branner and your laundry agency. The job will support you."
>
> "No, sir!" responded Hoover, emphatically. "If I accept this nomination and get elected, there's one thing sure. I take no salary. Otherwise, they'll say I'm backing the new constitution just to get a paid job!" (Irwin, 1928, 54)

The "3-H" ticket won. Sosh Zion opposed the salary. Hoover refused to take it, though he worked like a demon for the remaining two years at Stanford as treasurer. The new student government got the student body to pass the new constitution.

Hoover spent the following summer working again for Dr. Lindgren, who put Hoover's name with his own on the various maps and reports. "Years later, Hoover confessed to a friend that no subsequent honor had puffed him up so much as this."

The next autumn, Hoover's junior year, he was busy running a lecture series, keeping the records and accounts for athletic events, and generally making himself useful. As Will Irwin recalled:

> In the conferences over this or that problem of our bijou party in a toy state he seemed hesitant of advancing an opinion. Then, when everyone else had expressed himself, he would come in with the final wise word . . . After all, ours was the world in miniature. I lived to see him in councils whose decisions meant life or death for millions; yet it was always the same mind and the same method. (Irwin, 1928, 62)

Hoover, in other words, was one of the boys, but at the edges of the group in most of their activities. He was the reliable treasurer, the arranger of meetings, the hard-working but shy and restrained person. He was valued for his virtues, particularly his energy and carefulness, his thoroughgoing honesty. He was never a charismatic leader at Stanford. In nearly all of his activities, someone else — usually someone older like Professor Branner or Professor Lindgren or Sam Collins or Lester Hinsdale took the lead, and Hoover followed and served. Things got solved at Stanford in the caucus and Hoover took his part there. But there is not, in all of this student political and business activity, any record of his ever having spoken to a large gathering of his classmates. He was the man behind the scenes. He made friends, but many were the sort of friends whose respect is stronger than their affection.

In words, then, Hoover was restrained and not very expressive. In work he devoted all his energies to concentrated effort. In his personal relations he was a quiet, behind-the scenes coordinator, not a leader. And so he was as President of the United States.

A Summary of Main Themes

The links between each style at the time of first independent political success and in the presidency are clear in these two cases. Briefly put:

For Coolidge, *rhetoric* in the presidency consisted of (a) serious, abstract, epigramatic addresses, full of themes from Garman, delivered much like his serious debates and speeches at Amherst and (b) witty banter with reporters, much like his funny speeches to his fellow undergraduates. As president he avoided as much of the *business* of the office as he could; work on detail had played little or no part in his Amherst success. As president he avoided close personal relationships, keeping others at a distance with mildly aggressive wit; at Amherst intimate friendship or close cooperation had never been his style.

For Hoover, *rhetoric* was impossibly hard, and he failed at it, as words had so often failed him at Stanford. Forced to speak, he fell back on his mother's Quaker mysticism and his uncle's phoney advertising. His whole soul was poured into the *business* of the office, meticulous attention to detail, and careful designs for the arrangement of things. At Stanford very similar efforts had brought him money, independence, respect and acceptance. In *personal relations,* President Hoover tried desperately, in conference after conference, to repeat his success at Stanford in gaining cooperation by mastering details and presenting his plan.

The similarities are evident. Analyzed retrospectively here, they seem amenable to discernment in their earlier forms by an analyst attuned to the role demands of the presidency.

Presidential Style and First Independent Political Success

There are fundamentally three steps in this argument. One is that there is such a thing as presidential style, in the sense of habitual patterns of performance in response to recurrent role demands. I have tried to illustrate how the flow of energy and affect in three channels captures, within a broader typological framework, the major dimensions of such styles. Presidents tend to solve their rhetorical problems, their problems of managing business, and their problems of adapting in close personal relations in characteristic, patterned ways, not randomly or simply as flexible, rational responses to historical events.

Second, there is an identifiable formative period, that of first independent political success, in which the major elements of presidential style are exhibited. Personality formation is a long, developmental process, subject to change before and after this period. But the *main, adaptively strategic, politically-relevant action patterns* are evidenced most clearly when a young man, drawing together themes from his past, present and anticipated future, answers for himself the question, "What works for me?" The fit between presidential style and the style of the formative period is not vague or mysterious, but direct: in rhetoric, business management, and personal relations presidents tend to behave as they did when they first found a way to succeed with these tools.

The third step in the argument is less clear. Why does this congruence occur? The answers are speculative. Most probably, the strength of the adaptive pattern derives from the confluence, in its original formation, of (a) satisfaction of strong needs for compensation for earlier deprivations, (b) at least some resources from the past applicable to present achievement, and (c) a favorable set of opportunities. At a deeper level of analysis, this pattern's staying power derives from a solution to the Eriksonian identity crisis; it may represent the behavioral manifestation of an intensely emotional late-adolescent trial and victory. The outward signs of the formative period are a new surge of success on one's own, a new way of linking oneself to others and a new fame. To the psychoanalyst, these may be signs only, referents to much deeper developments in the meanings of work and luck, love and hate, thought and word. Psychoanalytic data would reveal, one suspects, such factors contributing strongly to habit formation in this critical period.

At an even more speculative level, the analogy between being president and emerging as a successful young adult with an individual style can be posed. Both are in some sense culminations of preparatory stages, modes in the curve of life, high points of achievement beyond which one may never go. Both are unique experiences, in the double sense that neither ever happens twice in the same life and that no two persons work them out in the same ways. Both highlight the lone individual discovering what he can make of a situation in which a great deal depends on his personal choices. A new president, scanning (though seldom consciously) his life's repertoire of successful strategies, might well turn to those which had worked so well for him as he became a man.

A few cases plus speculation do not make a theory. Yet as these ideas are refined they may find application in stylistic analysis not only of past presidents but also of men yet to be presidents. At that point we may be able to move beyond some of the many uncertainties of prediction, to guess better than we have, and before the fact, what the most powerful politician in the world will do with that power.

REFERENCES

Barber, James David. *The lawmakers: recruitment and adaptation to legislative life.* New Haven: Yale University Press, 1965.
Barber, James David. Leadership strategies for legislative party cohesion. *Journal of Politics,* 1966, **28.**
Coolidge, Calvin. *The autobiography of Calvin Coolidge.* New York: *Cosmopolitan,* 1929.

Cornwell, Elmer E. Jr. *Presidential leadership of public opinion.* Bloomington: Indiana University Press, 1965.

Fuess, Claude M. *Calvin Coolidge: the man from Vermont.* Hamden, Conn.: Archon Books, 1965.

Hinshaw, David. *Herbert Hoover: American Quaker.* New York: Farrar, Straus, 1950.

Hoover, Herbert. *The memoirs of Herbert Hoover: 1874–1920, years of adventure.* New York: Macmillan, 1951.

Hoover, Herbert. *The memoirs of Herbert Hoover: 1920–1933, The cabinet and the presidency.* New York: Macmillan, 1952.

Irwin, Will. *Herbert Hoover: a reminiscent biography.* New York: Century, 1928.

Joslin, Theodore G. *Hoover: off the record.* Garden City, N.Y.: Doubleday, Doran, 1934.

Lasswell, Harold D. *Psychopathology and politics.* New York: Viking Press, 1960.

Lasswell, Harold D. *Power and personality.* New York: Viking Press, 1962.

Liggett, Walter N. *The rise of Herbert Hoover.* New York: H. K. Fly, 1932.

Lowry, Edward G. *Washington close-ups: intimate views of some public figures.* Boston: Houghton Mifflin, 1921.

Lyons, Eugene. *Our unknown ex-president: a portrait of Herbert Hoover.* Garden City, N.Y.: Doubleday, 1948.

McCoy, Donald R. *Calvin Coolidge: the quiet president.* New York: Macmillan, 1967.

Meyers, William Starr. (Ed.) *The state papers and other public writings of Herbert Hoover.* Vol. 2 (Oct. 1, 1931 to March 4, 1933). New York: Doubleday, Doran, 1934.

Schlesinger, Arthur M. Jr. *The age of Roosevelt: the crisis of the old order, 1919–1933.* Boston: Houghton Mifflin, 1957.

Shapiro, David. *Neurotic styles.* New York: Basic Books, 1965.

Warren, Harris Gaylord. *Herbert Hoover and the great depression.* New York: W. W. Norton, 1967.

Wolfe, Harold. *Herbert Hoover: public servant and leader of the loyal opposition.* New York: Exposition Press, 1965.

Wood, Clement. *Herbert Clark Hoover: an American tragedy.* New York: Michael Swain, 1932.

A. Lincoln, Politician

David Donald

I

The statesmanship of Abraham Lincoln is so widely recognized as to require no defense. But it is not always realized that Lincoln's opportunities for statesmanship were made possible by his accomplishments as a politician. Perhaps it is too cynical to say that a statesman is a politician who succeeds in getting himself elected President. Still, but for his election in 1860, Lincoln's name would appear in our history books as that of a minor Illinois politician who unsuccessfully debated with Stephen A. Douglas. And had the President been defeated in 1864, he would be written off as one of the great failures of the American political system — the man who let his country drift into civil war, presided aimlessly over a graft-ridden administration, conducted an incompetent and ineffectual attempt to subjugate the Southern states, and after four years was returned by the people to the obscurity that he so richly deserved.

Lincoln's fame, then, was made possible by his success as a politician, yet in many of the techniques used by present-day political leaders he was singularly ineffectual. He never succeeded in selling himself — to the press, to the politicians, or to the people. To a public-relations expert, the Lincoln story would seem a gift from heaven. Like a skillful organist playing upon the keyboard of popular emotion, he could pull out the sentimental tremolo for Lincoln's humble origins, for his hard-scrabble Kentucky and Indiana childhood, for his Illinois rise from rags to respectability. A good publicity man would emphasize Lincoln's sense of humor (but, as a recent campaign has demonstrated, he should not overemphasize it), his down-to-earth folksiness, his sympathy for the oppressed. Appealing to the traditional American love of a fighter, especially an underdog, he could capitalize upon the virulent assaults of Lincoln's political enemies. The whole campaign, if managed by a Batten, Barton, Durstine & Osborn agent, should have been as appealing, as saccharine, as successful as the famous 1952 television appearance of our current Vice President.

In Lincoln's case, however, astonishingly little use was made of these sure-fire appeals — and when they were used, they backfired. The President said that he was a man of humble origins — and his opponents declared that, as Southern poor white trash, he was still cowed by the slaveholders and afraid of vigorously prosecuting the war. Lincoln stressed his sense of humor — and even his supporters protested: ". . . I do wish Abraham would tell fewer dirty stories." Mrs. Lincoln regularly visited the wounded in Washington's hospitals — and hostile newspapers hinted that she was really passing along military secrets to the Confederates.

Lincoln never succeeded in making his own case clear. He had no sounding-board. While Congressmen orated in the Capitol, the President sat gagged in the White House. In the 1860's, convention had it that a President must pretend not to be a politician. After wirepulling for a lifetime to secure the nomination, the successful candidate must be surprised when a committee from his party officially notified him that he was the lucky man. In the campaign that followed, he was supposed to sit indifferently at home, pretending to be a Cincinnatus at the plow, while his fellow citizens, unsolicited, offered him the highest post in the land. And, once in the Executive Mansion, he was to be muffled and dumb.

Like most self-made men, Abraham Lincoln was very conventional, and he never challenged the rules of the political game. A strict view of the proprieties prevented President Lincoln from going directly to the people. Although he had made his fame as a public speaker, he never once addressed the Congress in person, but, following Jefferson's example, submitted written messages that dreary clerks droned out to apathetic legislators. Rarely after 1861 did Lincoln make any speeches or public pronouncements. "In my present position," he told a Maryland crowd in 1862, "it is hardly proper for me to make speeches." Later, as candidate for re-election, Lincoln still further limited his utterances. "I do not really think," he said in June 1864, "it is proper in my position for me to make a political speech. . . ." ". . . I believe it is not customary for one holding the office, and being a candidate for re-election, to do so. . . ." During the four years of civil war, the people could hear every strident and raucous voice in America, but not the voice of their President.

The President's negative attitude discouraged support from the press. Although he gave a number of informal interviews, Lincoln held no press conference; reporters were still not considered quite respectable, certainly not worthy of private audience with the President. Newspapermen go where there is news. When a Washington correspondent found the White House well dry, he turned naturally to those running streams of gossip and complaint and criticism and intrigue, the Congressmen, whose anti-Lincoln pronouncements all too often agreed with the prejudices of his editor. Most of the leading American newspapers were anti-Lincoln in 1860, and they remained anti-Lincoln till April 15, 1865, when they suddenly discovered that the President had been the greatest man in the world. There were some notable exceptions, of course — the *Springfield Republican* and the *New York Times,* for example — but even these were handicapped by Lincoln's negative attitude toward the press. As one editor complained: ". . . it is our great desire to sustain the President, and we deplore the opportunity he has let go by, to sustain himself."

But most newspapers had no desire whatever to sustain the President, and they berated Lincoln with virulent obscenity that makes even the anti-Roosevelt campaigns of our own day seem mild. The sixteenth President was abused in the newspapers as "a slang-whanging stump speaker," a "half-witted usurper," a "mole-eyed" monster with "soul . . . of leather," "the present turtle at the head of the government," "the head ghoul at Washington."

President Lincoln was no more successful with the politicians than with the press. One of the saddest aspects of Civil War history is the sorry failure of Lincoln's appeals for bipartisan support. The Copperheads, outright antiwar Democrats, he could not hope to win, but the enormous mass of the Democratic party was as loyal to the Union as the President himself. On all crucial issues Lincoln was closer to George B. McClellan or Horatio Seymour than to many members of his own party. "In this time of national peril," Lincoln kept saying to such War Democrats, he hoped to meet them "upon a level one step higher than any party platform." He did not expect them to endorse every measure of a Republican regime, but he did wish that " 'the Government' [might] be supported though the administration may not in every case wisely act." So earnestly did he desire the support of an energetic War Democrat like Governor Seymour of New York that in 1862 he sent him a message: if the Governor would help "wheel the Democratic party into line, put down rebellion, and preserve the government," Lincoln said, "I shall cheerfully make way for him as my successor."

Such hopes for bipartisan co-operation were blighted at birth. Governor Seymour regarded Lincoln's offer as a trap, and he spent most of his term in Albany denouncing the corruption and the arbitrary methods of the Lincoln administration. Far from co-operating, Democratic politicians took out time to compare Lincoln with the "original gorilla," a baboon, and a long-armed ape; the more scurrilous elements of the opposition party suggested that the President suffered from unmentionable diseases or that he had Negro blood in his veins.

If the President's failure with the Democrats was to be expected in a country with a vigorous two-party tradition, his inability to influence leaders of his own party was a more serious weakness. In Washington, reported Richard Henry Dana, author of *Two Years before the Mast,* "the most striking thing is the absence of personal loyalty to the President. It does not exist. He has no admirers, no enthusiastic supporters, none to bet on his head." Republican critics openly announced that Lincoln was "unfit," a "political coward," a "dictator," "timid and ignorant," "pitiable," "too slow," a man of "no education," "shattered, dazed, utterly foolish." "He is ignorant, self-willed, & is surrounded by men some of whom are almost as ignorant as himself," historian George Bancroft declared. Republican editor Murat Halstead thought Lincoln "an awful, woeful ass," and a correspondent of the *Chicago Tribune* said that "Buchanan seems to have been a granite pillar compared to the

'Good natured man' without any spinal column. . . ." Republican Senator James W. Grimes of Iowa felt that Lincoln's "entire administration has been a disgrace from the very beginning to every one who had any thing to do with bringing it into power."

From the beginning the President and his own party leaders in Congress were often at loggerheads. Radicals and Conservatives, former Whigs and ex-Democrats, Easterners and Westerners, all viewed Lincoln with suspicion. Such a situation is, of course, fairly normal in American politics. As our major parties consist of conflicting interest groups bound together by political expediency rather than by ideology, a President is bound constantly to disappoint nine tenths of the voters who elected him. But in Lincoln's case the situation was more serious because he seemed unable to build up any personally loyal following. Nearly every important Republican leader — Chase, Sumner, Greeley, Stevens, Wade, Davis, Chandler, Browning, Grimes, Weed — doubted the advisability of a second term for Lincoln. When a Pennsylvania editor visited the Capitol in 1864 and asked to meet some Congressmen who favored the President's renomination, old Thad Stevens stumped over to Representative Isaac N. Arnold of Illinois, announcing: "Here is a man who wants to find a Lincoln member of Congress. You are the only one I know and I have come over to introduce my friend to you."

A failure with the press and the politicians, Lincoln is said by sentimentalists to have won the favor of the common people. This stereotype, so comforting to those who like to believe in the democratic dogma, started with Lincoln himself. When Congressmen and editors erupted in a frenzy of anti-Lincoln fury, the President liked to reflect that the "politicians" could not "transfer the people, the honest though misguided masses" to their course of opposition. Lincoln felt that he understood the mind of the masses. Day after day he greeted the throngs of visitors, petitioners, and office-seekers who besieged him in the White House, and he claimed that these "public-opinion baths" helped him sense the popular will. In return for his sympathy, the President felt, he received popular support. His private secretary, John Hay, echoed Lincoln's belief: "The people know what they want and will have it" — namely, a re-election of the President in 1864.

In fact, though, the evidence for Lincoln's enormous popular appeal during the war is sketchy and unreliable. One could quote, for instance, Congressman Lewis D. Campbell's opinion of the 1864 election: "Nothing but the undying attachment of our people to the Union has saved us from terrible disaster. Mr. Lincoln's popularity had nothing to do with it. . . ." More convincing, however, than such impressionistic evidence are the actual election returns. Lincoln was a minority President in 1861. His party lost control of the crucial states of New York, Pennsylvania, Ohio, Indiana, and Illinois in the off-year elections of 1862. And in 1864 — when all the Southern states were out of the Union and, of course, not voting — Northerners, given a chance to demonstrate their alleged enthusiastic support for the President, cast forty-five per cent of their ballots against Lincoln and for a Democratic platform that called both his administration and the war for the Union failures. A change of only eighty-three thousand votes — two per cent of the total — could have meant Lincoln's defeat.

II

Although Lincoln failed to win the press, the politicians, and the people, he was nevertheless a successful politician. He kept himself and his party in power. He was the first President since Andrew Jackson to win re-election, and his administration began an unbroken twenty-four years of Republican control of the Presidency.

The secret of Lincoln's success is simple: he was an astute and dextrous operator of the political machine. Such a verdict at first seems almost preposterous, for one thinks of Lincoln's humility, so great as to cause his opponents to call him a "Uriah Heep"; of his frankness, which brought him the epithet "Honest Abe"; of his well-known aversion for what he termed the "details of how we get along." Lincoln carefully built up this public image of himself as a babe in the Washington wilderness. To a squabbling group of Pennsylvania party leaders he said ingenuously: "You know I never was a contriver; I don't know much about how things are done in politics. . . ."

Before breaking into tears of sympathy for this innocent among thieves, it is well to review Lincoln's pre-Presidential career. When elected President, he had been in active politics for twenty-six years; politics was his life. "He was an exceedingly ambitious man," his Springfield law partner wrote, "a man totally swallowed up in his ambitions. . . ." "Rouse Mr. Lincoln's peculiar nature in a point where he deeply felt — say in his ambitions — his general greed for office . . . then Mr. Lincoln preferred Abm Lincoln to anybody else." But during his long career in Illinois politics Lincoln had never been chosen to major office by the people of his state; state legislator and one-term member of Congress he was, but never Senator — though he twice tried unsuccessfully — and never governor. Lack of appeal at the polls did not, however, prevent him from becoming the master wirepuller who operated the state political organization first of the Whig party and, after its decay, that of the Republicans. Behind that façade of humble directness and folksy humor, Lincoln was moving steadily toward his object; by 1860 he had maneuvered himself into a position where he controlled the party machinery, platform, and candidates of one of the pivotal states in the Union. A Chicago lawyer who had known Lincoln intimately for three decades summarized these pre-presidential years: "One great public mistake . . . generally received and acquiesed in, is that he is considered by the people of this country as a frank, guileless, and unsophisticated man. There never was a greater mistake. . . . He handled and moved men remotely as we do pieces upon a chess-board."

Lincoln's Illinois record was merely finger exercises to the display of political virtuosity he was to exhibit in the White House. He brought to the Executive office an understanding of the value of secrecy. So close did Lincoln keep his ideas, it can be said that no one of his associates understood him. Herndon concluded that this man was "a profound mystery — an enigma — a sphinx — a riddle . . . incommunicative — silent — reticent — secretive — having profound policies — and well laid — deeply studied plans." Nobody had his complete confidence. His loyal Secretary of the Navy was kept as much in the dark about Lincoln's views as the veriest outsider. "Of the policy of the administration, if there be one," Welles complained, "I am not advised beyond what is published and known to all." Lincoln moved toward his objectives with muffled oars. After ninety years historians are still arguing whether Lincoln arranged for Andrew Johnson to be nominated as his vice-presidential running-mate in 1864. Impressive and suggestive evidence can be cited to show that the President picked the Tennessean — or that he favored someone else entirely.

Lincoln's renowned sense of humor was related to his passion for secrecy. Again and again self-important delegations would descend upon the White House, deliver themselves of ponderous utterances upon pressing issues of the war, and demand point-blank what the President proposed to do about their problems. Lincoln could say much in a few words when he chose, but he could also say nothing at great length when it was expedient. His petitioners' request, he would say, reminded him of "a little story," which he would proceed to tell in great detail, accompanied by mimicry and gestures, by hearty slapping of the thigh, by uproarious laughter at the end — at which time he would usher out his callers, baffled and confused by the smoke-screen of good humor, with their questions still unanswered.

Akin to Lincoln's gift for secrecy was his talent for passivity. When he arrived in Washington, he was faced by a crisis not of his own making. Fort Sumter, provocatively located in the harbor of Charleston, the very hotbed of secession, had to be reinforced or evacuated. Reinforcement would be interpreted, not merely by the Confederates but also by large peace-loving elements at the North, as an aggressive act of war; withdrawal would appear to other Northerners a cowardly retreat on the part of a spineless administration. Lincoln considered both alternatives. Characteristically, he sought clear-cut written opinions from his Cabinet advisers on the course to follow — but left his own ideas unrecorded. Characteristically, the whole episode is muffled in a fog of confusion which has produced an interesting argument among later historians. But characteristically, too, Lincoln's final decision was neither to reinforce nor to withdraw; he would merely send food and supplies to the beleaguered Sumter garrison and sit back and wait. His passivity paid off. Confederate hotheads were unable to wait so long as the cool-blooded Northern President, and they fired the first shot at Sumter. To Lincoln's support all elements of Northern society now rallied. "At the darkest moment in the history of the republic," Ralph Waldo Emerson wrote, "when it looked as if the nation would be dismembered, pulverized into its original elements, the attack on Fort Sumter crystallized the North into a unit, and the hope of mankind was saved."

Repeatedly, throughout the war, Lincoln's passive policy worked politically. Because any action would offend somebody, he took as few actions as possible. Outright abolitionists demanded that he use his wartime powers to emancipate the Negroes. Border-state politicians insisted that he protect their peculiar institutions. Lincoln needed the support of both groups; therefore, he did nothing — or, rather, he proposed to colonize the Negroes in Central America, which was as near to nothing as he could come — and awaited events. After two years of hostilities, many even in the South came to see that slavery was doomed, and all the important segments of Northern opinion were brought to support emancipation as a wartime necessity. Only then did Lincoln issue the Emancipation Proclamation.

Along with secrecy and passivity, Lincoln brought to his office an extraordinarily frank pragmatism — some might call it opportunism. Often while in the White House he repeated an anecdote that seemed to have a special meaning for him — how the Irishman who had forsworn liquor told the bartender that he was not averse to having a spot added to his lemonade, "so long as it's unbeknownst to me." Again and again the President showed himself an imitator of his Irish hero. When the Pennsylvania miners broke out in open rebellion against the operation of the draft law in their section, worried Harrisburg officials inquired whether Lincoln would send troops to execute the law. Entrusting nothing to paper, Lincoln sent a confidential messenger to A. K. McClure, the aide of the Pennsylvania governor: "Say to McClure that I am very desirous to have the laws fully executed, but it might be well, in an extreme emergency, to be content with the appearance of executing the laws; I think McClure will understand." McClure did understand, and he made no more than a feeble effort to subdue the miners' revolt, but let the agitation die out of its own accord. Thus, the Lincoln administration won the credit both for preserving the peace and for enforcing the draft.

Lincoln enjoyed a similar pragmatic relationship with his unpleasant and irritable Secretary of War, Edwin M. Stanton. There was a sort of tacit division of labor between these two dissimilar men. Lincoln himself explained the system: ". . . I want to oblige everybody when I can; and Stanton and I have an understanding that if I send an order to him which cannot be consistently granted, he is to refuse it. This he sometimes does." The President then had the pleasant and politically rewarding opportunity of recommending promotions, endorsing pension applications, pardoning deserters, and saving sleeping sentinels, and Stanton, who was something of a sadist, took equal pleasure in refusing the promotions, ignoring the petitions, and executing the delinquent soldiers. While the Secretary received the blame for all the harsh and unpopular acts that war makes necessary, the President acquired a useful reputation for sympathy and generosity.

III

Valuable as were these negative traits of secrecy, passivity, and pragmatism, Lincoln understood that it was not policies or principles which would cause Congressmen to support his direction of the war. To mobilize votes in Congress, the Head of State must be a practicing Party Leader. Lincoln was a political realist, and he worked with the tools he had at hand. He understood that in a democratic, federal government like ours, patronage is the one sure way of binding local political bosses to the person and principles of the President, and for this reason he used and approved the spoils system.

Lincoln's entire administration was characterized by astute handling of the patronage. Even in picking his Cabinet, he took leaders from all factions of his own party, giving all groups hope but no group dominance. The result was that Cabinet members were so suspicious of each other that they hardly had time to be jealous of the President. It was not efficient administration, for the Secretary of State met with the President privately — to regale him, enemies said, with vulgar stories; the Secretary of War would not discuss his plans in Cabinet meeting because he thought — with some justice — that his colleagues could not be trusted with secrets; and the Secretary of the Treasury finally refused to attend the "so-called" Cabinet meetings at all. Of all these men, outstanding political leaders in 1860, not one ever became President; in Lincoln's Cabinet they ate one another up.

Even without such competition, a Cabinet officer found his political activity necessarily curbed. The fading of Salmon P. Chase's presidential hopes provides an illuminating insight into Lincoln's use of the appointing power. Self-confident, upright, and able, Chase thought that he had deserved the Republican nomination in 1860, and from the first the Secretary of the Treasury looked upon Lincoln as a well-meaning incompetent. He never saw reason to alter his view. Chase was not a modest man; he was sure of his ability and his integrity, sure that he would make an admirable President. As a senator said: "Chase is a good man, but his theology is unsound. He thinks there is a fourth person in the Trinity" — namely, himself.

The day he became Secretary of the Treasury, Chase began scheming for the 1864 nomination, but he found himself hampered by his ambiguous position in the Cabinet. If his financial planning went wrong, he received the blame; but whenever he achieved a success, in the issue of greenbacks or the sale of bonds, the credit went to the Lincoln administration, not to Chase alone. He converted his numerous Treasury agents into a tightly organized and highly active Chase-for-President league, but as long as he remained in the Cabinet, he could not openly announce his presidential aspirations. To relieve himself from embarrassment, to go into outright opposition to Lincoln, Chase needed to get out of the Cabinet, but an unprovoked resignation would be political suicide, a cowardly evasion of his duties. All through 1863 and 1864, then, Chase wriggled and squirmed. Time after time he cooked up little quarrels over patronage, squabbles over alleged slights, and the like, so that he would have an excuse for resigning. Every time Lincoln blandly yielded the point in dispute and refused to accept Chase's withdrawal. But in June 1864, just after the Republican national convention at Baltimore had renominated Lincoln, Chase once again tried his obstructionist tactics that had worked so well in the past, and he threatened to resign from the Cabinet. This time, to his vast chagrin, it was different, and Lincoln accepted his withdrawal. Now that the race was over, Chase was free to run.

If patronage could close a Cabinet member's mouth, it could open the lips of an editor. James Gordon Bennett, the sinful and unscrupulous editor of the *New York Herald,* was one of the most powerful newspapermen of his day. Spiced with sex and scandal, the *Herald* had the largest circulation of any American newspaper, and it was a potent agency in shaping public opinion. Bennett had opposed Lincoln in 1860, and throughout the war he kept up a criticism that was all the more painful to Lincoln because it was well informed and witty. In 1864 Bennett hoped that Grant would run for President, and he also flirted capriciously with the Democratic nominee, General McClellan. For Lincoln he had no use.

> President Lincoln [read a typical *Herald* editorial] is a joke incarnated. His election was a very sorry joke. The idea that such a man as he should be President of such a country as this is a very ridiculous joke. . . . His inaugural address was a joke, since it was full of promises which he has never performed. His Cabinet is and always has been a standing joke. All his State papers are jokes. . . . His title of "Honest" is a satirical joke. . . . His intrigues to secure a renomination and the hopes he appears to entertain of a re-election are, however, the most laughable jokes of all.

The vote in New York was going to be close, and Lincoln needed the *Herald's* support. Emissaries went up from Washington to interview the canny Scottish editor and ascertain his price. Bennett's terms were high. "The fact is B. wants attention," Lincoln's agent reported. "He wants recognition — & I think it will pay." A newspaperman before he was anything else, Bennett promised to give the administration's views "a thorough exposition in the columns of the Herald," provided Lincoln and his advisers "would occasionally confidentially make known to him [their] plans." Then, too, the editor, who was barred from polite New York society because of his flagrant immorality and was generally considered "too pitchy to touch," had a hankering for social respectability. When Lincoln's agents approached him, the editor "asked plumply, 'Will I be a welcome visitor at the White House if I support Mr. Lincoln?'" The answer was unequivocally affirmative, and, as proof of his good faith, the President promised to the totally unqualified Bennett an appointment as minister to France. Bennett did not want to go abroad, for he was too busy with his paper, but he did want the social recognition that such an offer implied; he wanted to be able to refuse. The bargain was complete, and the *Herald* abandoned its criticism of the President.

As a practical politician, Lincoln understood that election victories required more than the support of Cabinet officers or newspaper editors. Like a famous New York politician, he knew that "Parties are not built up by deportment, or by ladies' magazines, or gush." In the United States, party machinery is more important than public opinion, and patronage more influential than principles. In recent years American liberal historians, scorning the sordid realities of political life, have pictured Lincoln as somehow above the vulgar party apparatus that elected him, unconcerned with the greasy machinery of party caucuses, conventions, nominations, and patronage. This idea is the political equivalent of the doctrine of the immaculate conception. Lincoln himself would have been astonished at it. Politics was his life, and he was a regular party man. Long before he became President, Lincoln said that "the man who is of neither party is not, and cannot be, of any consequence" in American life. As Chief Executive, he was a party President, and he proudly claimed that his had "distributed to its party friends as nearly all the civil patronage as any administration ever did."

Lincoln believed in party regularity. In 1864 there was much discontent in New York with Representative Roscoe Conkling, a Radical Republican who sought re-election, and more moderate party members threatened to bolt the ticket. Conkling was no personal friend of Lincoln's. Boasting the "finest torso" in American political life, he used to descend upon the harried inmate of the White House and, with his wilting contempt, "his haughty disdain, his grandiloquent swell, his majestic, supereminent, turkey-gobbler strut," proceed to lecture the President on how to conduct the war. But Conkling in 1864 was the regular nominee of the New York Republican Party, and the President wrote a public letter to aid him:

> . . . I am for the regular nominee in all cases; . . . and no one could be more satisfactory to me as the nominee in that District, than Mr. Conkling. I do not mean to say that there [are] not others as good as he is in the District; but I think I know him to be at least good enough.

Lincoln made the politicos pay for his support. They could vote against administration bills and they could grumble in Capitol cloakrooms about presidential "imbecility," but he expected them to support his renomination. Those who refused were cut off from patronage and promotion. When Senator Samuel C. Pomeroy of Kansas tried to organize the Chase boom in 1864, every patronage plum in his state was snatched from his greedy hands. After a few months of dignified hostility, Pomeroy sidled up to the White House and begged forgiveness. But Lincoln, who could be so forgiving to sleeping sentinels and deserting soldiers, had no mercy for defecting politicians, and Pomeroy went hungry.

Using the sure goad of patronage, Lincoln's agents early in 1864 began lining up delegates to the Republican national convention. Before the other presidential hopefuls knew that the round-up had begun, Lincoln had corralled enough votes to insure his renomination. The work of the Lincoln men in a state like New Hampshire is instructive. Dignified Salmon P. Chase was making eyes toward this state where he had been born, but while he was still flirting at a gentlemanly distance, New Hampshire eloped with Lincoln. Shrewd Lincoln agents, dispensing patronage to the faithful and threats of punishment to the disobedient, moved in on the state convention at Concord in January 1864 and rushed through a resolution calling for Lincoln's renomination. They permitted New Hampshire Republicans to mention their native son, Chase, in the state platform — but only in order to urge that he clean up the corruption in his Treasury Department.

Everywhere it was the same — Connecticut, Pennsylvania, New York, and even Chase's own Ohio. From state after state Chase's friends protested: "I have never seen such an exhibition of office holders in any convention before." But, packed or not, these conventions chose the delegates to the national assembly at Baltimore. By March Lincoln's renomination was assured, and, with poor grace, Chase was compelled to withdraw from a hopeless contest.

Patronage had helped defeat Lincoln's enemies within the Republican party, and patronage would help defeat the Democratic nominee, George B. McClellan. No one knows how much money the Republicans spent in the 1864 campaign — indeed, no one knows how much either major party has spent in any campaign — but it is certain that a large part of the sum came from assessments levied upon Federal officeholders. A man who received a job from Lincoln might expect to contribute regularly ten per cent of his income to the Republican campaign chest; some gave much more. Henry J. Raymond, chairman of the Republican National Committee, planned systematically to levy upon war contractors, customs officers, and navy-yard employees. When the upright Secretary of the Navy protested this proposal "to take the organization of the navy yard into their keeping, to name the Commandant, to remove the Naval Constructor, to change the regulations, and make the yard a party machine for the benefit of party, and to employ men to elect candidates instead of building ships," Raymond summoned him into the President's office in the White House and gave the Secretary a little lecture on the political facts of life, with Lincoln silently approving each word.

In the long run, though, it took not merely delegates and money but votes to carry the election. During the summer of 1864 the war was going badly. "I am a beaten man," Lincoln said in August, "unless we can have some great victory." As late as October he calculated that he would carry the electoral college by only six votes — three of them from the barren desert of Nevada, which Lincoln leaders in Congress had providently admitted to the Union precisely for such an emergency.

Although propriety prevented him from campaigning, the President personally concerned himself with the turn-out of Republican voters in key states like Indiana, Ohio, Pennsylvania, and New York. Seeing that the Northwestern states were going to show a closely balanced vote, Lincoln wrote in September to General Sherman, whose army was in a tight spot in Georgia: "Any thing you can safely do to let [your] soldiers, or any part of them, go home to vote at the State election, will be greatly in point." Although he added: "This is, in no sense, an order," Lincoln was clearly giving a directive, and it was one that Sherman promptly obeyed. The Republicans carried the Northwest by narrow majorities.

In the East, too, the soldier vote was crucial. Pennsylvania Republicans, fearing defeat, persuaded the President to furlough thousands of soldiers just in time to return home and vote. When the ballots were counted, Lincoln had carried the state by only twenty thousand and would have lost it entirely but for the army. In New York the soldier influence on the election was somewhat different. There, allegedly to prevent rioting, daredevil Republican General Benjamin F. Butler was put in charge of Federal troops and, over the protests of New York officials, he stationed plainclothesmen at the polling-places and had four regiments of troops waiting on ferryboats, ready to "land and march double quick across the island" — just in case there were Democratic disturbances. Some years later, reviewing his career, Butler denied that he had earned his military laurels in the Louisiana campaign. ". . . I do not claim," he said modestly, "to be the hero of New Orleans. Farragut has that high honor; but I do claim to be the hero of New York city in the election of 1864, when they had an honest election, the only one before or since." A Democrat might question the "honesty" of the proceedings, but, under the protection of Federal bayonets, New York went Republican by seven thousand votes.

November 8 was a "rainy, steamy and dark" night in Washington, but politicians gathered in the War Department to await the telegraphic election returns. Most of the visitors were tense, but Abraham Lincoln was relaxed, "most agreeable and genial all the evening." At a little midnight supper he "went awkwardly and hospitably to work shoveling out the fried oysters" to others, and more than once he was reminded of a little story. A mishap to one of the guests brought to mind an anecdote about wrestling which began: "For such an awkward fellow, I am pretty sure-footed. It used to take a pretty dextrous man to throw me." His political management of the Civil War demonstrated that Abraham Lincoln was still sure-footed. By dominating his party, securing a renomination, and winning re-election, a superb politician had gained the opportunity of becoming a superb statesman.

The Dynamics of Decision

Arthur M. Schlesinger, Jr.

Franklin Roosevelt's two years in the White House had done much to transform potentiality into actuality. On the verge of power, he had been a man of charm, courage, craftiness, and faith who had survived a terrible personal ordeal but so far had been untried by ultimate public responsibility. Now he had undergone the testing of crisis. The result was a process of hardening and deepening which was changing a genial and enigmatic gentleman into a tough, forceful and still profoundly enigmatic President. . . .

VI

Beyond the cabinet there stretched the Executive Branch of the government — an endless thicket of vested usage and vested interest, apportioned among a number of traditional jurisdictions, dominated by a number of traditional methods and objectives. This was, in the popular understanding, the government of the United States — the people and departments and agencies whose office it was to carry out the national laws and fulfill the national policies. The President had few more basic responsibilities than his supervision and operation of the machinery of government. Little fascinated Franklin Roosevelt more than the tasks of presidential administration. And in few things was he more generally reckoned a failure.

This verdict against Roosevelt derived ultimately from a philosophy of public administration — a philosophy held for many years after by Civil Service professionals, expounded in departments of political science, and commending itself plausibly to common sense. This school's faith was in logical organization of government, founded on rigid definitions of job and function and maintained by the sanctity of channels. Its weapons were the job description and the organization chart. Its unspoken assumption was that the problems of administration never change; and its consuming fear was improvisation, freewheeling or unpredictability — which is nearly to say creativity — in the administrative process. From this point of view, it need hardly be said, the Roosevelt government was a textbook case of poor administration. At one time or another, Roosevelt must surely have violated every rule in the sacred texts of the Bureau of the Budget.

And this conventional verdict found apparent support in much of the

Reprinted by permission of the author and publisher, Houghton Mifflin Company from Arthur M. Schlesinger, Jr., *The Age of Roosevelt — The Coming of the New Deal*, Vol. II (Boston, 1958), pp. 511, 520–525, 527–532, 534–542, 583–588. © 1958 by Arthur M. Schlesinger, Jr.

literature written by men who worked for Roosevelt. Though these reports differed on many other things, one thing on which they very often agreed was in their complaint about Roosevelt as an administrator. They agreed on one other thing too — the perspective from which they were written. Nearly all exhibited the problems of the Presidency from below — from the viewpoint of the subordinate rather than from that of the President. The picture created by this mass of individual stories, while vivid and overwhelming, was inevitably distorted and too often querulous. For no subordinate ever got what he wanted or thought he needed. In later years, George C. Marshall would talk of "localitis" — the conviction ardently held by every theater commander that the war was being won or lost in his own zone of responsibility, and that the withholding of whatever was necessary for local success was evidence of blindness, if not of imbecility, in the high command. "Localitis" in one form or another was the occupational disease of all subordinate officials and, in a sense, it had to be, for each of them ought to demand everything he needed to do the best job he can. But "localitis" offered no solid ground for judgment of superiors, whose role it must inevitably be to frustrate the dreams of subordinates. The President occupied the apex of the pyramid of frustration. The essence of his job was to enforce priorities — and thereby to exasperate everybody. And, in Roosevelt's case, there is little left in the literature to emphasize the view from the summit, where any President had to make his decisions. As Grace Tully (whose book does something to redress the balance) commented on other memoirists, "None of them could know that for each minute they spent with the President he spent a hundred minutes by himself and a thousand more with scores of other people — to reject, improvise, weigh and match this against that until a decision was reached on a public policy."

The question remains whether the true test of an administrator may be, not his ability to design and respect organization charts, not his ability to keep within channels, but his ability to concert and release the energies of men for the attainment of public objectives. It might be argued that the essence of successful administration is: first, to acquire the ideas and information necessary for wise decisions; second, to maintain control over the actual making of the decisions; and, third, to mobilize men and women who can make the first two things possible — that is, who can provide effective ideas and information, and who can reliably put decisions into effect. It is conceivable that these things may be more important than preserving the chastity of administrative organization — that, indeed, an excessive insistence on the sacredness of channels and charts is likely to end in the stifling of imagination, the choking of vitality, and the deadening of creativity.

VII

Franklin Roosevelt, at any rate, had some such philosophy of administration. The first task of an executive, as he evidently saw it, was to guarantee himself an effective flow of information and ideas. And Roosevelt's first insight — or, at least, his profound conviction — was that, for this purpose, the ordained channels, no matter how simply or how intricately designed, could never be enough. An executive relying on a single information system became inevitably the prisoner of that system. Roosevelt's persistent effort therefore was to check and balance information acquired through official channels by information acquired through a myriad of private, informal, and unorthodox channels and espionage networks. At times, he seemed almost to pit his personal sources against his public sources. From the viewpoint of subordinates, this method was distracting when not positively demoralizing. But Roosevelt, with his voracity for facts and for ideas, required this approach to cross-check the official system and keep it alert as well as to assure himself the balanced and various product without which he could not comfortably reach decisions.

The official structure, of course, maintained a steady flow of intelligence. Roosevelt was, for a President, extraordinarily accessible. Almost a hundred persons could get through to him by telephone without stating their business to a secretary; and government officials with anything serious on their minds had little difficulty in getting appointments. In addition, he read an enormous number of official memoranda, State Department cables, and government reports, and always tried to glance at the *Congressional Record.* The flow was overwhelming, and he sought continually to make it manageable. "I learned a trick from Wilson," he remarked to Louis Brownlow. "He once told me: 'If you want your memoranda read, put it on one page.' So I, when I came here, issued a similar decree, if you want to call it that. But even at that I am now forced to handle, so the oldsters around tell me, approximately a hundred times as many papers as any of my predecessors." Certainly his subordinates paid little attention to the one-page rule.

What gave Roosevelt's administrative practice its distinctive quality was his systematic effort to augment the official intelligence. The clutter of newspapers on his bed each morning marked only the first stage in his battle for supplementary information. In this effort, reading was a useful but auxiliary weapon. Beyond government documents and newspapers, he read little. So far as current magazines were concerned, the President, according to Early, "sketches the field," whatever that meant. As for books, Roosevelt evidently read them only on holiday, and then not too seriously. When Frances Perkins sent him the Brookings study *America's Capacity to Produce,* he replied, "Many thanks. . . . I am taking it on the trip and will guarantee to browse through it but not of necessity to read every word!" On the whole, he preferred to acquire both information and ideas through conversation.

Many visitors, it is true, left Roosevelt with the impression that he had done all the talking. This was markedly less true, in his first term, however, than it would be later. Indeed, Henry Pringle, reporting the Washington view in 1934, wrote, "He is a little too willing to listen." And the complaint against Roosevelt's overtalking meant in some cases only that a visitor had run into a deliberate filibuster (thus William Randolph Hearst's baffled lament after a session with Roosevelt in 1933, "The President didn't give me a chance to make suggestions. He did all the talking"). "Words are a good enough barrage if you know how to use them," Roosevelt told one visitor. Like many talkers, moreover, Roosevelt absorbed attitudes and ideas by a mysterious osmosis on occasions when the visitor complained he hadn't got a word in edgewise.

Conversation gave him an indispensable means both of feeling out opinion and of clarifying his own ideas. He talked to everybody and about everything. His habits of conversation out of channels were sometimes disconcerting. He had little hesitation, if he heard of a bright man somewhere down the line in a department, about summoning him to the White House. Ickes complained bitterly in his diary about "what he does so frequently, namely, calling in members of my staff for consultation on Department matters, without consulting me or advising with me." And often he bewildered visitors by asking their views on matters outside their jurisdiction. "He had a great habit," said Jesse Jones, "of talking to one caller about the subject matter of his immediately preceding interview." "I would go to see the President about something," wrote James P. Warburg, "and the fellow who was there before me talking about cotton would be told by the President, 'Well, why don't you stay.' Before we were through the guy who was there talking about cotton was telling him what to do about gold." All this, irritating as it was to tidy minds, enlarged the variety of reactions available to him in areas where no one was infallible and any intelligent person might make a contribution. . . .

IX

If information was the first responsibility of the executive, the second was decision. American Presidents fall into two types: those who like to make decisions, and those who don't. One type designs an administrative system which brings decisions to him; the other, a system which keep decisions away from him. The second technique, under its more mellifluous designation of "delegation of authority," is regarded with favor in the conventional theory of public administration. Yet, pressed very far, "delegation of authority" obviously strikes at the roots of the Presidency. One can delegate routine, but one cannot delegate any part of the serious presidential responsibility. The whole theory of the Constitution makes the Chief Executive, in the words of Andrew Jackson, "accountable at the bar of public opinion for every act of his Administration," and thus presumably accountable in his own conscience for its every large decision.

Roosevelt, in any case, was pre-eminently of the first type. He evidently felt that both the dignity of his office and the coherence of his administration required that the key decisions be made by him, and not by others before him. He took great pride, for example, in a calculation of Rudolph Forster's that he made at least thirty-five decisions to each one made by Calvin Coolidge. Given this conception of the Presidency, he deliberately organized — or disorganized — his system of command to insure that important decisions were passed on to the top. His favorite technique was to keep grants of authority incomplete, jurisdictions uncertain, charters overlapping. The result of this competitive theory of administration was often confusion and exasperation on the operating level; but no other method could so reliably insure that in a large bureaucracy filled with ambitious men eager for power the decisions, and the power to make them, would remain with the President. This was in part on Roosevelt's side an instinct for self-preservation; in part, too, the temperamental expression of a restless, curious, and untidy personality. Co-existence with disorder was almost the pattern of his life. From the day of his marriage, he had lived in a household of unresolved jurisdictions, and it had never occurred to him to try to settle lines finally as between mother and wife. As Assistant Secretary of the Navy, he had indulged happily in the kind of administrative freewheeling which he was not much concerned to penalize in others now. As his doctor once said, Roosevelt "loved to know everything that was going on and delighted to have a finger in every pie."

Once the opportunity for decision came safely into his orbit, the actual process of deciding was involved and inscrutable. As Tugwell once put it, "Franklin allowed no one to discover the governing principle." He evidently felt that clear-cut administrative decisions would work only if they expressed equally clear-cut realities of administrative competence and vigor. If they did not, if the balance of administrative power would not sustain the decision, then decision would only compound confusion and discredit government. And the actualities of administrative power were to be discovered, not by writing — or by reading — Executive orders, but by apprehending through intuition a vast constellation of political forces. His complex administrative sensibility, infinitely subtle and sensitive, was forever weighing questions of personal force, of political timing, of congressional concern, of partisan benefit, of public interest. Situations had to be permitted to develop, to crystallize, to clarify; the competing forces had to vindicate themselves in the actual pull and tug of conflict; public opinion had to face the question, consider it, pronounce upon it — only then, at the long, frazzled end, would the President's intuitions consolidate and precipitate a result.

Though he enjoyed giving the impression of snap decisions, Roosevelt actually made few. The more serious complaint against him was his weakness for postponement. This protraction of decision often appeared a technique of evasion. And sometimes it was. But sometimes dilemmas did not seem so urgent from above as they seemed below — a proposition evidently proved when they evaporated after the passage of time. And Roosevelt, in any case, justified, or rationalized, delay in terms of his own sense of timing. He knew from hard experience that a person could not regain health in a day or year; and he had no reason to suppose that a nation would mend any more quickly. "He could watch with enormous patience as a situation developed," wrote his wife, "and would wait for exactly the right moment to act." When people pressed proposals on him, he often answered (as he did to Frank Walker in 1936), "You are absolutely right. . . . It is simply a question of time." The tragedy of the Presidency in his view was the impotence of the President. Abraham Lincoln, Roosevelt said, "was a sad man because he couldn't get it all at once. And nobody can." He was responding informally to an important young questioner. "Maybe you would make a much better President than I have. Maybe you will, some day. If you ever sit here, you will learn that you cannot, just by shouting from the housetops, get what you want all the time."

Yet his caution was always within an assumption of constant advance. "We must keep the sheer momentum from slacking up too much," he told Colonel House in 1934, "and I have no intention of relinquishing the offensive." Woodrow Wilson had given him a cyclical conception of social change in America. Roosevelt told Robert H. Jackson that he had once suggested that Wilson withhold part of his reform program for his second term. Wilson replied in substance: We do not know that there will be a second term, and, if there is, it will be less progressive and constructive than the first. American history shows that a reform administration comes to office only once in every twenty years, and that its forward impulse does not outlast one term. Even if the same party and persons remain in power, they become complacent in a second term. "What we do not accomplish in the first term is not likely to be accomplished at all." (When Roosevelt told this story to his press conference in the first year of his second term, he lengthened the period of possible accomplishment from four to eight years.)

X

This technique of protraction was often wildly irritating to his subordinates, enlisted passionately on one side or another of an argument and perceiving with invincible clarity the logic of one or another course. It was equally irritating to his opponents, who enjoyed the advantages of oversimplification which comes from observation without responsibility. But the President's dilatory tactics were, in a sense, the means by which he absorbed country-wide conflict of pressures, of fears, of hopes. His intelligence was not analytical. He did not systematically assess pros and cons in his own mind. What for others might be an interior dialogue had to be externalized for Roosevelt; and it was externalized most conveniently by hearing strong exponents of divergent viewpoints. Listening amiably to all sides, watching the opposing views undergo the test of practice, digesting the evidence, he gradually felt his way toward a conclusion. And even this would not often be clear-cut. "He hated to make sharp decisions between conflicting claims for power among his subordinates," noted Francis Biddle, "and decided them, almost always, in a spirit of arbitration: each side should have part of the morsel." Quite often, he ordered the contestants to work out their own compromise, as in NRA and on farm policy. In this connection he liked to cite Al Smith: "He said if you can get the parties into one room with a big table and make them take their coats off and put their feet up on the table, and give each one of them a good cigar, you can always make them agree."

With the conclusion, however reached, a new phase began. When Garner once tried to argue after Roosevelt had made up his mind, the President said, "You tend to your office and I'll tend to mine." ("I didn't take offense at that," said Garner, "because he was right.") "You could fight with Roosevelt and argue with him up to a certain point," said Morgenthau, " — but at no time during his waking hours was he anything else but a ruler." Wayne Coy, who was a Roosevelt assistant for some years, observed that one could say exactly what one thought to Roosevelt, so long as he was saying only "in my judgment" or "I think." When he said "The President thinks," the time for discussion was over. To another assistant, James Rowe, who insisted that he should do something in a particular way, Roosevelt said, "I do not have to do it your way and I will tell you the reason why. The reason is that, although they may have made a mistake, the people of the United States elected me President, not you."

Often he announced his decisions with bravado. He liked to tell advisers, "I'm going to spring a bombshell," and then startle them with novel proposals — or rather with proposals novel to them, not perhaps to another set of advisers. "He delights in surprises — clever, cunning and quick," said Hugh Johnson. "He likes to shock friends as well as enemies with something they never expected." But he seems rarely to have supposed that any particular decision was in a final sense correct, or even terribly important. "I have no expectation of making a hit every time I come to bat. What I seek is the highest possible batting average." He remembered Theodore Roosevelt's saying to him, "If I can be right 75 per cent of the time I shall come up to the fullest measure of my hopes." "You'll have to learn that public life takes a lot of sweat," he told Tugwell, "but it doesn't need to worry you. You won't always be right, but you mustn't suffer from being wrong. That's what kills people like us." After all, Roosevelt said, suppose a truck driver were doing your job; 50 per cent of his decisions would be right on average. "You aren't a truck driver. You've had some preparation. Your percentage is bound to be higher." And he knew that the refusal to decide was itself a form of decision. "This is very bad," he said to Frances Perkins, "but one thing is sure. We have to do something. We have to do the best we know how to do at the moment." Then, after a pause: "If it doesn't turn out right, we can modify it as we go along."

This dislike of firm commitments, this belief in alternatives, further reduced the significance of any single decision. As Miss Perkins observed, "He rarely got himself sewed tight to a program from which there was no turning back." The very ambiguity of his scheme of organization — the overlapping jurisdictions and duplicated responsibilities — made flexibility easy. If things started to go bad, he could reshuffle people and functions with speed which would have been impossible in a government of clear-cut assignments and rigid chains of command. Under the competitive theory, he always retained room for administrative maneuver.

Only a man of limitless energy and resource could hold such a system together. Even Roosevelt at times was hard put to keep it from flying apart. But he did succeed, as no modern President has done, in concentrating the power of executive decision where the Constitution intended it should be. "I've never known any President," said W. M. Kiplinger, "who was as omnipresent as this Roosevelt." "Most people acting for Roosevelt were messenger boys," said Ed Flynn. "He really made his own decisions.". . .

II

To guarantee the scope, Roosevelt had to revamp the structure of government. By orthodox administrative theory, the antidepression activities should have been brought in under the appropriate old-line departments — Agriculture, Commerce, Labor, the Treasury. But Roosevelt felt that the old departments, even with new chiefs, simply could not generate the energy and daring the crisis required. "We have new and complex problems. We don't really know what they are. Why not establish a new agency, to take over the new duty rather than saddle it on an old institution?" Hence the resort from the start to the emergency agency, an essential instrument in the Rooseveltian technique of administrative improvisation. If the obvious channel of action was blocked and it was not worth the political trouble of dynamiting it open, then the emergency agency supplied the means of getting the job done nevertheless. And the new agencies simplified the problem of reversing direction and correcting error. "We have to be prepared to abandon bad practices that grow out of ignorance. It seems to me it is easier to use a new agency which is not a permanent part of the structure of government. If it is not permanent, we don't get bad precedents.". . .

The new agencies were plainly indispensable. They tended to have an administrative dash and *élan* which the old departments, sunk in the lethargy of routine, could not match. Yet the theory could be pushed too far. At times Roosevelt acted as if a new agency were almost a new solution. His addiction to new organizations became a kind of nervous tic which disturbed even avid New Dealers. By 1936 we find Tugwell pleading with him not to set up new organizations. "My experience — and Harry's — is that it takes almost a year to perfect a country-wide administrative organization and that while it is being done there is political turmoil over the jobs, criticisms of procedure from the field, jealousy on the part of old organizations which fancy their prerogatives are threatened and other sources of irritation."

Each new agency had its own distinct mission. But in many cases jurisdictions overlapped each other and even spilled into cabinet departments. This was sloppy and caused much trouble. Yet this very looseness around the joints, this sense of give and possibility which Henry Stimson once called the "inherently disorderly nature" of Roosevelt's administration, made public service attractive to men of a certain boldness and imagination. It also spurred them on to better achievement. Roosevelt liked the competitive approach to administration, not just because it reserved the big decisions for the President, but perhaps even more because it enabled him to test and develop the abilities of his subordinates. How to tell which man, which approach was better? One answer was to let them fight it out. This solution might cause waste but would guarantee against stagnation. "There is something to be said," Roosevelt once observed, ". . . for having a little conflict between agencies. A little rivalry is stimulating, you know. It keeps everybody going to prove that he is a better fellow than the next man. It keeps them honest too. An awful lot of money is being handled. The fact that there is somebody else in the field who knows what you are doing is a strong incentive to strict honesty." One can see, for example, in the diaries of Harold Ickes how the overhanging presence of Hopkins and Morgenthau caused Ickes to spend hours and days in intrigue and invective. One can also see how the feuding stimulated him and them to more effective accomplishment and kept every part of the relief and public works effort forever on its toes.

Sometimes the competitive theory could meet political needs too. Roosevelt, as the leader of a coalition, had to keep a variety of interests satisfied, or at least hopeful. What better way than to give each representation where decisions were made? Some agencies seemed to be staffed on the ancient Persian theory of placing men who did not trust each other side by side, their swords on the table. Everywhere there was the need to balance the right and the left — let Cohen and Corcoran write the act establishing the Securities and Exchange Commission, but let Joe Kennedy administer it, but flank him with Jim Landis and Ferdinand Pecora. Rather than sitting on creative vitality anywhere, give each faction something of a head and try to cope with the results. "He had an instinct," wrote Frances Perkins with insight, "for loose, self-directed activity on the part of many groups."

Competition in government, inadequately controlled, would mean anarchy. Adequately controlled, it could mean exceptional creativity. One consequence under the New Deal was a darkling plain of administrative confusion, where bureaucrats clashed by night. Another was a constant infusion of vitality and ideas. In a quieter time, when problems were routine, there would have been every reason to demand tight and tidy administration. But a time of crisis placed a premium on initiative and innovation — and on an organization of government which gave these qualities leeway and reward.

III

Getting bold and imaginative subordinates, however, by itself hardly solves the problems of execution. The worst error a President can make is to assume the automatic implementation of his own decisions. In certain respects, having able subordinates aggravates that problem, since strong personalities tend to have strong ideas of their own. Civil government operates by consent, not by command; the President's task, even within his own branch of government, is not to order but to lead. Students of public administration have never taken sufficient account of the capacity of lower levels of government to sabotage or defy even a masterful President. Somehow, through charm, cajolery, and the communication of ideals, as well as through pressure, discipline, and coercion, the President must make the Executive Branch *want* to carry out his policies.

The competitive approach to administration gave Roosevelt great advantages. It brought him an effective flow of information; it kept the reins of decision in his own hands; it made for administrative flexibility and stimulated subordinates to effective performance.

At the same time it exacted a price in morale. It placed those close to him under incessant strain. Even for men who could have operated in no other way, it was at best nerve-wracking and often positively demoralizing. Yet this too Roosevelt turned to his own purposes of control. Their insecurity gave him new opportunities for manipulation, which he exploited with cruel skill, while looking blandly in the opposite direction. He pretended not to know what was going on around him; but, said Tugwell, "those who knew his weakness for not grasping really nasty nettles knew from small signs that he was peeking through his fingers." In a way he liked the agony below: "he gave" said Cordell Hull a bit dolefully, "the impression almost of being a spectator looking on and enjoying the drama." "If he seemed to ignore the heaving bosoms presented to him," said Tugwell, "it did not mean that he did not know all about the agitation, or . . . did not enjoy it."

"You know," Harry Hopkins once said, "he is a little puckish." Puckish at times must have seemed an inadequate description. What Roosevelt could regard with equanimity from his place at the summit was often unbearable for those beneath. And it was not just that he seemed oblivious or entertained; at times he appeared to take a light and capricious pleasure in intensifying anxieties. His sometimes unfeeling ribbing of his associates expressed a thin streak of sadism of which he was intermittently aware and for which he was intermittently remorseful. "However genial his teasing," said Francis Biddle, "it was often . . . pointed with a prick of cruelty, because it went to the essence of a man, hit him between the ribs into the heart of his weakness, which might often be his unreasonable affection for his chief." Others shared Biddle's apprehension "that if we came too close I might suffer from his capacity to wound those who loved him."

No one came closer than Henry Morgenthau, and no one suffered more. Selfless devotion, as Biddle observed, sometimes became a bore; "one had to dissipate the irritation — the mild irritation — by stroking Henry against the grain in public now and then. One could not tease a man in private." Roosevelt himself once confessed to Morgenthau, "I was so tired that I would have enjoyed seeing you cry or would have gotten pleasure out of sticking pins into people and hurting them." As almost a member of the family, Morgenthau bore more than his share of Roosevelt's excess irritability. But the President had his way of tormenting everybody. Against others, indeed, the very closeness to Morgenthau was itself a weapon. The intimacy demonstrated in their weekly Monday luncheons created heart-burning and indignation among other top officials who saw (or affected to see) nothing of talent or interest in the underrated Secretary of the Treasury. As Richberg said, "This relationship between the President and Secretary Morgenthau caused a great many jealousies." "For one thing," said Tugwell, "everyone else by contrast felt himself neglected; for another, no one could understand it."

And so the President went around the cabinet table. He played Ickes like an expert fisherman, giving him plenty of line, watching him fight and flap with fury and occasionally hauling him in. To each Attorney-General he would at some point outline an objective and say: "If you are a good Attorney General tell me how I can do it." "They always give him a silly laugh," said Morgenthau, "and go out and tell him how to do it." He bypassed Hull, limited his relations to Farley, kept Wallace at arm's length, and blew hot and cold on a dozen others. "He watched his subordinates at their games," said Tugwell, "checked them when necessary, contributed to their build-up when it was convenient, reprimanded them effectively by non-recognition, rewarded them by intimacies."

No one ever could be sure where he stood. Ickes once burst out at him: "You are a wonderful person but you are one of the most difficult men to work with that I have ever known." Roosevelt said, "Because I get too hard at times?" "No," Ickes replied, "you never get too hard but you won't talk frankly even with people who are loyal to you and of whose loyalty you are fully convinced. You keep your cards close up against your belly. You never put them on the table." (Roosevelt, Ickes added, "took all of this frank talk in a perfectly friendly manner.")

As Roosevelt saw the Presidency, no President could ever afford to lay his cards on the table. His way of playing the game frightened his subordinates. He had a genius for being indirect with people. Nearly all around him had the chilling fear, generally shoved to the back of their minds, that he regarded them as expendable. As Frances Perkins said, "He reserved the right not to go out and rescue you if you got into trouble." "It was your battle," said Tugwell, "and you were expected to fight it. If you ran to the President with your troubles, he was affable and even, sometimes, vaguely encouraging, but he never said a public word in support." In a bitter moment, Jerome Frank proposed a principle of liberal politics: "A liberal leader can always count on the active support of certain persons, because of their belief in his major policies, regardless of how badly he treats them. (Item: Some of them are masochists who apparently work harder when they are ill-treated.) Therefore rewards should not be wastefully bestowed upon them but should be saved for potential enemies."

The more self-centered among Roosevelt's subordinates furiously resented this attitude and took it out on the President when their time came. The more philosophical regarded it as inevitable. "If this made you indignant," said Tugwell, "and it practically always did, there was nothing you could do and, when you thought it over, nothing of any use that you could say. The President was not a person; he was an institution. When he took political chances, he jeopardized not himself but the whole New Deal. And the New Deal could not afford to be responsible for practitioners who threatened its life — that is, who might lose it votes." It was up to the President to judge what endangered his essential objectives, and he made the judgment "in the recesses of his own considering apparatus which no one ever penetrated." Morgenthau, looking back, observed with insight, "He never let anybody around him have complete assurance that he would have the job tomorrow." Morgenthau added, "The thing that Roosevelt prided himself the most about was, 'I have to have a happy ship.' But he never had a happy ship."

IV

Yet, as Morgenthau in other moods would freely admit, it was not altogether an unhappy ship either; for, if the manipulation of insecurity was part of Roosevelt's method, the provision of charm and consolation was an equally indispensable part. Probably no President was ever more skilled in the art of persuasion. He used every trick in the book, and most of them with the relish of a virtuoso. He had, as Biddle said, an intuitive grasp of people's weaknesses; and he employed this with stunning effect, not only to make them sad or scared, but to make them happy as well. As William Phillips put it, "He had a rare capacity for healing the wounded feelings which he had inadvertently caused." Roosevelt called this process "handholding." To it he devoted considerable energy and talent. "The maintenance of peace in his official family," Grace Tully reports, "took up hours and days of Roosevelt's time."

Hand-holding emerged as naturally from his complex personality as did the instinct to tease. His concern for people was perfectly spontaneous and genuine — and immensely disarming. After telling Morgenthau that he had been so tired he would have enjoyed seeing him cry, he added, "We both must take regular vacations . . . and never permit ourselves to get so tired again." Such messages were addressed again and again to all his associates. "When he detected signs of nerves or overwork," said Grace Tully, "he was quick to propose rest trips to Warm Springs or irregular vacations. More than once, he picked up substantial doctors' bills for members of his personal staff." Thus in January 1934 we find him urging Ickes and Wallace to go away. "He was quite insistent about it," Ickes reported. "He told me that it was beginning to worry him just to look at me and that if I didn't go away he would get mad." In May he ordered Wallace and Ickes to go to Santa Fe for a few days' rest ("The continued concern for my well-being," said Ickes, "really touched me"). In June, he ordered Hopkins on a trip abroad for his health. In December he wrote Richberg, "I am terribly sorry that you are still feeling so wretchedly and all I can do is to give you a definite order from old family Doctor Roosevelt. . . .

Don't think about my 'problems' until you have a chance to come and talk them over with me." (Richberg commented, "The calming influence of such a communication as this can be imagined.")

He could not bear to fire anybody — perhaps his best noted and most conspicuous administrative failing. He shrank from disagreeable personal interviews and pronounced himself "a complete softy" in face-to-face relations. In 1936 he described as "probably much the hardest decision I have had to make since coming to Washington," not any great issue of domestic or foreign policy, but his failure to reappoint his old friends Adolph Miller and Charles Hamlin to the reconstituted Federal Reserve Board. In addition, he could hardly bear to have people resign. Harold Ickes, who resigned often, came fuming away from one conference with Roosevelt, "The reason I wanted to send in my resignation right away was because I was afraid the President would do just what he did do. He side-tracked me. It is almost impossible to come to grips with him." Richberg, another chronic resigner, once was defeated when Roosevelt said gently to him, "You aren't going to let the old man down, are you, Don?"; and was equally defeated another time when Roosevelt, who thought his grievance trivial, said satirically, "I have just had some bad news, Don. Secretary Hull is threatening to resign. He is very angry because I don't agree with him that we ought to remove the Ambassador to Kamchatka and make him third secretary to the Embassy at Svodia." ("I felt thoroughly chastened after this conversation," said Richberg, "and very grateful that the President had betrayed only friendly amusement instead of the stern displeasure which a Chief Executive with a poorer understanding of human nature or less of a sense of humor might well have shown.")

The President spent a good deal of time dealing with what he called his "prima donnas" — the people who felt neglected and kept demanding attention and sympathy. Ickes and Morgenthau, of course, were pre-eminent in the cabinet. The Secretary of the Interior, whom Roosevelt used to refer to privately as "Donald Duck," at times made himself so unbearable with his self-righteous insistence that Roosevelt for long periods avoided seeing him; at other times, the President soothed his hurt feelings with flattery. As for Morgenthau, if the Secretary of the Treasury took more punishment than most, he also received more balm. Once when Roosevelt was telling his staff how he wanted his naval prints in his office, Marvin McIntyre said, "You are right, Mr. President, you ought to have them hung to suit yourself. After all, you are in this office more than anyone else except Henry Morgenthau."

There were always minor personal squabbles requiring attention. Once Morgenthau denounced Ickes in cabinet for some jurisdictional transgression. Roosevelt scribbled on a piece of paper, "You must not talk in such a tone of voice to another cabinet officer," showed it to Morgenthau and tore it up. But the argument continued, Roosevelt finally saying, "Don't you understand, Henry, that Harold said he knows nothing about it and that ends the matter." Morgenthau replied, "I am afraid that I am very dull, Mr. President, I do not understand." Roosevelt answered coldly,

"You must be very dull." That evening Roosevelt called Morgenthau and was, as Morgenthau put it in his diary, "most sympathetic and kind." He finished by saying, "Stop worrying, Henry, go to bed and get a good night's rest." He made a similarly tranquilizing call the same evening to Ickes, deprecated Morgenthau's attitude and hoped Ickes hadn't minded; "he was plainly," Ickes noted in *his* diary, "trying to apologize for Morgenthau." By such efforts, Roosevelt kept the peace. . . .

VI

At work or at play, the defenses remained intact. He appeared almost deliberately to surround himself by incurious people — the Earlys, McIntyres, Watsons — as if to preserve his inner sanctuaries. "It sometimes seems," Tugwell has perceptively noted, "that those who were closest to him for the longest time were kept there because they did not probe or try to understand but rather because they gave an unquestioning service."

Some pressed too hard, of course. They were too curious or insensitive or cared too much. It was when Roosevelt was thus pressed that he resorted — almost, it would seem, as if he considered himself entitled to do so — to deviousness and to deceit. Those who did not press rarely complained of being cheated. "I knew Roosevelt for twenty years," said Molly Dewson, "and never once did he give me double talk. In human intercourse, if a person shies off from a subject, it is common sense not to press him and force him into an evasive answer." Frances Perkins, who ordinarily restrained herself, said, "It is my final testimony that he *never let me down.*" Those who plunged ahead invited their own punishment. "It was evident," wrote Richberg, "that he often regarded the use of a deceptive statement as justified, particularly in discussions with someone who was trying to get him to commit himself to a position he did not wish to take."

There is no question that he took a certain relish in misleading those who seemed to him to deserve it. What may have begun as a necessity became on occasion a pleasure. "He was apt to see the importance of immediate ends," said Tugwell acutely, "more readily than the consequences of doubtful means" — and this myopia became a pervading weakness of his Presidency. For Roosevelt, the result tended to grow more essential than the method; and he never adequately recognized that casualness over methods might jeopardize or corrupt results. "Never let your left hand know what your right is doing," he once told Morgenthau. "Which hand am I, President?" Morgenthau asked. Roosevelt said, "My right hand, but I keep my left under the table." ("This is the most frank expression of the real F.D.R. that I ever listened to," Morgenthau noted, "and that is the real way he works — but thank God I understand him.") Once, rehearsing a speech, Roosevelt read a passage in what he called the T.R. manner. Tom Corcoran spoke up (as Richberg recalled it): "Oh, but Mr. President, the difference between you and T.R. is that you never fake." Roosevelt replied, "Oh, but Tommy, at times I do, I do!"

He did, of course; it became the last resort of his system of defense.

Those who impaled themselves on it felt bitter resentment in consequence. Some never forgave him. Others, who adored him, were deeply upset and angry. "It is pretty tough when things like this can be said about the President of the United States," wrote Harold Ickes after a Democratic congressman remarked to him that Roosevelt might have a hard time disproving Huey Long's charge that he was a liar, "and when members of his own official family and of his own party in Congress feel that his word cannot be relied upon. It hurts me to set down such a fact, but it is the fact, as I have had occasion to know more than once."

Roosevelt enjoyed mystification too much. But perhaps a measure of mystification is inherent in the Presidency. "There isn't enough time," Tom Corcoran once said, "to explain everything to everyone, to cajole everyone, to persuade everyone, to make everyone see why it has to be done one way rather than another. If a President tried to do this, he would have no time left for anything else. So he must deceive, misrepresent, leave false impressions, even, sometimes, lie — and trust to charm, loyalty and the result to make up for it. . . . A great man cannot be a good man."

VII

There are two sorts of greatness — the foursquare, all-of-a-piece, unitary, monolithic kind, possessed by Washington, Jackson, Winston Churchill; and the glittering, elusive, pluralistic, impalpable kind, possessed by Jefferson, Henry Clay, Lloyd George, where levels of personality peel off with the delusive transparence of the skins of an onion, always frustrating the search for a hard core of personality underneath. The greatest statesman may perhaps, like Lincoln, combine both kinds: in the phrase of Archilochus, he is both hedgehog and fox. Franklin Roosevelt clearly belongs in the second category. He had, not a personality, but a ring of personalities, each one dissolving on approach, always revealing still another beneath.

Yet one cannot exhaust the Roosevelt mystery by saying that he was complicated. For, though the central core of personality remained impossible to pin down, one felt, nevertheless, beneath the dazzling variety on the surface, behind the succession of masks, a basic simplicity of mind and heart. His complexity was infinite, but it all pertained to tactics. On questions of essential purpose, he retained an innocence which was all the more baffling because of its luminous naïveté. "He sometimes tries to appear tough and cynical and flippant," Hopkins once told Sherwood, "but that's an act he likes to put on. . . . You and I are for Roosevelt because he's a great spiritual figure, because he's an idealist." This was true. It was his tactical deviousness which got him into trouble; it was the fundamental, tantalizing, intermittent but ultimately indestructible idealism which saved him.

He was complicated everywhere except in his heart of hearts. There he perceived things with elementary, almost childlike, faith. "What is your philosophy" asked the young man. "Philosophy?" Roosevelt replied. "Philosophy? I am a Christian and a Democrat — that's all." And for him, his church and his party implied a series of lucid commitments — respect for persons, respect for nature, respect for freedom. He held to these commitments with a confidence he never questioned and a serenity which never faltered.

This inner well of serenity was the unending source of spiritual refreshment. Anne O'Hare McCormick called him "apparently the least worried man in the country." Gerard Swope once said to him that he marveled at the calm with which he carried the presidential load. "I'll tell you, Gerard," Roosevelt replied, "at night when I lay my head on my pillow, and it is often pretty late, and I think of the things that have come before me during the day and the decisions that I have made, I say to myself — well, I have done the best I could, and turn over and go to sleep." "More than any other person I have ever met," said Dr. McIntire, ". . . he had equanimity, poise and a serenity of temper that kept him on the most even of keels." As Eleanor Roosevelt summarized his attitude: "You made up your mind to do a thing and you did it to the best of your ability. If it went sour, why then you started in all over again and did something else, but you never spent time repining." And she added significantly: "I have never known a man who gave one a greater sense of security. . . . I never heard him say there was a problem that he thought it was impossible for human beings to solve." "Roosevelt was a man," said Tugwell, "with fewer doubts than anyone I had ever known."

What was the source of this serenity? He himself offered no clues; he was, he used to say, "the least introspective man in the world." In part, of course, it was character, temperament, experience, triumph over catastrophe. "F.D.R. was very tough," said Francis Biddle. "He had got on top of life. Nothing could touch him." But it was something more than this. "He had," said Tugwell, "a source of detached exaltation which could not be touched by the outcome." "He felt guided in great crises," said Eleanor Roosevelt, "by a strength and wisdom higher than his own." Hugh Johnson put it more forcibly, perhaps too forcibly: "That he has some sort of messianic complex, none who is near him will deny."

Roosevelt unquestionably had a deep sense of religious assurance, though its character remains a puzzle. His faith was unanalyzed, nontheological, a matter of tradition and propriety, something which he felt but did not care to formulate. "I think it is just as well not to think about things like that too much!" he admonished his wife. He was by no means a regular churchgoer; "by the time I have gotten into that pew and settled down with everybody looking at me, I don't feel like saying my prayers at all." The divisiveness of dogmatic theologies bothered him: "in our religious worship we should work together instead of flying off on different tangents and different angles." Though a Senior Warden of St. James's Church at Hyde Park, he personally preferred Presbyterian, Methodist, or Baptist sermons to Episcopalian, and on Christmas tended to go to one of the big Methodist or Baptist churches in Washington ("What's the matter? I like to sing hymns with the Methodys"). For a time, he had even omitted his Episcopalian affiliation from his biography in *Who's Who*, not restoring it until 1924. Yet, as Robert Sherwood said, "his religious faith was the strongest and most mysterious force that was in him." He once wrote, "I doubt if there is in the world a single problem, whether social, political, or economic, which would not find ready solution if men and nations would rule their lives according to the plain teaching of the Sermon on the Mount." If nothing ever upset him, if his confidence seemed illimitable, it was because he deeply believed, with full reverence and humility, that he was doing his best in the eyes of God, that God was blessing his purposes, that he was at one with the benign forces of the universe.

VIII

In the end, a President of the United States must stand or fall by his instinct for the future as well as by his understanding of the past and his mastery of the present. Implanted within him, there must be an image, not necessarily — or even desirably — explicit or conscious, but profoundly rich, plastic, and capacious, of the kind of America he wants, of the vision of the American promise he is dedicated to realize, of the direction in which he believes the world is moving. Without such a sense, his Presidency will be static and uncreative. As Franklin Roosevelt's successor once put it, "The President's got to set the sights." This vision of the future becomes the source of his values; it justifies his strivings; it renews his hopes; it provides his life with its magnetic orientation.

It was this astonishing instinct for the future which above all distinguished Roosevelt, his extraordinary sensitivity to the emergent tendencies of his age and to the rising aspirations of ordinary people — a sensitivity housed at the same time within a personality and intelligence sufficiently conventional to provide in itself a bridge holding together past and future. Indeed, his very position on the breaking point between an old world and a new one gave him a special freedom and spontaneity which only a man can possess who is nourished by older values. When Roosevelt accepted the inevitability of change, he did so, not by necessity, but by conscious choice. He had made a deliberate decision, both temperamental and intellectual, in favor of adventure and experiment. "My impression of both him and of Mrs. Roosevelt," wrote H. G. Wells, "is that they are unlimited people, entirely modern in the openness of their minds and the logic of their actions." Nothing could daunt him, very little surprised him, he was receptive to everything, and not in a passive sense either, he received, not to accumulate, but to act; the future which he perceived was (this he deeply believed) to be in part his own creation. Wells summed him up: "The most effective transmitting instrument possible for the coming of the new world order. He is eminently 'reasonable' and fundamentally implacable. He demonstrates that comprehensive new ideas can be taken up, tried out and made operative in general affairs without rigidity or dogma. He is continuously revolutionary in the new way without ever provoking a stark revolutionary crisis."

The essence of Roosevelt, the quality which fulfilled the best in him and explained the potency of his appeal, was his intrepid and passionate affirmation. He always cast his vote for life, for action, for forward motion, for the future. His response to the magnificent emptiness of the Grand Canyon was typical: "It looks dead. I like my green trees at Hyde Park better. They are alive and growing." He responded to what was vital, not to what was lifeless; to what was coming, not to what was passing away. He lived by his exultation in distant horizons and uncharted seas. It was this which won him confidence and loyalty in a frightened age when the air was filled with the sound of certitudes cracking on every side — this and the conviction of plain people that he had given them head and heart and would not cease fighting in their cause.

POWER

Power

Robert A. Dahl

In approaching the study of politics through the analysis of power, one assumes, at a minimum, that relations of power are among the significant aspects of a political system. This assumption, and therefore the analysis of power, can be applied to any kind of political system, international, national, or local, to associations and groups of various kinds, such as the family, the hospital, and the business firm, and to historical developments.

At one extreme, an analysis of power may simply postulate that power relations are one feature of politics among a number of others — but nonetheless a sufficiently important feature to need emphasis and description. At the other extreme, an analyst may hold that power distinguishes "politics" from other human activity; to analysts of this view "political science, as an empirical discipline, is the study of the shaping and sharing of power" (Lasswell & Kaplan 1950, p. xiv).

In either case, the analyst takes it for granted that differences between political systems, or profound changes in the same society, can often be interpreted as differences in the way power is distributed among individuals, groups, or other units. Power may be relatively concentrated or diffused; and the share of power held by different individuals, strata, classes, professional groups, ethnic, racial, or religious groups, etc., may be relatively great or small. The analysis of power is often concerned, therefore, with the identification of elites and leadership, the discovery of the ways in which power is allocated to different strata, relations among leaders and between leaders and nonleaders, and so forth.

Although the approach to politics through the study of power relations is sometimes thought to postulate that everyone seeks power as the highest value, analysts of power generally reject this assumption as psychologically untenable; the analysis of power does not logically imply any particular psychological assumptions. Sometimes critics also regard the analysis of power as implying that the pursuit of power is morally good or at any rate that it should not be condemned. But an analysis of power may be neutral as to values; or the analyst may be concerned with power, not to glorify it, but in order to modify the place it holds in human relations and to increase the opportunities for dignity, respect, freedom, or other values (Jouvenel 1945; Lasswell & Kaplan 1950; Oppenheim 1961, chapters 8, 9).

Indeed, it would be difficult to explain the extent to which political theorists for the past 25 centuries have been concerned with relations of power and authority were it not for the moral and practical significance of power to any person interested in political life, whether as observer or activist. Some understanding of power is usually thought to be indispensable for moral or ethical appraisals of political systems. From a very early time — certainly since Socrates, and probably before — men have been inclined to judge the relative desirability of different types of political systems by, among other characteristics, the relations of power and authority in these systems. In addition, intelligent *action* to bring about a result of some kind in a political system, such as a change in a law or a policy, a revolution, or a settlement of an international dispute, requires knowledge of how to produce or "cause" these results. In political action, as in other spheres of life, we try to produce the results we want by acting appropriately on the relevant causes. As we shall see, power relations can be viewed as causal relations of a particular kind.

It therefore seems most unlikely that the analysis of power will disappear as an approach to the study of politics. However, the fact that this approach is important and relevant does not shield it from some serious difficulties. These have become particularly manifest as the approach has been more earnestly and systematically employed.

Origins

The attempt to study and explain politics by analyzing relations of power is, in a loose sense, ancient. To Aristotle, differences in the location of power, authority, or rule among the citizens of a political society served as one criterion for differentiating among actual constitutions, and it entered into his distinction between good constitutions and bad ones. . . . With few exceptions (most notably Thomas Hobbes) political theorists did not press their investigations very far into certain aspects of power that have seemed important to social scientists in the twentieth century. . . . For example, most political theorists took it for granted, as did Aristotle, that key terms like *power, influence, authority,* and *rule* (let us call them "power terms") needed no great elaboration, presumably because the meaning of these words was clear to men of common sense. Even Machiavelli, who marks a decisive turning point from classical–normative to modern–empirical theory, did not consider political terms in general as particularly technical. Moreover, he strongly preferred the concrete to the abstract. In his treatment of power relations Machiavelli frequently described a specific event as an example of a general principle; but often the general principle was only implied or barely alluded to; and he used a variety of undefined terms such as *imperio, forza, potente,* and *autorità.* . . .

From Aristotle to Hobbes political theorists were mainly concerned with power relations within a given community. But external relations even more than internal ones force attention to questions of relative power. The rise of the modern nation-state therefore compelled political theorists to recognize the saliency of power in politics, and particularly, of course, in international politics (Meinecke 1924).

Thus political "realists" found it useful to define, distinguish, and interpret the state in terms of its power. Max Weber both reflected this tradition of "realism" and opened the way for new developments in the analysis of power. . . . " 'Power' (*Macht*) is the probability that one actor within a social relationship will be in a position to carry out his own will despite resistance, regardless of the basis on which this probability rests" (Weber [1922] 1957, p. 152). This definition permitted Weber to conclude that "the concept of power is highly comprehensive from the point of view of sociology. All conceivable . . . combinations of circumstances may put him [the actor] in a position to impose his will in a given situation" (p. 153). It follows that the state is not distinguishable from other associations merely because it employs a special and peculiarly important kind of power — force. In a famous and highly influential definition, Weber characterized the state as follows: "A compulsory political association with continuous organization (*politischer Anstaltsbetrieb*) will be called a 'state' if and in so far as its administrative staff successfully upholds a claim to the *monopoly* of the *legitimate* use of physical force in the enforcement of its order"(p. 154).

In his well-known typologies and his analyses of political systems, however, Weber was less concerned with power in general than with a special kind that he held to be unusually important — legitimate power, or authority.

Later theorists, practically all of whom were directly or indirectly influenced by Weber, expanded their objectives to include a fuller range of power relations. In the United States attempts to suggest or develop systematic and comprehensive theories of politics centering about power relations appeared in books by Catlin (1927; 1930), an important essay by Goldhamer and Shils (1939), and numerous works of the Chicago school — principally Merriam (1934), Lasswell (1936), and, in international politics, Morgenthau (1948). In the decade after World War II the ideas of the Chicago school were rapidly diffused throughout American political science. . . .

ELEMENTS IN THE ANALYSIS OF POWER

Power terms evidently cover a very broad category of human relations. Considerable effort and ingenuity have gone into schemes for classifying these relations into various types, labeled power, influence, authority, persuasion, dissuasion, inducement, coercion, compulsion, force, and so on, all of which we shall subsume under the collective label power terms. The great variety and heterogeneity of these relations may, in fact, make it impossible — or at any rate not very fruitful — to develop general theories of power intended to cover them all.

At the most general level, power terms in modern social science refer to *subsets of relations among social units such that the behaviors of one or more units* (the responsive units, R) *depend in some circumstances on the behavior of other units* (the controlling units, C). (In the following discussion, R will always symbolize the responsive or dependent unit, C the controlling unit. These symbols will be used throughout and will be substituted even in direct quotations where the authors themselves have used different letters.) By this broad definition, then, power terms in the social sciences exclude relations with inanimate or even nonhuman objects; the control of a dog by his master or the power of a scientist over "nature" provided by a nuclear reactor would fall, by definition, in a different realm of discourse. On the other hand, the definition could include the power of one nation to affect the actions of another by threatening to use a nuclear reactor as a bomb or by offering to transfer it by gift or sale.

If power-terms include *all* relations of the kind just defined, then they spread very widely over the whole domain of human relations. In practice, analysts of power usually confine their attention to smaller subsets. One such subset consists, for example, of relations in which "severe sanctions . . . are expected to be used or are in fact applied to sustain a policy against opposition" — a subset that Lasswell and Kaplan call power (1950, pp. 74–75). However, there is no agreement on the common characteristics of the various subsets covered by power terms, nor are different labels applied with the same meaning by different analysis.

Despite disagreement on how the general concept is to be defined and limited, the variety of smaller subsets that different writers find interesting or important, and the total lack of a standardized classification scheme and nomenclature, there is nonetheless some underlying unity in the various approaches to the analysis of power. In describing and explaining patterns of power, different writers employ rather similar elements (compare Cartwright 1965). What follows is an attempt to clarify these common elements by ignoring many differences in terminology, treatment, and emphasis.

Some Descriptive Characteristics

For purposes of exposition it is convenient to think of the analysis of power in terms of the familiar distinction between dependent and independent variables. The attempt to understand a political system may then be conceived of as an effort to *describe* certain characteristics of the system: the dependent variables; and to *explain* why the system takes on these particular characteristics, by showing the effects on these characteristics of certain other factors: the independent variables. Some of the characteristics of a political system that analysts seek to explain are the *magnitude* of the power of the C's with respect to the R's, how this power is *distributed* in the system, and the *scope,* and *domain,* of control that different individuals or actors have, exercise, or are subject to.

Magnitude. Political systems are often characterized explicitly or implicitly by the differences in the "amounts" of power (over the actions of the government or state) exercised by different individuals, groups, or strata. The magnitude of *C*'s power with respect to *R* is thought of as measurable, in some sense, by at least an ordinal scale; frequently, indeed, a literal reading would imply that power is subject to measurement by an interval scale. How to compare and measure different magnitudes of power poses a major unsolved problem; we shall return to it briefly later on. Meanwhile, we shall accept the assumption of practically every political theorist for several thousand years, that it is possible to speak meaningfully of different amounts of power. Thus a typical question in the analysis of a political system would be: Is control over government highly concentrated or relatively diffused?

Distribution. An ancient and conventional way of distinguishing among political systems is according to the way control over the government or the state is distributed to individuals or groups in the systems. Aristotle, for example, stated: "The proper application of the term 'democracy' is to a constitution in which the free-born and poor control the government — being at the same time a majority; and similarly the term 'oligarchy' is properly applied to a constitution in which the rich and better-born control the government — being at the same time a minority" (*Politics*, Barker ed., p. 164). Control over government may be conceived as analogous to income, wealth, or property; and in the same way that income or wealth may be distributed in different patterns, so too the distribution of power over government may vary from one society or historical period to another. One task of analysis, then, is to classify and describe the most common distributions and to account for the different patterns. Typical questions would be: What are the characteristics of the *C*'s and of the *R*'s? How do the *C*'s and *R*'s compare in numbers? Do *C*'s and *R*'s typically come from different classes, strata, regions, or other groups? What historical changes have occurred in the characteristics of *C* and *R*?

Scope. What if *C*'s are sometimes not *C*'s, or *C*'s sometimes *R*'s, or *R*'s sometimes *C*'s? The possibility cannot be ruled out that individuals or groups who are relatively powerful with respect to one kind of activity may be relatively weak with respect to other activities. Power need not be general; it may be specialized. In fact, in the absence of a single world ruler, some specialization is inevitable; in any case, it is so commonplace that analysts of power have frequently insisted that a statement about the power of an individual, group, state, or other actor is practically meaningless unless it specifies the power of actor *C* with respect to some class of *R*'s activities. Such a class of activities is sometimes called the range (Cartwright 1965) or the scope of *C*'s power (Lasswell & Kaplan 1950, p. 73). There is no generally accepted way of defining and classifying different scopes. However, a typical question about a political system would be: Is power generalized over many scopes, or is it specialized? If it is specialized, what are the characteristics of the *C*'s, the elites, in the different scopes? Is power specialized by individuals in the sense that C_a and C_b exercise power over different scopes, or is it also specialized by classes, social strata, skills, professions, or other categories?

Domain. *C*'s power will be limited to certain individuals; the *R*'s over whom *C* has or exercises control constitute what is sometimes called the "domain," or "extension," of *C*'s power (Lasswell & Kaplan 1950, p. 73; Harsanyi 1962*a*, p. 67). Typical questions thus might be: Who are the *R*'s over whom *C* has control? What are their characteristics? How numerous are they? How do they differ in numbers or characteristics from the *R*'s not under *C*'s control?

Given the absence of any standard unit of measure for amounts, distributions, scopes, domains, and other aspects of power, and the variety of ways of describing these characteristics, it is not at all surprising that there is an abundance of schemes for classifying political systems according to some characteristic of power. Most such schemes use, implicitly or explicitly, the idea of a *distribution of power over the behavior of government.* The oldest, most famous, and most enduring of these is the distinction made by the Greeks between rule by one, the few, and the many (*see* Aristotle, *Politics,* Barker ed., pp. 110 ff.). Some variant of this scheme frequently reappears in modern analyses of power (e.g., Lasswell & Kaplan 1950, p. 218). Often, as with Aristotle himself, the distribution of power is combined with one or more other dimensions (e.g., Dahl 1963, p. 38). Rough dichotomous schemes are common. One based on "the degree of autonomy and interdependence of the several power holders" distinguishes two polar types, called autocracy and constitutionalism (Loewenstein 1957, p. 29). American community studies have in recent years called attention to differences between "pluralistic" systems and unified or highly stratified "power structures." . . . In one study that compares four communities the authors developed a more complex typology of power structures by combining a dimension of "distribution of political power among citizens" with the degree of convergence or divergence in the ideology of leaders; the four types of power structures produced by dichotomizing these two dimensions are in turn distinguished from regimes (Agger et al. 1964, pp. 73 ff.).

Some Explanatory Characteristics

Given the different types of political systems, how are the differences among them to be explained? If, for example, control over government is sometimes distributed to the many, often to the few, and occasionally to one dominant leader, how can we account for the differences? Obviously these are ancient, enduring, and highly complex problems; and there is slight agreement on the answers. However, some factors that are often emphasized in modern analysis can be distinguished.

Resources. Differences in patterns or structures of power may be attributed primarily, mainly, or partly to the way in which "resources," or "base values," are distributed among the individuals, strata, classes, and groups in different communities, countries, societies, and historical periods. This is an ancient, distinguished, widespread, and persuasive mode of explanation, used by Aristotle in Greece in the fourth century B.C., by James Harrington in seventeenth-century England, by the fathers of the American constitution in the late eighteenth century, by Marx and Engels in the nineteenth century, and by a great many social scientists in the twentieth century. A central hypothesis in most of these theories is that the greater one's resources, the greater one's power. Although explanations of this kind do not always go beyond tautology (by defining power in terms of resources), logical circularity is certainly not inherent in this mode of explanation. However, there is no accepted way of classifying resources or bases. Harold Lasswell has constructed a comprehensive scheme of eight base values which, although not necessarily exhaustive, are certainly inclusive; these are power (which can serve as a base for more power), respect, rectitude or moral standing, affection, well-being, wealth, skill, and enlightenment (Lasswell & Kaplan 1950, p. 87). Other writers choose more familiar categories to classify resources: for example, in trying to account for the patterns of influence in one community, the author described the patterns of social standing; the distribution of cash, credit, and wealth; access to legality, popularity, and control over jobs; and control over sources of information (Dahl 1961, pp. 229 ff.).

Skill. Two individuals with access to approximately the same resources may not exercise the same degree of power (over, let us say, government decisions). Indeed, it is a common observation that individuals of approximately equal wealth or social status may differ greatly in power. To be sure, this might be accounted for by differences in access to other resources, such as the greater legality, bureaucratic knowledge, and public affection that fall to any individual who is chosen, say, to be prime minister of Britain or president of the United States. Another factor, however, one given particular prominence by Machiavelli, is political skill. Formally, skill could be treated as another resource. Nonetheless, it is generally thought to be of critical importance in explaining differences in the power of different leaders — different presidents, for example, as in Neustadt's comparison of presidents Roosevelt, Truman, and Eisenhower (1960, pp. 152 ff.). However, despite many attempts at analysis, from Machiavelli to the present day, political skill has remained among the more elusive aspects in the analysis of power.

Motivations. Two individuals with access to the same resources may exercise different degrees of power (with respect to some scope) because of different motivations: the one may use his resources to increase his power; the other may not. Moreover, since power is a relationship between C's and R's, the motivations not only of the C's but also of the R's are important. One person may worship authority, while another may defy it. A number of writers have explored various aspects of motivations involved in power relations (e.g., Lasswell 1930; Rogow & Lasswell 1963; Cartwright 1959).

Costs. Motivations can be related to resources by way of the economists' language of cost — a factor introduced into the analysis of power by a mathematical economist (Harsanyi 1962*a*; 1962*b*). In order to control *R*, *C* may have to use some of his resources. Thus *C*'s supply of resources is likely to have a bearing on how far he is willing to go in trying to control *R*. And variations in *C*'s resources are likely to produce variations in *C*'s power. *C*'s *opportunity costs* in controlling *R* — that is, what *C* must forgo or give up in other opportunities as a result of using some of his resources to control *R* — are less (other things being equal) if he is rich in resources than if he is poor in resources. In concrete terms, to a rich man the sacrifice involved in a campaign contribution of $100 is negligible; to a poor man the sacrifice entailed in a contribution of $100 is heavy. *C*'s willingness to use his resources to control *R* will also depend on the value to *C* of *R*'s response; the value of *R*'s response is, in turn, dependent in part on *C*'s motivations. The relationship may also be examined from *R*'s point of view. *R*'s opportunity costs consist of what he is then unable to do if he complies with *C*. In *R*'s case, as in *C*'s, his supply of resources and his motivations help determine his opportunity costs. Thus a power relation can be interpreted as a sort of transaction between *C* and *R*.

PROBLEMS OF RESEARCH

Like all other approaches to an understanding of complex social phe-nomena, the analysis of power is beset with problems. At a very general level, attempts to analyze power share with many — perhaps most — other strategies of inquiry in the social sciences the familiar dilemma of rigor versus relevance, and the dilemma has led to familiar results. Attempts to meet high standards of logical rigor or empirical verification have pro-duced some intriguing experiments and a good deal of effort to clarify concepts and logical relationships but not rounded and well-verified ex-planations of complex political systems in the real world. Conversely, attempts to arrive at a better understanding of the more concrete phe-nomena of political life and institutions often sacrifice a good deal in rigor of logic and verification in order to provide more useful and reliable guides to the real world.

There are, however, a number of more specific problems in the analysis of power, many of which have only been identified in the last few decades. Relevant work is quite recent and seeks (1) to clarify the central concepts, partly by expanding on the analogy between power relations and causal relations, (2) to specify particular subsets that are most interesting for social analysis, (3) to develop methods of measurement, and (4) to under-take empirical investigations of concrete political phenomena.

Power and Cause

The closest equivalent to the power relation is the causal relation. For the assertion "*C* has power over *R*," one can substitute the assertion, "*C*'s be-havior causes *R*'s behavior." If one can define the causal relation, one can define influence, power, or authority, and vice versa (Simon [1947–1956] 1957, p. 5).

Since the language of cause is no longer common in the formal theoretical language of the natural sciences, it might be argued that social scientists should also dispense with that language and that insofar as power is merely a term for a causal relation involving human beings, power-terms should simultaneously be dispensed with. But it seems rather unlikely that social scientists will, in fact, reject causal language. For the language of cause, like the language of power, is used to interpret situations in which there is the possibility that some event will intervene to change the order of other events. In medical research it is natural and meaningful to ask, Does cigarette smoking cause lung cancer and heart disease? In social situations the notion of cause is equally or even more appropriate. What makes causal analysis important to us is our desire to act on causes in the real world in order to bring about effects — reducing death rates from lung cancer, passing a civil-rights bill through Congress, or preventing the outbreak of war.

To interpret the terms *power, influence, authority,* etc., as instances of causal relations means, however, that the attempt to detect true rather than spurious power relations must run into the same difficulties that have beset efforts to distinguish true from spurious causal relations. Some analysts have confronted the problem; others have noted it only to put it aside; most have ignored it entirely, perhaps on the assumption that if social scientists tried to solve the unsolved problems of philosophy they would never get around to the problems of the social sciences. Yet if power is analogous to cause — or if power relations are logically a subset of causal relations — then recent analyses of causality must have relevance to the analysis of power.

In the first place, properties used to distinguish causation also serve to define power relations: covariation, temporal sequence, and asymmetry, for example. The appropriateness of these criteria has in fact been debated, not always conclusively, by various students of power (e.g., Simon [1947–1956] 1957, pp. 5, 11, 12, 66; Dahl 1957, p. 204; Cartwright 1959, p. 197; Oppenheim 1961, p. 104).

Thus, the problem whether *A* can be said to cause *B* if *A* is a necessary condition for *B*, or a sufficient condition, or *both* necessary *and* sufficient, has also plagued the definition of power-terms. Some writers have explicitly stated or at least implied that relations of power mean that some action by *C* is a necessary condition for *R*'s response (Simon 1953, p. 504; March 1955, p. 435; Dahl 1957, p. 203). Oppenheim has argued, however, that such definitions permit statements that run flatly counter to common sense; he holds that it would be more appropriate to require only that *C*'s action be sufficient to produce *R*'s response (1961, p. 41). Riker has suggested in turn that "the customary definition of power be revised . . . to reflect the necessary-and-sufficient condition theory of causality" (1964, p. 348). However, Blalock in his *Causal Inferences in Non-experimental Research* has shown that defining cause in terms of necessary and sufficient conditions leads to great practical difficulties in research. "In real-life situations we seldom encounter instances where *B* is present if and only if *A* is also present" (1964, p. 30); moreover, specifying necessary and sufficient conditions requires the researcher "to think always in terms of attributes and dichotomies," whereas "there are most certainly a number of variables which are best conceived as continuously distributed, even though we may find it difficult to measure them operationally in terms of a specified unit of some kind" (p. 32). "The use of 'necessary and sufficient' terminology . . . may work well for the logician but not [for] the social scientist" (p. 34). Blalock's criticism, and indeed his whole effort to explore problems of causal inference in nonexperimental research, are highly relevant to the analysis of power.

Aside from these somewhat rarefied philosophical and definitional questions, which many social scientists are prepared to abandon to metaphysicians or philosophers of science, the analogy between power and cause argues that the problem of distinguishing cause from correlation, or true from spurious causation, is bound to carry over into the analysis of power. And indeed it does. The difficulty of distinguishing true from spurious power relations has proved to be quite formidable.

The most rigorous method of distinguishing true from spurious causation is, of course, experimentation, and this would be the most rigorous method for distinguishing true from spurious power relations, provided the proper experimental conditions were present. Unfortunately, however, as in many areas of the social sciences, so too in the analysis of power, experimental methods have so far been of limited value, and for similar reasons. In nonexperimental situations the optimal requirements for identifying causal relations seem to be the existence of satisfactory interval measures, a large supply of good data employing these measures, and an exhaustive analysis of alternative ways of accounting for the observations (Blalock 1964). Unfortunately, in the analysis of power, existing methods of measurement are rather inadequate, the data are often inescapably crude and limited, a variety of simple alternative explanations seem to fit the data about equally well, and in any case the complexity of the relations requires extraordinary complex models.

The shortage of relevant models of power may disappear in time. In fact, the causal analogue suggests that the development of a great array of carefully described alternative models to compare with observations is probably a prerequisite for further development in the analysis of power. Again, the analogy between power and cause readily reveals why this would seem to be the case. In trying to determine the cause of a phenomenon it is of course impossible to know whether all the relevant factors in the real world are actually controlled during an investigation. Consequently, it is never possible to demonstrate causality.

> It is possible to make causal *inferences* concerning the adequacy of causal models, at least in the sense that we can proceed by eliminating inadequate models that make predictions that are not consistent with the data. . . . [Such] causal models involve (1) a finite set of explicitly defined variables, (2) certain assumptions about how these variables are interrelated causally, and (3)

assumptions to the effect that outside variables, while operating, do not have confounding influences that disturb the causal patterning among the variables explicitly being considered. (*ibid.*, p. 62)

If power relations are a subset of causal relations, these requirements would also be applicable in the analysis of power.

In analyzing power, why have analysts so rarely attempted to describe, in rigorous language at any rate, the alternative causal models relevant to their inquiry? There seem to be several reasons. First, students of power have not always been wholly aware that distinguishing true from spurious power relations requires intellectual strategies at a rather high level of sophistication. Second, the crude quality of the observations usually available in studying power may discourage efforts to construct elegant theoretical models. Third, until recent times the whole approach to power analysis was somewhat speculative: there were a good many impressionistic works but few systematic empirical studies of power relations. Of the empirical studies now available most are investigations of power relations in American communities undertaken since 1950. These community studies have provoked a good deal of dispute over what are, in effect, alternative models of causation. So far, however, investigators have usually not described clearly the array of alternative models that might be proposed to explain their data, nor have they clearly specified the criteria they use for rejecting all the alternatives except the one they accept as their preferred explanation.

Theories about power relations in various political systems are of course scattered through the writings of a number of analysts (e.g., Pareto 1916, volume 4; Mosca 1896, passim; Lasswell & Kaplan 1950, chapters 9, 10; Mills 1956; Dahl 1961; Rossi 1960; Polsby 1963; Parsons 1963*a*; 1963*b*). But a straightforward presentation of an empirical theory of power relations in political systems is a rarity. A notable exception is offered by March's formulation of six models of social choice that involve, in some sense, relationships of power.

The analogy between cause and power calls attention to one further point: any attempt to develop an empirical theory of power will run headlong into the fact that a causal chain has many links; that the links one specifies depend on what one wishes to explain; and that what one wishes to explain depends, in part, on the theory with which one begins. In causal analysis, it is usually

. . . possible to insert a very large number of additional variables between any two supposedly directly related factors. We must stop somewhere and consider the theoretical system closed. Practically, we may choose to stop at the point where the additional variables are either difficult or expensive to measure, or where they have not been associated with any operations at all. . . . *A relationship that is direct in one theoretical system may be indirect in another*, or it may even be taken as spurious. (Blalock 1964, p. 18)

Some of the links that a power analyst may take as "effects" to be explained by searching for causes are the outcomes of specific decisions; the current values, attitudes, and expectations of decision makers; their earlier or more fundamental attitudes and values; the attitudes and values of other participants — or nonparticipants — whose participation is in some way significant; the processes of selection, self-selection, recruitment, or entry by which decision makers arrive at their locations in the political system; the rules of decision making, the structures, the constitutions. No doubt a "complete" explanation of power relations in a political system would try to account for all of these effects, and others. Yet this is an enormously ambitious task. Meanwhile, it is important to specify which effects are at the focus of an explanatory theory and which are not. A good deal of confusion, and no little controversy, are produced when different analysts focus on different links in the chain of power and causation without specifying clearly what effects they wish to explain; and a good deal of criticism of dubious relevance is produced by critics who hold that an investigator has focused on the "wrong" links or did not provide a "complete" explanation.

Classifying Types of Power

Even though the analysis of power has not produced many rigorous causal models, it has spawned a profusion of schemes for classifying types of power relations (e.g., Parsons 1963a; 1963b; Oppenheim 1961; French & Raven 1959; Cartwright 1965).

Among the characteristics most often singled out for attention are (1) legitimacy: the extent to which R feels normatively obliged to comply with C; (2) the nature of the sanctions: whether C uses rewards or deprivations, positive or negative sanctions; (3) the magnitude of the sanctions: extending from severe coercion to no sanctions at all; (4) the means or channels employed: whether C controls R only by means of information that changes R's intentions or by actually changing R's situation or his environment of rewards and deprivations. These and other characteristics can be combined to yield many different types of power relations.

As we have already indicated, no single classification system prevails, and the names for the various categories are so completely unstandardized that what is labeled power in one scheme may be called coercion or influence in another. Detached from empirical theories, these schemes are of doubtful value. In the abstract it is impossible to say why one classification system should be preferred over another.

Nonetheless, there are some subsets of power relations — types of power, as they are often called — that call attention to interesting problems of analysis and research. One of these is the distinction between *having* and *exercising* power or influence (Lasswell & Kaplan 1950, p. 71; Oppenheim 1961, chapters 2, 3). This distinction is also involved in the way anticipated reactions function as a basis for influence and power (Friedrich 1963, chapter 11).

To illustrate the problem by example, let us suppose that even in the absence of any previous communication from the president to Senator *R*, or indeed any previous action of any kind by the president, Senator *R* regularly votes *now* in a way he thinks will insure the president's favor *later*. The senator calculates that if he loses the next election, he may, as a result of the president's favorable attitude, be in line to receive a presidential appointment to a federal court. Thus, while Senator *R*'s voting behavior is oriented toward future rewards, expected or hoped for, his votes are not the result of any specific action by the president.

If one holds that *C* cannot be a cause of *R* if *C* follows *R* in time, then no act of the incumbent president *need* be a cause of Senator *R*'s favorable vote. Obviously this does not mean that Senator *R*'s actions are "uncaused." The immediate determinant of his vote is his expectations. If we ask what "caused" his expectations, there are many possible answers. For example, he might have concluded that in American society if favors are extended to *C*, this makes it more likely that *C* will be indulgent later on. Or he may have acquired from political lore the understanding that the general rule applies specifically to relations of senators and presidents. Thus, the causal chain recedes into the senator's previous learning — but not necessarily to any specific *past* act of the incumbent president or any other president.

This kind of phenomenon is commonplace, important, and obviously relevant to the analysis of power. Yet some studies, critics have said, concentrate on the exercise of power and fail to account for individuals or groups in the community who, though they do not exercise power, nonetheless have power, in the sense that many people try assiduously to anticipate their reactions (Bachrach & Baratz 1962). This failure may be a result of certain paradoxical aspects of having power that can make it an exceedingly difficult phenomenon to study.

For in the limiting case of anticipated reactions, it appears, paradoxically, that it is not the president who controls the senator, but the senator who controls the president — i.e., it is the senator who, by his loyal behavior, induces the president to appoint him to a federal court. Thus, it is not *C* who controls or even attempts to control *R*, but *R* who attempts to control *C* — and to the extent that *R* anticipates *C*'s reactions correctly, *R* does in fact control *C*. It is, then, not the king who controls the courtier but the courtier who controls the king.

Now if we examine this paradox closely we quickly discover that it arises simply because we have tried to describe the relationship between king and courtier, president and senator, *C* and *R* by distinguishing only one aspect, namely, the exercise of power. The courtier does indeed exercise power over the king by successfully anticipating the reactions of the monarch and thereby gaining a duchy. But it was not this that we set out to explain. For it is the king who has, holds, or possesses the capacity to confer that dukedom, and even though he does not *exercise* his power, he gains the willing compliance of the courtier.

What is it, then, that distinguishes having power from exercising power? The distinction could hinge upon the presence or absence of a manifest intention. We could define the *exercise* of power in such a way as to require C to manifest an intention to act in some way in the future, his action to be contingent on R's behavior. By contrast, C might be said to *have* power when, though he does not manifest an intention, R imputes an intention to him and shapes his behavior to meet the imputed intention. If one were to accept this distinction, then in studying the *exercise* of power, one would have to examine not only R's perceptions and responses but also C's intentions and actions. In studying relationships in which C is thought to *have* power, even though he does not exercise it, one would in principle need only to study R's perceptions, the intentions R imputes to C, and the bearing of these on R's behavior. Carried to the extreme, then, this kind of analysis could lead to the discovery of as many different power structures in a political system as there are individuals who impute different intentions to other individuals, groups, or strata in the system.

The distinction between having and exercising power could also turn on the directness involved in the relation between C and R and on the specificity of the actions. In the most direct relationship R's response would be tripped off by a signal directly from C. In this case, C is exercising power. But some relationships are highly indirect; for example, C may modify R's environment in a more or less lasting way, so that R continues to respond as C had intended, even though C makes no effort to control R. In these cases, one might say that although C does not exercise control over R, he does *have* control over R. There are a variety of these indirect, or "roundabout," controls (Dahl & Lindblom 1953, pp. 110 ff.).

Measuring Power

Even more than with power terms themselves, notions of "more" or "less" power were in classical theory left to the realm of common sense and intuition. Efforts to develop systematic measures of power date almost wholly from the 1950s. Of those, some are stated partly in mathematical formulas, some entirely in nonmathematical language. Since the essential features can be suggested without mathematics, we shall describe these measures in ordinary language. (The reader should consult the sources cited for the precise formulations. Most of the best-known measures are presented and discussed in Riker 1964.)

In a rough way, the various criteria for measuring power can be classified into three types: game-theoretical, Newtonian, and economic.

Game-theoretical Criteria. Shapely, a mathematician, and Shubik, an econometrician, have jointly formulated a "method for evaluating the distribution of power in a committee system" (1954). This is intended to measure the power accruing to a voter where the outcome or decision is determined exclusively by voting. In these cases the rules prescribe what proportion of votes constitutes a winning proportion (e.g., a simple majority of all committee members). Thus each member has a certain abstract probability of casting the last vote that would be needed to complete a winning coalition, in other words to occupy a pivotal position with respect to the outcome. By adding his vote at this crucial juncture, a voter may be conceived of as having made a particularly decisive contribution to the outcome; thus, gaining his vote might have considerable value to the other members of a coalition that would lose without his vote. Shapley and Shubik proposed measuring the power of a voter by the probability that he would be the pivotal voter in a winning coalition. Because their measure is entirely limited to voting situations and excludes all outcomes other than the act of voting itself, the utility of the measure is limited to cases where most of the other familiar elements of political life — various forms of persuasion, inducement, and coercion — are lacking. . . .

Newtonian Criteria. On the analogy of the measurement of force in classical mechanics, a number of analysts propose to measure power by the amount of change in R attributable to C. The greater the change in R, the greater the power of C; thus C_a is said to exert more power than C_b if C_a induces more change in R_a than C_b induces in R_a (or in some other R). Measures of this kind have been more frequently proposed than any other (Simon 1947–1956; March 1957; Dahl 1957; 1963, chapter 5; Cartwright 1959; Oppenheim 1961, chapter 8).

"Change in R" is not, however, a single dimension, since many different changes in R may be relevant. Some of the important dimensions of the "change in R" brought about by C that have been suggested for measuring the amount of C's power are (1) the probability that R will comply; (2) the number of persons in R; (3) the number of distinct items, subjects, or values in R; (4) the amount of change in R's position, attitudes, or psychological state; (5) the speed with which R changes; (6) the reduction in the size of the set of outcomes or behaviors available to R; and (7) the degree of R's threatened or expected deprivation.

Economic criteria. Where the game-theoretical measure focuses on the pivotal position of C, and Newtonian measures on changes in R, a third proposal would include "costs" to both C and R in measuring C's power. Harsanyi has argued that a complete measure of power should include (1) the opportunity costs to C of attempting to influence R, which Harsanyi calls the *costs* of C's power, and (2) the opportunity costs to R of refusing to comply with C, which Harsanyi calls the *strength* of C's power over R (1962a, pp. 68 ff.). The measure Harsanyi proposes is not inherently limited to the kinds of cost most familiar to economists but could be extended — at least in principle — to include psychological costs of all kinds.

Designing Operational Definitions

Empirical studies discussed by Cartwright (1965), March (1965), and others, and particularly community studies, have called attention to the neglected problem of designing acceptable operational definitions.

The concepts and measures discussed in this article have not been clothed in operational language. It is not yet clear how many of them can be. Yet the researcher who seeks to observe, report, compare, and analyze power in the real world, in order to test a particular hypothesis or a broader theory, quickly discovers urgent need for operationally defined terms. Research so far has called attention to three kinds of problems. First, the gap between concept and operational definition is generally very great, so great, indeed, that it is not always possible to see what relation there is between the operations and the abstract definition. Thus a critic is likely to conclude that the studies are, no doubt, reporting *something* in the real world, but he might question whether they are reporting the phenomena we mean when we speak of *power*. Second, different operational measures do not seem to correlate with one another (March 1956), which suggests that they may tap different aspects of power relations. Third, almost every measure proposed has engendered controversy over its validity.

None of these results should be altogether surprising or even discouraging. For despite the fact that the attempt to understand political systems by analyzing power relations is ancient, the systematic empirical study of power relations is remarkably new.

BIBLIOGRAPHY

Agger, Robert E., Daniel Goldrich, and Bert Swanson 1964 *The Rulers and the Ruled: Political Power and Impotence in American Communities*. New York: Wiley.

Aristotle, *The Politics of Aristotle*. Translated and edited by Ernest Barker. New York: Oxford Univ. Press, 1962.

Bachrach, Peter, and Morton Baratz 1962 Two Faces of Power. *American Political Science Review* 56:947–952.

Blalock, Hubert M. Jr. 1964 *Causal Inferences in Nonexperimental Research*. Chapel Hill: Univ. of North Carolina Press.

Cartwright, Dorwin (editor) 1959 *Studies in Social Power*. Research Center for Group Dynamics, Publication No. 6. Ann Arbor: Univ. of Michigan, Institute for Social Research.

Cartwright, Dorwin 1965 Influence, Leadership, Control. Pages 1–47 in James G. March (editor), *Handbook of Organizations*. Chicago: Rand McNally.

Catlin, George E. G. 1927 *The Science and Method of Politics*. New York: Knopf; London: Routledge.

Catlin, George E. G. 1930 *A Study of the Principles of Politics, Being an Essay Towards Political Rationalization*. New York: Macmillan.

Dahl, Robert A. 1957 The Concept of Power. *Behavioral Science* 2:201–215.

Dahl, Robert A. (1961) 1963 *Who Governs? Democracy and Power in an American City*. New Haven: Yale Univ. Press.

Dahl, Robert A. 1963 *Modern Political Analysis*. Englewood Cliffs, N.J.: Prentice-Hall.

Dahl, Robert A., and Charles E. Lindblom 1953 *Politics, Economics, and Welfare: Planning and Politico-economic Systems Resolved Into Basic Social Processes*. New York: Harper. → A paperback edition was published in 1963.

French, John R. P., and Bertram Raven 1959 The Bases of Social

Power. Pages 150–167 in Dorwin Cartwright (editor), *Studies in Social Power*. Research Center for Group Dynamics, Publication No. 6. Ann Arbor: Univ. of Michigan, Institute for Social Research.

Friedrich, Carl J. 1963 *Man and His Government: An Empirical Theory of Politics*. New York: McGraw-Hill.

Goldhamer, Herbert, and Edward Shils, 1939 Types of Power and Status. *American Journal of Sociology* 45:171–182.

Harsanyi, John C. 1962*a* Measurement of Social Power, Opportunity Costs, and the Theory of Two-person Bargaining Games. *Behavioral Science* 7:67–80.

Harsanyi, John C. 1962*b* Measurement of Social Power in *n*-Person Reciprocal Power Situations. *Behavioral Science* 7:81–91.

Jouvenel, Bertrand de (1945) 1952 *Power: The Natural History of Its Growth*. Rev. ed. London: Batchworth. → First published in French.

Lasswell, Harold D. (1930) 1960 *Psychopathology and Politics*. New ed., with afterthoughts by the author. New York: Viking.

Lasswell, Harold D. 1936 *Politics: Who Gets What, When, How?* New York: McGraw-Hill.

Lasswell, Harold D., and Abraham Kaplan 1950 *Power and Society: A Framework for Political Inquiry*. Yale Law School Studies, Vol. 2. New Haven: Yale Univ. Press. → A paperback edition was published in 1963.

Loewenstein, Karl 1957 *Political Power and the Governmental Process*. Univ. of Chicago Press.

March, James G. 1955 An Introduction to the Theory and Measurement of Influence. *American Political Science Review* 49:431–451.

March, James G. 1956 Influence Measurement in Experimental and Semiexperimental Groups. *Sociometry* 19:260–271.

March, James G. 1957 Measurement Concepts in the Theory of Influence. *Journal of Politics* 19:202–226.

March, James G. (editor) 1965 *Handbook of Organizations*. Chicago: Rand McNally.

Meinecke, Friedrich (1924) 1957 *Machiavellism: The Doctrine of Raison d'État and Its Place in Modern History*. New Haven: Yale Univ. Press. → First published as *Die Idee der Staatsräson in der neueren Geschichte*.

Merriam, Charles E. 1934 *Political Power: Its Composition and Incidence*. New York: McGraw-Hill. → A paperback edition was published in 1964 by Collier.

Mills, C. Wright 1956 *The Power Elite*. New York: Oxford Univ. Press.

Morgenthau, Hans J. (1948) 1967 *Politics Among Nations: The Struggle for Power and Peace*. 4th ed. New York: Knopf.

Mosca, Gaetano (1896) 1939 *The Ruling Class (Elementi di scienza politica)*. New York: McGraw-Hill.

Neustadt, Richard E. 1960 *Presidential Power: The Politics of Leadership*. New York: Wiley. → A paperback edition was published in 1962.

Oppenheim, Felix E. 1961 *Dimensions of Freedom: An Analysis*. New York: St. Martins; London: Macmillan.

Pareto, Vilfredo (1916) 1963 *The Mind and Society: A Treatise on General Sociology*. 4 vols. New York: Dover. → First published as *Trattato di sociologia generale*. Volume 1: *Non-logical Conduct*. Volume 2: *Theory of Residues.* Volume 3: *Theory of Derivations.* Volume 4: *The General Form of Society.*

Parsons, Talcott 1963a On the Concept of Influence. *Public Opinion Quarterly* 27:37–62. → A comment by J. S. Coleman appears on pages 63–82; a communication by R. A. Bauer, on pages 83–86; and a rejoinder by Talcott Parsons, on pages 87–92.

Parsons, Talcott 1963b On the Concept of Political Power. American Philosophical Society, *Proceedings* 107:232–262.

Polsby, Nelson W. 1963 *Community Power and Political Theory.* Yale Studies in Political Science, Vol. 7. New Haven: Yale Univ. Press.

Riker, William H. 1959 A Test of the Adequacy of the Power Index. *Behavioral Science* 4:120–131.

Riker, William H. 1964 Some Ambiguities in the Notion of Power. *American Political Science Review* 58:341–349.

Rogow, Arnold A., and Harold D. Lasswell 1963 *Power, Corruption and Rectitude.* Englewood Cliffs, N.J.: Prentice-Hall.

Rossi, Peter H. 1960 Power and Community Structure. *Midwest Journal of Political Science* 4:390–401.

Shapley, L. S., and Martin Shubik 1954 A Method for Evaluating the Distribution of Power in a Committee System. *American Political Science Review* 48:787–792.

Simon, Herbert A. (1947–1956) 1957 *Models of Man: Social and Rational; Mathematical Essays on Rational Human Behavior in a Social Setting.* New York: Wiley.

Simon, Herbert A. 1953 Notes on the Observation and Measurement of Political Power. *Journal of Politics* 15:500–516.

Weber, Max (1922) 1957 *The Theory of Social and Economic Organization.* Edited by Talcott Parsons. Glencoe, Ill.: Free Press. → First published as part 1 of *Wirtschaft und Gesellschaft.*

Bargaining and Overload:
An Essay on *Presidential Power*

Peter W. Sperlich

I

Richard E. Neustadt's *Presidential Power* was first published in 1960,[1] and two paperbound editions have been published since.[2] The volume received favorable reviews and ready acceptance [3] and has now come to

Printed by permission of the author.

[1] Richard E. Neustadt, *Presidential Power* (New York: John Wiley & Sons, 1960).

[2] Wiley Science Editions, 1962; Signet Books, 1964.

[3] The major reviews were: Don K. Price, *The American Political Science Review,* LIV (September 1960), pp. 735–736; Harvey Walker, *Western Political Quarterly,* XIII

be regarded as one of the few truly significant statements about the American presidency. Indeed, it is well on its way toward becoming a classic of modern political science.

The office with which it deals is of immense importance. The fate of all mankind, as well as the welfare of the nation, is tied to it with strong bonds. It is not difficult to argue that works on the presidency should be closely inspected and thoroughly evaluated. However, there have been few serious analyses of *Presidential Power*.[4] This essay hopes to contribute to a critical understanding of Neustadt's propositions. Above all it hopes to stimulate the long overdue serious examination and testing of a very important work.

II

The purpose of *Presidential Power* is to instruct.[5] Neustadt wants to indicate how a President can become a powerful leader and what a President must do if he wants to have influence. There is an immediate objection to this purpose: a President *is* powerful. He must be elected, of course, but once in office, his position guarantees him influence. From a formal-constitutional perspective, the objection is reasonable enough. The perspective, however, is at fault. As Neustadt demonstrates, "the probabilities of power do not derive from the literary theory of the Constitution." (43)[6] Neustadt's perspective is empirical and his purpose is didactic. His observation of the working presidency has convinced him of the need for the lesson.

At mid-century, as Neustadt sees it, the President must perform many functions and provide many services. The demands made upon him have increased greatly during recent decades and continue to increase. The

---

(December 1960), pp. 1096–1097; Edward H. Hobbs, *The Journal of Politics*, 23 (February 1961), pp. 146–147; John H. Millett, *Midwest Journal of Political Science*, V (February 1961), pp. 89–90.

4 It should be noted that one aspect of *Presidential Power* has received detailed inspection: its value orientation. William T. Bluhm's recent *Theories of the Political System* (Englewood Cliffs: Prentice-Hall, 1965) contains a comparative study of Neustadt and Machiavelli. The confrontation is interesting and apt. The precepts for Princes and the precepts for Presidents show remarkable similarities of substance and purpose. Bluhm's central critique of Machiavelli, and to even greater extent of Neustadt, is that they have separated politics from ethics and have changed politics to a "purely technical affair." In both cases, Bluhm says, there is a lack of concern with goals and values, the advice is incomplete, and leadership is reduced to "the art of manipulation." The lessons are incomplete; but at least in Neustadt's case, this was intended. In an entirely aware and self-conscious manner, Neustadt set out to provide a President with *means*. Ultimately, of course, studies of political leadership require an integrated approach to means and ends. Still, it does seem possible to focus attention on one, without at the same time also considering the other. To claim, as Bluhm does, that such procedure necessarily reduces the whole of politics to its technical part, is to deny analytic separability of interacting factors.

5 The great wealth of descriptive materials has a purely illustrative function. *Presidential Power* is not intended as a historical treatise.

6 Figures in parentheses refer to page numbers in the 1960 edition of *Presidential Power*.

President's service functions (his "clerkship") are demanded and accepted by the many other actors in the political arena because they could not do their jobs without them. But this is not enough to make the President a leader in fact; services do not guarantee influence. (6)

If a President provides important services for others, why is he not assured of their support? The answer is that none of the other actors has his obligations or his outlook. The persons for whom he performs services and upon whom he depends in turn to have his wishes carried out — cabinet officers and other members of the executive branch, legislative leaders, party leaders, and other political figures at home and abroad — have their own obligations, their own constituencies, their own jobs to do. Because of the way in which they perceive their responsibilities, they may not assent to presidential wishes. (7–8)

Decisions are not self-executing; someone must do something. A President cannot execute many of his resolutions by himself. The task is physically impossible. Besides, in many cases the President lacks the proper power for such an undertaking. In the last analysis, the measure of a President's leadership is not so much his own actions but his influence on the actions of others. Not what he does, but what he gets done, indicates his true powers. (2)

Of course, an impressive array of formal powers is attached to the presidential office. Cannot the President simply issue an order? Not necessarily, says Neustadt. To begin with, these formal powers are effective only within a relatively narrow range because our system is one of shared powers. To employ formal powers in the form of a direct command is very costly. (10) Neustadt uses three examples of the actual use of command — Truman's conflict with MacArthur, Truman's seizure of the steel mills, and Eisenhower's sending of federal troops to Little Rock — to demonstrate the severe limitations on the President's use of formal powers. These incidents also show that even when the formal powers of the President are sufficient, certain other conditions must prevail if a command is to produce compliance. (19) In any case, formal orders are a President's last resort, to be employed only after "softer means" have failed. (27–30) Viewed realistically, "presidential power is the power to persuade." (10)

It is important that the President's persuasive arguments be phrased in terms of the interests of those whom he must persuade. "The essence of a President's persuasive task is to convince such men that what the White House wants of them is what they ought to do for their sake and on their authority." (34) The best way — perhaps the only way — to convince these men that their own interests are involved in presidential requests is to make the President's services dependent on their help. "A President's authority and status [formal powers] give him great advantages in dealing with the men he would persuade. Each 'power' is a vantage point for him to the degree that other men have use for his authority." (35) A President's formal powers do not in themselves bring about the execution of his decisions. They are, however, crucial ingredients of his persuasive efforts. "Power is persuasion and persuasion becomes bargaining." (38) Presidential power is the capacity to trade advantages and *"the power to persuade is the power to bargain."* (36)

To be a powerful leader, to have influence in fact as well as in theory, a President must be a successful bargainer. All his formal powers, all his status, all his well-reasoned arguments, all his charm will not secure his influence if he does not know how to bargain. Neustadt's lesson for Presidents is a lesson based on the premise that the structure of our political system and the nature of our time define the role of a President as that of a bargainer, not a commander.

Of all of Neustadt's rules, the following is the most basic: a President must want to maximize his power. If he does not, whatever his other qualities, he is not fit for the office. Presidents must have a will to power.[7] Mid-century politics contains constant emergencies and crises and results in enormous strain on the intellectual and material resources of policy-makers in the government. Proper — decisive, imaginative — political leadership is of vital importance to the welfare of the nation and the world. Only the President is in the position to furnish such leadership, which cannot be effected in the absence of true power and influence. Power and influence, however, are not guaranteed to a President. He must actively seek them. "A President's constituents, regardless of their party (or their country for that matter), have a great stake in his search for personal influences." (183)

Neustadt's principles are "content-free." The efficacy of the means is not dependent on the nature of the goals. Whatever a President's substantive aims might be, to reach them he must meet two criteria: he must want power and he must know how to bargain.

III

It is important in the following discussion to keep in mind that Neustadt's focus is on strategy rather than tactics. He is interested in the problem of how to secure a President's overall power stakes, how to make him influential in a general way. Neustadt is not concerned in any direct sense with particular persuasive efforts, such as persuading a given Senator in respect to a certain issue. (2) Neustadt's presentation of the detailed rules for successful bargaining is quite complex and precise relationships are somewhat obscured by many illustrations, although the descriptive materials are presented in a most readable and altogether spellbinding fashion. The diagrams in this section will permit simultaneous inspection of Neustadt's specific principles for successful bargaining. Hopefully they will help to clarify the interrelations of these principles.

A President, in any given bargaining situation, can be a successful bargainer only if he has taken care to guard his power prospects — his generalized influence — in previous bargains. To bargain means to make

[7] See Neustadt, *Presidential Power*, Chaps. 1 and 8.

choices.[8] To guard power prospects in bargaining means to make the right choices and the right choices are those that improve general power prospects while achieving a favorable bargain in the immediate situation. (56) A President's choices "are the only means in his own hands of guarding his power prospects for effective influence." (57)

Neustadt raises and considers the following two questions: How does making right choices guard a President's power prospects, and what must a President do in order to make the right choices? A pattern of choices emerges from a President's past choices. (61) From this pattern, not from any particular successes or failures, the men a President must persuade — the Washingtonians [9] — will take their cues as to his skill and his will to use his advantages.[10] (58) Tenacity can count for as much as technical skill in shaping the expectations of the Washingtonians about presidential bargaining behavior. These expectations constitute a President's professional reputation. The quality of his reputation has a significant effect on his ability to achieve good bargains and to guard his power prospects. (62–63)

Most Presidents must settle for a reputation short to some degree of an ideal one. A President, however, should at least try to minimize the uncertainties of reward for prospective support and maximize the uncertainties and risks of future opposition. In many ways, his reputation will depend on his ability to do this. (64) But whatever the nature and quality of this reputation, it is squarely based on his choices. (84)

Aside from professional reputation, a President's influence, or power prospects, also depends on his popular prestige. (85) He must not ignore the public at large. Although "the people" are not partners to presidential bargaining, those who are — the Washingtonians — take into account a President's public standing in their dealings with him. To some degree, most Washingtonians are dependent on public support and their constituents' views of the President are important factors in their calculations. (86) Thus, popular prestige gives a President leverage with the Washingtonians; the greater his popular prestige, the more difficult it is for them to resist him. (90)

What determines popular prestige? The right kind of personality is one component. The qualities — positively or negatively evaluated — that the public perceives in the President are not without consequence for his prestige. (94–95) But public perception of these qualities does not make the major contribution, nor is it a very dependable element in determining popular prestige. The prime determinant of a President's prestige is

---

[8] "Choice" refers to the President's decision to act or not to act in a given way in regard to a certain matter. (56)

[9] Neustadt defines the Washingtonians as "members of Congress and of [the President's] Administration, governors of states, military commanders in the field, leading politicians in both parties, representatives of private organizations, newsmen of assorted types and sizes, foreign diplomats (and principals abroad)." (58)

[10] The perceptions of the Washingtonians of presidential choice patterns may not always be correct, of course. Until demonstrated wrong, however, these perceptions constitute the reality upon which Washingtonians will act. (59)

the public's perception of his job performance. The satisfactions and frustrations in their personal lives that are linked to presidential performance determine his prestige. (95) Similarly events and happenings that frustrate large parts of the public are the most serious threat to a President's prestige. (95–98) A president does not control these happenings, however, and all he can work with are men's hopes and expectations. He must prepare the public for the frustrations that are bound to occur. "If he can make them think the hardship necessary, and can make them want to bear it with good grace, his prestige may not suffer when they feel it." (99)

What the President needs, however, is not a Madison Avenue public relations approach. To minimize popular frustrations in the face of adverse events and conditions — in the face of disappointed hopes and unwelcome hardships — a President must teach realism. (100) The real enemy of presidential prestige is unreality: unrealistic hopes and expectations. (106) The President can teach realism in only one way. He must make the right choices. "His choices of what he will do and when and how — his choices, also, of whom he will tell and in what way and words — are *his* means to protect this source of influence, just as they are his means to guard those other power sources: bargaining relationships and professional reputation." (107)

The circles are closed. Only by making the right choices can a President guard his power prospects. The connection between choices and power prospects is threefold. They are directly related in the immediate bargaining situation, in the President's professional reputation, and in the President's popular prestige. The last relationship is effective largely because of its influence on the second.

Diagram 1 traces the pattern of the answer to the first question raised above. There are three independent variables: choices, events and conditions, and personality. All three, of course, have their own antecedents but Neustadt considers only the factors that lead to making right choices since the remaining antecedents are outside the explanatory scope of his investigation.

The stage is set now for the second question: What must a President do in order to make right choices?

"Influence," says Neustadt, "adheres to those who sense what it is made of." (120) To guard his power prospects, a President, first of all, must understand the nature of power. If his choices are to be right — if they are to guard his power prospects — a President must perceive his power stakes in these choices. (122) He cannot rely on others to alert him to the personal power implications of his choices, nor will the issues necessarily provide guidance. A President must see the power implications by himself; he must be his own power expert. (148–151)

To be his own power expert, a President needs meaningful information. He needs the data his advisors will provide, but "he also needs to know the little things they fail to mention." (153) "To help himself he must reach out as widely as he can for every scrap of fact, opinion, gossip, bearing on his interests and relationships as President. He must become

Dɪᴀɢʀᴀᴍ 1

Success as a Bargainer

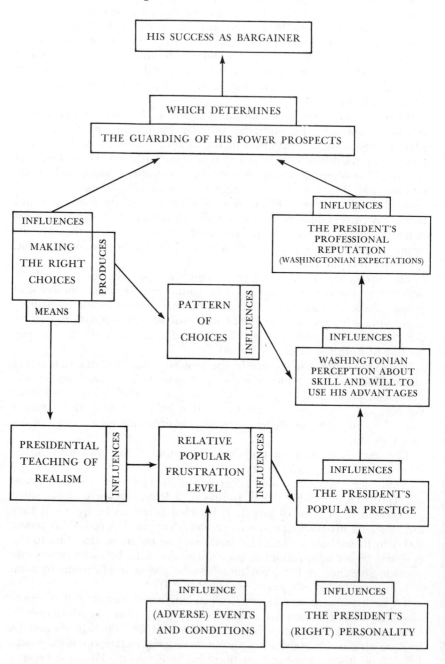

his own director of his own central intelligence." (154) A President needs all the facts — and interpretations of the facts — that he can get, but they will not be brought to him. To obtain facts he must actively be involved in the political processes in which they generated. A President cannot afford an Olympian posture. He must actively participate in the details of political work. (154)

If a President is to make right choices, the choices must be in his hands. (154–155) They are not his automatically, and they may be pre-empted or foreclosed by others. One commodity a President needs to obtain the ability to make choices is time. (155) A President's timetable is always crowded, and it is structured by deadlines imposed from the outside, by persons or events. To make time for himself, a President must set deadlines of his own and add these self-imposed deadlines to the others. (156) To get the choices into his hands, a President also must introduce competition into his administration because competition among his aides helps a President make choices of his own, and gives him time to make his decisions in a proper fashion. (157–158) Competition also helps a President in the gathering of meaningful information. (156–157)

Actively participating in the political process, setting his own deadlines, and fostering competition among his aides are the prime elements of presidential self-help. (161) Presidential self-help, in turn, rests upon a President's interior resources, the most important of which are a sense of power,[11] self-confidence, and a sense of direction. (171) By and large, however, these resources are available only to those with the right background, that is, to those who possess the right temperament [12] — personality — for the job and who have had sufficient political experience. (181–183) The most relevant type of experience is holding governmental office. Organization and party work do not offer the same benefits. To make right choices, a President must also know how to use the advantages — vantage points — that derive from his position and stature. This skill comes most easily to those who have had ample and proper political experience. (179)

The answer to the second question is outlined in Diagram 2. The dependent factor is "making right choices." The independent variables are vantage points, personality, and experience. For convenience, Neustadt's lesson has been presented in two parts, but this should not obscure the fact that his instructions form a well-integrated whole. The full set of components and component relations is presented in Diagram 3. As can be seen in this diagram, Neustadt's schema contains four truly independent variables: personality, experience, events and conditions, and vantage points. These determine in various ways such intermediate factors as a President's perception of his power stakes, his ability to get choices into his hands, and his professional reputation. Ultimately the four variables, in interaction, determine the final dependent factor of the model: a President's actual power.

11 "Will to power" and "understanding of power."
12 Neustadt is silent on the precise characteristics of a fitting temperament, although he does casually suggest that "humor and perspective" may be among them.

DIAGRAM 2

Making Right Choices

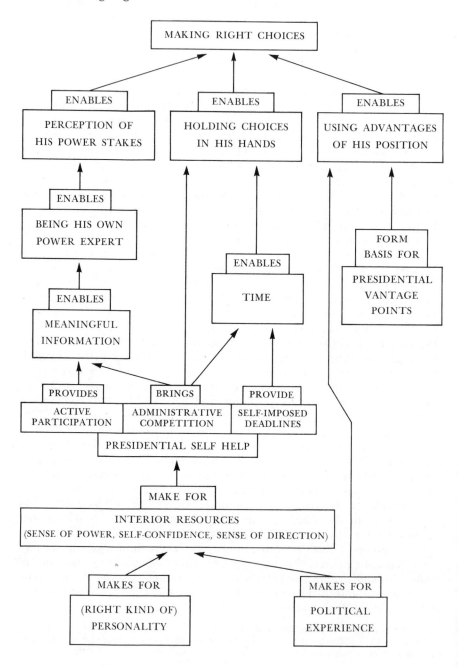

DIAGRAM 3
The Complete Schema

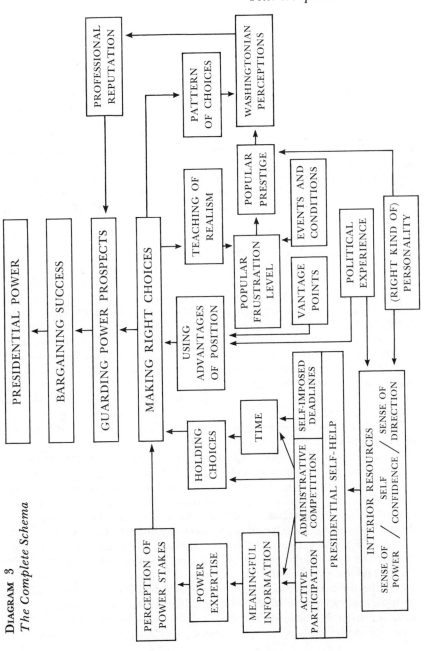

IV

It is a common observation that the quality and quantity of the literature on the American presidency, apart from strictly biographical materials, is exceedingly poor.[13] Systematic analyses of the office and officeholders are rare. Neustadt's efforts are welcome indeed, particularly for their empirical qualities. Although the empirical nature of Neustadt's model of presidential power is clear since in principle, all its assertions are subject to observational testing, the model has not yet been empirically verified.[14] Constructing a model, however empirico-inductive, does not include testing the model. For proper verification, the construct must be checked against a set of data other than that from which it was derived.

Neustadt's presentation has a most persuasive ring. In part, however, its persuasive power testifies to an ultimate weakness in the argument; for, like other systems, it does not consider alternative explanations. One of the basic problems involved, to use statistical language, is that of spurious correlations. For example, an author may be entirely correct in his observation of the association of A and B. Consistently, if A then B. But this observation ignores possible factor C, which might be producing A as well as B. The observation also ignores the relative strength of the association. Again, perhaps the author is quite right to state that the variation in A explains some of the variation in B. But what about D, which remains unconsidered, and which explains a good deal more of B's variation? My basic point is that Neustadt's model remains to be tested and indeed should be tested. Nothing could be more unkind to *Presidential Power* than to put it on the shelf as a classic. Neustadt chose to enter the empirical arena and he has a right to challengers.

The challenge, of course, must come from new research, not a review essay, which can only record what forms such investigations might take. The most appropriate first step would be an extensive analysis of historical data on American Presidents. Vast, if unsystematic, information on their personal characteristics, their conduct of office, their accomplishments, and their failures is available. We also have substantial knowledge about social and political conditions since Independence. In short, it would be quite feasible to check the model against most, if not all, American Presidents. Although Neustadt's schema is constructed against the background of a single culture, it is not culture-bound in its intent and foreign political executives can provide additional historical data. The essential procedure in such a historical investigation would be to independently measure Neustadt's antecedents and consequents and then see whether there is in fact a regular association between certain states of the former and certain states of the latter.[15] Theoretically, pre-

[13] Despite the current increase in writings on the American presidency, few writers contribute to a systematic knowledge of the presidency.

[14] In other words, there has not yet been an attempt to falsify the model.

[15] The problem of operationalization could be quite severe. Neustadt's analysis does not specify precise operationalizations. The criteria, for example, for determining the

dictive testing is also possible, although it would be quite difficult in practice, particularly since in general there is only one new case every eight years.

Two other approaches, more rigorous than historical analysis, are also possible. The first is laboratory experimentation, including various forms of human simulation. Small-group research has shown that the psychological laboratory can contribute significantly to the understanding of even highly complex social — interactional — phenomena.[16] Second, computer simulation has proven helpful in systematic explorations of models of social reality.[17]

Historical, and experimental, or predictive, tests of Neustadt's model, to the knowledge of this reviewer, have not yet been undertaken. This is a great handicap, but it does not preclude all evaluation of his work. The validation and critical examination of any theory or model includes tests of internal and external coherence. Indeed, they take logical priority to the other tests. As validation criteria they are, of course, not quite as powerful as tests of correspondence or pragmatic and predictive tests. Still, they do permit at least a preliminary critical evaluation. And while they do not suffice to verify or falsify a construct, they are essential to any analysis.[18]

To test a model for internal coherence means to probe for the internal consistency and for the parsimony of a construct. The first is a matter of formal logic, the second of descriptive simplicity. One probe has been executed already in Section III, where the crucial ingredients of Neustadt's model were made explicit. Several diagrams traced their relationship and revealed no inconsistencies or contradictions. The probe for parsimony depends upon comparative criteria as it is difficult to assertain

---

relative magnitude of a President's popularity (not to speak of his power sense) are not clear. There is also the problem of deriving precise theoretical definitions for key concepts. However, these difficulties can be resolved.

16 Cf. Allen L. Edwards, "Experiments," in Gardner Lindzey, ed., *Handbook of Social Psychology*, Vol I. (Reading, Mass.: Addison-Wesley, 1954); Leon Festinger, "Laboratory Experiments," in Leon Festinger and Daniel Katz, eds., *Research Methods in the Behavioral Sciences* (New York: The Dryden Press, 1953); Harold H. Kelley and John W. Thibaut, "Experimental Studies of Group Problem Solving and Process," in Lindzey, ed., *Handbook of Social Psychology*, Vol. II; Morris Zelditch, Jr., and Terence K. Hopkins, "Laboratory Experiments with Organizations," in Amitai Etzioni, ed., *Complex Organizations* (New York: Holt, Rinehart & Winston, 1961); Karl E. Weick, "Laboratory Experimentation with Organizations," in James G. March, ed., *Handbook of Organizations* (Chicago: Rand McNally, 1965).

17 Cf. Dorothy L. Meier and C. H. Bradford, "Creating a World for Research," *Trans-Action*, 3 (March/April 1966), 37–39; Harold Guetzkow, ed., *Simulation in Social Sciences* (Englewood Cliffs: Prentice Hall, 1962); Sidney C. Rome and Beatrice K. Rome, "Computer Simulation Toward a Theory of Large Organizations," in Harold Borko, ed., *Computer Applications in the Behavioral Sciences* (Englewood Cliffs: Prentice-Hall, 1962); Oliver Benson, "Simulation of International Relations and Diplomacy," in Harold Borko, ed., *Computer Applications in the Behavioral Sciences* (Englewood Cliffs: Prentice-Hall, 1962); Kalman J. Cohen and Richard M. Cyert, "Simulation of Organizational Behavior," in March, ed., *Handbook of Organizations*.

18 Cf. Abraham Kaplan, *The Conduct of Inquiry* (San Francisco: Chandler Publishing Co., 1964), Chap. VIII.

the degree of descriptive simplicity attained in a single model. The second probe cannot be attempted here. It will have to wait until alternative models of the same reality become available.

V

To test a model for external coherence means to check its propositions against those currently accepted in relevant disciplines. External coherence lends credibility to new constructs, although the lack of such coherence does not necessarily falsify them since it is conceivable that the established positions might be in error. Perhaps the best approach is to assume with Kuhn and others that all theories are at least partially wrong.[19]

By Neustadt's own testimony, his model's range of applicability goes beyond Presidents. Other political figures must guard their power stakes in very similar ways. Protection of power stakes "is a problem also for the heads of private 'governments,' for corporation presidents, trade union leaders, churchmen." (viii) The literature germane to testing for external coherence is large and diverse. The relevance of organization theory is evident and its propositions about managements, bureaucracies, administrations, and similar public or private social systems are of great interest. These propositions are particularly important in relation to such matters as influence, leadership, decision-making, and bargaining. Also relevant are the data relating to persuasion and attitude change, role behavior, communication, and conflict behavior. Without much trouble, this list of relevant information could be lengthened by a good measure.

The first step in testing for external coherence is to check for concept comparability. This is of more than routine importance in the social sciences, which are burdened by multiple-meaning terms. A minimal listing of Neustadt's key concepts includes leadership, power or influence, bargaining, choice-making, persuasion, personality, and experience. Few of these are given explicit definitions. Thanks to lucid writing, however, Neustadt's meanings can be specified with a good deal of precision. When this is done, it becomes clear that most terms are used according to currently dominant conventions. For example, by power Neustadt means the ability of a President to get someone else to do something that he wants him to do, but which that other person would not do otherwise. (2, et passim) This definition is very similar to most presently accepted views of power in the field of political science.[20] It also agrees with current socio-psychological definitions.[21]

[19] See Thomas S. Kuhn, *The Structure of Scientific Revolutions* (Chicago: University of Chicago Press, 1962).

[20] Cf. Robert A. Dahl, "The Concept of Power," *Behavioral Science*, 2 (July 1957), 201–215; David Easton, *The Political System* (New York: Alfred A. Knopf, 1959), pp. 143–144; also see Harold D. Lasswell and Abraham Kaplan, *Power and Society* (New Haven: Yale University Press, 1950), pp. 75–76.

[21] Compare John R. P. French, Jr., and Bertram Raven, "The Bases of Social Power," in Dorwin Cartwright and Alvin Zander, eds., *Group Dynamics* (Evanston, Ill.: Row, Peterson and Co., 1960), pp. 608–610; also Daniel Katz and Robert L. Kahn,

Another term that is conventionally defined is bargaining. Neustadt sees bargaining as the trading of advantages with persons of influence — the Washingtonians — but not with the public at large. This is almost identical to the view of bargaining given by Dahl and Lindblom's classic *Politics, Economics, and Welfare:* "Bargaining is a form of reciprocal control among leaders." [22] With slight adjustments, Neustadt's usage of the term is also compatible with that of Schelling.[23] In both cases, the central notion about bargaining is the existence of a common interest and of mutual, but not necessarily equal, advantages.

The term leadership is the single exception and has a different meaning for Neustadt than it has for other writers on the subject, most of whom are social psychologists. Neustadt defines leadership in terms of power and it is not by accident that *Presidential Power* is subtitled "the politics of leadership."

In the hands of social psychologists the term leadership has experienced a rather mixed fortune. Three epochs can be distinguished.[24] The oldest and now discredited is the trait approach, which saw leadership as the personal property of the leader by virtue of certain specific characteristics of mind or body. A newer tradition is the functional approach, which defines leadership without any reference to a leader. The needs of the group and the requirements of the situation determine leadership, and any category of behavior can be an act of leadership, provided it meets current needs. "In principle, leadership may be performed by one of many members of the group." [25] In principle, also, a given leadership function may be executed through any number of different behaviors. Most recently, a third tradition of leadership, which limits leadership functions to acts of particular importance or unusual significance, has begun to emerge out of the second. This last approach is the relatively most sensitive to the relational aspects of leadership,[26] but the basic functional orientation remains.[27]

In spite of many studies and approaches, the number of well-founded propositions of leadership has remained small.

> Anyone at all familiar with the literature of sociology and social psychology will readily grant that the topic of leadership has

The Social Psychology of Organizations (New York: John Wiley & Sons, 1966), pp. 218–220.

22 Robert A. Dahl and Charles E. Lindblom, *Politics, Economics, and Welfare* (New York: Harper Torchbooks, 1963), p. 324.

23 Thomas C. Schelling, *The Strategy of Conflict* (New York: Oxford University Press, Galaxy Books, 1963), Chaps. 1 and 2.

24 Cf. Cecil A. Gibb, "Leadership," in Lindzey, ed., *Handbook of Social Psychology,* Vol. II; Dorwin Cartwright and Alvin Zander, "Leadership and Group Performance: Introduction," in Cartwright and Zander, eds., *Group Dynamics.*

25 Cartwright and Zander, "Leadership and Group Performance: Introduction," p. 492.

26 A fine example of the new approach is found in Katz and Kahn, *The Social Psychology of Organizations.*

27 While the trait approach defines leadership as that which leaders do, the functional approach defines the leader as the person who leads. Both definitions have certain maddening qualities.

commanded considerable attention from students in these fields. However, it is not unfair to say that these disciplines have distinguished themselves more by accumulating *studies* on leadership than by cumulating *knowledge* on leadership.[28]

Power has played a very minor role in these studies.[29] As Janda has observed:

> The first thing to be noted in a comparative review of the literature on leadership and that on power is that there is almost no overlap between the two. Studies of leadership and studies of power have been conducted almost independently of each other.[30]

There are exceptions of course. Most notable for their integrative approaches to leadership are John French [31] and Dorwin Cartwright.[32] Most studies, however, have seen leadership as somebody doing something about an important group need, without paying much attention to the requisite power bases for such behavior. At least from the point of view of political science, Neustadt's deviance from common usage, then, is a step in the right direction, and in testing Neustadt's propositions about presidential leadership for external coherence, we will consider only those theories that define leadership to some degree in terms of power.

We discussed Neustadt's basic observations and assumptions in section II. There is general agreement on his view that mid-century politics is full of emergencies and crises that make enormous demands upon governmental resources, that many governmental functions could not be performed adequately in the absence of presidential leadership, and that a President must have influence if he is to fulfill his leadership function. For an adequate understanding of this assertion we must examine Neustadt's propositions on the nature of presidential power and how it can be obtained and secured.

Most fundamental in Neustadt's account, and closely related to each other, are the two propositions that *presidential power is the power to persuade,* and that *the power to persuade is the power to bargain.* Neustadt considers two ways in which a President can influence the action of

[28] Kenneth F. Janda, "Toward the Explication of the Concept of Leadership in Terms of the Concept of Power," *Human Relations,* 13 (November 1960), p. 347.

[29] Some of this is due to ideological self-indulgence and poor logic: Power is undemocratic.

[30] Janda, "Toward the Explication of the Concept of Leadership," pp. 353–354.

[31] John R. P. French, Jr., and R. Snyder, "Leadership and Interpersonal Power," in Dorwin Cartwright, ed., *Studies in Social Power* (Ann Arbor: Institute of Social Research, 1959); John R. P. French, Jr., and Bertram Raven, "The Bases of Social Power," and John R. P. French, Jr., "A Formal Theory of Social Power," in Cartwright and Zander, eds., *Group Dynamics.*

[32] Dorwin Cartwright, "A Field Theoretical Conception of Power," in Cartwright, ed., *Studies in Social Power;* Cartwright and Zander, "Leadership and Group Performance: Introduction," in Cartwright and Zander, eds., *Group Dynamics;* and Dorwin Cartwright, "Influence, Leadership, Control," in March, ed., *Handbook of Organizations.*

others: command and persuasion. Command means giving a direct order and persuasion is the trading of advantages, or bargaining. As far as Neustadt is concerned, bargaining is the only "real" means for the exercise of presidential influence and he rejects the use of command as a suitable method except as a last resort. In testing for external coherence, then, we shall consider the following: Do command and persuasion constitute the full range of influence alternatives? Is command as unworkable as Neustadt says it is, and is bargaining in fact as good a tool as he would have it? A convenient place to begin testing for external coherence is an investigation of the bases of presidential power.

Neustadt's presidential power bases are vantage points, experience, and personality.[33] Vantage points are the formal powers of the presidency and the abilities and opportunities to perform needed services that the office supplies to its occupant. Experience and personality are not altogether separable. They concern the personal element — a President's knowledge, skills, drive, etc. Command is based on formal powers only, while bargaining requires the activation of all three power bases.

How do Neustadt's power bases compare with those of others? John French and Bertram Raven distinguish five sources of power: [34] (1) reward power (P accepts O's influence because O is able to manipulate P's attainment of positive values); [35] (2) coercive power (P accepts O's influence because O is able to manipulate P's attainment of negative values); (3) legitimate power (the "power which stems from internalized values in P which dictate that O has a legitimate right to influence P and that P has an obligation to accept this influence"); (4) referent power (P accepts O's influence because he identifies with O); and (5) expert power (P accepts O's influence because he attributes knowledge or experience to P). Most alternative systems [36] are similar to French and Raven's. Divergencies are a matter of finer or larger slices more often than of different categories. Thus, for example, reward power is subdivided occasionally into material and psychic satisfactions. The present writer prefers a simplified three-fold classification of sources of power: [37] (1) instrumental (O is able to manipulate P's rewards and punishments); (2) internalized-authoritative (P has internalized values that require him to accept O's influence whenever O is seen as possessing attributes — legitimacy and expertise, for example — relevant to these values); and (3) libidinal (P accepts O's influence, indeed seeks it, because he has cathected libido on O — in mild cases this can be an admiring identification, in severe cases a surrender of P's ego to O's charisma).

That Neustadt's power bases cover the same ground as French and

---

[33] See Diagram 3. The fourth independent variable — events and conditions — is not a systematic power base, although, of course, certain events may create occasional opportunities for influence.

[34] John R. P. French, Jr., and Bertram Raven, "The Bases of Social Power."

[35] In this symbolism, "O" represents the influencer, "P" the recipient of influence.

[36] For a comprehensive review see Cartwright, "Influence, Leadership, Control."

[37] The categories are similar to those in Herbert C. Kelman, "The Process of Opinion Change," *Public Opinion Quarterly*, 25 (Spring 1961), 57–78.

Raven's five, or as the reduced three, except for referent or libidinal power, has important consequences for Neustadt's presidential power model. The first consequence is that the model does not include certain variables relevant to a determination of presidential influence. Neustadt does not consider the possibility that a person might accept influence and will do what is requested of him because he has come to identify with the individual who makes the request.[38] Not included among Neustadt's many prescriptions, then, is that a President, within the limits set by other criteria, should select his associates on the basis of personal loyalty and identification, and that he should attempt to create feelings of subjective identification in those in whose selection he had no voice. In practice, opportunities to do this might be somewhat limited, but at least in the case of cabinet officials and other members of the executive staff, identification could be a power basis of some force.[39] The greatest amount of identification is likely to take place outside the Washingtonian circle, but these contributions would be indirect and probably minor.[40]

The second consequence of the absence of referent power in Neustadt's prescriptions is an unnecessarily sharp restraint in the use of command. Formal powers are not the only possible base for commands. They can also be given on the less-costly grounds of interpersonal identification. Neustadt's de-emphasizing of command follows current organizational thinking.[41] However, as a result of neglecting identification as a power

[38] Neustadt gives less adequate treatment to psychological and ideological variables than to political and sociological ones. For consideration of the contributions of various types of identification in social systems see Katz and Kahn, *The Social Psychology of Organizations,* pp. 365–368; Amitai Etzioni, "Organizational Control Structure," pp. 651–654; Herbert A. Simon, "Authority," in Conrad Arensberg, *et al.,* eds., *Research in Industrial Human Relations* (New York: Harper & Row, 1957), pp. 104–106; James G. March and Herbert A. Simon, *Organizations* (New York: John Wiley & Sons, 1958), pp. 73–75.

[39] It is interesting to note that in *Presidential Power* very little advice is offered on staff selection. The lack of identification considerations may be connected to this. Of course, Professor Neustadt, an authority on matters of staff, in several publications has addressed himself to the specific problem of the staffing of the presidency. How a President might get the help he needs has always been one of his major concerns. The points of view put forth, and the positions taken, in these writings will be noted occasionally. They diverge in certain ways from the dominant theme of *Presidential Power.* Such divergent positions, however, will not be used to modify in any way the propositions now under review since only *Presidential Power* is the subject of the present discussion. Representative of Professor Neustadt's views on staffing are "Presidency and Legislation: Planning the President's Program," *The American Political Science Review,* XLIX (December 1955), 980–1021; "Staffing the Presidency: The Role of White House Agencies," a lecture given at the Indian Institute of Public Administration, New Delhi, January 13, 1962, reprinted in *Administration of National Security, selected papers prepared by the Subcommittee on National Security Staffing and Operations, of the Committee on Government Operations, United States Senate* (Washington, D.C.: U.S. Government Printing Office, 1962), 855–864; and "Approaches to Staffing the Presidency: Notes on FDR and JFK," *The American Political Science Review,* LVII (December 1963).

[40] In elections to presidential office they could be of great importance, of course.
[41] Cf. Douglas McGregor, *The Human Side of Enterprise* (New York: McGraw-Hill, 1960), Chap. 4; or Dahl and Lindblom, *Politics, Economics, and Welfare,* pp. 106–109.

base, he may have limited command employment more severely than actually required. Another reason for this limitation may lie in the illustrations selected by Neustadt. Less dramatic examples or influence attempts in matters of less importance might have produced a more positive picture of the use of command.[42]

Although Neustadt does consider the internalized-authoritative power base, his treatment is not fully adequate. He sees it only in the form of legitimacy and attributes very little importance to it. Altogether missing, for example, is a discussion of organizational ideology. Various studies have noted that mutual role expectations and shared norms and values can be an important and powerful source of request, command, compliance.[43] There is no reason to think that ideology, at least within the executive branch, could not function as a power base. As with identification, a command based on shared norms and values is not likely to carry the same price as one based exclusively on a formal right to issue the command. Again, since Neustadt does not consider this factor in *Presidential Power*, he offers no advice to the President about creating and sustaining a proper ideological climate among his associates.[44]

Neustadt's almost exclusive emphasis on bargaining as a tool of influence seems a direct result of his equally exclusive focus on instrumentalism. The assumption is that people, or at least those people a President might want to influence, are susceptible only to instrumental appeals. As far as the model is concerned, instrumental rewards and punishments are practically all; libidinal power is ignored, and internalized-authoritative power is discounted. Politics as bargaining is a presentation, of course, that has gained wide acceptance — and rightly so. In one sense, this is precisely the point Neustadt wants to make. There is no doubt that "the others" can be motivated by services performed, but even in politics, instrumental relationships may not tell the whole story.

So far, then, our examination of command and persuasion has led to the conclusion that the former is underrated and the latter is overrated in Neustadt's schema. Now it is time to shift the focus of investigation to consider whether command and persuasion are the only ways of exercising influence.

It is helpful to turn to Dahl and Lindblom's system of control relations.[45] They distinguish four "basic control techniques," three "roundabout control techniques," and six "conditions for effective control."

---

[42] In *Presidential Power*, Neustadt does not often distinguish degrees of importance or significance. All matters seem to have equal weight.

[43] Cf. Theodore R. Sarbin, "Role Theory," in Lindzey, ed., *Handbook of Social Psychology*, Vol. I; also Katz and Kahn, *The Social Psychology of Organizations*, pp. 48–57. Some comments on norms and role expectations are found in Neustadt's "Presidency and Legislation: Planning the President's Program," particularly on pp. 1011 and 1013.

[44] On the function of ideology as a "coordination tool" see Aaron Wildavsky, *Dixon-Yates: A Study in Power Politics* (New Haven: Yale University Press, 1962), p. 314 *et passim*.

[45] Dahl and Lindblom, *Politics, Economics, and Welfare*. Unless otherwise indicated, the following discussion is based on Chapter 4.

These various control relations are cast fully in instrumental language. However, it is interesting to note the appearance of terms that can be interpreted as symbolic, or non-instrumental, influence techniques. Specifically, they are appeals on the basis of legitimacy, appeals on the basis of identification, and appeals on the basis of feelings of duty or pride. *Presidential Power* gives only limited attention to legitimacy and none to identification or duty or pride.

Dahl and Lindblom's system also suggests a shortcoming in *Presidential Power* on the strictly instrumental side. Dahl and Lindblom's basic instrumental control techniques are: (1) spontaneous field control; (2) unilateral and bilateral manipulated field control; (3) command; and (4) reciprocity. "Command" has much the same meaning in *Presidential Power* as in *Politics, Economics, and Welfare.*[46] Neustadt's "bargaining" corresponds closely to Dahl and Lindblom's "reciprocity" and "bilateral manipulated field control." What is missing from Neustadt's list is "unilateral manipulated field control." [47] Neustadt identifies unilateral manipulated field controls exclusively with command. Dahl and Lindblom, by contrast, suggest that command is the particular case of unilateralism that is based on threats of punishment for non-performance and on the removal of those threats when compliance has been obtained.

Neustadt is right in thinking that opportunities for non-command unilateral presidential action are limited. Yet, it cannot be ignored that many presidential requests are acted upon without bargaining and without commanding. As noted earlier, the dramatic nature of the examples in *Presidential Power* may have contributed to the neglect of the rather substantial area of routine compliance.

The inference must be drawn, then, that bargaining and command are not the only two usable techniques of influence available to a President. This is clearest perhaps when attention is focused on symbolic manipulations. Influence attempts based on appeals to duty, pride, role-conception, ideology, conscience, interpersonal identification, etc., are notoriously non-reciprocal. There is no reference to instrumental rewards or deprivations. There is no bargaining activity. The influence attempt appeals to internalized values. The power of the charismatic leader over his followers may be regarded as the extreme case of such non-instrumental, non-reciprocal control relationships. Appeals to internalized values may also be thought of as a form of persuasion. If bargaining is instrumental persuasion, this is symbolic persuasion.[48]

46 Also, in both volumes "command" is regarded as a marginal technique for control.
47 Neustadt also does not deal with "spontaneous field control." In view of his purposes, this exclusion is justified. While in some ways it is a most effective control technique, it is not one that can be formalized in a set of rules.
48 The last two decades have seen the growth of a rich literature on the relative efficacy of various forms and methods of persuasion. For some good summaries see Carl I. Hovland, Irving L. Janis, and Harold H. Kelly, *Communication and Persuasion* (New Haven: Yale University Press, 1953); Carl I. Hovland and Irving L. Janis, eds., *Personality and Persuasibility* (New Haven: Yale University Press, 1959); and Theodore M. Newcomb, Ralph H. Turner, and Philip E. Converse, *Social Psychology: The Study of Human Interaction* (New York: Holt, Rinehart & Winston, 1965), especially Chaps. 4 and 9.

The extent of opportunities available to a President for symbolic persuasion is an empirical question. However, we have noted that at least within the executive branch opportunities are quite plentiful.[49] They will be more so if a President is alert to the possibilities for role-conception and personality reshaping and for properly selective recruitment. Personal loyalty or a role-based sense of obligation may not count for much among bargainers, each of whom is eager to maximize his power. The basic point, however, is that all of the presidential universe does not consist of such bargainers.[50]

This brings to its end the very limited test for external coherence that could be attempted here. The major conclusion is that Neustadt's model of presidential power seems to reflect "reality" quite correctly in its heavy emphasis on instrumental bargaining, but that, at the same time, it is not accurate in its almost complete disregard of unilateral instrumental controls other than command and of non-instrumental influence relationships. The lack of recognition accorded to these latter items has important consequences for Neustadt's schema in its practical and prescriptive role.

VI

The last aspect of *Presidential Power* to be scrutinized is its contribution as a practical guide for Presidents and presidential electorates. In many ways, this is the crucial test of the volume since Neustadt's fundamental aim is prescriptive. Successful advice takes priority over correct historical observation. It is well known that "understanding" and "prediction" stand in a highly flexible relationship.

Advice to the electorate is the concern of lesser importance and we will consider it first. Four factors determine the bargaining success of a President: vantage points, events and conditions, experience, and personality. At any given point in time, the first factor is identical for all candidates. Events and conditions during a President's term in office — the second independent variable — cannot be predicted with any assurance. Only the last two factors can enter the voters' equations in their choice among candidates. Diagram 3 reveals that if the electorate wants a successful — powerful — President, they should vote for the man with the greater and better political experience and with the right kind of personality. Neustadt says that "if we want Presidents alive and fully useful, we shall have to pick them from among experienced politicians of extraordinary temperament." (195) Of course, Neustadt is quite aware that more is required than experience and personality. (192–193) It is all, however, that he can state systematically. Of how much help, then, is *Presidential Power* to the electorate?

[49] It is the view of Dahl and Lindblom that there exist opportunities for unilateral control in "administration" that do not exist in "politics." Cf. *Politics, Economics and Welfare,* p. 334, *et passim.*

[50] The argument that in pluralistic societies bargaining has to be the key technique for social control is most persuasive. The question is to what degree a President's "household" is, or has to be, a pluralistic society.

First, Neustadt's advice is not altogether new. Experience and right temperament have been deemed beneficial and important for political leaders for a long time.[51] Second, and more importantly, the advice lacks specificity. Neustadt offers very little detail, and even where he does provide specifics, he does not provide operational translation. The voter still lacks guidance. The matter is particularly severe in respect to personality. Neustadt says a President should have a sense of power, a sense of direction, self-confidence. (171–179) How does the voter ascertain the relative power sense of competing candidates? How does he measure their respective degrees of self-confidence? Neustadt does not say.

"The Presidency is no place for amateurs." (180) In other words, a prospective President should have had political experience. Among the various types of political experience, Neustadt prefers executive to non-executive experience. (173) Those "men of politics who specialize in organization work and party office scarcely qualify at all; governmental office is the relevant experience." (181) "Yet expertise in presidential power does not follow automatically from such experience." (182) What else besides previous executive office does Neustadt tell voters, then, to demand of candidates? They should demand a first-rate temperament. (182) In short, *Presidential Power* is of relatively little help. It will aid the electorate only in eliminating rank amateurs and out-and-out psychopaths.

Neustadt's primary prescriptive aim is to advise presidential incumbents. Basically, *Presidential Power* is a set of rules for successful presidential conduct. How good and workable are they?

We must distinguish between the prescription to bargain and the prescriptions for successful bargaining. The former follows from the propositions that "Presidential power is the power to persuade," and that "the power to persuade is the power to bargain." The latter are all of the remaining rules — a President must teach realism, he must be his own power expert, he must actively participate in the details of political work, etc.

For the present evaluation, it is crucial to note that both prescriptions are stated essentially without reservation. All presidential behavior must be bargaining behavior. All bargaining behavior must follow specific rules. Given the universalistic scope of the prescriptions, and given the great demands on resources that they make, close adherence can lead to only one outcome: overload and breakdown.

Bargaining strategies may be more productive of the desired outcome than any other alternatives. In a variety of contexts, especially in the realm of presidential politics, this is likely to be the case. But the bargaining strategy that Neustadt provides for Presidents is enormously

---

[51] The emphasis on experience and character is as old as Western political philosophy. It is found in Plato as well as in Aristotle. To document this emphasis, in effect, would be to list practically every political theorist since. Besides, the opposite argument is somewhat hard to imagine. It has, in any case, not been encountered by this writer.

costly in resources, even though the probabilities for success are quite reasonable. The weakness of the system lies in its cost calculations. One suspects that the costs have not really been calculated at all. Neustadt gives no evidence that he is aware of any difficulties that might result from his simultaneous prescription of a highly complex and expensive strategy and a reduction in the scope of personnel resources. The more a President opts for bargaining, the more he must do by himself. To strike the right bargains, a President must be "his own executive assistant." (154) The President as bargainer can really depend or rely on no one. He cannot trust anybody but himself.

If bargaining makes almost superhuman demands on Presidents — and there is no better testimony for this point than *Presidential Power* — the following questions become important: Must a President always bargain? Can the expense of bargaining be reduced?

The investigations in Section V led to the conclusion that bargaining is not as exclusive a tool in the strategic repertoire of a President, as Neustadt believes. Alternative strategies exist to both bargaining and command. And even command can have a considerable range of effectiveness. There are two additional corrective factors. Issues, or power objectives, vary in importance.[52] Not all potential recipients of presidential influence are equally independent. This means that the need for bargaining strategies varies directly with the importance of the issue and the independence of the influence recipient. Some requests will be carried out without bargaining by almost anybody because very little is at stake, and some persons will execute requests of almost any importance without bargaining because they have very little independence vis-a-vis the source of the request.

As noted earlier, Neustadt's selection of dramatic examples may have contributed to the lack of attention to the variables of issue importance and recipient independence. In any case, this lack of attention made it possible to attribute universal validity to a set of rules with a large, but decidedly partial range. If a President were to follow Neustadt's prescriptions at all times, there would be very little difference in his approach to his director of the Bureau of the Budget about a minor item and his approach to an opposition Senator in respect to a major new policy.[53] He would, of course, offer instrumental rewards of different magnitudes. The persuasive strategy, however, would be exactly the same.

Neustadt's prescription to bargain is an example of what Herbert Shepard terms the "primary mentality." [54] Order and goal accomplish-

---

[52] Analysis could proceed in terms either of "objective" or "subjective" importance. However, the results would be essentially the same, and the distinction will not be made here.

[53] Some agencies even within the executive apparatus, of course, have a good deal of independence. It must be emphasized, however, that the F.B.I. and the Corps of Engineers are not typical. Cf. Robert L. Peabody and Francis E. Rourke, "Public Bureaucracies," in Marsh, ed., *Handbook of Organizations*, pp. 818–827.

[54] Herbert A. Shepard, "Changing Interpersonal and Intergroup Relationships in Organization," *ibid.*, 1115–1143.

ment are thought to be possible only on grounds of coercion or instrumental bargaining, or compromise. But this approach, while quite real, does not represent all of human experience. It describes only that part in which people either are a threat to each other or have some use for each other.[55] Beyond strict instrumentalism are "secondary mentality" and "secondary relations," the areas that were discussed above in terms of mutual confidence, trust, and identifications.[56]

In their recent major work on organizational psychology, Katz and Kahn noted three bases for system cohesion and productivity. People will support each other and cooperate because of functional interdependencies, normative requirements, or value internalizations.[57] As the authors point out, in any given organization emphasis may be on one or another of these bases. They also come in different "mixtures." Neustadt's system, however, is constructed almost exclusively on grounds of functional interdependence. Once this restrictive grounding is accepted, the universalistic bargaining prescription follows logically.

The fundamental weakness in Neustadt's system is a lack of attention to psychodynamics, especially to the non-instrumental motivations among the recipients of presidential requests.[58] Just as not everyone in the presidential environment can be a bargainer, not everyone wants to be a bargainer. There is a tendency in *Presidential Power* to picture the President as a lonely fighter against all others. The people with whom the President must deal are seen as "them," as his natural opponents or enemies. Is it so inconceivable that some persons may genuinely want to help a President? [59]

A second and related weakness lies in the volume's failure to appreciate the potentialities of the environments in which those "others" have to operate. In spite of basically instrumental motivations, a person might carry out a request without bargaining if group standards and group pressure point in that direction.[60] A President can free himself from bargaining if he knows how to create and sustain supportive norms and ideologies. Mobilization of "ecological control" [61] will permit a President to employ strategies of influence less expensive of his personal resources than bargaining.

All this, of course, is not to deny that bargaining remains indispensable, perhaps even in the great majority of cases. The range of cases

---

[55] *Ibid.*, pp. 1124–1125.

[56] See also Likert's Principle of Supportive Relationships. Rensis Likert, *New Patterns of Management* (New York: McGraw-Hill, 1961).

[57] Katz and Kahn, *The Social Psychology of Organizations*, p. 38 *et passim.*

[58] The only exception is Neustadt's consideration of the affects of commands.

[59] Among recent examples of "help-oriented" staff, the Kennedy assistants come to mind most readily.

[60] Cf. Morton Deutsch and Harold B. Gerard, "A Study of Normative and Informational Social Influences upon Individual Judgment," and Leon Festinger, Stanley Schachter, and Kurt Black, "The Operation of Group Standards," both in Cartwright and Zander, eds., *Group Dynamics.*

[61] The term is Cartwright's in "Influence, Leadership and Control," p. 19.

optimal employment of the bargaining tool would include is not known, but whatever its size, the crucial question is whether bargaining must indeed be as costly as it is in Neustadt's model. The answer hinges on two points. One is the persistent problem of the instrumentality or non-instrumentality of human relationships. The other is the question whether anyone else can see things as the President does.

It is quite clear that a President cannot be his own executive assistant, his own director of intelligence, etc., etc., for all the cases in which he must resort to bargaining strategies, particularly if these constitute the greater part of his activities. Even "experienced politicians of extraordinary temperament" are subject to certain limitations. Their days, too, have no more than twenty-four hours. Their mental and physical resources are not inexhaustible. But it also seems that a President need not be all these things to himself and by himself; for it is possible for him to receive good and dependable help.

In Neustadt's schema, even the closest associates of a President, his own appointees, his personal friends, become part of the oppositional "they." Cases are not unknown, of course, where close associates have turned into opponents. But what is the frequency of such occurrences? How deep and extensive are the splits? Neustadt's assumptions are maximal on all dimensions. This is not justified. Partials of partials are raised to universal absolutes. Neustadt's approach requires modification and moderation by its opposite: treating as axiomatic such forces as loyalty, trust, and identification, and trying to explain pure instrumentalism as deviation.

An example of a practical alternative to unmitigated "self-help" can be given. Instead of trying to be his own director of intelligence, his own executive assistant, his own watchdog of the calendar, a President can create new staff positions and fill them with competent people of known loyalty. These would be persons employed only at the pleasure of the President and responsible only to him. Neustadt writes that all the individuals with whom a President must deal have their own and specific constituencies, non-identical with his. What is overlooked is the possibility of the President as constituency.[62]

Even where bargaining is the best strategy, a President may not be able to employ it, if all the tasks associated with it must be performed by himself. The first goal of a President who would be a successful bargainer would be an increase in resources of personnel. There still will be tasks that cannot be delegated, but some of those that Neustadt enumerates could well be handled by capable and loyal assistants. The exact amount of potential help is not crucial at the moment. The point is that a

---

[62] It is time perhaps to point out once more that only *Presidential Power* is the subject of discussion. In many of his other writings, Professor Neustadt deals most explicitly with such matters as staff loyalty and ideological climate. For some examples see "Staffing the Presidency: The Role of White House Agencies," pp. 133–134; and "Approaches to Staffing the Presidency: Notes on FDR and JFK," pp. 857–858 *et passim.*

President following the recommendations of *Presidential Power* in full would not be oriented and motivated to explore these, and other, means to lighten his work burdens.

Assuming that it is possible to find loyal and competent helpers, there remains the problem of perspective. Neustadt asserts that no one can see things as does the President because no one can stand exactly in his place. No doubt, this is true, but it is a matter of degree. There is nothing mystical about the "presidential perspective." It is generated by a unique composite of inputs. With certain exceptions, what is unique is the composition rather than the constituent elements. It would not seem impossible for a President to share many of these inputs with selected assistants. Indeed, by way of such dynamics as close interpersonal identifications, it may even be possible to create in these assistants a considerable appreciation and understanding of the unique composite, that is to say, of the great responsibilities and pressures that are entailed in the presidential office.

A President who would always bargain and who would carry out by himself all the tasks associated with successful bargaining will not be a President for very long. An immense and consistent overloading of his physical and mental apparatus will produce a breakdown in short order. His search must be for alternative strategies and loyal help, and he must be alert to the ideological and personal bases upon which such strategies can be employed and upon which such help can be obtained.

This section has stressed limitations in the usefulness of *Presidential Power* as a guide for presidential behavior. This should not, however, obscure the basic fact that this volume is a handbook of immense usefulness. Neustadt's advice is nowhere faulty as such. The shortcomings and possible dangers in Neustadt's set of rules result from the universalistic mood in which they are offered. Although the area for valid applications of these rules is likely to be large, it is a restricted and partial one nevertheless. The President who would always govern by bargaining may soon not govern at all.

The Presidency at Mid-Century

Richard E. Neustadt

I

There are many ways to look at the American Presidency. It can be done in terms juridical or biographical, political or managerial: the office viewed primarily as a compendium of precedents, a succession of personalities, a fulcrum for party politics, a focus for administrative management. This essay denies the relevance of none of these approaches and makes use, incidentally, of them all, but aims at observation from a rather different point of view. This is an effort to look at the Presidency *operationally*, in working terms, as an instrument of governance in the middle years of the twentieth century; as man-in-office, that is to say, in a time of continuing "cold war," spiralling atomic discovery (and vulnerability), stabilized "big government," and stalemated partisan alignment — the *policy* environment capsuled by Clinton Rossiter as "new economy" and "new internationalism"; the *political* environment billed by Samuel Lubell as "politics of twilight." [1]

This calls for an examination of the President at work within the Presidency in a setting bounded on the one hand by the final phases of the last World War and on the other by the unknowns of the next decade — the setting for Harry S. Truman's term in office and for Dwight D. Eisenhower's up to the fall of 1956. Given that contemporary focus, there is less need for emphasis on presidential tasks, per se, than on the means and methods of performance; the theme, here, is less "what" than "how." The modern Presidency's powers and responsibilities — the "what," that is to say — are widely known, however we may differ on their import for our form of government, and anyone in doubt has only to review numerous recent writings in the field. But the "how" is relatively unexplored terrain for which there are no ready references outside the realm of selective particulars in press reports, case studies, memoirs, and the like. Granting the President his modern "roles," how does the work get done? What are his means? How may these be employed? Under what limitations? At what cost? With what effect? In what degree sufficient to the Presidency's purposes?

Reprinted by permission from a symposium, "The Presidential Office," appearing in *Law and Contemporary Problems*, Vol. 21, No. 4 (Autumn 1956), published by the Duke University School of Law, Durham, North Carolina. Copyright 1957 by Duke University.

[1] These terms are taken from Rossiter's *The American Presidency* (1956) and from Lubell's *The Future of American Politics* (1952).

These are the central questions I should like to pose — to pose, note, not to "answer." The search for answers is a task I am prepared, at this writing, to acknowledge as ambition, not accomplishment.

The emphasis on ways and means suggested by these questions has special pertinence, it would appear, for a symposium prepared in 1956. For 1956 is, after all, the year of cardiology in politics, the year of Great Debate about the on-the-job demands of being President, a debate which revolves around not powers but performance; a matter, in short, of means. Indeed — the Brickerites aside — most of the current arguments over presidential "powers" that agitate observers, both professional and lay, seem to involve at bottom the same sorts of issues; not change the job, but better its doing. Thus, the majority of recent schemes for legal and institutional reform are aimed avowedly (though sometimes disingenuously?) at aiding execution of the Presidency's mandates, not their alteration. This seems to be the sense of demands for a tightened disability provision, of blueprints for new staffs, new cabinets and the like, of plans to enhance the Vice Presidency (or add another one), even of those perennials on the congressional side, the four-year term, the item veto, the question period, and the right of dissolution. Quite obviously, there is relevance in emphasizing means, in asking "how," when one engages to survey the Presidency at mid-century!

There is, though, a prerequisite: If one would focus on the doing of the presidential job, one needs a characterization of the job, as such, that lends itself to operational appraisal; a characterization that defines what need be done in terms approaching those in which the doer does it. For working purposes, the President is never "many men," but one; the Presidency, as an instrument of givernment, is indivisible; the White House has no separate rooms for the "Chief Legislator," "Chief of Party," "Chief Administrator," et al. Observations on the doing of the job must build upon a statement of what exists to be done in terms other than these.

Hence, having stressed an emphasis on means and advertised its claims, I must begin where everyone begins, with a review of presidential powers — a review of the Presidency's place, that is to say, in the contemporary governmental scene.

II. The Presidency in Government

"His is the vital place of action in the system," wrote Woodrow Wilson of the President toward the close of TR's term.[2] And this, a new discovery for Wilson's generation, is now, at mid-century, a matter of course. Presidential leadership is now a matter of routine to a degree quite unknown before the Second World War. If the President remains at liberty, in Wilson's phrase, "to be as big a man as he can," the obverse holds no longer: he *cannot* be as small as he might choose.

[2] Woodrow Wilson, *Constitutional Government* 73 (1908).

Once, TR daringly assumed the "steward's" role in the emergency created by the great coal strike of 1902; the Railway Labor Act and the Taft-Hartley Act now make such interventions mandatory upon Presidents. Once, FDR dramatically asserted personal responsibility for gauging and guiding the American economy; now, the Employment Act binds his successors to that task. Wilson and FDR became chief spokesmen, leading actors on a world stage at the height of war; now UN membership, far-flung alliances, the facts of power, prescribe that role continuously in times termed "peace." Through both World Wars, our Presidents grappled experimentally with an emergency-created need to "integrate" foreign and military and domestic policies; the National Security Act now takes that need for granted as a constant of our times. FDR and Truman made themselves responsible for the development and first use of atomic weapons; the Atomic Energy Act now puts a comparable burden on the back of every President. In instance after instance, the one-time personal initiatives, innovations of this century's "strong" Presidents, have now been set by statutes as requirements of office. And what has escaped statutory recognition has mostly been absorbed into presidential "common law," confirmed by custom, no less binding: the unrehearsed press conference, for example, or the personally-presented legislative program.

The "vital place of action" has been rendered permanent; the *forms* of leadership fixed in the cumulative image of *ad hoc* assertions under Wilson and the two Roosevelts; past precedents of personality and crisis absorbed into the Government's continuing routines. For the executive establishment and for the Congress, both, the Presidency has become the regular, accustomed source of all major initiatives: supplier of both general plans and detailed programs; articulator of the forward course in every sphere of policy encompassed by contemporary government. Bold or bland, aggressive or conciliatory, massive or minimal, as the case may be, the lead is his.

Thus, we have made a matter of routine the President's responsibility to take the policy lead. And at the same time, we have institutionalized, in marked degree, the exercise of that responsibility. President and Presidency are synonymous no longer; the office now comprises an officialdom twelve-hundred strong. For almost every phase of policy development, there is now institutional machinery engaged in preparations on the President's behalf: for the financial and administrative work plan of the Government, the Budget Bureau; for the administration's legislative program, the White House counsel and the Budget's clearance organization; for programming in economic and social spheres, the Council of Economic Advisers (and to some degree the cabinet, Eisenhower-style); in foreign and military fields, the National Security Council; in spheres of domestic preparedness, the Office of Defense Mobilization; these pieces of machinery, among others, each built around a program-making task, all lumped together, formally, under the rubric, "The Executive Office of the President," an institutional conception and a statutory entity less than two decades old.

These are significant developments, this rendering routine, this institutionalizing of the initiative. They give the Presidency nowadays a different look than it has worn before, an aspect permanently "positive." But the reality behind that look was not just conjured up by statutes or by staffing. These, rather, are *responses* to the impacts of external circumstance upon our form of government; not causes but effects.

Actually or potentially, the Presidency has always been — at least since Jackson's time — a unique point of intersection for three lines of leadership responsibility: "executive" and partisan and national. The mandates of our Constitution, the structure of our political parties, the nature of the President's electorate, fused long ago to draw these lines together *at that point and there alone:* the Presidency at once the sole nationally elective office,[3] independently responsible to a unique constituency; sole centralizing stake of power, source of control, in each party (as a glance at either party out of power shows); sole organ of foreign relations and military command; sole object of the "take care" clause and of the veto power; and with all this, sole crown-like symbol of the Union.

By Wilson's time, that combination, in the context of world power stakes and status, had brought a fourth line of leadership into play, a line of leadership abroad, its only point of intersection with the other three the White House, once again. Since then, there have been revolutionary changes in the world and in American society and in the character of government's commitments toward both; changes productive of fast-rising expectations and requirements for leadership transmitted toward the Presidency along each line — four streams of action impulses and obligations converging on the President, whoever he may be, their volume and their rate of flow varying with events, a source which never, nowadays, runs dry.

The contemporary President, in short, has *four constituencies,* each with distinctive expectations of him and demands upon him. One of these is his "government" constituency, comprising the great group of public officers — congressional as well as executive — who cannot do their own official jobs without some measure of performance on his part. A second is his "partisan" constituency, comprising at once his own party's congressional delegation, and its organization leaders, workers, even voters, all those whose political fortunes, interests, sentiments, are tied, in some degree, to his performance. A third is his "national" constituency, comprising all those individuals and groups among Americans who look to him, especially when crises come, for an embodiment and an expression of government's relationship to its citizenry, for a response to their needs, purposes, endeavors. And fourth, is his "overseas" constituency, comprising not alone the officers of foreign governments, but the political oppositions, the opinion molders, even the plain citizens to some

---

[3] Discounting the Vice Presidency, which I am prepared to do.

degree, in every country where our power, policies, or postures have imposed themselves upon domestic politics.

In respect to the first three of these constituencies, membership is not a mutually exclusive matter. A number of American officials — among them cabinet officers and congressmen, are members of all three. And most Americans hold membership in two, as at once partisans and citizens. But whatever its effects on individual or group behavior, multiple membership does not preclude distinctly differentiated sets of Presidency-oriented expectations and demands, identifiable with each constituency, arising in the circumstances of mid-century from the pervasive needs of each for governmental action.

In these terms, it appears no accident that at a time when stakes of government are high for all the President's constituents, to him has passed, routinely, the continuing initiative in government. That role is both assured him and required of him by the very uniqueness of his place at the only point of intersection, the sole juncture, of those four lines of leadership responsibility and the constituencies they represent.

Yet, the demands and expectations pressing in upon the President propel him not alone toward enunciation, but delivery. Executive officials want decisions, Congressmen want proposals, partisans want power, citizens want substance, friends abroad want steadiness and insight and assistance on their terms — all these as shorthand statements of complex material and psychological desires. These things are wanted *done;* given our Constitution and our politics, that means done by, or through, or with assistance from, or acquiescence of, the President. The very factors that contribute to his unique opportunities — and routinized responsibilities — as an initiator, make him essential also as protector, energizer, implementor, of initiatives once taken. His special place in government requires of him, indeed, thrusts upon him, a unique responsibility — and opportunity — to oversee and assure execution.

But while responsibility for the initiative has now been routinized and even institutionalized, authority to implement the courses set remains fragmented in our system. In most respects and for most purposes, the President lacks any solid base of assured, institutionalized support to carry through the measures he proposes. His four constituencies are capable of constant pressure, but not of reliable response to downward leads. The "executive" is not a unity with a firm command-and-subordination structure, nor is the Government, nor is the political party, in Congress or out, nor is the nation, nor the alliance system overseas. All these are feudalities in power terms; pluralistic structures every one of them. Our Constitution, our political system, our symbolism, and our history make certain that the President alone assumes, in form, the leadership of each; and guarantee, no less, that he will not have systematic, unified, assured support from any. Indeed, precisely the conditions vesting him alone with leadership responsibility for all prevent the rendering of any one of them into tight-welded followings. The constitutional separation of powers — really, of institutions sharing powers — the federal separations of sovereignty, hence politics, the geographic separations of electorates, these and their consequences at once have helped the Presidency to its special place and hindered the creation of a strong supporting base. And, at a time when the executive establishment has grown too vast for personal surveillance, when Congress is controlled in form by narrow, shifting partisan majorities, in fact by factional coalition, weighted against the President's electorate, the hindrances are bound to be enhanced. Ours is that sort of time.

This does not mean that Presidents are powerless; far from it. Their four-way leadership position gives them vantage points aplenty for exerting strength in Government, in party, in the country, and abroad; collectively, by all odds, an array of strong points quite unmatched by any other single power-holder in our system. It does mean, though, that presidential power must be exercised *ad hoc*, through the employment of whatever sources of support, whatever transient advantages can be found and put together, case by case. It means the President can never choose a policy with certainty that it will be approximated in reality or that he will not have it to unmake or make again. It means he cannot, as he pleases, moderate, adjust or set aside the rival, overlapping, often contradictory claims of his constituencies. *He has no option but to act, at once, as agent of them all, for their conjunction in his person is the keystone of his potency;* none is dispensable, hence the demands of none are automatically disposable at his convenience. Events, not his free choices, regulate their pressures and condition his response.

Dilemmas, consequently, are the Presidency's daily bread. The President must now initiate specific policies and programs for all fields of federal action; he has become the focus for all forward planning in our system; whatever leads the Government and country and his party (and indeed, the opposition also) are to have, will stem from him. Yet, not his preferences only, but events in an inordinately complex world, not his reasoning alone, but his constituencies' felt requirements, contradictory as they may be, mold his determinations, limit his choices, force his hand. What he initiates he must attempt to implement. He must try so to manage the executive establishment, and Congress, and his party oligarchs, and the other party's also, and "public opinion," and overseas support, that the essential things get done — so far at least as government can do them — to keep administration reasonably competent, the country reasonably prosperous, the cold war reasonably cold, and his party in the White House; objectives which will seem to him synonymous (no President in memory, Mr. Eisenhower naturally not excluded, has ever thought his policies could best be carried forward by the other party's men). Yet, none of these agencies of action, of execution, are subject to his management by fiat; not even those closest to home, his own administration, his own party, are constructed to provide him with assured support. Rarely can he order, mostly must he persuade. And even were his controls taut and sharp, there would remain, of course, those agencies beyond his power to command, events.

No doubt, in times of great emergency, sharp crisis seen and felt as such throughout the country, the Presidency's measure of assured support from public, party, and administration tends to increase dramatically, if temporarily, while "politics as usual" abates, at least until the sharpness wanes; witness the situation circa 1942. But it is characteristic of our circumstances at mid-century — in all the years since the Second World War — that while our Government's responsibilities retain a trace of every prior crisis, no comparable sense of national emergency pervades our politics. If this is an "era of permanent crisis," it is one in which Presidents must manage without benefit of crisis consensus.

Given the underlying situation here described, the balance of this paper is, perforce, a study of dilemmas; dilemmas nurtured by disparities between the Presidency's obligation to initiate and its capacity to achieve, the one nailed down, the other relatively tenuous, both bound to be so by the nature of our institutional adjustment, up to now, to the complexities of governing this country at mid-century.

What, currently, is the American Presidency? A cat on a hot tin roof.

III. THE PRESIDENT IN THE PRESIDENCY

So far in this discussion, "President" and "Presidency" have been used almost interchangeably; the man and his office equated in an effort at capsule characterization. But since it is our purpose to appraise the man *in* office, the *President* at work, we must now differentiate between the individual and his official tasks, between the work done by the White House occupant and that performed by others in his name.

What does the President, himself, contribute to the conduct of the Presidency? What, in an office now so institutionalized that it encompasses six hundred "professional" aides, has he, himself, to do? What, in a government of vast and complicated undertakings, in a substantive environment demanding every sort of expertise, can there be *left* for him to do? To put the case in current terms, what is there that no "chief of staff" can do without him?

There are two ways to approach answers to these questions. One is to abstract the person of the President from office at a given point in time; the other is to note what occupies his working day when he is on the scene. Both methods, it appears, produce equivalent results, as may be seen by trying them in turn.

The Eisenhower illnesses provide us with illustrations ready-made for speculation on the Presidency *sans* the President, to wit: Three days after his heart attack, Cairo announced its arms deal with the Czechs, thereby upsetting the whole power balance in the Middle East.[4] By all accounts, this action, far-reaching in implications, did not catch the State Department unawares. For months, American diplomacy had sought to head it off. Once it occurred, however, we confined ourselves for a long period to verbal protests and to indecisive consultations. There were no prompt moves made either to force reversal or to take countermeasures of decisive

---

[4] The President was taken ill on September 24, 1955; the Egyptian-Czech agreement was announced on September 27.

sort. Some persons outside Government have speculated that had Mr. Truman then been President, the Sixth Fleet might have steamed to the Aegean with orders to halt shipments of Czech arms by sea or air. One wonders if in office his response would have been so Draconian. One can be sure, however, that had he, like his successor, then been hospitalized, critically ill, under a regimen of absolute quiet, no orders of this sort would have gone to the Navy. (Indeed, in the far starker, more extreme, hence simpler instance of Korea, can one imagine Louis Johnson taking Dean Acheson's view on anybody's say-so but the President's?)

This is not to suggest that Eisenhower, healthy, would have approved — much less been urged to sanction — any forcible reaction to the Czech-Egyptian deal; it seems unlikely on the public record, though one cannot know for certain from outside. Nor is it implied that some such response should have been attempted; policy is not the issue here. What *is* suggested, here, is that the option was not open to our Government because the President himself was not available to choose. It is suggested that the risk of action, the onus of decision, in this case could have been shouldered only by the President, by him or not at all; *the Presidency's functioning dependent on his individual performance as maker of the residual choices no one else will make.*

Turn now to Eisenhower's second illness for a moment. Three weeks after last June's ileitis operation, while he was still recovering at Gettysburg — allowed to work, by press reports, but one hour a day — the House of Representatives rejected the School Construction Assistance bill, thereby seeming to terminate all chances of substantial federal aid to education in the current presidential term.[5] The bill was lost in circumstances complicated partly by its contact with the segregation issue, partly by its Democratic sponsors' preferences for certain sums and formulae unlike those forwarded from the Republican administration. And on the latter ground, or nearly so, a number of Republicans seem to have justified "nay" votes. But Eisenhower's actions and pronouncements over three years' time had long made it appear he strongly wanted some measure of aid to education by 1956. Indeed, this bill, reportedly, might not have reached the floor save for the Democratic leaders' understanding that he was in earnest and would not let his House Republicans forget it. Yet, when the ultimate test came, he was not there to remind them.

To quote the correspondent of the *New York Times:* [6]

> There is hardly an observer in Washington who doubts that a personal appeal from a healthy Dwight Eisenhower — or even some last-minute personal letters from Gettysburg — would have changed enough Republican votes to make the difference.

Perhaps, of course, the President in full health would have foregone that appeal. We do not know his private views upon the final bill in

[5] Surgery was performed on June 9, 1956. The final House votes on the School Aid Bill (H. R. 7535) came on July 5.

[6] Anthony Lewis in "The News of the Week in Review," *N.Y. Times,* July 8, 1956, p. E9.

terms either of substance or of Senate tactics. We do not know what private tallies were run or what was reasoned from them; the problem, after all, was scarcely his alone, for party lines broke sharply on both sides of the aisle. But whatever he might have done, if well, he *could not* act, one may believe, when ill. Were this conceived a proper matter for the patient and as such worth exclusion of all else, an hour's working day scarcely suffices for the requisite persuasive phone calls to the Hill or for the substitute of letter writing (in the circumstances only done convincingly longhand). And in this case, if Eisenhower could not institute his own appeals, no one could make them for him. The option of a final presidential exhortation is not open to the White House save as the man himself can serve; *the Presidency's functioning dependent on his personal performance as persuader of those otherwise indifferent or unmoved.*

There are numbers of other illness illustrations, but these suffice to make the point: the President's own specialties within the Presidency, the contributions none can make without him, consist of acts of choice and of persuasion; choices not in foreign policy alone, but in all spheres of action and of men as well as measures; persuasion not only of Congressmen, but of administrative officers and politicians, of private interests and "the public" generally, of foreign governments and their publics; choice and persuasion exercised, in short, throughout the range of problems and of persons covered by his four constituencies.

These things are his to do because he is the sole, accountable human embodiment of an office which, in turn, is uniquely the center of responsibility and motive-power in our system. No President, of course, takes to himself more than a fraction of the choices, efforts at persuasion, made on his authority and in his name. But beyond a certain point — a point, of course, that varies case by case — choice-making and persuasion become personalized, of necessity, because his aides and auditors insist that it be so; because no one will accept others' choices, because no one will heed others' persuasions, because no others dare or care to run his risks on their discretion or their risks on his authority. Beyond another point — which may or may not coincide — persuasive acts and choices become ripe for his personal attention as a matter of desirability in his own interest, because his personal perceptions of that interest are ultimately untransferable; because save second-hand, by empathy, not even Harry Hopkins, Sherman Adams, can know fully what it feels like to sit where he sits (endowed with his intelligence, his temperament) at the solitary juncture of his four constituencies, "President of the United States" — hence, no one else can bring to bear precisely his own "feel" for risks to him, to the totality of his unique position, inherent in alternatives of doing and not doing.

If a look at the Presidency without a working President shows choices and persuasion as the man's own occupation, that impression cannot be strengthened by a glance at what takes up his time when on the job. Nowadays, the normal presidential working week revolves around a series of fixed sessions: one set meeting apiece with the National Security Council, and the cabinet, and (when Congress is on hand) the legislative leaders,[7] and the press, each preceded and followed by appropriate staff briefings, consultations; one set appointment apiece with the Secretary of State, the Secretary of Defense, the Chairman of the Joint Chiefs of Staff, and (an Eisenhower innovation, now suspended) the Chairman of the Council of Economic Advisers. Truman had, besides, a daily morning conference with his principal staff aides to make *ad hoc* assignments and receive routine reports; such sessions Sherman Adams has conducted under Eisenhower.

When one includes the chores of getting ready, cleaning up, these regularly scheduled consultations pre-empt a substantial portion of the President's own working hours, week by week. In the case of a President like Eisenhower, who finds these mechanisms to his taste and uses them to the exclusion of much else, that share of hours occupied mounts high. And what is the object of this outlay of his time? Such sessions serve, in part, as occasions for others to put their concerns, their views before him; partly as occasions for him to impress his personality and attitudes *on* others. Which of these parts has major place will vary with each sort of session, influenced by subject matter, membership, and *his* proclivities. But whatever their variation, the components are the same: one part material for choice-making, the other part the stuff of personal persuasion.

As for the balance of the presidential working week, the bulk of it is turned to comparable account; the documents signed, the persons seen, the places filled, the arguments resolved, the messages sent, the speeches made, the ceremonies held, all these are characteristically acts of choice or efforts at persuasion, often both at once — even the formal ceremonials contributing a portion of his power to persuade, even their performance contingent on his choice.

The preoccupations of the presidential week will vary with the seasons of the presidential year, from budget and message seasons in the fall, through early, middle, and late stages of the legislative season, through the rush of adjournment and enrollments, to that precious period, the post-adjournment lull (if any), season for recovery and repairs, and so to fall again — a round, successively, of planning to decision, campaigning to compromise, recuperating to resumption; a peacetime rhythm set primarily to legislative tasks but liable constantly to interruptions on account of mishaps and emergencies in operating spheres. Inevitably, presidential choices, efforts at persuasion, reflect in their intensities, their objects, and their scope these swings of emphasis throughout the year. And even more they reflect swings in the cycle of the presidential term, from early groping through a first consolidation and a forward push up to the test at midterm, then regrouping and a second forward effort dwindling toward haitus in the final year.[8] But whatever their application

---

[7] With the Senate and House leadership, that is to say, of the President's own party, whether in the majority or not.

[8] The cycle, that is, of first terms in these years. As for second terms, new style, under twenty-second amendment, all is unknown.

in a given context, choice-making and persuasion remain the components of the President's own work; comprising what he does himself, both on the insistence of others and at his own inner promptings.

These are, in short, his means; the means by which he, personally, exercises influence within his office and upon the course of government; the means by which he makes his own mark on the tasks of office sketched in part II, above. As such, these "means" are not for him mere instruments employed at will to carry out those tasks. Rather they are the concrete manifestations of the tasks themselves, applying to him personally; the work he has to do, no act of will required. In literary terms, one may say that he sets the tone, provides the lead in government by choosing and persuading. In operating terms, though, one must put it in reverse: that acts of choice and of persuasion cumulated over time produce an ultimate effect of tone and lead which may or may not correspond to any prior blueprint, purpose, or intention. Such is the consequence of disentangling the President from the Presidency.

That ultimate resultant labelled "leadership" will be compounded of two types of actions by the President: those he may reach for in his own discretion and those thrust on him of necessity; the one type, opportunities, the other, compulsions. And, as the compound will be viewed by his constituents and history, more than these enter in; the multifarious things done or left undone by others in his name, or the Government's, and happenings beyond the Government's discretion, plain events.

No President is free to concentrate upon his opportunities at the expense of his compulsions; he can but hope to find room for the things he may do amidst all things he must. Nor is he free to wave away those other actors on the scene; he can but hope to channel and deflect their impacts on his audience. To the extent he wants to make his own will dominate the conduct of his office, his regime, he has no recourse but to choices and persuasion exercised within these narrow limits. The purposeful President, his face set against drift (and any President, these days, will so regard himself), is thus confronted by an operating problem of immense complexity and large proportions, or more precisely by two problems tightly linked: Given those limits and in furtherance of his own purposes, how is he to maximize the efficiency of his choice-making? How maximize the efficacy of his power to persuade?

The proportions and complexities of these two connected problems it now becomes our object to explore.

IV. THE FREEDOM TO CHOOSE

If Presidents were free to choose the matters they made choices on, their problems of choice-making would be relatively simplified; but Presidents are not. The flow of issues they must face cannot be turned off like a water tap; to know that, one has but to note its sources.

Why do men in government and politics (and in the country and the world) bring issues to a President, invoke his act of choice? To amplify the foregoing analysis, it may be said that they do so for one, or another, or all of three reasons. First, there are matters that by law or custom require some sort of personal performance on his part, his signature, his presence or his voice. Second, there are matters on which others, theoretically competent to act, want the loan of his potency or the cover of his prestige, his impetus behind their preferences, his brand on their performance. Third, there are the matters he himself wants made his own, that on his own initiative he has marked "count me in," matters on which he exercises the discretion we have already discussed. And in the circumstances of mid-century, no President will lack for quantities of matters of each sort.

In the first of these three categories, volume is adjustable, at least to a degree. A President who does not like to sign his name hundreds of times a day, can ease that chore somewhat, by turning over to department heads his formal exercise of statutory powers; so Eisenhower has done in some routine instances. A President who dislikes handshaking *ad infinitum* may find excuses for curtailment of big White House social functions, as FDR did with the war and Truman with repairs and Eisenhower with his heart attack. But such adjustments are mere nibbles at the fringes; they may save time or energy but not the mind and heart. No President can delegate the formal exercise of constitutional prerogatives, and it is from those that the greatest number of tough, touchy signatures derive. No President can be excused from all political speechmaking, disaster visiting, fireside chatting, dignitary dealing, least of all from the big ones, sources of greatest strain.

As for the second category, the most a President seriously can hope to do is slow the rate of flow, shut out the marginal case. He may pound tables at associates, demanding that they mind their business on their own responsibility; he may set obstacle courses for them to run, complete with committees, secretariats and Sherman Adamses — and still there will be persons, plenty of them, spurred by their convictions or their fears, their sense of others' power or of their own insufficiency, who press on him the matters in their bailiwicks, or in their neighbors'. So Secretary Benson took care to get Eisenhower's affirmation (on a partial presentation) of his plan to fire Ladejinsky. So Administrator Stassen took pains, it appears, to gain presidential sanction for the course of action which then put Ladejinsky back to work. And when matters partake in some degree of both these categories — as oftener than not they do — when his distinct prerogatives become involved, however marginally, in choices his associates are loath to make (or to let others make) themselves, the pressure for a presidential take-over can push the White House hard; witness the Dixon-Yates affair or the 1947 tankers case immortalized by Louis Koenig.[9]

---

[9] The reference is to the "Sale of Tankers," a case study included in Harold Stein, *Public Administration and Policy Development* (1952).

There remains the third category, where interventions come at *his* initiative. There, he has the option, theoretically, of moving not at all. But this is fatal; also quite impracticable. No doubt, some Presidents may relish, others shy away from forcing matters into their own hands. No doubt, each will evolve some special preferences according to his particular competences, interests. But every President will find some issues that he wants to seize and ride — Truman on Point Four, Eisenhower on Atoms for Peace — and each will find a plenitude he feels *impelled* to take upon himself: so Truman took the fate of Lamar Caudle out of that worthy's hands and the Attorney General's, so Eisenhower acted in the Talbott case. When Mrs. Hobby panicked over polio vaccine, when Secretary Stevens got entangled in his own inanities regarding Zwicker and Peress, when Adam Clayton Powell blasted Public Health and Navy on account of segregation, the President moved in. Had he an option? To sense imperatives, one need but scan the "inside" stories Robert Donovan supplies.[10]

Since acts of choice are often negative, there are, of course, more instances of such "enforced" discretion than will appear in current press reports: Eisenhower choosing time and again, as Donovan records, *not* to blast McCarthy; Truman choosing — as he sometimes did — not to leap, guns blazing, into loyalty cases that aroused his ire; so forth, *ad infinitum*. The "I don't know about that" in press conference is deceptive as a guide to presidential doings. In most such cases, this would remain the expedient response, assuming he did know. Yet every President, one may suppose, will now go out of office wishing that is some respects he had pushed further still, discretion *un*enforced, toward taking over at times and in places where contemporary happenings did not push him.

One wonders whether Truman never wished that he had intervened more actively in the affairs of his Attorneys General. One wonders whether Eisenhower may not come to wish that he had done the same regarding some of *his* department heads. No President finds pleasure in waiting upon "messes" for his cue to intervene. But none can be sure, either, that initiatives of others will suffice to flash a warning to him in good time. There is an obverse of the second category named above: those issues men bring to the President out of their fears, uncertainties, are matched by those kept from him out of confidence, or cussedness, or independent power (even ignorance). Surely, Secretary Weeks was guilty of astigmatism, at the very least, in firing Dr. Astin [11] as a departmental matter. Or, in an instance of much greater moment, the Wage Board's public members, circa 1952, surely were guilty of too broad a view of their role and too narrow a conception of the Government's, in rendering their famous Steel decision without sounding out the White House. For other illustrations one can point, as always, to the classic record of the Corps of Engineers or to the Pentagon's routines for waging inter-

---

10 The reference is to Robert J. Donovan, *Eisenhower: The Inside Story* (1956).
11 The Chief of the Bureau of Standards in 1953.

necine warfare. Far from reducing his discretionary range, a President is bound to end by wishing he could widen it.

But time stands in his way. He cannot afford to do nothing at his own discretion; but neither can he manage to do everything. Priority of place on his choice-making production line belongs of sheer necessity to matters with *deadlines* attached. And in most days of his working week, most seasons of his year, a President has quite enough of these to drain his energy, crowd his attention regardless of all else. It is not "policy" but pressure that determines what comes first.

What makes a "deadline"? For one thing, constitutional or statutory obligations: the President must send his annual messages to Congress, must sign or veto its enactments. Or, for another, items on political agendas all across the country: the nomination and election contests over offices, both partisan and public, the distribution of the patronage, the management of national conventions and campaigns. Or, for a third, turns of events in diplomacy or war: the approach to the "summit" spurring a disarmament departure, "open skies"; the outbreak in Korea forcing a new Formosan policy. Or, for a fourth, "outside" events at home: a sharpened economic trend (whether up or down), a dragged-out strike, a natural disaster, a race riot; not necessarily the great things only but the small-with-bite, as when a Texas waitress would not serve the Indian Ambassador. Or, finally, for a fifth, such operational disorders in administration, day by day, as dot the preceding pages — plus, of course, their congressional counterparts. Dates-certain make for deadlines, so does heat; dates generated by our laws, our politics, and our diplomacy; heat generated by events impacting on the needs and expectations of presidential constituents. Singly or together — though most readily inflammable combined — dates and heat start the fires burning underneath the White House.

The President, of course, has influence on deadline-making and unmaking, but only to a limited degree. He sets or evades dates when he voluntarily decides upon a message or a meeting or a speech. He turns heat on when he permits himself to arouse expectations, as Eisenhower did in his press conferences before Geneva. He turns heat aside, if not off, when he finds plausible grounds, proper-looking means for "further study," as was done so notably in 1953. But these are marginal endeavors relative to the totality of dates and heat potentially imposed upon him from outside. And even these are usually reactions or responses to pressures not intrinsically his own. For the most part, even deadlines self-imposed are only nominally self-engendered. Save in rare instances, a mid-century President, however talented, simply has not time to man both ends of the choice-generating process.

The result is to put him in a paradoxical position anent the whole discretionary range of his choice-making. To reach out and take over *before* the dates are nigh or the heat on — publicly at least — can be crucially useful in his interest; yet, he always has to deal first with deadlines already at his desk. As has been said above, he cannot count on the initiatives of others to spur him into interventions timely in *his* terms; yet he is poorly placed to be his own self-starter. He needs to be an actor, yet he is pre-eminently a reactor, forced to be so by the nature of his work and its priorities. Since Eisenhower made Atoms for Peace his response to the heat expressed by cries for "candor" and to the dates required for a UN presentation in 1953, one may suppose he has not been entirely happy with its slowness to get off the ground. One may suppose, besides, that had he arrogated to himself all implementing choices and given them first call upon his time, the matter might have moved a little faster. Similarly, in the case of Truman and Point Four: had he, not State and Budget, implemented his inaugural's fourth point and made of this his first priority (as it never was for them), the sixteen months after his 1949 inauguration might have produced more results than one meager piece of legislation newly on the books. But whatever these Presidents might have done differently or "better" than they actually did, one thing they could *not* do: accord that hypothetical priority in terms of their own time.

Washington correspondents frequently complain that Eisenhower talks a better line than his administration takes; that he proposes better than his own regime disposes. Complaints of the same sort were made in Truman's time, oftener than not by the same correspondents. And these complaints — along with the realities behind them — symptomize the underlying problem here described. For in a time of routinized responsibility to take the policy lead, a President himself will have few deadlines more compelling than those clustering around the choice of measures to *propose,* of policies to *state.* Except, perhaps, in general war or comparable emergency, these gain and take his time more surely and more regularly than the general run of operating choices bound to follow in their wake. The weight which Robert Donovan's book gives to the *proposing* side of Eisenhower's "story," presumably reflects that skewing of the latter's workaday preoccupations. And if there is an implication that the White House sometimes came to look on messages and speeches as ends in themselves, delivery equated with accomplishment, such is a natural by-product, one not unknown in Truman's time, a point of view, indeed, by no means wholly unrealistic.

Ideally, a President concerned for the efficiency of his own choice-making in furtherance of his own purposes as *he* conceives them, should have free rein in choosing what to choose — and when — within the range of matters subject to his choice at his discretion. In practice, though, that is precisely what he *cannot* have. His discretionary range, while not a sham, is nowhere near as open as the term implies. Only his compulsions are potentially unbounded; his opportunities are always limited. Ideals apart, he is in no position to do more than seek some finite widening of those confines; he has no chance to break them down. But paradoxically, the only practical direction which his search can take — given the conditions here described — is toward some means of putting pressure on himself, *of imposing new deadlines on himself,* to come to grips with those things he would want to make his own if only he had time to contemplate the world about him, interfering at his leisure. And it is ironic that the very measures that a President may take to spare himself for "bigger things" by staffing out the "small," tend to work in the opposite direction. Of this, more later.

The limitations upon "what" and "when" which so restrict freedom of choice are reinforced by certain other limits of a different sort: limits on the substance of alternatives in choices actually made. The President's discretion is restricted by these limits also; they, too, are features of his landscape subject to some rearrangement but beyond his power to remove. What are these limitations on alternatives? Mainly three: limits of presentation, of substantive complexity, and of effectuation, each term loosely descriptive of a whole array of complications worth a chapter to themselves, though necessarily denied it here.

By "presentation" is meant time, form, and manner in which issues reach a President for his determination. If his desk is where the buck stops, as Truman liked to say, by the same token, it is the *last* stop on the line. Most matters reach him at a late stage of their evolution into issues calling for his choice; and many when they reach him warrant action fast. Wherever they occur, lateness and urgency — singly or combined — are bound to narrow options and to curtail chances for fresh looks or second thoughts. As for the *form* which issues take, the *context* of their presentation to a President, his settling of a budget sum, or phrasing of a speech, or soothing of a legislator, each in its own terms may mean disposal of an issue multi-faceted in terms of but one facet, thereby foreclosing options anent others. There is no counting the occasions on which Presidents have backed themselves — or been backed — into corners by this route. Moreover, those who brief a President, who can appeal to him, who can argue before him, have interests of their own which grow remote from his with every increment of organizational distance, institutional independence. Rarely will they see an issue wholly in his terms; oftener in some hybrid of his and theirs, sometimes in theirs alone. And Presidents are no less vulnerable than others (rather more so, in the circumstances) to the lure of wrong answers rightly put.

A tracing out of many of the illustrations posed above would show the workings of these presentation limits; signs of their presence are, of course, no novelty to readers of the *New York Times*. Nothing is intrinsically new about them nowadays, nor anything particularly obscure, though they are none the easier for being old and obvious. But when it comes to limits raised by substantive complexity, the case is rather different. Though not by any means a mid-century invention unknown to earlier times, the magnitude (and durability) of complications in the substance of issues with which Presidents must deal, these days, is greater in degree, to some extent in kind, than we have known before.

Take the question of the military budget which has haunted Eisenhower as it haunted Truman. That budget represents more than half the dollars of federal outlay year by year, four-fifths of the persons on all federal payrolls, half the Government's civilian personnel. It represents a mainstay of deterrence and recourse in the cold war, a bed-rock stabilizer in the national economy. Its annual determination raises issues of strategy, of economics, politics, administration, and (emphatically) technology; none of which are really manageable in annual or financial terms (the limit of form, again); none of which are really soluble by reference to anybody's certain knowledge, for nothing is certain save uncertainty in these spheres. To estimate what the American economy can "stand" is not to answer what Congress and interest groups will "take" (or what would be required to equate the two). To estimate what new weapons may do is not to answer what may be demanded of them, or opposed to them, years hence. To estimate the Russians' *capabilities* is not to answer what are their *intentions.*

Yet, on some sorts of "answers" to these questions must military budgets now be built. And limited in terms of what is knowable, a President has no recourse but to select among the "guesstimates" of others — or to compound a compromise among them — by way of searching for his answer-substitutes. In such a search, the signs most readily discerned are bound to be those rendered most concrete by visibility, or pressure, or personal proclivities, or "common sense." No doubt a President needs better signposts in times of cold war, technological revolution; but given the uncertainties these generate, whence are such signs to come?

Parenthetically, it may be said that whatever the answer to that question, the "experts" are unlikely candidates. For if the real technicians see far more than a President can see, the record up to now suggests that they, least of all, show a capacity to ask themselves, out of their expertise, the questions pertinent to him; to translate their vision (and language) into his terms. Shifting the illustration, one thinks in this connection of an aspect of the thermonuclear "crash-program" controversy during 1949, as rendered by the transcript in the Oppenheimer case: that for weeks AEC's consulting scientists debated what the President should do in terms rendered obsolete, for him, by the mere fact of their debate.

Finally, there is the problem of effectuation, the third of the stated factors limiting alternatives in choice. How is a President to make "no" stick; to translate "yes" into performance, actuality? He is not bound to make each choice dependent on his response to these questions, but in the normal course he cannot fail to ask them and to give the answers weight. When Truman chose intervention in Korea, it happened that the necessary military means lay near at hand across the Sea of Japan; a factor, surely, in his choice. The obverse holds, of course, for our passivity in the last days of Dien Bienphu; the means that *were* at hand were scarcely suited to the circumstance. But to cite instances of capability in military terms is to belittle the complexity of the how-to-do-it factor; in other terms, there are few choices blessed by aspects so nearly absolute or so readily calculable. Mostly the problem for the President is both more tenuous and more complex in character: how far can he hope to carry matters by persuading those whom he cannot command to do those things he lacks capacity to compel?

"I sit here all day," Truman used to remark, "trying to persuade people to do the things they ought to have sense enough to do without my persuading them." And on each posed alternative, in every act of choice, the question becomes whether to that workload he should add one thing more; with what prospect, at what risk. That question asked and answered may suffice to cancel options of all sorts; the President's choice-making ultimately interlocking with his power to persuade.

V. THE POWER TO PERSUADE

Concrete acts of choice engender concrete efforts at persuasion. Persuasion of whom? In general, of the President's constituencies, any or all as the case may be. In particular, of those who do the daily chores of governing this country: administrators, Congressmen, and organization politicians. To these one might add certain foreign notables and private persons prominent at home, on whom the Government depends for something in particular, a boost, a service or a sacrifice; but since such dependence is *ad hoc,* intermittent, their case can be ignored for present purposes.

In the main, day by day, it is the public officers and party politicians whom a President must reach to get his choices rendered into government performance. He may move toward them indirectly through public or interest-group opinion, sometimes his only routes, but they remain his objects because they, not the "public," do the close work; his preferences conditioned on their doing. To influence these men at work, he has at his disposal a quantity of instruments — refined and crude in varying degree — derived from his prerogatives of office as filtered through his personality.

Those instruments of influence, tools of persuasion, are common knowledge, no mystery about them and none pretended here: There is the aura of his office, coupled to the impact of his person and prestige, such as they may be. There are the varied forms of help, concrete and psychological, that Congressmen want from the White House in dealing, as they must, with the executive establishment. There are, in turn, the various assistances desired by executive officialdom in dealing with the Congress. There are also the loyalties, varying in depth, of administrators to their chief, of party members to the boss, of Congressmen (and citizens) to the head of State and Government. In party terms, there are, at once, supplies of federal patronage, such as it is, a presidential record which no party nowadays can shake, the prospect of a renewed candidacy (for first termers, anyway), and — save for Democrats, perhaps — a constantly replenished campaign chest, centrally controlled. These things, among others, are available to Presidents for use, reversibly, as carrots and as sticks in aid of their persuasion.

This listing has a formidable ring. In theory, it deserves it. For if a President could bring to bear that whole array effectively and all at once upon a given point, one may presume he would be irresistible. But practically speaking, such conjunctions are not easily arranged; far from it. Oftener than not, one or another of these tools will turn out ineffective of itself or in the hands of its prospective user, unsuited to use, by him, in any combination of resources he contrives. Why should this be so? What dulls their cutting edge and limits their employment? These questions become our immediate concern. Full answers would run far beyond the compass of this essay; no more can be attempted here than a suggestion of some factors that seem specially significant in the contemporary setting.

First among these factors — in order of discussion, not importance — is the uncertainty of a President's own hold upon his instruments of influence. They may attach to his office but can slip away from *him*. One doubts that at any time since 1935, or thereabouts, and not often before, have Presidents got half the mileage out of patronage the textbooks advertise. One doubts that Eisenhower can be sure from day to day of his control over the stockpile of administrative actions sought by congressmen. Most of these, certainly, are not under his sole lock and key. Others than he have the arts of persuasion to practice, and keys of their own. The story is told that a powerful House Democrat was traded off the same dam twice; once in Truman's time and once in Eisenhower's. If so, the Budget Bureau ought to be commended for its careful husbanding of presidential trading-stock. But such care is by no means universal in this Government (not even in the Budget). Moreover, a supply of trading-stock may prove insufficient just when the need is greatest. Appetites are insatiable and fears short-lived; a situation summed up in the phrase "What have you done for me lately," as amplified by "or *to* me."

In addition, sources of supplies to aid persuasion on one front may be endangered by the very effort at persuasion on another. A great share of a President's potential trading-stock with Congress is actually in the hands of the executive departments: jobs, expertise, publicity, administrative actions of all sorts. No less a share of his potential leverage with the departments is actually in the hands of his congressional supporters: protection or defense, consideration or support, in every sort of legislative situation. Too many sticks applied too often on the Hill may tend to uproot the supply of carrots growing there for use downtown, and vice versa.

A second factor is the tendency of certain presidential tools to cut in opposite directions, thereby impairing their simultaneous employment. It is not easy for a President to combine partisan approaches with attempts to crystallize support around the symbol of his office. He courts trouble when he tells his party's congressmen that his proposals will help them at the polls and simultaneously exhorts the other party's men to do their patriotic duty by their President. He courts trouble when he tries to draw upon the loyalties of subordinate officials and at the same time offers up their kind as human sacrifices on the altar, say, of adequate appropriations for their work. Such troubles come in infinite varieties; in every instance, they will tend to limit hypothetical effectiveness of each paired instrument. To say this is not to suggest, of course, that all these troubles are escapable. Carrying water on both shoulders — plus, perhaps, in both hands, also strapped around the waist — is frequently imperative for Presidents, a natural resultant of their four-way leadership position. But the complications are no less for often being unavoidable. So Truman found on many memorable occasions and even Eisenhower, now and then, especially in those first years of turmoil over "cleaning out the Communists" and Senator McCarthy.

A third factor complicating the persuasion process can be stated, most simply, as general dissatisfaction with the product to be "sold." It is difficult, in other words, to press a course of action intrinsically lacking much appeal to *any* of the persons whose support is being sought. Instruments of influence, however handled, are poor substitutes for genuine enthusiasm on the part of somebody among the movers and shakers in the case. And if the substitution must be made, as not infrequently occurs, the limits on the efficacy of persuasive tools will tend to be severe. The President's health-reinsurance scheme of 1954 is very much in point. So is the complex struggle over foreign aid in the 1956 session of Congress. There, Eisenhower pitted his own personal prestige, plus other sorts of pressure, against the disappointments, disenchantments, irritations, and forebodings which had penetrated every corner of both Houses. The result was a sharp check to the President — how serious in program terms one cannot know from the outside — a check administered, moreover, by traditional supporters of his course among the Democrats, together with a great proportion of *his* party's membership, election year or no. It is quite conceivable, in all the circumstances, that another President, in another year, might have done worse. But why did this President in this year not do better?

No doubt, his ileitis operation and its aftermath blunted Eisenhower's own persuasive influence at a crucial time.[12] Perhaps there were things poorly done or left undone at other times as well. But however healthy and adroit he might have been last summer, there are no indications — not, anyway of public record — that by then his persuasion could have bettered the result in any *marked* degree. For the great lack, apparently, was not of influence in mechanistic terms, but of program in substantive respects. A sense of changing world relationships pervaded the debates, providing ammunition for old enemies of Mutual Security and worries for old friends. Yet, the administration's program appeared cast from the same mold as all its predecessors back to 1951, when the world wore

[12] Eisenhower was hospitalized on June 8, 1956, and did not return to the White House until July 16. In the interim, the Mutual Security authorization went through floor debate in House and Senate, through conference, and on to signature, $800 million short of his request; the following appropriation, completed after his return to Washington, fell $300 million shorter still.

a very different look. And Eisenhower's troubles in July seem, by hindsight, an inevitable outcome of his choices in December; the efficacy of persuasive instruments conditioned, in their turn, upon the exercise — and limits — of choice-making.

Alongside these three factors there is need to place a fourth, which looms at least as large under mid-century conditions: the factor of too many things at once, as represented, classically, by FDR's fight for reorganization powers amidst controversy over his "court-packing" plan. In that instance, Roosevelt was criticized for moving for his management reform at a time when his influence was mortgaged to another cause. Perhaps he had an option then — though that can be debated — but not so his successors. In 1956, in a relatively quiet time at home and abroad, the Eisenhower influence has been demanded in three closely spaced, competing, legislative fights of first importance to his regime — farm, education, foreign aid — to say nothing of those headed off, like tax reduction, or of the many other issues on which White House labels were affixed to controversial aspects: Hells Canyon, highway aid, social security amendments, the civil rights commission, and numbers more. In Truman's time, the list was often longer, the controversial aspects sharper, the presidential temperature higher, and, besides, in many of his years, such legislative struggles were accompanied by operational involvements — military, diplomatic, economic, or administrative — also calling his persuasion into play on a grand scale.

A President's tools of persuasion are put under great strains when used on many projects simultaneously. Look at the tools themselves, and that becomes quite obvious. Yet, such use is the normal practice, nowadays; often mandatory, always wanted. No more as persuaders than as choice-makers are contemporary Presidents at liberty, discretion unconfined, to choose the "what" and "when" of their endeavors to persuade.

Four factors have been named, so far, as limiting the efficacy of persuasive instruments. But there remains a fifth, a factor so important as to dominate the rest, continually affecting the dimensions of all four. This is the element of "setting" in persuasion, a matter not of instruments, as such, but of the *background* against which they are employed. As a rough rule, it may be said that for a fraction of the persons on whom Presidents depend, continuing exposure to the White House and its occupant provides a background favoring — though not, of course, determining — effective exercise of presidential influence upon them. The bigger the "staff system," the smaller the fraction; but even an open door could not enlarge it into a preponderance. For most officials, both public and partisan, a favorable background will be differently derived. Derived from what? To this we may now turn.

In the case of executive officials, all sorts of variables of time, place, situation, substance, tend to affect actual responses to a particular pressure from the President. But there would seem to be one variable always present, always influential: their own instinctive estimate of his prestige with Congress, his potency on Capitol Hill. This may not square with visions conjured up by the tag "Chief Executive"; it is, however, entirely natural. For Congress, day in and day out, means life or death to programs, institutions, personnel. Putting the matter in its crudest terms (and thus rather larger than life): if Presidents can make much difference in these respects, either way, their own officialdom will be well disposed toward their wishes; if not, so much the worse for them; many a bureaucrat, like many a congressman, was there before and will be after.

Of course, such bureaucratic estimates of presidential prowess will vary from time to time. George Kennan once remarked that diplomats must rethink foreign policy each morning; so bureaucrats must reappraise their attitudes toward a President, and so they do, day after day. Such estimates will vary, also, from place to place. The weaker an agency, in terms of institutional entrenchment, program support, the more its officials will tend to view the President as a resource, no matter what the state of his congressional relations; thus Labor is traditionally a "tame" department. And every agency, however "strong," will make its calculations with reference, mainly, to those elements in Congress and those issues before Congress that affect it the most; even as between Army and Air the President is not appraised alike.

This does not mean that there is any one-to-one relationship between a President's congressional prestige and agency compliance with his wishes — though sometimes, certainly, the correlation is that close — but rather that a favorable background for persuasive efforts at his end of Pennsylvania Avenue is markedly dependent, over time, upon his prestige at the other end, with Congress. And in precisely the same sense — no more, no less — a favorable background for persuasion of the Congress is provided by his prestige with the country. As in the bureaucratic case. Senators and Congressmen differently situated, institutionally and electorally, will not see that matter all alike; place, time, party, and electorate make for differing appraisals, though by no means along strict party lines: witness Republican and Democratic attitudes in the Eighty-fourth Congress. No more than with the bureaucrats are estimates of this sort to be taken as controlling the congressional response in given instances of presidential pressure, but there can be no doubt that they contribute most significantly to the background against which such pressure is applied.

As for a President's own party's politicians outside Congress, they are quite comparably circumstanced, with the important qualification that at certain moments in the cycle of his term, their own enforced commitment to his record and his name may enhance their responsiveness regardless of his momentary popular prestige; a qualification applicable, equally, to certain of their brethren on the Hill.

In short, the President's persuasive power with those who do the daily chores of governing, is influenced by a sort of *progression of prestige,* a sequence culminating in the regard of the "general public," the country-at-large. Woodrow Wilson once wrote, in an academic vein, that a President "may be both the leader of his party and the leader of the nation or he may be one or the other." [13] Whatever the case fifty years ago, no such option is open to him now. He must endeavor to lead "party" (for which read public officers as well), since "nation" does not run the government machine, cannot itself effectuate his choices. But if he is to manage those who make the wheels go 'round, he needs public opinion at his back, must seek consensus as his context for persuasion. And in that dual compulsion lies the *ultimate dilemma* of the presidential operation at mid-century.

How describe this dilemma? One may begin by pointing to the sources of that popular prestige which so affects the President's own power to persuade. His general public — in our terms, national and partisan constituencies combined — actually comprises a diversity of presidential publics, their expectations nurtured variously by claims on him as "government," by respect for his office, or by ties to his personality: "interest" publics, "capacity" publics, and "personal" publics, each subdivided many times, all linked by the crisscrossing lines of overlapping membership, collectively encompassing the country, or that part of it which cares about the President.

His national prestige, therefore — which congressmen and politicians watch and weigh — is simply the net balance of favorable response these many groups, in sum, accord their varied images of him (a matter always to be gauged, not scientifically determined, the result influenced, of course, by the affiliation of the gauger). Those images and the responses to them are not static; they can and do vary over time. And what are the determinants of variation? Happenings, mainly, or the appearance of happenings, ascribable — or anyway ascribed — to him: the reward or frustration of a bread-and-butter want, an ethical attitude, a psychological identification; to such as these his publics will react wherever and in whatever degree they see his office or his person as the cause. Inevitably, every concrete choice he makes, both positive and negative, and every effort at persuasion will set off some reactions of the sort, and not all of one kind; if somebody is pleased, then someone else is bound to be offended.

For the President to give offense is to risk blurring his own image in the eyes of those offended, hence to risk lowering their favorable response to him. But on a maximum of such response, as aggregated all across the country, must he depend for the effectuation of his choices. And on choice-making he depends for the impression of his person on the product of his office. But the conduct of office is liable to require policy initiatives in all directions, not as free will, but as constituency pressures and events decree. Hence, acts of choice and of persuasion become mandatory, inescapable. Yet, they are bound to give offense.

This, then, is the ultimate dilemma, the vicious circle Presidents must tread by virtue of their unique placement in our system, the personal equivalent for them, as individuals, of that disparity which haunts their

[13] Woodrow Wilson, *op. cit., supra* note 2, at 69.

office, routinely responsible for programming without assured support to carry through. No President, of course, is wholly helpless in this situation. He gains from office when he enters it a sizable initial fund of favorable response; if he is fortunate enough to be an Eisenhower, he brings still more *to* office. Once installed, his actions bring him gains as well as losses. Approbation, no less than offense, is bound to follow, from some quarter, everything he does or fails to do. And nobody in government is better placed than he to focus public interest and attention where he wants it, to foster certain images, obscuring others, to make desired happenings occur, to give events a nudge.

These are not insignificant resources. Particularly in a time of sharp emergency — which a preponderance of publics see or can be made to see as such — their use with skill, accompanied by luck, should help a President to break out of that circle altogether, in a fashion advantageous to his person and his cause; enabling him to gain from what he does far more by way of favorable response than negative reaction. For such a time, a crisis-time, tends to put premiums on affirmative action, to make the very act of doing almost its own reward, not doing almost its own penalty; so Hoover found to his discomfiture and Roosevelt to his taste a quarter-century ago. Of course, if circumstances are precisely opposite and times all peace and quiet, the outcome may be no less advantageous for a President; so Coolidge made a virtue of *not* doing and was well rewarded for it.

But our situation at mid-century fits neither of these models; the years since the Second World War have neither been perceived, widely, as crisis times, nor have they been, in fact, peace-times in any familiar sense. And nowadays, the things that Presidents must do and those they may be called upon to do expose them regularly to the penalties of *both* such times with no assurance that they can gain the rewards of either. These days, both doing and not doing give offense in indeterminate proportion to offsetting approbation; almost all actions now *tend* to produce a negative reaction more concrete than favorable response. Both forms of action are abrasive; from neither can our Presidents now *count* upon a bonus of response. Yet, they are constantly impelled to actions of both sorts and so it has to be, these days, their preferences notwithstanding.

Consider what a President must do in times we now call "peace": keep taxes relatively high, armed forces relatively large, the budget "swollen," the bureaucracy "outsize"; inject himself into labor disputes just when tempers grow highest, into defense of overseas constituents just when they seem, at home, most irritating or unwise. And so the list goes on. Consider, also, what a President now may be called upon to do: intervene with arms in Korea, Indo-China; intervene with counsel in Southern school segregation; back the Benson plan for aid to farmers; endorse the Hobby plan for aid to schools; accept the Rockefeller plan for aid abroad; impose the New York Bar committee plan for personnel security; keep Nixon or take Herter; choose silence on McCarthy or attack; these among others. Such "musts" and "mays," as manifested in his acts of doing or not doing, are bound to outrage some among his publics (and anger may last long), to be accepted grudgingly by many as unpleasant facts of life, to warm the hearts of an uncertain number whose warmth may be short-lived. Whichever way he acts, his penalties may outrun his rewards in prestige terms. And rarely can he calculate with certainty, in advance, the net balance either way. Yet act he must.

By virtue of his unique place in government, a President gains unequalled opportunities to mold the images his publics have of him. But, for these opportunities, he pays a heavy price. Even for Eisenhower, immune, so far, to many of the payments levied on his predecessors, there is now the real price his illnesses exact: the issue of his health in the 1956 campaign; an issue taking its dimensions from the nature of his office at mid-century.

This observation instantly suggests a qualification upon everything that has been said so far: the ultimate dilemma for a President — and with it all the intermediate dilemmas here described — takes shape and form, in actuality, from the particulars of his own personality and of the situations he confronts throughout his term. This paper has presented up to now an outline, in the abstract, of the operating burdens thrust on Presidents, in general. Now, before we can consider what, if anything, ought to be done in consequence, we need note how these burdens, these dilemmas have been manifested in real-life and what the real-life men in office have made of them, each in his way and time. That becomes necessarily a first step toward conclusion.

VI. PERSONALITIES AND SITUATIONS

Two men have held the Presidency at mid-century, Truman and Eisenhower. While Franklin Roosevelt's shadow is upon them and their office, he is not counted of their number because he served in different times, faced different partisan and governmental situations; only from 1938 to 1941 had he a foretaste of the situations scheduled for his final term. For present purposes, Truman and Eisenhower stand alone.

In some respects, their personalities and circumstances are more similar than either might admit. Their likenesses of personality have been canvassed with dash and perceptivity by Richard Rovere in the final essay of his recent book; there is no need to retrace all his ground.[14] Suffice it to say here that both appear to have displayed in office an optimistic faith in progress, a confident, uncynical approach, no less sustaining and heart-warming for being late Victorian. So far, the White House at mid-century has been home to men formed, essentially, before the First World War, the Great Depression. No mid-century man, product of the Second World War and of the Great Prosperity, has yet lived in the place; for that there is, perhaps, some reason to be grateful.

Their situations, too, are much alike in numerous respects, those respects which give unity to times here termed "mid-century." Truman

14 See Richard H. Rovere, *The Eisenhower Years* 346–49, 8–10 (1956).

and Eisenhower, both, have had to deal with cold war and a full employment mandate; with inflation and recession, high taxes and high debt; with large armed forces, entangling alliances, atomic power, and "brush" warfare; with a bureaucracy two million strong; with a deeply split congressional party, sometimes in the minority, rarely more than nominally a majority; with notable discrepancies between each party's presidential and congressional electorates; with crises and with politics-as-usual combined.

These similarities of situation are accompanied by certain likenesses in approach, also. Both Presidents have been men rather narrowly acquainted outside their own professions, tending to rely for stimulation, counsel, and advice primarily on their official associates; neither has had anything like FDR's acquaintance, nationwide. Moreover, both have tended to put special credence in successful products of an idealized career line other than their own: military men in Truman's case; business men in Eisenhower's. To these and others among their subordinates both Presidents have delegated vastly, though in different spheres, and both have seemed to take ideas and issues as they come; to see what reaches them, often with sharpness and great common sense, but not to reach out constantly in restless search; displaying, so it seems, neither the intellectual's disquiet nor FDR's pervasive curiosity.

These similarities, of person, situation, and approach may well appear, historically, no less significant than many of the differences between their Presidencies. But if we are to set their own reactions in the office against our generalized discussion, differences become our main concern. In what do these consist? In respect to personality, of course, the public record is replete with information, not all of it informative, which scarcely needs rephrasing in this paper. It is enough, here, to identify those facets seemingly of special influence upon the styles of these two men as presidential operators: Eisenhower temperamentally a mediator, Truman disposed to put his head down and charge; Truman the politician, professional thick-skinned and relatively acclimated to abuse, save of his family, as against Eisenhower, the Supreme Commander, thin-skinned, apparently, and touchy at barbed questioning of his official conduct. These things, quite clearly, have affected and have differentiated *style*.

Yet, style in the abstract helps us very little; what counts, for present purposes, is application in the situations faced by these two Presidents, as actually experienced and met by each in turn. How differentiate their situations and responses? By focusing upon three crucial, common, inter-related aspects of their Presidencies: initial unpreparedness, pressure of events, and portions of prestige.

First is the matter of unpreparedness. Both men came to office inexperienced but ignorant of different things in differing degrees. Truman had been ten years in Washington, not close to the White House, not part of the executive establishment, but thoroughly accustomed to the search for and the uses of elective office; knowledgeable in the whole milieu of politics and in the power game, at least as played on the Hill; knowledgeable also, in a senatorial way, anent the divisive homefront issues of the past decade bound to project themselves into his Presidency; yet, almost wholly uninformed in the strategic spheres of foreign policy and military operations, his first concerns on taking office. At every point, the Eisenhower contrast is both plain and sharp. And when one notes their early opportunities for learning on the job, contrasts again are clear. Eisenhower, had, at least, the warm-up of campaign and preinaugural; Truman had two hours. Truman, on the other hand, inherited a going concern, albeit not of his contriving; Eisenhower had to build a new regime from scratch out of a party twenty years in opposition to the White House, its legislative oligarchy recently opposed to *him*. Yet, he did fall heir to a relatively stable home economy, a relatively viable position abroad, while Truman was confronted at the outset by immediate and drastic consequences of the shift from total war to general "peace."

This brings us to the matter of events, their tempo, and their context, not only at the start but throughout all the years of these two Presidents. Waves of inflation and industrial unrest, threats to the welfare-state, Soviet expansionism and intransigence and armament, European weakness, Chinese collapse, the aftermath of Alger Hiss, the outbreak in Korea and its consequences — these, among others, were themes sounded harshly and insistently in Truman's years; evoking a long line of *overt* events, almost all of them intense in pressure for affirmative, abrasive action, many of them thoroughly devisive in their social and political results. In Eisenhower's term, thus far (the early fall of 1956), some of these themes have been submerged, or nearly so; the rest have been productive of a lesser number of such overt events and at longer intervals.

To be sure, Eisenhower's years have not been without incident. The worst of McCarthy, the imminence of Bricker, the fall of farm income, the risks of renewed war in the Far East, the death of the European Defense Community, threats in the Middle East, convulsions in North Africa; these and others and, besides, those steps toward the future: in great power relationships, the coming of "competitive coexistence"; in their defense, the integration of tactical atomic weapons; in social policy at home, the Supreme Court decision on desegregation; and in home industry, the turn toward automation. Yet, unlike Truman's time, there have been virtually no national emergencies as a result of strikes, no spiralling price upswings (and only the mildest of recessions off the farm), no frontal assaults on the Roosevelt revolution, no *new* spy scares, no imminent collapses in Europe, no Americans fighting in Asia, no overt threats or acts of force from Moscow. Stalin, after all, turned ugly in Truman's first year; he died in Eisenhower's. And without these, the din of Truman's time has been muted indeed, for in his day, these made the greatest noise.

This does not mean the one man's problem of choice-making and persuasion were *intrinsically* much "harder" than the other's. That is a judgment the historians will have to render in due course; contemporary evidence appears to cut both ways. When Truman came to office, the New Deal inheritance remained to be secured; by Eisenhower's time, that had been done, the argument pushed to another level, the *Fair* Deal in dispute but the hallmarks of Roosevelt's revolution well entrenched: witness social security. Clearly, this eases Eisenhower's situation relative to Truman's. On the other hand, it seems less difficult, in terms both intellectual and political, to counter Stalin than to coexist with his successors. Building "situations of strength" in the face of intransigence and military threat is bound to be more concrete, more congenial, hence more manageable than using them, renewing them once built; especially when guns and money turn out insufficient, of themselves, as maintenance materials, and when the purpose loses shape, specific or short-run. Korea interrupted Truman's regime in preliminary grapplings with that harder task, and programs then frozen in a military guise have yet to be thawed out. But long before Eisenhower came to office, it appeared clear that should the Soviets, someday, mellow their manners, if not aims, our Government would be hard put to fashion adequate response.

Still, if one cannot strike a balance of intrinsic hardship in the troubles which events decreed for Truman and for Eisenhower, one can note certain things about the *context* of events which rendered Truman's handling of his troubles relatively harder. On the one hand, it happened in his time, as against Eisenhower's, that a lesser number of events had government and public impacts gradual, postponable, or transient: contrast Korea with Indo-China; the Steel dispute of 1952 with that of 1956, the rise of "neutralism" with the fall of dollar balances. On the other hand, it is distinctively different to respond to events as "Fair Dealer" than as "dynamic conservative"; different in terms of ideological commitment; different in terms of attitude about the Presidency's four constituencies, their diverse and conflicting expectations; differences only of degree, perhaps, but no less definite for that. So many things might Truman not have done, or held himself above, or dissociated himself from, had he been leader of the Eisenhower coalition instead of heir to Roosevelt's (and had he not been Truman, matters might have gone still otherwise; style counts in application).

Obviously there are connecting links between these two aspects of the context of events in Truman's time and in his later years, both are related to another: by June of 1950, this country to all public appearances, was launched upon a period of relative tranquility, assured, it seemed, by nice adjustments between the not-too-heavy burdens of a stabilized world leadership and the growing pleasures of a resurgent, expanding home economy; a period of calm protected, also, by the tranquilizing stand-off between reformism represented at the White House and conservatism dominant in Congress. After two decades of depression, World War, post-war readjustments, there we were, millions of us, savoring another gilded age. Then Korea and its prolongation and its side effects blasted the happy scene, upsetting expectations on every hand. With Eisenhower's advent and Korean truce, the happy prospects were revived;

by this he has gained greatly. Meanwhile, in proportion, Truman took the rap.

This raises the whole question of prestige, the third of those situational matters requiring review. Truman, of course, gained what he had to start with from his office, not his person. He suffered always from the prestige handicap of "daring," as an unknown and a commoner, to fill the regal shoes of FDR, a handicap increased, at first, by images of a lost little man, which his own "moon and stars" remarks did nothing to reduce. Those early images were to be overlaid in time, especially in 1948, but the more positive impressions which then took their place were of the sort, mostly, to blur at once with any undesired happenings, and these, perforce, were plentiful for many of his publics. In terms of the uncertainties of public prestige for a mid-century President as characterized above (part V), the Truman case is classic to the point of caricature. As the enormous variations in his Gallup polls suggest, he sometimes seemed assured a net balance of negative reaction no matter what he did or failed to do.

With Eisenhower, it has all been otherwise; almost the opposite at every point. Throughout his term, his own progression of prestige has culminated, constantly, in an extraordinary popular response. It may be that his images, like Truman's, have been changing over time; that he is now more nearly "grandfather" than a "crusader" to his publics; so Louis Harris suggests.[15] But, if so, there has seemed to be no diminution of response, at least up to the start of the 1956 campaign. For evidence, one need but note the polls, or trace the *tactics* and the *expressed* views (which is not to say votes) of his congressional opponents on both sides of the aisle as good a rough gauge of his popular prestige as once of Truman's. Eisenhower, therefore, has enjoyed at all times what was rarely Truman's lot: a hospitable climate for the making of those choices that impose the greatest strain upon the power to persuade.

And yet it has been Truman, far more typically than Eisenhower, who made that sort of choice, this past decade, interjecting the divisive issue, imposing the stiff commitment, calling for the drastic action by administration, Congress, party, and the country; Truman with his fluctuating, always limited prestige, which he endangered in the very act of drawing on it; not Eisenhower with his vast supply which has yet to be plumbed, much less drawn down. Truman treated prestige as a weapon to be brandished; Eisenhower treats it as an asset to be preserved. Yet we may not assume that either of them thought he had an option. For Truman seems to have regarded advocacy as *the* obligation of his office; while Eisenhower, seemingly, acts in the conviction that beneficence is its own reward.

No matter what his thoughts, of course, events and their context narrowed Truman's option; this we have seen above. But where he did have

---

[15] See, Harris, "How Voters Feel About Ike's Health," *Collier's,* July 20, 1956, pp. 17 ff.

leeway, his concept of his role disparaged an interpolation of the prestige factor into choice. In all that he has said and written on the Presidency, his emphasis always is on its constitutional and statutory
obligations; the duty to decide, the responsibility to state; the initiative
primary, implementation secondary; the *focus* on choice-making, not effectuation. "The President's got to set the sights," he once remarked.
"What the country needed in every field . . . was up to me to say . . .
and if Congress wouldn't respond, well, I'd have done all I could in a
straightforward way." [16] And this seems to have been not posture, but
precept, allowing little room for concern over personal prestige. What we
have termed his ultimate dilemma never seemed to faze this President;
indeed, he never would have granted its existence in our terms. In his
own outlook, he resolved it without having to acknowledge it, by ignoring the dimension he could do the least about.

Events in another context have been easier on Eisenhower; to that
degree, his option has been greater. But one gains the impression from
outside that he attributes much of the eased pressure of events to his
prestige, per se. To be, becomes then, a great act of doing in itself; to do,
or not to do, must be adjudged in its relationship to being, to those
images which calm and quiet by the very fact of their existence. Of
course, great prestige from the start permits considerable flexibility; this
standard — if it is the standard — does not call for frozen immobility, assuming such were feasible these days, which it is not; rather, what seems
to be at stake is a fixed attitude that in so far as possible, things others
might have done — not all, but many things — should not be done, or done
a different way: so with overt approaches to the Congress; hassles in the
executive, disputes in the party, wrangles in the country, crises abroad.
Save in extremity, the calming images must not be blurred. And up to
now, this standard (if it is the standard) must seem practical and workable to its adherents. In 1954, McCarthy hangs himself: in 1955, a Democratic Congress remains reasonable; in 1956, the Congress does no less
than usual in an election year, while a steel strike evaporates without
emergency; and so it goes. This Presidency, up to now, belies its supposed
ultimate dilemma, for where — save in two illnesses by act of God — are
the hard enforced acts of doing and not doing which may evoke more
negative reaction than favorable response? Apparently, they have been
calmed away. To all appearances, indeed, beneficence *is* its own reward.

These observations are by way of a trial balance on the operational
approaches of two Presidents. A "trial" is all that can be offered here.
History permits of no more now, particularly in Eisenhower's instance;
also, an observership conducted inside one administration, not the other,
puts comparison in double jeopardy. Moreover, in a perfectly objective
sense, the value of comparison is jeopardized as well by the disparate
tenures of Truman and of Eisenhower. The Truman style which we

16 Interview with former President Truman, Kansas City, Mo., Dec. 27, 1955.

remember now, the Truman staff which is familiar in our recollections, date at the earliest from 1947. In Eisenhower's case, the comparable date might be, say, January 1954. A good eight months, or more, of Truman's term in 1948, again in 1952, were lost for forwarding policy endeavors by virtue of election-year uncertainties, preoccupations. A comparable pause in Eisenhower's term would date from the early spring of 1956. And in the four preceding months, of course, he was either hospitalized or convalescent. We are comparing, then, one man's activities in office during four and two-thirds years with another's during twenty months, at most. Even if one assumes that the Eisenhower regime might have tended less than Truman's to suspend its forward planning long before the election, the ileitis operation helps redress the balance. The shortness of the working term for a new President, discounting both his first year(s) and his last, does not get from our literature the notice it deserves. But note it here we must; for as applied in these two instances, it limits the utility of our comparison.

Still, such as it is, we have run a trial balance. What does it show? It indicates, at first glance, that one of these Presidents worked at his tasks as though they posed no "ultimate dilemma," while the other has managed in a fashion to dissipate it, up to now. These findings do not signify that the dilemma, as abstractly stated, lacks reality, in the concrete. Truman may have ignored it, but it haunted his Presidency none the less and manifested itself, at the last, in Eisenhower's election. As for the latter, history will have the final word about beneficence; the record yet is incomplete. Besides, we have no precedents since Washington, if then, for so remarkable a showing of popular prestige diffused so widely, for so long. National heroes do not come a dime-a-dozen; the hero in our momentary concord of events remains unique, by definition. One may expect the cardinal dilemmas of the Presidency in our time to re-enter the White House upon its next change of occupant, if not, indeed, before.

What then is to be learned from our trial balance? Essentially that every President will meet and measure those dilemmas according to the dictates of his situation, his personality. It is a good and necessary thing that this be so. Had Truman seen his problems in what seem to be his successor's terms, it well might have destroyed him as an integrated individual, the task beyond his powers, in his circumstances, to perform; but had he seen things so he would not have been Truman. And on the other hand, had Eisenhower willingly aroused the sort of criticism taken by his predecessor, one wonders what would have become of him; but had he done so, he would never have been Eisenhower. It follows, therefore, that whatever we conceive to help our Presidents shoulder their burdens at mid-century, we must be wary of diminishing their freedom to define those burdens after their own fashion, in their situations as they see them, each in his turn and time. That freedom is already tightly circumscribed by laws and institutions and constituency expectations. No need for students and observers to make the crowding worse.

VII. Prospects and Proposals

"Mid-century" will not endure forever. If the cold war holds its present course and if our national economy continues, generally, to climb, we may face six, eight, even ten years, perhaps more, that will bear an affinity, in presidential terms, to the decade just past. Beyond another decade, though, our population, science and resources, our industrial development, urbanization, regional realignments, will have brought us to such a point that even if affairs abroad held constant — which they cannot do — what has been described here may be wholly out of date. Even a decade may turn out too long a period to bracket as a portion of "our times." But there is likelihood, at least, that the next two, perhaps three, presidential terms will have much in common with the three since the Second World War.

How then might the next few Presidents be helped to ease the likely operating problems of the office? The answer, plainly, is that nothing fundamental can be done to help them. Nothing short of really revolutionary party centralization bids fair to eliminate that basic and dilemma-nurturing disparity between the Presidency's obligation to initiate and its capacity to achieve. Of course, were our parties fully nationalized and centralized, the party oligarchs might well command the capacity and would tend to assume the obligation, relieving the Presidency, as such, both of burdens and of unique place. But it has been six years now since a committee of the American Political Science Association summoned the revolution to commence, and I am prepared to predict that our parties will endure, for one more decade anyway, substantially unnationalized as in the last.

Barring fundamentals, one can try to nibble at the fringes of the Presidency's problems via piecemeal structural reforms. But those a President might find most fun cannot be had, as a practical matter: witness the item veto. And those most certain to affect him for the worse are only too likely to be thrust upon him: as now we have the two-term amendment and still might find ourselves some day with Bricker's or with Mundt's. As for the many proposed statutory changes which fit neither of these two extremes, opinions differ; their proponents, though, would be well advised to reflect upon Rossiter's admonition: "Leave Your Presidency Alone." [17] In my own view, that caution makes great sense and applies equally to all proposals of a structural and statutory sort. For all of them — all, anyway, of which I am aware — incur a common risk: that they will produce *wayward side-effects,* however unintended by their sponsors, which may make matters worse, or at least put new problems in the place of old. Even the twentieth amendment, widely heralded as an essential modernization, made matters difficult for Eisenhower his first year, and scarcely would have aided FDR, and easily might have been ruinous in Lincoln's time, the classic case of grave emergency it is intended to

---

17 See Rossiter, *op. cit., supra* note 1, at 161–62.

Richard E. Neustadt   225

relieve. This is not to suggest we should repeal the "Lame Duck" amendment, or even alter its required starting-dates for the congressional and
presidential terms; the point, rather, is that if so logical and seemingly so
slight a change produces wayward side-effects, it might be well to avoid
others more complex or more obscure.

Some risks, of course, accompany all change; this is no argument for
never changing anything. But when one can forsee a wayward consequence, however unintended by proponents, then is the time, it seems
to me, to move on their proposals very cautiously indeed. So, in the legislative cabinet scheme, as recently revived by Professors Corwin and
Koenig,[18] one is confronted with the prospect, all other things aside, that
formal cabinet rank for leading senators would transfer from an Eisenhower to Knowland, say, and Bridges, some part of his privacy, prestige,
and nominal authority, without in any way diminishing their independent power base, or guaranteeing him improvement in the quality
of counsel and advice they have provided up to now. If there should be
a President who wished to try this one-way transfer, he could find means
without a statute. The privilege remains his; why then impose a mandate? Of course, if one's concern is less with easing operational dilemmas
than with checking arbitrary power, the matter wears a wholly different
look. But if the Presidency now is dangerously powerful, this essay's
premises and argument are all awry.

In terms of easing burdens, hence of strengthening the President, by
means externally imposed, there is but one proposal that in all good
conscience I could urge without equivocation, a proposal once made (but
not patented) by a former Roosevelt aide: to guarantee new Presidents
a solid partisan majority in both Houses of Congress, composed of men
dependent on the President's own electorate. But in the circumstances of
mid-century, this, above all, is never to be guaranteed; indeed it is not
even to be hoped for.

Where does this leave us then? It leaves us with the Presidents themselves, with what they might do for themselves in their own self-defense,
within the confines and environs of their office.

To make suggestions to them, without knowing them or their specific
situations, imposes certain limitations on would-be suggestors, one limit
above all: that each suggestion be adaptable for use by an incumbent,
whatever his work-habits and his style; that each be usable by men so
various in those respects as Eisenhower, Truman, FDR. Truman's White
House rather resembled a senatorial establishment, writ large: the staff
informal, almost family-like, assignments shifting casually among jacks-of-
all-trades, organization plastic, hierarchy slight, and anything liable to be
mulled over with the President. Eisenhower, one supposes, could not have
abided it. But no more could Truman have abided — much less politically afforded — the military sort of staff system as adapted and on display
in Eisenhower's White House. Yet this is the way Eisenhower works and

18 See Edward S. Corwin and Louis W. Koenig, *The Presidency Today* 90–99 (1956).

that was the way Truman worked and the next President may want to work like one, or the other, or like neither. There is no point in urging upon any of them a suggestion he could not adopt without foregoing his accustomed way of work.

To illustrate the sort of thing thereby put out of bounds, a number of observers assert that the current regime is a "regency" and urge that Eisenhower should dispense with Sherman Adams. But if this were a regency, then Eisenhower and not Adams must be presumed First Regent. The military have their rules for chiefs of staff, and those who cannot keep them do not long retain the place. There is no evidence that Eisenhower lacks acquaintance with these rules or that his principal assistant has not learned to work within them. If Adams were to vanish overnight, no doubt there would soon appear in his place another such abrasive, intense concentrator. That is the Eisenhower way, and so it was long before 1953. In terms of personal performance, we might as well accept the moral and forbear to debate here whether Eisenhower's system, in the abstract, is a good thing or a bad. Some Presidents will find they cannot stand it, others that they cannot get away with it politically, while others, still, may try to proceed as much as he has done.

I have stressed Eisenhower's case because among those of all recent Presidents his most restricts the range of the suggestible. Our need is for things Presidents might do to help themselves, on their initiative, at their discretion. Suggestions that seem reasonably practicable for a man of military background, entrenched behind the paraphernalia of elaborate staff, are likely to be usable, as well, by those schooled in more fluid, personalized, working-ways of civil government and politics, whence one supposes the next Presidents will come. But having so delimited the field of search, what remains to be found? In such a narrow ground, what is there to discover that may help a President resolve — or live with — his dilemmas? Tentatively, I would hazard the following response.

First, the fewer a President's illusions about the limitations on his power stakes and status in our system, the better his performance on the job. The more nearly he sees his power problem as I have endeavored to describe it here, the greater his chance to master his circumstances or at least hinder them from overwhelming him. Of course, a man wants the illusions that sustain him at his work, and if he needs to look upon the world in terms other than jungle, then so he must. It might help, though, if Presidents who felt impelled to find identification with a forerunner, would look to Lincoln, not as myth or symbol, but as man-in-office. For in their wartime crises, FDR and Wilson seem more removed from our mid-century state than Lincoln does, despite the fact of war. In its operational dilemmas, he was a very modern Presidency, contrasts notwithstanding. And should they seek such parallels, I suggest that the image of his operating burdens and his power problem, rather than, say, Washington's (or Jackson's or a Roosevelt's), be graven on the minds of our next Presidents.

Second, of all the self-perceptions that can help a President, nothing helps so much as an awareness of his absolutely unique place — of his aloneness at the only juncture of his four constituencies — and an alertness, consequently, to the fact that he can count on no one else in Government to sense his interests in precisely his own terms. To stress the "team" and teamwork is a fine thing for morale and useful, too, in binding others to one's cause. But any President who regards the blithe spirit all-for-one-and-one-for-all as a reality which may assume full right-and-title to his interests is assured disenchantment and distortion of his aims.

It follows that he needs to widen, so far as he can, the confines of his own freedom to choose what he himself would think he were well advised to make choices on and undertake persuasion on and when. As we have seen, he cannot hope to widen these confines more than a little; how might even that little be accomplished? On the one hand, I would suggest, by rendering the regular assistance he receives more representative of the totality of his constituencies; on the other hand, by building into government and his own staff the sorts of competitions which will create "deadlines" for him at times and on issues useful in his terms.

Perhaps we do not recognize sufficiently the deep distortions, in constituency terms, of staff assistance now officially available to a President. Without exception, his department heads and institutional staff aides are tightly linked to, actually are part of, his "government" constituency. The same thing can be said for his legislative leaders and for such White House aides as he may draw from agency or congressional sources to help with liaison in both directions. Many of these people also represent, in varying degree, some portions of his "partisan" constituency; so, of course, does the National Committee Chairman, whose office is more or less part of presidential staff facilities. And all of them can claim to be in some sense representative of "national" constituency as well. But taking them together as a collectivity, their representative character is decidedly different than his own; greatly overweighing the governmental element, especially its executive side, while relatively slighting partisan, underweighing national, and virtually ignoring overseas components. Even in the White House staff, none but the Press Secretary is free of institutionalized routines which pull particularly in the government direction (perhaps explaining why that post becomes so powerful when manned by a superb technician).

To compensate for these distortions, Presidents must break out of their official families and so they do, with ceremonials and visitors, with trips, and tête-à têtes, with consultations and with confidants, each in his fashion. But I submit that these are frail reliances which need the utmost buttressing by Presidents themselves in conscious, purposeful awareness of official insufficiencies. And not the means but that awareness becomes crucial in this case; if that be strong enough, the man makes his own means. His aides, of course, can help and so they will, provided his insistence is incessant, but their reach is no *substitute* for his, nor their awareness either.

As for the matter of "created" deadlines, this was a specialty with FDR which, suitably adapted, I commend to his successors. Roosevelt is commonly supposed a "poor" administrator; lines of authority confused, the same assignments in the hand of numerous subordinates, doors opening and closing unpredictably, nobody knowing everything of anybody's business and everybody horning in on everything. Yet with all this and *by* it, he kept in his own hands more power of judgment and decision than most Presidents before or since. In the administration of the Presidency, what could be more important? This is not to suggest that future Presidents should try to play by ear, *ad hoc,* in Roosevelt's special way. They cannot if they would — nor could he either, at the end — for government has grown too big, its scope too broad, their own responsibilities too routinized, their office far too institutionalized. What is suggested, rather, is a search for substitutes compatible with their more complex circumstances. The building-in of competition seems to me the key.

Without attempting an exhaustive exploration, let me mention two means by which competitive relations might be fostered: namely appointments and reorganizations. The President who wishes to enhance his prospects for free choices in an area of policy will do well to arrange that opposed attitudes in country or in Congress, or in his own mind are represented among appointees charged institutionally with its consideration *and* administration. By "represented" is meant not in form alone, but in a balance what suffices to force underlying issues on the table, up the line, and in good time, without exhausting institutional support for a decision *either* way. Thus, Eisenhower seems to run tremendous risks of foreclosed freedom in the sphere of foreign aid, when all the posts of massive institutional power are held by men reportedly conservative in view, with "balance" furnished mainly by a brace of White House aides.

One sympathizes with the wish of both Roosevelt's successors to avoid such unseemly public struggles as were carried on from inside his regime. But foreclosed freedom can be harder on a President than struggling subordinates. Indeed, unless they are sufficiently well-matched to carry controversies to the press, he loses one among the early warning signals built-in-competitions can provide. If he is lucky and adroit and granted a respectful opposition, perhaps he can hold down the public outcries though he keep his fighters matched, and can devise internal signals as a substitute. But if, to keep the public peace, he rigs fights overmuch, he pays an exorbitant price, or so it seems to me. Indeed, under the circumstances of mid-century, an outward look of total harmony in a regime might well be taken as itself a warning sign.

As for reorganization, it is obviously useful, often essential, as a supplement to the appointive power in building or in equalizing institutionalized competitions. There is one disability, however: my colleague, Wallace Sayre, has propounded the sound "law" that any benefits of a reorganization are immediate, while disadvantages are cumulative over time. To this I would append the simple corollary that as for a President's own freedom, gains are short-range, risks long-run. And this applies with greater force the closer one approaches his own person. The moral appears plain. It cannot be enough to reorganize, one must keep on with it. In their relations to each other and the President, his official associates need stirring up; not with such frequency that they shrink into immobility, but just enough so that they are never absolutely confident in unchecked judgment of their chief's own judgment, or of their colleagues' either.

With that I would conclude. These several imprecise suggestions of what Presidents might do in their own self-defense are neither very bold nor very new; assuredly, they are neither my own last testament nor anybody's. In that regard, one final word: if we, as citizens, cannot rescue our Presidents from their dilemmas but must leave them to help themselves as best they can, there is one thing that we, as students and observers, might do to render their self-help a little easier. We might take more care in the future than sometimes in the past, lest we foster stereotypes and expectations not within their capacities or even their own interests to fulfill.

In the two decades since the report of the President's Committee on Administrative Management, great numbers of experts, in universities and out, have been hard at work seeking solutions for the managerial dilemmas of the federal government. And whether the focus be on budgeting, on organization, or on personnel — in order of prevailing fashion, then to now — the outcome tends to be the same: "The President, himself, must take command."

Faster than perhaps we realize, the frame of reference underlying such investigations, such solutions, becomes popularized (and oversimplified), eventuating in those plain truths nobody learns but everybody knows: "The President, of course! As in business, so in government; the title is the same and so should be the function." Perhaps it would not be amiss to remind the managerial enthusiasts of Woodrow Wilson's wise prognosis half a century ago: [19]

> . . . as the business of government becomes more and more complex and extended . . . the President is becoming more and more a political and less an executive officer . . . incumbents will come more and more [to be] directors of affairs and leaders of the nation — men of counsel and of the sort of action that makes for enlightenment.

For so it has turned out; these and not management are the great objects of their work and sources of their troubles at mid-century.

[19] Woodrow Wilson, *op. cit., supra* note 2, at 66, 81.

The Two Presidencies

Aaron Wildavsky

The United States has one President, but it has two presidencies; one presidency is for domestic affairs, and the other is concerned with defense and foreign policy. Since World War II, Presidents have had much greater success in controlling the nation's defense and foreign policies than in dominating its domestic policies. Even Lyndon Johnson has seen his early record of victories in domestic legislation diminish as his concern with foreign affairs grows.

What powers does the President have to control defense and foreign policies and so completely overwhelm those who might wish to thwart him?

The President's normal problem with domestic policy is to get congressional support for the programs he prefers. In foreign affairs, in contrast, he can almost always get support for policies that he believes will protect the nation — but his problem is to find a viable policy.

Whoever they are, whether they begin by caring about foreign policy like Eisenhower and Kennedy or about domestic policies like Truman and Johnson, Presidents soon discover they have more policy preferences in domestic matters than in foreign policy. The Republican and Democratic parties possess a traditional roster of policies, which can easily be adopted by a new President — for example, he can be either for or against Medicare and aid to education. Since existing domestic policy usually changes in only small steps, Presidents find it relatively simple to make minor adjustments. However, although any President knows he supports foreign aid and NATO, the world outside changes much more rapidly than the nation inside — Presidents and their parties have no prior policies on Argentina and the Congo. The world has become a highly intractable place with a whirl of forces we cannot or do not know how to alter.

THE RECORD OF PRESIDENTIAL CONTROL

It takes great crises, such as Roosevelt's hundred days in the midst of the depression, or the extraordinary majorities that Barry Goldwater's candidacy willed to Lyndon Johnson, for Presidents to succeed in controlling domestic policy. From the end of the 1930's to the present (what may roughly be called the modern era), Presidents have often been frustrated

Reprinted by permission of the publisher from *Trans-Action*, Vol. 4, No. 2 (December 1966). Copyright 1966 by the Community Leadership Project of Washington University, St. Louis, Missouri.

in their domestic programs. From 1938, when conservatives regrouped their forces, to the time of his death, Franklin Roosevelt did not get a single piece of significant domestic legislation passed. Truman lost out on most of his intense domestic preferences, except perhaps for housing. Since Eisenhower did not ask for much domestic legislation, he did not meet consistent defeat, yet he failed in his general policy of curtailing governmental commitments. Kennedy, of course, faced great difficulties with domestic legislation.

In the realm of foreign policy there has not been a single major issue on which Presidents, when they were serious and determined, have failed. The list of their victories is impressive: entry into the United Nations, the Marshall Plan, NATO, the Truman Doctrine, the decisions to stay out of Indochina in 1954 and to intervene in Vietnam in the 1960's, aid to Poland and Yugoslavia, the test-ban treaty, and many more. Serious setbacks to the President in controlling foreign policy are extraordinary and unusual.

Table 1, compiled from the Congressional Quarterly Service tabulation of presidential initiative and congressional response from 1948 through 1964, shows that Presidents have significantly better records in foreign and defense matters than in domestic policies. When refugees and immigration — which Congress considers primarily a domestic concern — are removed from the general foreign policy area, it is clear that Presidents prevail about 70 per cent of the time in defense and foreign policy, compared with 40 per cent in the domestic sphere.

TABLE 1

Congressional Action on Presidential
Proposals from 1948–1964

Policy Area	Congressional Action		Number of Proposals
	% Pass	% Fail	
Domestic policy (natural resources, labor, agriculture, taxes, etc.)	40.2	59.8	2499
Defense policy (defense, disarmament, manpower, misc.)	73.3	26.7	90
Foreign policy	58.5	41.5	655
Immigration, refugees	13.2	86.0	129
Treaties, general foreign relations, State Department, foreign aid	70.8	29.2	445

Source: Congressional Quarterly Service, *Congress and the Nation,* 1945–1964 (Washington, 1965).

WORLD EVENTS AND PRESIDENTIAL RESOURCES

Power in politics is control over governmental decisions. How does the President manage his control of foreign and defense policy? The answer does not reside in the greater constitutional power in foreign affairs that Presidents have possessed since the founding of the Republic. The answer lies in the changes that have taken place since 1945.

The number of nations with which the United States has diplomatic relations has increased from 53 in 1939 to 113 in 1966. But sheer numbers do not tell enough; the world has also become a much more dangerous place. However remote it may seem at times, our government must always be aware of the possibility of nuclear war.

Yet the mere existence of great powers with effective thermonuclear weapons would not, in and of itself, vastly increase our rate of interaction with most other nations. We see events in Assam or Burundi as important because they are also part of a larger worldwide contest, called the cold war, in which great powers are rivals for the control or support of other nations. Moreover, the reaction against the blatant isolationism of the 1930's has led to a concern with foreign policy that is worldwide in scope. We are interested in what happens everywhere because we see these events as connected with larger interests involving, at the worst, the possibility of ultimate destruction.

Given the overriding fact that the world is dangerous and that small causes are perceived to have potentially great effects in an unstable world, it follows that Presidents must be interested in relatively "small" matters. So they give Azerbaijan or Lebanon or Vietnam huge amounts of their time. Arthur Schlesinger, Jr., wrote of Kennedy that "in the first two month of his administration he probably spent more time on Laos than on anything else." Few failures in domestic policy, Presidents soon realize, could have as disastrous consequences as any one of dozens of mistakes in the international arena.

The result is that foreign policy concerns tend to drive out domestic policy. Except for occasional questions of domestic prosperity and for civil rights, foreign affairs have consistently higher priority for Presidents. Once, when trying to talk to President Kennedy about natural resources, Secretary of the Interior Stewart Udall remarked, "He's imprisoned by Berlin."

The importance of foreign affairs to Presidents is intensified by the increasing speed of events in the international arena. The event and its consequences follow closely on top of one another. The blunder at the Bay of Pigs is swiftly followed by the near catastrophe of the Cuban missile crisis. Presidents can no longer count on passing along their most difficult problems to their successors. They must expect to face the consequences of their actions — or failure to act — while still in office.

Domestic policy-making is usually based on experimental adjustments to an existing situation. Only a few decisions, such as those involving large dams, irretrievably commit future generations. Decisions in foreign affairs, however, are often perceived to be irreversible. This is expressed, for example, in the fear of escalation or the various "spiral" or "domino" theories of international conflict.

If decisions are perceived to be both important and irreversible, there is every reason for Presidents to devote a great deal of resources to them. Presidents have to be oriented toward the future in the use of their resources. They serve a fixed term in office, and they cannot automatically count on support from the populace, Congress, or the administrative apparatus. They have to be careful, therefore, to husband their resources for pressing future needs. But because the consequences of events in foreign affairs are potentially more grave, faster to manifest themselves, and less easily reversible than in domestic affairs, Presidents are more willing to use up their resources.

THE POWER TO ACT

Their formal powers to commit resources in foreign affairs and defense are vast. Particularly important is their power as Commander-in-Chief to move troops. Faced with situations like the invasion of South Korea or the emplacement of missiles in Cuba, fast action is required. Presidents possess both the formal power to act and the knowledge that elites and the general public expect them to act. Once they have committed American forces, it is difficult for Congress or anyone else to alter the course of events. The Dominican venture is a recent case in point.

Presidential discretion in foreign affairs also makes it difficult (though not impossible) for Congress to restrict their actions. Presidents can use executive agreements instead of treaties, enter into tacit agreements instead of written ones, and otherwise help create *de facto* situations not easily reversed. Presidents also have far greater ability than anyone else to obtain information on developments abroad through the Departments of State and Defense. The need for secrecy in some aspects of foreign and defense policy further restricts the ability of others to compete with Presidents. These things are all well known. What is not so generally appreciated is the growing presidential ability to *use* information to achieve goals.

In the past Presidents were amateurs in military strategy. They could not even get much useful advice outside of the military. As late as the 1930's the number of people outside the military establishment who were professionally engaged in the study of defense policy could be numbered on the fingers. Today there are hundreds of such men. The rise of the defense intellectuals has given the President of the United States enhanced ability to control defense policy. He is no longer dependent on the military for advice. He can choose among defense intellectuals from the research corporations and the academies for alternative sources of advice. He can install these men in his own office. He can play them off against each other or use them to extend spheres of coordination.

Even with these advisers, however, Presidents and Secretaries of Defense might still be too bewildered by the complexity of nuclear situations to take action — unless they had an understanding of the doctrine and concept of deterrence. But knowledge of doctrine about deterrence has been widely diffused; it can be picked up by any intelligent person who will read books or listen to enough hours of conversation. Whether or not the doctrine is good is a separate question; the point is that civilians can feel they understand what is going on in defense policy. Perhaps the most extraordinary feature of presidential action during the Cuban missile crisis was the degree to which the Commander-in-Chief of the Armed Forces insisted on controlling even the smallest moves. From the positioning of ships to the methods of boarding, to the precise words and actions to be taken by individual soldiers and sailors, the President and his civilian advisers were in control.

Although Presidents have rivals for power in foreign affairs, the rivals do not usually succeed. Presidents prevail not only because they may have superior resources but because their potential opponents are weak, divided, or believe that they should not control foreign policy. Let us consider the potential rivals — the general citizenry, special interest groups, the Congress, the military, the so-called military-industrial complex, and the State Department.

COMPETITORS FOR CONTROL OF POLICY

The Public. The general public is much more dependent on Presidents in foreign affairs than in domestic matters. While many people know about the impact of social security and Medicare, few know about politics in Malawi. So it is not surprising that people expect the President to act in foreign affairs and reward him with their confidence. Gallup Polls consistently show that presidential popularity rises after he takes action in a crisis — whether the action is disastrous as in the Bay of Pigs or successful as in the Cuban missile crisis. Decisive action, such as the bombing of oil fields near Haiphong, resulted in a sharp (though temporary) increase in Johnson's popularity.

The Vietnam situation illustrates another problem of public opinion in foreign affairs: it is extremely difficult to get operational policy directions from the general public. It took a long time before any sizable public interest in the subject developed. Nothing short of the large scale involvement of American troops under fire probably could have brought about the current high level of concern. Yet this relatively well developed popular opinion is difficult to interpret. While a majority appear to support President Johnson's policy, it appears that they could easily be persuaded to withdraw from Vietnam if the administration changed its line. Although a sizable majority would support various initiatives to end the war, they would seemingly be appalled if this action led to Communist encroachments elsewhere in Southeast Asia. (See "The President, the

Polls, and Vietnam" by Seymour Martin Lipset, *Trans-action*, Sept/Oct 1966.)

Although Presidents lead opinion in foreign affairs, they know they will be held accountable for the consequences of their actions. President Johnson has maintained a large commitment in Vietnam. His popularity shoots up now and again in the midst of some imposing action. But the fact that a body of citizens do not like the war comes back to damage his overall popularity. We will support your initiatives, the people seem to say, but we will reserve the right to punish you (or your party) if we do not like the results.

Special Interest Groups. Opinions are easier to gauge in domestic affairs because, for one thing, there is a stable structure of interest groups that covers virtually all matters of concern. The farm, labor, business, conservation, veteran, civil rights, and other interest groups provide cues when a proposed policy affects them. Thus people who identify with these groups may adopt their views. But in foreign policy matters the interest group structure is weak, unstable, and thin rather than dense. In many matters affecting Africa and Asia, for example, it is hard to think of well-known interest groups. While ephemeral groups arise from time to time to support or protest particular policies, they usually disappear when the immediate problem is resolved. In contrast, longer-lasting elite groups like the Foreign Policy Association and Council on Foreign Relations are composed of people of diverse views; refusal to take strong positions on controversial matters is a condition of their continued viability.

The strongest interest groups are probably the ethnic associations whose members have strong ties with a homeland, as in Poland or Cuba, so they are rarely activated simultaneously on any specific issue. They are most effective when most narrowly and intensely focused — as in the fierce pressure from Jews to recognize the state of Israel. But their relatively small numbers limits their significance to Presidents in the vastly more important general foreign policy picture — as continued aid to the Arab countries shows. Moreover, some ethnic groups may conflict on significant issues such as American acceptance of the Oder-Neisse line separating Poland from what is now East Germany.

The Congress. Congressmen also exercise power in foreign affairs. Yet they are ordinarily not serious competitors with the President because they follow a self-denying ordinance. They do not think it is their job to determine the nation's defense policies. Lewis A. Dexter's extensive interviews with members of the Senate Armed Services Committee, who might be expected to want a voice in defense policy, reveal that they do not desire for men like themselves to run the nation's defense establishment. Aside from a few specific conflicts among the armed services which allow both the possibility and desirability of direct intervention, the Armed Services Committee constitutes a sort of real estate committee dealing with the regional economic consequences of the location of military facilities.

The congressional appropriations power is potentially a significant resource, but circumstances since the end of World War II have tended to reduce its effectiveness. The appropriations committees and Congress itself might make their will felt by refusing to allot funds unless basic policies were altered. But this has not happened. While Congress makes its traditional small cuts in the military budget, Presidents have mostly found themselves warding off congressional attempts to increase specific items still further.

Most of the time, the administration's refusal to spend has not been seriously challenged. However, there have been occasions when individual legislators or committees have been influential. Senator Henry Jackson in his campaign (with the aid of colleagues on the Joint Committee on Atomic Energy) was able to gain acceptance for the Polaris weapons system and Senator Arthur H. Vandenberg played a part in determining the shape of the Marshall Plan and so on. The few congressmen who are expert in defense policy act, as Samuel P. Huntington says, largely as lobbyists with the executive branch. It is apparently more fruitful for these congressional experts to use their resources in order to get a hearing from the executive than to work on other congressmen.

When an issue involves the actual use or threat of violence, it takes a great deal to convince congressmen not to follow the President's lead. James Robinson's tabulation of foreign and defense policy issues from the late 1930's to 1961 (Table 2) shows dominant influence by Congress in only one case out of seven — the 1954 decision not to intervene with armed force in Indochina. In that instance President Eisenhower deliberately sounded out congressional opinion and, finding it negative, decided not to intervene — against the advice of Admiral Radford, chairman of the Joint Chiefs of Staff. This attempt to abandon responsibility did not succeed, as the years of American involvement demonstrate.

The Military. The outstanding feature of the military's participation in making defense policy is their amazing weakness. Whether the policy decisions involve the size of the armed forces, the choice of weapons systems, the total defense budget, or its division into components, the military have not prevailed. Let us take budgetary decisions as representative of the key choices to be made in defense policy. Since the end of World War II the military has not been able to achieve significant (billion dollar) increases in appropriations by their own efforts. Under Truman and Eisenhower defense budgets were determined by what Huntington calls the remainder method: the two Presidents estimated revenues, decided what they could spend on domestic matters, and the remainder was assigned to defense. The usual controversy was between some military and congressional groups supporting much larger expenditures while the President and his executive allies refused. A typical case, involving the desire of the Air Force to increase the number of groups of planes is described by Huntington in *The Common Defense:*

> The FY [fiscal year] 1949 budget provided 48 groups. After the
> Czech coup, the Administration yielded and backed an Air Force

TABLE 2

Congressional Involvement in Foreign and Defense Policy Decisions

Issue	Congressional Involvement (High, Low, None)	Initiator (Congress or Executive)	Predominant Influence (Congress or Executive)	Legislation or Resolution (Yes or No)	Violence at Stake (Yes or No)	Decision Time (Long or Short)
Neutrality Legislation, the 1930's	High	Exec	Cong	Yes	No	Long
Lend-Lease, 1941	High	Exec	Exec	Yes	Yes	Long
Aid to Russia, 1941	Low	Exec	Exec	No	No	Long
Repeal of Chinese Exclusion, 1943	High	Cong	Cong	Yes	No	Long
Fulbright Resolution, 1943	High	Cong	Cong	Yes	Yes	Long
Building the Atomic Bomb, 1944	Low	Exec	Exec	Yes	No	Long
Foreign Services Act of 1946	High	Exec	Exec	Yes	No	Long
Truman Doctrine, 1947	High	Exec	Exec	Yes	No	Long
The Marshall Plan, 1947–48	High	Exec	Exec	Yes	No	Long
Berlin Airlift, 1948	None	Exec	Exec	No	Yes	Long
Vandenberg Resolution, 1948	High	Exec	Cong	Yes	No	Long
North Atlantic Treaty, 1947–49	High	Exec	Exec	Yes	No	Long
Korean Decision, 1950	None	Exec	Exec	No	Yes	Short
Japanese Peace Treaty, 1952	High	Exec	Exec	Yes	No	Long
Bohlen Nomination, 1953	High	Exec	Exec	Yes	No	Long
Indo-China, 1954	High	Exec	Cong	No	Yes	Short
Formosan Resolution, 1955	High	Exec	Exec	Yes	Yes	Long
International Finance Corporation, 1956	Low	Exec	Exec	Yes	No	Long
Foreign Aid, 1957	High	Exec	Exec	Yes	No	Long
Reciprocal Trade Agreements, 1958	High	Exec	Exec	Yes	No	Long
Monroney Resolution, 1958	High	Cong	Cong	Yes	No	Long
Cuban Decision, 1961	Low	Exec	Exec	No	Yes	Long

Source: James A. Robinson, *Congress and Foreign Policy-Making* (Homewood, Illinois, 1962).

of 55 groups in its spring rearmament program. Congress added additional funds to aid Air Force expansion to 70 groups. The Administration refused to utilize them, however, and in the gathering economy wave of the summer and fall of 1948, the Air Force goal was cut back again to 48 groups. In 1949 the House of Representatives picked up the challenge and appropriated funds for 58 groups. The President impounded the money. In June, 1950, the Air Force had 48 groups.

The great increases in the defense budget were due far more to Stalin and modern technology than to the military. The Korean War resulted in an increase from 12 to 44 billions and much of the rest followed Sputnik and the huge costs of missile programs. Thus modern technology and international conflict put an end to the one major effort to subordinate foreign affairs to domestic policies through the budget.

It could be argued that the President merely ratifies the decisions made by the military and their allies. If the military and/or Congress were united and insistent on defense policy, it would certainly be difficult for Presidents to resist these forces. But it is precisely the disunity of the military that has characterized the entire postwar period. Indeed, the military have not been united on any major matter of defense policy. The apparent unity of the Joint Chiefs of Staff turns out to be illusory. The vast majority of their recommendations appear to be unanimous and are accepted by the Secretary of Defense and the President. But this facade of unity can only be achieved by methods that vitiate the impact of the recommendations. Genuine disagreements are hidden by vague language that commits no one to anything. Mutually contradictory plans are strung together so everyone appears to get something, but nothing is decided. Since it is impossible to agree on really important matters, all sorts of trivia are brought in to make a record of agreement. While it may be true, as Admiral Denfield, a former Chief of Naval Operations, said, that "On nine-tenths of the matters that come before them the Joint Chiefs of Staff reach agreement themselves," the vastly more important truth is that "normally the *only* disputes are on strategic concepts, the size and composition of forces, and budget matters."

Military-Industrial. But what about the fabled military-industrial complex? If the military alone is divided and weak, perhaps the giant industrial firms that are so dependent on defense contracts play a large part in making policy.

First, there is an important distinction between the questions "Who will get a given contract?" and "What will our defense policy be?" It is apparent that different answers may be given to these quite different questions. There are literally tens of thousands of defense contractors. They may compete vigorously for business. In the course of this competition, they may wine and dine military officers, use retired generals, seek intervention by their congressmen, place ads in trade journals, and even contribute to political campaigns. The famous TFX controversy — should General Dynamics or Boeing get the expensive contract? — is a larger than life example of the pressures brought to bear in search of lucrative contracts.

But neither the TFX case nor the usual vigorous competition for contracts is involved with the making of substantive defense policy. Vital questions like the size of the defense budget, the choice of strategic programs, massive retaliation vs. a counter-city strategy, and the like were far beyond the policy aims of any company. Industrial firms, then, do not control such decisions, nor is there much evidence that they actually try. No doubt a precipitous and drastic rush to disarmament would meet with opposition from industrial firms among other interests. However, there has never been a time when any significant element in the government considered a disarmament policy to be feasible.

It may appear that industrial firms had no special reason to concern themselves with the government's stance on defense because they agree with the national consensus on resisting communism, maintaining a large defense establishment, and rejecting isolationism. However, this hypothesis about the climate of opinion explains everything and nothing. For every policy that is adopted or rejected can be explained away on the grounds that the cold war climate of opinion dictated what happened. Did the United States fail to intervene with armed force in Vietnam in 1954? That must be because the climate of opinion was against it. Did the United States send troops to Vietnam in the 1960's? That must be because the cold war climate demanded it. If the United States builds more missiles, negotiates a testban treaty, intervenes in the Dominican Republic, fails to intervene in a dozen other situations, all these actions fit the hypothesis by definition. The argument is reminiscent of those who defined the Soviet Union as permanently hostile and therefore interpreted increases of Soviet troops as menacing and decreases of troop strength as equally sinister.

If the growth of the military establishment is not directly equated with increasing military control of defense policy, the extraordinary weakness of the professional soldier still requires explanation. Huntington has written about how major military leaders were seduced in the Truman and Eisenhower years into believing that they should bow to the judgment of civilians that the economy could not stand much larger military expenditures. Once the size of the military pie was accepted as a fixed constraint, the military services were compelled to put their major energies into quarreling with one another over who should get the larger share. Given the natural rivalries of the military and their traditional acceptance of civilian rule, the President and his advisers — who could claim responsibility for the broader picture of reconciling defense and domestic policies — had the upper hand. There are, however, additional explanations to be considered.

The dominant role of the congressional appropriations committee is to be guardian of the treasury. This is manifested in the pride of its members in cutting the President's budget. Thus it was difficult to get this crucial committee to recommend even a few hundred million increase in defense; it was practically impossible to get them to consider the several billion jump that might really have made a difference. A related budgetary matter concerned the planning, programming, and budgeting system introduced by Secretary of Defense McNamara. For if the defense budget contained major categories that crisscrossed the services, only the Secretary of Defense could put it together. Whatever the other debatable consequences of program budgeting, its major consequence was to grant power to the secretary and his civilian advisers.

The subordination of the military through program budgeting is just one symptom of a more general weakness of the military. In the past decade the military has suffered a lack of intellectual skills appropriate to the nuclear age. For no one has (and no one wants) direct experience with nuclear war. So the usual military talk about being the only people to have combat experience is not very impressive. Instead, the imaginative creation of possible future wars — in order to avoid them — requires people with a high capacity for abstract thought combined with the ability to manipulate symbols using quantitative methods. West Point has not produced many such men.

The State Department. Modern Presidents expect the State Department to carry out their policies. John F. Kennedy felt that State was "in some particular sense 'his' department." If a Secretary of State forgets this, as was apparently the case with James Byrnes under Truman, a President may find another man. But the State Department, especially the Foreign Service, is also a highly professional organization with a life and momentum of its own. If a President does not push hard, he may find his preferences somehow dissipated in time. Arthur Schlesinger fills his book on Kennedy with laments about the bureaucratic inertia and recalcitrance of the State Department.

Yet Schlesinger's own account suggests that State could not ordinarily resist the President. At one point, he writes of "the President, himself, increasingly the day-to-day director of American foreign policy." On the next page, we learn that "Kennedy dealt personally with almost every aspect of policy around the globe. He knew more about certain areas than the senior officials at State and probably called as many issues to their attention as they did to his." The President insisted on his way in Laos. He pushed through his policy on the Congo against strong opposition with the State Department. Had Kennedy wanted to get a great deal more initiative out of the State Department, as Schlesinger insists, he could have replaced the Secretary of State, a man who did not command special support in the Democratic party or in Congress. It may be that Kennedy wanted too strongly to run his own foreign policy. Dean Rusk may have known far better than Schlesinger that the one thing Kennedy did not want was a man who might rival him in the field of foreign affairs.

Schlesinger comes closest to the truth when he writes that "the White House could always win any battle it chose over the [Foreign] Service; but the prestige and proficiency of the Service limited the number of battles any White House would find it profitable to fight." When the President knew what he wanted, he got it. When he was doubtful and perplexed, he sought good advice and frequently did not get that. But there is no evidence that the people on his staff came up with better ideas. The real problem may have been a lack of good ideas anywhere. Kennedy undoubtedly encouraged his staff to prod the State Department. But the President was sufficiently cautious not to push so hard that he got his way when he was not certain what that way should be. In this context Kennedy appears to have played his staff off against elements in the State Department.

The growth of a special White House staff to help Presidents in foreign affairs expresses their need for assistance, their refusal to rely completely on the regular executive agencies, and their ability to find competent men. The deployment of this staff must remain a presidential prerogative, however, if its members are to serve Presidents and not their opponents. Whenever critics do not like existing foreign and defense policies, they are likely to complain that the White House staff is screening out divergent views from the President's attention. Naturally, the critics recommend introducing many more different viewpoints. If the critics could maneuver the President into counting hands all day ("on the one hand and on the other"), they would make it impossible for him to act. Such a viewpoint is also congenial to those who believe that action rather than inaction is the greatest present danger in foreign policy. But Presidents resolutely refuse to become prisoners of their advisers by using them as other people would like. Presidents remain in control of their staff as well as of major foreign policy decisions.

How Complete Is the Control?

Some analysts say that the success of Presidents in controlling foreign policy decisions is largely illusory. It is achieved, they say, by anticipating the reactions of others, and eliminating proposals that would run into severe opposition. There is some truth in this objection. In politics, where transactions are based on a high degree of mutual interdependence, what others may do has to be taken into account. But basing presidential success in foreign and defense policy on anticipated reactions suggests a static situation which does not exist. For if Presidents propose only those policies that would get support in Congress, and Congress opposes them only when it knows that it can muster overwhelming strength, there would never be any conflict. Indeed, there might never be any action.

How can "anticipated reaction" explain the conflict over policies like the Marshall Plan and the test-ban treaty in which severe opposition was overcome only by strenuous efforts? Furthermore, why doesn't "anticipated reaction" work in domestic affairs? One would have to argue that for some reason presidential perception of what would be successful is consistently confused on domestic issues and most always accurate on major foreign policy issues. But the role of "anticipated reactions" should be greater in the more familiar domestic situations, which provide a backlog of experience for forecasting, than in foreign policy with many novel situations such as the Suez crisis or the Rhodesian affair.

Are there significant historical examples which might refute the thesis of presidential control of foreign policy? Foreign aid may be a case in point. For many years, Presidents have struggled to get foreign aid appropriations because of hostility from public and congressional opinion. Yet several billion dollars a year are appropriated regularly despite the evident unpopularity of the program. In the aid programs to Communist countries like Poland and Yugoslavia, the Congress attaches all sorts of restrictions to the aid, but Presidents find ways of getting around them.

What about the example of recognition of Communist China? The sentiment of the country always has been against recognizing Red China or admitting it to the United Nations. But have Presidents wanted to recognize Red China and been hamstrung by opposition? The answer, I suggest, is a qualified "no." By the time recognition of Red China might have become a serious issue for the Truman administration, the war in Korea effectively precluded its consideration. There is no evidence that President Eisenhower or Secretary Dulles ever thought it wise to recognize Red China or help admit her to the United Nations. The Kennedy administration viewed the matter as not of major importance and, considering the opposition, moved cautiously in suggesting change. Then came the war in Vietnam. If the advantages for foreign policy had been perceived to be much higher, then Kennedy or Johnson might have proposed changing American policy toward recognition of Red China.

One possible exception, in the case of Red China, however, does not seem sufficient to invalidate the general thesis that Presidents do considerably better in getting their way in foreign and defense policy than in domestic policies.

THE WORLD INFLUENCE

The forces impelling Presidents to be concerned with the widest range of foreign and defense policies also affect the ways in which they calculate their power stakes. As Kennedy used to say, "Domestic policy . . . can only defeat us; foreign policy can kill us."

It no longer makes sense for Presidents to "play politics" with foreign and defense policies. In the past, Presidents might have thought that they could gain by prolonged delay or by not acting at all. The problem might disappear or be passed on to their successors. Presidents must now expect to pay the high costs themselves if the world situation deteriorates. The advantages of pursuing a policy that is viable in the world, that will not blow up on Presidents or their fellow citizens, far outweigh any temporary political disadvantages accrued in supporting an initially unpopular policy. Compared with domestic affairs, Presidents engaged in world politics are immensely more concerned with meeting problems on their own terms. Who supports and opposes a policy, though a matter of considerable interest, does not assume the crucial importance that it does in domestic affairs. The best policy Presidents can find is also the best politics.

The fact that there are numerous foreign and defense policy situations competing for a President's attention means that it is worthwhile to organize political activity in order to affect his agenda. For if a President pays more attention to certain problems he may develop different preferences; he may seek and receive different advice; his new calculations may lead him to devote greater resources to seeking a solution. Interested congressmen may exert influence not by directly determining a presidential decision, but indirectly by making it costly for a President to avoid reconsidering the basis for his action. For example, citizen groups, such as those concerned with a change in China policy, may have an impact simply by keeping their proposals on the public agenda. A President may be compelled to reconsider a problem even though he could not overtly be forced to alter the prevailing policy.

In foreign affairs we may be approaching the stage where knowledge is power. There is a tremendous receptivity to good ideas in Washington. Most anyone who can present a convincing rationale for dealing with a hard world finds a ready audience. The best way to convince Presidents to follow a desired policy is to show that it might work. A man like McNamara thrives because he performs; he comes up with answers he can defend. It is, to be sure, extremely difficult to devise good policies or to predict their consequences accurately. Nor is it easy to convince others that a given policy is superior to other alternatives. But it is the way to influence with Presidents. For if they are convinced that the current policy is best, the likelihood of gaining sufficient force to compel a change is quite small. The man who can build better foreign policies will find Presidents beating a path to his door.

FURTHER READING SUGGESTED BY THE AUTHOR

The Common Defense, by Samuel P. Huntington. New York: Columbia University Press, 1963. The best study of presidential participation in the making of defense policy.

Congress and the Presidency, by Nelson W. Polsby. Englewood Cliffs, New Jersey: Prentice-Hall, 1965. A fine short study of executive-legislative relationships.

Mass and Attentive Opinion on Nuclear Weapons Tests and Fallout, 1954–1963

Eugene J. Rosi

American policy on nuclear-weapons testing from March 1954, when the fission-fusion-fission bomb blanketed a large area of the Pacific with fallout, to August 1963, when the partial test-ban treaty was signed, was made within a context conditioned by domestic public opinion. Public opinion was hailed by some advocates of test cessation for bringing about the suspension of tests in 1958 and 1963; it was condemned for the same reasons by some opponents of test suspension, who criticized policy makers for bowing to its demands.

This study investigated public opinion on testing and fallout as it was reflected in national opinion surveys over the decade.[1] The intention was to characterize opinion on these issues and, hopefully, to shed some light on opinion-policy relationships. An attempt was made to differentiate between the mass public and the "attentive public" of Almond's model,[2] that more informed and analytical audience which has seldom been empirically located and traced on a single issue over a period of years.

The discussion will proceed as follows: first, general opinion and the events judged to be significant (special attention was paid to the pronouncements of the President), with a brief structural breakdown according to sex, age, region, education, and political party; second, information and opinion on radioactive fallout; third, an attempt to depict the opinions of the attentive public; and, finally, inferences and speculative observations.

GENERAL OPINION

This section presents general opinion within a setting of significant events, thereby laying the groundwork for subsequent conclusions and

Reprinted by permission from the *Public Opinion Quarterly*, Vol. XXIX, No. 2 (Summer 1965), pp. 280–285, 296–297.

[1] The opinions of interest groups, mass media, and various elite individuals will not be examined; for such an investigation from 1954–1958, see the writer's Ph.D. thesis ("Public Opinion and Foreign Policy: Non-governmental American Opinion Concerning the Cessation of Nuclear Weapons Tests 1954–58," Columbia University, 1964, unpublished), from which part of the present study was derived.

The analysis is based chiefly on responses to questions from 18 national opinion surveys, conducted by the American Institute of Public Opinion (AIPO, 13 surveys); National Opinion Research Center (NORC, 4 surveys); and the Survey Research Center (SRC, 1 survey).

[2] Gabriel Almond, *The American People and Foreign Policy*, New York: Harcourt, Brace, 1950; Praeger, 1960.

inferences. Two generalizations about national opinion are suggested by an examination of the accompanying chart and table:

1. From 1954 to 1958 the American public seemed to differentiate between multilateral and unilateral test cessation (i.e. cessation by agreement of all the nuclear powers or by the United States alone without such an agreement), strongly opposing unilateral American cessation while generally approving, by fairly large majorities, a multilateral agreement.

2. Numerous and wide fluctuations of opinion occurred: (a) shortly after the 1956 presidential election, approval of a multilateral agreement dropped twenty points to a minority, only to climb back to a majority the following April; (b) in November 1959, 77 per cent of the people approved a continuation of the testing moratorium that had begun the year before; (c) in mid-1961, attitudes plummeted to disapproval of continued cessation; (d) in November 1961 and January 1962, the nation was evenly divided on the issue of America's resuming atmospheric tests; (e) two months later, 67 per cent of the public favored resumption of such

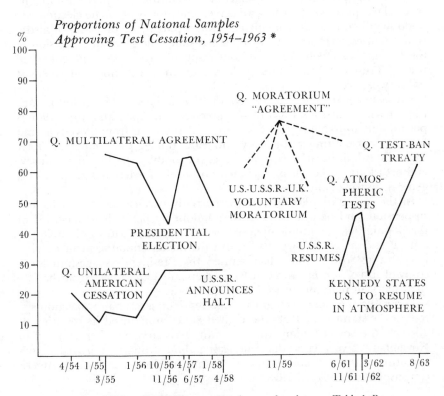

*Proportions of National Samples Approving Test Cessation, 1954–1963 ***

Based on AIPO and NORC surveys. For the complete data, see Table 1. Responses to "resumption" questions in 1961-1962 have been reversed.

tests; (f) and seventeen months after that (August 1963), a majority swung to approval of the partial test-ban treaty.

These swings in opinion must now be placed in the context of events. Between 1954 and early 1956, the public could scarcely have understood the implications of test cessation. Most likely, unilateral suspension was equated with unilateral disarmament or surrender of the nuclear weapons that were the primary defense of the West; the main appeal of a test-ban agreement may have been the need for co-operation in view of the special nature of the atomic bomb or the overtones of the word "agreement." Cues supporting both positions could have been derived from the Administration's emphasis on the importance of nuclear weapons, continued testing, the insignificance of fallout, and its goal of a comprehensive disarmament agreement to control nuclear weapons.

The opinion shifts around election time in 1956 seemed due largely to party affiliation: during the campaign, Democratic candidate Adlai Stevenson proposed a cessation that, in its original form, could have been interpreted as unilateral American suspension; the Republicans tended to oppose cessation in any form that did not provide "fool-proof" inspection and comprehensive disarmament. In addition to partisanship, the reversal of opinion concerning an agreement shortly after the election was undoubtedly due to the convincing "expert judgment" of the Administration on an esoteric subject; the Suez crisis and the Russian repression of the Hungarian revolution; and, as a result of these crises, the enhanced role of President Eisenhower as leader of all the people and foremost military expert.[3]

Partisanship subsided in the months that followed. The swing in attitudes back toward approval of an agreement in April and June 1957 is possibly attributable to the dissociation of the issue from Stevenson and from the extremism exhibited by both sides during the campaign. Moreover, the Administration appeared more favorable: the President on several occasions in the spring included approval of a test ban as part of a general disarmament agreement.

In the spring of 1958, despite (or partially because of) the Soviet test suspension, and despite concern over fallout by more than one-third of the population, the public opposed American test cessation 61 to 28 per cent. President Eisenhower had called the Soviet announcement a "gimmick." The Soviet Union had refused the President's suggestion for a study of inspection measures (it later accepted it) and rejected in the UN the American plan for inspection in the Arctic.

Following the Geneva technical conference on a test-ban inspection system in the summer of 1958, the United States announced its cessation of all tests; the Soviet Union, after resuming tests in September, stopped in November. A year later the American public strongly approved a continuation of the test moratorium, in contrast to the disapproval of American suspension in April 1958.

---

[3] During the campaign, large percentages of "Don't Know" (DK) responses appeared. Before October 1956 the public had opined with ease; the "No Opinion" responses only hinted at the extent of uninformed and unstructured opinion.

TABLE 1

National Opinion on Test Cessation, 1954–1963
(in per cent)

Date	Unilateral American[a]				Multilateral[b]			
	For	Against	DK	(N)	For	Against	DK	·(N)
4/ 6/54[c]	21	72	7	(1,435)				
1/21/55[d]	11	84	5	(1,209)				
3/11/55[d, e]	15	80	5	(1,225)	65	28	7	(1,225)
1/26/56[d, e]	12	83	5	(1,238)	62	29	9	(1,238)
10/16/56[c]	28	53	19	(1,049)				
11/15/56[d]					42	52	6	(1,286)
4/23/57[c]					64	28	8	(1,602)
6/25/57[c]					64	22	14	(1,515)
7/16/57[c, f]								
1/22/58[c]					49	36	15	(1,543)
4/14/58[c]	28	61	11	(1,433)				

Date	For	Against	DK	(N)
11/10/59[c, g]	77	10	13	(1,636)
6/21/61[c, h]	27	53	27	(1,625)
11/15/61[c, i]	44	42	14	(1,523)
1/ 9/62[c, i]	45	45	10	(1,618)
3/ 6/62[c, i]	25	67	8	(1,600)
8/13/63[c, j]	61	18	21	(1,246)

[a] Most questions asked something like "Should the United States stop nuclear (atomic, hydrogen bomb) tests?" or "continue tests?"

[b] Most questions asked something like the phrase in footnote a, but added, "if all other nations, including Russia, stop."

[c] Date sent out by the American Institute of Public Opinion (AIPO).

[d] Date sent out by the National Opinion Research Center (NORC).

[e] This question first asked if the United States should continue tests, then asked those who wished tests to continue if they favored an agreement by all countries, including the United States and Russia, to stop tests. The total in favor of the multilateral ban here includes those who stated their approval first of unilateral American cessation, the assumption being that they would also approve of an agreement.

[f] This ambiguous question did not specify multilateral or unilateral cessation; the results: 40 per cent for (5 per cent qualified); 43 per cent against (3 per cent qualified); 17 per cent DK.

[g] The testing moratorium was misleadingly called an "agreement" in this question.

[h] ". . . should the U.S. resume tests at this time?"; responses reversed.

[i] ". . . U.S. should or should not start tests in the atmosphere"; responses reversed.

[j] Those who heard or read about "the agreement with Russia to have a partial ban on the testing of nuclear weapons" (78 per cent of the sample) were asked, "Do you think the Senate should vote approval of this ban or not?"

Several reasons for the shift to approval suggest themselves. The Administration was continuing to endorse the moratorium, albeit cautiously, conditional upon the success of the Geneva talks, and this may have given the cessation a kind of official sanction. Additional support might have stemmed from the question wording, which mistakenly called the moratorium a Soviet-American "agreement" (presumably the public would not be sophisticated enough to consider the implications of "tacit" agreements).

By June 1961, however, the majority had reversed, now favoring resumption of American testing 53 to 27 per cent. Tension was mounting over the Berlin crisis following Chairman Khrushchev's June ultimatum, and public doubts were expressed by the Kennedy Administration over adhering to a test halt without progress toward a treaty or assurance that Russia was not testing clandestinely. The President ordered a scientific inquiry to determine whether evidence indicated a Soviet violation of the moratorium.

With the passage of four months, the issue became the resumption of atmospheric tests by the United States, since underground operations had begun after the Soviet Union resumed tests in the atmosphere in September. The American public was split evenly. Significant events included Soviet explosions up to 56 megatons, the Berlin crisis, and President Kennedy's order for preparations to test in the atmosphere if it became necessary. Radioactive fallout was apparently not decisive at this time, since a majority of the people (61 per cent) did not consider it a danger. Opinion remained deadlocked in January 1962, as the Geneva talks seemed headed for a dead end.

But in March 1962 a large majority (67 per cent) emerged in favor of American testing in the atmosphere. A survey had been made shortly after President Kennedy's national television address announcing the U.S. decision to resume atmospheric explosions.

The final reversal of opinion occurred seventeen months later, when, in August 1963, a majority (61 vs. 18 per cent) approved Senate ratification of the partial test-ban treaty signed in Moscow. The President had called the treaty a "victory for mankind" and the Administration strongly supported it in Senate hearings being conducted during the survey interviewing period. . . .

5. These findings have implications for the opinion-policy relationship. To a considerable extent, the major fluctuations in opinion — from disapproval of American cessation in April 1958 to approval in November 1959 to disapproval in June 1961–March 1962 to approval in August 1963 — seem explainable as responses to cues from political elites as they debated and modified policy (coupled with events and elite interpretation of events). Mass opinion did not "enfeeble . . . the executive [at the] . . . critical junctures," which usually occurred in this century according to Walter Lippmann,[4] and force the United States to stop tests contrary to

4 Walter Lippmann, *The Public Philosophy*, New York: New American Library, 1956, pp. 19, 23. For a critique of his approach, see David B. Truman, "The American System in Crisis," *Political Science Quarterly*, Vol. 84, December 1959, pp. 481–497.

national security interests (recall, for example, that the Administration decided to halt all tests in 1958 when the public had recently opposed cessation unless by agreement). Nor was public opinion ahead of its leaders.[5] If anything, in this case — one with greater technical ramifications than many foreign policy issues — the public would very likely have looked to experts (governmental and nongovernmental) for guidance more than they would on less esoteric domestic issues. The Administration was apparently able to mobilize opinion in support of policy, whether the policy was to resume or halt nuclear tests (e.g. (1) the strong approval of test resumption in March 1962 after several months of closely divided general opinion, with the Administration evidently reaching and reversing the opinions of even the most inattentive groups; (2) the approval of the test-ban treaty in August 1963 and the communication of its limited scope).

To conclude, mass opinion did not compel the government to be "too pacifist in peace"[6] at the "critical junctures" examined here. Instead, the attentive public seemed responsive to discriminating leadership, being more flexible, less volatile, and less prone to absolute means and goals. While the greatest support for policy stemmed from the informed sector that attended the elite debate, there was generally support also from majorities of the inattentive mass, and radical cleavages did not occur.

To the extent that the permissiveness of public opinion in this case is generalizable to foreign-policy-making in the nuclear age,[7] the responsibility rests heavily upon elites — political, communications, interest group, individual — to offer relevant criticism of Administration policies and to generate new alternatives. For both policy and the democratic process would seem best served if the public is mobilized in support of policy that has benefited from the intelligent debate of governmental and nongovernmental elites rather than policy that has been decreed by either philosopher-kings or "the Queen of the World" (public opinion).[8]

[5] Reviewing the foreign policy attitudes of the American people in *American Credos* (New York: Harper, 1962), Stuart Chase wrote that "the United States government followed the wish of the city-dwellers and resumed testing" (59 per cent of the respondents in New York City, Chicago, and Los Angeles favored American testing in August 1961).

[6] Lippmann, *op. cit.*, p. 24. Similarly, it may perhaps be inferred that when faced with limited conflict the public may be less inclined to compel the government to be, in Lippmann's words, "too bellicose in war."

[7] Other instances of permissiveness in recent public opinion have been noted by Bernard C. Cohen, *The Political Process and Foreign Policy: The Making of the Japanese Peace Settlement*, Princeton, N.J.: Princeton University Press, 1957; Samuel P. Huntington, *The Common Defense*, New York: Columbia University Press, 1961; Almond, *op. cit.*; Campbell *et al.*, *op. cit.*; and Key, *op. cit.*

[8] Pascal's phrase, as quoted in Key, *op. cit.*, p. 7.

Presidential Action in Congressional Nominations

William H. Riker and William Bast

In his recent work, *Presidential Power*, Richard E. Neustadt poses the question of what a President "can do to make his own will felt within his own Administration." [1] This question, so reminiscent of the "prince-books" or "kings' mirrors" of early modern times, is wholly appropriate again in this century, which has witnessed the remarkable and world-wide revival of popular expectations of effective executive leadership. For political scientists with a practical interest in good government, questions similar to Neustadt's are probably more appropriate than those questions of constitutional structure and political behavior with which they have conventionally been concerned. At least for us it was a conviction of the need for more concentrated executive power that informed the inquiry reported here into an especially sensitive area of presidential action.

I. Presidential Endorsements of Candidates in Congressional Primaries

The constitutional separation of powers, which renders it difficult for Presidents to influence congressmen, is only partially modified by party allegiance. As Neustadt properly remarks, the continuing effectiveness of the forms of this eighteenth-century constitutional theory is due to the fact that the President and his congressional partisans are elected in different ways:

> The White House has too small a share in nominating Congress-men, and Congress has too little weight in nominating Presidents for party to erase their constitutional separation. Party links are stronger than is frequently supposed, but nominating processes assure the separation.[2]

This separation is in sharp contrast to the unification often achieved through party control in parliamentary regimes. In England, for example, the Prime Minister has a great deal to say about who gets nominated for the safe seats of his party and thereby can often exercise a continuing control over both those members of his party who have such seats and those who would like to have them.

While American Presidents cannot easily exercise such control over congressmen, they have often tried to do so. In the sense that they attempt

---

Printed by permission of the authors.

[1] Richard E. Neustadt, *Presidential Power* (New York: John Wiley & Sons, 1960), p. vii.

[2] *Ibid*, p. 34.

to formulate a popular ideology to which others will adhere simply because it is popular they are in an indirect way also attempting to control the kind of people who are nominated for Congress. But in addition to this general ideological leadership, many of the more capable or ambitious or activist Presidents have tried to influence nominations directly. Ever since Jefferson's time, Presidents have urged their personal or ideological allies to seek nominations and often have helped them to form local coalitions for this purpose. From Jackson's time until the early twentieth century, many Presidents extensively manipulated patronage to affect congressional nominations. But in recent years, especially since the passage of the Seventeenth Amendment and later the Hatch Act, such manipulation has been more difficult. Not only is there relatively less patronage and not only is the civil service somewhat isolated from party politics, but also the character of the nominating process has changed. What formerly was done in caucus and convention, where coalitions could be constructed in the privacy of the hotel room, is now done in primary elections. While the President is not debarred from sending agents to help make alliances for his ideological friends whom he hopes to nominate for Congress, often his influence is non-existent unless he speaks out publicly. And this he is loath to do for reasons that we will examine in detail.

Between 1913 and 1960 there were — so far as we can discover — 39 instances in which Presidents have publicly endorsed candidates in congressional primaries of their own parties. Since two of the instances were re-endorsements of already endorsed candidates, in fact there were only 37 public interventions in primaries. In each party during this period there were about 12,000 nominations, mostly by primary elections. Thirty-seven is only an infinitesimal fraction of these. Even if one considers only the thirty-one instances in which Presidents endorsed candidates in senatorial primaries, this number is less than 5 per cent of the approximately 800 senatorial nominations in each party. Even subtracting from 800 the nominations made in years of presidential elections in which the incumbent was not a candidate, 31 is still less than 5 per cent of the senatorial nominations. It seems fair to say, therefore, that Presidents have been deeply reluctant to attempt, at least publicly, to control congressional nominations.

Considering that, as Neustadt observes, the curtailment of presidential power by the separation of branches is maintained as a viable constitutional form owing to the President's lack of control over congressional nominations, considering further that the acquisition of control over nominations would greatly enhance the President's power to influence the whole process of government, and considering finally that Presidents seem to have been exceptionally reluctant to attempt to exercise control over congressional nominations, we are led to ask two questions:

1. Why have Presidents so seldom endorsed candidates in congressional primaries? and

2. Is there any way, given the present state of American politics, that a

President might obtain some control over congressional nominations in his own party?

While the first question probably cannot be answered definitively, some of the compelling considerations can be surmised from historical and analytical evidence. As for the second question, which is a matter of practical invention or political engineering, only Presidents themselves can answer it, although the concerned political scientists may make suggestions on the basis of an examination of the outcome of instances of presidential endorsements.

The basic data for answering both questions is, of course, information about public presidential activity in congressional primaries. This we have obtained by examining all entries under both presidential and state politics in the index of the *New York Times* from 1913 to the present. Whenever an entry in the index even hinted at public presidential endorsement of a candidate in a primary, we examined the news story. If it recorded such an endorsement, we then examined the regional press. A summary of the thirty-nine instances of endorsement that we discovered is set forth in the Appendix. The same material is arranged somewhat differently and even more summarily in Table I. Incidentally, we used 1913 as the base year for that was the year the Seventeenth Amendment became operative and thereby took senatorial nominations out of the privacy of the legislative caucus and into (usually) the public arena of the primary.[3]

II. The Reasons for Presidential Reluctance

There undoubtedly exists an old and persuasive tradition in American politics that a congressional nomination is exclusively the business of the state or district the congressman represents. The constitutional provision that each congressman be a resident of the state he represents was undoubtedly intended to prevent that centralized control of nominations that since Tudor days had been a striking feature of the English political system. Similarly, the almost never violated tradition, which seems to have been in force from 1788 onwards, that Representatives be residents of the districts they represent seems to be an elaborating detail on the constitutional provision about residence.

[3] Several writers have recognized the crucial character of presidential endorsements in congressional primaries, especially in connection with the so-called purge of 1938: William H. Riker, *Democracy in the United States* (New York, 1953), pp. 285–93; Austin Ranney and Willmoore Kendall, *Democracy and the American Party System* (New York, 1956), pp. 286–9; V. O. Key, Jr., *Politics, Parties, and Pressure Groups* (New York, 1958, 4th ed.), pp. 484–7; J. B. Shannon, "Presidential Politics in the South," *Journal of Politics*, Vol. 1 (1938), pp. 146–70, 278–300; and James M. Burns, *Roosevelt: The Lion and the Fox* (New York, 1956), pp. 360–64. None of these discussions is completely systematic, however, and none is therefore able to throw much light on our questions, especially since they emphasize the purge of 1938, which is the most dramatic but not the most typical incident in the series. Surprisingly, Neustadt does not discuss the maneuver of presidential endorsement at all, possibly because it did not occur dramatically during the two administrations he studied in detail.

TABLE 1

*Success and Failure of Presidentially Endorsed
Candidates in Congressional Primaries, 1913–1959*

Presidential Action	Candidate Succeeded*	Candidate Failed
President Endorsed Incumbent	4 (Tillman, 1918); 8 (Lewis, 1918); 10 (Tillman, 1918); 11 (Freinghuysen, 1922); 13 Reese, 1930); 16 (Pepper, 1938); 17 (Thomas, 1938); 19 (Bulkley, 1938); 20 (Thomas, 1938); 21 (Barkley, 1938); 22 (Caraway, 1938); 37 (Kilgore, 1952)	12 (Lenroot, 1926); 23 (McAdoo, 1938); 30 (Wheeler, 1946)
President Endorsed Incumbent's Opponent	5 (Slayden, 1918); 6 (Vardaman, 1918); 9 (Hardwick, 1918); 27 (Fay, 1938); 31 (Slaughter, 1946)	7 (Huddleston, 1918); 18 (Gillette, 1938); 24 (George, 1938); 25 (Lewis, 1938); 26 (Smith, 1938)
President Endorsed a Candidate when no Incumbent was in the Primary	1 (Underwood, 1913); 2 (Palmer, 1914); 3 (Ford, 1918); 14 (Burke, 1934); 15 (Fish, 1936); 28 (Johnson, 1941); 29 (Gillette, 1944); 33 (Carrol, 1950); 34 (Loveland, 1950); 35 (Disalle, 1950); 36 (Granger, 1950); 39 (McKay, 1956)	32 (Hennings, 1950); 38 (Symington, 1952)

* Each entry consists of a reference number to an item in the Appendix, plus, parenthetically, the name of the chief congressional figure and the date of the endorsement.

Presidents have generally felt the force of this tradition. In nearly all the thirty-nine instances we have collected, Presidents in one way or another apologized for intervening in a "local" affair. When Wilson endorsed a candidate in the Georgia senatorial primary of 1918 as part of a general program of eliminating Southern Democrats not sufficiently enthusiastic about the war, he still contrived to make it appear that the impulse for the endorsement originated in Georgia, not in the White House. Thus the endorsement was given in response to an (undoubtedly inspired) request from the editor of the *Atlanta Constitution*:

> Your letter, I observe, is addressed to me by you in your capacity as a member of the National Democratic Committee, and I assume that it is proper for me to answer the question in the interests of the party as a national unit. . . . I have never undertaken and I would not presume to undertake to dictate to the voters of any state the choices they must make, but when

my views have been sought by those who seem to have the right
to seek them, I have not hesitated to give them. . . .[4]

Most of the other endorsements Wilson made during that summer had
the same form, a local request, followed by a joint explanation and endorsement. Similarly, when Franklin Roosevelt began the purge of 1938,
he prefaced his action with a fireside chat that was both a justification
and an apology:

> As head of the Democratic party . . . charged with carrying out
> the definitely liberal declaration of principles set forth in the
> 1936 Democratic platform, I feel I have every right to speak in
> those few instances where there may be a clear issue between the
> candidates for a Democratic nomination involving those princi-
> ples or involving a clear misuse of my own name.[5]

The earlier Roosevelt, who was, if anything, more eager than his younger
cousin to acquire power over his congressional partisans, drew back quite
sharply when it came to "interfering" in "local" nominations. Much as he
disliked Senator Teller (Democrat, Colorado), T.R. would do nothing to
help Colorado Republicans agree on a candidate. Perhaps as a result, a
few Republican legislators defected to Teller, who was then reelected.
Writing to his close friend, Philip B. Stewart of Denver, Roosevelt said,
"Of course, now [since his elevation to the presidency over a year previ-
ously] I can take no part of any shape or kind in the senatorial contest.
The President has no business to interfere." [6] Furthermore, although he
was a constant behind-the-scenes manipulator of New York politics, although indeed one of his great achievements as President was to wrest
control of the New York Republican party from the Platt stalwarts, still
in 1906 at the height of his self-assurance and popularity T.R. refused to
speak out publicly for Hughes for the New York Republican gubernatorial nomination:

> Most of the people whom I have consulted feel very strongly
> that such action as you suggest [a public endorsement of Hughes]
> would be a harm instead of a benefit. . . . They feel that I have
> gone as far as I can safely go, and that an utterance from us
> [Roosevelt or his Secretary of War Elihu Root] would have di-
> rectly the opposite effect of what is anticipated.[7]

This persistent reluctance by Presidents to intervene in congressional
primaries is matched by a jealous defense of local autonomy by, of course,

---

[4] *New York Times*, August 12, 1918, p. 9; *Atlanta Constitution*, August 12, 1918, p. 1.

[5] *The Public Papers and Addresses of Franklin D. Roosevelt* [*1938*], vol. 7 (New
York, 1941), p. 399.

[6] Letter of November 24, 1902, *The Letters of Theodore Roosevelt*, ed. E. E. Morison,
vol. 3 (Cambridge, Mass.: 1951–54), p. 378.

[7] *Ibid.*, vol. 5, p. 466. True, this was a gubernatorial rather than congressional
campaign; but, at least with respect to a President's own state, the tradition of non-
interference does not sharply distinguish between them.

those whom the President might oppose. When President Hoover endorsed Representative Reese of Knoxville in 1930 (see Appendix, item 13), Reese's opponent in the primary responded with a blast of rhetoric reminiscent of an earlier era of American politics:

> The time has not yet come in this district when any man, before offering himself for office, must make a pilgrimage to the distant shrine of a great political boss and humbly climb up the golden stairway to the throne and kiss His Majesty's great toe and beg to be annointed with the privilege of asking the voters of his district to support him. . . . I am taking my case to the people of this district. They know me and I trust them.[8]

A few years later, when the White House endorsed his opponent, Senator Gilette of Iowa's (see Appendix, item 18) most telling argument was that "Tommy Corcoran and his crowd of non-Iowans" were trying to tell the people of Iowa how to vote; and Georgia Senator George described Roosevelt's attempt to purge him by endorsing Lawrence Camp (see Appendix, item 24) as "a second march through Georgia." [9]

Both presidential reluctance and the sense of outrage displayed when Presidents do actually endorse in congressional primaries combine to demonstrate the viability of the tradition that congressional nominations are local affairs into which Presidents ought not to intervene. To demonstrate that the tradition exists does not, of course, explain why it does. We can, however, offer some explanation of its genesis and persistence, without, naturally, having any absolute evidence that our explanation is correct.

The kind of federalism invented in Philadelphia in the summer of 1787 consisted of the creation of a central government endowed with adequate authority to make and carry out national policy along with a bribe to the local politicians who would give up power when the new central government came into existence. This bribe was the guarantee that local politicians would both continue to have offices and continue, despite the transfer of duties and functions to the center, to have a considerable voice in the selection of national officials. The constitutional provisions for the election of the President, for the election of Senators, for the residence of congressmen, and the implied provisions for control of the process of election by state legislatures were part of the content of the bribe.[10] Although these provisions have been greatly modified, especially with

[8] *Knoxville Sunday Journal*, July 27, 1930, p. 4. The orator was Sam W. Price and the district was near Buncombe County, North Carolina.

[9] *New York Times*, June 3, 1938, p. 2. In a dramatic story of Roosevelt's attack on George, the *Atlanta Constitution* wailed, "Never before had a President entered Georgia and called for the defeat of one of its leading political figures." The journalist perhaps did not know that his own editor had arranged for Wilson to do almost the same thing in 1918. See the *Atlanta Constitution*, August 12, 1938, p. 1.

[10] For an elaboration of this explanation of American federalism, see William H. Riker, *Federalism* (Boston, 1965), *passim;* William H. Riker, *Soldiers of the States* (Washington, 1958), Chaps. 1–2; and William H. Riker, "The Senate and American Federalism," *American Political Science Review,* vol. 49 (1955), pp. 452–69.

respect to the election of Presidents and Senators, the basic content of the bribe still exists today. For example, President Eisenhower was moved to remark after five years in office, "There are no national parties, but forty-eight state parties and they have a right to put in office whom they want." [11] While our kind of federalism allows for repeated centralization of function, it nevertheless maintains a variety of political independence at the periphery. And it is this independence, we believe, that accounts for the presidential reluctance to engage in nominating congressmen.

Given the political independence of states in our federalism, consider the position of any President who endorses a partisan in a congressional primary. By the very act of endorsement, he transfers the popular decision from one on the candidates to one on himself. Thus, endorsement renders presidential prestige a subject for electoral decision in a contest in which the President himself has neither a legal nor a traditional role. No prudent man, we believe, would lightly risk prestige in this way, especially considering, as Neustadt points out, that prestige, imprecise as it is, is still one of the main components of presidential power.[12] If a presidentially endorsed candidate wins both the primary and general election, the President may perhaps enhance his prestige. But if the candidate loses either one, the President is quite likely to tarnish himself. Assuming all candidates have an equal chance of winning, the *a priori* probability that a presidentially endorsed candidate will win both elections is at most one-fourth and may be much less. Historically, presidentially endorsed candidates have won both elections, seventeen out of thirty-seven times or about 46 per cent. If the odds that endorsed candidates would win were somewhat better than even, many Presidents might frequently have endorsed. But, probably owing to the structure of our federalism, the odds are not very good; and this fact undoubtedly partly explains the presidential reluctance.

Complicating all this, moreover, is the structure of our electoral system. A non-incumbent candidate for President can hardly endorse persons in congressional primaries, for the presidential candidate has not ensured his own candidacy until after most congressional primaries are held. Furthermore an incumbent presidential candidate for renomination may often and justifiably fear that endorsements in congressional campaigns may hurt his own chances. Hence, regardless of the odds on endorsed candidates, most Presidents have apparently felt that they can endorse only in congressional elections occurring in years without presidential elections. Thus, thirty-two of the thirty-seven endorsements we counted occurred during mid-term elections.

Our explanation of presidential reluctance to endorse is thus twofold. Both the structure of our federalism and the temporal involvement of congressional elections with presidential ones render Presidents reluctant to enter congressional primaries publicly.

11 *New York Times,* October 12, 1957, p. 1.
12 Neustadt, *op. cit.,* Chap. 5.

III. Can a President Influence Congressional Nominations?

From the point of view of states' righters — whether racial or commercial conservatives, both of whom fear national action — and from the point of view of exponents of the separation of powers — who are conservatives of the same two sorts who fear governmental decisions of any kind — the tradition that excludes Presidents from congressional nominations is a morally valuable constitutional restraint. Not surprisingly, therefore, since 1913 the Presidents with conservative ideology have displayed far less interest in manipulating nominations than have those with a more radical orientation. Harding, Coolidge, Hoover, and Eisenhower publicly endorsed candidates in Republican congressional primaries only once each. Wilson, on the other hand, publicly entered ten Democratic congressional primaries; Franklin Roosevelt entered sixteen; and Truman entered nine. While complete information on the behavior of earlier Presidents in this century is not available, it appears that this dichotomy holds true for them also. The conservative Taft attempted to manipulate only two nominations,[13] while the radical Theodore Roosevelt, so one infers from his letters, maneuvered behind the scenes in perhaps dozens of congressional nominations.

In this essay we reject the moral view of the advocates of states' rights and the separation of powers. We adopt instead the morality implicit in Neustadt's work and in the behavior of Wilson, Truman, and the two Roosevelts. In this latter and activist morality, increases in the President's power to compel congressional decisions are regarded as morally desirable and the constitutional tradition that restricts presidential participation in primaries is interpreted as an impediment to good constitutional structure. Adopting, as we do, this activist morality, our practical question is: Can a President evade the restrictive tradition that keeps him out of congressional primaries and lessens his ability to influence congressmen?

Manifestly, a President can force himself into any and all congressional nominations simply by announcing a preference among candidates. Such announcements are unlikely to awe congressmen, however, unless they also believe that the President's actions significantly influence the outcome of primaries. Hence, to break the restrictive tradition, a President must not only participate, but also participate successfully. "Successfully," means, of course, both that the President's candidate wins and that congressmen infer — whether correctly or incorrectly is irrelevant — that the voters were influenced by the President's announcement. So our question really is: How can a President achieve a reputation for successfully influencing congressional nominations?

Historically, Presidents have tried in two ways, clandestinely and publicly. The clandestine method is to send emissaries, who are often well supplied with the currency of high politics — judgeships, donors of funds, organizers of campaigns, etc. — to participate in local campaigns. The

---

[13] See Riker, *Democracy in the United States,* p. 292.

advantage of this method is that if the supported candidate wins, the exaggerations of rumor may gain a President credit for far more than he actually accomplishes, while at the same time, if the candidate loses, the President's prestige is probably not diminished. This method has two disadvantages, however. The currency of high politics is today in limited supply, and the decision in primaries is sufficiently public that the significance of clandestine aid is always disputable. No ambitious and activist President can ignore clandestine methods. Indeed, all of them in this century have apparently used them to a considerable degree. Nevertheless, the drawbacks of the method are today such that a reputation for influence can probably be acquired only by the public method of endorsement. So we reduce the question further: How can a President gain a reputation for successful endorsements?

To answer this question, we distinguish three kinds of endorsements: (1) endorsements of incumbents; (2) endorsements of opponents of incumbents; and (3) endorsements of candidates in primaries in which incumbents are not running. Further, we point out that in the present state of American politics, the incumbent has a considerable advantage, except perhaps when he is very old or is a first-termer who has not yet acquired leadership in his state or district.[14] Assuming then that incumbents have a great advantage, the effects of endorsements may be analyzed in six cases.

Case 1a: A presidentially endorsed incumbent wins the primary. Since the presumption is that the incumbent will win anyway, the fact of endorsement will probably be thought to have relatively little significance. Only if it is widely believed that the incumbent is likely to lose his seat can the President be given much credit for the success. This may have occurred in the Kentucky Democratic senatorial primary of 1938, when Senator Barkley, although endorsed, barely beat off the challenge of Governor Chandler.[15] (See Appendix, item 21.)

Case 1b: A presidentially endorsed incumbent loses the primary. Because of the presumption of success for the incumbent, the fact that he loses may well reflect negatively on the President's prestige. It will be said, for example, that the President was too weak to help a friend or that the voters definitively rejected the President himself. This clearly occurred in 1926 when Coolidge reluctantly and ineffectually endorsed Senator Lenroot of Wisconsin who promptly lost the primary by a wide margin. (See Appendix, item 12.) On the other hand, Senator McAdoo's failure in California in 1938 passed largely unnoticed among the more dramatic events of the purge. (See Appendix, item 23.) And Truman's defense of Senator Wheeler in 1946 probably did not detract from the President's prestige when Wheeler lost since Truman then had little prestige to lose. (See Appendix, item 30.)

Case 2a: A presidentially endorsed opponent of an incumbent wins the primary. Since the presumption of success lies with the incumbent, his opponent's victory may well be regarded as quite surprising and thereby

14 Key, *op. cit.,* pp. 489 ff.
15 Shannon, *op. cit.*

will reflect much credit on the President. It may be believed — whether rightly or wrongly is irrelevant — that the President provided the margin of victory. This seems to have occurred for Wilson in the events mentioned it items 6 and 9 of the Appendix. Fay's victory in 1938, however, did not enhance Roosevelt's prestige greatly for it was overshadowed by other events in the purge of that year. (See Appendix, item 27.) Nor did Axtell's victory in 1946 greatly enhance Truman's prestige since the primary was in Truman's own district where he might be expected to have much influence. Furthermore Axtell lost the general election. (See Appendix, item 31.)

Case 2b: A presidentially endorsed opponent of an incumbent loses the primary. Since the presumption of success lies with the incumbent, his victory does not necessarily reflect great discredit on the President. Wilson was apparently not greatly hurt by Huddleston's victory in Birmingham in 1918. (See Appendix, item 7.) On the other hand, Roosevelt certainly did lose some prestige by the success of incumbents he opposed in 1938. (See Appendix, items 18, 24, 25, and 26.) Yet this loss derives from some of the unique features of the purges rather than from the inherent nature of the events themselves. After much hesitation, Roosevelt undertook the purge with the maximum amount of publicity, aiming, presumably, to unseat a number of partisans. After a brave beginning, the purge rather fizzled out and in the end only the least important of the five endorsed opponents of incumbents won. Quite probably it was the bad batting average after so much publicity that hurt Roosevelt in these instances.

Case 3a: A presidentially endorsed candidate wins in a primary without an incumbent. In this case there are no guide lines for expectations about the outcome. Since the main unusual feature of such a primary is the President's endorsement, he may well be popularly credited with his candidate's victory. Of course, if there is only one candidate the credit is trivial. (See Appendix, items 2, 15, and 29.)

Case 3b: A presidentially endorsed candidate loses in a primary without an incumbent. As the exact converse of *Case 3a,* here it may be expected that the President will lose some prestige.

Having distinguished these cases, we are now able to lay down some elementary canons of behavior for a President who desires to win a reputation for successfully influencing primaries.

Our first canon is that a President ought quite frequently to try to influence primaries either clandestinely or publicly. The most striking feature of Table I is, we believe, the paucity of entries, only thirty-nine events in all (really only thirty-seven, for two pairs relate to the same primary). Presidents have been too cautiously bound by tradition, unaware that sometimes — even with bad planning — their predecessors have influenced a primary.

Our second canon is that a President ought to avoid *Case 1* endorsements. If his endorsed candidate is successful, the President is given little credit, as indeed happened in 1938. The purge of that year is almost universally interpreted as a failure although five of the six endorsed incumbents were renominated. (See Appendix, items 16, 17, 19, 20, 21, 22, and 23.) On the other hand, if the President's candidate fails, the failure may be credited to the President rather than the candidate, as happened when Coolidge endorsed Lenroot. (See Appendix, item 12.) In short, in *Case 1* endorsements, the President stands to lose very much and gain almost nothing.

It has been the fashion among political scientists to poke fun at the political ineptitude of President Eisenhower. Yet in one instance, at least, he showed a fine sense of political strategy. Despite substantial pressure to endorse Senator Wiley in Wisconsin in 1956 when he was in great danger of losing the nomination to a Representative of the McCarthy wing of the Republican Party, the President refused to endorse his fairly reliable congressional supporter when the state Republican convention endorsed Wiley's opponent. Shortly before this, however, Eisenhower had publicly endorsed Secretary McKay in the Oregon Republican senatorial primary in which no incumbent was involved. The contrast between the endorsement and the refusal to endorse suggests that Eisenhower believed (a) that, if Wiley won, the President would have exactly the same influence whether or not he endorsed; (b) that, if Wiley lost after presidential endorsement, the President would have a hostile partisan in Wiley's opponent; (c) that, if McKay was endorsed and won, the President would have a reliable ally; and (d) that, if McKay lost after presidential endorsement, the winner would not greatly resent the President's endorsement of a cabinet officer. If these were Eisenhower's opinions, then his strategy was very good. It is, indeed, an excellent operative instance of our second canon of presidential behavior.

Parenthetically, it might be observed that Presidents are under great pressure to make *Case 1* endorsements, especially when the incumbent is a faithful congressional ally who faces a difficult time in the primary. Sometimes the pressure may be so great that the President cannot resist it and indeed there may even be occasions when he may not wish to. If he does decide to endorse an incumbent, however, he should do it long enough in advance and with sufficient material aid to avoid the debacle of the incumbent's defeat. Contrast Wilson's endorsement of Tillman of South Carolina in 1918 or Roosevelt's endorsement of Thomas of Oklahoma in 1938 with Coolidge's endorsement of Lenroot of Wisconsin in 1926. In the former two instances the President acted far enough in advance and with sufficient planning to force the withdrawal of the main opponent from the primary. (See Appendix, items 4, 10, 17, and 20.) In the latter instance Coolidge hesitated and fumbled, watched five of his strongest supporters in the Senate lose in primaries, and then, rather panic-stricken, ineffectually praised Lenroot in a speech that came too late to have any possible influence on the Wisconsin primary.[16] So we add to the second canon this proviso: If the President decides to violate the

16 The fallen allies were: Pepper of Pennsylvania, Cummins of Iowa, Stickney of Vermont, Stanfield of Oregon, and McKinley of Illinois. Lenroot was the last — and probably least important — of these. See the *New York Times*, May 23, 1926, p. 3; June 5, 1926, p. 3; July 11, 1926, p. 1; and Appendix, item 12.

canon, he ought to do so with planning and care and, above all, he ought not to allow last-minute considerations to move him to an imprudent position.

The third elementary canon we lay down is that in making *Case 2* and *Case 3* endorsements, a President ought to be reasonably sure that his endorsed candidate will win. If he cannot thus assure himself, he should be silent. In both categories of endorsement, the success of the candidate reflects credit on the President, while in most *3b* and *2b* instances the failure detracts from his prestige. Elementary prudence suggests, therefore, that these endorsements be made only when the President has assured himself that his candidates can win.

To justify this canon we will contrast instances of *Cases 2a* and *3a* endorsements with instances of *Cases 2b* and *3b*. What makes the difference between them? Since only Wilson, Franklin Roosevelt, and Truman made endorsements in both categories, we will examine only their experience.

In 1918, Wilson undertook to unseat several Southern Democrats who, he believed, were not supporting the war program. In a letter to a significant Democratic official of the district, Wilson denounced Representative Slayden of San Antonio. While he did not endorse a specific candidate, one of Slayden's opponents was Carlos Bee, a brother-in-law of Postmaster-General Burleson. Slayden withdrew and Bee was nominated and elected. Given the Burleson-Bee relationship, there can be hardly any doubt that all this was carefully anticipated in advance by Wilson or his advisors. (See Appendix, item 5.) By letters to prominent Mississippi Democrats, Wilson denounced Senator Vardaman whose only opponent, Pat Harrison, won the seat and held it for many years. This too was a well-prepared action, for Wilson's candidate was also endorsed by the main figures in Mississippi politics including the other Senator. (See Appendix, item 6.) In an obviously inspired and already quoted letter to Clark Howell, Wilson denounced Senator Hardwick and endorsed his opponent William J. Harris, who was nominated and elected. As in the previous case, Wilson was clearly acting in concert with important Georgia politicians. (See Appendix, item 9.) On the other hand, Wilson's one significant failure involved Representative Huddleston of Birmingham, whom Wilson denounced in a letter to a minor party official. (See Appendix, item 7.) Since Huddleston had several opponents, Wilson's inferential blessing was scattered among them in a way that could do no good. Wilson's planning was so ineffectual in this instance that, in response to his letter, the Democrats of Bessemer promptly and with apparent confusion endorsed both Wilson and Huddleston.[17] It thus appears that Wilson's candidate succeeded when the President allied with leading local politicians and concentrated his blessing on one candidate. When the President did neither of these things, his candidate failed.

The same proposition holds for the *Case 3* events in which Wilson was involved. In one instance he arranged for an opponent of Representative

[17] *Birmingham Age-Herald*, August 10, 1918, p. 1.

Underwood to withdraw from the Alabama senatorial primary. Since Underwood, a national figure, was also the leading politician of the state at the time, Wilson was clearly in alliance with the dominant forces of Alabama politics. (See Appendix, item 1.) Much the same thing can be said of his other *Case 3* endorsement where, in effect, Wilson acted as a recruiting agent to obtain the strongest possible candidates. (See Appendix, items 2 and 3.) For Wilson the moral is clear. When he acted with significant local forces and concentrated his strength, his candidate won, quite possibly thereby enhancing his strength in Congress.

Much the same generalization can be uttered about Franklin Roosevelt. In those *Case 2* events in which his endorsed candidate lost to an incumbent, Roosevelt opposed a well-entrenched local leader and did not make adequate preparations for his action. (See Appendix, items 18, 24, 25, and 26.) In every one of these instances, the incumbent had lined up a substantial amount of local support *before* Roosevelt endorsed. The most significant episode of this sort was in Georgia, where Roosevelt decided to endorse Camp *after* Senator Russell had already announced his own support of the incumbent, Senator George. Many observers at the time believed that, had Roosevelt acted earlier, he could have obtained Russell's endorsement of Camp or at least his silence. As it was, however, Russell was committed to working for his senior colleague throughout the campaign. The same sort of belatedness characterized Roosevelt's endorsement of Olin Johnson against Senator "Cotton Ed" Smith of South Carolina, of Representative David Lewis against Senator Tydings of Maryland, and of Representative Wearin against Senator Gillette of Iowa. On the other hand, the single instance of *Case 2* in which Roosevelt's endorsed candidate won involved a — probably unanticipated — alliance with a significant local force. While Representative O'Connor was supported by Tammany, his opponent, James Fay, was supported by the Workers' Alliance, a union of WPA workers that had the personnel and the energy to make a full canvass of the district. (See Appendix, item 27.) For these *Case 2* events, the clear conclusion is that Roosevelt's candidate won when he had the support of significant local interests and lost when he did not.

The same is true of Roosevelt's *Case 3* endorsements. In item 15 of the Appendix, Roosevelt's candidate won trivially, for there was no opposition, but in items 14, 28, and 29 his candidates won against significant opponents. In each of these instances Roosevelt sided with dominant local forces. When he endorsed Representative Burke of Nebraska against Governor Bryan in the Nebraska senatorial primary of 1934, he supported an advocate of national relief against one of its main opponents in the Democratic Party. When he endorsed Lyndon Johnson in the Texas senatorial primary of 1941, he sided with Speaker Rayburn especially against the notorious party irregular, Martin Dies. When he endorsed ex-Senator Gillette in Iowa in 1944, he made peace with the man who had proved in 1938 that he dominated the Iowa Democracy. Thus, like Wilson's, Roosevelt's candidates won when he allied with local strength and concentrated his blessing.

Finally, the same observation holds true of Truman's endorsed candidates. When in his own district he endorsed Enos Axtell against Representative Slaughter, he was, of course, acting with his own intimate political friends who had long demonstrated their ability to control the local Democratic Party. (See Appendix, item 31.) When, on the other hand, he endorsed candidates in the Missouri Democratic senatorial primaries in 1950 and 1952, he was attempting to extend the influence of his friends in the northwestern portion of the state through the state as a whole. (See Appendix, items 32 and 38.) Since there had always been tension between the northwest and the rest of the state in the Democratic party, his candidates' failures may be attributed to the fact that Truman did not ally with the dominant state leaders. Truman's greatest success in endorsements occurred in 1950, when, so he several times hinted in the fall and winter of 1949–1950, he had planned a reenactment of Roosevelt's entry into Democratic primaries. Instead of attacking the South, however, Truman apparently intended to build up the party in the northern Midwest. This was the area he had so triumphantly carried by his whistle-stop tour in 1948. Presumably, he intended in 1950 to use the same means to elect a number of Democratic Senators. He started by picking candidates for the primaries. Thus, he appointed the governor of Colorado to a judgeship, leaving the way clear for Representative Carroll. He encouraged Undersecretary of Agriculture Loveland, to enter the Iowa primary. He endorsed Michael Di Salle in Ohio. And he announced that he hoped that Walter Granger would be unopposed in the Utah primary. (See Appendix, items 33, 34, 35, and 36.) These men all won in the primaries, but lost in the general election, perhaps because Truman never made the anticipated campaign trip. The sudden eruption of the Korean War diverted Truman's energies from domestic politics to international affairs. Had he been able to make the trip, this planned participation in senatorial nominations and elections might have significantly changed the relation of President and Congress. No permanent consequences flowed from it, however, for the plan was aborted. Nevertheless it is sufficient to point out that Truman's candidates succeeded in the primaries when he carefully planned his strategy and, in Colorado and Utah especially but in the other two states also, allied with the strongest local leadership.

On the basis of these *Case 2* and *3* events we reaffirm our third canon: a President ought endorse only when he has made reasonably sure that his endorsed candidates can win. This means that, unlike Roosevelt in 1938, he must start planning his action many months in advance. It also means that he must have a staff of political secretaries both to inform him about possible endorsements and to help elect his endorsed candidates.

We started with the question of how a President might obtain greater influence over Congress and subsequently we reduced this to the more specific question of how he might obtain a reputation for influencing the outcome of congressional primaries. This latter question we answered with three canons of Presidential behavior: (1) a President ought to try to influence nominations; (2) he ought not endorse an incumbent; and (3) he ought to endorse a candidate only when he has made reasonably sure that the candidate can win. While the latter two canons are quite restrictive, even within the restrictions an activist President has the opportunity to substantially revise the American Constitution. As the nation becomes more centralized, in fact, it may well happen that voters increasingly turn to the President for leadership in congressional nominations. If so, and if several activist Presidents should follow the conservative and cautious canons here set forth for long enough and with enough frequency to destroy the federalistic tradition of non-interference, it might indeed happen that presidential endorsements would be expected in every congressional primary as a matter of course. Should this occur, the canons we have set forth would be completely superseded, for they are canons of behavior in a transitional situation.

APPENDIX

List of Instances in Which Presidents Have Endorsed Members of Their Own Parties for Nomination for the House or the Senate *

1. Wilson, by letter, asked Representative Henry C. Clayton to withdraw from the special senatorial primary in Alabama, thereby leaving the field clear for Representative Oscar Underwood. In effect, Wilson chose Underwood over Clayton for the senatorship. Clayton withdrew and Underwood was nominated and elected. *Montgomery Advertiser,* October 12, 1913, p. 1.

2. Wilson, by interview, requested Representative A. Mitchell Palmer to withdraw from the Pennsylvania Democratic gubernatorial primary and to enter the senatorial primary. In effect, Wilson recruited a candidate where there had been none. Palmer was nominated but lost the election. February 5, 1914.

3. Wilson asked Henry Ford to run for the Democratic as well as the Republican nomination for Senator from Michigan. Ford did so, winning the Democratic, but not the Republican, nomination and losing the general election. *Detroit News,* June 14, 1918, p. 1.

4. Wilson asked Representative Lever to withdraw from the South Carolina Democratic senatorial primary, thus leaving the field open for the reelection of Senator Tillman. Lever withdrew on June 14, 1918. *Charleston News and Courier,* June 14, 1918, pp. 1 and 3.

5. Wilson, by letter, denounced Representative James Slayden of Texas (San Antonio) as an enemy of the administration, but did not endorse either of the other two candidates. Slayden withdrew and Carlos Bee was nominated and subsequently elected. July 26, 1918. *San Antonio Express,* July 25, 1918, p. 1.

* Dates are those on which the endorsement is reported by the *New York Times.* For those instances in which the regional press gives more detail than the *New York Times,* the names and dates of the appropriate newspapers are added.

6. Wilson, by letter, denounced Senator Vardaman of Mississippi, thereby indirectly endorsing Pat Harrison, the only other candidate in the Democratic senatorial primary. Harrison won. August 10, 1918. *Natchez Democrat*, August 11, 1918, p. 4.

7. Wilson, by letter, denounced Representative Huddleston of Alabama but did not endorse any of his opponents in the primary. Huddleston was renominated. August 10, 1918. *Birmingham Age-Herald*, August 10, 11, 1918, p. 1.

8. Wilson, by letter, publicly requested (and thereby inferentially endorsed) Senator J. Ham. Lewis of Illinois to seek renomination and reelection. Lewis won the primary but lost the general election. August 12, 1918.

9. Wilson, in a letter to Clark Howell, endorsed William J. Harris for the Georgia Democratic senatorial nomination against Senator Hardwick. Harris won. August 12, 1918. *Atlanta Constitution*, August 12, 1918, p. 1.

10. Wilson, by letter, denounced the claims of Governor Cole Blease, candidate for the South Carolina Democratic senatorial nomination, to be a friend of the administration, thereby inferentially endorsing Senator Tillman, who won. August 17, 1918.

11. Harding in a speech praised the political services of Senator Frelinghuysen of New Jersey, thereby presumably endorsing him for renomination against George L. Record. Frelinghuysen won the primary and general elections. September 4, 1922.

12. Coolidge in a speech at Washington mildly praised Senator Lenroot of Wisconsin, thereby presumably endorsing him for renomination against Governor Blaine. Blaine won the primary and the general election. September 6, 1926.

13. Hoover, by letter, endorsed Representative B. Carroll Reese of Knoxville, Tennessee, for renomination against Sam Price. Reese won the primary and general elections. July 27, 1930; *Knoxville Sunday Journal*, July 27, 1930, p. 1.

14. Roosevelt, by quoting extensively and with approval in a Green Bay, Wisconsin, speech from the speeches of Representative Edward Burke, a candidate for the Nebraska Democratic senatorial nomination against Governor Charles Bryan, allowed the press to infer that he (Roosevelt) preferred Burke to Bryan. Burke won the primary and general elections. August 10, 1932.

15. Roosevelt specifically endorsed the unopposed candidate for the Democratic nomination for the House of Representatives in Dutchess County, New York. The Republican incumbent, Hamilton Fish, was reelected. September 25, 1936.

16. James Roosevelt, presumably acting for his father, specifically endorsed Senator Claude Pepper of Florida for renomination against a former governor and representative. Pepper won. February 7, 1938.

17. Roosevelt, by interview, persuaded Representative Disney to withdraw from the Oklahoma Democratic senatorial primary, thus

clearing the way for the renomination of Senator Thomas who was reelected. February 13, 1938.

18. Harry Hopkins, presumably acting for the President, endorsed Representative Otha D. Wearin for the Iowa Democratic senatorial nomination against Senator Guy Gillette, who won the primary but lost the general election. May 27, 1938.

19. After a fireside chat in which he said, "I have every right to speak . . . where there may be a clear issue between candidates for a Democratic nomination," Roosevelt began a campaign tour, the first step of which was to indirectly endorse Senator Robert Bulkley of Ohio for renomination against a former governor. Bulkley won the primary but lost the general election. July 9, 1938.

20. Roosevelt, in a speech, mildly endorsed Senator Thomas of Oklahoma for renomination against Governor Marland and Representative Gomer Smith. Thomas won the primary and general election. July 10, 1938.

21. Roosevelt, in a speech, strongly endorsed Senator Alben Barkley of Kentucky for renomination against Governor Chandler. Barkley won the primary and general election. July 9, 1938.

22. Roosevelt, in a speech, mildly endorsed Senator Hattie Caraway for renomination against Representative John McClellan. Mrs. Caraway was renominated and elected. July 10, 1938.

23. Roosevelt, in a speech, strongly endorsed Senator McAdoo of California for renomination against Sheridan Downey. Downey won the primary and the general election. July 17, 1938.

24. Roosevelt, in a speech, strongly endorsed Lawrence Camp for the Georgia Democratic senatorial nomination against Senator Walter George. George won. *Atlantic Constitution,* August 12, 1938, p. 1.

25. Roosevelt strongly endorsed Representative David Lewis for the Maryland Democratic senatorial nomination against Senator Millard Tydings, who won. August 17, 1938.

26. Roosevelt, without mentioning either of the South Carolina Democratic senatorial candidates by name, discussed them in such a way that his words could easily be interpreted as an endorsement of Olin Johnson again "Cotton Ed" Smith. August 31, 1938.

27. Roosevelt condemned Representative O'Connor of New York City as an enemy of the administration thereby indirectly endorsing James Fay, O'Connor's opponent in the primary. Fay won the primary and general elections. August 17, 1938.

28. Roosevelt praised Representative Lyndon Johnson, running for the Texas Democratic senatorial nomination in a field of twenty-five candidates. Johnson won. April 3, 1941. *Houston Post,* April 23, 1941, p. 1.

29. Roosevelt indirectly endorsed ex-Senator Guy Gillette for the Iowa Democratic senatorial nomination. Gillette won both the primary and general election. April 9, 1944.

30. Truman, in a press conference, defended Senator Burton Wheeler

from charges made against him by an opponent, Leif Erickson, in the Montana Democratic senatorial primary. Erickson won the primary and lost the election. July 12, 1946.

31. Truman announced that he opposed the renomination of Representative Roger Slaughter of Missouri, thereby indirectly endorsing Enos Axtell, who won the primary but lost the election. July 19, 1946.

32. Truman announced that he supported Emery Allison for the Missouri Democratic senatorial nomination. Former Representative Thomas C. Hennings won the nomination and general election. January 6, 1950. *Kansas City Star,* January 7, 1950, p. 3.

33. Truman appointed Governor W. Lee Knous of Colorado to the federal bench, presumably to withdraw the governor from the Colorado Democratic senatorial primary and leave the way clear for the nomination of John A. Carroll, who won the primary but lost the general election. March 2, 1950.

34. Truman encouraged, but did not clearly endorse, Albert Loveland for the Iowa Democratic senatorial nomination. Loveland won in a field of five but lost the general election. March 4, 1950. *Des Moines Register,* March 4, 9, 1950.

35. Truman, by announcement, endorsed Michael Di Salle in the Ohio Democratic senatorial primary where he had only token opposition. Di Salle won the primary but lost the election. Frebruary 5, 1952.

36. Truman announced in a press conference that he hoped Representative Walter Granger would be unopposed in the Utah Democratic senatorial primary. He was, but Granger lost the general election. January 25, 1952.

37. Truman announced he would regard the loss of Senator Harley Kilgore to the Senate as a loss to the country, thereby in effect endorsing Kilgore against Representative Andrew Edmiston. Kilgore won both the primary and the general election. February 13, 1952.

38. Truman endorsed J. E. Taylor for the Missouri Democratic senatorial nomination, against Stuart Symington and James Slaughter. Symington won the primary and the general election. May 25, 1952.

39. Eisenhower endorsed Douglas McKay for the Oregon Republican senatorial nomination. McKay won the primary but lost the general election. March 10, 1956.

Patronage and Presidential Legislative Leadership

Stanley Kelley, Jr.

Richard Neustadt, writing in 1955, noted the emergence of the presidential legislative program as a concept and examined the procedures associated with planning the President's legislative program in particular cases.[1] Both the concept and the procedures were creatures of the Truman and Eisenhower administrations. Truman and Eisenhower were of course not the first Presidents to take stands on legislative issues, but they were the first routinely to prepare comprehensive and detailed statements of legislative needs for annual presentation to Congress. Neustadt believed that he was holding up a newly born constitutional custom for public inspection, and he was correct in that belief. The legislative programs of Presidents Kennedy and Johnson have been at least as comprehensive in scope, and detailed in statement, as those of their immediate predecessors.

Concurrent with the changes described by Neustadt were other important developments in the relations between the President and Congress that have received less attention. One was the appearance on the White House staff of persons specializing in the handling of requests by congressmen for favors. They appeared first in the Truman administration, which, in its later years, had specially designated liaison officers in the White House for both the Senate and the House of Representatives. The Eisenhower administration increased the size of this congressional relations staff to near its present level,[2] and, more significantly, enlarged its activities. Under President Eisenhower, and later under Presidents Kennedy and Johnson, the congressional liaison group in the White House concerned itself not only with acting on requests for favors, but also with the content of legislative proposals and with shepherding measures sponsored by the administration through Congress. During the Eisenhower

Printed by permission of the author. This article is a revised version of a paper prepared for delivery at the 1962 Annual Meeting of the American Political Science Association in Washington, D.C. The author is grateful for criticisms of it in its earlier form by professors Jameson W. Doig and Walter F. Murphy of Princeton University and by Professor Laurin Henry of the University of Virginia. He is also indebted to Mr. Richard Ayres of the Yale Law School for surveying the case literature on the legislative process and discussions of the use of patronage in mustering support for legislative measures.

[1] Richard E. Neustadt, "Presidency and Legislation: Planning the President's Program," *American Political Science Review*, XLIX (1955), pp. 980–1021.

[2] When President Eisenhower left office, his congressional liaison group included a deputy assistant to the President for congressional affairs, a Senate man, a House man, a "backfielder" assigned to neither house, a research man, and one or two others.

administration steps were taken also to coordinate the work of congressional liaison men with that of White House staff members charged with clearing political appointments with members of Congress; once again, the Kennedy and Johnson administrations followed this practice. When Kennedy was President, one man, Lawrence F. O'Brien, was his special assistant both for congressional affairs and for personnel.

What these developments mean is relatively clear. They mean a centralization, rationalization, and institutionalization of responsibility for dispensing all forms of presidential patronage,[3] and the close integration of that activity with administration lobbying. Why these changes have occurred is less easy to say; nor is it easy to evaluate their significance. I hope that the discussion that follows will cast light on both these points. Many of those who have interested themselves in presidential leadership in legislation have given either skeptical or negative appraisals of the developments just described. For some time political scientists have been equivocal in their statements about the importance of patronage as an instrument of presidential leadership. Discussion, both scholarly and popular, has also suggested that administration lobbying may be counterproducing, stimulating resentment rather than inducing cooperation, and that a White House congressional relations staff may build into the structure of the White House Office a group so sensitive to legislative interests that it neglects the administration's own.

THE WASHINGTON PATRONAGE MARKET

Assessment of the significance of the recent innovations in handling presidential patronage and in arrangements made for liaison between the President and Congress may best begin with some very general observations. First, the importance of either patronage or lobbying in a President's relations with Congress clearly depends on the legislative goals a President sets himself. "You can water bills down and get them by," President Kennedy once told reporters. "Or you can have bills which have no particular controversy to them and get them by. But important legislation, medical care for the aged and these other bills, farm programs, they are controversial, they involve great interest, and they are much more difficult." [4] In other words, a President's difficulties as a legislative leader arise when his program does not command the support of natural majorities in the two houses of Congress, and when he is unwilling to make the concessions on the substance of his program that would win such support.

---

3 The word patronage is used here to mean "the offices, contracts, honors, etc. which an official may bestow by favor." *Webster's Collegiate Dictionary.* This is one of its commonly accepted definitions, and the words "etc." and "by favor" are important to the definition. Any action undertaken by an official as a favor may serve as an inducement for the individual who receives that favor to act in accordance with the official's desires.

4 Statement made in his press conference of June 28, 1962.

It is then that he must try to persuade individual legislators to his point of view, or to induce them to support his program by granting or withholding favors, or, in unusual cases, to activate pressures on them from constituents.

Second, probably no President is able to make more than marginal changes in the alignment of legislators on most legislative issues either by persuasion or by exchanging favors for support. That, at any rate, seems the most reasonable conclusion to draw from the meager evidence that exists on this subject. In the accounts of legislative actions in both case studies and the press intensive lobbying by an administration is reported almost entirely in connection with situations where the vote on a major administration measure was expected to be close.[5] Experienced observers of Congress also judge the votes that can be changed by deals and lobbying to be few in number, even if the votes are critical. A prominent Washington attorney, who has himself been involved in several administration lobbying efforts, has said that "favors are done for powerful members of Congress. This means committee chairmen and the occasional member who has that one necessary vote." [6] A former congressman similarly sees the number of negotiable votes at any given time to be quite limited. "Most of the support you get for your program is from people who will support you anyway. Others, however, can be given a reason to vote with you. You probably can't change forty votes, but you can give twenty people a good reason to vote for you and make it easier for twenty more to do so." [7]

Third, when a President makes appointments with an eye to winning support for some part of his legislative program, he is not doing something sui generis; the trading of favors is a practice that pervades the legislative process. Members of Congress, heads of administrative agencies, and lobbyists continually do unto others in the hope that others will do at least as well by them. The President as a manager of patronage is simply one trader in a market system. To a large extent his problems as a trader are like those of any other trader in the system, and to understand them, one must appreciate some of the peculiar features of the market in which he must deal.

In some respects the Washington patronage market is like the markets that normally occupy the attention of economists. It arises because pairs of participants in the legislative process find that they can mutually better their positions if each will render a service that he values relatively less in return for the other rendering a service that he values relatively more.

---

[5] For some descriptions — albeit sketchy ones — of administration lobbying in cases of this kind see Hugh Douglas Price, "Race, Religion, and the Rules Committee," in Alan F. Westin, *The Uses of Power* (New York: Harcourt, Brace and World, 1962), pp. 1–71; Richard L. Lyons, "Complex Forces Beat Farm Bill," *Washington Post*, June 23, 1962; William M. Blair, "Johnson Phone Effort Credited with House Victory on Farm Bill," *New York Times*, April 10, 1964; and John D. Morris, "Rights Bloc Sees New Johnson Aid," *New York Times*, April 12, 1964.

[6] Statement made in an interview with the author, July 5, 1962.

[7] Statement made in an interview with the author, July 11, 1962.

These situations are frequent because participants are specialized in powers and competences: a President, a speaker, and a chairman of an important committee, for example, are in positions to perform quite different kinds of services for others. In the patronage market, as in any market, traders are aware that there are alternative bargains to be struck. The exchange values — or "prices" — of services thus become a function, at least in part, of the intensity of the demand for them and the scarcity or abundance of their supply.

But, as suggested, the patronage market also differs in important particulars from the market described in economics textbooks. The interdependence of the traders is undoubtedly less. In spite of all the pressures on legislators and on the President to get results that they cannot get by their own efforts, probably no legislator and no President has to trade to survive in the same sense that a business firm does. Trading among participants in the legislative process is more like the trading that arises in primitive societies where each member of the tribe satisfies basic subsistence needs by his own labor and trades mainly for luxury items. The legislator may be able to better his position by trading, either with his constituents or with his colleagues, but trading is not a sine qua non of his existence as a legislator.

The patronage market is also one without money; it involves no generalized medium of exchange or standard unit of account. It is a barter market, and the traders must deal in rough equivalences. They may equate an appointment at a given level with a vote on a bill, for example, in the same way that a person may equate two invitations to cocktails with one invitation to a soiree.[8] They will find it far more difficult to arrange mutually satisfactory trades than if this were not the case. They also may have to do much trading speculatively and on credit. That is, they may have to perform a service now with the understanding, and on the chance that, a comparable service will be performed in return at some time in the future.

Further, the patronage market is not entirely respectable. Our mores will not permit a congressman to advertise publicly that his vote on an issue about which he cares little is negotiable and that he is willing to trade it for something he and his constituents value more.[9] Because this is

[8] In "Passing out the Patronage," *The American Magazine* (August 1933), p. 77, James A. Farley described the relative values he assigned to various kinds of patronage appointments: ". . . recommendations are being made equitably among the states. If one state, for example, gets several important appointments, while a state next door, of equal size and importance, receives less important appointments, the latter will receive a larger number of minor jobs. Also, in the quota arrangements, jobs which have much influence count just as largely as jobs which have large salaries. For example, a small cabinet position, paying perhaps only $6,800 per year might count in the quota just as much as two obscure jobs paying $10,000 a year each."

[9] Occasionally members of Congress will talk publicly about the exchange of favors. When Senator Frank Lausche of Ohio proposed a measure providing for what he called "special" tax relief for Minnesota's Twin City Rapid Transit Company in a Senate debate in August 1962, for example, he was taken to task by the late Senator Kerr, who said that he [Kerr] had just put through the Senate another "special re-

true, knowledge of who wants to trade what and on what terms is not readily available to traders, and such knowledge becomes of great value in and of itself. Its possession helps give to leaders their ability to lead. As Gus Tyler has observed,

> "The leadership knows where there are Congressmen — House or Senate — in search of votes to put over favored projects. Often, the sponsors of bills do not find a natural majority behind the proposal. Sometimes, they go shopping for the needed votes on their own. But at other times, they secure the active help of the leadership who act as intermediaries, composing the necessary majorities by picking up votes for one measure in exchange for votes pledged to another measure." [10]

Finally, and this is another consequence of the difference between the mores of the Washington political community and the greater community in which it exists, traders in the patronage market have a mutual interest in hiding its existence. Ordinarily they do not strike bargains in crude terms. A congressman may simply plead to a prospective trading partner that a problem is keeping him so busy that he is not sure that he will have time to look into the matter that the other has put before him. Or ideas may be put together as if by chance. One legislator makes a request of another legislator who discusses the matter on its own terms and then apparently as an afterthought goes on, "Oh, by the way . . . ." Trading in patronage, in short, normally proceeds only according to certain rules of etiquette. These rules may not greatly inhibit trading among initiates but they probably perplex some freshman legislators and certainly perplex the outsider who wants to find out what is going on.[11]

THE MARKET POSITION OF THE PRESIDENCY

The position of a President in the patronage market is clearly one of great strength. He undoubtedly has greater patronage resources at his disposal than any other single participant in the legislative process, and

---

lief" measure as a "favor" to Lausche. According to Robert Albright in the *Washington Post*, August 31, 1962, "Lausche said he had spent 30 years building up a reputation in public service, and he would not let Kerr make him 'appear as a base individual' . . . . Kerr said he . . . had mentioned nothing about 'iniquities' . . . he had merely done Lausche a 'favor.' 'It is not a favor to me,' said Lausche. 'Strike it from the bill.' 'That may be done,' said Kerr. He added coldly that he would not again seek 'to do a favor for the Senator from Ohio. He may seek his own.'"

10 Gus Tyler, *A Legislative Campaign for a Federal Minimum Wage* (New York: McGraw-Hill Book Co., 1955), p. 9.

11 The elliptical manner in which the trading of favors may be discussed should not be totally unfamiliar to academic politicians, however, or, at any rate, to readers of F. M. Cornford's discussion of "squaring" in his delightful *Microcosmographia Academia: Being a Guide for the Young Academic Politician* (London: Bowes and Bowes, 1964). The object of "squaring," says Cornford, is to "emphasize the fact that there is absolutely *no connection whatever* between my supporting your Job and your supporting mine." *Ibid.,* p. 30.

the sympathy that Presidents have received because of the decline in the amount of job patronage is probably misplaced. While the supply of that kind of patronage has shrunk greatly, the demand for other services that a President has within his power to give or withhold has probably grown more than enough to make up his loss. Donald Matthews observes, for instance, that "a large majority of the time of every senator's staff" is devoted to case work on favors.[12] Some of this work, perhaps the most important parts of it from the legislator's standpoint, will involve Senators or members of their staff with the White House.

In addition to having greater patronage resources than any other trader in the patronage market, a President also has a greater variety of resources, giving him the opportunity to better his own position by serving as a middleman in transactions between other traders. For example, legislator A may require a service from legislator B, while he is unable to do the sort of favor that would induce B to render that service. The President, with a diversified supply of patronage, is more likely to have something B wants. Thus, A will do a favor for the President, the President will do a favor for B, B will return the President's favor by doing what A requests, and the President has built up credit with both A and B for facilitating the transaction.

If a report by George Dixon in his column, "Washington Scene," is reliable, Lawrence F. O'Brien suggested his readiness to involve the White House in this kind of trading operation rather explicitly in an encounter with a Republican member of the House, James F. Battin of Montana. According to Dixon,

> Mr. Battin, an innocent freshman, went to a cocktail party at the home of Democratic Representative Edward P. Boland, who comes from O'Brien's hometown of Springfield. The White House lobbyist [Mr. O'Brien] hoisted a couple of canapes with Battin, then said, "We can't expect you to support us. But we can be friends. If you ever have a bill you want to get out of committee, and onto the floor, maybe we can help you." Battin recounted to me later: "I was pleased, but flabbergasted. I hadn't known the Executive Branch ran the Legislative." [13]

The bargaining advantages that a President can derive from his great resources, however, are not so great as one might at first imagine. His trading of favors for support can rarely be a straightforward business because the patronage market is not a straightforward market. The etiquette of trading in the patronage market and the fact that much trading must be done on credit means that there is always a good deal of room for misunderstanding about the terms of trade. Favors may not be seen as favors by those who receive them and attempts to collect may bring resentment. And, as already noted, trading in the patronage market may be advan-

---

[12] Donald R. Matthews, *U. S. Senators and Their World* (Chapel Hill: University of North Carolina Press, 1960), p. 225.
[13] *Washington Post*, June 27, 1962.

tageous but not crucial; it will occur only when potential traders see themselves as better off for it. Thus "arm twisting" — meaning forced sales — is not a strategy available to a President. If a legislator or a committee chairman does not want to play the trading game, there is no way he can be forced to do so.[14]

Nor are these a President's only problems. A President's ability to use patronage advantageously in support of his legislative program will depend on the kind of patronage at his disposal, the demand for that kind of patronage, and where that demand arises. To clarify just what this may mean for a President intent on "buying" support, let us suppose the following situation to exist: There is to be a vote on a measure in which the President is very much interested. A preliminary vote count tells him that 180 members of the House of Representatives are inclined to vote for his bill, that 180 are inclined to vote against it, and that 75 are relatively indifferent to the outcome. The President's most rational strategy, obviously, will be to seek votes for patronage among those who are indifferent to the fate of his bill. To do otherwise would be to waste patronage by "buying" votes that do not need to be bought or by "buying" votes from among members who will require relatively greater inducements to abandon their initial positions. Now, if all 75 "doubtful" legislators should come from districts anxious for reclamation projects, for example, and if presidential influence can enable them to get such projects, the President will be in a very good position to carry the day. A high demand for patronage will have coincided with his ability to supply it, and that demand will have come from those who will be his least expensive source of "purchased" support.

But one must suppose that a floor voting situation this favorable — from the President's point of view — will be rare. It involves too many happy coincidences. We can do little more than suppose, however, since there are few data on the demand for patronage. We lack any systematic knowledge of the wants and intensity of wants among legislators for various kinds of favors, although undoubtedly this varies a great deal from legislator to legislator, although such knowledge would be critically important to knowing what a President could do with his supply of patronage.

Moreover, even a situation relatively favorable to effective use of patronage as an instrument of presidential leadership will pose at least two serious problems for the President. If the reasoning above is correct, he will have to allocate a disproportionate part of his patronage to legislators who are relatively indifferent to the success of his legislative program. While the interests of the President's allies in Congress may be furthered

14 President Kennedy and the chief of his legislative liaison group, Lawrence F. O'Brien, found this to be true in the case of Representative James Delaney, who in 1961 joined opponents of Kennedy's Aid to Education Bill to vote it down in the House Rules Committee. According to Theodore Sorenson in *Kennedy* (New York: Harper and Row, 1965), p. 361, "No amount of pleading or pressures by the President or Ribicoff could budge him. More adamant than many leaders of his church, he had no interest in bargains or trades on other subjects. 'He didn't want a thing,' said O'Brien. 'I wish he had.' "

by his diverting patronage from them to doubtful or hostile legislators, they are likely to be disgruntled at such a diversion unless they can be made to see the balance of forces and interests as the President sees them. If they cannot be induced to see legislative realities as the President does, he may be faced with foot dragging or revolts in his own camp. In any case, "buying" votes from doubtful legislators involves a President in a kind of contradiction. The desire to see his program enacted into law leads him to spend his patronage with them while this expenditure of patronage may increase both their electoral security and the probability that these relatively "expensive" legislators will return from election campaigns for yet another year of trading.

Finally, when a President attempts to "buy" favorable action by a committee on a bill, he is likely to be in a much worse position than when he is trying to "buy" favorable action on the floor of Congress. There are fewer individuals in a position to "sell" the service he seeks and their preferences on any given issue — because of the differing natures of the constituency of the President and the constituencies of committee chairmen — are likely to diverge greatly from his own. Doing favors to secure committee action may thus be exceedingly costly, if a chairman or enough committee members are even willing to bargain at all.

MAXIMIZING PRESIDENTIAL CONTROL OF LEGISLATIVE OUTPUT

Some of the difficulties Presidents may encounter if they attempt to use patronage to win support for legislation have been listed. What can Presidents do about them? There is a curious scarcity of published speculation on this subject. Newly elected Presidents have been advised by some writers to withhold nominations to posts in the executive branch until they have secured action on as much of their legislative program as possible. Giving priority in the exercise of the appointing power to their oldest and closest political friends has also been suggested as sound practice.[15] Both these principles, however, involve only the disposition of patronage in jobs and neither takes us very far. There are at least a few additional measures by which a President can increase the usefulness of patronage in furthering his legislative interests.

First, a President by his own action can increase or decrease the amount and kind of patronage at his disposal. When President Eisenhower gave his Cabinet officers a free hand in choosing their subordinates, for example, he was destroying part of his potential patronage resources; when President Kennedy instituted the practice of giving advance notice to legislators of the awarding of defense contracts, he was creating a patronage resource.[16] The possession of almost any kind of discretionary power cre-

[15] Farley, "Passing out the Patronage," pp. 20–22, 77.

[16] According to George Dixon in the *Washington Post*, December 20, 1963, one of the first tasks Lyndon Johnson assigned himself as President was to plug "bureaucratic holes through which scoops [on the announcements of federal projects] intended for Democratic members of Congress have been leaking — often to politically undeserving Republicans."

ates the opportunity for its possessor to use it to play favorites. Including items in the budget, ordering the actual spending of appropriated monies, authorizing studies of postal services, deciding on the location of government installations, interpreting civil service regulations, granting audiences to important constituents of legislators, helping in campaigns — any of these actions may become patronage, or may not, depending on the spirit in which a President undertakes them. Other things being equal, of course, Presidents should seek to make patronage of services that are in high demand among legislators.

Second, a President can enhance his chances to control legislative output by centralizing the direction of trading operations carried on in his name. The fewer the number of voices speaking for him, and the less *ad hoc* trading operations are, the more likely it is that patronage will be spent in a manner that will maximize support for the presidential program as a whole and do so in accordance with the priorities the President has set for particular parts of it.

Third, a President should avoid short-circuiting the centralized machinery he has established for trading. If he himself makes bargains without the knowledge of the staff he has delegated that responsibility to, or allows anyone outside that staff to do so, he must be prepared to handle future trading himself, set up a new staff with powers to trade for him, or see the centralized machinery for trading break down.[17]

Finally, a President can take steps to decrease some of the communication difficulties that beset any trader in the patronage market but are particularly acute for him. A comprehensive and detailed legislative program by its very nature is vague about priorities. These priorities must be defined if legislators are to know what actions on their part can earn them the greatest credit and if interest in trading is to center on matters of greatest concern to the President. Favors must also be defined, a far more subtle business than it might seem. Thanking a legislator for some action of his is one way to define a favor and one that increases the legislator's confidence that any services he chooses to render in the future will be noticed and will earn him credit. Similarly, withholding action on a request can be a way of defining that class of requests as favors and of informing a legislator that action on them will depend on a return favor from him.[18] A President can also take measures to discover the distribu-

---

17 Charles Roberts in *LBJ's Inner Circle* (New York: Delacorte Press, 1965), p. 122, reported that Lawrence F. O'Brien continued in his job as head of the White House lobbying group in the Johnson administration on the understanding that his authority would remain the same as it had under Kennedy. Johnson understood, according to Roberts, that "to deal with members of Congress on equal footing, not as a messenger, he [O'Brien] had to be recognized as *the* link between the White House and Capitol Hill."

18 Thus, in the Spring of 1963, according to columnists Rowland Evans and Robert Novak, in the *Washington Post*, May 26, 1963, the failure of several liberal Republicans in the House of Representatives to support the Kennedy administration on several bills earned them a "lack of cooperation" from the White House on requests for such things as invitations to bill-signing ceremonies.

tion of preferences, the demand for particular kinds of patronage, and the obligations legislators have outstanding. Accurate knowledge on these points is essential to his ability to make the right trades at the right time with the right people and not to make unnecessary expenditures of resources. A President can take action to minimize discontent with the way in which he allocates patronage by making his allies see the rationale of that allocation and by simple courtesies. Finally, he can take care to coordinate bargaining on the substance of legislation with favor trading. From the President's point of view, amending a bill or doing a favor may be alternative means of accomplishing the same purpose, and actions of one kind cannot be taken in disregard of actions of the other kind without either making unnecessary expenditures of patronage, unnecessary concessions on substantive issues, or both.

Concluding Observations

An ability to take most of the steps just suggested presupposes some kind of organized and fairly extensive staff specialized in legislative trading. And so, in concluding, I return to the subjects I discussed in the beginning. Recent Presidents have formalized arrangements for liaison with Congress and have centralized the handling of presidential patronage. Analysis suggests that they have done so for good reason. In assuming the responsibility for securing the enactment of a comprehensive program, because of the differences between their own constituency and that of Congress, they have had to become harder bargainers than their predecessors were. They have marshalled their resources and rationalized the procedures for putting hem to work in influencing legislative action. The new dimension of the President's role as legislative leader heralded by Neustadt, and the new arrangements for liaison with Congress that I have noted, have thus not only been concurrent developments but also integrally related ones.

PUBLICS

THE PRESIDENCY
AND THE PEOPLE

More on Children's Images of the President

Fred I. Greenstein

Although political socialization has long been an underdeveloped area of the behavioral sciences, in 1960 reports of two independent studies of the political orientations of grade school children appeared virtually simultaneously. In their central finding the reports were mutually reinforcing. Robert Hess and David Easton, studying second- through eighth-grade children in a Chicago suburb, reported in these pages that young children have highly positive, idealized views of the President of the United States. Their data were elicited by multiple-choice items comparing the President with "most men" in terms of such attributes as his honesty, his "liking for people," and "how hard" he "works." [1] At the same time, in another journal, this writer reported responses of New Haven fourth- through eighth-grade children to a differently constructed item — an open-ended question asking simply for a description of the President's duties. This item evoked spontaneous references to the President's "good" qualities, references which had a strikingly close fit to those stemming from the fixed-choice Chicago items.[2]

For the purpose of determining the degree of juvenile idealization of the President, items of the sort used in Chicago seem more appropriate. The New Haven procedure (which included content analysis of the children's written descriptions of the President and other public officials), on the other hand, has obvious advantages for producing a reasonably precise characterization of "the child's image of the President" and how it changes with age. The following paragraphs briefly summarize a number of additional Hess-Easton observations about the

Reprinted by permission from the *Public Opinion Quarterly*, Vol. 25, No. 4 (Winter 1961), pp. 648–654.
[1] Robert D. Hess and David Easton, "The Child's Changing Image of the President," *Public Opinion Quarterly*, Vol. 24, 1960, pp. 632–644.
[2] Fred I. Greenstein, "The Benevolent Leader: Children's Images of Political Authority," *American Political Science Review*, Vol. 54, 1960, pp. 934–943. Responses to multiple-choice items, asking the child to rate the President on a scale ranging from "very good" to "bad," also are reported. The New Haven questionnaires were administered between January and March 1958. Mr. Hess informs me that the Chicago field work was done in the spring of 1958.

child's developing conception of the President, indicating where the New Haven data support their findings, where they modify them, and where they are inconsistent with them.

Since the Hess-Easton study was conducted in a "middle class" suburb, I shall compare the Chicago findings with the responses of the New Haven upper-socio-economic-status subsample, a group consisting almost exclusively of children of white-collar parents. The accompanying table shows the ways those of the upper-SES New Haven children responding to the question "What kinds of things does the President do?" described his role. The number of respondents at each grade level is small, but the findings relevant to the following remarks also obtained with the larger lower-SES subsample.[3]

1. The "child's initial point of contact . . . with elected political figures," Hess and Easton report, "[seems to be] with the President." [4]

In New Haven, by fourth grade (age nine), children were universally aware of *two* elected officials, the President and the Mayor. Both these individuals, in fact, were known by name by more than 90 per cent of the fourth-graders. However, New Haven was probably atypical in having an extremely popular and dynamic mayor, a man who, among other things, makes a practice of visiting every classroom in the city each year! Pre-tests in a fifth-grade classroom in a nearby town, where only 40 per cent of the children knew the first selectman's name, suggest that for most localities the Chicago finding would hold.[5]

2. "We propose . . . that the first step of political socialization is initially completed with essentially no information about the political figure himself except that he is an authority figure whose status exceeds that of the authorities with whom the child has been familiar." The child seems first to acquire from the adult world an "evaluative [definition of political authority] presented in terms of positive or negative emotional tone." [6]

This assertion, which Hess and Easton base on the exploratory interviews which preceded the design of their multiple-choice items, is amply supported in the New Haven questionnaire data. By fourth grade only 30 per cent of the upper-SES children were able to give specific, reasonably accurate meaning to their general awareness of the existence of the President. But 98 per cent of them were willing to evaluate the President, and 96 per cent judged his performance to be very or fairly good.

---

[3] The following items in the table vary by SES: lower-SES children are less likely to describe the President in "budgetary" terms; they are more likely at the fourth- and fifth-grade levels to make use of "benevolent" imagery; and their tendency to refer to the President's international duties remains low until sixth grade, rather than increasing at fifth grade. For fuller data, see Fred I. Greenstein, "Children's Political Perspectives: A Study of the Development of Political Awareness and Preferences among Pre-Adolescents," Yale University Library, 1959, Chap. 6, unpublished doctoral dissertation.

[4] Hess and Easton, *op. cit.*, p. 634.

[5] Greenstein, "The Benevolent Leader," p. 937.

[6] Hess and Easton, *op. cit.*, p. 643.

TABLE 1

Statements Made by Upper-socio-economic-status New Haven Children Who Were Able to Describe the President's Role, by School Grade (in per cent)

Image	School Grade				
	4	5	6	7	8
Executive: "He supervises the country"	9	25	42	31	32
Budgetary: "He takes care of the expenditures, . . . taxes"	0	7	5	41	26
Legal: "He vetoes bills, . . . makes laws, . . . enforces laws"	21	11	13	25	47
Communicative: Makes speeches; goes to meetings	6	9	8	9	12
Individual: "Plays golf, . . . paints pictures, . . . goes to the hospital"	6	16	3	0	9
International: "Takes care of threatening wars, . . . deals with foreign countries"	12	32	28	50	68
Benevolent: "Gives us things, . . . takes care of us"	24	7	8	3	6
Normative: "Does good things, . . . tells the people what is good"	6	14	16	3	12
Miscellaneous*	30	18	18	22	26
Mean images per child	1.14	1.39	1.41	1.84	2.38
(Total N)	(33)	(44)	(38)	(32)	(34)

* All responses not codable in the above categories were classified as miscellaneous. These include the vague or inaccurate statements of young children ("The President is in politics") and the detailed elaborations better-informed older children were capable of making ("He meets with members of the Cabinet." "He is Commander-in-Chief of the Army.") Since only one "miscellaneous" response was coded per child and older children made more such statements, the estimate of the increase with age in "mean images per child" is conservative.

3. At an early stage, the child's "socialization is to an image viewed in personal terms. . . ." [7] Then, the President becomes "increasingly seen as a person whose abilities are appropriate to the demands of his office — a differentiation of role functions with increasing age of respondent." [8] "The demands and expectations of the office, rather than the characteristics of the occupant, [now] influence the child's definition of the President." [9]

It is at this point that the New Haven procedure becomes particularly useful for complementing and modifying the Chicago observa-

[7] *Ibid.*, p. 634.
[8] *Ibid.*, p. 640.
[9] *Ibid.*, p. 644.

tions. In addition to relying on their exploratory interviews, Hess and Easton document the credible hypothesis that the President's role becomes increasingly differentiated by a rather complex, indirect inference: they note that with age children evaluate the President more favorably in areas which the authors feel are directly related to the performance of his duties ("hard work" and "knowledge") and less favorably with respect to attributes which any individual might share (his "honesty," the degree to which he "likes people," whether he is a "good person").[10]

Our table permits us to describe childhood conceptions of the President in a way which is much closer to the child's cognitions. We see that differentiation does indeed increase (note the steady progression from fourth to eighth grade in the number of "images" in each child's response), and we see the kinds of distinctions made more often by older than younger children. From the vague, often affectively tinged, statements of the nine-year-old child, there is a generally consistent advance in the direction of greater awareness of the President's executive and legislative functions, for example. Moreover, the table makes it possible to specify ages which seem to be thresholds for greater awareness. Between fourth and fifth grades there is a substantial increase (from 12 to 32 per cent) in the proportion of children portraying the President in the way which most distinguished his image from those of the Mayor and Governor — as the country's representative in foreign affairs, or as the man who "keeps us at peace." There is another substantial increase between grades 6 and 7.[11]

The table also suggests one respect in which the indirect inferences made from the Chicago questionnaire responses and the results of the Chicago exploratory interviews may be misleading. We see that references to the President as an individual were *not* particularly common among fourth-graders and that they did not vary consistently with age. (The New Haven children were even less likely to describe the Governor and Mayor in personal terms, though a large proportion of them had met or seen the latter, and many seemed to know where in the city he lives, the size of his family, etc.) The developmental progression in the President's image seems rather to be from a fuzzy conception of his duties to a more accurate and variegated conception. But at all ages (beginning at least with age nine) there is an awareness of him as a public figure.

4. A final aspect of the New Haven findings which may be used to elaborate further on the Chicago observations relates to the interesting speculations by Hess and Easton about the connection between conceptions of the President and conceptions of other political roles. To the child, they suggest, "the President stands as a symbol of undifferentiated government that includes all levels and holds essentially all governmental authority . . . the President serves as a central orientation point

---

[10] *Ibid.*, pp. 639–640.

[11] President Eisenhower was, of course, probably more likely to evoke this class of imagery than other White House occupants would be.

for an increasing awareness of other elements of the political system. These other elements are initially seen in terms of their assumed relationship to the President himself. Thus, [for example] to the very young child . . . Congress is viewed as a group that takes orders from the President and performs certain tasks at his command." [12]

The New Haven data suggest that not only the President but also other elected leaders may serve as "orienting" figures for children. The data further suggest that at least two types of psychological mechanism may help to determine the ways in which children relate one political role to another. Three classes of New Haven responses and the mechanisms which may account for them are worth noting:

1. "A small percentage of the [New Haven] respondents (but some in each of the four schools which make up the sample) coped with the problem of organizing their fragmentary political information by using hierarchical concepts. They saw politics, even in the case of individuals and institutions which are formally co-ordinate, in terms of a chain of command." [13] Some of these children described the President as giving orders to the Mayor and Governor; others described a less complete chain of command, placing the Governor over the Mayor, but not relating the President to the two. A potentially testable hypothesis, following from the speculations of both Hess and Easton and this writer, is that the mechanism underlying such responses is a transfer of, or reaction to, the child's perceptions of the power structure of his family.

2. Another even smaller group of New Haven respondents incorrectly attributed to one aspect of the political environment features of another aspect. In New Haven this did not involve extensions of the President's image. Rather, it was the President and Governor who were seen in terms of aspects of the Mayor's role. Mayor Lee was widely and accurately perceived by many of the children as the initiator of the city's massive urban redevelopment program. Occasional children then went on to explain that the President or Governor "cleans up slums." When one political phenomenon presents an especially vivid impression, simple cognitive mechanisms may tend to generalize this perception to other roles.

3. An additional New Haven finding is closely related to the Hess and Easton description of how the young child links the President and Congress. A surprising number of New Haven children, particularly in the upper-SES subsample, spontaneously responded to the open-ended questions asking for a description of the functions of the Board of Aldermen, the State Legislature, and Congress by implying that these bodies are subordinate to the executive at the same level of government. The most common statement was, "They are the people who help the Mayor (etc.)." About 30 per cent of the children describing the Board of Aldermen, 10 per cent of those describing the State Legislature, and 15 per cent of

---

[12] Hess and Easton, *op. cit.*, p. 635.
[13] Greenstein, "The Benevolent Leader," p. 939*n*.

those describing Congress used such language.[14] Since at each age level more children are informed about the executive than about the legislative body at the same level of government, it is possible that cognitive dynamics again help to account for such perceptions. The child learns first about the President. When he becomes aware of Congress, he assumes that its members must be the President's underlings. However, experiences with family authority also may be at work here. Assumptions have sources, and the home is one possible source of the assumption that individuals and groups relate to each other in terms of one telling the other what to do.

It should be emphasized that all the foregoing classes of political imagery were evident in only a minority of the New Haven responses. However, when some children spontaneously make statements of the types described here (especially statements of the first and third type above), when they have been asked only what the President does, it is reasonable to assume that more would make such statements in response to items explicitly designed to evoke them. (For example, "Does anyone tell the President [Congress] what to do? Who?")

Thus the Hess and Easton hypothesis about how the child's awareness of the President influences his conception of other political roles is partially supported by the New Haven data, but the latter suggest that the hypothesis needs further modification. As Hess and Easton make clear, we still know very little about the child's developing conception of politics, the ways this varies over time and through space, and the factors which determine it. But as we progress in putting together the pieces of such jig-saw puzzles, and as our capacity to relate early experience to adult behavior increases, new dimensions should be added to our growing understanding of political man.

14 It is conceivable that these findings are an artifact of the questionnaire, since items about legislative bodies followed items about the executive at the same level of government. That only one child in a sample of 659 described an executive as subordinate to a legislature suggests that this is not the case, however. It is worth noting that the class of perceptions described here did not seem to be a function of being a very young child. Although the number of children describing legislative bodies in the lower grades was not enough to compute stable percentages, there seemed to be no age variation in assertions that the legislative body was "under" the executive. An additional point may be noted: lower-SES children were substantially less likely than upper-SES children to describe legislatures in this fashion. This may be a function of level of information. Lower-SES children were as likely as upper-SES children to describe legislatures reasonably accurately. However, they produced consistently shallower descriptions, in the sense of the number of images per child (see Greenstein, "Children's Political Perspectives," Chap. 6).

Popular Images of the President

Fred I. Greenstein

The question "What is the nature of popular orientations to the American President?" has two ingredients which make it compelling. First, it is addressed to an exceedingly important matter. Secondly, it is problematic — the evidence necessary to answer this question fully is not now available, and the fascinating pattern of evidence which *is* at our disposal has its puzzling aspects. Let me expand on each of these points.

You do not need a specialist in American government to remind you of the importance of the Presidency itself. The President is the fulcrum of our domestic political system and a central force in the international political arena. A little reflection will make it clear why public orientations to him are important. In what some consider an ambiguous phrase, the President often is called the most powerful democratic leader in the world. The ambiguity in this characterization lies in both of the qualifying terms, "powerful" and "democratic." The complex and extended debates which have arisen over the definitions of these terms — and over how one determines the degree to which an individual is powerful, or democratic — have made at least one thing clear. Both terms refer to interpersonal relationships, not merely to qualities which reside in a single individual such as the President. When we say that the President is powerful, we are saying that he has been empowered by others. To understand this power relationship we must be attentive not only to the President's actions, but also to others' reactions to him. When we say that the President is democratic, we may mean a number of different things, one of which is the closeness of fit between the President's actions and popular desires. Again knowledge of public orientations becomes a necessary part of our assessment of the Presidency.

Public dispositions toward the President have their most directly observable effects in electoral behavior, the White House mail, the activities of those specialized publics we call interest groups and politicians and, sadly, in occasional isolated outbursts such as that of Lee Harvey Oswald. These dispositions have a less visible but equally important effect in the public's acceptance of the system of government, including the Presidency, as legitimate. In the United States, the standing decision of the citizenry to accept its leaders as authoritative has an unrecognized, almost atmospheric quality. But we can see the importance of this standing public commitment to the existing political order by

Reprinted with an addition by permission from the *American Journal of Psychiatry*, Vol. 122, No. 5 (November 1965), pp. 523–529. Copyright © 1965 the American Psychiatric Association.

reminding ourselves of instances where it has not existed — for example, France of the Third and Fourth Republics, the contemporary Congo, the United States in 1860.

In spite of the importance of public dispositions toward the President, we do not have systematic knowledge of their nature. What is puzzling in the existing pattern of evidence can be indicated briefly. Most citizens, under most circumstances, seem to display a remarkable lack of interest in even the most conspicuous features of the governmental and political process, including the public actions of the President. Yet under certain circumstances — notably following the death of an incumbent Chief Executive — the President becomes the object of extraordinary outbursts of deeply felt and widely shared emotion. Response to such an event far exceeds what might have been expected from the respondents' prior demeanor.

The response to a Presidential death is so profound that for many people it entails somatic symptoms. The National Opinion Research Center (NORC) survey of public reaction to President Kennedy's death found, for example, that 43 per cent of a national sample of adults experienced loss of appetite during the four days following the President's assassination, 48 per cent reported insomnia, 25 per cent headaches, 68 per cent general feelings of nervousness and tenseness, and substantial numbers of people reported such anxiety symptoms as "rapid heart beats" (26 per cent) and perspiring (17 per cent). All of these percentages, it should be noted, are substantially above the normal prevalence of such signs of distress(22).[1]

Intense emotion was felt by Kennedy's opponents as well as by his supporters. Indeed, the former were sometimes taken aback at the magnitude of their own responses. The *main* immediate stimulus for this flood of spontaneous feeling does not seem to have been the violent circumstances of the President's death, nor does the feeling seem to have been a result of John F. Kennedy's personal characteristics — his youth, his appealing manner and so forth. Rather it is that *the President* has died. The historical record suggests that comparable public responses have followed each of the Presidential deaths in office since Lincoln — Roosevelt, McKinley, Garfield and even Harding(18). Further, nothing like this emotional outpouring ensues following the deaths of other figures in public life, including ex-Presidents.

We all know individuals who are attentive to national and internaltional affairs and who regularly become exercised about these aspects of the remote environment. For such people, strong emotional responses to an event like the President's death would not be puzzling. Most of us know many people who display strong political affect, since political involvement increases with level of education, and we tend to associate

[1] Two to five days after the President's funeral, reports of these symptoms had declined to the following levels: loss of appetite, 12 per cent; insomnia, 18 per cent; headaches, 9 per cent; nervousness and tenseness, 24 per cent; rapid heart beats, 6 per cent; perspiration, 4 per cent.

with highly educated segments of the population. What must be emphasized, however, is the degree to which concern with politics is a minority preoccupation. For example, a full 80 per cent of the electorate do not regularly engage in political conversations, while 90 per cent fail to write public officials(10, p. 11). A recent (November 1964) Gallup poll showed that 30 per cent of the electorate had paid no attention to the fighting in Viet Nam, and of those with some awareness of this military action a third were unable to supply any explanation of why the United States was participating in these events.[2] Yet, as the NORC survey clearly shows, distress at President Kennedy's death was virtually universal.

These rather extended preliminary remarks on why popular conceptions of the President are important and why they are puzzling have already made it possible to exhibit a portion of the available evidence about the public and the President. The series of statements which follow serve to fill in the picture further and provide the basis for a number of observations and speculations about the meaning of the Presidency to Americans.

1. *The President is by far the best known figure on the American political scene.* I have already commented on the capacity of a substantial proportion of the electorate to insulate itself from well-publicized aspects of political life. One consequence of this is that political leaders have great difficulty in making themselves known to the electorate. A not untypical public opinion poll conducted in 1945 found, for example, that 15 per cent of the electorate could not identify the Republican candidate of the previous year (Thomas Dewey); 34 per cent could not identify Henry Wallace, who a year earlier had been Vice President. A number of other leading figures — members of Congress, Cabinet officials and governors — were familiar to only well under half of the sample. But there was almost no one (a mere 5 per cent) who could not name President Truman. The President even exceeded a number of almost universally known popular entertainers in his visibility (10, p. 13). A point emerges from these findings which I shall return to in my concluding remarks: the President is not only the best known American political leader. For some people he is the *only* known leader, and for others one of the few. (This goes far to explain why only two 20th century Presidents, Taft and Hoover, were defeated for re-election.)

2. *The status of President is accorded great respect in American society.* Americans tend generally to deprecate and distrust individuals who carry the label "politician." Nevertheless, when we ask people to rank occupations in terms of their importance and respectability, certain high political roles, such as Senator and Supreme Court Justice, regularly appear at the top of the rankings. Unfortunately, the Presidency has not

[2] By July 1965, after American involvement in the Viet Nam conflict had substantially increased, the inattentive segment of the public had shrunk considerably. Nevertheless, 15 per cent of a Gallup national survey still admitted that it was not following events in Viet Nam and 33 per cent had no opinion about what United States policy on Viet Nam should be.

been included in these occupational prestige studies, but if this office were included the likelihood is that it would rank at or near the peak of the listing(11, pp. 28, 63).

3. *The President ordinarily is the first public official to come to the attention of young children.* It is one of the anomalies of scholarship that more is presently known about young children's images of the President than about how adults conceive of him. By the age of nine (and, evidently earlier) virtually every child is aware of the Presidential role and the name of the incumbent President. Children of this age resemble the least informed members of the adult population in that they have almost no further political information. For example, most of them have not heard of Congress and cannot provide even a vague specification of what the President's duties are(11, Chs. 3 and 4).

4. *Even before they are substantively informed about the President's functions, children believe that he is exceptionally important — and that he is benign.* Children as young as nine have been asked to rank occupations in terms of importance. The President stands at the top of their rankings, ahead, for example, of physicians, school teachers and clergymen. Children of this age describe the President as a kindly, benevolent figure. Throughout the childhood years, the conception of the President has an overwhelmingly positive quality, although there is some decline in idealization of him between early childhood and age 13(9, 11[pp. 31–43], 13). It has been argued that these early, favorable images of the Presidential role color children's subsequent learning about politics, contributing to a generally positive orientation toward the political system and fostering tacit assumptions about the importance of the Presidency vis-à-vis other political institutions, such as Congress.[3]

5. *Adult assessments of the performance of incumbent Presidents fluctuate from time to time and differ from group to group, but in spite of this variation, adults normally have a favorable view of the President's performance* (although not so automatically positive a view as that held by children). The most convenient index of ebb and flow in Presidential popularity is the question asked regularly since the 1930's by the Gallup poll: Do you approve or disapprove of the way President X is handling his job? Most of the time a clear majority of the electorate (not just a majority of the 80 to 90 per cent responding to the question) approve. Roosevelt's score never dropped below 50 per cent and Eisenhower's did so only once (to 49 per cent). Positive assessments of FDR ranged as high as 84 per cent; those of Eisenhower reached 79 per cent. Kennedy's popularity in office ranged from a low of 57 per cent to a high of 69 per cent. Only Truman, who just after entering office achieved the record rating of 87 per cent, ever experienced substantial disapproval. At one point there was only 23 per cent favorable response to him. The strong supporters of the opposition party are probably the most consistent source of disapproval of the President's performance, but at one time

---

[3] Children of other countries also seem to perceive their national leaders in an idealized fashion, but the absolute levels of idealization vary from nation to nation(12).

or another all of the Presidents I have referred to were the recipients of substantial bipartisan backing(2).

6. *There is a significant tendency for citizens to rally to the support of the President, particularly when he acts in times of international crisis.* During the month in 1950 when the decision was made to resist the Communist invasion of South Korea, President Truman's popularity rose from 37 per cent approve — 45 per cent disapprove, to 46 per cent approve — 37 per cent disapprove. President Eisenhower's popularity rose from 67 per cent to 75 per cent during the month of the Suez crisis, from 52 per cent to 58 per cent after sending the Marines to Lebanon in 1958. Interestingly, even those international actions which are viewed by informed observers as fiascos have led to increases in Presidential popularity. Eisenhower's popularity rose by 6 percentage points after the U-2 incident and the collapse of the summit meetings; Kennedy's rose by 10 points after the Bay of Pigs invasion(19, p. 28). Another event which usually produces substantial increases in Presidential popularity is the President's election, or re-election. Perhaps the most striking instance of this effect can be seen in the case of President Kennedy, who in November 1960 was favored by barely more than half of the electorate, but who, by inaugural day, had the approval of 69 per cent of the electorate(3). A number of studies provide accounts of the almost self-conscious process of rationalization through which the winning candidate's former opponents "improve" their opinions of him(11, p. 29). We have already noted a further occasion for the channeling of sympathetic feeling toward the Presidency — the death of the Chief Executive. It remains to be noted that at such a time the Vice President becomes the beneficiary of an impressive display of support and good will.

7. *Citizens seem to perceive and evaluate the President as a person, rather than in terms of his policy commitments or his skill in the specialized tasks of leadership.* When people are asked to indicate what they like or dislike about the President, they most commonly refer to aspects of his personal image — for example, his sincerity and integrity, his conscientiousness, his warmth or coldness, his physical vigor, his religious background and practice. There are, of course, some references to his policy positions and his leadership qualities, but together these references are less frequent than statements about the President's personal qualities. I must hasten to add, however, that the evidence for this series of assertions is still a bit shaky, since it is based on studies of public perceptions of the single recent President about whom one would most expect people to have such diffusely personal conceptions — President Eisenhower(4).[4] Nevertheless, it is consistent with the general picture of electoral motivation which has emerged from the voting research of recent decades. For example, early in 1948, a three-state sample of voters who had indicated their preferred Presidential candidate were asked: "What are the qualities that you think would make him the best man (for President)?" References

---

[4] Parallel data from France reveal the same emphasis on the personal characteristics of President DeGaulle.

to personal qualities exceeded ideological references by more than four-fold(14).

8. *Finally, there is some scattered clinical evidence that, at least for a portion of the population, the President is the unconscious symbolic surrogate of childhood authority figures.*

Up to now, all of the evidence I have discussed about public orientation toward the President has been based on readily observable behavior and on explicit or implicit public attitudes which are ascertainable by simple public opinion poll interviews. Any comprehensive explanation of public dispositions toward the President will have to encompass these phenomena that appear at the conscious level. I have so far avoided referring to the familiar psychoanalytic proposition that responses to civil authority are a function of — and capture some of the affect derived from — experiences with parental authorities(e.g., 6, 7, 8). Some hypothesis of this sort would contribute usefully to an explanation of the seeming paradox in public orientations toward the President. Whenever — as in the case of reactions to a President's death — an individual's response to a stimulus seems out of proportion to his prior demeanor, we find ourselves revising our estimate of what his prior demeanor "really" was. And these are the circumstances under which psychiatry has accustomed us to look for over-determined motivation, a component of which is unconscious.

Social scientists have been reluctant to accept such psychiatric explanations of public orientations toward authority, partly for reasons which have already been suggested in my remarks about the level of public political interest. Because of the seeming lack of cathexis of politics for most people, it becomes difficult to accept theories which assume that orientations toward public authority serve deep psychological functions. Further, the findings of the scattered quantitative research on the generality of attitudes toward authority(e.g., do people perceive their employers in the same terms as their fathers?) are at best ambiguous(11, pp. 50–51). There *are* clinical reports which fit the psychoanalytic hypothesis. Some of these reports are of psychiatric patients' reactions to the extraordinary stimulus of the deaths in office of Presidents and other chief executives. A number of analysands are reported, for example, to have responded to FDR's death in a manner which indicates that they symbolically equated the President with their own fathers(5, 23). There also is at least one report in the literature by an analyst who found similar symbolic associations among his patients under less extreme circumstances of national election campaigns of 1948, 1952, and 1956(20).

Although we have had a number of such clinical reports of patients who symbolically link the President with parental authority, there is no evidence as to the frequency with which this linkage occurs among psychiatric patients, much less in the general population. Nor do we have a clear indication of the variation in form that such linkages might take from individual to individual. As Lasswell has pointed out, if images of objects in the secondary environment (such as the world of politics) acquire meaning from experiences in the primary environment (such as the family), it does not follow that the former will be simple extensions of the latter. Generalization may be compensatory, taking the shape, for example, of reaction formation(17, pp. 156–159). To complicate matters, both types of generalization may be at work. For some people, orientations toward secondary environment authorities may be extensions of primary environment orientations; for others the generalization may take a compensatory form. (This may account for the lack of significant correlation between attitudes toward different authorities in the quantitative research on this topic.) [5] Moreover, linkages beween primary environment experience and orientations toward the President may differ from President to President. Thus, for example, it is difficult to believe that many adults would treat a youthful President such as Kennedy as a father surrogate,[6] even though there is some evidence that for children he may have unconsciously been perceived in these terms(1).

These last observations provide the transition to an obvious concluding remark. More research on public orientations toward the President clearly is needed. Some of this presently is being done by political scientists using survey research techniques, notably Professors Aaron Wildavsky and Peter Sperlich of the University of California at Berkeley. Certain complementary contributions might well come from psychiatrists. Nearly 30 years ago, in a paper entitled "What Psychiatrists and Political Scientists Can Learn from One Another," Harold Lasswell commented that "Psychiatrists do not, as a rule, record the role of secondary symbols (such as political attitudes) in relation to the personality structure which they observe. Once they understand the nature of the problem to which these data are precious, they may take care to preserve, rather than to ignore or to discard, material which is so fully exposed by their special procedure(16)." And, I might add, to elicit more such material.

Until more psychiatric research is done the possible deeper motivational significance of the President for citizens will remain unclear. However, the existing evidence — especially the public opinion polls — provides a basis for suggesting several closely related ways in which citizens seem to make psychological use of the Chief Executive. To varying degrees, citizens probably draw on the President in the following ways.

1. *As a cognitive aid.* The existence of a single, highly publicized national figure who combines the roles of political leader of the nation and symbolic head of state provides citizens with an enormously convenient vehicle for taking cognizance of government and politics. Even for the politically sophisticated, the existence of this central figure in the political arena helps provide a focus for ordering one's thoughts and

[5] The handful of clinical reports are consistent with this suggestion, in that they describe psychological processes of considerable complexity and idiosyncratic distinctiveness.

[6] However, there is a report that this was the case in one group of patients in therapy(15). Also see(21, p. 282). For a psychoanalytic statement which emphasizes unconscious perception of the President in maternal, as well as paternal, terms, see de Grazia(5).

perceptions about public affairs. For the politically inert, the Presidency may provide virtually the only basis for connecting the citizen to his government. In the case of young children, the Presidency becomes the instrument of initial socialization into national citizenship.[7]

2. *As an outlet for affect.* Apart from the obvious emotional response to Presidents by their more articulate supporters and adversaries, it seems likely that Presidents (and their families) serve certain more general — and more diffuse — emotional functions. The detailed preoccupation in the mass media with the President's personal interests and activities has become an American equivalent of the more dignified displays of symbolic activity associated elsewhere in the world with monarchs. Attention to this aspect of the Presidency probably cuts across more segments of the population than does interest in any of the other celebrities publicized by the mass media. A remarkable variety of Presidential styles has proved to be almost equally fascinating to the mass media — and presumably also to the public which attends to the media. But there also are limits to what will be accepted as consistent with the Presidential role.[8]

3. *As a means of vicarious participation.* By personifying the complex process of government and politics, the President becomes a potential object of identification. To the degree that the President's actions are effective, citizens who identify themselves with him may experience heightened feelings of potency — of being in a world in which one is not completely dependent upon external circumstances and events. In addition to whatever attachments there may be to the President at the deeper motivational levels, it seems quite likely that, under some circumstances, a variety of people "identify" themselves with the President at least in the superficial fashion of our "identifications" with the heroes in novels and films. This probably occurs especially during international crises, such as the bombing of Pearl Harbor, when the President provides a ready outlet for patriotic feelings.

4. *As a symbol of national unity.* For this and the next point we may return to the research on responses to the President's death. It is striking to see how complete the consensus was on that occasion among such diverse segments of the population as pro-Kennedy Northern Negroes and anti-Kennedy Southern Whites(22). Although there were group differences in the intensity of response to the assassination, our overwhelming impression is of the homogeneity of public opinion — a homogeneity fostered, albeit in a macabre fashion, by the Presidency.

5. *As a symbol of stability and predictability.* We may assume that

[7] The Presidency may serve a similar function for hitherto politically inactive adult groups, which are in the process of becoming politically active. I am indebted for this point to Donald Matthews, a University of North Carolina political scientist who is studying Negro political participation in the South.

[8] It is difficult to state these limits precisely, but in general they seem to be connected with expectations about what is and is not consistent with the dignity of the Presidential office. Among recent Presidents, Truman probably was most often perceived as going beyond these limits. The connection between this and his low public opinion poll ratings seems obvious.

the Presidency normally helps to signify social stability, since for so many people one of the most disturbing aspects of President Kennedy's assassination was that it carried implications of domestic and international disorder. Again, the ease with which even the most apolitical citizen can personify the government in the President is probably significant. Our own lack of interest in the details of how the nation is governed becomes more acceptable if we feel that *someone* is attending to such matters. The assumption is that events are being controlled, that life is not whimsical and dangerous.[9] This assumption is easier to entertain in the contemporary world because of the existence of institutions like the American Presidency.[10]

REFERENCES

1. Alpert, A.: "A Brief Communication on Children's Reactions to the Assassination of the President," *Psychoanal. Stud. Child* 19:313, 1964.
2. American Institute of Public Opinion news releases.
3. American Institute of Public Opinion news release, Jan. 25, 1961.
4. Converse, P., and Dupeux, G.: "Eisenhower et de Gaulle: Les Généraux devant l'Opinion," *Rev. Franc. de Science Politique* 12:54–92, 1962.
5. de Grazia, S.: "A Note on the Psychological Position of the Chief Executive," *Psychiatry* 8:267–272, 1945.
6. Freud, S.: *Totem and Taboo* (1913). Standard Edition, *The Complete Psychological Works of Sigmund Freud*, vol. 13. London: Hogarth Press, 1955.
7. Freud, S.: *Group Psychology and the Analysis of the Ego* (1921). Standard Edition, *The Complete Psychological Works of Sigmund Freud*, vol. 18. London: Hogarth Press, 1955.
8. Freud, S.: *Moses and Monotheism*. New York: Alfred A. Knopf, 1939.
9. Greenstein, F. I.: "More on Children's Images of the President," *Publ. Opin. Quart.* 25:648–654, 1961.
10. Greenstein, F. I.: *The American Party System and the American People*. Englewood Cliffs, N.J.: Prentice-Hall, 1963.
11. Greenstein, F. I.: *Children and Politics*. New Haven: Yale University Press, 1965.

[9] The need to believe that events are controlled (and therefore controllable) helps explain why conspiracy theories — theories of the "power elite," as well as Who Killed Kennedy? theories — are so easily produced and have such widespread appeal. This is not to say, of course, that all such theories have no basis in fact.

[10] Since 1965 a second American President, Lyndon B. Johnson, has joined Truman in receiving favorable assessments by less than half of various national samples. Significantly, Johnson's low popularity — which contributed to his decision not to run for reelection — like Truman's, occurred during a period of persistently stalemated limited warfare. For data on Johnson's popularity see various numbers of the *Gallup Political Index*. Another reference to be consulted is the following paper published in 1968, which reports on a specialized sub-group of children from a region in which political leaders are widely distrusted — Appalachia: Dean Jaros, Herbert Hirsch, Frederic J. Fleron, Jr., "The Malevolent Leader: Political Socialization in an American Sub-Culture," *Amer. Pol. Sci. Quart.* LXII:564–575, 1968.

12. Hess, R. D.: "The Socialization of Attitudes toward Political Authority: Some Crossnational Comparisons," *Int. Soc. Sci. J.* 15:542–559, 1963.
13. Hess, R. D., and Easton, D.: "The Child's Image of the President," *Publ. Opin. Quart.* 24:632–644, 1960.
14. Hyman, H. H., and Sheatsley, P. B.: "The Political Appeal of President Eisenhower," *Publ. Opin. Quart.* 17:443–460, 1953.
15. Kirschner, D.: "The Death of a President: Reactions of Psychoanalytic Patients," *Behav. Sci.* 10:1–6, 1965.
16. Lasswell, H. D.: "What Psychiatrists and Political Scientists Can Learn from One Another," *Psychiatry* 1:33–39, 1938.
17. Lasswell, H. D.: *Power and Personality.* New York: W. W. Norton and Co., 1948.
18. Orlansky, H: "Reactions to the Death of President Roosevelt," *J. Soc. Psychol.* 26: 239–266, 1947.
19. Polsby, N. W.: *Congress and the Presidency.* Englewood Cliffs, N.J.: Prentice-Hall, 1964.
20. Renneker, R. E.: "Some Psychodynamic Aspects of Voting Behavior," in Burdick, E., and Brodbeck, A. J., eds.: *American Voting Behavior.* Glencoe, Ill.: The Free Press, 1959.
21. Rokeach, M., *Three Christs of Ypsilanti.* New York: Alfred A. Knopf, 1964.
22. Sheatsley, P. B., and Feldman, J. J.: "The Assassination of President Kennedy: A Preliminary Report on Public Reactions and Behavior," *"Publ. Opin. Quart.* 28:189–215, 1964.
23. Sterba, R.: "Report on Some Emotional Reactions to President Roosevelt's Death," *Psychoanal. Rev.* 33:393–398, 1946.

Image of the American Presidency:
Part II of An Exploration into
Popular Views of Presidental Power

Roberta S. Sigel

The nature of political leadership in the United States has become a subject of increased interest for political scientists and political sociologists. Crucial though their studies have been to our understanding of American governmental system and of American politics, most of them have told us little about the nature of the presidential image among

Reprinted by permission from *Midwest Journal of Political Science*, Vol. X, No. 1 (February 1966), pp. 123–137. Copyright 1966 by Wayne State University Press.

those people on whose behalf presidential leadership is exerted, namely the public.

The concurrent persistence of two themes in popular discussion, the dislike of authority and power, and the contradictory admiration for dynamic leadership suggests that Americans are highly ambivalent regarding power. They admire power and yet they fear it.[1]

Our study was designed on the basis of this ambivalence theory. Following from it we developed three hypotheses which we tested in a public opinion survey administered in Detroit, Michigan.[2] Our first hypothesis was: *Voters want strong presidents who know how to lead and how to make their will prevail.* They want them to be far more than chief executives.[3] They want them to be people with programs and ideas of their own, with the power to carry them out. *In case of conflict between president and Congress or president and public opinion, they want to see the president's will prevail.*

The second hypothesis takes account of apparent contradictions in our political tradition. *Because Americans are afraid of political power and precisely because they have accorded the president so much of it, they also wish to curb his power lest he abuse it.* A suitable device for curbing power might be the imposition of a limit on the length of time he may occupy the office. This second hypothesis we proved previously in these pages when we showed that the 22nd Amendment was very popular with respondents because it was seen as a time limit on otherwise almost unlimited presidential power and as an effective bar to dictatorship.

Our third hypothesis was based on the assumption that acceptance of a powerful president would incline *voters to prefer traits in a president which are characteristic of power* rather than homey human traits or virtues. Power-related traits would be all those traits which are judged to help a president meet the demands of his role, such as independence of judgment, intelligence, resistance to pressure, capacity for innovative thinking in contrast to such characteristics as honesty, humility, friendliness, etc.

In line with this thinking we further hypothesized that the public would pay scant attention to a President's background or qualifications, and skills which are not directly relevant to the role-demands of the presidency (such as great poverty or wealth as a child, ancestral background, self-education, etc.). To be sure, the last part of our hypothesis contradicts the so-called log cabin myth which historians and journalists

---

[1] Wm. C. Mitchell, "Ambivalent Social Status of the American Politician," *Western Political Science Quarterly*, v. 12, pp. 683–698.

[2] For a description of the sample, methodology, etc. please refer to Roberta S. Sigel and David J. Butler, "The Public and the No Third Term Tradition: Inquiry into Attitudes toward Power," *Midwest Journal of Political Science* VIII (February 1964), pp. 43–44.

[3] Of course we do not really presume to speak for all Americans, but just for Detroiters. Further research needs to be done to see if our findings will hold up for a national sample.

have found recurring through American presidential politics. This myth holds that early childhood poverty, rural origin, and a propensity for hard work and education (preferably self-education) are experiences and skills Americans value very highly in a president.[4]

Finally, we are assuming that this view of the presidency is held by most groups in the population irrespective of class, sex or age, but not race. We assumed that the strong leadership image would be most pronounced among Negroes. We hold this for two major reasons: (1) The Negro's political experience — especially in Detroit and perhaps the rest of the industrial North — has been that he fares better at the hands of Presidents than at the hands of Congress, state legislatures, and public opinion. (2) Negroes for the most part belong to socio-economic and religious groups not adverse to strong, even authoritarian, leadership ideals. Negroes tend to be predominantly of lower socio-economic status, and there seems to be a tendency among lower-class individuals to accept authoritarian concepts.[5] As for religious affiliation, Negroes belong predominantly to those Protestant denominations and sects which are usually classified as fundamentalist (such as the Baptist), and which politically are conservative even though not necessarily authoritarian.[6]

In summary, we predict that for all groups, the same image of the presidency will prevail: Wanted is a man who is strong, who has ideas of his own on how to solve problems, and who will make his ideas prevail even if Congress or the public should oppose him. The personal qualities most desired in a president are those which would enhance his leadership potential rather than those which would make him a pleasant neighbor. Finally this powerful man should exit from his office after eight years lest he become too powerful.

To test our leadership-power hypothesis we used three questions, all inquiring into the extent of leadership respondents wanted to see in a president. Two questions were phrased to juxtapose two different presidential images for the respondent's choice: one, the chief-administrator type, anxious to take his guidance from the people's and Congress's will; the other, the strong leader type, the man with ideas of his own which may be in conflict with Congress or public opinion. Of these two questions, one dealt with presidential leadership in general and the other, more specifically with presidential leadership in foreign affairs. Question one read:

> Now, which of the two statements comes closest to your own ideas: "The President is an inspired leader; he has ideas of his own how to help the country. He should be able to make the people and Congress work along with him." or "It is up to the

[4] W. B. Brown, *The Peoples Choice*, Baton Rouge, 1960.

[5] See, for example, Lipset's essay on "Working-class Authoritarianism," S. M. Lipset, *Political Man* (1960, pp. 97–130).

[6] Robin H. Williams, Jr., *American Society*, rev. ed. (1960, p. 359) documents the orthodoxy and conservatism of some Protestant denominations as contrasted to others.

people through their Congressman to find solutions to the problems of the day. The President should stick to carrying out what the people and Congress have decided."

Question two, the foreign affairs question, read:

Now, suppose that fighting is breaking out somewhere abroad, and the President thinks it's *important* to send American troops there. He knows, however, that most Americans are *opposed* to sending our troops there. Now, what do you think: Should he *send* these troops, which he may *legally* do as President, or should he *follow* public opinion and keep them home?

To discover what kind of qualities or qualifications or both voters consider most essential for a president, we constructed a list of ten personal traits a president could possess and asked respondents to select *three* of these traits they thought were most important in a president. Based on the hypothesis that people would prefer those qualities which would be indicative of leadership, the list included attributes such as intelligence, independence, and "a man with lots of ideas of his own on how to solve problems." In addition, we included such homey, personal attributes as humility and friendliness. We predicted that intelligence, independence, and "a man with lots of ideas . . ." would be among the most frequent choices. To test for the log cabin myth we also gave respondents a list of ten different personal backgrounds (such as having "grown up in a small town" or having "had to work as a young boy") and asked voters to tell us if any of these backgrounds would be good or bad for a president to have. Respondents had the opportunity to answer "indifferent" in order to permit us to test our third hypothesis that voters were concerned with leadership-connected traits and not much with quasi-private personality traits.[7]

RESULTS

Our predictions proved correct for all three hypotheses. Results indicate that majorities of our respondents want strong presidents but want a time-limit on their terms of office. (Tables 1, 2.) The public was found to be most willing to hand over power to the president in the realm of foreign affairs. The decisiveness with which people ask for leadership in foreign affairs in particular becomes truly impressive when we bear in mind that in that question we had deliberately pitted the president against public opinion when we asked if the president should send troops abroad even if "*most* Americans are opposed to sending troops there." Nonetheless 75% wish to see the president prevail *in spite of public opinion.* Here we seem

---

[7] The questions testing the log cabin myth were contained in an appendix which was administered to only one-third of the total sample of 1350 respondents. The one-third was, of course, randomly selected. Much of the appendix was the work of Professor Paule Verdet of Monteith College, Wayne State University, who is currently preparing a paper on religion and the presidency.

to be confronted with an instance of the public abdicating decision making. The reasons given for such abdication — and not just in the realm of foreign affairs — ran as follows: "that is his job"; "that is what we elected him for"; and then over and over again: "He knows more than the people." A major reason for this faith in the president's superior knowledge seems well expressed in the rhetorical question one respondent poses: "How are we to know? We don't have the facts." The overwhelming impression one gets from reading the protocols is that of an electorate which feels uninformed, does not trust its own judgment, and thinks the whole business of governing is very complicated and far beyond the comprehension of the average man. The respondents persistently tell us that they don't understand these matters and that they do not have access to the crucial information. One gets the impression of an electorate that either is not able or not willing to make crucial decisions itself. In this connection it must also be pointed out that the willingness to delegate decision making to the president stems not only from the public's view of his superior ability to do so because of his better knowledge (either innate or due to better access to information) but also from the public's trust that as a rule presidents are not wont to abuse their decision-making power. Rarely did a respondent suggest that the president might send troops abroad needlessly or otherwise act irresponsibly or selfishly. Whatever doubts our sample had with regard to the wisdom of granting a president much power does not stem from lack of faith in the president's dedication to the public interest.

When the question regarding presidential power did not deal with foreign affairs but with domestic issues, the willingness to let leadership rest with the president is sharply reduced, as we also predicted. It may be recalled that in this question both Congress and the people are joined together and put in juxtaposition to the president. Even so, 52% still want decision-making to rest exclusively with the president; 40% prefer to leave it with Congress and the people. (Table 1.) Figures such as these do not demonstrate that the public wishes to be the chief decision-makers, or for that matter that it wishes its Congressional representatives to act in this capacity. Nor does it wish to see the president's role confined to that of chief executive. Findings from a 1959 national poll conducted by the Survey Research Center corroborate our findings. When the Center asked people who they thought was in the best position to see what the country needs [8] 61% chose the president and only 17% chose Congress. We must, however, bear in mind that in both surveys respondents were asked to tell *how they would like* to see decision-making power allocated, not how they perceived it to be allocated *in reality*. *That* question was also asked by the Survey Research Center in their 1958 study. The question read: "In

[8] The exact wording of the question ran as follows: "Some people say the president is in the best position to see what the country needs. Other people think the president may have good ideas about what the country needs, but it is up to the Congress to decide what ought to be done. How do you feel about this?" (Survey #31, Election Survey, Survey Research Center, University of Michigan, Ann Arbor, Michigan.)

general, which do you think has most to say in the way our government is run — the Congress, the president, or are they about equal?" 52% thought Congress had most to say, 10% thought the president, and 24% said it was about equal.[9] This distribution is in direct opposition to the one we get from the questions which inquire into respondents' preferences.

TABLE 1

Power Attributes

Question I*	Percentage of Agreement
Presidential leadership preferred	51.5
Public and Congressional leadership preferred	39.6
Combination of both preferred	6.0
No answer	3.0
Question II*	
President should send troops in spite of public opposition	75.0
President should not send troops over public opposition	20.8
No answer	4.0
n = 1342	

* For the exact wording of the questions, see above.

The impression would not be justified that our respondents favor a powerful presidency totally immune from political or public influence. The majority of respondents express themselves in favor of letting appropriate people try to influence presidents should they so desire. Respondents were asked which people had the right to try to make the president change his mind once he has made up his mind on a matter of public policy. As Table 2 shows, no objection exists should the Cabinet, Congress, or public try to exert such influence. Apparently it is felt that these three have a legitimate stake in politics and hence a right to try to exert influence. No such right is accorded to some other people, such as his wife, spiritual leaders, or leaders of business and labor. These answers too indicate that the public's view of the presidency is essentially a political one. In summary then we can say that the public's preference for the presidential *office* is one of broad scope and wide powers but that excess of power should be guarded against by the imposition of limited tenure.

And what of the *personal* qualities considered to be important in a president? It will be recalled that we predicted that people would choose those qualities which would enable the president to be a powerful leader. Hence, we predicted voters would put most emphasis on independence,

[9] Depends 2%. Don't know 10%. Not ascertained 2%.

TABLE 2

Permissible Outside Influences on the President

Question:

Once the president has made up his mind on a matter of public policy do any of the people below have a right to try to make him change his mind?

A. NEGRO-WHITE DIFFERENCES

	Respondents Answering in the Affirmative		
	Total	Negroes	Whites
His wife	14%	11%	16%
The cabinet members	71%	55%	78%
The White House assistants	31%	23%	33%
Past presidents and senior statesmen	36%	27%	40%
The Congress and Congress leaders	69%	49%	76%
Business leaders and union leaders	21%	22%	22%
Spiritual leaders	19%	20%	18%
The American public	67%	50%	72%
	n = 416	n = 101	n = 315

B. NEGRO-WHITE DIFFERENCES WITH CONTROL FOR EDUCATION

	Respondents Answering in the Affirmative					
	Negroes with education in:			Whites with education in:		
	Grade School	High School	College	Grade School	High School	College
The cabinet members	35	69	33	79	76	87
The Congress and Congress leaders	29	64	33	67	78	82
The American public	41	52	67	66	75	73
Total n = 416	n = 34	n = 58	n = 9	n = 73	n = 182	n = 60

intelligence, and "a man with lots of ideas of his own on how to solve problems." These would rank as the three frequently given choices. From Table 3 we can see we were only partially correct; intelligence ranks second and independence third, but honesty is first; in fact is selected considerably more often than all other possible choices.[10]

Emphasis on the importance of honesty may be interpreted in several ways. It may just reflect a stereotypic and hence, meaningless choice. After

[10] Roper in a national survey found a rather similar distribution of preferences. Voters' first four choices were: Honesty, intelligence, experience, and independence. However, the margin he obtained for intelligence was considerably smaller. (American Institute of Public Opinion, Poll #412, April 1948.)

TABLE 3

Personal Qualities of President

Question:

Here's a list of qualities. Tell me which you think are the most important in a president. Try to list the three most important.

	Percentage of Choice
a. Honesty	78.4
b. Careful spender of public money	35.8
c. Friendly	8.2
d. Independent, a man who is not run by others	44.8
e. Good speaker	7.5
f. Intelligence	55.2
g. Sympathy with the lot of the little man	20.2
h. Good television personality	1.5
i. A man with a lot of ideas of his own on how to solve problems	23.9
j. Humility	9.7
Other (Specify)	5.2
No answer	1.5
Total	291.9*

---

* Percentages are based on n = 1342 (number of respondents), not on n = 3922 (number of responses), and therefore exceed 100.

all, who would not value honesty? Who would not be for virtue? However, since the respondents were presented with a list of ten qualities of which at least six can be classified as virtues and the respondents could choose three, we can point out that other "virtues" are ignored by many while honesty is not. This finding seems in keeping with Murray Levine's in Boston (Levine, 1960) which indicates how upset voters are about the lack of honesty and morality they think they find among public officials.

The importance to respondents of morality in politics can also be seen in the answers on the previously discussed appendix. Inquiring into the president's moral character, 79% express themselves in favor of a man whose private and public life is exemplary; only minorities feel that his public life alone is of concern to people, and just 2% expect little morality from politicians.[11] When this answer is viewed in conjunction with the strong preference for honesty, one may speculate whether to the pub-

---

[11] The exact wording of the question and response distribution are as follows: "The following opinions are like a ladder. On which step of the ladder do you think it is reasonable to stand?" This is about a president's moral character. "A president should give a perfect example for all Americans, at all times" (62%). "A President should not do any wrong in his public or in his private life" (17%). "A president should not give public scandal, but his private life is his own business" (21%). "You can't expect a politician to be too moral" (2%).

lic the term "honesty" is not perhaps a rather all-inclusive term covering a wide spectrum ranging from public rectitude to personal righteousness.

When we look at the three traits deemed most essential in a president as a constellation, we get a definite feeling for the type of man wanted: honest, intelligent, and independent. He is the strong knight in shining armor, the "Mr. District Attorney" or Teddy Roosevelt as folklore or television picture them: smart enough to figure out new solutions, and honest and independent enough to pursue them no matter what the intimidation.

It is interesting to note that the three top qualities are job relevant. As we had predicted, the qualities we might refer to as more personalized, such as friendliness (chosen by 8.2%) and humility (chosen by 9.7%) receive but scant attention. One may infer that respondents may value friendliness in a man but do not give it the same priority in a president since they do not judge it as crucial for him as those qualities which they judge to be job-relevant in a president — a man who has to be a leader and perhaps a fighter.[12]

Even less crucial are external characteristics, such as good speaking ability or good television personality. They rank lowest. *Appearance,* it would seem from this hierarchy of preferences, counts far less than *performance.*

In view of this emphasis on role-relevant traits, it is not surprising that respondents do not seem particularly concerned about the personal background from which presidents arise. It may be recalled that one-third of the sample was offered a list of ten background statements (see Table 4) and asked whether it is good, bad, or indifferent for a president to have come from such backgrounds. In eight instances the respondents are indifferent. In two they care: Voters think it is important for a president "to be very highly educated" (88%) and "to have had to work as a young boy" (81%). The magnitude of these two preferences is all the more impressive in view of the indifference to the remaining eight items. It is well to point out that of the two, one — education — is clearly job-relevant.

By considering the other eight background items a matter of indifference, voters apparently say that it does not matter whether a president is raised in a big city or small town; whether he is rich or poor, etc. These findings would lead us to suggest that the log cabin myth (that is, the desirability of a humble and rural but respectable background) may or may not have played a role in presidential politics at one time but that it does not seem to play a role today in an urban electorate such as the one we studied. Rather the overwhelming impression is one of voters' indifference to a president's personal background which in turn tends to confirm our assertion that the public concerns itself predominantly with role-relevant traits.

The picture which emerges from the above is that of a president pos-

[12] We may well have overestimated the importance of personality in politics. In a study of public school students Hess and Easton (1962) noted that the older a child was the more he was concerned with the "role-demands" of the presidency and the less with personal characteristics.

TABLE 4

Background Desires for Presidents

Question:

In your opinion, which of the following things would be good, or bad for a president to have?

Item	Indifferent	Percentage of Choice Good	Bad	No Answer
To have grown up in a small town	67	26	5	2
To be very highly educated	7	88	2	2
To come from a large family	45	41	2	2
To have lived through great personal suffering	45	38	10	5
To be *independently* wealthy	55	24	17	5
To have been raised among important people	41	45	7	5
To come from *old* American stock	57	31	7	5
To have grown up in a big city	69	17	10	5
To feel called by Providence to be president	38	26	26	10
To have had to work as a young boy	14	81	2	2

n = 419

sessed of those qualities which will enable him to make decisions, to make them independently, intelligently, and with integrity (honesty). These personal qualities truly fit in well with the leadership attributes discussed previously in which respondents always express preference for the president who is the leader and even molder of public opinion and Congress, not the chief-executive or errand-boy type.

Negro-White Image Differences. As we had predicted, this view of the presidency is held by all sub-groups in our population. When we control for such demographic variables as sex, age, occupation, etc. the image varies very little from group to group. All share the image of the president as a strong leader. No sub-group wants the president to be co-equal with the Congress, let alone to be weak.

However, the degree with which people want a strong president varies somewhat with groups. Most emphatically in favor of strong presidents are Negroes, which is as we had predicted. Even more than whites do they prefer presidential over public or Congressional leadership,[13] and their enthusiasm for the 22nd Amendment, the curb on presidential power, is considerably less. 58% favor it as contrasted with 69% of the

[13] In their suspicion of Congressional and public leadership Negroes are very similar to the most highly educated group in our sample, those with a college education. This latter group, however, is numerically small and has been treated elsewhere (Sigel and Butler, 1964).

whites. Those who favor it do not cite fear of one-man rule as frequently as do the whites. Nor do they see much virtue in change *per se* as did so many whites.

There also seems to be a *qualitative* difference in their image of the ideal president. Unlike whites, they tend to prefer a president insulated from most other outside influences. Whereas the population at large is quite willing to let people with a stake in government such as Congress, the Cabinet, and the public (see page 300), try to make the president change his mind, Negroes are very reluctant to concede them this right. For example, 51% of the Negroes compared with 24% of the whites would deny Congress this right. (See Table 2.)

In their preference for a strong, outside-pressure-free president, they seem to ask for one who is almost divinely inspired. Thus 45% of the Negroes thought it would be good for a president to feel called to the office by Providence (whites 20%). (See Table 4.)

The question immediately arises whether this preference for the strong, divinely inspired leader could be a function of the generally lower socio-economic standing of the Negro — which is what we had predicted. Controlling for socio-economic status proved unsatisfactory because we did not have enough Negroes in the upper and middle SES cells to make comparisons with any degree of confidence. Controlling for education, however, showed that Negro preference for strong presidents cuts across educational level. To be sure, it drops somewhat with each increment of education (see Table 2 B) but it does not drop nearly as rapidly as it drops among whites. We were right then in attributing preference for strong, charismatic leaders among Negroes in part to educational level (as an index of social status) but we underestimated the appeal such a leader had among Negroes of *all* social levels. Given the fact that even today preponderant proportions of Negroes are lower and lower middle class, it is safe to generalize that strong presidents have particularly great appeal for Negroes. Part of the explanation may lie in the fact that they partake of the general ethos of lower class culture in which predilection for strong leaders runs high (Lipset, 1960). In part this preference may also be a function of the Negro's suspicion of Congress, state legislatures, politicians, and public opinion, none of whom he has found to be friendly to his cause. His desire for strong executives thus may be grounded in the realities of the political situation as they affect him.

The Negro's image of the ideal president is very similar to that of the white but again shows some differences in emphasis. While Negroes prefer the same three qualities in an ideal president (honesty, intelligence, independence) as the whites, they do not rate intelligence and independence quite as highly as the rest of the population.[14] Part of the

[14] The figures for Negroes and whites are as follows:

Qualities	Whites	Negroes
Honesty	78.9%	77.7%
Intelligence	57.7%	45.0%
Independence	47.1%	38.3%
Sympathy with the little man	17.3%	29.6%

explanation for this may lie in the fact that more Negro than white re-spondents appear interest group oriented and hence the ability to sympa-thize "with the lot of the little man" competes with intelligence and independence in their list of priorities.

On the surface these lower margins for intelligence and especially inde-pendence seem to contradict our previous statement that Negroes, even more than whites, want strong presidents. This contradiction may well have an inner logic of its own and may be due to the community from which our sample was drawn and to the realities of the American experi-ence as it affects Negroes. For example, data from another part of our interviews indicate that Negroes, when voting for president, are less interested in the man and more in the party (49% of the Negroes and 30% of the whites tell us that they mostly vote the party not the man). How does this fit with the previously documented demand for strong, independent presidents? The answer might well be that presidential independence from Southern Congressmen is one thing but independence from the Democratic Party and its program is quite another thing.[15] Negroes, particularly those residing in the industrial non-Southern states, such as our Detroit Negroes, may well have come to look to the Demo-cratic party and upon governors and presidents as those political institu-tions most likely to be sympathetic to them. Hence, considerations of party and party loyalty rank high. This however does not preclude Ne-groes from wishing to have a president who is exceedingly strong, enough so to be leader of his own party and to resist the councils of Congressmen, Cabinet ministers, and older statesmen, to cite just a few, whom the Negro suspects of not being solicitous of his welfare. After all, from the point of view of self-interest why should Negroes wish a president to listen to Senator Eastland or a Cabinet member from North Carolina, and why on the other hand, should they not insist that he listen to the councils of the Democratic Party, especially in such states as Michigan?

The responses of Negroes then may be explained by their political ex-periences and do not deter us from reiterating that the overall image pre-ferred by the Negro is that of an extremely strong president — but that this image is tempered by considerations of party and ideology (sympathy with the little man).

DISCUSSION

The results of our survey confirm the hypothesis that the public has rather ambivalent attitudes toward power and power-holders. In the case of the president, it wants to endow him with very full powers while he is in office. In fact, the grant of power — at least in the realm of foreign affairs — amounts almost to an abdication of popular and Congressional decision-making. However, in line with our ambivalence theory, it was also

15 For documentation that presidents are often seen in the image of the party they represent, see Roberta S. Sigel, "Partisanship and Non-Partisanship and their Effect on the Perception of Political Candidates" (1964).

discovered that Detroiters were genuinely concerned over a possible abuse of power and hence preferred a time limit set on the exercise of power.

It would seem that our respondents reject the idea so eloquently stated by Spitz (1960, pp. 82–93) that "it is the business of a democratic state to give the people what they want, to satisfy their stated desires rather than their objective needs (what some wise men conceive their needs to be). This is why, in principle, all the people, and not just a few of them, are given political rights."

If our sample is any indication, the people apparently do not wish to exercise these political rights to the fullest, but rather wish to have their representative, the president, exercise these rights. The political right they do wish to retain is the privilege of choosing the correct representative.

Unfortunately our study was not designed to probe deeply into the reasons for this quasi-abdication of decision-making. Yet it is precisely such a probe which we think is urgently needed. The temptation is too great to explain such quasi-abdication on the basis of political apathy, alienation, and anomie on the one hand, or on the basis of the masses' alleged need for charisma and elitism on the other — to suggest some of the most obvious. Such temptation should be resisted — at least at this early stage. We have neither the theory nor the data to offer such explanations. Nor should we dismiss, as yet, from consideration the possibility that apathy, etc. are merely labels (possibly incorrect ones) characterizing basic — and perhaps quite positive — attitudes toward authority and power, experts, and decision-making. Attitudes toward authority and power may well be the relevant variable to be investigated in studies of political leadership. We would like to suggest that a fruitful approach for such investigations might be a study in depth which distinguishes between attitudes toward power as an abstract concept and toward power in a contextual setting. If such a study would relate power to the public's view of the role of government and the role of the citizen, we would undoubtedly gain much needed insight into the role representative government plays in the eyes of people. Not until we know this can we begin to understand what politics really means to the people of an highly industrialized nation.

REFERENCES

1. William Burlie Brown, *The People's Choice* (Baton Rouge: Louisiana State University Press, 1960).
2. Robert D. Hess and David Easton, "The Role of the Elementary School in Political Socialization," *The School Review*, Vol. 70, pp. 257–265 (1962).
3. Murray B. Levine, *The Alienated Voter* (New York: Holt, Rinehart and Winston, 1960).
4. Seymour M. Lipset, *Political Man* (New York: Doubleday and Company, 1960).

5. William C. Mitchell, "The Ambivalent Social Status of the American Politician," *Western Political Quarterly*, Vol. 12, pp. 683–698 (1959).

6. C. Perry Patterson and Harvey Walker, *American National Government* (Boston: D. C. Heath & Co., 1949).

7. Roberta S. Sigel, "Partisanship and Non-Partisanship and their Effect on the Perception of Political Candidates," *Public Opinion Quarterly*, Vol. XXVIII, pp. 483–496 (1964).

8. Roberta S. Sigel and David Butler, "The Public and the No Third Term Tradition: Inquiry into Attitudes Toward Power," *Midwest Journal of Political Science*, Vol. VIII, pp. 39–54 (1964).

9. David Spitz, "Power and Personality: The Appeal to the 'Right Man' in Democratic States," *American Political Science Review*, Vol. 52, pp. 92–93 (1960).

10. Robin M. Williams, Jr., *American Society*, rev. ed. (New York: Knopf & Co., 1960).

THE PRESIDENCY
AND THE PRESS

Presidential News:
The Expanding Public Image

Elmer E. Cornwell, Jr.

That the presidency has increasingly occupied the center of the national governmental stage in this century is apparent to the most casual observer. This fact raises a series of basic questions about the evolving pattern of American government in the mid-twentieth century.

It seems apparent that the center of gravity of the system is being shifted toward the White House. Students of the President's legislative role, for example, have unearthed considerable evidence, both institutional and in terms of changed patterns of expectations within the government, to document the fact that the President is becoming chief legislator.[1] Specialists and nonspecialists alike are aware of the expanded potential for opinion leadership which came with the advent of the regular Presidential news conference, the radio fireside chat and the medium of television.[2] The problem remains, however, of giving some more precise contours to this expanding Presidential image and the evolutionary process through which the expansion has taken place.

If this process of the expansion of the Presidential image has really gone on to the extent suggested, as focus of the public's attention and expected source of initiative, an analysis of the news content of the mass media relating to the President should reveal the fact. One is justified in inferring that a content analysis of this kind, which showed a rising curve of prominent Presidential news, reflected a rising tendency for the public to focus primary attention on the President at the expense of other parts of the national government.[3] There are two general justifications for this inference. In the first place, it is axiomatic that the great bulk of the

Reprinted by permission from *Journalism Quarterly*, 36 (Summer 1959), pp. 275–283.

[1] *Cf.* Richard E. Neustadt, "Presidency and Legislation: Planning the President's Program," *American Political Science Review*, December 1955, pp. 980–1021.

[2] *Cf.* such general works as James E. Pollard, *The Presidents and the Press*, The Macmillan Co., New York, 1947.

[3] For a general discussion of this kind of inference drawn from the results of content analyses *cf.* Bernard Berelson, *Content Analysis in Communications Research*, The Free Press, Glencoe, Ill., 1952, pp. 90–108.

electorate's knowledge about government must come from the mass media. (The only alternative, face to face contact, must be of almost negligible importance in a nation the size of the United States.) If, therefore, the media contain a rising proportion of Presidential news, it can be assumed that many of those exposed thereto will draw the obvious conclusion about the President's relative importance. In the second place, there is undoubtedly a feedback process involved. Since the President (unlike Congress) is an interesting individual doing interesting things, one can readily assume that a demand for Presidential news developed naturally and inevitably, and in turn was catered to and thus enhanced by the press.[4] In any event, this study proceeds on the assumption that a measure of Presidential news content in a representative sample of the media can be taken as a rough measure of the relative public preoccupation with the Presidential office.

THE NEWSPAPERS USED

The problem of securing a representative sample of the media next posed itself.[5] Ideally a cross section of all the important media, taking into account their successive emergence on the scene, would produce the best results. Practical considerations, however, dictated the use of the one which has existed substantially unchanged in general technique and format since the latter part of the nineteenth century — the newspaper. It was necessary for the study to cover a period roughly from the 1880s to date in order to embrace the 20th-century era of strong Presidents and enough of the preceding period to provide a basis for comparison. Practical considerations dictated the choice of two newspapers, the *New York Times* and the *Providence Journal*. Both were accessible in the form of complete files for the period, and both had been in continuous daily publication on substantially the same basis since well beore the 1880s.[6]

It happened that availability and usefulness for sampling purposes coincided to a considerable extent, in that the *Times* represents the nearest thing the United States has to a "national" newspaper in news orientation,[7] while the *Journal* is a medium-sized daily with statewide circulation in its area and a normal preoccupation with state and local news. If data from these two at least roughly correspond, a degree of general validity can be assumed for the findings.

The next problem was the selection of a sample. Ideally a sample tak-

---

[4] This idea closely parallels Bagehot's when he wrote in *The English Constitution:* "The best reason why Monarchy is a strong government is, that it is an intelligible government . . . the action of a single will, the fiat of a single mind, are easy ideas: . . . ." (D. Appleton and Co., New York, 1884, p. 101).

[5] Berelson, *op. cit.*, and Harold D. Lasswell et al., *Language of Politics*, G. W. Stewart Inc., New York, 1949, both contain extensive discussions of sampling problems in content analysis research.

[6] That is, both retained the same name and general reputation during the period and roughly the same policies as regards the quality of the news coverage they attempted to provide.

[7] *Cf.* Lasswell, *op. cit.*, p. 116.

ing every nth day during the approximately 70-year time span involved might have been used, but this would have posed enormous problems: handling several hundred bound volumes (the need to measure column inches militated against the use of microfilms), and turning thousands of fragile pages. However, anything other than a random sample of this sort, unless carefully devised, would risk distortion because of the complex cyclical patterns involved in the Presidency. The basic cycle is a four-year one, with, however, some Presidents serving one term and others more than one. Within this, before adoption of the lame-duck amendment, there was a two-year cycle containing a long and a short Congressional session, and since 1934 a series of annual cycles starting with the January convening of Congress.

With these considerations in mind the *New York Times* sample was planned to include every eighth year, that is the year following every second Presidential election year, beginning with 1885 and ending with 1957, or a total of ten years. Within each year, the first full week (starting with Sunday) in the months of January, March, May, July, September and November was used, or a total of 60 weeks comprising 420 daily papers. The choice of the weekly unit [8] was dictated in part by the impracticability of using individual days, and also to make possible observation of the weekly cycle within which the President has operated particularly since the start of the regular news conference, as the sample was tabulated.

THE RESEARCH PLAN

It was next decided arbitrarily to limit the examination of these 420 papers to the front page of each on the assumption that front pages tend to attract more reader attention than the average inside page and that the front page was reserved in the two newspapers studied for the most important news during the period under examination.[9]

The final decisions involved the actual means used to identify the news items to be tabulated. It was apparent that both Presidential and Congressional news would have to be recorded to provide a basis for assessing both the absolute and relative increase of the former. Hence headlines

[8] Lasswell (*op. cit.,* p. 136 f.) compares the accuracy of using weekly units rather than non-consecutive days and finds that the latter gives somewhat better results. For purposes of the current study, however, the loss of accuracy seemed likely to be minor in comparison with the labor that a non-consecutive day sample would have entailed. Berelson (*op. cit.,* p. 183) cites examples of studies in which both types of samples have been used.

[9] Some limited distortion was doubtless introduced in the early figures drawn from the *Journal* sample by this limitation to front pages. In the earlier years studied two or three columns of advertisements on page one were not uncommon. The distortion is probably not very great because of the fact that entire articles appeared on page one much more frequently than in later years when the practice of continuing articles to inside pages became common. Hence, though the presence of ads on page one tended to reduce somewhat the probability of a given category of news finding space on the same page, when an article did appear there its entire length would be included in the tabulation.

were examined for the words "President," "Presidency," "White House" or the *name* of the incumbent President; and for the words "Congress," "Senate," "House" (the last two only when they referred to the national legislature, of course) and the names of specific Congressional committees. Headlines containing "Congressman" or "Senator" were not tabulated if none of the other words appeared since usually the articles involved related only to one individual and not to Congress as a corporate entity. If one or more of the above words appeared in any of the levels of headlines before the dateline of the article the story was included and its column inches on the front page recorded.[10]

Several additional problems had to be taken into account in the research plan. First, when headlines contained both a Presidential word and a Congressional one, the article was put into a separate "both" category. Second, though there were obviously some articles of either Presidential or Congressional news whose headlines did not contain one of the words being tabulated, they were not included in the count.[11] It is reasonable to assume that stories of this sort would have been fairly evenly distributed between the two categories with little distortion therefore resulting. Third, the column inches of headlines that extended more than one column were recorded as these began to appear in later years, when the multi-column head contained a key word. Column inches occupied by pictures of the President also were included on the theory that such pictures had at least as much impact as a comparable number of inches of headline and text.[12] Finally, the use of measured column inches itself can be justified on the ground that this represented one means of assessing the relative impact of the story and its subject matter on the consciousness of the reader.

Thus far discussion has been of the handling of the *New York Times* sample. In order to maximize the usefulness of the *Journal* analysis as a "control," several aspects of the selection of the sample were varied, though the method of tabulating the individual issues remained the same as outlined above. It was decided to relate the *Journal* sample to the pattern of successive Presidents, rather than to arbitrary eight-year intervals.[13] Consequently one year was selected from the term in office of each of the

[10] Though the form which headlines took did change over the years, the number of words and ideas contained in the headlines, and the likelihood that they would represent a summary of the contents of the story, seem not to have changed enough to present a problem.

[11] The purpose of the study was to attempt a measurement of the impact of the Presidency (and Congress) on the consciousness of the newspaper reader. This suggested a limitation to words that would immediately suggest either of the institutions even if little more than those headlines were read.

[12] Obviously a picture of Congress could hardly have appeared for tabulation unless one were printed showing Congress in session. This suggests the publicity advantage the President enjoys by virtue of the fact that he is one man rather than a group, suggested above.

[13] The rationale behind this decision lies in the fact that the Presidency is an office peculiarly subject to modification to suit the personality, skills and philosophy of each succeeding occupant. In particular, succeeding Presidents have varied markedly in their "publicity sense" and skill in molding public opinion.

12 individuals who occupied the White House from 1889 to the present. In most instances the year chosen was that following the year in which the President was first inaugurated, that is, the first even-numbered year of his first term. In the case of McKinley, 1899 was used instead of 1898 to avoid the impact of the Spanish War; the year 1926 was used for Coolidge as the comparable year following his first election in his own right; and for Truman, though 1950 should have been used on the same principle, 1949 was substituted because of the Korean War. In each of the years chosen the same months were sampled as for the *Times* but a different week in each — the *last* full week in the month.

THE RESULTS

The data obtained from the two samples are to be found in Table 1 and are arranged on bar graphs in [Figure 1]. As might be expected, the *New York Times* data show the anticipated pattern most clearly. This sample naturally reflects both the preoccupation of the *Times* with national news and the fact that each year chosen was an inaugural year and hence, presumably, a year of abnormally high interest in Presidential doings.

TABLE 1

| | Times sample | | | Journal sample | | |
	Pres.	Both	Cong.	Pres.	Both	Cong.
1885	169.0	149.0	129.5			
1890				90.0	0	947.5
1893	191.5	197.5	75.5			
1894				136.0	36.0	80.5
1899				160.0	0	51.5
1901	320.5	16.0	30.5			
1906				300.0	0	129.5
1909	223.5	192.0	92.5			
1910				462.5	69.0	187.5
1914				210.0	9.0	82.0
1917	804.5	413.0	428.5			
1922				513.0	58.5	233.0
1925	588.0	257.5	290.0			
1926				285.0	53.0	264.0
1930				253.0	70.5	309.0
1933	1369.0	332.0	213.0			
1934				571.5	185.5	202.0
1941	762.0	255.0	444.5			
1949	437.0	278.0	536.5	378.0	175.5	368.0
1954				313.5	111.5	304.0
1957	889.0	270.0	317.0			

FIGURE 1

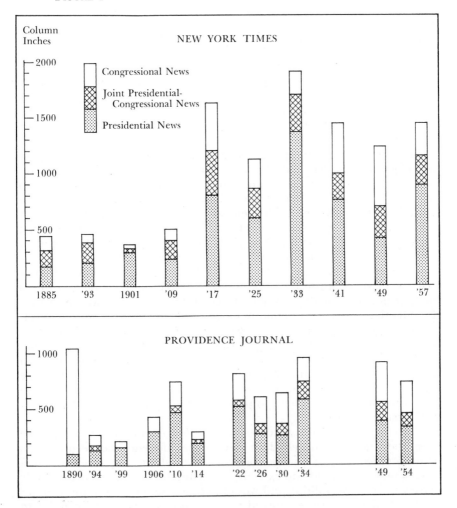

Furthermore, no effort was made to eliminate years which might, because of a crisis situation, find the President particularly prominent. The *Times* portion of [Figure 1] shows the pattern graphically: the very marked upward trend of Presidential news in contrast with the limited increase of Congressional news and less consistent upward trend of the latter.

One of the most striking features of [Figure 1] is the sharp rise in *overall* national government news. A comparison of the column inches tabulated (Table 1) with the total column inches represented on front pages in the sample examined for each year,[14] shows that up through 1909 the Presi-

14 For the *Journal,* fluctuations in column length and the shift from eight to seven and back to eight front page columns produced the following totals of front page columns (for the 42 issues tabulated each year): 1890 through 1899, 6720; 1906 through

dential plus Congressional news never reached 10% of the total (the high point was 8.5% in 1909). From 1917 on, however, the bars on the graph only twice represented less than 20% of total front page column inches. Specifically, the percentages were: 24.5 in 1917, 17.0 in 1925, 28.5 in 1933, 22.0 in 1941, 18.5 in 1949, and 22.0 in 1957.

The study shows clearly that Presidential news increased more rapidly than either national government news as a whole or Congressional news. In all but one of the years sampled following World War I, straight Presidential news represented more column inches than the other two categories combined, while this was only true in one of the first five years under study. This, in spite of the fact that in the last five years checked, Congress was in session (and presumably making news) for an average of about seven and a half months each year, and only in session about five and a half months on the average during each of the first five years. In other words, much of the increase in Congressional news during the total period can be attributed to the general increase in governmental activity and public interest in government, and to the increase in Congressional activity particularly. At the same time, preoccupation with the President and news about him outstripped all of these other trends.

The picture presented by the *Journal* data is not as clear-cut as that of the *Times,* due both to the differences in sample construction and to the local/regional orientation of the former. (While the *Times* averaged 16% Presidential plus Congressional news on page one, the *Journal* only averaged 10%.) The vast amount of Congressional news recorded for 1890, followed by a precipitous drop during the next years, reflects no more than a changed policy in the location of the daily two or three column discussion of congressional happenings. In 1890 it was generally on page one, and in ensuing years, frequently on an inside page. It was not until later that Congressional news appeared in the *Journal* in the form of several separate stories.

The crucial question is as to whether the *Journal* findings *parallel* those from the *Times.* As suggested, in view of the differences between the two papers, differences in sample construction, and the like, even a rough correspondence would indicate that conclusions drawn from the study have some general validity and would not need serious alteration if other reputable dailies [15] were sampled and the results compared. In order to facilitate analysis of the degree of correspondence of the two, a combined graph was prepared using the total column inches of Presidential news plus the news involving both President and Congress — in other words, the two categories that involved some headline Presidential reference.

1922, 5292; 1926 through 1934, 6048; and 1949 and 1954, 6720. In the *Times* the total for each year from 1885 through 1909 was 5880, and from 1917 to the present, 6720.

[15] By reputable daily is meant a newspaper that makes some serious efforts to feature news in relation to its relative importance, rather than one which follows "tabloid" policies. Presumably, however, even in a tabloid, analysis would turn up patterns roughly similar to those found in this study.

FIGURE 2

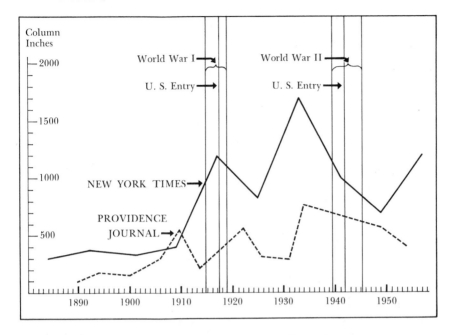

An inspection of [Figure 2] indicates a very close parallelism between the two samples. In both instances there is a consistently low level of Presidential news until the advent of Theodore Roosevelt, both exhibit a post-World War I dip, both reach their highest peak in the early Franklin Roosevelt administration, and though both fall off from this peak, both remain at a level considerably above the previous average. In short, both show patterns that fluctuate similarly but with an unmistakable marked upward tendency.

There is one major area in which the lines do not correspond at all aside from the period of the Eisenhower administration which may reflect no more than the difference between 1954 and the inaugural year 1957. Close analysis suggests that the World War I discrepancy is in fact easily explainable and in itself significant. The year 1914 was used for the *Journal* sample, while the year 1917 was used for the *Times*. In the former year Wilson was quite apparently making fewer headlines than students of his vigorous legislative and opinion leadership might lead one to expect. Furthermore, in the final two months of the sample the beginnings of the war in Europe pushed virtually everything else off the front page. The first four months of 1914 sampled yielded 208.5 column inches of Presidential and joint Presidential-Congressional news, while September and November yielded only 10.5 inches. On the other hand, 1917 produced a vast amount of Presidential and "joint" news for the simple reason that this year embraced the rapid-fire exchange of notes and accusations immediately preceding our entry into the war and, of course, the initial months of war mobilization.

The fact that Wilson achieved a column-inch score in the *Times* sample second only to that of F.D.R. in 1933 (and a higher score than F.D.R. made in the closely comparable year 1941) suggests the same conclusion reached by the author on the basis of another study.[16] Wilson's contribution to the enhancement of the Presidency in the public eye, and as platform for opinion leadership, was much more the result of his wartime role and the way it was portrayed than of his preceding peacetime activities.

The foregoing suggests further possibilities for generalization about the pattern which the 20th-century expansion of the Presidential image followed. The three crucial points appear to have been the impact of T.R.'s popularity, the much greater impact of World War I, and the still greater impact of F.D.R. and the Great Depression. In each instance, the tide of publicity receded somewhat following the peak, but tended to establish a new norm higher than the previous one. Thus the pattern is one of short term fluctuations but a long term upward trend in overall Presidential news, both in absolute terms and relative to news about Congress. Other evidence suggests that this overall upward movement was due in part to the use that succeeding Presidents since World War I made of new mass media as they emerged.[17] It doubtless was also the result of a kind of cumulative impact on the public which must in turn have translated itself into a heightened demand for Presidential news.

This cumulative factor (or delayed reaction) can best be seen in the graph based on the *Journal* sample [Figure 2], avoiding as this sample does the direct effects of national crises. Such a delayed reaction must explain the fact that both Taft and Harding scored higher than their immediate predecessors, generally assumed to have far surpassed them as strong and newsworthy Presidents. Note the *Journal* figures for 1910 (and the *Times* figures for 1909). President Taft frequently made the headlines because his name was linked with that of ex-President Roosevelt who was either preparing for his sojourn in Africa (1909) or involved in a widely reported quarrel with his chosen successor over policy (1910). In other words, the full impact of the Roosevelt popularity apparently came *after* he had left office and found part of its expression in the form of heightened interest in President Taft.

The same hypothesis is doubtless relevant in explaining Harding's greater popularity than either Coolidge and Hoover on the one hand, or even the pre-War Wilson, on the other. The extraordinary publicity given Wilson once war came seems to have rubbed off on his otherwise exceedingly colorless successor. In both instances, some, though significantly not all, of this heightened interest died down in another few years.

F.D.R. seems to belie this theory but perhaps does not in reality. Atten-

---

16 Manuscript article entitled "Wilson, Creel and the Presidency," which [appeared] in the *Public Opinion Quarterly*, Summer 1959, pp. 189–202.

17 *Cf.* the author's "Coolidge and Presidential Leadership," *Public Opinion Quarterly*, Summer 1957, pp. 265–278.

tion was focused upon him following March 4, 1933 with an intensity and urgency unmatched in any inaugural year since 1861. This preoccupation which diminished only slightly during the rest of his first term is clearly evident in both samples. Involved, in other words, was a much more abrupt build-up of interest in the White House occupant than in the case of either T.R. or Wilson. In addition, during Franklin Roosevelt's unprecedented 12 years in office the tide of interest in his Presidency had time to recede somewhat from the peak reached in the early '30s and before his successor took over. As a result the Truman administration coincided with the downswing in interest encountered earlier. Taft and Harding, on the other hand, scored higher than their more impressive predecessors because they came into office before the tide of interest in the men they followed had had time to recede.

One final pattern, observable on [Figure 1], is worth underscoring. That is the fairly consistent expansion of the portion of the bar which represents news dealing with both Congress and the President. One assumed characteristic of the 20th-century Presidency has been an increase in Presidential legislative leadership. Obviously news items in this "both" category deal with some kind of contact between the executive and legislature, and frequently with participation by the President in the legislative process. An expansion in this category of news would hence be significant. In the *Journal* data, only twice were such items tabulated at all up to the Harding administration, but from Harding on they are consistently present and increasingly prominent. This trend is somewhat less pronounced in the *Times* sample, but none the less present. In each of the *Times* bars from 1917 on, the "both" category is larger than in any of the four preceding years sampled. Whether this limited evidence indicates increased Presidential legislative leadership or generally accelerated governmental activity, or both, the findings are significant.

SUMMARY

The data presented indicate that Presidential news, and by inference the public's image of the Presidency and its relative governmental importance, has increased markedly and more or less steadily in this century, particularly since World War I. The average column inches of straight Presidential news even in the *Journal* sample, following the Great War, ran at a rate nearly double the earlier period — and in a newspaper, like most American city dailies, unwilling to devote more than a portion of its front page to other than local news. In the nationally oriented *Times,* the post-War average was nearly quadruple that of the pre-War period.

This trend is the result of the interaction of strong Presidents and periods of national crisis, in large part. The story is more complex, however. Weak Presidents in between have both basked in reflected publicity and utilized the developing media for their own more limited purposes.

The Washington Correspondents

Leo C. Rosten

The Washington correspondents, more familiarly known as "the capital press corps," enjoy a semi-official status. They are listed in the *Congressional Directory*. They have access to conferences with the officers of the government from the President of the United States down. They have special quarters set aside for their exclusive use in all government buildings, including the White House. Official documents, statements, reports, statistics, are made available to them. They receive advance copies of speeches and announcements. They have special sections reserved for them in the galleries of the House of Representatives and the Senate, and at Congressional Committee hearings. A committee of their own choice governs them in the press galleries, formulating rules for admission and enforcing discipline.

The Washington correspondents consort with statesmen. They dine with Ambassadors and Cabinet members. They are fêted at the White House in a special reception and ball. They are not strangers to full dress or the perquisites of social status. Their help is sought by persons and organizations trying to publicize an issue; their displeasure is avoided. They are aware, by virtue of the deference paid to them and the importance attached to their dispatches, that they are factors of political consequence. They have launched Congressional investigations and wrecked political machinations. They are the antennae of newspapers all over the nation. They are private citizens working for private employers; yet their status is such that they are granted quasi-official prerogatives. The agencies of the federal government co-operate with them, with varying degrees of efficiency and ingenuousness, in the process of informing the United States about what is going on in its capital.

The press corps is a professional skill-group with a high morale, a strong tradition, a vigorous if unarticulated code of ethics, and a body of specialized techniques. Now a profession may attract personalities of a generic type by its very nature, and a community of interest, experience, and skills tends to stamp professional perspectives with an identity of form. Despite the anonymity which journalism usually imposes upon its practitioners, newspapermen do not live in either a social or an intellectual vacuum. The journalist is sensitized to the observation of aspects of the real world, with a talent for translating segments of reality into the grammar of "news stories." In the inflections which creep into his recording of events there is imbedded, however obscurely, a personality — and an autobiography. "Objectivity" in journalism is no more possible than

Reprinted by permission from Leo C. Rosten, *The Washington Correspondents* (New York: Harcourt, Brace & World, Inc., 1937), pp. 3–6, 47–49, 51–53, 55–57, 250–254.

objectivity in dreams. Even under the mobilization of arid facts in a dispatch on the Budget there is a structure of professional reflexes and individual temperament. . . .

The circumstances under which President Roosevelt took office were peculiarly auspicious. After the negativism of Calvin Coolidge and the intransigence of Herbert Hoover, an executive with an engaging manner, a modicum of wit, and an appreciation of newspaper problems was destined to receive an enthusiastic welcome from the Washington press corps. Mr. Roosevelt's insight into publicity techniques effected a revolution in White House press relations. The social setting in 1933 was, of course, made to order for a man who knew how to dramatize himself and his program in terms understandable to the common man. From 1933 through 1934, news dispatches from the capital publicized his talents and extolled his political astuteness. The newspapermen who swarmed to press conferences at the White House were convinced that "here was a politician to make Machiavelli, Mark Hanna, Talleyrand, and Boies Penrose hang their heads in utter shame." Publishers began to complain that Mr. Roosevelt had hypnotized their reporters with his charm and misled them with his "propaganda.". . .

At his first meeting with the newspapermen, on March 8, 1933, Mr. Roosevelt announced that the correspondents would be free to ask direct oral questions. The President's advisers had warned him against oral questioning as an unnecessary and hazardous procedure; they awaited it with anxiety, the correspondents with skepticism. The President's technique and the spirit which pervaded that first press conference are worth describing in detail; they have become something of a legend in newspaper circles. Mr. Roosevelt was introduced to each correspondent. Many of them he already knew and greeted by name — first name. For each he had a handshake and the Roosevelt smile. When the questioning began, the full virtuosity of the new Chief Executive was demonstrated. Cigarette-holder in mouth at a jaunty angle, he met the reporters on their own grounds. His answers were swift, positive, illuminating. He had exact information at his fingertips. He showed an impressive understanding of public problems and administrative methods. He was lavish in his confidences and "background information." He was informal, communicative, gay. When he evaded a question it was done frankly. He was thoroughly at ease. He made no effort to conceal his pleasure in the give and take of the situation.

The correspondents were exhilarated. Mr. Roosevelt's first interview with the reporters of the capital ended in a spontaneous outburst of applause, a phenomenon unprecedented in White House annals. One of the oldest and most respected correspondents in Washington, Henry M. Hyde of the *Baltimore Evening Sun,* called it "the most amazing performance the White House has ever seen."

> The press barely restrained its whoopees. . . . Here was news — action — drama! Here was a new attitude to the press! . . .
> The reportorial affection and admiration for the President is

unprecedented. He has definitely captivated an unusually cynical battalion of correspondents.

Even the editor of *Editor and Publisher* was ebullient.

> Mr. Roosevelt is a great hit among newspapermen at Washington. I rubbed my ears (*sic!*) and opened my eyes when I heard hard-boiled veterans, men who had lived through so many administrations and been so disillusioned that there are callouses in their brain, talk glibly about the merits of the White House incumbent. If Mr. Roosevelt fails the craft, by any false word or deed, he will break a hundred hearts that have not actually palpitated for any political figure in many a year.

The reasons for this hero-worship by presumably "hard-boiled" newspapermen are not difficult to isolate. Mr. Roosevelt's colloquial manner soothed journalistic egos still smarting under the rebuffs of his predecessor. The laughter at press conferences was in the nature of a catharsis: in it was vented some of the hostility which Mr. Hoover had aroused. Newspapermen admired President Roosevelt's adroit handling of questions. He won professional approbation for his news sense, his ability to "time" a story so that it broke with maximum force, his skill in investing even routine affairs with news value. "He never sent the reporters away empty-handed . . . and reporters are all for a man who can give them several laughs and a couple of top-head dispatches in a twenty-minute visit." Above all, the positivism and range of Mr. Roosevelt's action, pouring climax upon climax in a remarkable sequence of political moves, won newspapermen, no less than lay citizens, after the obstinate inertia of the last White House occupant. . . .

The Washington correspondents were pleased by Mr. Roosevelt's obvious efforts to win their good-will. They were flattered by "off the record" comments. Their professional ethic was gratified by the fact that Mr. Roosevelt cultivated them as a group, playing no favorites and breeding no "trained seals." Many of them were won by the hospitality shown at picnics, receptions, and Sunday afternoon teas at which the President and Mrs. Roosevelt played host to the press.

Mrs. Roosevelt broke the tradition of Presidential wives and became a personality of consequence in her own right. She held press conferences with women correspondents; in her way she was often more effective than her husband. She won widespread respect and affection.

The President's influence permeated every department and bureau of the government. . . .

. . . When one executive in NRA refused to co-operate with the press he was discharged on orders from the White House. When Major Dalyrymple of the liquor division of the Internal Revenue Office (the Alcohol Tax Unit) rebuked newspapermen and told them "not to hang around my office," he was chastised in a manner certain to win the correspondents' hearts. When Henry Morgenthau, Jr., on becoming Acting Secretary of the Treasury, issued his General Order Number 1, on November 20, 1933, ruling that all departmental news must come directly from him or his press agent, the Treasury Correspondents Association wired their protest to Hyde Park and got a modification of the rule. There was general agreement among the Washington correspondents that the New Deal was trying to provide accurate news, and that the press agents of the various governmental agencies were doing a commendable job. Even handouts, later the subject of considerable criticism, were praised for their veracity and the service which they afforded hard-pressed newspapermen.

It was "a newspaperman's administration." Arthur Sears Henning, head of the Washington bureau of the *Chicago Tribune,* stated that never had relations between the press and the White House been so happy. George R. Holmes, bureau chief of International News Service, praised the President for his policy, called him "his own best press relations man," and said that in the twenty years he had been in Washington he had "never known a time when the administration seemed more honest in giving out news." Arthur Krock, of the *New York Times,* said that Mr. Roosevelt was the greatest reader and critic of newspapers he had ever seen in the Presidential office; and, the final accolade, "He could qualify as the chief of a great copy desk."

The honeymoon could not last. The Washington correspondents had propagated the impression that Franklin D. Roosevelt was a paragon of talents and a repository of supreme political skills. Events which shattered this idea released that iconoclasm which is the successor to faith.

In 1935 dispatches began to reveal a more aggressive and critical journalistic temper. In Washington newspaper circles one encountered less hero-worship, more skepticism of both the President's personal graces and his political acumen. Ashmun Brown of the *Providence Journal,* honorably mentioned in the 1936 Pulitzer Prize awards, wrote an astringent article in the *American Mercury* for April, 1936, and insisted that "the Roosevelt Myth" was no more. Other newspapermen in the capital began to write caustically of Mr. Roosevelt's "dictatorial" aspirations, the menace of his "propaganda" or the various follies of the New Deal.

The correspondents began to falter in their emotional allegiance as the structure of the New Deal began to totter. In some dismay they were driven to the conclusion that Mr. Roosevelt's More Abundant Life was overdue. Unemployment figures began to worry them — particularly since they could not get exact ones from government sources. Some began to murmur that, for all the ballyhoo, the New Deal was less an integrated program than a series of adventures in the realm of political economy. Many newspapermen found it difficult to reconcile the politics of Mr. Farley, for whom they had a genuine personal affection, with Rooseveltian moral purpose.

At a press conference in February, 1935, the President was asked whether he would support state NRA legislation. He answered in the negative. The correspondents hastened to send off their dispatches and in some places special editions appeared. That afternoon Governor McNutt of Indiana, campaigning to stimulate NRA legislation in his state, called the White House by telephone; Mr. Roosevelt assured him that he (the President) had been misquoted. He sent a telegram to the Governor which was made available to the press. It read, in part:

> I have no hesitation in making perfectly plain to you the extraordinary misinterpretation put upon my reply at press conference.

At his next press conference Mr. Roosevelt chided the correspondents for their "misinterpretations." He warned the corps not to draw unwarranted inferences from his failure to comment on "pending legislation," since "80 per cent" of such conjectures were incorrect. The newspapermen were surprised. They felt that the President had wriggled out of a difficult situation, leaving them to hold the bag.

After the "Dred Schechter decision," to use one of H. L. Mencken's more palatable phrases, Mr. Roosevelt delivered his famous "horse and buggy" stricture against the Supreme Court, in the press conference of May 31, 1935. Some correspondents thought the comments petulant and impolitic. Those who regarded the Constitution as a parchment of divine origin called the President's comments heresy. To others it was simply the most unforgivable of political sins: bad strategy.

On June 24, 1935, the President held an emergency conference with congressional leaders. When it was over, Senators Harrison and Robinson, spokesmen for the administration, declared that a decision had been made to push through the President's recommendations for so-called "Soak the Rich" legislation, by attaching them as a rider to a bill pending on excise taxes. A howl of protest went through the editorials of the land. At his next press conference, June 26, 1935, Mr. Roosevelt announced that he had *not* recommended such legislation. "The correspondents . . . gasped in amazement. The questions which followed reflected their anger and incredulity."

Several blunders of another caliber saddened correspondents who had come to believe in their own reports of Mr. Roosevelt's infallible political acumen: his letter of July 7, 1935, to Representative Sam Hill, apropos the Guffey Coal Bill ("I hope your committee will not permit doubts as to constitutionality, however reasonable, to block this legislation."); his public reversal of attitude on the propriety of corporation gifts to charity; the flagrant error involved in the cancellation of the air-mail contracts, permitting the Army, with inadequate resources, to fly the mails — with tragic consequences; the affair of the "preacher letters," in which it was discovered that by some colossal carelessness the White House secretariat had sent out an inquiry to several thousand clergymen which was in part a verbatim copy of a letter sent six months earlier by Governor La Follette of Wisconsin. . . .

Other sources of irritation were less explicit, but no less corrosive. The correspondents were disillusioned when the President, in answering one newspaperman who had persisted in asking an embarrassing question, said tartly: "This isn't a cross-examination." To newspapermen who had come to feel that they had a right to cross-examine the President on matters of policy, if not on affairs of state, this was a distressing blow.

Newspapermen began to feel that the exercise of Presidential wit to evade a question was less of a novelty than an irritant. The use of correspondents' first names was resented by some as a form of psychological bribery. Mr. Roosevelt's debonair manner offended those newspapermen who thought the dignity of the office called for lugubrious intonations, or those who could not forgive a personality exuberant in the face of adversity. Liberal correspondents mourned the President's compromises with the Right; conservatives, his flirtations with the Left. The Roosevelt smile was maliciously likened to a faucet, turned on and off with calculated purpose. One heard repeated displeasure with Mr. Roosevelt's facial gestures ("mugging").

There was growing antagonism to the "off the record" remarks. They were called "silly" or "unnecessary"; it was said that they no longer divulged really confidential information, but more often acted "to sew up a story" which some correspondents were ready to write. Arthur Krock, after praising the President and his aides for their newspaper policy, and after granting the great service of the press releases, suggested that the administration was guilty of "more ruthlessness, intelligence, and subtlety in trying to suppress legitimate unfavorable comment than any other I have known."

With the spread of critical sentiment, Mr. Roosevelt was charged with faults for which his responsibility was questionable. For instance, at each press conference the same group of correspondents (generally from the press associations) stand in the front row, directly before the President's desk. These men, it was darkly hinted, "play the stooge": they laughed too heartily at Mr. Roosevelt's puns. The "front row" ordinarily supplies the "Thank you, Mr. President" which is the informal signal for the end of the conference; some newspapermen suggested to this writer that the technique was being used to rescue Mr. Roosevelt from embarrassing situations. It was said, too, that reporters in "the front row claque" permitted themselves to be used for "planted questions" (i.e., questions suggested to them by one of the President's secretaries) for which Mr. Roosevelt was primed with a ready and devastating answer.

Now some of these charges were legitimate, some absurd. The whole array, including many which must seem picayune, is given here because it is undeniable that there are newspapermen in Washington who harbor a resentment against Mr. Roosevelt, for one or another of these reasons, which is reflected in the tenor of their news dispatches. In the very fervor with which he was delineated in the first days of his administration lay part of the animus for that reversion of sentiment which took place once it became clear that not even Mr. Roosevelt could fulfill the extravagant expectations of the newspapermen. They had accepted as real not merely their glorification of a man, but their fabrication of a superman. No agnostic is so bitter as one disenchanted of a desperate and adolescent faith.

In the myth about Mr. Roosevelt which the Washington correspondents propagated, and in the energies devoted to the later deflation of it, there is an illuminating lesson for analysts of public opinion. Neither the myth-making nor the myth-destroying was an inexplicable or unique phenomenon. The same journalistic process has operated before; and it will be repeated with future Presidents and by future correspondents. The dynamics of that process form a study in the psychology of journalists. . . .

. . . Reporters often come to believe in the fictional qualities which they assign to public figures during that professional delirium which characterizes the daily meeting of deadlines. Newspapermen are driven to overstatement because they are competing against overstatements. And men who operate in the realm of words unconsciously assign to the words they use a reality which transcends their intentions. In this context it was not Mr. Roosevelt who hypnotized the Washington correspondents: it was the Washington correspondents who hypnotized themselves.

The one measure of value which most newspapermen possess is the rod of success. Ashmun Brown has stated that, for the Washington correspondent, "The man who gets away with it is a good politician." This empirical standard does not create analytic judgments which have validity beyond the immediate day and the successes thereof. The press corps vested a great deal of emotional faith in Mr. Roosevelt; as long as he was a politician "getting away with it" that faith was justified. But when he began to meet formidable opposition from the Supreme Court, Congress, the Republicans, the elders of the Democratic Party, and the wide front of private groups who fought the President tooth and nail, when he began to meet with a series of defeats or temporary setbacks, some of the Washington correspondents began to falter. The corps had greeted Mr. Roosevelt with frenzy in 1933; in it there was a will-to-believe which, because it ignored future possibilities and past experience, would end by tearing down the myth it was creating.

The "disillusionment" with the President by newspapermen represented an externalization of guilt. For the Washington correspondents were naive, rather than hard-boiled, in the adulation which, upon their own initiative, they showered upon Mr. Roosevelt. Having "betrayed" the objective function which they felt they must observe, the conscience of the correspondents acted with doubled vigor. Newspapermen added to a situation for which they held the President responsible those discontents which might more legitimately have been directed against themselves. This was improper, for in inter-personal relations as in commerce the admonition *caveat emptor* throws responsibility upon the gullible. A healthy proportion of the antagonism to Mr. Roosevelt was over-reaction by reporters who would have preferred that their earlier exaltations of the man might be removed from the record. They could not wipe out the emotional commitments of the past, but they intensified their efforts to compensate for them.

The emotional affect of the Washington correspondents travels along cyclical lines. It has happened so often before that, given the demands of journalistic writing, the face-to-face relationship of the press conferences, and the personality types who are attracted to newspaper work, there is every reason to believe it will happen again. Adulation — guilt — debunking. Newspapermen greet the new statesman with a deep hope that here, at last, is the great man incarnate. There is evidence to support this in the traditional honeymoon psychology of the first months. The great man's talents are sung, over-sung in the struggle for journalistic existence. Then "incidents" occur, a political compromise of not admirable hue, a political setback, attacks from the opposition. The newspapermen begin to see the pedal clay. They have been "taken in." Their faith has been outraged. How did they ever "fall for the stuff"? The demon on the desk in the home office sends them sarcastic reminders of their first euphoria. Other newspapermen, columnists, editors, publishers cry that the press corps was hamstrung by phrases. The correspondents are hurt; they are irritated; and they feel guilty. The breaking of the myth begins, by the men who erected it.

This writer inclines to the view that had Governor Landon been elected to the Presidency in 1936 he would have been hailed by many correspondents as the Fox from Kansas ("the greatest President since Calvin Coolidge") in 1937, that articles called "Is Landon Slipping?" (written for the Sunday pages) would appear in 1938, that public recantations by newspapermen would mount in 1939, and that — assuming no spectacular boom — the majority of the correspondents would be dreaming of "a *real* leader" in 1940.

The Presidential Press Conference

Fauneil J. Rinn

Regularly during the last half century since the presidential press conference took root as a Washington custom strident demands have been made for its abolition. The loudest complaints have come from the Washington press corps itself. Some reporters have grown impatient with what they see as a chasm-like gap between the promise of the conference of inform-

Printed by permission of the author.

ing them — and through them, the public — of everything worth knowing and the reality that at a press conference Presidents tell only as much as they think it is in the public interest to tell. Occasionally, particularly during national crises, Presidents, too, have shown signs of disenchantment with the conference. Their displeasure has concerned the reporters' failure to appreciate that Presidents, not the press, are in the best position to determine what is necessary, safe, or wise to make public.

These considerations point to the main barrier to the smooth running of the conference. By most accounts, trouble is caused by the opposing expectations that the press and Presidents bring to their meetings. The reporters come in order to get the news, and they often think that Presidents hinder rather than help them. The recipe for what makes news is as closely guarded a secret as the formula for Coca-Cola, and it consists of mysterious proportions of novelty, controversy, and significance. When blended, these ingredients can create a mixture that is distasteful to Presidents, who do not mind novelty or significance but often think newsmen season their stories with too much controversy. For the public the inclusion of rival interests in the conference may be beneficial if the interplay uncovers something that the public can use to judge whether or not a President is doing what he should. Conflict can also benefit the public if the President takes the reporters to task and makes them examine their standards and practices.

The problems of the conference, however, do not center on the friction between reporters and Presidents. A little verbal sniping from both sides can be a healthy thing — the public may be able to see through the holes. Problems derive from the dispute between those on the press side who want total access to the details of administration plans and projects and those on the government side who know that premature publicity can spoil policy-in-the-making. The question is where does the public's best interest lie in individual cases of press-President contention? The nature of the question forbids any once-and-for-all answer. The constant trumpeting by the press that it alone can protect the people's right to know is not an answer but merely a slogan that helps little toward clarification or solution. But the President cannot automatically be given the benefit of the doubt. His potential control over information is already so vast that it would be foolish never to question his decisions about what the public needs to know in order to make an intelligent assessment of the government's performance.

Critics of the conference, who see little hope of shaping it so that it can live up to its promise as a vehicle for informing the public, have set goals for the conference that are beyond its competency and have missed or undervalued some worthwhile tasks that it can and does perform. The best way to see how their criticisms have been poorly grounded is, first, to describe the main attributes of the conference and, second, to evaluate the various claims for what it accomplishes or should accomplish. These two efforts may provide a better basis for proposals to improve conference theory and practice.

The President can meet the press anywhere from the site of a new dam to a vacation spot although most conferences have taken place in Washington. A conference can be held at any time during the day or night and can last from three minutes to two hours. Its proceedings can be fully and even instantaneously publicized or firmly and completely off the record. There is no fixed format, and there has never been uniformity among Presidents as to the time, manner, and place of conferences. Decisions about these matters are strictly up to the President, although he may consult the press about its preferences. Most Presidents have found some congenial format and stuck fairly closely to it. Others have tried various types. Lyndon Johnson, for example, has held surprise conferences, off-the-record conferences, and "live" TV conferences. He even tried "walka-thon" conferences during which he responded to reporters while the group strolled around the White House lawn.

For all the variations possible on the conference theme, however, there are four requisites that must be present for there to be a conference: the President must be present; there must be a sizeable contingent from the Washington press corps present; there must be some questions and answers; and there must be a considerable degree of spontaneity. The need for the first three is self-evident. Spontaneity is also essential because there would be no real exchange of views — and, hence, by definition no conference — if the proceedings were wholly rehearsed and done by rote.

The four essential attributes do not include making the proceedings public. The press might include that as another necessity, but if one were to insist on it, most of the conferences in the last half century could not be called conferences. It is only since the end of Truman's term that nearly full publicity has been given to the conference exchange. This question of whether and to what extent publicity is a requirement of the conference has been the most persistent and serious source of trouble between the President and the press.

Six categories of purposes of the conference have been postulated by various journalists, historians, and political scientists: (1) it holds the executive accountable and, thus, does for the United States what the Question Hour, the means by which Members of Parliament hold their Cabinet to account, does for England; (2) it is another method of fulfilling the check and balance function of our constitutional system; (3) it offers a way to get a valid portrait of the President; (4) it demonstrates the vigor and pervasiveness of democracy in America; (5) it furnishes a means for the President to hear what is on the minds of some knowledgeable observers of government who have fewer axes to grind than most of those with whom he associates; and (6) it is a channel for presidential leadership. The list reveals a considerable lack of agreement among those who have thought about the significance of the conference although the first four categories view the press as the most important element in the conference. Discussion of each category may reveal their differences and similarities more sharply as well as aid in articulating the true potential of the conference.

THE CONFERENCE AS QUESTION HOUR

Those who see an American Question Hour in the press conference are struck by the grave lack elsewhere in the American system of any method by which the executive may be called upon formally to explain administration policy or by which he may be forced to debate it to the satisfaction of his opponents.[1] A common assumption of those who see the conference as a Question Hour is that no democracy deserving of the name should be without some device like the Question Hour. This belief, however, leads them to overlook some decisive differences between the conference and the Question Hour in the participants, in format and procedure, and in their disparate ends.

Reporters do not and cannot approach the conference as persons who may some day have the responsibilities of government. Reporters, unlike Members of Parliament, are not in any sense political equals of the executive. The most dramatic difference between the Question Hour and the press conference is that the Question Hour can topple the government while the press conference has no such impact on the government. At his last conference, President Eisenhower was asked, "During these eight years . . . did you feel that reporters had been fair to you . . . in their questions?" His reply was: "Well, when you come down to it, I don't see what a reporter could do much to a President, do you?" [2]

Also, the Question Hour is held with unremitting regularity as a formal governmental procedure while the scheduling of press conferences is entirely up to the President. Another marked difference in format concerns the questioning. Parliament's questions are written and submitted far in advance to afford the Cabinet ministers time for research and reflection. Supplementary questions may be posed once the subject of the written question has come to the floor. The press conference for more than thirty-five years has allowed only oral questions and the opportunities for follow-up questions have dropped as attendance has soared. This difference is significant because the supplementary question is responsible for the Question Hour's success in holding the Cabinet to account for its actions.

1 Among those who favor this view of the conference's prime purpose are S. S. Douglass Cater, Jr., *The Fourth Branch of Government* (Boston: Houghton Mifflin Company, 1959), 142–55; Erwin D. Canham, "Democracy's Fifth Wheel," *The Literary Digest,* CXIX, No. 1 (January 5, 1935), 6; Max Lerner, *America as a Civilization* (New York: Simon and Schuster, 1957), 753; Arthur M. Schlesinger, Jr., *The Coming of the New Deal* (Boston: Houghton Mifflin Company, 1958), 562; Richard L. Strout, "President and Press," *The Christian Science Monitor,* April 2, 1955; Bernard A. Weisberger, *The American Newspaperman* (Chicago: University of Chicago Press, 1961), 174. Lindsay Rogers takes strong exception to this idea, calling it "a silly assumption" in a review of Cater's book, *Saturday Review,* XLII, No. 23 (June 6, 1959), 21. Louis Brownlow did not regard the conference as doing a complete job but thought that, coupled with the congressional power to investigate, it performs the Question Hour function. *The President and the Presidency* (Chicago: Public Administration Service, 1949), 89.

2 Dwight D. Eisenhower, *Public Papers of the Presidents* (Washington, D.C.: U.S. Government Printing Office, 1961), conference of January 18, 1961.

This "power of pursuit" is a necessary, although not a sufficient, attribute if the press conference is to be a comparably effective tool for accountability. Only on rare occasions have reporters put a President on the spot. For instance, it seemed as if they had consulted beforehand to take Eisenhower to task over his Attorney General's charge that the Truman administration had not been alert to Communist influence in the government. Occasionally a single reporter has tenaciously held the floor until he finished a string of questions on one subject. On September 13, 1962, for example, Jack Raymond of the *New York Times* asked three questions in a row to draw out Kennedy's views on calling up army reserves.[3] Reporters have sometimes brought up the same subject in conference after conference until they got satisfaction or the question became obsolete. An example of this concerned Kennedy's campaign pledge to end racial discrimination in federally aided housing "by the stroke of a pen." He was asked quite pointedly at three conferences — on March 23, 1961, January 15, and July 5, 1962 — when he was going to do this, and after he announced on November 20, 1962, that he had done so, a reporter asked "Why have you taken so long?" Kennedy's rather lame reply was that it had not been "in the public interest" to act earlier.[4]

The conference and the Question Hour are alike in that both seek to put the government on the spot. But this resemblance is mainly superficial; for each institution has different fundamental aims behind that common one. The goal of reporters at the press conference is to get the news. The purpose of the Question Hour is to compel the government to explain itself. It is true that, in getting news, reporters may receive explanations and, in getting explanations, M.P.'s often make news. But the primary ends are nonetheless importantly different, and any analysis that overlooks or tries to minimize the differences sacrifices too much in order to gain the comforts of comparison.

THE CONFERENCE AS ANOTHER CHECK AND BALANCE

Anthony Leviero of the *New York Times* disagrees with the notion that the conference is best understood as a counterpart of the Question Hour. He sees the conference as "a sort of extra safety valve in our system of checks and balances." [5]

The Constitution gives the President some legislative powers — the veto is the most striking example — so that he can check Congress. The legislature also has some powers that are executive in their nature — for example, the involvement of the Senate in the appointment process — and that can be used against a President who appears to be upsetting the con-

---

[3] Harold W. Chase and Allen H. Lerman, *Kennedy and the Press* (New York: Thomas Y. Crowell Company, 1965), 322–33.

[4] *Ibid.*, 56, 157, 284, 334, 337.

[5] Anthony Leviero, "How to Live in a Fish Bowl," *The New York Times Magazine*, November 30, 1952, 33.

stitutional balance among the three branches. The power of publicity can be said to furnish another means by which the President and Congress can check one another. Although in the conference setting this power has operated mostly from the executive on Congress, congressmen and newsmen often have a closer link with each other than Presidents do with either. One reason is the more desperate need of the congressman — only one among many — for the correspondents of his district's newspapers and radio and TV outlets to remind the people back home that he is alive and doing well for them in Washington. Occasionally congressmen encourage reporters to question a President on some touchy subject, but more often Presidents have used the conference either to take the publicity spotlight away from Congress or to needle a congressional committee into some course of action. In this respect, the check function is closely allied to the leadership function of the conference, because the check most often occurs when a President speaks out strongly on a proposal that is having rough going in Congress with the hope of generating public pressure on the House and Senate to do presidential bidding.

On occasion the conference has also afforded the President a check on the Supreme Court. The conference was the setting that President Truman chose in 1952 during the "steel seizure" crisis to tell the Court in public that he did not think much of the majority opinion's narrow view of the President's emergency powers. President Eisenhower's unenthusiastic remarks whenever the school desegregation decision came up at his conferences lessened the decision's impact.

That the conference as check has operated mainly from the executive on the legislature rather than the other way around is a further reason for rejecting the notion that the conference can be best understood as a version of the Question Hour.

The Conference as a Portrait of the President

The *New York Times* once said that "the principal function of the White House press conference [is] . . . to provide the nation with a contemporary portrait of its President." And Arthur Krock wrote that "fortunately for contemporary public estimates and future biography, the real man inevitably emerges in news conferences. . . ." [6] These are two statements of yet another view about the value of the conference.

Of course it is important for the public to know what a President is "really" like so that it can make a sound judgment about whether to keep him in office, but the assumption that the conference gives a true and complete picture of a President's character and ability is questionable. The conference does give those who follow it a chance to speculate about a President's effectiveness in an area of human relations where the advantages are not all on his side. What things strike him as funny? What annoys or angers him? Is he courteous, rude, or cool to reporters? Is he

6 *New York Times*, February 22, 1953, Section IV, and June 2, 1959.

authoritarian, cooperative, or obsequious in their presence? Does he express himself well and think rapidly? The answers to these questions are often highly speculative and, therefore, much open to error. If, for example, Eisenhower had really become angry during his conferences as many times as reported, it is doubtful that his heart could have sustained him through two terms.

How adequate, then, is the reporting of a President's conference behavior? The concept of "news" as conflict or controversy colors the accounts of conference happenings and determines what shall be included and what left out. German reporters were said to have been surprised to see how dignified and composed President Eisenhower was when he met with them in Bonn. The newsreel excerpts that they had seen from Eisenhower's conferences had left the impression that he was short-tempered, irritable, and always vehement in manner.[7] Another question worth raising is whether or not a spontaneous event gives the best picture of a man's character and ability. Ever since "the Freudian slip" became a household expression, it has been largely taken for granted that a person's truest self is shown when he is caught off guard and not when he has said or done something after reflection. This is an assumption that needs examination.

When judging the ability of a President, his behavior at conferences is one factor to be weighed along with others such as his policies, his formal addresses, and his messages to Congress. But how a President appears in a conference has no necessary bearing on his competence. The evidence suggests that Warren G. Harding — responsive, kind, and humorous, but hardly competent — would have been an excellent performer in the press conference.

The Conference as a Demonstration that the United States Is a Full-fledged Democracy

This idea has three variations. One is that the conference is a ritualistic reminder to the American people and to other nations that this is a society in which the power-holders are treated with a minimum of deference and are responsible to the public. Thus, the *New York Times* has commented editorially:

> . . . so long as the institution of the Presidential press conference prevails we can feel that we are truly a democracy. Who can imagine Stalin or Franco or Péron meeting so frankly and unceremoniously with representatives of all the various shades of opinion in the nation's press? [8]

The conference may be a symbol that equality is an operating principle in our society domestically but is it also a symbol for foreign countries? Few persons living under totalitarian regimes are allowed to see the films or read the transcripts of conference proceedings.

7 *New York Times,* August 28, 1959.
8 "No Comment and All That," *New York Times,* November 16, 1951, 24.

The second variation of the idea that the conference demonstrates American democracy is that the conference attracts public attention to the government. As one commentator wrote:

> . . . every conference tends to have something dramatic about it. It has been said that democracies stagnate if voters lose interest. That will not happen in the United States so long as press conferences continue to be held.[9]

Presidential advisor Theodore C. Sorensen agreed with the notion that the aim of the conference is to capture the interest of voters when he wrote that the "primary purpose" of the televised conference is "to inform and impress the public more than the press." [10] But the press is needed, if only for transmission, if the conference in any of its forms is to affect the public. Although an audience estimated at 18 million watched Kennedy's televised conferences, indicating that a large segment of the public was interested in them, the news media have either not believed the estimates or have not wished to acknowledge the interest, as shown by their spotty conference coverage.

The third variation that this concept of the conference takes is that through the conference the President can learn what is on the public mind. In a lead editorial, the *New York Times* said of reporters at the conference:

> They are more than ever a fourth estate, a third branch of the legislature, a court of not quite last resort, a town meeting, a group of customers in a corner drugstore or, more grandly, the people of the United States. They would have no right to be there at all unless it was supposed, and correctly, that . . . they spoke for and listened for the nation.[11]

This aspect of the conference differs from that of informing the President. It values gaining knowledge of what is on the minds of the people because this knowledge can help the President ascertain the popular will so that he can follow its bidding, not because it may enable him to judge better where public thinking needs re-direction or reinforcement.

The Conference as an Antidote for the President's Isolation

Observers have noticed that the President is largely sealed off from outside contacts and that too many matters reach him only after having been filtered and perhaps distorted. The press conference may help to inform him about subjects that his advisors have not, for one reason or another, told him about. Pre-conference briefings by his staff may also aid in making sure the President knows what is happening in his administration.

[9] A. L. Goodhart, "The President's Press Conference," *The Listener* [London], Vol. LIX, No. 1518 (May 1, 1958), 725.

[10] Theodore C. Sorensen, *Kennedy* (New York: Harper and Row, 1965), 322.

[11] "Chorus: 'Mr. President,'" *New York Times,* April 29, 1955.

Presidents Franklin Roosevelt, Truman, and Eisenhower have all re-marked that they found the conference enlightening. Nonetheless, often in both briefings and conferences the President hears for the first time information that may really be inconsequential and may take time and energy away from vital issues. Conference records abound with instances of trivial questions that either find the President unprepared with an answer or simply replying with a clever rebuke to publicity seekers.

THE CONFERENCE AS A CHANNEL FOR PRESIDENTIAL LEADERSHIP

Whether off the record or fully publicized the conference's plainest poten-tial is as a leadership tool for the President. He may choose the conference as the place to lash opponents or push favorites. He may use it as a forum for pronouncements designed to get or test policy support from the nation as a whole. He can try to stimulate the public to pressure Congress. He can stir his own bureaucracy or discuss the citizens and governments of other nations. When news from opposition headquarters has been getting a lot of space, a President may, by way of the conference, recapture the limelight. He can rely on coverage of the conference to give him at least some attention in even the most unfriendly newspaper. All twentieth-century Presidents have used the conference for some of these purposes; most of them have used it for all.

Louis Brownlow has called the press "the principal engine which the President uses to influence public opinion, to maintain discipline in his own party, and to spread dissension among the opposition." [12] The most important aspect of the conference is that it gives the President one op-portunity for employing the press for leadership purposes. When used for this purpose the conference stirs the most anxiety in the press. News-men prefer Presidents to treat the conference as their prerogative, not his, and occasionally Presidents have honored this preference. But to let reporters run the conference would be quite unwise. Presidents do not have to initiate every conference topic, although they may sometimes do so to good effect, as Kennedy did when he took out after "Big Steel" for raising its prices. But Presidents should use the questions as springboards for things that they think need to be said, rather than simply react to the questions and not go beyond them. President Truman often made the mistake of simply reacting to questions, letting the press determine the contours and direction of the discussion. Lyndon Johnson's conference of August 18, 1967, furnishes an example of seeming press dominance but actual presidential initiative. He had no prepared announcements at the outset but when the inevitable questions came about the "ghetto riots" of that summer, Johnson took off from the question and made a spirited pitch for his urban programs — rent supplements, model-cities, urban re-newal, and rat control — that had been stalled in congressional commit-

12 Brownlow, *The President and the Presidency*, 81.

tees or mistreated by the House.[13] Examples abound of Presidents using the conference in a similar way for similar purposes. There is not necessarily anything underhanded or shady about this use of the conference. The feeling that there is stems from the conviction that the conference should belong to the press and that former press secretary James C. Hagerty was wrong when he said that "the press conferences by the President of the United States are the press conferences of the President of the United States, and no one else." [14]

This excursion through the purposes claimed for the conference was begun because some critics, having misjudged the conference's capabilities, have been unduly harsh in their judgment of its worth. Presidents also have erred in their ideas about what the conference can accomplish. Unrealistic expectations are inevitably frustrated, leading to discontent. But if conference participants and observers see more clearly what the conference can and cannot do, they will have more sensible ideas about ways to improve conference design and practice. They will know better what to add and what to rearrange, what to omit and what to leave alone.

[13] *New York Times*, August 19, 1967.

[14] Fifteenth Annual Memorial Lecture, American Newspaper Guild, AFL-CIO, and the School of Journalism, University of Minnesota, Minneapolis, Minnesota, November 9, 1961, 14.

THE PRESIDENCY
AND THE PARTIES

Which Road to the Presidency?

Daniel J. Elazar

On July 10, 1960, James Reston wrote in the *New York Times:*

> As world problems and Federal problems have increased there
> has been a shift, too, in the type of candidate [for President of
> the United States] from the solid administrative characters in
> the State Governors' mansions to the men trained in world and
> national affairs in Washington, most of them in the Senate.

Reston was simply giving expression to a growing feeling among the politically articulate in that year, that the old order of state-based, decentralized American national politics was beginning to give way to a new
order of nationalized politics, an order in which the erstwhile parochial
political leaders of the states were no longer to dominate the national
scene as candidates for the nation's highest elective office and, hence, as
leading spokesmen for their parties and articulators of political issues in
the country as a whole. This feeling — and Reston's forecast — was at least
partly based on a view of the presidential race of 1960, a race in which
neither candidate was selected from the ranks of the state governors and
in which both had gained their nominations through careers on the national scene which had given them national reputations. Not only that,
but their respective opponents for the nominations had also, with one
exception, become contenders because of activity in Washington rather
than as a consequence of position in one of the fifty states. Thus Senator
John F. Kennedy was nominated over Senators Lyndon Johnson, Stuart
Symington, and Hubert Humphrey, with a fifth contender, Adlai Stevenson eight years removed from the governorship of Illinois. Similarly, Vice
President and former Senator Richard M. Nixon was nominated over
Senator Barry Goldwater and the one gubernatorial contender in either
camp, Nelson Rockefeller.

Senator Kennedy's triumph in November of that year only sharpened
the feeling that the United States Senate was coming to replace the office
of governor as an important way station on the road to the White House,

Reprinted by permission from *Southwestern Social Science Quarterly* (June 1965),
pp. 37–46.

as columnists all over the country were quick to point out. The analysis went as follows: the increased role of the United States in world affairs and the growth of federal power domestically have finally combined to eliminate another vestige of the old federal system by reducing the role of the states as providers of presidential candidates from the ranks of their governors. New times, which demand experience with matters beyond the borders of the states, have made experience on the national and international level well-nigh indispensable for potential presidents; hence the locally oriented governors have had to give way to nationally oriented senators as presidential timber.

If this analysis were accurate, it would indeed indicate a shift of some significance in the informal operation of the American political system, with consequences far beyond those implied in a simple shift of springboards to higher office. Whole patterns of political careers and party organization would have to be redrawn and the nation would have to expect not only different kinds of men to occupy the presidential office but different kinds to become governors and state leaders as well.

The historical record, however, generally belies the foregoing analysis in its view of the past and in its projections for the future. As many a presidential candidate has said, "Let us look at the record." What have been the various sources for recruiting presidential candidates in the American past and why have different sources served at different periods?

Since 1824, when the present system of popular election of presidents began to take on meaning, through 1956 there have been forty-two different major party candidates contesting for the office of president in a total of thirty-four separate elections, excluding incumbent presidents seeking re-election. If their immediate past political experience is defined to include all public offices held by them in the eight years immediately prior to their nominations for the presidency, the relative importance of gubernatorial office as a road to the presidency is seen in its proper light. Using the most gross calculations, only sixteen, or 33 per cent, of the forty-nine nonincumbent presidential nominees in the thirty-four presidential elections held state office at the time of their nomination or immediately prior to it. Twenty-six of the nominees held or had just retired from positions in the federal government; and seven were nominated after extensive periods spent in private life.

Of the sixteen candidates holding state office, fourteen were governors. But in only ten cases did the governorship represent a step upward in their careers on the road to the presidential nomination. James K. Polk, William McKinley, and James M. Cox went to the governorship directly from the House of Representatives; Polk and McKinley, after they had been defeated in bids for re-election to Congress. McKinley, at least, was encouraged to run for the governorship by Mark Hanna to remain in the public eye in order to be in a better position to secure the presidential nomination in 1896. Adlai Stevenson's previous service was exclusively in the federal executive branch and in the field of foreign affairs at that.

Only ten of the governors had not had experience in national politics in the years immediately preceding their election to the governorship.

Of the other two candidates nominated from state office, William Henry Harrison held a county sinecure as clerk of the court of common pleas in Hamilton County, Ohio, secured by his party comrades to provide him with a means of support after a number of years of service ʼat the federal level in the army, in Congress, and in the executive branch. Only Judge Alton B. Parker, the Democrats' compromise candidate in 1904, had a career confined to his state (New York) before and after his nomination. It may be said with considerable justification that only eleven (or slightly better than one-fifth of all the candidates) of the sixteen erstwhile state-rooted candidates actually developed their candidacy on the state level only. The other five all had substantial, and no doubt critically important, experience in the national government prior to their nomination. In four of the five cases it is no exaggeration to say that their reputations were made in national politics.

The backgrounds of the twenty-six candidates selected after direct prior federal level experience are also revealing. Twelve were nominated either directly from Congress or after recent service in that body. Nine of these were Senators and three were Representatives. Of these twelve, none had served as governors in the decade prior to their nomination. If the historical record is any guide, it may be concluded that, statistically, at least, it is somewhat more likely for a person with national legislative experience and no recent state service to be nominated for the presidency than for a person with a record of state service and no national legislative experience. Even Charles Evans Hughes, the only member of the federal judiciary ever nominated for the presidency, had spent the six years immediately preceding his nomination (1916) on the federal bench, though he was governor of New York from 1906 to 1910.

The choice of presidential candidates has been further slanted toward candidates with professional military backgrounds, by definition "national" experience. Seven professional soldiers have been nominated, only one of whom, John C. Fremont who served briefly as United States Senator from California from 1850 to 1852, had any previous political experience. Since Andrew Jackson and William Henry Harrison were military heroes and at least semiprofessional soldiers, they may also be considered national figures and, indeed, it was in consideration of their national military roles that they were nominated and elected. Nine candidates, then, were selected after gaining public recognition for military service which meant service to the nation through the federal government.

The federal-level experience of all the candidates in the eight years before their nominations (Table 3, p. 346) is also very revealing. Sixteen candidates were drawn from Congress, eleven were Senators and nine were Representatives (some served in both houses). Despite the erstwhile isolationism of the United States, ten candidates had had recent experience in the administration or execution of American foreign policy, either as secretaries of state or as ministers to foreign governments.[1] This number would be increased to thirteen if the three professional soldiers whose reputations were won in foreign wars (Taylor, Scott, Eisenhower) were included. Contrast this to the fifteen (including Hughes) who served as governors and it is clear that the governorship has not been substantially more important as a stepping stone to the presidency than foreign service in the over-all pattern of American political history.

Nevertheless, with all these qualifications and exceptions, there is a basis for the theory that the trail through the governorship provides a good road to the presidency. The first governor to be nominated for the presidency solely because of his gubernatorial background was Horatio Seymour of New York, the Democratic candidate in 1868. His nomination was precedent-setting since thirteen of the fourteen men nominated for the presidency directly from the governor's chair were nominated after the Civil War. Of these thirteen, eight were Democrats, nominated in roughly two periods. Three (Seymour, Tilden, Cleveland) were candidates over the five presidential elections between 1868 and 1884, and four (Wilson, Cox, Smith, Roosevelt) were nominated in the twenty-year period that included six elections between 1912 and 1932. Similarly, three of the five Republicans nominated while governor (Landon and Dewey twice) were selected to run in the four elections between 1936 and 1948.

In each of these three periods, the party which repeatedly selected governors as its presidential nominees was nationally the minority party, not only in terms of the presidency, but in the Congress as well. When Horatio Seymour was nominated in 1868, the Democrats had not had a majority in the Senate since 1861 and in the House of Representatives since 1859. When Samuel Tilden was nominated four years later, the Democrats had managed to gain control of the House but were still a minority in the Senate. They had also failed to elect a president in twenty years. By 1884, when Cleveland was nominated, the Democrats had briefly gained control of the Congress for one term (1879–1881) and then had lost control of the Senate again, which they did not regain until 1893. Not only that, but none of the leading members of Congress in that period were Democrats. Similarly, when Woodrow Wilson was nominated in 1912, the Democrats had not controlled the Senate since 1895, had just gained control of the House for the first time in fourteen years, and had not elected a Democratic president in two decades. James Cox, nominated in 1920, was somewhat of an exception coming as he did at the beginning of a new era of Republican-controlled Congresses that began in 1918. By the time Al Smith was nominated in 1928, however, the number of consecutively Republican-controlled Congresses had grown to five and even Franklin D. Roosevelt's nomination in 1932 came in the face of the seventh consecutive Republican-controlled Senate and a small new Democratic majority in the House.

[1] This number would be greatly increased if the pre-1824 presidential candidates were also included, at least half of whom had foreign affairs experience immediately prior to their candidacy.

On the Republican side, Alf Landon was nominated in 1936 after the two most one-sided Democratic Congresses to that date, and Thomas E. Dewey's nomination in 1944 came after six successive Democratic Congresses. In 1948, Dewey was nominated to defend the record of that first Republican-controlled Congress in sixteen years and that election reaffirmed the minority position of the Republican party in the national legislature as well as its inability to win control of the White House.

The conclusion should be clear. The choice of governors to be presidential candidates was not a search for "the solid administrative characters in the State Governor's mansions" but an indication of a party's reliance on state chief executives when it had no prominent and acceptable national figures to draw upon. The exceptions prove the rule. Among the three candidates nominated from the governor's chair and not included above, Polk was nominated in 1844 after the Democrats had lost control of the Congress in 1841 for the first time in twelve years and had been a minority in the Senate for four years. McKinley had been a Congressman who had been defeated in his bid for re-election in 1890 because of his position on the tariff question. He was then elected governor through the efforts of Mark Hanna to keep him in the public eye preparatory to nominating him for president. The one possible exception is Adlai Stevenson, nominated in 1952 after a period of renewed Democratic ascendency. Stevenson is indeed the one candidate who fits the classic image of a governor nominated for the presidency as a consequence of his career as governor. Virtually unknown to the general public during his federal service, his reform administration in Illinois put him in the national limelight at a time when the Democratic-controlled Congress had its own share of distinguished Democratic leaders. Yet, even in the case of Stevenson, who appeared too recently on the American scene to have set any recognizable precedents, his sole previous (and subsequent) political experiences have been in the field of foreign affairs.

Indeed, the governorship was not the best route to the presidential nomination even for a member of the minority party. While the Whigs were in the minority, they chose their candidates from the United States Senate (Henry Clay) and from the ranks of the military heroes (William Henry Harrison, Zachary Taylor, Winfield Scott). The ante-bellum Republicans chose their first candidate (John C. Fremont) for his military appeal and their second candidate (Abraham Lincoln) was plucked from private life. Between 1864 and 1932 the Democrats, as a minority party, selected as many candidates from the army (George B. McClellan, Winfield S. Hancock), the Federal executive (Cleveland, John W. Davis), and from private life (Horace Greeley, William Jennings Bryan — three times) as they did from the governorship. Since 1932, the Republican minority has also balanced its nominations from the governorship with those from these other walks of life (Wendell Willkie, Dwight D. Eisenhower, Richard M. Nixon).

It is even more revealing to look at the winners. Five of those nominated from the governor's chair and one ex-governor nominated after a brief retirement have won the presidency. Congressmen have fared equally well. Prior to 1960 three of their number moved directly from the Congress to the White House while another three did so after first spending a few years in private life. The governors' edge is thus challenged by the Congressmen. In addition, four military men have been successful and five presidents have been elected from other positions in the executive branch. With one possible exception (Ulysses S. Grant) the military men have been elected from the minority party and have served as vehicles for the minority party to capture the presidency. Even Grant was nominated by the Republicans at a time when they were not certain of their majority status. By the same token, all five presidents elected from the executive branch were elected as members of the majority party who were "handed" the "succession."

It is true that there has been a decline in the number of nominees chosen from Congress since the Civil War. Indeed, their decline as potential presidential candidates began after 1848. This brief article cannot attempt to indicate why this is so. It does seem that the Senators served much the same function as vehicles for the minority party on the antebellum political scene as have the governors in the post-bellum period. This is at least partly because the balance between the two parties between 1824 and 1852 was very close and both parties were represented in the Senate by national figures able to command widespread support. It is apparent that the nature of a presidential candidate's politicial position, not his prior governmental experience, is what counts in securing the nomination for the presidency. The record shows that those governors who have been elected to the presidency were really political heads of state, able to command political prestige and following both within and beyond their state's borders during their tenure as governors. They have not been chosen as candidates because of their services as chief executives (narrowly defined) in the administration of their state governments.

The evidence from the past indicates that future patterns are not clearly predictable insofar as selection of presidential candidates from particular lower offices is concerned. The "tradition" of nominations from the governor's chair is no tradition at all. Consequently, it is not possible to conclude that the 1960 presidential election broke tradition. It can be said that no particular office has an advantage for the presidential hopeful, except insofar as the minority party candidate will most likely be chosen from the ranks of the governors who have inherited the party's political power unless a military hero is available. On the other hand, the majority party is much more likely to choose a candidate identified with its previous record and administration, one who is already in politics at the national level.

So much for the past. What of the period since 1960? If anything, it seems to indicate that the governors staged a slight "comeback." In the Democratic camp there was, of course, no question in July 1964 as to who the nominee would be in August. Barring death, disability, or some entirely unforeseen occurrence, President Johnson was to run for a full term. On the Republican side, the field remained open until the California primary. Ironically enough, this was in no small measure due to Richard Nixon's earlier failure to capture the governorship of that state as a springboard to renomination. Barry Goldwater was the only Senator under consideration. Rockefeller, Romney, and Scranton — the other possibilities — were all under consideration by virtue of their successful efforts at capturing the governors' chairs in their respective states. Since Goldwater's defeat, GOP interest in gubernatorial office has increased. This is as it "should" be according to the theory. The Republicans have not controlled the Congress in more than ten years. Lacking members of Congress who can successfully project themselves as national figures and with no control over the federal executive branch, they may have to turn once again to the office of governor to recruit potential presidential candidates.

Table 1

Previous Political Experience of Presidential Candidates

Year	· Non-Incumbent Presidential Candidate (winners in italics)	Previous Political Office
1824	*John Quincy Adams* (D)	U.S. Sec. of State (1817–1825)
	Henry Clay (D)	U.S. House of Reps. (1811–1825)
1828	*Andrew Jackson* (D)[a]	U.S. Senator (1823–1825)
1832	Henry Clay (W)	U.S. Senator (1831–1842) and Sec. of State (1825–1829)
1836	*Martin Van Buren* (D)	U.S. Vice President (1833–1837) and Sec. of State (1829–1833)
	William Henry Harrison (W)[b]	Clk. Common Pleas Ct., Hamilton Co., Ohio (1829–1836) U.S. Minister to Colombia (1828–1829) U.S. Senator (1825–1828)
1840	*William Henry Harrison* (W)[b]	Clk. Common Pleas Ct., Hamilton Co., Ohio (1829–1836) U.S. Minister to Colombia (1828–1829) U.S. Senator (1825–1828)
1844	*James K. Polk* (D)	Governor of Tenn. (1839–1841) U.S. House of Reps. (1825–1839)
	Henry Clay (W)	U.S. Senator (1831–1842)
1848	Lewis Cass (D)	U.S. Senator (1844–1857) U.S. Minister to France (1836–1842)
	Zachary Taylor (W)	General Officer, U.S. Army
1852	*Franklin Pierce* (D)[c]	U.S. Senator (1837–1842) U.S. House of Reps. (1833–1837)
	Winfield Scott (W)	General Officer, U.S. Army

Year	Non-Incumbent Presidential Candidate (winners in italics)	Previous Political Office
1856	*James Buchanan* (D)	U.S. Minister to Great Britain (1853–1856) U.S. Sec. of State (1845–1849)
	John C. Fremont (R)[d]	U.S. Senator (1850–1852) U.S. Army
1860	Stephen A. Douglas (D)	U.S. Senator (1847–1861)
	Abraham Lincoln (R)[e]	U.S. House of Reps. (1847–1849)
1864	George B. McClellan (D)	General Officer, U.S. Army
1868	Horatio Seymour (D)	Governor of N.Y. (1862–1864, 1852–1854)
	Ulysses S. Grant (R)	General Officer, U.S. Army
1872	Horace Greeley (D)[f]	Private Citizen
1876	Samuel J. Tilden (D)	Governor of N.Y. (1874–1876)
	Rutherford B. Hayes (R)	Governor of Ohio (1874–1876, 1868–1872)
1880	Winfield S. Hancock (D)	General Officer, U.S. Army
	James A. Garfield (R)	U.S. House of Reps. (1863–1881)
1884	*Grover Cleveland* (D)	Governor of N.Y. (1882–1884) Mayor of Buffalo (1881–1882) Sheriff of Eric County (1869–1881)
	James G. Blaine (R)[g]	U.S. Sec. of State (1881) U.S. Senator (1876–1881)
1888	*Benjamin Harrison* (R)	U.S. Senator (1881–1887)
1892	*Grover Cleveland* (D)	U.S. President (1885–1889)
1896	William Jennings Bryan (D)	U.S. House of Reps. (1891–1895)
	William McKinley (R)	Governor of Ohio (1891–1895) U.S. House of Reps. (1883–1891)
1900	William Jennings Bryan (D)[h]	Private Citizen
1904	Alton B. Parker (D)	Chief Justice, N.Y. Court of Appeals (1888–1904)
1908	William Jennings Bryan (D)	Private Citizen
	William Howard Taft (R)	U.S. Sec. of War (1904–1908) Gov. of the Philippines (1901–1904)
1912	*Woodrow Wilson* (D)	Governor of New Jersey (1911–1912)
1916	Charles Evans Hughes (R)	Assoc. Justice, U.S. Sup. Ct. (1910–1916) Gov. of N.Y. (1906–1910)
1920	James M. Cox (D)	Gov. of Ohio (1912–1914, 1916–1920) U.S. House of Reps. (1908–1912)
	Warren G. Harding (R)	U.S. Senator (1915–1921) Lt. Gov. of Ohio (1904–1906)
1924	John W. Davis (D)	U.S. Ambassador to Great Britain (1919–1921) U.S. Solicitor General (1913–1918) U.S. House of Reps. (1911–1913)
1928	Alfred E. Smith (D)	Governor of N.Y. (1919–1921, 1923–1929)
	Herbert Hoover (R)	U.S. Sec. of Commerce (1921–1929)
1932	*Franklin D. Roosevelt* (D)	Governor of N.Y. (1929–1933)

Year	Non-Incumbent Presidential Candidate (winners in italics)	Previous Political Office
1936	Alfred M. Landon (R)	Governor of Kansas (1933–1937)
1940	Wendell L. Willkie (R)	Private Citizen
1944	Thomas E. Dewey (R)	Governor of N.Y. (1943–1955) N.Y. Dist. Atty. (1937–1943)
1948	Thomas E. Dewey (R)	Governor of N.Y. (1943–1955)
1952	Adlai E. Stevenson (D)	Governor of Ill. (1949–1953) Fed. Govt. Service (1933–1934, 1941–1947)
	Dwight D. Eisenhower (R)	General Officer, U.S. Army
1956	Adlai E. Stevenson (D)	Private Citizen

a Jackson was nominated and elected in his capacity as military hero after a brief "retirement" from public office between 1825 and 1828.

b Harrison was nominated and elected in his capacity as military hero. His county office was in the nature of a sinecure. Between 1836 and 1840 he was semi-retired.

c Pierce was engaged in the private practice of law at the time of his nomination.

d Fremont was engaged in private business at the time of his nomination.

e Lincoln had not held public office for over a decade at the time of his nomination.

f Greeley, a newspaper editor, had no previous experience in elective office.

g Blaine had been in brief "retirement" from public office.

h Bryan held no public office between 1895 and 1913, except as Colonel of the Nebraska Volunteers in the Spanish-American War.

TABLE 2

Presidential Candidates: Previous Political Experiences

Number of Elections		34
Number of Non-Incumbent Candidates[a]		49
State Offices[b]	16	
Federal Offices[c]	26	
Private Life[d]	7	

a Candidates nominated more than once are counted separately for each nomination.

b Includes holders of state office at least three years prior to nomination (Harrison, Polk, Seymour, Tilden, Hayes, Cleveland, McKinley, Parker, Wilson, Cox, Smith, F. D. Roosevelt, Landon, Dewey (2), Stevenson).

c Includes positions in all branches, civil and military (J. Q. Adams, Clay (3), Jackson, Van Buren, Cass, Taylor, Scott, Buchanan, Fremont, Douglas, McClellan, Grant, Hancock, Garfield, Blaine, Harrison, Cleveland, Byron, Taft, Hughes, Harding, Davis, Hoover, Eisenhower).

d Includes those in private life for at least four years prior to nomination (Pierce, Lincoln, Greeley, Byron (2), Willkie, Stevenson).

TABLE 3

Federal Positions Held by Presidential Candidates [1]

U.S. Congress		20	Federal Executive		15
Senate[a]	11		Sec. of State or Foreign		
House of Reps.[b]	9		Service[c]	10	
			Other Cabinet[d]	2	
			U.S. Army[e]	7	
			Judiciary[f]	1	
			Other[g]	3	

[1] Total exceeds 28 since all positions held in preceding eight years are included.

[a] Jackson, Clay (2), W. H. Harrison, Cass, Pierce, Fremont, Douglas, Blaine, B. Harrison, Harding.

[b] Clay, Polk, Pierce, Lincoln, Garfield, Bryan, McKinley, Cox, Davis.

[c] Adams, Clay, Van Buren, W. H. Harrison, Cass, Buchanan, Blaine, Taft, Davis, Stevenson.

[d] Taft, Hoover.

[e] Taylor, Scott, Fremont, McClellan, Grant, Hancock, Eisenhower.

[f] Hughes.

[g] Van Buren, Cleveland, Davis.

Some Dynamic Elements of Contests for the Presidency

Donald E. Stokes

Despite the measured pace of American elections, there have now been a number of presidential campaigns since the advent of survey studies of voting. However sparingly, political history slowly has added to the set of distinct configurations of men and events which comprise a contest for the Presidency. The set is still small, whatever the impression created by massed thousands of interviews or by the accompanying files of election returns. Yet it is now large enough to be pressed hard for evidence about the sources of electoral change.

A primary virtue of measurements extended over a series of elections is that they can throw light on the problem of change. So long as the earliest voting studies were confined to cross-sectional relationships, they

Reprinted by permission from the *American Political Science Review*, 60 (1966), pp. 19–28.

could deal only very inadequately with changes super-imposed on these relationships or with changes in the relationships themselves. In the case of Lazarfeld's enormously influential Erie County study in 1940, the natural limitations of a single-election study were compounded by the investigators' misfortune in choosing a campaign whose dominant personality and principal issues differed little from those of preceding elections. I have often wondered whether the static social determinism of *The People's Choice* would have emerged from a campaign in which the tides of short-term change were more nearly at flood.[1]

I shall examine here some sources of change which are richly evident in the presidential elections of the last two decades. In doing so I shall utilize several time series which can be extracted from the Survey Research Center's interview studies of the American electorate. The presidential contest of 1964 marked the fourth occasion on which the Center's national electoral studies have recorded the public's response to the issues and personalities of a presidential campaign.

This lengthening interval of electoral history contains material enough for the analyst of change. From the Eisenhower victories of the early 1950's, the high-point of presidential Republicanism since the Great Depression overwhelmed Hoover's party, the strength of Eisenhower's successors ebbed away in 1960 and sank in 1964 to a level which can only be regarded as one of the extreme lows of American national party competition. I shall examine some of the attitudinal factors in this extraordinary decline, focusing especially on the importance of changes in the issues and leaders which the electorate is asked to appraise. The relation of these "inputs" to the "output" of the presidential vote is exceedingly complex, but the moral of my piece is that this relationship introduces more dynamism into contests for the Presidency than the stability of party identification or of the social bases of party preference might lead us to expect.

In the course of the discussion I shall utilize a statistical model which has proved useful for measuring various attitudinal forces on the nation's vote. Dealing with a type of behavior which is notoriously subject to multiple influences, this model seeks to discern the relative importance of several dimensions of attitude both for individual choice and for the nation's collective decision.[2] The model treats the behavior of the individual voter as governed in an immediate sense by the direction and strength of his attitudes toward the several political objects he is asked

---

[1] Paul F. Lazarsfeld, Bernard Berelson, and Hazel Gaudet, *The People's Choice* (New York: Duell, Sloan and Pearce, 1944). It is paradoxical that Lazarsfeld and his associates should have come to so static a view of party preference, since the desire to observe changes of preference was so central to their original intentions. Had they worked within the context of an election such as that of 1952 it is entirely unlikely that they could have ignored the presence of a massive inter-election change, overlaid on the social bases of preference summarized in the Index of Political Predisposition.

[2] For a report of the application of this model to the Eisenhower elections see Donald E. Stokes, Angus Campbell, and Warren E. Miller, "Components of Electoral Decision," *American Political Science Review*, 52 (June 1958), 367–387.

to appraise, attitudes which we have probed in these presidential elections by asking a series of free-answer questions about the parties and presidential candidates. Since a presidential campaign confronts the voter with four main objects — the two parties and the two candidates — it is natural to place each respondent along four dimensions of attitude, and many of the findings reported below will rely on such a four-dimensional model. For other purposes, however, it is more revealing of the content of political attitude to place each respondent along six attitudinal dimensions: (1) attitude toward the Democratic candidate as a person; (2) attitude toward the Republican candidate as a person; (3) attitude toward the parties and candidates which relates to the benefit of various groups; (4) attitude toward the parties and candidates which relates to domestic policy; (5) attitude which relates to foreign policy; and (6) attitude which relates to the general performance of the parties in the nation's affairs. A detailed account of the procedure by which respondents are assimilated to these several dimensions appears in the appended note.

The appendix also describes the statistical operations by which we obtain definite estimates of each dimension's contribution to the winning majority — the means by which, in effect, the nation's collective decision is resolved into a set of attitudinal components. These methods must of course be regarded as approximate, for reasons of sampling if no other, and I advance no claim to exact measurement; none is really necessary to the central conclusion which I shall draw from the analysis. Nevertheless, the model's success in estimating the direction and size of the winning majority in each of a series of elections does increase our confidence that we have measured dimensions of popular feeling which are deeply involved in changes of party fortune.

The several dimensions of attitude, however, have by no means been equally involved in electoral change. Just as the various components of electoral decision can be very different in their direction and strength at a given point in time, they can exhibit a very different tendency to change over time. In the period of our research some have been relatively stable, others not. By examining the role of each attitude component over twelve years we form several time series which are extraordinarily suggestive of the sources of change during this interval of our national politics.

The Attitudinal Components over Time

The curves described by the components of the six-dimensional model arrange themselves into three interesting pairs. The first of these is a pair whose values have consistently favored the Democrats over the entire period. As shown by Figure 1, partisan evaluations relating to domestic issues and to group benefit have uniformly helped the Democrats more than the Republicans, although the extent of this aid has fluctuated from year to year.[3] To an unusual degree these elements of the party images have roots in the past, extending back at least to the Roosevelt New Deal. Indeed, the benefit to the Democrats from their party's sponsorship of disadvantaged elements of American society is an antique theme of our party politics. Even in the mid-1950's and the early 1960's the volume of comment approving the Democrats and disapproving the Republicans in terms of the interests of the common man was impressive. In the two most recent elections, however, these class-related comments were diminished somewhat and were accompanied by references to religious and racial groups in which the arithmetic of group size was less favorable to the Democrats. For these reasons the group curve in Figure 1 shows the party's advantage to be somewhat less in 1960 and 1964.

It will be apparent that the concept of "group" is defined here in a very inclusive manner. Likewise, our net has been cast very widely in coding references relating to domestic issues. In particular, many of the comments giving substance to the domestic issue dimension are "valence" or "image" issues, in which the parties or candidates are linked with something which is uniformly approved or disapproved ("the Republicans are the party of depression") rather than "position" issues on which there are genuine differences of party policy. The leading image issue of domestic politics throughout this period was the association of the Democrats with good times, the Republicans with bad. This association, which probably had weakened steadily from the height of the Great Depression to the election of 1952, was further attenuated by the prosperity of Eisenhower's first term. But it revived again in the recession of 1958, before the Republican administration had left office, and it has been given fresh substance by the rising prosperity of the Kennedy and Johnson years.

The domestic issue dimension has not, however, been altogether lacking in genuine position issues. One of the peculiar qualities of the Goldwater candidacy is that it converted into position issues a number of image issues on which a broad consensus had hitherto existed between the parties. This fact was not lost upon the general public. Under the Goldwater challenge, the Democrats were rewarded more generously in 1964 than in any of the three prior elections for their sponsorship of social security and of the circle of other social and economic welfare policies which had wide popular approval. Primarily for this reason the

[3] The vertical coordinate of Figure 1, as well as of Figures 2 and 3, gives the value of the quantity

$$b_i(\overline{X}_i - X_i^0)$$

defined in the Appendix. As explained there, this quantity may be interpreted either at the individual level as the average amount by which a given dimension has increased (or lessened, in the case of negative values) the probability of the individual's voting Republican or at the level of the whole electorate as the proportion of the total two-party vote by which a given dimension has increased (or lessened) the Republican share.

FIGURE 1

Continuing Democratic Advantage:
Groups and Domestic Policy

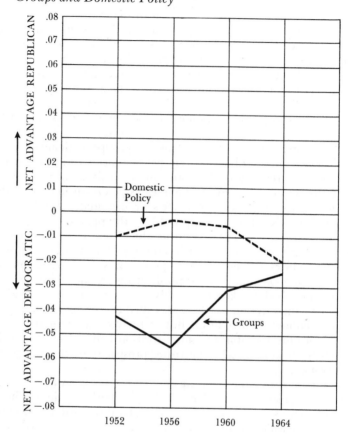

domestic issue curve of Figure 1 shows a greater Democratic advantage in 1964 than in the years before.

A second pair of curves is traced by the movement of two components in which a strong initial Republican advantage is seen to have vanished over these four elections. As shown by Figure 2, the Republican party under Eisenhower enjoyed a substantial lead over the Democrats on foreign affairs — preeminently in terms of the great image issue of peace and war. This lead was not greatly lessened when Eisenhower's deputy sought the Presidency in 1960, but Nixon's legacy dissolved altogether in the contest of Goldwater and Johnson. It would be a misreading of the 1964 value, however, to suppose that widely-held foreign policy beliefs consistent with Goldwater's were nicely balanced by widely-held beliefs consistent with Johnson's. According to our evidence, foreign affairs did intrude on the public's consciousness in the 1964 campaign more than in any election since 1952, but popular references to foreign issues in 1964 still had only about a fourth the frequency of references to domestic issues. The loss of Republican advantage on this dimension was due to final collapse of the belief that the party under Goldwater was more likely to bring peace than were the Democrats under Johnson.[4]

FIGURE 2

Decaying Republican Advantage: Foreign Policy and Party Performance

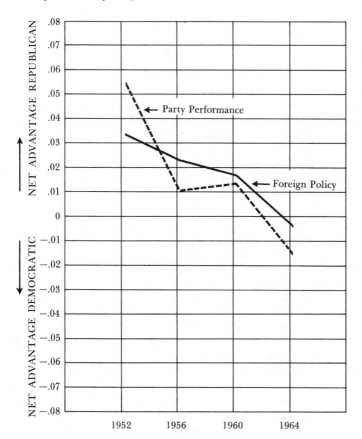

[4] For direct additional evidence on this point see Philip E. Converse, Aage R. Clausen, and Warren E. Miller, "Electoral Myth and Reality: The 1964 Election," *American Political Science Review,* 59 (June 1965), p. 332.

The loss of Republican advantage in foreign affairs is paralleled by the decay of the party's advantage in popular assessments of party performance. The Republicans began this series of elections immensely aided by the mood for a change in 1952. There is no more striking element in all of our attitudinal materials than the public's anger and frustration with the outgoing Democratic administration in that year. Whatever the validity of the public's grievance, it was real enough in motivational terms and contributed handsomely to Eisenhower's first victory. The force of this feeling was easily spent, however, once the Democrats had been driven from office. Yet in 1956 and again in 1960 the Republicans still enjoyed an edge in terms of the electorate's general evaluations of current party performance, a fact which is the more remarkable in view of the stronger hold of the Democrats on the nation's underlying party identifications.[5] By 1964, however, this lingering advantage had been swept away, and the Democrats by a modest margin were now seen as the party better qualified to conduct the country's affairs.

The third pair of curves is traced by the components having to do with popular reactions to the personal attributes of the candidates. As shown in Figure 3, there has been remarkable variety in the appeal of the Republican candidates. The values of this component in 1952 and 1956 attest to General Eisenhower's personal hold on the electorate, an attraction which, if anything, was even more wholly personal after Eisenhower had served four years as President. Mr. Nixon's appeal in 1960 was somewhat less, although his personal appeal to the electorate, especially the sense of his broad experience, was marked. If the eventual account given by the political histories is that Nixon was a weak candidate in 1960, it will be largely myth.

The response to Goldwater, however, was something else again. Whereas Nixon's personal stature helped bring his party to the verge of a third presidential victory against a party enjoying a clear advantage in the country's partisan identifications, popular reaction to Goldwater contributed to his party's electoral ruin. The detailed references to Goldwater are an impressive amalgam of doubts — a wild and erratic campaigner, muddled and unclear, unstable, poorly educated, and so on — with these themes very little offset by references to the advertised qualities of integrity, sincerity, and decisiveness. If our estimates are right, the transition from Nixon to Goldwater cost the Republicans something like 7 per cent of the total vote.

Despite immense differences of personal style, the appeal of three successive Democratic candidates was much more nearly equal. And except for Stevenson's second campaign, the response to each of these candidates added to his strength at the polls. Certainly the movement of the Democratic curve in Figure 3 shows Johnson to have been an asset to his own candidacy in 1964: the response to Johnson's attributes apparently did

---

[5] For evidence on the distribution of party identification in this period see "The Concept of the 'Normal Vote,'" in A. Campbell, P. Converse, W. Miller, and D. Stokes, *Elections and the Political Order* (New York, 1966), Ch. 1.

FIGURE 3

Greatest Variation: Appeal of Candidates

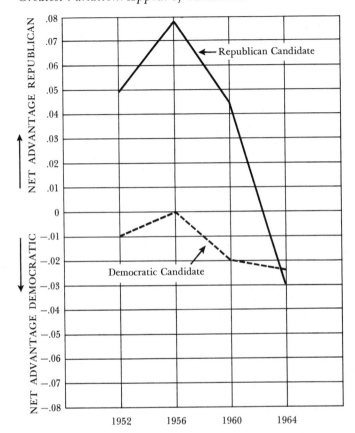

the Democrats about as much good as the response to Goldwater's did. The combined effect of both appears to have moved the two-party vote roughly 5 percentage points toward Johnson.

To emphasize the dynamic implications for party competition of pairing successive candidates for President, Figure 4 combines the effect of the personal appeals of the two men seeking the office in each of these elections.[6] The variation of this summary curve is impressive indeed. From a maximum Republican advantage of nearly 8 per cent in the re-match of Eisenhower and Stevenson, the curve falls through more than

---

[6] The individual and aggregate interpretations of the quantity represented by the vertical coordinate of Figure 4 are the same as before, but the quantity itself is the sum of the components measuring the increment or decrement to Republican strength due to personal attributes of the Republican and Democratic candidates.

FIGURE 4

Net Impact of Candidates

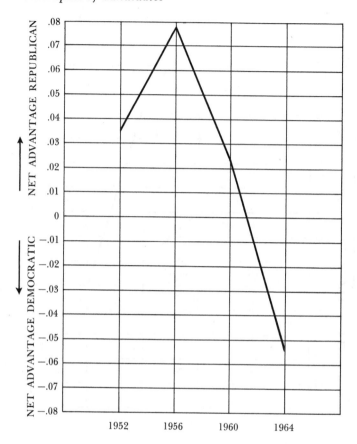

13 percentage points to a maximum Democratic advantage of more than 5 per cent in the contest of Johnson and Goldwater. A more eloquent statistical comment on the personal contribution which candidates for President can make to electoral change could hardly be given.

It would be a mistake to read into these figures too simple an explanation of the impact of candidate personality on the mass public. Certainly it would be grossly wrong to suppose that the properties of these "stimulus objects" are somehow immediately and directly impressed on the electorate's response. The relation of stimulus and response is remarkably complex, involving an interplay of several quite different factors. Before drawing some general conclusions about the problem of change, it would be well to consider the interaction of the "actual" properties of the stimuli to which the electorate responds, certain response dispositions which the electorate has already learned, and some properties of the communication processes by which the electorate is informed of the objects of presidential politics.

STIMULUS PROPERTIES AND RESPONSE DISPOSITIONS IN THE ATTITUDE COMPONENTS

Although the comments below extend to the full range of stimuli to which the public is exposed, some of the subtleties of electoral response can most readily be observed in connection with candidate effects. The men seeking the Presidency bring to a campaign certain "real" properties as stimulus objects. Some of these belong to the past — the candidate's role as war hero, his success as governor or senator, his marital difficulties, and so on — although the communication of these things to much of the public may lie ahead. Other properties have to do with appearance, behavior, and personal style — the candidate's smile, the timbre of his voice, his smoothness in dealing with the teleprompter, his willingness to suffer fools gladly — knowledge of which can reach the electorate in numberless ways.

Impressions of these things, however, do not fall on wholly unprepared ground. Voters display a variety of response dispositions as they form their evaluations of the candidates. One type of response disposition is so evident as to require little comment. A wealth of research evidence, as well as familiar observation, attests the profound influence which partisan loyalties may have on the voter's perceptions of the men seeking office. The stronger the voter's party bias, the more likely he is to see the candidate of his own party as hero, the candidate of the other party as villain. No one who has talked with a sample of voters during a presidential campaign can have failed to note at every hand the processes by which cognitive balance is achieved.[7]

The voter's perceptual predispositions are not, however, limited to party bias. We are confronted at times by striking evidence of other identifications exerting a like influence on candidate images. A vivid example of these is the influence of religion on perceptions of John F. Kennedy during the 1960 election campaign. Because Kennedy was the Democratic candidate, voters identifying with the Democratic party tended to view him more favorably than did voters identifying with the Repub-

---

[7] Certainly evidence of it is plentiful enough in the Center's studies. See, for example, Angus Campbell, Philip E. Converse, Warren E. Miller and Donald E. Stokes, *The American Voter* (New York: John Wiley and Sons, 1960), pp. 120–145. An excellent general review of the achievement of cognitive congruence in political attitudes is given by Robert E. Lane and David O. Sears in their *Public Opinion* (Englewood Cliffs, N.J.: Prentice-Hall, 1964). An interesting application of these concepts to attitude change may be found in Denis G. Sullivan, "Psychological Balance and Reactions to the Presidential Nominations in 1960," in M. Kent Jennings and L. Harmon Zeigler (eds.), *The Electoral Process* (Englewood Cliffs, N.J.: Prentice-Hall, 1966), pp. 238–264.

lican party. But Kennedy was seen by the electorate not only as a Democrat; he was seen as a Catholic as well. As a result, at every point along the party identification continuum, Catholics tended to perceive Kennedy in a more favorable light than did Protestants.

A demonstration of the joint biasing effects of religion and party in 1960 may be found in Figure 5. In that campaign we placed each of our sample respondents along a standard party identification scale, represented here by five ordered groups: Strong Republicans, Weak Republicans, Independents, Weak Democrats, and Strong Democrats. At the same time we placed each of our Protestant and Catholic respondents on a scale of religious identification defined here by four ordered groups: persons strongly identified with a Protestant church, persons weakly identified with such a church, persons weakly identified with the Catholic Church, and persons strongly identified with the Catholic Church. These two forms of psychological identification are moderately correlated in American society (that is, Catholics are more likely than Protestants to be Democratic) but not more than moderately so. Crossing the two here yields twenty groups defined by religion and party at once in which we may examine the distribution of attitude toward Kennedy. Figure 5 displays the mean attitude toward Kennedy within each of these twenty groups.[8]

The means exhibit a remarkable pattern. The fact that the curve for each religious group slopes upward to the right shows that, whatever the voter's religious identification, he is more likely to have perceived Kennedy favorably the closer he was to the Democratic end of the party identification dimension. And the march of the four religious curves up the figure shows that, whatever the voter's party identification, he is more likely to have perceived Kennedy positively the closer he was to the Catholic end of the religious dimension. There is even a pattern to the partial discontinuities: the regularity of the curves for weak Protestants and weak Catholics suggests that the biasing tendencies of party identification were generally effective among the mildly religious while the irregularity of the curves for strong Protestants and strong Catholics suggests that party loyalty could have a marked impact on the strongly religious only if a party faith were itself strongly held.

Figure 5 is so rich in evidence of selective perception that we may easily miss what it has to say about the element of Kennedy's image which was not the result of response dispositions based on religion and party. The fact that this element was a favorable one ought not to be obscured by the strong pattern of the figure. Any reasonable operation by which we might seek to reconstruct a mean attitude among persons who are religiously and politically neutral would show that Kennedy was

[8] In order to standardize the metric used in these comparisons, I have divided each of these means by the sample standard deviation of attitude toward Kennedy. Because the sample contained only seven Weak Catholic Weak Republicans and only seven Weak Catholic Independents the means for these two groups have been adjusted to reduce the probable effect of sampling error.

FIGURE 5

*Influence of Party and Religious Identifications
on Perceptions of Kennedy*

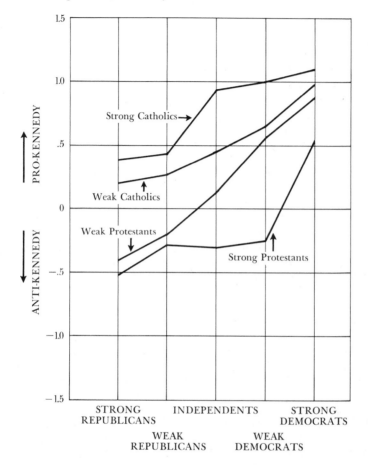

likely to be positively seen when his image did not fall prey to strong negative bias. For example, persons who were politically independent perceived Kennedy favorably even if they were weakly identified with a Protestant church.

We ought not to conclude from this that partisan and religious dispositions were the only response biases involved in the electorate's response to Kennedy or that, these dispositions aside, Kennedy was in some absolute sense an attractive candidate. In 1960, as any campaign year, many other kinds of response dispositions underlay the private impressions of the candidates formed by tens of millions of voters. We have identified two of the most important. It would not be difficult to suggest other factors which may have predisposed voters to react positively or negatively to something in the youthful, vigorous, Ivy-educated, Boston-accented stimulus which Kennedy presented.

Perhaps this point can be stated even more forcefully in terms of popular reaction to General Eisenhower, the most attractive presidential candidate since Franklin Roosevelt. The point is simply that "attractive" implies more than something about the candidate himself; it also implies something about the response dispositions of the electorate. Given the dominant values of contemporary American society, Eisenhower was enormously appealing. But we can at least imagine his having done very badly before an electorate less resonant to the military conqueror and less susceptible to the charm of a supremely other-directed personality who nevertheless evoked many of the traditional virtues. We might suppose, for example, that Eisenhower would have done very badly indeed before an electorate whose dominant values are those of American university faculties of social science.

Attitudes already formed toward some political objects are of course among the dispositions which can influence response to others. This seems especially true in the case of attitudes toward the candidates. When one rival for the Presidency already is well known, as an incumbent President will always be, the public's attitude toward his opponent will inevitably be colored by its response to the established figure. Thus, in 1940, Roosevelt-haters were quick to discover the virtues of Wendell Willkie when he was thrust onto the presidential stage, as Roosevelt's partisans were quick to discern Willkie's vices. And in the early 1950's, Adlai Stevenson had the misfortune to be paired with a much better-established rival who already enjoyed the highest public regard.[9]

Of course the complex relation of candidate stimulus to the public's response also involves important communication factors. In a sense, the only real candidate stimuli are those' which reach the voter via the mass media and interpersonal conversation, stimuli which only rarely are complemented by direct voter contact with the candidate. Therefore, the benefit or harm done to a candidate's cause by his actual personal attributes is mediated not only by the response dispositions of the electorate; it is mediated as well by the manner in which these attributes are communicated to the electorate. It is not hard to believe that some of the disarray of Goldwater's popular image was due to his extraordinarily bad press. The candidate properties communicated to the public are not a pure fiction of the media. But neither are they a pure reflection of the candidate himself, as he might have been seen at home in the desert.

What has been said of candidates can be said of any object which has

---

[9] The voter's attitude toward a given political object may be influenced by the presence of other objects in his perceptual field even when no question of order is involved in the formation of attitude. In such a case, however, it is more reasonable to think of these effects as belonging to the configuration of stimulus objects, rather than to the voters response dispositions.

electoral effects. Certainly the political role of domestic and foreign issues involves a similar interplay of stimulus properties, response tendencies, and communication processes. The Korean War's immense profit for the Republicans in 1952, for example, depended on much more than a set of objective events in the Far East and the parties' stand on those events. It depended too on a welter of response dispositions in the electorate — general isolationist or internationalist attitudes, hostility to communism, latent militarist tendencies, the anxieties of farmers over having sons away at harvest time, and the like — as well as the way in which the public was informed by the communications media of what was happening half a world away.

If the political effects of issues and personalities in the wider environment depend partly on what the electorate hears and how it is disposed to react to what it hears, it follows that changes in communication and response tendencies can at times alter the political effects of a stimulus which has not itself changed. A clear example of this is the rapid build-up of a candidate by the mass media when he steps into the charmed circle of leading contenders — or the opposite experience, which many potential candidates have had, of falling through the medias' trap door to oblivion. Instances of marked change of response dispositions while political objects remain unchanged are more difficult to discern, but they undoubtedly occur. Herbert Hoover's high starched collars, a symbol of middle class prosperity in the booming twenties, probably looked quite different from the bread-lines of 1932.

Although changes of communication and of response dispositions can alter the electorate's response to a given political object, it is nevertheless true that a turnover of objects — of the personalities, issues, and events of national politics — is the more important source of short-term electoral change. This is the more true since a stimulus object can affect communication and response dispositions themselves. For example, quite apart from the sort of man he "really" is, a candidate can have wide influence on his treatment by the mass media. If the newspapers gave Mr. Goldwater extraordinarily rough treatment for a Republican candidate, Goldwater's own posture toward the press was part of the reason. Similarly, different candidates engage different response dispositions in the mass public. Unlike any Democratic candidate since Al Smith, Kennedy activated response dispositions based on Catholic and Protestant religious identifications, as we have seen. And candidates can lead the electorate to learn new dispositions, as Kennedy helped make the country receptive to a whole new generation of youthful, vigorous candidates for national and state office.

This type of change is vividly mirrored in the components of electoral decision given here for the past four presidential elections. The evidence of the changing personal impact of the candidates is especially impressive. Yet in a presidential system the turnover of candidates has implications reaching beyond sheer personal appeal. A candidate for the nation's great office is a focus for popular feeling about issues and questions of group benefit as well, and our measurements should be extended to take this fact into account.

RELATIVE CHANGE IN CANDIDATE AND PARTY ATTITUDE

It is hardly surprising that candidates for the Presidency should attract attitudes which are somewhat distinct from those attaching to the parties themselves. The platforms adopted by the nominating conventions are much less binding than the election manifestoes of a British party, for example, and a presidential candidate is notoriously at liberty to take his own stands on major issues and the problems of major social groupings. Equally, on matters requiring congressional action he is free to contradict positions taken by his party in the Senate and House. And on matters of foreign policy, the country is largely dependent on the candidate's record and views to know what his administration would be likely to do in the world. This is the stuff of which a presidential system is made.

Therefore, it is of interest to compare the variability of attitudes toward the parties and their presidential candidates. Neither has been constant over the period of our research, but the two have shown vastly different propensities to change. When we turn from a six- to a four-dimensional model, summarizing popular feeling according to the party or candidate toward which it is directed whether or not it concerns domestic or foreign issues, questions of group benefit, or other matters, the candidate components are found to have moved much more strongly from Republican to Democratic advantage.

This contrast is shown by Figure 6, in which each pair of party and candidate components of the four-dimensional model is added together at each election. The combined party curve has not by any means stood still. The public's full assessment of the parties showed a marked Republican advantage in the mood of 1952. But by 1956 the comparison of parties had moved to the Democrats' benefit, and this trend continued over the later two elections.

The combined candidate curve, however, describes a very much greater change. The public's full assessment of Eisenhower and Stevenson, including issue and group perceptions as well as perceptions of personal qualities, was strongly Republican in 1952 and even more decisively so four years later. In the 1960 election, the comparison of candidates still favored the Republicans, although much more moderately. But between the Kennedy-Nixon campaign and the Johnson-Goldwater campaign the combined candidate component moved a most remarkable distance to the Democrats' advantage. In each contest the candidate curve was the farther removed from the zero-point: indeed, its average displacement from the neutral point has been more than 6 per cent, whereas the average displacement of the party curve has been about 2 per cent. But the really arresting comparison has to do with relative change: over

FIGURE 6

Variation of Party and Candidate Components

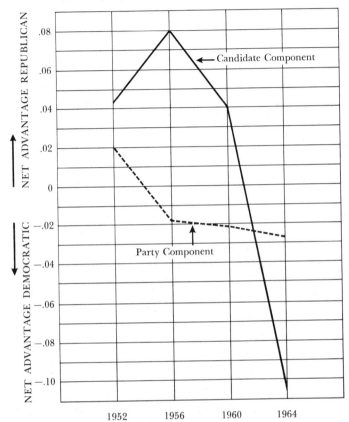

these elections the variance of the candidate curve has exceeded that of the party-curve by more than 10 to 1.

It is therefore evident that the dynamism of popular attitude is peculiarly tied to the emergence of new candidates for the Presidency. The attitudes toward the parties are not inert. The shift in the relative assessment of the parties over the period of this research has been enough to alter the parties' strength by something like six million votes on a turnout equal to that of 1964. But this change, impressive as it is, nevertheless is moderate by comparison with the change induced by succeeding pairs of candidates. The fluctuations of electoral attitudes over these elections have to a remarkable degree focused on the candidates themselves.

All of this is quite out of keeping with the static perspective of the earliest studies of voting. Even if our findings are no more than approximately true, they argue strongly the dynamic implications of changes of the stimulus objects of national politics. This source of change has in fact brought spectacular shifts of presidential voting despite the fact that over the same period there has been almost no perceptible shift in the single most important type of response disposition, the electorate's enduring party loyalties. It may also be noted that the variations of attitude recorded here have been largely independent of secular changes in the structure of American society, although, as we have seen, a turnover of stimulus objects can alter dramatically the facts of social structure which are relevant to political choice. Taken together, changes in the several stimulus objects of presidential politics in this span of years have been quite enough to bring a change of party control, indeed to have induced a drastic transformation of party fortune in the contest for the Presidency.

APPENDIX: A NOTE ON THE STATISTICAL MODEL

Since the number of positive and negative comments which a given voter makes about a given political object depends on the direction and strength of his feeling toward the object, we have placed a respondent on any given attitude dimension by forming the arithmetic difference of his pro-Republican and pro-Democratic responses whose content relates to the dimension. A pleasing variety of evidence can be marshaled to support the assumptions involved in this technique. That the resulting scales measure the intensity of attitude is borne out by the monotonic (indeed linear) relationships they exhibit with a host of other partisan variables, including the vote itself. That the neutral point is correctly located is indicated by the fact that a majority of those placed at the first scale position to the pro-Democratic side of the zero-point of each dimension do in fact vote Democratic; a majority of those at the first scale position to the pro-Republican side, Republican. The correct location of the neutral point is also attested by the model's success in estimating the direction and magnitude of the winning majority, as explained below. That the distances between scale positions are roughly equal (an assumption necessary to the further statistical operations) is also supported by the linearity of the relationship between the attitude scales and individual voting choice. Indeed, the proportion of the variance of the vote explained when individual choice is treated as a linear regression (as measured by the square of the product moment correlation) is almost identical with the proportion of the variance due to differences between the scale classes (as measured by the correlation ratio). That only a modest amount of error is involved in forming these relative-frequency measures of the direction and intensity of attitude is indicated by the success of the scales in accounting statistically for voting choice. Interestingly, the possibility that large errors have resulted from differences of verbal behavior can be partially discounted on the basis of experimental permutations of the order in which respondents were invited to comment on the two parties and the two candidates. Despite the reasonableness of the suspicion that either "warm-up" or "fatigue" effects might produce large differences in the volume of response according to the order in which the parties and candidates were presented, changes of order in fact seem not to make a particle of difference.

A linear probability model is used to describe the relation of these scales to voting choice, with a Republican vote scored 1 and a Democratic vote 0. If the probability of voting Republican, $Pr(R)$, is expressed as a linear regression on the dimensions $X_1, \ldots, X_I$:

$$Pr(R) = b_0 + b_1X_1 + \ldots + b_Ix_I, \tag{1}$$

where I is either four or six according to the model used, the coefficients $b_1, \ldots, b_I$ of this linear combination measure the relative dependence of partisan choice on each of the dimensions. For some purposes it is useful to standardize these coefficients by measuring each attitude dimension in terms of sample standard deviations, yielding a new set of coefficients $b_1^*, \ldots, b_I^*$, as defined in a manner:

$$b_i^* = b_is_i \qquad (i = 1, \ldots, I) \tag{2}$$

which removes the effect of differences in the extent of variation along each of the dimensions. These standardized coefficients are not, however, the familiar beta coefficients of a regression equation in which both the dependent and independent variates are measured in sample standard deviations about their respective means. Scoring the dependent variable 0 and 1 is necessary to the probability interpretation of estimated scores. And each attitude scale is measured about its neutral point since this constitutes a theoretically meaningful origin.

The multiple correlation of the several predictors with partisan choice has varied in the range of .72 to .75 over the four presidential elections studied. There is reason to believe that most of the remaining "error" variance is due to the dichotomous nature of the dependent variate and that the multiple correlation of the attitude dimensions with some underlying *propensity* to vote Republican or Democratic would be substantially higher. Of the alternative ways of describing this relationship, I have given most attention to a multivariate probit model under which the probability of voting Republican varies according to the cumulative normal ogive. Such a model has aesthetically pleasing formal properties, especially the fact that it will never give probability estimates less than zero or exceeding unity. In practice, however, its performance differs little from that of the model used, since the relation of voting choice to the several dimensions is so nearly linear over the range of attitude actually found in our samples. The distribution of the electorate along an attitude dimension is much more easily summarized under the linear model, a fact which counts greatly in its favor.

To estimate the average amount by which a given dimension has increased (or lessened) the probability of the individual's voting Republican, we combine the information about its relation to voting choice, as measured by the multiple regression coefficient, with information about the mean location of voters on the dimension, as measured by the displacement of the observed mean from the theoretical neutral point, forming for each attitude dimension the product

$$b_i (\overline{X}_i - X_i^0) = b_j{}^* \frac{\overline{X}_i - X_i^0}{s_i} \tag{3}$$

where b_i and $b_i{}^*$ are as defined above and X_i^0 is the neutral point of the ith dimension. If the neutral point is taken as the origin, this product of course simplifies to

$$b_i \overline{X}_i = b_i{}^* \frac{\overline{X}_i}{s_i}. \tag{4}$$

It is these quantities which I have called "attitudinal components" of the vote. The rationale for taking account of the mean's displacement from the neutral point is of course that a given dimension will benefit one party or the other only as its mean departs from the neutral point.

On the assumption that a dead heat would be the outcome of an election in which neither party was advantaged along any of the dimensions of attitude, the test of the model's ability to estimate the winning majority consists in seeing how well this relation is satisfied by the actual vote:

$$P_R - .5 = \sum_{i-1}^{I} b_i \overline{X}_i \tag{5}$$

where P_R is the proportion of the two-party vote actually polled by the Republican candidate for President and each attitude factor X_i is measured about its theoretical neutral point. Over the four elections studied the maximum departure of this relation from equality has been about two per cent, despite the fact that the Republican proportion of the two-party vote has varied over an interval from 58 per cent to less than 40 per cent. Indeed, the correlation of estimated and actual majorities over these four contests is .98, a figure which increases our confidence that we have faithfully measured many of the immediate attitudinal forces on the electorate's decision.

Winning the Election and Governing the Nation

Aaron Wildavsky

One man sniffs the air of American politics and detects a significant change in the prevailing winds. Another man notices only some turbulence that is bound to be smoothed out as the traditional flow of party politics reasserts itself. Most of us feel that something is happening, but we do not know exactly what. Will the Presidential election be decided by the normal criteria — the amount of party support and the candidates' popularity? Will the next government undertake radical changes in foreign and domestic policies? Will this election be a harbinger of fundamental alterations in the American party system?

If we want to know whether we have some understanding of the future, we shall have to risk making predictions now. For one test of knowledge is prediction — anyone can see how an election turns out and then propose an *ad hoc* explanation that appears to fit the facts. The best way to know if we have a grip on the future is to say what it will be. By allowing the election itself to pass judgment on the theories that underlie our predictions, we will better be able to determine whether we have any insight into current trends in American political life. And we shall then be in a stronger position to speculate about the future shape of the American party system.

I predict that 1968 will witness a Republican sweep throughout the nation. The Republican Party will gain a substantial majority in the House of Representatives. As for the Senate, although present Democratic majorities make the loss of Democratic control unlikely, Republicans will improve their position there as well. Any Republican Presidential nominee will win the Presidential election. In Richard M. Nixon's case, however, his relative lack of personal popularity means that in most states he will run behind the Congressional Republicans. (For those who cannot contemplate the prospect that their old antagonist might become chief executive, I suggest this simple procedure: Every day, when you wake up in the morning, just say, "Richard Nixon, President of the United States." This may help avoid culture shock in November.)

THE (DEMOCRATIC) PARTY REJECTION THEORY

The theory underlying these predictions is deceptively simple. People are unhappy about the Vietnam war. They are much more unhappy about

Reprinted by permission from *Trans-Action*, 5 (October 1968), pp. 8–15.

racial conflicts and violence at home. To manifest their displeasure, people will take the Democratic Party, which is in, and throw it out, and take the Republican Party, which is out, and put it in. This instinctive and convulsive changing of the guard need not be caused by a popular belief that the candidate or leaders of one party are better than another. All that is necessary is widespread dissatisfaction and a consequent desire to give a new team a chance.

The Vietnam war has divided and embittered the Democratic Party. A large percentage of its activists, intellectuals, and students are opposed to the policies of the Democratic Administration and to Hubert H. Humphrey, who has been identified with it. While these people will not vote for Nixon, they will not campaign for the Democratic candidate and thus will not perform their usual function of stimulating the turnout in a Democratic direction. Indeed, in some states the anti-Vietnam-war Democrats may end up supporting a fourth-party candidate.

The dissatisfaction of Democratic activists will work changes in the present voting preferences of those who identify themselves with the Democratic Party. There is unlikely to be a rapprochement between the young, white, middle-class activists supporting Senator McCarthy and the backers of Hubert Humphrey. McCarthy people are fierce in their opposition to the Vietnam war. Their hostility to Lyndon Johnson knows no bounds. They want to make Vice-President Humphrey suffer for "selling out the cause of peace" through his loyal support of the President. In talk and in print, Humphrey will be derided, castigated, and blasphemed. These feelings against the Vice-President will be aggravated by charges that the Democratic convention is rigged and that Senator McCarthy's supporters have been shabbily treated. [*This article was written during the second week in July, before either convention.* — Editor's Note.] The anti-Johnson buzzing in the ears of these party activists will prevent them from hearing Humphrey's views on foreign policy, which are similar to their own. The one thing they might hear — an angry rejection of Johnson and his Vietnam policy — will not come from the vice-president. The crescendo of disapproval of Hubert Humphrey by a large portion of the élite of his own party will become deafening after the national convention has exacerbated deep-seated resentments.

Some white Democrats (especially those in blue-collar occupations) may defect from their party on racial grounds. These are the people who directly feel pressure from Negroes. They believe it is their neighborhoods that are threatened, their jobs that are in dispute, and their safety that is being undermined. These white Democrats find it difficult to accept compensatory measures designed to help Negroes.

The major beneficiary of this racial protest may be Governor Wallace. Should a big Wallace vote throw the election into the House of Representatives, however, the large Republican majorities predicted by the Democratic Party Rejection Theory would still make Nixon President.

Nor is there any reason to believe that the Democratic Party's loss of whites will be made up — in critical states — by an increase in black votes.

Many Negroes have not been happy with the policies of the Johnson Administration. In the absence of Senator Robert F. Kennedy, the one Democratic leader who commanded their loyalty, Negroes are likely to turn out in lower percentages, thus hurting Democratic chances.

I will try to be precise in specifying the causal mechanisms that will lead to a Republican victory.

As the summer goes on and the campaign builds up in the fall, there are bound to be racial rebellions. Working-class and lower-middle-class Democrats, together with white Independents, will react to fresh evidence of racial violence by defecting towards a Republican Party perceived to be stronger on the issue of law and order — or by supporting Governor Wallace.

The Vietnam issue is tearing the Democratic Party apart. The hatred many activists have for Lyndon Johnson (extended through him to Humphrey) will sharply reduce the normal polarization effect through which Democrats would have intensified their loyalty during the campaign. The polarization phenomenon depends upon a reinforcement of one's views by hearing friends, neighbors, and élites support the party and belittle the opposition.

The hostility of Democratic activists to their Presidential candidate will be expressed in many ways. For one, the talk among activists will be highly derogatory to Humphrey. This chain of personal communications will reach large portions of Democrats now supporting Senator Mc-Carthy. Then too, these word-of-mouth blasts at Humphrey will be reinforced and amplified through the communications media. The alienated Democratic activists, though not a large percentage of party voters, occupy strategic positions. They include reporters, news broadcasters, writers for the literate "monthlies," and liberal political magazines. The bad impression of Humphrey these publicists leave with their listeners and readers will prevent party support among Democrats from reaching its usual peak.

As of this writing, these predictions of Republican victory are *not* supported by evidence from the polls, although I expect the results to change so as to confirm the Democratic Party Rejection Theory. According to Gallup, Democrats have the support of 58 per cent of the voters in the Congressional elections. Both Humphrey and McCarthy appear to be leading Nixon in the Presidential contest. A different theory, stressing traditional party support, would explain these findings.

The (Democratic) Party Support Theory

According to the Party Support Theory, the strongest tie between a man and his vote is his party identification. That is, most of the time people vote for the candidate of their party. Therefore, if an election is decided on the basis of existing party loyalty, the Democrats will win because they have many more supporters than the Republicans do. The large Democratic majority of 58 per cent projected for 1968 Congressional elections is just what one would expect if party identification were the only consideration in the election. For what good reason, it might be asked, should there be this normal party vote in what otherwise seems to be an abnormal political year?

One answer: Neither Nixon nor Humphrey appears to excite any great interest in the electorate. Thus, there will be no swing away from one party or towards another because of the popularity of one candidate or the unpopularity of another. When President Johnson removed himself from the Presidential race, he deprived the Republicans of an opportunity to center their campaign on a rejection of him. The fact that he will not run also makes it more difficult to mount a campaign centered on opposition to the party in office.

No doubt there is widespread dissatisfaction about the Vietnam war. But according to the Party Support Theory, the war will not push voters in any single direction. Some people would like the United States to get out of Vietnam immediately. Others would like the United States to escalate the war even further and *then* get out. Still others are confused. Since there is unlikely to be a great difference between the candidates on the issue of Vietnam, it will not be possible for the voters to choose on the basis of this issue, even if they know in which direction they wish to move. The candidates of both major parties will promise to bring the war to an end, and voters will have to decide who is better able to do this under the most satisfactory conditions. Under these conditions, the Republican Party will not be able to gain enough votes on the Vietnam issue to overcome the normal Democratic lead in the electorate.

The position of both parties on racial conflict is also likely to be similar. They will come out for law and order. They will call for measures to deal with poverty. While some voters may find the Democrats too favorable to Negroes, they would not find the Republican candidate sufficiently unfavorable to justify a switch in party vote. It is far more likely that these Republicans would take the opportunity to vote for George Wallace. The polls have shown, however, that Wallace takes two votes from the Republicans for every one he gets from the Democrats. Hence the anti-black vote would do more harm to the Republicans than to the Democrats.

If the voters were divided along party lines now, the proponents of the Democratic Party Support Theory would argue, these differences will be even more pronounced at election time. All of the forces agitating the nation's political life will cancel one another out. Beset by doubt, overwhelmed by perplexity, American voters will reaffirm their traditional party positions.

GOVERNING THE NATION: NIXON

Whether one chooses to project current polls predicting a Democratic victory, or whether, like myself, one expects future change leading to a Republican triumph, is determined as much by intuition as by science.

No one has to remind an American living in 1968 of the contingent nature of political events. What is certain is that the next President of the United States will face grave difficulties in governing the nation. Since I have predicted a Republican victory, let's begin with the dilemmas facing Richard Nixon.

Predicting the Nixon Administration's foreign policy is relatively easy because internal political forces will produce substantially the same results, no matter who is elected. It is difficult to imagine any President's maintaining 500,000 troops in Vietnam through the 1970 Congressional election. To do so would lead his party to a crashing defeat. To maintain much more than the Air Force and Navy presence in Vietnam past the 1972 presidential election would be an admission that Nixon's term in office has been a failure. While the American people may not agree on what to do about Vietnam, they are in overwhelming agreement that we should get out. The only difference is that the doves wish we had gotten out yesterday and the hawks want to force the enemy into submission tomorrow. Virtually everyone is agreed that the Vietnam war must be ended or vastly diminished.

Each major-party candidate will say that he is the better man to bring the war to an end, and he will know that he must make good on that promise. Senator McCarthy might try to arrange a speedy withdrawal, but he would discover that the lives of millions depend upon his negotiating an agreement for their safety. Vice-President Humphrey can be expected to attempt a gradual withdrawal of American troops over a period of four years. Richard Nixon might once have liked to maintain the American commitment over a longer period, but now he recognizes that he cannot. The election of one or another of these men, therefore, will lead to similar patterns of slow withdrawal.

Nixon will, however, enjoy greater flexibility in pursuing a new Vietnam policy than his Democratic opponent. McCarthy has centered his campaign on the Vietnam issue. He would be dreadfully embarrassed by any inability to show immediate results in obtaining the withdrawal of American armed forces. Humphrey is bound by the necessity of placating the furious opposition to the war within his own party. He must call for an immediate cessation of bombing North Vietnam and show actual withdrawal of troops within a few months. Nixon is in the best position because he is broadly acceptable to Republican activists who have never been strongly opposed to the Vietnam war as their Democratic counterparts. As President, Nixon could afford to wait longer and bargain for more acceptable conditions of American withdrawal.

The party unity that Nixon has labored so hard to bring about is his strongest resource, and yet it might turn out to be his gravest weakness. A unified base of support in the country will surely help Nixon govern. The great question is whether he will have to pay too high a price to his most conservative supporters on domestic policies.

Disaster would follow if the Republican Party interpreted its victory as a mandate for racial repression and an abandonment of welfare policies. Then it could no longer hope to recapture the allegiance of part of the Negro population, the only major new group from which it could hope to gain long-lasting support. A Republican government would not be prepared to cope with the vast conflicts its policies unleashed. The combination of racial and class conflicts would be too much for it, and might even threaten the survival of our political system. There are radical revolutionaries who count on just this kind of development to leave the people no alternative but a basic transformation of social life (before the rise of Hitler, Communists called this policy "The worse, the better").

Yet there is another course of action that is compatible with traditional Republican views and that holds out much greater promise of free political life. A Republican President and a majority of Republican Congressmen could look upon the election as a mandate to try conservative solutions to major social problems. Instead of a welfare-state apparatus directed from Washington, they could come out for decentralization of authority, with large block grants going to cities, states, and neighborhood governments — in which Negroes would play a dominant part in the areas where they predominate. Instead of a guaranteed annual wage, Republicans could insist on vast job programs, with the idea of providing work at good wages for every American. The old virtues about which so much is heard — hard work, local control, citizen participation — could be made the foundation of promising new policies. The nation has a large stake in which alternative the Republican activists choose.

GOVERNING THE NATION: HUMPHREY

The overwhelming problem faced by Hubert Humphrey is not winning the election, however insuperable the odds, but governing the country should he happen to win. To lose may merely turn out to be allowing Nixon to suffer. But to win, and to be unable to lead the country, would be the worst thing that could happen.

The danger is that Hubert Humphrey would take Lyndon Johnson's place as a beleaguered President, unable to travel among his people, a prisoner in Washington without a loyal core of followers in his party, in Congress, or in the bureaucracy. We know that racial conflict has deep roots in our society and will not soon be mitigated. No President, however determined or well-intentioned, will be able to prevent racial rebellions. Though Humphrey will try to bring the Vietnam war to an end, that process is bound to take several years. He will not be able to satisfy people who want a fast end to hostilities. Nor will there be an immediate release of the vast funds tied up in the war, funds that might be used to make a massive attack on racial and urban problems.

Humphrey might face a Republican House of Representatives dedicated to thwarting him at every turn. Even the best he could hope for, a small Democratic majority in the House, would leave control with the conservative coalition. The frustrations of the first two Kennedy years, during which the late President was unable to get most of his program enacted, would be repeated under much more dangerous and disadvantageous circumstances. In the first two or three years of his Administration, therefore, Humphrey would be unable to achieve the miracles necessary to win a reservoir of good will. On the contrary, his term in office would probably begin amidst a sullen and angry popular mood. For undertaking the same good policies that would have given Kennedy credit, Humphrey would be abused.

It is important to understand that the nation faces a crisis of legitimacy surrounding its political institutions and leaders. Many blacks who have been treated badly in this country say that they are no longer certain they wish to think of themselves as Americans who give allegiance to national political symbols, institutions, and officials. White opponents of the Vietnam war feel that the President, by escalating the war, has betrayed his promise to limit the conflict. An unsettling series of events — the Kennedy assassinations, Johnson's decision not to run, Rockefeller's refusal to enter the primaries when he still had a chance — has deprived many political activists of both symbols of hope and targets of hostility. Instead of blaming fate, they tend to turn against existing political institutions and Hubert Humphrey, the man who epitomizes their frustrations.

It is critically important that the next President not only do good but get credit for it. If he is constantly under bitter attack, he will not be able to mobilize the resources to create and carry out wise policies. Yet Humphrey may find that history has placed him in a position that will thwart his most noble impulses. That is why his stress of winning the nomination, instead of gaining the support of McCarthy's people for governing the country, seems misplaced. Humphrey has not taken the actions — extreme generosity in allocating delegates to McCarthy's supporters, granting them a preponderant voice in writing the platform, entering into sustained discussions — that would not only improve his chances of electoral victory but give him a fighting chance to govern effectively.

Only gross miscalculation and grave error could have led Humphrey to denounce McCarthy supporters as brown shirts and suggest they are already determined to set up a fourth party. Humphrey is not supposed to be a political prognosticator but a Presidential statesman. His task is not to make it impossible for McCarthy supporters to turn to him but to leave every door open to every man who can go with him during and especially after the Presidential campaign. The task is to govern. Perhaps the best parallel is Abraham Lincoln's good sense and forbearance in accommodating leaders of hostile party factions in his Administration. He gave away Cabinet positions and offered Vice-Presidential posts to keep his party and nation together. We also face internal rebellion; our unity is threatened. Humphrey should do no less than Lincoln did.

Humphrey's suggestion that Edward Kennedy would be welcome as Vice-President may have been a proper symbolic gesture to a tragic family, but it evidences a deplorable insensitivity to the need of obtaining widespread reconciliation. Dissent within the Democratic Party is rooted in disagreement over foreign policy, not over whether there should be deference to the Kennedy family. A Vice-Presidential candidate known to have been opposed to the Vietnam war, like Senator McGovern, together with a platform dedicated to that end, are essential first steps toward healing the party's wounds. McCarthy supporters require acknowledgment that their crusade has merit; they need guarantees that their views and their men will help determine the nation's foreign policy; above all, they require evidence that their leader and his views will be respected. It is unlikely that McCarthy would respond to even such overtures by warmly endorsing Humphrey and the Democratic Party. But if he made clear his intention to remain with the party, most of his supporters would follow his lead. If McCarthy's wishes are given special consideration during the Presidential term, persuading him to give the party a chance to perform, Humphrey will have gained immeasurably in authority to govern. If Humphrey's Presidency were to become "hell on wheels," we cannot forget that his personal tragedy would also be a national disaster.

The Future of the American Party System

Preoccupied with the coming election and its immediate impact upon national policy, we lose sight of the long-run implications of this contest for the Presidency. The outcome of the 1968 election may be of critical importance in determining the shape of the future party system and the content of American political life.

Though we are in the habit of talking about the American two-party system, it might be more accurate to say that there is at present a party-and-three-quarters system. By the usual tests of party identification, the Democrats command the support of approximately 46 per cent of the voting population, whereas the Republicans are down to about 27 per cent. This is a gap so huge that it would not require much for the Republican Party to go *below* the minimum voter allegiance required for effective opposition in national elections.

The dilemma of the Republican Party may be seen by posing the basic question about its disastrous defeat in 1964: Why did the party nominate a man who was disliked by most Republicans and despised by an overwhelming number of Democrats? The major clue was discovered by Herbert McClosky, who found that Republican Party activists were immensely more conservative than ordinary Republican voters. In the absence of a moderate candidate commanding widespread public support in primaries, the convention delegates, who represent Republican Party activists, just nominated a man like themselves.

The Republican Party may be on the verge of a downward spiral in which the tension between party activists and general voters leads to ever-decreasing support.[1] Let us suppose that in 1972 and 1976 the Republicans nominate candidates who represent the conservative activists and not the more moderate voters. Finding the Republican Party with a candidate they cannot support, large numbers of voters begin to move to the Democrats. As the Republican Party becomes smaller, its activists make up a larger percentage of the whole. Hence they continue to nominate candidates who are extremely popular with the hard-core conservatives but are less and less able to attract popular support. The spiral continues as the Democratic Party grows larger and the Republican Party grows smaller. The inevitable result would be the conversion of the Republican Party into a small sect concerned with maintaining its ideological purity, but not with winning elections. Nor would this outcome necessarily be advantageous for the Democratic Party, which would become so large that it would lose whatever cohesion it now has and would most probably disintegrate into warring factions.

The future stability of the Republican Party requires that it be able to win with a candidate who is clearly identified with its traditions. The 1968 election presents the party with an extraordinary opportunity to capitalize upon the unpopularity of the Johnson Administration. If a real Republican like Nixon cannot win under present favorable circumstances, there would not appear to be much hope for the Republican Party as it is now constituted.

A defeat for Nixon would split apart the Republican Party. Its most conservative elements would conclude that since they cannot win through compromising their position, they might as well form a new party and stand up for what they believe. The possibility of an amalgamation with Governor Wallace's followers would not be entirely out of the question. (Seymour M. Lipset has observed that frustration at losing an election they expected to win in 1948, after decades out of office, led some Republican leaders to give support to Joe McCarthyism.) Conservative Republicans might find their body infected by a racist virus. As for Republican liberals and moderates, to understand what they might do, we must first consider the situation in the Democratic Party.

A defeat for Hubert Humphrey would leave the Democratic Party without a national leader in office. The strategy of the dissident Democrats, therefore, would be to defeat their party in hopes of picking up the pieces after the election. Then it would be possible for the dissidents to take over the party from the inside. The fourth-party movement designed to defeat Hubert Humphrey would dissolve after the election in order to carry on its struggle within the Democratic Party.

[1] In social-science terminology, this downward spiral is called an "unstable equilibrium." Imagine that a husband and wife are in bed, covered with an electric blanket. Unknown to either of them the electric controls have become switched. He is too warm and moves the indicator to a colder temperature. She is too cold and moves her indicator to a warmer temperature. The colder she gets, the warmer he becomes; the warmer he feels, the colder she gets. Carried to its ultimate conclusion, this unstable equilibrium could burn him to a crisp and freeze her into a block of ice.

Our future sight is dim. But it does appear that the emergence of a Republican President holds out the best hope for the maintenance of the two-party system. Republicans would unite behind Nixon to enjoy the fruits of office, while Democrats fought for the right to use the old party name. Both parties (though this prediction is more like prayer than prophecy) would shift somewhat to the left. Republicans would become more reconciled and responsive to conditions of modern political life, and Democrats would be more consistently dedicated to political innovation.

If Humphrey were to win the election, however, the Republican Party might break up in despair, and the Democratic Party might split out because of the dissidents' anger at winning with a "tainted" candidate. The most conservative Republicans, as noted, might join the Wallace forces to create a new rightist Republican Party, while the more radical McCarthy supporters might unite with some of the New Left activists to form a party of their own. Liberal Republicans would then have no alternative but to join the Democrats, the one remaining moderate party.

This three-party system — moderates and radicals of the left and right — would likely prove unstable. As Michael Leiserson has suggested, the right-wing party might find itself increasingly regarded as irrelevant to the times. In response, the center and left would unite, and the system would finally change itself into a two-party system defined along radical-versus-gradualist lines. The fulcrum of political life would have shifted dramatically to the left.

Another possibility is that the leftist party would somehow discredit itself, leaving the electoral field effectively to the moderate and right-wing parties. Political life would have moved sharply to the right.

My guess is that a three-party system would lead to perpetual rule by an oversized moderate majority as the right and left parties become too extreme to command public confidence. The alienation of radical right and left parties that could never hope to govern would become serious national problems. The majority party would be torn between its need for unity to prevent the extremes from winning and its desire to break up into more cohesive blocks. We would indeed be in a time of trouble.

After speculation upon speculation, the mind boggles at proceeding so much further than the eye can see. What is clear is that the 1968 election will affect our national political life far after the issues, personalities, and perhaps even the political parties involved have disappeared from our consciousness.

Election 1968 — The Abortive Landside

Walter Dean Burnham

The 1968 election marks a turning point in American political history. Richard Nixon won the presidency but the ambiguity of the vote reached proportions unusual even for American electoral politics.

By following a rigid periphery vs. center campaign strategy, Nixon lost what was probably a golden opportunity to win the commanding victory the polls had once forecast. The Republicans won the presidency and a dominant majority of state governorships yet they failed to significantly improve their congressional position. The Democratic labor-urban coalition in the industrial states worked surprisingly well but in the end not quite well enough. Humphrey fought a superb campaign in the last six weeks and gained prestige but still he could not overcome the long anti-Administration electoral build-up. And while those supporters of Senator McCarthy who believed Humphrey's defeat essential to their purposes got their wish, their enemies from the Chicago convention remain firmly astride the party saddle. George Wallace, in the end, was quietly dispatched to Alabama but even in defeat he led one of the most impressive third-party showings in the history of the two party system.

These ambiguities faithfully reflect the totality of missed chances, major policy disasters, dissipated majorities, abortive candidacies and exceptionally narrow political choices which have dominated American politics for the last several years. Although deadlock politics has been the norm since 1938, the muffled results of the 1968 election seem even more paradoxical. In the past, *immobilisme* has been a heavy contributor to the survival of American political structures. Whether it will have the same positive effect this time is one of the most significant questions this election has left unanswered.

Even though analysis at this stage is necessarily fragmentary, the cloud of ambiguity can be penetrated and some of the dynamics beneath it perceived. It is worth recalling that just four years ago the Republican party had come dangerously close to losing its position as a usable opposition to which swing voters could feel free to move if they grew disenchanted with the incumbents. President Johnson's 61.3 per cent of the vote was a landslide that seemed to foreshadow a long Democratic ascendancy, as did the 1964 party identification in the electorate — 53 per cent Democratic, 25 per cent Republican, 22 per cent Independent. Usually such landslides presage victory for the winning party for at least the next two presidential elections. In 1964, Democratic auguries looked

Reprinted by permission from *Trans-Action*, 6 (December 1968), pp. 18–24.

even more favorable since the Goldwater candidacy seriously damaged traditional Republican party loyalties in the Northeast. It seemed clear that a solidly partisan-identified Republican could never win the presidency in any foreseeable future.

Viewed over a time span extending back to 1964, the most dramatic aspect of 1968 was the magnitude and speed of voter defection from the Democratic coalition. Between 1964 and 1968, the net swing to the Republican party was exceptionally high, out-ranked in a list of 18 election pairs only by the shift from Hoover to Roosevelt and Wilson to Harding (see Table 1).

TABLE 1

1968 Was a Year of Massive Democratic Defection

Net Partisan Swing in American Presidential Elections, 1892–1968 (Ranked by Magnitude)

Election Pair	Swing	Election Pair	Swing
1928–1932	17.1 D	1924–1928	3.9 D
1916–1920	14.6 R	1892–1896	3.7 R
1964–1968	11.5 R	1932–1936	3.3 D
1960–1964	11.2 D	1952–1956	2.3 R
1956–1960	7.8 D	1944–1948	2.1 R
1936–1940	7.2 R	1940–1944	1.2 R
1948–1952	7.1 R	1896–1900	0.9 R
1900–1904	6.3 R	1920–1924	0.5 D
1912–1916*	5.9 D	1908–1912*	0.1 R

* For analytical purposes the Republican and Progressive percentages of the total vote are combined in Tables 1 and 2.

Clearly, the 1964–1968 swing falls into a special category of election type: the landslide which is a vote of no confidence in the incumbent party. Such landslides are rare, and historically have been associated with traumatic experiences felt with abnormal intensity by large numbers of voters.

At first blush it seems anomalous to classify 1968 as a "landslide" since it obviously was not in terms of a two-party division. But examination of the gross shifts in each party's share of the total vote, as well as other factors, suggests that it was in fact a landslide — albeit a negative one.

This is the important reality of the 1968 election. While the magnitude of the gross *Democratic decline* can only be compared with the Republican collapse of 1932, the *Republican gain* over 1964 was so small that Nixon was barely able to win.

TABLE 2

*A Negative Landslide — 1968 GOP Gains Were
Small Compared to Large Democratic Losses*

Shifts of 4.9% or More in Winning and Losing Party's
Percentage of the Total Vote, 1892–1968

Losing Party		Gaining Party	
Election Pair	Shift	Election Pair	Shift
1928–1932	−18.6 (R)	1928–1932	+16.6 (D)
1964–1968	*−18.2 (D)*	1916–1920	+14.2 (R)
1916–1920	−15.1 (D)	1924–1928	+12.0 (D)
1960–1964	−11.1 (R)	1960–1964	+11.3 (D)
1900–1904	− 7.9 (D)	1948–1952	+10.0 (R)
1956–1960	− 7.8 (R)	1936–1940	+ 8.3 (R)
1920–1924	− 6.3 (R)	1892–1896	+ 8.0 (R)
1936–1940	− 6.1 (D)	1956–1960	+ 7.7 (D)
1948–1952	− 5.1 (D)	1904–1908	+ 5.5 (R)
		1964–1968	*+ 4.9 (R)*

This result reflects not only the massive impact of the Wallace vote, but also the decline over the past generation in the Republican party-identified electorate, the dislocation of 1964, and Nixon's failure to capitalize on Democratic and Independent disaffection. Granted all these factors, it seems evident that only a political upheaval of near-cataclysmic proportions could have created the conditions in which his election was possible at all.

That this election shares something in common with earlier no-confidence landslides is also suggested by the uniformity of the anti-Democratic shift outside the South, whether measured on a two-party or a three-party basis. The combined effect of the Wallace candidacy and the uniformity of the anti-Democratic swing elsewhere produced three regional bulwarks of support: the Deep South for Wallace, the plains and mountain states for Nixon and New England for Humphrey. These regional polarizations appeared in the 1964 election.

Barry Goldwater's campaign quite clearly polarized the country, not only ideologically but sectionally. In a real sense the Goldwater campaign was an insurrection of local or parochial elements in the American elector-ate against the cosmopolitans who since the 1930s had controlled the presidential politics of both parties. While the polarization which Gold-water forced upon the American electorate was not widely perceived at the mass base in ideological terms, it was clearly responded to through the social values associated with regional political subcultures. The result was the production of a massive regional tilt from West to East and from

South to North. Goldwater's Southern-Western strategy had the expected results, with one important exception: most of "Goldwater country" remained below the 50 per cent level of electoral support. This strategy also had massive and perhaps permanent adverse effects on the Republican party particularly among traditional Republican supporters in the more cosmopolitan regions and sectors of American society.

The results of the 1968 election clearly indicate that this regional tilt has persisted. In an obviously volatile election year, the campaign strategy which Nixon adopted had, it seems, a lot to do with regional persistence. His strategy was, in fact, surprisingly close to Goldwater's, with two major exceptions. First, the extreme racist element associated with the Goldwater effort in the South was, for the most part, cut off from the 1968 Nixon coalition by the Wallace candidacy. And while the Nixon periphery vs. center coalition strategy was still based on the West and South, it was structured by the pragmatic calculations of political technicians rather than by ideological fervor. The fact remains that Nixon, given a once-in-a-generation opportunity to win over large numbers of disaffected cosmopolitans from the Democrats, instead chose a remarkably consistent coalition strategy based upon the more remote areas of American society. With the addition of just enough traditional Republican metropolitan support, he won narrow victories in some industrial states. Although Democrats have occasionally won presidential elections on a similar regional base — Wilson in 1916 and Truman in 1948 — 1968 marks the second time that Republicans have tried such a coalition, and the first in history in which it produced a Republican victory. The 1964 election may have had more significant long-term consequences for the political system than is often supposed.

One of the elements which made the 1968 election unexpectedly close was Nixon's refusal to make a serious bid for the cosmopolitans who had defected so massively from Goldwater, and the resultant refusal of many of them to give Nixon their support. One indicator of this is Nixon's relatively poor showing in the suburban reaches of the northeastern megalopolis. Lower Merion Township, a bedroom suburb of Philadelphia which is still very "Main Line" in its socioeconomic characteristics is probably typical. As Table 3 implies, the Republicans are emerging as a party of defense of peripheral social strata and regions against the threat of change. The Democrats, on the other hand, are progressively broadening their base in these social strata and areas which have a vital interest in political modernization and structural transformation. Despite its ambiguous result, the election of 1968 may speed up this process of differentiation.

The emergent Democratic coalition is increasingly based on the deprived and nonwhite at the bottom, the younger and better-educated — along with academics and other intellectuals — in the middle, and corporate and financial interests who have accepted the "new economics" and are major partners in the welfare-warfare state at the top. Yet such a coalition of the top and the bottom against the middle still heavily

TABLE 3

GOP Strength in a Bedroom Suburb

Political Patterns in Lower Merion Township, 1948–1968:
Transfer of Cosmopolitan Loyalties?

	Percentage of Vote				Difference From National Percentage			
Year	D	R	Oth.	% D, 2-party	D	R	Oth.	% D, 2-party
1948	22.2	76.4	1.4	22.5	−27.4	+31.3	− 3.9	−29.9
1952	22.9	77.1		22.9	−21.7	+21.7		−21.7
1956	24.2	75.8		24.2	−18.0	+18.0		−18.0
1960	35.6	64.4		35.6	−14.5	+14.5		−14.5
1964	52.7	47.3		52.7	− 8.6	+ 8.6		− 8.6
1968	42.0	55.7	2.3	43.0	− 0.9	+12.3	−11.4	− 7.1

depends on the support of the middle stratum that is growing technologically obsolescent and is also directly on the front lines of our contemporary social wars. Even though George Wallace's penetration of these white-collar and blue-collar workers was substantially checked at the end, they clearly remain among the most potentially volatile elements in the American electorate. Their future partisan allegiance is by no means certain, for as the election returns show, the Republican party has a fundamental problem with its present "image": When the unionized working class becomes disaffiliated from the Democratic party, it does not see Republicanism as a viable option, and hence turns to a third party candidate or to abstention.

The Republican coalition is increasingly becoming composed of the "middle" and technologically-obsolescent peripheries of American society allied against the top and bottom. For many of these voters, significant change in any direction is threatening, and with good reason. But periphery-centered coalitions based on declining social strata have rarely been successful. When they have been, their winning candidates have invariably won less than half of the total vote. Such victories, moreover, have not paved the way for coalitions with great staying power.

Richard Nixon thus faces some extremely tricky political problems, even apart from the overhanging social tensions which alone made his accession to power possible. Governing, which involves both the need to acquire highly skilled personnel to fill key positions and the need to make side-payments to coalitional allies in his first and foremost problem. Skilled personnel are found more and more in the higher reaches of the technical-academic complex. Out of all proportion to their numbers, this complex has in the main contributed to Democratic programs and policies. Whether enough of these people will be available to a Nixon administration will depend, to a large degree, upon the coalition and policy strategies the new President chooses to adopt. Perhaps the President may govern with some effectiveness without the substantial positive support of opinion-leaders, academics and the technologically sophisticated. But the collapse of the Johnson administration is a warning to any incumbent of the real dangers he may bring upon himself if he follows policies that evoke passionate hostility in most of them. If the periphery-centered strategy of the Nixon campaign is continued and converted into policy, such hostility is very likely to mushroom. If it is abandoned in favor of policy choices which such groups would be likely to at least tacitly support, the periphery-centered elements in his coalition will be tempted to defect.

NIXON'S OPTIONS SEVERELY LIMITED

Policy choices and coalitional strategies are intimately related to each other. The need to expand his base of coalitional support, and expand it broadly, is the second of Richard Nixon's problems of choice. Yet his range of options appears to be remarkably limited. A move toward the middle-class political modernizers in both parties is conceivable, but would be a calculated risk carrying very uncertain payoffs with the strong possibility of mass defections within the coalition which elected him. A Whiggish Eisenhower strategy of administrative laissez-faire would probably be ideal from many points of view; however, Nixon is not Eisenhower and the year is not 1955. Any overt movement toward the Wallace following would increase internal tension to the bursting point and destroy any possibility of a positive relationship between the President and the key cosmopolitan influentials whose acquiescence he must have to govern. A policy strategy of calculated ambiguity is probably the most likely way out of these coalitional dilemmas. It remains to be seen whether the press of events will permit the Nixon administration that luxury.

From start to finish, the 1968 election exhibited exceptionally high-levels of public alienation from the old political routines and structures of American electoral politics. Two of the obvious centers of alienation this year were the college-educated young in revolt over Vietnam and a good deal else, and those Southern and blue-collar white elements caught up in the emotions of Negrophobia. There is much evidence, however, that the mood of disenchantment is pervasive.

In the past four years the proportion of Independent identifiers in the electorate have risen rapidly to an all-time high: Independents are to be found among the young, the better-educated and the more affluent. That 43% of the American electorate according to the CBS pre-election poll, would have preferred a choice among candidates different from the one given it is another indicator of alienation. So is the decline in turnout which occurred in many parts of the country. In Massachusetts, for example, turnout declined from 77 per cent in 1960 to 72.5 per cent in 1964 to 68.5 per cent in 1968. Interestingly enough, the decline which appears to have occurred in much of the country this year conforms to a long-standing historical uniformity in American politics. With the exception of the 1856–1860 period, every election in which major third-party candidacies have occurred has been associated with declines in voter participation. The two are probably interrelated: the same widespread public dissatisfaction with the alternatives presented by the two major parties might be expected to manifest itself in abstentions as well as third-party voting.

When all is said and done, the size of the Wallace *ressentiment* movement remains as the most impressive feature of this election; it dramatically shows the disruption of electoral politics through which the country is now passing. While Wallace was not able to win the 20 per cent of the vote projected by the surveys, his total of ten million votes — 13.7 per cent of the total cast — was more than enough to mark his American Independent Party as one of the most significant third-party insurrections in American political history.

TABLE 4

In This Century Only Lafollette's and Roosevelt's Progressives Fared Better Than Wallace's AIP

American Third Parties, 1832–1968*

Year	Party	Per Cent of Total Vote
1832	Anti-Masonic	8.0
1848	Free Soil	10.1
1856	American (Know-Nothing)	21.1
1860	Southern Democrat	18.2
1860	Constitutional Union	12.6
1892	Populist	8.5
1912	Progressive	27.4
1912	Socialist	6.0
1924	Progressive	16.6
1968	American Independent	13.7

*Parties winning less than 5% of the total national vote are omitted.

Even though its popular support was concentrated in the thirteen states of the greater South, where it won about 57 per cent of its nationwide total, the Wallace movement received about 7.5 per cent of the vote outside of this region — a not insignificant share of the whole vote. The AIP is also the first American third party — with the possible exception of the Breckinridge Democrats in 1860 — to constitute a major movement on the right rather than on the left.

Definitive academic study of the 1968 election will center most probably on the Wallace movement's impact on American electoral politics. At this time we can only surmise that Wallace's overall effect was to deny Nixon and the Republicans a real rather than an abortive landslide by "spoiling" the major domestic issues (law and order, Negro-white tensions) that were the focal points of greatest discontent with the incumbent Democrats. Such an interpretation tends to support the view that the 1968 election was a partly aborted no-confidence landslide, with the added proviso that both the gross profile of the returns and the limited survey information available suggest a vote of no confidence on the part of many Americans in electoral politics as a whole. The view that the Wallace candidacy further frightened an already unsettled electorate, and frightened a good many voters away from the hard line on law and order, also goes far in explaining Humphrey's near-success in patching the old northern Democratic coalition back together. It is quite understandable that in an abnormally unstructured context, where no candidate is able to develop a differentially positive and reassuring electoral appeal, the voters move back to the safety of established reference groups and traditional routines of electoral behavior.

Large third-party uprisings against the established two-party system have been closely and typically associated with critical political realignments. Realignment comes about in the American context because political party structures and behavioral routines associated with them tend to be static and repetitive over long periods of time. But while politics in America is inherently non-developmental — parties in this country adapt but they do not evolve — the economy and the society evolve rapidly and unevenly. In the process, the disadvantaged and disaffected become more and more numerous, and their demands for political action become more insistent. Eventually the gap between the "old politics" and political demand arising from the consequences of unplanned social change produces a rupture in traditional voting alignments. More often than not, such disruption takes the form, in its earlier stages, of a massive protest movement against established policies, parties and leaders. Third parties reflect politically organizable maladjustments in society which the established order has been unwilling or unable to cope with. In the past they have tended to be way-stations for millions of voters who are *en route* from one major-party coalition to the other.

WALLACE AND THE REPUBLICANS

The Wallace movement was centered upon the most explosive and indigestible set of social dislocations the country has had since the Civil War. These dislocations, with racial antagonisms at their core, have raised the few issues in American history which resist incremental or disaggregated solutions. In this respect Wallace's strength in the South, while much more massive than in other parts of the country, is less significant than his penetration of the North — now the vortex of the racial cold war. For it seems clear that the issues involved are going to be fought out at the center of modern American society, in the metropolitan complex rather than at its periphery. With each passing year it seems less likely that the explosive tensions of racial polarization can be settled in the classical American incremental pattern. The New York school strike, after all, may be part of the wave of the future. But to say that these tensions cannot be resolved incrementally is also to say that they will not be resolved at all within the traditional American institutional structure, in which case they will continue to increase. Of course, it is possible to resolve them by fiat. This, however, requires that Americans face up to certain hard questions of sovereign power whose avoidance is the very heart of the American political tradition. It is also possible to resolve these issues through decentralization linked to participatory democracy at the local level. This too would be, in effect, a quasi-revolutionary change in American ways of transacting political business.

Thus the mixture of issues that come from disruptive and unplanned social change, the fruit of millions of private decisions, confronts American politics with very basic challenges. The American political system is Whiggish to its core. It is predicated upon the assumption that fundamental polarizations among antagonistic groups will not often become a cluster of political demands, and that if they do, they can be successfully individualized, fragmented and processed into incremental policy outputs. The political system as a whole can work with minimal success only when this conversion process functions and produces results accepted by the combatants. It seems to be structurally incompatible with any use of political power for authoritative planning and control over the socio-economic system. If problems involving social collectivities cannot be evaded and cannot be adequately resolved in terms of incremental policy outputs resting on individualist social assumptions, the system as a whole will undergo the most profound crisis. So it was in the Civil War era; so it seems to be now.

The Wallace movement or one like it will continue to exist indefinitely as long as the cold war between black and lower-middle-class white communities continues to generate social strains on the current order of magnitude. Only if the Republican party moves toward a semi-Wallaceite position would its political entrepreneurs be absorbed into the existing two-party system. But this kind of movement would not only produce a huge political realignment, it would also augment the potential for civil-war that already exists in this country. If neither party makes a serious effort to win over Wallace's ten million, a racist-populist third party will most probably survive for the indefinite future. From what we know about the political behavior of threatened lower middle-classes, further escalation of our domestic social wars may well ensure a surprisingly bright future for such a third party — that is if the appropriate leadership skills become available.

Nixon has emphasized his commitment to solving metropolitan problems through the medium of private enterprise. But if the domestic policies of 1938 seem to be irrelevant to this problem, it is unlikely that those of 1928 will be any more relevant or productive of viable policy results. Nixon's commitment is, of course, an act of faith in disaggregated individualism as a substitute for social policy; it is a belief that fundamental social problems involving intractable groups can be resolved within the established individualist framework. As such he is touchingly, almost embarrassingly, in the mainstream of the American political tradition. It serves as a convenient reminder that you probably can't get there from here without making a clear break from that tradition.

And so the first clearly partisan Republican president has been elected in this country since 1928 at a time when the disenchantment with traditional American political structures and leadership is pervasive and seems to be growing. If the incoming administration permits its ideology to get the better part of its discretion in foreign policy, and if its private-enterprise policies toward the metropolitan centers provide only palliatives or worse, it will prove not to have been a usable opposition after all. Indeed, it will not have been an opposition at all. The consequences that would follow from this admission, following hard on the heels of the collapse of the Johnson consensus, are not pretty to contemplate. We·might then be faced with a really massive popular repudiation of electoral politics as such, and the rise of a popular-totalitarian movement which would seek to destroy the barriers to central political control of society while professing to uphold or restore them. Confronted by accumulated social dislocations so deep and so intractable that no resolution of them is in sight, we have approached the verge of the deepest and most comprehensive crisis in our national history. The way out or through this crisis remains as murky and ambiguous as the results of the aborted landslide of 1968.

Titular Leadership of the Presidential Parties

Ralph M. Goldman

A persistent anomaly of the American party system is the lack of a formal organizational status for the "titular" leaders of the presidential parties. Like any rank-and-filer, the President and his most recently de-

Printed by permission of the author. The problems discussed here were first investigated while the author was a research associate at the Brookings Institution in Washington, D.C., whose support he gratefully acknowledges.

feated opponent are formal members of their party only to the extent that they may enroll at registration time, pay a membership fee, make a financial contribution, or serve, through appointment by some party official, on a party committee — for example, Adlai Stevenson's service on the Democratic Advisory Council. Incumbency in the presidency or recent service as the party's presidential nominee carries no special status in the formal party organization. Yet, these men are perceived as and expected to behave as leaders of the national presidential parties. Such leadership is indeed "titular"; it is an elusive political resource for the incumbent, the party, and the nation. The responses of particular titular leaders to their role is the subject of the present report.

While the major national parties in the United States have much of the appearance of systematic formal organization from national committee to precinct captain, it is a well-established fact that neat organizational charts hardly fit either the organizational or the political realities. Party structure at the national level, for example, is a fragmented array of sometimes cooperating, sometimes hostile, sometimes active, sometimes dormant organizational units. On the congressional side, these units include the party leaders of the House (Speaker, Majority and Minority Leaders, Whips) and the Senate (President pro tempore, Majority and Minority Leaders), the senatorial policy committees, and the senatorial and congressional campaign committees. On the presidential side, these units include the national convention, the national committee, the national chairman and his headquarters, and the nominee's campaign headquarters, which need not necessarily work with national headquarters. In recent years the Governors' Conference has become a leading national center of systematic consultation among fellow-partisans.

The party organizational fragments over which the President and the out-party leader presumably preside stretches across the nation in a complex network of regional conferences, state committees, county and city chairmen, congressional district committees, ward and precinct units, semi-independent clubs, etc. But, in more localities than either party is happy to admit, absolutely no semblance of organization exists. This decentralized, confederal approach to American partisan organization is as "ancient" as Sam Adams's Boston Caucus Club and the committees of correspondence during the Revolution. Most analysts agree that the adaptability, representativeness, capacity for growth, and ease of meaningful dissent *within* the two major American parties have been among the desirable consequences of loose organizational structure. On the other hand, a price has been paid for this structure, including the all-too-frequent emasculation of leadership, indecision in crises, inarticulate oppositions, and the incapacity to achieve even a minimal coordination of national party affairs. The story of the titular leaders — presidential and out-party — is one of the more prominent and significant illustrations of the problem.[1]

1 The distinction between presidential and congressional parties is convincingly drawn by James M. Burns, *The Deadlock of Democracy* (1963).

A Partisan Typology of
Post-Convention Titular Leaders

The national convention, endowed with the power to bestow its party's presidential and vice-presidential nomination upon men of its own choice, appeared in 1832 upon a national political scene previously dominated by the Cabinet and one or the other house of Congress. These conventions, by their nominating decisions, usually clarified the question of presidential party leadership, at least from convention time to election day.[2] After the inauguration of a new President, how have the titular leaders, both "in" and "out," responded to their unofficial party roles? Have they renewed their partisan activity or sublimated partisanship for either statesmanship or retirement?

A survey of the behavior of titular leaders since the beginning of the convention system suggests a variety of responses to this special leadership situation. Table 1 lists the four types and the Presidents in each category. Somewhat unusual typological names have been adopted to facilitate the reader's recollection of the different characteristics emphasized by this classification: nonpartisan; subpartisan; transpartisan; and partisan. The typology identifies four general attitudes or approaches to the party leadership role by particular titular leaders. Because of the exploratory character of the typology, we shall eschew formal definition in favor of a simple enumeration of some of the characteristics that are particularly evident among the cases within each type.

The *nonpartisan* titular leader becomes his party's presidential nominee without a long background of party involvement and identification. In the presidency, he stands "above party" in the George Washington tradition. As a defeated nominee, he retires from politics entirely or into the role of an elder statesman.

The *subpartisan* titular leader is well identified as a member of his party, most often as a leader of one of its factions. While titular leader, he finds it difficult to pull the party together or to do very much with its organization and management. Eventually, he retreats to the subordinate role of factional leader, hence the term subpartisan.

The *transpartisan* titular leader is one whose party identification and leadership role is ambiguous, either by background or design. He may shift from one party to become the titular leader of another. He may deny or suppress references to his party affiliation in order to help create a new political coalition. He may maintain his party affiliation while encouraging the development of another party.

---

[2] Fourteen Presidents have been in office while their party's next nominee was campaigning for election. These incumbent Presidents have not always been willing to take a "back seat" in the campaign, sometimes creating confusion in the campaign's management as did Theodore Roosevelt's participation in Taft's campaign and Truman's in Stevenson's campaign.

Finally, the *partisan* titular leader makes much of his party affiliation, takes an active if not directive interest in the management of his party's organizational affairs, and seizes as many opportunities as possible to exercise his titular leadership in the promotion of party policies and the solicitation of popular support for the party.

Table 1 offers a subjective classification of titular leaders according to these four categories. No interjudgmental test of the classification was made, nor did it seem necessary for the purposes of this analysis. The principal utility of the typology is to reveal the various patterns of response to the titular leadership situation, particularly those responses indicating an intensity of involvement and concern for party fortunes. The responses of the partisans are of particular interest for the problem of strengthening the organizational aspects of the presidential party system.

THE NONPARTISANS

Typically, the nonpartisan titular leader is a national military hero, drawn into presidential politics late in his career at the invitation of a coalition of state and local party leaders. Seven of the eight men in this category were of this background. The most recent illustration is General Eisenhower. Even the exception, Hoover, achieved early political popularity as a consequence of his war-relief activities during World War I. He acquired a reputation as an expert and social engineer rather than as a politician, and this reputation placed him "above politics" like military service did for the others.

The tenure of Presidents Harrison and Taylor as titular leaders was cut short by their early deaths after taking office. However, given the nonpartisan background of these men and the strong exercise of leadership by their party colleagues in state organizations or Congress, it is not likely that either would have exercised the titular leadership with vigor. Both men were nominated by divided Whig national conventions, and both prevented Henry Clay from getting the nomination. A coalition of strong state party leaders against a strong congressional leader again appeared in 1952 when General Eisenhower grasped the nomination from "Mr. Republican," Senator Robert A. Taft.

The analogy between Grant and Eisenhower has often been drawn. Each man was far more popular than the party that nominated him. Each man's popularity rested upon distinguished, almost heroic, military service to the nation. As President, however, each man deferred to the greater party experience of others. In Grant's case, this consisted of the leadership of the Stalwart faction in Congress. The Stalwarts were, in effect, the Radical Republicans of the Lincoln-Johnson era grown older. At the center of the "Directory" or "Stalwart Cabal," as the group was known, were: Roscoe Conkling of New York, Zachariah Chandler of Michigan, Simon Cameron of Pennsylvania, and Oliver P. Morton of Indiana, each a leading member of the Senate as well as undisputed boss

TABLE 1

*The Partisanship of Titular Leaders
Under the National Convention System
(Dates indicate beginning of leadership.)*

Type of Partisan	Presidents	Nominal Opposition Leaders
Nonpartisan:	W. H. Harrison (1840) Taylor (1848) Grant (1868)* Eisenhower (1952)*	Scott (1852) McClellan (1864) B. Harrison (1892) Hoover (1932)
Subpartisan:	Pierce (1852)* Buchanan (1856)* Hayes (1876)* Arthur (1881)* Taft (1908)* Harding (1920)	Cass (1848) Hancock (1880) Cleveland (1888) Parker (1904) Taft (1912) Hughes (1916) Cox (1920) Davis (1924) Landon (1936) Goldwater (1964)
Transpartisan:	Tyler (1841) Fillmore (1849) Lincoln (1864) A. Johnson (1865) Cleveland (1892) T. Roosevelt (1901)*	Fremont (1856) Greeley (1872)
Partisan:	Jackson (1832)* Van Buren (1836) Polk (1844)* Lincoln (1860) Garfield (1880) Cleveland (1884) B. Harrison (1888) McKinley (1896) Wilson (1912)* Coolidge (1923)* Hoover (1928) F. D. Roosevelt (1932) Truman (1945)* Kennedy (1960) L. B. Johnson (1963)* Nixon (1968)	Clay (1832) Van Buren (1840) Douglas (1860) Seymour (1868) Tilden (1876) Blaine (1884) Bryan (1896) Smith (1928) Willkie (1940) Dewey (1944) Stevenson (1952) Nixon (1960) Humphrey (1968)

* In office while party's next presidential nominee was campaigning
for election.

of his state party organization. For most of Grant's administration this group managed the party's legislative program and patronage distribution.

Senator Taft was clearly the leader of the Republican party in Congress, a status built upon his years of service as chairman of the Senate Republican Policy Committee. During the election campaign, in a well-publicized meeting at Eisenhower's residence in Morningside Heights, New York, the general and the Senator presumably arrived at agreements that placed the Taft following solidly behind the Republican nominee. Upon election, President Eisenhower turned matters of congressional party management over to Senator Taft and Speaker Martin. Other party affairs were handled by Eisenhower's special assistant, former Governor Adams of New Hampshire, Attorney General Herbert Brownell, and others. That President Eisenhower kept a light hand on party affairs became particularly evident during the Republican nominating conventions of 1956 and 1960 when Vice President Richard Nixon was left to fight his own way.

The nonpartisans of the out-party usually promptly retired from party politics after election defeat. General Winfield Scott's nomination and defeat in 1852 brought the Whig party to the end of its career and led to the departure of his principal adversary for the nomination, ex-President Millard Fillmore, into the short-lived American party. General McClellan simply went to Europe and remained there.

The difficulties of Benjamin Harrison, who had just served four years in the White House, began with the resistance to his renomination from supporters of James G. Blaine and William McKinley. After the nomination, there were protracted maneuvers to gain the national chairmanship and the management of the campaign. After his defeat, ex-President Harrison returned to his law practice in Indiana, wrote books and lectures commenting on the history of the nation, and retired from active party involvements.

Despite the Depression and the New Deal landslide, ex-President Herbert Hoover was less willing than other defeated titular leaders to retire from the political scene. He felt a strong obligation to liquidate the $200,000 deficit left after his unsuccessful campaign, to keep control of the party machinery out of the hands of the Old Guard, and to help in the search for a successor to the titular leadership. In June 1934 Hoover made it clear to a number of his political friends that he would not be a candidate for renomination in 1936 but that he hoped that he could continue to exert his influence in party affairs and contribute to its campaigns. Through associates on the Republican National Committee, Hoover played an important part in its reorganization just prior to the mid-term elections.[3] Thereafter, the ex-President lent himself and his name to Republican events; with each brief appearance at many succeeding national conventions, Hoover's stature as an elder statesman grew.

3 *New York Times,* May 6, June 5, and June 8, 1934.

However, 1934 marked the end of his active interest in the management of party affairs.

THE SUBPARTISANS

Table 1 shows six Presidents and ten defeated nominees in the subpartisan classification. The prefix "sub" suggests that these titular leaders were the product of or beholden to some subordinate or subsidiary element or faction in their party. Thus, several — Cass, Hancock, Parker, Landon, and Goldwater — became nominees as a consequence of the temporary ascendency of their particular faction within the party. The status of these titular leaders dissipated as rapidly as did the fortunes of their respective factions. Other subpartisans were the second or third choice among convention candidates; several were "dark horses" upon whom stalemated conventions eventually agreed — Pierce, Hayes, and Harding among the Presidents, and Cox and Davis among the nominal opposition leaders. The subpartisans have not been titular leaders for any length of time and they have not had persisting majority support.

Presidents Pierce, Buchanan, Hayes, and Arthur were unable to win a renomination from their national conventions. Only after a thirty-four-ballot deadlock at the 1852 nominating convention was Pierce's name added to the list of candidates. It required another fifteen ballots for him to receive the nomination. Pierce's administration was devoted mainly to the search for a position of neutrality between the rapidly polarizing North and South. As civil war raged in the Kansas Territory, the flimsy support Pierce had within the Democratic Party disappeared.

In 1856 the Democratic national convention vote on the sixteenth ballot stood 168 for Buchanan and 122 for Stephen Douglas. Twenty-two years Buchanan's junior, Douglas agreed to step aside in favor of the older leader. Although nominated by the withdrawal of a Westerner, Buchanan won the election mainly as a result of Southern electoral votes. His administration suffered the same North-South incapacitation as Pierce's. Douglas broke with Buchanan, and Buchanan later gave tacit support to the Southerners who bolted the 1860 Democratic convention and subsequently bolted the Union.

Hayes was another President with somewhat doubtful credentials. Tilden won a majority of the popular votes in 1876, but Hayes was elected as a result of a special electoral commission's judgments regarding the set of election returns to be counted in South Carolina, Louisiana, and Florida. The tenuous mandate of Hayes's one-vote majority in the Electoral College was further undermined by his commitment to liquidate Reconstruction in the South. Against the judgment of major segments of the Republican party, Hayes pursued his policy of troup withdrawal, non-intervention, and Southern conciliation in the expectation that enough conservative Southern Democrats would be converted to the Republican cause in time to produce a natural two-party division in the electorate. Republican defeats in the congressional and state elections of 1878 and 1880 demonstrated the extent of Hayes's misjudgment.

President Arthur, who succeeded to the office after Garfield's assassination, had been a minority faction's vice presidential nominee who never mustered sufficient support within his party to assure himself a renomination.

Taft was the chosen successor of President Theodore Roosevelt, whose personality dominated the Taft election campaign and who, within four years, lead the Progressives out of the Republican party in order to prevent his successor's reelection. Taft never perceived himself to be a party leader and, by 1912, was the instrument of a coalition of Republican leaders in Congress.

The 1920 Republican national convention was almost entirely dominated by Senate leaders. Out of the Wood-Lowden stalemate came a retreat to "dark horse" Harding. There was little enthusiasm for Harding, and the convention chose the Ohio Senator only after much conferring about the possibility of naming National Chairman Will Hays. As President, Harding exerted little political leadership over his administration, found himself very shortly surrounded by corruption, and mercifully died in office in 1923.

Among the nominal opposition leaders, Cass's nomination represented a temporary victory of the Northwestern region within the Democratic party, Hancock's was a one-time victory of the anti-Tilden forces, Parker's was a reaction to Bryan's ascendancy, Landon's was a concession to the Midwestern Republican leadership in 1936, and Goldwater's was a similar short-term victory of the conservative wing of the Republican party. Although Cass allowed his name to be used again as a regional candidate in 1852, he attempted no active leadership in the interim. Hancock and Parker withdrew without fanfare to other activities after their defeats. Landon and Goldwater continued to attract public attention as individuals but did not endeavor to maintain a factional organization.

President Cleveland's defeat by Benjamin Harrison in 1888 was close enough to be "honorable." Cleveland returned to his law practice and only moderately pursued party affairs. He took an active but not decisive interest in the selection of a Democratic national chairman in 1889. Watching the free silver movement grow, Cleveland issued a public letter in which he declared unqualifiedly that the free coinage of silver was a "dangerous and reckless experiment." He thus took a firm position on the most controversial issue of his day, and the Southern and Western press promptly heaped abuse upon him for it. Cleveland, however, remained silent regarding his availability for a third nomination. The last President to lose an election after a second nomination had been Van Buren, who sought but failed to receive a third. Anti-Cleveland leaders continued to be active until the very end of the first 1892 national convention ballot, which resulted in Cleveland's renomination. At best, Cleveland's interim titular leadership had been ambiguous.

No defeated presidential nominee has retired from titular leadership as promptly and emphatically as Charles Evans Hughes in 1916. Supreme Court Justice Hughes was the only public figure upon whom the Taft and Roosevelt forces could agree in 1916, and his nomination did much to re-unite the deeply divided party. His hair's breadth defeat by an incumbent President — a few thousand votes put California into Wilson's column — made him the inevitable candidate for 1920. However, Hughes's withdrawal of 1916 was complete. According to his biographer, Hughes "dropped the role of standard-bearer as completely as he had dropped the practice of law when he became governor and politics when he went to the Supreme Court." He never spoke as the leader of an opposition party, "thinking it absurd for a defeated candidate to retain any such prerogative." Reluctant in the first place to leave the Supreme Court to accept his party's nomination, Hughes completely banished from his mind any idea of being President. He returned to the full-time practice of law. In 1920 he firmly refused to deliver the keynote address of the Republican national convention and, when urged to become a candidate again, requested "that my name be not even mentioned." [4]

THE TRANSPARTISANS

The six transpartisan Presidents and two nominal opposition leaders had ambiguous party status: (a) they had membership in either party; (b) they had created a new party; or (c) they were a coalition-maker for the two major parties. In these situations none could exercise titular leadership explicitly or influentially. Yet, several were highly skilled as national politicians, albeit not as party leaders. This type of leader is apparently a phenomenon of the first hundred years of the party system, during which well-established parties disappeared, new ones were created with frequency, and popular attachments to parties had not yet achieved their twentieth-century stability.

President Tyler succeeded to office upon the death of William H. Harrison. The Harrison-Tyler ticket had been an inter-party coalition, a Whig-Democratic ticket. Tyler, a Virginia Democrat, accepted the Whig vice presidential nomination to demonstrate growing Southern dissatisfaction with President Van Buren's slavery policies. The Democrats, in fact, had become so divided by 1840 that Van Buren ran with three different vice presidential nominees to attract votes in different sections of the country. When he became President in 1841, Tyler, a states' righter, promptly devoted himself to the defeat of the centralizing programs of Clay on the Whig side and Van Buren on the Democratic. With the help of Senator Robert J. Walker, the "Wizard of Mississippi," and Speaker George C. Dromgoole of Virginia, President Tyler was able to prevent Van Buren's renomination in 1844. Tyler then contributed to Polk's victory over Clay in the election by withdrawing his own candidacy and

---

[4] Merlo J. Pusey, *Charles Evans Hughes* (1951), Vol. I, pp. 367–68, 403.

placing the Tyler-Calhoun press and organization behind the Polk-Dallas ticket.[5]

A similar complication of titular leadership resulted from the Union party ticket of President Lincoln and Andrew Johnson in 1864. Lincoln was the first President of the new Republican party and Johnson was a Democratic leader of a border state that had remained loyal to the Union. With both parties deeply divided on the issue of the war, the Lincoln-Johnson ticket was designed to attract conservative Republicans and War Democrats, leaving the Radical Republicans without a candidate of their own and the Peace Democrats in the anomalous position of supporting General McClellan.

After Lincoln's assassination, President Johnson found himself in the impossible position of, on the one hand, dealing with a Congress controlled by the Radical Republicans, and, on the other, of reestablishing the Democratic party in the South where, as a War Democrat, he had little political credit. Confusion reigned in the leadership of both major parties. During the mid-term congressional election campaign, President Johnson committed himself to no more than the election of a pro-Johnson Congress. For this he drew support from both parties, encouraged the calling of unprecedented pro-Johnson mid-term conventions, and embarked upon an unusual stumping tour of the country in support of pro-Johnson candidates. Meanwhile the Radical Republicans captured control of Congress, the Republican national party machinery, and, with Johnson's near-impeachment, almost captured the presidency. Johnson's attempt to build a "personal party" had failed; he was barely mentioned at the 1868 Democratic nominating convention and totally ignored in the Republican convention.

President Fillmore, who succeeded upon Taylor's death in 1849, failed to win the Whig nomination in 1852 and led as many of his followers as he could into the new, nativistic American party.

Under different circumstances, ex-President Theodore Roosevelt became dissatisfied with the direction of the administration of his successor, President Taft. In 1910 the inimitable Roosevelt permitted his name to be used as a rallying point for the progressive forces within the Republican party. When Taft refused to withdraw from the race in 1912, Roosevelt became the nominee of the new Progressive party and contributed thereby to Wilson's victory as a minority President.

During his second term, President Cleveland's titular leadership was marred by the widening division between silver and gold Democrats. The panic of 1893 was generally blamed upon the operations of the Sherman Silver Purchase Act, and Cleveland responded by calling a special session of Congress to repeal the act. The silverite South and West characterized the President as "a tool of Wall Street." The Democratic defeat in the mid-term elections of 1894 was as much due to the Populists as the Republicans. A struggle to control the Democratic national committee and

[5] Walker to Polk, June 18 and July 11, 1844, and Jackson to Polk, July 26, 1844, James K. Polk Papers, Library of Congress.

the Democratic nominating convention of 1896 went on for more than two years. The 1896 convention nominated ardent silverite William Jennings Bryan. Throughout, President Cleveland remained adamant against free silver: "We can survive as a party without immediate success at the polls, but I do not think we can survive if we have fastened upon us, as an authoritative declaration of party policy, the free coinage of silver." [6]

With the adoption of a free silver plank by the 1896 Democratic convention, 162 sound-money delegates refused to vote in the presidential nominating ballots and 260 delegates were absent or declined to vote on the vice presidential nomination. By September 2, the National Democratic party had been organized and a Palmer-Buckner ticket nominated, but only after President Cleveland had declined the new party's invitation to be its candidate. Among the principal financial angels were such long-time Cleveland associates as William C. Whitney and Abraham S. Hewitt. Cleveland and many of his Cabinet gave as much support as they could to the new Democratic ticket; only the necessity of conducting further legislative business with Congress kept Cleveland from making a public campaign.[7]

The two out-party transpartisans achieved temporary titular leadership as the result of almost accidental coalitional factors. During the fragmentation of political parties that took place between 1852 and 1856, former Jacksonians, ex-Whigs, emergent Midwestern Republicans, and Northeastern Free Soilers sought eagerly for a new party and a new candidate who could serve as a common denominator. The Republican party filled the first need.

A key figure in the search was Francis P. Blair, the venerable former member of Jackson's Kitchen Cabinet and co-founder of Van Buren's Free Soil Party. In Blair's opinion, the "natural" candidate was General John C. Fremont, the famous "Pathfinder of the West," enough of a novice in politics to be unburdened by views and enemies. Thurlow Weed, architect of the William Henry Harrison and Zachary Taylor nominations, found the attraction of another military hero irresistible. Thus, Fremont's nomination on the first Republican presidential ticket, brought together within the new Republican tent leading elements of the moribund Whig party, the declining Free Soil party, and many Northern and Western elements of the Democratic party. None but Fremont took his prospects seriously, and all but Fremont remained after the election to carry on a new factionalism within the Republican national party.

Horace Greeley, the life-time Whig-Republican editor of the *New York Tribune,* became the Democratic presidential nominee in 1872. His nomination originated in the creation of the Liberal Republican party during Grant's first administration. In Congress, independent Republi-

---

[6] Cleveland to Dickinson, March 25, 1896, Grover Cleveland Manuscripts, Library of Congress.

[7] Allan Nevins, *Letters of Grover Cleveland, 1850–1908* (1933), p. 457; Cleveland to Judson Harmon, September 13, 1896, Grover Cleveland Manuscripts, Library of Congress.

cans promoted several investigations of the administration. As these investigations began to reveal abuses, Greeley's *Tribune* led the criticism of President Grant. In states such as Missouri, New York, Illinois, Massachusetts, and Indiana reform Republicans were cut off from the patronage and other perquisites available to the Stalwarts running the Grant administration. Meanwhile, the Democrats floundered in confusion, with severe divisions in the New York organization and without a man of presidential stature. Several of the Liberal Republican prospects — Supreme Court Justice David Davis, and Lincoln's old associates, Charles Francis Adams, of whom Democratic National Chairman August Belmont spoke highly — were attractive to the more conservative Democrats. The Liberal Republican convention, however, divided between "politicians" from Illinois, New York, and Pennsylvania on the one hand and "the great quadilateral" of reform editors (Bowles, Halstead, White, and Watterson) who firmly opposed Davis on the other. To head off the editors, the politicians came up with their own editor, Horace Greeley, who won a surprise nomination. With no candidate of its own in the wings, the Democratic convention also reluctantly endorsed its old-time foe. Southern Democrats found little difficulty in accepting Greeley, who had long campaigned for a lenient Reconstruction program. Greeley's defeat and death before the Electoral College met added a personal tragedy to a partisan one.

THE PARTISANS

According to Table 1, this is the category with the greatest number of cases: there were sixteen presidential partisans and thirteen out-party partisans. Yet, each of these totals is equal to or less than the combined totals of sixteen presidential and sixteen out-party cases for the other three types. Presumably, a party system typically should produce partisan leaders. The American system has done so half of the time or less.

The partisan Presidents were those who, during their incumbency, concerned themselves actively with the organizational development and future course of their party. These men, although willing to defer to the concept that the President of the United States serves all of the people, were rarely reluctant to assert their own party affiliation and actively support their party's interest. A number of these Presidents were nominal opposition leaders at other times but their titular leadership in the presidency serves as the basis for their classification among partisans.

Jackson's second term was filled with partisan and factional battle as he inveighed against the National Bank, Daniel Webster's federalist policies, Calhoun's Nullifiers, and Clay's personal ambition. Meanwhile, the Kitchen Cabinet, under Vice President Van Buren's direction, carefully distributed available federal patronage in order to build up Jacksonian organizations in selected states. These same party organizing efforts were carried on under Van Buren's administration, complicated by the ancient rivalry between Calhoun and Van Buren and by the sharpening struggle over slavery. At the national convention of 1840 the Jacksonians dropped the Republican part of their Democratic-Republican name, thus founding the modern Democratic party.

The Polk Cabinet was staffed almost entirely with key party leaders: Robert Walker was Secretary of the Treasury, New York's William L. Marcy was Secretary of War, Massachusetts's George Bancroft was Secretary of Navy, Tennessee's Cave Johnson was Postmaster General, and James Buchanan was Secretary of State. Unfortunately for Polk's peace of mind, several of these men were lively presidential prospects. Polk insisted upon keeping his one-term pledge, holding his Cabinet officers within bounds regarding the succession, and strengthening the party organization wherever possible. Gideon Welles of Connecticut complained, "The Administration has endeavored to acquire for itself a strong party character, but has failed to create a party attachment. It has trusted too much to organization, insufficiently mindful of principles." [8] Through Senator Jesse D. Bright of Indiana and other congressional allies, President Polk exerted substantial influence on the national convention of 1848, which selected Polk's preferred candidate, Lewis Cass, as its nominee and created the first formal national party committee and national chairman, in keeping with Polk's insistence upon improved organization.

The surprise nominee of the 1860 Republican convention, Lincoln devoted much time to the reconciliation of his opponents at that convention and subsequently to constraining the aggressive and disruptive tactics of the Radical Republicans in Congress. Only toward the end of his first term did Lincoln begin to feel an obligation to recognize the contribution of the War Democrats to his conduct of the struggle with the South. His transpartisan responses in 1864 were primarily due to the efforts of the conservative Republicans and War Democrats in the Northeast to create a "Union" party.

Several of the presidential partisans had long careers in party politics and were conversant with organization leaders and problems. Dark horse nominee Garfield, a potent leader in the Midwest, promptly reconciled the principal opposition faction by agreeing to the nomination of Chester Arthur, an Eastern machine product. Cleveland built upon Tilden's national coalition and carefully chose the partisan battles into which he threw himself. Harrison was constantly preoccupied with and receptive to the demands and machinations of such Republican state bosses as Matthew Quay of Pennsylvania and Thomas C. Platt of New York. Coolidge and Hoover did much, against the wishes of a stubborn Old Guard, to purify the Republican party image following the Harding scandals and to maintain an internal balance among Republican factional interests.

From the national organizational point of view the contributions of McKinley and Franklin D. Roosevelt are of special interest. McKinley

[8] "Selection of Candidate for President in 1848," Memorandum in Gideon Welles Papers, Library of Congress.

chose and encouraged the first of the modern national party chairmen, Mark Hanna, who turned the normally dormant national committee into an instrument of campaign and interim effort that became the model for later national party operations. Similarly, Roosevelt brought James Farley to the national chairmanship with the result that the Democratic national committee and national headquarters became permanently organized on a year-round basis. In addition both McKinley and Roosevelt became lasting symbols of leadership for their respective parties.

It remained for a college professor, Woodrow Wilson, to make the philosophical case for presidential leadership of his party. In *Constitutional Government in the United States,* published in 1908, Wilson observed that the President automatically becomes leader of his party as a consequence of his selection by a nominating convention. Once a nominee is chosen, he stands before the country as the symbol of the party, and the party must be led by its presidential candidate during the campaign. Once a President is elected, "he cannot escape being the leader of his party except by incapacity and lack of personal force, because he is at once the choice of the party and of the nation. He is . . . the only party nominee for whom the whole nation votes."

Regarding the selection of a Cabinet, Wilson wrote:

> Self-reliant men will regard their Cabinets as executive councils; men less-reliant or more prudent will regard them as also political councils, and will wish to call into them men who have earned the confidence of their party. The character of the Cabinet may be made a nice index of the President's theory of party government; but the one view is, so far as I can see, as constitutional as the other.

Historians and political scientists have portrayed Wilson as a strong party leader. The Democratic leaders of his day, however, would probably have testified otherwise, for Wilson repeatedly undercut or otherwise complicated the lives of state, national, and congressional leaders of his party by behaving as though he were the titular leader in a parliamentary rather than a presidential system.

The nation can be characterized as having a Democratic electorate following the New Deal. Most opinion polls showed this to be a 3-to-2 majority. Under such circumstances, a Democratic presidential candidate needed only to bring out the normal Democratic vote to win. Thus, Truman, Stevenson, and Kennedy strongly identified themselves as Democrats in their election campaigns. This worked well for Truman and Kennedy in closely won contests, but it failed for Stevenson, who faced a popular military hero in two campaigns.

Lyndon Johnson has had a somewhat different partisan situation in which to work. Always active as a party leader, both in Congress and in the presidency, Johnson has minimized his party identification. Although he was Democratic Majority Leader in the Senate for many years, he and Speaker Sam Rayburn avoided excessive partisan controversies during the Eisenhower years. Johnson came to be perceived more as a *Senate* leader than a *Democratic* leader. This carried over into his first campaign for President in 1964 as he sought to attract the Republicans disaffected by the Goldwater campaign.

The thirteen losers, or the out-party, are characterized by the fact that they remained systematically active in party affairs after election defeat for the presidency, although there existed every usual expectation that each would retreat, retire, or revert to pre-nomination status. The activity of each was in part sustained by a continued interest in the nomination, with all the attendant organizational effort that goes with such a motivation.

Clay had a remarkable record for more than thirty years, from the time of his leadership of the War Hawks to the great slavery Compromise of 1850. His leadership in the House of Representatives as Speaker culminated in his naming a President in 1824. His partisan leadership in the Senate was capped by his successful effort to have the Whig caucus read President Tyler out of that party shortly after the latter assumed office. In September 1841 the caucus issued a manifesto regretting that the President ". . . by withdrawal of confidence from his real friends in Congress and from the members of his Cabinet . . . has voluntarily separated himself from those by whose exertions and suffrages he was elevated to that office. . . ." [9] However, Clay's achievements were strictly as the head of his congressional party. He never worked well with the presidential wing or the presidential electorate.

Upon his defeat in the presidential race of 1840, ex-President Van Buren left little doubt regarding his interest in a renomination. In fact, Van Buren was the first nominal opposition leader under the national convention system who had previously been President. In his *Autobiography,* Van Buren himself reports his view that party organization is the greatest need of a party in defeat. "Always under similar circumstances, the rank and file of a political party, taught by adversity the folly of their divisions, looked to a discontinuance of them to soothe its mortification, and long delays in accomplishing a cordial reconciliation are invariably attributed to the policy inhibition of leaders." [10] Van Buren's home in New York became the center of out-party activity in national politics. "Lindenwald was becoming another Monticello," according to some contemporary observers. As Democrats gained in local and congressional elections during 1841 and 1842, congratulations poured in to Lindenwald.[11] Van Buren held on to the titular leadership up to the moment of his narrow defeat by the two-thirds rule and Polk's dark horse candidacy in 1844.

[9] Robert J. Morgan, *A Whig Embattled; The Presidency Under John Tyler* (1954), p. 158.

[10] Leon W. Cone, Jr., "Martin Van Buren: The Architect of the Democratic Party, 1837–1840" (Ph.D. dissertation, University of Chicago, 1950), pp. 193–94.

[11] Dennis T. Lynch, *An Epic and a Man; Martin Van Buren and His Times* (1929), pp. 477–83.

Senator Stephen Douglas of Illinois most dramatically demonstrated his party loyalty by stepping aside for the nomination of James Buchanan in 1856. Again in 1860, after his break with the Buchanan administration, Douglas approached the issue of the presidential nomination as one involving the very survival of the party and the nation. It could not have been a felicitous year for the Democrats, with Southern extremists insisting upon the defeat of *both* Douglas and the Black Republicans. The Buchanan forces lined up behind Vice President Breckinridge, while most other Democrats acknowledged that it was Douglas's turn for the nomination. A slight Douglas majority prevailed at Charleston in the making of the platform, but the price was a Southern walk-out. After 57 ballots, Douglas still remained short of the 202 in 303 convention votes needed to nominate. The Charleston convention adjourned to meet again six weeks later in Baltimore. Despite another Southern walk-out at Baltimore, Douglas received the nomination of the "regular" convention while Breckinridge became the nominee of the Constitutional Democrats. President Buchanan then suggested that every Democrat make his own choice; ex-President Pierce indicated that he would himself support the Breckinridge ticket. As efforts to create a fusion ticket dragged on, Douglas himself despaired of winning and began a final tour of the South — where he was least likely to gain electoral votes — in a bold and patriotic, but unsuccessful, attempt to dissuade his countrymen from taking the dangerous road to secession. His death in 1861 left the Democrats without a titular leader.

With the Southern Democrats gone, the major responsibility for the care and nurture of the national party rested with New York Democrats. Former Governor Horatio Seymour, at age fifty-eight, was the state organization's elder statesman, although Democratic State Chairman Samuel Tilden repeatedly mentioned his name as a possible presidential nominee. Seymour served as permanent chairman of the 1868 national convention, which divided among Pendleton, Hancock, and Hendricks. As the convention went into its twenty-second ballot, the factions in the Ohio delegation reached an agreement to return the care of the party for another four years to New York. As Ohio led the convention in shifting votes to Seymour, he shouted, "Your candidate I cannot be!" But caretaker candidate he was. With the help of State Chairman Tilden, he established a vigorous new organization of clubs called the Order of the Union Democracy to supplement the lethargic official party machinery. Although Seymour's own campaign was unsuccessful against General Grant, his party-building effort did pave the way for the subsequent successes of Tilden.

Tilden remained out of sight during the Greeley catastrophe in 1872 and successfully ran for the governorship of New York in 1874. At a time when the Grant administration was being tarred with the brush of corruption, Governor Tilden successfully destroyed the New York Canal Ring which had for years been collecting fraudulent fees for repairing the state's canals. In the Spring of 1876, Tilden, always his own campaign manager, set up a campaign organization outside of party channels, as he had for Seymour. Later loss of the disputed election of 1876 and the subsequent revelation of corruption within his own campaign group left Tilden with a large but relatively damaged titular leadership. His agreement was necessary for Hancock to receive the nomination in 1880. He turned what remained of his organization and national alliances over to Grover Cleveland when the latter became available for the nomination in 1884. Never a healthy man, Tilden and a small group of associates nonetheless maintained an active role in party affairs for more than a generation.

As Speaker of the House, James G. Blaine's long service nearly brought him the Republican nomination in 1876 and again in 1880. He won the nomination in 1884 only to lose the election in a close vote. Blaine considered the campaign a disaster "personally, politically, pecuniarily." [12] The Plumed Knight travelled in Europe, prepared a second volume of his *Twenty Years of Congress,* and continued work on still another book. For the Republican party, Blaine's defeat meant the loss of the presidency for the first time in a quarter of a century as well as the creation of the solid Democratic South. Blaine, however, did not withdraw from politics completely; his associates remained in control of the national party machinery during the interim between 1884 and 1888. Blaine engaged President Cleveland in public debate over the tariff issue and seemed the most available nominee for 1888. However, in February of that year he announced this his name would not go before the national convention. Most Republican leaders, as they turned to other prospects, remained skeptical and ready for Blaine's renomination by acclamation. However, Blaine's former campaign manager, Stephen B. Elkins, put himself in touch with the Harrison forces, and Harrison took the convention away from Sherman on the ninth ballot. Upon his election, Harrison promptly called Blaine out of retirement to serve as Secretary of State.

Possibly the most tenacious of the partisan nominal opposition leaders was William Jennings Bryan. A loner for most of his political career, Bryan, at the age of thirty-six, snatched the Democratic nomination from the hands of older silver Democrats, who never forgave him his skill and presumption. Although defeated by a landslide, Bryan continued to run for the presidency between 1896 and 1900. His post-election mail ran into several hundred thousand pieces. He embarked upon a lecture circuit that carried him over a total of 92,720 miles in three years and earned him the name The Chautauqua King. He wrote a lengthy exposition of the 1896 campaign, *The First Battle,* which brought a substantial income. He practiced his profession as a lawyer only once, to argue and win the famous Nebraska Railroad rate case before the United States Supreme Court. Wherever he went, Bryan endeavored to supplement grass-roots party organization and to raise party funds. He stimulated the development of the National Association of Democratic Clubs, of which William Randolph Hearst accepted the presidency in 1900.

[12] David S. Muzzey, *James G. Blaine* (1934), p. 326.

If the sound-money men and Eastern regulars in the Democratic party expected to capture the national organization after Bryan's second defeat, they reckoned poorly with their leaders. "I am not a candidate for any office," Bryan said in 1901. "However, I would not enter into a bond never to become a candidate." [13] Bryan was not about to relinquish his titular leadership and turn his party over to its conservative wing. Instead, he inaugurated a weekly newspaper called *The Commoner,* began a book entitled *The Second Battle,* and continued his speaking engagements, in which he made more frequent reference to religious subjects. In *The Commoner,* Bryan kept up a barrage of reformist and democratic philosophizing that helped cement the political alliance he had forged in his previous campaigns between agrarian and labor elements.

Bryan supported William Randolph Hearst for the nomination in 1904, but at that national convention the Hearst boom collapsed fairly rapidly. The convention was not Bryan's to control, but he did manage to keep a sound money plank out of the platform and have the rules set aside when he wished to address the convention at a time of his own choosing. Ascending the platform, Bryan revealed how much he considered the titular leadership an active responsibility. "Eight years ago," he said, "a Democratic national convention placed in my hand the standard of the Party and commissioned me as a candidate. Four years later that Commission was renewed. I come tonight to this Democratic Convention to return the commission."

However, the Democratic Party had not yet heard the last of William Jennings Bryan. During the Summer, Bryan explained his support of Democratic nominee Alton B. Parker although the nominee was "wrong" on the money question, the anti-trust issue, and the problems of the working man. His concluding comment was that "as soon as the election is over, I shall . . . undertake to organize for the campaign of 1908." A few days later, he announced in *The Commoner* a program for a radical Democracy, reiterating that "immediately after the close of the campaign I shall start out to reorganize the Democratic Party along radical lines." [14]

From Fall of 1905 to Summer of 1906, Bryan conducted an extensive world tour, followed by reporters wherever he went. The trip was extremely valuable in assuring him publicity at home. Democratic leaders, particularly National Chairman Tom Taggart, once again began to consider Bryan as a candidate. Bryan's homecoming in August 1906 was the occasion for a mammoth Democratic rally at Madison Square Garden in New York City attended by eighteen governors, fifteen Senators, and nearly every prominent Democrat in the country. In 1908 Bryan received the party's nomination once again.

Bryan's third defeat, a distinction that only Henry Clay could match, still did not tear the toga of titular leadership from his shoulders. He took another newsworthy foreign tour, this time to South America. He campaigned for Democratic and Progressive candidates during the mid-term

13 New York *Tribune,* July 31, 1901.
14 July 15 and 22, 1904.

elections. He made himself highly visible during the pre-convention maneuvers of 1912, from which Speaker Champ Clark of Missouri, Oscar Underwood of Alabama, Governor Judson Harmon of Ohio, and Governor Woodrow Wilson of New Jersey emerged as the leading candidates. Bryan sent questionnaires to the candidates to test their orthodoxy as progressives. He made speeches eliminating all but Clark and Wilson as acceptable candidates, although withholding his own preference between these two. By convention time, Bryan's intentions had become a source of great uneasiness among Democratic politicians. Bryan was a master of the national convention process and thoroughly familiar with the strategies for producing a stalemate. That Bryan should wish to capture still another nomination from the emerging divisions was not beyond possibility.

Since Bryan was the senior titular leader, the convention managers invited him to make the keynote speech. He declined on grounds that he might be accused of trying to stampede the convention. The managers turned to the next in seniority, Alton B. Parker. When the national committee voted to give the honor to Parker, Bryan decided to go into the Convention to nominate John W. Kern, his vice presidential running-mate in 1908, for the temporary chairmanship. Kern declined and, after seeking a compromise, nominated Bryan as keynote speaker. The floor vote ran 579 for Parker and 508 for Bryan. As expected, the Underwood and Harmon support went almost entirely for Parker. Most of the Wilson delegations went to Bryan. The Clark delegates were almost evenly divided. In a single stroke, Bryan had succeeded in measuring the progressive strength in the convention. His action also generated some 100,000 telegrams from followers across the nation who decried the conservatives' tactics.

Later in the convention Bryan offered a resolution calling for the withdrawal of any candidate associated with the "privilege-hunting and favor-seeking class," namely, the leaders of the New York conservatives. The delegates became so distraught that one went so far as to offer a $25,000 reward to the person who would assassinate Bryan. Nevertheless, a significant part of the resolution was carried, and it became clear that Bryan would name the party's nominee. With Wilson's election, Bryan became Secretary of State.

Another perennial candidate for the presidential nomination was Alfred E. Smith of New York. A leading prospect in the catastrophically divided Democratic conventions of 1920 and 1924, Smith finally won the nomination in 1928. The first Catholic to be nominated for the presidency, Smith's candidacy drove much of the Democratic South into the Hoover column. On the other hand it also attracted into national politics the formerly non-voting urban masses in most Eastern and Midwestern metropolises. An old hand at party organization, Smith and his colleagues, particularly multi-millionaire National Chairman John J. Raskob, maintained control of the national party machinery in the expectation of another chance in 1932. That expectation was crushed when

Smith's former associate and the newly-elected Governor of New York, Franklin D. Roosevelt, became his principal contender. Denied the re-nomination in 1932, Smith retired from Democratic politics entirely.

Wendell Willkie was another nominal opposition leader without a party rostrum from which to speak after his defeat in 1940. The Republicans, in fact, found themselves with *three* titular leaders: former President Hoover, Landon, and Willkie. Believing that the party needed revitalization and new views on the issues, Willkie, on November 11, 1940, spoke over the combined radio networks of the country to ask his fellow-partisans to maintain American unity and to devote themselves to service as a vigorous but loyal opposition. Without mentioning the more than 10,000 Associated Willkie Clubs of America that had campaigned for him, Willkie declared that it would be entirely appropriate for his supporters to remain active.

The leaders of the "regular" Republican organization were outraged. The isolationist-interventionist battles within the party broke forth once again. Speaker Joe Martin announced his intention to resign as national party chairman. Journalist David Lawrence suggested that Willkie himself take the chairmanship as a vehicle for serving as spokesman of the "loyal opposition." Elsewhere Senator Robert A. Taft, in a Lincoln Day address, denied that Willkie did or could speak for the Republican party. Taft saw "no justification in precedent or principle for the view that a defeated candidate for President is the titular leader of the party."

Meanwhile, Willkie joined a law firm, continued to issue statements on foreign policy, urged all-out aid to the allies, declared that he would take an active part in the 1942 mid-term elections on behalf of candidates supporting internationalism, and agreed to make a world tour as the representative of President Roosevelt. He returned in mid-October in time to make a well-publicized nationwide broadcast reporting on his tour.

In September 1943 writing for *Look* magazine, Willkie indicated his willingness to seek the 1944 nomination on a "liberal" platform. However, the field was soon crowded with such names as MacArthur, Dewey, Stassen, Bricker, and Taft. The national party machinery was in anti-Willkie hands. Ex-titular leader Landon predicted, even before the Wisconsin primary, that the nomination would go to Dewey on the second ballot, which it did. Willkie withdrew from the race entirely after his resounding defeat by the Dewey forces in the Wisconsin presidential primary.

Despite his defeats in 1944 and 1948, Dewey did have a formidable rostrum from which to maintain his titular leadership, the governorship of New York. The national organization that he built through two presidential campaigns was relatively intact and deliverable in 1952 when Dewey declared his intention to support the candidacy of General Eisenhower. With Senator Taft the front-runner for the nomination, the Dewey-Eisenhower forces needed every vote they could muster in the hotly contested convention.

Perhaps the first attempt to construct a formal organizational status for the nominal opposition leader took place in the Democratic party after the defeat of Adlai Stevenson in 1952. The day after the election President Truman, in a telegram to Stevenson, expressed the hope that "you may see your way clear as the head of our party to initiate steps as soon as possible to revitalize the national committee and set the wheels in motion toward a victory in 1954." The telegram was a significant clarification regarding the position of titular leader. Stevenson also heard proposals that he assume the national chairmanship in order to have a formal position from which to speak out, but he declined. National Chairman Mitchell then indicated that he would stay on as chairman, serving under Stevenson as "the Party Leader." Senator Richard Russell of Georgia, one of the contenders for the 1952 nomination, added his comment on Stevenson's status. "Titular," said Russell, means "title without authority." Stevenson was indeed titular head of the party, Russell went on, but Democratic policy would be established in Congress over the succeeding four years. Russell referred to the fact that formal congressional leadership rested in the strong hands of Sam Rayburn and Lyndon B. Johnson, both of Texas.

Fully aware of the political and organizational difficulties of the Nominal Opposition Leadership, Stevenson wrote:

> In our country this role is an ambiguous one. . . . the titular head has no clear and defined authority within his party. He has no party office, no staff, no funds, nor is there any system of consultation whereby he may be advised of party policy and through which he may help shape that policy. There are no devices such as the British have developed through which he can communicate directly and responsively with the leaders of the party in power. Yet he is generally deemed the leading spokesman of his party. And he has — or so it seemed to me — an obligation to help wipe out the inevitable deficit accumulated by his party during a losing campaign and also to do what he can to revise, reorganize, and rebuild the party.[15]

Elsewhere, he observed "that opposition leadership rests in the Congress, except that it is assumed by individuals for the most part ambitious to be heard." [16]

In a small office in Chicago, Stevenson made arrangements to exercise his ambiguous duties. An informal advisory group began to meet with him at irregular intervals to discuss public policy issues. The group included former Secretary of the Air Force Thomas K. Finletter, historian Arthur Schlesinger, Jr., Harvard economists Kenneth Galbraith and Seymour Harris, former Ambassador Chester Bowles, W. Willard Wirtz, and others.

The Democrats regained control of both houses of Congress in 1954, placing Rayburn in the Speakership and Johnson in the positions of Majority Leader and chairman of the Democratic Policy Committee of

[15] Adlai E. Stevenson, *What I Think* (1956), pp. ix–x.
[16] Letter to author, August 30, 1955.

the Senate. Within a few weeks National Chairman Mitchell, Stevenson's personal appointee, indicated his intention to retire. Mitchell led a campaign for the election of Paul M. Butler of Indiana. Butler won in a sharply contested election, and the Stevenson people remained in control of the national headquarters during 1955 and 1956. Butler promptly set about to strengthen the national party organization and particularly to formalize the activities of the Finletter seminar as a device for creating a distinctive Democratic Program as well as an aid in communication between the party leadership in Congress and out.

In 1956, Stevenson found himself challenged for the nomination by Senator Estes Kefauver, Governor Averell Harriman, and others. He won the nomination only after hard campaigning and Kefauver's last-minute withdrawal in his favor. His second nomination was followed by his second defeat at the hands of Eisenhower. In anticipation of another Stevenson claim to the titular leadership, congressional leaders were quick to comment. Senator Hubert H. Humphrey predicted that party leadership "will be essentially Congressional." Senate Majority Leader Johnson observed, "Mr. Stevenson can speak for himself." [17]

National Chairman Butler was not to be dissuaded. Pursuing his pre-election reorganizational efforts, he announced plans to create a consultative committee that could coordinate the policy and strategy decisions of the party leadership in the Senate, the House, state houses, city halls, state organizations, national headquarters, and leading Democrats in private life. On November 27, 1956, the executive committee of the national committee approved plans to create such a high-level advisory board to shape legislative proposals in keeping with the party's "progressive, forward-looking platform." Butler was authorized to appoint not more than seventeen senior Democrats to the board. A week later, he announced the names of twenty leaders who had been invited to serve on the new Advisory Council. He also announced eight acceptances: Truman, Stevenson, Harriman, Williams of Michigan, Kefauver, Humphrey, Tucker of St. Louis, and Representative Green of Oregon. From his office in Chicago, Stevenson added his own announcement: he would not again run for President.

On December 9, Speaker Rayburn wired Butler from Texas that he had consulted with Representatives McCormack, Albert, and Kirwan. On behalf of all four, Rayburn declined membership on the Advisory Council. In Rayburn's opinion it would be "a mistake" for these party leaders to accept a place on a non-congressional policy-making body. The Speaker thought that the 233 party members in the House would undoubtedly resent it if the four leaders were to develop legislative policies on any committee outside of the House. A few days later, Senator Johnson announced his declination, saying that "legislative processes are already very difficult, and the necessity of dealing with an additional committee not created by Federal Law before taking action will only cause delays and

[17] *New York Times,* November 7, 8, 10, 11, 18, 1956.

confusion." Johnson, as had Rayburn, expressed his willingness to consult informally with the Advisory Council.

National Chairman Butler received the declinations with regret, insisted that the purpose of the Advisory Council had been misrepresented, and declared that there had never been an intention to dilute the powers of the leaders in Congress nor to question their responsibilities in legislative actions. Nevertheless, he said, the Advisory Council would be composed in such a way as to give "some form of national representation to the millions of Democrats who are not represented" by a Democratic Senator or Representative. Butler expected the Council to provide "progressive and effective political leadership . . . by a continuing study of the inter-convention problems that are constantly arising and suggesting programs to deal with them." Stevenson endorsed his statement and supported the Advisory Council as an aid to making the party "an effective opposition." [18]

The Advisory Council was given a permanent staff and developed a number of task forces to study specific public policy areas. Former President Truman went out of his way to endorse the Advisory Council as an instrument of party policy-making. On February 16, 1957, the Advisory Council issued the first of its official statements, with comments on civil rights legislation, statehood for Alaska and Hawaii, and Eisenhower's foreign policy. During the rest of the year, the Council issued approximately twenty-three statements on national policy. In February 1958 while members of Congress gathered for the new session, the Advisory Council issued its own "State of the Union Message." In 1959, as part of the preparation for the 1960 platform, the Advisory Council issued a 10,000-word policy statement for the consideration of the party.

With the 1960 nomination, the Kennedy-Johnson ticket became heir to the accumulated policy wisdom of the advisory council and its numerous task forces, many of which moved directly into the Kennedy campaign organization. The Democratic Advisory Council was dissolved in March 1961 leaving a body of experience for the other party's new nominal opposition leader, Richard M. Nixon.

Nixon returned to his partnership in a Los Angeles law firm after the 1960 election while, in Washington, the Republican national committee became occupied with the production of a series of television broadcasts called "The Loyal Opposition," featuring congressional leaders Everett Dirksen and Charles Halleck. The press dubbed it "The Ev and Charley Show." In time, Nixon ran for and lost the race for the governorship of California, declaring somewhat bitterly that this would be his last political race. The nominal opposition leadership was thus once again a vacancy.

On January 11, 1965, Senate Minority Leader Everett Dirksen and House Minority Leader Gerald Ford announced the creation of the Republican Coordinating Committee to stimulate communication among

18 *New York Times,* December 4, 9, 13, 14, 16, 19, 1956, and January 4, 1957.

Republican leaders, set up task forces to study public policy problems, and broaden the advisory base for the development of Republican national policy positions. With the Republican national chairman as its presiding officer, the Coordinating Committee consists of: all former Republican Presidents and presidential nominees; seven party leaders from the Senate and nine from the House; eight members of the Republican Governors Association; one representative of the Republican Legislators' Association; five officers of the national committee; and staff support provided by the national committee. Meetings are held every three months to consider position papers presented by the task forces.

Significantly, in contrast to the arrangements for the Democratic Advisory Council, the initiative for the Republican Coordinating Committee came from the congressional — rather than the presidential — party leadership. The most recently defeated presidential nominee, Nixon, was "out of politics," unlike Stevenson, and posed no threat to new presidential aspirants. Above all, the policy papers published by the Coordinating Committee made no distinction between congressional and presidential wings of the Republicans, a divisive trap into which the Democratic Advisory Council had fallen. The Republican Coordinating Committee has in effect become an institutionalized national platform-writing committee. From the point of view of overt titular leadership, the "Ev and Jerry Show" replaced the "Ev and Charley Show," at least until the election of President Nixon. In a fragmented and confederal party system, two or three heads may, at times, be better than one.

CAN THE TITLE BE FORMALIZED?

Can — and should — the titular leadership of the presidential parties be formalized and reinforced? Can — and should — the political contract consummated between the national convention and the nominee be extended? These questions require extrapolations of trends in the development of titular leadership, estimates of the political feasibility of creating an appropriate formal position, and judgments about the desirability of such formalization within the special framework of the American national party system. They also require analysis of substantial organizational complexity. This may be seen by simply enumerating the many semiautonomous components of the national parties: the party-in-the-Senate; the party-in-the-House; the national convention; the national committee; the quadrennial and often separate presidential campaign organization; the national party chairmanship; the party-in-the-electorate; and the titular leadership itself.

TRENDS IN THE PARTISANSHIP TYPES

The Founding Father's conception of the presidency as a nonpartisan position in the model of a Whig King is well known. Even such astute partisans as Jefferson and Madison carefully observed the rituals of legislative supremacy and classified partisanship as an appropriate and necessary congressional activity while they were in office. The achievement of the Jacksonian Kitchen Cabinet, with the acquiescence of Jackson himself, was to elevate the newly enfranchised elements in the presidential electorate to a new importance in American politics. One instrument for doing so was the national nominating convention. The national conventions, created in 1832, radically changed the character of titular leadership in the presidential parties.

Of the four suggested types of partisanship among titular leaders, the least likely to appear again is the transpartisan. Quite unlike the national parties during their early decades, the modern major parties will probably, between them, retain the loyalty of most politicians and voters in the years to come. Indeed, individual politicians, such as Wayne Morse and Strom Thurmond, will continue to cross party lines, as will individual voters by the millions. However, all or most of the shifting is likely to be between the Democratic and the Republican parties. New third parties will probably continue to fail to attract large portions of the presidential electorate, although such parties will remain significant in pivotal areas of the country where their existence may lead to the defeat of one or the other major party. The weaknesses and confusions of changing party organization and affiliation, occurring so often in the nineteenth century, is likely to disappear in an older and more stabilized party system.

The nonpartisan President, however, is likely to appear from time to time, particularly when the presidential party organizations go outside their ranks for leadership talent. While nonpartisans tend to be famous military figures, in a more peaceful world the nonpartisan might also be drawn from among famous businessmen, engineers, entertainers, and similar non-party occupations. The nonpartisan is likely to be more attractive to a minority party-in-the-electorate, as it tries to draw to itself the weak party-identifiers among the opposition. Such minority parties are likely to prefer to retain the ambiguous character of the titular leadership.

The subpartisan is a type of titular leader who is likely to appear with increasing frequency as the factions within the two presidential parties become more fully and durably organized. Bifactionalism has been a fact in Republican presidential politics for some time. The repeal of the two-thirds rule has increased the frequency and prospect of bifactionalism in the Democratic party. Dark horses and temporary factional victories are likely to be one consequence of these developments. Such factors contributing to the emergence and disappearance of subpartisan leaders are likely to inhibit formalization tendencies; factions creating subpartisans prefer fluid leadership situations.

The partisan titular leader, however, is here to stay — and for most of the time. In Woodrow Wilson's phrase, this role is "inescapable" for the President. It is also increasingly compelling for the nominal opposition leader, who has gathered together for his nomination fight a substantial campaign organization, a campaign debt resulting from his election effort, a status that the press is not likely to allow him to forget, and a responsibility for projecting the party image.

If this is the historical tendency, how, then, may or will the two major parties deal with it? The question seems less urgent for the partisan President with all the resources of that office and all of the assurances that the formal organs of the national party will be fully staffed and supported. However, it may be precisely during the incumbency of a partisan President that the opportunities for strengthening the titular leadership both in and out of office may best exist. The anomaly is typified by President Truman's firm "bestowal" of the nominal opposition leadership upon Stevenson in 1952 and the former President's steady endorsement of the activities of the Democratic Advisory Council.

The experience and performance of Tilden, Bryan, Willkie, and Stevenson seem to confirm the growing inescapability of the nominal opposition leadership. The recent creation of the Democratic Advisory Council and the Republican Coordinating Committee strongly suggest a felt need among out-party leaders for some kind of organization instrument to deal with the leadership void.

THE GROWING AWARENESS OF A NEED

A number of probable developments in the national party system over the coming decades is likely to compel increased attention to the problems of presidential titular leadership.

The first of these is the increasingly competitive character of the party system, particularly at the national level. The Solid South and other one-party regions in the country are rapidly disappearing and are likely to become competitive two-party constituencies within a single generation. To deal with across-the-board competition, each party will need to sharpen its capacity to respond promptly to changes in constituency characteristics and attitudes. With this need will come the demand for improved coordination of party activities from titular leader down to precinct worker.

The demand for top-to-bottom coordination will inevitably bring with it a demand for improved coordination among the national-level agencies of each party, as attempted by the Democratic Advisory Council and the Republican Coordinating Committee. It is unlikely that such coordination will eliminate the built-in constitutional competition among the branches of government. It will, however, simply by providing channels of communication, eliminate the surprises, circumventions, and embarrassments created by the fear of consultation that exists among competing leaders of the same party, in or out of Congress.

A third tendency that will probably influence the notice given the titular leadership is the growth in the size and activity of the national electorate. This is likely to happen in absolute numbers as a consequence of normal population growth. It is also likely to happen relatively, as an increasingly educated and politically organized electorate — both assured by our system of free education and the mass media of communication — raises its rate of participation. This growth will place demands upon intermediate levels of party leadership, which in turn will require a more systematic set of relationships among the top leaders.

A fourth tendency is the stabilization of factionalism within each of the parties. Since Reconstruction, the Republicans have had their conservative and liberal wings, although the particular policy dividing the party has changed from decade to decade. The Democrats, on the other hand, primarily as a consequence of the two-thirds rule in the national conventions, have tended to generate more numerous factions. Repeal of the rule in 1936 was first felt in a significant manner in the nomination of Harry Truman in 1948. Subsequent presidential nominations have taken the form of the front-runner against the field, although there is evidence of a growing isolationist-interventionist type of division within the Democratic Party. Whatever the issue or the particular factional leadership, the persistence of particular factions and the tendency to transfer resources from old to new factions suggests that these subsidiary elements of the parties will eventually need to be harnessed more firmly to the larger interest of the party as a whole. There are substantial grounds to believe that a well-institutionalized system of factional conflict can contribute to the integration, unity, and growth of a political party. Often positions of leadership in large-scale organizations may, as the object of such competition, become the instruments for so harnessing the competition.

Finally, there is the almost overriding concern for the protection of a loyal opposition in a one-sided presidential system of government. The objective here is to preserve a minority fit to govern should it suddenly be called upon to do so and to permit such a minority to produce leaders competent for such an onerous task. If the titular leadership of the presidential parties does come under active public consideration, as anticipated here, the nominal opposition leadership will present some difficult challenges to the architectural ingenuity of American politicians.

THE PRESIDENCY
AND CONGRESS

The Presidency and the Hill

James Sterling Young

STATECRAFT

To assert that the constitutional framers intended to prevent the President from exercising influence over men and policies on Capitol Hill would be an overstatement. But it seems beyond argument that the Constitution provided a wholly inadequate vehicle for presidential leadership of Congress. That the framers made the Chief Executive independent of the representative body was no inconsiderable accomplishment in a nation whose colonial experience gave every reason for mistrusting executive power. Nothing would have been more out of keeping with the post-Revolutionary political mood nor out of character with the organizing principles of the Constitution than for the framers to have admitted into it the concept of presidential leadership of the legislative branch.

As ratified, the Constitution indeed opened fewer and less promising avenues for legislative influence to the head of government than it did to ordinary citizens outside government. If the Constitution gave the President the authority to propose action and recommend measures to Congress, it gave not only this but more to the citizenry: upon citizens but not upon the President it conferred the right to petition Congress — in modern usage, to mount "pressure" campaigns — and an all but unlimited freedom to organize as need dictates for the pursuit of legislative objectives. If the President was given a potentially important source of influence in the conditional veto over measures passed, the ultimate sanction against unwanted legislation was given to the voters, not to the President. None of the framers' objectives was more explicit than to deny the head of government any influence over the selection, tenure, or career advancement of legislators. If the Constitution gave the President authority to summon Congress in extraordinary session, nothing in the Constitution ensured a hearing for the President's views. Upon citizens and states, but not upon the President, the Constitution conferred the

Reprinted from James Sterling Young, *The Washington Community: 1800–1828* (New York: Columbia University Press, 1966), part IV, pp. 157–210.

411

opportunity and the right to have spokesmen on Capitol Hill. Far from providing legislative representation for the President's interest, the framers took special pains to avoid it. The ingenuity of their devices for ensuring disharmony or at least divergence of viewpoint between Congress and President — devices ranging from staggered elections to different constituencies for the two — was matched only by the elaborateness of their schemes to ensure frustration of action when different viewpoints proved irreconcilable. There remained, as a potential instrument of leadership, the President's appointive power; but this was shared with the Senate for all those executive positions which were, at Congress' option, made subject to confirmation.

Of legal authority for presidential leadership of Congress, then, the Constitution was nearly as bare as Mother Hubbard's cupboard.

No more promising avenues to presidential leadership were opened by the social structure of the governmental community. If the Constitution preferred constituents over the President for access to the legislative branch, the retreat of legislators into a separate and exclusive community of their own, and their deployment inside their community into boardinghouse fraternities, ensured priority to the influence of their associates over the influence of the White House across the swamp. The Constitution and the structure of the Washington community together thus tended to relegate the President to third place in the hierarchy of influence over the legislative branch, after constituents and colleagues. And, just as the Constitution legally defined the President's position as an outsider to Capitol Hill, the structure and values of the governmental community defined the President socially as an outsider. Tacit rules reinforcing social segregation were especially stringent in the case of the President, and community custom, more explicitly than anything in the Constitution, kept the presidential tiger from the gates of Capitol Hill. Etiquette forbade the Chief Executive to set foot inside the legislative compound for any purposes but inauguration, attendance at a few other ceremonial functions, and to sign bills on the last day of the session, the last being an accommodation to Congress and one which must have gone far toward neutralizing the political feasibility of the pocket veto. Early-rising legislators might glimpse President Adams trotting around the Capitol on his dawn constitutionals, and President Jefferson might be seen on rare occasions at the Sunday sermon in the Hall of Representatives; but confinement in the White House was a rule never broken by any Jeffersonian President for missions of persuasion, political negotiation, or leadership to Capitol Hill.

The morass of the Tiber swamp intervening between the Capitol and the executive mansion, and the rutted causeway pretending to bridge it, were fitting symbols for what the community arrangements of the governing group offered the President by way of access to power on the Hill.

What, then, was left to the President for providing that "rallying point" which his party, and that stabilizing force which the Congress, so sorely needed? There remained precisely what presidential power in Congress has always largely, though not exclusively, depended upon: the exercise of political skill, of statecraft, by the occupant of the White House. The means and tools of leadership which the Constitution and the community culture all but denied to him the President had to improvise out of wit and ingenuity, as his political talents, circumstance, statutes, and good fortune permitted. Possibly the framers of the Constitution intended it this way — intended that leadership be politically achieved rather than legally ascribed. Probably they did not intend leadership at all. Probably they believed they had invented a system of government that would make leader-follower relationships unnecessary within the ruling establishment. More likely they never comprehended the risks of government by "separate and rival interests," never foresaw a Congress unable to control conflict within itself, and never foresaw that the Presidency would have to supply the unifying influence needed to secure the Congress and the fragments of the nation it represented against disintegration. For it would tax the imagination to believe that the framers intended so much to depend so largely on the chance of having a skilled politician for a President.

. . . Were there in the Jeffersonian era any circumstantial aids to the winning of presidential influence on the Hill? . . . what were the means devised and used by Presidents for this purpose? . . . were the means sufficient? Did they allow Presidents to perform from a distance and as outsiders the task of political management that legislators themselves would not regularly perform? . . . what explanations does a community study of the governing group suggest for the success or failure of presidential leadership in the period 1801–28? . . .

There was, first, the predominance of foreign affairs over the domestic work of the governmental community. Except for the admission of new states and the administration of territories, the attention of the Washington community during the period 1801–28 was principally absorbed in that area of activity which has traditionally given large scope to presidential initiative, namely, foreign affairs: the war against the Barbary pirates; the acquisition of Louisiana from France; the tortuous negotiations with Spain for the acquisition of West Florida; the Seminole War; the working out of a policy toward the emerging nations of Latin America and the formulation of the Monroe Doctrine; the readjustment of relationships with France in the aftermath of her revolution, during a period which saw Napoleon's rise and fall; and the prosecution of the second war against the colonial parent of the young nation, the War of 1812. Predominance of foreign policy issues by no means assures a President of influence in Congress. But the tendency of such predominance, recognized generally by students of American politics, is to increase the political risks of opposition to the President, to elicit whatever forces there be for unity, and to heighten that dependence of legislators upon the President (in this case, for policy initiative and information) which is the keystone of presidential influence on the Hill.

Second, Presidents of the Jeffersonian era faced only negligible competition from organized citizen groups for access to, and influence among, legislators. The negligibility of organized citizen demands upon Congress was, to be sure, a mixed blessing. For if it tended to reduce the President's competition and saved Congress from what might well have been, in the Jeffersonian era, divisive influences the community could not have begun to cope with, it also denied the President the important supplementary source of support for his legislative objectives that lobbyists may provide. Nonetheless, the virtual absence of organized "pressure-group" representatives at the seat of government heightened the chances for the President to dominate the communication channels to Congress. It saved the voice of the White House from being lost in a general noise of lobbying.

Third, the method of presidential nomination by congressional caucus (and of presidential election by the House of Representatives when, as in 1801 and 1824, no candidate received an electoral majority) assured Jeffersonian Presidents of some degree of personal support on Capitol Hill at the time of their accession to office. . . .

Last, all Presidents of the Jeffersonian era had service experience in Congress prior to entering the White House. Jefferson served four years as presiding officer of the Senate, moving directly from one of the largest boardinghouse groups on Capitol Hill to the executive mansion. Madison was a Republican leader in the House for a considerable period before moving to the Secretaryship of State and thence to the Presidency. Monroe had served four years, and John Quincy Adams five, in the Senate. All Jeffersonian Presidents were members of the governmental community at Washington when they were elected to the Presidency, and none came into the office without having had the opportunity to learn at firsthand the facts of political life on Capitol Hill.

With these more or less favorable auguries, among the several unfavorable ones mentioned earlier, how did Presidents go about the work of preserving and enlarging that sphere of influence with which they came into office? The record indicates four presidentially improvised practices directly or indirectly related to the acquisition of influence in Congress: the selection of confidential agents among legislators themselves; the deputizing of cabinet members for political liaison with Congress; "social lobbying" of legislators at the executive mansion; and the use of a presidential newspaper. A dubious fifth may have been the political use of the President's appointive power. Of the Presidents holding office from 1801 to 1828, the first was the only one to employ all the techniques mentioned above and the only one, it seems, to pursue with vigor the task of leading Congress. Any exploration of presidential leadership of Congress must therefore have to do principally with Thomas Jefferson's eight years in the White House.

Jefferson's enlistment of legislators to act as his agents on the Hill has been noted. . . . The practice was to single out individual legislators for "confidential" communication who, privy to the President's wishes and presumably acting under his guidance, would steer desired bills through the legislative process. What Jefferson had to gain by this innovation in presidential-congressional relations is obvious enough to require no elaboration. So long as enough legislators — and the right legislators — could be persuaded to undertake the job, the President acquired not merely that legislative representation of his interest which the Constitution denied but also an indirect participation in internal legislative processes where direct participation was constitutionally proscribed. Equally important must have been the advantages to the President of having confidential sources of political intelligence from the Hill. Jefferson's apparently impressive record of legislative successes, which is widely believed to have resulted from "drilling" the membership in party caucuses, may well have been due instead to his foreknowledge of congressional sentiment afforded in part by these confidential agents, and the resulting opportunity to adjust the timing, language, and content of his legislative proposals accordingly. . . .

As previously noted, it is questionable whether the term "leaders" accurately denotes the relationship of these men to their fellow party members on the Hill. "Spokesmen" for the President would appear better to describe the legislative role of men whose position was not legitimated by seniority or by election of their colleagues, as leadership in the modern Congress is; of men who, on the evidence of the written record, enjoyed no opportunities for influence over legislative procedure that were not available to any other legislator; and whose only distinguishing characteristic indicated by the historical record was their special relationship to Jefferson.

. . . Recent understanding of the historical and functional relationship between the Presidency and the congressional party . . . would indicate rather that Presidents are more the beneficiaries than the victims of organized congressional parties with self-elected leaders. That it was an advantage for the President to be able to choose the individuals with whom he would deal in Congress seems likely. But the circumstance which gave him his choice — namely, the failure of the congressional party to organize and select its own leaders — seems just as likely to have canceled out this advantage. The fact that his congressional agents were not legitimated as leaders meant, for one thing, that they could not speak authoritatively to President Jefferson for the party membership. Nor could they, on the President's behalf, approach the party's membership with the authority and the bargaining leverage that accrue to the elected leadership positions of organized congressional parties. Far more significant, the fact that these agents were not legitimated as leaders by their own colleagues must have heightened, to the President's great disadvantage, the conflicts inherent in a role which required loyalty to the White House in a community where independence of the White House tended to be a measure of a man's personal integrity. Lack of an elective base or other recognition of their legitimacy must, in other words, have made Jefferson's spokesmen far more sensitive to intralegislative pressures and sentiments adverse to the President than to party leadership in the modern

Congress, which combines spokesmanship for the President with a demonstrated base of support within the congressional community. . . .

The troublesome problem of divided loyalty was not so apparent, at least, in the case of cabinet members, and this may have been one of the reasons why all Jeffersonian Presidents used them for political liaison with Capitol Hill. Not only because they were members of the President's own executive community and formally subordinate to him, but also because the President had no staff of his own to dispatch on political missions to the Hill, department heads figured prominently as intermediaries between President and Congress in every administration. Secretary of the Treasury Albert Gallatin was President Jefferson's principal executive agent for congressional relations, and he is the only high-level executive officer known to have resided permanently on Capitol Hill. . . .

President Madison regularly instructed his department heads to take advice concerning legislation to Congress and to discuss policy matters with congressmen, commenting as follows:

> I remarked that the intention was honest and the object useful, the convenience of facilitating business in that way was so obvious that it had been practiced under every past administration, and would so under every future one.

Although President Monroe privately objected to official communications from Congress directly to department heads and bypassing the President, he and his successor in office encouraged direct communication from department heads to legislators, extending their instructions to include political liaison with congressional committees:

> It has always been considered as a practical rule [wrote Secretary of State Adams] that the Committee of Foreign Relations should be the confidential medium of communication between the Administration and Congress. . . . The Chairman . . . has always been considered as a member in the confidence of the Executive . . . [and] the President has . . . directed me to communicate freely to him.

To the extent that Presidents utilized cabinet members from choice rather than because they had no personal staff, the practice conceivably had some advantages over direct presidential liaison with legislators. The use of "front men" allowed Presidents to maintain, for what it was worth, the outward appearance of conformity to community norms which decreed social distance between the President and Congress. It also gave them a medium of influence perhaps more palatable to lawmakers than direct confrontation with the President himself, since cabinet members had inferior social status to elected persons; and it gave Presidents particularly good access to the congressional committees with which department heads had, then as now, much business. The use of executive agents also permitted what neither public messages to Congress nor personal transactions between the President and legislators did: a means for presenting and pressing upon Congress legislation in which the President did not want or could not afford to be directly implicated. . . .

A third power technique was the wining and dining of legislators at the executive mansion. If etiquette restrained the President from crossing the Tiber to make the acquaintance of congressmen, he could lure them across to the White House. Like the enlistment of congressional spokesmen for the President, legislative dinners were Jefferson's innovation and a device conspicuously employed by him alone among Presidents. Before and after his two terms in office, the President's after-hours social life was restricted almost exclusively to obligatory dinners and state functions, a once or twice weekly White House levee, and holiday receptions. Jefferson abolished the levee immediately upon assuming office and substituted small dinners held almost nightly when Congress was in session, with legislators predominating among the guests. The dinners were the talk of Washington. In the judgment of observant diplomats from abroad, for whom food and wine were standard accessories of political persuasion, they were the secret of Jefferson's influence.

Political purpose pervaded the conception and execution of Jefferson's legislative dinners, and if no one but foreign emissaries seemed to perceive the fact, that was but testimony to their political success. Rarely more than a manageable dozen guests were invited at the same time, and each evening's dinner group was selected "not . . . promiscuously, or as has been done [by Jefferson's successors], alphabetically, but . . . in reference to their tastes, habits and suitability in all respects, which attention had a wonderful effect in making his parties more agreeable, than dinner parties usually are." Guests received invitations penned in the President's own hand, often with a personal note; hundreds of mementos sent over the Tiber in those eight years later found cherished places in family albums. All legislators were invited, most more than once during the course of a session. Jefferson apparently made more of a distinction between Federalists and Republicans than did the legislators themselves in their own community. While Federalists received their share of invitations, the President seems never to have invited them at the same time with legislators of his own party, save for a maverick like Senator Adams, whom he regularly surrounded with Republicans at the dinner table, and who subsequently defected to the Republican fold. "He ought to invite them without regard to their political sentiments," a Federalist Senator grumbled; "the more men of good hearts associate, the better they think of each other." But nothing would have been more out of keeping with Jefferson's desire to cultivate a sense of comity among his partisans on the Hill. Not only did he avoid mixing Federalists with Republicans, but fragmentary evidence suggests that Jefferson made it a practice to bring Republicans from different boardinghouses together around his dinner table, while Federalists were invited by boardinghouse bloc. Nor did Jefferson ordinarily mix cabinet members with his congressional guests. The field was reserved for the Chief Executive and legislators.

The dinners could not have been better staged. A round table was used, thus avoiding a place of precedence for the President and putting him among peers, at the same time that it prevented separate, private conversations. The risk of distraction and eavesdropping by waiting servants was averted by Jefferson's installation of a dumbwaiter situated near his elbow, bringing up victuals and potables from belowstairs to be served by the President himself: "You see we are alone," he announced, "and *our walls have no ears.*" A French chef was "his best ally in conciliating political opponents" and the finest of imported wines put "all their tongues . . . in motion." "You drink as you please and converse at your ease," a bedazzled Senator wrote home. The President's uniform for the occasion was nondescript, marking his for a humble station: slippers down at the heel, faded velveteen breeches, hairy (not quite threadbare) waistcoat. Politics seemed somehow the one subject never discussed, talked around but not about, with the conversation adroitly steered away from shoptalk: enough of that in the boardinghouses from which the guests had now escaped. An Adams might, however, come away with an idea of what the President's views were on a question of national boundaries; another congressman on a prospective presidential appointee. Dominating the situation but never the conversation, Jefferson "took the lead and gave the tone, with a *tact* so true and discriminating that he seldom missed his aim; which was to draw forth the talents and information of each and all of his guests and to place every one in an advantageous light and by being pleased with themselves, be enabled to please others. Did he perceive any individual silent and unattended to, he would make him the object of his peculiar attention and in a manner apparently the most undesigning would draw him into notice and make him a participator." To farmers he talked of agriculture; to classicists, of philosophy; to geographers, of Humboldt; to lawyers, of Blackstone; for naturalists he brought out his elegantly illustrated bird books from Europe. Raconteur extraordinary, he played the buffoon with zest, and improved upon the Baron Münchhausen himself. "You can never be an hour in this man's company without something of the marvellous. . . . His genius is of the old French school." . . .

Why Jefferson's three successors in office failed to continue the tradition can only be speculated upon. Perhaps the usefulness of the dinners lay in their novelty, and maybe there was little political mileage left in them by the time of Jefferson's retirement. Perhaps their usefulness derived from the lack of competition elsewhere in the executive community; for in the administrations of Jefferson's successors, as will later be shown, congressmen did not want for a multitude of eager hosts and hostesses along executives' row. Perhaps the ever-swelling ranks of Congress, with reapportionment and the admission of new states, made small dinners impractical and dictated large receptions for congressmen (as in Jackson's time), invited in alphabetical segments according to the first letter of their last names. Perhaps none of Jefferson's successors had the inclination or the stamina to spend long hours nightly listening to congressmen after a hard day's work. Perhaps none saw the political opportunities in it. . . .

As to patronage, the definitive work on early public administration states unequivocally that "the institution of bartering patronage for legislation . . . did not exist." Leonard White has found that before Jackson "no President . . . undertook to buy leadership with patronage. . . . The practice of using patronage to get votes in either House was rare and would have been thought corrupt." As White implies, then, community attitudes and values tended to foreclose the use of patronage as an instrument of pressure upon Congress. More than this, they did not offer any but the most equivocal sanction for the partisan use of the President's removal and appointive power. No President before Jackson either subscribed to or practiced on more than a small scale the principle that vacancies ought to be created to make way for partisan appointments. Such a practice would, as Jefferson saw it, "revolt our new converts, and give a body to leaders who now stand alone." . . .

It is "probable," as White also points out, that no President "failed on occasion to smooth the path of legislative accommodation by a suitable appointment." But even where community values did not restrict partisan use of the President's appointive power, it is certain that availability of positions did — and not alone because "the number of vacancies was relatively small." Another reason was that the principal responsibility for staffing the appointive offices did not rest with the President. Precisely how many of the appointive positions were the President's to dispose is not known. . . .

What principally remained to the President seems to have been therefore the relatively small number of district attorneys and marshals (only 24 each in 1801), territorial governorships, diplomatic and cabinet posts, and judgeships. . . .

But here the President's choice was by no means free, for all these positions required Senate confirmation. This fact, considered together with the President's implicit or explicit political obligations to legislators deriving from the mode of presidential nomination by congressional caucus, makes it not at all surprising that legislators figured very prominently among the presidential appointees to high-level executive positions. . . . As to cabinet posts, two of every three appointees from the administration of John Adams through Jackson's second administration had seen previous service on Capitol Hill, and well over half of the 49 cabinet appointees during this period (28, or 57 per cent) were initially brought into the executive branch from a last preceding government service in Congress. Not all of these went immediately to cabinet posts; ten of the 49 appointees were elevated to cabinet rank after first serving in other executive posts, most of them diplomatic. Of the remaining 39 who were appointed directly to the cabinet from outside the executive branch, 23 (59 per cent) were appointed from a last preceding government service in Congress, 20 being members of the congressional community at the time of their appointment; 14 (36 per cent) were appointed from a last preceding service in state government; and only two (5 per cent) were appointed directly from private life without recorded previous government service.

The practice of appointing legislators to high executive places, considered together with a presidential nominating procedure which put incoming Presidents under obligation to legislators for having won the Chief Magistracy, would seem to indicate that the prestige patronage available to Jeffersonian Presidents was employed more to repay their own pre-inaugural political debts on Capitol Hill than to create congressional indebtedness for purposes of winning influence on the Hill.

Indeed, the choice of legislators personally as beneficiaries of this patronage may have hindered more than it facilitated presidential leadership of the legislative branch. Consider the dilemmas posed for the President in thus bringing about the transfer of important men in Congress from one to the other side of the Tiber. If executive appointments were given to repay political services pre-inaugurally rendered, who would be left behind on Capitol Hill to render party services to the President after inauguration? How helpful was it to Presidents in mobilizing party majorities and winning friends on the Hill to have removed from the congressional community, by executive appointment, the very men who had helped organize the congressional backing that had given them the Presidency? No wonder Jefferson was constantly on the search for men to replace his congressional spokesmen, and resorted to letter-writing campaigns imploring trusted friends to run for Congress where they might act on his behalf. . . .

POWER WON AND POWER LOST

All studies of the period are agreed on Thomas Jefferson's successful leadership of Congress — on "the extraordinary compliance that Jefferson drew from his party followers in the two Houses." . . .

. . . Congress made no major forays against the President's executive subordinates, through investigations or otherwise. Assertions of congressional supremacy thus remained harmlessly verbal, receiving no institutional implementation. Jefferson furthermore succeeded, against a ground swell of citizen discontent, in carrying the congressional party with him on a series of progressively harsher measures to implement the embargo during his last year in office. It does the record no violence, then, to say that during the better part of Jefferson's two administrations a relatively successful ad hoc experiment in party government under presidential leadership was being undertaken at Washington.

But this experiment lasted at the longest for only seven of the twenty-eight years of the Jeffersonian era, and came to an abrupt end ere its leader had departed Washington. All historical studies are equally agreed that there occurred in 1808–9 a sudden and drastic decline in the influence of the Presidency which was never recouped for the remainder of the Jeffersonian era. . . .

Madison inherited the wreckage. "New subdivisions and personal factions [in Congress] equally hostile to yourself and the general welfare daily acquire additional strength," Secretary Gallatin advised the President from his post on Capitol Hill;

> measures of vital importance have been and are defeated; every operation, even of the most simple and ordinary nature, is prevented or impeded; the embarrassments of government, great as from foreign causes they already are, are unnecessarily increased; public confidence in the public councils and in the Executive is impaired, and every day seems to increase every one of those evils. . . . [It is impossible] to produce the requisite union of views and action between the several branches of government. . . .

While the House simultaneously demanded war and economy, the Senate busied itself in seizing control over presidential appointments. A Senate clique refused Madison's choice for Secretary of State and installed an incompetent to handle the nation's diplomacy at a time when diplomatic talent alone might have saved the nation from a war it was not prepared to fight. Madison was given a Secretary of State who breached cabinet security, intrigued against him on Capitol Hill, and who was so inept that he had to be instructed to conduct all diplomatic dialogue in writing so that the President could be certain of what was being communicated and could ghost-write the Secretary's papers. Opportunity to negotiate a settlement, presented by Russia's offer of mediation, was all but foreclosed to the President by the Senate when it rejected Secretary Gallatin, its erstwhile political guide, as the President's special envoy to St. Petersburg. Confirmation was refused after Gallatin was already on the high seas, and notice of his lack of authority to act for the United States was not received until after he had presented his credentials to the Tsar. . . .

Congress had become "unhinged," Madison wrote to Monticello. "I know of no government which would be so embarrassing in war as ours," brooded the former President. His prophecy was fulfilled, and what ensued seems, in the twentieth century, like a nightmare from the nation's childhood. With a politically disabled President and congressmen scuffling among themselves for the helm, the nation drifted leaderless into war, utterly at the mercy of events. . . .

The disorganization of the government and the discord of the populace communicated itself to the military and made the nation's capital a monument to the greatest disgrace ever dealt to American arms. One year after Congress had fiddled while Alexandria burned, the enemy was all but made a gift of Washington, funds for the defense of which had been provided on the eve of attack — not by congressional appropriation but by local Washington banks. . . .

If the invaders had thought to lay siege to the government they were bound to have been thwarted in any event. For the government was not merely physically absent from the capital. It was politically nonexistent. Congress had responded to the emergency by disbanding for summer vacations. The cabinet had dispersed to all points of the compass. The

President roamed alone in the countryside while Washington burned, a tragic figure among a receding tide of deserting troops. And a perverse citizenry who demanded a magician for a President, and expected victory without sacrifice or inconvenience to themselves, found voice enough for revilement. A country housewife refused sanctuary to Mrs. Madison and cursed her out of the house because the President had called her husband's militia unit into service. Insulting remarks about Madison were inscribed on the blackened stone rubble of the Capitol. . . .

Except for disunion itself, Madison's administration saw the fulfillment of every worst prophecy of the governmental community's structure, its attitudes toward politics and power, and its remoteness from the citizenry. Jefferson's leadership having already collapsed, the Presidency was restored politically to the place defined for it constitutionally and structurally in the community — a position as outsider to, and lacking leadership authority over, the establishment on Capitol Hill. This unifying influence removed, all the divisive forces inherent in the social organization and values of the congressional community were loosed. The party shattered to pieces and Congress could not govern, plunging into factional strife at the very moment of rejecting presidential leadership. Leadership of the nation thus fell to a legislative body whose organization and values rendered it wholly unequipped to lead, and obliged it to follow, a distant and divided citizenry. Policy initiative thus passed to a Congress unable to mobilize itself, much less the populace, for the pursuit of any consistent policy. A nation on the brink of military disaster was thus embarked upon erratic and mutually contradictory courses of action dictated by transitory factional combinations at the seat of government. It was total victory for the principle of government by "separate and rival interests." The Presidency slept; effective power resided nowhere; an anarchy of groups reigned over the nation. As a wise historian put it, "government, in the sense hitherto understood, became impossible."

. . . Why should Jefferson's experiment in party government under presidential leadership have withered on the vine? A fundamental explanation is that the experiment was conducted in a hostile institutional, psychological, and national cultural setting. Its objective was basically at cross-purposes with the constitutional order of the government establishment, at cross-purposes with a social and political order inside the governmental community that had been created by the governors themselves, and at cross-purposes with deep-seated values and attitudes which sustained both these structures. It would be too much, perhaps, to say that the experiment was doomed from the beginning. But it is a real wonder that, with such a powerful combination of factors against it, the experiment worked for even a brief while.

Yet something more than this general explanation seems necessary to account for the sharp contrast between Jefferson's experience in dealing with Capitol Hill and that of the three succeeding Presidents. Despite the odds against the perpetuation and institutionalization of presidential leadership, Jefferson's administration did demonstrate that Presidents could command significant influence on the Hill. What, then, is the explanation for the very marked *change* in the power position of the Presidency vis-à-vis Congress that began in Jefferson's last year in office?

. . . Jefferson . . . was the only President to employ all the tools or techniques of power. He was the only President who was persistent and innovative in statecraft. He was the only President to 1829 whose performance in office indicates anything remotely approaching aptitude or liking for the politics of leadership. A subjective evaluation, based on the persistence and ingenuity of his efforts to influence Congress, would be that Jefferson alone achieved that psychological liberation from his party's and his culture's attitudes toward executive power which seems an essential precondition for the development of personal expertise in the pursuit of power. . . .

Granted the importance of political skill and granted Jefferson's distinction in this respect, the "great man" theory still falls short as a total explanation of the drastic change in the power position of the Presidency beginning in 1808. It is most obviously inadequate because the change occurred not after but during Jefferson's incumbency. Not only the time but also the circumstances of Jefferson's loss of power on the Hill challenge an interpretation which would attribute changes in presidential power exclusively to variations in the leadership skill of Presidents. The circumstances were that Jefferson had insisted upon continuance of a policy, the embargo, which was arousing clamor in the constituencies. Being the only policy of Jefferson's administration which aroused widespread interest and significant opposition outside the capital, the embargo provided the only test of presidential leadership under conditions comparable to those prevailing in modern times. Jefferson's leadership failed that test. Congress abandoned the unpopular embargo policy just as it abandoned the unpopular compensation policy in 1816: the energetic efforts of a politically skilled President to preserve the one policy had no more impact upon Congress than utter presidential indifference on the other policy. For all Jefferson's virtuosity as a politician, it counted for nothing on the Hill when good political reason arose for legislators to resist the President's lead.

One is therefore obliged to seek a further explanation for the fact that the collapse of presidential leadership in 1808–9 established the pattern for the next twenty years. In the author's opinion, two factors claim equal consideration with lack of political skill in Jefferson's successors. One was the weakness of the President's resources for leading Congress: the weakness of the early Presidency as a bargaining position. The other was internal institutional changes on Capitol Hill which were beyond control from the White House and which in all probability rendered any degree of political skill useless to Presidents for recouping leadership of the legislative branch.

The President's leadership resources were weak in the sense, first, that they were not exclusive to the Presidency. Enlistment of congressional agents to promote and protect one's interests, entertainment of legislators at home after hours, use of public media of propaganda, and employment of departmental patronage to discharge and create congressional obligations were every one of them resources of influence available equally to cabinet-level executives. In Jefferson's time there is no evidence that these resources were being utilized by any executive but Jefferson himself. After Jefferson . . . their utilization became common practice among cabinet members. The point to note here is that the usefulness of these resources to the President was largely dependent upon the failure of his subordinate executives to exploit them in their own interests.

The President's leadership resources were weak in the further sense that, however adequate for eliciting affirmative responses from a permissive Congress, they were not of the sort that enables a President to "pressure" affirmative responses out of a reluctant or resistive Congress. Persuasion is the necessary tactic for leading an independent legislature whose support a President cannot command; and the principal source of a President's persuasiveness is the strength of his bargaining position. It follows that the Chief Executive must have "currency" with which to bargain if his leadership is to survive the sorts of challenges to be expected from an independent Congress. Rewards must be available for inducing legislators to cooperate with the President, and risks must be posed for noncooperation: the self-interest of the legislators must, in some degree, be made to connect with "going along" with the President. Precisely this essential ingredient seems to have been lacking in the leadership resources of the Jeffersonian Presidents. Only one of the tools of influence used by them touched the self-interest of the legislators, namely, patronage; and use of patronage for bargaining purposes was eschewed by Jeffersonian Presidents. Threat of veto was another possible sanction, also unused, however, for bargaining purposes.

Nothing else seems to have remained, nothing, certainly, remotely comparable to the sources of pressure which a twentieth-century President can summon in behalf of his legislative objectives. Reference has earlier been made to the absence of organizational resources for exerting pressure upon Congress. Jeffersonian Presidents had no personal staff — no king's men — to carry on the work of lobbying; they were dependent upon department heads having obvious political and organizational interests of their own to promote on Capitol Hill. There were no organized interest groups whose bargaining resources a President might have enlisted in bringing pressure to bear upon legislators. There was no national party committee to supplement, with its own tools of influence, a President's efforts to secure congressional party support. There was no organized party within the Congress, with its tools of influence over the rank and file, to lend aid to a President.

Moreover, the opportunities to perform useful services for legislators — no inconsiderable source of leverage for a modern President — were negligible. The practice of presidential endorsement of legislators running for reelection did not exist. The opportunity to direct campaign aid to legislators at election time — money, publicity, personnel — was precluded by the absence of a national party committee or any other organ with such services to dispense. The minimal involvement of national gov ernment in the domestic affairs of the country precluded any significant opportunities to reward cooperative legislators with "pork" for their con stituents; and what local patronage was available was most of it dispensed by department heads and service chiefs. Detailing of staff and experts to help congressional committees or legislators who supported presidentially endorsed legislation was unheard of: there were no executive experts or staff to detail for the purpose; there was no technically complex legisla tion requiring expert service. The Washington bureaucracy was too small and too accessible to make legislators dependent upon the Chief Execu tive's help in expediting their administrative requests.

The impressive bargaining advantages a modern President has as repre sentative of a national citizen constituency were precluded altogether be cause the Jeffersonian Presidency had no popular electoral base. Protégés of kingmakers on the Hill, Jeffersonian Presidents could not claim popu lar backing for their candidacies. None could even lay claim to having won his own election, since whatever campaign work was involved was presumably carried out by a caucus committee of legislators. No President ever went on a campaign tour. Stumping was unknown; exposure to the people was negligible.

It follows that no Jeffersonian President could exploit the bargaining advantages of citizen spokesmanship, and none tried to claim such a role for themselves. This role was preempted by legislators, inevitably to the disadvantage of the President in a community where citizen spokesman ship provided the most acceptable cover for power claims. It follows, too, that the President could not benefit from any aura of popular prestige or charisma, as President Jackson did: "Were it not for the fear of the out door popularity of General Jackson," Senator Webster observed in 1830, "the Senate would have negatived more than half his nominations." No President could claim a popular mandate for policies requested of Con gress. None could plead campaign commitments to a party platform in support of his legislative objectives; rather it was legislators who were in the better position to claim policy commitments from Presidents, all of whom got into office by the pleasure, as it were, of the men on the Hill. Even more important, the absence of public campaigning meant that no Jeffersonian President could claim the independent electoral strength and the popular following which today tie the vocational security of many congressional party members to the presidential coattails. This source of legislators' dependence upon the President was lacking in Jeffersonian times, and with it was lacking what is today one of the most important incentives for party members on the Hill to cooperate with the Chief Executive: the incentive of building a legislative record that will enhance his, and therefore the party's, chances for victory at the next election.

"Nor," as Leonard White has noted, "did any President 'go to the coun try.' The facilities for such a course were almost wholly lacking, and prob ably none of the four [Jeffersonian] Presidents . . . possessed the personal qualities that would have made such an appeal either feasible or success-ful." No Jeffersonian President sought forums outside Washington for communicating his views; and in an isolated capital where reporters were rarely to be found press releases and press conferences could not be. The ability to reach the outside public and the opportunity to guide opinion; the ability to appeal over the heads of Congress to their constituents; the chance to command national attention for himself and his policy objectives: these important sources of leverage were denied to the President of a nation still in the predawn of the communications revolution.

Against this background, the Jeffersonian Presidency seems to have been in no bargaining position at all. Leadership was, to be sure, possible without carrots or sticks: Jefferson demonstrated that. But leadership without services or sanctions, without coattails or a constituency, and without organizational resources or access to mass communications could hardly have survived serious challenge from Capitol Hill. Truer insight was never shown than by a legislator who observed, even as Jefferson's power was at its zenith, that the President's techniques of influence were "temporizing expedients the [ultimate] success of which is doubtful. If a really trying time should ever befall this administration, it would very soon be deserted by all its troops, and by most of its principal agents." Small wonder that the President's leadership collapsed so swiftly in 1808 and so permanently for the remainder of the Jeffersonian era. It was dependent on little more than the charms and wits of the man in the office; on the political naïveté — or unhuman self-denial — of the President's cabinet members in not utilizing in their own interests the techniques of influence demonstrated by the President himself; and on the pursuit of policies which did not arouse widespread controversy in the constituencies. In a word, continuance of Jefferson's leadership largely depended on the continuance of circumstances that were abnormal in American politics.

Internal institutional changes on the Hill further contributed to the political incapacitation of the Presidency after Jefferson. These changes were of two sorts. First, there were changes in the number, size, and composition of the fraternity blocs, changes which enormously complicated the task of securing party cohesion. There was, second, the development of the committee system, which made the mobilization of party majorities increasingly insufficient for purposes of attaining leadership over Congress. . . .

Jefferson, then, had the double advantage of a relatively few groups to deal with on the Hill and a fraternity group composition in which state delegation ties and fraternity ties were generally in harmony. For Jefferson's successors, increase in the number and decrease in the size of boardinghouse groups diminished the possibility of concerting them sufficiently to maintain a working majority; while the possibility of mobilizing the bloc strength of state delegations, as an alternative, was diminished owing to burgeoning sources of cleavage within the delegations, one of them being an increasing diversity and disparity of fraternal obligations within the delegation memberships.

What happened, in brief, was that the congressional community became afflicted with a politically dysfunctional "metabolism" which created an ever more acute need for the stabilizing influence of presidential leadership but which at the same time made any possibility of presidential leadership ever more remote. Trends the Presidency was helpless to arrest and which it lacked the tools to counteract tended progressively to diminish the hope of successfully utilizing the two — probably strongest — types of group ties in the congressional community for purposes of rallying majority support. Without any compensatory growth in leadership resources, it seems doubtful that any President after Jefferson could have preserved his congressional party from these disintegrative trends in its host community. Political virtuosity, surely, could not alone have stabilized a social system undergoing fission. Considering the circumstances, Presidents after Jefferson may have been political realists, after all, in eschewing the effort to lead Congress.

The rise of the committee system, coming on top of these developments, sealed the doom of presidential leadership. Beginning in earnest during the War of 1812, the evolution of the committees from *ad hoc* advisory groups into permanent "little legislatures" paced the decline of presidential leadership. By 1825 the committee system had taken on most of its modern features — seniority rule and the House Rules Committee excepted — and had absorbed broad powers of initiative, amendment, and quasi-veto in legislation, as well as supervision of executive administration. By Jackson's first term, foreign visitors to Washington were making the same observations about the committee system that American scholars were to make half a century later:

> These committees have separate apartments, in which the real business of the country is carried on . . . no bill connected with any branch of public affairs could be brought into Congress with the smallest prospect of success, which had not previously received the initiative approbation of these committees. . . . the members of the cabinet are, in truth, nothing better than superintending clerks in the departments over which they nominally preside. . . . [The] standing committees . . . in fact, manage the whole business of the executive departments.

That committee preeminence challenges the preeminence of the White House as a claimant for influence on Capitol Hill is widely enough accepted to require no argument here. . . .

In creating sublegislatures Congress practically liberated itself, also, from even the weak bonds of dependence upon the Presidency which Jefferson had been able to exploit for leadership purposes. Committees provided Congress with its own organs for exercising policy initiative, investigating policy alternatives, obtaining background information, and supervising the administration of measures passed. Dependence upon the

President for these functions was correspondingly reduced; and in so far as information or guidance was wanted from the executive branch at all, committees provided the means for getting it directly from the departments themselves.

Finally, the committee system pushed the Presidency into the background and brought cabinet members to the forefront of executive dealings with Congress. With the establishment of congressional agencies for overseeing the work of the executive departments and passing upon substantive legislation affecting these departments, it was unavoidable that interaction should be intensified between the department heads and their superintending committees on the Hill — intensified to the degree that, as one scholar has observed, cabinet-committee relationships became the principal "medium of intercommunication" between the two branches of government. Thus it was that a subsystem of political relationships between department heads and their supervising congressional committees came to supplant, as the principal arena of confrontation between the executive and legislative establishments, the direct relationship between the President and his congressional party that Jefferson had enjoyed. The committee system caused the President to lose dominance over the communication channels to the community he needed to lead, and gave executive subordinates better access to the vital centers of legislative decision than the President himself had. Men whose positions made them "the natural enemies of the President," as department heads have been called, became the principal spokesmen for the executive branch before Congress.

The committee system, in short, ensured the end of a political relationship between President and Congress which was fundamentally at odds with the structure and values of the governmental community to begin with, which was impossible to maintain in the face of systemic trends within the congressional community, and which existed as long as it did only because a permissive Congress tolerated it. For the second half of the Jeffersonian era, the whole question of presidential leadership of Congress was "academic": nothing short of dramatic innovations in the style and in the political resources of the Presidency would make it possible again. The important question, after Jefferson, was whether the President could maintain the loyalty and cohesion of his own executive branch in the face of committee pressures from Capitol Hill — in the face of assault upon the executive establishment by a Congress so divided, so leaderless within itself.

It is a weak Presidency, then, that emerges from this exploration of presidential-congressional relations in the Jeffersonian era. A brief taste of power under Jefferson, and then the Presidency was reduced to political impotence, failing to provide that leadership of the legislative branch which the Constitution did not intend the executive branch to provide and which the congressional community did not provide within itself. . . .

Shortage of leadership skill and resources in the White House, as on Capitol Hill, was partially the manifestation of antipower attitudes among the power-holders themselves. A community ethos hostile to leadership and followership roles per se was especially hostile to any effort toward supplanting the constitutionally orthodox relationship between President and Congress with a superordinate-subordinate relationship. A community inclined to equate citizen spokesmanship with virtue itself provided little rationale for leadership of citizen spokesmen by an office which could not claim citizen spokesmanship for itself. A pervasive mistrust of power-seeking, among the governors themselves, must have inhibited the desire of Presidents to lead as well as the willingness of legislators to follow; and an underlying sense of the wrongness of presidential influence over the legislative branch made presidential leadership a covert affair which could neither be acknowledged in practice nor defended in principle on either side of the Tiber.

Antipower attitudes nourished a community structure hostile to presidential leadership. Community arrangements, reflecting the preferences of the governors themselves, went far beyond the Constitution in isolating the President from those he would lead in Congress, assigning the Chief Executive and legislators to separate camps as members of mutually exclusive social entities. A subcommunity structure on Capitol Hill split the President's potential followership into organized minority blocs, introducing durable sources of cleavage among them that were unknown to the Constitution, that were independent of disagreements on passing policy issues, and that were destructive in tendency of the one instrumentality on Capitol Hill — the political party — which might have facilitated presidential leadership. These built-in sources of cleavage proliferated, moreover, as the Jeffersonian era advanced. A 350 per cent increase, from 1801 to 1828, in the number of primary-group voting blocs and an increase of nearly 50 per cent in the size of Congress created purely mechanical and communication problems of rallying majority support which the early Presidency clearly lacked the resources to surmount. Changes in the composition of these voting blocs, furthermore, introduced new sources of cleavage and lessened any realistic hope of mustering majority voting strength on the alternative basis of state delegation solidarity. And the development of the committee system, besides adding still another source of cleavage to the congressional community, created a new arena of policy-making that was elusive of influence even by a President who might succeed in rallying majority support on Capitol Hill.

Studying the Jeffersonian experience in its community context thus opens new perspectives upon the nature and role of the Presidency as a leadership position.

The resistiveness of the American governmental system to presidential leadership, first of all, has been much greater than the conventional legal, historical, or institutional analyses of the Presidency would suggest. The problem of presidential leadership was not merely to find ways around the language and intent of a Constitution which did not equip the presidential office for leadership. The task was to find ways of counteracting or circumventing the manifest attitudes, the preferred organizational behavior, and the systemic trends of the governing society itself. The Jeffersonian Presidency was wholly unequal to that task. As a leadership office, the Presidency was therefore a failure. It could not have been, under the conditions prevailing in the Jeffersonian era, anything but a failure.

Second, it would seem, from the perspective of a community study, that converting the presidential office into a vehicle for leadership of Congress required basic changes in the style and structure of American national politics. Passing crises and other empowering events were not, as the Jeffersonian experience amply demonstrates, sufficient. The preeminence of foreign policy; war and the gravest threats to national security; lack of organized opposition outside government and political quiescence in the country; consistent dominance of Congress by the President's party; overwhelming landslides at the polls for the presidential candidate: none of these sufficed to convert the early Presidency into a leadership position. To confer enduring leadership capacity upon the White House, nothing less than the revolution in government-citizenry relationships that came with Jacksonian democracy would seem to have been adequate. Continuing attention and interest on the part of the citizenry would liberate the Presidency from psychological bondage to antipower attitudes and from institutional bondage to a kingmaking Congress. Democratically exploited, an attentive citizenry would give the Presidency coattails and a constituency, and a role of citizen spokesmanship equal to that of Congress. It would give the Presidency a forum for appealing over the heads of a resistive Congress. An articulate and demanding electorate would sustain a party organization outside of government which would provide the President with services and sanctions to use in his dealings with Congress. It would lay the groundwork for the organization of congressional parties and it would ultimately bring organized citizen interests into the political arena, each equipped with resources for persuasion which a President might enlist in behalf of his legislative objectives. Giving the Presidency a national citizen constituency would never suffice to guarantee presidential leadership of the legislative branch. But the Jacksonian revolution, which marked the beginning of a major constituency-building effort, would seem to have been a necessary prerequisite for leadership in the White House — as much so as it seems to have been for the emergence of leadership in Congress.

Third, the need for presidential leadership would seem, from the perspective of the Jeffersonian experience, far more acute than is generally recognized. The eclipse of the Presidency after Jefferson signified the loss of the only stabilizing influence then available upon a governing society on the Hill that was inherently unstable. Had the loss of presidential leadership been compensated by the development of self-leadership or other stabilizing devices within the congressional establishment, the long-range viability of that establishment as a governing institution would be less subject to question. But theories to this effect cannot be reconciled with the community record of the legislative branch. New leadership did not arise on Capitol Hill to supplant that of the President. The congressional party did not change masters, as some have argued: it ceased to have masters. The party did not evolve toward an organized action group, toward greater cohesion, once Jefferson's leadership had collapsed. On the contrary, loss of presidential leadership was attended by disintegration of the majority party into warring factions, by an accelerating fragmentation of the social and political system on Capitol Hill, and by the development of a committee system which not merely introduced new divisive forces but also offered legislators a means of exercising power which minimized the need for building stable majorities.

If, therefore, presidential leadership made the difference between a Congress capable of managing major social conflict and one incapable of doing so, the failure of presidential leadership after 1808 must be interpreted as an event of profound significance in the political history of the republic. Until such time as presidential leadership was regained, or until new stabilizing influences developed on Capitol Hill, one-third part of the government had failed in one of the fundamental tasks of government. Well beyond the halfway point from 1789 to the Civil War, a congressional community doggedly committed to its own internal democracy, progressively anarchic within itself, and jealous of its independence from the President had failed to provide security against the rupture of the Union itself. . . .

The Presidency

Henry Jones Ford

According to the intention of the constitution it is the business of the President to run the government. It is the business of other branches of the government to condition the operation of the executive department in accordance with the constitutional principles on which the government is founded; but to take care of the government, to attend to its needs, to shape its policy, and to provide for its responsibilities is the special business of the President.

This might seem to be a better statement of the duties of the British ministry than of the President of the United States; but the constitutional provision requiring the President to "recommend" to the consideration of Congress "such measures as he shall judge necessary and expedient" contemplated the discharge of just such duties of foresight and provision

Reprinted from Henry Jones Ford, *Rise and Growth of American Politics*, chapter XXII (New York: The Macmillan Company, 1898), pp. 275–293.

as are performed by the British ministry. Gouverneur Morris, who did the actual work of draughting the constitution, gave precisely this illustration of the functions of the presidency when the office was under discussion. "Our President," he said, "will be the British minister." [1] There was no dissent as to that; the controversies of the convention turned upon the mode of constituting the office, and the means by which it should be confined to its appointed sphere and at the same time be protected in it. The fathers knew very well that the king himself had been superseded by the ministry as the actual agency of government. In the same debate Morris referred to the fact that "the real king" was "the minister." At that period the interception of royal duty by ministerial combinations, based upon parliamentary interest, was regarded as an aberration from the principles of the English constitution and as the chief source of political corruption. The framers of the constitution took special pains to guard against a parliamentary control. The President himself was to carry on the administration. In order that he might be able to impress his policy upon Congress with vigor and effect, the patronage of the government was placed in his hands. Appointments to office were referred to as "the principal source of influence." The fathers did not mince words in speaking of such matters; Morris bluntly declared that "the loaves and fishes must bribe the demagogues." [2] It should be borne in mind that the very object in view in framing the constitution was to enlist the passions and selfish interests of men on the side of social stability and public order.

This duty of management was fully conceived by Washington and was habitually acted upon by him in his relations with Congress and in his use of the patronage of his office. The President's responsibility for national policy was the ground on which Hamilton appealed to Jefferson to exert his personal influence to secure votes to carry the assumption bill through Congress. Jefferson reports him as saying "that the President was the centre upon which all administrative questions ultimately rested, and that all of us should rally around him, and support with joint efforts measures approved by him." [3] It was from the same point of view that Rufus King, one of the framers of the constitution, criticised Jefferson's behavior in the presidential office. Commenting upon the political situation in 1806, King remarked: "It is scarcely credible that the public honor and safety, instead of being well guarded by well-concerted and prudent arrangements, should be suffered to become the sport of the casual, intemperate, and inefficient measures of inexperienced individuals; and yet the several messages of the President look as if every subject were to be submitted to Congress, without the disclosure of the views of the executive, which by the letter and spirit of our government is charged with our foreign affairs." [4]

---

1 Madison's Journal, July 24.
2 *Ibid.*, July 2.
3 *Writings of Jefferson*, Vol. I., p. 163.
4 *Life and Correspondence, Rufus King*, Vol. IV., p. 481.

The growth of parliamentary control which went on during the Virginia dynasty impaired the original conception of presidential duty, but did not extinguish it. It was still the usage for Congress to respect the President's initiative and provide for it. When this tradition of congressional behavior was ruptured by the violence of party strife during the administration of John Quincy Adams, there was a shock to conservative sentiment. Benton, himself a leader of the Jacksonian party, whose work this was, said, "The appointment of the majority of members in all committees, and their chairmen, in both Houses, adverse to the administration, was a regular consequence of the inflamed state of parties, although the proper conducting of the public business would demand for the administration the chairmen of several important committees as enabling it to place its measures fairly before the House." [5]

The direct representative character imparted to the presidential office, when the machinery of the electoral college passed under the control of a system of popular election, gave the office a much firmer foundation than it originally possessed, and invigorated all its functions, so far as the independent powers of the executive department sufficed to give them efficiency. This condition was completely satisfied in the case of the veto power, but the correlative function, the legislative initiative, still dependent as it is upon congressional acquiescence, has shown no access of strength. It is complicated with the ordinary activities of Congress, and the operation of the presidential office in this respect has been obscure. Nevertheless, the fact is clear that the basis of administrative control is not Congress but the President. Possession of that office is the great object of party struggles. It is impossible for a party to carry out even a purely legislative programme unless it embodies a policy accepted by the President and sustained by the influence of his office.

The agency of the presidential office has been such a master force in shaping public policy that to give a detailed account of it would be equivalent to writing the political history of the United States. From Jackson's time to the present day it may be said that political issues have been decided by executive policy. The independent treasury system introduced during Van Buren's administration was a measure formulated by the President and forced upon Congress. Tyler, although his congressional following was so weak that it was known as "the corporal's guard," prostrated Whig plans for the reëstablishment of the Bank of the United States and controlled the tariff policy of Congress. The annexation of Texas, which was the issue of the election of 1844, originated as an executive proposal, and was consummated by Tyler before he retired from office. Polk's administration is associated with tariff reform and the Mexican War, both measures originating in executive policy. The slavery agitation, whose growing intensity was the chief feature of the administrations of Fillmore, Pierce, and Buchanan, presented issues which the executive department was, above all things, anxious to

[5] *Thirty Years' View,* Vol. I., p. 92.

avoid, so that presidential influence strongly supported a policy of adjustment and compromise by negotiation among the congressional factions; but nevertheless the issues which arose were shaped by executive policy, as the inevitable result of its trenchant nature. In the presence of emergency it is necessary to do one thing or another, and the decision stands out for condemnation or approval, thus furnishing a dividing line for party formation. The election of 1860 turned on issues raised by executive policy in Kansas. The administration of President Lincoln saw the opening of a new arsenal of presidential authority in the war powers, whose extent is still quite unmeasured. The President levied an army without authority of Congress, and before Congress had met. He assumed and exercised the right of suspending the writ of *habeas corpus.* The crowning event of his administration — the emancipation of the slaves — did not take place in pursuance of any act of Congress, but was done on his own authority as President, and was as absolute an exercise of power as the ukase of the Czar which freed the serfs of Russia. President Lincoln was able to do these things by the direct support of public opinion, irrespective of the volition of Congress. Although in the case of his accidental successor, Congress was strong enough to enforce its own programme of reconstruction, it instinctively recognized the fact that it was not able to do so from its inherent authority. Senator Sherman put the case exactly when he said, "The recent acts of Congress, those acts upon which the President and Congress separated, were submitted to the people, and after a very full canvass and a very able one, in which great numbers of speeches were made on both sides, and documents were circulated, the people, who are the common masters of President and Congress, decided in favor of Congress." [6] That is to say, Congress prevailed not by virtue of its ordinary representative capacity, but by express delegation for that special purpose.

While all that a President can certainly accomplish is to force a submission of an issue to the people, yet such is the strength of the office that, if he makes a sincere and resolute use of its resources, at the same time cherishing his party connection, he can as a rule carry his party with him, because of the powerful interests which impel it to occupy ground taken for it by the administration. Many instances of this tendency may be found in our political history. A noted case in our own times is the result of General Grant's veto in 1874 of the bill providing for an additional issue of legal tender notes. Later on, the same Congress passed an act providing for the redemption in coin of the outstanding issues.

On the other hand, unless a measure is made an administrative issue, Congress is unable to make a party issue. Colonel W. R. Morrison, when the Democratic leader of the House, was unable to accomplish the passage of a tariff bill although there was a party majority. His explanation of his failure is that "my bills all lacked the influence of administration and party support and patronage." Colonel Morrison's successor, Mr.

[6] *Congressional Globe,* January 8, 1867.

Mills, was more fortunate in his leadership of the House, because "when Mr. Cleveland took decided ground in favor of revision and reduction he represented the patronage of the administration, in consequence of which he was enabled to enforce party discipline, so that a man could no longer be a good Democrat and favor anything but the reform of the tariff." [7]

If, in default of a definite administrative policy vigorously asserted, Congress is left to its own devices, issues are compromised and emergencies are dealt with by makeshift expedients. The complex entanglements of the currency situation were brought about in this way. But even then, the presidential authority, however passive its condition, continues to be a factor of great importance. The passage of the silver bullion purchase act of 1890, according to its framer, Senator Sherman, was thus the result of the President's attitude, although the President had nothing directly to do with it. Senator Sherman says: "A large majority of the Senate favored free silver; and it was feared that the small majority against it in the other House might yield and agree to it. The silence of the President in the matter gave rise to an apprehension that if a free coinage bill should pass both Houses, he would not feel at liberty to veto it. Some action had to be taken to prevent a return to free silver coinage, and the measure evolved was the best obtainable." [8] The repeal of this law in November, 1893, after a memorable struggle in the Senate, affords a conspicuous example of the efficiency of the presidential office in influencing legislation when in earnest about the discharge of that duty.

The evidence which our history affords seems conclusive of the fact that the only power which can end party duplicity and define issues in such a way that public opinion can pass upon them decisively, is that which emanates from presidential authority. It is the rule of our policies that no vexed question is settled except by executive policy. Whatever may be the feeling of Congress towards the President, it cannot avoid an issue which he insists upon making. And this holds good of presidents who lose their party leadership as with those who retain it. Tyler, Johnson, and Cleveland, although repudiated by the parties which elected them, furnished the issues upon which party action turned.

The rise of presidential authority cannot be accounted for by the intention of its presidents: it is the product of political conditions which dominate all the departments of government, so that Congress itself shows an unconscious disposition to aggrandize the presidential office. The existence of a separate responsible authority to which questions of public policy may be resigned opens to Congress an easy way out of difficulty when the exercise of its own jurisdiction would be troublesome. Its servitude to particular interests makes it chary of issues which may cause dissension. It goes only so far as it is compelled to go in obedience to a party mandate, and is apt to leave as much as possible to executive dis-

[7] *New York Sun* interview, September 12, 1893.
[8] *Sherman's Memoirs*, p. 1070.

cretion. So it happens that important determinations of national policy are reached in ways that seem to ignore congressional authority, although the circumstances imply congressional acquiescence. A curious case in point is the well-known fact that the gold reserve fund, which became the base of the monetary system of the nation, was the creation of the executive department. There is no law on the statute books which directed or authorized the establishment of a gold reserve fund. The act of 1875 for the resumption of specie payments authorized the Secretary of the Treasury to sell bonds to enable him to redeem in coin the legal tender notes of the United States. Under the authority of that law Secretary Sherman collected $100,000,000 in gold which was designated as the reserve fund, and its existence has been only indirectly recognized by subsequent legislation.

When the reserve fund was depleted during the panic of 1893–1894, the administration was reluctant to take the responsibility of selling bonds to replenish the fund, and submitted to the Senate Committee on Finance the draught of a bill, specially authorizing the sale of bonds for that purpose. The party leaders, however, advised the executive department to proceed upon its own responsibility, on the ground, as given by Senator Voorhees, chairman of the Finance Committee, that "it will be wiser, safer, and better for the financial and business interests of the country to rely upon existing law with which to meet the present emergency rather than to encounter the delays and uncertainties always incident to protracted discussion in the two Houses of Congress." [9] This confession of the incapacity of Congress in the presence of an emergency, made with such exquisite candor, gave no sting to parliamentary pride, and excited no comment. The opposition of course promptly denied the right of the administration to issue bonds, but it did not seem to occur to any one that the abased attitude assigned to Congress was at all unfitted to its dignity. The whole debate turned upon points of law.

The strong disposition of Congress to extend the scope of federal duty powerfully stimulates the development of presidential authority. That authority may emerge with startling vigor from the implications of laws enacted without any idea of producing such results. A memorable instance is the manner in which the last vestige of the old state sovereignty doctrine was obliterated from practical politics by the agency of the interstate commerce act. In assuming to regulate interstate commerce, Congress put upon the national administration the responsibility of maintaining interstate railroads as national highways. The significance of this never dawned upon the country until the railroad strikes of 1894 took place, when the arm of federal power was suddenly extended to suppress riot and quell disorder. The popular belief had always been that the national government could not act in such cases until requested by state authority, but now state authority was not only ignored, but its protests were unheeded. Time was when such action would have con-

9 Statement furnished to the Associated Press, January 16, 1894.

vulsed the nation and might have caused collision between state and federal authority, but the act was hailed with intense gratification both North and South; the governors who took up the old cry of state rights were loaded with derision, and a Congress, Democratic in both branches, passed resolutions by acclamation approving the action of the executive.

Such vigor, in an authority which the framers of the constitution erected with painful misgivings as to its stability, becomes the more impressive when it is contrasted with the lot of the institution upon which it was patterned. The Federalist makes a detailed comparison between the powers of the President and the British crown, so as to exhibit the more stringent limitations and the inferior authority of the presidency. Since then every power ascribed to the king has withered; but there is no authority conceded to the President, at the time the duties of the office began, that is not flourishing with unimpaired vigor. Moreover, authority which the early Presidents would not have ventured to assume is now regarded as belonging to the ordinary functions of the office. This aggrandizement of presidential authority has gone on under all parties since Jackson's time, and in the hands of men of widely varying capacity. The tendency is so powerful that it sustains itself against the great weakness of the vice-presidency in our constitutional system. That office, of such small, ordinary importance that it is disposed of as an incident in the struggle for the presidential nomination, serving as a make-weight on the ticket, or as a sop to faction, may at any time produce a President. Men have been raised to the presidency who never would have been thought of as a candidate for that office; but its powers have sustained no permanent loss thereby. Although once executive power, in the hands of an accidental President, was bent and held down by the weight of a huge congressional majority, its springs were unbroken, and it sprang up unhurt when the abnormal pressure was removed. Incidentally the history of Andrew Johnson's administration discloses the fact that the extraordinary check provided by the constitution — the process of impeachment — is practically worthless. It remains in the armory of Congress, a rusted blunderbuss, that will probably never be taken in hand again.

Another check upon the power of the President, which has been made obsolete by the peculiar turn taken by our constitutional development, is the power of the House to refuse supplies. Madison said: "The House of Representatives cannot only refuse, but they alone can propose the supplies requisite for the support of the government. . . . This power over the purse may, in fact, be regarded as the most effectual weapon with which any constitution can arm the immediate representatives of the people, for obtaining a redress of every grievance, and for carrying into effect every just and salutary measure." [10] Such an opinion was fully warranted by English constitutional history, but it has been falsified by American experience. As a means of coercing the administration, con-

10 The *Federalist,* No. 58.

trol of supply failed so completely when the test was made that it is not likely that such an use of it will ever be made again. Probably the attempt would not have been made at all had it not been for the extraordinary circumstances of the presidential election of 1876 and the moral weakness of President Hayes' position. The House attempted to reduce federal control of elections by annexing conditions to appropriation bills; but the demands of the House were baffled by a series of vetoes, and in the end Congress had to pass the appropriation bills without the extraneous legislation to which the President objected. It is now a fact recognized by all parties that the idea of stopping the government by withholding supplies cannot even be considered seriously. As a practical expedient, such a check upon executive authority no longer exists. The federal election laws that were attacked in 1876 were repealed in 1894, but that was not until the people had put a President in office who was favorable to the repeal.

Although the power of making appointments to office has been, to a large extent, practically taken over by the Senate, under the exercise of the authority to confirm or reject nominations, yet in this respect also, the executive department possesses abundant power for the protection of its constitutional rights. The President has power "to fill up all vacancies that may happen during the recess of the Senate, by granting commissions which shall expire at the end of their next session." As he has absolute power of removal, he can select his own time for making vacancies, and the commissions which he shall issue will hold good to the last day of the expiring session, whereupon, in case of a rejection, another commission may be issued of like duration. Precedents for such action go back to the early days of the republic. Robert Smith acted as Secretary of the Navy during the whole period of Jefferson's second administration without his appointment to that office being confirmed by the Senate, or any known authority except the verbal request or permission of the President.[11] The appointment of Taney to be the Secretary of the Treasury, in which office he carried out the financial policy of the administration, was never confirmed by the Senate. Jackson did not send in the nomination until the last week of the session, when Taney had finished all that he entered the office to do. There are numerous precedents for the appointment and retention of minor officials in the face of senatorial refusal to confirm the nominations. There were a number of such cases during President Cleveland's term of office.

The strongest and most unqualified statements of the powers of the presidential office come from experienced statesmen who have had the best opportunity of scrutinizing its operation. John Quincy Adams, at a time when presidential authority was less developed than now, said, "It has perhaps never been duly remarked that, under the constitution of the United States, the powers of the executive department, explicitly and emphatically concentrated in one person, are vastly more extensive

---

[11] Adams' *History of the United States*, Vol. III., p. 12.

and complicated than those of the legislature." [12] Secretary Seward told a *London Times* correspondent, who was interrogating him as to the nature of our government, "We elect a king for four years, and give him absolute power within certain limits, which after all he can interpret for himself." [13] Quite as strong were the expressions used by ex-President Hayes to a publicist who applied for information on the subject. "Practically the President holds the nation in his hand." [14] Hare, the leading legal authority on this subject, sums up the case as follows: —

> A chief magistrate who wields the whole military and no inconsiderable share of the civil power of the state, who can incline the scale to war and forbid the return of peace, whose veto will stay the force of legislation, who is the source of the enormous patronage which is the main lever in the politics of the United States, exercises functions which are more truly regal than those of an English monarch.[15]

It should be carefully noted, however, that this power of the presidential office does not proceed from its strength as an embodiment of royal prerogative as conceived by the framers of the constitution. Their expectation was that in the ordinary working of the machinery of election they had devised, there would be numbers of candidates in various states — "favorite sons," to use the modern phrase. Therefore the electoral college of each state was to vote for two persons, one of whom should not be an inhabitant of that state, so that, at least in one instance, the vote of each state would be likely to "fall on characters eminent and generally known." [16] The Federalist speaks of this scheme with a complacency rare in that sombre treatise; but it was a complete failure. It never worked according to the design, except in the election of Washington, when the work of the electoral college was really done for it in advance, and it had simply to register an unanimous consent. The greatness of the presidency is the work of the people, breaking through the constitutional form.

The truth is that in the presidential office, as it has been constituted since Jackson's time, American democracy has revived the oldest political institution of the race, the elective kingship. It is all there: the precognition of the notables and the tumultuous choice of the freemen, only conformed to modern conditions. That the people have been able to accomplish this with such defective apparatus, and have been able to make good a principle which no other people have been able to reconcile with the safety of the state, indicates the highest degree of constitutional morality yet attained by any race.

[12] Discourse on the Jubilee of the Constitution.
[13] Jennings' *Republican Government in the United States*, p. 36.
[14] Stevens' *Sources of the Constitution*, pp. 167–170.
[15] *American Constitutional Law*, p. 173.
[16] Madison's Journal, September 5.

The President, Congress, and Legislation

Lawrence H. Chamberlain

Since the turn of the century the increasing importance of the president in the legislative process has received almost continuous discussion. The emergence of the chief executive as a force in the initiation and formulation of legislation is, in fact, primarily a twentieth-century phenomenon. When Woodrow Wilson wrote his classic treatise, *Congressional Government,* in 1885, he detected little tendency on the part of the president to take an active hand in shaping legislation.

It is true that some earlier presidents had conceived their responsibility broadly enough to include legislative leadership. During the administrations of both Washington and Jefferson executive influence was an important factor in shaping legislative policy. Secretary of the Treasury Alexander Hamilton, acting in the capacity of President Washington's personal representative, enjoyed singular success in gaining congressional acceptance of a comprehensive legislative program. Jefferson, as president, employed methods strikingly different to achieve similar results. He was truly the leader of his party at a time when party lines in legislation were much more clearly drawn than is the case today.

Thus, within the first twenty years, forceful and skilled executives demonstrated that our system of mechanical checks and balances need not constitute an insurmountable barrier to executive-legislative coöperation in legislation. During the succeeding years, however, the lessons so effectively presented at the threshold of our governmental development were largely wasted. Only occasionally did we have a president who consistently chose to seize the initiative and guide the Congress in the formulation of a legislative program for the country. In different ways and with varying degrees of success Jackson, Lincoln and Cleveland, as well as some others, sometimes sought to exert strong pressure in legislative matters. But these occasions occurred infrequently and the presidents concerned made no effort to assume general responsibility for legislative leadership.

It was only when Theodore Roosevelt came into office that the philosophy of the executive dominant in legislation received conscious application. During his seven years in the White House, Roosevelt invested the presidency with a dramatic and aggressive personal spirit. After the Taft interregnum, Woodrow Wilson's particular contribution was a more deliberate and a more effective party leadership. Finally, the multidimensional leadership of Franklin Roosevelt did much to create the

Reprinted by permission from the *Political Science Quarterly,* Vol. LXI, No. 1 (March 1946), pp. 42–60.

impression that the congressional rôle in legislation had become definitely secondary.

Those who insist that the president has indeed become "chief legislator" [1] can offer persuasive evidence to support their thesis. Theodore Roosevelt's record in railroad and conservation legislation, Wilson's successful efforts on behalf of tariff, banking and business regulation, and Franklin Roosevelt's achievements in many fields of legislation are common knowledge. All of these men were forceful personalities who refused to accept a limited view of their duties and responsibilities. Each came into office at a time when the social and economic development of the country had rendered existing laws inadequate and the need for forward-looking legislation was acute. Congress, alone, was seemingly unable to produce results. In each instance the advent of the new president was accompanied by significant legislation, and there can be no question concerning the genuineness of his contribution. Without his catalyzing influence Congress would not have succeeded in bringing its own labors to fruition. It should be kept in mind, however, that the president's contribution was fundamentally that of making Congress effective, rather than that of creating something himself.

In the United States, legislation is characteristically a collegial process in which the rôle of the Congress is no less important than that of the president. During the periods when the chief executive assumes the lead, the partnership between the executive and the Congress usually operates more efficiently. This does not mean that Congress has become less important. The legislative process is not like a seesaw where as one end goes down the other must automatically go up. It is, rather, like a gasoline engine which operates most efficiently when all of its cylinders are functioning. When the president becomes unusually active, there is a tendency to assume that the congressional cylinder has ceased to function. Such is not necessarily the case.

It does not detract from the importance of the president to point out that the tendency to magnify his participation to the exclusion or neglect of Congress may create impressions that not only are false but may be dangerously misleading. The spectacular examples afforded by taking a few highly publicized cases from the careers of our most aggressive presidents should not be given undue emphasis. Further investigation might show that the impressions created by these headline incidents lose some of their substance when considered in their proper context. With this thought in mind the writer undertook a detailed study of the legislative history of several major laws passed during the last fifty years for the purpose of identifying more sharply the persons who exercised greatest influence upon their form and substance. In this way it was hoped to indicate more clearly the relative contribution of the president and Congress in the formulation of at least some of our most important laws.

[1] The term was given general currency by Howard Lee McBain in his trenchant book, *The Living Constitution* (New York, 1927).

The period chosen has been the most significant so far as the rôle of the federal government is concerned. Except for a few important laws, among which might be mentioned the Morrill Act of 1862, the reconstruction legislation of the sixties, and some currency legislation, the period of federal intervention in economic and social matters does not antedate the 1880's. By examining a cross-section of recent federal legislation on a relatively broad front, it was hoped that an accurate picture of the legislative process might be obtained. Consequently, approximately ninety major enactments of the past half-century were studied for the purpose of discovering their origins.

It is, of course, realized that in the final analysis the ideas for legislation originate with neither the president nor the Congress. Most legislation is in reality the product of forces external to any governmental agency. The proposal for governmental intervention, whether it comes from the president, the Congress, or the department concerned, may generally be understood to have originated with some group much more directly interested in the specific results of the proposal than are any of these agencies of government. The governmental agency thus becomes, as the term implies, merely the agent through which the proposal is made rather than the true initiating body; but this does not mean that it is entirely unrealistic to allocate responsibility as between the president and the Congress. Granting the thesis that most legislation in varying degrees has its origins in some private group rather than in any governmental body, the fact remains that pressure groups for all their importance cannot enact laws themselves. This is a prerogative which continues to be the exclusive possession of the legislative and executive departments of the government. Unless and until they act, the pressure groups fail to accomplish their objectives. For this reason the measures surveyed were not attributed to pressure groups unless the president and Congress abdicated so completely that the outside interests did in effect write the legislation in question.

The laws studied fall into ten categories: agriculture, banking and currency, business, government credit, immigration, labor, national defense, natural resources, railroads, and tariff. Within each of these general fields several federal laws of national import have been passed during the period under investigation. Some have been passed under the stress of emergency conditions, others in periods of comparative quiet. Some have been enacted during the administrations of aggressive presidents, others have come into being under presidents whose attitude toward legislation was more or less passive. The fields chosen do not embrace all federal legislation but they were selected because they embraced legislation extending over the greater part of fifty years and thus provided a basis broad enough to make possible the drawing of useful comparisons.

The specific acts within each of these fields are necessarily selective. The number of important laws passed in several of these fields has been large. Any attempt to select the ten most important is to invite challenge because it is impossible to establish a completely objective standard.

Every effort was made, however, to select those acts which seemed to constitute a representative cross section of each particular field.

On the basis of the detailed study of the ninety laws selected they were allocated to four categories: laws in which the influence of the president was dominant; laws in which the influence of Congress was dominant; laws in which the influence of both the president and the Congress was sufficiently great that they must be given joint credit; and laws in which the influence of outside groups transcended that of either the president or the Congress. These categories are not absolute. Few laws are so unmixed in their origins that they can be arbitrarily catalogued in any one of the above categories without a bit of straining. To a certain extent any measuring stick which may be developed must be subjective. No single formula can be devised which when applied to widely varying combinations of legislative action will automatically produce the correct answer, because each law presents special problems. Although the chronology of events from introduction to ultimate approval may indicate a superficial similarity, significant factors vitally affecting the finished product frequently defy sharp identification.

The allocation is based upon a weighing of the relative influence of the president and Congress in its total effect upon the particular law in question. In some cases the initial impetus has come from one, but the preponderant influence in the completed statute has been ascribed to the other after a careful weighing of all the evidence. Unless the impact of the president or the Congress when judged in terms of its total effect upon the form, substance and operation of the statute in question is sufficiently clear cut to remove reasonable doubt, the dilemma has been avoided by classifying the act as "joint." If this method is defective because it fails to accord sufficient weight to the more subtle factors present in all legislative activity, it has the merit of removing doubtful allocations from the area of controversy and of restricting conclusions to those statutes about whose origins the facts can be fairly definitely established.

The following tabulation indicates the classification assigned each law.[2] Of the ninety major laws studied, approximately twenty per cent fall to the credit of the president; roughly forty per cent were chiefly the product of Congress; about thirty per cent fall into the joint presidential-congressional category; and slightly less than ten per cent are identified as primarily the handiwork of external pressure groups.

This tabulation demonstrates the joint character of the American legislative process. Significant as this fact is, the tabulation fails to reflect another aspect of congressional participation in legislation which is equally fundamental. By allocating each law to the instrumentality chiefly responsible for its passage in final form, it has not been possible to indicate the origin of the proposal in the first place. One of the points

[2] An asterisk indicates that one or more bills dealing with this subject had been introduced without administration support and had received substantial consideration in Congress before administration backing led to the enactment of the measure here listed.

TABLE 1

Origin of Legislation

PRESIDENTIAL INFLUENCE PREPONDERANT

Agriculture	1	Agricultural Adjustment Act of 1933.*
Banking	3	Silver Purchase Repeal Act of 1893; Emergency Banking Act of 1933; Gold Reserve Act of 1934.*
Business	3	Securities Act of 1933; * Securities and Exchange Act of 1934; * Public Utilities Holding Company Act of 1935.*
Credit	3	War Finance Corporation Act of 1918; Reconstruction Finance Corporation Act of 1932; Home Owners' Loan Corporation Act of 1933.*
Immigration	0	
Labor	1	Second Employers' Liability Act of 1908.*
National Defense	6	Militia Act of 1903; General Staff Act of 1903; Selective Service Act of 1917; Naval Construction Acts of 1901–1905; Naval Construction Act of 1916; Navy Act of 1938.*
Natural Resources	0	
Railroads	0	
Tariff	2	Underwood Act of 1913; * Reciprocal Trade Agreements Act of 1934.*

<u>19</u>

CONGRESSIONAL INFLUENCE PREPONDERANT

Agriculture	2	Capper-Volstead Act of 1922; * McNary-Haugen bills, 1924–1928.*
Banking	6	Currency Acts of 1873; * 1878; * 1890; * 1900; * 1908; * Glass-Steagall Act of 1933.*
Business	1	Sherman Act of 1890.*
Credit	3	Federal Farm Loan Act of 1916; * War Finance Corporation Revival Act of 1921; * Agricultural Credits Act of 1923.*
Immigration	9	Chinese Exclusion Act of 1882; * Chinese Exclusion Act of 1892; * General Immigration Acts of 1882; * 1903; * 1907; * 1913; * 1917; * 1921; * 1924.*
Labor	3	Department of Labor Act of 1913; * Second Child Labor Act of 1919; * Norris-LaGuardia Act of 1932.*
National Defense	4	National Defense Act of 1916; * National Defense Act of 1920; Selective Service Act of 1940; * Naval Disarmament Act of 1920–21.*
Natural Resources	2	Carey Act of 1894; * Act of 1897.*

CONGRESSIONAL INFLUENCE PREPONDERANT (*Continued*)

Railroads	3	Interstate Commerce Act of 1887; * Valuation Act of 1913; * Transportation Act of 1920.*
Tariff	2	Wilson Act of 1894; * Payne-Aldrich Act of 1909.*

35

JOINT PRESIDENTIAL-CONGRESSIONAL INFLUENCE

Agriculture	3	Agricultural Marketing Act of 1929; * Soil Conservation Act of 1936; Agricultural Adjustment Act of 1938.*
Banking	4	Federal Reserve Act of 1913; * Thomas Silver Amendment of 1933; * Silver Purchase Act of 1934; * Banking Act of 1935.*
Business	2	Clayton Act of 1914; * National Industrial Recovery Act of 1933.*
Credit	2	Federal Home Loan Bank Act of 1932; * Emergency Farm Mortgage Act of 1933.*
Labor	4	First Employers' Liability Act of 1906; * First Child Labor Act of 1916; * National Labor Relations Act of 1935; * Wages and Hours Acts of 1938. *
National Defense	3	Army Act of 1901; * Naval Construction Act of 1929; * Naval Construction Act of 1934.*
Natural Resources	7	General Revision Act of 1891; * Newlands Act of 1902; * Weeks Act of 1911; * Migratory Bird Act of 1913; * Migratory Bird Treaty Act of 1918; * Migratory Bird Refuge Act of 1929; * Taylor Grazing Act of 1934.*
Railroads	4	Hepburn Act of 1906; * Mann-Elkins Act of 1910; Emergency Railroad Transportation Act of 1933; Transportation Act of 1940.*
Tariff	0	

29

PRESSURE GROUP INFLUENCE PREPONDERANT

Labor	1	Railway Labor Disputes Act of 1926.*
Natural Resources	1	Clarke-McNary Act of 1924.*
Railroads	1	Elkins Act of 1903.
Tariff	4	McKinley Tariff Act of 1890; * Dingley Tariff Act of 1897; * Fordney-McCumber Tariff Act of 1922; * Hawley-Smoot Tariff Act of 1930.

7

brought out most clearly by the case studies was the depth of the legislative roots of most important statutes. For instance, a law is hailed as something new at the time of passage, but further examination reveals that the proposal had been discussed more or less continuously in Congress for several years. Presidential attention had led to its elevation from the obscurity of just another bill to the prominence of an administration measure. Administrative experts had participated by drafting a new bill but there was not very much in the new bill that had not been present in one or more earlier drafts. At all events, driven by the power now behind it, the bill becomes law without great difficulty or delay, while in the absence of presidential action years might have gone by without its adoption. The law is allocated to the category of presidential influence because its passage in final form was certainly not assignable to any other instrumentality. But the influence of what had taken place in Congress cannot be ignored. Had the initial proposal not been introduced and discussed, the final act might not have come when it did or it might have emerged in quite a different form. There is no way in which this preliminary activity can be assessed and it would be futile to attempt its measurement, but its importance is genuine. It is at least possible to indicate which of the ninety laws included in the survey was the end product of a bill or bills initiated within Congress and the subject of hearings and discussion there prior to the events leading to its final passage.

Of the entire ninety laws no less than seventy-seven (marked with an asterisk) trace their ancestry directly to bills which originally had been introduced without administration sponsorship. These bills or their successors had been the subject of hearings and committee consideration for periods ranging from a few months to a dozen or more years before they were passed with or without administration support. Presidential influence was dominant in the case of nineteen laws, but twelve of these had been originally initiated by Congress and had been the subject of extensive hearings. Among the twenty-nine laws classified as the joint product of the president and Congress, twenty-six trace their origin to bills which had been introduced without benefit of administrative support and had served as the basis for committee hearings and discussion.

These figures do not support the thesis that Congress is unimportant in the formulation of major legislation. Rather, they indicate, not that the president is less important than generally supposed, but that Congress is more important.

An examination of the legislative history of the past ten years indicates a somewhat more one-sided distribution, but the influence of Congress was by no means negligible. Of the twenty-three laws in this survey which were passed after 1932, the president is credited with eight, Congress with only two, and the president and Congress jointly with thirteen. When the backgrounds of these laws are examined, however, the contribution of Congress assumes substantial proportions. For example, the Agricultural Adjustment Act of 1933 may be classified as presidential but the struggle for farm legislation which virtually monopolized the attention of several sessions of Congress during the twenties had left its mark. The almost continuous series of hearings had provided a clearing house for the various agencies, governmental and private, which were seeking some new formula for putting the farmer back upon his feet. The domestic allotment plan of 1933 did not spring into being overnight. Its lineal ancestry can be traced directly back to the earlier plans of the McNary-Haugen era. Congress acted in response to executive pressure in its speedy approval of the agricultural adjustment bill, and it did so in spite of the opposition of the two committee chairmen handling the bill, because the congressional mood at this time was one of coöperation. In this sense the priority of presidential influence was incontrovertible. On the other hand, the influence of previous congressional activity upon the substance of the bill requested by the president, while impossible to measure or weigh in exact terms, was no less important.

Similar influences can be pointed to in the case of the securities and exchange legislation of 1933–1934. The technical details of the two acts were not written in Congress, but the sentiment for regulation along these general lines had been growing steadily for more than twenty years. The legislative history of the holding company bill of 1935 reveals a parallel period of legislative preoccupation preceding presidential concern. Moreover, in several instances where bills have been classified as joint in influence, it is Congress and not the president that deserves the lion's share of credit not only for originating the idea in the first place but also for the drudgery of grinding out the provisions of the bill itself. The National Labor Relations Act of 1935, the Fair Labor Standards Act of 1938, the Taylor Grazing Act of 1934, and the Transportation Act of 1940, all owe much of their present substance to the efforts of Congress.

Viewing the entire ninety laws from the standpoint of subject matter, what do the figures reveal? Can generalizations be made regarding the presence or absence of presidential domination in certain fields? What about Congress? Does its influence run chiefly to certain categories or does it cover the entire panorama? What has been the history of pressure group dominance? Answers to these questions are suggested by the case studies.

The president has been consistently strong in the field of national defense legislation. Of the thirteen major laws included in this study, six have clearly been the handiwork of the president or his representatives. (Secretary of War Elihu Root rather than Theodore Roosevelt was the focal point of two important army laws passed during the latter's administration.) Even in this admittedly executive domain, however, Congress has made contributions of vital importance. Of the four acts wherein its influence was paramount, two were particularly important. These two, the National Defense Act of 1916 and the Selective Service Act of 1940, came during pre-war periods and both were passed during the administrations of presidents noted for their aggressive leadership. It is not only in post-war periods of reaction that congressional leadership comes to the fore. Neither do such events occur only when the White House is occupied by weak presidents.

Of the six laws regulating business, included in the survey, presidential influence dominated in the case of four. These figures are somewhat misleading, however, because all four of these laws came during the first two years of Franklin Roosevelt's administration. The National Industrial Recovery Act, the Securities Act, the Securities and Exchange Act, and the Public Utility Holding Company Act, all bear the imprint of the president. Congress passed them by healthy majorities but they are what they are because the president backed them even though his decisions reflected the influence of earlier congressional activity. This is a break with the past, for historically the president has not taken the lead in this field. The Sherman Act of 1890 was born without benefit of executive support. Despite the enthusiastic outbursts of Theodore Roosevelt about trust busting, no significant legislation was enacted during his stay in office. Wilson entered the White House with a program of business reform. The Clayton Act of 1914 and its sister statute, the Federal Trade Commission Act, may be cited as evidence of his influence. But the Clayton Act, popular legend to the contrary notwithstanding, was not an unqualified presidential victory. While it probably could not have been passed without Wilson's support, the substance of the final product was at least as much the work of Congress as it was that of the administration.

Those areas in which the influence of the president has been noticeably weak are no less interesting. In five fields — agriculture, immigration, labor, natural resources and railroads — presidential leadership has been unsteady. Six major statutes have been passed in the field of agriculture; of these only one, the Agricultural Adjustment Act of 1933, is credited to the president and then, as has been said, with qualifications. Two were primarily the work of Congress and three were the joint product of both. The most striking example of presidential weakness is found in the record of immigration legislation. Ten important immigration acts were passed during the period under study; not a single one of these was substantially influenced by the president. Several of them were outright defeats for him.

Only one of the nine important labor laws studied in this report owes its existence chiefly to the president. None of the ten laws dealing with natural resources conservation are credited principally to him. This seems surprising in view of the fact that Theodore Roosevelt's name is intimately associated with conservation in this country. Only one major conservation act, the Newlands Act of 1902, came during his administration. Roosevelt took a great interest in this bill, and his contribution to its final enactment was not inconsiderable. On the other hand, the contribution of Congress was not less important, and any just appraisal must classify the measure as of joint parentage. Finally, the president has not been a powerful figure in railroad legislation. Major enactments in this category during the period under study total eight. Not one of these eight can be classified as primarily executive. Three of them — the Interstate Commerce Act of 1887, the Valuation Act of 1913, and the Transportation Act of 1920 — are listed as chiefly the work of Congress. The Hepburn Act of 1906, the Mann-Elkins Act of 1910, the Emergency Transportation Act of 1933, and the Transportation Act of 1940 came from both ends of Pennsylvania Avenue. Though the Elkins Act of 1903 came in the administration of Theodore Roosevelt, who was vitally interested in railroads, it was almost entirely the work of the railroads themselves.

In those areas where Congress has consistently played a major rôle, banking and currency and immigration stand out, with labor legislation only a few steps behind. Six acts — the Currency Acts of 1873, 1878, 1890, 1900 and 1908, and the Glass-Steagall Banking Act of 1933 — owe most of their substance to Congress. Three others — the Federal Reserve Act of 1913, the Thomas Amendment of 1933, and the Silver Purchase Act of 1934 — were at least as much influenced by Congress as by the president. Four statutes — the Silver Purchase Repeal Act of 1894, the Emergency Banking Act of 1933, the Gold Reserve Act of 1934, and the Banking Act of 1934 — are classified as executive. Only in the case of the first two, however, was the influence of Congress negligible. The Gold Reserve Act of 1934 was virtually extorted from the administration by pressure from within Congress. In the case of the Banking Act of 1935, it was the Federal Reserve Board Chairman, Marriner S. Eccles, rather than the president who held the central rôle; the bill was approved by Congress only after substantial modifications had been written into its provisions.

Throughout the entire period under study, immigration legislation has been the exclusive prerogative of Congress. From the initial steps toward developing our national policy in the early eighties, congressional interest and activity have transcended that of the executive. When the president has attempted to impose his views he has received sharp rebuffs. The Act of 1913 became law over the veto of Taft; the Act of 1917 came into being under similar circumstances except that the president who suffered defeat this time was Wilson. The Act of 1924 was signed by Coolidge only after he had tried unsuccessfully to have certain of its provisions eliminated. One may argue that American immigration legislation would have been improved had the president been able to make his influence felt. For our purposes that is a point on which an opinion need not be expressed. The record shows that whatever immigration policy we have is the handiwork of Congress and not of the executive.

The conspicuous position of Congress in labor legislation may occasion some surprise. Particularly since the New Deal the impression has prevailed that the president stood as labor's champion against an indifferent if not a hostile Congress. Events since 1939 have indeed followed a pattern not inconsistent with this impression. Nevertheless, the record shows that from the very beginning Congress has taken a more active part in legislating in the interest of labor than has the president, and the record of the past ten years of New Deal hegemony has not upset the historic pattern. Nine major labor laws were passed between 1890 and 1940. Congress was chiefly responsible for three of these — the Department of Labor Act of 1913, the Second Child Labor Act of 1919, and the Norris-LaGuardia Act of 1932. Four others were the joint product of president and Congress — the First Employers' Liability Act of 1906, the First Child Labor Act of 1916, the National Labor Relations Act of 1935, and the Fair Labor Standards Act of 1938. In the case of employers' liability, Congress had been at work on such legislation for several years before a bill was finally pushed through with the aid of President Theodore Roosevelt. Not only was his contribution one of motive power; he also took an active interest in the substance of the bill, and its final form was in part due to his efforts. So far as the other three laws are concerned, the story is quite different. Wilson finally threw his support behind the child labor bill, and this was the deciding factor in its eventual passage. His aid was belated, however, and was supplied only after the real sponsors of the bill had overcome many difficulties that would have never occurred had he taken a strong position from the beginning. It is something less than fair to Congress to classify such a law as the joint product of president and Congress. A situation not essentially different accompanied the passage of the National Labor Relations Act when the admittedly indispensable presidential support was tardy in making itself felt. The history of the Wages and Hours Act presents a somewhat stronger record of executive participation. Of all the laws in this category it comes closest to being truly joint in authorship.

Natural resources legislation deserves special comment. Analysis of the ten laws falling within this broad grouping indicates that seven have been the result of joint activity of the president and Congress. Actually, this is not quite the case. "Administrative agency" would be more accurate than "president." The fount of much of our most far-sighted conservation legislation has been the man or men charged with the administration of the particular activity in question. In some cases it has been as far up the hierarchy as the department head, a man of cabinet rank. Just as frequently it has come from farther down the pyramid. Often men at the bureau level have been the real inspiration of much needed law. Men such as these, working hand in hand with members of Congress on the one side and with representatives of private interests on the other, have been the real pioneers of America's stumbling efforts toward a conservation policy.

A final word on a field in which the outside interests have prevailed — tariff legislation. Eight major tariff acts have been passed during the last fifty years. Half of these have been almost completely dominated by pressure politics: the McKinley Act of 1890, the Dingley Act of 1897, the Fordney-McCumber Act of 1922, and the Hawley-Smoot Act of 1930. Two — the Wilson Act of 1894 and the Payne-Aldrich Act of 1909 — were influenced by Congress, more particularly by individual congressmen.

At the outset the Wilson Act was an embodiment of a principle — a tariff for revenue only. Before it became law it had been subjected to a withering attack by numerous interest groups and much of its initial symmetry had been twisted out of shape by special concessions which its sponsors had been powerless to prevent. Even in this distorted condition the law retained a substantial proportion of its original substance. By comparison, at least, it can be stamped a congressional rather than a pressure group bill.

The Payne-Aldrich Act of 1909 is also classified as congressional, although its parentage was exceedingly complex. The original Payne bill was the answer of the House Ways and Means Committee to President Taft's plea for a general reduction of tariffs. As such it was written by the committee and it complied with the spirit of the president's message. By the time the bill emerged from the House it had lost some of its noble character, and when it reached the Senate Finance Committee it underwent almost total metamorphosis under the influence of Senator Aldrich and his associates. Its policy of moderation was transformed into a sharp restatement of the principle of protection. During Senate consideration representatives of special interests obtained so many additional increases in certain schedules that the bill lost all semblance to its original form. At the last moment President Taft interceded and managed to obtain a few relatively minor reductions in certain schedules. Yet, viewing the bill as a whole, one may say that its final form seems to have rested chiefly with Congress.

Two tariff laws, the Underwood Act of 1913 and the Reciprocal Trade Agreements Act of 1934, are definitely presidential. These two instances are important chiefly because they demonstrate that tariff legislation is no different from other legislation. When the president takes a strong stand and is willing to use the weapons of persuasion at his disposal, he can compete with the most powerful economic combines on more than equal terms.

The preceding pages fall short of being an unqualified tribute to Congress. It has upon occasion yielded ground to the chief executive; it has been guilty of rubber stampism for brief intervals; on some of the occasions when it has insisted upon making its influence felt the results have been unfortunate. Nevertheless, its record, even during the past ten years when its independence was at the ebb, compares not unfavorably with that of the president in terms of significant legislation achieved. The Banking Act of 1933, the National Labor Relations Act of 1935, and the Selective Service Act of 1940 have been inseparably bound up with the country's recent history. No three executively inspired laws hold a more prominent place. Furthermore, measured in terms of influence upon many executive proposals which have ultimately become law, the impact of Congress has been consequential. In some instances congressional initiative spurred the president to action when he would have preferred to wait; in others presidential inactivity was compensated for by independent congressional action. But of even greater importance, viewed in terms of its long-range effects, has been Congress' service as a center for the origination and maturing of innovative legislation.

Even the most severe critic of Congress would not deny that it has been sensitive to the ever-increasing areas demanding recognition by the federal government. Most of the great mass of regulatory legislation of the past decade, popularly dubbed New Deal legislation, had a well-defined prenatal history extending back several years before it was espoused by the Roosevelt administration. This is true not only of the more conventional fields such as banking, railroads and taxation, but of the newer areas of social security, holding company regulation and securities control. Congressional attention to these new fields had not been absent prior to the time the president made his specific recommendations. The normal process has been fairly uniform: an initial reference by one or a few individuals, then a gradually increasing volume of comment accompanied by numerous specific proposals coming from widely divergent sources. In some cases legislation has resulted in a very short time, but more frequently the initial flurries of interest have subsided, to be revived from time to time until finally culminating, perhaps with the help of the president, in a law.

The long germinative period detectable in the genesis of most laws is of the utmost importance; it constitutes one of the most valuable contributions that a legislative body can make. No other agency in a democracy is so well equipped by composition and organization to discharge this function. The accessibility of Congress, coupled with its ever-changing personnel, tends to guarantee a maximum of responsiveness to the varied but always moving currents of thought. One cannot examine the official records of a single session of Congress without becoming deeply impressed with the substantial contribution which the individual congressman frequently makes when it comes to locating the weakness and gaps in our legislative fabric and initiating action to fill the breach. The piecemeal character of our national legislative program which results from the individualistic nature of the initiation process has frequently been criticized for its lack of unity and coherence. Without arguing the accuracy of this assertion it does seem worth while to emphasize the unusual place the individual senator or representative holds in the sagas of many of our most valued laws. To go no further than the single field of labor legislation, such outstanding examples as those of Shipstead, Norris and LaGuardia in anti-injunction legislation, Wagner in the field of collective bargaining, and Black in the regulation of wages and hours may be cited. These men were the authors as well as the sponsors of the bills and laws bearing their names. Had it not been for their persistent efforts and their unwillingness to give up in the face of administration indifference or hostility, it is probable that, even if the laws would have eventually been passed, their enactment would have been much longer delayed and their content would have been much less definite than they actually are. This is an important factor to bear in mind when attempting to allocate credit between the president and the Congress for legislation that has been passed. It frequently appears that the president is the initiating agent of a particular law when as a matter of fact he is little more than the conveyance — sometimes even the reluctant one — upon which it moves to fruition, and is not entitled to credit for anything more than that.

President Roosevelt's approach to the problem of legislative leadership was more imaginative than that of most of his predecessors. He was not only willing but eager to make suggestions regarding the laws which he deemed necessary. Yet in several notable instances, for example, the National Labor Relations Act and the Selective Service Act, even he demonstrated a strange reluctance to request or support legislation that was both necessary and desired. The simple fact is presidential leadership has been and probably will continue to be uneven. Such being the case, the value of congressional initiative, whether as a stimulant or as an irritant, is and will continue to be exceedingly important.

Congress has been criticized for its inability to take a long-range, comprehensive view. Because of its method of selection, Congress is inclined toward localism rather than nationalism. The executive, so it is said, has supplied a more integrated and better balanced point of view. Even if this is the case the atomized nature of the congressional approach to our legislative needs has supplied something without which executive leadership would be less effective.

From the half-thousand individualists who make up the two houses of Congress the annual harvest of legislative proposals continues uninterrupted. That many of these ideas may be impractical is beside the point. The constant replenishment of the supply is the important thing. This inexhaustible flood of observations, suggestions and proposals constitutes a fairly accurate barometer of prospective as well as prevailing pressures. General concern with any particular aspect of our economy is usually preceded by a gradually increasing tide of comment in Congress. From these suggestions come not only the stimulus for positive action but also much of the substance that will eventually become law.

Functional Interdependence: The Elective Leaders, the White House, and the Congressional Party

David B. Truman

LEADERSHIP OF THE PRESIDENT'S MAJORITY

Generalized in the baldest terms these data demonstrate that the "program" of the President had a centripetal effect upon the majority Congressional parties that gave coherence to their leadership structures and meaning to the roles of the leaders, especially those in the principal "elective" positions. In other words, and somewhat more extreme ones, the Democratic majority parties in the Congress worked as groups because of and in response to the initiatives of a Democratic Administration.

This conclusion, given the complexity and the crudity of the underlying data, calls for some qualification. What, precisely, is the nature of the relations implied by the data? Do they mean more, for example, than the familiar characterization of the Presidency as involving the role of "Chief Legislator"? This term has no very explicit or precise meaning, but it usually denotes an aspect of the President's relations with the Congress as an inclusive institution and hence does not make the point that is here intended.[1] The response of interest here is not that from the Congress as a whole but rather the response from the Congressional party. Nor is the same sense conveyed by the notion of the President as "party leader," since this ascription normally implies no distinction between the electoral party and the Congressional party or, more accurately, parties. It is not even very helpful to refer to the President as the "leader" of the House and Senate parties. These groups have their own leaders, whose roles, as the data on the Eighty-first Congress have shown, are real ones. These roles are not, however, independent of the Presidency, and their occupants do not have resources of power equal to those of the President.

What is needed to describe the relations between the President and the leaders of his Congressional majority that are pointed to in these data is perhaps a slightly modified conception of leadership in the context of the Congressional party. In contemporary social science precise notions of leadership have grown primarily from the close observation of relatively small groups, in which the leader is defined operationally as one

Reprinted with permission from *The Congressional Party* (New York: John Wiley & Sons, 1959), pp. 289–316.

[1] See, for example, Edward S. Corwin, *The President: Office and Powers*, 3d Edition, New York: New York University Press, 1948, chap. 7, and Clinton Rossiter, *The American Presidency*, New York: Harcourt, Brace, 1956, p. 14 and *passim*.

who characteristically initiates action for the other members of the group. These studies, for understandable reasons of research manage-ability, have tended to treat the small group — committee, neighborhood clique, trade union local, factory work-group — in isolation rather than as a unit in a more inclusive system or organization. In consequence they do not throw much light on more complex situations in which initiative does not have its origins within the membership of the group.[2]

For it is a commonplace that the President is not a member of the Congressional party. Without attempting to draw a sketch that is more precise than the materials warrant, one may surmise that in the com-plexities of the Presidency and the Congressional parties one is dealing with mutually dependent sets of relations, the Congressional party leaders with their rank-and-file members and the President with his more in-clusive audience going beyond the Congress and the executive branch to the nation and the world. The relations of the President with the leaders of the Congressional party at the convergence of these sets are typically not symmetrical, since the power resources of the President generally ex-ceed those of the Congressional party leaders, but they are mutually dependent because the initiatives of the President are necessary for his performance of his role in his larger constituency and are also essential in the Congressional leaders' performance of their roles within the legislative party.

An analogy that implies a clear hierarchy in this pattern is not en-tirely fortunate, but one may think of the President as resembling, not the leader in the small group, but a plant manager who may lead a work-group through its foreman. The parallel is not close, but it suggests the essential point that the President's initiatives, though indispensable to the effective functioning of the legislative party, are not normally equivalent to the direct leadership of that group.[3] The analogy to the plant manager is also helpful in its suggestion that the common enter-prise of the electoral party, though possibly less completely absorbing than an industrial enterprise, encourages a convergence of view that otherwise would not occur.

The President, as these comments suggest, does something more than merely provide an agenda for the Congress or even for the legislative parties. If that were all he did, the policy differences between the two parties and between their respective elective leaders, which have been identified here, would not be accounted for. The minority parties and

[2] For critical comments on the shortcomings of observation of small groups *in vacuo* and on the distortions resulting from projecting inferences about small groups upon large and complex systems, see William F. Whyte, *Patterns for Industrial Peace*, New York: Harper and Brothers, 1951.

[3] The Woodrow Wilson of 1907 made a number of the distinctions indicated here, though the points were not elaborated and, in a sense, they could not be until after his Administration. (In Woodrow Wilson, *Constitutional Government in the United States*, New York: Columbia University Press, 1908, see, for example, pp. 72 ff. and 107 ff. Compare also Arthur N. Holcombe, *Our More Perfect Union*, Cambridge: Harvard University Press, 1950, pp. 236–283.)

their leaders would not have diverged so consistently from the majority. The President's initiatives and preferences do set an agenda, to be sure. This has become one of the unwritten components of his role, regardless of whether his party is in the majority in the Congress and almost regardless of his personal conceptions of the position. But, especially if his is the majority party in the legislature, his preferences also provide leverage useful if not absolutely essential to the principal elective leaders of the legislative party in the performance of their roles.

This distinction between setting an agenda for the Congress as a whole and providing leverage for the elective leaders of the President's legislative party permits some clarification of the different senses of the term "program" in these pages. The word appeared first . . . as a means of characterizing the tendency toward a voting pattern in the majority party that showed elements of coherence along substantive policy lines. This tendency was treated as evidence of the "program" of the majority legislative party, and the data in this chapter indicate that it had more than a little to do with both the initiatives and the agenda of the President. But the agenda of the President, composed of his public requests to the Congress, clearly is not identical with the program of the legislative party or even with the President's own program. Some occupants of the White House demand much of the Congress and some relatively little, but none, with the possible exception of Franklin Roosevelt in the first months of his first term, is granted all that he asks for. (No Congress, however compliant, could reasonably be expected even to act on, to say nothing of granting, the range of requests making up Harry Truman's agenda for the Eighty-first.) The actions he most wants the legislature to take, his program, presumably fill a considerably shorter list, approximating the items he judges he can or must get, and the program of the Congressional party is likely to be still less comprehensive. The principal elective leaders, on the basis of their own preferences and their estimates of what they in turn can expect from the committees and from their chambers, arrive at what the legislative schedule and the voting indicate as the program of the Congressional party. But the emergence of this program of the legislative party is a function of the mutual dependence of the President and the principal leaders of the Congressional party, in which the leverage provided by the President's preferences is crucial.

The importance for the principal elective leaders of their relations with the President, especially if the Congressional party is in the majority, is fundamentally traceable to the peculiar characteristics of these groups. As earlier chapters have argued, the legislative parties are marked by a paradoxical set of attributes: fractionation and, in some instances, structural fluidity, but also a tendency toward shared attitudes and expectations, even in substantive policy matters, and an apparent interdependence of role among the members, both of which testify to their persistence as groups. These attributes have been summarily described in these pages by designating the Congressional parties as "mediate" groups, meaning that the relations constituting the groups are distinctively affected but not wholly determined by their members' affiliations with and dependence upon other groups.[4] The latter would include primarily interest groups and constituency parties but would of course not be confined to these.

One of the implications of the mediate character of the Congressional party is that the risks to which its members are subject are not fully integrated into the shared attitudes and goals of the group, as they would be in an immediate group such as a militant labor union, a military combat group, or even a well-managed business firm. Its members' fortunes are not identical with those of the legislative party, but at the same time they are not completely independent of it. The degree of independence, as has been suggested earlier, is probably less in the House than in the Senate. In addition, the degree of independence is not a fixed quantity but is subject to fluctuation with various circumstances — the nature of emergent issues, the timing and imminence of the re-election contest, the vigor and popular standing of the President, and the like. These fluctuations usually are not highly predictable or subject to precise ranking. Hence the distribution of risks as between those produced by the performance and fortunes of the legislative party and those more closely related to "outside" groups is often decidedly unclear and ambiguous.

This ambiguity of risk and the mediate function of the legislative party seem to be the keys to the roles of the principal elective leaders. Ambiguity may help to support the demands of the Floor Leader if he is able, unconsciously or by design, so to define the context in which the party's members make their choices that the apparent risks involved in opposing the leadership are emphasized. The ambiguity of risk also places a premium on being close to the centers of communication within the legislative party, for to be "in the know" concerning impending events in and outside the Congress is to be better prepared to minimize the risks they may imply. In consequence, the influence of one who, like the Floor Leader, occupies a position at the center of such communication can hardly fail to be enhanced.[5]

---

[4] The implication desired here is that of a relation that is dependent upon "outside" influences and hence is derivative and supplementary rather than direct and inclusive. As applied to a group, "mediate" obviously must be a term of degree. In justification of this excursion into the coining of labels, note that neither the sociologists nor the social psychologists concerned with "group dynamics" have developed a satisfactory typology of groups and that, in particular, they have paid relatively little attention to identifying variations in the characteristics of groups dependent on differences in their settings and their functional relations with other groups in the society. Robert K. Merton (*Social Theory and Social Structure*, revised edition, Glencoe, Illinois: The Free Press, 1957, pp. 308–326) has developed a suggestive "provisional list of group-properties." Most relevant to the concept of the mediate group are those he labels as "degree of engagement of members in the group," "degree of expected conformity to norms of group," and "autonomy or dependence of the group."

[5] Presumably much the same inference is to be drawn from the apparent value of belonging to what William S. White calls "the Inner Club" in the Senate (*Citadel*, New York: Harper, 1957, chap. 7). Voorhis makes the same point in discussing the "select circle" in the House. "I confess," he says, "to having had a deep desire to have the friendship and understanding — if not the agreement — of certain of these men." (Voorhis, *Confessions of a Congressman*, pp. 31–32.)

Given the mediate function of the Congressional party, the powers of its leaders, especially its principal elective leaders, cannot be expected, except in very small measure, to be formalized, codified, and at all times fully adequate for meeting the vicissitudes of their roles. Rather they are for the most part informal, personal, interstitial, and — somewhat like those of the President — often less extensive than the range of expectations they must meet. For reasons that have already been discussed, there appear to be differences in this respect between the House and Senate party leaders, but in both chambers the influence of the principal leaders depends heavily upon their recurrently improvising effective combinations among fragments of power of the most varied sorts.

A former leader, commenting upon this aspect of the role, reported that he had on occasion persuaded a "lobbyist" whom he knew to be close to a wavering member of his party to influence the latter to vote with the party and its leadership. This testimony illustrates both the mediate character of the party and the kinds of fragments of power on which the elective leader must often rely. The fragment in this instance was formally outside the party group. It thus resembled the kind of leverage with which a President's initiatives may provide a Majority Leader, for clearly the leader of a mediate group, who almost by definition ranks little above his colleagues, must, if he chooses to perform his role with maximum effectiveness, avail himself of any outside resources that may be converted into influence within the legislative party.

This potential of presidential initiatives as leverage for the leadership of the Congressional party has already been referred to in discussing the relations of the President and the leaders of his Congressional party in terms of convergence of interdependent sets of leader-follower relations. The basic point is that the imperatives of the Presidency and the peculiarities of leadership in a Congressional party with the characteristics of a mediate group make collaborative relations between the President and the principal elective leaders of his legislative party functionally useful for both participants.

Illustrations of this utility are not hard to find. A key leader in the House, who has been Majority Leader both when the President was of his party and when he was not, described his efforts under the latter circumstances to negotiate with the standing committee chairmen, individually, in order to develop an agreed program for a Congressional session. When asked whether the President's being of his party made any difference in the performance of this task, the immediate reply was, "Much easier, much easier." [6] A respected and experienced member of the Senate's staff, commenting on his own observation of the relations of Floor Leader and President, noted their tendency toward collaboration

[6] Programming is not equivalent to implementation, as Neustadt has pointed out, but in this context the two may be regarded as closely related. See Richard E. Neustadt, "Presidency and Legislation: Planning the President's Program," *American Political Science Review*, Vol. 49, no. 4 (December 1955), p. 1016.

and emphasized particularly the inclination of Senate elective leaders not only to acquiesce in but to encourage presidential initiatives. He cited the case of a Floor Leader, not publicly known for his dependence on his party's President, who increasingly during his tenure solicited White House intervention with wavering senators in aid of agreed legislative projects.

The utility of the collaborative relation between the President and the leaders of his legislative party is further suggested by the fact that the regular White House meetings of the President and the "Big Four" or "Big Six" of the Congressional parties, meetings which in the past two decades have become a normal feature of governmental operation, provide the most regular contact between President and Congress and the only institutionalized point of meeting for the leaders of the parties in the Senate and House. Other communication between them takes place, of course, but apparently more casually and in a more restricted context. The White House meetings are not highly formalized, their results normally are not recorded except in the limited replies to inquiries from the press or in accounts of later discussions in the policy committees, and there is in the public domain little information concerning precisely how they operate. Some former participants have stated in interviews that at least occasionally the meetings involve considerable give and take and some effort to achieve common ground.

From the standpoint of their value for the performance of the elective leader's role, however, the precise character of the meetings is probably less important than their regular occurrence and the comparative privacy surrounding them. Some reporting of the discussions is usually made in the meetings of the policy committees and other sessions of the legislative party leaders, but if all that occurred in them immediately transpired, their utility would be considerably reduced, both as a locus of genuine negotiation and as a source of leverage for the Congressional party's leaders. The mere fact of the meetings, uniquely composed as they are and normally conducted without even the presence of staff, presumptively gives the Congressional participants "inside" intelligence concerning both the President and the other chamber that, whether communicated subsequently or not, in the context of the mediate group can be a source of influence.[7]

These comments should not be interpreted as suggesting that the elective leaders of the Congressional party do or can have a monopoly of information, especially concerning the President's intentions. Individual seniority leaders, perhaps especially in areas where the President's

---

[7] Informants report a more formalized arrangement during most of the Eisenhower Administration, with attendance at the meetings by the Assistant to the President and the Deputy Assistant to the President, and apparently with minutes taken at least concerning the agreements reached. The effect of this formalization, especially the presence of presidential staff, may be to reduce the utility of the meetings for participants on both sides. One suspects that such alterations would not be acceptable to some Democratic leaders, such as Speaker Sam Rayburn.

prerogatives and responsibilities are large, such as foreign policy, may enjoy a high degree of intimacy. But these are inevitably single areas, however important, and the data on the seniority leaders and the principal elective leaders would support the inference that they probably do not extend very far over the interconnections among all the parts of the legislative program. Moreover, the suspicion is strong that if these relations with the committee chairmen do not supplement but steadily bypass the elective leaders, they may reduce rather than augment the President's influence. Given the tremendous range of demands on his time and energies, to say nothing of the obstacles inherent in the Congressional institution, the President probably cannot successfully attempt to become regularly the direct leader of the Congressional party, working exclusively through the committee chairmen or directly with the rank and file. If this interpretation is correct, Franklin Roosevelt's reliance upon the leaders of the Congressional party and his refusal to bypass them by creating an alternative structure of communication with the Congress showed more wisdom than some of his critics are willing to grant.[8] He could and did attempt to influence the legislative party's choice of elective leaders, but had he not relied upon them, once they were chosen and regardless of whether they were his favored candidates, his effectiveness almost certainly would have been reduced.

Experienced members of both parties testify to the desirability of being "in on things," of knowing what is going on, and the importance of such information is suggested by the regular, but frequently unsatisfied, demands of the more junior members of the rank and file on both sides of the aisle for more meetings of party members. . . . essentially this point was offered in explanation of the functions of the policy committees in the Senate. Those who stand at major junction points in an important communication network may acquire power from that fact alone. Even the appearance of being on the inside, however little it corresponds to reality, may have value for the leadership of a mediate group.

Other things being equal, therefore, the elective leaders of the President's legislative party have a stake in their regular meetings at the White House and a corollary interest in the President's political standing. As leaders, they lose if he loses. Other things, of course, may not be equal. Attachment to the role of elective leader may be less than that to other opportunities and aspirations. Personal and political animosities may be too strong to be submerged in even the semblance of a collaborative effort. Participants on either side may be insensitive to the subtleties of the relation. Or a President's missteps and misfortunes may make association with him an embarrassment rather than a reliance. Proximity to the White House is not the only fragment of power available to the leaders of the Congressional party, and circumstances may reduce it to unimportance despite a general tendency in the other direction.

8 See James M. Burns, *Roosevelt: The Lion and the Fox*, New York: Harcourt, Brace, 1956, pp. 348–350 and *passim*.

The benefits of a fruitful collaboration, however, are not all on one side. They accrue also to the President's account. In the thundering crises that are the normal lot of Presidents in times when "normalcy" exists only in the past, the clock provides no hours for the cultivation of rank-and-file legislators which direct leadership of the Congress would require. But in addition the President is dependent upon the principal elective leaders of the Congressional party in much the same way, if not to the same degree, as are their colleagues on the Hill. If the agenda he sets is to emerge in a product he favors, he must have the information and the means for day-to-day assessment, if not actual guidance, of Congressional activity. The elective leaders wield no monopoly here, but, standing at strategic communication points, they are, for the President much as for their legislative associates, an important source of intelligence, entirely aside from their capabilities as facilitators or obstructors of his program. And on the score of obstruction, the lengths to which as adroit a tactician as Franklin Roosevelt went in 1937 to forestall the selection of an uncongenial Senate Majority Leader are illustrative enough of this aspect of the mutually dependent relation.[9] But the President, save in exceptional instances, must rely on the leaders of the Congressional party. If means exist by which he can do without them on a continuous day-by-day basis, the record does not reveal what they are. Relations with the leaders of the Congressional party can be supplemented, as they often have been, but no substitutes have appeared on which he can rely with equal confidence. To the degree that the mechanism of the Congressional party is relied upon, however, it must be taken as it is, with the leaders it has produced. For a President to attempt to act directly as the leader of the Congressional party almost certainly would be to destroy, for the time being, this valuable, if variable, governing instrument.

To call the relations between the President and the leaders of his Congressional party collaborative and mutually useful is to raise the problem of whether occupants of these legislative positions are to be viewed primarily as "his" or as the leaders of their respective houses and Congressional parties. The formal answer, that their principal loyalties must be toward those whose suffrage they hold, their colleagues in the Congressional party, is not very helpful since it avoids the underlying realities. The question itself would lack point, in fact, if an answer were given categorically either way.

The fundamental complexity and subtlety of the role lie in the fact that the elective leaders are, and probably must be, both the President's leaders and the party's leaders. However, if the analysis developed in these pages is valid, it follows that, in order to be fully effective as leaders of the Congressional parties, they must above all be effective spokesmen for the President; or at least, excepting the most unusual circumstances, they must appear to be his spokesmen. The data on the Floor Leaders in the Eighty-first Congress clearly point in this direction.

9 *Ibid.,* pp. 309, 361–362.

Senator Lucas, it will be remembered, appeared somewhat to the "left" of the center of his party largely because of his position on the Administration support votes, and Representative McCormack apparently went to considerable lengths to avoid being recorded in opposition to the President, even when the overwhelming majority of the House Democrats were opposing the White House. Open opposition to the President — as distinguished, perhaps, from covert failure to press his programs aggressively — apparently was something to be avoided.

The position that support for the President is a pivotal element in the roles of the principal elective leaders of the President's Congressional party is not accepted by some observers, especially as it applies to the Senate. William S. White, whose discerning observations on the upper chamber cannot be dismissed lightly, places chief emphasis on the requirement of loyalty to the views of legislative colleagues. Noting that in the Senate there is little agreement on what a Floor Leader ought to do but a broad consensus on what he ought not to do, White argues that "in all but those rare and comparatively brief periods when it is thrust into the background by extraordinary circumstances" the Senate "expects" that the Floor Leader of the party holding the White House "will not so much represent the President as the Senate itself." At the height of Franklin Roosevelt's prestige, White observes, "there arose a highly oversimplified public notion of the duties of Senate leadership based on the assumption that a leader of Democrats in the Senate *necessarily* owed obedience to a Democratic President. The compulsive actions of the Senate itself . . . for a time had the effect of promoting what the Senate felt to be a profound heresy." [10]

In these comments White correctly calls attention to the element of variability in the role of the Senate leader. The broad discretionary range implied in the expectations composing it, inevitably reflecting changes in the external setting of the legislative party, is unquestionable. The data in these pages amply demonstrate that in attempting to reach an understanding of leadership in the Congressional party one must beware of beguiling absolutes. One must seek central tendencies, not constants. Nor can one quarrel with the proposition that a Leader not in sympathetic communion with his legislative colleagues will in most circumstances fail to perform his functions effectively.

One must acknowledge also a reality of structure and of attitude in the separation of Senate from House and especially of both from the President.[11] The patterns of risk are not the same. They do converge, but

[10] White, *Citadel,* pp. 96–98. Italics in the original.

[11] The restraining impact of this reality is suggested by President Truman in a comment on relations between a President, on the one hand, and the Speaker and Vice President, on the other. "The President cannot afford to have his confidential matters discussed in Senate cloakrooms. A leak from the White House to the Senators and Representatives is always worth a headline, and that compels a President always to be on guard when he is being interviewed by members of Congress. That is also one of the reasons why it is very difficult for a President to take the Vice President completely into his confidence." (Harry S. Truman, *Memoirs,* Vol. I, *Year of Decisions,* New York: Doubleday, 1955, p. 54.)

convergence does not produce identity. Nevertheless, if the findings of this study are in any degree representative, the imperatives of presidential politics produce more than an echo in the Congressional party, and the partisan responses at either end of Pennsylvania Avenue have a detectable mutual resemblance.

Within the Congress the contrasts between the Senate and the House, rooted in differences of risk and in the related factor of the size of the two bodies, are real and perceptible. They supply additional reason for the elective leaders to avoid too open emphasis upon their ties to the President. These contrasts are reflected in the rules of the two chambers, in the relative "visibility" of senators and representatives, in the attitudes of the members and even of the professional staff in one house toward the other, and in a variety of other ways. The two chambers are not totally unlike, but they are quite different groups. In consequence, the legislative parties within them do not impose the same requirements on their leaders, and preservation of the leaders' base of influence assumes sensitivity to these differences in demand.

The disposition of the elective leaders to play down their spokesmanship for the President also follows from the fact that the Congressional party as a mediate group affords its leaders little opportunity for command, in the strict sense. Their influence in either house is only slightly the product of hierarchy and, because the limits on their influence are ambiguous, their power may in fact be more extensive than any of their followers would be willing to grant in a formal delegation of authority. Actions propose definitions, and in a loosely integrated structure — perhaps in any structure — action that explicitly proposes to invoke the outer limits of implied power is likely to fail, and the resulting definition to fall short of what had previously received *de facto* acknowledgment.[12] If the elective leaders only rarely can command, they also can publicly commit their followers to a given action only after elaborate preparation.

An instance that can be interpreted as illustrating the caution imposed on the leaders of the legislative party by the requirements of their roles was provided by the events surrounding the creation of a Democratic advisory committee following the election of 1956. Meeting shortly after the election, in which the Democrats retained control of the Congress despite a landslide victory for President Eisenhower that included marked gains in most of the large metropolitan areas, the executive committee of the Democratic National Committee decided to create an advisory committee to develop a legislative program for the party. Early in December Chairman Paul Butler named twenty members to the group, including the seven principal elective leaders in both houses: from the Senate, Majority Leader Lyndon Johnson, Whip Mike Mansfield, and Chairman of the Campaign Committee George Smathers; from the House, Speaker Sam Rayburn, Majority Leader John McCormack, Whip Carl Albert,

[12] This appears to be the real significance of the "overthrow" of Speaker Joseph Cannon in 1910–1911.

and Campaign Committee Chairman Michael Kirwan. Despite some press reports that Butler's invitations were merely a formality and that acceptance had been assured before the list was announced, within ten days all seven of these leaders declined to serve. Since the movement for the committee was known to have been sponsored by the national committeemen from California, Pennsylvania, and Illinois, and since some of its proponents presented it as an effort to produce a "liberal" legislative program and, at least by implication, to bypass the Congressional leadership, interpretations of Mr. Butler's somewhat comic embarrassment almost inevitably talked about "liberals" against "conservatives" in the party and about challenges to the Congressional leaders.

Although party factions and the status of the Congressional leaders obviously were relevant, the debacle can be interpreted in quite different terms. Even if the seven leaders of the Congressional party were in sympathy with the substantive objectives of the movement, which is well within the realm of the possible, and even if the preliminary arrangements had been made more adroitly so that the announcement could have come as the result of negotiations between the National Committee and the Congressional leaders rather than as a proposal from the Committee to the legislative leaders, Messrs. Johnson and Rayburn and their associates would have been ill advised to enter the group.

For if its decisions were made public, as the proposals of the subsequently reconstituted committee have been, the leaders of the Congressional party would have assumed a position of command that they may have by implication and after maneuver and negotiation but that they can rarely announce in open forum. Even after conferences with the President the leaders of his legislative party, though they may head a majority, normally avoid specific public commitments about what the Congressional party will do. Rather they report what the President wants and indicate an intent to help get it for him if they can. What they do not do as spokesmen for the White House they clearly cannot appear to do as members of a group created by the National Committee.

Matters would not be much different if the decisions of such an advisory committee were not made public. In their negotiations within the Capitol the principal elective leaders would not seem to be speaking in the comfortably ambiguous name of an unspecified "party" majority composed of colleagues similarly situated and with equivalent political risks, nor would they be speaking for a President with at least contingent claims upon their support. Rather they would appear to be acting for an "outside" agency without status or legitimacy.[13]

In either case, with or without publicity, the party leaders recurrently

13 Even when acting on behalf of the President, a Congressional leader cannot afford to appear to be speaking exclusively to rather than from his colleagues. Thus after the Eighty-third Congress (1953–1954) the view was common on Capitol Hill that Representative Martin was stronger in the House than Representative Halleck, who, as Majority Leader, had become so completely and so dogmatically a spokesman for the Administration that he had lost some of his effectiveness in the House.

would be placed in a position, whether justifiably or not, of asking or commanding without success. Given the mediate character of the legislative party and its attendant factionalism, commitment of the party by the elective leaders normally must follow internal negotiation, not precede it, and, if negotiation fails, the leaders will be better off in most cases if they are not too frequently and openly identified with the losing side. In his dealings with the Congress, a President may be able without net loss to make public demands that are repeatedly denied by the legislature, if he makes compensating gains within the electorate. The leaders of the Congressional party are not situated in the same way. Repeated failure of their public initiatives, even if enunciated in the name of the President, is more likely to destroy them entirely. They can, as Senator Johnson did in declining membership on the advisory committee, invite the views of an "outside" group, but if these views commit the leaders, the implied initiatives are likely to produce a restricted rather than a broadened definition of their power.[14]

The two requirements, that the principal elective leaders of the Congressional party support a President of their own party and that they function as the spokesmen for their colleagues in the Congress, are not always cleanly compatible. At the same time it seems clear that they are generally interdependent, in the sense that representing the President provides a focus and part of the leverage for leadership of the Congressional party, and sympathetic reflection of the problems of legislative colleagues is an essential in advancing the President's program. One or the other element may be more conspicuous from time to time. Apparently, moreover, the Congressional base is generally nearer the surface; it is more openly expressed. But the element of support for the Administration is normally present, if only implicitly and though often reflected in ambivalent terms.

The implicitly acknowledged interdependence of these two features of the role and the resulting ambivalence concerning them, especially in the case of the Floor Leader, can be easily illustrated. They are evident, for example, in estimates of the special hazards associated with the position. When a number of senators, representatives, and staff people were asked whether they felt a Floor Leader ran any special risks, the almost unanimous response was in the affirmative, the normal explanation being that as Leader he was obliged to act and to vote as he would not act and would not vote if he were an ordinary member of the Congress.

The typical illustrations for this reply were the cases of Majority Leader Lucas and Majority Whip Myers, both of whom failed to be re-elected in 1950, and the case of Majority Leader McFarland, who was defeated in the election of 1952. There may well be doubt whether

[14] This account is based on the reports and interpretations published in the *New York Times* for November 28, December 6, 13, 14, 19, and 23, 1956, and January 16, 1957. It should not be construed as a negative assessment of the utility of the reconstituted committee, but only of the original plan to include the Congressional party leaders.

holding these positions and being identified with the Administration in fact contributed significantly to the defeat of these men. The important point is that in and around the Congress a strong belief persists that this was the case. There is evidence that Senator Lister Hill for just this reason was persuaded, after the departure of Lucas, not to become Majority Leader, as he might easily have done. The choice of McFarland, although undoubtedly it owed much to the sponsorship of Senator Russell, can be traced in part to the reluctance of more vigorous members of the party to accept a post that would inevitably involve representation of an Administration increasingly regarded as a political liability.

The criticism of McFarland as Senate Majority Leader in the Eighty-second Congress and even some of the explanations of his shortcomings illustrate the ambivalence concerning the dual aspects of the role.[15] The Arizona Senator, though personally popular, was regarded as insufficiently aggressive, as unable to be "tough" with his colleagues. But in extenuation it is said that, even had he chosen to be less complacent, McFarland could not have been much more effective because of the declining prestige of President Truman. In other words, he was expected to be aggressive, and the basis for such behavior normally would be the White House program.

The conflicts, ambiguities, and ambivalences in the role of the Senate Majority Leader are particularly well illustrated by the case of Senator Knowland in the Eighty-third Congress and especially in 1954. In February, 1954, Knowland spoke and voted against President Eisenhower's position on the so-called Bricker amendment to the Constitution, which proposed to place restrictions on the treaty power. During the summer he advocated a declaration that the United States would withdraw from the United Nations if the Communist government of China were admitted to membership and also called for breaking diplomatic relations with the Soviet Union. Finally, in November he called for a Congressional review of the Administration's entire policy in the "cold war." [16]

These actions provoked a good deal of comment. The press carried reports of intense resentment in the White House, of suggestions that Knowland should resign as the Republican Leader, and even of rumors that he would resign.[17] Commenting on these responses, White says that ". . . men very high in the Eisenhower Administration honestly felt that Senator Knowland of California simply had no *right* as the Republican leader to denounce Administration policy on China. The Senate itself has been wholly unimpressed; . . . Knowland, . . . far from overextending his credit in the Institution as Republican leader, became in a way ever more acceptable to it during the Eisenhower years." [18]

---

15 Compare White, *Citadel,* p. 106.

16 A good summary of these events and the text of Senator Knowland's speech demanding a review of foreign policy appeared in the *New York Times,* November 16, 1954.

17 *New York Times,* July 1, November 17 and 21, and December 2 and 3, 1954.

18 White, *Citadel,* p. 98.

Criticisms of Knowland were not confined to "outsiders," however. In an interview some time later a former Senate Majority Leader, albeit a Democrat, stated flatly that he would have resigned as Floor Leader if he felt that he could not get along with a President of his own party, especially on a matter of foreign policy. Knowland himself, moreover, said that he would resign his post if the Administration ever granted diplomatic recognition to the Communist government of China. By this statement, as Arthur Krock noted in the *New York Times,* the Republican Senate Floor Leader conceded implicitly "that there are limits to the usefulness of a party leader in Congress who opposes a major policy of a President of that party." [19]

More significant than this implied acknowledgment by Knowland of the dual character of his role was the dramatically explicit gesture that the Republican Leader made early in this series of events. This came after the Bricker amendment had been altered by the Senate's adopting changes proposed by Senator Ferguson and acceptable to the President and by its passage of alterations sponsored by Senator George that were not approved by the White House. Just as the final roll call was about to be taken on the modified Bricker resolution, when, after five weeks of debate, senators were calling for a vote, Mr. Knowland exchanged desks with Senator Saltonstall, the Republican Whip, and addressed the chair:

> Mr. President, I know the hour is growing late, and I do not wish to detain the Senate. . . .
> I have left the desk of the majority leader because I wish to make it very clear that what I say is not said as majority leader, but is said in my capacity as an individual Senator of the United States. . . .
> So far as I know, the President of the United States has not changed his view that the only amendments acceptable to the administration were those which were presented by the distinguished Senator from Michigan [Mr. Ferguson]. . . . I say that in order that there may be a clear understanding that there has been no change in the situation, and in order that no Senator may vote under a misapprehension.
> I have left the desk of the majority leader because I feel that I have an obligation, while speaking in my individual capacity, to make that very clear.[20]

He then went on to an account of his prolonged efforts at reaching a compromise satisfactory to the President and to the sponsors of the measure, explained his concern over the issue, and announced that he would vote for the resolution.

Although Senator Knowland did not repeat this gesture in his later estrangements from the President — when no votes were involved — he

19 *New York Times,* May 3, 1955. Krock added that the chief difference between Knowland and his critics was that they thought these limits had already been passed.
20 *Congressional Record,* 83d Cong., 2d sess., 100:2 (February 26, 1954), 2371.

here clearly demonstrated the point that, subject to some variations in the conceptions of individual incumbents, the role required him to be also the President's leader if he was to be the Senate party's leader.[21]

These are requirements of the Leader's role, but the precise definition of those requirements lies within the discretion of the man performing it at the time. His background, his skills, his energy level, and his own policy preferences will determine his conception of the role and, in general, his effectiveness in performing it. He may easily be satisfied with exploiting the potentialities of the role at a minimal level, especially if the President's own skills in this realm are not an inducement to vigorous activity.

It is also possible that practice, resting on convention alone rather than on a full appreciation of possibilities, encourages performance at levels well below the full potential. Thus the data on the importance of the state delegations in the House . . . raise the question whether the influence of these intradelegation relations reflects a sort of power vacuum within the party or rather an inevitable restriction on the influence of the leaders. The data of the present study will not permit an adequate answer to this question, but, to the extent that the unity of the delegations is a response to ambiguity in the House rather than to claims from the constituency — and some of the evidence points in the former direction — it may indicate a failure of the leaders to realize the full potential of their roles.[22]

Some circumstantial evidence carries the same implication. Interviews with representatives in both parties indicate that communication of the policy preferences of the party leaders is frequently badly timed, inadequate, and ambiguous. Representatives on one side of the aisle, more-

21 The Knowland example sharpens the implications of Senator Barkley's resignation as Majority Leader following Franklin Roosevelt's veto of the 1944 tax bill, for the implied relations were not clear on the face of that incident. Barkley's vigorous speech of denunciation was in response to what he regarded as a gratuitous insult to the Congress, yet in discussing the case later he referred to himself as "the Administration's floor leader" and expressed his conviction that he was obliged to resign in the event of a "fundamental and irreconcilable disagreement with the President." (Alben W. Barkley, *That Reminds Me,* New York: Doubleday, 1954, p. 173.) Roosevelt's action undermined Barkley's value as the Administration's leader by treating him, implicitly, as exclusively that. Barkley's resignation and immediate re-election as Majority Leader restored the emphasis on his ties to his colleagues and re-established the dual relationship, though not, apparently, in identical form. Illustrations such as these occur more readily in the Senate than in the House in part because of the circumstances that make the Leader's behavior in the upper chamber more conspicuous. Since in the House the Speaker does not vote and neither he nor the Majority Leader takes as open and prominent a part on the floor as does the Senate Leader, their positions are less obvious and their apparent commitments more ambiguous. There is every reason to assume, however, that duality is as central to a definition of their roles as it is in the Senate.

22 H. Bradford Westerfield, *Foreign Policy and Party Politics: Pearl Harbor to Korea,* New Haven: Yale University Press, 1955, pp. 92 and *passim,* offers the opinion that House Democratic leaders did not utilize the full resources of their positions.

over, many of whom have served several terms in the House, support this point implicitly by exaggerating the quality of performance on the other. Though an adequate sample has not been taken, scattered testimony indicates that many Republican legislators regard the Democrats as better organized and more aware of their leaders' policy views than are those on their own side, and many Democratic legislators have a similar view of the Republicans. These symptoms are hardly conclusive, but, if they are reliable, they suggest the possibility that the roles of the elective leaders may one day, as a result of the skill and imagination of a single incumbent, break with existing practice and move to a new level of effectiveness. Such a level, once achieved, would likely remain the norm, even for less talented successors, as long as the underlying conditions remained unchanged. A Lyndon Johnson, under whom the office of Floor Leader apparently became a clearance point for the whole Senate party to an unprecedented degree, might, after long occupancy of the position, bequeath to his successor a role whose dimensions had been materially altered.

Whatever the extent of the gap between performance and potentiality, it is important to emphasize that these inferences concerning the role of the principal elective leaders, especially in their relations with the White House, do not and almost certainly could not span the whole range of the legislative agenda. Inevitably they refer to major items and to leading proposals. Most of what is routine, uncontested, or only narrowly controversial — probably the bulk of Congressional business — and some of what is highly explosive is left to the committees, their chairmen, the executive departments and agencies, and the relevant interest groups, except as one of the elective leaders may have a personal stake in them. Within these circles, of course, commitments and prerogatives become established, and, as in almost any complex organization, intervention from unaccustomed quarters in matters that have suddenly been projected from the obscurity of custom into the center of controversy may provoke resistance that places restrictions on any leadership, even if it has the prestige of presidential endorsement.

The Congressional party, in the form of the President's majority, is a governing instrument of great, possibly growing, value, but it is important to remember that it is not the only mechanism for determining legislative action. The structure described and analyzed in these pages demonstrates that the Congressional party has meaning as a system of relations extending over a wide range of the voting behavior in both Senate and House. But, as the cleavages on the low-cohesion votes indicate and as the material . . . on the state delegations testifies, there are other patterns of Congressional action in which the mechanism of the legislative party plays no part or only a minor one. Coalitions and alliances, operating *ad hoc* or more or less continuously through the leadership of particular committee chairmen, along lines of sectional and interest-group affiliation, are a normal feature of the Washington scene, and they may provide patterns of action entirely outside those of the legislative party on matters of grave importance.[23] The Congressional party, however, is a system of relations at least as important as these and probably more lasting than any of them.

PERPLEXED MINORITIES AND TRUNCATED MAJORITIES

The explanatory comments offered in the preceding pages have dealt with the majority Congressional party whose presidential candidate occupied the White House. What can be said of the minority? What, further, can be conjectured about a "truncated" Congressional majority, one without partisan ties to the President? And what about the legislative party that is in the minority on Capitol Hill but is "in power" in the White House? The data of the Eighty-first Congress, of course, bear on only the first of these questions, but, assuming the validity of the broad scheme of explanation offered in this chapter, it should be possible to suggest answers to the others.

The conspicuous characteristics of the minority Congressional party in the Eighty-first Congress have been described in earlier chapters and need not be repeated in detail here. In general the Republican structure in both houses was more fluid, at times almost kaleidoscopic, in appearance. This fluidity was paralleled by a lower rate of agreement among the principal elective leaders of the minority and by much less evidence of accommodation between the Republican Floor Leaders and the several seniority leaders than appeared on the Democratic side. The latter peculiarities may have been primarily a consequence of the personalities and skills of the Minority Leaders, but the similar behavior of Senator Taft and Representative Halleck suggests, among other things, that, though personal differences were not wholly irrelevant, if accommodation were to occur it had to be through the Floor Leader. Its absence reflected less urgency among the minority and less opportunity to effect agreement.

In other words, the minority Congressional party, out of power in the White House, seems to have encountered special obstructions to coherent and programmed voting behavior. Since the minority were limited in their influence upon the agenda, program — as distinguished from isolated efforts on a small number of issues — was of little or no relevance for them. This conjecture is consistent with the apparent fact that the minority party in the Senate was able to function without conspicuous evidences of internal conflict although its Floor Leader, Senator Wherry, inadequately satisfied what would seem to be one of the basic requirements of the role, a middle position in the voting structure of the party. It also helps in interpreting the kinds of disagreements that occurred between the House Minority Leader and, respectively, the Whip and the ranking member of the Rules Committee. These would not be remark-

[23] David B. Truman, *The Governmental Process*, New York: Knopf, 1951, chaps. 11, 13, and *passim*.

able if there was in the minority a general unconcern with a coherent program.

The suspicion is strong that perhaps the major reason for these Republican peculiarities in the Eighty-first Congress was that the minority Congressional party and its principal leaders reflected, but not precisely in reverse, the importance of the White House for the effective working of the legislative group.[24] Given the presidential program, they did not mirror in opposition the pattern of the majority. . . . Presidential initiatives distinguished minority from majority, but not in exact opposition presumably in part because the Minority Leaders lacked the leverage supplied by partisan association with the President, though they shared with their colleagues of the majority the agenda provided by the White House.

The nature of the Presidency itself probably contributes to the awkward position of the minority leaders. For the President of the United States is not, and is expected not to be, merely a partisan figure. Some Presidents more and some less, but all to a degree, speak for and to the nation as a whole. When they do, they increase the relative strength of their own Congressional leaders and threaten that of the opposition leaders, who normally lack not only most of the means of developing an alternative program but also the leverage of an alternative "outside" source of legitimacy. In a substantive area, notably foreign affairs, in which the propriety of presidential initiative is generally conceded, this predicament of the minority is particularly evident, as others have noted.[25] This view of the minority helps to explain as well both the frequency with which the seniority leaders on the Foreign Affairs and Foreign Relations Committees disagreed with the Minority Leaders and also the frequency with which the rank-and-file Republican members of those committees supported the seniority leaders on those disagreements.

The effect of the President's position on the Minority Leader's ability or inclination to establish a successful alternative program makes understandable the curious pattern of Representative Martin's top scores. . . . Apparently Martin's kind of "middle" position was acceptable to a fair proportion of the more senior members of the minority and those elected at the midpoint of a Democratic President's term — or at least his preferences resembled theirs — but it was less acceptable to those elected for the

[24] It is worth noting that in these respects the minority wing of the majority party bore a resemblance to the minority party. Especially in the House, its structure showed similar symptoms of fluidity and presumably for comparable reasons. Except in policy areas such as those involving race relations, it seems to have lacked a legitimizing focus for opposition, with the result that variously composed splinters of the wing broke off from it, and the remaining segment of the wing showed a changing membership from one issue to another.

[25] For example, George L. Grassmuck, *Sectional Biases in Congress on Foreign Policy*, Baltimore: The Johns Hopkins Press, 1951, pp. 134–136, 172 and *passim*, demonstrates the tendency for a Congressional party without a President in the White House to shift its position on foreign policy matters when it becomes the President's party, and he argues that the minority lacks the focus provided by the President's foreign policy program.

first time in recent presidential years. The latter stood a good deal to the "left" or "right" of the Minority Leader in their voting on Administration issues. Unlike their Democratic counterparts, they could not respond to the structuring influence of a known President and a known program bearing their partisan label. Lacking the leverage of the White House, Martin was unable, or disinclined, to develop a substitute focus within the minority party.

These tendencies of the Republican minority probably were accentuated by the circumstances of the Eighty-first Congress. Had these been different, this particular minority's behavior might not have shown the assumed general tendencies so conspicuously. In the first place, the relative size of the Congressional minority almost certainly was a matter of some importance. A tiny minority, confined to a few constituencies in which it held unchallenged supremacy, would be likely to show a somewhat more structured voting pattern. In the Eighty-first Congress, the Republican contingent in the House was not remarkably small, and in the Senate it held more seats than in the last Congress in which it had been a minority (1945–1946).[26]

Second, though there are apparent limits to what can be accomplished by a minority leadership deprived of the political assets of the White House, a dedicated and skilled leadership acceptable to almost all factions of a party plainly can do much toward checking looseness in the voting structure, and its absence can have the opposite effect. In the Eighty-first Congress the Republicans, especially in the Senate, were not blessed with great skill on the part of their principal elective leaders.

Third, the immediate political conditions and the issues confronting a particular Congress clearly make a difference in the performance of any legislative party. A minority demoralized by an unexpected electoral defeat, as the Republicans apparently were after 1948, and confronted with a series of issues that are controversial within the party because they are connected with disputed explanations of the defeat, is certainly likely to show more fluidity in its voting structure than a party that is assured and confident that the issues are working in its favor.

Finally, the way in which the majority's President and his associates exploit the issues and influence the legislative program may contribute to the fractionation and fluidity of the minority while at the same time favorably affecting the structure and coherence of the majority. Whatever may be said of its skill, the Administration during 1949 and 1950 was unmistakably aggressive in its demands upon the Congress, and many of the issues it raised, not only in the realm of foreign policy, but on the domestic front as well — public housing, social security extension, minimum wage increases — scarcely contributed to the coherence of the minority.

It seems likely, however, that the tendencies of the minority Congres-

---

[26] There had been more House Republicans in the 78th, 79th, and, of course, the 80th Congresses, but the number elected in 1948 was larger by 9 seats than the number chosen in 1940 (77th Congress). In the Senate there were 9 fewer Republicans than there had been in the 80th Congress, but 4 more than in the 79th.

sional party are considerably altered when its candidate has successfully gained the White House. At any rate, the logic of the general explanation offered in these pages suggests that inference. Provided that it has not been temporarily discredited and that its occupant does not entirely neglect the opportunity to set the legislative program, the Presidency should be a source of leverage to the minority's leaders even though their position does not permit exercising control over the precise schedule of the Congress or influence upon the timing of reports from committees and the form in which bills are reported. Depending on the skill of the leadership in both legislative parties, as well as on that in the White House, the responses of the minority in these circumstances would be expected to resemble those of a party in the majority at both ends of Pennsylvania Avenue. Testing this expectation lies outside the scope of the present study, but, as comments in earlier chapters have suggested, there were signs of behavior in the Eighty-fourth Congress (1955–1956) consistent with the hypothesis. For example, the frequent meetings of the Republican Policy Committees in both houses and their evident importance as centers of communication testified to President Eisenhower's role as a focus for the Congressional minority.

By the same token, a truncated legislative majority, nominally dominant in the Congress but facing a President of the other party, should display much of the same unprogrammed, fluid appearance identified here in the case of the Congressional minority. During the 1948 campaign President Truman vigorously denounced the Republican Eightieth Congress for its alleged "do-nothing" record. The charge was, of course, exaggerated, but it was not wholly unwarranted. If, moreover, the line of analysis pursued in this chapter is valid, any Congress situated as the Eightieth was, that is, any Congress in which the majority is truncated, is likely to appear as a "do-nothing" body. Between 1930 and 1959 there were four such Congresses: the Seventy-second (1931–1933), in which the Republicans had a nominal Senate majority but were in a clear minority in the House, the Eightieth, the Eighty-fourth (1955–1956), and the Eighty-fifth. The political situation confronting the majority in each of these was, of course, somewhat different, but they all seem to have shared the dual characteristic of being unable to make use of the President's initiatives and being unable, or at least disinclined, to develop a coherent alternative program. Ineffectiveness rather than unified opposition is likely to characterize a truncated majority. The Seventy-second Congress suffered from the special peculiarity that party control was not the same in both houses. Its record, moreover, was written in another era of American government; and its closing months were those of a "lame-duck" legislature, unresponsive to the President and as yet not guided by the President-elect. In the absence of compelling initiatives from the White House, it produced many proposals, but no program.[27]

[27] Arthur M. Schlesinger, Jr., gives an excellent account of these years in *The Crisis of the Old Order*, Boston: Houghton Mifflin, 1957, chaps. 25, 26, 34, and 35.

The Republican majority in the Eightieth Congress, the first since the Hoover landslide of 1928, was supremely confident, as its Democratic counterpart had been in 1931. The election of 1946 was regarded generally in the country as a repudiation of the Administration. President Truman was a mere place holder for the Republican who would surely occupy the White House in January, 1949. His initiatives thus could be ignored with impunity, though in fact they were not entirely passed over, even in the domestic sphere. This was the Congress that supported the so-called Truman Doctrine, designed to keep Greece and Turkey from falling into the Soviet sphere, and gave effect to the Marshall Plan for European economic recovery. In the domestic field it is usually associated with the passage of the Taft-Hartley Act over a presidential veto, but it also voted a token anti-inflation measure in response to the President's demand for a strong program which included selective wage and price controls. During its critical second year, however, the Eightieth Congress was bombarded, both in its regular second session and in the special session convened after the two national party conventions, with a steady succession of demands dealing with both foreign and domestic policy. It was the limited response to these that became the target of the President in the 1948 campaign.

Though the response was limited, the important point in the present context is that there were efforts within the Congressional majority to develop and enact an alternative program. In particular, Senator Taft, as Chairman of the Senate Majority Policy Committee, sponsored and secured Senate passage of a comprehensive housing bill and one extending Federal aid to education. Neither, however, was passed in the House. As one perceptive observer has noted, ". . . the cumulative impact of these messages [from the White House] — indeed of the whole Truman offensive — would have been very considerably diluted had not the House leadership frustrated Senator Taft's own program for Congressional achievement. . . ." [28] The fact of the Ohio Senator's aspirations to the Republican nomination in 1948 complicates but does not otherwise alter the inference that a truncated Congressional majority lacked an effective focus, an "outside" point of leverage sufficient to produce a coherent, programmed performance.[29]

The Democratic majority that took over in January, 1955, was in a highly ambiguous position, since the midterm elections of 1954 by no means indicated a diminution in President Eisenhower's prestige. It had in the House the familiar leadership of Rayburn and McCormack and in the Senate Lyndon Johnson, one of the new virtuosos of legislative maneuver. Almost at once, however, and particularly in the House, an absence of policy guidance was noted by members of the majority whose

---

[28] Richard E. Neustadt, "Congress and the Fair Deal," *Public Policy*, Vol. 5, Cambridge: Harvard University Press, 1954, p. 364, n. 20.

[29] In an interview, one of the key leaders in the House volunteered the judgment that, lacking the advantages of the White House, the inability of the Republican leaders to develop a program for the Eightieth Congress was a major factor in the debacle of 1948.

service dated back six years or more but who were not yet high in the formal hierarchy of the party. By comparison with their experience in earlier Congresses in which the Democrats had been in the majority, they received little communication on what the "party program" was. Several of them were inclined in interviews to attribute this to the leaders' having grown accustomed to a Democrat in the White House, but to an outsider the parallel to other truncated Congressional majorities is more impressive.

In the Senate, Majority Leader Johnson exerted his energies toward an accommodation among the dissident Democratic elements. As White describes the effort, Johnson's ". . . first necessity was to find *some* areas upon which all could agree, and these areas when found, were necessarily somewhat thin, sometimes rather dusty with age, and always deeply traditional." [30] Noting that as these efforts at unifying the Senate Democrats succeeded, members of the party outside the Senate began to complain of the unaggressive performance of the Senate majority and of its apparent reluctance to do battle with the Administration, White continues:

> The non-Senatorial Democrats began to make complaint that Democratic unity in the Senate was all very well; but what of the millions of non-Senatorial Democrats as against the few in the Institution? What of the national, the state, the county and city and ward organizations? What sort of record was being made in the Senate for these sinews, these repositories of the blood and guts, of the party? Who could win a campaign in '56 on co-operation? [31]

White's principal explanation of this performance, which he thinks involved a more than ordinary amount of bipartisan accommodation, is that Johnson, partly unconsciously but partly by design, was reestablishing and even extending the Senate's "historic claim" to an "independent political life." [32] There is no reason to quarrel with this explanation. The reality of the Senate as a group and as an object of loyalty is clear. But, granting this point, one may yet inquire whether it was the only or even the major factor, especially as the House majority presented much the same appearance. Many motives could be assigned to Johnson in the situation and many undoubtedly were guiding him, but, although he was probably not guilty of an excess of zeal for the national party record, it is clear that his range of alternatives was narrow. A new Majority Leader, relatively junior in Senate service, working with a divided party and the narrowest of majorities, yet ambitious to make a record, would not have been very impressive in a policy of relentless attack upon a popular Administration. But, given the nature of the Senate party and particularly, perhaps, the Democratic party, any Leader of a truncated majority who was more disposed toward positive action than toward obstruction or inaction would have been pushed toward a moderate position because

---

30 White, *Citadel*, p. 103.
31 *Ibid.*, pp. 103–104.
32 *Ibid.*, pp. 101 ff.

he lacked the outside leverage that would permit his doing otherwise. Even a popular President of the other party could not, except in the most extreme sort of crisis, adequately provide such leverage. The main stream of politics in the United States is presidential politics, from Washington to the whistle stops. A legislative leader may not play this game very consciously or with great effectiveness, but he can rarely ignore it to the extent of calling for unity in the Congressional party on the grounds of loyalty to a President who belongs to the other side.[33]

Johnson's "resources," therefore, were concentrated on Capitol Hill. There, even had he not had political and personal ties to the Southern wing of the party, he could hardly have avoided being drawn toward the Southerners in any effort to develop the semblance of a program likely to be acceptable to most Senate Democrats. The weakness of even this sort of effort at avoiding a "do-nothing" appearance was evident, however, when, in November, 1955, shortly before the opening of the second session of the Eighty-fourth Congress, Johnson announced a thirteen-point "program." Although he apparently felt sufficiently sure of his position in the Senate to make such an announcement, his reach did not go much beyond the north wing of the Capitol. In the House Speaker Rayburn indicated that he had not been consulted about the "program" proclaimed by his Senate colleague.[34] The actors were different, and the setting was not identical, but the situation was reminiscent of the Taft debacle of 1948. These events, moreover, were of a piece with the initial miscarriage of the Democratic National Committee's proposal at the opening of the Eighty-fifth Congress to include the leaders of the Congressional party in an advisory committee created to develop a party program. The negative response from Speaker Rayburn, Senator Johnson, and their immediate associates had its roots in 1957 in the dilemma of the truncated majority; the divergence of Johnson and Rayburn two years earlier had essentially the same source.

[33] Rarely can an opposition leader say, as did the Republican Floor Leader during the House "debate" on emergency banking legislation in March, 1933: "The house is burning down, and the President of the United States says this is the way to put out the fire." (Quoted in Pendleton Herring, *Presidential Leadership*, New York: Farrar and Rinehart, 1940, pp. 57–58.) Moreover, if this analysis of the dilemma of a truncated majority is valid, more than partisan advocacy may be cited in justification of Eisenhower's pleas for a Republican Congress in the elections after 1952. Without a majority of his own persuasion the President lacked a valuable instrument of governing. In this connection it is worth noting that no public or journalistic protests greeted Eisenhower's requests in these campaigns. Since the days of the allegedly widespread criticism of Wilson for the same action in 1918, attitudes apparently have altered. The continuance of truncated majorities in successive elections from 1958 onward, however, would suggest that popular appreciation of the handicaps imposed on a President by a party distribution of this type is still inadequate.

[34] *New York Times*, November 22 and 23, 1955. In the Eighty-fifth Congress the deepening foreign policy crisis after October, 1957, and the onset of economic recession seemed to provide enough leverage to the Democratic Leaders, enough centripetal pressure, to permit the development of a fairly coherent program, but many of the characteristic earmarks of the truncated majority were still evident.

Larry O'Brien Discusses White House Contacts with Capitol Hill

Q. Larry, how do you see the function and scope of the White House liaison?

A. Well, it's certainly developed into an important element, the operation of the White House, when you think back on the history of Congressional relations, the fact that to some extent it was not only non-existent White House-to-the-Hill in the days of Wilson and through a period following President Wilson we had the situation of no rapport between the two branches of Government. They seemed to be at cross purposes, and in the era of Roosevelt, the first hundred days, of course, a massive legislative program was enacted. The situation at the moment called for it, and following that, however, after the so-called "court-packing" period, there was a slackening off again in this area. I think this went on to a considerable extent until a point in the Eisenhower Administration, where it was, if you will, reformalized and put on a departmental level in the White House.

With us, of course, it was the problem that we were faced with after the 1960 election, while we had secured the White House; nevertheless, we lost 21 seats. Solid, voting Democrats had been defeated in the '60 election, and it was immediately apparent that we were going to have great difficulties. So we had to take a very close look at the type of operation we might put into effect, and what procedures we could follow. We were hard put to it — the realities of the situation were that the New Frontier Program was massive, and we were in a tight bind in the Congress, particularly in the House.

So my view now in the fifth legislative year I've been in the White House is that it has been awfully productive to us. It really made an impact on the program, and I think finally it has been determined that within the Constitutional limitations, it is feasible and proper to have a close rapport with the Legislative Branch of Government; that this

Reprinted by permission from *Congressional Quarterly Weekly Report* for week ending 7/23/65, Vol. XXIII, no. 30, pp. 1434–1436. © 1965 Congressional Quarterly, Inc. [This article is a] transcript of a television interview in which one of President Johnson's key assistants discussed the role of the Administration in initiating and lobbying for legislation in Congress. The interview was with Lawrence F. O'Brien, special assistant to the President for Congressional affairs; O'Brien has served in the post since the beginning of the Kennedy Administration. The National Educational Television Network produced the show, titled "From the White House to the Hill," as part of its series entitled "The Changing Congress." The program was shown on the NET network the week of July 11. The complete interview with O'Brien is printed . . . not all of the material was used in the television program. Paul Duke, a reporter for NBC, conducted the interview.

doesn't in any sense violate the constitutional provisions or the historic concept, if you will, of the relationship of the two branches. It's just the human element is present, as it is in all activities in life, and the closer the relationship, the better the understanding, the greater the possibilities of ultimate enactment of the White House proposals.

After all, we recognize that the President proposes, and it is up to the Legislative Branch of the Government to dispose. But certainly there is no known barrier to constantly advocating our program . . . to the people and to the Congress.

So I would have to say that in retrospect — viewing the situation in January '61 and thinking back today to that period — that obviously there has been real progress. I don't think perhaps there's been a five year period in our history similar to the five years here in the White House in this Democratic Administration. I think not only in the number of legislative proposals that have been enacted, but when you look at the substance of these proposals, the far-reaching impact of many of the bills that have been enacted during the period — hopefully will be enacted before this session comes to an end — it all points to a permanancy, I think, in relationships of this nature. It is a department of the White House, it involves a variety of individual contact with Members of Congress, and I must say it's developed into a two-way street up and down Pennsylvania Avenue. There's not any hesitancy I'm able to observe on the part of the Member of House or Senate to contact the White House to discuss matters of mutual interest, nor is there any hesitancy on our part to do the same. And as far as I can determine, it's worked out quite well.

Liaison Office Formalized

Q. You mentioned the formalization of the liaison office under President Kennedy. I think it's quite true. How did he come to do this? How did he come to set up a liaison chief with one man delegated for the House and one man delegated for the Senate under you? Were there any recommendations for this . . . any studies made that this would be a feasible thing to do?

A. There were discussions involving Professor Dick Neustadt and others. I think, however, that the President's judgment to a great extent, as I indicated, was based, if you will, on the political reality of the situation when we moved into this building — that we had a difficult situation ahead of us and just what conceivably could be done about it. And I recall President Kennedy at one time saying to me, "I see a great deal — Members of Congress individually and in groups — we seem to have a great deal of contact with them"; and he said, "I recall my fourteen years on the Hill, and I cannot recall during that fourteen-year period having any direct or meaningful contact with a Member of the White House staff."

Now, when you think about it for a moment, his years on the Hill were split between the House and the Senate — I believe six and eight. And I can see how that would occur, that in that period the concentration contact-wise was pretty much confined to the top leadership, and the average Member, if you will, seniority-wise, probably wasn't exposed to any great extent to this type of contact. And I think it struck President Kennedy that on this end of the Avenue he found that this was a meaningful, daily activity. And when you look at the statistics of contact and realize the extent of his activity, I imagine he thought back to his years on the Hill and wondered just what took place during those years.

But I think if he had been a committee chairman, or had, say, fourteen years plus seniority in one body, perhaps he would have been exposed to the White House contact. But that wasn't the case, at least, as he remembered the years, and it intrigued him. And then furthermore, it was, as we have said, rather informal, and it was not departmentalized and placed on the level operationally that it has been placed over the last five years.

And again I feel that there are pluses and minuses in the views of observers, some political scientists and others in this activity, but we feel the pluses far outweigh the minuses that conceivably could be conjured up. And I therefore think that as the years go on, this type of contact and relationship will continue — perhaps be further refined — but I think it's here to stay now. It represents an historic breakthrough in this relationship.

Use of Agency Personnel

Q. Well, with a limited staff and more than 500 members, how can you keep up with your job?

A. Well, that entered our minds when we started this operation, but of course there are Congressional liaison chiefs in each department and agency of the Government. Our feeling was that we had to unify this activity, we had to centralize it in the sense that it would be a team effort, and we inaugurated a new procedure. And that is that each department and agency would provide to us by Monday noon of each week a written report of the department's activity with the Congress over the prior week and the projection for the current week.

Now, we take those reports and review them on Monday afternoon and present an analysis to the President for his night reading on Monday, along with a suggested agenda for his use, if he so desires, of the leadership meetings that are held on Tuesday mornings.

In addition, we have these Congressional relations people — there are about forty of them — they're in these key roles in departments and agencies — in periodically to the White House to discuss our mutual legislative problems. And the emphasis constantly is on the President's program, that all elements of this program really in the final analysis are part of a single program, that the downtown in this building . . . the only man I'm aware of who's been elected to office is the President of the United States. And he has proposed to the people what he conceives his program to be. The people made a determination that he should be their President.

Furthermore, you have the Democratic Party Platform, and it is, as we see it, a mandate for action.

So by establishing this team and working very, very closely with these people in the departments and agencies, it gave us additional manpower, and it insured that our activities would be properly channeled for maximum results, and we would not have cross-wires and individuals going off in separate directions and working with the Congress.

Now, President Johnson has emphasized and re-emphasized this, as you know, and on many occasions at Cabinet meetings he re-states his concern about the progress of his program, the Great Society program: his intention that every member of the Executive Branch be involved, the responsibility of the Cabinet member in this area. He has stated to them on several occasions in my presence that no person in his respective department could ever be any more important than the head of the Congressional relations activity. And he places the responsibility directly on the Cabinet member in that regard.

So there is a total awareness that we've developed over these years that as I said is re-emphasized constantly by President Johnson — awareness that this team effort is a continuing, day in and day out effort.

For example, we would anticipate that the Secretary of Agriculture would have a great interest in our education program, although it does not come directly under his activities in his department. Nevertheless, he has friends and associates on the Hill, and he would be an advocate of our educational legislation whenever an opportunity presented itself. And likewise across the board the entire program.

And in addition to that, even here on the White House staff, the special assistants to the President who are working in other areas are under Presidential direction always available to us for assistance and support as we move along through the legislative year. Nothing has a greater priority in the President's view than the legislative program, and I think when you look at the program and analyze it, you can understand that, because we are at this moment engaged in most meaningful legislative activity, again in the field of education — with all the progress that we have made, with the great elementary-secondary education bill that was enacted earlier this year. We still have additional proposals in this area. There will always be an unfinished agenda.

We are still working on our "medicare" program, and our voting rights legislation. And we have several meaningful proposals in the field of health and research. And all of this is so important that you have to bring into focus every element of potential that you can possibly bring in to help promote the program.

'ARM TWISTING . . . DOES NOT EXIST'

Now, they talk about arm twisting and all that sort of thing. And I read these stories with great interest, because this just does not exist. The fact of the matter is that what we have by way of strength, if we do have anything in promoting the program, is the attitude of the average member of Congress toward the President. This has applied to President Kennedy, and it applies to President Johnson, that there is a good feeling on the Hill, if you will, toward the President. There is a realization of his massive problems, there is an attitude of general acceptance of his basic proposals in the legislative area, and therefore we find that doors are open to us. The members are interested in hearing our views, we are equally interested in having their views, and their views are extremely important.

So I think that basically is what you have going for you, to use the vernacular. This suggestion that you trade the bridge or the dam or some project for a vote, and that sort of thing, well, it's just not the case.

I think that we can continue to make progress in this area and our relationships with the Congress if we never lose sight of one important factor (the fellows on the staff here remind themselves constantly of this, and all those in key roles in the Executive Branch remind themselves constantly) that there are on the Hill 535 *elected* officials. They have been elected by the people; they have been in the ballot box, so to speak, and we must recognize this. All of us are appointed, and in our form of government we must constantly be aware of the role of the elected office holder, appreciate his problems, understand his responsibilities. And as long as we continue to have that clearly in mind, we're in no position, nor should we be, nor would we want to be, to dictate in any sense — that this is a matter of firm belief in a program that affects all of America — and that belief in this program is shared generally on the Hill. Individual members have individual views relating to various aspects of the program, but we can work together, and again, we can only propose and advocate. The decision is made on the other end of Pennsylvania Avenue, and we recognize and respect it.

POWERS AVAILABLE; RULES COMMITTEE FIGHT

Q. Well, you certainly have certain powers that you can use to help get your program across. James McGregor Burns once said that a President not only has the right but the duty to use political power in getting his program through, and I recall the instance of 1961 when the Rules Committee fight came along, and the Administration became involved in that. So isn't it true even if there isn't the over-arm-twisting, that every Administration has certain power which it can use? A President can go out and make a speech for a member of Congress, for example.

A. Yes, of course. I think that what you are really saying, however, is that, is the President a strong advocate? Is he firm in his convictions? Is he, therefore, a man that the elected office holders on the Hill respect in the sense that he *is* the nation's leader, elected by *all* the people of the country? And, if they can be sure that he means it, they can be sure that therefore it's in the national interest, and he can persuade, in that context.

I think in the final analysis, that *is* what you have going for you, as I suggested, and I think that you could court disaster in a relationship such as this if at any time the average Member of Congress determined that we were trying to move beyond our constitutional situation, that we felt that the Congress should be a "rubber-stamp" Congress, for example (you hear that reference often). This Congress is not a "rubber-stamp" Congress, I can assure you. And anyone that works with the Congress on the subcommittee and committee level, day in and day out, knows that the independent judgments and views of those Members are expressed without reluctance, and oftentimes we are pressed back a few yards in the struggle. But I think basically they have to be convinced, and that they look to the President for leadership, and I think that many times these decisions are made up on the Hill, when they're very close, on the basis of a feeling of loyalty, desire to support their own leaders on the Hill in the House and the Senate, support the President in his proposals. And you mention the Rules fight of 1961. It was our first struggle, and it was a close one. And as a matter of fact, my recollection is that the vote was postponed twice until we felt we had sufficient troops marshalled. It was a real challenge to us; it was a real test. It was, however, sort of a blessing in disguise, because, having been put through that and winning it, I believe by five votes after a *great* deal of activity on our part and on the part of our leaders on the Hill, it certainly was the evidence that we needed to show what we had suspected was the case. And that is that we were in for a continuing struggle, and all decisions would be made by very, very, very small margins. But also, if we had lost the Rules struggle in '61, obviously the opportunity to have the Kennedy program voted up or down would have disappeared, and you would have seen a Congress spend two legislative years here with no progress.

So a great deal was at stake, and thank goodness we got by that first one, because we wouldn't be able to point with pride, as I think we can legitimately do, to the progress of the last several years, if the first one hadn't been won.

REACTION OF LEADERSHIP

Q. The Administration was heavily involved in the Rules Committee fight right after it came into power in 1961, and you obviously spent a lot of your time on the House side then. What was the reaction of the leadership toward your lobbying activities?

A. Well, of course first of all, this activity was all new to me. And we moved cautiously and carefully. We had to explore reaction. And the distinguished Speaker at that time, Speaker Rayburn, was of course a major point of contact. And I can remember in those early days and weeks as I went to the Hill (being somewhat concerned that we would be accepted, that we would have the freedom of movement in contact with the leadership and the Members, that we would not step on someone's toes), and as I recall those early days, it was not unusual to have a considerable wait to see the Speaker. And I think I was always filled with a certain degree of concern, trepidation, if you will — I found as time went on that there was a warm relationship, one of the great periods of my time here has been in the association that I always remember with Speaker Rayburn. But I must say at the outset I don't know how the Speaker felt about us, but I do know that we were very, very careful not to cross that barrier that we felt existed constitutionally. I don't think we ever have crossed it, but we have found you can talk across it, if you will. You can get together quite easily. But the early days — it wasn't that the Speaker made it difficult — I think we were concerned, nervous about the whole thing, and perhaps the Speaker was wondering a little bit about us, because he hadn't had the experience as a leader up there of having that kind of continuing contact from the White House and the President on down. But it worked out awfully well, and during the Rules fight, of course, it put us to the test, because we had to press. We were awfully concerned; so was the Speaker and the other leaders.

But I think that it was one of the, as I see it, one of the breakthroughs, and I think the awfully warm relationship between President Kennedy and Speaker Rayburn developed over those years, until the Speaker's death, is the best evidence that I have that it worked out without any serious problems coming about.

ROLE OF MEDIA, CITIZENS' GROUPS

But there's another area of contact. We've talked about the departments and agencies, trying to put as vigorous and able a team as you can — numerically strong team into the field from day to day. But of course we have a reliance upon the activities oftentimes of citizens' groups, you might call them. The great trade bill struggle during the course of that period we were aided tremendously by the citizens' group that was established here in Washington and spread throughout the country.

Media is awfully important to us. If the media generally in the country determines to support our position, that of course can be helpful. The trade bill was a good example of the combination of media support, citizen support across the board, which without question made a real impact on that legislation, had a great deal to do with its ultimate passage.

And you have a variety of citizen activity, and many legislative proposals are made by us — bring into action interested groups throughout the country that can be helpful. The business community on the tax cut is another example in that area.

And then we do have a close and continuing relationship with the labor groups here in Washington. They're represented legislatively by former Congressman Biemiller; President Meany of the AFL-CIO maintains a full-time interest in the legislative program. Generally speaking labor is in support of most every — all elements of our program. We have a lot in common, so oftentimes it's really a joint effort, and we're coming into labor legislation a little later on this session, and in the meantime, labor's working closely with (us) on "medicare" and voting rights, and pretty much the entire program, so that a citizens' group, if you will, representing millions of members throughout the country has a continuing relationship with us. But I think all of that is important. And we try to cultivate it, we try to cooperate with these groups, because after all, they are grass roots, and their interests at a given moment mean much to us, and by the same token, the President's interest in their specific problem of the moment means a great deal to them. And so it can be mutually cooperative and helpful.

INFLUENCE OF THE PRESIDENT

Q. Why is the Administration's help needed to get most major legislation through these days?

A. Why, I think that over this five years you have to go back again to a strong President who exerts leadership, who was willing to step out and propose, who was willing to put the weight of his office behind the proposals, who was at all times attempting to encourage the average citizen to join with him. All of this places you, I think, in a much stronger position, because with — the President, after all, gets the attention of the people to a far greater extent than any other leader, and they are interested in his views. They will listen to him. He commands massive audiences on television and radio, and public appearances. And I think that it's an important element in legislative success, the success of the program, to have a President not only advocating initially, but constantly reminding, if you will, everyone of the program and its meaning, and giving proof positive that he is not only proposing, but he is vitally concerned personally.

And that transmits to the public, and in turn, from our point of view, is helpful to us on the Hill, because we have to anticipate that these Members, as I've said before, elected to office, are going to react to the views of their constituency. And that's in the nature of things the way it should be, and we can only hope the constituency view transmitted to them by letter and personal contact will be more often than not our view, and therefore becomes everyone's view.

I think the difference between initiating on the Hill and initiating here is obvious, because the initiation by the President makes for greater impact, greater citizen interest, and consequently, I think ultimately, closer attention on the Hill.

PROBLEMS OF CONGRESSMEN

Q. Larry, one final question. You get hundreds of calls coming in here from Members of Congress. Your office is really a kind of reservoir of complaints and problems. What's a typical problem or complaint you have to deal with?

A. Well, oftentimes a Member has a problem that is serious in his view, because it involves constituent interests. This is a rather massive Government, many departments and agencies and subdivisions, and we find at times we can encourage quicker action, an earlier decision, or perhaps we can express the Presidential view directly to his constituents. It would indicate what his close relationship is to the White House. That type of thing is a daily occurrence. The Member of Congress does not contact us and say: This is important to me; I want it done this way. The contacts we get generally are: Gosh, it's been a long period of time has elapsed. I have a difficult situation, because my constituents can't understand why this decision hasn't been rendered before this. Can you help us move it along to a decision? And also, interestingly enough, during the course of an average day, you have Members who contact us on matters such as — simple matters such as a White House tour.

As you know, we have tremendous numbers of people going through the White House daily. There are tours in the early morning that are conducted that we try to be helpful to Members of Congress, having their constituents join in these tours. And you can understand, the Congressman on the Hill would have half a dozen important constituents arriving in Washington, and he has difficulty setting a schedule for them so they can view the White House at their leisure — that could be an embarrassment to him.

Those things don't sound awfully important, but I mentioned earlier human relations, the human element, and we are constantly aware of the need and the right of the Congressman to receive reasonable service from the Executive Branch. After all, most of those fellows give us great service, because they support the program, and again — always recognize — recognizing they're elected to office. It provides a variety of opportunities here to be of some meaningful service, but as I say, there's no single element of it that is overridingly important, but the over-all activity day to day in putting the package together over a period of years can only hope the Member up there has the view that the White House is interested in him and his problems. That's really — and therefore when we have our problems — we will get favorable reaction at least from the sense of giving us a hearing, seriously considering our viewpoint, if he feels that we in turn understand his problems.

Well, to sum it up, and I think you can succinctly, why let me just say that no one here in this building will ever suggest to a Member of Congress that he commit political hari-kari. That's not the realistic approach to this problem, and as long as we don't reach that point where we feel a Member just must darn well be with us or all bets are off — then, I think that we have good mutual understanding and rapport.

We just have to recognize the problems of the Members of Congress, their constituent, or, if you want to term it that way, political problem. As long as we have a clear understanding of that, and most of us here have been engaged over a long period of time in the political arena, and I think we do have that understanding, and that is the major asset that we have, in my view, in working with them.

THE PRESIDENCY AND
THE EXECUTIVE BRANCH

Presidential Executives or
Congressional Executives?

David B. Truman

The variety of lines of access to the government that have developed through the separation of powers and the clashes and deadlocks that normally occur between the president and the legislature encourage a competition between them for control of the operating agencies of the executive branch. Such a struggle has been fought more or less from the beginning,[1] but as the discretionary powers delegated to administrative units have grown, its importance has increased. The ambiguities of the Constitution are such that there can be constant dispute over whether control of administrative decisions is to take place directly through the authorizing and appropriating functions of the legislature or through the executive power with which the president is vested.

Because the interests that enjoy privileged access to the legislature are not ordinarily the same as those to which the president is most sensitive, the administrative agencies are exposed more or less constantly to competing and frequently incompatible demands. Despite the "awesome terms" in which the formal powers of the chief executive are formally described, he can have no confidence that the conflict will be resolved in his favor.[2] The position of the administrative official is consequently a most delicate one. The bureaucrat may be withdrawn and aloof under some systems, but in the American scene, especially at the national level, he is often as exposed to changes in the pattern of power as any elected official. His position, moreover, may be far more vulnerable. The conflict resulting from what Herring calls "the presidential versus the congressional theory of responsibility for administrative action" may not often be open and declared, since on both sides the consciousness of role implies the imperative of compromise. Nevertheless, the difference between the two

Reprinted by permission from *The Governmental Process*, by David B. Truman, pp. 404–410. Copyright 1951 by Alfred A. Knopf, Inc.

[1] W. E. Binkley, *The Powers of the President* (Garden City, N.Y.: Doubleday, Doran & Company, 1937), pp. 296–8.

[2] V. O. Key, Jr., "Legislative Control," in Fritz Morstein Marx, editor, *Elements of Public Administration* (New York: Prentice-Hall, Inc., 1946), pp. 339, 349.

486

theories "lies like a submerged reef," and the administrator cannot ignore it.[3]

The struggle over which influences shall control administrative agencies is reflected, often very sharply, in the cabinet, though it is by no means confined there. It is inherent in the make-up of the cabinet, for, although nominations to his "official family" are rarely rejected, the president's choices are not free. His selections to head the great "clientele" agencies, such as the Departments of Agriculture, Labor, and Commerce, must be acceptable to the principal interest groups affected, and in some cases are virtually selected by them. The Senate will not necessarily reject a cabinet appointee unacceptable to the affected groups, but both the president and the secretary are likely to suffer unless he is or becomes *persona grata* to these groups. In these and other cabinet appointments the president must satisfy the claims of factions within the coalition that has nominated and elected him. He must recognize the dominant interests in various sections of the country in which an agency's functions are important, as those of the Department of the Interior are to the arid West. Where he wishes to emphasize his role as a unifying national symbol, he may have to include the opposition party, as Franklin Roosevelt did in 1940 by appointing Henry L. Stimson as Secretary of War and Frank Knox as Secretary of the Navy. If the president composes his cabinet exclusively of personal supporters and sympathetic minds, he may secure loyal counsel, but he will sacrifice influence with the Congress and with interest groups.[4]

Consciously or unconsciously the members of the cabinet will "speak for" the elements that have had to be considered in their selection, some as vigorous "members" of these interest groups and others reluctantly as personal adherents to the president's cause. It is not just that different points of view will be expressed, but in many cases competing claims and aspirations will be asserted. Under the circumstances, the cabinet is primarily a means of consolidating the president's political strength and only secondarily an advisory council for the development of policy. Presidents who have aspired to fulfill the expectations focused upon the office and who have been able to meet the requirements of the role have paid little or no attention to the cabinet as a general council. They could not. There are additional reasons why cabinet meetings are so confined to trivialities that they are generally regarded as a waste of time, but the factors that control cabinet appointments are probably the most fundamental.[5]

[3] Herring, "Executive-Legislative Responsibilities," p. 1157. Cf. Norton E. Long, "Power and Administration," *Public Administration Review*, Vol. 9, no. 4 (Autumn, 1949), pp. 257–64; Paul H. Appleby, *Policy and Administration* (University, Ala.: University of Alabama Press, 1949).

[4] Edward Pendleton Herring, *Presidential Leadership* (New York: Farrar and Rinehart, 1940), p. 100. Cf. Key, "Legislative Control," p. 355.

[5] Herring, *Presidential Leadership*, pp. 92 ff.; cf. Henry L. Stimson and McGeorge Bundy, *On Active Service in Peace and War* (New York: Harper and Brothers, 1947), pp. 44, 561–2, and *passim;* Arthur W. Macmahon and John D. Millett, *Federal Administrators* (New York: Columbia University Press, 1939), pp. 4–5.

The president must use his department heads, or rather their influence with legislators and with interest groups, as Lincoln successfully used a cabinet including two men who had been his competitors for the White House. He must compromise and defer as well as dominate, but he cannot be guided by such a motley council. Individually they must have access to him, and such access is valuable. The efforts of various interest groups to achieve cabinet rank for the heads of agencies with which they deal indicates the importance of getting the president's ear even in a formal way. Efforts to achieve departmental status for an agency, however, may be guided quite as much by a desire to achieve independence of the president as by a solicitude for closer integration with his program. The ambiguities concerning the dominance of legislative or presidential control over the administrative agency ordinarily give more room for maneuver to one of cabinet rank than to one of subordinate position.

The continuing, unanswered question of where the responsibility for administrative action shall lie and the expediencies that consequently must guide the president's cabinet appointments turn department heads in varying degrees into political opponents. The institutionalized relationships between an established agency and its attendant interest groups and legislators may make even a personal supporter act as the president's "natural enemy" when he heads a major department. For, as Appleby says of the president: "He acts subject to subordinates dealing directly with Congress and playing off Congressional forces against Presidential power." [6] The situation is an old one. When John Adams retained the cabinet that he had inherited from Washington, he was surrounded by men who felt themselves responsible to the President's political enemy, Alexander Hamilton, then a private citizen. More recent examples are numerous. Henry C. Wallace, Harding's Secretary of Agriculture, "cooperated actively" in the effort of the Farm Bureau and the "farm bloc" of 1921 to force the Administration's hand. In 1942 the Secretary of Agriculture, Claude Wickard, quietly supported a Farm Bureau amendment to pending price-control legislation, although Roosevelt opposed it. Jesse Jones, as Secretary of Commerce and head of the Reconstruction Finance Corporation, operated with almost complete independence of Roosevelt, thanks to his following among important business elements and among the members of the Texas delegation in Congress and their allies.[7]

The president's constitutional power of removal has little relevance to his control over his cabinet. There are no legal limitations upon his power to discharge a department head, whatever restraints may apply to his removing others of his appointees. But if the president is not free to choose whom he will as department heads, he is equally constrained in their removal. Any member of the cabinet who is strong enough with groups in and out of the Congress to act in a fashion independent of the

[6] Appleby, *Policy and Administration*, pp. 113–14. Copyright 1949 by and used with the permission of University of Alabama Press.

[7] Kile, *The Farm Bureau Through Three Decades*, pp. 101–2; Herring, "Executive-Legislative Responsibilities," pp. 1159–60.

president's wishes can be removed from office only at a political price. The opposition of the interest groups and legislators with whom an official is affiliated may make the price too high, unless the president can gain more strength than he loses by the action or unless he can weaken the offending official's following before taking action. Roosevelt did not drop Jesse Jones from the cabinet until there was gossip indicating that the Secretary of Commerce had not supported the national ticket in the 1944 campaign.[8] When Truman asked for Henry A. Wallace's resignation as Secretary of Commerce in 1946, he lost less support in Congress and among interest groups outside than he would have if Secretary of State Byrnes had resigned in protest against Wallace's public statements. But a skillful department head who maintains strong support among the interest groups affected by his agency and among members of Congress can be virtually free to ignore the preferences of the chief executive.

Just as the president cannot use his removal power freely, he cannot take a position on every major controversy over administrative policy, not merely because his time and energies are limited, but equally because of the positive requirements of his position. He cannot take sides in any dispute without giving offense in some quarters. He may intervene where the unity of his supporters will be threatened by inaction; he may even, by full use of the resources of his office, so dramatize his action as to augment the influence he commands. But he cannot "go to the country" too often, lest the tactic become familiar and his public jaded. Rather than force an administrative issue, he may choose to save his resources for a legislative effort. The effectiveness of a group's access to the president, therefore, is always subject to a priority rating that may be set by him or by circumstances. He must preserve some of the detachment of a constitutional monarch.[9]

The president's decision to intervene or not in a conflict over administrative policy reflects a choice among competing interests, including those reflected in widely held expectations concerning the other aspects of his role. Thus when Franklin Roosevelt during World War II avoided taking sides in controversies that had implications for the extension or consolidation of the New Deal and concentrated on matters directly affecting strategy and war production, he was emphasizing his role of commander in chief and chief of state. He narrowed his role partly because his time and energy were limited and partly because his information on conflicts within the executive branch was inadequate, but also probably from deliberate attention to being "Dr. Win-the-War."

The president's necessary detachment from numerous issues of administrative policy inevitably imposes a large measure of independence upon department heads, whether or not they are personally attached to his policies. Moreover, it increases the concentration of organized interest-group effort upon administrative agencies, either directly or through leg-

---

8 See, for example, *Business Week*, January 27, 1945, p. 16, and I. F. Stone, "Wallace In, Jones Out," *Nation*, Vol. 160, no. 4 (January 27, 1945), pp. 89–90.
9 Herring, *Presidential Leadership*, pp. 111–12; Key, "Legislative Control," p. 344.

islators and congressional committees. The department head must handle relations with interest groups and their congressional spokesmen largely on his own, knowing that if he gets into difficulty he may have to solve it without aid from the White House. In turn the cabinet officer's tactical position imposes a similar detachment from many intradepartmental problems. This detachment helps to insulate bureaus and divisions from the lines of presidential policy and to increase control of administrative action by way of the Congress. On a matter of any considerable controversy the head of an administrative agency, whether at the cabinet, bureau, or even divisional level, must repeatedly choose between "faithfully going down the line of presidential policy" at the risk of antagonizing competing interests with effective access to the legislature and acting in opposition to the president in order to preserve harmonious relations with key elements in the Congress.[10]

The patterns of interaction among officials of the executive branch do not necessarily show a dominant hierarchical pattern reaching its apex in the presidency. Even in noncontroversial activities the patterns may not take this form. The equilibrium reflected in lack of controversy may be founded, not on executive leadership, but on an accepted practice of responding to the initiative of organized interest groups, to elements in the legislature to which these have effective access, or to both. Within limits this situation is an inevitable and, from any point of view, a desirable consequence of delegated authority. It is quite reasonable, for example, that there should be close and cordial relations between the Chicago Board of Trade and the local employees of the U.S. Department of Agriculture who help administer the laws regulating trading in grain futures; it is also reasonable that many matters of administrative policy should be settled without recourse to the formal hierarchy of the department of the executive branch generally.[11] It is equally appropriate that administrative agencies accept a measure of guidance from members of Congress. Such relationships can "promote stability and continuity in policy." [12] Patterns of this sort occur in governments other than the American . . . .

The peculiarities of the system of control over administrative agencies in the United States appear when a controversy, a conflict between interest claims, arises. Then it is never certain whether the pattern of decision will be set via the lines of interaction between administrators and the interest groups with access to key points in the legislature or whether it will emerge from the channels of what is usually thought of as the formal hierarchy. Organized interest groups with privileged access either to the legislature or to "superior" points in the executive will attempt to make one or the other of these patterns dominant. Legislators and administrators who are acting for organized groups or for unorganized interests in-

---

[10] Key, "Legislative Control," pp. 344–6. Cf. Wayne Coy, "Basic Problems," *American Political Science Review*, Vol. 40, no. 6 (December, 1946), p. 1129.

[11] Cf. David B. Truman, *Administrative Decentralization* (Chicago: University of Chicago Press, 1940), pp. 175–7 and *passim*.

[12] Key, "Legislative Control," p. 346.

volved in a policy controversy will attempt to strengthen whatever lines of influence they possess in and outside the executive branch. A department head or a chief executive may find in standing aloof from some policy conflicts a higher expediency than in committing his full resources to achieving a dominant position. The outcome of a policy controversy, therefore, may not represent a test of the full potential of either side. In any case the movement to a decision may be either "horizontal" through the legislature or "vertical" through the executive. In many instances the decisive relationships will reflect a compromise the details of which are obscure even to the close observer. The continuing pattern of administrative controls in the United States is a compromise of alternations, a "maze of crisscrossing relationships." [13]

The President's Cabinet

Richard F. Fenno, Jr.

DIMENSIONS AND TYPES OF PRESIDENTIAL INFLUENCE

It is a first lesson of this study that the Cabinet is dependent on the President. It is a first lesson of history that no two Presidents will behave exactly alike. We can expect to find, therefore, that the President's importance to the Cabinet will be manifested in as many different ways as there are Presidents. Short run variations in actual Cabinet behavior are, in fact, traceable more to the influence of the President than to any other single factor — and traceable ultimately to the differences in temperament, ability, desire, experience, and habit which distinguishes one presidential personality from another. The impact of presidential behavior runs, however, within some broad institutional limits which need to be located before an examination of dimensions and types of influence is undertaken.

In the first place, the structure of the American Executive fixes a lower limit to Cabinet activity. The President's power to use or not to use it is complete and final. The Cabinet is his to use when and if he wishes, and

[13] Herring, "Executive-Legislative Responsibilities," p. 1159. On this whole problem see Herbert A. Simon, Donald W. Smithburg, and Victor A. Thompson, *Public Administration* (New York: Alfred A. Knopf, Inc., 1950), esp. chaps. 18, 19.

Reprinted by permission of the publishers from Richard F. Fenno, Jr., *The President's Cabinet*, Cambridge, Mass.: Harvard University Press, Copyright 1959, by the President and Fellows of Harvard College.

he cannot be forced into either alternative. He has the power of life or death over it at this point. He is a policeman with sole and unlimited control over the traffic signals. Without the green light which only he can flash, and for reasons largely of his own choosing, the Cabinet cannot even begin to function; whatever it does, it is always subject to his desire to change the signal from green to red. Here is the point at which the rock-bottom dependence involved in the power-responsibility relationship becomes most strikingly obvious. It is the point at which the time-honored anecdote about Lincoln's decision which was taken contrary to the unanimous vote of his Cabinet ("seven noes, one aye — the ayes have it") is applicable. In this formal sense, Jonathan Daniels' statement is accurate, that "No institution is more a body of one man's men than the American President's Cabinet."

In the second place, the nature of the presidential function sets certain upper limits to Cabinet activity, limits which varying presidential attitudes cannot alter. The President can render the Cabinet useless, but he cannot mold it to any use he may desire. That is to say, there are real limits to the kind and the extent of assistance he can get from the Cabinet. A widespread tendency exists, however, to assume otherwise. Thus it is a commonly accepted platitude of Cabinet commentary that "An able Cabinet will go far to make up for the deficiencies of a weak President." This expression of what might be labeled "the compensatory Cabinet theory" carries with it no implication of upper limits to Cabinet usefulness. In the light of at least two cases during the period under study, it is a theory which stands in need of some revision.

Warren Harding repeatedly expressed the idea that his Cabinet was comprised of the "best minds." Implicit in this concept was a self-awareness of his own personal inadequacies. He felt that he could compensate for them by surrounding himself with men who possessed the talent and the experience which he lacked. One reviewer put the compensatory Cabinet theory succinctly in this fashion: "He could not be a Mellon, but he got Mellon; he could not be a Hughes, but he got Hughes; he could not be a Hoover, but he got Hoover; he could not be a Hays, but he got Hays." This comment fails to consider the total picture.

In the very act of constituting the Cabinet, Harding began to display weaknesses of inconsistency and lack of direction. He not only "got" Hughes, Hoover, and Mellon, but he also made the less happy appointments of Daugherty, Denby, and Fall. Harding's compensatory Cabinet was an extremely heterogeneous one. Furthermore, the "best minds" concept required that someone integrate the diverse contributions of the group: firm principles and clear policy direction were required of the President. Warren Harding could furnish neither. The lack of a consistently thought-out program, the dearth of general constructive principles on which to base action, the personal qualities which produced poor appointments — all of these were Harding's own weaknesses. They were fatal, and no Cabinet could compensate for them. Under these circumstances, the "best minds" idea was in its consummation a dream-wish, a mythical conception of a superstructure which well qualified builders might construct on a perilously shaky foundation. A President who aspires to be only the simple sum of his Cabinet advisers will be hardly anything at all.

The pre-presidential experience of Herbert Hoover was of a type that eminently fitted him for some of the tasks of the Presidency, but which did not equip him for others. His jobs in engineering, in the Food Administration, and in the Department of Commerce required organizational talent, the ability to plan and direct large enterprises. He came to the Presidency, therefore, prepared and trained to organize and administer the governmental business as he had done in lesser areas. He brought with him well digested plans for construction and development. No one in the nation was more abundantly endowed with the necessary qualifications, but the fields in which he had labored before differed from those of his new office. His previous activities had not been exposed to constant public scrutiny and political debate. His success had not depended upon his own participation in the give and take, the pressures, and the conflicts that characterize the democratic process. He had not been required to sell his basic purposes or his program to Congress, or to his party, or to the public at large to the degree which became necessary in the Presidency. In these respects, his experience and his temperament did not equip him for survival in the new environment — especially so considering the magnitude and the novelty of the problems which arose to upset all his preconceived plans.

Commentaries on Hoover as President confirm his difficulties in providing democratic leadership. "This job," he said, "is nothing but a twenty ring circus — with a whole lot of bad actors." And the President, he felt, should not descend to the role of ringmaster. "This is not a showman's job. I will not step out of character." With this attitude, he was bound to be less effective in working where there was a conflict of wills, in persuading Congress and party, or in guiding public opinion in the midst of controversy. On these grounds, a uniform complaint arose from his Cabinet members, from his party leaders in Congress, from political commentators of all convictions, from newspapermen, and from private citizens — phrased differently, but always with the same dominant theme. William Allen White summed it up: "President Hoover is a great executive, a splendid desk man. But he cannot dramatize his leadership. A democracy cannot follow a leader unless he is dramatized. A man to be a hero must not content himself with heroic virtues and anonymous actions. He must talk and explain as he acts — drama."

There is no evidence at all that Hoover, like Harding, recognized a personal shortcoming and attempted to offset it in selecting his Cabinet. There is some evidence to support the proposition, true in Harding's case, that the President's personal deficiencies are as likely as not to be mirrored in the composition of his Cabinet. The uniform tenor of commentary on the Hoover Cabinet stressed its homogeneity and its undramatic quality — "a solid and impregnable and [journalistically speaking] dismally unsensational Gibralter," "solidity and dependableness," "serenity and tranquillity, and stability and loyalty and reliability," "cooperators rather than individualists," "no solo performers," "little of the spectacular," "averageness," "efficient and machinelike," "solid and substantial internal harmony." When Hoover selected men of political experience for the Cabinet, he failed to rise above his own source. The two "politicians" whom he chose were uninspiring and workmanlike, ordinary individuals without any popular appeal. They were "pinnacles of composure" rather than men of distinction. They were singularly unqualified to save the President from the effects of his awkwardness in public political relations. Most important, they could not have done so under any circumstances.

The Harding and the Hoover experiences serve equally well to support the following conclusion: there are certain fundamental qualities and abilities which the President and he alone must possess and for which no Cabinet can compensate. He is, after all, more than the leader of the Cabinet. He is the leader of the nation. If he lacks the basic equipment to fill this primary role, the Cabinet can be of only patchwork assistance. Indeed, Presidents may not be able to rise above their own inadequacies in the act of Cabinet selection. As Harding's case shows, the Chief Executive must give a steady purpose and a direction to his administration, choosing wisely from among competing policies where he himself has none. As Hoover's difficulties demonstrate, the President must dramatize issues, lead and persuade his party, guide and shape public opinion. These requirements form the essence of successful democratic leadership. Conversely, they establish some irreversible limits to Cabinet usefulness. The implications of the compensatory Cabinet theory must be held strictly within the boundaries set by the necessities of presidential leadership.

The President's influence on Cabinet activity is circumscribed by lower and upper limits, both of which spring not from personality factors but from the basic nature of the presidential function. As an independent executive, he has absolute power over the use of his advisory group, and it represents an institutional impossibility to expect the Cabinet to pull itself up by its own bootstraps. The President's leadership function also sets irreversible limits to what the Cabinet can do to help him; the Cabinet cannot act as a surrogate for him where the quintessence of leadership is involved. Within this broadly limiting framework lies the permissive realm of actual Cabinet performance. It is here that the President's personal influence comes into play and manifests itself in the varieties of Cabinet activity.

The precise relationship between presidential personality and Cabinet activity is impossible to gauge, especially given the memoir, manuscript, public, and secondary materials available for this study. The diffused, refractory, and uneven nature of the sources makes an elusive subject even more slippery. One can, however, indicate what seem to be the relevant areas of presidential behavior and suggest their likely effect on the Cabinet.

At a most general level, it is probable that particular presidential interpretations of the Presidency will affect the activity of the Cabinet. Theodore Roosevelt's ideas about the necessity for vigorous presidential leadership led to a certain reluctance to consult with his Cabinet before taking important action. As he put it, "A council of war never fights, and in a crisis the duty of a leader is to lead and not to take refuge behind the generally timid wisdom of a multitude of counsellors." Woodrow Wilson developed a theory of strong executive leadership, according to which the President devined the popular will and then led the other organs of government. From his twin-pronged faith in public opinion and in his own ability to plumb its depths, he developed a "teacher-tribune" conception of presidential leadership. Whenever he assumed this role, he was markedly unreceptive to words of reconsideration, compromise, or, indeed, advice of any kind. During the struggle over the League of Nations, for instance, he turned a deaf ear not only to the protestations of the Senate, but also to the pleas of his own Cabinet. Several of these individuals urged a more conciliatory course, but to no avail.

Warren Harding, on the other hand, explicitly attacked the broad Wilsonian concept of leadership, which Harding labelled "personal government, individual, dictatorial, autocratic or what not." During his campaign speeches he claimed that he would introduce "plural leadership" into the administration, and that he would substitute government by men of the "best abilities" for "one man government." He repeatedly said that his own view of the job placed emphasis upon building a Cabinet comprised of the "best minds" in the nation. In his acceptance speech, he lost no time in declaring: "Our vision includes more than a Chief Executive; we believe in a Cabinet of the highest capacity, equal to the responsibilities which our system contemplates." Referring to this recurrent theme, one observer summarized: "Mr. Harding gave signs during the campaign of believing that almost any Republican of good standing would do well enough as President, but that the Cabinet was the place for men of great mental force."

One kind of interpretation looks toward a full realization of the potentialities of the Presidency for leadership; the other deliberately underplays these possibilities. Historically, an emphasis on the Cabinet is frequently associated with a set of attitudes and beliefs which minimizes strong executive leadership. Individuals of this persuasion are apt to accent "the men around me," "the best minds," or "the team," to the relative detraction of the presidential office. President Eisenhower, whose cautious attitude toward the powers of the Presidency in a system of "coordinate" powers falls somewhat nearer that of Harding than that of Wilson, has placed a heavy emphasis on "the team" and on "the Cabinet" as opposed to "my Cabinet." Historical reactions to "excessive" presidential activity have been paralleled in many cases by assertions of devotion to the Cabinet. The Whig theory of the Presidency may have as a corollary a Whig theory of the Cabinet — a relationship which did, in fact, hold for the Whigs, and is strikingly evident in such sequences as the Wilson-Harding one. The likelihood is that Wilson and Presidents whose attitudes approximate his will tend to rely on the Cabinet less than Harding and those whose attitudes approximate his.

The generic function of the President's Cabinet is to advise the President. To say that every President takes advice is true but meaningless, for within the limits of such a truism there remains ample room for variety in application. The Cabinet has no one stereotyped and immutable role to play in presidential decision-making, and the President's own desire for, receptivity to, and use of advice is a key variable in determining that role for any particular Cabinet.

A gross distinction between Presidents who require a great deal of advice and those with a greater intellectual self-sufficiency might be useful. Thus we have Harding's constant self-depreciation, as revealed graphically in this outburst to a friend.

> John, I can't make a damn thing out of this tax problem. I listen to one side and they seem right, and then God! I talk to the other side and they seem just as right, and there I am where I started. I know somewhere there is a book that would give me the truth, but hell, I couldn't read the book. I know somewhere there is an economist who knows the truth, but I don't know where to find him and haven't the sense to know him and trust him when I did find him. God, what a job.

Harding's attitude might be contrasted with that of Wilson and Hoover, the two men during the period who were frequently accused of not taking (nor, indeed, wanting) much advice. The extreme indictment will not stand up in either case, but the preference of the two men for intellectual self-sufficiency was marked. Such a preference might lead to less Cabinet activity than, say, the Harding position.

In a slightly different vein, we might contrast Harry Truman's receptivity to advice given "whether he liked it or not" with Herbert Hoover's sometime sensitivity to adverse criticism. Truman wrote: "I made it a point always to listen to Cabinet officers at length and with care, especially when their points of view differed from mine. . . . I would ask the Cabinet to share their counsel with me, even encouraging disagreement and argument to sharpen up the different points of view." Hoover, on the other hand, evinced only the mildest enthusiasm for the single Cabinet member who did differ vigorously with him, Henry Stimson. There is no evidence that any of his Cabinet advisers advised him to alter his direction or his pace or presented him with counter proposals during the economic crisis, and perhaps this willingness to follow stemmed from a reluctance to criticize.

Presidents may be more amenable to some kinds of advice than to others. As between what we have called "expert" and "political" advice, Wilson and Franklin Roosevelt accommodated the first much more readily than the second. Where specialized advice of a military, economic, administrative, or narrowly partisan nature was concerned, Wilson utilized experts, yet in the delicate synchronization of diplomatic maneuvering with domestic public opinion preceding World War I, he acted alone and over the protests of many of his advisers. Likewise, too, in the matter of political timing in pushing his legislative program, he made the major decisions himself and in the face of advice to the contrary. Similarly, Roosevelt deferred to such groups as the Chiefs of Staff and the "Brain Trust," but when a decision involved the subtleties of public political relations, he relied mostly on his own abilities and instincts. The efforts of Henry Stimson and Harold Ickes to prod Roosevelt to more decisive action in 1941 and 1942, in the face of what they considered to be the President's exasperating deliberateness at this time, provides an excellent example. Ickes' agitated concern over Roosevelt's handling of the 1936 presidential campaign is another. Depending on what kind of advice a Cabinet is best equipped to furnish, differences in attitudes such as these may have consequences for Cabinet activity.

Probably the most important of all factors relating to advice is that complex of presidential attitudes and habits which goes to make up his distinctive pattern of decision-making.

Herbert Hoover's decision-making procedure was characterized by the extent to which he dominated it through a personal involvement at all levels. His secretary writes that "He had to originate every last recovery program put forward by his administration." Hoover "had to" not because others were incapable of doing so, but because this was the method which best suited his ability and temperament. In all of his prior executive experience he had stressed the necessity of tight one man control over an organization. It was, for instance, almost a conditioned response to the onset of a new problem for Hoover to call a conference of specially qualified experts. But he did not call it until after he had first formulated a set of proposals, laying out the line of approach he desired.

"Whatever the plan or program, he always prepared it to the last detail prior to holding the conference at which he was to project it." The group discussion was designed not to initiate, but to explore ramifications and consequences, to bring about a meeting of the minds, and to enlist voluntary cooperation — all based on Hoover's original propositions. The tempo of decision-making as well as the substance of policy was controlled by him. On the way to a decision, he planned and organized his moves with a constitutional deliberateness which impatient advisers could not alter. He wanted, above all, to know exactly where he was going before he rendered a decision. The gradual reduction of alternatives was a slow process, accompanied by long hours of intellectual application to the problem. His decision on the moratorium on war debts is a case in point. It is difficult to imagine Hoover going before his advisory body with the unadorned question: "What shall I do?" If they did hash over a proposal, it was likely to be strictly his own, and more than likely to have been rolled over in his own mind for a long time previously.

Woodrow Wilson, like Hoover, had a distinctive method of decision-making, intellectually structured and carried through with enough consistency to provide an important clue to his Cabinet relations. In the earliest stages, before he had made up his mind and settled on a course of action, he was receptive to advice, even though, as Colonel House said, "it mostly comes gratuitously and not by his asking." He was anxious to listen to all sides of an argument, to obtain a complete picture of each issue, and to make certain that he lacked no pertinent facts or information. His attitude and behavior in the controversy over plans for the army in 1916 is a case in which he had no preconceived ideas. Here, he was open-minded to the point of being indiscriminating about the alternatives. Once he had availed himself of the necessary preliminary information and arguments, he reached his decisions by himself, after lengthy, painstaking, and solitary deliberation. He did not make up his mind in the presence of conflicting voices, and very often characterized his own procedure as that of a man with a "one track mind."

Once Wilson had thought a problem through to a decision, his attitude hardened almost to intransigeance. William McAdoo, Secretary of the Treasury, and Colonel House put it succinctly: "He listens quite patiently, and makes up his mind and then stays put." Franklin Lane concurred, that "Once he has reached a conclusion, that conclusion becomes a part of his nature. He is inflexible." Given this pattern, Wilson's Cabinet could at best be effective as an advisory body only at that stage in the decision-making process where Wilson felt he needed to delineate and document a problem requiring his decision. Between this point and his announcement of a decision his advisers were not likely to be involved. This does not mean that Wilson would be averse to submitting some of his final conclusions to their discussion, but it does indicate that when he did so his mind usually would be well fixed. At this point, he would be testing out their reactions or seeking their reassurances, but not inviting debate.

Franklin Roosevelt's decision-making procedure was quite different from Hoover's or Wilson's. His personal involvement was regular only in its irregularity, and predictable only in its unpredictability. This is because his decision-making habits were essentially experimental, grounded in his own subtle sense of timing. His advisers could and did complain alternately about his slowness in making up his mind and his "weakness for snap decisions." He would make exploratory decisions, sometimes in the form of trial balloons, which he did not consider final and irrevocable. He would make a quick tentative decision and then change direction, as in the case of the Morgenthau plan. Or, he would pursue a course of watchful delay as in the third term and the cross-channel invasion decisions.

Roosevelt frequently delayed in making difficult decisions because he disliked argument and hoped that differences of opinion could be compromised. Indeed, he commonly reached decisions by simply withdrawing to "hold the ring" while the disputants debated to some outcome. He would step in himself, listening to advice and deciding, only if there were no other recourse. Yet, "He would take a suggestion from anyone, anywhere." All of these decision-making methods tended toward one result — keeping his advisers off-balance, unable to forecast or rationalize their own advisory role, and uncertain as to whether he was or was not taking their advice.

Calvin Coolidge's decision-making procedure was, by contrast with Roosevelt's, conducted in the most explicit conformity with the canons of regularity. It was neither impulsive nor imaginative, but "calculated, direct, safe, and sure." It was studied in its avoidance of executive initiative and in its eager deference to the Cabinet. Coolidge's strategy of control over decision-making was to "sit down and keep still" in the face of problems rather than to confront them, to "remain silent until an issue is reduced to its lowest terms, until it boils down to something like a moral issue." "If you see ten troubles coming down the road," he philosophized, "you can be sure that nine will run into the ditch before they reach you and you have to battle with only one." He followed this prescription in two of his biggest decisions as an administrator, the Boston police strike and the firing of Harry Daugherty. He followed it with respect to his public policy decisions on the farm problem. Indeed, as his most sympathetic biographer says: "The one important occasion when Coolidge did not keep his mouth shut . . . proved to be the most unfortunate blunder he ever made." Coolidge consciously prescribed extensive Cabinet participation in decision-making, and he stated flatly that "I rarely failed to accept their recommendations." But his calculated inactivity and his general reluctance to set in motion the machinery of decision-making indicates that the members would probably be given relatively few opportunities to exercise influence.

Probably the best example of a decision-making procedure with extensive, built-in Cabinet reliance is that of President Eisenhower. He is, unlike Roosevelt, not addicted to "snap or unconsidered decisions." His tempo of decision-making is slow and deliberate, sometimes painfully so. His "compelling desire to have his decisions turn out right" dictates not only the pace of the process but also his receptivity to the advice of others. "Before reaching his conclusions," said one of his Cabinet-level officials, "he wants to be sure that he has considered the views of all those who properly have something to contribute." His use (unlike Hoover) of representative study committees to lay the foundation for his programs is evidence of this fundamental desire. The study group device is evidence too of another personal characteristic, his preference for having the groundwork thoroughly laid and the issues boiled down before he finally confronts them.

As he nears the point of final decision, there is still much room for advisory activity. This is mostly because Eisenhower, unlike Wilson, "likes to reach his conclusions by talking out his thoughts rather than brooding." "He likes to take in by ear all that he can." This means that he will pass problems around for discussion among his advisers, listen carefully to their debates, and use them as a sounding board for his own ideas. He is apt, in other words, to do his thinking in the presence of others, in a group meeting. Most important of all, he frequently if not usually makes his final decision on the spot. When he is ready to act, he wants to make certain that his decision is clear, understood by all and concurred in by all, conditions which are best secured in a meeting rather than afterward. On-the-spot decision-making is easy for him since, as he has said, "I have trained myself as soon as a matter is finished and a decision is made to put it out of my mind and to go on with the next subject." Eisenhower's procedure is not characterized by tight personal control over it.

It is a generalization worth considering, perhaps, that other things being equal, a President who exercises a tight control at many points in the decision-making sequence will tend to rely on his Cabinet less than one whose intervention in the process is more limited.

A President's administrative habits and attitudes are related to, but distinguishable from, those regarding decision-making procedures, and they are equally crucial in their effect on the Cabinet in action. Especially is this true of the techniques and extent of delegation. Should the President employ a haphazard, nonhierarchical, or highly personalized method of delegation, his Cabinet subordinates may be accorded no special emphasis. If he delegates regularly through the chain of command, a greater Cabinet reliance may be indicated. Similarly with the extent of delegation: in those areas where he is reluctant to delegate, the participation and the value of the member or members involved may be diminished in the policy-making process. Delegation which proceeds, however, to the point of abdication is equally likely to impair Cabinet usefulness, by depriving the President of any control over it.

Calvin Coolidge's administrative behavior followed, in every respect, the tenets of orthodoxy. His philosophy concerning delegation was formalistic and simple. He was especially lavish in the field of foreign affairs. "The only way to succeed when there is a job to be done," he said, "is to look around and find the best man to do it and then let him do it." To those sent on foreign missions he gave a virtual *carte blanche*. He placed the task of directing and coordinating our foreign policy almost wholly in the laps of Secretaries Hughes and Kellogg. The all-important matter of timing, for instance, in the Kellogg-Briand negotiations he left entirely to the discretion of Kellogg. Nor would Coolidge weaken or subvert the formal hierarchy of responsibility and authority. Psychologically, he found it necessary to keep his friend Frank Stearns around him as a kind of buffer-companion-confessor, yet he would not work through him or consult him in any way. During a conversation about Colonel House, the President made clear the strict limitations of his friend's role. " 'Mr. Stearns, an unofficial adviser to a President is not a good thing and is not provided for in our form of government.' Stearns replied, 'Did I ever try to advise you?' 'No,' was the reply, 'but I thought I had better tell you.' " "I have never relied on any person to be my unofficial adviser. . . ."

Coolidge said, "My counsellors have been those provided by the Constitution and the law."

Harry Truman, too, attached special importance to the Chief Executive's ability "to delegate responsibility and then back up those he trusts." And he underscores, in his writings, the inherent connection between his techniques of delegation and his claim to have "revived the Cabinet system." He looked upon his Cabinet as "a board of directors appointed by the President to help him carry out the policies of the government," or, alternatively, as "the principal medium through which the President controls his administration." Truman learned through experience, however, that he could not delegate too much without losing control of his own job. Having begun by delegating copiously to his Secretary of State, he finally wrote to Secretary Byrnes:

> I have been considering some of our difficulties. As you know, I would like to pursue a policy of delegating authority to the members of the Cabinet in their various fields and then back them up in the results. But in doing that and in carrying out that policy, I do not intend to turn over the complete authority of the President, nor to forego the President's prerogative to make the final decision.

He followed this practice with Secretaries of State Marshall and Acheson, freely delegating authority (as in Marshall's China mission), and interfering only occasionally (albeit sometimes impulsively, as with the proposed trip to Moscow by the Chief Justice), but retaining throughout "his own basic power of decision and direction."

It has been said that "the Eisenhower and Truman administrations . . . are a good deal alike . . . in their patterns for the delegation of authority." In the case of President Eisenhower the germinal influence is, again, his military habituation to the chain of command. "He imported from the army a form of the staff system in which all functions and responsibilities flow in a more or less fixed order and sequence from the President on down." As a general rule, it may be suggested, those presidents like Coolidge, Truman, and Eisenhower, who have most frequently expressed their resolution to delegate, who have been hyperconscious of this particular administrative virtue, and for whom it forms an integral part of their administrative philosophy, can be expected to delegate in large measure through their Cabinet members. This, in turn, will facilitate (should they wish) useful, informed, and informative Cabinet discussions. This does not mean that these men were, in fact, equally reliant upon the Cabinet. For instance, the contrast between Coolidge's admitted penchant for "avoiding the big problems" and Truman's unflinching attitude in the face of the big foreign policy decisions of 1945–1952 probably indicates that Truman was less "Cabinet-reliant" than Coolidge. Such differences are hard to calculate. But it is useful to contrast the attitude of the three Presidents listed above with, for example, that of Woodrow Wilson in the field of foreign affairs, to isolate one kind of influence on the Cabinet in action. On the evidence, Wilson wanted to be, and was, his own Secretary of State. His relationship with Robert Lansing was a product of this desire; it neutralized Lansing's Cabinet performance and helped to remove the Cabinet from the center of activity in this area.

Franklin Roosevelt's approach to delegation was noteworthy both for its technique and for its extent. He "was a great believer in alternatives. He rarely got himself sewed tight to a program from which there was no turning back." He sought always to preserve his discretionary "freedom of action." He accomplished this by delegating responsibility and authority in small, vague, and sometimes conflicting fragments, to a point where only he could contribute consistency and direction. "Nothing whatever counted in the entire administration," said Henry Wallace, "except what went on inside FDR's head." The result was an essentially unpatterned technique of administration. It resulted in fuzzy lines of responsibility, no clear chain of command, overlapping jurisdictions, a great deal of personal squabbling, and a lack of precision and regularity. It was, in short, a"fantastically complex administrative mechanism," so labelled by Henry Stimson who protested vigorously over its sometime sterilizing effect on Cabinet officers.

In the field of foreign affairs, for example, Roosevelt confided to a friend that he felt it was necessary to be his own Secretaries of State, War, and Navy. He did this by personal intervention and by delegating tasks to his own personal representatives and to others outside the direct chain of command. No Secretary of State with a different temperament and who was not as mild-mannered and patient as Cordell Hull could have suffered as much circumvention of his proper authority as Roosevelt's personal leadership in foreign affairs involved. First Raymond Moley and later Sumner Welles, as subordinates of Hull, were given direct lines of access to the White House. Each of them embarrassed and undercut Hull on numerous occasions — the most famous denouements coming at the London Economic Conference of 1933 and the Rio Conference of 1942. Furthermore, Roosevelt sent personal envoys on foreign missions (Hopkins, Harriman, Wallace, Hurley, Donovan, Davies) who consequently reported to him and not to the State Department. Some of our ambassadors, like William Bullitt, were encouraged to report directly to FDR rather than via State Department channels. Hull was not taken to any of the meetings of the Big Three (in sharp contrast to Truman and Byrnes). The President handed over State Department functions to other departments, as when he authorized Henry Morgenthau to initiate conversations leading to the recognition of Russia. The entire procedure irritated Hull, who complained feelingly in his *Memoirs,* but he was able to console himself somewhat naively with the thought that things were not really as bad as they seemed. Yet they clearly affected Hull's ability to contribute usefully to Cabinet discussions.

In domestic affairs, too, the technique was similar though the extent of delegation was greater. "He is bypassing me right and left," complained the Secretary of the Interior, whose grievance was shared especially by the

Secretary of the Treasury. When Roosevelt did delegate, it was common for him to do so in a trial and error way, dividing responsibility yet not basing his delegation on any preliminary job analysis. He might set up a two-headed program like work relief with Hopkins and Ickes, or institute two-headed agencies like the National Defense Advisory Commission. He set up other agencies in which there was no concentrated responsibility, like the War Production Board. He conceived of the CCC program and then delegated the details wholesale to a committee representing three separate departments. This method of delegation left jurisdictional boundaries to be mapped out by conquest or agreement. It promoted much "stimulating" inter-departmental conflict which could and did eventually land in his own lap.

Neither Roosevelt nor Wilson harbored Coolidge's scruples against unofficial advisers, which helps to explain why Harry Hopkins and Colonel House performed so many important administrative functions. Both men remained outside of the formal hierarchy. Colonel House was offered a Cabinet position but declined. Hopkins was made Secretary of Commerce for a while but, significantly, this coincided with the period when he was being built up as an independent figure, and when his influence with the President was least important. Each man served the President informally as buffer, communication line, sounding board, coordinator, listening post, and mouthpiece abroad. Their activities affected the Hoover Commission's prescribed "clear line of command" and the Cabinet members' formal position as "chief assistants" or "chief lieutenants" of the Chief Executive. In short, Hopkins and House performed some functions and provided some types of assistance that might be associated *a priori* with the Cabinet. Thus, to some degree, a President's working habits with respect to unofficial advisers do affect his Cabinet activity.

A final aspect of administrative behavior which has relevance to Cabinet activity concerns the exercise of the removal power. Here, as in the other areas discussed, the institutional prescriptions are broad, the expected patterns of behavior are few, and the opportunity for the exercise of personal presidential influence is correspondingly great. In the controlling Supreme Court decision of *Meyers* v. *United States,* the unimpeded legality as well as the administrative imperatives of the removal power were established by Chief Justice Taft, speaking as he was from both judicial and executive experience. For a variety of reasons, however, Presidents have exercised this authority with extreme moderation. Where discretion does operate, the ultimate determination most often centers upon the nexus of loyalty, both personal and programmatic, which binds the two individuals involved. A decision to remove or not to remove will depend upon the limits of toleration which the participants place upon this relationship.

Franklin Roosevelt, for example, tolerated a greater amount of personal and programmatic "non-loyalty" than any of the other Presidents studied. When Harry Woodring was Secretary of War, he and his Assistant Secretary "were at swords' points all the time" over policy decisions. Woodring was basically isolationist, while Louis Johnson, in company with the President, believed in pushing an armament program. As a result, Roosevelt instructed others to treat Johnson as if he were Secretary of War, bypassing Woodring. War Department functions were allocated to the State and Treasury Departments for accomplishment. Other Cabinet members (Ickes, Morgenthau, and Farley at least) were fully aware of the anomalous situation, called it "a public scandal . . . bringing no credit to the Administration," and recommended removal. Some put the argument squarely in terms of loyalty. Roosevelt, however, would not fire his recalcitrant Cabinet official. He forestalled resignations and was almost unable to remove several other members who were totally ineffective or in whom he had no confidence; yet removal might have promoted cohesiveness, smoothed out working relationships, and it almost certainly would have lifted the morale of his Cabinet. By keeping the group intact he left it as a chain with several weak links. Behavior such as this would seem to be some measure of a President's disregard for the Cabinet as a working team.

Calvin Coolidge's attitude was governed by a narrow and inflexible sense of propriety. When Harding died Coolidge proclaimed that it was "a sound rule" and "the duty" of the successor "to maintain the counsellors and policies of the deceased President." Acting on the basis of this principle, he repeatedly declined to ask for the resignation of Harry Daugherty — in spite of the fact that Daugherty's presence was seriously damaging the prestige of his administration. He finally removed Daugherty when the situation had become absolutely intolerable, but he based his request for resignation purely on the grounds of legality. Of the entire Harding Cabinet, only Daugherty was ever requested to leave, and none of those who resigned did so in protest. Coolidge's formalistic deference to a preceding President's Cabinet, with the indifference to personal allegiance inherent in such an attitude, does not demonstrate a very complete grasp of that group's potentialities as a flexible instrument of the President.

Harry Truman's reaction to his inherited advisers was strikingly different. He understood, as Coolidge had not, the essential principle that "every President must have a Cabinet of his own choosing" and that "when there is a change in administration, there are bound to be some changes in the Cabinet." In six months time, six Cabinet positions had changed hands, whereas Coolidge did not reach that figure for five years. Discounting the differences in external conditions, it is clear that Coolidge and Truman did not place the same emphasis on personal loyalty. Truman's biographer notes his habitual use of the aphorism "politics is not a one-way street" to punctuate the idea of loyalty as the superlative human virtue. Its importance had probably been impressed upon him during his long apprenticeship in the political ranks. He required a close loyalty, and he reciprocated in full measure when any of his subordinates (like Dean Acheson) were under fire from the outside.

Whenever he generalized about the nature of his office, Truman stressed the idea of loyalty to his decisions.

> I never allowed myself to forget that the final responsibility was mine. . . . I expected Cabinet officers to be frank and candid in expressing their opinions to me. At the same time I insisted that they keep me informed of the major activities of their departments in order to make certain that they supported the policy once I had made a decision. If a Cabinet member could not support the policy I had laid down, I tried to work out an understanding with him. But I could not permit, any more than any President can, such differences of opinion to be aired in public by a dissenting member of the Cabinet.

It was within this context that he viewed the "resignations" of Secretaries Byrnes, Ickes, and Wallace. In none of these cases was removal related to the ability of the member involved. All turned on the question of loyalty, personal and programmatic seamlessly joined. An index to the strict construction which Truman placed on loyalty is the fact that whereas Harold Ickes' two resignations proffered to Roosevelt were quickly rejected, a similar "gesture" to Truman was summarily accepted. Probably Truman's behavior indicates a more serious attention to his Cabinet as a developer of, in his words, "teamwork wisdom."

Presidential interpretations of the Presidency, receptivity to advice, kinds of advice accommodated, decision-making procedures, habits of delegation, use of the removal power — all these represent relevant areas in which the personal impact of the President on Cabinet activity may be examined. In no particular situation is there a one-to-one relationship between presidential attitude and Cabinet behavior.

No attempt has been made here to predict which types of presidents will utilize their Cabinets most and how. For the person who wishes to develop such a calculus there are, perhaps, some clues in this section. For the more casual observer, there are some suggested areas into which he might probe in trying to explain the behavior of any given Cabinet at a given time. Ultimately, however, the students' task is not this simple. The President-Cabinet nexus is subject to the impingement of other forces. The presidential personality cannot be "the answer" to Cabinet activity because the President is only one relevant factor among many. His influence on the Cabinet is always crucial, but it is always being shaped, counter-balanced, and transformed by other influences in the American political system. . . .

CABINET AND DEPARTMENTAL ADMINISTRATION: POSSIBILITIES AND LIMITATIONS

The most ambitious and talented department head confronts a formidable complex of situational limitations on his activity. The new appointee finds himself amid a framework of established relationships, of goals already fixed and of forces long since set in motion. He faces an impersonal bureaucratic structure with great resistance to change. Most of his organization is staffed with career personnel, relatively unaffected by changes in high-level policy. Power relationships among constituent elements of the department, or between departmental units and clusters of interest outside the department, tend to be in an equilibrium which reflects an optimum adjustment for all concerned. Their desire to survive may confront the Secretary with serious limitations. He has, of course, some formal controls with which to countervail departmental resistances, but these are frequently minimized by the very forces he is trying to combat.

One control, for instance, which is a prerequisite to successful departmental management is the power of appointment. Yet the Secretary frequently operates under considerable restriction — statutory or otherwise. Harold Ickes complained that, "Without the power to appoint subordinates there is no power of control at all. I think this power should lie with the Secretary because, at least in the public mind, he is charged with the responsibility. As it is now, he has the responsibility without any authority, and that makes for bad administration, bad morale, and misunderstanding."

The appointments of the Under Secretary and Assistant Secretaries are subject to many non-Secretarial influences. During party turnovers these positions are eminently suited for the payment of political rewards. Both President and Congressmen may press personal favorites upon the department head. In any case, the result may be unfortunate from the standpoint of internal administration, as, for example, Stimson's experience with Under Secretary Castle will attest. Or, interested groups may lay claim to some of these positions. The desire of the AFL and the CIO for one Assistant Secretaryship of Labor apiece is a case in point. With regard to Bureau Chiefs, the Secretary operates under severe statutory handicaps. Inability to remove these officials follows where the power of appointment is lacking.

The department head's formal managerial weapons may be further blunted by organizational inflexibilities. We have already noted the historical evolution of the so-called "holding company" type of department, which includes Interior, Defense, Commerce, and Health, Education and Welfare. Many constituent units of these departments have their own separate statutory bases, thereby helping to establish an authority with non-departmental roots. Since built-in unity is lacking, it can come to the "holding company" organization only by super-imposition from above, yet it is part of the organizational pattern that such authority is hard to come by. In an "integrated" type of organization the Secretary has substantive grants of authority over the constituent units, whereas in the more loosely structured department he has a vaguely defined responsibility to "direct and supervise" them. In practice, however, such a mandate is "an almost meaningless generality."

This limitation is most obvious in terms of authority to reorganize the relationships of the subordinate units. Frequently, he cannot transfer activities from one unit to another, make adjustments in his field organization, or alter the budget so as to make organizational changes possible. Congress may want to exercise minute supervision over all such organizational changes. When Chairman Carl Vinson of the House Armed Services Committee proposed that the Secretary of Defense should consult his Committee before making any organizational changes, Secretary Louis Johnson exclaimed, "Why, you would become the Secretary of Defense. That completely ties the hands of the Secretary." Said Vinson in reply, "We don't want Congress by-passed."

What appear, from a bird's-eye view, to be limitations on the Secretary's managerial discretion appear from another perspective as the phenomenon of "bureau autonomy." Hoover described the Commerce Department as "a congeries of independent bureaus . . . all old establishments created prior to the Department itself. . . . Each was an inbred bureaucracy of its own. There was little department spirit or *esprit de corps*. Some of the bureaus even placed their own names on their letterheads, without mentioning the Department." Franklin Lane described the Interior Department as "a rather disjointed department [in which] the bureaus have stood up as independent entities." The independence of the Army Corps of Engineers is a classic instance of the pattern of relationships which may develop, and it has been admirably related in another place. The important thing to be noted about bureau autonomy, for our purposes, is that its dynamics are by no means explainable in wholly organizational terms. An administrative organization like a bureau does not hang motionless in a political vacuum waiting to be directed according to statute and hierarchy. In order to gain and hold any degree of autonomy, its position must be shored up by sufficient political support. This usually derives from those groups in the political system to whose advantage it is to maintain such autonomy. In addition to bureau personnel, these groups will ordinarily include the clientele for whom the bureau provides services, and members of the legislature who have an interest, corporate or otherwise, in controlling the activities of an administrative agency. The intimate *rapprochement* which the Corps of Engineers have established with local organizations and with influential Congressmen is a key to their continued administrative independence.

Considered in these broad situational terms, the problems raised by bureau autonomy may arise to some degree in every executive department. Even though a departmental executive may possess considerable authority, a bureau will possess its own independent base of support to which it may appeal. In fact, and this is the point, it must do so in order to get the power to operate. Regardless of statutory relationships with Congress (though these help), direct bureau-legislature relationships will be legion, including appropriations, investigations, appointments, etc. Every governmental bureau has one vested interest, one constant preoccupation — survival. And in the interests of survival, it must cultivate sympathetic attitudes and support on the part of those who can do it harm, which most often means the legislature. In the interests of control, the legislative unit whose relations with the agency are most frequent will encourage and attempt to enforce responsibility to it. This mutuality of interests may create a concentration of power which can undermine the authority of the Secretary over his department.

Interwoven with the bureau-legislature "sub-system," and operating on both parties to it, are the interested private groups. Regional labor groups interested in employment may work with both bureau admirals and pork-barreling Congressmen to keep the control of naval shipyard and supply contracts out of the hands of an economy-minded Secretary of the Navy. In the process of administration, policy is made by the operating bureaus. Each bureau develops its own clientele — people interested in the policy questions within the bureau's area of discretion. Thus, "a structure of interests friendly or hostile, vague and general, or compact and well defined encloses each significant center of administrative discretion." If the bureau is to survive and develop a program, it must have support from these sources. To the private groups, on the other hand, the bureaus "represent the institutionalized embodiment of policy, an enduring organization actually or potentially capable of mobilizing power behind policy." Here again, mutual dependence dictates a close relationship, one which may not be logically consistent with the policies or desires of the Secretary. Little can be known about these informal power clusters by studying the formal intradepartmental hierarchy, yet they may be in direct competition with it. Where this is so, they impair the Secretary's ability to manage his department and to provide the President with good administration just as surely as any lack of adequate formal authority.

Time is still another complicating factor for every Cabinet official. If he wishes to help the President by rendering him good departmental administration, he must focus his energies downward into the department. But as he provides this kind of negative assistance, he has little time left for positive and constructive assistance. Men of large vision and extra-departmental enthusiasms like Secretary of the Interior Franklin Lane will often leave, like him, a testament of frustration in office: "Ability is not lacking, but it is pressed to the point of paralysis because of an infinitude of detail. . . . Every man is held to details, to the narrower view which comes too often to be the departmental view or some sort of parochial view . . . there was little opportunity to think of anything more than the immediate." William Redfield, the man who received Wilson's letter of praise for efficient departmental administration, admitted that "I looked at my duties too much as a busines matter — too little as the creative counsellor." But, he explained in defense, "My nose is kept closely to the grindstone in my own Department." The tendency to become sucked in and submerged by routine or detail or immediacy has been called "the most insidious hazard both to the executive and his organization." He cannot lift up his head often enough to look at things from a government-wide, i.e. presidential, standpoint. If he is to be of help to the President, his time is a precious resource, easily exploited and difficult to conserve.

Department Secretaries live in a world which has many extra-presidential dimensions. We have seen the multiplicity of forces within the political system which impinge upon him — forces built into his department by its history, by forces of the appointment process, by forces emanating from Congress, and by forces generated by the publics which the department serves — forces of interest, of authority, and of partisanship. Up to this point in our discussion we have discussed what might be called a series of objective factors which affect departmental administration, with potentialities for lightening or increasing the President's burden. They are objective factors in the sense that the assumption is made that the overriding concern of the Secretary is to manage the internal affairs of his department in the interests of the President. The implicit image of the Cabinet member thus far has been something akin to that of a person whose administrative life history is one ceaseless struggle to surmount a veritable network of obstacles, personal and situational, in an effort to act as the agent and servant of his superior. Such may, indeed, be the case. The Secretary may be exclusively President-oriented, and instances where he fails to help the President may be written off as the result of forces which he cannot bring under control. But it is an equally likely possibility, in view of the department head's problems of success and survival, that he may deliberately assume postures and adopt positions that are department-oriented, and which may not accord with presidential desires.

Secretaries of Agriculture have frequently faced the problem of reconciling the views of the Farm Bureau with their loyalty to the Chief Executive. Secretary of Labor James Mitchell has lived amid similar cross-pressures from his union constituency and from President Eisenhower on such matters as right-to-work laws and FEPC legislation, and he has taken positions on them which the President himself refused to take. There is present, almost always, this dilemma of competing responsibilities, loyalties, and demands, bringing with it the potentiality of conflict. Conflict may, of course, be avoided, but its presence colors the Secretary's whole pattern of behavior. Every department head finds himself caught and torn between alternatives of action — President-oriented or department-oriented — in an environment where the rationale, the means, and the incentives for pursuing either are readily available.

His very position as head of one executive establishment among several carries with it certain attitudes and organizational necessities non-presidential in character. He inherits an immense bureaucratic structure with its own traditions, its own *raison d'être*, and its own operating methods. None of these depend on him, nor will he be able to alter them very significantly. He cannot help but become a part of this particular organization, supporting its vested interests, concerned for its *esprit de corps*, and speaking for it in all of its conflicts.

A Secretary of the Interior will predictably contest the location of the Forest Service (now in Agriculture) with the Secretary of Agriculture. He will do it not because it is a personal or partisan matter, but because it is a long-established, organization tenet within Interior that the Forest Service belongs there. Secretaries may "defend or [be] governed by bureaus they themselves do not control," which in turn may lead them to "take positions hostile to presidential needs and policy."

The department head is not to be viewed as the unwilling captive of his organization or as someone who "fronts" for bureaus against his own subjective inclinations. No admiral of the navy ever defended bureau autonomy more stubbornly, more vigorously, and more willingly than did Secretary of the Navy Josephus Daniels. If a Secretary is to accomplish any of his goals, he must cultivate the support of his own organization. He cannot, as the Hoover Commission seems to think, trade exclusively on the influence of the President in his operations. Beyond his own organization, he must locate his support within the legislature and with interested private groups. Without non-presidential support of this kind, his department may be decimated — as the Secretary of Labor lost some of his bureaus by congressional action in a period when these units and the department in general had insufficient support from organized labor.

Harold Ickes' attempt to change the name of his Department from "Interior" to "Conservation and Public Works" illustrates how impotent a Cabinet official can be when he operates on the assumption that presidential support is all that he needs to run his department. Relying on Roosevelt's assurances that he was interested, that he would request other executive departments (Agriculture, War, and Navy) not to oppose it, and that he would urge congressional leaders to take favorable action, Ickes introduced his measure. When the bill failed to pass even a congressional subcommittee, Ickes was shocked, and interpreted the result as an act of personal perfidy by the President. What happened, actually, was that other executive departments which felt their interests threatened by the change were able to muster congressional support in the person of the Chairman of the subcommittee, and external support from the farm organizations. The President could not have made the difference in any event. More than this, it is not realistic to expect the President to give strong support to those pet projects of a Cabinet member which affect so many of his fellows. The Cabinet member is left on his own most of the time simply because the President, for most of his time, must remain relatively detached as between competing departments. And where Congress is concerned, if the President exerts his power too frequently he may, by virtue of a familiar political paradox, lose it.

In the interests of effective departmental administration, most Cabinet members will be led at one time or another to exploit the presence of the competing lines of authority, running vertically to the President and horizontally to the Congress. The spectacle of Secretary of War George Dern supporting the Corps of Engineers in their autonomous operations is explainable only by looking behind the vertical, hierarchical rationale. Dern did everything he could to resist integrated planning on water resources because he felt it would dilute the functions of one of his bureaus. He even went so far as to claim that the Corps was "an agency of the legislative branch," thereby protecting his department by renouncing his own control over it! Many Secretaries, like him, have nourished the notion of horizontal responsibility in order to preserve their organizations. The point is that conflict between President-oriented actions and department-oriented actions inheres in the American political system. It is as evident in the administrative realm as in the legislative. The Cabinet member is subject to strong non-presidential or extra-presidential influences, creating a gap between fact and theory in the formal power-responsibility relationship. . . .

THE CABINET AND POLITICS: SOME CONCLUSIONS

The investigations which we have made into Cabinet-member activity in the areas of public prestige, party, Congress, and departmental administration lead to a few conclusions about the Cabinet and the political system in which it operates. One striking circumstance is the extent to which the Cabinet concept breaks down in the course of the members' activities outside the Cabinet meeting. In matters of prestige, partisan politics, and legislative relations alike, the Cabinet as a collectivity has only a symbolic value, a value which readily disappears when the need for action supersedes the need for a show window. In the day-to-day work of the Cabinet member, each man fends for himself without much consideration for Cabinet unity. His survival, his support, and his success do not depend on his fellow members. His performance is judged separately from theirs. This condition is but another result of the combination of the centrifugal tendencies in our political system with the low degree of institutionalization which characterizes the Cabinet.

The political help which the President receives comes not from the group but from individual Cabinet members, who can and do augment the President's effectiveness in his leadership roles. It would be a serious mistake not to emphasize the possibilities for crucial assistance by individuals. But probably most striking is the fact that the possibilities for such assistance are very frequently negated by the number of limitations which surround them. There are pervasive limitations of a personal or a situational nature, and there are limitations inherent in the political system — all of which make it neither easy for a Cabinet member to help the President nor axiomatic that he should do so. In the final reckoning, the President receives much less assistance of a positive, non-preventive type from his individual Cabinet members than one might expect. This fact serves to accent the high degree of success which is represented by preventive assistance. It also helps to underline the tremendous gap which separates the presidential level of responsibility from that of his subordinates. It demonstrates, too, the extent to which the two levels are subject to the pulls of different political forces.

The President-Cabinet power-responsibility relationship is, according to the analysis of this chapter, inadequate as a total explanation for the extra-Cabinet performance of the individual member. As a group the Cabinet draws its life breath from the President, but as individuals the Cabinet members are by no means so dependent on him. In many instances, we are presented with the paradox that in order for the Cabinet member to be of real help to the President in one of his leadership roles, the member must have non-presidential "public" prestige, party following, legislative support, or roots of influence in his department. And in any case, the problems of his own success and survival will encourage him to consolidate his own nexus of power and will compel him to operate with some degree of independence from the President. For his part, the President's influence over the Cabinet member becomes splintered and eroded as the member responds to political forces not presidential in origin or direction. From the beginnings of his involvement in the appointment process, the President's power is subject to the pervasive limitations of the pluralistic system in which he seeks to furnish political leadership.

One final conclusion takes the form of a restatement of the pluralism of American politics. In every area we have noted the diffusion, the decentralization, and the volatility of political power. The same kaleidoscopic variety which characterized the factors influential in the appointment process is evident in the political processes which engulf the Cabinet member. Each member interacts with a great variety of political units, interest groups, party groups, and legislative groups, and each has his own pattern of action and his own constellation of power. The feudal analogy is an apt one. It frequently makes more sense to describe the Cabinet member as part of a "feudal pattern of fiefs, baronies, and dukedoms than . . . an orderly and symmetrical pyramid of authority."

Here, then, is an underlying explanation for Cabinet-meeting behavior. Departmentalism is a condition whose roots are grounded in the basic diversity of forces which play upon the individual member. By the same token, this pluralism generates centrifugal influences which help to keep the Cabinet in its relatively non-institutionalized state. The greatest problems for Cabinet and President, like the greatest problems in American politics, are those which center around the persistent dilemmas of unity and diversity.

Testimony of Richard Neustadt Before the Senate Subcommittee on National Security Staffing and Operations

. . . You have asked me to comment on basic issues in national security staffing and operations. This is a vast field and a very complex one, where troubles are hard to track down and "solutions" come harder still. The field is full of genuine dilemmas, many of them quite new to our governmental system but all of them quite likely to endure as far ahead as one can see. Durability is a common characteristic. So is difficulty.

Perhaps the chief of these dilemmas is the one placed first in the subcommittee's recent, cogent staff report on "Basic Issues." To quote from that report:

> The needs of a President and the needs of the departments and agencies are not identical.
>
> What does a President need to do his job?
>
> Essentially . . . to keep control . . . to get early warning of items for his agenda before his options are foreclosed, to pick his issues and lift these out of normal channels, to obtain priority attention from key officials on the issues he pulls to his desk, to get prompt support for his initiatives, and to keep other matters on a smooth course, with his lines of information open, so that he can intervene if need arises.
>
> What do the officials of our vast departments and agencies need to do their jobs?
>
> Essentially . . . orderly, deliberate, familiar procedures — accustomed forums in which to air their interests, a top-level umpire to blow the whistle . . . written records of the decisions by which they should be governed.
>
> . . . middle-level yearnings for some equivalent of the OCB [originate] in the desire to have one's views heard through some set, certain, reliable procedure which binds the highest levels as well as other agencies.

A President needs flexibility, freedom to improvise, in dealing with those below. Officialdom needs stability, assurance of regularity, in dealing with those above. To a degree these needs are incompatible; hence the dilemma. As your staff report notes:

> It is not surprising that the departments often find a President's way of doing business unsettling — or that Presidents sometimes view the departments almost as adversaries.

Reprinted by permission of Dr. Neustadt and the Subcommittee on National Security Staffing and Operations of the United States Senate.

In considering the problems now before you, I find it the beginning of wisdom to face this dilemma candidly. That is what I hope to do today.

THE PRESIDENT VERSUS OFFICIALDOM

So much of our literature and everyday discussion treats the executive branch as though it were an entity that effort is required to visualize the President apart from the departments, in effect a separate "branch," with needs and interests differing from those of "his" officialdom. Yet constitutional prescription, political tradition, governmental practice, and democratic theory all unite to make this so. In all these terms the separateness of presidential need and interest are inevitable — and legitimate.

The man in the White House is constitutional commander of our military forces, conductor of foreign relations, selector of department heads, custodian of the "take care clause" and of the veto power. No other person in our system has so massive a responsibility for national security. At the same time he is the one executive official holding office on popular election, and save for the Vice President he is our only public officer accountable directly to a national electorate. He is, besides, a relative short-timer in our Government. Members of Congress and career officials often hold high places for a generation. He, at most, holds his for just 8 years. The first year is a learning time, the last year usually a stalemate. Whatever personal imprint he can hope to make is usually reserved to the short span between. Yet his name becomes the label for an "era" in the history books; his accountability widens as time goes on. Schoolchildren yet unborn may hold him personally responsible for everything that happens to the country in "his" years.

The constitutional responsibility, the political accountability, the time perspective, the judgment of history: all of these adhere to the President himself, not as an "institution" but as a human being. In this combination his situation is unique. No one else in the executive branch — or for that matter in the Government — shares equally in his responsibility or feels an equal heat from his electorate and history. It is no wonder that his needs can be distinguished from, and actually are different from, the needs of most officials in executive departments.

Cold war and nuclear weapons make the difference greater. A new dimension of risk has come upon American decisionmaking. Its effect has been to magnify the President's responsibility, and to intensify his needs for flexibility, for information, for control. This new dimension first began to manifest itself in President Eisenhower's second term. Mr. Kennedy is the first President to live with it from the outset of his administration.

THE PRESIDENT AS RISKTAKER

What a President now lives with is the consequence of a substantial nuclear delivery capability acquired by the Soviet Union as well as the United States. It is the mutual capability which pushes our decision-making — and theirs, too, of course — into a new dimension of risk. In an article included in your volume of selected papers, I have termed this the risk of "irreversibility," the risk that either bureaucratic momentum in a large-scale undertaking or mutual miscalculation by atomic adversaries, or both combined, may make it infeasible to call back, or play over, or revise, an action taken in our foreign relations, at least within the range of the cold war. But the term "irreversibility," standing alone, does not really suffice to convey what is new in this dimension. Bureaucratic momentum and multiple miscalculations made a German emperor's snap reaction after Sarajevo "irreversible" as long ago as July 1914. Therefore, to amend the term: what is new since the Soviets acquired their ICBM's is the risk of irreversibility become irremediable. Unlike the problems facing Kaiser Wilhelm 50 years ago — or those of President Roosevelt in World War II, or even those of President Truman in Korea — a possible result of present action is that nothing one does later can ward off, reduce, repair, or compensate for costs to one's society.

Let me underscore this point; it goes to the heart of my presentation today. Last October we all glimpsed the new dimension in a President's risktaking. But the Cuban confrontation seems to me a relatively simplified affair: geographically, in the issue raised, in the number of contestants, and in duration. What if there were two or three such issues simultaneously, or stretched over 2 months instead of 2 weeks? What if there were — as Mr. Kennedy told us last week there may be 10 years hence — a multiplicity of nuclear powers, a multiplicity of possible miscalculators, each capable of setting off irreparable consequences? Consider the next President's risktaking, let alone Mr. Kennedy's. This new dimension deepens year by year.

The consequences for the Presidency are profound.

One consequence is that the sitting President lives daily with the knowledge that at any time he, personally, may have to make a human judgment — or may fail to control someone else's judgment — which puts half the world in jeopardy and cannot be called back. You and I will recognize his burden intellectually; he actually experiences it emotionally. It cannot help but set him — and his needs — sharply apart from all the rest of us, not least from the officials who have only to advise him. As Mr. Kennedy remarked in his December television interview: "The President bears the burden of the responsibility. The advisers may move on to new advice."

A second related consequence is that now more than ever before his mind becomes the only source available from which to draw politically legitimated judgments on what, broadly speaking, can be termed the political feasibilities of contemplated action vis-a-vis our world antagonists: judgments on where history is tending, what opponents can stand, what friends will take, what officials will enforce, what "men in the street" will tolerate; judgments on the balance of support, opposition, indifference at home and abroad. Our Constitution contemplated that such judgments should emanate from President and Congress, from a combination of the men who owed their places to electorates, who had themselves experienced the hazards of nomination and election. The democratic element in our system consists, essentially, of reserving these judgments to men with that experience. But when it comes to action risking war, technology has modified the Constitution: the President, perforce, becomes the only such man in the system capable of exercising judgment under the extraordinary limits now imposed by secrecy, complexity, and time.

Therefore as a matter not alone of securing his own peace of mind, but also of preserving the essentials in our democratic order, a President, these days, is virtually compelled to reach for information and to seek control over details of operation deep inside executive departments. For it is at the level of detail, of concrete plans, of actual performance, on "small" operations, to say nothing of large ones, that there often is a fleeting chance — sometimes the only chance — to interject effective judgment. And it is at this level that risks of the gravest sort are often run. "Irreversibility become irremediable" is not to be considered something separate from details of operation. If, as reported, Mr. Kennedy kept track of every movement of blockading warships during the Cuban crisis of October 1962, this is but a natural and necessary corollary of the new dimension of risk shadowing us all, but most of all a President.

The net effect is to restrict, if not repeal, a hallowed aspect of American military doctrine, the autonomy of field commanders, which as recently as Mr. Truman's time, as recently as the Korean war, was thought to set sharp limits upon White House intervention in details of operation. The conduct of diplomacy is comparably affected. So, I presume, is the conduct of intelligence. Also, we now rediscover that age-old problem for the rulers of States: timely and secure communications. The complications here are mind stretching.

The only persons qualified to give you a full appreciation of the President's felt needs in such a situation are Mr. Eisenhower, keeping his last years in view, and Mr. Kennedy. Mr. Khrushchev might now be equipped to offer some contributory evidence. The situation is so new and so unprecedented that outside the narrow circle of these men and their immediate associates one cannot look with confidence for understanding of their prospects or requirements as these appear to them. I do not advance this caution out of modesty — though my competence suffers along with the rest of the outsiders — but to suggest that there remains, at least for the time being, a further source of differences between the President and most executive officials: the former cannot fail for long to see what he is up against; the latter have not seen enough of men so placed to have much sympathy or a sure sense for how it feels these days, in these conditions, to be President. What they see with assurance is what they in their jobs want of him in his, a very different matter. Such differing perceptions of the Presidential task are bound to widen differences of perceived need between the White House where responsibility is focused and officialdom where it is not.

The same phenomenon of differing perceptions seems to play a part in other Presidential relationships. No doubt it has some bearing on the current difficulties of relationship between the White House and its counterparts in certain allied capitals where political leaders, in their own capacities, have not experienced the risk to which our President is heir because they lack the power which produced it. Presumably some of the sore spots in congressional relations have a comparable source. Certainly this is the case with some of the complaints voiced against Messrs. Eisenhower and Kennedy, in turn, by private groups intent upon particular action programs.

The lack of common outlook increases the Presidency's isolation and thus reinforces the dictates of common prudence for a man who bears the burden of that office in our time, namely, to stretch his personal control, his human judgment, as wide and deep as he can make them reach. Your staff report is quite right in its catalog of Presidential needs.

OFFICIALDOM VERSUS THE PRESIDENT

The cold war, however, and the pace of technology have not affected only Presidential needs. They also have affected departmental needs, and in a very different way.

Well before the Soviets achieved ICBM's the pace of change in our own weaponry combined with our wide-ranging economic and political endeavors overseas were mixing up the jurisdictions of all agencies with roles to play, or claim, in national security: mingling operations along programmatic lines, cutting across vertical lines of authority, breaching the neat boxes on organizational charts. Defense, State, CIA, AID, Treasury, together with the President's Executive Office staffs, now form a single complex — a national security complex, if you will — tied together by an intricate network of program and staff interrelationships in Washington and in the field. AEC, ACDA, USIA are also in the complex; others lurk nearby, tied in to a degree, as for example Commerce.

As early as the National Security Act of 1947 we formally acknowledged the close ties of foreign, military, economic policy; these ties had been rendered very plain by World War II experience. But in the pre-Korean years when ECA was on its own, when CIA was new, when MAAG's were hardly heard of, while atom bombs were ours alone and military budgets stood at under $15 billion, a Secretary of Defense could forbid contacts between Pentagon and State at any level lower than his own, and within limits could enforce his ban. That happened only 14 years ago. In bureaucratic terms it is as remote as the stone age.

While operations now have been entangled inextricably, our formal organizations and their statutory powers and the jurisdictions of congressional committees remain much as ever: distinct, disparate, dispersed. Our personnel systems are equally dispersed. In the national security complex alone, I count at least seven separate professional career systems — military included — along with the general civil service which to most intents and purposes is departmentalized.

These days few staffs in any agency can do their work alone without active support or at least passive acquiescence from staffs outside, in other agencies — often many others. Yet no one agency, no personnel system is the effective boss of any other; no one staff owes effective loyalty to the others. By and large the stakes which move men's loyalties — whether purpose, prestige, power, or promotion — run to one's own program, one's own career system, along agency lines not across them.

These developments place premiums on interstaff negotiation, compromise, agreement in the course of everybody's action. This subcommittee has deplored the horrors of committee work: the wastes of time, the earstrain — and the eyestrain — the "papering over" of differences, the search for lowest common denominators of agreement. I deplore these horrors, too, and freely advocate "committee killing," periodically, to keep them within bounds. But given the realities of programing and operations, interagency negotiation cannot be avoided. To "kill" committees is, at most, to drive them underground. Officials have to find at least an informal equivalent. What else are they to do?

One other thing they can do is push their pet issues up for argument and settlement at higher levels. Once started on this course, there is no very satisfactory place to stop short of the White House. In logic and in law only the Presidency stands somewhat above all agencies, all personnel systems, all staffs. Here one can hope to gain decisions as definitive as our system permits; congressional committees may be able to supplant them, special pleaders may be able to reverse them, foot-draggers may be able to subvert them — even so, they are the surest thing obtainable.

Accordingly officials urged to show initiative, to quit logrolling in committee, to be vigorous in advocacy, firm in execution, turn toward the White House seeking from it regular, reliable, consistent service as a fixed and constant court of arbitration for the national security complex. This means, of course, a court which knows how courts behave and does not enter cases prematurely. Your staff report rightly describes the sort of service wanted; in the circumstances of officials they do well to want it.

Their need for such a service is unquestionable, and legitimate. To flounder through the mush of "iffy" answers, or evasions; to struggle through the murk of many voices, few directives; to fight without assurance of a referee; to face the Hill without assurance of a buffer; or on the other hand, to clean up after eager amateurs, to repair damage done by ex parte proceedings; to cope with happy thoughts in highest places — these are what officialdom complains of, and with reason. For the work of large-scale enterprises tends to be disrupted by such breaches of "good order" and routine. Not bureaucrats alone but also Presidents have stakes in the effectiveness of the Executive bureaucracy. From any point of view, officials surely are entitled to want White House service in support of their performance.

But if a President should give this service to their satisfaction, what becomes of him? While he sits as the judge of issues brought by others — keeping order, following procedure, filing decisions, clearing dockets — what happens to his personal initiative, his search for information, his reach for control, his mastery of detail? What happens to his own concerns outside the sphere of national security? In short, where is his flexibility? The answers I think are plain. Thus the dilemma with which I began: to a degree — a large degree — his needs and theirs are incompatible.

HELP FROM THE SECRETARY OF STATE?

It is tempting to assert that this dilemma could be resolved at a stroke by the appointment of a "czar," a Presidential deputy, to serve as court-of-first-resort for all disputes within the national security complex except the ones the President preempted out of interest to himself or to the Nation. The "solution" is tempting but I find it quite unreal. I do not see how this role can be built into our system. I share the reservations put on record by the reports of your predecessor subcommittee.

Setting aside grandiose solutions, what might be done to ease the tension between presidential and official needs, to keep the pains of this dilemma within bounds? The answer I believe — insofar as one exists — lies in careful and selective augmentation of the Presidency's staff resources. A President may not need deputies, writ large, to keep decisions from him but he certainly needs ready and responsive staff work in the preparatory phases of decisionmaking and followup. The better he is served thereby, the better will officialdom be served as well. In this their needs run parallel: effective staff work for him cannot help but put some firm procedure under foot for them; such staff work promises that bases will be touched, standpoints explored — with rocks turned over and the worms revealed — positions traced, appeals arranged, compromises tested. When this prospect is seen ahead official hearts are glad.

In the nature of the case, a President's assistants at the White House cannot do that sort of staff work by themselves except — they hope and so does he — on issues having top priority for him in his own mind and schedule, day-to-day. Preparatory work on issues not yet in that class and followup on issues which have left it must be done, if done at all, at one remove through staff facilities less dominated by the President's immediate requirements. Hence the distinction introduced a quarter-century ago between personal staff at the White House and institutional staff, mainly career staff, in the executive offices across the street, of which the longest-lived example is the Bureau of the Budget.

But in the sphere of national security there is no Budget Bureau. Its nearest counterpart remains the Office of the Secretary of State. This is the traditional source of "institutional" assistance for a President in what was once the peacetime sum of foreign relations: diplomacy. And while the Office has not kept pace with the meaning of that term, no full-scale substitute has been built in its stead. I hope none will be. I hope, rather, that the Secretary's Office can be rebuilt on a scale commensurate with the contemporary reach of foreign relations.

Reliance on the Secretary's Office as an institutional staff resource seems to have been envisaged at the start of Mr. Kennedy's administration. On the White House side Mr. Bundy was named to the necessary personal assistantship, filling a post established in the previous administration: "Special Assistant for National Security Affairs." But formalized committee structures and secretariats built up around his post during the 1950's were scaled down or disestablished by the new administration. This was done with the expressed intent of improving staff performance by transferring staff functions to the Office of the Secretary of State. OCB is a case in point. As Mr. Bundy wrote your chairman on September 4, 1961:

> It was and is our belief that there is much to be done that the OCB could not do, and that the things it did do can be done as well or better in other ways.
> The most important of these other ways is an increased reliance on the leadership of the Department of State . . . the President has made it very clear that he does not want a large separate organization between him and his Secretary of State. Neither does he wish any question to arise as to the clear authority and responsibility of the Secretary of State, not only in his own Department, and not only in such large-scale related areas as foreign aid and information policy, but also as the agent of coordination in all our major policies toward other nations.

For a variety of reasons, some of them beyond my range of observation, this staffing pattern has not been set firmly up to now: the White House side, the "personal" side, seems firm enough but not the other side, the "institutional" side. So far as I can judge, the State Department has not yet found means to take the proffered role and play it vigorously across the board of national security affairs. The difficulties here may be endemic; the role may ask too much of one department among others. But I think it is decidedly too soon to tell. State, I conceive, should have the benefit of every doubt and more time for experiment.

This seems to be the view of the administration. It is striking that in all these months the White House staff has set up no procedures or "machinery" which would interfere in any way with building up the Secretary's Office as a Presidential "agent of coordination." It is striking also that the Secretary has moved toward enhancement of his Office by equipping it with a strong No. 3 position in the person of Mr. Harriman, who preceded me at your hearings. The burdens of advice-giving and of negotiation weigh heavily these days not only on the Secretary but also on the Under Secretary. This position thus comes into play as in effect their common deputyship. Mr. Harriman, I take it, with his new authority as second Under Secretary has more opportunity than they to be a source of guidance and of stiffening — and interference-running — for careerists in the State Department, as they deal with one another and with staffs outside. If he actually can do this, if he too is not weighed down by other duties, then the ground may be prepared now for substantial further movement toward development of central staff work in the national security sphere.

Until now, I gather, no one has had time to make himself consistently an energizer, catalyst, connective for the several sorts of planners, secretariats, task forces, and action officers now scattered through the upper floors of our vast new State building. The Secretary may sit at the center of this vastness, but his Office has almost no staff which he can call his own. To weld together such a staff out of these scattered pieces, to imbue it with cohesion and a government-wide outlook, to implant it as a Presidential agent of coordination for the sweep of national security affairs: all this is far from done. I need not tell you why I think the doing will take time.

THE SECRETARY VERSUS THE OTHERS

But I must not mislead you. What I offer here is "conventional wisdom," my hopes are conventional hopes. To call for augmentation of the Presidency's staff resources is to echo what has been prescribed for almost every governmental ailment these past 30 years. To fasten on the Secretary's Office as the means is to follow the footsteps of innumerable study groups intent upon improving something in particular within the range of foreign operations. The Herter Committee very recently, concerned for personnel in Foreign Service, charged the Secretary's Office with coordination of civilian career systems. Now I come along to charge the Office with coordinative staff work in the realm of policy. Such unanimity is dangerous.

The danger is that as we try to make the Secretary's Office serve the needs of personnel directors, or of action officers, or White House aides, or Presidents, we may forget the Secretary's needs. The danger is that as we try to make him a strong instrument for other people's purposes we may forget that he will have some purpose of his own. The modern secretaryship of state is not merely a Presidential staff resource — or a personnel agency for that matter — nor can it be used simply to bridge differences between the President and officialdom. This Office has its own compelling and divergent needs apart from theirs; it has its own dilemma differing from theirs. To seek the best of both worlds from the Secretary's Office, to intend effective staff work for both President and Secretary, is to present as delicate a task of institution building as the Executive has faced in modern times. Because it is so delicate the outcome is uncertain. The danger is that in our advocacy we forget the delicacy, the uncertainty, or both.

Consider for a moment the responsibility of any modern Secretary of State. Always in form, usually in fact, the man becomes a very senior personal adviser to the President, a source of brainpower and judgment for him both as one man to another and at working sessions of his chosen inner circle — currently the executive committee of the National Security

Council. Perhaps this was not Mr. Bryan's role — to reach far back — or Mr. Hull's, but certainly it was the role of Messrs. Marshall, Acheson, and Dulles, among others. Under conditions of cold war, this role is sharpened, rendered more intense by emergence of the Secretary of Defense, an officer with roughly equal claim but necessarily different focus, as a source of judgment in the foreign relations sphere. Balance of advice becomes important on each issue every day.

The Secretary of State is much more than a personal adviser. He also is our ranking diplomat at large for sensitive negotiations just short of the summit. Furthermore, he serves as an administration voice to Congress, to the country, and abroad whose public word is weighty in proportion to his rank. At the same time he is actively in charge of a complex administrative entity. He is "Mr. State Department" and "Mr. Foreign Service," leader of officials, spokesman for their causes, guardian of their interests, judge of their disputes, superintendent of their work, master of their careers.

The Secretary of State has a dilemma all his own. These roles are mutually reinforcing: his advice gains weight because he represents the whole Department, his public statements and internal orders gain in potency because he is so often at the White House. But these roles are also mutually antagonistic: fronting for officials strains his credit as an adviser, advising keeps his mind off management, negotiating preempts energy and time. No modern Secretary has performed the miracle of playing all these roles at once so skillfully and carefully that he obtains the benefits of all and pays no penalties. Presumably there is no way to do it.

A Secretary cannot wriggle out of this dilemma by ditching his department and retreating to the White House, although at least one Secretary may have wished he could. His job cannot be done from there, nor is he needed there. Another man can serve, and does, as White House aide for national security affairs; like others of his kind the aide stays close at hand to deal with action issues on the President's agenda when and how the President's own mind, interests, and work habits require as he meets his own time pressures and priorities. No doubt this personal assistantship includes a role as personal adviser. The Secretary also is a personal adviser. But this coincidence does not make them the same, nor would it help the President to have two such assistants and no Secretary.

The Secretary's usefulness as an adviser lies precisely in the fact that he is more than just another aide whose work is tied entirely to the President's. The Secretary has work of his own, resources of his own, vistas of his own. He is in business under his own name and in his name powers are exercised, decisions taken. Therefore he can press his personal authority, his own opinion, his adviser's role, wherever he sees fit across the whole contemporary reach of foreign relations, never mind the organization charts. He cannot hope to win all arguments in such a sphere, nor is he in position to contest them indiscriminately. But his status and the tasks of his Department give him every right to raise his voice where, when and as he chooses. To abandon his Department in an effort to escape its burdens and distractions is to cloud his title as adviser.

Yet to concentrate on running his department — combating weaknesses, asserting jurisdictions, adjudicating feuds — is no better solution for a Secretary's problem. With the President absorbed, as Presidents must be, in foreign operations, in diplomacy, defense, no Secretary worth his salt would spend much time on management while others drafted cables in the Cabinet room. And if he did he would not long remain effective as a personal adviser.

The modern Secretary of State, whoever he may be, deserves more sympathy than most receive. He lives with his dilemma but he cannot take the comfort which officials, facing theirs, draw from longevity: "This too shall pass." Nor can he take the comfort which a President derives from being, for a fixed term, No. 1. The Secretary's only consolation is to share with Gilbert's Gondoliers "the satisfying feeling that our duty has been done." But "duty" is exceedingly ambiguous for him. What about the duties he has slighted?

Two Notes of Caution

Under these circumstances it would add insult to injury if this man were asked to serve in any simple sense as the Director of a Presidential staff facility on the model of the Bureau of the Budget. For self-protection he would have to shirk the task if it were his. Otherwise he would be kept so busy checking on the work of his resentful Cabinet colleagues that every present role might suffer more than it does now. What is the gain from that? But if we simply move the upper reaches of the State Department out from under him and tie them to the Presidency apart from him, where does he get his staff work done, who bulwarks his initiatives, supports his roles? Yet if we leave his departmental aides to serve him only and turn elsewhere for the Presidency's service — if, as some have urged, we simply set up a new "Office of National Security Affairs" in the Executive Offices beside the Budget Bureau — what happens to the Secretary's status and utility in doing what he now does for our Government?

I pose these questions to be cautious, not equivocal. I hope that through the Secretary's Office we can build an institution serving both the Presidency and the Secretary himself. I hope thereby that we can ease the tension between President and officialdom, and at the same time ease the Secretary's own dilemma. In my opinion we should try to realize these hopes. But I would not pretend to you that such a course is either safe or certain. And assuredly it is not simple.

In closing let me add a second caution: even with time, even with good use of it, even if we master complex institution building, we can expect no miracles from policy. Even if the Secretary's Office should become a partner with the White House in the Presidency's business while the Secretary's business is protected and enhanced, even then both sorts of business would be botched on numerous occasions. For methods and procedures at their best cannot abolish the deep difficulties of perception, of analysis, of judgment, of persuasion which confront our policymakers now and in the future. Organizational arrangements at their most ingenious cannot rub out the underlying differences of duty, interest, role, perspective, separating Presidency from officialdom — and separating both from Congress, for that matter.

These difficulties, differences, lie at the root of most "botched business" we have witnessed in the past and will experience in future. Machinery may confine the damage or enlarge it, but to see the source of damage as the vehicle in use is to ignore the driver, and his passengers, and road conditions, and the other drivers. To claim that it could be made damage-proof by redesign is to divert attention from the human condition. I would make no such claim. Machinery is important; our President and our executive officials need the most effective mechanisms they can get. Still, this remains emphatically a government of men who face in national security affairs unprecedented problems mostly not of their own making.

They dare not hope for too much from machinery, nor should we. To do so is to court unnecessary disappointment. As the world goes these days I see no need for that. There seems to be quite enough necessary disappointment. . . .

. . . If you feel that I kept shifting from foot to foot in the last half of my statement, you are absolutely right. Let me put it as candidly as possible: I don't like the thought that we may have to come to another fairly large-scale institutionalized office in the President's own neighborhood. I think we ought to avoid it if we can. I am not, as you can see, prepared to come here as a student and say to you, "It can be avoided." I don't know if it can be. You have suggested reasons why it is going to be extremely difficult to do it.

Let me simply say that staff facilities around the Presidency are not an unmixed blessing for the President. The man needs the kind of flexibility, the kind of reach, that staff is supposed to give him, the kind of balanced advice that staff is supposed to be able to procure for him by careful watching and airing of difficulties and differences and grievances and information which may not appear upon the surface of advice from the departments.

But staff itself can become, all too quickly, another "department," another complicating echelon in a very complex system. There are two ways one could build up the staff now in the President's neighborhood; both ways have disadvantages. The first way is to markedly enlarge the Bundy office. But the more one does that, the more one threatens Mr. Bundy's utility as a personal aide. He is pushed toward the troubles that your predecessor subcommittee treated in its staff report on super-Cabinet officers and superstaffs, the troubles Mr. Rockefeller evidently found himself in 8 years ago, or Mr. Stassen and others, when their personal service, their ability to be personal agents, to move quickly, to keep abreast of the President's mind — in short, their intimacy — was compromised by all the second-level work their staffs were doing, all the fights their staffs were getting into. The personal assistant begins to bog down as a personal watchdog and intimate servant, once he starts presiding over 50, 80, or 100 subordinates.

A second way of building staff is to create an Office of National Security Affairs detached from the Bundy office, manned by careerists across the street, like the Budget Bureau. We may come to this in time. But, in doing so, we must remember that we are adding another echelon, another level for clearances, another level for negotiations, another set of career officials who have to relate every day with Pentagon and State and the domestic economic agencies; thus, to a degree, we are throwing more pressure on the White House for personal staff work to protect the President's interest in these new interagency interrelationships. My feeling is we should resist this as long as we can. . . .

Mr. NEUSTADT. There is one other difficulty, Senator, and without spending a lot of time on it, let me put it before you. It underlies my caution and it complicates your hopes, I think.

In my experience, the most effective kind of staff organization is an organization built around what I would call an action-forcing process, by which I mean a steady stream of actionable issues, concrete issues, that have to be attended to, issues where something has to be done, a decision has to be reached.

In this national security area, you have a number of these processes: the budget process with its statutory deadline is one of these; action cables coming in from Embassies abroad requesting answers and instructions, are another; requests for instructions from military assistance groups, the flow through ISA is another. In wartime, the conduct of hostilities creates still others.

Wherever you build staff, you ought to try to build it around one or another of these streams of action, issues that have to be attended to. Otherwise, you just get planners floating in a void, as you suggest. Now, most of these action streams do flow through the departments. The action cables come through the State Department or, if the military are involved, through the Pentagon.

One reason why the Bureau of the Budget, as an institution, is stronger and has lasted longer than others at the Presidential level, is that it is built around just such a stream of actions, budget deadlines, apportionment deadlines, which belong to no department but are imposed routinely and directly on the President himself. If you compare the strength of this entity with the strength of the Council of Economic Advisers, which has much less of an action orientation, I think you will see the difference.

One of the reasons why I keep backing away from an Office of National Security Affairs is that if the staff work there were to be effective, it seems to me you would have to lift up to the President's level, on a routine basis, a great part of the action issues and the action officers now located in Pentagon and State. Otherwise, the Office of National Security Affairs would be a kibitzer, another echelon of planner-kibitzers, on the business, the day-by-day business, of the two Secretaries and their subordinates.

So if we build the new office and then try to insure its success, we tend to pull away from the two Secretaries a lot of relatively routine action-taking, decision-taking before we are done. If we don't pull it away, we run the risk that we just have this other layer, this waffle layer of planners and kibitzers operating in a void. If we do pull it away what have we done to the President?

This is very tricky, in my opinion, and it is the underlying reason why I would like to see the preparatory staff work and the followup on everything the White House now can't handle kept down as close to the present operators as possible.

I grant you that if we took the new Office of Science and Technology, instead of the Budget Bureau, as a model for staff up above the Departments, the case for an Office of National Security Affairs might look a lot better, at least on the surface. Mr. Wiesner and PSAC and OST, taken together, have made quite an impact even though they aren't organized around an action-forcing process they can call their own. But I think this is partly because their full-time staff is still rather small. I don't think I would want to be in Mr. Wiesner's shoes when his staff gets big as it will surely tend to do. More importantly, he and his associates have been able, up to now, to reach out and hook onto action-issues in other people's bailiwicks for a rather special reason: his office has been able to do this with others because it can claim special expertise, because it can lay hands on technical resources, judgments, better or more readily or more confidently than they can. An Office of National Security could never hope to be in such a good position vis-a-vis the expert claims and confidence of others, especially not others like the Pentagon, or CIA, or State — or Treasury, the Fed, and even Commerce, for that matter, if you want to talk about economics. This is part of the problem of the Council of Economic Advisers.

Senator MILLER. Let's say we have an Office of National Security Planning set up. Would you prefer to see it set up along the lines of the Council of Economic Advisers, or would you prefer to set it up along — let's talk about action.

Would you prefer to see it confined to actions of the type, if you want to call them that, the Council of Economic Advisers performs, or such as the Bureau of the Budget performs?

Mr. NEUSTADT. If you are going to have a strong staff office, you have to build it around actions. You have to build it around the process of receiving and answering requests for instructions from diplomatic and military missions abroad. There is something solid, a solid core of work to build a staff around. If you build it around that, what have you done to the work of the Office of the Secretary of Defense and the Office of the Secretary of State? . . .

Mr. TUFTS. You speak in your statement of the Secretary of State's peculiar, compelling needs, and you say something about where these needs arise — in his role of special adviser to the President, chief negotiator for the Government, and so forth. In your consideration of the Secretary's many roles, how do you think he should assign his priorities? What roles should receive priority?

Mr. NEUSTADT. I think a Secretary, unless he is hired specifically for a different purpose as Mr. Stettinius was, a Secretary hired for the job in the more normal course will and should try to put first his role as a senior adviser to the President. I think he must put immediately after that, really as part of it, the role which I didn't specifically mention but implied of collegial relations with that other senior adviser, the Secretary of Defense. I believe Mr. Harriman singled this out for you the other day as a special Cabinet relationship. I think that is quite right.

If a Secretary of State takes fully seriously his mandate as expressed by the Bundy letter of September 1961, then he would have to put next his role of attempting to stand at the center of the group of Cabinet officers concerned with national security affairs, while attempting to act as agent of coordination.

This would leave him very little time for all the roles assigned him and demanded of him within his own organization, but it would seem to me that a Secretary who started off to be a President adviser would have to put ahead of department management these other obligations.

Mr. TUFTS. It seems to me as I listened to the discussion this morning, repeatedly we have come to the point that it is the State-Defense relationship that is the key, and where the big problems of coordination arise. The Secretary of State, after all, already has, by law and tradition and practice, the authority for supervision of the aid program and the information program, the disarmament agency, and so on.

It seems to me that the State-Defense role is where the major problems of coordination arise. Therefore, I wondered whether by performing your second role, the collegial relationship with the Secretary of Defense, he is not getting at the heart of his third task.

Mr. NEUSTADT. He is getting at the heart of it, but there are two other aspects that a buddy-buddy relationship with the Secretary of Defense will not automatically take care of. One is the aspect that in form is within his departmental mandate; coordinating with the traditional bureaus those autonomous units, AID, ACDA, USIA which takes policy advice from him, and so forth. This is really a matter of interagency relations, even though in form some of these agencies are within the Department.

The other aspect involves the Secretary of the Treasury. Treasury is our third Foreign Office. The only exception I would take to Mr. Harriman's remarks — and I agree that one should put the Defense relation first — is that I think in these times, so long as the balance of payments and all it represents is with us, and so long as the Secretary in his internal job of debt financing is heavily and delicately involved in a host of external relations, involved among other things in banking community interrelations around the world — one can never afford to regard Treasury as a marginal agency in the national security sphere.

On some issues the State-Treasury relationship will be as crucial as it is all the time in the State-Defense area. . . .

Mr. ENGBERG. You don't feel, then, that there would be, in sort of a de facto sense, the development of a super-State Department agency?

Mr. NEUSTADT. Well, it depends on what you mean by "super."

Mr. ENGBERG. If it is a prime adviser to the President on security problems and if he depends upon State for this type of thing and State has to either by informal or formal means get the necessary information on all of these highly important and related fields in determining the policy that it is recommending, wouldn't there be a tendency to think of it as being a superagency, a top agency?

Mr. NEUSTADT. If all these things followed precisely as you put them, yes; but I don't think there is any chance that they will. The Secretary of Defense is unlikely to be a shrinking violet; neither is the Secretary of the Treasury. I can't make promises about personalities in the future, but their institutional positions are such that they will be able to make their voices heard and their subordinates will have strong rights and will push to get them exercised. As for the White House I am most doubtful that it would depend on staff in the Secretary's Office to bring up all the papers which the President's aides would merely scan for proper form and then have the President sign. This seems to me a most unlikely eventuality.

All one really wants from State is this: On issues which a Bundy office cannot handle because they aren't at the top of the President's own list, or after a decision is made because he shifts off to something else while they have to be tidied up and tended to, all one wants — all I hope — is that staff in the Secretary's Office will conscientiously and carefully, and with a sense of serving the whole Government, make sure that all the people with a right to know, all the people with a right to be involved, to express opinions, will get a crack at the right time and place.

This is asking a lot, but this is all I am asking. The better State is able to do this, the more confidence will develop in the Pentagon and in the Treasury. The more effective this begins to be, the less will be the tendencies to do the things Mr. Tufts and I were talking about, to hide information.

If other agencies find the State Department staff a good resource for them, a good avenue for them, they will use it. In the best of all possible worlds, it is still a far cry from czardom or from the single or sole source of advice. This is merely a means of getting the preparatory work done, putting advice in shape, everybody's advice in shape, and getting the followup work done, passing the word, checking on what has been done, getting both kinds of work better handled beyond the range where White House staffers can do it themselves on an ad hoc basis. . . .

The Presidency, Executive Staffing, and the Federal Bureaucracy

Laurin L. Henry

Students of the presidency tend to be a little puzzled by the perennial underdevelopment of the personnel function of the office. Although aware that the appointment process is necessarily highly political and inevitably somewhat personal in nature, observers have often felt that decision-making about appointments was unnecessarily casual and that Presidents tolerated personnel staff work that was disfunctional from almost any point of view. Would not just a little more White House sophistication and attention to filling the top political and career posts produce substantial benefits for the President, both in improved management and leadership of the various executive agencies and in greater responsiveness to presidential direction of the bureaucracy?

My purpose here is to examine current methods of filling the most strategic executive positions in light of newly available data from other studies and my own limited inquiry into recent developments that have not been fully reported. My initial suspicion — hypothesis if you will — was that changes of permanent significance for the power position and institutional apparatus of the presidency might be occurring. My findings are that developments in the political and administrative position of the presidency since World War II have opened the way to an important expansion of the presidential role in the personnel area. The current President [Lyndon B. Johnson] is striving by personal effort and sponsorship of institutional innovations to take advantage of these opportunities. How far he can go, how firmly he can establish these innovations, will depend on a number of things including the duration and future political standing of the present administration. Proceeding at least partly along lines that have had expert and bipartisan support for years, the President's efforts have not become sharply controversial so far, although certain aspects of his strengthened control are producing some partisan and bureaucratic anxieties. These anxieties may increase and lead to a pause and possible retrenchment by the President's successor, whoever and whenever he may be. However, my own feeling is that any retrenchment is likely to be modest and temporary and that much of what has happened will last. We are seeing another of those accretions of presidential role, responsibility, and apparatus with which each incumbent endows and partially binds his successors.

Printed by permission of the author. This article was delivered before the American Political Science Association in Chicago, September 1967.

Let us look first at some of the characteristics of the executive bureaucracy and some previous efforts to define and advance the President's interest therein; then we will turn to recent developments in executive staffing.

THE FEDERAL BUREAUCRACY AND
THE PRESIDENTIAL INTEREST

This article will concentrate on the two groups of executives that are most crucial for the President. First, we will consider the principal political executives of the administration. These include the department heads, under- and assistant-secretaries, principal members of the White House and Executive Office staffs, heads and deputies of the leading non-Cabinet agencies, chiefs of a few of the major bureaus or services within the departments, and, for some purposes, the members of the principal regulatory commissions. Depending on the strictness of one's definition, there are perhaps as many as 300 of these principal officials. Below them lies a zone of several hundred lesser presidential appointees such as ambassadors, federal attorneys, members of minor boards and commissions, and some others who are traditionally considered more important for patronage than for policy reasons. The White House staff currently calculates that the President appoints 526 full-time executive branch officers, 489 judicial branch officials, and almost 1700 "others" including members of 145 part-time and temporary advisory bodies, for a grand total of about 2700 presidential appointees.[1] This of course excludes several thousand foreign service officers and members of uniformed corps whose presidential commissions are routine and nominal.

Second, we will consider the so-called "supergrades" — the 4,400 positions at levels GS-16, -17, and -18 of the classified civil service. According to Civil Service Commission tabulations, about three-fourths of the supergrades are occupied by career men appointed under full merit procedures — the elite of our permanent civil service. The remaining thousand or so are in various special schedules and exempt categories; the incumbents range from those who are essentially careerists despite their formal classification to some very political birds of passage. (We will leave aside the three or four thousand positions comparable to the supergrades in "other pay systems" outside the General Schedule such as the FBI, AEC, TVA, postal field service, VA medical service, and overseas agencies; these special categories have defied systematic study and rationalization for years.)

Characteristics of Executives. In recent years several research studies have greatly enriched our understanding of the backgrounds, career lines, appointment processes, and actual jobs held by top federal executives. In 1957, Paul David and Ross Pollock produced an interesting

[1] In the preparation of this article I have had the benefit of interviews during the summer of 1967 with several members of the White House staff and other governmental officials whose anonymity probably should be preserved.

analysis of alternative systems for staffing the political and career executive positions, with special attention to the tendency of the two kinds of jobs to blur into one another with respect both to functions and to status.[2] Marver Bernstein's study of the functions of political executives provided valuable insights into the political-administrative milieu at upper levels of the executive branch. It emphasized the demanding nature of the jobs, the increasing requirements for substantive and managerial expertise, and the complexity of the relationships incumbents must maintain with the White House, department heads, congressmen, "opposite numbers" in other agencies, interest representatives, and career staffs.[3] John Corson and Shale Paul recently have scutinized the functions of upper career executives and identified an interesting trichotomy of types — program managers, supporting staff managers, and professionals who are essentially practicing within the government.[4]

There is a great deal of new data about the social and educational origins of government executives. In 1963, Warner, Van Riper, Martin, and Collins published a study of over 10,000 political and career civilian executives and over 2,000 top-ranking military officers.[5] Two years later, the Brookings Institution issued a study by Dean Mann and Jameson Doig of the careers and processes of appointment of political executives at the assistant-secretary level since the New Deal,[6] and two years later released a more detailed analysis by David Stanley of some of the same data, widened to include regulatory commissioners and extended through President Johnson's early appointees.[7] We also have further data on top career executives in a separate study by Stanley.[8]

These studies are not precisely comparable because of differences in methods, but the results are quite consistent. Warner and associates found that although somewhat over 20 per cent of the civilian executives were "upwardly mobile" sons of tenant farmers, laborers, and skilled workers, and about the same number were sons of white collar workers and independent farmers, over half were from business and professional families. The separation of data on political and career executives in Warner's study is not complete, but the data seem to indicate that the political executives include a considerably greater proportion of the sons

[2] Paul T. David and Ross Pollock, *Executives for Government* (Washington, D.C.: The Brookings Institution, 1967).

[3] Marver H. Bernstein, *The Job of the Federal Executive* (Washington, D.C.: The Brookings Institution, 1958).

[4] John J. Corson and R. Shale Paul, *Men Near the Top* (Baltimore: Johns Hopkins Press, 1966).

[5] W. Lloyd Warner, Paul P. Van Riper, Norman H. Martin, and Orvis F. Collins, *The American Federal Executive* (New Haven: Yale University Press, 1963).

[6] Dean E. Mann with Jameson W. Doig, *The Assistant Secretaries* (Washington, D.C.: The Brookings Institution, 1965).

[7] David T. Stanley, Dean E. Mann, and Jameson Doig, *Men Who Govern: A Biographical Profile of Federal Political Executives* (Washington, D.C.: The Brookings Institution, 1967).

[8] David T. Stanley, *The Higher Civil Service* (Washington, D.C.: The Brookings Institution, 1964).

of large business owners, executives, and professional men, while the career executive group has a flatter social profile with more persons of farmer, working class, and white collar origins. Even among the civil service executives, however, sons of businessmen were overrepresented by a factor of five as compared to the general population, and sons of professional men were overrepresented by a factor of four.[9] These findings of relatively high family occupational backgrounds of the upper bureaucrats are consistent with data on religious preferences from the Brookings study showing a disproportionately high percentage of Protestants — and especially the so-called "high status" Episcopalian and Presbyterian denominations — among political executives.[10]

The key to advancement — the process through which even the well-born have to qualify and the less advantaged young men have their chance to catch up — is education. Warner and his associates reported that as of 1959, 78 per cent of the career executives and 90 per cent of the political executives had graduated from college, and that 45 per cent of the career executives and 74 per cent of the political executives had graduate or professional degrees. The big difference in advanced degrees was largely accounted for by the high proportion (39.9 per cent) of law school graduates among the political executives.[11] The Brookings and the Corson and Paul data show even higher levels of education for the two groups in more recent samples.[12]

Federal political executives not only have many degrees, but they have them from good institutions. Considering the large number of degree-granting colleges in this country, it is remarkable that data on undergraduate colleges of political executives since 1933 show that 19 per cent came from Yale, Harvard, or Princeton, 6 per cent were from other Ivy League institutions, and 15 per cent more were concentrated in a dozen other colleges including such leading private universities as Chicago, Stanford, and Northwestern, and such major state universities as Wisconsin, Michigan, California, North Carolina, and Minnesota. The convergence at major private and state universities was even sharper among those earning graduate or professional degrees.[13]

To be sure, many poor lads manage to graduate from high-status institutions. Nevertheless, the implication in these figures of predominantly high socio-economic status origins is supported by the report that 17 per cent of the political executives studied by Brookings received pre-college education at one of a list of eighteen select preparatory schools in the Northeast.[14] A boy who goes to Groton and Harvard is far more likely to become an assistant-secretary than one who attends his local public high school and the average state or private college. What accounts for

9 Warner, et al., esp. pp. 12–13.
10 Stanley, Mann, and Doig, pp. 14–16.
11 Warner, et al., pp. 107–110; Table 33B, p. 354; Table 36B, p. 357.
12 Stanley, Mann, and Doig, pp. 17–20.
13 Ibid., pp. 21–23.
14 Ibid., pp. 20–21.

this? No doubt it is partly a qualitative difference in the education at the elite insitutions; partly a matter of acquiring motivation, outlook, and expectations for a career that may lead to high public position; and partly a matter of making the friendships and connections that will ease the way to the sort of career expected. Elements of "merit" and "privilege" are inextricably mingled in such a career line.

Career executives are educated at a somewhat different and more diverse set of institutions than political executives, with much heavier concentration at public rather than private universities. Warner's comparison of the colleges at which members of the two groups received bachelor's degrees showed that after George Washington and City College of New York — important for both groups — the leading producers of career executives were the big state universities. No Ivy League institution ranked among the top ten producers of career executives, and only such fringe members of the Ivy League as Cornell and Pennsylvania placed in the second ten — along with New York University and Benjamin Franklin of Washington, D.C. On the political executive side, the state universities were shoved downward in the ranking to make room for Harvard, Yale, Princeton, and Pennsylvania in the first ten, and Chicago, Georgetown, Cornell, and Northwestern in the second ten. The concentration of career executives at public institutions continued, although less strikingly so, at degree levels above the baccalaureate.[15]

The pathways to the top are also fairly clearly marked, especially for the career executives. The great majority of those who reach supergrades enter the service relatively young and arrive at the supergrades in their late 40's or early 50's after a career in one or two agencies. According to Stanley's data, less than 5 per cent had served in more than three federal agencies, and Corson and Paul pointed out that a high percentage of the interagency transfers occur relatively early in a civil service career.[16] The narrowness and "closed" nature of the multiplicity of career ladders comprising the federal service is illustrated by what career executives say about how they got their present jobs. Most report either straight promotions or movements outward and upward to higher positions as a result of prior acquaintance or service with people who were in position to hire them.[17]

Political executives, of course, often enter federal service after establishing other careers. Although there have been some variations from administration to administration, the distribution of prior occupations of political executives has been quite stable. From Franklin Roosevelt through the early Johnson appointees, 24 per cent of all the political executive appointees had primary occupations in business, 26 per cent in law practice, 7 per cent in education, 2 per cent in science or engineering, and 6 per cent in miscellaneous private pursuits. However, 35 per cent came from primarily public service careers, including 4 per cent from

[15] Warner, *et al.*, pp. 131–136, 367–373.
[16] Stanley, pp. 31–33; Corson and Paul, p. 106 and Appendix B.
[17] Stanley, pp. 56–57.

elective public service, 22 per cent from federal appointive service, and 9 per cent from state or local appointive service. Until recently, the main variations from these patterns have been in the administrations of President Truman, who relied unusually heavily on appointees with long government service, and of President Eisenhower, who drew less from government and more from business.[18]

Other breakdowns of Brookings data emphasize the tendency for political executive appointments to go to individuals who have pursued "in and out" if not continuous federal careers. Out of 1,567 appointments (some individuals receiving two or three), 29 per cent of the individuals had held other political executive posts in the same agency, 8 per cent had held political executive jobs in other agencies, 24 per cent had held lower level non-career appointments in the same agency, 37 per cent had held lower level non-career posts in other agencies, 14 per cent had held career jobs in the same agency, 11 per cent had held career jobs in other agencies, 6 per cent had been in Congress, 1 per cent had been on the federal bench, and 7 per cent had held national party office. Only 15 per cent had had no discernible national-level political or administrative experience.[19]

The Mann-Doig study sheds important light on the typical route to political executive office. It has been mainly a departmental system. Despite their formal status as presidential appointees, most assistant-secretaries and the like have been appointed as a result of prior service in the agency, personal acquaintance with other departmental officers, and other experience and connections revolving around the agency's substantive program. Despite efforts of most Presidents to put a personal stamp on their administrations in the initial staffing, their later appointees have tended to be program rather than President or party oriented.[20]

Our information is perhaps least satisfactory concerning the personalities of political and career executives and the attitudes they have about their careers and roles. The Brookings study by Stanley indicates that the very top career executives have strong positive motivations for "getting things accomplished" in the public service and feel that although they might make more money elsewhere their work would be less interesting professionally and lack the satisfactions of service. Stanley found a remarkable amount of satisfaction of top career executives with the basic outlines of the system in which they had risen to the top, and surprisingly few ideas about how it might be improved — except of course by more pay. The attempts to develop psychological profiles of federal executives in the Warner book are perhaps the least satisfactory aspect of that study.[21]

The federal high bureaucracy is overwhelmingly white and male and

18 Stanley, Mann, and Doig, pp. 31–33 and Table E-1, p. 132.
19 *Ibid.*, pp. 41–42 and Table E-5, p. 137.
20 Mann and Doig, pp. 64–124, esp. pp. 91–99.
21 Stanley, pp. 59–65; Warner, *et al.*, pp. 191–250.

predominantly Protestant in its composition. Although a considerable number of men of blue and white collar family origins manage to qualify by educational achievement, a greater number come from upper-middle business and professional class families who find it relatively easier to inspire and finance their sons through a few of the nation's leading universities whose alumni dominate the service. The non-tenure political executives who are supposed to keep the career services responsible are even less socially, economically, and educationally representative of the nation as a whole than the career men. The careerists tend to rise to the top on narrow ladders of departmental or functional specialization. The political executives tend to have broader experiences, but there are increasing elements of careerism in this group as well, and the appointment process often has amounted to presidential acceptance of the man who rose to the top of the whirlpool of departmental interests.

How has the legitimacy of such a group been maintained? In large part, no doubt, it is because federal executives, although not mirroring the nation, have represented much of what the nation has admired and aspired to. Whether that is still true, in this year of rising discontents, is not entirely clear. Although the bureaucracy is also responsible to Congress and the courts, the nation's most active supervisory agent is the popularly elected President. How does the system for choosing these men affect the President's ability to direct and lead the executive establishment?

Defining the President's Interest. A strong presidential interest in the higher appointments has always been recognized, but views of how that interest should be defined and advanced have been constantly changing and frequently controversial. For the most part, nineteenth-century Presidents used the appointing power to reward electoral supporters and consolidate their partisan and factional positions. The rise of the merit system removed increasing numbers of lower level appointments from the patronage area, which was generally acceptable to the President as long as scandal was avoided, a sufficient number of appointments were available for his own purposes, and the remainder were denied his enemies. Both the presidential appointments and the non-presidential but exempt positions continued to be used primarily for patronage purposes well into the New Deal period.

Franklin D. Roosevelt's Committee on Administrative Management — the Brownlow Committee — defined the President's interest largely in terms of an extension upward of the merit system and sharp curtailment in the number of presidential appointees. The committee's staff study of personnel administration, by Floyd Reeves and Paul T. David, called for limiting the presidential appointments in each department to the secretary, under-secretary, and possibly a handful of staff assistants. A sharp line was to be drawn between these political appointees and the career service, which in each department was to be represented by an executive officer — the equivalent of the permanent under-secretary — supported by assistant executive officers and bureau chiefs all on a career basis.[22] The political assistant-secretaries apparently were to be eliminated altogether.

The committee itself did not go quite so far. It affirmed the need for a "sufficient number of high policy-determining posts at the disposal of a newly elected President to enable him and his administration to control the service." [23] The committee defined the policy determining posts as including the department heads and under-secretaries, assistant-secretaries, and the most important bureau chiefs. It also discussed the ill effects on both the President and the department head of having the President make subordinate appointments within the department. It proposed to extend the merit system upward within the departments, with exceptions to be made "only in the case of such of the highest positions as the President may find to be principally policy-determining in character." The committee recommended further that all positions in the departments then filled by presidential appointment should be filled by the department or agency head "except under secretaries and officers who report directly to the President or whose appointment by the President is required by the Constitution." [24] By implication, the assistant-secretaries were to be the department head's appointees. For control of the departments, the committee apparently was willing to rely mainly on the President's hierarchical authority running to the department heads and to leave appointments below that to either the department head or the merit system. Although the committee recommended that the staff of the central personnel agency and the personnel offices of the operating departments "should be regarded collectively as a unified career service of personnel administration," [25] there was little to suggest that the committee thought of the whole civil service as anything but a collection of departmental career services. Indeed, the proposed permanent executive officer at the apex of each department would have strengthened the departmental career service.

Subsequent history unfolded in several unforeseen ways. Although the next twenty years saw a gradual reduction in presidential appointments at lower levels, the number of top departmental officers appointed by the President did not shrink. Continued growth of the government and the experience of World War II and Korea led to recognition of need for more assistant-secretaries, not less, and by the mid 1950's the typical department had four or five where it had had one or two in the 1930's.

Moreover, the nature of the political executive jobs was changing, reflecting trends in the character of the bureaucracy and the position of the President. The growing size and complexity of the government required more substantive knowledge and managerial skill in top appointees. The political talents needed were sensitivity to programmatic

---

[22] President's Committee on Administrative Management, *Report With Staff Studies* (Washington, D.C.: Government Printing Office, 1937), pp. 121–122.

[23] *Ibid.*, p. 8.

[24] *Ibid.*, p. 9.

[25] *Ibid.*, p. 10.

and interest group considerations and capacity for delicate executive-legislative maneuvers, rather than old-fashioned credentials based on party organization and campaign service. At the same time, changes in party organization were lessening the need to use critical executive positions for strictly partisan purposes. The President increasingly dominated the party apparatus and had to make fewer concessions to it; he also had new and perhaps less costly forms of "recognition" at his disposal, such as appointments to advisory groups and invitations to White House dinners for visiting leaders of newly independent countries. There was a brief resurgence of interest in patronage at the advent of the Republican administration in 1953, but this soon spent its force, and by the end of the Eisenhower era it was widely recognized that traditional considerations were becoming almost irrelevant in the filling of these jobs.

The Personnel Task Force report and subsequent recommendations of the Second Hoover Commission in 1955 crystallized the implicit agreements of the previous twenty years and set many of the goals for the next twenty, although there remained much disagreement about the particular methods. The experience of the Eisenhower transition had demonstrated, and the commission affirmed, that the continuity and neutrality of the career service could be preserved only by the insulation of a substantial number of political appointees who could take the heat and change with the administration. The Task Force's use of the term "political executive" and its spelling out of his functions served to legitimatize the existence and need for such people. The Task Force also emphasized that political executives should be considered agents of the President; there were no worries about diluting the department head's authority with presidential appointees serving under him.[26]

With reference to the career employees, the commission stated forcefully an idea that had been creeping into the discussion for some time — the need for increased mobility among agencies and if possible the development of a corps of career executives of government-wide orientation and experience rather than narrow departmental outlooks. About the methods to achieve these objectives there was and still is considerable disagreement. The commission's wish to draw a sharp line between political and career executive positions, and to establish a senior civil service of career executives who would hold rank in their persons like military or foreign service officers and be subject to a centralized involuntary assignment process designed to provide mobility and diversity of experience, proved controversial and impossible of realization.

Search for an Organizational Link. During this evolution of doctrine about the President's interest in the personnel system, efforts to establish an organizational focal point to guard that interest have taken a variety of forms — none of them long lasting.

The Brownlow Committee, seeking "positive personnel management,"

26 Commission on Organization of the Executive Branch of the Government, *Personnel and Civil Service,* and *Task Force Report on Personnel and Civil Service* (Washington, D.C.: Government Printing Office, 1955).

recommended converting the three-man, bipartisan Civil Service Commission into a Civil Service Administration, which would be one of the principal staff arms of the President in the new Executive Office. The agency would be headed by a single administrator chosen under merit procedures but serving at the pleasure of the President; a seven-man board attached to the administration would provide advice and serve as watchdog over the merit system but would have no direct responsibility for personnel management. The functions prescribed for the administration had to do entirely with the consolidation, extension, and management of the career services. Staff work in connection with presidential appointments presumably would be left to the departments or handled by the expanded White House staff, but the committee did not describe these arrangements.[27]

The bipartisan commission proved to be politically untouchable. Even when establishment of the Executive Office was finally authorized, in 1939, the commission was excluded from the President's reorganization authority and left intact. One of FDR's six new administrative assistants was designated as Liaison Officer for Personnel Management with responsibility for linking the President and the commission and for coordination of personnel matters not under commission jurisdiction. This office was manned by a former civil servant and seems to have confined its attention to the career services. In Roosevelt's time, presidential appointments were managed by other White House functionaries — or the President himself.

In the Truman administration, White House staff work on political and career personnel was merged under a presidential assistant, Donald Dawson, who does not seem to have dealt very strongly with either, although there were attempts toward the end of the administration to develop a set of files and procedures to put the screening of presidential appointees on a somewhat more rational basis than ever before. The first Hoover Commission in 1949 recommended more presidential involvement with the career services and a reorganization of the Civil Service Commission to place responsibility for its administration on the chairman, who would also be designated personnel adviser to the President. Later in 1949 the "strong chairman" scheme was installed at the commission by a reorganization plan, but the chairman was not given additional duties as presidential adviser.

The "two-hat" arrangement was officially established early in the Eisenhower administration when commission chairman Philip Young was also designated as personnel adviser to the President. In his White House capacity Young took over the aspects of merit systems coordination that had been handled by the Dawson office. Although according to some reports he had more to do with patronage and presidential appointments than met the eye, Young's White House duties were mainly with the various career services. Meanwhile, a succession of other White House

27 President's Committee on Administrative Management, pp. 11–12.

special assistants had primary responsibility for the political appointments. However, under the Eisenhower doctrine, which placed primary responsibility on the department and agency heads for recommending appointments in their bailiwicks, the White House office never developed into a powerful force in its own right, serving for the most part as a checkpoint for recommendations and political clearances.

The second Hoover Commission Personnel Task Force, reporting in 1955, criticized the "two-hat" system, alleging at least potential incompatibility of the two roles. As chairman of the commission the incumbent must symbolize and guard the merit system; as presidential adviser he "must consider all sorts of personnel questions which may be far afield from the career service, and he is subject to more patronage pressure than he would be as Chairman of the Civil Service Commission alone." [28] Perhaps in response to this criticism, a little later in the administration when Young resigned and the chairmanship of the commission was awarded briefly to a congressional lame duck, the two functions were split again. A former assistant-secretary of Labor, Rocco Siciliano, served as White House special assistant for personnel matters for most of the remainder of the Eisenhower administration, dealing primarily with the career services. About 1958, when a bill sponsored by Democratic Senator Joseph Clark proposed to establish a single personnel administrator similar to the old Brownlow recommendation, the administration backed away.

President Kennedy did not keep a White House assistant for personnel in a role like the one Siciliano had played. He looked to his Civil Service Commission chairman, John W. Macy, Jr., both for administration of the commission and the classified service under its jurisdiction and for general advice on career systems (with some help from the Budget Bureau). Kennedy, however, did institutionalize the President's interest in presidential appointments to a greater extent than any of his predecessors. Before his inauguration, Kennedy used the frequently described talent scout group to help identify potential appointees for his administration. He interested himself not only in the top but in what he considered the crucial appointments at second or third levels in some departments. By inauguration day the talent scout group was scattered, but one of the chief scouts, Ralph Dungan, was established as a special assistant on the White House staff.[29] Dungan gradually built up a staff of several professional level people to assist in the screening and recruitment of presidential appointees. Personnel, however, was not Dungan's exclusive concern; he had other more or less standing areas of interest, including foreign aid and Latin American affairs. At least in the beginning, there was an attempt at functional separation between the aides under Dungan who were supposed to be concentrating on identification of quality talent for

---

[28] Commission on Organization of the Executive Branch of the Government, *Task Force Report on Personnel and Civil Service*, p. 144.

[29] Laurin L. Henry, "The Transfer of Power" and "The New Administration" in Paul T. David (ed.), *Presidential Election and Transition, 1960–61* (Washington, D.C.: The Brookings Institution, 1961); Mann and Doig, pp. 269–270.

the crucial policy and administrative posts, without too much regard for patronage considerations, and another group that was primarily concerned with routine patronage operations in jobs of lesser importance, including classified positions in the departments and a considerable number of presidentially appointed part-time and advisory posts — some strictly honorary and others of substantial importance.

When Dungan left the White House after the Johnson succession and the 1964 election, arrangements were recast in their present form. Although he did not receive an additional commission or White House title, chairman Macy was given special duties as the President's chief adviser on presidential appointments. Macy now has primary responsibility for White House staff work on appointments at all levels, including both the "quality" and the "political acceptability" aspects.

Thus we now have, unofficially, a federal personnel administrator and adviser with wider scope of responsibility than any predecessor seen in the flesh or envisaged. Although Macy is commonly said to wear two hats, by comparison with Brownlow's Civil Service administrator or such previous figures as Philip Young, he wears three or four. That is, he combines (1) his official role as chairman and principal administrator of the general classified service under the Civil Service Commission, with (2) additional duties as presidential adviser on civil service problems in other merit systems, (3) identifier and preliminary recruiter of presidential appointees at all levels, and (4) staff man with responsibility for securing most of the evaluations and political clearances on prospective appointees. Macy performs these functions under the continuous scrutiny of a President whose interest in personnel matters, both political and career, is such that it is only slight exaggeration to say that the President himself is the government's chief personnel officer.

STAFFING THE PRESIDENTIAL APPOINTMENTS

Apparently all modern Presidents have felt occasional impulses to improve the appointment process. Franklin Roosevelt is said to have complained about the "same old names" that always turned up when vacancies arose and to have urged his staff to get out into the country and find some fresh talent. But no one seemed to have time or means to do this, and FDR continued to rely on the personal contacts of himself and a few insiders, plus risky recommendations from Democratic political sources.[30]

President Truman, who usually suffered from weakness in factional and public support, had to cope with both the problem of effective distribution of patronage and an apparently genuine shortage of well-qualified people willing to accept important posts in the military, foreign affairs, and economic mobilization agencies during the Korean period. It

[30] This is the author's recollection from conversations several years ago with James H. Rowe, Jr., who worked on appointments as a Roosevelt administrative assistant.

was about this time that the "government executive problem" first began to be cast in modern terms.[31] The job of, say, assistant secretary of the Air Force, demanded so much substantive or managerial ability that traditional sources of political recruitment could not produce qualified candidates; but the qualified prospects who could be located by other means tended to be unmotivated for the job, sometimes had potential conflicts of interest, and usually showed little or nothing in the way of political credentials. It was in this period that Truman's aide, Donald Dawson, made the first important attempt to build up a set of files on individuals who had been brought to White House attention. According to Dean Mann, this office never became effective with respect to the hard-to-fill jobs. It served mainly as a clearinghouse for information and did little in the way of evaluation or active recruitment. "Moreover, it focused attention on meeting the demands of those whose stakes were political in nature rather than on the promotion of effective policy leadership." [32]

The Eisenhower administration's efforts in this area suffered from changing objectives and were largely abortive. In the pre-inaugural Hotel Commodore period, some of Eisenhower's associates, with the aid of a management consulting firm, attempted to identify the key jobs that would have to be filled and to locate high quality prospects — usually businessmen who combined Eisenhower support credentials and executive talent — to fill them. This operation had a good deal of success in making the first round of executive appointments. However, the key people in it did not join the White House staff, and shortly after inauguration control of appointments began to slip in two directions. On the one hand, in the interest of party harmony Eisenhower committed himself to greater attentiveness to party and congressional sources in the making of appointments, so that powerful Senators and committeemen were increasingly in a position to exercise vetoes and occasionally to virtually demand that certain people be taken care of. On the other hand, Eisenhower firmly believed in the administrative principle of giving subordinates control of the means to fulfill their responsibilities, so that it was increasingly left to the department heads to find and evaluate prospects, carry on the necessary political maneuvers, and make recommendations to the White House, which ordinarily were followed. The center of gravity on appointments remained in the departments, and the White House personnel office, as before, served mainly as a clearinghouse with occasionally some wider latitude in presidential appointments that did not clearly fall within the scope of a department. The effect of this was to accent the natural centrifugal tendencies of the system. It produced in the first Eisenhower administration a considerable number of appointees who were politically incongruous with the objectives being enunciated from the White House, and in the second administration,

[31] John J. Corson, *Executives for the Federal Service* (New York: Columbia University Press, 1952).
[32] Mann and Doig, p. 269.

after partisan and patronage pressures had eased, an aggregation of appointees who were mainly department or agency oriented and inclined to look with suspicion on White House efforts at policy leadership.[33]

The Kennedy Experience. The Kennedy inner circle set out with enthusiasm and a fair measure of sophistication to place what were usually referred to as "our kind of guys" in the principal positions. I have already referred to the pre-inaugural talent scout operation in which Robert Kennedy, Lawrence O'Brien, Sargent Shriver, Ralph Dungan, and other staff men extended the search for prospects beyond the usual political sources to include foundations, universities, unions, and non-profit organizations, as well as the best law firms and business organizations. The talent scouts scattered after inauguration but were replaced by a lower-keyed personnel activity at the White House under Dungan's supervision. In the summer of 1961, Dan H. Fenn, Jr., a young faculty member from the Harvard Graduate School of Business, joined the staff as the principal executive recruiter. Fenn, in turn, gathered a staff that varied from two to four assistants — mostly relatively young men from the career service.[34]

Fenn's group set as its goal the identification of "quality" prospects for the principal policy and managerial posts, and some additional positions in which the President had a special interest, like AID mission directors. The lower-level, traditional patronage posts, "honoraries," and the usual political referrals were to be left to others. This was to be a recruiting effort, not simply a process of sorting through and evaluating names suggested by others, and partisan or presidential political considerations, while obviously to be borne in mind, were not to be the prime concern of this operation.

It was recognized that, next to the President, the department head had the strongest interest in the appointment. Typically, Fenn or someone from his group — and, if the appointment were significant enough, Dungan — would visit with the secretary, agency head, or commission chairman to find out what he felt he needed in the job and how his own recruiting efforts were coming. (Departmental efforts were often found to be minimal and on a hit-or-miss basis.) Then the White House group would consult other sources, such as the Budget Bureau, about the kind of person who should be recruited. At various stages of the process Fenn's group would check with the department head, trying out different possibilities with him. There was a continuing effort to work in cooperation with the head of the agency, and in almost every case this arrangement worked out to everyone's satisfaction. Only very occasionally did a department head resist this kind of relationship; sometimes, of course, they would deal directly with other White House staff members simultaneously, which would make the Fenn operation somewhat murky! The White House recruiters felt that their major departmental problems were

---

[33] Laurin L. Henry, *Presidential Transitions* (Washington, D.C.: The Brookings Institution, 1960), pp. 639–686; Mann and Doig, pp. 87–123.

[34] This account of the Kennedy staff operation is based on interviews with Fenn and others who participated, August 1967.

resistance from the career establishment and the unwillingness of the top non-career — political — officials to make decisions and stand by them under pressures from their own bureaucracies. On the whole, department heads welcomed the kind of White House role in recruiting that was provided and seemed to feel that, while decisions clearly remained with the President, their concerns and views were being systematically fed into the selections made.

Prospects for consideration were identified in various ways — scrutiny of lists of persons active in politics, business, education, and public affairs; personal suggestions by department and White House staff members; political referrals; and an occasional volunteer who was sufficiently impressive to be taken seriously. Also, as an aid in checking the qualifications of prospects and securing new suggestions when needed, Fenn developed a list of trusted persons all over the country who were used as contacts and references. Dossiers on individuals who had passed at least preliminary screening went into a file of several hundred prospects that was supposed to be kept up to date. The "ready file" was classified by general fields of interest but it emphasized individuals with wide experience and general managerial talent who might be fitted into a variety of posts. There was a special category of "bright young men" of limited experience but high motivation and adaptability.

Typically, when the prospects for a vacancy had been narrowed down to two or three, a more intensive check of references and credentials was made, someone in the White House — usually not of the Fenn group — was asked to determine political acceptability, and inquiries were made as to the prospect's likely availability. Whenever possible these things were done quietly and indirectly, to avoid disappointing the unsuccessful, but occasionally there was no alternative to calling a man in to discuss the possibility of an appointment. When a tentative choice had been made or ratified by the President, someone on the staff would talk to the candidate to make sure he would accept the appointment if formally offered; the idea was to avoid the embarrassment of a direct refusal of a presidential offer. Actually, according to the staff, turndowns at the late screening stage were rare; if the staff work was done right, people who pretty clearly would not be available were spotted early and removed from consideration.

Although one cannot be certain on the basis of the limited information available, it appears that the Dungan-Fenn recruiting activity functioned with a fair degree of success through most of the Kennedy administration. The presidential interest, as conceived by the staff, was made operative in the appointment process in a stronger way than ever before. A considerable number of promising under- and assistant-secretaries, deputy assistant-secretaries, commissioners, and directors of special programs were seeded into the federal system. The office also proved its utility in special projects of particular interest to the President, such as attempts to get more Negroes into upper administrative levels and to restaff the much battered foreign aid agency.

Nevertheless, it must be noted that the Fenn staff operated under some conditions that definitely limited its impact. For one thing, it appears that although President Kennedy understood the importance of placing *his* men rather than the department's, the Senate's, or the interest group's men in the important jobs, his personal interest in appointments tended to be selective rather than comprehensive and sustained. He might take great pains with the choice of, say, the civil administrator of Okinawa, but deal rather casually with an assistant-secretary of the Navy. For another thing, Fenn did not ordinarily deal with the President directly, but usually through Dungan, who had several responsibilities in addition to personnel and, although an old and trusted Kennedy staff man, may not have had quite the access to the President enjoyed by such persons as O'Donnell and O'Brien — or Robert Kennedy. Under these circumstances, the Fenn group never established an exclusive right to the inside track with the President on appointments. The President continued to permit — or perhaps encourage — other members of his staff to dabble in recruiting on occasions, and more than once the Fenn group discovered that an important position had been committed to someone they had not realized was under consideration. Finally, the Fenn activity suffered from blurred jurisdiction with another White House personnel group under somewhat vague supervision. Usually referred to as "the Dorothy Davies operation," this was a staff activity and set of files from which names were pulled for lesser presidential appointments, more or less honorary commissions and advisory bodies, and the presidential patronage generally. The distinction in principle between executive recruiting and political appointments proved difficult to maintain in practice and in the minds of the clienteles with which the White House had to deal.

These factors may or may not have had something to do with the fact that shortly before President Kennedy's death it was announced that Fenn was leaving the White House for a seat on the U.S. Tariff Commission. For several months thereafter Fenn's staff carried on under Dungan's direct supervision. Late in 1964, Dungan was appointed Ambassador to Chile and it was announced that chairman Macy of the Civil Service Commission would assist President Johnson with the restaffing of the administration that would be required as the President entered the full term to which he had been elected. Although, as noted above, Macy received no White House title, he did assume direction of Dungan's personnel staff. Since then there have been some changes of methods and an almost complete turnover of men on that staff, with only one of the principals going back to Dungan's time.

The Johnson Approach. The Johnson-Macy recruiting effort, as developed through mid-1967, differs in several ways from the operation under Kennedy.[35] Much of the change is with the President himself. Mr. Johnson's involvement with appointments seems to be more intense and

[35] This account of the Johnson staff operation is based on interviews with several participants and close observers, August 1967.

comprehensive than that of any of his predecessors. According to his associates, Johnson feels strongly that his appointees represent the President in more than just a nominal sense. This leads him to careful scrutiny of not only the top-level nominations but also many minor and more or less honorary appointments heretofore left largely to the departments concerned. It also causes him to seek appointees whose support of the administration will extend beyond their own areas of programmatic responsibility and across the entire range of its policies — a difficult principle to apply literally. And there is plenty of corroboration for reports that the President often becomes furious at leaks of public speculation about impending appointments that he regards as intended to probe his intentions or force his hand.

The President's strong interest has led to high status for his personnel man. Macy deals directly with the President. He and his staff have established, if not their right to the last word with the President, at least an expectation that they will get their word in most personnel decisions. The department heads increasingly check their personnel recommendations to the President with Macy and work with the Macy staff to reach joint proposals. Suggestions reaching the President from other sources often are sent to Macy's staff for comment and further evaluation. However, the President has not put himself completely in Macy's hands or denied himself an occasional highly personal impulse. The recent bestowal of a sinecure on the Subversive Activities Control Board to a young lawyer with no apparent qualifications except marriage to a former LBJ secretary is ample evidence of that.

As before, the departments are encouraged to take thought of their own personnel needs. Such trusted department heads as Robert McNamara, who has a reputation for competence in this as in so many areas, are given a good deal more latitude than others. But it is clear that the center of gravity on personnel decisions has shifted noticeably toward the White House.

Previous attempts at distinction between responsibility and procedures for handling the major and minor, the "quality" and the patronage, presidential appointments have been given up. The same staff processes all the appointments including the investigation of both personal ability and political factors. Although this may mean more politics in some appointments, it means less in others. The custom of congressional clearance — or at least prior notification — is still followed, but the routine and mechanical clearances of all appointments through the national committee and state organizations that have been customary in some administrations are not part of the process. The President dominates the party organization and is determined to control the administration; *he* issues the political clearances.

In addition to Macy, who divides his time between the commission and the White House, the present staff consists of four men who have more or less standing assignments to keep in touch with and recruit for particular clusters of agencies, plus a fifth man who is responsible both for overseeing the files and records and for dredging up names in large batches for various part-time and temporary advisory boards, commissions, and delegations. As before, the staff is composed of relatively young career types who do not expect long tenure in these jobs; turnover in about two years is the norm.

The procedural core of the system is a set of files on some 30,000 people, of which about half are considered active and kept more or less up to date. The present staff considers that one of its principal accomplishments has been the consolidation into a single system of the several sets of files on prospective personnel that previously had been officially and unofficially kept around the White House. The Macy group claims now to be tied into the presidential paper flow in such a way that every White House communication that might bear on personnel gets scanned for information that may be used to start a new file or add to an existing dossier. Recommendations and evaluations are cross-filed both by recommender and recommendee. Other inputs come from scanning newspapers, documents, and other sources in which significant information about the lives and careers of prospects might be recorded. Files on individuals who have been under active consideration are of course heavier with informal notes and evaluations.

Although insiders credit the idea to Dungan, the Macy staff has installed the most publicized innovation in the process — a computer. The key to the files is a set of computer tapes that store basic information on each individual in the files. The computer holds mostly standard and public biographical data, with each individual coded for fields of interest by the job code used in the Census of Manufactures. The evaluative material is in the files, not the computer. Thus it is an exaggeration to suggest, as some have done, that the Johnson administration is "selecting people by computer." The personnel staff may start the canvass of possibilities for a given position by asking the computer for names of, say, Midwest college presidents, or electronics executives with Department of Defense experience. When the list is compiled, the staff then can pull the files to see which ones merit further scrutiny. But there still remain the problems of knowing what kinds of lists to ask the computer for, how to obtain and weigh evaluations and judgments about the individuals whose names are spewed out, and when to shift the search into new categories of personnel. And it is not unreasonable to suspect that when the computer produces a long list the staff will begin by pulling the files on those whose names bring instant recognition because they have previously been brought to attention in some way.

In addition to the "talent bank" of prospects the office also has — for the first time, it is claimed — a complete current inventory of presidentially appointed positions, and a matching list of incumbents, both on computer tape.

Recent Johnson Appointees. What effect is the Johnson system having? The nature of the linkage between the system for screening appointees and the qualitative character of the product is to some degree conjectural. Some might argue that the kinds of appointees who emerge are determined by the President's predilections, his political situation, and the nature of the market in which he seeks to recruit, and that the personnel recruitment system has at most a marginal influence. Personally, I suspect that the system itself does have some independent effect. At any rate it is clear that the Johnson appointees now being produced by the system differ in some discernible ways from the Eisenhower, Kennedy, and early Johnson appointees.

The Stanley-Mann-Doig data recently published by Brookings analyzes the backgrounds of over 1,000 principal political executives since the New Deal, with comparisons of the Roosevelt, Truman, Eisenhower, Kennedy, and Johnson appointees through April 30, 1965.[36] Using definitions and methods as nearly identical to Brookings as possible, Mr. Joseph R. Rudolph, Jr., has analyzed 100 Johnson appointments between April 1, 1965, and June 30, 1967. This overlaps very slightly with the group of earlier Johnson appointees analyzed by Brookings and includes virtually all appointees at the defined levels in the period indicated.

It is commonly said in Washington that Johnson has a preference for people he regards as fellow professionals in the running of the government. This is borne out by data on the recent Johnson appointees showing a sharp rise over the Eisenhower, Kennedy, and early Johnson appointees in the proportion whose prior careers had been primarily in some form of public service. Tabulation of principal prior occupations showed "public service" for 43 per cent of the later Johnson appointees, which is 6 per cent higher than for his earlier appointees, 10 per cent higher than Kennedy's, and 14 per cent higher than Eisenhower's.[37] Although exceeding FDR, Eisenhower, and Kennedy in the proportion of appointees with long experience in public office, Johnson still is not relying on insiders to quite the same extent as Truman, who made 52 per cent of his appointments from public service careerists.

[36] The data on previous appointees, with which Johnson's recent appointees are compared in the immediately following paragraphs, are from Stanley, Mann, and Doig, *op. cit.*

[37] By our tabulations, the "public service" group consisted of 38 per cent former federal appointive officials, 3 per cent former elective political careerists, and 2 per cent non-federal appointive careermen. Although the categories are different, these figures are roughly consistent with a breakdown provided by a White House staff member, who indicated that through 1966 the origins of all Johnson's appointees in all categories were:

Federal Government		44%
Civil Service	21%	
Foreign Service	19%	
Legislative Branch	2%	
Military	2%	
Business		15%
Law		16%
Universities		14%
Unions		1%
State and Local Government		9%

[Percentages add up to only 99% because of rounding off.]

Johnson's recent appointees also show some important difference from previous groups in the distribution of occupations of those who were drawn from the private sector. Business and law practice are sharply down, while education, science and engineering are up as sources of talent.

Analysis of the kinds of federal positions previously held by recent Johnson appointees shows a distribution rather similar to previous appointee groups, with perhaps a slightly greater tendency to appoint political executives from both career and subordinate political posts within the same agency rather than across agency lines. The percentage of recent Johnson appointees from career to political ranks was 31 per cent — about the same as for the Truman, Kennedy, and early Johnson groups but much higher than for Eisenhower.

The conclusion that Johnson is relying to an increasing extent on persons who are essentially Washington careerists in either political or civil service is bolstered by data on the geographic regions in which recent Johnson appointees had their principal careers prior to appointment. The percentage from the south Atlantic region, which includes Washington, D.C., was up to 57, which is an all-time high for any administration, including Truman's. Washington itself accounts for 55 per cent of Johnson's recent appointees — as compared to 45 per cent for Truman, 19 per cent for Eisenhower, 31 per cent for Kennedy, and 34 per cent for early Johnson appointees. Of the other regions, only New England is holding its own as a source of Johnson appointees. Even the west south central area, which includes Texas, is not faring well.

The trend toward higher levels of education that has been apparent for the political executives of all recent administrations continues through the Johnson appointees. The men who never went to college, a group that has been dwindling rapidly among political executives in recent years, are completely unrepresented in the recent Johnson appointees, 96 per cent of whom have at least a bachelor's degree. Even more impressive is the fact that 75 per cent of the recent group have graduate or professional degrees. Of the recent Johnson appointees, 43 per cent are law graduates, which corresponds to the average of recent administrations. But there has been a sharp increase, even over the Kennedy administration, in those who have master's and doctor's degrees of various kinds, including science, engineering, medicine, social science, business, and public administration. A full 26 per cent of Johnson's recent appointees have earned doctorates, as compared to 19 per cent of the early Johnson appointees, 18 per cent of Kennedy's appointees, and much lower figures for previous administrations.

Tendencies toward educational elitism are continuing under one of our more equalitarian Presidents. As compared to other appointee groups, Johnson's recent executives show even higher concentration of undergraduate preparation at the leading colleges. The percentage from the "Big Three" — Yale, Harvard, and Princeton — was 25.5 per cent, which is similar to the early Johnson appointees and substantially higher than previous administrations, including Kennedy's. The percentage from the whole Ivy League, including the Big Three, was up to 36.2, higher than ever before. And the concentration from a list of eighteen leading private and public institutions reached 50 per cent. Among the leading institutions in the most recent set of appointees Yale declined and lost first place to Harvard but remained ahead of Princeton, which declined but still held third place. Of the other private institutions, Stanford, Columbia, and Cornell were up, while Dartmouth and Chicago were down. Among the public universities, Wisconsin, California, and Michigan held their places, several others declined or were unrepresented altogether, and only one — Texas — increased significantly. The concentration at the leading institutions for graduate and professional degrees was about the same as for previous groups, about three-quarters coming from one of the eighteen leading schools. Thus, the quest for quality seems to lead inevitably to the establishment.

THE PRESIDENCY AND THE CAREER SERVICES

Now let us look briefly at the higher levels of the civil service, where some important developments have occurred in the past decade and a half and even more important ones may be in the making. In retrospect, one of the crucial events was the creation of the super-grades — the addition of levels GS–16, –17, and –18 at the top of the civil service. Established in very limited numbers in 1949 and steadily increased to the present 4,400, these positions have provided appropriate recognition, pay, and status for obviously important jobs near the apex of the federal establishment that are not filled by presidential appointment. Without them, the promotion and salary structure of the civil service would have been so compressed that the service could not have retained personnel of the caliber it has, and the number of presidential positions would have had to be greatly enlarged. Because they are by definition special, the establishment and filling of each supergrade position is subject to scrutiny and approval by the Civil Service Commission on a case by case basis. The commission is required to make sure that appropriate procedures have been followed in every appointment to the three-fourths of the supergrade jobs that are under full merit coverage, and even for the remainder that are exempt or occupied at the pleasure of the agency head, the commission must be satisfied that the agency's choice has reasonable credentials for a job at that level of responsibility. Thus we have an identifiable group of elite positions, large enough to justify systematic attention but small enough to permit fairly effective central supervision. Small wonder that the second Hoover Commission thought of creating a presidentially commissioned corps of civilian officers to occupy these positions as a solution to many of the problems of status, tenure, mobility, and policy fragmentation.

As Roger Jones has pointed out in a recent summary and commentary on the trends of the past decade, the Government Employees Training

Act of 1958 was the key to many subsequent developments.[38] This act provided the first general authorization of government sponsored and financed training throughout the federal service. It encouraged not only job-related skill training at lower levels but also special training and development for higher professional and executive personnel, to be provided either in-service or in appropriate academic institutions. Under the stimulus of this act and follow-up nagging by the Civil Service Commission, many agencies, in the course of examining and justifying their needs for higher level training, began for the first time to take stock of their career executive personnel, their qualitative and quantitative needs in future years as compared to the replacements coming up the ladder, and the problems of quality recruiting, turnover, and attrition. This not only stimulated a great burst of new training activities but placed them in a context of serious manpower planning and efforts in most agencies to institutionalize the delicate processes of identifying, developing, promoting, and using the top career executives. Examination of the attractiveness of the service and problems of recruiting and attrition helped clinch the argument for another landmark act, the Federal Salary Reform Act of 1962, which declared the principle that federal pay rates should be comparable to private enterprise pay for the same levels of work and actually brought that principle close to realization for most of the service, although falling somewhat short at the highest career levels.

Although they lent at least nominal presidential support to these measures, the Eisenhower and Kennedy administrations both worried, although in different ways, about the responsiveness of the career service to legitimate political control. The Republicans feared at the outset that their policies might be sabotaged for ideological reasons and established Schedule C to enlarge the number of positions at the top of the service occupied at the pleasure of the department heads. As time went by, the Eisenhower administration found that civil servants in most cases were at least as tractable as Republican patronage appointees, and lived increasingly comfortably with the bureaucrats. Kennedy and his associates began with little burden of ideological suspicion but became increasingly frustrated by what they regarded as plain bureaucratic immobility in many agencies. They went along with the idea of improving the quality of the higher civil service but they remained dubious about getting effective policy leadership from this group and convinced of the necessity of a sizable and vital corps of political executives.

As compared to his predecessors, President Johnson has far more faith and interest in the careerists. He has promoted many career men to presidential posts and indicated that he thinks this is a good thing to do. He presides over special recognition and awards ceremonies with obvious enjoyment. He has stepped up the pressure on the commission and the agencies to employ more Negroes and more women. One might also interpret as evidence of presidential interest the custom begun in this administration of treating civil servants being promoted to supergrade

[38] Roger W. Jones, "Developments in Government Manpower: A Federal Perspective," *Public Administration Review*, XXVII (June 1967), pp. 134–141.

jobs to a visit to the White House and an interview with presidential aide Marvin Watson. Administration sources aver that these visits come only *after* the individual has been chosen and are not part of any kind of political clearance procedure; this, it is said, is merely positive personnel management because it builds morale and reminds departmental officers of their tie with the President who symbolizes the government as a whole. History entitles the observer to remain a little skeptical on this point.

President Johnson also supports some important proposals still pending as of late 1967. Two bills before Congress would greatly increase public service training at all levels. One calls for a national program of graduate fellowships for public service training, in some respects analogous to the NDEA program for increasing the nation's supply of college teachers, plus an auxiliary program of grants to educational institutions for the development of their resources and training programs. Another bill, which owes much to the sponsorship of Senator Muskie of Maine, would authorize sizable federal grants to state and local governments for training and other improvements in their civil services, as well as permit intergovernmental cooperation in training and occasional detailing of personnel. If these bills do not fall victim to wartime economy impulses, they should produce important long-range benefits for the public service — not to mention a boom in academic public administration programs.

Training and executive development activities are to be stepped up within the service. In April 1967 President Johnson issued an Executive Order that put into effect most of the recommendations of a blue ribbon presidential task force on this subject.[39] Perhaps the most interesting provision is for a new federal executive institute to provide advanced study on a full-time residential basis to selected civil servants at the highest levels. This institution, for which the Civil Service Commission is now planning actively, will climax several years of discussion of the "federal staff college" concept.

The latest development to be noted is a new executive assignment system for supergrade positions that went into effect in November 1967 after a year of Civil Service Commission preparation.[40] Although the details are complex, the essentials of the system are as follows:

1. No involuntary assignment of personnel by a central agency; continued recognition of the right of agencies to make basic decisions, following merit procedures, about recruiting and promotion to their supergrade jobs; corresponding right of individual employees to hold tenure in their existing jobs and make their own decisions about accepting other jobs if offered.

[39] Presidential Task Force on Career Advancement, *Investment for Tomorrow* (Washington, D.C.: U.S. Civil Service Commission, 1967); Executive Order 11348 and accompanying statement by the President, April 20, 1967.

[40] Executive Order 11315 and accompanying statement by the President, November 17, 1966; U.S. Civil Service Commission, "The Executive Assignment System," and "Questions and Answers on the Executive Assignment System" (mimeographed releases, November 1966). Interview, Mr. Seymour Berlin, director, Bureau of Executive Manpower, August 8, 1967.

2. Continued Civil Service Commission scrutiny of agency decisions, with a prospect of increased pressure on the agencies not to promote from within to supergrade levels without careful examination of alternatives who might be available through outside recruiting or voluntary transfer from other agencies.

3. Requirement that agencies periodically submit and review with the commission executive staffing plans covering current and long-range needs and steps to be taken to meet them by executive development, training, outside recruiting, and promotion.

4. Staffing of a new Bureau of Executive Manpower at the commission in sufficient depth to permit a responsible officer to work closely and continuously with each agency on the preparation and implementation of its staffing plan and on filling its key vacancies at supergrade levels.

5. Establishment of an executive inventory containing personnel data on all individuals holding positions at levels GS–15 through 18 — and counterparts in other pay systems; this information to be coded both to permit rapid identification by computer of all individuals who might be referred to an agency for a particular vacancy as well to facilitate general analyses of the characteristics of the top-ranking federal work force.

6. Recognition, through a sub-category of non-career executive assignments, of the continuing need for a small number of supergrade positions to be filled by special procedure and occupied at the pleasure of the agency heads — although appointees must still stand Civil Service Commission quality inspection.

The commission now has received and coded the personally prepared questionnaires from most of the 26,000 executives who are to be included in the inventory. However, one hears in Washington a certain amount of grumbling about the length and personal nature of some parts of the questionnaire, as well as reports of foot-dragging by a few well-established old timers who are not particularly interested in having their credentials handed about or being urged to change jobs. The appeal of the system is mainly to those who are young, ambitious, and don't mind another FBI full field investigation.

How much new interagency mobility this will produce is of course conjectural. Undoubtedly it will make additional opportunities available to career men who might be interested in moving and will help break up some of the more outrageously closed agency promotion systems. However, the prevailing thought today is more tolerant of the one-or-two-agency career than it used to be; the ideal of the broadly competent general executive seems harder and harder to realize. Although the computerized inventory attracts the most attention, my personal guess is that the agency staffing review and the rapport between the agency and its liaison officer at the commission are more crucial. According to the commission, career executive staffing at the upper levels is now an active concern of top-ranking political executives of most agencies, under steady pressure from both chairman Macy and the President. One hopes that the pressure continues until the habit is formed.

The executive assignment plan and related developments mark a significant shift of ground from most of the debates and reform efforts aimed at the higher civil service since World War II. The essence of it is that we have ceased trying to reform the civil service by tinkering with *formal status*. Politicians, civil servants, and reformers are all relatively unconcerned about the line between political and career appointments. National affluence has dulled both partisan hunger for patronage and the wariness of bureaucrats, and department heads will take good men from wherever they find them. No one is pushing for a system that will force either civil servants or agencies to accept involuntary interagency transfers. There is little interest in providing either greater formal tenure security for individuals, as in the rank-in-the-man senior civil service scheme proposed by the second Hoover Commission, or taking some of it away as proposed by the Committee for Economic Development.[41] In effect, we have decided to rely for mobility on a combination of natural turnover — the commission tells us that almost one out of every four supergrade jobs turns over each year anyway — and the working of an expanded, better informed, less monopolistic, better policed free market in which agencies and potential employees can find each other. And regardless of how much interagency movement this leads to, improved training and agency executive development plans will make everyone better off and happier with what he has.

What will all of this do for the President? Mr. Johnson apparently regards these things as making an important contribution to the development and better utilization of the upper career service. To the extent that they lead to more intelligent, more broadly trained, more potentially mobile civil servants with a government-wide rather than parochial view, they should strengthen the presidency against the centrifugal forces we know so well. But the benefits to the President will be indirect. It seems to have been decided, implicitly or explicitly, that an essentially agency-based system will suffice and that no specific organizational link to the presidency is required except through the Civil Service Commission. Although presidential aides may dabble in career appointments from time to time, the President's own regular and formal involvement is best in the form of support for general institutional improvements. If this seems less presidential direction than some might wish, it might be as much as the system can survive politically.

SUMMARY AND PROSPECT

As we have seen, our current President participates actively in personnel matters, both political and career, and has concentrated responsibility for overseeing federal personnel administration on his behalf under a single subordinate. Although some aspects of President Johnson's interest may be peculiar to him personally, much of this presidential involvement

41 *Improving Executive Management in the Federal Government,* a statement by the Research and Policy Committee of the Committee for Economic Development (New York: Committee for Economic Development, 1964), p. 48.

— especially the centralization of staff work on presidential appointments — continues a trend visible under his predecessors.

The trend of recent Presidents toward greater domination of their party has expanded political latitude in making top executive appointments, but at the same time the increasingly complex nature of the executive branch has limited the sources from which effective subordinates can be chosen. The last two Presidents have developed and begun to mechanize a more systematic canvass of the areas where potentially effective appointees may be found. It is not clear that these efforts are bringing much greater diversity in the body of appointees, although they are lessening somewhat the long-time dependence on lawyers. So far, they have accelerated a trend toward the domination of the government by a highly educated group, many of whose members began with distinct socio-economic advantages. They also have accelerated a trend toward careerism in the holding of presidential appointments, and an increasing fusion of the top of the career system with the presidentially appointed group. Although President Johnson shows more signs than his predecessors of wishing to identify with the higher civil service and make it his personal instrument, the reforms he is sponsoring, significant as they are, amount to the acceptance and improvement of the inherited basic system; the sometime dream of a government-ranging presidential corps of high career officers seems to be fading rapidly.

How firmly may one project these trends into the future? Another four years of Democratic control might set much of current practice into presidential concrete. On the other hand, although members of the administration resent the suggestion, there are many indications that the present administration is rapidly running out of political steam. If a party turnover should occur in 1968, it would probably bring about a resurgence of interest in patronage, new concern about the neutrality of the higher career service, and the installation of a more diverse set of less experienced presidential appointees in the top positions. Macy's multiple-hat role would probably be fragmented.

Yet I suspect that any successor administration, whatever its initial impulses, will soon find itself approximately where we are now. The requirements of running the executive branch become more and more stringent, and qualified executives no more plentiful. Active presidential control of political appointments, backed up by White House staff work, is a feasible and perhaps necessary means of finding talent and countering centrifugal tendencies of the system. This much, I believe, is a presidential job from now on. Whether it will give future Presidents significantly more control over the executive branch than was enjoyed by their predecessors is not clear. I doubt that many personnel officers have found that routinization of their function leads to greater personal discretion and control of events.

TABLE 1

Principal Occupations of Political Executives Prior to Appointment: A Comparison of President Johnson's Recent Appointees with Previous Appointee Groups

Occupation	Appointed by					
	Roosevelt	Truman	Eisenhower	Kennedy	Johnson through Apr., 1965	Johnson Apr., 1965–June 1967
Business	20%	20%	34%	17%	20%	15%
Law	24	22	26	25	20	12
Education	10	2	5	12	11	16
Science or Engineering	2	1	1	4	3	9
Other Private	6	4	5	9	9	5
Total Private	62	48	71	67	63	57
Public Service, Elective	5	4	4	3	3	3
Appointive, Federal	23	41	18	22	20	38
Appointive, Non-Federal	9	7	7	8	13	2
Total Government	38	52	29	33	37	43
Number of Persons	269	317	347	191	147	100

Note: Adapted from David T. Stanley, Dean E. Mann and Jameson W. Doig, *Men Who Govern* (Washington, D.C.: The Brookings Institution, 1967), Table E. 1, Appendix E. Data in columns for Roosevelt, Truman, Eisenhower, Kennedy, and Johnson through April 1965 are from The Brookings Institution. Data for Johnson, April 1965 through June 1967, are by Joseph R. Rudolph, Jr., University of Virginia. Percentages may not add to subtotals or 100 per cent because of rounding.

TABLE 2

Location of Principal Occupation of Political Executives Prior to Appointment: A Comparison of President Johnson's Recent Appointees with Previous Appointee Groups

Census Region	Appointed By					
	Roosevelt	Truman	Eisenhower	Kennedy	Johnson through Apr., 1965	Johnson Apr., 1965–June 1967
Pacific	3%	5%	8%	10%	10%	4%
Mountain	3	2	4	3	3	1
West North Central	4	2	11	4	5	2
East North Central	14	7	15	9	8	3
West South Central	6	5	4	4	2	2
East South Central	3	1	1	2	1	0
South Atlantic	33	51	22	34	37	57
Washington, D.C.	(28)	(45)	(19)	(31)	(34)	(55)
Other S. Atlantic	(5)	(6)	(3)	(3)	(3)	(2)
Middle Atlantic	22	18	22	19	18	14
New England	9	4	6	9	9	9
Foreign and other	4	5	7	6	8	8
Number of persons	264	314	345	191	147	100

Note: Adapted from David T. Stanley, Dean E. Mann and Jameson W. Doig, *Men Who Govern* (Washington, D.C.: The Brookings Institution, 1967), Table D.2, Appendix D. Data in columns for Roosevelt, Truman, Eisenhower, Kennedy, and Johnson through April 1965 are from The Brookings Institution. Data for Johnson, April 1965–June 1967, are by Joseph R. Rudolph, Jr., University of Virginia. Percentages may not add to subtotals or 100 per cent because of rounding.

TABLE 3

Post-Baccalaureate Degrees Earned by Political Executives: A Comparison of President Johnson's Recent Appointees with Previous Appointee Groups

Appointed By	Law Degree	Master's	Doctorate
Roosevelt	39%	17%	11%
Truman	48	16	8
Eisenhower	42	17	9
Kennedy	46	18	18
Johnson through April 1965	45	23	19
Johnson April 1965–June 1967	43	35	26

Note: Data on Roosevelt, Truman, Eisenhower, Kennedy, and Johnson through April 1965 are adapted from David T. Stanley, Dean E. Mann, and Jameson W. Doig, *Men Who Govern* (Washington, D.C.: The Brookings Institution, 1967), Chart 2.3, p. 19. Data on Johnson, April 1965–June 1967, are by Joseph R. Rudolph, Jr., University of Virginia.

TABLE 4

Undergraduate Colleges and Universities Attended by Political Executives: A Comparison of President Johnson's Recent Appointees with Other Appointee Groups [a]

Appointed By	Big Three[b]	Ivy League[c]	Top Eighteen[d]	Others[e]	Number
Roosevelt	15.6%	20.8%	35.7%	64.3%	269
Truman	18.0	22.1	36.6	63.4	317
Eisenhower	22.2	31.1	46.7	53.7	347
Kennedy	21.5	26.2	44.5	55.5	191
Johnson through April 1965	25.2	29.2	44.9	55.1	147
Johnson, April 1965 through June 1967	25.5	36.2	50.0	50.0	94

[a] Data on Roosevelt, Truman, Eisenhower, Kennedy, and Johnson through April 1965 appointees from David T. Stanley, Dean E. Mann and Jameson W. Doig, *Men Who Govern* (Washington, D.C.: The Brookings Institution, 1967), Table D.10, Appendix D. Data on Johnson appointees, April 1965 through June 1967, by Joseph R. Rudolph, Jr., University of Virginia.

[b] Yale, Harvard, and Princeton.

[c] Big three plus Dartmouth, Columbia, Cornell, Brown, and Pennsylvania.

[d] The top eighteen in the Brookings analysis included the big three, plus Dartmouth, Columbia, and Cornell of the Ivy League, plus Wis-

Presidency and Legislation:
Planning the President's Program

Richard E. Neustadt

Early in 1954, President Dwight D. Eisenhower presented to the Congress — and the country and his party — some 65 proposals for new legislation, over and above appropriations.[1] This presentation was a massive affair. First came six weeks of well-publicized preliminaries: cabinet deliberations, congressional briefings, press conferences, and a fireside chat. Then, in three annual messages to Congress — a State of the Union Address, a Budget Message, and an Economic Report — the President set forth his bundle of proposals, elaborating certain aspects, outlining the rest. Along with these came seven supplementing special messages, each filling in

---

consin, California (Berkeley), Michigan, Stanford, Chicago, North Carolina, Minnesota, Nebraska, Northwestern, Kentucky, Texas, and the U.S. Military Academy (West Point).

[e] In each administration, some schools in the "other" category outranked some members of the top eighteen. For example, in the recent Johnson appointees such schools as Williams, Pittsburgh, DePauw, Florida, Emory, and Catholic had over 2 per cent each, while such top eighteen schools as Chicago, North Carolina, Minnesota, Nebraska, and Kentucky were unrepresented.

Reprinted by permission from the *American Political Science Review*, Vol. 49 (1955), pp. 980–1021.

[1] The exact number of these Eisenhower proposals was computed differently by different observers depending on varying definitions of what constitutes a separate item. Thus Peter Edson cited the figure 110 (*Washington Daily News*, July 14, 1954), while Cabell Phillips wrote of "over 200" (*New York Times*, May 30, 1954), and *Congressional Quarterly* reported a total of 214, reached partly by counting separately each point in the Administration's agriculture recommendations. The writer prefers to count separately only those proposals, or groups of related proposals, which would normally be enacted and/or considered in separate bills. Exceptions are made where — as in the case of public housing, for example — the conventions of publicity and politics very sharply differentiate items incorporated in the same bill. It is on this basis that internal Executive Office status reports on the President's program are now compiled and have been in the past. Note that the total of 65, cited above, excludes not only appropriation requests, as is the general custom, but also international treaties and conventions subject to Senate ratification and those few agency proposals not called for in a presidential message but cleared in bill draft form by Budget as "in accord with the President's program" (which under present practice means *specifically* approved by the White House for addition to his program list). Both of these latter categories *are* included in Executive Office status reports which now circulate on the Hill and therefore may have been the basis for some press compilations.

details on some particular: Taft-Hartley, farm price supports, social security, health, housing, atomic energy, foreign aid, and trade. And following the messages Administration-approved bills, conveyors of the ultimate details, were introduced in Congress.

Throughout, one theme was emphasized: here was a comprehensive and coordinated inventory of the nation's current legislative needs, reflecting the President's own judgments, choices, and priorities in every major area of Federal action; in short, his "legislative program," an entity distinctive and defined, its coverage and its omissions, both, delimiting his stand across the board. And — quite explicitly — this stand was being taken, this program volunteered, in order to give Congress an agenda, Republicans a platform, and voters a yardstick for 1954.

Thus, one year after his inaugural, Eisenhower espoused a sweeping concept of the President's initiative in legislation and an elaborate mechanism for its public expression; developments which no one seemed to take amiss. Both in governmental circles and in the press, the whole performance was regarded almost as a matter of course, a normal White House response to the opening of Congress. The pattern, after all, was quite familiar; the comprehensive program expressed in ordered sequence, with some sort of publicized preliminaries and detailed follow-up, had been an annual enterprise in Truman's time. Indeed, while Eisenhower had undoubtedly improved upon the earlier mechanics, his 1954 procedure seemed expressive less of innovation than of reversion to accustomed practice. In 1953, he had been criticized in many quarters for failing to produce a defined program of this kind; now that "failure" was made good, a general expectation satisfied in the "customary" way.

Customary, perhaps; yet as recently as 1946 an informed observer had remarked, accurately enough, on the "absence of cohesion in the legislative program of the chief executive — absence, in fact, of a program clearly designated as such." [2] Presidential reports and recommendations to Congress were as old as the Constitution; presidential sponsorship of specific measures, highlighted in special messages and spelled out in Administration bills, had been a commonplace in Franklin Roosevelt's time and by no means unknown much earlier. But the elaborate paraphernalia of a comprehensive and specific inventory, contents settled and defined as regards substance no less than finance, *presented in detailed fashion and packaged form at the opening of each session of Congress —*

---

[2] V. O. Key, "Legislative Control," in F. Morstein Marx, *Elements of Public Administration* (New York, 1946), p. 351. Lest semantic difficulties arise, note that the term presidential "program" as used throughout this paper connotes the comprehensiveness, specificity, and defined boundaries characteristic of contemporary annual presentations in the legislative sphere. This is the current connotation of the term within the government (and quite generally in press reports). As such, this is a term of art, to be distinguished from the looser usage long employed by scholars, journalists — and Presidents themselves — to cover legislative issues with which particular Presidents somehow became identified, pro or con. In the latter sense, of course, there have been presidential "programs" since Washington's time, notably under the "strong" Presidents.

this was a "custom" scarcely nine years old, a postwar phenomenon evolving under Truman and now carried forward under Eisenhower.[3]

Here is an institutional development of no mean proportions, with a great preparatory effort obviously involved in advance of every session. Three questions are suggested: First, currently, what are the mechanics of this program preparation; how is the job done and by whom? Second, historically, what gave rise to such institutionalization in the postwar decade; how did it evolve and how did it survive the change of Administration? Third, prospectively — and speculatively — what may the whole development imply regarding powers, opportunities, of President and presidency in the legislative process? This paper attempts answers to these questions; its starting point is the making of the Eisenhower program of 1954.

I. Preparing the Eisenhower Program of 1954

"The presentation of a legislative program," wrote Truman in his farewell message to the Congress, "falls properly to my successor, not to me . . . and I would not infringe upon his responsibility to chart the forward course." [4] This was easier said by the outgoing President than done by the incoming, with his first Congress already in session (courtesy the Twentieth Amendment). In 1953, for the first time in years, there was no "legislative program," no charting of the course in the specific sense conveyed by Truman's words and prior practice.

At the outset, Eisenhower did present to Congress his own report on the State of the Union, but he chose throughout that address to keep most of his legislative references general to the point of homily.[5] The new regime, while reducing appropriations requests — as in the case of the Air Force — forebore to present a complete new budget document and message; while revising some economic policies — as in the case of credit and controls — it attempted no new Economic Report. During the spring of 1953, a number of Administration stands on legislation were developed and expressed, piecemeal, in special messages or bills, or both. But for the most part these encompassed only inescapable necessities — like foreign aid, taxation, reciprocal trade — where scheduled expirations of authority forced the presidential hand. More characteristic were the sur-

---

[3] Note that the Eisenhower program presentation of early 1955 to the first session of the 84th Congress followed the pattern of 1954, despite the change in party control of Congress. During January and February, 1955, three annual and nine special messages, all interlocking, conveyed a defined, comprehensive, relatively integrated legislative program from President to Congress, buttressed in most instances by specific Administration bills. The message on Formosa, January 25, was, of course, a thing apart.

[4] State of the Union Message, Jan. 7, 1953. This principle was followed also in the 1953 Economic Report and Budget Message (conveying the fiscal 1954 budget), which Truman submitted to Congress just before leaving office. With minor exceptions, these two messages carried no recommendations for new legislation.

[5] Address of Feb. 2, 1953.

veys, investigations, and study groups brought forward by the President or his subordinates in lieu of action recommendations on numbers of great issues, foreign and domestic.[6]

What accounts for this lack of firm programming in the congressional session of 1953? Wherefore the failure to exploit, in action terms, the President's election victory at this, his surest time of legislative honeymoon? Ultimate explanations wait, of course, on the historians. Meanwhile, two tentative answers, superficially opposed, may be suggested here. On the one hand, note the circumstances of the new regime's accession to its seats of power in the White House and the great departments — and the Republican party. Looking back on early 1953, a White House aide remarked in private conversation:

> We were prepared before inauguration only for the budget [cutting] drive and some executive reorganization, especially in the military. It would have been impossible to plunge into a full program the first session [of the 83rd Congress]. The Cabinet people had to learn their way around and get settled in . . . the staff here had to learn the issues . . . and a lot of these things go back to the year one. . . . And the President had to lay a groundwork of personal acquaintance and persuasion on the Hill. Our people up there expected him either to push them around or lie down and be walked on. Neither one! Instead, he has made every effort to reach out, get to know, seek personal contact. . . .[7]

In these terms, program gaps become by-products of the "newness" of the Eisenhower "team"; an explanation reinforced when one recalls the time squeeze of the Twentieth Amendment together with such matters as the learning problems of a Charles E. Wilson, say, or the predominance of Taft men among the Republicans in Congress — or, for that matter, the preeminence of Senate leader Taft himself. Of course, this implies that a full-scale program presentation was consciously intended from the start, then deliberately — indeed necessarily — postponed in 1953, while education and persuasion had their day. "We always meant to have a program," said this same White House aide, "but these other things came first."

On the other hand, no such symmetry of purpose and postponement

6 No less than 14 such surveys, undertaken with either executive or congressional authorization, were listed as matters of direct presidential concern and sponsorship in a special appendix to the authoritative Executive Office report on the status of "presidential measures at the close of the first session of the 83rd Congress." Bureau of the Budget, Office of Legislative Reference, "Legislative Status of Recommendations of the President, 83rd Congress, 1st Session (excluding Appropriation Requests)," Final Report, Aug. 8, 1953.

7 A comment made to the writer in the spring of 1954 during one of a number of interviews with members of the White House and Budget Bureau staffs, and with certain agency and congressional officials and Washington reporters. These interviews were conducted in March and May, 1953 and in April and December, 1954. The information presented in this section is drawn principally from those sources. Judgments and interpretations are, of course, the writer's own.

was publicly avowed in 1953; nor easily to be read into any signs and portents then emanating from the White House. Quite the contrary; this was the time when numbers of old Washington hands of both political persuasions in press corps, Congress, and the agencies explained the lack of program in terms of a fixed presidential policy stemming from some basic attitudes attributed to Eisenhower: a distaste for his predecessor's overt — and combative — exercise of the initiative in legislating; a feeling that to Congress, not the President, belonged the overt lead; an impulse to break sharply with the past by demonstrating presidential adherence to "proper" principles of "balance" between branches (or at least between the Republican President and "Mr. Republican" in the Senate leadership). These — or something like them — may, in fact, have been the President's own fixed beliefs; alternatively, their dissemination in that guise may have been engineered deliberately as an aid to "persuasion." Conviction or gambit or a blend of both — one cannot know from the outside.

But whatever Eisenhower's personal position, there seems no doubt that certain members of his entourage were then distinctly predisposed against a comprehensive program presentation along anything like Truman's lines. "We always meant to have a program," appears a considerable overstatement, at least if "we" refers to the whole White House entourage in 1953. Conciliating Congress was the order of the day; by some, apparently, this was interpreted as *not* doing whatever Truman might have done. Moreover, some of the new White House aides appear to have been seriously concerned about the constitutional proprieties; others disturbed about the range of Democratic intervention in domestic spheres; still others doubtful of the need for further emphasis on lawmaking, *per se*. Such attitudes as these add up to general bearishness toward widespread volunteering of firm presidential stands on current or prospective legislation — especially when controversial. "Let Congress struggle with it; keep us out." Here was, reportedly, an often-sounded White House theme through most of the first session of the 83rd Congress.[8]

---

[8] It is important to understand that in terms both of backgrounds and of ideologies, the aides whom Eisenhower brought into the White House — and has retained — were a rather heterogeneous group. On the legislative policy and liaison side, they included mainly: Adams, the Assistant to the President, an Eisenhower-before-Chicago man, former governor of New Hampshire and one-term Republican congressman; Shanley, the original special counsel, a New Jersey lawyer and former Stassen campaign manager; Rabb, the present Cabinet Secretary, for years ex-Senator Lodge's legislative aide; Hauge, the "economic" Administrative Assistant, a Harvard-trained economist and McGraw-Hill editor; Persons, the chief congressional liaison officer, an army careerist and long-time head of Army's legislative liaison (highly regarded as such, by the congressional oligarchs of both parties with whom it had been his job to smooth Army's path); and Persons' three original assistants — Morgan, a Washington lawyer, former Taft consultant, and longtime member of the House Office of Legislative Counsel; Harlow, former staff member of the House Armed Services Committee; and Gruenther, the General's brother, Senator Wherry's former secetary. For purposes of the 1954 legislative program, there should be added to this list the Chairman of the Council of Economic Advisors, Arthur M. Burns, Columbia economist at the time of

Yet scarcely five months after that session's close, there came the Eisenhower legislative program of 1954. Whether as an outcome of deliberate plans, or of changed attitudes, or both, this represents a distinct alteration in approach from one session of Congress to the next. How did it come to pass? How was the newness tempered, the bearishness reduced, the program put together?

In May, 1953, the Bureau of the Budget sent to the multilith machines — in preparation for June 30 distribution — its annual call for estimates from Federal agencies, in this case for fiscal 1955. Included in that document as an instruction to each agency was Section 86, entitled "Legislative Program":

> A statement will be submitted [by September 15] describing the preliminary legislative program of the agency for the forthcoming session of Congress. This statement should include *all* items of legislation [other than appropriations] which the agency contemplates proposing during the ensuing twelve months. . . .
> The statement should be in three parts:
>
> 1. Those items in the President's legislative program which have not yet been enacted . . . limited to proposals . . . specifically identified by the President as a part of his program, or specifically held [by Budget through central clearance] to be "in accord with the program of the President."
> 2. Legislative proposals not included in part 1 . . . which would cause no increase in budgeting requirements.
> 3. Legislative proposals not included in part 1 . . . which would cause an increase in budgeting requirements . . . arranged to reflect relative priority among items on the list and also . . . with respect to other portions of the budget. . . .
>
> With respect to each item of proposed legislation, this statement should set forth (1) the subject matter . . . together with a summary statement of the objectives . . . and the need . . . (2) the state of readiness of legislative drafts and other supporting material; (3) a reference to the numbers of pertinent bills and . . . reports [in recent sessions] . . . together with a brief appraisal . . . (4) a forecast of both the appropriations and the expenditures required . . . and (5) the names of other [interested] departments and agencies. . . .[9]

---

his initial appointment to the Eisenhower entourage; also Robert Cutler, then Special Assistant to the President for National Security Affairs and Chairman of the NSC Planning Board, a Boston banker and one-time CIA representative on the Planning Board's precursor, the Truman-era Senior Staff; finally, I. Jack Martin, Senator Taft's former assistant, who joined the Persons group after Taft's death.

[9] Budget Circular A-11, "Instructions for the Preparation and Submission of Annual Budget Estimates," June 30, 1953, Sec. 86. This section also called for an indication of the "nature and status" of legislative items under discussion but not yet in firm program stage and for a report on all provisions of law "of interest to the agency" scheduled for expiration in the coming year. Note that this section has remained a feature of the Budget's calls for estimates in 1954 and 1955.

This language was identical with that included in the 1952 call for estimates issued a year earlier before the close of Truman's term. Indeed, section 86 and its requirements had been a feature of each Budget call since 1949. Their renewal in 1953 marks not an Eisenhower innovation but a bureaucratic continuum, an attempted restoration of routines, an action taken on the Budget's own initiative without advance assurance as to either agency response or ultimate White House reaction.

This was a venture with no guarantees attached; it was, however, something more than a leap in the dark. The Budget Bureau's renewal of section 86 was powerfully reinforced by two other acts of initiative, one preceding, one following preparation of the new call for estimates.

The first of these involved the agencies. As early as January, 1953, the new Budget Director, Joseph M. Dodge, had corralled cabinet colleagues, one by one, for orientation briefings by his career aides. In a number of cases these sessions were held even before Inauguration Day, providing several cabinet members-designate their first glimpse from inside into the complexities of their new assignments. And at each briefing Budget staffers took occasion, with Dodge's assent, to inform the department head about "his" legislative program (compiled the preceding fall), its existence in form and fact, its usefulness for orientation, its potential for planning and control, its liability to renewal on Budget's call.[10]

Thereby, a piece of left-over machinery idling in the departmental depths was impressed on the consciousness of new department heads at a uniquely favorable moment. This had its due effect; by late summer 1953, when lower-level bureaucrats began preparing agency responses to Budget's new call, their top superiors, in almost every case, were reasonably well acquainted with the departmental "program," quite acclimated to its presence as a fact of departmental life, and quite prepared to oversee its renovation and renewal in advance of 1954.

Meanwhile the Budget had taken a further act of initiative, this time involving the White House. Early in July, 1953 President Eisenhower had voiced some concern about means to bring together, well in advance, data and suggestions for his January, 1954 State of the Union message. Budget aides were asked to brief him on his predecessor's practice; they took the opportunity to urge some White House recognition for the programming requirement in section 86 of the new call for estimates. In Truman's time it had been customary for the President to write each agency in early autumn, requesting message data and, at the same time,

[10] An earlier article has noted the importance of Dodge's personal role in carrying the Budget Bureau's legislative staff work through the 1953 transition from the old to the new regime. Here is another demonstration of the point. Given the White House attitudes outlined above, Dodge might well have chosen to let cabinet officers discover for themselves and make what they chose of legislative programs inherited from their predecessors. Instead he chose to impress legislative clearance regulations generally, and legislative programs in particular, upon the new department heads at this first advantageous opportunity. See Richard E. Neustadt, "Presidency and Legislation: The Growth of Central Clearance," *American Political Science Review*, Vol. 48, pp. 641–71, at pp. 655–56 (Sept., 1954).

reiterating over his own signature the main terms of section 86. Message and program requests had long been joined; that was made clear to the new President.

The result was an identical letter to each cabinet officer over Eisenhower's signature and bearing signs of his own dictation. Dated July 30, 1953 — a month after formal issuance of Budget's call — the letters asked for substantive ideas appropriate to the State of the Union Message, these ideas to be based on a "thorough rethinking of the mission of your department and the . . . means to achieve it." And, quite explicitly, that review was to "complement attention you are giving the 1955 budget and the formulation of a carefully planned, specific legislative program." [11]

If there were any doubts remaining at top departmental levels about the propriety — and the priority — of Budget's legislative call, this missive from the President appears to have resolved them. By mid-September, 1953, agency legislative programs were flowing to the Budget. By early October, departmental message memoranda were en route to the White House, many of them referencing or appending these programs to concretize suggested points of emphasis. The President had called for a "thorough rethinking." Here, in this double-barrelled presentation, was the visible response.

Cumulatively, it was an astonishing response, at least to those White House staffers disinclined toward executive initiatives in legislation. For here were departmental declarations of intent to sponsor literally hundreds of measures great and small, *most of which the President was being asked to make his own by personal endorsement in a message.* And among these were dozens of proposals, espoused now by one or another of Eisenhower's own department heads, closely resembling — in general purpose, if not always precise form — predecessor measures urged in Truman's time and bearing then a Fair Deal label: an expansion of social security, an increased minimum wage, a revision of immigration laws, a broadening of unemployment compensation, and many more. Mostly these represented improvements in going programs long advocated by career administrators (and their clientele) to modernize or clarify the application of public policies in their charge. Agency legislative programs in 1953 were not sheer replicas of those in 1952 and earlier — some items were stricken, others added, still others revised — but their content makes plain that

[11] Reportedly the first draft of these letters was written largely by the President himself, at his volition, as a personal adaptation and improvement in his terms of the prior procedure on which he had been briefed by Budget. The mechanism of formal letters and their referencing of budget and legislative programs seem to have been direct outgrowths of that briefing. On the other hand, the call for a "thorough rethinking" appears to reflect Eisenhower's personal views on a paramount duty of his Administration, a duty stated in most unbureaucratic language in the opening paragraph (not quoted above). That opening language designedly lent a personal flavor to the whole proceeding, a flavor emphasized by subsequent presidential references in cabinet meetings. Note that noncabinet agencies were approached in a briefer, much less personal vein, receiving requests over Sherman Adams' signature, dated July 31, 1953, for any "ideas appropriate for the State of the Union message."

mixed with the rethinking from on high was a good deal of educating from below.

For eight years past — save only 1953 — there had been a presidential charting of the course in Truman's terms: an executive inventory of specifics (agenda and yardstick both) for action by the Congress. Now, in October, 1953, these agency submissions forecast that some such executive charting would be done in 1954 — if not by Eisenhower comprehensively, then by his cabinet members piecemeal; if not in his name, then in theirs. At his own invitation they had defined their ambitions, drawn their plans, and these now turned out to encompass controversial innovations of national concern, inextricably involving the President's position and prestige. Were he therefore to influence scope, scale, priorities, and presentation, he needs must act upon their requests for endorsement, thereby asserting his own role in program-making, *his* plans, *his* charting of the course as against theirs.

The implications were not lost for long upon the presidential staff.

Within the Budget Bureau — whose initiatives had helped bring matters to this pass — the disposition was to move no further without guidance from the White House. During October and November, 1953 Dodge forebore to channel departmental legislative programs into the main stream of estimates review. Instead the budgeteers concentrated upon going operations, leaving proposed legislation in the air for last-minute juggling independently of the balance of the budget. This was precisely what section 86's call for agency programs purported to avert, but Dodge displayed no interest in asserting *for the budget process* title to the task of reconciling the regime's first-session legislative stance with the logic of the situation these created. Having made certain that the issues would be posed, he was content to let others take first crack at them — this, anyway, under the special circumstances of 1953.

Within the White House, on the other hand, there was no escaping action upon agency submissions. By mid-October it was generally conceded that whatever major issues they might raise would have to be acknowledged in some form or fashion — negatively, at the very least — by or before Eisenhower's annual messages. This necessitated first of all a close look at the contents of the pile well in advance of message preparation. And by early November, such examination was preoccupying half the members of the White House entourage.

Their initial "look-see" became a rather elaborate affair. Under the aegis of the Assistant to the President, Sherman Adams, with his deputy, Wilfred E. Persons, and the then Special Counsel, Bernard M. Shanley, actively in charge,[12] anywhere from six to ten members of the entourage

[12] General Persons had originally been appointed Special Assistant to the President for legislative liaison rather than Adams' general deputy, a change in designation (and to some extent in role) which took effect after the close of the first session of the 83rd Congress. Early in 1955 Shanley left the post of Special Counsel to become Appointments Secretary and was succeeded by Gerald Morgan, one of Persons' original assistants.

— depending on subject-matter — joined in an item-by-item review around the conference table; over a two-week period this involved some 12 meetings of two to three hours apiece.[13]

At the outset, the purpose of that exercise was educational. Every White House aide with any role to play in policies or tactics on the legislative side had a stake in developing the staff's position upon agency particulars; hence the collaborative conference approach. But up to that time none but Shanley had been exposed to the substantive aspects of anything like the range of measures reached by agency programs — the result, in his case, of nine months' contact with the Budget's legislative clearance work, especially on enrolled bills [14] — and now he and his colleagues faced a welter of substantive needs and remedies presented by the agencies, with antecedents tracing back, in the already quoted phrase, "to the year one." In consequence, these conferences assumed the aspect of a cram course on the issues, a guided tour through the past histories of agency proposals.

The guide in this case was Roger W. Jones, career chief of the Budget Bureau's Office of Legislative Reference, control center for legislative clearance. Jones took as his text a checklist of almost 300 "major" proposals, culled mostly from agency programs, and these were systematically reviewed in subject-matter groupings as staff sessions proceeded.[15] In each case it became Jones' role to sketch pre-history and pros and cons, both substantive and tactical, in "institutional" terms, leaving policy judgments and partisan aspects for his hearers to argue out among themselves. "There came about," he later recalled, "almost a fierce dedication [on the part of the White House staff] to keeping me in the role of telling both sides of the story." Given the staff's spread of interests and attitudes, some of those stories sparked a great deal of question-raising and discussion. That the process was educative, there seems to be no doubt.

This seminar approach tended to generate its own next steps. As key problem areas emerged from the discussion, particular aides took up *ad hoc* assignments to dig deeper and report: checking Jones' version of the facts, sounding departmental attitudes and conflicts, judging congressional and "outside" opinion, and generally feeling out what open issues — substantive, or tactical, or sheer mechanical — remained for resolution in each case. These preliminary inquiries were not confined exclusively to items in agency programs or on Jones' list. Several matters raised within the White House were researched in this fashion at this point. (Some of them ultimately found their way into the President's

---

[13] Participants were drawn mostly from among the staff members listed in note 8, above. Hauge and Burns, for example, attended all sessions involving matters of "economic" significance, which included virtually everything in the social welfare field.

[14] See Neustadt, *op. cit.*, pp. 666–67.

[15] Agency legislative programs, message suggestions, and lists of expiring legislation, supplemented by Jones' informed guess-work, provided the field from which items were selected for this list. See "Checklist of Major Proposals for the 83rd Congress, 2nd Session," Bureau of the Budget, Office of Legislative Reference, Nov. 1, 1953.

January program, *e.g.,* voting at eighteen, and loss of citizenship for Smith Act violators.)

In terms of the advices thus obtained, the White House staff group turned next to determining by what means necessary steps toward resolution should be taken. At this stage there was a good deal of checking with the President. As a result, certain proposals simply dropped out of sight, at least for 1954; others were assigned to staff members for handling with the agencies and ultimate informal presentation to the President; still others were allotted to the Budget for handling and presentation alongside departmental estimates; finally, a number of complex and controversial measures, high in policy and partisan significance — among them social security, taxation, agricultural assistance, foreign aid — were earmarked for formal presentation to the cabinet (or alternatively, the National Security Council) by the sponsoring department head.

These cabinet presentations — which grew in number as the first experiments succeeded — were a striking feature of the preparatory effort on the 1954 program. Procedurally, they ran about as follows: first, each cabinet officer concerned was asked to ready a comprehensive visual presentation explaining and justifying his proposals in detail. Next, this presentation was tried out before the White House staff group (Jones still included), these "dry-runs" giving staff an opening for criticism or advice on both substance and presentation-technique. Finally, when the staff was relatively satisfied — and the President briefed accordingly — a full cabinet session was convened, the formal presentation made, discussion held, and general concurrence invited. (It was forthcoming in each case, accompanied sometimes by alterations of detail.) All told, there were some seven such full-scale presentations in the last week of November and the first two weeks of December, led off by what staff aides termed a "magnificent performance" in the social security field.[16] On each occasion Eisenhower was in the chair, not merely presiding, but actively participating; his questions, suggestions, and advice sparked most of the changes made.

This formalized proceeding had been improvised by President and staff, perhaps less out of abstract deference to the cabinet, *per se,* than as a concrete response to immediate felt needs arising in the course of program review. By this means it was hoped to check and test not alone substance, but also the selling-power of proposals and the status of their packaging for sale, each presentation being taken as a test of departmental readiness to go up on the Hill in what for many cabinet members would be their first full-scale approach to a legislative committee. By this means it was hoped as well to gain commitments at the cabinet table on which Budget could base effective interagency coordination of actual bill drafts and testimony; hoped, also, that the formal circumstances of their giving would help to keep commitments green in cabinet memories

[16] Note that the Cabinet Secretary's present duties of agenda preparation, decision minuting, and follow-up first took contemporary form as an outgrowth of these presentations.

through the spring; hoped, finally, that exposure to each other's plans and problems would combat members' tendencies toward "parochial" views.

Education was the order of the day. And as an educative venture, in these several respects, this cabinet mechanism proved a handy instrument, producing results satisfying, on the whole, to its initial sponsors. "We never could have got as many things done half as well, in any other way," remarked a White House aide, ". . . those cabinet members put a lot of effort into this and it paid off. Besides they were floored by each other's presentations . . . and also by the chief's own grasp, and interventions, and ideas. . . . The whole effect was very good." Of course, one's needs and circumstances change with time. This venture was conceived and carried out by a new regime facing its first annual message season. A year later preparation of the 1955 program was marked by rather less wide-ranging cabinet consultation.

In the course of these various proceedings late in 1953 — staff reviews, presidential briefings, cabinet presentations, and attendant negotiations — the White House grew increasingly committed to an Eisenhower legislative program, the more so as its practicable scope and character came clear. By the end of November there was no longer any question that a program would ensue, or that it should appear in annual messages, or that it should be at once comprehensive and concrete. Amidst the concentration on specifics, these things came to be taken for granted. In part, this is attributable to the sheer momentum of those staff and agency proceedings once started on their way. In part, it seems related to the intra-party power struggle in which Senator McCarthy had engaged with increasing directness since the death of Senator Taft the preceding summer. On December 2 and on December 16 the President at press conference took pains to assert that his own forthcoming program, *not* McCarthy's chosen issue, would measure Republican performance in the election year of 1954; this hard upon the Senator's press statements to the contrary.[17] The presidential program, once, perhaps, a questionable undertaking or a necessary chore, was now become a prime political imperative, its relative readiness a godsend, one expects, to the regime.

In this context, the work of program preparation was carried toward completion through the last weeks of December, traditional peak-period of message season. With some significant exceptions, most substantive decisions had been taken by the middle of that month. But other tasks were still far from complete: transforming the decisions into messages and bills, and "warming up the customers" before their presentation. These tasks now took the center of the stage.

On December 17, 18, and 19, 1953, Eisenhower formally unveiled his program to the Republican congressional leadership, in an unprecedented series of carefully staged briefings at the White House. With the

17 For the Eisenhower and McCarthy comments, respectively, see *New York Times*, Dec. 3, Dec. 17, and Nov. 25, 1953.

President presiding, these ran a full eight hours daily, covering a subject-matter agenda fixed in advance and rigidly enforced from the chair. The Vice-President, the Speaker, the Majority Leaders, and the Whips were in attendance at all times, as were most members of the cabinet and the White House entourage. Committee chairmen and their ranking (Republican) associates participated when their subjects were discussed, arriving and departing on a pre-determined schedule; so did a number of executive officials below cabinet rank. In deference to Eisenhower's own communiques, issued each afternoon, and honoring his personal request, those moving in and out avoided detailed comment to the press; thereby, the White House got ideal publicity in presidential terms — headlines about Eisenhower and his program but no scoops on particulars.

The briefings themselves followed a set form. Typically, as a subject was reached, the President would open with some appropriate remarks, then call on the department head (or in some cases the staff member) most concerned; the latter responding with what was, in effect, a redo or refinement of his cabinet presentation (or equivalent), complete with visual aids. Everything was visual and oral; no written summaries, much less bill or message drafts, were passed around. Language, it was explained, remained in a preliminary stage, pending these consultations. During the presentation the President himself would interpose a running commentary; at its close he would invite reactions (not concurrence) from the leaders — equally calling time rather shortly, and passing on to the next subject.

In a few instances, the leaders expressed prompt and uniform concern about advancing a particular proposal at the coming session. When this occurred, the President was generally quick to accept their advice and strike the measure. (One senses that some of these may have been paraded for the purpose.) Mostly, however, the legislators looked and listened, with much to absorb, nothing to ratify, and little time for argument. This does not seem to have been inconsistent with the President's intent.

The White House did not ask that they approve. It hoped, however, that they would be impressed by what was set before them. A prime purpose of the whole affair was education, once again; this for good reason and, apparently, with good results. "Most of the people from the Hill were dazzled, very much enthused," reported an *executive* observer of these gatherings. "Some of them discovered things they hadn't known about the President . . . he was fast on his feet, and on top of the issues . . . very quick and very shrewd . . . a lot of people realized that for the first time. And then it turned out that his program had real substance and real saleability . . . something they could really use . . . packaged and ready . . . a very great attraction and they weren't prepared for it . . . they were bowled over by it. . . ." Or, as a Democratic congressman remarked, "I wasn't there and I don't know, but [Speaker] Martin and [Majority Leader] Halleck came out and told the press they were behind the 'program' and would push it and they really must have meant that — just look at the record. . . . Certainly they got religion somewhere; maybe there." [18] Of course the chances for and profits from such formal education grew out of particulars of time and situation. A year later, Eisenhower's 1955 program was previewed for the leaders in much less elaborate fashion — consisting mainly of a presidential listing, on successive days, to the majority and minority leadership — partly, of course, because it was to go before a Democratic Congress; partly, perhaps, because its (prospective) main *new* features — aid to Asia, schools, and roads — were nowhere near "packaged and ready" by, much less before, the time Congress convened.[19]

Less than three weeks intervened between these leaders' meetings in December, 1953 and the President's State of the Union address to Congress; it was a busy season for the message drafters. In policy terms there was by this time little left to be decided, but the contents of the several messages remained to be coordinated, their relative scope and coverage fully defined, specific drafts agreed upon — or, indeed, written — and final language snarls worked out. In carrying these matters forward, actual drafting of the Budget Message was left largely to the Budget Bureau, the White House checking mainly general tone and precise wording of concrete proposals. Similarly, drafting of the Economic Report remained largely in the hands of the Economic Council chairman, himself a prime participant in earlier staff consultations. But for the psychologically most important annual message, the President's personally delivered State of the Union address, the drafting was from first to last a White House undertaking.

Initially, the work on that address was done by members of the Persons-Shanley staff group — utilizing agency submissions where they could — with Bryce Harlow, a "speech and message" Administrative Assistant, as rhetoric expert and editorial coordinator.[20] When it came to elaboration of particular proposals, a tentative division of responsibility had been planned in advance between their product and the other annual messages, *e.g.*, taxes in the Economic Report, postal rates in the Budget Message. Even so, the first consolidated State of the Union draft was so crowded with specifics that it would have taken some three hours to deliver. In consequence, large portions were pulled out to form the

[18] Another comment worth quotation came from a one-time Truman aide with long experience in matters legislative: "That conference with the leaders seems to have been a good show. Perhaps 'we' should have tried something like it. I wonder, though, if anyone could have gotten the comparable *Democrats* to sit still in the White House for three days."

[19] Regarding the 1955 program, Eisenhower met with the prospective minority (Republican) leadership December 13, 1954 and with the prospective majority (Democratic) leaders the next day. These meetings, relatively *pro forma* in character, followed by six weeks the mid-term elections of 1954.

[20] Harlow, a former House Military Affairs Committee aide, has functioned more recently as an additional Persons assistant on the legislative liaison side; his speech drafting and editorial duties, temporarily assumed in 1953, are now (1955) performed mainly by Eisenhower's biographer, Kevin McCann, another Administrative Assistant to the President and successor, in effect, to Emmett Hughes, of *Life* Magazine, who functioned in that capacity during the first six months of 1953.

first five of Eisenhower's 1954 special messages, his personal address becoming in the end a sort of preparatory note and table of contents for the supplementing documents to follow.[21]

Meanwhile, the departments concentrated on bill drafting in order that each definite proposal conveyed by these messages might be backed promptly by a detailed draft of legislation bearing an Administration label and ready for transmission (formally or not) to Congress. With most policies decided earlier and elsewhere, Jones in Budget's clearance office was enabled to ride herd on these drafts, their preparation, interagency coordination, presidential clearance, and transmission, his priorities keyed to the subject-matter emphasis of the successive messages as scheduled by the White House.[22]

Considering the number and diversity of documents involved, both messages and bills, the product of these last weeks' work was remarkably integrated: the messages reasonably consistent internally and with each other; their ambiguities mostly deliberate, not unconscious; their main affirmative proposals packaged in bill form, approved and ready-to-hand. That this was managed by a new regime to whose top echelons each operation was a new experience is tribute partly to the underlying bureaucratic structure and partly to the thoroughness of preliminary preparations — and sheer education — at staff and cabinet levels. In only one respect did final documents display a notable deficiency, or gap, in advance preparations: the logic of requests for legislation sometimes failed to jibe with that of budget estimates for going operations — on the one hand were proposed increments in present powers, and on the other budget cuts in present programs, e.g., grants for hospital construction. The last weeks of December were not long enough, it seems, to synchronize in all respects the results of that separation between budget and legislative planning on which Dodge had determined, not without reason, the previous September.

But if — with this exception — the documents conveying Eisenhower's program were consistent and coordinated, they were voluminous as well; if the program was coherent, it was also bulky and diffuse, devoid of

---

[21] See State of the Union Address, January 7, 1954; Budget Message, January 21; Economic Report, January 28; also the special messages carved out of the early State of the Union compendium: Taft-Hartley and farm, January 11; social security, January 14; health, January 18; housing, January 25. Two other special messages, drafted somewhat later, completed the initial program presentation: atomic energy, February 17; foreign economic policy, March 30, this last including the substance of the Randall Committee's recommendations on tariff legislation, as well as the Administration's proposals for further foreign aid.

[22] Note one principal exception: Eisenhower's proposals for general tax reductions were not made the subject of a consolidated bill draft cleared by Budget and introduced in Congress prior to and as a basis for committee consideration. Instead, Treasury presented draft language, piecemeal, to the House Ways and Means Committee as a "technical drafting service" in elaboration of the President's proposals preparatory to the framing of a *committee* bill. This is the usual course with tax reductions as a matter of traditional committee preference (not so tax increases, where an Administration bill, as such, is usually very welcome at the start).

single focus or outstanding theme. Among the many things proposed to be done, or not done, or held for study, none was so striking as to dominate the rest, while impacts of particular proposals were muffled by sheer numbers and diversity. And style of presentation did nothing to make up the lack; the messages were basically compendia, high in plain exposition, low in excitement.

Neither by content nor tone were documents like these well suited to the task of dramatizing for the country and his party the President's own personality and purposes. Yet if there was but little drama in the messages themselves, there was, perhaps, much to be gained by focussing attention on their presentation as a collectivity, seeking dramatic impact in the sheer fact of "program," aside from the nature or the statement of its parts. To this the White House — President and staff together, it appears — devoted a great deal of thought and care during December, 1953.

In the five weeks before the State of the Union address, there emanated from the White House a steady stream of press communiques and dope stories concerning the program's preparation. Specific plans were guarded rather carefully — the aim, no doubt, to generate suspense — but generalized official comments on the special cabinet sessions, and in particular the legislative leaders' meetings, were arranged and facilitated by the White House press office with all the fanfare usually reserved for first-rank international conferences.[23] After the conclusion of those meetings, December 19, the President removed to Georgia over Christmas, whence came almost daily stories of last-minute conferences on the impending messages with officials flown down from Washington. On January 4, 1954, all this was capped by a radio and television address to the nation, in which Eisenhower plugged his program and urged everyone's attention to its imminent unveiling. In dramatic appeal this discourse was scarcely an unqualified success; trying to reach the country in the evening hours without depriving Congress of its first crack at details, he avoided scooping his congressional address at the expense of over-generalizing. Nevertheless, the notion that something portentous impended, Eisenhower's own, received top billing once again in newscasts and the press.

On January 5, the President met minority legislative leaders at the White House for a courtesy preview of his recommendations; thereby the press got one last "program" story before the opening of Congress. Then on Thursday, January 7, came the President's State of the Union address to the Congress, another radio and television presentation, if at noon. There followed on three successive Mondays and Thursdays no less than seven of his supplementing messages, spaced for optimum press play and in a sequence obviously intended to strengthen the impression of a vast executive creation, highlight its most generally appealing features, blur the rest: Taft-Hartley and farm messages sent up at the same time on

23 See especially the official White House communiques and participants' statements to the White House press corps during and after the three-day meeting with the Republican congressional leaders. *New York Times*, Dec. 18, 19, 20, 1953.

the same day (with a Korean defense treaty sent the Senate simultaneously); social security, health, and housing messages each featured in a separate package on a separate day; housekeeping and limited-interest requests buried by the dozen in the Budget Message; tax reduction dominant in the Economic Report.

All this elaborate staging for the 1954 program was in its way no less an educative effort than the cabinet and legislative leaders' presentations which had gone before. Like them it was improvised to meet the special needs and opportunities of the regime's first venture into legislative program-making; like them it was to be reduced in scale — of buildup, not of messages — the following year. All three were quite distinctly first-time undertakings, each aiming to inform and to convince a different audience of propositions which would hardly need such emphasis a second year: that Eisenhower had assumed a new degree of leadership in course-setting for Congress and his party, and that the course was to be, as he later termed it, "moderate progressivism," or "dynamic conservatism," its salient domestic feature a conservative consolidation of the human welfare side of the New Deal, *viz.*, 1954's social security, housing, and health proposals.

Whether by accident, accretion, or design, those propositions had emerged as something on the order of a presidential policy by the time White House staff got deep into reviewing agency programs. Subsequent cabinet sessions, leaders' meetings, press build-ups did not create a course of action but served rather to test, trim, "package," and persuade. And the fact that such processing was conceived to be necessary, indeed was actually employed, needs to be understood not merely as an outgrowth of prevailing notions on "efficiency" or "public relations," but as an attribute of the divided counsels, attitudes, traditions attendant on the first Republican Administration in 20 years, whose head — and the Republican party's head — had previously been a professional non-partisan.

The presidential role anent Congress, cabinet, and party; the party's general posture anent oppositional gambits of other days, these things were by no means become matters of course or common understanding during 1953 — not even, perhaps, in the White House at the time those staff reviews began. Yet the regime's first venture into legislative programming, while in no sense determinative on all scores, was bound to come to grips with such unknowns more directly and on a wider scale than any prior undertaking in the Eisenhower term. The form and content of the annual messages for 1954 thus became matters of considerable moment to Republican office-holders — and their clientele — of all shades of opinion at both ends of the Avenue. The very elaborateness of program processing devices suggests the amount of potential party cleavage they were relied on to contain. The very moderateness of the final product disguises a not inconsiderable amount of prior disputation among protagonists variously placed along the regime's right-left spectrum of opinion (a spectrum obviously centered to the right of that in Truman's time, or in F.D.R.'s, but distinctly observable nonetheless).

If a number of "liberal" projects were earmarked for further study, as with immigration, education, minimum wage, or watered down, by prior *Democratic* standards — as with public health and housing — what remained by way of progressive measures and what failed to appear by way of schemes for "turning back the clock," both represent reportedly the fruits of hard-pressed argument "within the family" at the crucial early stages of departmental programming and White House staff review. And were the outsider to question what could have been so disputatious in the final product, how could less have been recommended by a modern President — mindful of his national constituency, facing a mid-term election — the rejoinder would seem to be that this regime began in company with all the attitudes and symbols of long opposition; their shedding was no light task.

Presumably — and pending the researches of historians — it is in this perspective that one ought to view the course of program preparation during 1953. Much of what was done procedurally becomes, then, specialized and perhaps transitory, rooted in particular times, persons, circumstances. But clearly there is nothing transient about the venture as a whole, the compilation of an inclusive bill of particulars for presentation annually by President to Congress. This is now (mid-1955) no less a matter of course in Eisenhower's time than formerly in Truman's; the practice which survives such a change of regime is likely to endure. And clearly its most institutionalized features as of now are also those whose prior presence on the scene helped signally to push a new Administration toward resuming and elaborating Truman patterns: the departmental inventorying in September submissions and the presidential inventorying in January messages. It was then caught between the actuality of agency programs and the nearing of no less than three required annual messages (inventories all, each year from 1946 through 1952), that Eisenhower's White House turned in earnest to developing his 1954 program. It was upon these pre-existing institutional foundations that there arose that programming machinery sketched in the previous pages.

This suggests an obvious question: where did these foundations come from; what brought them into being in pre-Eisenhower years? For answers it is necessary to look back at least as far as the preceding transition period, the early presidency of Harry S Truman.

II. The Use of Annual Messages in Truman's Time

The first of these developments, alike in time and in importance, is that described above as presidential inventorying, the use of annual messages buttressed by special messages and bills to take specific legislative stands across the board. In its contemporary form this practice may be said to have originated in the three-year period immediately following World War II, arising out of circumstances which are now to be defined.

In January, 1944, five months before D-Day, President Roosevelt had proclaimed an "Economic Bill of Rights," a generalized statement of his postwar goals which served to reaffirm and to elaborate prewar assertions of the government's responsibility for peacetime economic development and social welfare, as well as to dramatize the presidency as prime source of ideas and initiative in this vast area of home affairs.[24] In February, 1946, six months after V-J Day, the underlying concepts of both governmental and of presidential duty were written into law, receiving permanent institutional expression in the Employment Act of 1946:

> . . . the Congress declares that it is the continuing policy and responsibility of the Federal Government to . . . promote maximum employment, production and purchasing power. . . . The President shall transmit to Congress at the beginning of each regular session . . . a program for carrying out [this] policy. . . .[25]

Here was a pressing charge upon the postwar White House, in terms of public expectation — and of anticipated postwar needs — a mandate no less meaningful before than after its enactment into law. To F.D.R.'s successor in the presidency this was perforce an immediate obligation of office. For him as heir to Roosevelt's coalition it was, moreover, a political imperative. And from the moment "peace" arrived with unexpected suddenness in August, 1945, releasing all manner of public hopes and fears and expectations, Truman showered upon Congress literally dozens of recommendations, great and small, for legislative action in the economic and welfare spheres his predecessor had marked out.[26]

Beginning with his "21-point program" of September 6, 1945 — which launched what became known as the "Fair Deal" — the new President sent Congress seven special messages in 10 weeks' time requesting a melange of reconversion aids, administrative improvements, and long-range reforms, their number and diversity measuring not only social but governmental changes called for, in his view, to meet the needs of peace. Then in January, 1946, at the opening of the new session, the more significant of these were rearranged and bundled together, inventory style, into a single package, presented to Congress by an enlarged Budget

[24] The Economic Bill of Rights was set forth in the State of the Union Message, January 11, 1944, as a matter not of specifics but of general postwar objectives to which Roosevelt pledged himself and his regime and, as the year wore on, his party. These objectives figured prominently in F.D.R.'s fourth-term campaign with Truman as his running mate.

[25] A glance at any Economic Report of the President since 1946 — Eisenhower's as well as Truman's — will show that the Act's mandate regarding "employment, production and purchasing power" has drawn from Roosevelt's successors recommendations (of varying scope) for economic and social legislation in every area encompassed by his "economic rights."

[26] Indeed, most of the major Truman proposals had been foreshadowed by F.D.R. during the 1944 campaign, especially in his Chicago address, October 28, 1944. And Roosevelt's Special Counsel has recorded that the Truman messages on social security, education, and health grew out of preparatory work commissioned by F.D.R. before his Yalta trip. Samuel I. Rosenman, *Working with Roosevelt* (New York, 1952), pp. 514–15. Whether Roosevelt would have followed his own commission in so faithful a fashion remains unknown.

Message, and to the public by radio address.[27] This presentation anticipated by a month final passage of the Employment Act; the annual message of 1946 was, among other things, an Economic Report in embryo.[28]

In Roosevelt's time, the President's address to Congress on the State of the Union had usually sounded some general, introductory theme, warmly personal, even philosophic, with definite proposals left for later, piecemeal presentation when, as, and if the President chose. Now, in attempted response to the post-war push of office and constituency, Truman used that address, experimentally combined with his Budget Message, to tidy up and restate his long list of post-V-J Day particulars. And whereas Roosevelt, when the time came for particulars, was usually both dramatic and concrete, Truman confined himself to rapid-fire listing of everything at once, impacts diffused and loose ends flying. "Where Roosevelt had been criticized for sending prepared bills to Congress Truman dumped mere proposals in batches." [29] In 1946, except for international agreements there were but few bills bearing a reliable Administration label. On the generality of Truman's own proposals, authoritative information — to say nothing of general understanding — was almost wholly lacking as regards his order of priorities, his preferences and tolerances, bill by bill, his outlook on specifics urged by other Democratic spokesmen.

The presidential silence on these matters may be explained in part by reference to the former Senator — a junior in the New Deal's palmy days — who used to say, during his first year in the White House, that Presidents should state their case and then leave legislating strictly up to Congress. But something more was operating here than anybody's personal proclivity. For not alone in public were these things unsettled but in private also. Truman's "batches" of "mere proposals" had been produced, of course, in the aftermath of Roosevelt's death and enemy surrender, a time of greatest difficulty for the White House. The presidential staff was thoroughly disoriented, its composition and relationships in flux. The cabinet abounded in new faces. The government was plagued by all the woes of demobilization, reconversion, and deteriorating overseas alliances. Meanwhile, the Congress strained toward its first postwar political campaign — from which, incidentally, the President was to ab-

[27] For further observations on the content of Truman's post-V-J Day program and on the personal and political motivations behind it, see Richard E. Neustadt, "Congress and the Fair Deal: A Legislative Balance Sheet," *Public Policy*, Vol. 5 (Cambridge, Mass., 1954), pp. 349–81, at pp. 355–60.

[28] Truman's annual message went to Congress January 25, 1946. It combined the State of the Union and Budget Messages into a single document which included gross national product analysis, discussion of the economic outlook, and a sweeping program of "economic" legislation. The Employment Act, which became law March 2, was still under consideration in Congress and it was hoped by some of the President's advisors that the example of a single, consolidated message would head off prescription of a separate Economic Report. That hope was vain and the consolidated message disadvantageous on several counts, its bulk precluding, among other things, a face-to-face report to Congress on the State of the Union. The experiment was not repeated. Since 1946 three separate messages have gone annually to Congress.

[29] Wilfred E. Binkley, *President and Congress* (New York, 1947), p. 278.

sent himself by urgent invitation of his party. In this situation there was scarcely room or opportunity for careful White House definition and elaboration of a presidential view on details of the varied legislation Truman felt impelled to recommend.

If in January, 1946 the President did little more than spread bare-bones endorsements on the record, in January, 1947 even this activity was circumscribed. There intervened, of course, the congressional elections. Under the initial impact of Democratic reverses the Administration lost, for a time, its sense of domestic direction; in home affairs all budding plans were rendered obsolete. Here was a tremendous shock for a regime which, 19 months in office, had still to catch its breath. Within the President's own entourage a first reaction was compounded of uncertainty and hesitation; twin themes which can be read between the lines of Truman's annual messages to the newly-convened — and Republican-controlled — 80th Congress, documents prepared in the immediate aftermath of the election.

In January, 1947, there were for the first time three of those messages: a State of the Union Address, a Budget Message, and an Economic Report (the first under the Employment Act). In one respect at least these three, taken together, recalled their single counterpart of 1946: subject-matter ran the gamut of government concerns. But where in 1946 each subject introduced was capped by one or more demands for legislation — emphatic, if not necessarily specific — the discourses of 1947 concluded mostly with requests for "study" or "consideration," gently, even ambiguously phrased, not so much calls for action as warnings and appeals to the congressional Republicans.[30] Far less than in 1946 did these three messages — or any later statements during 1947 — convey a specific presidential "program" in anything like Eisenhower's current terms.

But while 1947 began on a note of hesitation for the Truman regime, it ended with most doubts resolved. By Fall the White House was preparing to make Congress' domestic legislative record a prime issue in the coming presidential campaign. By that time also the Administration was well started on a foreign policy — bipartisan in origins and application — which would require legislative execution, via authorizations and appropriations, all through Truman's hoped-for second term. In practical effect, the Truman Doctrine and the Marshall Plan tied foreign policy to legislation and added new specifics on which Truman was now bound to exercise his constitutional authority to recommend, *thereby extending to the foreign field something approaching the Employment Act's mandate in home affairs.*

For reasons, then, of policy and politics alike, Truman's three annual messages of January, 1948 were quite different in tone and content from those of the year before, the subject-matter no less broad, but everywhere much more specific, with most affirmative proposals delineated much

---

[30] Especially was this the case with that year's pressing issues of inflation, tax reduction, and labor relations. See Address on the State of the Union, Jan. 9, 1947; Economic Report, Jan. 11; and Budget Message, Jan. 14.

more sharply.[31] And where in early 1947 many presidential references had been left dangling, to be defined as anybody pleased or not at all, in 1948 an amplifying special message went to Congress almost every week, usually with an approved draft bill hard on its heels.[32] Save in foreign and defense fields, the motivation here was mainly issue-making, record-building through congressional *non*-performance on the widest possible range of liberal measures; in their domestic aspects these measures reformulated and elaborated every controversial segment of the 1946 program. On the domestic measures, therefore, no less than the Marshall Plan, it was essential that there should be clear lines, sharply drawn — with more than mere proposals needed in the record, since, if not this Congress, hopefully the next would have occasion to respond. Thus specificity became the order of the day. Despite their very different settings — and with regard to form, not substance — the prototype of Eisenhower's presentation *circa* January, 1954 was Truman's effort in the spring of 1948.

It was the rush of public needs and expectations after enemy surrender which prompted Truman's first resort to presidential inventorying in 1946's annual message. It was the Truman strategy for 1948 which renewed and confirmed this practice, at the same time transforming a previously imprecise and unelaborated presentation into a relatively defined and detailed bill of particulars. And always in the background were the postwar President's vast legislative programming responsibilities, expressed and symbolized by the Employment Act and cold-war foreign policy.

The patterns set in 1948 were to be followed — and indeed elaborated further. During Truman's second term his 1949 and 1950 program presentations tended toward more comprehensive coverage, more specificity, more rationalization of sequential messages and bills; his post-Korean presentations stabilized along 1950 lines. Politically there was, or then seemed to be, good reason every year for staking out anew — or anyway not overlooking — unenacted portions of his pre-election program.[33] And governmentally there was no slackening of social, economic, foreign-policy involvements to generate new needs for legislation in those years of initial recession, subsequent inflation, partial mobilization, military alliance-building, and dragged-out Korean war. Moreover, in the process of recurrent use the practice of presenting annual programs acquired a momentum and survival power of its own, each year more generally regarded throughout government as the accustomed way of doing business, each year more nearly built into the institutional arrangements, expecta-

---

[31] State of the Union Address, Jan. 9, 1948; Budget Message, Jan. 11; Economic Report, Jan. 14.

[32] *E.g.*, civil rights, Feb. 2, 1948; rent control and housing, Feb. 27; reciprocal trade, March 1; European recovery and national defense, March 17; Alaska development, April 24; agriculture, May 14; social security, May 24.

[33] For discussion see Neustadt, *op. cit.*, in *Public Policy*, Vol. 5, pp. 349–81, at pp. 366–81.

tions, of Congress, agencies, and presidential staff alike. Policy and politics aside, perpetuation of the practice during Truman's second term owes much to the fast rise of institutional stakes in the game.

Nowhere was this more striking than in the case of presidential staff. In Truman's time, at least before Korea, the main thrust of Administration effort and attention was less operational than legislative; this in those notable domestic spheres where policies once cast in legislative guise remained so for lack of commensurate congressional response; likewise in crucial foreign fields where new infusions of authority and funds were periodically required. The great issues of policy, oftener than not, revolved around what Congress should be asked to do. For White House aides and budgeteers and economic advisers there were, therefore, no better ways to reserve policy decisions to the President — or, indeed, to get them taken — than those afforded by presidential messages to Congress. Nor were there any ways more likely to bring staff facilities and talents into play; nor any better suited to set President (and entourage) astride department heads' negotiations with one another and with the Hill. The greater the spread of *presidential* requests for legislation, the wider the President's own reach as decision-maker — and the deeper staff's participation in essentials of decision-making. Protection for the President *and* for the work of staff — both motives, variously combined, helped markedly to incline numbers of key Truman aides toward ever more elaborate legislative program presentations.

The institutional factor's influence upon the course of presidential inventorying cannot be better illustrated than by reference to the growth of a related, if subsidiary, practice, where institutional concerns were paramount from first to last: with the development, that is to say, of the other of the two inherited foundations on which Eisenhower's programming was to be based, namely the *departmental* legislative programs. To that development we may now turn, its starting point not again presentation, but rather preparation of the President's program in Truman's early years.

III. The Emergence of Departmental Legislative Programs

The custom of compiling formal agency programs as a preliminary stage in presidential program-making owes very little to procedural initiatives from the departments, deriving, rather, from White House requirements imposed upon them in the four years after World War II. Those requirements, in turn, reflect a step-by-step accumulation of *ad hoc* responses on the part of Truman's aides to various felt needs arising in the course of readying his annual messages, especially as they assumed their "inventory" cast. What were these needs, and what the character of staff response? For answers it is necessary to review some facets of the staff work at successive message seasons from 1945 through 1949.

In Roosevelt's time, the actual drafting of Budget Messages — then mostly discourses on going programs — had been left to the Budget Bureau under varying degrees of presidential supervision. State of the Union preparations, on the other hand, had remained pretty much the President's affair, with Samuel I. Rosenman, his Special Counsel, as chief continuing assistant in the process.[34] Over the years the drafting of these latter addresses came to depend in considerable part on the availability of proposed texts and of supporting data emanating from the agencies;[35] with little or no prompting, their contributions and advices flowed regularly to Rosenman through well-worn channels, part of the routine of annual message season.

That routine and those channels were not much disturbed during 1945, despite Truman's accession in mid-April and his trial combination, nine months later, of the State of the Union address with the Budget Message. For Rosenman, who had remained with the new President, was on the scene in his accustomed place during the drafting of that omnibus affair; his opposite number from the Budget side was Harold D. Smith, another Roosevelt holdover. Whatever the consolidated document's demerits, presentation-wise, its drafting under their joint management assured a single — and, to the bureaucracy, familiar — focus both for staff work and for departmental liaison.

Not so the following year. By message season 1946 both Rosenman and Smith had left the government; their replacements were new men in Washington. By then more institutions had appeared within the White House orbit: a Council of Economic Advisors under the Employment Act, and an office of Assistant to the President, residual legatee for OWMR. By then, too, there were to be three separate annual messages. And adding to the other troubles of the time — sketched in section II above — these three became the object of four quasi-independent drafting operations. The Budget, reverting to custom, held pretty tightly onto that year's Budget Message. The Economic Council tried its best to follow suit on the first Economic Report, its virgin — and uncertain — efforts being duplicated, meanwhile, closer to the throne, by what remained of OWMR. And elsewhere in the White House, State of the Union drafts were put together, cut-and-paste, by the new presidential counsel, Clark M. Clifford, utilizing diverse agency suggestions and some borrowed Budget staff.[36]

[34] A relationship on all major speeches which dated back to Albany. For illuminating details see Rosenman, *op. cit.*, especially Ch. 1.

[35] For illustrations, *ibid.*, pp. 262–65; 510–12.

[36] Clifford, a St. Louis attorney before the war, was appointed Counsel in July, 1946 after a year's duty in the White House as assistant Naval Aide. Smith's successor, James E. Webb, previously a Sperry Gyroscope official and wartime Marine specialist, was appointed Budget Director that same month, after a short stint as an executive assistant to the Under Secretary of the Treasury. The original members of the Council of Economic Advisers, Nourse, Keyserling, and Clark, were not appointed until August, 1946, six months after passage of the Employment Act; of the three, only Keyserling had had previous government experience. The new Assistant to the President, Steelman, on the other hand, was a government official of long standing, who had served as OWMR's last Director, assuming his new White House post upon that agency's termination in the aftermath of the November, 1946 election, and keeping with him, for a time, a remnant of his former staff.

Reflecting the scatteration of these enterprises, a multiplicity of overlapping calls for plans, suggestions, and advice went from them to the various departments. On November 14, 1946, the OWMR Director — soon to be Assistant to the President — wrote all the agencies, inviting views on legislation they desired at the coming session. The next day Truman asked in cabinet for suggestions on the subject-matter of his State of the Union address; this request was conveyed later to a number of non-cabinet agencies by letter from Counsel Clifford. Meanwhile, similar requests regarding subjects for the Economic Report had gone out more informally from CEA. And in the course of budget hearings, Budget staff had asked each agency for information on its legislative plans. In all of this and in the results of it all there was, of course, confusion and waste motion, with presidential staff-work afflicted no less than departmental. Ambiguities and uncertainties there were bound to be in the Administration stand of January, 1947. This rather gilded the lily.

Time helps, however. By the Fall of 1947, staff and personality relationships in Truman's entourage had shaken down somewhat, all parties more accustomed to their jobs, each other, and the President. By then also the regime had begun to crystallize its goals, in home affairs no less than overseas. And facing preparation of the annual messages for 1948, both President and staff were conscious of a crucial corner to be turned. The tightening of preparatory staff work was a natural result, though scarcely one preplanned.

Procedurally, that tightening began in an attempt to deal with the preceding year's most obvious mechanical defect — those tangled requests to the agencies. In September, 1947, White House and Budget aides accepted a suggestion from the Economic Council that they combine such inquiries for the forthcoming message season; the upshot, on September 26, was a formal letter from the President himself to the head of each major agency. There Truman asked that he receive by November 1 "such material as you would propose for inclusion in the 1948 State of the Union Message or the Economic Report of the President," and in addition a report "showing the character of legislation of concern to [the agency] which you anticipate may be considered by the Congress," this latter "not [to] be in great detail but [to] contain sufficient information to identify the subjects upon which legislation may be introduced or requested." And as a closing note, "the White House staff, the Council of Economic Advisers or the Bureau of the Budget may make additional requests for material or arrange for discussions with your representatives to whatever extent may be required." [37]

Here was a first approach to those elaborate calls for departmental legislative programs now issuing each year from Budget as a matter of course. This letter may be said to mark the start of annual agency programming in contemporary terms. But no one could have told that at the time, nor sense it now from the loose wordage then employed.

[37] Quoted passages in this and similar presidential requests annually through 1954 are from texts or notes in the writer's files.

The imprecision of the words reflects the fact that drafters of this letter were much clearer in their minds about the need to send it than about the uses they might make of agency replies. Message suggestions were requested because it was traditional to have them, a tradition reinforced by data needs attendant on that new affair, the Economic Report. Legislative intentions were canvassed in the hope, from the White House side, that message drafters might be safeguarded against ignoring, inadvertently, items either attractive to the President or wholly counter to his aims. To complement this hope there was the notion, from the Budget side, that advance word on departmental plans might sharpen current estimates reviews and expedite next-session legislative clearances. All staffs concerned were pleased by the idea of placing agencies on record with the President regarding plans their bureaucrats were brewing. And institutional staffs were pleased as well by the explicit presidential recognition of their roles in message making, together with the general hunting licenses officially bestowed upon them. This last, especially; it is no accident that the initiative in presidential letter-writing came from the late-on-the-scene, least institutionally secure staff element, the Economic Council.[38]

But all of these were rather preconceptions than specific undertakings as regards the actuality of agency replies. Precisely what was to be done with them and for what purpose and by whom remained unsettled in advance, with no one in the presidential entourage sure of results to be expected or desired. The proceeding was new and the 80th Congress in its second session was an unpromising occasion for breast-baring by departments on behalf of the perhaps shortly-to-be-retired President.

Truman's 1947 letter was a fishing expedition; results are hard to classify. Most agencies consolidated answers to his two requests, blurring or ignoring distinctions between them, with legislative projects mostly buried in suggested language drafts. However, there was one thing notably concrete about these agency replies: the pile they made on White House desks November 1, or thereabouts. By that time, staff work was already underway in Budget and CEA on preliminary drafts of the two secondary messages; as for the State of the Union address, a White House-Budget drafting team had been lined up by Clifford, though not yet put to work. While there was little disposition to rely on departmental prose, *per se,* each staff engaged, or soon to be engaged, in message preparation needed to know what was contained in agency submissions — for the sake of the record, if nothing more — but none had time or means to plow straight through the pile, much less sift substantive suggestions from the

---

[38] This is not to suggest, of course, that Executive Office staffs lacked working-level channels to the agencies or informal advice on agency interest and intentions. Quite the contrary. The purpose of the quoted language in the letter of September 26, 1947 was not to obtain data otherwise inaccessible to staff, but rather to put agency heads responsibly on record pro or con departmental ideas more probably than not already known or sensed by presidential aides, while at the same time giving the latter a formal — even constitutional — rationale for their own attempts at follow-up, coordination, and review.

rhetoric in which they were conveyed. By common consent, heartfelt if *ad hoc*, that task went to the Budget's newly-expanding legislative clearance organization, then titled the Division of Legislative Reference.[39]

There, informal appraisals were solicited from specialists in Budget and in CEA,[40] and the results highlighted in an annotated checklist of action-recommendations, including legislative issues ignored by the agencies but not by staff critiques.[41] Here, in a single document, was an inventory for the message-drafters, a handy guide to problems needing resolution and to potential gaps or overlaps among the messages. As an aid to coordination, this mechanical contrivance was supplemented in two ways: there was much interchange of drafts — and some of drafters — among staffs working on the messages, while every phrase concerning legislation was centrally reviewed in Legislative Reference. (By these means wording was coordinated and much substance also; for it was mainly in the course and guise of actual message drafting that 1947's open issues were brought before the President for his decision.) Thereafter, once the message drafts were put in final form, White House and Budget legislative staffs — maintaining the collaboration forged in message season, seeking the new degree of specificity for 1948 — joined in a review of "developmental" work still to be done, of actions needed to give full effect to presidential tone and purpose: interagency disputes to be resolved, special messages prepared, bills and amendments drafted, departmental testimony set. And with these clean-up tasks identified, those staffs turned jointly to the doing of them, utilizing in experimental fashion both legislative clearance channels and *ad hoc* staff-and-department working teams.[42]

[39] For a discussion of that expansion and the motivations behind it see Neustadt, *op. cit.*, *American Political Science Review* (Sept. 1954), pp. 659–63.

[40] As a matter of sheer improvisation, Legislative Reference established a number of *ad hoc* staff "working teams," drawn from other Budget divisions and to some extent from CEA, to comment on the adequacy and utility of departmental recommendations and to point up major issues of substance or finance raised by, or omitted from, agency submissions. See Budget Bureau inter-office memorandum from Elmer B. Staats, then chief of the Division of Legislative Reference, to Messrs. D. C. Stone, J. W. Jones, Martin, and Rice, Nov. 17, 1947. In two weeks' time there were prepared some 20 staff critiques combining agency responses into subject-matter fields. Considering the time and circumstances, these were reasonably thorough jobs of summarization and analysis, generally of higher quality, certainly much more specific, than the original agency documents. As such they served in lieu of most originals as working papers for the drafting staffs on all three annual messages. Note that in this 1947 experiment CEA's participation in the Legislative Reference "working teams" was marginal. General inclusion of CEA specialists came as a refinement the following year. For this subsequent elaboration of the procedure see Budget Bureau inter-office memorandum from Elmer B. Staats to Messrs. Stauffacher, Martin, J. W. Jones, and Gross (CEA), Dec. 6, 1948.

[41] "Checklist of Recommendations for Presidential Messages in January, 1948," Bureau of the Budget, Division of Legislative Reference, Dec. 3, 1947 (duplicated).

[42] Note that in this 1947 sequence message drafting, itself, became the central focus for policy decision as regards the legislative program, with detailed elaboration of particular policies a later, subsidiary undertaking. This more or less inverts the sequence and focus of Eisenhower's program-making during 1953. Of course, that is to compare Truman's third programming effort with Eisenhower's first. In 1947, while a

These staff procedures and relationships evolving in the course of 1947's message season were relatively crude and unelaborated by contemporary standards. They were, however, a considerable improvement over what had gone before, sufficiently successful to attract attention and adherents for the future. Of course, the White House aides who had provided leadership and drive were scarcely bent on setting precedents nor much concerned about procedural trends. In 1948, their horizons were to be limited, perforce, by the forthcoming presidential election; their interest, time, and energy absorbed, increasingly, by preparations for convention and campaign. Within the Budget Bureau, on the other hand — divorced from the campaign, acutely conscious of the presidency's durability, mindful of its own — the 1947 effort was regarded as a promising beg'nning of what ought to be a long-run undertaking; a step toward staff and agency relationships potentially of great significance for budgetary review no less than legislative clearance. And while the White House staff turned to full-time electioneering in late summer, 1948, the Budget made an effort to preserve, as nearly as might be, one concept introduced the year before: the formal annual canvass of agency intentions in the legislative sphere. To that end an innocuous inquiry was slipped into the call for estimates of July, 1948. Were the presidency to change hands, so ran the reasoning, this would already have been institutionalized, at least in theory, as part of the budget process.[43]

But on November 3, 1948, Washington officialdom awoke to find itself executor of the "outgoing" President's election victory. Truman would remain, with Democrats controlling Congress; in every Federal agency caretaker attitudes were hurried out of sight. On the legislative front, a vast array of talk-stage ideas for the coming session were recast, overnight, as current, actionable issues. In home affairs, especially, the character of Truman's campaign and election combined to rouse great expectations, in and out of government. There was no dearth of raw materials to go into a Truman program for the Congress which had shared his victory. Quite the contrary; in the 60 days between election's end and session's start the problem was not to create, but rather to rationalize, to gain some order

---

checklisting of possible proposals had negative, coordinative uses, the White House was by no means faced with first-time issues new or strange or unexplored politically. Moreover, in domestic spheres the 1948 program, unlike the 1954, was not constructed with an eye to maximizing short-run congressional response.

[43] In July, 1948, the call for estimates for fiscal 1950 requested, for the first time, some report on departmental legislative plans. The agencies were asked to include with their budget estimates, due September 15, a brief statement "calling attention to any recommendations for proposed legislation . . . which should be taken account of in preparing the Budget Message . . . or in arriving at budget totals. . . ." Information of this sort had long been wanted by the Budget for purposes of estimates review; in 1946, verbal requests at budget hearings had brought relatively few results; in 1947, agency responses to the presidential call had arrived relatively late. But nobody expected either cabinet officers or their career subordinates to go on record candidly in mid-September, 1948. This innovation in the Budget call was scarcely designed to gain much information; nor did it do so in fact. Rather, it was an expedient, a pre-election gambit, designed to give Budget a precedent for possible application in a new regime.

of priority, some measure of coherence overall, some semblance of agreement on details, for inventory in the customary annual messages, topped off this time by an Inaugural Address.

Here was a heavy load for presidential aides — especially for a White House contingent just off the campaign train. To make a start, they hastily revived and amplified their improvised machinery of a year before, beginning with the presidential letter to the agencies.

On November 5, three days after election, Truman told his cabinet members to review his campaign speeches and to ready legislation on the pledges these contained. The next day he sent a formal request to all major agencies, asking advice on his messages and on their legislative plans. This was something more than a repeat performance of his 1947 letter. Reflecting the changed circumstances, this new document departed from its predecessor's terms in two significant respects. On the one hand, the request for message data was trimmed down in an evident desire to avoid new piles of departmental prose.[44] On the other hand, the request for legislative information was much more elaborate than in 1947, also much more precise, its wordage a first approximation of that employed by Eisenhower's Budget Bureau five years later.[45]

And as regards this legislative inquiry, it is doubtful that either before or since did any Truman broadside receive faster or more generally responsive answers. Most agency replies were relatively complete, well organized, informative, and marked by evidences of review at upper echelons. While formats varied, as did depth and specificity of information on particulars, there was, in fact — as time would show — quite general coverage of agency intentions all the way from major policy affairs to matters of administrative routine.

There was only one trouble with these departmental documents: they came too late for great effect on presidential program-making. December, 1948 was scarcely a propitious month for measured applications of staff "expertise" through paper channels. In no event was there much room for staff (or agency) debate about the general range of measures to be recommended at the opening of Congress. Past history and present cir-

---

44 The agencies were simply asked to name ". . . the subjects which you would propose for inclusion in the State of the Union Message and the Economic Report . . . together with a brief explanation of each. . . ."

45 In 1948 Truman asked for "a report on the proposed legislative program of your department [which] should show (1) the subject-matter of all legislation which you desire to propose . . . [to Congress] . . . , (2) the state of readiness of legislative drafts and supporting material, (3) references to the bills and . . . reports in the 80th Congress concerning the subjects covered . . . with a brief appraisal of the adequacy of these bills, (4) your views on the timing of introduction and . . . consideration, and (5) the names of other departments and agencies . . . interested in the same subjects." Necessarily, the time for response to this request was very limited. The President's letter asked that message suggestions be sent directly to the White House by November 29, 1948; legislative programs were to be sent him by that date "through" the Bureau of the Budget, with the proviso that supplemental listings would be accepted up to December 15; as regards that time-extension, the letter voiced an expectation that each agency program "will be fully developed by that date," a scarcely enforceable directive to make "all" mean "all."

cumstances made it plain that at a minimum the 81st Congress would be asked for everything the 80th had denied. As for the all-important details — how much of what to recommend, in terms of what specifics, at what dollar cost and when — deep cross-currents kept sweeping such things far beyond the reach of formal papers or their processors: [46] the military seeking more security "in being"; Budget and Treasury trying to cut "inflationary" spending and the public debt; Fair Dealers, momentarily in seventh heaven, demanding action, fast, on all their aims at once. Relatively few of the proposals prized by high officials and their clientele were wholly free of impacts on the budget. The rest became involved in tugs of war between expansive social purpose and conservative financial policy; each view with departmental and staff advocates to jostle one another for the presidential ear by means more personal — and more emphatic — than mere submission or review of agency programs.[47] Given the time factor and the message framework, there was, perforce, a certain lack of order in this process. Inevitably, some of the results were arbitrary, mutually inconsistent, even, in the course of time, embarrassing to the regime. To take just one example, the rural telephone program — which Truman came to list in later years among his regime's great accomplishments for 1949 — was kept out of his January messages and once thereafter held "not in accord" by Budget as a matter of financial stringency.

The 1948 message season, taken as a whole, left in its wake among the staffs concerned less satisfaction than frustration: White House and CEA programmers conscious of a disadvantageous tactical position on price-tag issues late in budget season; legislative clearance aides concerned lest their home institution's role as a cost-cutting advocate endanger their desired "neutral" standing and new White House links; the budgeteers bemused by failures once again to bring new legislation into focus soon enough for rational review alongside going programs. Everybody's troubles turned on timing; the cure, apparently, an earlier beginning and more integration of both plans and planners. And in the relatively simpler circumstances of 1949 — a non-election year to be succeeded by a second session — an early start became the central feature of staff preparations for 1950's program presentation.

In July, 1949, the Budget call for estimates for fiscal 1951 replaced

---

[46] In 1948, reversing 1947's procedure, Legislative Reference had produced a "preliminary" checklist for the message drafters (based on campaign materials and staff anticipations) two weeks *before* the agency programs arrived. Elaborate working teams were drawn from Budget and CEA to review those submissions on arrival. But by that time such a review process was bound to involve more activity than result.

[47] The well-known Budget-Forrestal dispute over the fiscal 1950 military budget was, of course, a very vital background factor in the legislative program conflicts of this period. As a practical matter, only with that argument settled in Webb's favor were there funds for Fair Dealers and budgeteers to quarrel about. By the same token, universal training legislation then assumed a higher relative priority for the President than most of his supporters, in and out of Congress, were ever willing to concede it at either end of the Avenue — a circumstance since echoed in the reserve training controversy during the congressional session of 1955. Indeed, the broader conflict over military force levels since Eisenhower's accession is reminiscent in many ways of those of 1948 and 1949.

1948's mere for-the-record inquiry on legislation with a full-blown replica of Truman's post-election request for departmental legislative programs. This time the agencies were to submit "preliminary" legislative programs to the Budget along with their annual estimates; "final" programs would then be in order later as responses to the "usual" message season letter from the President. This new feature of the Budget call — a fixture each year since — required presentation by the agencies of the same range of data specified in Truman's letter of November 6, 1948.[48] This scheme of departmental double-jeopardy on legislative programs was motivated partly by uncertainty about prospects for change in agency intentions during the fall months, a concern proved groundless, largely, especially in 1949. And, partly, the motivation was political in bureaucratic terms: a demonstration to the agencies that no loss of "presidential" status was involved in the shift to an earlier submission on Budget's call.[49] Results were as desired; the preliminary programs which reached Budget in September, 1949 were generally no less comprehensive than had been the presentations of December, 1948 — indeed, reflecting first-session turn-downs and delays, they were in large part carbon copies.

With these at hand so early in the game, the paper processing arrange-ments improvised in 1947 were renovated and enlarged as means of

[48] To the 1948 language there were added requests for cost estimates and a listing of laws due to expire. Bureau of the Budget, *Instructions for the Preparation and Submission of Annual Budget Estimates,* June 30, 1949, Sec. 86. The purpose of the expiration list is obvious, its need made sharp by the fast-rising congressional practice of authorizing long-term programs on a short-run, review-and-extend basis. Lest this request receive less than just due from the agencies, the Budget Director followed his formal call with an explanatory memorandum for department heads. "The request," he wrote, "is intended to give the Budget Bureau and the President as much informa-tion as possible about your plans . . . for the next legislative session in time to be considered in the early stages of budget review." With this in hand it would ". . . be possible to inform you, when we discuss your budget allowance, of the President's views on the relationship between items in your legislative program and the·total budget outlook at that time." These programs, coming to the Budget in September, might be — in part — outdated by events before Congress assembled. Therefore, ". . . we anticipate that the agencies will be asked to present final legislative programs late in the year, in conjunction with suggestions for the annual messages." However, since preliminary programs were to provide better opportunity ". . . for proper integration of legislative proposals with the President's budget recommendations," agencies were urged that they ". . . should not hold back, for later presentation, any items which can possibly be foreseen at this time." Bureau of the Budget, Bulletin No. 50-5, Aug. 31, 1949.

[49] The presidential letter foreshadowed by the 1949 call for estimates followed in short order. Dated Sept. 26, 1949, the President's request for message suggestions paralleled the language used in 1948. On the legislative side, the agencies were asked to transmit through the Budget, by November 1, a "final" program which would ". . . restate and bring up to date the preliminary legislative program submitted . . . in accordance with the Call for Estimates." This was to include "all" agency desires for the coming session, as regards bills pending or to be proposed, with indications of departmental urgency and "views on the timing of congressional consideration." If a bill or proposal in December's program had not appeared in September's precursor, there was to be a statement of ". . . the circumstances which led to its addition"; this last a fine flourish, scarcely enforceable.

minimizing the difficulties encountered in 1948. For the first time most de-partmental legislative plans received considerable going-over in the normal course of estimates review, with relatively timely entrée assured interested White House aides. Meanwhile, reviews of form and substance and priority outside the range of budgeting *per se* were somewhat disen-tangled from the chores of message drafting, defined and organized in their own terms and in advance, with all the staffs concerned drawn into working-team arrangements under White House auspices. There were, of course, but few *new* measures of a controversial cast proposed by the departments or conceived by staff for 1950's program presentation. For the most part, these preparatory efforts dealt with carry-overs previously recommended to the Congress, things easily contained in paper channels. And as regards new elements, where more intensive staff collaboration was required, their number was so limited and time so free, relatively speaking, that procedural improvements sufficed to avert any major repetition of 1948's last-minute controversies and confusions.[50]

Under the circumstances, 1949's budget and message seasons ran rela-tively smoothly in terms of staff and agency relationships, the mechanics regarded in most quarters as advances on what had gone before and har-bingers of better still to come. But in the event there was to be no further innovating. Every plan for planning was abruptly pushed aside by the Korean outbreak and its aftermath, both military and political.

During the budget and message seasons of 1950–52 both agencies and staffs went through the motions more or less along the lines marked out in 1949. As a matter of form, these remained frozen in their pre-Korean cast; as a matter of fact, they became every year more marginal among the key concerns of policy officials.[51] In part, such stalemating was a reflection of reduced Democratic majorities in the 82nd Congress combined with stepped-up oppositional attacks against a regime fast declining in prestige

[50] The eventual "new" features of Truman's 1950 program included official en-dorsement of the so-called "Brannan Plan," which the Secretary of Agriculture had presented to congressional committees the preceding spring, along with aids to small business, assistance for middle-income housing, and general revision of the internal revenue code. On these, there were arguments, of course, but relatively quietly re-solved "within the family."

[51] It had been planned before Korea to eliminate eventually the duplicative factor in requests for "preliminary" and for "final" programs. After Korea, though, no easy opportunity was found to do so, nor a compelling need; the dual system continued, for lack of time or energy to change it. The Budget Bureau's call for estimates in 1950, 1951 — and 1952 — reiterated the terms of Section 86 in 1949's call for preliminary legislative programs, with some elaboration of reporting requirements. The language was identical with that used under Eisenhower in 1953. (See above.) Bureau of the Budget, *Instructions for the Preparation and Submission of Annual Budget Estimates* (June 30, 1950; June 30, 1951; June 30, 1952), Sec. 86. Presidential calls for final legislative programs patterned on Truman's request of 1949, with some new terminology to take account of the emergency, went forward in the form of letters from the President on October 4, 1950, asking for submissions December 1 (after the mid-term election), and on October 5, 1951, again with a December 1 date for replies. There was no *presidential* call in 1952 regarding agency proposals for the 83rd Congress.

and coherence, driven to the defensive on almost every front. In part, it reflected preoccupation by both principals and staffs with complex, *ad hoc,* and unprecedented issues of economic and of military management attendant upon partial mobilization and limited war. In part, too, it reflected the attendant diminution in developmental efforts on Fair Deal particulars, once prime stimulators of programming machinery. Post-Korean advocacy of large-scale commitments lacking mobilization flavor at home or abroad — like general school construction or expansion of Point IV — met stiff resistance from the Budget and also, for the most part, from the President himself. Save for emergency measures, the presidential program, like the mechanisms for its preparation, remained relatively fixed in Truman's final years.

It may be said, then, that the departmental programming requirement now carried forward under Eisenhower emerged out of successive pressures in and on the Truman entourage, originating as a modest part of one attempt to pull together hitherto haphazard staff work in the face of a grave test, the 1948 election-year program; expanding and becoming institutionalized, increasingly, as a departure-point for efforts to hold staff coordination firm against the strains imposed by post-election clashes of Fair Deal and fiscal policies; stabilizing and becoming routinized as government's key policy preoccupations turned more operational than legislative, while mobilization bit at home and fighting wore on in Korea. And from the great departments — executors, *not* instigators of that programming requirement — there came, in Truman's time, a comparable sequence of responses.

In 1947, the President's first, hesitant request to them was met mostly by pro-forma rejoinders compiled at bureau levels with a minimum of higher echelon review — while Budget's muffled inquiry of July, 1948, was scarcely even noticed outside departmental budget offices. But with Truman's election, the replies to his November, 1948 request received careful review, even some reconsideration and reworking, at levels up to and including the department heads themselves; this last, especially, in those domestic agencies administering or ambitious for promotional programs. Partly as a carry-over, partly in awareness of their growing use by presidential staff, the responses to Budget's first full-scale request of 1949 were also given a considerable going-over at top departmental levels. Then with Korea, and thereafter, came a tendency to treat these annual exercises as increasingly routine affairs, the more so every year.

The very fact that *presidential* inventories were by then the norm insured that departmental compilations would remain of some significance to agency executives as means to stake out claims against the President's program; "routine" does not imply sheer departmental abdication to the bureau-level bureaucrats. Rather, what was involved for most departments in the final Truman years amounted to a diminution of top-level interest in assuming the initiative on those recurrent, largely repetitive, bills of particulars. Negatively, upper echelons were for the most part relatively conscientious in their screening and consolidation into proper form of propositions annually put forward by their bureaus. Some — notably Interior's then Program Staff — tried hard to enforce department-wide standards of readiness, consistency, coherence, priority. Almost everywhere, in some degree or other, there was a certain scrutiny of what came from below. But affirmatively, there was very little innovating at the instance of department heads.

In general, then, department heads and their top staffs accepted pro-gramming responsibility in Truman's second term, but rather passively as a requirement for proper compilation, than actively as an excuse for posi-tive coordination. To this, however, there was one notable — and natural — exception: 1947's "unified" armed forces organization, the National Military Establishment, since 1949 the Department of Defense.

There White House-Budget calls were seized on very actively indeed and used as both a weapon and a rationale to help force the three military services into coordination of their legislative plans. This was among the most determined, if least known, attempts at unifying in the period of Forrestal's — and subsequently Johnson's — tenure as Secretary of Defense. Spurred by Marx Leva, then Assistant Secretary, their office actually extracted from the services much of the initiative and most of the control on plans for forward legislation. This was accomplished in successive stages, mainly during 1948 and 1949, its virtual completion signalled late the latter year by a combined "preliminary" and "final" Defense Department legislative program for the 1950 session of Congress, this in the form of a book of 80-odd bill drafts and justifications sub-mitted to the Budget, not alone for message purposes but for clearance also, in one lump and before the session's start. Since 1949, such consoli-dated, detailed, neatly packaged presentations have been standard at the Pentagon, renewed each year as a distinctly departmental matter, for purposes alike of internal coordination, Administration clearance, and ordered presentation on the Hill.

It is no accident, of course, that this exceptional response to presiden-tial calls should have come from the office of the Secretary of Defense, whose problems of internal coordination and control were more nearly akin to the President's own, also much more acute — this at the start, especially — than those of any other department head. For Forrestal's and Johnson's aides and their heirs and assigns, it has been natural to find in departmental programming advantages not unlike those sought by presi-dential staff. In Truman's time, there were a few sporadic efforts made by members of his entourage to lure or push other departments toward an equivalent response. But lacking the incentives of the Secretary of De-fense there was, elsewhere, no comparable internal drive in that direction; nor, after Korea, much pressure from above. During Truman's last years, the Defense Department program remained what it had been before Korea, a unique undertaking.

While the development of departmental programming was checked on all fronts in the three years after 1949, mere repetition of that year's pro-ceedings had significance for 1953's transition to a new regime. By 1953 the agency bureaucracies were thoroughly habituated to an annual call from White House precincts for their legislative programs; habituated, also, to conceiving of those programs as inclusive inventories of precise proposals. Repetition robbed these things, in varying degree, of interest or excitement in high places, but at the same time gave them status and tradition as among the built-in patterns of agency routine. And in the Budget Bureau, also, there were some traditions built, especially some habit-forming ways of working with the White House. Year after year its legislative clearance aides had served as back-up staff to Truman's Special Counsel,[52] drafting the programs call, checklisting agency responses, identifying open issues, stimulating working teams and acting as their secretariat, collating phraseology in message drafts, providing linkages among their drafters — all this done by the prospective interpreters of presidential programs: the clearance agents gaining a firm footing for their clearances. Long before 1953 these Budget aides became accustomed to seek out and stimulate conflicting judgments in the legislative field; accustomed also to the role of "institutional" exponent in interchanges with the White House "politicians." That year, in his capacity as career chief of Budget's clearance operations, this was the background brought by Roger Jones to his first contacts with the new regime anent the forward course in legislation.

IV. Legislative Programs and Presidential Leadership

Survival is the acid test of institutional development within the White House orbit. At this writing, in 1955, the Budget's call for estimates for fiscal 1957 has just gone to the agencies, a Section 86 included as before. The President may now abandon letters of request for message data — in 1954, a reminder at cabinet table served instead — but there is every expectation in his entourage that 1955's budget and message seasons will proceed along the lines of prior years, with January, 1956's annual messages conveying to the Congress and the country a comprehensive program presentation, Eisenhower's third — thus marking the tenth anniversary of Truman's trial compendium of 1946.

Looking back upon the intervening development, as traced above, one might easily gain a sense of busy bureaucrats entangling Presidents — Truman and Eisenhower both — in processes expressive more of institutional concerns than presidential personality, the product rather of the office than of the men. Of course, this may turn out, historically, to be but commentary on the personalities of those two Presidents. Even so, the record here presented demonstrates that year by year staff interests and initiatives have had — or, if one prefers, were allowed to have — a

---

[52] Charles S. Murphy, who succeeded Clifford early in 1950, carried on the combination of speech-and-message drafting with legislative policy duties which characterized the Counsel's post in Truman's time (and F.D.R.'s).

major, frequently decisive influence in shaping the *particulars,* the ways and means of current presidential programming.

This is not to suggest that either now or in the past have these particulars reflected *merely* needs and circumstances of the staffs as entities distinct from sitting Presidents. No doubt that brand of institutionalism plays a part in the proceedings here described — witness the Budget's interests *circa* 1948 and 1953 or CEA's in 1947 — but a part powerfully reinforced at every turning point by what then seemed a crucial undertaking in the President's own terms: Truman in 1945, attempting to discharge the trust and meet the situation he inherited; in 1948, trying to rally North and West against Republicans (and Henry Wallace); or Eisenhower in 1954, seeking, it would appear, to fix the label "middle of the road" on his own party's right-wing-dominated delegation in the Congress. If not, perhaps, the personal initiatives of Presidents, then at least their own circumstances and felt needs have markedly affected programming techniques. In that sense the personal equation is not to be discounted.

Yet in a deeper sense, neither personal proclivities nor, for that matter, bureaucratic busyness suffice to explain this development's direction overall, however much accounting for particulars. Perhaps two different Presidents, differently trained, motivated, staffed, might have proceeded in a rather different way. Conceivably, both presidential and staff needs might have been formulated and expressed in terms other than those actually employed. But it is difficult to see how any postwar President — whether Truman or Dewey, or Eisenhower or Stevenson — could have avoided some kind of approach to legislative program-making on a comprehensive scale. Behind the momentary situations molding presidential conduct, there have been other pressures, far less transient: the mandate of the Employment Act, the policy of Soviet containment, and, as concomitants, perpetuation of big government, big budgets, and big debt — at home, the heritage of Roosevelt's revolution; abroad, cold war in the atomic age — all this accompanied politically by alternating Democratic and Republican majorities in coalition-dominated Congresses, along with notable discrepancies between each party's presidential and congressional electorates.

In such a context, the executive establishment was bound to generate large-scale requirements for substantive — and controversial — legislation; the presidency no less bound to take the lead. In spheres of foreign policy and of defense, the constitutional position of the President left him no room to stand aside. In home affairs there were specific statutes to compel his lead, the Budget and Accounting Act of 1921 and the Employment Act of 1946, this last but formally expressive of a role which F.D.R.'s example had already rendered virtually inescapable. And only interventions by the party leader in the White House could set tone and limits for that necessary *modus operandi,* "coalition" government *without* political truce. These ultimately were the pressures on the presidency at mid-century which gave rise to the programming endeavors here recorded;

that record measuring successive, improvised responses on the part of real-life Presidents and staffs in their own terms and time.

Traditionally, there has been a tendency to distinguish "strong" Presidents from "weak," depending on their exercise of the initiative in legislation. The personal appearances in the hall of the House, the special messages, the drafted bills, the public appeals, so characteristic of contemporary program presentation, have all been represented in the past — no farther back than Franklin Roosevelt's time — as signs of a President's intention or capacity to "dominate" the Congress. If these were once relevant criteria of domination, they are not so today. As things stand now they have become part of the regular routines of office, an accepted elaboration of the constitutional right to recommend; as such, no more indicative of presidential domination than the veto power, say, in Herbert Hoover's time.

Indeed, from the congressional point of view, "service," not domination, is the reality behind these presidential undertakings. In practical effect, they represent a means whereby Congress can gain from the outside what comes hard from within: a handy and official guide to the wants of its biggest customer; an advance formulation of main issues at each session; a work-load ready-to-hand for every legislative committee; an indication, more or less, of what may risk the veto; a borrowing of presidential prestige for most major bills — and thus a boosting of publicity-potentials in both sponsorship and opposition.

That Congress wants these things and finds them useful for its purposes may be judged from the almost total absence nowadays of vocal criticism or surprise at annual presentations of the President's program; an indicator reinforced by irritated comments, privately expressed on both sides of the aisle, when Eisenhower stayed his hand in 1953. Outcries against "dictatorship" and "speeches-from-the-throne" have long been stilled in responsible quarters. In 1947, Senator Taft told a Budget aide that as a matter of orderly procedure Republican committee chairmen *ought* to have the Democratic President's own views across-the-board and in detail, else the committees would lack solid ground from which to gauge the pleadings of departments and their clientele.[53] In 1953, the very senior chairman of a major House committee reportedly admonished an Administration witness, "don't expect us to start from scratch on what you people want. That's not the way we do things here — *you* draft the bills and *we* work them over." [54]

As that remark suggests, the Congress deals not in abstract ideas but in bills. It comes to grips with substance in terms of phraseology. The process cannot start without a draft. And since executive expertise is often

[53] An observation dating from the early part of the first session of the 80th Congress, as then reported to the writer by Taft's auditor.

[54] A remark made at an executive session of the House Foreign Affairs Committee in April, 1953, as reported to the writer by a committee member present. In question were the new Administration's views on form and character of legislation to extend the foreign aid program.

indispensable, while executive wishes are data to be weighed — though quite conceivably ignored — a "downtown" draft has tangible advantage as the starting point. But more than drafting service is provided by contemporary presidential programs. Annual programming serves also to identify, to render timely, in effect to choose, most *legislative* issues on which serious attention is to center at a session; the President becomes agenda-setter for the Congress, the chief continuing initiator of subject-matter to reach actionable stages in committee and on the floor, whether or not ultimately passed. Of course, as Lawrence Chamberlain and others have made plain, most major measures are the product of long germination, much cross-fertilizing. Quite so; the service of contemporary Presidents has been less creativity than crystallization; a matter less of seeding new terrain than of tracing new lines in old ground, thereby to mark the field for current cultivation.

In this respect, the presidency is performing for the Congress a task apparently beyond that body's institutional capacity to carry on its own account. When one looks at the legislative record of the last decade, the major controversial measures brought to focus, debate, and near-passage or enactment on congressional initiative *alone,* are small scatteration relative to those highlighted by — or with assistance from — the President: most prominently, perhaps, the Taft-Hartley Act, the two McCarran Acts, and the perennial Bricker Amendment.[55] Of these, at least Taft-Hartley may be ascribed actually to a reverse sort of presidential initiative — Truman choosing *not* to propose action in an area where momentary public sensitivity was certain to evoke response of some sort from the 80th Congress. Indeed, such a "reverse" initiative on issues known to generate more current heat than a Congress was likely to withstand has relevance for other instances as well, if more a matter of necessity than choice in, say, the Bricker case. Of course, where heat is less intense, a withholding of the initiative is likely to be *directly* effectual. Had Eisenhower's 1954 program called, say, for substantial reform of the immigration laws, one may assume that facing an election there would have been a ruckus in the Congress; lacking a White House lead, reformers' efforts did not make a dent. In such cases, the presidential silences no less than statements may serve to delineate the actionable issues.

But note that setting an agenda is not the same thing as enforcing it; selecting issues for consideration is not equivalent to having bills enacted into law. For evidence one has but to review the course of any recent congressional session. As a matter of fact, the most institutionalized aspects of the President's involvement in the legislative process are precisely

---

55 Other items which reached the point of passage include the tax reduction measures of 1947 and 1948, the first tidelands bill in 1947, and the natural gas and basing point bills of 1949. Of course, there have been infinite numbers of amendments to, adjustments in — and sheer denials of — Administration proposals, over the years, as matters of distinct congressional initiative, oppositional to presidential purposes or claimed intent. But these are in a different category. The fact that Presidents are now so largely raisers of the issues does not signify that they are safe from penalties for having done so; quite the contrary, both in and out of Congress.

those least concerned with actual campaigning for his program once presented: legislative programming and legislative clearance, *not* legislative in-fighting and signal-calling, day-by-day. To be sure, periodic White House meetings with congressional party leaders have become the norm; agendas prepared for the President in Truman's time; minutes kept as well in Eisenhower's. And Eisenhower has established in his entourage an Army-type liaison operation, its several staff aides covering each corner of the Hill on regular patrols.[56] But formal leaders' sessions tend to be ambassadorial encounters; organized liaison tends to create its own chores, if not, indeed, to confuse liaisoners' loyalties. So far as one can judge from the outside, it remains true in Eisenhower's time — as in Truman's and F.D.R.'s before him — that when the chips are down, there is no substituting for the President's own footwork, his personal negotiation, his direct appeal, his voice and no other's on the telephone. Naturally, such methods cannot guarantee success; to overwork them would be self-defeating; to institutionalize them may well be impossible. Yet these, not programming devices, must bear the weight, provide the test, of presidential "domination" over Congress.

Indeed, a presidential purpose to control the congressional *product* may actually be impeded, not advanced, by legislative programming as presently evolved. Those massive, annual presentations have a tendency to blur the public impact of particulars, scatter attention, divert interest — as with Eisenhower's messages of 1954, or Truman's, year by year. Regularized repetition tends to dilute the dramatic, focussing effects of personal appearance and appeal. White House sponsorship spread wide tends to reduce the import of each presidential label. Manifold commitments tend to complicate the task of striking particular bargains. Multi-item programs tend to encourage score-keeping by parties, press, and public, ordinarily with the result of stressing losses over gains on a strict by-the-numbers basis.

For a President pledged to adventuring in controversial areas and anxious to obtain results at given sessions, these can be handicaps; a case in point is the Truman situation *circa* 1946 (or 1949). On the other hand, of course, a President desirous of holding new departures within bounds may find sufficient compensation in a practice which permits him to stress his program's sum more than its parts, to express caution on particulars in a context of general affirmation: Eisenhower's case, apparently, in 1954. And when a President is in a position to use Congress less as action-instrument than whipping-boy, the compensations may be great indeed; so Truman found before the 1948 election.

In Truman's second term there were some unavailing doubts expressed

---

56 These liaison aides also engage in special forays on particular legislative and personality problems. Rarely if ever before has White House staff coverage of congressional moods, wishes, activities, and foot-dragging spread so wide, so consistently. Of course this enterprise has yet to stand the "acid test" of repetition in a new regime. Roosevelt, in his later years, and Truman were distinctly cool to organized, continuing staff effort of this sort.

within his entourage about the practical advantage of proceeding, post-election and then post-Korea, with a presentation technique improvised initially for 1948. But Eisenhower's aides now seem entirely satisfied. "The program layout is a good thing for a President," one of them told the writer, "it keeps him from looking too negative when he has to op-pose some grandiose scheme cooked up on the Hill. This way there's his own roster of affirmative positions to point back to . . . the country knows he's not just 'agin' things." Of course in Truman's years the shoe was mostly on the other foot, the "grandiose schemes" coming from the President, expressions of resistance from the Congress. One's aims and circumstances make one's case. It is quite understandable that skepti-cism should have grown in Truman's entourage after 1949, while dwin-dling in Eisenhower's after 1953. As a commentary on programming's variable contribution to the art of presidential leadership, that difference speaks volumes.

But whether or not always advantageous in those terms, the annual presidential inventory and its attendant mechanics have now become so rooted in responsibilities of office, so customary in the view of press and public, so satisfactory to the Congress, so institutionalized in the executive, that major alteration of the present pattern, much less its permanent abandonment, would appear no light matter for a President, nor likely. The present incumbent can be presumed to lack incentive for a break-away; quite the contrary, to judge from what occurred in 1953. Of course, one or another of his successors may not turn out so comfort-ably circumstanced — imagine F.D.R. in his first years encumbered by such ponderous proceedings. Yet that a future President could simply shoulder them aside remains improbable on all the evidence accumulated in the last decade. The F.D.R. of 1946 would have been subject to com-pulsions virtually unknown (or unrecognized) in 1933, many of his own making. And these are backed now by accustomed practices each year becoming more entrenched — not only as responses to congressional and public expectations, but as prime means to policy decision and control in the executive. To disavow them now might be to trade more flexibility with Congress for fewer hand holds on departments — this difficulty among others.

Still, in such matters these are never certainties. Conceivably, the time will come when a new President, pressing the Congress hard for measures of great moment and high controversy, finds it imperative to dramatize that enterprise by ostentatiously departing from the tradition of formal, comprehensive programs. Past Presidents have focussed national attention on their aims by introducing novelties in presentation: Wilson's recapture — and F.D.R.'s resumption — of the personal appearance before Con-gress; Roosevelt's special messages, bill drafts, and fireside chats. Now that all prior innovations have been lumped together into customary practice, what else remains for innovation's sake, than its abandonment? A para-dox, perhaps, but paradoxes have been commonplace in the development of legislative programming.

V. Presidency and Legislation:
an Afterword

In this paper, together with its predecessor on the growth of legislative clearance, an effort has been made to trace the institutionalization of certain aspects of the President's role in the legislative process, involving essentially elaboration of three constitutional prerogatives: his duty to recommend, his power to veto, and his right to the opinions of department heads. Among other things, this tracing can be taken as a case study in presidential staff development. And while that has not been the major purpose of these papers, a few notations on the point appear in order by way of addendum to them both.

Two things emerge from the whole history of legislative staff work in this area: First, there are no laws requiring a President to build or use the staff facilities as actually evolved, or any other, for that matter; the growth which has occurred and now survives has been organic, not a graft. Second, the central feature of that growth is nicely balanced inter-action between an intimately associated member of the personal entou-rage and a particular segment of the institutional entourage, the latter constantly in touch with other segments and with agencies — on the one hand, the Special Counsel to the President, and on the other, Budget's office of Legislative Reference.

With regard to the lack of legal form, contrast the Budget Bureau as originally established in-but-not-of Treasury, or the Council of Economic Advisers, or the National Security Resources Board of recent memory, or the National Security Council, each thrust into the presidential orbit from outside, fixed in form and in form changeable only by act or ac-quiescence of the Congress. Experience with all those organizations sug-gests the relative inflexibility, sheer awkwardness, of such arrangements amidst changing circumstances, needs, and Presidents: the Budget finally dislodged from the Treasury after eighteen years of ambiguity; the CEA worked into satisfactory patterns of association after seven years of inter-nal uncertainty and external hostility, or plain indifference; the NSRB painfully evolving, first by statute, then attrition, finally disestablishment, from a cabinet committee to a staff unit differently empowered and differ-ently named; the NSC growing in stature — possibly more than utility — ever since the Soviet's first atomic explosion, and thereafter subjected to much mechanical tinkering in efforts, so far vain (a judgment from outside), to make a cabinet mechanism approximate staff.[57]

57 The Budget Bureau, originally created in the Budget and Accounting Act of 1921, was formally transferred to the newly-established Executive Office of the Presi-dent by congressionally-approved reorganization plan in 1939. The Council of Economic Advisers, established under the Employment Act of 1946, was revised by reorganization plan in 1953 to the extent of vesting administrative powers and ad-visory responsibilities in the chairman rather than the membership. Some changes in CEA's external relationships were accomplished less formally at the same time. The

That CEA's *external* relations were ultimately altered quite informally in 1953, that NSC may yet be turned, somehow, into a staff equivalent — such things would simply seem to reinforce the point. New times and new personalities are bound to call forth adaptations in the presidency's ways and means; power *without* organizational prescription makes the process infinitely easier and — to judge from legislative programming and clearance spheres — the product no less adequate. Naturally, there are numbers of pragmatic reasons why Congresses and sometimes Presidents may be attracted or impelled toward statutory forms, but one doubts there are any reasons justifying cheers from political scientists. In terms of organization for policy "development," "coordination," and "control," it might be well to let our Presidents alone; here is an instance where they have not done so badly.

Turning to that other aspect of legislative staff work, the interaction between White House and institutional aides, note the careful balancing of functions and relationships. Legislative Reference can assure the Special Counsel ample research and negotiatory assistance, ready-to-hand, for purposes of planning or reviewing legislation. He, in turn, can assure Legislative Reference a direct channel to the President, a steady source of political advice, and, as need be, political protection or a place to pass the buck. He keeps his intimacy as a personal assistant, without the incubus of a large staff; Legislative Reference keeps its distance as an institutional establishment, without losing close contact. Legislative Reference also retains independence as executor of its own (technically, the Budget's) presidential mandate, serving other members of the entourage on call, or, if need be, the President himself, and keeping school no matter what. Meanwhile, the Counsel retains freedom to consult whom, how, and when he pleases, working out his own salvation in the legislative sphere and undertaking manifold *ad hoc* assignments from the President for other services besides.

This staffing pattern is not precisely typical, but it appears remarkably protected from disabilities afflicting those more generally in vogue. The large-scale, special-purpose staff group in the White House proper is likely to find itself in an anomalous position, the more so with each increment of personnel. That certainly was the case with the Harriman office in 1950–51. One wonders about Stassen's enterprise, and Rockefeller's

---

National Security Resources Board, created by the National Security Act of 1947, was altered by the National Security Act Amendments of 1949 which transferred all administrative and advisory powers from the ex-officio departmental members to the presidentially-appointed chairman. In December, 1950, NSRB's post-Korean coordinating powers were transferred by executive order to the Office of Defense Mobilization, established for the purpose by the President. In 1953, remaining NSRB functions went to ODM by reorganization plan. The National Security Council was also established by the National Security Act of 1947. Its heightened activity after 1949 followed a significant legal change, reduction of the Pentagon's statutory membership from four to one (and statutory addition of the Vice-President) by the National Security Act Amendments of 1949. Since then, there have been various non-statutory elaborations of working membership and methods.

at the present time.[58] Such units risk becoming neither fish nor fowl, their intimacy compromised by the activities of numerous subordinates, their initiative and freedom for maneuver cramped by lack of institutional independence. On the other hand, the pattern of a sub-cabinet committee-with-secretariat, presided over by a White House aide — as with the present NSC Planning Board, the Council on Foreign Economic Policy, or the Operations Coordinating Board [59] — does not appear, by all accounts, free from that bane of interdepartmental undertakings: the search for lowest common denominators of agreement as substitute for an appraisal in approximately *presidential* terms. Perhaps this can be cured by lively applications of White House initiative in committee discussion and debate, but past experience is scarcely reassuring.

Whatever the demerits of the legislative pattern — for such, review the record previously presented — these, in particular, seem to have been avoided. That is no mean advantage for a presidential staff pursuit; an advantage enhanced by the fact that it has involved no large-scale organizational creations. Legislative Reference, from within the Budget, has been able to draw upon a wide variety of other staff resources both on its own account and for the White House, thus notably enhancing its capacities without enlarging its personnel. Given a staff total of some 500 "professionals" in Eisenhower's entourage *outside* the White House proper, there is much to be said for a device which can regroup and utilize, *ad hoc,* those already on hand — this not for sheer economy, but to shield Presidents from suffocation by the presidency.

And it may be suggestive that the staff innovation under Eisenhower which this writer, at least, would count currently most rewarding approaches very closely — though not consciously, perhaps — the main lines of the pattern in the legislative field: namely, the relationship prevailing between Gabriel Hauge, Administrative Assistant to the President for matters economic, and Arthur M. Burns, Chairman of the Council of Economic Advisers: another tandem operation, balanced, mutually beneficial, quiet in its workings, and, apparently, effective.

These notations are put forward here for what they may be worth to any interested machinery-makers in or out of government. In that regard a final note appears in order. Among other things, what gives this legislative staff work its vitality and staying power, year after year, Administration after Administration, is its orientation toward one of the

[58] Averell Harriman functioned for somewhat more than a year as a Special Assistant to the President, with considerable staff of his own, before receiving institutional status and statutory workload as Director for Mutual Security under the Mutual Security Act of 1951. Harold Stassen and Nelson Rockefeller were appointed Special Assistants to the President in 1955, the former to work in the reduction-of-armaments field, the latter in an undefinable area of foreign relations. Both have recruited sizeable staffs of their own.

[59] Dillon Anderson, a Special Assistant to the President, now heads the Planning Board of NSC. Joseph M. Dodge, the former Budget Director, heads the CFEP, also as a Special Assistant; Nelson Rockefeller is a member of the OCB; its chairman, though, is the Undersecretary of State, for obvious reasons of relationship.

cardinal decision-and-action-forcing processes in contemporary government. Involved are matters flowing to and fro between executive and Congress, rising toward the surface of attention as they break branch lines, which have to (or then can be made to) cross the President's own desk for definite decisions *by dates certain:* the content of his legislative program, the phrasing of his congressional messages, the legislative views of his department heads, the enrolled bills requiring his signature or veto. It is hardly to be wondered at that during Truman's years such matters became focal points for policy development, especially in the domestic sphere. Save for the operational compulsions of diplomatic crisis, or hot war, or home emergency, there are no other work-flows so compelling of decision *on a constantly recurrent basis* — except, of course, those in the budget process. And it would seem no accident that the sole staff facility with a still longer history of demonstrated staying-power is the estimates arm of the Bureau of the Budget.

Presidency and Legislation: The Growth of Central Clearance

Richard E. Neustadt

Ten months after President Eisenhower's inaugural, an article in *Fortune* extolled a presidential aide in terms which would have seemed familiar ten months before; [1] the picture of his role in Eisenhower's entourage might easily have been drawn in President Truman's time. The subject of this piece was Roger W. Jones, an Assistant Director of the Bureau of the Budget and chief of its Office of Legislative Reference. In *Fortune's* terms, here was a confidential, if "non-political," member of the White House circle performing tasks of great importance to the President, trusted, respected, and relied upon by all of his associates. As an analysis of governmental functions and relationships, this testimonial was scarcely definitive, but its mere publication testifies to the continuation of the Budget Bureau's so-called legislative clearance operations, handily surviving the Great Transition of 1953.

What are these clearance operations? Essentially they amount to central

Reprinted by permission from the *American Political Science Review,* Vol. 48 (1954), pp. 641–671.

[1] Katherine Hammill, "This is a Bureaucrat," *Fortune,* Vol. 48, pp. 156 ff. (Nov., 1953).

coordination and review of stands taken by the various federal agencies at three successive stages of the legislative process.

Large numbers of the public measures introduced in Congress are formally proposed by agencies of the executive branch; departmental drafts officially en route to Congress first have to clear the Bureau of the Budget for interagency coordination and approval on the President's behalf. Once bills are introduced, regardless of their source, congressional committees ordinarily solicit views from interested agencies; official agency responses — in whatever form, to whomever addressed — first channel through the Budget Bureau for coordination and advice on each bill's relation to the President's program. When enrolled enactments come from Congress to the President for signature or veto, the Budget Bureau, as his agent, obtains, coordinates, and summarizes agency opinion on the merits, preparing in each case a presidential dossier complete with covering recommendation.

These are the components of "legislative clearance" as the term is normally employed.[2] In practice, these operations are much more complex and a good deal less absolute than this simple recital would indicate. But generally speaking, central clearance has proceeded along these lines for many years.

Last year, despite the change of Administration, 380 agency drafts, 3,571 agency reports on pending bills, and 525 enrolled enactments were processed by the Budget Bureau.[3] In 1954, the Bureau's Office of Legislative Reference, control center for clearance operations, is handling an even larger volume — with President Eisenhower and Budget Director Hughes earnestly supporting clearance regulations in effect since 1948, signed by a Budget Director long out of office, issued "by direction" of the President whose term expired January 20, 1953.[4]

Here is presidential machinery to coordinate a vital aspect of executive policy development; machinery to control, in some degree at least, the means by which the diverse elements of the executive express and implement their own designs. In Truman's time this mechanism was, as one observer put it, "the only clearing house that operates regularly between the multitudinous departments and bureaus . . . sometimes the only possible way to get government agencies working together. . . ."[5] In the present Administration, it may well be that legislative clearance is losing

---

[2] Agency proposals for executive orders, proclamations, and certain other formal presidential actions are also coordinated and cleared through the Bureau of the Budget, as are feasibility reports on proposed public works requiring congressional action.

[3] Source: Office of Legislative Reference, Bureau of the Budget. In addition, there were 889 "direct referrals" from congressional sources asking Budget for views on pending bills.

[4] Budget Circular A-19, Revised, dated October 25, 1948 sets forth coordination and clearance procedures and requirements concerning proposed and pending bills. Budget Circular A-9, Revised, issued at the same time, deals with enrolled enactments. Both circulars codified and brought up to date earlier usage and regulations.

[5] Bertram M. Gross, *The Legislative Struggle* (New York, 1953), p. 169.

this particular distinction. Elsewhere in the Executive Office of the President, new life has been breathed into the National Security Council, as an apparatus of policy coordination and control. Even the Council of Economic Advisers, with its revised chairmanship and interdepartmental advisory board, shows signs of institutional advance in these directions. So, indeed, does the Cabinet — though history suggests this may not last.

But if legislative clearance is no longer unique, it is by far the oldest, best intrenched, most thoroughly institutionalized of the President's coordinative instruments — always excepting the budget itself — receiving new stability and new significance by virtue of its demonstrated power to adapt and to survive. And this power is not something suddenly achieved and first displayed in 1953. The central clearance system has surmounted every governmental transition since the 1920's, preserving into Eisenhower's term not only the accretions of two Democratic decades, but even the inheritance from Harding, Coolidge, and Hoover.

What is the nature of this mechanism? How has it adapted? Why has it survived? These are the questions to which this paper is addressed.[6]

I. FINANCIAL CLEARANCE IN THE TWENTIES

When President Harding approved the Budget and Accounting Act on June 10, 1921, the federal agencies lost their historic freedom to decide for themselves what appropriations they should ask of Congress; now the President, alone, was to decide and to request, with a new staff agency, the Budget Bureau, to help him do it. Moreover, in accordance with the Act's intent, but one committee in each House of Congress was to receive and review appropriation requests.[7] Here, prescribed in law, was a new restrictive way of handling the life-and-death concerns of every agency — and most congressmen. And here were new organizations with a tremendous institutional stake in the successful assertion of that new way: the presidential Bureau of the Budget and the congressional Committees on Appropriations. Furthermore, these organizations had a clear mutuality of interest in closing off, as nearly as might be, all avenues to action on appropriations save their own. Substantive congressional committees, no less than executive agencies, were potential conspirators against the exclusive jurisdictions conferred by the new budget system. Facing common dangers, the system's beneficiaries made common cause. Central legislative clearance was a principal result.

[6] This article deals with legislative coordination and review centering in the Bureau of the Budget. At a later date the author hopes to deal with a related process, planning the President's own legislative program: a process but newly and incompletely institutionalized, centering more nearly in the White House than the Budget Bureau, yet also exhibiting a high degree of continuity from Truman's time to Eisenhower's.

[7] As an integral part of the budget reform, the House of Representatives changed its rules in 1920, at the second session of the 66th Congress, to reduce from eight to one the number of committees authorized to deal with appropriations. The Senate followed suit two years later, at the second session of the 67th Congress.

It is significant of this community of interest that the original proposal for some form of central clearance came not from the new Budget Bureau, but from the House Appropriations Committee. In November, 1921, less than a month before the first presidential budget went to Congress, the Committee Chairman voiced to the Budget Director his concern about two minor measures — introduced at an agency's request and referred to a substantive committee — which authorized diversion of appropriated funds from the purposes originally specified. In the Chairman's view, ". . . matters of this character should come through the Bureau of the Budget . . . I have called them to your attention in order that you may take . . . steps . . . to include [such] requests . . . in the control which the Bureau has over direct estimates." [8] It was this congressional observation which precipitated the first presidential effort to assert central control over agency views on proposed and pending legislation, an effort embodied in Budget Circular 49, issued December 19, 1921, "by direction of the President," after clearance with the House Committee.

This first approach to legislative clearance was a rather curious affair. The language of the Budget Circular was very sweeping, requiring — in accordance with the "spirit" of the Budget and Accounting Act — that all agency proposals for legislation or expressions of views on pending legislation "the effect of which would be to create a charge upon the public treasury or commit the government to obligations which would later require appropriations," be submitted to the Budget Bureau before presentation to Congress. The Bureau was to make recommendations to the President, ascertain the "relationship of the legislation to the President's financial program," and advise the agencies accordingly. Agency proposals for legislation were to go forward only if approved by the President; agency views on pending legislation, when presented to Congress, were to include a statement of the advice received from the Budget Bureau.[9]

Here, at least on paper, was a new assertion of presidential control over the agencies, a new form of continuing staff intervention between President and department heads, conceptually a radical departure in American

[8] Letter from Chairman Madden of the House Appropriations Committee to Budget Director Dawes, November 17, 1921. Budget Bureau central files; 1921–38: *Legislation No. 1.* The measures in question were Senate Joint Resolutions of very limited significance, affecting War Department obligating authority. Madden's concern was clearly not with these specifics, but with their procedural implications.

[9] In contrast with the asserted presidential veto over agency proposals volunteered to Congress, this circular and its successors have carefully refrained from claiming any right to stop or alter agency responses to congressional requests for views on pending bills. Formally speaking, the only requirement has been that the President's position, as expressed by Budget, be stated in an agency report along with the agency's own views. Furthermore, by long custom now acknowledged in current regulations, an agency's response to congressional requests for "technical drafting service" is exempt from clearance so long as it carries no official endorsement. Thus has the Budget tried to duck the charge of "interference" with congressional access to agency opinion or expertise. In practice, this means non-interference with agency calculation of the risks involved, if any, in holding to views which do not square with those of the Executive Office.

administration matched only by the new budget process. Yet the official sponsors of Circular 49 avowed no such intent. There is nothing in the record prior to the order's issuance to show that either the Budget Director or the President grasped these implications in the language they approved.[10] But there is plenty in the record demonstrating that the members of the Cabinet did not leave them long in ignorance, once the order had gone out. The subsequent course of legislative clearance in Harding's time is mainly a matter of apologies, concessions, limitations tacitly approved or self-applied, to soften agency reactions against Circular 49.

The agencies were aroused both by the Circular's potential coverage — broadly interpreted, its criteria reached virtually all subjects of legislation — and by interposition of the Budget Bureau between them and the President on such a range of measures. In beating his retreat, at the President's behest, Dawes did not try to find fixed subject-matter limits for his procedure; instead he let it be known that matters of importance could be cleared with the President directly. Only on routine affairs would the Budget act as agent.[11] In practice, Dawes went even farther, leaving interpretation and compliance to departmental discretion. The Budget Bureau neither guided nor protested; the agencies proceeded accordingly.

For two years Circular 49 remained in limbo. Then a new Administration seized on this empty order and within it built a strong and well enforced, if narrowly defined accessory to central budgeting. The forms of financial clearance are traceable to Harding's time. The actuality begins with Coolidge.

By early 1924, the presidential budget system was a going concern, veteran of three "budget seasons." The Budget Bureau had been staffed and organized, routines established, procedures set. The Bureau's leadership had passed from Dawes to his handpicked successor, General Lord, a zealot for the small economy.[12] And the presidency had passed to perhaps the most determined economizer ever to hold the office. "I am for econ-

---

10 Dawes obtained Harding's approval in advance, sending him the proposed circular on December 3, 1921, with the notation that it "needs no argument," being intended "simply to insure that all estimates and requests for appropriations [are] presented in the manner provided in the Budget and Accounting Act." Dawes may have said less than he believed, but there is no hint of this either in the official files or in his published memoirs, *The First Year of the Budget* (New York, 1923).

11 This modification was suggested by Harding himself at a conference with Dawes in January, 1922. A formal amendment to Circular 49 was actually drafted along these lines but was never issued; an oral clarification in Cabinet meeting appears to have been substituted, supplemented by explicit waivers of jurisdiction in Budget Bureau correspondence with particular departments. Budget Bureau, central files; 1921–38: *Legislation No. 1.* For detailed discussion of this and other aspects of the subject, see Richard E. Neustadt, "Presidential Clearance of Legislation," unpub. diss. (Harvard, 1950), pp. 28 ff.

12 Herbert Lord, an army careerist and wartime associate of Dawes, served as Budget Director from 1922 to 1929. It was his custom, in the search for economy, to inspect his subordinates' desk drawers after office hours, confiscating extra pencils, paper clips, and pads of paper. Note that the total full-time Bureau staff numbered less than thirty in 1924. Ten years later the total was still under forty.

omy and after that I am for more economy," so Coolidge put it, conceiving economy not merely as a matter of politics or economics, but as an exercise in personal morality, an ethical principle, a constitutional requirement, an end in itself.[13] In the Coolidge Administration the theme of budget policy was reduction: reduction of expenditures, of taxes, and of the public debt, with presidential budgeting mainly a means of cutting back on current outlays and avoiding new commitments. It is in this context that legislative clearance was revived.

Early in 1924, the Budget Bureau, with presidential support, began a vigorous campaign to activate Circular 49. For nearly two years, Lord peppered key departments with letters of warning, abjuration, and complaint, backed by a considerable amount of Budget staff investigation and analysis.[14] By 1926, he was able to report that agency compliance had become "practically universal." [15] Of course, the Coolidge clearance system, thus successfully asserted, was carried on within a very narrow frame of reference. Cabinet officers were constrained to accept Budget Bureau placement between them and the President, but only on proposals clearly costing money, and only with respect to cost, not substance. The Bureau's task of ascertaining the relationship of agency proposals to presidential program was rendered relatively safe and sure by virtue of the program's identification with recorded budget policies and estimates.

The purpose of the exercise is clear from Budget's rules of thumb for processing what came its way. An adverse agency report on a pending measure was usually taken as conclusive. An affirmative report resulted in careful scrutiny of relationship to the current budget and implications for future years. It was common practice to hold favorable agency reports "in conflict" with the President's financial program. Frequently, legislation was held "in conflict" unless the money authorization was reduced. This negative advice also applied wherever a semblance of prior legislative

[13] *Addresses of The President of the United States and the Director of the Bureau of the Budget at the Seventh Regular Meeting of the Business Organization of the Government* (Washington, G.P.O., 1924), p. 6. See also the corresponding releases for the ninth meeting (1925), and the eleventh meeting (1926). The Business Organization of the Government, including all department heads and bureau chiefs, met semiannually from 1922 to 1929 for purposes of presidential exhortation on, and departmental oaths of fealty to, economy in government. Coolidge's addresses on these occasions are classics of their kind. A Dawes innovation, becoming more ritualistic with each passing year, these meetings were abruptly terminated by Herbert Hoover when he assumed the presidency after years of attendance as Secretary of Commerce.

[14] For a detailed review of these efforts, see Donald A. Hansen, "Legislative Clearance by the Bureau of the Budget," unpub. staff monograph (Budget Bureau, 1940), pp. 10–19. For Lord's correspondence with departments, see Budget Bureau central files; 1291–38: *Legislation No. 1.*

[15] Bureau of the Budget, *Third Annual Report of the Director of the Bureau of the Budget to the President of the United States* (Washington, G.P.O., 1926), p. 28. Within his limited frame of reference, Lord's claim for compliance appears reasonably accurate. Apparently he was afforded the opportunity to see in advance those legislative reports and proposals that he and the President really wanted. See Hansen, *op. cit.,* pp. 19 ff.

authority could be found to render the current proposal "unnecessary." [16] When the Bureau was confronted with opposing views from two departments, its normal procedure was to endorse the negative position. If this were not feasible, an independent staff analysis was sometimes made the basis for decision. Changes in drafting were sometimes suggested to the agencies, but always as a Budget idea, not as the result of any effort at coordination. Occasionally, the Bureau would attempt to mediate major differences of opinion, but it never undertook to seek them out.

The Coolidge clearance system, then, was quite straightforward in its negative endeavor to buttress the President's control over his budget policies and his — or the Budget Bureau's — forward financial plans. In no sense did the system operate as a coordinative or developmental mechanism in areas of substantive policy. And what was true in Coolidge's Administration was also true in his successor's term. President Hoover not only inherited and applied this form of central clearance, he even refined its terms of reference, emphasizing more than ever its budgetary association and its negative cast.

Shortly after his inauguration, Hoover suggested that the Budget Bureau take no action on agency requests for clearance unless and until it received a clear intimation of congressional interest. The President intended personally to approve all clearance actions and saw no point in bothering with measures which were not going to receive action.[17] A further refinement followed late in 1929, when Hoover sanctioned a formal amendment to Circular 49 exempting from clearance all agency reports on private bills and all *unfavorable* reports on public bills.[18]

These minor changes simply put finishing touches on the edifice of Coolidge clearance; within these limits, the character of clearance actions remained unchanged through Hoover's term. His budgetary problems became immeasurably more difficult than Coolidge's had been. As the economic decline worsened after 1929 and federal revenues fell steadily, enormous pressures built up for increased federal spending. But the Hoover Administration remained unalterably opposed to deliberate deficit financ-

16 Hansen, *op. cit.*, especially pp. 17–20. See also Budget Bureau central files; 1921–38: *Legislation No. 1* for a variety of typical clearance letters in this period.

17 Budget Bureau central files; 1921–38: *Legislation No. 1*, Budget Director's Memorandum to the files, May 17, 1929. Hoover actually did review and initial virtually every Budget Bureau clearance letter issued during his term of office, an interesting commentary on the presidency of twenty-five years ago. The documentation behind such letters was relatively haphazard in those days, frequently lacking in summaries of the issues, or of agency positions, or even of the bills themselves. The President must often have had to plow through the legislative language to reach an understanding of the subject at hand.

18 Budget Circular 273, issued December 20, 1929. The Budget Bureau shortly found it expedient to issue supplementary instructions requiring that to qualify for the exemption, reports on public bills must be definitely unfavorable, not merely noncommittal. This amplifying note was contained in a "Memorandum to the Heads of all Departments and Establishments," issued April 10, 1930, "by direction of the President." In Coolidge's regime, these types of reports had received almost automatic clearance from the Budget Bureau, usually without referral to the President.

ing, and in its clearance operations the Budget Bureau tried harder than ever to ward off all possible legislative authorizations for unbudgeted expenditure.[19] Of course, after the mid-term elections of 1930 the President was unable either to develop a coherent budget policy and make it stick, or to avoid the opposition's criticism for his failure to do so. And in that painful situation, financial clearance became the least of remedies.

II. THE ROOSEVELT REVOLUTION AND POLICY CLEARANCE

President Franklin D. Roosevelt's inaugural in 1933 was accompanied by a clean sweep topside in all the departments, after twelve years of continuity under the Republicans. The procedures for financial clearance had grown up in those years and concern about them, or even understanding of them, seems to have been carried off with the outgoing Administration. The succeeding regime was enormously busy and very new.[20] Only the President himself was really familiar with governmental administration. His cabinet members were novices at it.[21] Moreover, they were moving at much too fast a pace to stop for the niceties of an auxiliary budget procedure.

They moved fast; they moved the federal government into unprecedented ventures, into new spheres of action on many different fronts. The first years of the New Deal released a torrent of measures for reform, and these were mingled with a host of shifting, often contradictory improvisations in the fight against depression. Roosevelt had pledged financial stringency in the 1932 campaign, attacking Hoover on home grounds. During the next two years "sound money" and "economy in government" remained on-again-off-again themes, but sounding ever fainter as the New Deal gathered impetus, their principal adherents mostly out of office before the end of 1934.[22]

[19] This theme appears strongly in Hoover's last three Budget messages. For example: ". . . we cannot afford to embark on any new or enlarged ventures. . . . There will be before the Congress many legislative matters involving additions to our estimated expenditures. . . . The plea of unemployment will be advanced . . . but Congress [should] give full due to our financial outlook. . . . In the absence of further legislation . . . we can close [the] year with a balanced budget." *Message of the President of the United States Transmitting the Budget for the Fiscal Year Ending June 30, 1932* (Washington, G.P.O., 1930), p. XIX.

[20] For sidelights on the "newness" of the incoming Cabinet see Frances Perkins, *The Roosevelt I Knew* (New York, 1946), pp. 228–30. See also Harold Ickes, *The First Thousand Days* (New York, 1953).

[21] Roosevelt's really extraordinary grasp of the tempo and politics of departmental administration comes clear in the meetings of the National Emergency Council, an enlarged Cabinet group which met under his chairmanship from 1933 to 1936. The verbatim transcripts of these meetings, available in the National Archives, preserve intact his "lectures" to his department heads on such subjects as how to manage bureau chiefs, congressional committees, and the press.

[22] Notably Roosevelt's first Budget Director, Lewis Douglas, and his first Undersecretary of the Treasury, Dean Acheson. Both returned to government with the coming of World War II.

The motives which led Coolidge's Administration to stress financial clearance were scarcely in the forefront of the new regime's concerns. Not until January, 1934 did the Budget Bureau take any steps to remind department heads of their continuing obligations under the old circulars. And then the Bureau's action was muted, almost apologetic. Taken by the staff, not the Director, it was a bureaucratic restoration of routines, not in any sense a presidentially-inspired campaign for compliance.[23]

Roosevelt's contribution to central clearance was of quite another order. Nearly a year after this Budget Bureau "restoration" of financial clearance, the President took the initiative in launching a different kind of clearance: clearance of all agency proposals for legislation, "policy" clearance in substantive terms.

Roosevelt brought the matter up on his own motion at a National Emergency Council Meeting in December, 1934, shortly before the convening of the 74th Congress. He told the assembled officials he had decided to stop the practice of uncoordinated agency requests for legislation. At the preceding session of Congress he had been "quite horrified — not once but half a dozen times — by reading in the paper that some department or agency was after this, that, or the other without my knowledge." [24] He wanted no more of that. In the future, agency officials should come to him with their proposals before taking them to Congress.

One Cabinet officer observed that the departments were already clearing through the Budget Bureau. Roosevelt brushed this aside. "That," he said, "was for appropriations. What I am talking about is legislation. . . . Coming down to legislation there has never been any clearing house . . . and, I think in the last analysis that has got to be tried in and go through the National Emergency Council . . . and up to me if necessary. In all probability it will come to me." [25]

On December 13, 1934, the secretariat of the Emergency Council followed up the President's remarks with a memorandum to all members, signed by Donald Richberg, then NEC's Executive Director. This instructed the agencies that at the forthcoming Congress all proposals for appropriations and all bills "carrying appropriations measures" should be cleared with the President through the Bureau of the Budget. All "other proposed legislation" was to be cleared through the Council's Executive Director, or in certain cases with special-purpose NEC committees.

---

[23] The Bureau's reminder was contained in a memorandum from the Budget Director's career assistant to the heads of all major agencies, January 22, 1934. It was a gently phrased affair and while most of the agencies replied in kind, the Bureau's records indicate that they were slow to take their duties very seriously. See Budget Bureau central files; 1921–38: *Legislation No. 1*. Budget Director Douglas seems to have had no part in this proceeding, nor much interest in the outcome. Two weeks later, when queried by a Cabinet member, he expressed himself as unfamiliar with the "old orders," and uncertain of their scope. See National Emergency Council, *Proceedings of the Fourth Meeting* (February 6, 1934), pp. 21 ff.

[24] National Emergency Council, *Proceedings of the Nineteenth Meeting* (December 11, 1934), p. 7.

[25] *Ibid.*

While this directive referred to proposals only and contained a caveat on appropriation matters, its language was far from precise. The result was widespread confusion over the relationship between the new procedure and the old Budget circulars. In April, 1935, the Acting Budget Director, Daniel Bell, protested to Richberg; the problem was raised at an Emergency Council meeting on April 23 and the President decided that clarifying instructions should go out.[26] These took the form of a new Budget Circular 336, issued "by direction of the President" on December 21, 1935.[27]

Circular 336 brought together and superseded outstanding NEC directives, as well as previous Budget circulars. It provided that all agency proposals for legislation and all reports on pending legislation should clear through the Budget Bureau "for consideration by the President," before submission to Congress; as before, private relief bills were exempted. Agency proposals or reports when subsequently sent to Congress were to include a statement as to "whether proposed legislation was or was not in accord with the President's program." This was also to apply to oral testimony before congressional committees.

Procedurally, the circular provided that the Budget Bureau was to check directly with the President on legislation "solely concerning fiscal matters." Legislation "solely concerning policy matters" was to be referred to the President through the Emergency Council staff. The two organizations were to clear with him jointly on legislation involving both "fiscal" and "policy" matters. The Council was to inform the Bureau of clearances which it obtained from the President independently; the Bureau was to inform the agencies in all instances.

In print — and in practice — these procedures had a very clumsy look; for obvious reasons they proved cumbersome and somewhat unrealistic. Two years later they were superseded. But while the mechanics were transitional, the basic requirements have remained in force, without essential change, for nineteen years.

The Roosevelt clearance system, thus established, incorporated its financial precursor but was no mere extension of the budget process.[28] On

---

[26] National Emergency Council, *Proceedings of the Twenty-sixth Meeting* (April 23, 1935), p. 8. Bell, at the time a senior career official in the Treasury Department, had taken the Budget Directorship on an acting basis after Douglas' departure. He held the job in addition to his duties as a special assistant to Secretary Morgenthau and this "temporary" arrangement was continued for nearly five years, until Harold Smith relieved him in 1939.

[27] This new order was discussed by the Emergency Council before issuance and the President then went to great lengths to emphasize his personal approval. See National Emergency Council, *Proceedings of the Twenty-eighth Meeting* (December 17, 1935), pp. 14–23.

[28] In 1937, when a revision of Circular 336 was under discussion, F. J. Bailey — soon to become the first Assistant Budget Director for Legislative Reference — wrote an undated memorandum pointing out that "there is no authority whatever in the Budget and Accounting Act for our procedure with respect to reports on legislation. And I would not try to make believe that there is. The authority we have over [these] reports comes from Executive authority and *not* from any Act of Congress." Budget Bureau central files; 1921–38: *Legislation No. 2*.

the contrary, in form and fact and terms of reference this was Roosevelt's creation, intended to protect not just his budget, but his prerogatives, his freedom of action, and his choice of policies, in an era of fast-growing government and of determined presidential leadership.

Roosevelt's statements make it plain that he sought to protect both President from agencies and agencies from one another. In the first place, he wanted the Administration's stand made known on agency proposals, not only in his own defense but for the sake of everyone concerned, including the congressional leaders. Of these proposals he remarked:

> They fall into three categories: first, the kind of legislation that, administratively, I could not give approval to — [clearance] will eliminate that; secondly, the type of legislation which we are perfectly willing to have the department or agency press for, but at the same time we do not want to put it in the [third] category of major Administration bills. Obviously I have to confine myself to what the newspapers called last year "the comparatively small list of *must* legislation." If I make every bill that the Government is interested in *must* legislation, it is going to complicate things . . . very much; and where I clear legislation with a notation that says "no objection" that means you are at perfect liberty to try to get the thing through, but I am not going to send a special message for it. It is all your trouble, not mine.[29]

In the second place, it was good business to have ideas and information contributed by all agencies concerned, not just the originating departments. Having bills cleared through a central agency would, in Roosevelt's words, give somebody else outside the department itself the opportunity to have happy thoughts." [30] Moreover, such exchanges in advance would prevent crossed wires within the Administration. The President did not want the agencies "stepping on each others' toes" and he definitely did not want them "stepping on mine . . . :"

> Just the other day a resolution was passed through Congress — a House resolution that did not even have to come to me — asking for a certain report on a very important matter from one of the departments. It was a policy matter. The department was asked to send the report up to the Committee and nobody outside the department knew about it. We happened to catch it. If the report had gone up in the form in which it was prepared, it would have been absolutely contrary to the policy of the Government.[31]

On pending bills which the Administration had not sponsored, he wanted the departments to keep out of each others' way:

> In all our testimony before Congress and in all our answers to questions, let us stick to our own last and let us be factual about

[29] National Emergency Council, *Proceedings of the Twenty-second Meeting* (January 22, 1935), p. 2.
[30] *Ibid.*, p. 3.
[31] National Emergency Council, *Proceedings of the Twenty-eighth Meeting* (December 17, 1935), p. 17.

it. This is one of the most important things that has been said for a long time . . . let us say the Secretary of Agriculture goes up there and he doesn't know much about the bill, but he knows that he is going to be asked about it. It might . . . [relate] . . . not only to Agriculture but to Interior and some other departments as well and he ought to in some way find out what the general attitude is through some kind of clearing house. . . .[32]

Thus Roosevelt expressed the purpose of his new clearance system: by and large a negative purpose, even as Coolidge's had been. An opportunity for "happy thoughts" apart, the system's new coordinative elements, no less than broadened clearances, were seen primarily as means to keep the many-voiced executive from shouting itself down in the legislative process.

Granting Roosevelt's purpose, what, in fact, did he obtain? Initially, not very much:

Clearance as practiced in the 74th Congress [1935–6] was restricted almost entirely to minor departmental bills . . . nearly all of the really important bills and many minor measures originating in the Executive Branch, did not pass through this machinery. . . . Matters discussed with the President in person by a department head were not submitted for clearance, except in a few cases . . . the President's approval, orally given or read into his statements was deemed sufficient . . . nearly all of the measures about which the President sent messages to the Congress [the major administration bills] . . . [were] . . . exempt from clearance . . . many lesser matters also escaped such checking.[33]

This appraisal was based on a study utilizing only Emergency Council records. A later survey of the period, based on Budget Bureau files, concluded that there was "less evidence of deliberate agency failure to comply . . . than of Bureau failure to follow the prescribed procedure in the clearance of policy matters." [34] Perhaps so — but there is nothing in print or on file to controvert the general tenor of the earlier view.

Yet by 1939 the Budget Director was talking confidently before Congress of the scope and general coverage of central clearance.[35] In 1943, an acute and experienced observer could write that Budget clearance was "frequently commanding," the Bureau's influence "very great." [36] For

---

32 *Ibid.*, pp. 19–21.

33 Edwin E. Witte, "The Preparation of Proposed Legislative Measures by Administrative Departments," *Studies on Administrative Management in the Government of the United States for the President's Committee on Administrative Management* (Washington: G.P.O., 1937), p. 56.

34 Hansen, "Legislative Clearance by the Bureau of the Budget" (cited in note 14), p. 34.

35 Testimony by Daniel W. Bell, Acting Director of the Budget, before the Treasury Subcommittee of the House Committee on Appropriations, *Hearings on the Treasury Department Appropriation Bill for 1940*, 76th Cong., 1st sess. (Washington, G.P.O., 1939), p. 936.

36 Roland Young, *This is Congress* (New York, 1943), p. 59.

this changed appraisal at least four things were responsible: the demise of NEC, the Budget Bureau's great expansion, the slowing down of New Deal creativity, and the formal marriage of central clearance to the veto power.

The Emergency Council was dying on the vine by 1936, commanding little presidential interest, or agency respect. Its diminished status and potential were accurately reflected in the Brownlow Committee's recommendation that the Council be abolished, and its staff activities discarded or dispersed.[37] Undoubtedly the Council's relative and growing weakness had much to do with the lax attitude of agencies and Budget Bureau toward the Executive Director's prerogatives under Circular 336. Had he been the sole institutional peg for "policy" clearance, that process might well have gone under also, retrievable with difficulty, if at all. But behind him stood the Budget. When he vanished, it inherited. This happened, actually, as a matter of course, a detail of administrative tidying, a minor item among all the major changes in the Bureau's status, role, and outlook envisaged by and following upon the Brownlow Committee Report of January, 1937.[38]

In the two years after publication of the Report, the Bureau moved, as never since the twenties, to strengthen and consolidate its clearance operations. In the spring of 1937, Director Bell loosed a stream of correspondence on the agencies, reminiscent of Lord's effort thirteen years before.[39] In December, 1937, Circular 336 was formally re-issued — renumbered 344 — as a means of removing reference to the Emergency Council in official clearance instructions.[40] Henceforth, the Bureau was to be in form and fact the President's sole institutional clearance agent, on matters of substance no less than finance. Internally, also, the Bureau acted — Brownlow Report in hand — to put new life and strength into the job. In 1938, Bell increased the staff assigned specifically to clearance work, reorganized it as a separate, full-time, undertaking and gave it status as a major Bureau function, autonomously organized in a Division of Coordination, precursor of the present Office of Legislative Reference.[41]

[37] See President's Committee on Administrative Management, *Report with Special Studies* (Washington, G.P.O., 1937), pp. 15–21.

[38] *Ibid.* The Report recommended essentially that the Budget Bureau become the President's chief staff agent for "administrative management," enlarged, revitalized, and formally made part of the President's own office. In passing, the report endorsed a staff proposal that NEC clearance functions devolve upon the Bureau, with Circular 336 simplified accordingly and then generally enforced. In so urging, the Committee simply followed the logic of events, which fitted neatly enough into its major theme: building up the Budget Bureau.

[39] See Budget Bureau central files; 1921–38: *Legislation No. 2*, especially entries between March and May, 1937.

[40] Circular 344 — virtually identical in its terms with 336, save for deletion of NEC's participation — was drafted in May, 1937, but for various reasons, mechanical and other, was not released to the agencies until December 17, 1937. Circular 344 was later renumbered A-19.

[41] In 1938, the President obtained from Congress a supplemental appropriation enabling the Budget Bureau to start tooling up for the new or redefined tasks envisaged in the Brownlow Report. For details on the ensuing reorganization and restaffing see

During 1939, in the first session of the 76th Congress, the Budget Bureau processed agency reports on 2,448 pending public bills. Four years before, in the days of financial clearance, only 300 pending measures had been covered by submissions to the Bureau. Again, in 1939 the Bureau handled 438 drafts of proposed legislation; this compares with 170 proposals sent by the agencies to NEC under the procedure of 1935, or 162 proposals sent to NEC and Budget both, under the procedure of 1936.[42] These figures are illustrative of the rise in clearance coverage after 1937, though nothing can be more elusive than the search for such objective measurements, nor anything more misleading than raw data of this type.[43] But there are other evidences also, in Budget Bureau files of agency and White House correspondence, and in transcripts of legislative hearings and debate, to demonstrate that central clearance was now reaching wider than before.[44]

The climate of the times, perhaps, contributed to this no less than did improved organization and procedure. The main thrust of New Deal innovation was long past by 1939. The emergency had lost its cutting edge; emergency agencies had either disappeared or dug roots into routine. In Europe and in Asia world war threatened. In Congress, the anti-New Deal coalition had become a formidable fact of life. In the executive, sails were trimmed accordingly. Real legislative ambitions for most agencies were now measured largely by consolidation and amendment — goals much more easily contained in clearance channels than the great, unprecedented ventures once hurried before relatively complaisant Congresses.

Bell's testimony, *Hearings* (cited in note 35), pp. 936–55. This preceded by a year the Bureau's formal transfer from the Treasury to the Executive Office of the President (Reorganization Plan I and Executive Order 8,248 of 1939). Before Bell's reorganization, clearance work had been handled almost entirely by the Bureau's estimates examiners as an adjunct of their other duties. The new Division of Coordination was conceived, both in the Brownlow studies and by its Bureau sponsors, as a small, full-time unit to guide and coordinate, but not supplant, the contribution of all other Bureau staff to legislative analysis and review. This has remained the concept, though since World War II not just the Bureau but the whole growing Executive Office has become the field from which staff contributions have been sought. By 1939, the Coordination Division's professional staff for legislation numbered five; in the fifteen years since, the comparable figure has never risen above nine. The unit's changes in title have had no substantive purpose or effect.

42 Source of Budget figures: Office of Legislative Reference, Bureau of the Budget. For NEC figures see Witte, *op. cit.*, p. 53.

43 To illustrate: In the 1939 session some 5,000 public bills were introduced in the two Houses of Congress; of these, 452 were passed by both Houses and enrolled that year. But only an item-by-item comparison — which no one has ever made — would show the relationship between the 2,400-odd bills cleared and the 5,000 introduced, or between the 438 drafts cleared and the 452 bills passed. To complicate the issue further, the figures on drafts cleared and on bills enrolled represent separate subjects in virtually all cases; not so the figures on bills introduced, where substantial duplications within or between the two Houses may run as high as forty per cent in the average first session. This is an estimate; firm data are not available.

44 For examples see Hansen, *op. cit.*, pp. 81–84.

And one thing more: in 1938, the Budget Bureau gained a new sanction and an unassailable rationale, for its clearance of proposed and pending measures. That year, the Bureau came into control of agency communications to the President on signature or veto of enrolled bills. Henceforth, Roosevelt's clearance agency was also his chief institutional advisor on the generality of measures passed by Congress. Within this combination lay real power, and the Bureau made the most of it.

III. POLICY CLEARANCE AND THE VETO POWER

Traditionally, Presidents have sought advice from their department heads on disposition of enrolled enactments. Until the thirties, though, this custom had some drastic built-in limitations. When an enrolled bill reached the White House, the President's Secretary or Executive Clerk would hazard a quick guess at the agencies concerned; the bill itself would then be passed by hand to each in turn — a document of state, handled with care — and their replies, filtering back, one by one, would get such correlation as hard-pressed White House aides might manage. All this went on during the ten days within which the President could veto. Frequently he was but poorly served, receiving very late, for fast decision, an ill-digested mountain of material.[45]

From its establishment in 1921, the Budget Bureau had been asked for views on each enrolled appropriations bill. In 1934, Roosevelt told his staff to get Bureau reactions on all private relief bills involving an expenditure of funds. His aides went one step further, urging — as a measure for their own relief — that on such bills the Bureau also seek and summarize the views of other agencies concerned. This worked, and presently, without fanfare, the White House staff began to send across the street all manner of substantive public bills as well, asking the Bureau to circularize agencies and correlate views. By 1938 almost all enrolled bills were going to the Bureau for this handling. That year, the few exceptions followed no clear line of demarcation; after 1939, there were no more exceptions. This process of pragmatic delegation took but five years, from start to finish.

So long as the original enrollments had to be handed around, the Budget Bureau was as helpless as the White House staff had been to make

---

[45] There were other hazards too: ". . . one enrolled bill was lost and once when we called up one of the new [New Deal] agencies and asked where the bill was, they said they had put it in the files." Testimony of Frederick J. Bailey, Assistant Director for Legislative Reference, Bureau of the Budget, before the House Committee on the Civil Service, 78th Congress, 1st sess. *Hearings Pursuant to H. Res. 16.*, Part 2 (Washington, G.P.O., 1943), p. 361. The writer is indebted to Bailey; to the late Maurice Latta, former White House Executive Clerk, whose tenure in subordinate capacities began with McKinley; to William J. Hopkins, Latta's successor as Executive Clerk; and to James H. Rowe, Jr., a Roosevelt Administrative Assistant, for data on the evolution of enrolled bill procedure. Information here provided is drawn from their recollections, from Roosevelt's enrolled bill files (now at Hyde Park), and from contemporary Budget Bureau records.

of this anything but a thankless, mainly ministerial performance. In 1938, however, the Public Printer was persuaded to prepare facsimile copies of each enrolled bill; these went directly to the Bureau at the same time the original went back to Congress for signature by Speaker and Vice President. Armed with these copies, the Bureau could put an official text before each agency simultaneously, hours or even days before the bill itself could reach the White House and the President's time began to run.

This was a simple, mechanical improvement, but what it gave was time, and time spelled opportunity. On January 19, 1939, the Bureau issued "by direction of the President" Circular 346, defining agency obligations under the new procedure. For the first time Budget was identified officially as presidential agent on all enrolled enactments. Bureau requests for agency opinions were to receive an absolute priority; agency replies were to be forthcoming within forty-eight hours, and were to include in each case a specific recommendation, backed by as much factual information as possible. Any recommendation against presidential signature was to be accompanied by a draft veto message or memorandum of disapproval (for use with pocket vetoes). In these terms Circular 346 formalized previous practice, giving it a mandatory application beyond anything remotely possible in absence of facsimile procedure.[46]

Within the Budget Bureau, corresponding steps were taken. The chores of asking agencies for views, pressuring the dilatory, correlating replies, reworking message drafts, were all put on a centralized and systematic basis. Summaries and covering recommendations to the President were now developed uniformly, carefully, and in much greater detail than before. All this took organization, specialization, and somebody's time and effort; by 1939, the Bureau had these at hand in its Division of Coordination. There full responsibility for enrolled bills was vested.

This new function quickly became the key element in central clearance. The Budget Bureau's work on agency proposals and reports built up a general, comprehensive record, unmatched elsewhere in government, to buttress its consideration of enrolled bills. At the same time, its mandate on enrolled enactments now lent special point and purpose to clearances of measures in proposed and pending stages.[47]

The veto power's potency in this connection depends, of course, upon its use, and Roosevelt was a constant user. "If the decision is close," he once remarked to his department heads, "I want to veto." [48] In 1939, he chose to veto sixteen bills despite approval by the Budget Bureau, remarking to an aide, "The Budget is getting too soft; tell them to stiffen

[46] "This is a splendid contribution," wrote Rudolph Forster, then White House Executive Clerk, "we could never have got half as far before." Budget Bureau central files; 1921–38: *Enrolled Bills No. 1*, undated memorandum from Forster to F. J. Bailey.

[47] In order to build up back-ground files for use on enrollments, private bills were brought back under clearance at the pending stage by Budget Circular 390, June 1, 1942.

[48] National Emergency Council, *Proceedings of the Twenty-eighth Meeting* (December 17, 1935), p. 17.

up." [49] Indeed, he was prone to call occasionally for "something I can veto," as a "reminder" to department heads and congressmen alike.[50] This was not frivolity; to F.D.R. the veto power was among the presidency's greatest attributes, an independent and responsible act of participation in the legislative process, and a means of enforcing congressional and agency respect for presidential preferences or programs.[51]

From the beginning, Roosevelt placed a great deal of reliance on the Budget Bureau's weighing and sifting of bureaucratic opinion. On the generality of measures he inclined to discount Cabinet, congressional, and interest group advices which found their joint and several ways directly to the White House. But he took care that there should be, between him and the Budget, some White House staff review to check the institutional approach against the personal, to balance off the presidency with the President. In 1943, that task went to Judge Rosenman, in his new post as Special Counsel to the President; there, with temporary lapses, it has remained, assumed by each of Rosenman's successors in Truman's time and Eisenhower's.[52]

The Budget Bureau took its staff work on enrolled enactments as seriously as Roosevelt did his veto power. Here, unchallengably in the Budget's hands, was all-important preparation for decisive acts of state, exclusively in presidential jurisdiction. Of course, on the great, controversial measures, the White House could expect appraisals and advice from many other sources and through many other channels. But usually on the general run of bills enrolled at every session, particularly the private bills, the Budget file was the "works." Within the Bureau, priorities were set accordingly.

In Roosevelt's later years, no other element of central clearance received half the attention, time, and effort which Bureau staff gave to enrolled enactments, especially to lesser issues where its word weighed the most. From 1940 on, coordination of proposed and pending bills was routinized increasingly, with stress on negative, protective aspects only, and great reliance on the written word. Rarely were agencies called in for face-to-face discussion; rarely were efforts made to conform clearance actions with the exigencies of the legislative timetable. If agencies and

---

49 Budget Bureau central files; 1921–38: *Enrolled Bills No. 1,* undated memorandum from Rudolph Forster to F. J. Bailey.

50 See note 45.

51 All Roosevelt aides consulted by the writer have been emphatically agreed on his conscious adherence to these views and his consistent application of them.

52 Review of Budget Bureau submissions on enrolled bills first became a distinct White House assignment in 1939, shortly after the Bureau's formal assumption of responsibility for their handling. Initially, this assignment went to James H. Rowe, Jr., one of the original Administrative Assistants to the President appointed under the Reorganization Act of 1939. Rowe had left the White House by the time Samuel I. Rosenman was appointed Special Counsel in 1943; this work then gravitated naturally to Rosenman, who had performed a similar service for F.D.R. in Albany, a decade earlier. Rosenman was succeeded as Special Counsel by Clark M. Clifford in 1946; Clifford by Charles S. Murphy in 1950; Murphy by Bernard Shanley, the present incumbent, who took office with the Eisenhower Administration.

committees wanted such advantages as clearance offered at the pending stage, they could ask and wait their turn; if not, they took their chances when the bills became enrolled.

IV. From Roosevelt to Truman

The coming of World War II confirmed this Budget Bureau tendency to concentrate on enrolled bills, its inescapable job, while energy, interest, and opportunity were diverted from staff work on proposed and pending measures. The war itself made operating policies and administrative actions the pivotal affairs of government. Congress lost the center of the stage; the legislative process ceased to be either the Administration's chief concern, or the nation's main measure of governmental progress.

"Dr. New Deal" was succeeded by "Dr. Win-the-War." The new physician prescribed far less than the old in the way of urgent home-front legislation — and most of this in war-related fields, now the concern of new emergency agencies. This was not the stuff, nor these the agencies, to stay confined in peacetime clearance channels. And once their operating conflicts forced establishment of an effective wartime instrument for mediation and control — the Office of War Mobilization — their legislative conflicts and ambitions gravitated toward the War Mobilizer, not the Budget Director.[53] The result, of course, was to down-grade all previous coordinators on the governmental stage — not least the Budget Bureau's clearance mechanism. OWM action in the legislative field was limited, deliberately, to matters of the highest policy or greatest urgency. But by the war's end, its successor's interests were proliferating through the government. Most Budget staff accepted, without much demur, OWM's wartime over-shadowing of their coordinating role; they took with far less grace OWMR's widening postwar interventions on the legislative front.

Meanwhile, Truman suddenly succeeded to the presidency. With this the Budget Bureau's role was shaken mightily amidst pangs of transition unmatched since 1933. The two years after Roosevelt's death were doubly transitional: the government was entangled in a complex shift from war to peace and back again to something in-between; the presidency was in process of adjustment from the old to a new personality, and to new work methods and interpersonal relationships. It was a complex, clouded, often contradictory time, climaxed by the congressional overturn of November, 1946. To the great alterations in the executive, there were now added many changes in personalities and power on Capitol Hill, profoundly affecting relationships and atmosphere at both ends of the Avenue.

In all this swirl, the Budget Bureau stumbled badly, its prestige and position challenged as rarely before or since. Most of the services Roosevelt had charged it to perform were little understood, at first, by the new

---

[53] The Office of War Mobilization (OWM) was established by Executive Order 9347, May 27, 1943. It was transformed into a statutory Office of War Mobilization and Reconversion (OWMR) by the War Mobilization and Reconversion Act of 1944. For an admirable summary of OWM-OWMR history, see Herman M. Somers, *Presidential Agency* (Cambridge, Mass., 1950), pp. 47–108.

President and his new team of close associates; legislative clearance least of all. "I simply do not see," allegedly remarked one high-placed Truman aide, "why [legislative] *policy* is any business of the *Budget* Bureau." [54] Truman's three successive OWMR Directors — Vinson, Snyder, and Steelman — were all, in varying degree, much closer to the President than were the hold-over Budget leaders, Smith and Appleby. And in the months after V-J day, it was to OWMR, not Budget, that Truman and his White House aides looked mainly for help on policy problems, legislative and other.

By mid-summer, 1946, the Budget Bureau's status in the presidential orbit had reached its lowest point. OWMR seemed superficially to be assured a strong, perhaps a permanent position. A new staff agency of unknown policy potential, the Council of Economic Advisers, had just been authorized by statute.[55] Between these two, the Budget's future role, particularly in the legislative sphere, appeared attenuated and uncertain.

Yet scarcely two years later the Bureau was entrenched as the prime source of presidential staff work on the Administration's legislative program, its clearance tasks, especially at proposed and pending stages, more actively developed and more central to the President's concerns than ever in their history. Three things, mainly, lay behind this change: reappearance of the legislative process as the key government preoccupation; attrition or demise of other institutional staff facilities; and the personality of James E. Webb, Truman's new Director of the Budget.

The first Truman term, be it remembered, was a time of executive retrenchment, of climbing down from wartime peaks. The early Fair Deal blueprinted many a large-scale peacetime venture in administration, but save for atomic energy and foreign aid — and the short-lived emergency housing program — these remained largely on paper. For this was a time, also, of congressional stalemate in home affairs, and these new ventures needed legislation. Numerous issues of domestic policy confronting the regime were, therefore, first cast up in legislative guise, then frozen in that status by an unresponsive Congress.[56] The operating tasks, which in their magnitude had called forth OWM, were finished; nothing comparable took their place. Presidential messages to Congress became the central focus for policy-making; legislative drafts the major means for translating policy into coordinated action. With Congress formally in opposition after 1946, the object of the game — save in the foreign field — turned into record-building, pure and simple. But more than mere demands were needed in the record; for someday there might be response, if not from the current Congress, then the next. Serious proposals had to be specific; specifics meaningful — and viable.

[54] A comment dating from the early spring of 1946, made by the then OWMR Director to a member of his staff and relayed by the latter to the writer.

[55] The Employment Act of 1946 was approved February 20, 1946. The Council did not begin to function until the following September.

[56] For a survey of Truman's domestic legislative program and the character of congressional response, see Richard E. Neustadt, "Congress and the Fair Deal: A Legislative Balance Sheet," in the forthcoming Vol. 5 of *Public Policy*, eds. Carl J. Friedrich and J. Kenneth Galbraith (Cambridge, Mass.).

This called for central staff work, continuous effort on a large scale. Where could it be obtained? The OWMR staff had been dispersed, abruptly, at the end of 1946; Steelman, its last Director, had returned to the White House in the new post of Assistant to the President.[57] The Economic Council was then untried, preoccupied, and short on staff, its product showing from the first the strains imposed by step-child status and divergent membership.[58] The White House Staff — the President's Assistant, Special Counsel, and the rest — could guide, review, and interject, but scarcely could engage in all the detailed and continuous endeavors these legislative tasks required.

This left only the Budget Bureau, or some new creation. And at the crucial moment the new Budget Director managed to reorient the Bureau's role anent the Truman White House, thereby giving the President the staff work he required.

By early 1947, Webb had become a principal adviser to the President, a full-fledged member of the Truman team. This built the Budget's entree and Webb made much of it, selling staff services as he sold himself. He broke precedent by making his subordinates freely available to White House aides, on their terms, for their purposes.[59] He cheerfully acceded to several full-time transfers of Budget staff to White House assistantships, thus building bridges which were bound to last.[60] Above all, Webb turned to his machinery for legislative clearance as a prime means of focussing staff efforts to help meet the President's needs. The clearance of proposals and reports had not been sensitive to congressional schedules; it was to become so. The emphasis of central clearance had been negative; it was to be made positive. It had interpreted policies and programs where it found them; it was to help create them. It had relied on Bureau staff resources; it was to draw, instead, on the expanding Executive Office as a whole.

Those were the goals Webb set for central clearance in Truman's time.

[57] OWMR was terminated by presidential action through Executive Order 9809 of December 17, 1946. Some of the factors leading to its demise are discussed in Somers, *op. cit.,* pp. 100–1. Steelman's principal lieutenants had planned to move the core of the whole organization to the White House with him, but they reckoned without his sensitivity to Cabinet and congressional resentment over late-coming, subordinate "empires" in the President's own office, especially after the 1946 election.

[58] Quite apart from the so-called "Nourse-Keyserling dispute," Budget, Treasury, and OWMR each had hoped and planned to assume the staff responsibilities ultimately conferred on the Council. Only the mutual jealousy of these three agencies stalemated executive opposition to the Council's creation. Their grievances did not yield, all at once, to the accomplished fact; and an uncertain performance on the first Economic Report did not enhance the Council's standing with its sister agencies, their heirs and assigns.

[59] The 1947 veto of Taft-Hartley, for example, was preceded by a special White House appraisal undertaken by the Special Counsel at the President's behest, with the fulltime assistance of three Budget staff members whom Webb turned loose entirely, requiring from them neither consultation nor report.

[60] A residual reflection of the then dependence on the Budget, which Webb so strongly aided and abetted in 1947–48, is found in the fact that in 1953 fully a third of the outgoing Truman assistants had come to the White House staff from the career service in the Budget Bureau.

To implement them he relied on a reconstituted Legislative Reference organization, now given status as a sort of institutional Executive Office secretariat for legislative policy development, formally within the Budget Bureau but serving, in effect, as back-up staff to Truman's Special Counsel, then chief White House officer in fields of forward policy.[61] Webb did not delegate all responsibility, nor abdicate all interest, but as a practical matter, Legislative Reference's White House ties became both real and generally respected.

V. The Character of Clearance in Truman's Time

All this involved great changes in the character of clearance at proposed and pending stages. After 1947, the Budget Bureau's war-encouraged passive attitude gave way, perforce, to much activity. A first step was the campaign begun early in 1948 to mesh these clearance actions with congressional requirements, and this despite the opposition character of the then Congress:

> We had found in the immediate post-war years that there were a great many situations in which the . . . clearance process was an annoyance to the Congress and properly so. . . . Consequently [in 1948] . . . Webb . . . specifically charged me with responsibility of talking with the staff directors and clerks of . . . major committees to see if our . . . process could be tied more closely into the committees' desires for the scheduling of items to come before them. On the other side of the coin, I was to acquaint the committees with the issues and items which . . . were being advanced in priority by the President, or . . . major departments. . . .
>
> With the . . . cooperation of the Public Works Committees it was possible for us to work out . . . almost a precise schedule of what [they] wanted . . . and when . . . and . . . then go back and hasten our clearance process.
>
> From the Public Works Committees this same kind of cooperative effort was extended to other . . . committees.[62]

Indeed, this operation steadily expanded; by 1950, the Budget was regularly and informally in touch with both majority and minority staffs of most major legislative committees, having by then a record of successful relations with committee chairmen of both parties.

In 1948, the Bureau also embarked on a wholly new approach to the coordinative aspects of its clearance tasks, subordinating negative protection of President and agencies to positive development and drafting of

[61] F. J. Bailey retired as Assistant Director of the Budget for Legislative Reference after the first session of the 80th Congress in 1947. His place was taken by Elmer B. Staats; in 1949, Staats was succeeded by Roger W. Jones, the present incumbent.

[62] Testimony of Roger W. Jones before the House Select Committee on Lobbying Activities, 81st Congress, 2nd sess. *Hearings Pursuant to H. Res. 298*, Part 10 (Washington, G.P.O., 1950). Note that the current version of Circular A-19 is printed with Jones' testimony.

Administration measures. Executive Office "working teams" came into being with "leadership" assigned to the White House, Budget, or the Economic Council, as the case might be, while Legislative Reference served as secretariat and stimulator of them all. Each unit of the presidential staff contributed its experts and its points of view; all agencies concerned were called on to confer.[63] A high proportion of the Fair Deal's later measures were worked out in detailed form through this new application of "coordination"; for example, the Housing Act of 1949, and the Social Security Act Amendments of 1950.[64] On many lesser proposals, involving fewer agency and private interests, or interests lower in importance to the President, the Budget's Legislative Reference staff led similar excursions on its own, sometimes merely tinkering with agency submissions, sometimes redoing the whole drafting job around the conference table.

This new technique — new, anyway, as an adjunct of central clearance — developed alongside and, in part, grew out of efforts to provide fixed meaning, concrete form, and better advance planning for the President's own legislative program. Toward that end, White House and Budget legislative staffs worked in close combination, after 1947, developing relationships which lent both strength and informality to team play on particulars.

Coinciding with these various endeavors came an external change which gave the clearance system a new dimension and new opportunity. In 1947, congressional committees began to ask Budget for its views on pending bills, at the same time that requests for views were sent to the agencies. These so-called "direct referrals" were an 80th Congress innovation; a means whereby Republican committee chairmen could gauge the intentions of the Democratic Administration. Whatever the initial motive, the practice became increasingly popular with the committees in each succeeding Congress, regardless of party coloration. During the 80th Congress there were 370 of these direct referrals; during the 81st, 974; during the 82nd, 1,102. In the 83rd Congress, there were 889 for the first session alone. Of course, this volume has not stemmed equally from all committees of each House in every Congress. For example, since 1947 the Senate Labor and Welfare Committee has referred nearly all bills to the Budget; not so its House counterpart.[65] Variations have their roots in

[63] After 1949, NSRB, ODM, and DMS staff, and occasionally NSC staff, were also drawn into or given leadership of such Executive Office teams.

[64] Of course, not all proposals were prepared in this way. For example, the so-called "Brannan Plan" was first set forth informally in the shape of "suggestions for study" put to congressional committees in testimony by the then Secretary of Agriculture. Truman's health insurance proposals were never translated into Administration-approved specifics; nor did the Administration ever commit itself to the details of bills introduced in Congress. As for revenue measures, their preparation, for the most part, was — and still is — dominated by the Treasury.

[65] Currently, the committees which engage most frequently in direct referrals are: Senate Interior, Labor, Public Works, Finance, Banking, Commerce, Civil Service, Government Operations; House Agriculture, Commerce, Merchant Marine, Public Works, Government Operations, Civil Service. Source: Office of Legislative Reference,

diverse compounds of committee composition, jurisdiction, clientele. But while they keep the practice less than universal, this has not altered one significant result: the Budget's growing opportunity to register a presidential view directly on a high proportion of the bills considered actively by both houses.

Moreover, since 1949 other direct channels have opened to the Bureau, further enhancing this opportunity. For example, during Truman's second term the Majority Leader of the House and the Democratic chairmen of several Senate and House committees — including the House Rules Committee — acquired the habit of checking with White House or Budget staff (sometimes both), by telephone or special note, for the current Administration stand on bills nearing the reporting stage.[66] Whereever addressed, these inquiries almost always passed through Budget hands; responses, however conveyed, afforded vital supplements to clearance actions and formal reports. While these particulars and others have altered since Eisenhower's accession, comparable avenues continue to link the clearance system not only with congressional committees but with the leadership as well.

Here are alternatives to the traditional approach of central clearance, wholly independent of agency action, and compensating for deficiencies in agency compliance, while naturally increasing the incentive to comply. Progressively, the Bureau has inclined to concentrate its energies upon its own responses and those it readies for White House staff use; these rather than agency reports become the key documents of clearance action at the pending stage. Of course, there have been instances — no doubt there will be more — where Budget's direct answers have reflected its own institutional concerns more nearly than the President's personal designs.[67] But Bureau advice via agency reports has been no less susceptible to such confusions. That problem is generic.

The new spirit of Truman's clearance system affected not only proposed and pending stages, but also operations on enrolled enactments. From 1947 on, the technique of the working team was frequently applied, with varying degrees of informality, to staff evaluation of the major measures passed by Congress and to preparation for the President's own action, especially where vetoes were involved. From time to time, this teamwork at the enrolled stage proved useful in the development of new

Bureau of the Budget. Note that the early adherence of the Senate Labor Committee reflects Senator Taft's own view of the need for a formal channel between President and committees on current measures.

[66] Also in 1949, the Senate Majority Leader arranged to have the Budget report to him the number of each bill cleared and the nature of the clearance given, week by week. These data were then tabulated by his staff for ready reference to Administration stands on the general run of pending bills. So routinized a transmittal of so much information proved of limited utility. After 1950, the practice was curtailed.

[67] A classic example is provided by Budget reports to the Senate Labor Committee on S. 614, the Hospital Construction Act Amendments of 1949. For details see Budget Bureau central files; Enacted Legislation, 81st Congress, *Hospital Construction*, R6–15/48.3.

proposals: alternatives to measures vetoed and additions to bills signed with reservations.[68] In this respect, a positive note was injected into the review of enrolled bills, equivalent in purpose, if not scale, to the new ventures in coordination of proposals and reports.

In Truman's time, work on enrolled enactments came to contribute in another way to policy development. On certain classes of enactments, the President found it possible to make consistency in signature or veto a potent instrument for setting and enforcing general policies. On veterans benefits, his vetoes drew and held a general line; on private immigration bills, his signatures held one last entryway wide open. These things were done despite unceasing protest from affected agencies, a testimonial not only to the President's determination, but to the Budget's constancy in finding counter-arguments to justify his action.

From 1947 to 1950, central clearance progressed vigorously in these various directions. New Budget circulars, while adding nothing to the substance of the old, provided literary — and official — recognition of the changed pace and emphasis.[69] Then in June, 1950 came Korea, and in November, full-scale Chinese intervention. Thereafter, throughout Truman's last two years, the Administration's crucial policy preoccupations were operational, no less than congressional, the legislative focus narrowing, meanwhile, from Fair Deal to defense.

Partial mobilization and limited war had an immediate impact on clearance operations, though the effect was less decisive than in the all-out conflict nine years earlier. During 1951 and 1952, central clearance did not lose its mandate, nor greatly shift its goals; it simply ceased to grow, mirroring thereby the "half-way" character of changes in the governmental climate. With the new Office of Defense Mobilization — nearest equivalent of the old OWMR — the Budget Bureau managed peaceful collaboration in the legislative field, easily adapting pre-existing patterns to the special case of economic controls. Here, by common consent, ODM took the Executive Office "lead," organizing and directing efforts to develop an Administration product, serving thereby as acknowledged "agent" of the central clearance system, and utilizing Budget clearance channels to fortify its interagency coordination.[70]

Aside from "defense production," only "mutual security" — consolidated, defense-packaging of foreign aid — emerged in Truman's final

[68] See, for example, Truman's message to Congress, July 13, 1951, announcing the signature of S. 984, a bill to aid recruitment of Mexican migrant workers, of which the President remarked: "I could not have given my approval had I not been assured . . . that supplementary [measures] would receive prompt attention." Truman then recommended a three-point supplementing program, produced by a staff team after the bill's passage.

[69] See note 4.

[70] The Office of Defense Mobilization was established by Executive Order 10193 on December 15, 1950 within the Executive Office of the President, to exercise direction and control over all aspects of the post-Korean mobilization program. ODM received permanent status through Reorganization Plan 2 of 1953, absorbing the war mobilization planning functions of the National Security Resources Board under the National Security Act of 1947.

years as a major, new legislative venture requiring sustained developmental staff work. And here the Bureau worked out arrangements with the Director for Mutual Security similar to those established with ODM. The Harriman Office took the lead, while Budget staff manipulated clearance channels on its behalf.[71] Otherwise, the Budget's clearance system carried on much as before, though with less emphasis on positive coordination, because there was less presidential need, relying heavily, by way of substitute, upon the store of plans worked out and positions clarified in pre-Korean years. The patterns of staff action and relationship which had emerged by 1950 were, in the main, consolidated during 1951 and 1952. But there was little new adventuring in the high policy arena.

Korea and its consequences were not the only factors responsible for this; there was, as well, the President's acute awareness that the presidency would soon change hands. In 1951, Truman appointed as Budget Director a top Bureau careerist, Frederick J. Lawton, charging him specifically, though not publicly, to batten down the institution, readying it for the transition ahead.[72] There was to be no more expansion in politically-charged directions. The Bureau's reputation for "non-political" expertise, its institutional respectability, were to be guarded at all costs, thereby preserving its utility to the next President.[73]

VI. The First Year Under Eisenhower

On January 20, 1953, the new President took office, his inauguration marking the first complete party turnover in twenty years. Superficially, this had a sweeping impact throughout the government. But paradoxically, perhaps, the Budget clearance system was affected less this time than in the previous transition years of 1945 and 1933; reasserting, not in years but in months, its old role in the new regime.

Why did this occur, and how? Why not the fall into drawn-out obscurity, the slow revival, that characterized both previous occasions? There seem to be three reasons: some relatively careful pre-inauguration planning on both sides; some vital accidents of personal relationship; and, underlying everything, a very real continuum in the outlook for government.

In November, 1952, immediately after Eisenhower's election, Truman took a number of specific steps toward the goal of orderly transition,

---

[71] In June, 1950, Averell Harriman was appointed Special Assistant to the President to coordinate various overseas affairs. Under the Mutual Security Act of 1951, his post was transformed into an Office of the Director for Mutual Security (DMS), within the Executive Office of the President. DMS was abolished by Reorganization Plan 7 of 1953 and its functions transferred to the Foreign Operations Administration.

[72] Lawton had been a senior Bureau official since 1935, number-three man under Webb, number-two man under Webb's successor, Frank Pace, Jr. He is serving presently as a member of the Civil Service Commission.

[73] It is an interesting sidelight on the longevity of Truman's concern for a smooth transition that a number of the preparatory actions Lawton took, both before and after the 1952 election, corresponded with arrangements planned by Webb on a "contingent" basis during the summer of 1948.

among them an invitation to the President-elect to have his representative participate as an observer in final preparation of the forthcoming (Truman) budget. During the nine weeks before inauguration, Eisenhower's Budget Director-designate, Joseph M. Dodge, worked full time in the Budget Bureau, conducting himself with great discretion, watching the staff at work, learning their problems and routines, winning their confidence as they gained his respect.[74]

Once installed in office, Dodge emerged as a strong member of the new inner circle. His influence, the value of his services, and his ability to act were enhanced, no doubt, by his acceptance, hence effective leadership, of the established staff at his disposal. This set the stage for firm and confident assertion of Budget Bureau functions in the new regime, central clearance no less than the rest. Even before Inauguration Day, most of the Cabinet members-designate were called into the Bureau for Dodge-sponsored indoctrination lectures on its prerogatives and their responsibilities. Clearance regulations received attention at that time. And after the inaugural, Dodge made a point of picking up initial failures to comply, taking a strong line with department heads, reminiscent of Lord's language thirty years before.

The new Budget Director did one thing more for central clearance: to his hold-over chief of Legislative Reference he gave the backing of his own unqualified endorsement, and a total delegation of authority surpassing anything experienced in Truman's time. Between these two men, Dodge and Jones, evolved a personal relationship of greatest moment for clearance's survival. Dodge used his own prestige unsparingly to break a path for Jones into the Eisenhower White House, overcoming tendencies to treat careerists with extreme reserve. He then cut Legislative Reference entirely loose to seek its lead from presidential staff, thus extending under Eisenhower an innovation Webb had introduced in Truman's first term.

It was one thing to open an acquaintance between White House and Legislative Reference; quite another to establish adequate patterns of staff interaction. The Budget's clearance operations were dependent, now more than ever, on guidance from the President and access to him, by and through his White House aides. All the well-worn Truman channels were erased; they had to be rebuilt from scratch around another President, new aides, new methods. That this was done in less than six months' time, as *Fortune* attests, is tribute partly to the sheer inescapability of so much of the matter grinding through the clearance mill. And partly it is tribute to the personality equation, once again: to Jones' success in work-

[74] Dodge was not precisely a newcomer to government, having organized War Department renegotiation activities in World War II and having carried out significant overseas assignments for the occupation authorities of both Germany and Japan. His attitude toward his new role was very healthy for the institution he would head, fairly free of the suspicion and uncertainty which plagued so many Eisenhower appointees and their career subordinates. Dodge resigned as Budget Director, April 15, 1954, and was succeeded by his deputy, Rowland Hughes. For information on this and other aspects of the 1953 transition, the writer is indebted to the many officials throughout the Executive Office who have answered his inquiries with candor and good will.

ing with the three key legislative policy officials in Eisenhower's entourage — Adams, Persons, and Shanley.[75]

Reinforcing these relationships were some deep strains of continuity in government's most basic problems. Only on the surface was transition sharp and sudden. There was neither 1945's dramatic plunge from total war to general peace, nor 1933's wholesale experimenting with new rules for the governmental game. True, by 1953 the emergency impacts of Korea were diminishing, economically, psychologically, militarily. The cold war was entering a new phase, the atomic arms race a new dimension, the American economy a new adjustment. But these remained the underlying problems, whatever their changed aspects, with the new President, no less than the old, pledged to collective security and full employment as goals of governmental action. And as the operating crisis faded, policy-making tended to resume its pre-Korean cast.

The new regime brought many alterations of detail, quick shifts of attitude, emphasis, approach, which in the longer course of time may prove profound. But in 1953, at least, the real conditions and commitments — and dilemmas — overhanging from the past left little room for sweeping change, save on the planes of people and "psychology." Particularly was this the case for a regime so "new" as Eisenhower's. The President was new to national politics and civil government, his Cabinet members mostly newer still, his congressional colleagues wholly unused to a Republican Executive. His campaign for election had been influenced by concepts and illusions bred of opposition; some basic a-b-c's had to be learned anew.

Combined with this inexperience, the continuity of problems confronted the new White House with two needs, sharply felt: the need for facts about the past to help project decisions for the future, and the need for caution in commitments until homework had been done. The Budget clearance system proved a handy instrument in both instances. Once the ice was broken, the White House staff, however much mistrusting bureaucrats in general — holdovers schooled for twenty years in Democratic policies — could turn to Budget's, in particular, to tap resources of careerist expertise through clearance channels everywhere in government.[76] Simultaneously, the White House could obtain from central clearance a series of continuing protections for presidential freedom

[75] Under Eisenhower, Sherman Adams, the Assistant to the President, has a formal, though not always operative, role in the coordination and direction of all White House staff undertakings. Wilton B. Persons, now Adams' deputy, had major responsibility for congressional liaison during Eisenhower's first year and is still heavily involved in legislative affairs. Bernard Shanley, Special Counsel to the President, acquired during 1953 a good share of his predecessors' tasks in policy development, especially on the legislative side, resuming, among other things, the Counsel's old role as regular channel between Budget and President on enrolled enactments and other clearance actions.

[76] The legislative clearance system was not, of course, the only means employed. The National Security Council Staff — especially the old Senior Staff reconstituted as the Planning Board — contributed importantly in some major areas. Certain of the presidential and agency study groups, among the many operating in 1953, helped also to build effective links between the new regime and its inherited experts; notably in the government organization, psychological warfare, social security, and housing fields.

to withhold decision. The congressional session of 1953 was a time for ducking and dodging on a wide range of legislative issues, while study groups studied and administrators felt their way.[77] As legislative clearance had once helped protect F.D.R.'s own choice of action, it now helped safeguard Eisenhower's choices of inaction.

The gathering of background facts, the sidestepping of new commitments, were the services commending central clearance to the White House staff in early 1953; initially the clearance system's *raison d'être* in the new regime. The fact that budget-cutting was one measure *not* deferred that year, soon gave the system added opportunities for service, harking back to purposes three decades old. And when, in August, 1953, the Eisenhower White House faced its first end-of-session flood of enrolled bills, its dependence on Budget aid — and Budget staff's dependability — was demonstrated forcefully, with due effect.

Thus, by midsummer, 1953, it was quite evident that legislative clearance would survive, remaining a close institutional adjunct of the White House staff, retaining a real role in the presidential orbit. But what kind of role, of what significance? The scope and character of Truman's clearance system evolved out of the drive to build a comprehensive legislative program, buttressed by specific measures bearing an Administration label. Nothing of the sort occurred while Congress was in session during 1953. And though the Truman forms remained, the substance of the clearance job, that session, bore less resemblance to postwar operations than to the narrower, more limited approach of Roosevelt's early years — or even, in some aspects, Coolidge's. "The key to this whole operation," remarked a Budget aide, "is whether Ike decides to have a legislative program. We can't interpret, much less help develop, something that isn't there."

In the event, that decision was emphatically affirmative, as demonstrated by the stream of presidential messages when Congress reconvened in January, 1954, and by the prompt introduction of Administration bills to carry out most Eisenhower proposals.[78] Thereby central clearance gained the last element required for a new start on its postwar course.

This did not bring full restoration of all Truman methods; naturally, there have been adaptations as to ways and means. However, most of the changes made in 1953 and early 1954 relate to a phenomenon which may prove transitory: the imperfect acquaintance, trust, relationship between

---

[77] Note that Eisenhower's inaugural marked the first change of party in the executive under the so-called "Lame Duck" Amendment; the new President was inaugurated only ten weeks after his election; the new Congress was in regular session two weeks before Inauguration Day.

[78] It has been the custom during 1954 for the White House to disavow Administration "sponsorship" of measures introduced by committee chairmen or other senior members after congressional receipt of presidential recommendations. But in the great majority of cases, as almost any *New York Times* account will show, these bills actually represent departmental drafts, conveyed with the Administration's blessing to competent authorities in Congress. This is the same route previously taken by most Truman "must" measures, which seldom traveled straight from White House to Congress. In all such cases, denials of Administration sponsorship are merely exercises in semantics, sometimes accepted at face value by the press, rarely, if ever, by congressmen, though giving all concerned a useful "out" for future reference.

the new principals and old staffs. No two departments are alike in this, but its effects are widespread still. Hence, much of the informal, day-by-day coordination once carried on through departmental bureaucrats is being handled by the Budget now — no less informally — through "little cabinet" officers or department heads themselves. Much of the developmental effort on main measures, once farmed out to staff-level working teams, now turns on full-dress departmental presentations to the Cabinet, dry-run for White House and Budget staffs well in advance; with essentials of agreement at the Cabinet table providing, then, the base for formal interagency accord through clearance channels. Even where something like a "Truman" working team has been employed — as with Taft-Hartley changes, for example — its membership has comprised principals rather than staff, save at the White House level.

It is too soon, of course, to be definitive about the Eisenhower pattern. As this is written — in the spring of 1954 — many things remain unsettled and unsure. To cite just one example, there has not been, so far, a single Eisenhower veto of the disciplinary, attention-calling kind which lent its sting to clearances in Roosevelt's time and Truman's.[79] But if one thing is certain, it is this: the pre-existing patterns show a hardy tendency to reassert themselves in Eisenhower's present circumstances.

VII. THE CIRCUMSTANCES OF SURVIVAL

For more than thirty years now, central clearance has persisted, its history marked by a long series of "accidental," unforeseen accretions. Nothing once absorbed has been wholly displaced; each new element somehow encompasses the old. There have been periods of relative stability, if not stagnation; times of obscurity, even decline. But overall, here is a record of great growth, successful adaptation — this under six successive Presidents, through every variation in national and governmental circumstances since Harding's term of office.

What contributes to this continuity? What explains this institutional survival and advance, particularly in the years since F.D.R. cut clearance loose from its "financial" moorings? There is no answer in the statute books; no law prescribes this system. There is no guide in partisan commitments; one finds no platform planks or campaign speeches, pro or con. As for old presidential orders on the subject, the signatures of Roosevelt, Truman, Smith, and Webb are not, *per se,* coin of the realm today. The explanation lies in many things, but in these least of all.

Part of the answer can be drawn directly from events recorded in this paper. Note the impact of personalities, among them Roosevelt himself, Webb, Dodge, Bailey, Jones. Their interactions helped to mold — and to sustain — the modern clearance system. Note also the close correspondence of that system's varied fortunes, since 1933, to shifting presidential policy preoccupations in an era of "big government," successive national emergencies, and changeable White House political prestige. It is not sheer

---

[79] This is not to say that the President subscribes to a Whig theory of the veto power. Staff aides contend otherwise and the evidence is not yet in.

happenstance that central clearance was but temporarily obscured by operational crises in depression and war; or that its greatest institutional expansions followed the political events of 1938 and 1946; or that its postwar growth, while checked by the Korean outbreak, seems to be resuming in Korea's aftermath, despite the change of Administration.

Note, finally, the clearance system's formal locale in the Budget Bureau, a fact of real significance for continuity and for survival. Here is the oldest, toughest organism in the presidential orbit. The making of the budget is still the prime general-purpose, decision-and-action-forcing process yet institutionalized in the executive. The budget process, as it stands, is so firmly a fact of governmental life, so thoroughly assimilated in legislative and administrative practice and expectation, that its continuation goes unquestioned; its institutional embodiment, "The Budget," commanding everywhere a healthy measure of respect, if not always regard. Perhaps, as students now are fond of pointing out, the Bureau is by no means the ideal locale — not, anyway, in theory — for policy staff work on the substantive side.[80] And yet, in practice, nothing is so vulnerable as the high policy performer dangling loose, a ready target and potential sacrifice at every turn in presidential circumstance (e.g., NEC, OWMR). The more immediate the clearance system's policy involvement, the more advantageous, at least for survival, its impersonal exterior, its undescriptive designation, its "budgetary" context.

Theoretically, perhaps, the combination of effective personal relationships, continuing White House requirements, and stable staff resources should suffice to explain survival of a presidential mechanism aimed at administrative agencies. So might it be, were Presidents, in fact, "administrators" of some neatly unified executive. But they are not; instead, the White House looks out on:

> . . . a protean agglomeration of feudalities that overlap and crisscross in an almost continual succession of changes. Some of the lines of control . . . terminate in the Presidency, some in . . . the legislature and some . . . 'outside' the government; a few lie in the hands of 'subordinate' executives; many more involve all of these in collegial arrangements so informal as to be but dimly recognized even by the chief participants.[81]

This is the context in which "central" clearance actually operates; its very terminology a contradiction of the feudal order. How then does it survive?

It lasts because most of the wielders of real power in this wilderness find in it net advantage to themselves. Of course, the agency secure in a strong "horizontal" power complex — buttressed by potent clientele and purposeful congressional committees — may have but little tolerance for clear-

---

80 For examples, see Somers, *op. cit.*, pp. 213 ff., Norton Long, "Popular Support for Economic Programs," *American Political Science Review*, Vol. 42, pp. 326–36 (April, 1948); Arthur Maass, "In Accord with the Program of the President?" in *Public Policy*, eds. Carl J. Friedrich and J. Kenneth Galbraith (Cambridge, Mass., 1953), Vol. 4, pp. 77–93.

81 David B. Truman, *The Governmental Process* (New York, 1951), pp. 437–38.

ance of its pet proposals. But every agency is not a Corps of Engineers; few, if any, are so "favorably" situated all the time. Most measures of most agencies face an uncertain future in the legislative process. Whatever clearance brings by way of support, even acquiescence, from President and Budget Bureau, from other agencies and, implicitly, their clientele, may help to reduce hazards, strengthen prospects in the Congress. Of course, advance accommodation is the purchase price. Whether to pay or not to pay involves a complex, variable estimate of cost and return, power and position, which bureaucrats must calculate afresh in every case. This does not produce absolute adherence to either the form or the spirit of clearance regulations; it does, at least, give most agency officials a real, long-term stake in the system's survival. And that is reinforced, for every agency, by virtue of the chances clearance brings to sit in judgment on the other fellow's viewpoints and designs.

As for senators and congressmen, they may show small concern for clearance niceties when potent sponsors or committees seize hold of an issue strongly backed by tough and vocal interests stimulating wide support. One thinks of Taft-Hartley, for example, or the McCarran Acts, or the Bricker Amendment. But Congress moves, perforce, on many measures of a very different character: on those the President stakes out for his own, and on a host of others which are neither "musts" for Presidents nor irresistibly appealing to members *en masse*. On the bulk of this business, overburdened legislators, in committee and out, need a handy criterion for choice of measures to take up, especially when faced with technical alternatives in which they have but little vested interest. They need, as well, an inkling of Administration attitude toward the outcome: how much, if at all, does the President care? What will he stand for when the bill comes down? What will he do thereafter, by way of budgetary follow-through? And save when they themselves choose otherwise, congressional committees need some measure of defense against time-wasting or discreditable cat-and-dog fights on their premises among the agencies concerned in pending bills. These services the clearance system can provide; that Congress wants them as a matter of practical self-interest is demonstrated by committee and leadership initiation of the direct referrals and other links to Budget now so integral a part of clearance operations.[82]

Naturally congressmen, like bureaucrats, incline to weigh the relative advantages of heeding or ignoring clearance actions, case by case. Particular results have varied greatly from issue to issue, from committee to committee, and even among personalities and between the Houses. But there

[82] Another service merits passing mention: favorable clearance gives a sponsor opportunities to wrap his project in the "presidential" mantle; unfavorable clearance lets him rise to defend Congress and the public interest — and his bill — against executive blundering or "interference." Each tactic has its uses in the legislative struggle; each may bring members and their measures within reach of the publicity inherent in the presidential office. For a recent illustration, see the press treatment of sponsors' complaints against an apparently adverse Budget report on several House bills depriving Alger Hiss of retirement benefits. *New York Times*, June 23–25, 1954.

can be few members who have not found some clearance actions to their taste, few legislative leaders or committee chairmen who have not seen some disregarded clearance warning rise to haunt them in a veto message or a bobtailed budget. Again, this does not make for uniform responses to the terms of clearance; it is productive, though, of genuine concern for the system's survival.

For all these reasons, the "feudalities" at both ends of the Avenue have found that it pays to tolerate the clearance system. They have, indeed, found it quite possible to do so without yielding to the President their underlying freedom to maneuver. Yet simultaneously the President, while also husbanding his liberty to move, has found in clearance means to make these gentry heedful of his powers when they exercise their own. The vitality of central clearance lies in the fact that it can satisfy, at once, both these conditions. The President, as he may choose, gains ample opportunities to make known his desires. But Congress and the agencies are not compelled to notice. And he, meanwhile, retains the right to alter course, or change his mind. The voice that speaks is not the President's; it is the Budget Bureau's. And when need be, the Budget serves as whipping-boy.

This is a neat arrangement; it helps preserve the enterprise. But it can do that only so long as the distinction remains more fiction than fact. Were there to be a demonstration, generally and over time, that Budget really spoke not for the President but for itself alone, then the whole game would lose its point and the participants soon cease to play. Here one is brought to a new set of questions: What is the "program of the President" that Budget claims to interpret in clearance actions? Does such a thing exist and if so how is it constructed, and by whom? These questions lie outside the scope of this paper, but they can serve, perhaps, as curtain-raisers for another study.

Presidential Leadership: The Inner Circle and Institutionalization

Lester G. Seligman

One of the significant trends of the past two decades is the development of the President's staff as an institution. "From a purely staff service it is

Reprinted by permission from the *Journal of Politics*, Vol. 18 (1956), pp. 410–426.

fast developing into an agency that also formulates and coordinates policies at the highest level." [1] The White House staff now employs 389 people. Since 1939 this immediate headquarters of the President's activities has been ringed by the Executive Office of the President. In the latter are now included the Bureau of the Budget, the National Security Resources Board, the Economic Adviser, the National Security Council, and the Office of Defense Mobilization. [2]

Each of these aforementioned agencies in the Executive Office of the President has been created by law and now constitutes an institutionalized part of the President's apparatus. [3] One of the principal functions of Presidential agencies is the formulation of plans and policies for executive action. In the first two terms of Franklin D. Roosevelt's administration the most pressing problems dealt with economic recovery and reform policies. When Roosevelt assumed office in 1933, there existed no staff agencies to supply advice to the President. As we shall more fully elaborate, Roosevelt relied upon his closest informal advisers to fill this need. Thirteen years later, in 1946, Congress enacted the Full Employment Act which expressed a new and historic commitment on the part of the federal government to the maintenance of full employment and economic stability. Under the provisions of that act, a new agency was created, the Council of Economic Advisers. [4] The CEA was by statute placed in the Executive Office of the President in order to fulfill the legislative intent that it serve as the President's staff of expert economic advice.

The Full Employment Act, both in its objectives and the organizational means it prescribed, attempted significant institutionalizations in the American government. This paper is concerned with the question of the relation among members of the President's (Roosevelt) inner circle of economic advisers, their rôle and activities as instruments of Presidential leadership, and the attempted institutionalizations prescribed by the Full Employment Act. What clues do developments in this specific area offer to the larger problems of the growth and development of institutionalized expectation of leadership? What are the motivations and purposes of Congressional attempts to formalize executive leadership? What is the effect of attempted formalization of the President's staff on the President? Finally, there is a broad question to which this paper is related. What is

[1] Clinton L. Rossiter, "The Constitutional Significance of the Executive Office of the President," *The American Political Science Review*, XLIII, No. 6 (December, 1949), 1214.

[2] For an historical review of the development of the executive office of the President, see Joseph P. Harris, "The Future of Administrative Management," in Leonard D. White, ed., *The Future of Government in the United States* (Chicago: The University of Chicago Press, 1942), and Fritz Morstein Marx, *The President and His Staff Services* (Chicago: Public Administration Service, 1947).

[3] It is fair to suggest parenthetically that the emergence of this large Presidential staff coupled with the general growth in executive agencies, may have made Presidential leadership less a personal entity than a corporate product.

[4] Hereinafter referred to as the CEA.

the relationship between political leadership and policy and administrative changes? [5]

I. The President's Inner Circle

Personal organizations surrounding positions of leadership are characteristic of executive leadership. A group of loyal personal aides who are incorporated into or retained alongside the formal organization [6] are characteristic of executive positions in many large-scale organizations. In the case of the President such a development is also apparent. Every President has had his inner circle of advisers and aides.[7] Sometimes called "kitchen cabinets," "tennis cabinets," or "inner circles," these are Presidential intimates whom the President treats not only as friends but as aides in fulfilling his many rôles. Among our recent Presidents such inner circles have assumed greater political and administrative significance.

What are the factors in the institutional conditions of the Presidency that make such inner circles necessary? Our modern Presidents have discovered that the formal organization of the executive is only apparently hierarchial. Cabinet members tend to pursue their own policies. Bureau chiefs tend to guard jealously their independence of action. "Left to himself, even the top executive, in the imposing plenitude of his directive power, may have the ugly feeling of perching atop an angry elephant firmly set to have things his own way." [8]

The President, not only in his relations with cabinet heads, but also in his relationship to Congress, his party, and interest groups, has no guaranteed support. The absence of institutional support forces the President to rely on negotiation and manipulation in order to gain his ends. It has been said that our system is unique in isolating the President.[9] This results in making his a bargaining relationship with other policy contestants. In this setting of fragile institutional support, the President's intimate advisers play a specialized rôle. As Pendleton Herring has stated, "Lacking the sanction of institutional controls or the stimulus of a party creed,

---

[5] See my "The Study of Political Leadership," *The American Political Science Review*, XLIV, No. 4 (December, 1950), 904–915.

[6] See David Cushman Coyle, for a discussion of inner circles around executive positions, in Albert Lepawsky's *Administration; The Art and Science of Organization and Management* (New York: Alfred A. Knopf, 1949), p. 317; and Roberto Michels' *First Lectures in Political Sociology*, tr. by Alfred de Grazia (Minneapolis: University of Minnesota Press, 1949), pp. 129–130.

[7] Data on the historical rôle of White House intimates are to be found in *The Intimate Papers of Colonel House*, arranged as a narrative by Charles Seymour (New York: Houghton Mifflin Company, 1926); Joseph P. Tumulty, *Woodrow Wilson As I Know Him* (Garden City: Doubleday, Page & Company, 1921); *Taft and Roosevelt: The Intimate Letters of Archie Butt, Military Aide*, Vols. I, II (Garden City: Doubleday, Doran & Company, Inc., 1930).

[8] Fritz Morstein Marx, ed., *Elements of Public Administration* (New York: Prentice-Hall, Inc., 1946), p. 301. The chapter on informal organization is perceptive.

[9] Woodrow Wilson, *The President of the United States* (New York: Harper & Brothers, 1916), p. 39.

we are thrown back upon the politics of persuasion and manipulation. . . . The formulation of a program has been left to the president and his informal advisers." [10]

Members of the President's inner circle play a number of functional rôles.[11] At times they are buffers to absorb pressures which the President must avoid or divert. Some serve as catalysts to expedite administrative or political action when it is in danger of being bogged down by resistances of various kinds. They are liaison men and fixers with the press, Congressmen, administrators, party leaders, doing the "cementing" job of negotiation and discussion for the President. They are "needlers" who, acting for the President, may expedite action at key points where bureaucratic resistance threatens. Others serve as communication experts in preparing drafts of Presidential addresses, handling relations with the mass media. They are policy-advisers and experts supplying data, advice, criticism, and suggestion for overall policy-thinking. They are sometimes ideologists, whose task it is to intellectualize the policies of the President.

This unique rôle of an inner circle or kitchen cabinet is hence a necessary part of Presidential leadership. Though its members are highly expendable, the group as such is indispensable to the President. As we shall observe, the very nature of their work on the firing line as buffers and shock troops to the President makes them highly vulnerable to attack and criticism. The political mortality rate in such positions is very high.[12] Changes in political alignments in the electorate and in Washington; changes in political, economic and social conditions at home and abroad; any and all of these affect the status of members of the inner circle. This, briefly sketched, is the setting of the Presidency and its inner circle.

II. Roosevelt's Inner Circle as Economic Advisers

Even before Roosevelt's nomination in 1932, he had selected a group of experts to advise him in various areas of public policy. This group, of whom a good number were academic people, included Raymond Moley, Rex Tugwell, A. A. Berle, Jr., S. Rosenman, Hugh Johnson, among others. It was the task of this "brain trust" to enlighten Roosevelt on matters of urgent national policy.[13] After Roosevelt's nomination they continued to give him active assistance, as, for example, in the prepara-

---

[10] Pendleton Herring, *Presidential Leadership: The Political Relations of Congress and the Chief Executive* (New York: Rinehart & Company, Inc., 1940), p. 24.

[11] The categories that follow can refer to collective rôles performed by the inner circle *as a whole,* as well as to the rôles of individual members.

[12] On this point see Raymond Moley, *After Seven Years* (New York: Harper & Brothers, 1939), p. 166.

[13] See Moley, *op. cit.,* p. 55; Rexford Guy Tugwell, *The Stricken Land: The Story of Puerto Rico* (Garden City: Doubleday & Company, Inc., 1947), p. 3 *et passim;* R. G. Tugwell, "The Preparation of a President," *The Western Political Quarterly,* I, No. 2 (June, 1948), 131–137; Gerald White Johnson, *Roosevelt: Dictator or Democrat?* (New York: Harper & Brothers, 1941), pp. 165–187; Ernest K. Lindley, *The Roosevelt Revolution: First Phase* (New York: The Viking Press, 1933), p. 24 *et passim.*

tion of campaign addresses in 1932. Roosevelt also consulted with them on national policy problems which he would have to face upon his assumption of office.

After Roosevelt's inauguration in March, 1933, he chose to disband the group as a structured unit,[14] while he assigned to many of its members formal positions in top administrative positions, where they could continue to serve as policy advisers. Much of the legislation of the early New Deal — NRA, CCC, AAA, FERA, and PWA — has been attributed in good part to the influence of this "brain trust." [15]

In the years 1935–37 the composition of Roosevelt's inner circle changed. Moley, Tugwell, and Hugh Johnson were replaced by Hopkins, Ickes, Cohen, Corcoran, Robert Jackson, Leon Henderson, Laughlin Currie, and others. The "shift to the left" in New Deal economic policy has been attributed to this change.[16] The "soak the rich" tax in 1935, the Public Utility Holding Company Act, and the Fair Labor Standards Act and the growing anti-monopoly orientation of New Deal are traceable to the influence of advisers in this circle. In 1937–38 a business recession occurred. Roosevelt was undecided as to whether to retrench government expenditures, as some advised, or to pursue a line of increased government expenditures to compensate for declining private expenditures.[17] It is the latter view, counseled by members of the inner circle, that prevailed. While a full and precise account of the influence of the President's advisers is difficult, all the evidence indicates that the main lines of economic policy, as well as many specific policies, were distilled through the inner circle.[18]

This being the case, when matters involving post-war planning for a peacetime economy came to the fore in Congress, it was inevitable that the experience between 1933 and 1940 would be borne in mind. The ac-

[14] Samuel I. Rosenman advised against this action, contending that the group should retain its informal, non-official status. See his *Working with Roosevelt* (New York: Harper & Brothers, 1952), pp. 87–88.

[15] The rôle of the brain trust and early New Deal legislation is described in the following: Moley, *op. cit.*, Chapters V, VI, VIII, IX; Frances Perkins, *The Roosevelt I Knew* (New York: The Viking Press, 1946), Chapter XVII; Rosenman, *op. cit.*, Chapter V; Johnson, *op. cit.*, pp. 165–187.

[16] See Eric F. Goldman, *Rendezvous with Destiny* (New York: Alfred A. Knopf, 1952), pp. 363–367. Edgar Eugene Robinson, *Roosevelt Leadership, 1933–1945* (New York: Lippincott, 1955), distorts the rôle of the inner circle to the point where it appears like a conspiratorial cabal.

[17] Joseph Wright Alsop and Robert Kintner, *Men Around the President* (New York: Doubleday Doran, 1939), pp. 119–195; Goldman, *op. cit.*, pp. 363–367.

[18] The rôle of the inner circle in shaping various policies is described in Robert Sherwood, *Roosevelt and Hopkins: An Intimate History* (New York: Harper & Brothers, 1948), *passim;* volume I of the Ickes diaries, *The First Thousand Days, 1933–1936* (New York: Simon and Schuster, 1954), *passim,* is invaluable. The rôle of the inner circle in the Supreme Court Packing Plan is described by Joseph Wright Alsop and Turner Catledge in *168 Days* (New York: Doubleday Doran, 1938) and in Wages Hours Legislation by James MacGregor Burns, *Congress on Trial: the Legislative Process and the Administrative State* (New York: Harper & Brothers, 1949), pp. 68–82.

tivities of the President's inner circle and the public attitude toward them thus figured significantly in the Congressional deliberations over the Full Employment Act of 1946 and its administrative provision.

III. FDR's INNER CIRCLE IN THE CONSIDERATION OF THE FULL EMPLOYMENT ACT

The guidance and direction Roosevelt and his circle gave to domestic economic policy since 1933 bore fruit in considerations of the Full Employment Act of 1946. This act expressed an historic governmental commitment in principle toward the maintenance of full employment.

> The Congress hereby declares that it is the continuing policy and responsibility of the Federal Government to use all practicable means consistent with its needs and obligations and other essential considerations of national policy . . . to coordinate and utilize all its plans, functions, and resources for the purpose of creating and maintaining . . . conditions under which there will be afforded useful employment opportunities . . . and to promote maximum employment, production, and purchasing power.[19]

The provisions of this statute established a Council of Advisers to the President to consist of three professional economists.

In the Senate version of the act, sponsored by Senator Murray, little provision was made for the creation of a special staff agency to assist in the preparation of diagnoses and recommendations for the President and Congress. The Murray bill called for the preparation of a National Budget and a program for balancing aggregate investment and spending with full employment needs. It suggested that plans be formulated "under the general direction and supervision of the President, and in consultation with the members of his Cabinet and other heads of departments and establishments." [20] Others (minority members) of the Committee saw the necessity of fixing responsibility for staff work in some specific agency like "an Office of the Director of the National Budget . . . and not by an anonymous group of economic planners." [21]

The House version of the bill was more definite in recommending a permanent, identifiable, and professional staff to carry out the research task. More than one witness in the House argued for such formal organization.[22] The opposition to an ambiguously defined staff responsible was clearly expressed in the testimony of George Terborgh, a former govern-

[19] Public Law 304, 79th Congress, 2d session, Chapter 33 (S380), Sec. 2.
[20] Edwin G. Nourse, *Economics in the Public Service: Administrative Aspects of the Employment Act* (New York: Harcourt, Brace and Company, 1953), p. 71.
[21] *Ibid.*
[22] The various proposals are to be found in Stephen Kemp Bailey's *Congress Makes a Law: The Story Behind the Employment Act of 1946* (New York: Columbia University Press, 1950), Chapter VIII; Edward Henry Hobbs, *Behind the President: a Study of Executive Office Agencies* (Washington: Public Affairs Press, 1954), pp. 94–96.

ment economist, who represented the Machinery and Allied Products Institute. Terborgh argued for the creation of a national economic commission.

> We believe that an official commission of this character, insulated so far as possible from political pressure, and commanding the attention and respect of the Nation, can make an invaluable contribution to public understanding of the complex and difficult art of economic stabilization, and can have a most salutary influence on public policy, now too often dominated, in the absence of popular comprehension of the problems involved, by the self-seeking demands of minority pressure groups, and by the opinions and philosophies of a changing coterie of Presidential advisers, operating in the obscurity of the Executive Offices.[23]

Earlier Terborgh stated

> . . . Both the economic analysis and the economic policy may be prepared and promoted by men unknown to the public, whose appointment has not been confirmed by Congress, and who have no formal public responsibility. This set-up invites behind-the-scenes manipulation by Presidential advisers of the moment, possessed, it may be, both by a passion for anonymity and a passion for controlling national economic policy. However able and high-minded these advisers may be, the arrangement is bad. If the Federal Government is really serious about developing and implementing a full-employment policy — as it should be — it ought to make better organizational provision than is made in this bill.[24]

According to Stephen Bailey, the view expressed in this testimony became an influential idea in the discussion of the bill culminating in the final decision to establish a permanent staff agency of professional economists.[25] Clearly, the argument for a specific, formal, statutory staff agency was designed *to prevent* the assignment of this function to the President's circle of personal advisers.[26]

Even the proponents of the bill argued that had Roosevelt been equipped with such a group of top professional economists as advisers, he might have avoided some errors in economic prognosis and policy. Thus, Henry Wallace testified before the House Committee: "I think it would have been a very great help to both President Hoover and President Roosevelt, and to the Congress, and to the country, if both of them had been under the necessity of complying with the processes of a bill like this. . . . If an economist, continuously working on this kind of a prob-

---

23 *Full Employment Act of 1945*, Hearings before the Committee on Expenditures in the Executive Departments, House of Representatives, Seventy-ninth Congress, first session on H.R. 2202, October 23, 1945 (Washington: Government Printing Office, 1945), p. 613.

24 *Ibid.*, pp. 612–613.

25 Bailey, *op. cit.*, p. 166; Nourse concurs that Terborgh's testimony was very influential in the final recommendations of the committee. See Nourse, *op. cit.*, p. 72.

26 Hearings, *op. cit.*, pp. 612–613.

lem could have been at President Roosevelt's elbow, he could have saved him from making such an unduly optimistic statement, perhaps,[27] in the fall of 1936." [28]

One of the drafts of the House bill that Representative Whittington prepared would have made the Council of Economic Advisers a completely independent agency in the Executive Branch. Fred Vinson, then head of OWMR, pointed out that such a provision would have prevented the President from assuming leadership in matters of economic policy.[29]

The bill as finally enacted incorporated the House of Representatives provision for a professional staff, to be called the Council of Economic Advisers and lodged in the Executive Office of the President. It was the first Congressional law to locate a statutory agency within the Executive Office of the President.[30] The bill specified that the Council must be composed of persons "who, as a result of . . . training, experience, and attainments, [are] exceptionally qualified to analyze and interpret economic developments, to appraise programs and activities of the Government in the light of the policy declared in section 2, and to formulate and recommend national economic policy to promote employment, production, and purchasing power under free competitive enterprise." [31] The bill further provided that council members were to be of high professional competence. The council was also to include a small but highly qualified staff to draw upon the work of professional economists throughout the government and outside.[32] The council was to be solely responsible to the President, but Congress was to set up a Joint Committee to consider its recommendations. Two new departures are noteworthy. First, this was the first Congressional law to locate a statutory agency specifically within the Executive Office of the President. Second, the Congress, by requiring Senatorial approval of all council members, departed from the precedent set when in setting up the positions of Director and Assistant Director of the Bureau of the Budget, it did not require Senatorial confirmation.[33]

IV. The Dual Significance of the Development

Thus, Congress intended that the economic advisory function which had been primarily performed by Roosevelt's inner circle should be performed by a statutory body of professional experts with prime responsibility to the President and co-ordinate responsibilities to Congress. Viewed as an historical development, this attempt at institutionalization of a function

---

[27] The reference is to Roosevelt's predictions of continuous prosperity in 1936, that were proved erroneous with the onset of the recession of 1937.

[28] Hearings, *op. cit.*, p. 849.

[29] Bailey, *op. cit.*, p. 170.

[30] Nourse, *op. cit.*, pp. 74–75.

[31] Public Law 304, *op. cit.*, Sec. 4 (a).

[32] *Ibid.*

[33] W. Coy, "Basic Problems," *The American Political Science Review*, XL, No. 6 (December, 1946), 1124–1136; Hobbs, *op. cit.*, p. 104.

hitherto residing primarily with an informal group of Presidential advisers is of considerable significance.

As a formal recognition that, in matters of economic policy, leadership was to be expected from the President, the Full Employment Act *reflects a confirmation of the leadership of President Roosevelt.* The President's leadership in economic policy was thus made an institutional feature of his office. A new and permanent expectation of Presidential leadership by Congress and the public was indicated. What was once largely a Presidential innovation was given statutory legitimacy by this act. A Roosevelt "initiative" became an established objective of policy-making. There is here expressed a consistent progression from Presidential initiative (or leadership) to institutionalization.[34]

On the other hand, there was another motive indicated in the considerations of the act. This motive was to *limit, restrict, and contain the President's leadership.* Those who advocated a staff of professional economists and insisted upon its relative independence and statutory definition were expressing an intention that the agency be beholden to Congress. On one occasion, a principal proponent of the Senate bill, Senator O'Mahoney of Wyoming, stated on the floor of the Senate: "Mr. President, this is a bill to vest in Congress the power and the responsibility of meeting the issue, instead of continually delegating the power to the executive branch of the government. This, Mr. President, is a bill to restore the functions of Congress." [35] These provisions made it evident that there was a Congressional view that strongly reacted to the galaxy of "invisible advisers," inner circles, and brain trusters, whose ideas were regarded as unorthodox, if not dangerous. The Act in this sense was designed to "contain" Presidential leadership.

In the prescriptions of Congress (1) defining the type of personnel the President might select, (2) requiring Senatorial confirmation, (3) insisting on co-ordinate responsibilities to Congress the attempt to restrict the President and his aides is evident. The requirement that the council be partially responsible to Congress was a device by which Congress could drive a wedge between the President and his staff. Such a policy could make the President the "victim" of this staff, for the President might be reluctant to arouse the inevitable Congressional criticism should he fail to follow their advice.[36] In this respect, the act was a qualified mandate for Presidential leadership.

---

34 See on change, conflict and the acceptance of changes in politics, the brilliant analysis by Arthur W. Macmahon, "Conflict, Consensus, Confirmed Trends, and Open Choices," *The American Political Science Review*, XLII, No. 1 (February, 1948), 1–15. The institutionalization of change is treated in various theories of leadership and social change, briefly summarized by D. R. Mathews, *The Social Background of Decision-Makers* (New York: Doubleday, 1954).

35 Quoted in Bailey, *op. cit.*, p. 120.

36 See Don K. Price, *The New Dimensions of Diplomacy* (New York: Woodrow Wilson Foundation, 1951), p. 20, for a discussion of this point. Parenthetically, the power implications of presidential dependency upon staff are worthy of greater attention than they have as yet received.

We must conclude that the attempt at the institutionalization of Presidential leadership in this case had double meaning. On the one hand, it represented confirmation of the new departures contributed by Roosevelt's dynamic personal leadership and his personal aides. On the other hand, it expressed a desire to confine and limit that personal leadership.[37]

V. CONGRESSIONAL INSTITUTIONALIZATION
AND PRESIDENTIAL LEADERSHIP

The intent of Congress having placed CEA in the Executive Office and having indicated by law that it wished the agency to be responsible to the President and Congress on matters of economic program was not realized. The background of this Congressional intention is worthy of attention.

The behavior of Congress toward executive leadership and reorganization has been revealing.[38] Congress has been reluctant to take the Presidential view of a need for overall executive programming and the necessity of a staff for such purposes.[39] Congress has tended to see in executive programming a challenge to its prerogative to declare and validate the lines of public policy. A more fragmented field facilitates the influence of Congressional committees in alliance with particular bureaus and interests. This suits the more particularistic conception of politics of Congress.[40] The activities of the President's staff in key programmatic rôles is thus a matter of critical moment to legislators. The power of the President's staff is considerable. Earlier in this paper we sketched some of the functional rôles that presidential staff members perform. It was evident that these rôles are at the heart of the President's political influence. To paralyze a White House staff would be to render the President relatively immobile. Flexibility, maneuverability, and vulnerability are essential to the effectiveness of such a staff.

Congress could view developments in the New Deal as the crystallization of new power. The President had armed himself with a core of advisers, and strong public following, and a new Civil Service. The heart of this whole complex was the President and his staff. Congressional resistance to the reorganization bills in 1937 and 1939 reflected this view.[41] Congress has not conceded that such a matter as the President's staff is an exclusively executive matter. It is note-worthy that since the statutory requirement of Senatorial confirmation of the CEA, the legislation creat-

---

[37] Such Congressional contradictions between policies and administrative means are discussed by Don K. Price in "The Presidency: Its Burden and Its Promise," in *The Strengthening of American Political Institutions* (Ithaca: Cornell University Press, 1949), p. 92.

[38] Herman Miles Somers, "The President as Administrator," *The Annals of the American Academy of Political and Social Science*, 283 (September, 1952), 105–106.

[39] Price, *The Strengthening of American Political Institutions*, p. 101.

[40] Avery Leiserson, "Political Limitations on Executive Reorganization," *The American Political Science Review*, XLI, No. 1 (February, 1947), 80. W. Coy, "Basic Problems," *op. cit.*, pp. 1129, 1130.

[41] Leiserson, *loc. cit.*, p. 70.

ing more recent executive staff agencies (the National Security Resources Board, the National Security Council, the Director of Defense Mobilization, and the Director of Mutual Security) has required Senatorial confirmation.[42] (The Hoover Commission took sharp exception to this policy.) [43]

If the President's economic advisers could be made a detached group delivering learned reports to the President and Congress alike, then the influence of the President [44] could be reduced. Congress knew well that a council of economic "bright boys" or a council of economic advisers who "looked at the President and reported to the country" could only enhance the political effectiveness of the President. In its attempt to delimit the CEA, perhaps Congress erred in supposing that at the level of the Presidency and in the circle of his immediate official family, the qualities of dispassion and objectivity could flourish. Equally fallacious was an expectation that the President could tolerate a group divorced from his political responsibility. The President needs in his closest circle "idea" men and political responsiveness. Detached expertness, if it is to remain detached, must be fed into policy formation at other levels.

The creation by Congress of a *Council* of Economic Advisers could not help being another anti-executive leadership proposal. A council almost by its very nature cannot integrate itself into the confidential relationships of the President. Committees and councils are too unwieldy and prone to disunity to mesh with such close relationships. The Hoover Commission proposals in recommending a single Economic Adviser were on firmer ground.[45]

In defining the CEA in the aforementioned manner, Congress attempted to rigidify the executive, neglecting the political responsibility and responsiveness of the President. Men who are "experts," beholden to Congress and resistant to political pressure, are incompatible with the executive rôle. The President has trouble enough changing governmental policy even with his own men. He would face greater difficulty with aides who are divided in their obligation to him.[46] The inevitable result of such rigidities is the emergence of informal lines of personal contacts that bypass formal institutions and operate parallel to them.

Such attempted Congressional institutionalizations fail for another reason. The President's interpretation of his rôle [47] is a key factor in deter-

[42] Hobbs, *op. cit.*, p. 104.

[43] General Management of the Executive Branch; a Report to Congress (February, 1949), PT. II, "The Executive Office of the President," notably recommendations 2 to 9 incl. See also the perceptive comments of John M. Gaus, "The Presidency," *The American Political Science Review*, XLIII, No. 5 (October, 1949), 952–958.

[44] On this point see George A. Graham, "The Presidency and the Executive Office of the President," *The Journal of Politics,* 12, No. 4 (November, 1950), 609.

[45] *Ibid.*, p. 610.

[46] The dangers of staff institutionalizations are illuminated by Louis Brownlow in his *The President and the Presidency* (Chicago: Public Administration Service, 1949), pp. 128–135.

[47] Herring, *op. cit.*, p. 29. The writer is elaborating on rôle interpretation and staff in a forthcoming monograph on Presidential leadership. See Harold Dwight Lasswell, *Power and Personality* (New York: W. W. Norton & Company, Inc., 1948); E. Hughes,

mining the relationships between the President and his staff. Formal institutions are rather elastic fences: they limit action, but they do not exhaust alternatives. Congress may set up a CEA, but it cannot compel the President to seek its advice often, nor listen to it when given. A façade of conformity to legislation may be maintained while the President seeks effective advice elsewhere. Expressed in terms of a dichotomy of rôle interpretations, a President may rely heavily upon prescribed staff organization to the point where he becomes the "victim" of his staff. In the other extreme, a President may recruit advisers from many sources, both inside and outside the government, and prefer a staff set-up of wide flexibility.

The experience with the CEA in Truman's administration indicated that Truman was more the latter type of President than the former. Edwin Nourse, writing after he terminated his service as first chairman of the CEA, stated that: "the success of the Council as an institution, the importance of the place it occupies and the value of its work will be just what the President makes them." [48] Mr. Truman did not wish the Council to serve as an independent agency "on the cabinet level" but rather to have the same flexible relationship to himself as "the rest of the White House aides." [49] But Nourse had no desire to play the rôle of a politically committed member of the palace guard.

As a result, after a lapse of a little more than a year, Nourse stated: "There has been no single case when he [Truman] has called upon us in any specific situation for counsel in his study of any matter of national economic policy." [50] It was evident that members of Truman's inner circle, like Dr. John Steelman and Clark Clifford, were to play a more important rôle in the economic formulation.[51] On the other side, the split between Dr. Nourse and Keyserling reduced itself to the unwillingness of the former to accept the premises of operation of an inner circle member, and the willingness of Keyserling to do just that.

Under the Eisenhower administration a number of significant changes have occurred in the structure and functioning of the CEA.[52] In the early days of his administration, President Eisenhower indicated his desire to continue the Council of Economic Advisers, though with some changes.

"Institutional Office and the Person," *American Journal of Sociology*, 43 (1937), 404–413; Theodore R. Sarbin, "Role Theory," in Gardner Lindzey, ed., *Handbook of Social Psychology* (Cambridge: Addison-Wesley Publishing Company, Inc., 1954), Vol. I, 223–258.

48 Nourse, *op. cit.*, p. 378.

49 *Ibid.*, p. 380.

50 *Ibid.*

51 Nourse, *op. cit.*, p. 380. See also W. Cikins, "The Council of Economic Advisers: Political Economy at the Crossroads," in *Public Policy*, a yearbook of the Graduate School of Public Administration (Cambridge: Harvard University Press, 1953), pp. 94–115.

52 The account that follows is based upon the January, 1954, *Economic Report of the President* (Washington: United States Government Printing Office, 1954), pp. 119–125, and personal interviews with various staff members of the CEA. See for an interpretation Ronald C. Hood, "Reorganizing the Council of Economic Advisers," *Political Science Quarterly*, LXIX, No. 3 (September, 1954), 413–437.

Congressional opinion was divided. Within the White House there was divided opinion. Some favored a single Presidential Economic Adviser integrated into the White House Staff. Others favored the continuation of the full Council. While the President was making up his mind, Congress, through the Appropriation Act of March, 1953, provided for the establishment of a single economic adviser to the President, rather than a continuance of the Council. The President appointed Arthur F. Burns to the position.

On June 1, 1953, President Eisenhower transmitted to Congress Reorganization Plan No. 9, in which he indicated his matured plans for CEA. The plan was considered in the House by a subcommittee on government operations. The committee was unanimous in approving the plan, and it was permitted to go into effect August 1, 1953. Under the reorganization plan responsibility for administration and policy of the Council was fixed with the Chairman. The Chairman was tied more closely to the President. The position of the vice-chairman was abolished. By centralizing authority in the Chairman, it was hoped that the endemic divisions in the CEA under the Truman administration would be vitiated. In July, 1953, Arthur Burns was appointed to the Council; and in August, 1953, he was designated its Chairman. Neil Jacoby and Walter Stewart were appointed to the other two council positions.

The relationship of the Chairman to the President and the cabinet was made more intimate. The Chairman met with the President for an economic advisory session at a fixed time each week. In addition, Arthur Burns, or his representative, sat in on cabinet meetings and occasionally at meetings of the National Security Council. Thus, the pro forma and often distant relationship that prevailed between Truman and Nourse was supplanted by closer relationships between the new Chairman and the new President.

The appointment of Gabriel Hauge, an economist, to be administrative assistant and economic adviser to the President in January, 1953, portended some complication. Evidently no friction has resulted from this arrangement, largely because Burns and Hauge get on well. Hauge has been particularly attentive to enlisting support from the business community and has been more "political." Moreover, Hauge, a Presidential intimate, serves as a channel for the CEA into the White House Staff.[53] Burns is thus made more free for the "non-political" staff work of CEA.

Generally speaking, CEA history to date supports the following observation. A political leader needs experts at some levels who furnish the most reliable data and diagnoses. He also needs no less a circle of politically committed policy advisers sensitive to political situations and equipped with refined skills in winning support for policies.

[53] Here again the rôle of the White House intimate is illustrated. It is this critical link personified by Frank Walker, Harry Hopkins, James Byrnes with FDR (for example) that makes the difference in staff rôles. The point is borne out in the Truman and Eisenhower staffs as well. See H. M. Somers, *Presidential Agency* (Cambridge: Harvard University Press, 1950).

VI. CONCLUDING OBSERVATIONS

Our study of this case instance would lead us to believe that inner circles play a rôle in the policy innovations and new departures of Presidential leadership. These innovations become with time and general acceptance regularized and institutionalized expectations of leadership. Attempts to build up a Presidential staff as an institution and to institutionalize the President's relationship to it may go through another pattern. The President who chooses to lead resists restrictions upon his staff organization.

The conflicts and frustrations of CEA to date are suggestively reminiscent of the history of the National Resource Planning Board. The latter agency was in its way an attempt to formalize the planning and advice that the brain trust furnished. The NRPB failed, among many other reasons, because it was not closely articulated with immediate Presidential needs and with the closest circle of Roosevelt's relationships.[54]

It would seem that Congress prefers to maintain the autonomy of the extremities of the executive by limiting the President and his staff. While it may have greater success in doing the latter, it has had less success in accomplishing the former. The reason lies principally in the fact that the more it may attempt to confine the President's staff, the more it makes necessary that a Presidential leader employ devices to make them elastic.[55]

We doubt that Congress alone can make a Presidency by staff. It takes the President's self-abnegation to accomplish that purpose. Hence, we return to the basic fact that a President who interprets his rôle as leading and responding to public expectations of leadership must resist any attempts to define the personnel of his staff and his relations to it. It is the heart of leadership to serve a dynamic function, generating activities that need planning and organizing. It is the demise of leadership to become *itself* completely *organized*.[56]

The President's inner circle among its rôles fulfills a function of leadership for innovation and "new thinking." We suggest that in this "groundbreaking" rôle, new policies may ultimately become institutionalized; but the ground-breakers cannot become institutionalized, lest leadership itself be stifled and hamstrung in the process.

[54] John D. Millett, *The Process and Organization of Government Planning* (New York: Columbia University Press, 1947), pp. 139–140, 142; Charles E. Merriam, "The National Resources Planning Board; a Chapter in American Planning Experience," *The American Political Science Review*, XXXVIII, No. 6 (December, 1944), 1075.

[55] Rossiter, *loc. cit.*, p. 1206.

[56] Joseph A. Schumpeter, in his *Capitalism, Socialism, and Democracy* (New York: Harper & Brothers, 1947), p. 133, wrote suggestively of a historic trend toward administrative arrangements *replacing* leadership.

The Politics of Economic Advice

Edward S. Flash, Jr.

THE BASIS OF POLITICALLY ORIENTED ECONOMIC ADVICE

. . . The Council [of Economic Advisers] has had no choice but . . . to become involved in presidential policy and leadership. Under the terms of the Employment Act it has had no identity except as adviser to the President. Everything it has done has been done in the name of the President and the President's program. If, as Sorensen maintains, presidential decision is influenced by "presidential politics," "presidential advisers," and "presidential perspective," then the Council as one set of presidential advisers (and nothing but advisers), has been linked with decisions, politics, and perspective. Operationally if not physically, the Council has become attached to the White House. Its work is part of what Neustadt describes as "the initiatives a President can take"; it belongs to the decisions, agendas, records, "helping hands," and "grinding stones," things right and things wrong. As Homan has expressed it, "A proposal made by the Council to the President is an invitation to him to make a political issue and the Council is no less involved politically because it is one step removed from the scene of actual political strife." The Council's interpretative and conceptual advisory operation constitutes the same sort of political creativeness and synthesis as that attempted by the President but for which he has so little time. Consequently, the Council stands in the center of the arena into which converge the great multitude of pressures, interests, opportunities, and problems of national government and from which emerge the major strands of political leadership.

The Council, however, is obviously by no means alone in its advisory association with the President. By responsibility and initiative, the operating departments are constant in their advice. In addition to the Council there is, of course, within the Executive Office of the President the White House staff, the Bureau of the Budget, and other components such as the National Security Council, the National Aeronautics and Space Council, the Office of Emergency Planning as the residual legatee of ODM, and the Office of Science and Technology established in 1962. There are in addition, two operating components, the second of which is of direct interest to the Council; the Central Intelligence Agency (CIA) and the new Office of Economic Opportunity established in 1964 to coordinate the government's antipoverty programs. With the Council they exist primarily

Reprinted by permission from Edward S. Flash, Jr., *Economic Advice and Presidential Leadership: The Council of Economic Advisors* (New York: Columbia University Press, 1965), pp. 308–319.

as advisers and assistants to the President. With the Council they comprise the "presidential bureaucracy" as distinguished from the bureaucracies of other agencies of the federal government. In their primary orientation to the President, their roots are not in the large operating departments with separate resources, recognized specialties, far-flung operations, separate clientele, and particular career interests. Rather, their perspective is more nearly governmentwide; it epitomizes the representative bureaucracy described by Long in 1952. With the Council, these components of the Executive Office comprise a presidential "medium for registering the diverse wills that make up the people's will and for transmuting them into responsible proposals for public policy." They reflect a presidential "sensitivity to long-range and broad considerations, the totality of interests affected, and the utilization of expert knowledge by procedures that ensure a systematic collection and analysis of relevant facts." The association with the President makes the medium and sensitivity all the more comprehensive — more so, that is, than those of operating departments or (as Long emphasizes) of Congress.

The educational background of the presidential bureaucracy appears to have been largely in comprehensive disciplines such as in economics, law, and political science. It is true that, among those who have made the federal government their career, many senior analysts and executives have had substantial experience in other segments of the federal government or even with the state and local organizations. Available evidence nevertheless suggests that experience and career development within the Executive Office have constituted their dominant pattern of employment. Economic and budget analysis, legislative clearance, planning, and liaison work have not paralleled or been confined to particular operating programs such as forestry, housing, or defense. Assignments have admittedly involved degrees of specialization toward certain activities and issues but not to the extent of transferred loyalties and motivations. Macroanalysis and advocacy have been preferred to micro-operation and production. The application of professional competence and policy involvement combined at the presidential level have provided more satisfactory fulfillment of career objectives than work at a relatively programmatic level. Top policy review and analysis within the surviving Victorian splendor of "Old State" have provided an atmosphere more closely resembling the unique air of the Presidency than the ordinary ozone of the field installation. Although maintaining a system of governmentwide contacts and associations with operating programs, the presidential bureaucracy is geared to the President's operations and to his deadlines. Its activities have his symbolic coloration. Whether he be a temporary appointee to the Council or a permanent member of the Budget Bureau staff, the presidential bureaucrat is a part of, not apart from, the White House.

The Operation of Political Conflict. Although the Council's association with the President and his bureaucracy is crucial, it is none the less activated and meaningful only in terms of specific issues. If, as Sorensen concludes, conflict is "the one quality which characterizes most issues likely to be brought to the President," then the Council as a group of presidential advisers is party to the conflict in issues of economic significance. In its varying roles of participant, representative, mediator, protector, and catalyst, it becomes involved in conflicts "between departments, between the views of various advisers, between the Administration and Congress, between the United States and another nation, or between groups within the country: labor versus management, or race versus race, or state versus nation."

In terms of economic philosophy, the Council has inherited the Employment Act's policy conflict. It has been swept up in the generalities and compromises of a statute in which Congress did not resolve conflict so much as give it statutory permanence. Some years ago, Leys wrote that " 'Moral gesture' legislation amounts to an instruction to do nothing specific, but most 'pass-the-buck' legislation is an instruction to resolve the conflict between groups who want definite but rival standards to be legalized." The Council has been faced with the opportunity and problem of living under a piece of legislation that is at once of both varieties. The Council's attempt to receive the "buck" and to give it some concrete interpretation has automatically involved it in the very conflict of "ideas, interests, institutions, and individuals," to use Bailey's terms, that could not reach agreement in the first place. Not only its analysis and advocacy but its methods of operations as well have become parties to the conflict. The passage of time may have mellowed the extent of the conflict, but it has not changed the conflict's basic nature nor diminished the significance of conflict in the Council's operations or in the praise or condemnation it has received for doing or not doing. The pro-and-con reaction to the Nourse-Keyserling feuds, the stretch-out of the Korean mobilization program over the objections of Keyserling, the feet-dragging reaction to Burns' 1954 step-up program, and the breadth of reaction to the 1963 tax revision proposals — to say nothing of the prolonged consideration of it — all attest to the enduring vitality of the ambivalence of the Council's enabling legislation.

Pervasiveness of Economic Policy. The inevitability of association with presidential leadership and the dominance of political conflict of which the Council is a part are doubly significant for the Council because of the relevance of economic considerations to such a wide area of governmental policy and operations. Fiscal and monetary policy are not mutually exclusive among themselves, nor do Treasury, Federal Reserve Board, and Budget Bureau monopolize concern for them. They represent broad categories of economic policies that contribute to and draw their significance from such disparate program areas as taxation, housing, foreign aid, international trade and finance, business regulation, defense, labor relations, natural resources, education, and agriculture. Moreover, such seemingly noneconomic issues as civil rights ramify into economic issues as varied as job security and urban expansion.

Where does the Council's potential involvement stop, for example, in the development of federal transportation policies? Both the Burns and Heller Councils were concerned with such an issue. Can objectives of pay-as-you-go financing, maintaining fair competition among different carriers, improving the economic viability of downtown areas, providing better commuting services, and satisfying defense transportation needs be considered apart from one another or from objectives of growth, stability, and decreased poverty? Can the Council rationalize or analyze apart from these considerations or without some form of collaboration with the Interstate Commerce Commission, Treasury, the Bureau of Public Roads, the Defense Department, the Urban Renewal Administration, and the Budget Bureau? Can it ignore the constituencies, views, committee assignments, and seniority of particular congressmen? Can it pass off as someone else's worry the pressures of cement makers, the railroad brotherhoods, beleaguered commuters, city councils, motorists, and so on, ad infinitum? Can it ignore matters of technical feasibility, obsolescence, and innovation?

To all these questions, the answer is "No." The confluence of economic and political aggregates at the presidential level has not delineated any distinct segment or level of government policy for the Council but rather exposed it to the length, breadth, and specifics of federal policy. Its economic analysis, whatever the base in economic theory, reflects the interdependent relationship between interests and institutions which are both initiators and reactors to national economic policy. It seems not without inverse relevance that the Council's relative abstention from involvement in agriculture policy reflects at least in part the considerable isolation of such policy within the Department of Agriculture and its organized clientele.

Subjectivity of Economic Analysis. Association, conflict, and pervasiveness have in turn been complemented by the subjectivity of economic analysis. Economic truth is not unitary; it does not admit of single and objective answers that, by virtue of such attributes, are automatically accepted. Rather, it involves sets of answers that are consistent with some sets of economic and noneconomic consequences, inconsistent with others, and reflective of different values. Sometimes they are automatically or hastily accepted, at other times only after the most careful and hesitant scrutiny. As Arthur Smithies has argued,

> Hardly any economic theory can be ideologically neutral. . . . The mere selection of economic problems for investigation involves value judgments. . . . Attempts to draw sharp distinctions between means and ends can be misleading and dangerous. . . . An economic problem of any importance is too complicated for all such judgments involved in its solution to be set out explicitly. An economist who is advising a President on whether or not to employ direct controls in time of inflation must base his advice largely on his views of the importance or unimportance of preserving a free market economy. Those views necessarily involve value judgments.

In reflecting upon his own experience, Burns has written, "Nor can the economist afford to forget that he is rarely able to speak with the impersonal authority of science. Not only is his ability to predict very limited, but in handling issues of policy he is inevitably influenced by his philosophic and ethical attitudes." Aside from any conscious interpretation of the Employment Act, the content and mode of the Council's economic service to the President has constituted an embracing of noneconomic values primarily because the Council's economics have themselves been rooted in values. Even Nourse's scientific objectivity was a reflection of conservative values. As Keyserling had his Wagner, so Burns had his Mitchell and Heller had his Commons. The aggregate projective nature of Keynesian analysis and prescription underpins convictions that government *ought* to be dynamic and active on behalf of national welfare, that it *should* provide a counterbalance to the non-self-regulating economy. The development of quantitative analysis techniques has itself contributed to these political values. The inductive nature of non-Keynesian analysis supports values of a more passive government role — of free (that is, non-regulated) competition, of wealth accumulation, and the preservation of small business. As a value-laden word, "welfare" connotes governmental responsibility to one group and governmental domination to the other. In principle, these combinations of different approaches to economics and different values have not been interchangeable.

The significance of this subjectivity both for the Council as an organization and for the individuals in it is that it has been a source of motivation rather than frustration, a form of security and not danger, and hence a strength and not a weakness. True, some Council personnel have differed in the degree of their willingness to become directly involved in advocacy as distinct from analysis, but this has not detracted from the values that attracted them to the Council and underpinned their analysis. To the Council economist absorbed in the daily process of analysis, of coping with problems and opportunities, of brokering ideas, of meeting deadlines, and of still taking time to think, economics and policy have not been consciously separated but have been naturally combined in a professional, political, and social equilibrium.

Analysis and advice have not gingerly walked some invisible but none the less calculated line between objective economics and substantive policy. Nourse's economic conservatism in a Fair Deal environment rather than his standards of objectivity made it impossible for him to achieve a viable equilibrium — which in turn contributed to his conflicts with his associates on the Council and to his estrangement from the White House. The compatibility of Keyserling, Burns, and Heller with their Presidents and administrations constituted an equilibrium that grew out of a mutual acceptance and understanding of economic and noneconomic values; it was not a compromise between politics and economics. The Council personnel who served as allies to the State Department during the NSC 68 considerations, participated in drafting the Defense Production Act, helped Burns make the National Bureau approach work, developed arguments on behalf of tax reduction were all acting on the equilibrium. Conflict for the professional Council economist has not developed from either political-economic or objective-subjective dichotomies but from consideration of policy values, the means of achieving them, and analyses of specific situations under a given political and economic framework.

The Competitiveness of Advice. If a multiplicity of advisers advise the President and his administration on issues characterized by conflict, if such issues are spread over a variety of policies and subpolicies and call forth subjectively based analysis, then advice is bound to be competitive. If the Council members and staff are not neutral regarding their advice, then it is natural that their advice be advocacy and their advocacy be competitive. From its inception, the Council has competed to have its advice considered, to say nothing of trying to have it accepted.

From the Council's viewpoint, the nature of advisory competition can be viewed as threefold:

1. Opposing economic advice, the acceptance of which would mean adoption of policies countering those recommended by the Council. In part this is an issue of economists differing as economists, as, for example, when Federal Reserve and Council economists differ on the relative efficacy of different monetary policy proposals toward the objective of economic growth. In more fundamental terms, it is an issue of economic policy advice being developed in particular and institutional terms. If specific rather than overall policy activates the relations among the President, Congress, the departments, and their respective publics, then such specificity monopolizes the President's leadership resources and fills his channels of information and advice. Recommendations on decisions to be made on such issues as defense expenditures, foreign aid, balance of payments, collective bargaining, and housing (each of which affects the economy as a whole and is therefore of concern to the Council) are delivered to the President in the package of the department involved, be it Treasury, Defense, State, Labor, or Housing. They are wrapped with the personality of a Marshall, a Humphrey, or a McNamara, insulated with layers of uniqueness, precedent, and constituent interest, and armed with the sponsor's own value-loaded economic analysis. Analysis and advice of departmental perspective, in which the part is allegedly related to the whole, compete with the Council's aggregative analysis and advice, which attempts to apply the whole to the part.

2. Opposing noneconomic advice, which does not necessarily refute economic advice as such but presses for preeminence of other factors of political, military, administrative, or other significance. Presumed production bottlenecks and assessment of the point of maximum danger of Communist aggression rendered Keyserling's arguments for economic expansion irrelevant in Truman's 1951 stretch-out decision. Similarly, in his commitment to a balanced budget in 1961 and his refusal to seek a tax cut in 1962, Kennedy was persuaded by noneconomic advice of the validity of largely noneconomic considerations. At the same time, he ac-

cepted the validity of economic considerations in committing his administration to seeking tax reduction in 1963.

3. Other demands upon the President's time and energies. These demands do not offer advisory competition as such but obstruct the transmitting and receiving of advice. In the day-to-day handling of issues and
events, the President has limited opportunity to see whom he would like,
to summon the Council for contemplative discussion of national policy,
or to consider the variety of advice he might like to have. Neustadt
sketches a President run largely by the daily pressures put upon him:

> A President's own use of time, his allocation of his personal at-
> tention, is governed by things he *has* to do from day to day: the
> speech he has agreed to make, the fixed appointment he cannot
> put off, the paper no one else can sign, the rest and exercise his
> doctors order. These things may be far removed from academic
> images of White House concentration on high policy, grand strat-
> egy. There is no help for that. A President's priorities are set
> not by the relative importance of a task, but by the relative
> necessity for him to do it. He deals first with the things that
> are required of *him* next. Deadlines rule his personal agenda.
> In most days of his working week, most seasons of his year,
> he meets deadlines enough to drain his energy and crowd his
> time regardless of all else. The net result may be a far cry from
> the order or priorities that would appeal to scholars or to col-
> umnists — or to the President himself.

If the President has little time for reflecting on grand strategy, he also
has little time for reflecting with grand strategists or over what the grand
strategists send him. Kennedy's voracity for information of all types was
undoubtedly more than met by the quantity and variety of memoranda,
reports, and analyses that came to him.

Depending upon the circumstances surrounding the issues involved, the
three competitive characteristics exist separately or complement one another; they vary in intensity and therefore in their impact upon the
Council.

The source of the Council's competition lies in the formal power and
operating involvements of agencies like the Treasury, the Federal Reserve
Board, ODM (while it existed), and the Budget Bureau. *Their* direct
access to the President, the impact of the immediate situation on *their*
operations, and the significance of *their* particular operations in the President's leadership responsibilities therefore all compete with the Council's advisory function. The power behind economic advice is for the
most part lodged with the Secretary of the Treasury. His department's
functions and traditions make him a preeminent force in fiscal matters.
Eisenhower may have welcomed Burns' briefings on economic developments, he may have asked Burns to coordinate countercyclical activities,
but he did not attempt to place Burns between himself and Humphrey,
nor, according to available evidence, did he directly overrule Humphrey
in favor of Burns during the 1953–54 period. By virtue of its indepen-

dence, the Federal Reserve Board has exerted control over monetary policy. For all intents and purposes, Keyserling was unable to storm these fortresses in order to take a direct part in the reaching of the Treasury-Federal Reserve accord. Heller had to await Dillon's acceptance in principle of the arguments on behalf of tax reduction, and, even when they came, the Secretary's specific proposals were less extensive than Heller had hoped for and were, contrary to Heller's advice, linked with the Treasury's reform proposals. The ODM's policy and operating control of partial mobilization made it invulnerable to Keyserling's advice and criticism.

In addition, the Council has had none of the operating carry-through normally associated with its chief competitor and colleague within the Executive Office, the Bureau of the Budget. Its major functions of budget preparation and legislative clearance make it an essential link in the executive function. They give it unparalleled knowledge of governmental operations, they put it squarely astride the policy-making process, and they enable it to develop a budgetary management hierarchy extending down into departmental and subdepartmental budget offices. The development over the past quarter-century of a Budget Bureau viewpoint has influenced its interpretation of what is and is not "consistent with the President's program." In short, the Bureau is the dominant advisory force within the Executive Office. It does not necessarily smother the Council; often their interests are complementary and their operations cooperative, but its functions give it a measure of power that the Council does not have.

Compared with this array of formal operating power, the Council has no equal powers to bring to the decision-making arena. It may "assist and advise the President," "gather timely and authoritative information," "analyze and interpret," "appraise," "develop and recommend," "make and furnish studies," "make an annual report," "constitute . . . advisory committees," and "consult with such representatives . . . as it deems advisable." It may not, however, require, coordinate, intercede, or accept delegations of authority; it may not impose its will. Executive Order 10161 of September, 1950, in which the Council was permitted to "furnish guides" and "obtain necessary information," and the creation of ABEGS under Burns and of the Cabinet Committee on Economic Growth under Heller stand out as slim façades before a vacant lot of power. Consequently, the Council's formal authority has been essentially passive; there is no expectation on the part of the President or operating agencies that the Council's judgment will necessarily be substituted for theirs. The Council has always enjoyed legitimacy as the President's economic adviser, even when Eisenhower had his own economic assistant in the White House. As a formal part of the Presidency, it has been able to establish and maintain operating relations, but this agency role has done little more than establish the Council as a *de jure* participant in advisory competition. Competitive success has demanded more potent ingredients.

The passive nature of the Council's formal role has obliged it as the President's economic agent to rely upon what reflected power it has been able to gain from him and upon the persuasive force inherent in the application of its expertise. That is, the competitive strength brought by the Council to the decision-making fray has grown out of the accuracy of its expert economic analysis relative to the economic conditions of the time, the explicit or implicit interpretation it has placed upon issues at stake, the appropriateness of the Council's analysis and interpretation to the President's perspective, and the application it makes (or attempts to make) of its analysis and interpretation to the decision-making process.

The analysis of the Council's performance in three particular situations indicates that the Council has experienced significant successes and has made a difference. The Council's powers, however, compared with those of other presidential advisers, have been so transitory, peripheral, and intangible that as a result its competitive position has been consistently weak. Presidential endorsement and persuasion have carried insufficient force to guarantee impact upon economic policy decisions. Indeed, although the President has depended upon his Council, he has depended upon others even more. As Seligman has noted, "Congress may set up a CEA, but it cannot compel the President to seek its advice often, nor listen to it when given." In his summary of pre-1953 Council experience, Robert C. Turner, a former Council member, attributed part of the Council's difficulty in influencing major policy issues to "the problems of muscling in." Sorensen asserts that the President will "pay more attention to the advice of the man who must carry out the decision than the advice of a mere 'kibitzer.'" The expert is normally presumed to be trapped by the narrowness of his own expertise, yet in point of fact the general and aggregative nature of the Council's expertise tends to hinder its applicability in specific decisions. Ideologies, expert analysis, and advice developed by a small staff and accepted at the general policy level often have difficulty surviving at the level of policy specifics that constitute the bread and butter of presidential leadership.

The net result of the Council's weak competitive position is that it has always been faced with the necessity of creating and maintaining a need for its services, in effect, of nurturing a demand for its supply of analysis and advice. The more its advice and analysis have been directed to the specifics of issues, the more such service has centered upon commitments to action involving one or at most a few operating programs, and the more that action has been hedged with obligation and limited discretion for the operating agency, then even more elastic has been the demand and the greater the resistance to the Council's participation. Conversely, the more circumstances have been marked by such characteristics as basic economic policy significance, policy nascence as compared to precedence, diffused leadership, emergency issues, the need for allies by operating agencies, and interdepartmental coordination, then the more inelastic has been the demand for the Council's involvement.

Truman's absorption during the Korean mobilization with military and international affairs, indirect controls, and decentralized mobilization responsibility created a demand for the Keyserling Council's services and influence that expired when partial mobilization and direct controls coalesced under Wilson's leadership. Burns could serve as leader in public works planning and as ally in the move to enlarge unemployment compensation, but he could be neither in the monolithic tax area nor could he implement his own step-up proposals. Not until economic growth abroad combined with the threat of another recession in 1962 to reveal the inappropriateness of traditional policy thinking (not only to Kennedy but also to advisers like Dillon and Mills) was Heller able to make headway with his arguments. The shift from the Keyserling period of making the *Economic Report* the "indispensable engine of consent" for economic policy recommendations to the articulation of more general and informal consensus, apparently typical of the Heller *Reports*, suggests the relative acceptance for general as distinct from specific advice.

The demand for the Council's services is also affected by the nature of their application. The demand for information and comment, for ammunition and rationalization, for drafting and verbalizing is generally greater (that is, less elastic) than the demand for direct participation in the creative and ratifying steps of decision-making. The relevance of the former as an essential supporting activity is by no means to be denied; in fact, its significance has previously been noted, but the distinction must be made in appreciating the competitive aspects of the Council's advisory activity.

Given the competitive situation, the Council has necessarily been responsive to the kaleidoscopic interplay of situational factors. In order to compete, to have their days in court, all three Councils attempted to anticipate issues and opportunities. Early involvement has often enabled the Council to influence issues and decisions before they reach the final ratification stage. In reflecting both its competitive position and the pressures that are upon the President, the Council also has on occasion assumed that half a loaf is better than none; it has tempered both its advice and its methods of operating to what, in the light of its assessment of economic and noneconomic factors, appears to have a reasonable chance of acceptance. It, too, has lived within what Sorensen calls "the outer limits of decision," the limits of "permissibility," "previous commitment," "available resources, time, and information." The Council's reliance upon an interpretive and opportunistic application of its expertise has been inevitable and natural. It is an outgrowth of the environment of presidential association and political conflict, of broad-scale involvement and subjective analysis in which the Council has lived and worked. The Council's performance and operating characteristics have represented the art of the politically possible. In a climactic sense, they have portrayed the relationship between economic knowledge and presidential power.

The Development of Political-Military Consultation in the United States

Ernest R. May

In the Cabinet room of the White House, every Thursday morning, the National Security Council gathers around a long, massive table. On the table are printed briefs reviewing some problem of national policy. Prepared by the Council staff, these briefs blend the views of many departments and agencies, but in Council discussions the members and advisers rehearse these views once again. The Secretary of State and others suggest desirable solutions to the policy problem, while the Secretary of Defense and the Chairman of the Joint Chiefs of Staff describe the military risks entailed in each alternative course of action. The President then reaches his decision, and the United States may acquire a new foreign policy or perhaps a new shading for an old policy.

Nearly all Americans agree on the need for this National Security Council. Everyone realizes that American policy has outgrown the Cabinet, just as the atom has outgrown the college laboratory. Where, fifty years ago, Secretary of State Elihu Root could disregard reports of a crisis in the Middle East, cabling the American envoy, "Continue quarrels with missionaries as usual," [1] a similar crisis today would call out instructions to diplomats all over the world, orders to military and naval commanders, anxious discussions in Washington, and an earnest session of the National Security Council. Living in a world as sensitive as a can of nitroglycerin, Americans accept the need for exact weighing of political and military factors before each policy decision.

The nation has acknowledged this need, however, for only a short time. Not before the 1940's would the majority of Americans have endorsed the rationale that underlies the National Security Council. Yet this rationale now seems self-evident: military forces are the rooks and bishops behind the knights and pawns of diplomacy; although the rooks and bishops move less frequently, their rôle in the game is no less decisive. Before the executors of foreign policy can decide what the nation ought to do, they must learn from political and military experts what the nation is able to do. They must lay objectives alongside capabilities, in the same way that business men compare the blueprints of design engineers with the estimates of cost accountants. In making foreign policy, in other words, ends must be measured against means.

Although this rationale won acceptance only recently, it is not new,

Reprinted by permission from the *Political Science Quarterly*, LXX (June, 1955), pp. 161–180.
1 Phillip C. Jessup, *Elihu Root* (New York, 1938), II, 109.

even in the United States. Nowhere, in fact, is it more vigorously summarized than in Number 23 of the *Federalist Papers*, written by Alexander Hamilton. But long years of isolated safety smothered the idea of political-military collaboration. It found no new spokesman until Captain Mahan began to preach, late in the nineteenth century. Even then, the idea was not translated into action until after the conquest of the Philippines, when a few Americans, looking across six thousand miles of water at their new colony, began to believe that the United States had grafted to itself an Achilles heel. They perceived that the safety of this faraway member could not, like the safety of the homeland, be entrusted to Providence.

Realizing the need for hard, far-sighted planning, this handful of Americans also realized their lack of any planning instruments. The State Department, as Tyler Dennett characterizes it in his life of John Hay, was an "antiquated, feeble organization, enslaved by precedents and routine inherited from another century, remote from the public gaze and indifferent to it. The typewriter was viewed as a necessary evil and the telephone as an instrument of last resort." [2] Although the Army and Navy had professionals, while the State Department had none, the armed services were still no better outfitted for strategy-planning than the State Department for policy-planning. Before the Army and Navy could produce coherent advice, they had to nurture brains or general staff organizations, and such brains developed slowly. The Army's General Staff, for instance, was "only just growing to man's estate" fifteen years after its founding, according to the 1918 report of its Chief of Staff.[3] This General Staff and the Navy General Board faced, in addition, the problem of welding Army and Navy differences, so that military advice on policy could be based on estimates of the total military power of the United States. Until a Joint Board of the Army and Navy and the State Department, too, perfected their internal workings, the coördination of strategy and policy could only be haphazard.

During the first two decades after the War with Spain, as a result, consultation among the State, War, and Navy Departments took the antique form of correspondence among the three secretaries. The Navy Secretary, advised by his General Board, would write to the Secretary of State, proposing acquisition of a certain naval base on foreign soil. After referring the proposal to such experts as he could collect, the Secretary of State would return his judgment, either killing the idea or pushing it up for final decision by the President.[4]

Like sophomore letters home, these begging communications from the Secretary of the Navy sometimes hinted casually at subjects under study. The Navy revealed its concern with Panama, for instance, by requesting

[2] *John Hay* (New York, 1934), p. 198.
[3] *Annual Report of the War Department, 1918: Report of the Chief of Staff*, p. 3.
[4] See Seward W. Livermore, "American Strategy Diplomacy in the South Pacific, 1890–1914," *Pacific Historical Review*, XII (March 1943), 33–51, and "American Naval Base Policy in the Far East," *ibid.*, XIII (June 1944), 113–135.

bases across all the sea approaches to the Isthmus — on the coast of Peru, off the Pacific coast of Panama, on Fonseca Bay, and in Cuba.[5] Never, before completion of the canal, did the Navy General Board say that the Isthmus was of vital importance to the military security of the United States. Alert eyes in the State Department might have detected this thought in the Board's selections of naval bases. And eyes even less alert might have perceived the concept in two bolder letters, reminding the State Department that no great Power should be allowed to perch on Ecuador's Galápagos Islands or on Haiti's Môle St. Nicholas.[6] But the Navy and Army rarely let fall such clues to their stategic thinking.

Neither did the State Department share its political thinking with the services. In the archives of the McKinley, Roosevelt and Taft Administrations, I have yet to find a letter from a Secretary of State asking for a military cost accounting before some diplomatic stroke. Although Taft's Secretary of State did occasionally ask the fleet to back up his diplomacy, he never inquired ahead of time about the fleet's location and make-up. Thus, in May 1912, when unrest was sweeping Cuba, the Secretary asked for "a considerable naval force . . . in the vicinity of Havana." Only by chance, or as a result of naval clairvoyance, did nine warships happen to be handy at Key West.[7]

Letter writing in the State, War, and Navy Departments failed to bring about effective coördination of policies. As a rule, in fact, diplomatic and military recommendations reached the White House separately, and the relationship between political aims and military capabilities had to be gauged, if at all, by the President. Although this rule-of-thumb system could work for a strategy-minded President like Theodore Roosevelt, it displayed its failings even in his time.

In the summer of 1907, for example, the budding American high command, the Joint Board of the Army and the Navy, discussed the hostility growing between the United States and Japan. Realizing that war, if it came, would find most of the American fleet in the Atlantic, the Board proposed a precautionary shift of battleships to the Pacific, then asked the Secretaries of War and the Navy to suggest such a shift to the Presi-

---

5 Livermore, "American Strategy Diplomacy in the South Pacific, 1890–1914"; Jessup, *op. cit.*, I, 326. The following from Record Group 80, the General Records of the Navy Department, in the National Archives (hereinafter cited as Navy Dept. Arch., RG 80): C. Darling (Acting Sec. of Navy) to J. Hay, Mar. 5, 1903 (carbon), 8480–8; G. v. L. Meyer to P. C. Knox, Feb. 23, 1910 (carbon), 8480–9; J. Daniels to R. Lansing, Feb. 28, 1920 (carbon), "Spindle File" — State Department. The following from Record Group 45, Naval Records Collection of the Office of Naval Records and Library (hereinafter cited as Navy Dept. Arch., RG 45): J. D. Long to McKinley, Dec. 13, 1901 (carbon), Confidential Correspondence, vol. III.

6 Livermore, "American Strategy Diplomacy in the South Pacific, 1890–1914." Rear Adm. H. C. Taylor to W. H. Moody, Nov. 10, 1902 (original), Confidential Corr., vol. III, Navy Dept. Arch., RG 45. Jessup, *Elihu Root*, I, 562–563; and the following from the General Records of the Department of State, National Archives (hereinafter cited as State Dept. Arch.): Daniels to Lansing, Jan. 2, 1920 (orig.), 822.014 0/287.

7 Knox to Meyer, May 25, 1912 (orig.); B. Winthrop to Knox, May 25, 1912 (carbon) — both in 27868–4, Navy Dept. Arch., RG 80.

dent. The Secretaries did so, writing to Roosevelt at Oyster Bay, and Roosevelt agreed, choosing, however, to disguise the movement as a good will cruise. Although he seems to have reached this decision without delay, Roosevelt waited from late June until mid-July before notifying his Secretary of State, who was still in Washington. For several weeks, therefore, the Secretary of State duelled with Japanese diplomats, wholly unaware, so far as the records show, of the Navy's preparations for a warlike gesture! [8]

The first advances from haphazard coördination-by-letter to coördination-by-conference were made, paradoxically, under an administration that would never have endorsed the rationale of political-military collaboration. President Woodrow Wilson may even have denied the need for long-range military planning. At any rate, two generals swore after World War I that Wilson had given verbal orders forbidding the Army and Navy to construct hypothetical war plans.[9] During his Administration, furthermore, a pacifist sat for two years as Secretary of State, a near-pacifist ruled the Navy Department, and a Quaker became Secretary of War.

Perhaps a prevailing attitude of the Administration was expressed on one occasion by this pacifist Secretary of State, William Jennings Bryan. Renewed tension with Japan had brought before the Cabinet another Joint Board recommendation for a fleet movement to anticipate the possibility of war. According to one member of the Cabinet, David F. Houston, this recommendation angered Bryan, who "flared up . . . got red in the face and was very emphatic. He thundered out that army and navy officers could not be trusted to say what we should or should not do, till we actually got into war; that we were discussing not how to wage war, but how not to get into war." [10]

Yet the Wilson Administration, with Bryan as Secretary of State, saw uniformed officers and black-tied diplomats sit down together to discuss questions of foreign policy. Tension with Mexico, during the first year of the Administration, brought Bryan himself to the White House for a conference with the War and Navy Secretaries, the Army Chief of Staff, and the head of the Navy General Board.[11] After war exploded over Europe, Bryan and his subordinates found a recurring need for special consultations with representatives of the Army and Navy. The uncertain character of neutral rights and duties brought into being a permanent

[8] Hermann Hagedorn, *Leonard Wood: A Biography* (New York, 1931), II, 79–81; Thomas A. Bailey, *Theodore Roosevelt and the Japanese-American Crises* (Stanford, 1934), pp. 211–227. Taft to Roosevelt, June 22, 1907, Private Papers of Theodore Roosevelt, Manuscripts Division, Library of Congress. Roosevelt to H. C. Lodge, July 10, 1907, in Elting E. Morrison *et al.* (eds.), *The Letters of Theodore Roosevelt* (Cambridge, Mass., 1951–1954), V, 709–710; Roosevelt to Root, July 13, 1907, *ibid.*, pp. 717–719.

[9] Frederick Palmer, *Newton D. Baker* (New York, 1931), I, 40–41; Hagedorn, *Leonard Wood,* II, 205.

[10] *Eight Years with Wilson's Cabinet* (Garden City, 1926), I, 66.

[11] Ray Stannard Baker, *Woodrow Wilson* (New York, 1926–1937), IX, 328–329.

Joint State and Navy Neutrality Board, an advisory body on diplomacy and international law. The amount of correspondence among assistant secretaries of the three departments increased three times over the pre-war average. And Bryan's successor, Robert Lansing, met almost daily, according to his desk diary, with officers from the Navy General Board and the Army General Staff.[12] Thus conferences, letters and committee meetings began to knit the three departments together.

But American policy failed to benefit from this increasing teamwork, for Wilson reached his decisions with little assistance from any of the three departments. Lansing had come into office, in Colonel House's words, as a man "to do the details intelligently," [13] and his Department's share in policy-making was never large. Meanwhile, the military planning agencies lacked not only the Administration's trust but also the ability to justify such trust if it were handed them. The Joint Board of the Army and Navy had virtually disbanded, because one of its recommendations had piqued the President.[14] The Army General Staff had slipped into torpor, while the Navy General Board languished as a casualty of Josephus Daniels' perpetual feud with his admirals. Collaboration among these powerless agencies could result, at best, in a coördination of futilities.

The idea of political-military collaboration nevertheless survived. Since the war had revealed defects in the State Department and in the Army and Navy, the post-war years saw reforms in all three: the Rogers Act for the State Department, reorganization of the Army General Staff, progressive change in the new office of Naval Operations, and creation of a new and stronger Joint Board of the Army and Navy. To some men in the War and Navy Departments experience had also proved the need for regular, official consultation with the State Department. And these men put forward two successive proposals for consultative organizations.

The first and most ambitious of these proposals came from Franklin D. Roosevelt, then acting as Secretary of the Navy. On May 1, 1919, Roosevelt wrote to the Secretary of State:

> It is a fundamental principle that the foreign policy of our government is in the hands of the State Department. It is also an accepted fact that the foreign policy of a government depends for its acceptance by other nations upon the naval and military force that is behind it. . . .
> It is probable that certain policies are of such importance to our national interests that they must be defended at all cost.
> On the other hand certain policies are not, by the expense they would entail, justified if they lead to war.
> Hence it is submitted that in the framing of our policies, it is

12 Private Papers of Robert Lansing, MS Div., Library of Congress.

13 E. M. House to Wilson, June 16, 1915 (orig.), Private Papers of Woodrow Wilson, MS Div., Library of Congress.

14 Diary of Josephus Daniels entry, for May 16, 1913, Private Papers of Josephus Daniels, MS Div., Library of Congress.

necessary for the State Department to know how much they will cost to maintain by force, in order to assign them their relative importance.

Conversely, it is necessary for the Navy Department to know what policies it may be called upon to uphold by force, in order to formulate plans and building programs.[15]

Enclosed with this letter was a giant sheet of blueprint paper, charting with boxes and arrows an organization for planning against all possible wars. Prepared by the Naval War College, this neat chart outlined duties for a State Department planning agency, for the Army General Staff, for a Naval General Staff, and for a Joint Plan Making Body, composed of officers from all three staffs. To this Joint Body was to go responsibility for estimating national resources, both American and foreign, and the key rôle of defining American objectives for each possible war and assessing the force needed for success.

Although this grandiose scheme was probably unworkable, hardheaded discussion of the Navy's proposal might have engineered some practical organization for national defense. No such discussion ever took place, and, in fact, Roosevelt's letter was not even acknowledged. The letter and its enclosure went, by mistake, to the State Department's Division of Latin American Affairs. After some misspent months in that Division's filing cabinets, the document was interred in the general records, never opened by the Secretary of State.[16] Indeed, when I found the original of Roosevelt's letter in the State Department archives, the blueprint was stapled to it, closed, and, as far as I could tell, the staple had never been removed, the blueprint never unfolded. Such was the fate of the first proposal for a National Security Council.

The second proposal came on December 7, 1921, this time sponsored jointly by the Secretary of the Navy and the Secretary of War. Considerably less pretentious than the original Navy blueprint, this joint proposal offered only the idea of collaboration between the State Department and the Joint Board of the Army and the Navy. But the reasoning in the service secretaries' letter closely resembled Roosevelt's.

They put forward three proposals. The State Department should designate "a responsible official" to sit in with the Joint Board when "questions involving national policy are under consideration." For similar discussions, one or more State Department people should sit in with the Joint Board's Planning Committee. Finally, the State Department should "refer to the Joint Board those national policies which may require the potential or dynamic support of the Army and Navy" and find out "whether the Army and Navy as at that time constituted and disposed are capable of supporting the policy in question. . . . All such opinions

---

[15] (Orig.), 110.7/56, State Dept. Arch. The copy in the Franklin D. Roosevelt library is described in Frank Freidel, *Franklin D. Roosevelt: The Ordeal* (Boston, 1954), pp. 19–20.

[16] Memo, Division of Latin American Affairs to Index Bureau, July 21, 1919, 110.7/56, State Dept. Arch.

and recommendations of the Joint Board," the Secretaries added, "will be referred to the Secretaries of State, War and Navy for approval." [17]

This letter at least reached the desk of Secretary of State Charles Evans Hughes, but Hughes brushed it into his "Out" basket, noting: "This appears to me to be in substance a suggestion that at least provisionally matters of foreign policy be submitted to the Joint Board. I question the advisability of this." Taking their lead from Hughes, the undersecretary and the assistant secretaries questioned its advisability even more seriously. Consequently, Hughes suavely replied: "The only officials of the State Department who can speak for it with authority on questions of national policy are the Secretary and Undersecretary of State, and it is impossible, in the existing circumstances, for either of them to undertake this additional duty." [18]

Since War and Navy Department officials believed their proposal to be of great importance, they refused to accept the Secretary of State's negative reply. They countered with a new suggestion: the Joint Board should inform the State Department "whenever a subject comes before them for consideration which in their opinion is interwoven with the international policies of the United States." The Secretary of State or his representative could then attend the Joint Board's meeting. To this proposal the Secretary of State gave perfunctory agreement, thus providing the Army and Navy with a valve for starting a flow of military-political discussion.[19] But the military leaders did not open this valve for over thirteen years.

Perhaps this long delay resulted from the series of slights administered to the military departments by the Secretary of State during the Washington Conference on Naval Limitation. Preparing for that conference, Secretary Hughes "worked closely with the Navy," his biographer says, and "was scrupulous in exploring the Navy's point of view while insisting that civilian statesmanship rather than naval strategy should guide the conference." [20] The General Board, anxious to push the Navy's ideas, presented Hughes with long, hard-thought essays on the questions apt to come up for negotiation. The Board advised that the United States fleet should equal the combined fleets of Britain and Japan, cautioned against any let-up in the naval building program, and portrayed the vital importance of fortifying Oahu, Guam and Manila Bay. But Hughes rejected each item of the Board's advice. In his opening speech to the conference, he not only proposed a 5:5:3 ratio among the three naval Powers but also offered to scrap thirty American capital ships. Later he

17 (Orig.) 110.7/123, State Dept. Arch.
18 Hughes to Fletcher, Dec. 12, 1921 (orig.); F. M. Dearing to Fletcher, Dec. 13, 1921 (orig.); W. J. Carr to Fletcher, Dec. 22, 1921 (orig.); Dearing to Fletcher, Jan. 4, 1922 (orig.), noted "(Mr. Fletcher concurs: JBS)"; Hughes to E. Denby and J. W. Weeks, Jan. 17, 1922 (certified carbon) — all in 110.7/123, State Dept. Arch.
19 Denby and Weeks to Hughes, Jan. 25, 1923 (orig.); Memo, Fletcher to Hughes, Feb. 20, 1922 (orig.); Hughes to Weeks and Denby, Mar. 14, 1922 (certified carbon) — all in 110.7/124, State Dept. Arch.
20 Merlo J. Pusey, *Charles Evans Hughes* (New York, 1950), II, 460.

proposed a general agreement not to fortify islands in the Pacific.[21] Undoubtedly, Hughes based these stands on careful reasoning and broad advice, but the Navy's feelings were badly hurt, and a sense of resentment over the Washington Conference colored the writings of Navy and Army officers for decades.

As a result, these officers became even more circumspect than before in dealing with political questions. Furthermore, they fell altogether from public favor, as, during the twenties, newspapers and magazines drummed disillusionment, isolationism, and new forms of pacifism and anti-militarism. Whereas to Secretary Hughes a suggestion for political-military collaboration had seemed only imprudent, to either of his successors a similar suggestion would have seemed rash and startling. When Hoover's Secretary of State was preparing for the new naval conference of 1930, for instance, he rejected out of hand suggestions from the General Board and took with him to the conference only one uniformed adviser, an admiral "carefully selected . . . by the administration's civilian leaders," one who "took a different position . . . from most of his colleagues." [22]

During these years, nevertheless, the general staffs were improving their minds by cloistered study of possible wars, and junior officers in the armed services were building friendly ties with their counterparts in the Foreign Service. They were exchanging intelligence data, a practice started soon after World War I, and they were meeting on various inter-departmental boards, like the Radio Advisory Committee and the committee on strategic raw materials. Early in the twenties, too, Foreign Service officers began to attend the Army and Navy War Colleges and to give lectures before War College classes.[23] Thus the future heads of divisions and branches within the three departments laid a foundation for later coöperation on questions of policy.

Over this foundation a structure began to rise shortly after Franklin D. Roosevelt became President. His Secretary of State, Cordell Hull, found himself dealing with a newly barbarous Germany, an emboldened Italy, and a hostile Japan. As Hull stated to the Pearl Harbor investigators:

> . . . soon after I came into the State Department, when I would be talking with the representatives of the thugs at the head of governments abroad . . . they would look at me in the face

[21] *Ibid.*, pp. 460, 462, 477.

[22] Henry L. Stimson and McGeorge Bundy, *On Active Service in Peace and War* (New York, 1947), p. 168.

[23] Memo, A. Dulles to "Mr. Merle-Smith," Sept. 21, 1920 (orig.), 110.72/8, State Dept. Arch. J. C. Grew to E. Young, Oct. 18, 1924 (orig.); Davis (Asst. Sec. of War) to Grew, Oct. 20, 1924 (orig.); Grew to Davis, Oct. 23, 1924 (certified carbon) — all in 110.72/29, State Dept. Arch. J. M. Wainwright (Acting Sec. of War) to Hughes, July 8, 1922 (orig.); W. Phillips to Weeks, Sept. 1, 1922 (certified carbon) — both in 110.72/13, State Dept. Arch. Rear Adm. W. V. Pratt to Grew, Feb. 25, 1926 (orig.); Grew to Pratt, Mar. 11, 1926 (carbon); T. Dennett to Grew, Mar. 8, 1926 (orig.) — all in 110.75/20–21, State Dept. Arch.

but I soon discovered that they were looking over my shoulder
at our Navy and our Army and that our diplomatic strength . . .
goes up or down with their estimate of what that amounts to.[24]

Consequently, Hull took more interest than his predecessors in military plans and opinions. Preparing for yet another naval conference, he
asked the Navy to detail its wishes, and he sent to London, not just a
"carefully selected" admiral, but the Chief of Naval Operations and a
sizable band of naval officers. In the same year, too, he named a high
State Department officer to sit in with the Joint Board's Planning Committee for a reëxamination of America's military position in the Far
East.[25] Early in his term, thus, Hull began to seat military and political
thinkers at the same tables.

As Europe's war drums beat more insistently, Hull drew the State,
War, and Navy Departments closer together. After suggesting special conferences on Axis infiltration of Latin America, he proposed a standing
interdepartmental committee to consider, among other things, "matters
of national policy affecting the three departments." He nominated Undersecretary Sumner Welles to represent the State Department. The
President chose the Chief of Naval Operations and the Army Chief of
Staff to be the committee's other members, and this three-man group took
the name Standing Liaison Committee. Thus was formed the first American agency for regular political-military consultation on foreign policy.[26]

The Standing Liaison Committee lasted until 1943. Though it handled
chiefly questions of hemisphere defense and Good Neighbor relations, it
still gave the military chiefs an opportunity to learn the trends of policy
thinking in the State Department. Later, too, it gave the State Department's second officer a chance to learn highly secret Army-Navy plans for
possible war, plans formerly withheld from State Department eyes.[27]

Rarely, however, did questions of policy come up for the Committee's
discussion, perhaps because the members had little time for talk. The
military chiefs were busy fabricating fleets, armies and air forces out of
raw metal and rawer men, while the undersecretary and his department
were swirling through diplomatic crises that absorbed their time and
powers. So the Liaison Committee failed to march with the perilous
times.

In only one instance did the Liaison Committee handle an important
issue of policy, and then it patched together a compromise instead of
building a solution. The issue came before the Committee in the summer
of 1940, when Hitler was looking acquisitively at the Vichy fleet. The
Army and Navy, fearing that Germany might seize control of the Medi-
terranean, proposed a shift of the American battle fleet from the Pacific

24 *Hearings before the Joint Committee on the Investigation of the Pearl Harbor
Attack,* 79 Cong., 1 sess. (hereinafter cited as *Pearl Harbor Hearings*), Pt. II, p. 455.
25 George H. Dern and Claude A. Swanson to Cordell Hull, Nov. 26, 1935 (carbon);
Hull to Dern, Nov. 27, 1935 (orig.) — both in WPD 3887, General Records of the War
Department, National Archives.
26 Mark S. Watson, *Chief of Staff: Prewar Plans and Preparations* (Washington,
1950), pp. 89–92.
27 *Ibid.,* p. 90.

to the Atlantic. But the State Department disagreed. More fearful of a Japanese attack on Southeast Asia than of German naval expansion and aware that Britain held the same fear, the State Department believed the fleet more effective stationed at Pearl Harbor, where it might deter Japan from rash aggression. Since the undersecretary and the military members all stood fast behind their differing views, the Liaison Committee's decision solved nothing. The fleet, they agreed, "should be withdrawn from Hawaii only if the Germans actually secured control of the French fleet." If that happened, of course, the issue would still exist and would simply be more urgent.[28]

Other than this decision, the Liaison Committee accomplished little that touched the great issues drawing the United States toward double war. After November 1940, furthermore, its functions shifted to other committee and council tables. A new Secretary of War started weekly conferences with his State and Navy counterparts.[29] The President began to deal directly with his chiefs of staff, by-passing not only the State Department but also the civilian Secretaries of War and the Navy. By the autumn of 1941, in the tempestuous twilight before Pearl Harbor, the President was convening a War Council, made up of his State, War, and Navy Secretaries, and his chiefs of staff.[30]

Despite the resemblance of this War Council to the present-day National Security Council, it hardly served as a palette for the mixing of military and political views. Rather, it provided the President with a platform from which to announce decisions already reached with the help of the chiefs of staff. After November 5, 1941, the War Council spent its time devising ways to carry out the strategic concept long ago devised by the Joint Board and now ratified by the President: "War between the United States and Japan should be avoided while building up the defensive forces in the Far East, until such time as Japan attacks or directly threatens territories whose security to the United States is of very great importance."[31] Then, when war broke out, the President stopped inviting Hull to the War Council's meetings, and the Council, while it lasted, became nothing more than a board of strategy.

The idea of coördinating strategy and policy seemed, indeed, to die out with the onset of war. The President began to consult only with his chiefs of staff and with a few para-military officials like Harry Hopkins. Not only was the Secretary of State excluded from meetings of the War Council, but he was left at home when the President went abroad to meet British and Russian leaders and even left outside when Roosevelt met with Churchill in Washington and Quebec.[32] During most of the war, as

---

[28] William L. Langer and S. Everett Gleason, *The Challenge to Isolation, 1937–1940* (New York, 1952), pp. 596–597.

[29] *Ibid.*, p. 10; Watson, *Chief of Staff*, p. 91; Stimson in *Pearl Harbor Hearings*, Pt. XXIX, p. 2065.

[30] *Pearl Harbor Hearings*, Pt. XXIX, p. 2066.

[31] *Ibid.*, Pt. XIV, p. 1062; William L. Langer and S. Everett Gleason, *The Undeclared War, 1940–1941* (New York, 1953), p. 846, and chapters xxvi–xxviii.

[32] *The Memoirs of Cordell Hull* (New York, 1948), II, 1109–1111.

a result, the State Department became almost an auxiliary arm of the military services.

Uniformed officers meanwhile filled the chairs left vacant by diplomats. Eisenhower, Stilwell and Wedemeyer negotiated with allied governments. The service chieftains, reorganized as the Joint Chiefs of Staff, met face to face with their allied counterparts and negotiated agreements that were, in effect, military treaties, requiring for ratification only the counter-signature of the President. Although the Joint Chiefs continually disclaimed any authority in political affairs, their decisions, in fact, directed American policy. When they concluded, for example, that Russian aid was essential to victory in the Far East, they said, in effect, that American diplomacy should subordinate other aims in order to bring about a Russian declaration of war on Japan. Had professional diplomats desired to challenge this ruling, they would have been unable to do so. In 1944, as a matter of fact, when the State Department wanted the Dumbarton Oaks conferees to begin discussions of post-war boundaries, the Joint Chiefs checked any such discussions.[33] Quarrels among the Allies might result, the chiefs asserted, and Russia might find cause for delaying her entry into the Pacific war. Thus, during World War II, the strategists took command, and the military-State Department relation was reversed. No longer were the military leaders seeking parity with diplomats; on the contrary, the diplomats were looking for space alongside the chiefs of staff.

Not until the last year of World War II did the State Department begin to regain its lost status. Then the need for military government directives and surrender terms caused the creation of the State-War-Navy Coordinating Committee, the National Security Council's immediate ancestor.[34]

This Coordinating Committee, composed of assistant secretaries, prepared the plans for occupying Germany, Austria and Japan, and pondered, in addition, many other questions of post-war policy. Since most or all of these questions involved fleets and forces in the theaters of war, the Coordinating Committee had to clear its decisions with the Joint Chiefs of Staff, and officers representing the Joint Chiefs sat in with the Coordinating Committee's staff groups. Before the Committee's recommendations went to the Secretary of State and the President, therefore, any differences with the Joint Chiefs had already been discovered and explored.

Such a process brought forth, as an example, the Committee's recom-

---

[33] See Department of State, *Post-War Foreign Policy Preparation, 1939–1945* (1949), pp. 276, 660–661.

[34] Howard W. Moseley, Charles W. McCarthy, and Alvin F. Richardson, "The State-War-Navy Coordinating Committee," *Bulletin* of the U.S. Department of State, XIII (Nov. 11, 1945), 745–747. Ray S. Cline, *Washington Command Post: The Operations Division* (Washington, 1951), pp. 326–330. John Carter Vincent, "The Post-War Period in the Far East," State Dept. *Bulletin*, XIII (Oct. 21, 1945), 644–648; "Germany and the Occupation," *ibid.*, XIV (May 26, 1946), 910–914; John H. Hilldring, Velma H. Cassidy, "American Policy in Occupied Areas," *ibid.*, XV (July 14, 1946). 47–48, (Aug. 18, 1946), 291–296.

mendations on post-war aid to China. Had these recommendations been compounded by the State Department alone, Herbert Feis tells us in his recent book, *The China Tangle,* they "would have subordinated the program of military aid to the satisfaction of . . . political ideas" — democratic government and political unity for China.[35] Recommendations drafted by the Army, Navy, and Air Forces, on the other hand, would have fixed on two different objectives — territorial unity for China and military strength for the Chinese government. Thus, while the State Department thought of aid for China as a means of exerting pressure on the Kuomintang, to force a political strengthening of the Nationalist government, the armed forces tended to think of this aid solely as a means for strengthening the battle capabilities of the Nationalist forces.

Since the choice between these points of view depended at all times upon detailed, expert information, the State Department and the military had to reconcile, or at least define, their differences before going to the White House with a program for immediate post-war aid for China. The State-War-Navy Coordinating Committee was an obvious arena where these views might be tested against each other.

The State Department drew up a statement of China policy, emphasizing the political objectives of unity and democratic government. Although this statement of policy has not been printed, an earlier model of it is visible in the MacArthur hearings, and the views of the State Department's chief Far Eastern planner, John Carter Vincent, have been published at length in the records of the McCarran committee.[36] In the final proposals of the State-War-Navy Coordinating Committee, quoted in Feis's book, one can therefore detect phrases written in with stubby blue pencils by the War and Navy Departments and the Joint Chiefs of Staff:

> The achievement of [American] objectives in China requires a friendly, unified, independent nation with a stable government resting, *insofar as practicable,* on the freely expressed support of the Chinese people. . . . The following should be established as policies of the United States: . . . .
>
> (b) *To assist and advise China in the development of modern armed forces, ground, sea and air, for the . . .*
>
> (1) *Maintenance of internal peace and security in China including the liberated areas of Manchuria and Formosa. . . .*[37]

One can see also the unaltered will of the State Department in such a sentence as: "The extent to which political stability is being achieved in China under a unified, fully representative government is regarded by the U.S. as a basic consideration which will at all times govern the furnishing of economic, military, or other assistance to that nation. . . ."

[35] Princeton, 1953, p. 374.

[36] *Hearings before Committee on Armed Services,* Committee on Foreign Relations, U.S. Senate, 82 Cong., 1 sess., "Military Situation in the Far East," Pt. IV, pp. 2929–2930. *Hearings before Subcommittee on Internal Security,* Committee on Judiciary, U.S. Senate, 82 Cong., 1 sess., "Institute of Pacific Relations."

[37] Feis, *China Tangle,* p. 375 (italics mine).

Thus were political and military views brought into line, through the agency of the State-War-Navy Coordinating Committee. That line admittedly jogged and wavered. And one can argue that events in the Far East would have followed a different course had the opinions of one department or the other prevailed. It remains true, nevertheless, that the State Department and the military departments disagreed, and this disagreement was due, not to a personal difference between John Carter Vincent and some general or admiral, but to a real difference between political and military perspectives. General Marshall, while Chief of Staff, opposed the State Department's idea of using aid to promote reforms in the Chinese government. Then, when he became Secretary of State, he defended this very idea against challenges voiced by the new chiefs of Staff.[38] Such real disagreements between the State and military departments had to be reconciled in some place like the State-War-Navy Coordinating Committee, or such a committee had to define the points at issue for the President's adjudication.

But the Committee had its limitations. It suffered, in the first place, from its inability to make policy. Although the Committee was capable of rapid staff work, as evidenced in its eight-day fabrication of a workable surrender instrument for Japan,[39] its mill of subcommittees hummed uselessly in the spring of 1945 when Marshal Tito threatened to march against Allied forces in Trieste. The question of American action simply fell beyond the powers of the assistant secretaries who made up the Coordinating Committee; and the Trieste decision had to be made by the President and his Cabinet Secretaries with little or no preliminary staff study.[40]

In the second place, the Committee went to work only when a question was referred to it by one of the departments. As a result, it failed to handle some questions well within its purview. The four-Power arrangements for occupation of Berlin were worked out hastily by soldiers and diplomats in the European Theater and approved by a nod from President Truman.[41] The Coordinating Committee never had a chance to examine these arrangements, and no provision was made for guaranteeing access to the city.

The nation needed the Coordinating Committee, but it also needed a policy-making agency with the power to review all questions. President Truman fully realized this need, and so did his Cabinet Secretaries, particularly Secretary of the Navy James Forrestal. Within two years after World War II, consequently, Mr. Truman, Mr. Forrestal, and a staff of experts had worked out a plan for a National Security Council. Bedded in the Unification Act of 1947, this plan received the approval of Congress, and the United States acquired a regular, legally established,

[38] U.S. State Dept., *United States Relations with China with Special Reference to the Period 1944–1949* (1949), pp. 251–252, 255–256, 269–273.

[39] *Hearings*. "Institute of Pacific Relations," *passim* (see index under "E. H. Dooman," "J. C. Vincent").

[40] Joseph C. Grew, *Turbulent Era* (New York, 1952), II, 1474–1485.

[41] Speech by Mr. Truman, *New York Times*, Oct. 5, 1952, p. 82. Speech by Mr. Eisenhower, *ibid.*, Oct. 8, 1952, p. 23.

cabinet-level agency for the coördination of political and military views on foreign policy.

Fifty years of growth and experiment lay behind this Council, and additional years of experiment lay ahead of it. The original Council showed signs, some said, of being dominated by its military members. As a result, Congress changed the membership in 1949, dropping out the Secretaries of the Army, Navy, and Air Force. And the composition of the Council has since been altered several times, by executive order or simply by invitation. Thus, for example, President Eisenhower has invited his Secretary of the Treasury to sit with every session of the Council, so that dollar costs may be reckoned with political and military costs.

These alterations, of course, reflect a change in the Council's functions. Still the patching and mending is all applied in one place, on the National Security Council, and with one aim — to perfect that Council. Instead of replacing one experiment with another, in other words, we are striving now to improve a working model.

Mechanically, of course, the National Security Council is still in its scraps-of-wire and bits-of-chewing-gum stage. While its general purposes are clear, its specific functions are not. There seems real doubt, particularly, whether the Council is meant to resolve differences of opinion or simply to bring them into the open. Is it to copy the British Committee of Imperial Defense, where variant ideas are exposed to endless debate, or Japan's pre-war Liaison Conference, where decision was the goal, and difference often resulted in resignation? Which direction the National Security Council means to take is, at this writing, far from sure.

A reflection of this uncertainty has been the tendency of the Council and its predecessors to work like church councils or party platform committees, rather than action groups. Compromises have been forged, it seems, simply for an inner feeling of righteousness and an outward appearance of unanimity. In the State-War-Navy Coordinating Committee paper on China quoted earlier, for example, the State Department and the military departments did not really reconcile differences. They simply agreed on an ambiguous formula. With easier consciences, thus, each department could do what it wanted to do in the first place. Forrestal's notes on subsequent National Security Council discussions, testimony at the MacArthur hearings, and Chalmers Roberts' reports in the Washington *Post and Times Herald* on the Indo-China and Quemoy mix-ups of 1954 suggest that there have been later instances of meaningless compromise.[42] Realization of the need for a coördinating committee has, in other words, sometimes obscured the truth that decision-making can become more realistic, but it cannot become easier. Coördination is no substitute for thought.

Neither has the problem of coördination itself been fully solved. While executive departments may treat one another with increasing frankness,

[42] Walter Millis (ed.), *The Forrestal Diaries* (New York, 1951), pp. 454, 517–518. Roberts synthesized his newspaper articles in "The Day We Didn't Go to War," *The Reporter*, XI (Sept. 14, 1954), and "Battle on 'The Rim of Hell': President vs. War Hawks," *ibid.* (Dec. 16, 1954).

the executive branch and the Congress retain the relationship of un-friendly sovereignties. Beside the monumental problem of harmonizing executive and congressional foreign policies, the relatively recent and minor problem of harmonizing executive views shades into insignificance. Even the simplest questions of executive-congressional coördination present absurd difficulty. "If you tell Congress nothing," as James Reston remarked, "they go fishing; if you promise nothing, they go fishing; if you tell them all, they go wild." [43] And, as Hanson Baldwin states the larger question: "Are national policies ever really forged in secrecy and by a small group? Do they not require the support and substantiation of Congress and public opinion?" [44]

These unsettled questions of function and competence, relations with Congress, and relation to public opinion ought not to cloud the progress that has been made. A committee that effects some political-military co-ördination has come into existence. Fifty years ago such a committee could not openly have existed in Washington. Had it existed in secret, it would very likely have been ineffective. During World War I, when a need for coördination was recognized, actual coördination was at best haphazard, and the new crises attending World War II saw one experi-ment tumble after another. The National Security Council is thus the product of a long and painful history. Whatever its present inadequacies and whatever the trials that lie ahead, it is still an institution. It answers an enduring need, and it is likely to be a permanent feature of American government.

The National Security Council Under Truman, Eisenhower, and Kennedy

Stanley L. Falk

The National Security Council, in the words of one observer, "constitutes the most ambitious effort yet made to coordinate policy on the cabinet level in the American federal government." [1] Created by the National

---

[43] Quoted in Millis, *Forrestal Diaries*, p. 444.
[44] Letter to the author.

Reprinted by permission from the *Political Science Quarterly*, LXXIX (1964), pp. 403–434.
[1] Paul Y. Hammond, "The National Security Council as a Device for Interdepart-mental Coordination: An Interpretation and Appraisal," *American Political Science Review*, LIV (1960), 899.

Security Act of 1947 and subsequently modified or expanded by Congress and the President, it represents an attempt to fill a long-recognized need for a single, top-ranking body to formulate and correlate national policy. Its roots lay in the British Committee of Imperial Defense, a Cabinet agency for coordinating national security matters, and in certain American attempts to provide a similar mechanism. The American efforts dated back to World War I but took form most notably in the Standing Liaison Committee of the early nineteen-forties and the State–War–Navy Coordinating Committee established in 1944.[2]

Yet the Committee of Imperial Defense was an arrangement more suited to Cabinet than to presidential government, and none of the American examples was extensive or effective enough to solve the pressing problems of policy formulation and direction that arose in the hectic days following World War II. It was at the height of the postwar unification struggle, then, that Ferdinand Eberstadt, in a study prepared for Navy Secretary James Forrestal, urged the establishment of a National Security Council as "a policy-forming and advisory" body of top government officials to assist the President in making and coordinating "over-all policies in the political and military fields." [3]

The National Security Act of 1947 accepted the Eberstadt recommendations for the establishment of the NSC. The Act created a Council consisting of the President, who would chair its meetings or, in his absence, designate another member to do so; the Secretaries of State, Defense, and the three Services; the Chairman, National Security Resources Board; and certain other officials whom the President, if he wished, might designate with the advice and consent of the Senate. A permanent staff would support the Council.

The function of the NSC, briefly stated, would be to assist the President in integrating and implementing national security policy. Specifically, the Council would examine American national security goals in relation to national power, study policies on areas of common interest to those departments and agencies concerned with national security, and suggest guidelines and courses of action to the President. To ensure the availability of an adequate intelligence basis for these deliberations, the 1947 Act also created a Central Intelligence Agency. This Agency, operating under NSC direction, would coordinate all government intelligence activities concerned with national security, would correlate and evaluate national security intelligence, and would advise and report to the Council on all matters within this field.

The National Security Council, while lacking executive authority or

---

[2] For these and other roots of the NSC, see *ibid.*, 899–901; U.S. Senate, Committee on Naval Affairs, *Unification of the War and Navy Departments and Postwar Organization for National Security, Report* to Hon. James Forrestal, Secretary of the Navy by Ferdinand Eberstadt, 79th Congress, 1st Session, 1945, 47–54 (hereinafter, *Eberstadt Report*); Ernest R. May, "The Development of Political-Military Consultation in the United States," *Political Science Quarterly*, LXX (1955), 161–80.

[3] *Eberstadt Report*, 7.

in fact any power other than to offer advice, was really an extension of the presidency. With the chief executive as its chairman, its decisions would become his decisions, and its members, as department heads, would be in a position to see that these decisions were carried out. Under a weak president, this sort of arrangement might tend to diminish or diffuse the powers of the chief executive; but under a strong one it would sharpen the decision-making process and render more efficient the implementation of decisions once made. In the final analysis, the personality and individual desires of each president would determine the role and scope of activity of the National Security Council.

Since the creation of the NSC, three strongly different individuals have occupied the White House. Each regarded the Council in his own way; each used it to satisfy his own needs and intentions. And in each administration, the organization of the NSC and its role in the formulation of national security policy have changed to meet the criteria imposed by the chief executive.[4]

I

President Truman's use of the National Security Council,[5] especially in the three years prior to the outbreak of the Korean War, reflected his strong concern for the authority, responsibility, and prerogatives of the chief executive. Congress had declared that the NSC would consist of certain officials whose function it would be to "advise the President . . . in matters involving the national security." [6] But Truman, among others, seriously questioned whether Congress had the constitutional power to require the President to seek advice from specific individuals before reaching decisions on certain subjects.[7] Truman also recognized that the wording of the National Security Act might be construed to establish the Council as an imitation of the British Cabinet, with similar powers and

4 The best source for a study of the birth and development of the NSC is the collection of hearings, studies, reports, and recommendations on the national security structure compiled by a group headed by Senator Henry M. Jackson and published as U.S. Senate, Subcommittee on National Policy Machinery of the Committee on Government Operations, *Organizing for National Security*, 3 Volumes (Washington, D.C., 1961). Especially useful is the "Organizational History of the National Security Council," prepared by James S. Lay, Jr., and Robert H. Johnson, two long-time staff members of the Council, which appears in Volume II of this collection. Unless otherwise indicated, this article is based on these volumes.

5 For this section, see also Sidney W. Souers, "Policy Formulation for National Security," *American Political Science Review*, XLIII (1949), 534–43; James S. Lay, Jr., "National Security Council's Role in the U.S. Security and Peace Program," *World Affairs*, CXV (1952), 37–39. These and some of the other articles cited below are also reproduced in *Organizing for National Security*, II.

6 National Security Act of 1947, Sec. 101 (a).

7 On this point, see Robert Cutler, "The Development of the National Security Council," *Foreign Affairs*, XXXIV (1956), 442–43; Hammond, "The National Security Council," 903. President Truman's views on his relations with the NSC are described in his *Memoirs*, II, *Years of Trial and Hope* (Garden City, N.Y., 1956), 59–60, and the quotations in the following paragraphs are taken from this source.

responsibilities, and a subsequent diminution of presidential authority.[8] Indeed, he recalls, "There were times during the early days of the National Security Council when one or two of its members tried to change it into an operating super-cabinet on the British model." This he strenuously opposed, as he did all ideas of adopting any aspects of the cabinet system. Under the British system, he wrote later, "there is a group responsibility of the Cabinet. Under our system the responsibility rests on one man — the President. To change it, we would have to change the Constitution. . . ."

As a means of emphasizing the advisory role of the NSC, Truman did not regularly attend Council meetings. After presiding at the first session of the Council on September 26, 1947, he sat in on only eleven of the fifty-six other meetings held before the start of the Korean War. In his absence, in conformity with Truman's view that the Secretary of State was the second ranking member of the Council and that the Department of State would play the major role in policy development, Secretary Marshall (and later Acheson) presided. Beginning in August 1949, when the Vice-President was added to the NSC, that officer took the chair in the President's absence.

Truman's lack of participation in NSC proceedings has often been explained as a means of permitting a free exchange of views that might otherwise have been inhibited by his presence. Some observers have also suggested that the President was simply too busy to attend. It is quite evident, however, that his absence was aimed at clearly establishing the Council's position with respect to the President and at preventing any apparent dilution of his role as chief executive.

This is not to say that Truman regarded the NSC as unnecessary or undesirable. On the contrary, he viewed it as "a badly needed new facility" in the government. "This was now the place . . . where military, diplomatic, and resources problems could be studied and continually appraised. This new organization gave us a running balance and a perpetual inventory of where we stood and where we were going on all strategic questions affecting the national security." But the Council was only "a place for recommendations to be worked out." Like the President's Cabinet, it did not make decisions or policy. A vote was "merely a procedural step." Only the President could determine policy and reach decisions, and these were functions he could not delegate to any committee or individual. Even when he sat as chairman of the Council and indicated his agreement with a specific recommendation, this did not become final until the NSC submitted a formal document to the President and secured his written approval. "When the President signs this document, the recommendation then becomes a part of the policy of the government." Here was Truman's understanding of the role of the President, and this firm belief determined his relationship with the National Security Council during the five years that it operated under his direction.

[8] For a fuller discussion of this question, see Hammond, "The National Security Council," 899–901.

For the first ten months of its existence, the NSC met irregularly in the Cabinet Room of the White House. Beginning in May 1948 meetings were scheduled twice a month, although not necessarily held, and special meetings were sometimes called. Only those officials specified by the National Security Act attended initially, with others invited to participate in discussions of particular interest to their agencies. The Director, CIA, also sat in as an adviser and observer. In January 1949 Truman directed the Secretary of the Treasury to attend all meetings, and, that summer, amendments to the National Security Act eliminated the Service Secretaries from Council membership, added the Vice-President, and, by designating the Joint Chiefs of Staff as the "principal military advisers" to the Council, opened the way for regular attendance by the Chairman, JCS, beginning in 1950.

Reorganization Plan No. 4 of 1949, effective in August of that year, placed the NSC in the Executive Office of the President, where it remains today. This move not only formalized a *de facto* situation, but was dramatic evidence of the position of the Council as an advisory arm of the President rather than as any sort of policy-making "politburo."

To assist the NSC in dealing with specific problems, the Council began to establish certain standing committees, normally representing agencies already participating in its activities but occasionally including members of non-Council agencies as well. These groups were usually created to handle some particularly sensitive matter or one of direct interest to only some agencies on the Council. Among the first of these were two committees concerned with internal security, the Interdepartmental Intelligence Conference and the Interdepartmental Committee on Internal Security, which reported to the NSC through the Council's newly appointed Representative on Internal Security.

The NSC staff, a small body of permanent Council employees and officers detailed temporarily from the participating agencies, was headed by a nonpolitical civilian executive secretary appointed by the President. An "anonymous servant of the Council," in the words of the first executive secretary, "a broker of ideas in criss-crossing proposals among a team of responsible officials," [9] he carried NSC recommendations to the President, briefed the chief executive daily on NSC and intelligence matters and maintained his NSC files, and served, in effect, as his administrative assistant for national security affairs.

The organization of the NSC staff [10] was flexible and, as the Council developed, changed to meet new needs. In general, during the pre-Korean period, it consisted of three groups. First was the Office of the Executive Secretary and the Secretariat, composed of permanent NSC employees, which performed the necessary basic functions of preparing agenda, circulating papers, and recording actions. Next was the Staff, consisting almost entirely of officials detailed on a full-time basis by departments and agencies represented on the Council, and headed by a

[9] Souers, 537.

[10] In this article, the word "staff" refers to the entire NSC staff organization. The "Staff" and later "Senior Staff" and "Staff Assistants" refer to parts of the "staff."

coordinator detailed from the State Department who was supported, in turn, by a permanent assistant. This body developed studies and policy recommendations for NSC consideration. The third group consisted of consultants to the executive secretary, the chief policy and operational planners for each Council agency. Thus, the head of the Policy Planning Staff represented the State Department, the Director, Joint Staff, represented the Department of Defense, and so forth.

While President Truman, in Walter Millis' phrase, had a "disinclination to make full use" of the NSC,[11] the Council was extremely active in its first years both as a discussion forum and as a medium for drawing up formal statements of national policy on a wide range of subjects. This latter effort was extremely significant. It represented the first attempt in the nation's history to formalize and set down specific national objectives and methods of achieving them in a series of carefully constructed policy papers intended to serve as guides to action for all government agencies. That in practice this attempt turned out to be less successful than many would have hoped is perhaps not as important as the fact that such an ambitious task was ever undertaken in the first place.

Policy papers developed by the NSC fell into four categories. First and most important were the basic comprehensive statements of overall policy, concerned with a broad range of national security problems and the political, economic, and military strategy to be pursued in meeting them. Next were papers bearing on large geographical areas of the world or specific countries. A third category dealt with functional matters such as mobilization, arms control, atomic energy, and trade policies. The final group of papers covered organizational questions, including NSC organization, the organization of foreign intelligence activities, and internal security organization. All of these documents would theoretically dovetail with each other to "form a basis for a balanced and consistent conduct of foreign, domestic, and military affairs related to our national security." [12]

Papers originated in a variety of ways. Some projects grew out of recommendations by the executive secretary, but most developed from suggestions by one or more members of the Council or by the NSC staff. For a while studies or reports prepared by the State–Army–Navy–Air Force Coordinating Committee served as a basis for NSC papers.[13] Initially the State Department was the most important single source of project requests, with the Defense Department a close second.

Most of the early papers developed were of the geographical type, with a basic overall policy document a continuing study under way concurrently. It was not until November 1948 that enough other work had been completed to allow NSC adoption of the first comprehensive basic na-

---

[11] Walter Millis, with Harvey C. Mansfield and Harold Stein, *Arms and the State: Civil-Military Elements in National Policy* (New York, 1958), 182.

[12] Souers, 539.

[13] The State–Army–Navy–Air Force Coordinating Committee had replaced the wartime State–War–Navy Coordinating Committee. Since its functions closely paralleled or even duplicated those of the NSC staff, the Coordinating Committee was dissolved in 1949.

tional security paper. Because this was a formative period for the Council, organizational policies drew next consideration, while few policies of a functional nature were considered. In the spring of 1949, shortly after the beginning of the second Truman administration, the Staff took on the dual job of preparing periodic general reviews of existing policies to determine what revisions were necessary and of drawing up papers on major problems that would discuss policy alternatives without making specific recommendations.

The first step in the development of a paper was usually a meeting of the Staff to consider the problem and define its scope. After each Staff member had obtained the views of his own agency on these questions, one individual would normally be given responsibility for preparation of a draft. The drafts of most of the early NSC papers were written by the State Department Policy Planning Staff, and a few were the products of a number of individual agency contributions integrated into a single report. Whatever its origin, the policy draft was then gone over by the Staff as a whole, which made necessary or desirable changes and attempted to reconcile or spell out any differences of opinion. The paper then went to the consultants who, without formally committing their respective departments, indicated their objections or general concurrences. On occasion, other agencies might also be asked to comment. With this accomplished, the draft, including any unresolved divergencies of view, was forwarded for formal Council consideration. If the subject had military implications, JCS views were also included.

Some papers were submitted to the Council merely for information, others solely as a basis for discussion. Those embodying policy recommendations, however, were forwarded to the President, together with any JCS views, by the executive secretary. The President would then reconcile whatever differences of opinion were still outstanding and, if he agreed, place his approval on the "Conclusions" section of the paper. The appropriate departments and agencies, as notified by the executive secretary, would then implement the new policy. President Truman developed the practice of designating one department head, normally the Secretary of State, as coordinator of all implementation, and periodic reports were also required by the Council.

Once the President had signed an NSC paper and directed that it be carried out, a new policy had, to all intents and purposes, been established and put into effect. But this did not necessarily make it policy in practice. What gave it reality was the President's "will and capability to get it executed." [14] This might mean a hard campaign on the part of the chief executive to educate or arouse public opinion, a long and arduous legislative battle, or a host of other problems to be met before the policy could truly take effect.

In addition to the formal development of policy papers, the NSC during this period also met a number of times to discuss current problems of

[14] Hammond, "The National Security Council," 907.

vital importance to national security. On these occasions, the Council convened without the formality of elaborate preparations or preliminary briefings. Some of these discussions, of course, served as the basis for policy papers, but in other cases the NSC was simply an intimate forum where the President's top-level advisers could thrash out questions requiring immediate action. The Berlin crisis and blockade of 1948 is a good example of this. With President Truman in the chair and General Lucius D. Clay, American commander in Germany, present to report, the Council met several times to discuss developments and make recommendations that the President could act on immediately.[15]

By the beginning of the Korean War, two years and nine months after the establishment of the NSC, the Council had become a well-integrated, functioning organization. It had held more than fifty meetings and taken over three hundred "actions" in the form of approvals, recommendations, and other deliberations. But the Council was still a long way from being the type of body that its creators had envisioned, and many problems, both functional and organizational in nature, were becoming evident.

In the first place, for all of its activities, the NSC could hardly be regarded as the top policy-formulating agency of the government, or even as the primary presidential adviser on national security. President Truman, jealous of his powers and unwilling to rely on the NSC simply because Congress had said he should, did not hesitate to turn to other advisers, in the Cabinet or executive office, or to solicit the advice of members of the Council as individuals in preference to the corporate recommendations of the entire group. The Secretaries of State and Defense were two officials whose counsel the President sought with increasing readiness. Especially important was the role of the Bureau of the Budget in establishing ceilings on defense spending, which gave that agency an impressive fiscal veto on any program recommended by the NSC.

Even the hundreds of policy papers produced by the Council failed to carry overriding weight. These, more often than not, avoided coming to grips with major issues, or when they did so, "lacked the precision and decisiveness necessary if they were to serve as guides to action." [16] Composed less as specific policy directives than as broad statements of principle, they were frequently too general for practical implementation.

In the field of policy-making, as Walter Millis put it, "The effect of NSC is not prominent; NSC no doubt considered the staff papers, debated policy and arrived at recommendations, but every glimpse we have been given of the actual policy-making process in this period shows Defense, State, the Budget Bureau, the White House, making the independent determinations — usually on a hasty if not extemporaneous basis — which really counted." [17] Before the Korean War, noted another observer, NSC actions, with or without presidential approval, "did not play a decisive or

15 Truman, II, 124–29.
16 Millis, 182.
17 *Ibid.*, 223.

a particularly significant role in the defense policy-making or the administration of the military establishment." [18]

If this situation was the result of Truman's unwillingness to use the NSC as Eberstadt had envisioned its use, there were other weaknesses in the system, a few reflecting the President's attitude but others probably the standard organizational growing pains to be expected in such a new and completely different agency.

In the first place, attendance at Council meetings, originally limited to the statutory members, had gradually broadened to include the consultants and other departmental advisers. This not only made for too large a group for free discussion, but also encouraged NSC members to look to their departmental advisers and to present their departmental rather than individual views of problems. In the absence of the President, moreover, discussion was more rambling and diffuse than if he had been present, and important actions were sometimes delayed or taken later outside the Council. Then, too, while the executive secretary briefed the President on the meeting, Truman could neither hear the direct expression of individual viewpoints nor, more important, could he discuss these with Council members. This sometimes led members to seek out the President after an NSC meeting and give him their ideas separately, a procedure that downgraded even further the relative importance of the Council as a corporate body.

There were also problems in the functioning of the NSC staff. Other agencies that detailed individuals to the Staff tended increasingly to look upon these people as "foreigners," out of touch with problems and attitudes of their parent organizations. The NSC consultants, on the other hand, heavily engaged in responsibilities within their own departments, were less and less able to devote attention to NSC matters. As a result, Council members began to by-pass the Staff, submitting their policy recommendations directly to the Council, and, at the same time, the Council tended to refer many of its problems not to the consultants but rather to *ad hoc* NSC committees. The absence of sound preliminary staff work frequently led to confusion and delay, as did the necessity for relying on *ad hoc* committees, unfamiliar with the overall national security picture and hampered by difficulties of coordination and perspective. An additional problem was the absence of JCS representation on the Staff, which made it hard to anticipate and allow for probable JCS views on papers before they reached the Council table.

And finally there was the growing anomaly of the Staff representative of the State Department holding the position of Staff Coordinator at a time when the bulk of matters coming before the Council was no longer concerned primarily with foreign affairs. With problems of atomic energy, internal security, defense mobilization, and military strategy becoming increasingly important, and with the consequent growth of the role and

[18] Paul Y. Hammond, *Organizing for Defense: The American Military Establishment in the Twentieth Century* (Princeton, 1961), 233.

responsibilities of other departments and agencies, the Staff Coordinator found himself torn between his duties as an impartial chairman and his function of advocating the State Department position. What was needed, clearly, was a Staff Coordinator without departmental ties and one, moreover, in close and constant contact with the President and thus personally familiar with his views and requirements.

Recognition of all these problems led, in late 1949 and early 1950, to considerable study of the role and procedures of the NSC. As a result of recommendations by the executive secretary, deliberations by the Council itself, further investigation by an *ad hoc* committee, the outbreak of the Korean War, and President Truman's own thoughts on the NSC, a number of functional and structural changes took place.

Within a few days after the beginning of the war in Korea, Truman directed that the NSC would meet regularly each Thursday and that all major national security recommendations would be coordinated through the Council and its staff. He himself began presiding regularly at these sessions, missing only nine out of seventy-one NSC meetings held from June 28, 1950, through the end of his administration in January 1953.

In late July 1950, in a directive again underlining the role of the Council in policy formulation, Truman ordered a reorganization and strengthening of the NSC. He limited attendance at NSC meetings to statutory members [19] plus the Secretary of the Treasury, the Chairman, JCS, the Director, CIA, the Special Assistant to the President (W. Averell Harriman), Sidney W. Souers (former Executive Secretary and at this time a Special Consultant to the President), and the Executive Secretary. No one else would be present without Truman's specific approval. The President also directed a reshuffling of the NSC staff. The permanent Secretariat remained, but the Staff and consultants were replaced by a Senior Staff and Staff Assistants. The Senior Staff was composed of representatives of State, Defense, NSRB, Treasury, JCS, and CIA, and shortly thereafter of Harriman's office, and headed by the Executive Secretary, an official without departmental ties. Members were generally of Assistant Secretary level or higher and in turn designated their Staff Assistants.

The Senior Staff participated closely and actively in the work of the Council. Not only did it continue the functions of the Staff, but it also took over responsibility for projects formerly assigned to *ad hoc* NSC committees. It thus provided the Council with continuous support by a high-level interdepartmental staff group. The Staff Assistants, who did most of the basic work for the Senior Staff, spent a large part of their time in their respective agencies, where they could better absorb agency views and bring them to the fore during the developmental phase of NSC papers. The position of the executive secretary, moreover, as chairman of the Senior Staff and also head of the permanent NSC staff in the White House, gave that official an intimate view of the President's opinions and

[19] The President, Vice-President, Secretaries of State and Defense, and Chairman, National Security Resources Board.

desires that he could bring to bear quite early in the planning process. And finally, JCS and Treasury representation on the NSC staff filled needs that had been long felt.

Other changes also took place on the heels of the 1950 reorganization. At the end of 1950, the President directed the head of the newly created Office of Defense Mobilization to attend Council meetings, and a few months later the ODM Director nominated a Senior Staff member. The Mutual Security Act of 1951, establishing a new foreign aid organization, made the Director for Mutual Security a statutory member of the Council, and he too nominated a member for the Senior Staff.[20] Also, at about the same time, a representative of the Bureau of the Budget began sitting in at certain meetings of the Senior Staff to provide fiscal advice and liaison. And finally, to coordinate the implementation of national security policy and ensure that the NSC was provided with current information, Truman directed the establishment of a unit within the NSC staff to receive and channel to the Council agency reports on the status of approved national security programs.

One other addition to the NSC system came into being in the spring of 1951. This was the Psychological Strategy Board, consisting of the Under Secretary of State, the Deputy Secretary of Defense, and the Director, CIA, with a full-time director and staff. The PSB would develop and coordinate psychological strategy and, as one writer put it, "was to be a sort of a general staff to plan and supervise the cold war." [21] While not actually a part of the NSC, it reported to the Council and its director attended NSC meetings as an observer and was represented by an adviser on the Senior Staff. It marked the first attempt to pull together the nation's psychological planning and operations amidst a growing recognition of the need to counter Soviet use of psychological and other unorthodox methods in the heightening cold war.

The 1950 reorganization did not change substantially the procedure of preparing NSC papers, although it did somewhat tighten up the process. Aside from policy matters concerning the Korean War and related security areas, most Council papers were of the regional policy type and these continued to be prepared in initial draft by the State Department. Depending upon the subject, of course, other agencies, the Staff Assistants, and the Senior Staff also contributed to or initiated the draft process. Although President Truman now presided at Council meetings, he did not make an immediate decision on NSC recommendations. This he reserved until after the executive secretary had formally presented him with the Council recommendations and actions.

---

20 The new Director was Harriman, already a member of the NSC as Special Assistant to the President and already represented on the Senior Staff. He and his representative simply remained at their respective Council assignments, although with different titles.

21 Colonel Wendell E. Little, *White House Strategy-Making Machinery, 1952, 1954,* Air War College Studies, No. 2 (Maxwell Air Force Base, Alabama, 1954), 20.

In the first year after the beginning of the Korean War, the NSC and its Senior Staff were quite active, with the Council meeting about three times each month and the Senior Staff getting together at least twice weekly. By the end of 1951, however, the Council was meeting on an average of a little less than twice a month, the Senior Staff about once a week, and NSC activity was generally lighter. For the most part, during the Korean War phase of the Truman administration, the NSC played a somewhat larger role in helping to formulate national policy. Yet as a body it was still not dominant, since the President continued to look to individuals or other agencies for advice and recommendations in the national security field. The NSC "provided a convenient mechanism" for staffing and coordinating interdepartmental views, but "its position was still somewhat casual." [22]

As summed up by the executive secretary near the close of President Truman's term of office:

> . . . the National Security Council provides the President a readily available means of ensuring that a policy decision he has to make for the security of the nation has been carefully considered from all points of view and by all of the responsible officials in the Executive Branch who are directly concerned. . . . The existence of the Council gives the President a permanent staff agency in his Executive Office which can . . . bring to bear on each grave issue of national security all the talents, resources, and considerations which will help him find the best possible solution.[23]

The NSC was there if the President wanted to use it. But it was no more nor less than he wished to make it.

II

If Harry S. Truman to a large extent limited the role of the National Security Council in policy formulation and integration, Dwight D. Eisenhower may be said to have institutionalized it. President Eisenhower "reactivated NSC and infused into it a greater responsibility than it had enjoyed under Truman." [24] He did this by formalizing, developing, and expanding the structure and procedures of the NSC and in effect creating an NSC *system* of which the Council was itself the primary but by no means the most significant portion. The NSC system consisted of the central Council supported by a grid of highly standardized procedures and staff relationships and a complex interdepartmental committee substructure. In its final form, this machinery was geared to support the executive decision-making process not as Truman or Kennedy would conceive of it, but, properly, as Eisenhower practiced it. Not surprisingly,

[22] Millis, 255, 388.
[23] Lay, 37.
[24] Millis, 182.

the Eisenhower NSC reflected the Eisenhower view of government and specifically of the role of the President.[25]

During the 1952 election campaign, presidential candidate Eisenhower criticized Truman's use of the NSC. He promised that if elected he would elevate the Council to the position originally planned for it under the National Security Act and use it as his principal arm in formulating policy on military, international, and internal security affairs. Accordingly, he asked Robert Cutler, the Boston banker who was soon to become the new President's Special Assistant for National Security Affairs, to make a study of the NSC and recommend ways and means of improving it. Cutler's report, submitted to Eisenhower in mid-March 1953, became the basis of an immediate structural and functional reorganization aimed at systematizing the NSC. Subsequently, these initial changes, and other studies, led to further adjustments during the eight years of the Eisenhower administration.

By 1960, the NSC had developed into a highly complicated but nonetheless smoothly operating machine, with clear lines of authority and responsibility and elaborate yet systematized staff work.[26] The heart of the machine was, of course, the Council itself, with its five statutory members: the President, Vice-President, Secretaries of State and Defense, and Director, Office of Civil Defense Mobilization.[27] The Council met regularly on Thursday mornings. In addition to the statutory members, as many as a score of others might be present. Normally, the Secretary of the Treasury and the Budget Director attended NSC meetings and, when items pertinent to their responsibilities were being discussed, so did the Attorney General, Chairman, Atomic Energy Commission, and Administrator, National Aeronautics and Space Administration. At the determination of the President, officials such as the Secretary of Commerce or the Chairman of the Council of Economic Advisers might also be present for specific items. Occasionally private citizens, appointed by the President as informal advisers to the Council, might appear to present and discuss their reports. And a large number of others, not formal participants, also attended regularly in various capacities. The JCS Chairman and CIA Director were there as advisers. The Assistant and Deputy Assistant to the President, the Director, USIA, the Under Secretary of State for Economic Affairs, the Special Assistants to the President for Foreign Economic Policy and for Science and Technology, and the White House staff secre-

---

[25] The literature on the Eisenhower NSC is more extensive than for the Council under Truman. Three NSC officials have written or spoken publicly on the Eisenhower NSC, as have many knowledgeable writers and critics, and extensive testimony was heard by the Jackson subcommittee. A considerable amount of the literature has been reproduced with the testimony in *Organizing for National Security*.

[26] For a step-by-step account of organizational developments, see Lay and Johnson, 23–52.

[27] With the abolition of NSRB in 1953, the Director, ODM, replaced the NSRB chairman on the NSC and in 1958 this NSC membership was assumed by the Director, OCDM. Membership in the NSC of the Director for Mutual Security (subsequently the Director, Foreign Operations Administration) was dropped in 1955.

tary all attended as observers. Staff representation was provided by the President's Special Assistants for National Security Affairs and for Security Operations Coordination and by the NSC Executive and Deputy Executive Secretaries.

As Chairman of the Council, the President was directly supported by two White House Staff members, the Special Assistants for National Security Affairs and Security Operations Coordination. The former was by far the more important. The principal supervisory officer of the NSC, he advised the President on the Council agenda and briefed him before each meeting, presented matter for consideration at the meetings, appointed (with the President's approval) special committees and consultants, and supervised the executive secretary in the direction of the NSC staff. He also had the major responsibility of chairing the Council's two major subsidiary organizations, the Planning Board and the Operations Coordinating Board.

The NSC Planning Board had essentially the same functions as the old Senior Staff and a similar, somewhat expanded, membership. It met regularly on Tuesday and Friday afternoons. Those agencies with permanent or standing representation on the Council itself were represented on the Planning Board by officials at the assistant secretary level, nominated by the department heads and approved by the President. Advisers from JCS and CIA as well as the Special Presidential Assistant for Security Operations Coordination also attended meetings, as did observers from other interested agencies. Staff representation consisted of the NSC Executive and Deputy Executive Secretary and the Director of the Planning Board Secretariat. Planning Board activities were supported by a staff of Board Assistants, the old Staff Assistants under a new name.

The second major staff agency of the NSC was the Operations Coordinating Board. "The OCB," wrote Robert Cutler, "arose like a phoenix out of the ashes of the old Psychological Strategy Board." The PSB "had been premised on the fallacious concept of an independently existing psychological strategy," whereas the members of the Eisenhower administration believed that psychological strategy was an integral part of an overall national security program and could not practically be separated.[28] The purpose of the newly established OCB was not only to coordinate and integrate psychological with national strategy, but also, and more importantly, to act as the coordinating and integrating arm of the NSC for all aspects of the implementation of national security policy.

The OCB met regularly on Wednesday afternoons at the State Department. Permanent membership included the Under Secretary of State for Political Affairs, Deputy Secretary of Defense, Directors, CIA, USIA, and ICA, and the Special Assistants to the President for National Security Affairs and Security Operations Coordination (who served as Chairman and Vice-Chairman respectively). The Chairman, AEC, Under Secretary

28 Cutler, 448.

of the Treasury, and Deputy Director of the Budget attended on a standing basis and other agencies participated on an *ad hoc* basis. An elaborate staff supported the Board, and several of its members normally attended OCB meetings. Despite the strong military representation in other parts of the NSC, no representatives of the JCS participated in the activities of either the OCB or its staff.

Completing the organizational structure of the NSC were the Interdepartmental Intelligence Conference, the Interdepartmental Committee on Internal Security, and other special and *ad hoc* committees, and the NSC staff, which included the Planning Board, OCB, and Internal Security Coordinating staffs.

President Eisenhower's concept of the NSC, as stated by him, was that

> the Council is a corporate body, composed of individuals advising the President in their own right, rather than as representatives of their respective departments and agencies. Their function should be to seek, with their background of experience, the most statesmanlike solution to the problems of national security, rather than to reach solutions which represent merely a compromise of departmental positions. This same concept is equally applicable to advisory and subordinate groups, such as the Joint Chiefs of Staff, the NSC Planning Board, and the Operations Coordinating Board; although the members of the latter two Boards are responsible also for stating the views of their respective departments and agencies.[29]

Within this concept, policy formulation followed a somewhat formalized pattern. A subject for consideration or action might be raised by any part of the NSC system, from the President on down. It might deal with a new problem area, the result of some particular development in world events; it might merely be a suggestion that a standing policy be reviewed; it might be a combination of these or other factors. Discussion or preparation of a preliminary staff study would then begin within the Planning Board. A first draft, prepared by the agency of primary interest, would next be considered, gone over by the Board Assistants working with others within their own departments, and then restudied by the entire Board. This procedure might be repeated several times, frequently in smaller subgroups and often in conjunction with outside consultants, and the whole process would constantly be monitored by the Special Assistant for National Security Affairs and the Executive Secretary. Before formal Council consideration, finally, each member would receive an advance copy of the paper, with JCS comments, and be individually briefed by his Planning Board representative.

Under the Eisenhower administration, NSC papers included a Financial Appendix, something they had not previously contained. This document, specifically called for by the President as a regular part of most NSC papers, was intended to indicate the fiscal implications of the pro-

---

[29] Quoted in *Organizing for National Security*, II, 129. See also Lay and Johnson, 32–33.

posed policy and was to be carefully considered by the Council in determining its recommendations.

President Eisenhower sometimes made his decision on these recommendations at the NSC meeting itself, but in most cases a formal record of actions was circulated for comment by the members before it was submitted for final presidential approval. Once the President had made his decision, it was the OCB's function to coordinate and integrate the activities of those departments and agencies responsible for executing the new policy.

The OCB had no authority to direct or control these activities, but it provided a means by which the responsible agencies could consult and cooperate with each other. The Board's own operations were limited to advising, expediting, and following up, although since OCB members were on the Under Secretary level they each had enough authority within their own agencies to see that agreements reached within the Board were carried out. Also, while it did not make policy, the OCB developed or initiated new proposals for action within the existing framework of national security policies. In practice, all of the Board's activities were limited to policies affecting international affairs, since other coordinating mechanisms already existed for the fields of internal security and defense mobilization.

The whole process of policy formulation and implementation has been described by Robert Cutler with a simple and arresting metaphor. The NSC was at the top of "policy hill." Policy recommendations moved up one side of the hill, through the Planning Board to the Council, where they were "thrashed out and submitted to the President." Approved by the chief executive, the new policy traveled "down the other side of policy hill to the departments and agencies responsible for its execution." A short distance down the slope was the OCB, to which the President referred the new policy for coordination and operational planning with the relevant departments and agencies.[30]

The neatness and mechanical order of this process was praised by its supporters as the most efficient means of transacting the heavy load of business with which the National Security Council concerned itself under President Eisenhower. During his first three years in office, for example, the Council met 145 times and took 829 policy actions, as opposed to 128 meetings and 699 policy actions in its more than five years under Truman. Critics, however, labeled this "mass production, packaging and distribution," and questioned whether truly effective policy could be developed by a form of standardized bulk processing.[31] In reply, supporters of the system pointed out that in times of emergency — President Eisenhower's two illnesses, for example — it had provided a "reservoir of accumulated policy guidance" that enabled agency and department heads

---

[30] Cutler, 448. For case histories of two hypothetical policy decisions, see Cutler's testimony, *Organizing for National Security*, I, 579–83, and Timothy W. Stanley and Harry H. Ransom, "The National Security Council," a study prepared for the Harvard University defense policy seminar, January 1957, in *ibid.*, II, 199–200.

[31] Millis, 390.

to continue functioning with the full knowledge that they were following approved guidelines within "the broad policy concept established by the President." [32]

This sort of exchange was typical of the growing controversy over the NSC that had developed by the late nineteen-fifties. Critics admitted that the Eisenhower NSC had "infused a new order and system into decisions which were once more various and chaotic," that it had "assisted in bringing the departments together in more orderly and cooperative effort" in areas of "comparatively minor importance," [33] and that its theoretical potentialities were great. But they also charged that the Council was incapable of dealing with large, basic problems, that it was overstaffed, excessively rigid, and unable to bring any real focus to bear on major aspects of national security policy.

Basically, they argued, the NSC was a huge committee, and suffered from all the weaknesses of committees. Composed of representatives of many agencies, its members were not free to adopt the broad, statesmanlike attitude desired by the President, but, rather, were ambassadors of their own departments, clinging to departmental rather than national views. Moreover, the normal interagency exchanges and cross-fertilization that should have taken place outside the NSC were cut off in favor of action within the Council system, where members engaged in negotiation and horse-trading in a process essentially legislative rather than deliberative and rational. The result, as former Secretary of State Dean Acheson charged, was "agreement by exhaustion," [34] with the ponderous NSC machinery straining mightily to produce not clear-cut analyses of alternate courses, but rather compromise and a carefully staffed "plastering over" of differences.

The Presidential decision, therefore, was based on no deliberate measuring of opposing views against each other, but on a blurred generalization in which the opportunity for choice had been submerged by the desire for compromise. Approved national policy statements, it was argued, were thus not only imprecise, but were also far too broad and sweeping to be applied to specific problems. They were, consequently, all things to all men, with each protagonist of a different line of action finding justification for his own view in the vague or general wording of an approved paper. Even with the best of intentions, an agency or department head often could not divine the precise meaning of an approved policy — with consequent and obvious difficulties in implementing it.[35]

[32] Cutler, 445; Dillon Anderson, "The President and National Security," *Atlantic Monthly*, CXCVII (1956), 46.

[33] Millis, 391. Critics and defenders of the NSC under Eisenhower, especially the former, are amply represented, in *Organizing for National Security*. See also Hammond, "The National Security Council," 903–10.

[34] Dean Acheson, "Thoughts About Thought in High Places," The *New York Times Magazine*, October 11, 1959, reproduced in *Organizing for National Security*, II, 292. The theme of the legislation of strategy is developed at length in Samuel P. Huntington, *The Common Defense: Strategic Problems in National Politics* (New York, 1961), 146–66.

[35] The implications of this for military commanders and especially for the JCS were explained by former Army Chief of Staff General Maxwell D. Taylor before the Jack-

Nor was the OCB of much use in solving the problem. An interdepartmental committee with no authority, it engaged in the same sort of bargaining and negotiation in interpreting and implementing policy as had the Planning Board and Council in creating it. Frequently by-passed or ignored, also, the OCB in the final analysis had little effect on the actual coordination of policy execution.

To make matters worse, the critics went on, the NSC system by its very nature was restricted to continuing and developing already established policies and was incapable of originating new ideas and major innovations. Council members were either too busy in their own agencies or too intent on promoting departmental viewpoints to take the free and unfettered approach to their work on the NSC that was necessary to initiate fresh and imaginative policies. NSC members were well aware, also, that much of national security policy was in fact developed and coordinated outside of the Council, through the Budget Bureau, the Cabinet, or separate policy groups that dealt with matters like disarmament, manpower and reserve policy, or executive organization, or through individuals like the Secretaries of State or the Treasury who exercised personal influence with the President. Frequently departments or agencies purposely by-passed the NSC system in order to ensure the success of critical proposals. Indeed, the whole question of whether national policy was best developed by an NSC consisting of the officials who would implement this policy, and could thus best understand the attendant problems, or by independent bodies of thinkers not limited by operational restrictions was sharply underlined by President Eisenhower's increasing use of outside committees of private citizens to study important problems in the national security field.

To all of these criticisms, the supporters of the NSC system replied vigorously, either denying the accuracy of the critics' premises or the validity of their conclusions or arguing forcefully that if the Council machinery were less than perfect, it was nevertheless an extremely effective means of developing national security policy and the one best suited to the ideas and methods of President Eisenhower.

Some critics, in disparaging the Eisenhower NSC system, had admitted that the policies it developed would probably have been the policies of the Eisenhower administration in any event. Gordon Gray, Special Assistant to the President for National Security Affairs during most of Eisenhower's second term, implied strong agreement with this view. "I suspect," he said, "that the unhappiness of any knowledgeable person with respect to the NSC and its procedures really derives, not from a concern about how the machinery works, but what it produces. This, then, is substantive disagreement. For those, the only solution would seem to be to elect a different President." [36]

---

son subcommittee and in his own book: *Organizing for National Security*, I, 787–99; Taylor, *The Uncertain Trumpet* (New York, 1960), 82–83 and *passim*.

[36] Gordon Gray, "Role of the National Security Council in the Formulation of National Policy," prepared for delivery to the American Political Science Association, September 1959, in *Organizing for National Security*, II, 189.

III

In April 1959, Senator Henry M. Jackson, in a memorable address to the students of the National War College and Industrial College of the Armed Forces, vigorously attacked the Eisenhower NSC system. Summing up many of the criticisms already voiced by others, he referred to the Council as it then functioned as "a dangerously misleading façade." He had, he announced, recently proposed a full-scale, nonpartisan congressional study of the whole problem of formulating national security policy with a view to making definite recommendations for "constructive remedies." [37]

Three months later Jackson found himself at the head of a Subcommittee on National Policy Machinery, a subgroup of the Senate Committee on Government Operations newly established to implement his proposal. The subcommittee's "inquiry" — to use its own term — lasted more than two years, until the fall of 1961. During this period, it heard testimony from nearly three dozen individuals who had participated in one way or another in the process of helping to formulate or execute national security policy. It also studied all the available literature on the problem and itself prepared studies, reports, and collections of background material. Its efforts constituted the first comprehensive review of the national security policy process since the period leading up to passage of the National Security Act of 1947.

By the winter of 1960–61, the Jackson subcommittee had advanced far enough in its work to come up with a number of conclusions and recommendations, which it published for the education of the incoming Kennedy administration. These findings and proposals dealt with many areas of the government, from the President on down to the individual private citizen in the national service, but the National Security Council was, of course, of prime concern.

The new President, said the subcommittee, could use the NSC either as "an intimate forum" to meet "with his chief advisers in searching discussion and debate of a limited number of critical problems" both long-range and immediate, or as "the apex of a comprehensive and highly institutionalized system for generating policy proposals and following through on presidentially approved decisions." [38] Based on its study, the subcommittee concluded that the "real worth of the Council to a President" lay in the former course. Only in this manner could he and his most important advisers "gain that intellectual intimacy and mutual understanding on which true coordination depends." Only thus could he "receive from his department and agency heads a full exposition of

[37] Senator Henry M. Jackson, "How Shall We Forge a Strategy for Survival," April 16, 1959, *Organizing for National Security*, II, 266–77.

[38] "The National Security Council," December 12, 1960, *ibid.*, III, 32–33. The material that follows is drawn from *ibid.*, 38–40. See also "Final Statement of Senator Henry M. Jackson," November 15, 1961, *ibid.*, 3–8.

policy alternatives available to him, and, in turn, give them clear-cut guidance for action."

To establish a National Security Council of true value to the President, "to 'deinstitutionalize' and to 'humanize' the NSC process," the subcommittee made the following recommendations:

(1) The Council should meet only to advise the President or receive his decision on specific major items. "Council meetings and the Council agenda should never become ritualistic."

(2) The Council should offer a clear expression on alternate courses of action and their implications and "not spare the President the necessity of choice."

(3) Council meetings should be "considered gatherings of principals" and restricted to top officials, with staff attendance "tightly controlled." A written record of decisions should be kept.

(4) The Planning Board should be replaced by a group "used mainly to criticize and comment upon policy initiatives developed by the departments or stimulated by the President." This body should not negotiate or secure agency concurrences. More use might be made of "informal working groups" or outside consultants.

(5) "The President must rely mainly upon the Secretary of State for the initial synthesis of the political, military, economic, and other elements which go into the making of a coherent national strategy." The Secretary was "crucial to the successful operation of the Council."

(6) The OCB should be abolished and "responsibility for implementation of policies cutting across departmental lines should, wherever possible, be assigned to a particular department or . . . action officer, possibly assisted by an informal interdepartmental group."

(7) The NSC staff should be reduced and more closely integrated. A small presidential staff, working "outside the system," should closely assist the chief executive by providing information, suggesting "policy initiatives," and "spotting gaps in policy execution."

(8) The membership on the Council of the Chairman, NSRB, subsequently replaced by the Director, OCDM, was intended to provide the NSC with perspectives on the domestic economy and resources. Since OCDM was less concerned with these problems than with civil defense, the statutory membership of its director on the NSC might well be dropped.

(9) Ways and means should be found of better integrating NSC recommendations with budgetary decisions made outside the Council.

IV

The views of the Jackson subcommittee found a ready audience in the new administration that arrived in Washington in January 1961, for in spirit and content they came very close to matching President John F. Kennedy's ideas of the nature and process of presidential decision-making. Within a very short period after taking office, the new chief executive dismantled the elaborate NSC system so carefully built by his predecessor and replaced it with a loose, flexible, fairly pragmatic set of procedures more suited to his own concepts and methods. Gone was the NSC Planning Board with its highly systematized development of papers, gone the formal, crowded, regularly scheduled meetings of the Council, gone the OCB with its elaborate, interdepartmental follow-up on NSC actions. In their place was a new method of decision-making for national security problems, one that seemed to combine the better features of the informal mechanism developed by Truman and the institutionalized system created by Eisenhower.[39]

Of the old NSC system, all that now remains is the statutory membership in the Council itself — the President, Vice-President, Secretaries of State and Defense, and Director, Office of Emergency Planning [40] — and the President's Special Assistant for National Security Affairs who, assisted by a Deputy and the Executive Secretary, runs the small NSC staff. The Director, CIA, and Chairman, JCS, continue as advisers. Other officials participate in Council deliberations as and when directed by the President, but their participation is on a much more informal and *ad hoc* basis than before.

Under President Eisenhower, the NSC was a form of superdepartment placed atop the traditional structure of executive departments and agencies to solve the problems that individual departments were unable to handle. Under Kennedy, the NSC became only one of several means by which problems may be solved. It took its place beside special Cabinet committees, informal groups of officials, and other bodies organized on an *ad hoc* basis to assist and advise in the national security process. Primary emphasis was returned to the regular departments and agencies and their planning and operational staffs. These, reinforced by interdepartmental committees or task forces and close working, and often personal, relationships between the operating officials, bore the heaviest workload in the national security process.

Normally the President assigned the preparation of a study or recommendation to a Cabinet official or one of his top subordinates. This official, in turn, was responsible for obtaining other departmental views and checking and coordinating with other responsible individuals. Sometimes he did this within small, interdepartmental groups, specially created to study the problem, sometimes by arranging for subordinates in each interested agency to develop the matter. Where appropriate, this included close consultation with the Budget Bureau. Fiscal matters were considered during the development of a study and in drawing up recommendations and proposals; papers no longer had separate financial

39 This section is based on the testimony of then Budget Director David E. Bell, Defense Secretary Robert S. McNamara, and Secretary of State Dean Rusk before the Jackson subcommittee and on a letter from Kennedy's Special Assistant for National Security Affairs, McGeorge Bundy, to Senator Jackson, reproduced in the published hearings, *Organizing for National Security,* I, 1173–81, 1215–27, 1323–33, 1335–38.

40 OEP replaced the former OCDM.

appendices. The completed report included not only the responsible official's own analysis and recommendations for action, but also a full statement of any differing views held by other agencies or individuals. This was true whether the report was prepared by one person or by a special task force.

The final version, presented to President Kennedy at a formal meeting of the NSC or within smaller or larger panel or subcommittee meetings, was then discussed and, if necessary, debated further before the President made his decision. Once the chief executive approved a specific recommendation, the responsible agency or department made a written record of the decision and the head of that agency, or a high-level action officer, was charged with overseeing its implementation. By placing in the same agency or individual — always the agency or official of primary interest — the responsibility for both planning and implementation, Kennedy deliberately eliminated the distinction between theory and operation that had existed under the Planning Board–OCB balance, a distinction felt by many to have been unrealistic and impractical. If the course of action decided upon was so broad that a single department did not have overriding responsibility, the decision was written up by the NSC staff and the President himself might direct its implementation. Presidential decisions, incidentally, were no longer recorded as part of elaborate position papers, but stated briefly in National Security Action Memoranda — referred to by the initiate as NSAM's — which merely indicated the issue at hand and what Kennedy had decided to do about it.

In an administration that placed great emphasis on individual responsibility, initiative, and action, as well as on personal relationships, probably the most important member of the NSC after the President himself was Secretary of State Dean Rusk. President Kennedy firmly established the primacy of the State Department in foreign policy matters and in all national security matters that come within this area. To the Secretary of State and his top deputies — in this context normally the Assistant Secretaries for the various geographic areas — fell the job of pulling together many of the elements of national security planning and implementation. In placing "increased reliance on the leadership of the Department of State," one NSC official has written,

> . . . the President has made it very clear that he does not want a large separate organization [such as the NSC] between him and his Secretary of State. Neither does he wish any question to arise as to the clear authority and responsibility of the Secretary of State, not only in his own Department, and not only in such large-scale related areas as foreign aid and information policy, but also as the agent of coordination of all major policies toward other nations.[41]

Next in importance to the Secretary of State was Secretary of Defense Robert S. McNamara, who bore a heavy burden of responsibility in

[41] McGeorge Bundy to Senator Jackson, September 4, 1961, *Organizing for National Security*, I, 1337–38.

advising the President and carrying out his decisions. He worked closely with Secretary Rusk, and the top action officers of both departments were in immediate and constant touch with each other. Such day-to-day relationships enabled the Defense Department to operate with a full awareness of current political guidance and the State Department to have a proper understanding of the military implications of any new or proposed policy. The end result was to increase the effectiveness and ease of action of the President's two top advisers on the National Security Council.

Another statutory member of the NSC is the Director, Office of Emergency Planning, Edward A. McDermott. Under the Kennedy reorganization of the national government, the OEP came much closer to filling the presidential staff role originally visualized for the NSRB in coordinating government-wide planning for emergency management of national resources. The membership of its director in the NSC thus answered to a considerable extent the criticism of the Jackson subcommittee of the participation in the Council of the OCDM Director. McDermott was present at formal NSC meetings and his staff prepared studies and analyses of the nation's resources as they affect the development and implementation of national security policy.

One regular participant in the NSC who is not a statutory member of the Council but whose position was obviously unique was the Attorney General. As the President's brother, Robert Kennedy had the trust and confidence of the chief executive and ready access to the White House. He participated actively in the national security process and served on subgroups or panels of the Council. He also received the reports of the Interdepartmental Intelligence Conference and the Interdepartmental Committee on Internal Security, which hitherto had been responsible to the Council through the NSC staff.

The Special Assistant to the President for National Security Affairs, McGeorge Bundy, also played an important role in the national security process. Not only was he a top presidential adviser, but as overall director of the NSC staff he participated in all Council-related activities. He and his assistants had a variety of responsibilities in addition to their normal secretariat functions. They suggested areas for consideration and the mechanisms for handling these and other problems; followed studies through the planning stage and saw that they were properly coordinated, staffed, and responsive to the needs and desires of the President; ensured that a written record was made of all decisions, whether they were reached at formal NSC meetings or at other top conferences; and kept tabs on the implementation of whatever policy had been adopted. In this work, Bundy and the NSC staff coordinated closely with other parts of the presidential staff and the Budget Bureau, performed whatever liaison was necessary, and met frequently with the President at regular White House staff meetings.[42]

---

[42] For an interesting comparison of Bundy with earlier "White House advisers," see Chalmers M. Roberts, "About Mr. Bundy," *Washington Post and Times Herald,* November 3, 1962, A-9. See also Joseph Kraft, "Kennedy's Working Staff," *Harper's,* CCXXV (December 1962), 31–32.

Formal NSC meetings were held often but irregularly, sometimes as frequently as three times a week and usually at least once every two weeks. In the first half year of the Kennedy administration, for example, the Council met sixteen times. Many matters that had been considered at regular NSC meetings under Eisenhower were now handled in separate meetings of the President with Secretaries Rusk and McNamara or with a single Cabinet officer, or in committees of the NSC that included only some of the statutory members but also several of their top deputies or other government officials, or at meetings below the presidential level. During the height of the Cuban crisis in October 1962, for instance, Kennedy met almost daily with the so-called Executive Committee of the NSC. This committee consisted of the Chief Executive, Secretaries Rusk and McNamara, Treasury Secretary C. Douglas Dillon, Attorney General Kennedy, CIA Director John A. McCone, JCS Chairman General Maxwell D. Taylor, Presidential Assistant Bundy, and the President's Special Counsel, Theodore C. Sorensen. Also in attendance at many of these meetings were Vice-President Johnson, Under Secretary of State George Ball, Deputy Defense Secretary Roswell L. Gilpatrick, Ambassador at Large Llewellyn E. Thompson, UN Ambassador Adlai E. Stevenson, and former Secretary of State Acheson.[43]

The NSC under President Kennedy, it is clear, was thus a flexible organization within the overall national security structure. Used pragmatically and in a variety of ways, it was only one of several tools that Kennedy employed to help him reach decisions on major issues affecting the security of the nation.

V

"Fundamentally," as Robert Cutler observed in 1956, "the Council is a vehicle for the President to use in accordance with its suitability to his plan for conducting his great office." A "peculiar virtue of the National Security Act is its flexibility . . . each President may use the Council as *he* finds most suitable at a given time." [44]

The history of the NSC under three chief executives amply bears this out. As a means of assisting the President in the difficult task of forming and implementing national security policy, the Council has played a varied role since its inception. Its role under future presidents may be equally changed, but the need for an NSC or for something similar would appear to be self-evident.

[43] Stewart Alsop and Charles Bartlett, "In Time of Crisis," *Saturday Evening Post*, CCXXXV (December 8, 1962), 15–20; *Washington Post and Times Herald*, November 1, 1962, A-13.
[44] Cutler, 442–43.

Salvation by Staff: Reform of the Presidential Office

Aaron Wildavsky

By all accounts, the presidency is the most important political institution in American life. To many people, Presidents symbolize the nation. It is not surprising, therefore, that citizens have large expectations concerning the man who fills the presidency. Presidents are expected to lead the nation. They must maintain prosperity, they must strive constantly to preserve a just and honorable peace, they must secure social justice, they must manage a vast governmental apparatus, they must exercise power without being overbearing, and they must act for all the people while building and furthering the fortunes of their own political party. Several years ago, when a national game was made out of defining national goals, it became apparent that even if the citizenry was unable to define its own goals, the President still was expected to define them.

It is clear that the public's expectations are so great that no man or institution can fulfill them. It is also clear that these expectations are often mutually inconsistent if not contradictory. The overwhelming expectations surrounding the presidency naturally have led many people to suggest that the President needs help and they have devised means ostensibly for helping him. Presidents, however, sometimes need to be more wary of their friends than their enemies. Some of these proposals for helping the President would take his job away. Others would help him by making him take advice from people he has not chosen and may not like. Thus, suggestions for lightening the burden of the presidency are many and often contradictory. Should help consist largely of simplifying the governmental structure in the hope that it will be easier to manage? Or should it take quite the opposite course and call on more people, more agencies, and more devices?

Before 1939, the President officially had only three assistants assigned to him. Today the Executive Office has some 4,000 functionaries and employees. It includes the Budget Bureau, the Council of Economic Advisers, and the National Security Council. There are numerous special presidential assistants, the regular White House Office personnel, and more. But despite the phenomenal growth in the number of people who are supposed to help the President, his job remains as difficult as ever.

In view of the confusion as to what causes the trouble, let's first briefly analyze the problems that the President faces. We can then turn to the question of what changes in the Executive Office might result in a real

Printed by permission of the author.

contribution toward easing the tremendously difficult job of being President.

The President of the United States needs — perhaps more than anything else — three things to help him in his task. He needs an immense supply of knowledge to enable him to make his plans and decisions wisely. He needs time to do his thinking and to perform the work essential to meeting the responsibilities of the presidency with greatest effect and success. And he needs support — from his Cabinet, from the Congress, from the people — if he is to carry out his program successfully. But these are the very things often denied him, at least in part. No man, no matter how wise, can possess within himself the knowledge that a President requires to deal with the countless number of problems and questions that confront him. He must rely heavily on the knowledge and information of others to help brief him.

The President's time tends to be gobbled up not only by essentials but by seeming nonessentials. Some of the demands on his time can perhaps be lightened by improvements in the organization of the government and of the office of the presidency itself, but it would be a grave error to suggest that the President give up all acts of symbolic importance, such as lighting the national Christmas tree and putting medals on the chests of those who have performed heroic acts. Presidents soon discover that many of the things they do lead to criticism; it is in the very nature of the job that everyone cannot be satisfied. It is all the more important, then, that Presidents appear occasionally in symbolic roles that enable them to act for all the people in a noncontroversial way. Presidents need all the support they can get.

No President can carry out a program simply by issuing orders. The carrying out of his program depends on the degree of support that he can muster for it. Nor can a President count on an assured basis of support for everything he wants to accomplish just because he has won the general support of the citizenry in the presidential election. Individuals and interest groups that support him on one policy may oppose him on another. Because of the fragmentation of power in the national political system, today's opponents are often tomorrow's indispensable allies, and Presidents try to enact their policies through the creation of a series of *ad hoc* coalitions varying from issue to issue and from time to time. They are well advised not to prematurely close off sources of support. A President has to be careful not to permanently antagonize important interests on any one issue because he may need their support when it comes to other issues.

Our vital federal system concentrates groups with special interests in various geographical areas. These groups demand and often receive special representation in Congress, which holds the vital power of the purse and has the general legislative authority that the President needs and without which can accomplish little. Yet the President is unable to control the actions of most legislators because he cannot either help or harm them by affecting their chances for nomination or election.

Presidential intervention would be resented on grounds of local autonomy and would likely prove ineffectual because the interests that Presidents represent are not mirrored exactly in many congressional districts around the country. Furthermore, the more influential men in Congress are the committee chairmen, from safe districts who are reelected year after year, whose power is based on the seniority that comes with continuous service. The result is that the President is dependent on congressmen whose tenure in office is relatively invulnerable to anything he can do and whose constituencies and interests are much narrower than his.

Even in making Cabinet appointments the President is not entirely free to follow his own preferences. He may have to "give away" appointments to placate an opposing wing of his own party, to secure the support of a powerful interest group, or to mitigate the antagonism of an influential congressman. Moreover, department heads are expected to champion the cause of the labor, commerce, veteran, and other clientele groups that they serve and represent. Indeed, Cabinet members must serve these interests to some extent if they are to serve the President; the President would not find it advantageous if many important interests became hostile to him at the same time, even if the excuse was that his Cabinet members were putting his preferences before those of their clientele. It is, therefore, a profound error in American politics to say that merely because the President has formal powers of appointment he necessarily controls a particular agency.

How can the President's degree of support be strengthened — and should it be strengthened? He already has the veto power, and extensive powers over the military forces and over foreign affairs. He can avail himself of some patronage in making appointments. He has unparalleled publicity facilities for letting the citizenry know his views. He wields great moral force as the symbol of the nation.

One way to increase the influence he now holds would be to give him powers to compel the allegiance of a majority of Congress. Another way would be to enable him to discipline members of his party who disagreed with his policies. It soon becomes apparent that the measures necessary to give the President significantly greater assured support would involve radical changes in the American system of government.

The fact that the President's time and knowledge are limited means that he can deal only with a small number of the thousands of issues that come up within the administrative apparatus.

So here is where the President can truly be helped by getting aid from other people. He can hire observers to tell him what is going on in the government and country. He can hire experts to supply information. He can use advisers to suggest courses of action. He can use negotiators to deal with others on his behalf. He can delegate areas of decision to others. Yet the President's use of other people to overcome some of his limitations creates serious problems.

The first problem that the President encounters in using the help of other people is related to the question of support of his policies. Although a Cabinet officer presumably handles decisions for the President, he may be beholden to others and fail fully to represent the President's policy preferences.

Furthermore, how can the President be certain that an adviser will perform or recommend actions in accord with the President's own preferences? If the President lays down detailed instructions, the problem is minimized. But the greater the detail which the President gets into, the greater the amount of time and effort he must expend. And the President is still dependent on his staff for initial advice as to what his preferences ought to be in cases where his knowledge is limited, his time is short, or he has not yet formed opinions.

A further problem is that in seeking "salvation by staff" the President runs into serious managerial difficulties. There is a limit to the amount of information or advice it is useful for the President to have or on which he has time to act. After a while, the addition of new staff just multiplies his managerial problems without giving him valuable service in return. Forcing a President to "count hands" all the time, by making him consider endless strings of alternatives, is a good way of rendering him useless.

The multiplication of staff members creates another problem. When these men discover that the President is receiving all the information and advice he can assimilate, they are apt to be left without enough to do. In this circumstance there is a tendency to make work by taking over the operational responsibilities of the regular agencies. But this tendency destroys the one quality above all others which the staff must have if it is directly and dispassionately to serve the chief executive: the ability to view problems from the broad perspective of the presidency rather than from the necessarily narrower perspectives of the operating agencies.

Still another problem stems from the protectiveness which staff members may come to feel for the President. They may try to shield him from unpleasant information or contacts. They may try to cheer him up by telling him what they think he wants to hear. Jealous of their access to him, they may screen out people whom they do not want him to see. It is up to the President to make certain that he has alternative channels of information and that the lines of access to him are not blocked. For if the President lets a staff man act as his Prime Minister, he will find himself relegated to the status of a constitutional monarch with only symbolic powers.

The President is not only served by his staff; he must also constantly guard against becoming its victim. There is no more certain way of controlling a President than controlling the people available to help him. President Truman recognized this in his relationship to the Council of Economic Advisers. The Council was established in 1946 to advise the President on general economic problems relating to the maintenance of a high degree of employment. The original structure provided for a three-man body appointed by the President subject to senatorial confirmation. The expectation was that men of differing points of view would be chosen, that they would be impartial, and that they would also serve as congressional advisers. But this scheme proved unworkable.

Difficulties arose when members of the council who did not share the preferences of the President sought to give him their advice. There were also council members who would give advice but would not tackle the critical task of seeking political support for their recommendations.

As for the council's dual function of serving also in advisory capacity to Congress, experience proved that no cohesive group of legislators in Congress could make effective use of the council to put through a unified program. The reason is that there is no group of men in Congress sufficiently small to be able to act, sufficiently cohesive to be able to agree, and sufficiently powerful to guarantee that their program will be adopted. There is a governing body that does all of these things — it is the cabinet under the British model. The Council of Economic Advisers' organization was changed so that the President appointed the chairman as its chief officer, responsible only to him.

Judging from what has been discussed, what are the conditions under which appointees or additions to the presidential staff are most useful to the President?

These criteria might serve as a rule of thumb:

First, staff members must represent the President's personal choice and not that of any other person or group. Second, they must accept political responsibility for mustering support behind his programs. Third, he must be able to use them as he sees fit and not as others dictate. Fourth, their value to him must be greater than the additional burden of management caused by their presence. Fifth, they must not relieve his burdens by also relieving him of the most important prerogatives of his office.

Let us review some proposals for reform in the light of these criteria. A perennial type of reform (advanced by the President's Commission on Administrative Management in 1937 and by the two Hoover Commissions in 1949 and 1955) calls for reducing the number of government agencies reporting to the President by putting them under a few great departments. The rationale behind these proposals is that the President would exercise greater control over government agencies by placing them directly under his line of command through faithful cabinet officers. The difficulty with plans of this kind is that they confuse clarity and simplicity on an organization chart with an actual increase of presidential control. All the President might get would be a paper integration, because his need for support would still necessitate giving away appointments to high positions and would still prevent him from controlling agencies with powerful congressional and interest group support. After all, if the President were able to be sure that Cabinet members would follow and enforce his preferences, he would not need the large Executive Office staff he has now. If all federal agencies were put within the Executive Office of the President, the result of this extreme move would be to create additional employment for sign painters, but not much else. For underneath the title on every office would have to be painted "of the Executive Office of the President." But it is easy to see that nothing else would happen because people would still remain in the same buildings and their relationships to the President would not have been changed at all.

Critics of American foreign and defense policies in the past have complained that the National Security Council subordinated our military position to budgetary requirements. They suggested reorganizing the NSC to give higher priority to national defense. Presumably, these critics believed that changing the NSC's structure would also change the President's policy preferences. Yet it is difficult to see how any organizational change will prevent the President from getting advice he wants to take from the Budget Director or the Secretary of the Treasury·unless he is forbidden to see these people. As is so often the case, what we have here are differences in policy masquerading in the more palatable guise of organizational reform. Trying to make the President adopt other people's policies is an odd form of aid.

Another type of reform is contained in the proposal that the President should be served by a new management staff with its personnel drawn largely from the civil service. But what would happen then to the role of the President as a political leader with an overwhelming need for responsiveness and support? How could the President afford to take advice from people who, because of their civil service status, could not become fully identified with his program and openly develop support for it? The result would be to compel the President to take advice from people whose preferences may differ from his, whom he has not had a completely free hand in choosing, but who are in a position to exercise great influence over the information he receives and the alternatives he considers.

In recent years there has been a rash of proposals for the appointment of an assistant President to take over some of the chief executive's responsibilities. For example, it has been suggested that a sort of super-secretary be created to handle the development and coordination of military and foreign policies. But this is precisely the President's greatest task at the present time. To delegate this task to someone else would virtually mean abdicating his office. If this person were a man of independent influence he could use his resources to thwart the President in cases of disagreement. Furthermore, if he had no considerable political support to bring to the job in order to get the program accepted, there is no reason to believe that he would be more successful at it than the President. Some people propose giving the Vice President extraordinary responsibilities. They forget that he often represents a different party faction than the President. He may very possibly not agree with the President on key policies. A more drastic proposal calls for the establishment of a plural executive — that is, three Presidents instead of one. They might each have more time to work (and perhaps to disagree) but the scheme would sacrifice what is probably the major asset of the President today — his ability to speak with a single voice and propose a single line of policy. At bottom, these proposals represent an abiding distrust of the President and a desire to protect the country against him if he should prove weak. But does guarding against weak Presidents by thwarting strong ones seem like a valid answer to the problem?

Another set of suggestions for helping the President involves proposals for saving the President's time so that he can have some moments for reflection. Giving him more staff, however, may actually insulate him from currents of thought he should be aware of in the agencies which have operating responsibility for meeting the nation's problems. The President might have more time to think at the expense of not having much to think about.

Virtually all proposals insist that the President needs help in coordinating the activities of the Executive Branch. There is considerable truth in this assertion. The Chief Executive does need people to report on glaring inconsistencies in policy or to point out activities which are carried on at cross-purposes. And he already has many (perhaps too many) coordinators assigned to this task. As long as the lack of coordination is a result of ignorance of other people's activities or the complexity of organization, there is a good chance of overcoming it by dedicated staff work. But in many cases lack of coordination is a result of conflicting views about policy which are held by men and agencies which have independent bases of influence in society and Congress. The only ways to secure coordination in these cases is for one side to convince or coerce or bargain with the other. When it is understood that "coordination" is often just another word for "coercion," the full scope of the President's difficulties becomes even more apparent. For he is frequently unable to coerce others and the use of staff personnel for this purpose cannot be expected to be any more effective than the President's personal intervention.

It has become fashionable to speak of helping the President as if everyone were agreed that this was a good idea. This is not necessarily so. Of course we all want the President to be able to do his very best both at home and abroad. But in a democracy like ours people have many conflicting interests and there exist legitimate differences of opinion over what the government should do. If the President is made more effective this means that the interests which he represents will have an advantage over competing interests which may find their views more fully represented in Congress. Strengthening the President is not a neutral goal; it has vital implications for the kinds of decisions the government makes.

Is there nothing, then, that we can do to help the President? One course of action is obvious yet rarely mentioned: we can give him our active political support if we believe he is right — not just be passive bystanders.

In regard to staffing the Presidency, the best rule to follow would seem to be letting the President help himself by allowing him the utmost flexibility in the choice, number, characteristics, and deployment of his staff. Every President has different personal needs and priorities. Compelling him to use staff as we should like him to is a means of forcing our preferences on him. We ought not be surprised if he resists this kind of "help."

THE PRESIDENCY
AND THE COURTS

Executive Power and Domestic Emergency: The Quest for Prerogative

John P. Roche

INTRODUCTION

The Supreme Court's decision in the Steel Seizure case [1] that President Truman had exceeded his constitutional *vires* when he ordered Secretary of Commerce Sawyer to take over the steel industry is in many ways a unique holding. Although executive prerogative has been a constitutional tradition since the foundation of the Republic, the Court's opinion in the steel case marks the first instance since Lambdin P. Milligan was unnoosed in 1866 that a President had been told that his exercise of prerogative power was unconstitutional. The decision is, of course, entirely without precedent in that Truman, unlike Lincoln, was alive to learn his lesson.

This is not to suggest that Presidents have not been called to task by the Court in earlier decisions, but rather to note that in such cases as *Panama Refining Company v. Ryan,*[2] or *Schechter Bros. v. United States,*[3] the Court included Congress with the President in its interdiction, while in *Rathbun v. United States* [4] the Court construed the statute establishing the Federal Trade Commission in such a manner as to forbid Roosevelt's dismissal of Humphreys on the ground utilized. In these instances, the President claimed a statutory basis for his actions, but neither Lincoln, in his original order suspending habeas corpus and establishing military commissions for the trial of disloyal civilians,[5] nor Truman, in

Reprinted by permission of the University of Utah, copyright owners, from the *Western Political Science Quarterly*, Vol. 5 (December 1952), pp. 592–618.
1 *Youngstown Sheet & Tube Co. v. Sawyer*, 72 Sup. Ct. 863 (1952).
2 293 U.S. 388 (1934).
3 295 U.S. 495 (1935).
4 295 U.S. 602 (1935). *See* the similar early case of *Little* v. *Barreme*, 2 Cranch 170 (1804).
5 Lincoln's Proclamation of September 24, 1862, suspended habeas corpus and ordered military trials for disloyal civilians. A year later Lincoln again suspended habeas corpus for such disloyal persons, but this time his action was based on the Habeas Corpus Act of 1863. However, this statute did not authorize trial by military commission. *See* Clinton L. Rossiter, *The Supreme Court and the Commander in Chief* (Ithaca: Cornell University Press, 1951), pp. 26–28.

his seizure of the steel industry, offered any statutory foundation for his action. Each felt that he was exercising inherent executive power — prerogative — in combating a domestic emergency.

Consequently, before analyzing what the Supreme Court said about President Truman's seizure, it will be worthwhile to examine in some detail the precedents that exist for presidential exercise of prerogative power in domestic emergencies. Once this has been done, the decision and its implications will be discussed, and finally, certain conclusions will be suggested.

THE QUEST FOR PREROGATIVE

The Court's opinion in the Steel Seizure case was preceded and accompanied by the most frenetic display of precedent-chopping that the American public has been subjected to since President Roosevelt's 1937 attempt to "pack" the Supreme Court. The supporters of President Truman invoked the shades of Presidents Jefferson, Cleveland, and Franklin D. Roosevelt, with Lincoln and Theodore Roosevelt to give an air of bipartisanship to the undertaking. The steel seizure was equated with the Louisiana Purchase, the Emancipation Proclamation, Franklin D. Roosevelt's "destroyer deal," and other successful exercises of executive authority. On the other hand, President Truman's opponents, while not issuing a call for regicides, compared him unfavorably with Charles I, denied that the United States Constitution endowed the executive with any "prerogative," and maintained that the seizure of the steel companies was one more step on the road to unconstitutional, unlimited government — government of "men and not of laws." However, it is interesting to note that, unlike some of the bitter judicial controversies of the thirties, the division of opinion on the legality of seizure did not fall into the neat categories of "left" against "right," or "liberal" versus "reactionary"; individuals and organizations of unquestioned "liberalism," such as Norman Thomas and the American Civil Liberties Union, while not accepting the position of the steel companies on the merits of the dispute, condemned the government's constitutional claims.

One of the major assertions of the steel companies was that the President's seizure order was without constitutional basis or precedent. On the other hand, the solicitor-general of the United States, in his plea before the Supreme Court, maintained that President Truman's action, far from being *sui generis*, was just another exercise of an authority that could be traced back to the administration of President Washington. To a student of constitutional law, this is a major, if not the crucial issue in the steel seizure litigation. Which, if any, of these antithetical claims does a dispassionate examination of American constitutional history support?

The question may be formulated in more precise terms: To what extent does an analysis of the American constitutional tradition buttress the assertion that there is, incorporated in the initial phraseology of Article II of the Constitution, an independent grant of executive power?

The exhaustive and definitive research of Professors Corwin,[6] Binkley,[7] Hart,[8] and Rossiter,[9] has well explored the main lines and byways of the argument. One school of constitutional theorists, accepting the view of prerogative so brilliantly expounded by Alexander Hamilton in 1793, has maintained that the President is endowed by the Constitution with a high degree of autonomy and discretion — with "the executive power of the United States" not with "the executive power herein granted." The other viewpoint, that of Madison in 1793 and of Jefferson-the-philosopher (who must be distinguished from Jefferson-the-President, who was occasionally prepared to "rise above" the principle of strict construction), has urged that the President, like the Congress, has only those powers enumerated in the Constitution, and that there is, consequently, no executive "prerogative."

It would be highly pretentious here to attempt a re-tread of the scholarship in this area. Suffice it to say that Professor Corwin has concluded that the Framers of the Constitution intended to establish a "balanced constitution," which "carried with it the idea of a divided initiative in the matter of legislation and a broad range of autonomous executive power or 'prerogative.' "[10] However, the intent of the Framers, while of antiquarian interest, does not control the present interpretation of the Constitution.[11] Thus, while one may accept as bona fide the birth certificate of prerogative, it is necessary to examine further the history of executive power in order to determine the usages of prerogative, how this concep-

[6] Edward S. Corwin, *The President: Office and Powers* (New York: New York University Press, 1948). This is the definitive study of the American presidency, and where Corwin has gone into some matter exhaustively, I have contented myself with citing his research rather than engaging in the conspicuous scholarship of citing each source, statute, or executive order separately. The historical section of this paper does not pretend to be more than a synthesis of the work that has been done on one facet of the presidency, although certainly the scholars who did the original investigation should not be held responsible for any interpretations advanced herein! For a different approach *see* Albert L. Sturm, "Emergencies and the Presidency," in *The Presidency in Transition,* ed. Robert S. Rankin (Gainesville, Fla.: *Journal of Politics,* University of Florida, 1949), pp. 121–44.

[7] Wilfred E. Binkley, *President and Congress* (New York: Alfred A. Knopf, 1947).

[8] James K. Hart, *The American Presidency in Action: 1789* (New York: The Macmillan Co., 1949).

[9] Clinton L. Rossiter, *The Supreme Court and the Commander in Chief; Constitutional Dictatorship* (Princeton: Princeton University Press, 1948), chap. 14.

[10] Edward S. Corwin, *The President, op. cit.,* pp. 15–16. Corwin's italics have been deleted. See the same author's concise analysis of this early period in *Twilight of the Supreme Court* (New Haven: Yale University Press, 1934), pp. 123–30.

[11] See the interesting dispute on this point between Chief Justice Hughes and Justice Sutherland in *Home Bldg. & Loan* v. *Blaisdell,* 290 U.S. 398 (1934). A cynical insight into the degree to which a "Framer" felt himself bound by the intent of the "Framers" can be found in the Circuit Court's opinion in *Collet* v. *Collet,* 2 Dallas 294 (1792). I have suggested, on the basis of internal evidence, that Justice James Wilson wrote this decision, but in any event he concurred in it. The decision purports to explain exactly what the Framers intended by the naturalization clause of Article I, Section 8, of the Constitution, and could not have been further from the truth. *See* John P. Roche, *The Early Development of United States Citizenship* (Ithaca: Cornell University Press, 1949), pp. 14–15.

tion has been applied in specific instances, and how it has been received by the Court. More particularly it is important to consider precedents in the field of *domestic emergencies* where the President has taken action independent of any specific constitutional or congressional authorization.

This formulation immediately excludes two rich seams of precedent from consideration: first, those actions taken by the President in the field of foreign affairs which, like the Louisiana Purchase, were not based on any affirmative grant of power; and, second, such actions as various Presidents have taken in domestic emergencies under specific congressional authorization; e.g., Wilson's activities under the Overman Act of 1918, or Franklin D. Roosevelt's actions under the War Labor Disputes Act of 1943. The first of these exclusions is automatic; domesticity has been imposed on the author. The second, however, is arbitrary, and requires some justification.

It is patent that most of the President's powers in domestic emergencies have grown out of congressional delegations of power. Nevertheless, there seems to be little point to an elaborate examination of these delegated powers because there are no existent criteria of limitation. In fact, when the President and Congress co-ordinately and co-operatively recognize the existence of an emergency, there appear to be no limits to the power that the legislature can constitutionally confer upon the executive to cope with the problem. For example, in 1942, when the President and Congress [12] were in agreement that the Japanese-Americans were a threat to the security of the West Coast, 70,000 American citizens were "relocated" in concentration camps because they possessed enemy chromosomes. When, three years later, this unparalleled emergency action finally came under the scrutiny of the Supreme Court, the majority could only observe, in effect, that war was hard on everybody. The Court refused to question, or even to examine the reality of the emergency.

Along the same line, it should be noted that there is a notable scarcity of cases in which the Court has substituted its evaluation of an emergency for that urged by the executive. In the Korematsu case,[13] alluded to above, the Court said that it had to accept the executive definition of emergency. However, in the Steel Seizure case, the Supreme Court, far from accepting President Truman's claim that a pressing emergency existed, rhetorically exorcised the menace of a steel shortage and invoked the Constitution against the President. It is submitted that the key difference between the Korematsu case and the Steel Seizure case was that, in the former, Congress and the President were in full accord on the existence of the emergency, while in the latter there was militant hostility on

---

12 Actually the President's action in issuing Executive Order 9066 on February 19, 1942, antedated Congressional action on the matter by a month. On March 21, 1942, Congress ratified the President's action and provided penalties for violating orders issued under the authority of Executive Order 9066. However, these two actions were treated as a unit by the Supreme Court, and we shall so consider them. *See Korematsu v. United States,* 323 U.S. 214 (1944); Rossiter, *The Supreme Court and the Commander in Chief, op. cit.,* pp. 42–54.

13 323 U.S. 214 (1944).

Capitol Hill towards the President's action. The judiciary is seldom willing, even with an overwhelming body of constitutional precedent behind it, to stand against a united front of the legislative and executive branches. This may sound like a truism, but it is significant in defining the term "emergency." It may be suggested that an emergency is not an emergency if the Court is prepared to do something about it; its reality is more or less subjective. Aided by retrospective omniscience, one may assert that there was no menace of a Spanish invasion in 1898, or of a Japanese rising in California in 1942; but the Court, while it can refuse to come to terms with a problem for a year or two, must judge emergencies in a contemporary frame of reference. And when the Court is asked specifically if *this action* is justified by this emergency, its doubts on the matter will be assuaged or encouraged more by the temper of Congress than by the phraseology of the Constitution.

It may be objected that the Court's activities during Franklin D. Roosevelt's first term, when it defied both President and Congress, disprove this interpretation. They do indeed cast some doubt on its validity. However, the peculiar, antediluvian composition of the Court puts this period in a special category. The heart of the Court's actions at that time seems to have rested on the premise that the Justices represented the best interests of the people, and that the striking down of New Deal legislation was what the people *really* wanted. Hence, the Court felt that it was the only truly representative branch of government, or, to put it differently, that it was sustained by real political power. What the Court did was to hold off the tide of radicalism until the electorate had another opportunity to put *real* representatives into office. Thus, the tremendous Roosevelt victory of 1936 seems to have been far more effective than the 1937 "Court-packing" scheme, or the series of Roosevelt appointees (the first of whom, Black, took office after *West Coast Hotel* v. *Parrish* and *Jones-Laughlin* v. *N.L.R.B.*), in forcing the Court to reassess its apprehension of the American climate of opinion.[14]

One more striking instance comes to mind. In 1867 there was considerable — and justified — doubt as to the constitutionality of the reconstruction acts. Here was a situation in which President Johnson,

[14] The theory that the Supreme Court was intimidated by Roosevelt's "Court-packing" scheme seems supported by chronology: no sooner did the President propose reform to Congress than the Court radically revised its views on state wage and hour legislation, *West Coast Hotel* v. *Parrish*, 300 U.S. 379 (1937), and shortly thereafter in *Jones & Laughlin Steel Co.* v. *N.L.R.B.*, 301 U.S. 1 (1937), sustained the Wagner Act. Professor Corwin was one of the first to question this *post hoc ergo propter hoc* logic, so beloved by primitive tribes and historians, and to suggest that the 1936 election, as well as the inability of the states to deal with labor disturbances, was a far more potent factor. *See* his *Constitutional Revolution, Ltd.* (Pomona, Cal.: Pomona College, 1941), pp. 73 ff. Recent research has revealed that the Court had reached its decision in the *West Coast Hotel* case *before* Roosevelt presented his project of judicial reform to Congress. *See* Merlo J. Pusey, *Charles Evans Hughes* (New York: The Macmillan Co., 1951), II, p. 757. Of course, this does not prove that the election induced the judicial change of heart, but this theory — although it too is suffused with *posthocianism* — seems to fit the facts somewhat better.

who had vetoed the measures on constitutional grounds and seen Congress override his vetoes without paying the slightest attention to his views, undoubtedly hoped that the Court would accept his view of the legislation and strike it down. However, the Court, doubtless realizing that the Radical Congress would stop at nothing in its drive to inflict vengeance on the South, neatly side-stepped — on two rather shabby pretexts — the whole question.[15] The real locus of political power was then in Congress, and the Court, aware that if the myth of judicial supremacy is to be maintained the judiciary must never ride forth on Quixotic ventures (cf. *Scott* v. *Sandford*), refused to invoke the Constitution against the Radicals.

The Supreme Court then will rarely, if ever, attempt to frustrate the exercise of real political power; and, since in the United States real political power normally is shared between the President and Congress, the Court has shown great respect for emergency powers given to the President by Congress no matter what constitutional substance may be involved. Consequently, there is little point to a lengthy analysis of emergency powers which Congress has put in the President's arsenal. To those who maintain that the Constitution is the same in time of emergency as it is in time of calm, the Court has replied that, indeed, emergencies "do not create power," but that they may create situations in which hitherto unused powers may be exercised.[16] This ingenious sophistry converts the Constitution into a platonic form which exists in its full development somewhere, but which is not fully apprehended by any given generation. As new problems create new constitutional needs, the Constitution is found by the philosopher-Justices to contain adequate instruments to deal with emergent requirements. While some cynics may denounce this process as judicial legislation, it is not the purpose of this paper to engage in that discussion;[17] suffice it to say that, however the process of adjustment may be justified, the Constitution will be found flexible enough to authorize almost any conceivable congressional delegation of emergency powers to the executive.

Once the analysis has been thus narrowed, it may be possible to find a residue of "domestic prerogative," a body of inherent presidential powers which may be utilized in domestic emergencies. That prerogative powers have long existed in the field of foreign affairs hardly needs reiterating; the President's exercise of autonomy in this area can be traced back to Washington's administration, and has repeatedly received endorsement by the Supreme Court. However, as Justice Sutherland pointed out in *United States* v. *Curtiss-Wright Export Corp.*,[18] this "ex-

15 *See Mississippi* v. *Johnson,* 4 Wall. 475 (1866) and *Georgia* v. *Stanton,* 6 Wall. 50 (1867).

16 For the classic exposition of this formula, *see* the Court's decision in *Home Bldg. & Loan* v. *Blaisdell,* 290 U.S. 398 (1934).

17 *See* the admirable treatment of this problem in Fred V. Cahill, *Judicial Legislation* (New York: Ronald Press, 1952).

18 299 U.S. 304 (1936).

ternal prerogative" grew out of inherent powers of sovereignty in the field of international relations which could not apply to the domestic scene. Certainly in the view of this Justice, who was more than any other man responsible for the full formulation of the concept of "external prerogative," there could be no "domestic prerogative." The whole point of the Curtiss-Wright decision was that the doctrine of the separation of powers, while an active limitation on congressional and presidential action in domestic affairs, was not applicable to foreign affairs where special rules existed. Consequently, it is necessary to seek a different rationale for domestic prerogative from that which serves as constitutional justification for external prerogative. The United States cannot, at least not legitimately, offer the Louisiana Purchase as a precedent for the steel seizure.

The conception of domestic prerogative is found in the thought of Alexander Hamilton, and Abel Upshur could observe in 1840 that it had been "gravely asserted in Congress that whatever power is neither legislative nor judiciary, is of course executive, and, as such, belongs to the President under the Constitution. . . ." [19] However, it is the administration of Abraham Lincoln which provides the first full display of non-constitutional, non-statutory authority applied to a domestic emergency.

President Lincoln assumed the role of Protector of the Union and maintained that any and all means were legitimate to sustain the Constitution and the Union.[20] Thus, when mobs of Confederate sympathizers interrupted rail and telegraph communications between Washington, D.C., and Annapolis, Maryland, Lincoln on April 27, 1861, seized the railroad and telegraph installations.[21] He enlarged the army, suspended habeas corpus, turned government money over to private individuals, and ordered a naval blockade of southern ports — all without the slightest statutory or specific constitutional warrant, and much in direct violation of the Constitution. To Lincoln, the Constitution was not a set of procedural instructions, but a mystical entity — a corpus of republican principles — and it was in the spiritual sense a betrayal of solemn responsibility for the President — the high priest of this republican rite — to allow the shadow of procedural legality to undermine the substance of "Sacred Union."

True, Lincoln was prepared to request congressional approval, a posteriori for his emergency actions, but he assured himself of a free hand in the immediate crisis by not calling Congress into special session until July 4, 1861 — eleven weeks after the bombardment of Fort Sumter. When the Congress of patriotic Unionists did at last assemble, there was little else it could do but provide by statute that "all the acts, proclamations

[19] Cited by Corwin, *The President, op. cit.,* p. 25.

[20] Details on Lincoln's activities may be found in Randall's definitive *Constitutional Problems Under Lincoln.* A brief cogent insight into the President's eleven-week dictatorship is contained in Rossiter's *Constitutional Dictatorship. See* James G. Randall, *Constitutional Problems Under Lincoln* (Urbana: University of Illinois Press, 1951), and Rossiter, *Constitutional Dictatorship,* op. cit., chap. 15.

[21] This seizure is noted by Justice Frankfurter in Appendix II to his opinion in *Youngstown Sheet & Tube Co.* v. *Sawyer,* 72 Sup. Ct. 863, 909 (1952).

and orders of the President respecting the army and navy of the United States . . . are hereby approved and in all respects made valid . . . as if they had been issued and done under the previous express authority and direction of the Congress of the United States." The implication here was that the powers exercised by Lincoln were the property of Congress, but that Congress in a burst of generosity ratified the President's actions. In effect, the statute asserted that the President was working for Congress all the time. That this was hardly Lincoln's view emerges from an examination of the President's activities as Commander-in-Chief of the armed forces. While Article I of the Constitution specifically enumerates the power to wage war among the attributes of Congress, Lincoln infused presidential war powers into the Commander-in-Chief clause of Article II. Although it is doubtful whether the Framers intended anything more than civil control over the military by this provision,[22] Lincoln employed it as the rationale for broad substantive powers of presidential war-waging and, indeed, based the Emancipation Proclamation upon his authority as Commander-in-Chief. Similarly, he promulgated General Order 100, incorporating Lieber's *Code of Instructions for the Government of the Armies in the Field,* without any reference to Congress, although the latter body is charged by the Constitution with the establishment of rules and regulations for the armed forces.

What did the Supreme Court think of this tremendous exercise of domestic prerogative? In *Ex parte Merrymen,*[23] Chief Justice Taney felt that the suspension of habeas corpus (and by implication the other concomitants of Lincoln's dictatorship) was thoroughly unconstitutional. But Taney's action, undertaken in his capacity as Circuit Judge, had no follow-up; the copy of the decision that the courageous old Chief Justice sent to Mr. Lincoln apparently did not inhibit the President in the slightest. With the exception of *Ex parte Vallandigham,*[24] which the Court burked by a devious semantic maneuver, the only wartime test of Lincoln's actions to reach the Court was the Prize cases,[25] in which the President's power to blockade the South and seize shipping which violated the blockade was questioned. This decision, which was not handed down until March 10, 1863, involved a certain amount of judicial legerdemain, for the Supreme Court — unless it was prepared seriously to embarrass the administration — had to sustain the blockade without in any way according the Confederacy belligerent status. There is no point in here examining the intricate problems in both municipal and international law that were raised in the litigation; suffice it to say that Justice Grier succeeded notably in extricating the Court from its difficult position. With respect to the President's exercise of domestic prerogative, the Justice asserted that it was the duty of the President to resist re-

22 *See* Corwin, *The President, op. cit.,* p. 276.
23 17 Fed. Cas. 144 (Circuit Court, 1861).
24 I Wall. 243 (1864). *See* Rossiter, *The Supreme Court and the Commander in Chief, op. cit.,* pp. 28–30, for a discussion of this decision.
25 2 Black 635 (1863).

bellion with all the force at his command "without waiting for Congress to baptize it with a name," thus in large part ratifying Lincoln's conception of his war powers. As Rossiter has noted, the Court's decision in the Prize cases encouraged President Lincoln

> to believe that his ever-broadening interpretation of the commander-in-chief clause would encounter no substantial restrictions in the future decisions of the Court. It was a fact of considerable importance for the conduct of the war that the Court, although clearly in a position to do all sorts of legal and moral damage to the cause, did not go out of its way to castigate Lincoln's theory of his powers . . . or invite other challenges to the effective prosecution of the war.[26]

The war over, Lincoln dead, and the need for constitutional protection of individual rights largely passed, the Supreme Court became conscience-stricken. Although the exegesis on *Ex parte Milligan*[27] has already reached formidable proportions, we cannot pass it by without comment for it is the only case prior to the Steel Seizure case in which the Court investigated an emergency exercise of domestic prerogative and found a President *ultra vires*. Milligan had been seized at his home in Indiana, and then tried and sentenced to death for disloyal activities by a military commission established under the *sole* authority of President Lincoln. Milligan claimed that his constitutional rights had been violated, and — it now being 1866 — the Court leaped to the defense of constitutional rights. No procedural difficulties such as had restrained the Court's conscience in the Vallandigham case appeared to becloud the issue.

The outcome is well known. A unanimous Court declared that President Lincoln had been beyond his constitutional and statutory authority in creating military commissions for the trial of civilians in areas where the civil courts were functioning. The majority, bellwethered by Lincoln's intimate friend David Davis, went further and claimed that even Congress did not have the authority so to limit the constitutional rights of individuals. These rights were immutable in calm or crisis, in peace or war. If one takes *Ex parte Milligan* at constitutional face value, it is obviously not worth much as precedent — although perhaps Corwin and Rossiter have gone too far in devaluing it. However, if the majority decision is taken as a political maneuver rather than as a constitutional homily, one can possibly understand it better. In effect, Davis and his four majority colleagues were admonishing the Radical Congress on constitutional power *without risking the danger of a face-to-face, power-to-power encounter.*[28] Such a maneuver, as it was employed

26 Rossiter, *The Supreme Court and the Commander in Chief, op. cit.,* p. 75.
27 4 Wall. 2 (1866).
28 This hypothesis requires some further justification. Rossiter refers to the majority opinion as an "exhibition of judicial self-hypnosis," *The Supreme Court and the Commander in Chief, op. cit.,* p. 37, and Corwin has described it as "sheer fustian," *Total War and the Constitution* (New York: Alfred A. Knopf, 1947), p. 79. If one looks at Davis' opinion in a legal vacuum, these judgments have some merit, but if one

by John Marshall in *Marbury* v. *Madison,* has long been enshrined in American constitutional history as a masterpiece of judicial strategy.[29] Unfortunately, the Radical Congress was not to be bluffed, and when the face-to-face encounter did result, the Court was forced to retreat to the high ground of refusing jurisdiction. One may wonder what Marshall would have done had Marbury brought his suit again to the Supreme Court through the proper channel!

But while judicial mind-reading is fascinating, it is tangential to the discussion of *Ex parte Milligan* as a limit on presidential power. Here we may agree with Rossiter that it "was important, even at that late date, to announce that there were, after all, some limits to the President's power over the civilian population well behind the lines." [30] In short, a President — although deceased — was called to order by a Supreme Court, and the doctrine of domestic prerogative was — perhaps on dubious and overstated grounds — subjected to scrutiny and limitation. In a sense the fact that *Ex parte Milligan* was decided may be more important as a constitutional tradition than the actual content of the decision; the myth of presidential limitation, as it has been reinforced by generations of young Americans reading excerpts from Davis' sonorous opinion in history texts, can assume almost autonomous force and itself serve as a limitation on the actions of contemporary executives. We need only cite here the genuine wave of public opposition that developed in 1937 when President Roosevelt attempted to bridle the Supreme Court, and note that it was certainly not based on public approval of the Court's decisions in New Deal litigation. The political scientist may scoff cynically at the conception that the Supreme Court is "above politics," but this myth was strongly enough embedded in the American tradition to frustrate a President who had just won the electoral vote of forty-six of the. forty-eight states. Similarly, we may confidently assert that in *Ex parte Milligan* the Court belabored a dead lion, but a concept of presidential limitation *did* emerge from the encounter. In the public mind, the President is "under the Supreme Court," and the Court keeps this myth in working order by rarely attempting to validate it.

The conception of domestic prerogative as an important strand in

---

puts the majority opinion in its historical framework, these harsh views appear somewhat naïve. In the first place, Davis was no political acolyte uncontaminated by an understanding of the political process; he was, on the contrary, Lincoln's former campaign manager and a notoriously shrewd politician. Consequently, while Davis may have been attempting to hypnotize someone, we can rest assured that he and his judicial brethren were not the proposed subjects. Furthermore, there was absolutely no need to discuss congressional power in deciding the case, for Congress had not authorized the military commission that tried Milligan. In sum, this was a wholly gratuitous judicial safari, and the conclusion emerges that Davis was using the Milligan case as a vehicle for lecturing the Radicals, who were destroying all that Lincoln and David Davis held dear — the "Union" and the spirit of compromise.

29 Chief Justice Marshall delivered his homily to President Jefferson rather than to the Congress, but the technique was identical.

30 *The Supreme Court and the Commander in Chief, op. cit.,* p. 36.

American constitutional law thus dates from the presidency of Abraham Lincoln. However, in the period from the close of the Civil War to the accession of President Franklin D. Roosevelt, this tradition, probably because of a notable absence of domestic emergencies, received little exercise. One might expect that World War I would have made some substantial contribution to domestic prerogative, but President Wilson's conception of the President as a Prime Minister led to plenary delegations of power by Congress (e.g., the Overman and Lever Acts) rather than to extensive exercises of presidential autonomy. Nevertheless, there were in this period of relative calm several presidential actions and Court decisions relevant to the discussion here.

One new aspect of domestic prerogative which is extremely significant for our purposes was the increasing intervention of the Chief Executive into industrial crises. Since Professor Rossiter has already subjected this area to painstaking scrutiny,[31] it needs no extended analysis here. Beginning with President Hayes' action in the railroad strike of 1877, Presidents have frequently utilized federal troops in suppressing industrial disorders — even, as was the case with Cleveland's action in the railroad strike of 1894, over the vigorous opposition of the governor of the state in which the disorder existed. As Professor Corwin has noted, the Presidents have in such crisis activities relied upon both delegated and inherent powers.[32] In another area of labor relations, President Wilson established in 1918, with no statutory authorization, the National War Labor Board to mediate industrial disputes; and in a famous instance when some machinists in Bridgeport, Connecticut, struck against a decision of the Board, the President initiated the tradition of "indirect sanctions" by threatening the workers with the draft. President Roosevelt perfected the technique of indirect sanctions in World War II when he, too, established machinery for industrial mediation on the basis of prerogative power.

The President's prerogative power to intervene and keep the peace received powerful support from two Supreme Court decisions. In the first case, *In re Neagle*,[33] the Court was asked — with a certain overtone of grim humor — whether the President had the inherent power to protect a Supreme Court justice from assassination. Certainly the President had not been explicitly endowed by either the Constitution or congressional enactment with the power to undertake this protection, but the Court held — sensibly enough — that open season on federal judges was hardly contemplated by either the Framers of the Constitution or the national legislature. This holding may have been predictable, but the Court's basis for the decision was unique: Justice Miller advanced the thesis that there is a "peace of the United States" and that the President is the keeper of the peace. Legally this is a very interesting decision, for it blew

[31] *See* "The President and Labor Disputes," in *The Presidency in Transition, op. cit.,* pp. 93–120.
[32] *The President, op. cit.,* p. 164.
[33] 135 U.S. 1 (1890).

new breath into the corpse of the federal common law — a conception beloved by Marshall, Story, and Kent, but — with one major exception in the area of commercial law [34] — destroyed by the Jeffersonians. Politically, the implications of the Neagle case were far-reaching, for it could serve as the rationale for almost any presidential intervention into domestic disorder.

Five years later, in 1895, the Court returned to this theme. In the course of the strike of the American Railway Union against railroads using Pullman cars, violence had occurred, and President Cleveland — apparently identifying corporate with national interest — sent in federal troops to maintain "order" and see that the mails went through. In addition, the United States Attorney in Chicago obtained a blanket injunction against the strikers and, when the strike continued, had Eugene V. Debs, the union president, imprisoned for contempt of court. The validity of the injunction was appealed to the Supreme Court, for nowhere was there any specific statutory warrant for such an exercise of executive power as requesting the injunction, or of judicial power as granting it. The Supreme Court agreed unanimously that, although there was no statutory authorization for his action, the President, i.e., the United States Attorney, was legitimately exercising prerogative power in seeking the injunction, and that the United States Circuit Court was correct in granting it. Said Justice Brewer, "The entire strength of the nation may be used to enforce in any part of the land the full and free exercise of all national powers and the security of all rights entrusted by the Constitution to its care." [35] A more thorough repudiation of the Jeffersonian theory that there could be no federal crime without a specific punitive statute could not be imagined; this was federal common law with a vengeance. As Rossiter has pointed out, "In the light of the Debs and Neagle cases, it might easily be argued that there are no judicial limits to the President's real or alleged 'inherent' power to protect the peace of the United States." [36]

President Theodore Roosevelt accepted the role of Protector of the

---

[34] The Jeffersonians objected to federal common law as violative of both the separation of powers within the national government and the division of powers between the national government and the states. The Federalists consistently favored it as an instrument of national power. In addition, great legal scholars like Story and Kent were disgusted by a legal system which permitted each state to establish its own rules of procedure and substantive law, and felt that only a system of federal common law could bring order to this judicial chaos. After an interval in which federal judges assumed the existence of a federal common law, see John C. Miller, *Crisis in Freedom* (Boston: Little, Brown & Co., 1951), *passim*, for one example; the Court ruled in *United States* v. *Hudson*, 7 Cranch 32 (1812), that there was no federal common criminal law. Oddly enough, it was the Taney Court, normally dominated by Jeffersonianism, that authorized the federal common commercial law, *Swift* v. *Tyson*, 16 Pet. 1 (1842), which continued in effect until the Supreme Court in 1938 belatedly declared it to have been unconstitutional all along, *Erie R.R. Co.* v. *Tompkins*, 304 U.S. 64 (1938).

[35] *In re Debs*, 158 U.S. 564, 582 (1895).

[36] *The Supreme Court and the Commander in Chief, op. cit.*, p. 41.

Peace as naturally as a loon takes to water. When a great coal strike imperiled national health and safety in 1902, Roosevelt immediately brought his moral force to bear on the situation, personally urged a settlement on the disputants, appointed a commission (including a trade-unionist disguised as an "eminent sociologist"!) to investigate the matter, and even planned, as a possible last resort, to seize the coal mines [37] — this in spite of Attorney-General Knox's advice that seizure would be unconstitutional.[38] A settlement was reached, and the President shifted his strenuous proclivities to other areas. Roosevelt's reminiscences on this episode give a concise presentation of his "Stewardship Theory" of the presidency. He observed in his *Autobiography* that his action in the coal strike

> illustrated as well as anything that I did the theory which I have called the Jackson-Lincoln theory of the Presidency; that is, that occasionally great national crises arise which call for immediate and vigorous executive action, and that in such cases it is the duty of the President to act upon the theory that he is the steward of the people, and that the proper attitude for him to take is that he is bound to assume that he has the legal right to do whatever the needs of the people demand, unless the Constitution or the laws explicitly forbid him to do it.[39]

It is interesting to note that Roosevelt's similar view of the powers of the national government vis-à-vis the states was repudiated by the Supreme Court in *Kansas* v. *Colorado*,[40] but his views of presidential prerogative were not judicially challenged. In 1916, former President Taft, in his work *Our Chief Magistrate and His Powers*,[41] denounced Roosevelt's conception in no uncertain terms, although later as Chief Justice he seemed, in his decision in the Myers case,[42] to backtrack considerably. The argument between the two centered around the very issue at stake in the Steel Seizure case. While Roosevelt maintained that the President had all executive powers not explicitly forbidden to him, Taft asserted that the President, like Congress, had only those powers enumerated in the Constitution. Roosevelt accepted completely the common law responsibilities of Protector of the Peace of the United States, while Taft rejected — despite his reverence for the judiciary — the whole substance of the Debs and Neagle decisions.

---

[37] *See* Rossiter, "The President and Labor Disputes," *op. cit.*, pp. 106–07.

[38] Opinion cited by Justice Frankfurter in his concurring opinion in *Youngstown Sheet & Tube Co.* v. *Sawyer*, 72 Sup. Ct. 863, 898, fn. 20 (1952).

[39] Theodore Roosevelt, *An Autobiography* (New York: The Macmillan Co., 1913), p. 504.

[40] *Kansas* v. *Colorado*, 206 U.S. 46 (1907). It had been urged upon the Court that the federal government had the power to intervene in areas where the states were incompetent to act, even when there was no specific constitutional basis for such intervention. This was a view originally fathered by James Wilson. The Court held it to be repugnant to the Tenth Amendment.

[41] (New York: Columbia University Press. 1916), pp. 139 ff.

[42] *Myers* v. *United States*, 272 U.S. 52 (1926).

Although President Wilson did establish some of the emergency agencies of World War I on the basis of his prerogative, notably the National War Labor Board, the War Industries Board, and George Creel's Committee on Public Information,[43] his whole approach to emergency power was permeated by his philosophy of unity between the executive and the legislature, rather than by the prerogative-conception of the autonomous President. Nor did his three Republican successors, all compulsive "normalists," make any lasting contribution to the tradition of domestic prerogative. We are thus able to move with great dispatch to the accession of President Franklin D. Roosevelt in March, 1933.

As Rossiter has pointed out, "In Roosevelt the voters had chosen the most crisis-minded public figure in American history, a man who thrived on crises, emergencies, dangers, perils, and panics. His long tenure of office was a continuous emergency, and not just for the Republicans." [44] In the eyes of the conservative element of the American community, Roosevelt's conception of the presidency and his full acceptance of the assignment of Protector of the Peace brought the United States to the edge of unconstitutional presidential dictatorship. True, in the Debs case, a Supreme Court composed of unimpeachable conservatives had given its unanimous approval of strong, autonomous executive action, but then Debs was a dangerous radical. The utilization of emergency prerogative powers *against* corporate interests fell into a different constitutional category: "a government of men and not of laws."

While Roosevelt's actions against the economic emergency of the thirties may have smacked of dictatorship to some elements in the community, it should be noted that the President followed the Wilsonian rather than the Lincolnian pattern; i.e., he relied upon huge delegations of congressional power rather than upon inherent executive authority. Although his March 6, 1933, proclamation of a "bank holiday" was based upon a thoroughly tenuous statutory foundation — the Trading with the Enemy Act of 1917 — it was nonetheless assigned legislative parentage. Similarly, in his First Inaugural Address, President Roosevelt informed the nation that he would propose certain measures to Congress and then added that "in the event that the Congress shall fail to take one of these two courses . . . *I shall ask the Congress* for the one remaining instrument to meet the crisis — broad Executive power to wage a war against the emergency. . . ." [45]

Indeed, the pattern of strong presidential leadership exercised within a framework of delegated authority remained unchanged until the eve of World War II. Then, in the period after the outbreak of hostilities in Europe, but before the United States entered the war, Roosevelt began to supplement delegated authority with actions based on prerogative. His activities in the field of foreign affairs, notably the so-called "Destroyer Deal" of 1940 with Great Britain, should be referred to in passing, al-

---

43 *See* Corwin, *The President, op. cit.*, p. 287.

44 *Constitutional Dictatorship, op. cit.*, p. 256.

45 *Public Papers And Addresses Of Franklin D. Roosevelt* (New York: Random House, 1938), Vol. II, p. 15. Italics added.

though they are not strictly relevant to the topic under discussion. In domestic affairs Roosevelt took equally strong action and made a notable contribution to the development of domestic prerogative.

The President's initial action was to proclaim, on September 8, 1939, the existence of a "limited" national emergency — a constitutional innovation which was expanded to an "unlimited" national emergency on May 27, 1940 [46] — and he then proceeded to establish a series of agencies to deal with the domestic aspects of the emergency. The first of these, the Office for Emergency Management, was founded on May 25, 1940, with statutory authorization but no statutory powers.[47] Thirty-five other agencies were subsequently created purely on executive authority, including the Board of Economic Warfare, the National Housing Agency, the Office of Civilian Defense, and the National War Labor Board.[48] Corwin suggests that Roosevelt was well aware of the lack of constitutional precedent for the creation of these many agencies, and attempted to circumvent the constitutional issue "through the device of grouping [the] various creations under the rooftree of the oldest of them, the Office of [sic] Emergency Management, which was in turn installed in the 'Executive Office of the President.' "[49] Corwin adds, somewhat acidly, that this process was "one that might have been dragged out to even greater length without impairing the force of the axiom that zero plus zero is zero still."[50]

There has been extensive treatment of Roosevelt's wartime actions,[51] most of which automatically fall beyond the purview of this discussion as they were grounded on extensive delegations of congressional authority such as the War Labor Disputes Act of 1943 or the Emergency Price Control Act of 1942. Here it will suffice to make a brief examination of three areas in which the President either exercised or threatened to exercise domestic prerogative: seizure of industrial facilities, employment of "indirect sanctions," and the famous threat to overrule a provision of the Price Control Act of 1942.

The seizure of industrial facilities for non-complyment with emergency needs was not an innovation of World War II. President Lincoln seized the railroads; President Wilson also ordered the railroads into national direction, and seized several munitions plants as well.[52] Nor were Roosevelt's claims of inherent executive seizure power new; Lincoln took over

[46] *See* Corwin, *Total War and the Constitution, op. cit.*, p. 23.

[47] The creation of the OEM was statutorily blessed, but it was not legislatively endowed with any substantive powers. For a thorough discussion of this and other problems of the period 1939–1941 *see* Louis W. Koenig, *The Presidency and the Crisis* (New York: King's Crown Publishers, 1944), pp. 67–96.

[48] *Total War and the Constitution, op. cit.*, p. 51.

[49] *The President, op. cit.*, p. 295.

[50] *Ibid.*

[51] *See* Herman M. Somers, *Presidential Agency* (Cambridge: Harvard University Press, 1950), and Eliot Janeway, *The Struggle for Survival* (New Haven: Yale University Press, 1951), and sources cited therein.

[52] *See* Appendix II to Justice Frankfurter's concurring opinion in *Youngstown Sheet & Tube Co.* v. *Sawyer,* 72 Sup. Ct. 863, 910–11 (1952) for a complete list of seizures during World War I.

at least one railroad before the passage of the Railroad and Telegraph Act of 1862, and there seems to be some doubt as to Wilson's statutory justification for seizing the Smith & Wesson Company in World War I.[53] However, Franklin D. Roosevelt utilized the seizure power, both on statutory and on "inherent" authority, to an unprecedented degree. In the period from the outbreak of war in Europe to the passage of the War Labor Disputes Act on June 25, 1943, the President seized eleven industrial facilities ranging from one plant of the North American Aviation Company to the whole soft-coal industry.[54] In no case did Roosevelt list any statutory authority for his action; he merely noted the "Constitution and laws" as the basis of seizure.[55] Eight of these seizures were occasioned by labor disputes, while three were based on inefficient management. In one instance, after the passage of the War Labor Disputes Act, the semi-comic seizure of Montgomery Ward & Company in 1944 which featured Mr. Avery being dragged before *Life*'s camera by United States troops, the President apparently acted on the basis of inherent authority.[56] While there was some litigation on the consequences of seizure, and at least one District Court judge stood up bravely against Leviathan and ruled seizure unconstitutional, in no instance was such a ruling upheld on appeal. The Supreme Court took no judicial cognizance of the *legality* of seizure whether the latter was based on law or on presidential authority alone.[57]

Since in a discussion of constitutional theory one cannot assume that silence gives consent — although in practice it most certainly does — the issue of the constitutionality of these prerogative actions is still an open one. However, Koenig in his study of *The Presidency and the Crisis* suggests that seizure is merely an extention of the power of a military commander to requisition supplies for his troops in an emergency — an authority which has the sanction of long judicial approval.[58] The principal issue then becomes the existence or nonexistence of an emergency and the concomitant problem of who is to decide this ticklish question. Legally speaking, the precedents here are unclear, but in practical terms an answer seems apparent: when there is a consensus on the existence of an emergency; i.e., when public and congressional agreement on presidential action are apparent, an emergency exists. Or an emergency may be said *really* to be an emergency when the Supreme Court refuses to question its existence but rather observes, as it did in the Korematsu case, that it cannot question an exercise of discretion by the executive. In the

---

53 *See* Frankfurter's opinion, *op. cit.*, p. 898, fn. 20.

54 *See* Frankfurter's Appendix II, *op. cit.*, pp. 912–14, 927.

55 *See*, for example, Executive Order 8773, 6 *Fed. Reg.* 2777 (June 9, 1941), which ordered the seizure of the Inglewood, Cal., plant of North American Aviation Co.

56 *See* Rossiter, *The Supreme Court and the Commander in Chief, op. cit.*, pp. 61–62.

57 As an example of the litigation on the consequences of seizure, *see United States* v. *Pewee Coal Co.*, 341 U.S. 114 (1950). The outstanding case in which a District judge held seizure to be unconstitutional was *United States* v. *Montgomery Ward & Co.*, 58 F. Supp. 408 (N.D. Ill., 1945).

58 Koenig, *op. cit.*, p. 79.

Korematsu case the Court refused an opportunity to replace the military general staff, but in the Steel Seizure case the Court intrepidly displaced the President's economic advisors and substituted its judgment for theirs on the reality of the emergency. Thus a conclusion, which will hardly satisfy the constitutional perfectionists, seems to emerge on the legality of prerogative seizure: The President can on the basis of his inherent power seize an industry if an emergency exists, and an emergency exists if the President is successful in his exercise of his prerogative. The real job of the Supreme Court, viewed from this standpoint, is to enforce government by discussion, to prevent the President from breaching the contract of consensus. In a political system where executive action is not necessarily an outgrowth of party decision or legislative discussion, but where the President can claim potentially dangerous authority as the elected spokesman of a presumed "national will," this function of the Court can be of great value to the democratic tradition. But, as the thirties demonstrate, this calls for justices with a high degree of sensitivity to the national climate of opinion.[59]

President Roosevelt's employment of "indirect sanctions" has been well described by Professor Corwin [60] and needs little elaboration here. The most famous instance of such presidential blackmail was the withdrawal of Post Office employees from Montgomery Ward's special post office, but "government by press release" also closed down the nation's race tracks and enforced a nationwide "dim-out." In effect, the administrators of various wartime programs employed every possible technique to enforce compliance with their "advice." The reason for this is not hard to find: most of these agencies had been established by presidential fiat without statutory *vires* and they had to make their own way in the world largely unaided by penal legislation. Indeed, rather than co-operating with these agencies, congressmen often went out of their way to make life difficult for them, usually stopping just short of open nullification of their decisions. Nevertheless, however motivated, such blackmail tactics are hardly in the tradition of constitutional government and should be re-

---

[59] Percentage-wise, very few Court decisions fall into this category — judicial review of state and national legislation or executive activities is nowhere near as continuous as popular mythology would have it. In effect, it is suggested here that the purpose of judicial review is to enforce a cooling-off period on a nation whose political system does not otherwise inhibit popular passions. The British party system acts as a formidable institutional block against sudden change and, because of the tight party organization of the House of Commons, the chances of public passion being enacted into law are slight. Here the operation of the judiciary under the separation of powers supplies an institutional chaperone. But, and this is the lesson of the thirties, the judiciary must never allow the defense against passion to become a prohibition of marriage. Once a measure has received genuine public acceptance, the Court must retreat. Thus, one might say that the political function of the Court is to maintain a certain *process of government* rather than any body of substantive governmental principles.

[60] See *Total War and the Constitution, op. cit.*, pp. 50–70. Those in search of an "inside view" of some of these sanctions should *see* Somers, *Presidential Agency, op. cit.*, pp. 165 ff.

placed by regular criminal legislation in the event of future need.[61] In one case the Supreme Court came to grips with "indirect sanctions" and upheld an OPA order prohibiting future fuel oil allocations to a company which had violated a rationing order.[62] The Court held, in Corwin's words, that "indirect sanctions were constitutional when the deprivations they wrought were a reasonably implied amplification of the substantive power that they supported and were directly conservative of the interests that this power was created to protect and advance." [63]

President Roosevelt's famous threat to nullify a congressional enactment, a farm parity provision of the Emergency Price Control Act of 1942, brought the *claim* of presidential prerogative to its all-time apotheosis. Speaking to the Congress on September 7, 1942, the President informed it that unless the objectionable section of the act were repealed by the first of October, he would repeal it! He continued: "The President has the powers, under the Constitution and under Congressional acts, to take measures necessary to avert a disaster which would interfere with the winning of the war. . . . When the war is won, the powers under which I act automatically revert to the people — to whom they belong." [64] This assertion goes far beyond Theodore Roosevelt's claim, and reverts to John Locke's definition of prerogative "as the power to act according to discretion for the public good, without the prescription of the law and sometimes even against it." [65] To a mind steeped in Continental logic the next step was obvious: a guillotine in the shadow of the Washington Monument.

But Congress repealed the parity provision, not merely because of the President's threat, but rather because the President's statement echoed public sentiment. Instead of marking the end of constitutional government in the United States, this declaration merely emphasized Roosevelt's superb ability to lead from political strength. From a constitutional point of view, it may be unfortunate that Congress bowed humbly before the President, but from the viewpoint of practical politics one can be almost certain that Roosevelt knew before he issued his manifesto that he would not have to put his claims to the test. Unlike his successor, Franklin D. Roosevelt scrupulously avoided bridges that he didn't want to cross. It should be noted that he never allowed his interest in civil rights to hinder unity in the Democratic party. Instead of recalling General MacArthur, he would probably have reassigned him as Military Governor of Samoa.

The President undoubtedly has inherent powers, but to assert that they can be exercised against the will of Congress is in realistic political

61 *See* Rossiter, "War, Depression, and the Presidency," *Social Research*, Vol. 17 (1950), pp. 417, 424–25. The homiletic overtones of this statement should not be allowed to obscure the fact that in a future emergency, "indirect sanctions" will unquestionably again be employed if Congress refuses to create normal statutory sanctions to deal with such situations.

62 *Steuart & Bro., Inc.*, v. *Bowles*, 322 U.S. 598 (1944).

63 Corwin, *Total War and the Constitution, op. cit.*, p. 61.

64 Cited in *ibid.*, p. 63.

65 *Ibid.*, p. 64.

terms nonsense.[66] One can, for instance, build an elaborate case to demonstrate in abstract terms the extent of the President's authority in foreign affairs, but, as Daniel S. Cheever and H. Field Haviland, Jr., have recently pointed out in their excellent *American Foreign Policy and the Separation of Powers*,[67] in practice the President must work closely with Congress if his authority is to be implemented. To make a claim is one thing: to implement it is something quite different. Thus it appears that Roosevelt's assertion that he could overrule Congress on a statute is an example of political poker-playing rather than a constitutional precedent. In domestic even more than in foreign affairs everything has a price tag, and the President must maintain close liaison with Congress if his policies are to achieve concrete fulfillment.

This highly abridged summary of a century of domestic prerogative brings us to the instant situation: the seizure by President Truman of the steel industry. What conclusions can be drawn from past experience to aid us in examining the steel seizure and the litigation that grew out of it? First, in the realm of constitutional theory, it appears that the President's prerogative power in domestic emergencies has been and will continue to be shaped by the extent and intensity of the emergency. If a real emergency exists, it seems unlikely that the Supreme Court will declare a presidential action unconstitutional. Although this runs contrary to the Court's view of its own activities, the refusal of jurisdiction in cases questioning presidential power is equivalent to a statement of *nihil obstat*, and it is this technique that lends itself most readily to avoiding pitfalls. Justice Jackson has, indeed, urged the Supreme Court to avoid litigation in which it may establish unfortunate constitutional precedents under the pressure of emergencies.[68]

Second, the danger of unconstitutional presidential dictatorship, based on vigorous excise of domestic prerogative, seems virtually nonexistent. In real terms, Congress and the public must agree with presidential emergency actions if they are to be effective. The silences of American constitutional history lend strong support to this proposition for, *with the exception of the seizure of the steel industry*, there has not been one single instance of a President actually taking prerogative action in a domestic crisis against the wishes of Congress.[69] While the nature of the presidential office ensures that the President will take the leadership in the

[66] It should be noted that Congress had its revenge on Roosevelt for the message threatening to disregard the parity provisions. The price F.D.R. paid for his moment of glory was the failure of the "Third War Powers Act." *See* Corwin, *The President, op. cit.*, p. 495, for further details.

[67] (Cambridge: Harvard University Press, 1952). The authors state that "both the Constitution and actual practice make it clear that the President does not have sufficient authority to control foreign policy without regard to the wishes of the legislative branch" (p. 11).

[68] Dissenting in *Korematsu* v. *United States*, 323 U.S. 214 (1944).

[69] Truman's defiance was *de facto*, if not *de jure*; both houses of Congress informed the President that he should invoke Taft-Hartley, and refused to supply him with the seizure powers he requested after the Court ruled the original seizure *ultra vires* the Constitution.

exercise of emergency powers, the Congress and the President are the Siamese twins of American "constitutional dictatorship." The real unity of powers in the United States, the degree to which, for example, congressional committees effectively control various branches of the Administration (the Passport Division of the State Department is virtually a bailiwick of Senator McCarran's Senate Judiciary Committee, and other examples could be cited at length), as well as the party screening process which makes it almost impossible for an extremist to be nominated for the presidency, impel the conclusion that a President could not become a dictator on the strength of his inherent powers. Conceivably, Congress could create a *Duce,* but it is inconceivable that the President could go it alone.[70]

THE SUPREME COURT AND THE STEEL CRISIS

With this background in mind, we can now turn our attention to the Supreme Court's decision in the Steel Seizure case. The immediate history of this litigation might briefly be recalled. On April 8, 1952, President Truman announced that the impending industry-wide strike of the United Steelworkers of America, CIO, would imperil the national defense. To avert this crisis, the President issued Executive Order 10340 [71] which vested title to the major steel companies in the United States and appointed Secretary of Commerce Charles Sawyer as government administrator. The President, as he clearly indicated in a nationwide radio address, took this action in lieu of utilizing the injunctive provisions of the Taft-Hartley Act because he felt that the steel masters were at fault in the breakdown of collective bargaining. He asserted that to employ an

[70] Those critics of bureaucracy who feel that the President and his "vast, centralized apparatus of tyranny" are fast usurping American freedom would do well to read Senator McCarran's reaction to President Truman's veto of the McCarran-Walter immigration bill. The Senator noted with great indignation that every branch of the administration concerned with immigration and naturalization had thoroughly approved his bill! It should be noted in fairness to the bureaucrats concerned that Senator McCarran is a far greater threat to their livelihood than is the President, their nominal boss, because Senator McCarran will be there next January and President Truman will not. The close connections that exist between congressional committees and various branches of the administration — while common knowledge in Washington — have not received adequate scholarly investigation. The implications of this functional nexus on the so-called "separation of powers" are far-reaching. Among the few scholars who have come to grips with this problem are Herman Somers, see "The President as Administrator," *Annals of the American Academy of Political and Social Science,* Vol. 283 (Sept., 1952), pp. 105 ff., and Don K. Price, *see The New Dimension of Diplomacy* (New York: Woodrow Wilson Foundation, 1951). Other writers have dealt with specific aspects of this clandestine administrative-legislative relationship; see James M. Burns, *Congress on Trial* (New York: Harper & Bros., 1949), pp. 89, 96, and Arthur Maass, *Muddy Waters* (Cambridge: Harvard University Press, 1951), *passim.* For Senator McCarran's comments *see New York Times,* June 26, 1952, p. 14, and for the similar views of Representative Walter, co-sponsor of the bill, *see New York Times,* June 27, 1952, p. 1.

[71] Included as appendix to Justice Black's opinion in *Youngstown Sheet & Tube Co.* v. *Sawyer,* 72 Sup. Ct., 863, 868–69 (1952).

injunction would unjustly penalize the steel workers, who had earlier postponed their strike at presidential request. The next day, April 9, 1952, President Truman informed Congress of his action, and, in effect, asked the legislature to approve his seizure order.[72] On April 21, the President again communicated with Congress on the matter, justifying his action to the President of the Senate but adding that "Congress can, if it wishes, reject the course of action that I have followed in this matter." [73] While there was considerable objection by individual congressmen to the seizure, and the customary desultory threats of impeachment were vented, Congress as a body took no official action.

Meanwhile, the steel companies had gone to Court, having requested Judge Holtzoff of the District Court, D.C., to issue a temporary restraining order on April 9, 1952. This judge held that the equitable remedy was not applicable as there was no evidence that the seizure would do irreparable injury to the companies, and added that "to issue a restraining order against Mr. Sawyer, and in effect nullify an order of the President of the United States, promulgated by him to meet a nationwide emergency problem, is something that the Court should not do, unless there is some very vital reason for the Court stepping in." [74] In late April, 1952, the steel companies tried again, requesting Judge Pine of the District Court, D.C., to issue a preliminary injunction restraining the continued seizure and possession of the steel properties. The qualms which troubled Judge Holtzoff had no impact on Judge Pine — on April 29 he issued the injunction and accompanied it with a vigorous denunciation of the President's unconstitutional action. This opinion reads more like a Liberty League tract than a realistic appraisal of the duties and responsibilities of the President of the United States in an era of permanent crisis. Its flavor can only be appreciated by a full reading, but one extract may supply the essence: The government's contention, observed the Judge, "requires a discussion of the fundamental principles of constitutional government, which I have always understood are immutable, absent [sic] a change in the framework of the Constitution itself in the manner provided therein." [75]

The Court of Appeals, D.C., by a five-four decision, immediately restrained the issuance of the injunction until the Supreme Court could have an opportunity to rule on the matter. Four members of the Court felt that Pine's injunction should have been sustained, but the majority held that the matter was so delicate and of such constitutional significance that the Supreme Court itself should make the substantive determination.[76] The Supreme Court granted certiorari on May 3, 1952, and handed down its decision on June 2, 1952.[77] It should be noted that

[72] *See* 98 *Cong. Rec.* No. 60, 3962–63 (April 9, 1952).
[73] *See* 98 *Cong. Rec.* No. 66, 4192 (April 21, 1952).
[74] *Youngstown Sheet & Tube Co. v. Sawyer,* 103 F. Supp. 978 (D.C.D.C., 1952).
[75] *Youngstown Sheet & Tube Co. v. Sawyer,* 103 F. Supp. 569 (D.C.D.C., 1952).
[76] *Sawyer v. Youngstown Sheet & Tube Co.,* 197 F. 2d 582 (C.A.D.C., 1952).
[77] *Youngstown Sheet & Tube Co. v. Sawyer,* 72 Sup. Ct. 863 (1952).

almost two months intervened between the seizure and the final determination of its legality, and in this interim it had become clear that Congress disapproved of the President's action, and the nation's leading newspapers [78] had editorially announced strong opposition to the move. This is conjecture, but it seems that congressional confidence that the high Court would interdict the seizure inhibited legislative action on the matter.

Before subjecting the views of the justices on the legality of seizure to internal analysis, it would be worthwhile to make some generalizations about the over-all picture. First, nine justices filed seven opinions: six of these were to the point that President Truman's action was unconstitutional, while the three dissenters united on a common opinion. Justice Black's "opinion of the Court" was accepted as a common denominator by Justices Jackson, Frankfurter, Burton, and Douglas, and Justice Clark accepted the judgment but apparently not the opinion of the Court. Justice Black's opinion was a sufficiently low common denominator that all those who concurred in it felt impelled to elaborate their differences in separate opinions. Professor John Frank has suggested that only by saying very little and avoiding many issues could Justice Black persuade any of his brethren to join him in an "opinion of the Court." [79] Needless to say, a decision advanced with so many well-aired and significant differences of opinion among the majority justices can hardly be a firm precedent.

Second, and in a sense implicit in the above, it should be noted that the Court did not share Judge Pine's naïve Manichaean approach to constitutional problems. One of the notable aspects of the majority opinions is the humility with which they were rendered. The justices were obviously aware of the thinness of the ice on which they were treading, and spoke with muffled vehemence and, in most cases, with a sensible appreciation of the role and responsibilities of the President in emergencies. This decision certainly bore very little resemblance to the ex cathedra thunderings of the 1932–36 Court. One of the reasons for the fragmentation of the majority appears to have been the desire of each majority justice to make perfectly clear his reasons for rejecting the President's claim and to demonstrate that he was no constitutional ingénue who

---

[78] A check of leading newspaper editorial opinion, which does not pretend to be exhaustive, reveals the following journals strongly opposing the President's seizure: *Atlanta Constitution, Boston Herald, Chicago Daily News, Chicago Tribune, Chicago Sun-Times, Cleveland Plain Dealer, Christian Science Monitor, Des Moines Register, New York Times, New York Herald-Tribune, New York Journal-American, New York World-Telegram-Sun, Philadelphia Inquirer, Pittsburgh Post-Gazette, San Francisco Chronicle, St. Louis Post-Dispatch, St. Louis Globe-Democrat, Washington Post.* Where one of the above papers is a member of a large chain; e.g., *New York World-Telegram-Sun* — Scripps-Howard, *New York Journal-American* — Hearst, the views of this paper may be taken as reflecting the outlook of the other journals in the chain. No paper was found giving editorial support to the seizure.

[79] John Frank, "The Future of Presidential Seizure," in *Fortune*, July, 1952, pp. 70 ff. I am deeply indebted to this incisive analysis.

would simply accept the doctrine of the separation of powers at face value. It would indeed be difficult to find a more sophisticated distillation of constitutional wisdom with regard to presidential power than is contained in the brilliant concurring opinion of Justice Jackson.[80]

Third, as Professor Frank has noted,[81] the decision was implicitly an exhortation of Congress to take action in the area of industrial emergencies. To Justices Clark, Frankfurter, and Jackson, the President's refusal to employ the provisions of the Taft-Hartley Act brought him into Court with dirty hands. But supposing the President *had* exhausted his legislative remedies by invoking the Taft-Hartley Act, and *then* the strike had been called? Would seizure have been justified in such a situation? Naturally the Court would not deal with hypothetical situations, but one has the distinct feeling that to at least the three justices enumerated above this fact might justify a change of position. If only two of them changed positions, a different majority would be created. To put this query another way: if a real emergency existed for the solution of which Congress had supplied no instructions, would seizure then be unconstitutional? Again, the Court gave no answer to this question, but to an analyst of domestic prerogative it is a question of vital significance. This points up a conclusion about the Steel Seizure case which might serve as the conclusion of this whole over-all analysis: it was a highly tentative decision. To use a somewhat illogical metaphor, it was only a partial decapitation.

Justice Black's opinion of the Court [82] was notable mainly for what it didn't say. The Justice tersely examined the President's action, found it without statutory foundation, dismissed the argument that it was based on a legitimate exercise of inherent power, and ruled it violative of the separation of powers as an usurpation of the functions of Congress. This opinion was a straightforward and unadorned exposition of the doctrine of the separation of powers which avoided the basic questions created by emergencies. Justice Black concluded simply: "The Founders of this Nation entrusted the law-making power to the Congress alone in both good and bad times." [83] This may be of interest to antiquarians, but it was hardly a realistic analysis of the activities of the American President since 1789 — to say nothing of the legislative role of the Supreme Court!

Justice Jackson wrote a superb concurring opinion [84] which, it is to be regretted, was not the "opinion of the Court." Cutting through the legalistic arguments of both parties, the Justice suggested that presidential actions might be placed in one of three categories: first, where the President acts on the basis of delegated congressional authority; second, where the President takes unauthorized action which does not run counter to the wishes of Congress; and, third, where the President "takes measures incompatible with the expressed or implied will of Congress." Actions

[80] 72 Sup. Ct. 863, 869–80.
[81] Frank, *op. cit.*, p. 70.
[82] 72 Sup. Ct. 863–67.
[83] 72 Sup. Ct. 867.
[84] 72 Sup. Ct. 869–80.

in the first category would have a very strong presumption of legitimacy; actions in the second would have to be judged "on the imperatives of events and contemporary imponderables rather than abstract theories of law"; while actions in the third must be subjected to strong judicial scrutiny for there the President's "power is at its lowest ebb" and "what is at stake is the equilibrium established by our constitutional system." [85] It is submitted that what Justice Jackson has here suggested is the replacement of the mechanistic approach to the separation of powers — which inspired several of his brethren — with the conception that it is the responsibility of the Court to maintain the "ground-rules" of government by discussion. Jackson then examined the President's action in detail, relegated it to the third of his categories, and agreed that it should be held an unconstitutional exercise of power. The Justice concluded by observing that "with all its defects, delays and inconveniences, men have discovered no technique for long preserving free government except that the Executive be under the law, and that the law be made by parliamentary deliberations. Such institutions may be destined to pass away. But it is the duty of the Court to be last, not first, to give them up." [86] Thus in Jackson's opinion, the critical point was not that presidential autonomy violated the principle of the separation of powers, but that *irresponsible* presidential autonomy, prerogative exercise which did not have its foundation in the democratic process, did breach a basic principle of American constitutionalism: that the actions of the executive must be based on community consensus.

There is little point to a seriatim examination of the opinions of the other majority justices. Three of them, Justices Frankfurter,[87] Burton,[88] and Clark,[89] devoted their opinions largely to statutory analysis. Justices Frankfurter and Burton emphasized the President's refusal to invoke the national emergency provisions of the Taft-Hartley Act and concluded, in their separate fashions, that this rejection of a solution recommended by Congress militated against the legality of seizure. Justice Clark devoted his brief opinion to demonstrating that, in addition to eschewing the Taft-Hartley remedy, the President had not fulfilled the requirements of any statute authorizing seizure of industry. In relying heavily on the President's non-employment of the Taft-Hartley Act as a justification for interdicting seizure, these justices seem to have seriously questioned the tradition, clearly enunciated in *Mississippi* v. *Johnson*,[90] that the President's actions are wholly discretionary. Their interpretation appears to have been that the President's activities are ministerial to the extent that he cannot attempt an unauthorized remedy for a crisis until he has exhausted the powers delegated to him by Congress. While the Chief Execu-

---

85 72 Sup. Ct. 871.
86 72 Sup. Ct. 880.
87 72 Sup. Ct. 888–99.
88 72 Sup. Ct. 880–82.
89 72 Sup. Ct. 882–86.
90 4 Wall. 475 (1866).

tive cannot be forced by mandamus to employ a congressional remedy, he can be punished for trying one of his own in its stead. It was this view that the dissenting opinion characterized, with some justice, as a "messenger-boy concept" [91] of the presidency. Justice Douglas,[92] the other member of the majority, wrote a brief, general and somewhat didactic essay on the nature of constitutional government. He concluded by noting: "Today a kindly President uses the seizure power to effect a wage increase and to keep the steel furnaces in production. Yet tomorrow another President might use the same power to prevent a wage increase, to curb trade unionists, to regiment labor as oppressively as industry thinks it has been regimented by this seizure." [93] This may be true, but it is interesting to recall that when President Cleveland employed domestic prerogative against the American Railway Union, both Houses of Congress applauded his action [94] and it was sustained by the Supreme Court.[95] Yet the precedent of *In re Debs* carried very little weight in the decision of the Steel Seizure case, and it was doubtful whether the holding in the latter case would inhibit a President *with public and congressional sentiment behind him* from employing inherent seizure power against a union in future. Precedent undoubtedly has considerable value, but its worth can be overly inflated.

The vigorous dissenting opinion, written by the Chief Justice,[96] denounced the frivolity of the majority in no uncertain terms. The blindness of the majority, insisted the minority, did not for one minute alter the fact that there was an acute national emergency, that the President was the Chief Executive of the United States and not an agent of Congress, and that the action he had taken to cope with the emergency was within his constitutional *vires* as President and Commander-in-Chief of the armed forces. In short, the dissenters asserted that this was a *real* emergency, and took the traditional judicial attitude towards executive action in *real* emergencies. The legal arguments between the two divisions of the Court were consequently of little significance; the vital disagreement was over premises. Granted the assumption that no emergency existed, the majority view fell into the tradition of limitation. Granted the assumption that an emergency existed, the minority opinion fell into an equally well-defined tradition of judicial restraint.[97] It is submitted that this agreement over premises is not one that can be solved by the process of legal ratiocination, but rather it must be determined through judicial insight into the attitudes and opinions of the American community — particularly as reflected in the views of congressmen. It is

[91] 72 Sup. Ct. 949.
[92] 72 Sup. Ct. 886–88.
[93] 72 Sup. Ct. 888.
[94] 26 *Cong. Rec.* 7281–84, 7544–46 (1894).
[95] See *In re Debs*, 158 U.S. 564 (1895).
[96] 72 Sup. Ct. 929–49.
[97] See Rossiter, *The Supreme Court and the Commander in Chief, op. cit.*, pp. 128–29.

essentially a problem in social psychology, not in law. An emergency is — like the middle class — more a state of mind than an objective socio-political phenomenon.

Conclusions

Since conclusions have been liberally sprinkled throughout the body of this paper, this section can best serve to highlight two major points that seem to emerge from a study of the impact of the decision in the Steel Seizure case on inherent presidential power in the field of domestic emergencies.

First, the Court accepted the view which is characteristic of the American people and the Congress today that the Korean crisis and the "Cold War" are not full-scale emergencies justifying the full invocation and exercise of presidential war-powers. In time of "all-out" crisis, the boundary between domestic and foreign emergencies disappears, but in the Steel Seizure case, the Court — over the vigorous protests of the minority — insisted on maintaining the line of division between the two. Whether this interpretation of the reality of the emergency is correct or not only time will reveal, but in the contemporary context the Court insisted that the view of the American community prevail over the views of government experts. In so doing, the Court insisted on the primacy of discussion, of pragmatic blunderings and successes, over *expertise* and autonomous insight.

Second, by doing this, the Supreme Court struck a blow for constitutional government for which we should all be grateful. As in the Milligan case, the content of the decision is less significant than the fact that it *was rendered*. While all students of government appreciate the complexities of presidential existence in the United States, and most will admit that the President requires a high degree of discretion and autonomy for the proper exercise of his function, it is also important that a line be drawn between responsible autonomy and irresponsible autonomy. While it is no easy task to draw this line, its general outline should follow the boundary between community consensus and elitist conviction. One is always faced by the dilemma that the elitists may be right and the community may be wrong, but the history of democratic government seems to support the conclusion that if the views of an elite are correct, the people will adopt them before it is too late. While historical graveyards are littered with the bones of nations that tried to short-cut consensus, democratic governments have survived. And this — while it is not conclusive proof of the validity of democratic principles — is a significant validation of the viability of government by discussion, of the view that for better or for worse democratic executives must accept, or be compelled to accept, restraint of their insights and prerogatives.

The Power of the President to Impound Appropriated Funds: With Special Reference to Grants-in-aid to Segregated Activities

Robert E. Goostree

Debate in the first session of the present Congress has raised the question of the power of the President or other executive officers to withhold funds appropriated for Federal grants-in-aid to impacted school areas, when the impacted areas operate segregated schools.[1] The debate centered about a proposed amendment to the school aid bill which would have forbidden specifically the impounding of grant-in-aid funds to segregated school districts.[2] The amendment was defeated, perhaps upon the assurance of Secretary Abraham A. Ribicoff of the Department of Health, Education, and Welfare that neither he as Secretary nor the Commissioner of Education possessed power to withhold funds for this reason.[3]

The question of the constitutional power (or duty) of the President to order impounding by the Bureau of the Budget of funds for segregated school districts arose only in passing, in the form of a research report favoring such power prepared by the American Law Division of the Legislative Reference Service, and inserted into the *Congressional Record* during the debate.[4] This report was clearly drawn at the request of a proponent of the power and presented only arguments supporting the power.

The issue is, of course, an aspect of the broader constitutional question of the President's power under any circumstances to withhold funds appropriated for governmental functions authorized by law. No such question exists where the appropriation act or the authorizing statute specifically delegates discretion to the President or another executive officer in regard to expenditure: the very grant of discretion confers

Reprinted by permission from the *American University Law Review*, Vol. 11 (January 1962), pp. 32–47.

[1] Senate consideration of S. 1021, providing Federal aid for public schools, began May 16, 1961.

[2] 107 *Cong. Rec.* 7522 (daily ed. May 16, 1961). The proposed amendment provided, in part, that "no department, agency, officer . . . of the United States shall withhold funds appropriated under authorization of this title from any State or School otherwise eligible because of any law, policy or practice of the State or school with regard to segregation or desegregation of the races in the schools."

[3] *Id.* at 7807 (daily ed. May 18, 1961).

[4] *Id.* at 7522–24 (daily ed. May 16, 1961).

power to spend or not to spend. Where no such delegation of discretion exists, however, is this power to be found either in the Constitution or in general statutory enactments about executive budgetary control? The broad issue as to whether an appropriation is a mandate to spend or merely permission to spend is not clarified by the Constitution and has been the subject of judicial scrutiny only in limited aspects. Apart from legislation regarding executive control of the budget, a claim that an appropriation is merely permissive or that the President may impound appropriated funds for reasons of his own would seem to rest upon the Constitutional requirement that the President "take care that the laws are faithfully executed" [5] or upon an inherent executive power. It would seem that both possible bases for this claimed Presidential power have been eliminated by Supreme Court decisions,[6] although no case is fully dispositive of the question.

On the other hand, strong arguments can be made upon the basis of other Supreme Court decisions [7] for the existence of a general power to withhold funds, either totally or in part, as a result of other aspects of the Executive power. Finally, regardless of the existence of the power to impound as a general proposition, it may well be that specific Constitutional prohibitions on activity by the National Government may necessarily imply a Presidential power to impound funds the spending of which would in effect amount to a violation of the prohibition. This aspect of the problem in its baldest form is: When Congress has authorized and appropriated funds to be spent in aid of segregated schools, does a national constitutional policy supporting desegregation require and permit the President to impound such funds? It would seem that any power to impound either must rest upon statutory authority, or upon authority to be derived from the "execution of the laws" clause, or must be an inherent Executive power. No serious contention can be made that the President's power as commander-in-chief could confer upon him the power to impound funds for non-military purposes. The unexercised treaty power, similarly, can have no relation to this matter. No exercise of the power of the President to issue reprieves and pardons is involved, nor is there a question of the exercise of the President's appointment power.

Examination of the facets of Presidential power in the area involves, then, consideration of existing statutory authority to impound funds, of the possible authority to be derived from the "execution of the laws" clause of the Constitution, of the potential authority to impound as an inherent Presidential power, and of authority to impound as a derivative of Constitutional prohibitions, especially of the equal protection and due

5 U.S. Const. art. II, § 3.

6 Principally, *Kendall* v. *United States ex rel. Stokes*, 12 Pet. (37 U.S.) 524 (1838) and *Youngstown Sheet & Tube Co.* v. *Sawyer*, 343 U.S. 579; 26 A.L.R.2d 1378 (1952).

7 Principally, *In re Neagle*, 135 U.S. 1 (1890) and *United States* v. *Midwest Oil Co.*, 236 U.S. 459 (1915).

process clauses and their relation to expenditures for purposes of segregation.

I. STATUTORY AUTHORITY FOR PRESIDENTIAL IMPOUNDING

The control which the President exercises over the budget for the Executive Branch is statutory in origin, having been established by the Budget and Accounting Act of 1921.[8] This Act provided for Presidential control over requests for funds for activities of the Executive Branch, but made no provision for such Presidential control over the expenditure of appropriated funds, regardless of whether such funds were requested or were in excess of Presidential requests. For twenty years, the only formal Presidential response to appropriations "not in accord with the President's program" was by veto, if any control was to be had over the amounts appropriated.

Even before the Budget and Accounting Act, however, the Anti-Deficiency Acts of 1905 and 1906 had established the requirement of agency apportionment of total appropriations into quarterly amounts, providing that no more than one-quarter of the total appropriation might be expended in any quarter of the fiscal year. This device was later used to effect savings when the required purpose was accomplished within the appropriation made for that purpose.[9]

The first impounding of appropriated funds occurred in 1941, when President Roosevelt ordered the impounding of funds appropriated for public works not thought to be of an essential defense nature.[10] Congressional protest was unavailing. Since that time, Presidents have utilized the impounding technique from time to time to reduce the level of expenditures for an authorized program, invariably accompanied by Congressional protest. The most important of such incidents occurred in 1949 when President Truman ordered the withholding of $615,000,000 which had been appropriated in excess of his request for a forty-eight group Air Force.[11] With this controversy historically recent, impounding to prevent deficiencies and to effect economies in governmental operations was authorized by the General Appropriations Act of 1951.[12] This provision that "[R]eserves may be established to provide for contingencies, or

---

[8] Budget and Accounting Act, 42 Stat. 20 (1921), 31 U.S.C. §§ 1, 2, 11, 13–24, 41–44, 46–50, 52–57.

[9] Anti-Deficiency Act, 33 Stat. 1257 (1905). Also see Williams, *The Impounding of Funds by the Bureau of the Budget* 6.

[10] Williams, *op. cit., supra* at 8–20.

[11] *Id.* at 30. Most recently, President Kennedy on October 28, 1961, ordered the impounding of some $780,000,000, appropriated in excess of his budget request for B-52 and B-70 bombers. Congressional protest from Senator John Stennis, Chairman of the Military Preparedness Subcommittee of the Senate Armed Services Committee, was immediate. *Washington Star,* October 28, 1961, p. 1.

[12] General Appropriation Act, 64 Stat. 595 (1951), § 1211; 31 U.S.C. § 665(c).

to effect savings whenever savings are possible by or through changes in requirements, greater efficiency of operations, or other developments subsequent to the date on which such appropriation was made available" [13] remains in force in 1961. The House Appropriations Committee specified that the bill was designed "to hold administrative officials responsible for the administration of an activity for which an appropriation has been made" by assuring that they "should bear final responsibility for rendering *all necessary service* with the smallest amount possible within the ceiling figure fixed by the Congress." [14] The purpose of the reserve section, according to the Committee, is "to require careful apportionment of all types of funds expended by Federal agencies and efficient administration of the Government's business." [15]

The outer limits of statutory authority of the President or Executive officers are described by these provisions for apportionment and reserves. It would seem clear that in the eyes of Congress an appropriation is more than a mere authorization to spend. Rather, when taken together with the statutory authorization of a program for which the appropriation is made, it is a mandate to perform the service for which the appropriation is made, with due regard to efficiency and economy.

Impounding for reasons other than economy and efficiency has no statutory sanction as a part of the general process of budget execution. Instances in which it has occurred, either as regards an entire appropriation or in terms of the reduction of the level of expenditure for a program, have been met with Congressional protest. That impounding between 1941 and 1961 has not been subjected to judicial scrutiny is undoubtedly the result of lack of standing to sue on the part of agencies to which funds were denied.[16]

The grant-in-aid to states or localities for purposes previously authorized by law does not differ in kind from the appropriation which is spent directly by an agency of the national government. The present system of monetary grants is largely a twentieth-century development, but grants of land to the States for public purposes are contemporaneous with the Constitution itself. The Congressional authority to grant land rests upon the power to dispose of territory or other property of the United States.[17] Authority for grants of money to the States is derived from the power of Congress to pay the debts and provide for the common defense and general welfare.[18] Challenges of the constitutionality of grants-in-aid were rebuffed at the outset by denial in *Massachusetts* v. *Mellon* and *Frothingham* v. *Mellon* to states and to individuals of standing to sue for this purpose.[19] This doctrine has been applied to uphold the legality of

---

[13] 31 U.S.C. § 665 (c) (2).

[14] H. R. Rep. No. 1797, 81st Cong., 2d Sess. 9 (1951). (Italics supplied.)

[15] *Ibid.*

[16] *Supra* notes 10 and 11.

[17] U.S. Const. art. IV, § 3, par. 2.

[18] U.S. Const. art. I, § 8, cl. 1.

[19] *Massachusetts* v. *Mellon, Frothingham* v. *Mellon*, 262 U.S. 447 (1923). Many instances of impounding of appropriated funds for governmental operations other than

a federal grant for the purpose of constructing a municipal power plant to operate in competition with the plaintiff.[20] The only exception to the *Mellon* rule has been permitted on the theory that a grant-in-aid statute creates a legal right to receive granted funds and that consequently a state has standing to sue to obtain such funds.[21]

The power of Congress to impose conditions upon grants-in-aid was inferentially upheld in *Steward Machine Co.* v. *Davis* [22] and was specifically approved in *Oklahoma* v. *Civil Service Commission*.[23] The requirement of the Hatch Act for abstinence from partisan political activity by persons administering federal highway grants was held to be a condition to continued receipt of the grant. "While the United States is not concerned with, and has no power to regulate, local political activities as such of state officials, it does have power to fix the terms upon which its money allotments to states shall be disbursed." [24]

Under the holding of the *Oklahoma* case, it would seem that a state or locality claiming to have complied with conditions for the receipts of grants-in-aid would have standing to sue in the Federal courts for vindication of a legal right. "Congress may create legally enforceable rights where none before existed. Payments were not made at the unfettered discretion of a federal disbursing officer or . . . agency, but according to statutory standards, compliance with which entitled Oklahoma to receive her proper share of the Federal appropriations." [25] Executive action to withhold grant-in-aid funds is subject to adjudication as to the existence of authority to withhold other than (1) for purposes of economy and efficiency, (2) in the exercise of delegated discretion, or (3) in the enforcement of a Congressionally-imposed condition precedent to receipt of the grant.

II. THE POWER TO EXECUTE THE LAWS
AND AUTHORITY TO IMPOUND

The President is empowered and required to take care that the laws are faithfully executed.[26] Whether this Constitutional provision conferred powers beyond the enumerated powers of the President, and whether it vested in him discretion as to the execution of Acts of Congress was argued in *Kendall* v. *United States ex rel. Stokes*.[27] Postmaster General Amos Kendall disallowed claims of Stokes for carrying the mails. Congress

---

for grants-in-aid could not be litigated because of lack of standing to sue on the part of a governmental agency. More remote potential beneficiaries would lack standing under *Massachusetts* v. *Mellon*.

[20] *Alabama Power Co.* v. *Ickes*, 302 U.S. 464 (1938).

[21] *Oklahoma* v. *United States Civil Service Commission*, 330 U.S. 127 (1947).

[22] 301 U.S. 548 (1937).

[23] *Oklahoma* v. *United States Civil Service Commission*, *supra* note 21.

[24] *Id.* at 143.

[25] *Id.* at 136.

[26] U.S. Const. art. II, § 3.

[27] 12 Pet. (37 U.S.) 524 (1838).

passed an act directing Kendall to credit claimant with the amount due, as determined by the Solicitor of the Treasury. Kendall again refused to pay the claim, contending that only the President, under the power to see that the laws are executed, could require that he pay the claims. The Supreme Court upheld a mandamus by the Circuit Court of the District of Columbia, ordering the payment, holding that the President was not empowered to dispense with the operation of law upon a subordinate executive officer. "The executive power is vested in a president; and as far as his powers are derived from the constitution, he is beyond the reach of any other department, except in the mode prescribed by the constitution through the impeaching power. But it by no means follows, that every officer in every branch is under the exclusive direction of the President." Where Congress imposes "upon any executive officer any duty they may think proper, which is not repugnant to any rights secured and protected by the constitution . . . in such cases, the duty and responsibility grow out of and are subject to the control of the law, and not to the direction of the President." [28]

The Court scouted the idea that the effect of the responsibility to see that the laws are faithfully executed is to create discretion in the President as to their execution. "To contend that the obligation imposed on the President to see the laws faithfully executed, implies a power to forbid their execution, is a novel construction of the constitution, and entirely inadmissible." [29] The President cannot dispense with the execution of the laws, under the duty to see that they are executed. To hold otherwise would be to vest completely the legislative power in the President or to confer upon him a veto power over laws duly passed and enrolled. To accord discretion to a President as to what laws should be enforced and how much would enable him to interpose a veto retroactively, perhaps even upon legislation in full force and effect for decades. That each successive incumbent of the Presidency is not to have a veto power retroactive to the earliest laws is attested by the words of the Constitution itself. The manner of exercising the veto is narrowly circumscribed.[30] Upon Presidential signature, or upon repassage by two thirds of each House of Congress, the bill "shall become a law." [31] It is these laws that the successive Presidents are required to see faithfully executed. No means are envisioned in the Constitution for a President to make objection upon his opinion of the constitutionality of existing law other than by urging its repeal on that ground.

The same is true if it be argued that the Constitution itself is one of the "laws" to be faithfully executed. It cannot be denied that the President may veto proposed laws upon the ground of unconstitutionality. The dispensing power which would exist under a claimed power to im-

28 *Id*. at 610.
29 *Id*. at 613.
30 U.S. Const. art. I, § 7.
31 U.S. Const. art. I, § 7, par. 2.

pound appropriations would, however, place the question of constitutionality in the hands of each successive President with the result of unimaginable instability and uncertainty as to the force of any law. The force of any law would thereby be at the whim of the current incumbent of the Presidency. Surely this result cannot have been contemplated by the Framers.

Viewing the "faithful execution" clause as vesting in the President the power to accomplish the duty, the Constitution provides that Congress may prescribe the way in which this power is carried out. Congress "shall have power to make all laws which shall be necessary and proper for carrying into execution the foregoing powers, and *all other powers vested by this constitution, in the government of the United States, or in any department or officer thereof.*" [32] Congress accordingly prescribes the way in which the President sees that laws are executed embodying in their context the determination that they are to be executed according to their terms. "The executive cannot see that the laws be executed but in the due forms of law." [33] This limiting view of the relation of the "necessary and proper" clause to the powers granted by Articles II and III received the express approval of the United States Supreme Court as to Article III in *Ableman* v. *Booth*.[34] It follows that the President may not exercise legislative powers as a means of carrying out his own powers. This does not, of course, refer to legislative powers which are a part of his express powers, especially the veto power, the manner of using which is constitutionally determined. To sanction withholding of appropriations upon the basis of the Presidential authority to see that the laws are faithfully executed would be to sanction the exercise of legislative power by the President as a means of carrying out an executive power, thereby permitting him to make the Constitution self-executing as to his powers. This the "necessary and proper" clause necessarily precludes.

Correlatively, if the President has no dispensing power, he likewise has no power to instruct a subordinate officer to dispense with the execution of a statute. This principle was established in the earliest days of the nation, when a written instruction of the President, directing a naval officer to seize vessels trading with French ports was declared invalid as being in conflict with statute.[35] That the President cannot authorize acts forbidden by law was held specifically two years later by Justice Paterson on circuit, in the trial of one who alleged that the President had authorized him to gather troops with the purpose of a military expedition against a nation with which the United States was not at war. "The president of the United States cannot control the statute, nor dispense with its execution, and still less can he authorize a person to do what the law forbids. If he could, it would render the execution of the laws dependent

[32] U.S. Const. art. I, § 8, cl. 18. (Italics supplied.)
[33] *United States ex rel. Stokes* v. *Kendall*, 26 Fed. Cas. 702, 748. (No. 15,517) (C.C. D.C. 1837).
[34] 21 How. (62 U.S.) 506, 521 (1858).
[35] *Little* v. *Barreme*, 2 Cr. (6 U.S.) 170 (1804).

on his will and pleasure."[36] As recently as 1956, Executive Order No. 10450[37] was found to extend beyond the provisions of law and hence not to authorize the discharge of incumbents in non-sensitive agencies. The discharging of such an incumbent from the Department of Health, Education, and Welfare by the Secretary was found not authorized, and in violation of the Veterans Preference Act.[38]

In short, the high Constitutional duty to see that the laws are faithfully executed does not confer upon the President the discretion to determine what laws shall be executed and how much. Whereas it may be a practical impossibility that all the laws be executed with equal vigor all the time, the Constitution seems to require no less. It is fallacious to argue that what appears a practical impossibility gives legal justification to acts in defiance of a plain duty.

The Constitution may create the paradox that the President is required to enforce laws that he believes to be unconstitutional. It is not, however, permissible to resolve this paradox by Presidential defiance of law.

III. INHERENT EXECUTIVE POWER AND AUTHORITY TO IMPOUND

Theodore Roosevelt, making perhaps the most general claim of Presidential power ever made for a Chief Executive, insisted upon "the theory that the executive power was limited only by specific restrictions and prohibitions appearing in the Constitution or imposed by Congress under its constitutional powers."[39] The Roosevelt theory was repudiated by the United States Supreme Court as contrary to the Tenth Amendment, viewing its words of reservation of powers not delegated as precluding inherent executive power.[40] Before Roosevelt's enunciation of the "stewardship" theory, the Court had pointed out that "We have no officers in this government, from the President down to the most subordinate agent, who does not hold office under the law, with prescribed duties and limited authority."[41]

The most recent and perhaps the most significant decision upon the nature and scope of Presidential power was that of *Youngstown Sheet and Tube Co.* v. *Sawyer.*[42] This landmark case grew out of President Truman's seizure of strike-bound steel mills in 1952. On April 8 of that year the President issued Executive Order 10340,[43] authorizing and directing Secretary of Commerce Charles Sawyer to take possession of and operate certain steel mills. The President rested this action on "the authority vested in me by the Constitution and laws of the United States, and as President of the United States and Commander in Chief of the armed

36 *United States* v. *Smith,* 27 Fed. Cas. 1192, 1230. (No. 16,342) (C.C.D.N.Y. 1806).
37 18 Fed. Reg. 2489.
38 *Cole* v. *Young,* 351 U.S. 536 (1956).
39 Roosevelt, *An Autobiography* 389 (1913).
40 *Kansas* v. *Colorado,* 206 U.S. 46, 89–90 (1907).
41 The Floyd Acceptances, 7 Wall. (74 U.S.) 666, 676 (1868).
42 343 U.S. 579 (1952).
43 17 Fed. Reg. 3139.

forces of the United States." [44] The holding in the *Youngstown* case is seemingly conclusive upon the question of inherent powers. Although there was no majority opinion of the Court, two groups of three Justices each arriving at the same result by different reasoning, there was no disagreement among the six as to the lack of inherent Presidential powers. The consensus was that the investiture of the executive power in the President combined with the "faithful execution" gave him no authority of a legislative nature. The Executive Order was an unconstitutional violation of the basic principle of separation of powers. The opinion of Justice Jackson formulated what has been widely accepted as the correct statement of the applicable constitutional principle: "When the President takes measures incompatible with the expressed or implied will of Congress, his power is at its lowest ebb, for then he can rely only upon his own constitutional powers minus any constitutional powers of Congress over the matter. Courts can sustain exclusive presidential control in such a case only by disabling the Congress from acting upon the subject." [45] Congress' power to spend for the national defense and general welfare is plenary, and includes the imposition of conditions for the receipt of grants.[46] Since the power of Congress to act in the area exists, the possibility of "exclusive Presidential control" is eliminated. Put another way, if Congress has power to make unconditional grants and power to make conditions at its discretion, there is no room for Presidentially added conditions. In short, where Congress has a power, there can be no inherent Presidential power.[47]

Against the holding of the *Youngstown* case must nevertheless be weighed two earlier Supreme Court decisions which seem to bespeak a Presidential power of different dimensions. These are *In re Neagle* [48] and *United States* v. *Midwest Oil Co.*[49] The former case arose out of the assignment of a United States marshal, Neagle, to protect Justice Stephen J. Field while on circuit in California, in the course of which assignment Neagle shot and killed a man who was attacking the Justice. Expressing the view that the Executive power was not limited to "the enforcement of acts of Congress or of treaties of the United States according to their express terms," [50] the Court found that it was within "the power of the President to take measures for the protection of a judge of one of the courts of the United States . . . while in the discharge of the duties of his office." [51] This broad language of the Court is thrown into confusion, however, by a later reference to Neagle's act as having been a duty "im-

---

[44] *Ibid.*

[45] *Youngstown Sheet & Tube Co.* v. *Sawyer, supra*, 637–38.

[46] *Oklahoma* v. *United States Civil Service Commission, supra* note 21.

[47] The converse of this proposition and the basic argument of the proponents of executive impounding to prevent segregation is considered in IV, *infra*. Concisely, this argument is that lack of Congressional power to provide for segregation by appropriation creates presidential power to prevent the use of appropriations for segregation.

[48] *In re Neagle*, 135 U.S. 1 (1890).

[49] 236 U.S. 459 (1915).

[50] *In re Neagle, supra* note 48, at 64.

[51] *Id.* at 67.

posed on him by the section of the Revised Statutes which we have re-cited, in connection with the powers conferred by the State of California upon its peace officers, which become, by this statute, in proper cases, transferred as duties to the marshals of the United States." [52] The *Neagle* opinion is at most inconclusive as to whether an inherent Presidential power or the statute is the source of the marshal's power. A convincing argument could be made that the case in actuality was decided upon the basis of the statute, in which event the *dicta* of the decision are no author-ity for the existence of an inherent Presidential power.

The *Midwest Oil* case [53] involved the question as to the power of the President to transfer lands from the public domain to the naval oil re-serve, thereby removing them from eligibility for homestead or lease. No statutory authority was given the President to accomplish such transfers. Nevertheless, the Supreme Court upheld the President in his action. The Court held that, although the President could not by his own course of action create a power, Congress might ratify his actions by acquiescence in them. Explicitly, the President is acting as an agent of the Congress.[54] Likewise, no private interest was injured because there was no private right denied, there having been conferred merely a privilege to occupy public lands.[55] An entirely different and easily distinguishable situation existed than in the *Oklahoma* case,[56] in which a legal right had been created by compliance with the conditions for receipt of grant-in-aid funds. It would seem that the *Midwest Oil* case is no authority for the existence of inherent Presidential powers which might include the im-pounding power. Congress has by no means acquiesced in a course of conduct in regard to impounding funds as it had done in regard to the land transfers. Similarly, in grant-in-aid cases legal rights rather than privileges are involved.

It would seem, therefore, that the overwhelming weight of authority is against the existence of any inherent Presidential power to impound appropriated funds.

IV. GRANT-IN-AID STATUTES AND "NATIONAL POLICY" AS SOURCES OF AUTHORITY TO IMPOUND

If, as has been suggested, existing statutes regarding the execution of the budget confer no general authority to impound grant-in-aid funds; if the "execution of the laws" clause of Article II confers no such power; and if there is no inherent power over expenditures in the President,

[52] *Id.* at 69. The statute referred to is Rev. Stat. § 788, 28 U.S.C. § 549, which pro-vides that "A United States marshal and his deputies, in executing the laws of the United States within a state, may exercise the same powers which a sheriff of such a state may exercise in executing the laws thereof."

[53] *Supra* note 49.

[54] *Id.* at 491.

[55] *Id.* at 471. It is possible that today the Midwest Oil Company would not have standing to sue, for this reason.

[56] *Supra* note 21.

any power to impound grants-in-aid of desegregation must be found either in the statutes which themselves authorize the grants or in a "national policy" of desegregation.

A detailed analysis of the multifarious grant-in-aid statutes involved is precluded by space considerations. The major grant-in-aid programs in the administration or results of which racial segregation or discrimination exist have been considered by the United States Commission on Civil Rights.[57] These include grants for library services,[58] for hospital construction,[59] for aid to [60] and construction of [61] schools in local areas where Federal establishments have caused a substantial impact on school systems, for public airports,[62] for vocational rehabilitation,[63] for urban renewal [64] and for public housing.[65] In none of the statutes authorizing grants is there a clear and unequivocal grant of authority to the President or to a subordinate executive officer to withhold appropriated funds upon a finding of racial segregation or discrimination in their administration by states or localities. The closest approach to such authority is found in the Library Services Act and in the Vocational Rehabilitation Act, both of which authorize the responsible administrator to withhold funds upon a finding of failure to comply with the conditions of the acts.[66] The former is to provide public library services, defined as serving "free all residents of a community, district or region," [67] and the latter is to provide for "rehabilitating physically handicapped individuals." [68] It is a fair inference that the responsible administrator could withhold funds under these programs if "all residents" were not served by participating libraries or if rehabilitation of "physically handicapped" were based on racial considerations. This interpretation is found by the Civil Rights Commission to be followed by administration regulation in respect to vocational rehabilitation.[69]

A second group of grant-in-aid statutes, of which the Federal Airport Act is illustrative, are silent upon the subject. It would seem that silence permits administrative discretion as to imposition of non-discriminatory

[57] 1961 Commission on Civil Rights Report; pt. IV, "Education" at 144–48; pt. V, "Employment" at 81–93, 111–26; pt. VI, "Housing" at 81–118. Hereinafter cited as *1961 Report*.

[58] Library Services Act, 70 Stat. 293 (1956), as amended, 20 U.S.C. §§ 351–58.

[59] Hospital Survey and Construction Act (Hill-Burton Act), 60 Stat. 1040 (1946), 42 U.S.C. §§ 291, 291a–291m. The Land Grant College Act, 26 Stat. 417, 7 U.S.C. §§ 321–26, 328–29 carries a similar provision at § 323.

[60] 64 Stat. 1100 (1950), 20 U.S.C. §§ 236–44.

[61] 64 Stat. 967 (1950), 20 U.S.C. §§ 631–45.

[62] Federal Airport Act, 60 Stat. 170 (1946), 49 U.S.C. §§ 1101–19.

[63] Vocational Rehabilitation Act, 41 Stat. 735 (1920), amended to 68 Stat. 652, 29 U.S.C. § 3.

[64] Housing Act, 63 Stat. 413 (1949), 42 U.S.C. § 1441; Housing Act, 68 Stat. 623 (1954), 42 U.S.C. § 1451.

[65] United States Housing Act, 50 Stat. 888 (1937), 42 U.S.C. § 1401.

[66] 20 U.S.C. § 356; 29 U.S.C. § 35 (c).

[67] 20 U.S.C. § 358 (c).

[68] 29 U.S.C. § 31.

[69] *1961 Report*, pt. V, "Employment" at 111, citing 45 C.F.R. § 401.14 (a) (2) (1960).

use of Federal funds as a condition precedent to their receipt. The Civil Rights Commission reports that this technique has been successfully followed in the administration of the Airport Act.[70] The *Midwest Oil Co.* holding, deriving executive authority from Congressional acquiescence in a course of executive conduct,[71] clearly supports the validity of the application of administrative pre-conditions to the receipt of grant funds, in the event that Congress does not correct such administrative interpretations.

A third group of statutes presents Congress' determination that the appropriated funds shall be spent regardless of segregation in the facilities provided. The Hill-Burton Hospital Construction Act provides that a State plan for hospital construction shall not be approved unless assurance is given that hospitals will be made available to all residents without discrimination on account of race, creed or color, *except* "in cases where separate hospital facilities are provided for separate population groups, if the plan makes equitable provision on the basis of need for facilities and service of like quality for each such group." [72] The statutes providing grants for direct aid and for school construction in federally impacted areas require that "no department, agency, officer or employee of the United States shall exercise any direction, supervision, or control over the personnel, curriculum, or program of instruction of any school or school system of any local or State educational agency." [73] Detailed formulae are provided under these acts, and admit of little, if any, administrative discretion in arriving at the amounts payable. No power is provided to withhold funds for failure to comply with the conditions of the acts, comparable to provisions in the Library Services Act and the Vocational Rehabilitation Act.[74] It is clear that the Congressional intent did not embrace authorization to impound funds upon the basis that they might be spent in support of segregation.

Finding no statutory authority to withhold funds in this third group of statutes necessitates consideration of the impact of the school desegregation decisions [75] upon them, since the acts in question were passed before these decisions. In the context existing since these decisions, two questions are posed: do the decisions in *Bolling* v. *Sharpe* and *Cooper* v. *Aaron* establish a national policy which empowers the executive to ignore statutory language; if not, may the statutes themselves be subjected to a construction different than their plain meaning by reason of these decisions?

---

[70] *Id.,* pt. V, "Employment" at 85, citing 14 C.F.R. § 550.24 (i) (2) and (5).

[71] *In re Neagle* and *United States* v. *Midwest Oil Co., supra* note 7.

[72] 42 U.S.C. § 291 (f).

[73] 20 U.S.C. §§ 242 (a) and 642 (a).

[74] See note 66, *supra.*

[75] *Bolling* v. *Sharpe,* 347 U.S. 497 (1954) and *Cooper* v. *Aaron,* 358 U.S. 1 (1958). *Brown* v. *Board of Education,* 347 U.S. 483 (1954) is not considered, since it dealt with limitations upon the *states* under the equal protection clause of the Fourteenth Amendment, while the present issue involves limitations upon the *National Government.*

Bolling v. *Sharpe* decided the unconstitutionality of segregation based on race in the District of Columbia, upon the basis of the due process clause of the Fifth Amendment. The Court's language tends to include the Fourteenth Amendment guaranty of equal protection of the law as an aspect of that due process of law which is protected against denial by the National Government.[76] Proponents of a Presidential power to withhold grant-in-aid funds from segregated schools argue that the Fifth Amendment as interpreted in the *Bolling* case requires such Presidential action. *Cooper* v. *Aaron,* the Little Rock School case, is adduced in support of this view. Speaking of the contention that the Governor of Arkansas was not bound by the decision in *Brown* v. *Board of Education,* the Court said: "State support of segregated schools through any arrangement, management, funds, or property cannot be squared with the [Fourteenth] Amendment's command that no State shall deny to any person within its jurisdiction the equal protection of the laws." [77] It follows, it is argued, that the expenditure of Federal funds for the support of segregated schools is unconstitutional under the Fifth Amendment. Granting the validity of this proposition, however, it does not follow that the power to withhold funds provided by law which may be used for this purpose is thereby conferred upon the President. It would seem, in the light of considerations regarding the scope of his legislative power raised earlier, that Presidential action is constitutionally limited to vetoing the entire appropriation which would be put to constitutionally proscribed uses in some states. To hold otherwise would be to argue that the President may act unconstitutionally to uphold a constitutional principle, the absurdity of which is manifest. The constitutional situation is aptly summarized by Senator Kenneth B. Keating: "This is a classic example of constitutional wrong for which no constitutional remedy exists, other than what we [the Congress] may provide by express enactment." [78]

Accordingly, it would seem that the Hill-Burton Act must await Congressional action to bring it into compliance with the constitutional mandate, since judicial review is precluded by existing doctrine as to lack of individual standing to sue. Resort to impounding based on a claim of a constitutional power to impound may, however, be unnecessary in order to deal with the problem of expenditures for segregated schools under the impacted areas legislation. An acceptable argument can be made that Congress never intended by the "non-intervention" clauses of the education acts to preclude administrative discretion as to the disbursal of funds for segregated schools. It will be recalled that the "non-intervention" clauses provide that "no department, agency, officer or employee of the United States shall exercise any direction, supervision, or control over the personnel, curriculum, or program of instruction of any school or school system of local or State educational agency." [79] The

---

[76] *Bolling* v. *Sharpe, supra* at 499.
[77] *Cooper* v. *Aaron, supra* at 19.
[78] 107 *Cong. Rec.* 7808 (daily ed. May 18, 1961).
[79] See note 73, *supra.*

ambiguity of the phrase "personnel, curriculum, or program of instruction" is obvious, and this phrase is susceptible of construction so as to eliminate what has been administratively interpreted as a prohibition of denial of funds to segregated schools. That the "non-intervention" clause has been incorrectly construed by the responsible administrators is demonstrated by the fact that the National Defense Education Act, containing the same phraseology,[80] was passed in 1958 *after* the school segregation decisions. If Congress did not intend the "non-intervention" clause to have an unconstitutional meaning in 1958, which may be assumed, it presumably would have changed the phrasing of the clause if the words were to carry a different intent than when used before the desegregation decisions. It follows that segregation was never intended to be embraced within the language "personnel, curriculum, or program of instruction." Administrative interpretation to this effect, and application of the education acts accordingly, would be subject to judicial review. Such a procedure would not, as would impounding by Executive Order, place the courts in the position of upholding an unconstitutional act in order to determine the unconstitutionality of Federal grants-in-aid for segregated schools.

V. Conclusions

The President has no general statutory authority to impound appropriated funds for reasons other than economy and efficiency of operation, the power to impound for which is a specific statutory grant of power. Nor can the President validly claim such authority as derived from the duty "to take care that the laws are faithfully executed." Still less can power to impound be attributed to inherent powers of the office. *Bolling* v. *Sharpe* and *Cooper* v. *Aaron*, in holding that the National Government might not segregate or support segregation under the Fifth Amendment, did not thereby confer upon the President power to impound portions of appropriations to prevent their use for the unconstitutional purpose. Certain grant-in-aid statutes permit sufficient administrative discretion to provide for the withholding of Federal funds for purposes involving racial segregation, and the impacted area acts are susceptible of construction to permit such discretion, although it would seem that the Hill-Burton Act is not. That Congress has not acted to correct unconstitutional legislation and that doctrines of standing to sue make it difficult to obtain court action, however, lend no support to the argument that an executive power to correct the law, specifically by the impounding device, need exist. The dangers of the impounding device, giving the President the power to dispense with the execution of the law and giving him a retroactive veto based upon his present opinion of the constitutionality of any statute, are so great as to require resort to alternative methods of bringing grant-in-aid statutes into conformity with the Constitution as respects segregation. An alternative method of procedure worthy of con-

[80] National Defense Education Act, 72 Stat. 1582 (1958), 20 U.S.C. §§ 401, 402.

sideration has been recommended by the Civil Rights Commission: treat grants-in-aid as contracts and impose a non-discrimination condition precedent to the receipt of funds as is presently the case with government contracts.[81] This proposal has the great merit that it does not strike at the separation of powers of government, which is basic to our constitutional system. The establishment of a Presidential power to impound funds goes too far upon this road. "The temptation of many men of good will is to cut corners, take short cuts, and reach the desired end regardless of the means. Worthy as . . . the ends are . . . the particular means [proposed is] unconstitutional." [82]

A 20th Century Emancipation Proclamation: Presidential Power Permits Withholding of Federal Funds from Segregated Institutions

Harry Kranz

I. INTRODUCTION

As the 100th Anniversary of President Lincoln's Emancipation Proclamation draws near,[1] it has been suggested [2] that President Kennedy issue a modern proclamation forbidding use of Federal funds in support of segregated institutions.[3]

---

[81] *1961 Report*, pt. V, "Employment" at 162, recommendation 3. The question as to Presidential authority to accomplish this recommendation is not, however, satisfactorily solved by the Commission report.

[82] Douglas, J., dissenting in *Hannah* v. *Larche*, 363 U.S. 420, 494 (1960).

Reprinted by permission from the *American University Law Review*, Vol. 11 (January 1962), pp. 48–78.

[1] Three dates have been mentioned. On July 22, 1862, President Lincoln presented an initial draft to his cabinet. On September 22, 1862, Lincoln issued his preliminary proclamation, declaring that if the seceded states did not lay down their arms and return to the Union by January 1, 1863, he would declare their slaves to be "forever free." The formal Emancipation Proclamation followed on the first day of 1863. 5 *The World Book Encyclopedia* 200 (Field Enterprises Educational Corp., 1961).

[2] See, *e.g.*, Dean Eugene V. Rostow of the Yale University Law School, "The Freedom Riders and the Future," *The Reporter*, June 22, 1961, p. 21; the Rev. Martin Luther King, *New York Times*, October 17, 1961, p. 1.

[3] Throughout this article the phrase "segregated institutions" includes Federal grants to state and local governments and school districts, as well as to private institutions, such as colleges and hospitals, and to private individuals who spend the money at segregated institutions. It is the author's contention that these indirect Federal expenditures in support of segregated operations are just as subject to Constitutional

Such a proclamation [4] would require that seekers of Federal financial aid, including state and local governments and private institutions, agree in writing that there shall be no discrimination or segregation based solely on race, color or religion in any Federally aided facility, program or service, and would direct appropriate executive departments to withhold grants from those who refuse to agree to or abide by the anti-bias requirement.[5]

That the President, without further action by Congress [6] or the courts,[7] has the statutory and constitutional power to issue such an executive order or proclamation,[8] is our thesis.

Although the United States Supreme Court has not ruled on this specific issue, its decisions in three separate fields — state-sanctioned segregation, Federal grant-in-aid statutes, and the President's express and implied constitutional powers — coalesce to support Presidential withholding of public funds from segregated institutions. To weave our pattern of Presidential power, we shall examine each of these three threads.

---

limitations and Presidential power as the more direct Federal spending on armed forces, government employee salaries and national contract-buying of goods and services, all of which have been covered by executive orders barring racial discrimination. See *Lawrence* v. *Hancock*, 76 F. Supp. 1004 (S.D. W.Va. 1948) (government can't escape its constitutional obligations by providing "the ways and means for a private individual or corporation to discriminate against its own citizens").

[4] A presidential proclamation or executive order is an appropriate means for promoting human rights. See, *e.g.*, President Franklin D. Roosevelt's order creating a wartime Fair Employment Practices Commission, Executive Order 8802, 6 Fed. Reg. 3109 (1941) and President Kennedy's Executive Order 10925, 26 Fed. Reg. 1977, Mar. 8, 1961, creating the President's Committee on Equal Employment Opportunity to assure nondiscrimination in Federal employment and on work performed under government contract. On the legal effect of Presidential proclamations, see *Lapeyre* v. *United States*, 17 Wall. (84 U.S.) 191 (1873); *United States* v. *Klein*, 13 Wall. (80 U.S.) 128 (1872). For the advantages of a single proclamation over piecemeal orders, see Leadership Conference on Civil Rights, *Proposals for Executive Action To End Federally Supported Segregation and Other Forms of Racial Discrimination*, August 29, 1961, pp. 2–3.

[5] Withholding of Federal grants from segregated institutions has been urged by the United States Commission on Civil Rights in its *Report*, 1959, p. 329; and in *Equal Protection of the Laws in Public Higher Education*, 1960, p. 250. See also Leadership Conference on Civil Rights, *op. cit. supra* note 4; Rostow, *op. cit. supra* note 2.

[6] Congressional rules make it unlikely that Congress will enact specific, affirmative pro-civil rights laws in the near future. It is enough that Congress, in the broad delegations of power written into many Federal grant-in-aid laws, has already authorized the executive to act against segregated institutions, as will be shown later. On the Senate filibuster rule, see Emerson and Haber, *Political and Civil Rights in the United States* 132, note 4 (1958).

[7] Litigation has been relatively ineffective in implementing the Supreme Court's 1954 decision outlawing school segregation. See Southern Education Reporting Service, *A Statistical Summary, State by State, of Segregation-Desegregation Activity Affecting Southern Schools*, 1954–1960, p. 2; Report of the United States Commission on Civil Rights 309 (1959); Blaustein and Ferguson, *Desegregation and the Law* 269 (1957).

[8] President Kennedy has said: ". . . we will use the tools now given us by the Constitution itself and the laws already passed to make the American promise come true for all its citizens. . . ." Meany, Kennedy Discuss the 1960 Election Issues, 67 *The American Federationist* 15 (November, 1960).

II. STATE-SANCTIONED SEGREGATION
Is UNCONSTITUTIONAL

From Supreme Court decisions over the past 80 years, it is clear that state-sanctioned segregation is unconstitutional. The development and current content of this doctrine may be summarily traced.

While purely private discrimination is not constitutionally proscribed, "state action" must be non-discriminatory.[9] "State action" under the Fifth and Fourteenth Amendments includes action by the Federal or state governments through any branch, including the courts, the Congress or Legislature, and the President, Governor or lesser executive officials.[10]

Compulsory racial segregation in state-supported schools violates the equal protection clause of the Fourteenth Amendment,[11] and school segregation financed by the Federal government violates the due process clause of the Fifth Amendment.[12] Neither the Federal nor state governments may support segregated schools "through any arrangement, management, funds or property." [13] "All provisions of Federal, state or local law requiring or permitting" racial segregation in public education are unconstitutional.[14]

Not confined to schools, the Supreme Court's historic decisions during the past seven years have signaled the end of all racial discrimination by law in the United States.[15] Laws separating the races in any public facility, including parks and playgrounds,[16] golf courses,[17] swimming pools and beaches,[18] restaurants,[19] transportation facilities,[20] and public housing,[21] have been stricken down as discriminatory "state action."

[9] Civil Rights Cases, 109 U.S. 3 (1883).

[10] 16 C.J.S. *Constitutional Law* § 544. See also *Cooper v. Aaron,* 358 U.S. 1 (1958).

[11] *Brown* v. *Board of Education,* 347 U.S. 483 (1954).

[12] *Bolling* v. *Sharpe,* 347 U.S. 497 (1954).

[13] *Cooper* v. *Aaron,* 358 U.S. 1 (1958).

[14] *Brown* v. *Board of Education* (Implementing), 349 U.S. 294 (1955).

[15] Blaustein and Ferguson, *op. cit. supra* note 7 at 198; Emerson and Haber, *op. cit. supra* note 6 at 1417–1419.

[16] *Dawson* v. *Mayor and City Council of Baltimore,* 220 F.2d 386 (4th Cir. 1955), *aff'd per curiam,* 350 U.S. 877 (1955); *Department of Conservation and Development of Virginia* v. *Tate,* 231 F.2d 615 (4th Cir. 1956), *cert. den.,* 352 U.S. 838 (1956); *Hampton* v. *City of Jacksonville* (S.D. Fla. Civil No. 4368-J, Dec. 7, 1960) (includes parks, playgrounds, pools, tennis courts, zoo and baseball and football fields).

[17] *Holmes* v. *City of Atlanta,* 350 U.S. 879 (1955); *Simkins* v. *City of Greensboro,* 149 F. Supp. 562 (M.D. N.C. 1957), *aff'd* 246 F.2d 425 (4th Cir. 1957).

[18] *City of St. Petersburg* v. *Alsup,* 238 F.2d 830 (5th Cir. 1956), *cert. den.* 353 U.S. 922 (1956); *Prymus* v. *High* (S.D. Fla. Civil No. 9545, Sept. 12, 1960).

[19] *Derrington* v. *Plummer,* 240 F.2d 922 (5th Cir. 1956), *cert. den.* 353 U.S. 924 (1957); *Burton v. Wilmington Parking Authority,* 81 S.Ct. 856 (1961); *Boynton* v. *Virginia,* 364 U.S. 454 (1960).

[20] *Gayle* v. *Browder,* 352 U.S. 903 (1956) (buses); *Henderson* v. *United States,* 339 U.S. 816 (1950) (trains); *Henry* v. *Greenville Airport Commission,* 284 F.2d 631 (4th Cir. 1960) (airports).

[21] *Banks* v. *Housing Authority of City and County of San Francisco,* 120 Cal. App. 2d 1; 260 P.2d 668 (1953), *cert. den.,* 347 U.S. 974 (1954); *Detroit Housing Commission* v. *Lewis,* 226 F.2d 180 (6th Cir. 1955).

The concept of "state action" goes beyond the mere construction, operation or maintenance of public facilities with public funds. It embraces within constitutional protection many activities by "private" parties, including instances where the state has actively lent its aid; [22] has conferred the power that has subsequently been abused; [23] has transferred one of its regular functions to other hands; [24] or has seemingly endorsed the objectionable action by declining to halt it.[25]

III. PRESIDENTIAL POWERS TO WITHHOLD GRANTS UNDER THE FEDERAL AID STATUTES

In the hands of a President desiring to halt state-sanctioned segregation, Federal grants-in-aid are a major tool. Their phenomenal growth in the past sixty years has created "the most powerful device in this century for reshaping national-state relations." [26] Today they comprise nearly 8% of total Federal cash payments,[27] and more than 14% of total state receipts from all sources.[28] They are of particular importance in helping to subsidize segregation in the eleven Southern states, where Federal contributions to state and local governments (excluding grants to individuals and institutions) constitute from 10% to 22% of state and local government expenditures.[29]

Grants to the states, with Congressional and executive strings attached,

[22] *Shelley* v. *Kraemer*, 334 U.S. 1 (1948); *Barrows* v. *Jackson*, 346 U.S. 249 (1953); *Hurd* v. *Hodge*, 334 U.S. 24 (1948); *Pennsylvania* v. *Board of Directors of the Phila. City Trusts*, 353 U.S. 230 (1957); *Kerr* v. *Enoch Pratt Free Library*, 149 F.2d 212 (4th Cir., 1945), *cert. den.*, 326 U.S. 721 (1945).

[23] *Derrington* v. *Plummer. supra* note 19; *Lawrence* v. *Hancock, supra* note 3; *Burton* v. *Wilmington Parking Authority, supra* note 19.

[24] *Steele* v. *Louisville and Nashville Railroad Co.*, 323 U.S. 192 (1944); *Tunstall* v. *Brotherhood of Locomotive Firemen*, 323 U.S. 210 (1944); *Syres* v. *Oil Workers International Union*, 350 U.S. 892 (1955); *Marsh* v. *Alabama*, 326 U.S. 501 (1946); *Department of Conservation and Development of Virginia* v. *Tate, supra* note 16. But *cf. Johnson* v. *Levitt & Sons*. 131 F. Supp. 114 (E.D. Pa. 1955); and *compare Connecticut College for Women* v. *Calvert*, 87 Conn. 421, 88 A. 633 (1913) and *Betts* v. *Easley*, 161 Kans. 459, 169 P.2d 831 (1946), *with Watchtower Bible and Tract Society Inc.* v. *Metropolitan Life Insurance Co.*, 297 N.Y. 339, 79 N.E.2d 433 (1948), *cert. den.* 335 U.S. 886 (1948).

[25] *Terry* v. *Adams*, 345 U.S. 461 (1953); *Public Utilities Commission* v. *Pollak*, 343 U.S. 451 (1952). See also *Miller* v. *Schoene*, 276 U.S. 272 (1928), and *Lynch* v. *United States*, 189 F.2d 476 (5th Cir. 1951). On the "state action" concept, see generally Gellhorn, *American Rights* 174–82 (1960); Greenberg, *Race Relations and American Law* 51–52 (1959); Antieau, *Commentaries on the Constitution of the United States* 144–145 (1960); Note, *The Impact of Shelley* v. *Kraemer on the State Action Concept*, 44 Calif. L.R. 718 (1956).

[26] Young, *Essentials of American Government* 55 (8th ed., 1959).

[27] Bureau of the Budget, *Special Analysis of Federal Aid to State and Local Governments in the 1962 Budget*, p. 3.

[28] *Ibid*.

[29] They constitute 22% in Alabama and Arkansas; 21% in Mississippi; 16% in Georgia; 15% in Louisiana, South Carolina and Tennessee; 14% in North Carolina and Texas; 11% in Virginia; and 10% in Florida. U.S. Department of Commerce, *Statistical Abstract of the United States* 410 (1960).

are almost as old as the nation.[30] Not only did the courts uphold Congressional power to condition grants of public land,[31] but they also viewed with "great liberality" the discretion exercised for more than a century by Presidents who made reservations of public lands for a variety of purposes — all without Congressional authorization — thereby "creating precedents which are available, and which have been used to justify an equally broad range of presidential discretion in other areas of substantive activity." [32]

In the case of monetary, as distinguished from land, grants to the states, court recognition of the constitutional authority of Congress to provide for the common defense and the general welfare of the United States was longer in coming.[33] Under decisions of the Supreme Court within the past twenty-five years,[34] however, Congressional power to make cash grants and to impose conditions on the Federal aid is today beyond dispute.

In enacting Federal aid legislation, Congress has neither been willing to give the states a blank-check appropriation free of Federal executive supervision,[35] nor has it been able to spell out in the law all of the conditions upon which the aid was predicated.[36] Leaving administration of the grant to the executive branch, Congress has delegated broad rule-making power to Federal administrators in every grant-in-aid law passed in the 20th Century.[37]

Whether the source of the Federal standards is the law or the administrator's regulations, the Federal statutes ordinarily authorize withholding of the grants from would-be recipients who do not meet the established standards.

However, on the issue of racial discrimination or segregation in the use of the Federal funds, Congress has never written a specific anti-segregation standard into the fifty-odd grant-in-aid laws. Most of them are silent

---

[30] Starting in 1802, Congress bestowed on newly-admitted states public land to be used for development of permanent school funds. Young, *op. cit. supra* note 26. See also Corwin, *Annotated Constitution of the United States* 113 (1953).

[31] *Stearns v. Minnesota*, 179 U.S. 223 (1900); *McGehee v. Mathis*, 71 U.S. 143 (1866).

[32] Schubert, *The Presidency In The Courts* 353 (1957). Presidents reserved public lands for military purposes, to conserve natural resources, to resettle Indian tribes, and even to create lighthouses and bird sanctuaries. *Ibid.*

[33] U.S. Const., art. 1, § 8, clause 1.

[34] *United States v. Butler*, 297 U.S. 1 (1936); *Carmichael v. Southern Coal and Coke Co.*, 301 U.S. 495 (1937); *Steward Machine Co. v. Davis*, 301 U.S. 548 (1937); *Helvering v. Davis*, 301 U.S. 619 (1937); *Oklahoma v. Civil Service Commission*, 330 U.S. 127 (1947); *United States v. Gerlach Livestock Co.*, 339 U.S. 725 (1950).

[35] Burns, *Social Security and Public Policy* 237–238 (1956); see also *Public Health Grant-in-aid Amendments of 1954*, H.R. Rep. No. 1543, 83rd Cong., 2d Sess. (1954).

[36] Burns, *op. cit. supra* note 35 at 258.

[37] No court has ever interfered with Congressional delegation of power under the Federal grant-in-aid statutes, and only two cases, *Panama Refining Co. v. Ryan*, 293 U.S. 388 (1935) and *Schechter Poultry Corp. v. United States*, 295 U.S. 495 (1935), which have since become historical oddities, have ever restricted Congressional power to delegate administrative authority to the executive in any field.

on the specific question of granting or withholding funds from segregated institutions. A few permit or require grants for segregated activities.

A. Grant-in-aid Statutes May Be Construed to Authorize Withholding

Where the statute, though silent on segregation specifically, has broadly delegated power to the executive, or where it can be construed to authorize a withholding of the grant from a segregated institution, the President has the necessary discretion to act,[38] and the courts will not interfere.[39]

To avoid the more serious constitutional issues, the courts will unhesitatingly uphold the President's action on statutory construction grounds.[40] They will not only affirm the executive's own interpretation of his powers under the statute,[41] but presume that he has complied with the statutory conditions that authorize him to take action or limit his power to act.[42] When the President declares that something was "necessary"[43] or "suitable,"[44] the courts merely nod "Amen."[45]

Among the majority of Federal grant-in-aid statutes which are silent on segregation, but which contain language that may be construed as impliedly authorizing executive withholding are those dealing with impacted area schools, vocational education, libraries, the employment service, airports and housing. In every one of these programs, the Federal government is currently subsidizing segregation or discrimination, even though a Presidential proclamation or executive order could halt it.

A few examples of the discretionary language, which could be construed to authorize withholding under the Federal aid statutes, will suffice.

1. *Aid to Impacted Areas.* The Federal Aid to Impacted Areas Act,[46] designed to provide Federal grants-in-aid for the construction and the operation of public schools for the education of children whose par-

---

[38] *Arizona* v. *Hobby,* 221 F.2d 498 (C.C.A.D.C. 1954); *United States* v. *Eliason,* 16 Pet. (41 U.S.) 291 (1842).

[39] *Kurtz* v. *Moffitt,* 115 U.S. 487 (1885); *Smith* v. *Whitney,* 116 U.S. 167 (1886). In *Wyoming* v. *Franke,* 58 F. Supp. 890 (D. Wyo. 1945), the court held that the question of Presidential compliance with Congressional standards in the case of a conflict between the President and a state was political in nature and refused to intervene.

[40] *United States* v. *Rumely,* 345 U.S. 41 (1953); *Crowell* v. *Benson,* 285 U.S. 22 (1932).

[41] *United States* v. *Antikamnia Chemical Co.,* 231 U.S. 654 (1914); *United States* v. *Query,* 37 F. Supp. 972 (E.D. S.C. 1941); *Fleming* v. *Mohawk Wrecking and Lumber Co.,* 331 U.S. 111 (1947).

[42] Schubert, *op. cit. supra* note 32 at 316–318.

[43] *Merritt* v. *United States,* 264 F. 870, 873 (9th Cir. 1920), *reversed on other grounds* in 255 U.S. 579 (1921).

[44] *Kansas or Kaw Tribe of Indians* v. *United States,* 80 Ct. Cl. 264, 313 (1934).

[45] While executive legislation far exceeds in quantity that of Congress, it is highly significant that in all United States history, the Supreme Court has invalidated presidential orders only 14 times, while it has declared 80 Congressional statutes unconstitutional in this same period. Schubert, *op. cit. supra* note 32 at 355.

[46] 20 U.S.C. 236 *et seq.*

ents are employed directly or indirectly by the Federal government, contains at least ten sections which may be construed as authorizing the Commissioner of Education to withhold funds from segregated school systems.

For example, in the school "assistance" Act,[47] four separate categories of Federal aid are established. Two categories are wholly discretionary. One [48] (payments in lieu of taxes for Federally-preempted land) delegates entirely to "the judgment of the Commissioner" the "determination" of what districts shall get what aid, if any. In the second category [49] (school enrollment increases due to Federal contracts in area) the "judgment," "determination," and "estimates" of the Commissioner of what is "necessary," "reasonable," "comparable," "substantial," "equivalent," etc., are to be conclusive.

The remaining two categories of Federal aid [50] (for children whose parents live *and* work, or live *or* work on Federal property) are also replete with discretionary authority for the Commissioner. Under these sections, broadened by the Civil Rights Act of 1960,[51] the Commissioner may determine that a segregated public school system is not "suitable" for the children of men in the armed forces of the United States or otherwise employed by the Federal government in essential defense and domestic activities. He can "determine" that it is both "appropriate" and "necessary" to make other arrangements for the free public education of these children,[52] and "through deductions from amounts to which the local educational agency is entitled under this Act" the Commissioner may recoup the cost of educating these pupils.[53]

The "construction" Act,[54] too, contains broad language which lends itself to interpretation by the Commissioner. For example, the Commissioner may determine that it is *not* the construction of additional facilities which creates "an undue financial burden" on a city,[55] but the maintenance of a segregated school system, requiring dual schools, teachers, administrators, and even toilets, gymnasiums and swimming pools, which creates the "undue financial burden." [56]

2. *Vocational Education.* Under the Vocational Education program,[57] providing training for those of less than college grade in agriculture, home economics, distributive occupations, trades and industries,

---

47 20 U.S.C. 237–239.

48 20 U.S.C. 237.

49 20 U.S.C. 239.

50 20 U.S.C. 238.

51 74 Stat. 86, P.L. 86–449 (86th Cong.) approved May 6, 1960.

52 For the broad discretion vested in the executive branch by these words, see *Merritt* v. *United States, supra* note 43 ("necessary"); *Kansas or Kaw Tribe of Indians* v. *United States, supra* note 44 ("suitable").

53 20 U.S.C. 241 (b).

54 20 U.S.C. 631–645 (1960 supplement).

55 20 U.S.C. 635 (c).

56 The Commissioner's broad authority to interpret this section of the Act was confirmed in *School City of Gary* v. *Derthick,* 273 F.2d 319 (7th Cir. 1959).

57 39 Stat. 929 (1917), 49 Stat. 1489 (1936), 20 U.S.C. 11.

the Commissioner of Education and the Department of Health, Education and Welfare are given broad rule-making power [58] and are authorized to withhold Federal grants from states not complying with the administrator's standards.[59] There is a very unusual provision permitting the states to appeal any withholding of funds to Congress.[60]

Although racial discrimination is nowhere mentioned in the law, the Department in 1948 issued regulations banning racial discrimination "in the expenditure of Federal funds and in the administration of Federally aided programs of vocational education." [61]

3. *Library Services.* The Library Services Act of 1956,[62] which authorized grants to states for the extension and improvement of public library services in communities with a population under 10,000, defines the term "public library" to mean "a library that serves free *all* residents of a community, district or region, and receives its financial support in whole or in part from public funds." [63] [Emphasis added.]

Since a whites-only library or a Negroes-only library does not serve "all" of the residents of a community, it falls short of the statutory definition of "public library." An administrator would be justified in withholding funds from a library which thus did not comply with the statute.[64]

4. *Employment Service.* Public employment offices, which aid unemployed workers to find jobs, have been established in all states under Federal law.[65] The Secretary of Labor and subordinate administrators are authorized to make rules and regulations for the Employment Service, and to determine what funds shall be allotted the states for "proper and efficient" administration.[66]

This authority has already been used to require farmers seeking temporary help through the U.S.E.S. to agree to maintain minimum job standards, and to prohibit the acceptance of discriminatory job orders from agencies of the Federal government.[67] Clearly, the maintenance of dual, segregated employment offices and other discriminatory practices is

[58] 20 U.S.C. 11–28.

[59] 20 U.S.C. 26.

[60] *Ibid.* The provision also appears in the Morrill Land Grant College Act, 7 U.S.C. 361 (g) (1958). If the Secretary of HEW withholds certification of funds for any state, he is required to report the facts and reasons to the President, and the amount involved must be kept separate in the Treasury until the close of the next Congress to permit the state to appeal to Congress. If the next Congress does not direct "such sum to be paid (to the State) it shall be carried to surplus." Thus, the act contains a built-in method of testing Congressional reaction to executive withholding of grants from states which maintain segregated institutions.

[61] 45 C.F.R. 102.18.

[62] 70 Stat. 295 (1956), 20 U.S.C. 355.

[63] 20 U.S.C. 358.

[64] Segregation in public libraries is unconstitutional. *Giles* v. *Library Advisory Committee* Civil No. 452 (W.D. Va., May 11 and Sept. 14, 1960).

[65] 48 Stat. 144 (1933), as amended, 29 U.S.C. 49(b)–(n) (1952).

[66] 29 U.S.C. 49(k). See also Greenberg, *Race Relations and American Law* 165–66 (1959).

[67] 20 C.F.R. 604.8(c).

not "proper and efficient" administration of the Act.[68] A Presidential order could so construe it.

5. *Airports.* Despite the silence of the Federal Aid to Airports statute [69] on the subject of segregation, the FAA Administrator has issued a regulation directing that no funds "will be made available for the development of separate facilities." [70] This furnishes another precedent for executive anti-segregation rule-making, even though Southern communities have gotten around the regulation by using the Federal funds for land, runways, lights, etc., while using their own funds to build and maintain segregated terminal buildings.[71]

There is ample statutory authority to ban such terminal segregation. The Civil Aeronautics Act [72] provides that no air "carrier" shall subject any person to "any unjust discrimination or any undue or unreasonable prejudice." While a terminal is not an air "carrier," similar language in the Interstate Commerce Act has already been construed by the Supreme Court to bar segregation in interestate bus terminal restaurants regardless of who operates the restaurant.[73]

6. *Housing.* The principal Federal aid housing laws are those providing grants for low-rent public housing [74] and for insurance of mortgage loans on private housing.[75] Although both laws are silent on the question of segregation, the Federal housing administrators have used their rule-making powers to require or permit segregated housing.[76] The same authority can be employed to require non-segregated housing.

In addition, a 95-year-old civil rights law provides further legislative sanction for outlawing racial discrimination in Federally aided housing.[77]

[68] The extent of current discrimination by the Employment Service is detailed in *New York Times*, July 2, 1961, p. 22. The effects of employment discrimination are described in Ginzberg, *The Negro Potential* 122 (1956); Ashmore, *An Epitaph for Dixie*, especially ch. 7 (1957); Hill, "Recent Effects of Racial Conflict on Southern Industrial Development," 20 *The Phylon Quarterly* 4 (1959).

[69] 49 U.S.C. 403 *et seq.*

[70] U.S. Department of Commerce, Civil Aeronautics Administration, *Airports Policy and Procedure Memorandum No. 41,* April 6, 1956.

[71] Segregated terminals are unconstitutional. *Henry* v. *Greenville Airport Commission,* 284 F.2d 631 (4th Cir. 1960). See also Greenberg, *op. cit. supra* note 66 at 129–130.

[72] 49 U.S.C. 484(b).

[73] *Boynton* v. *Virginia,* 364 U.S. 454 (1960).

[74] United States Housing Act of 1937, as amended, 50 Stat. 888, 42 U.S.C. 1401.

[75] National Housing Act of 1934, as amended, 48 Stat. 1246.

[76] See, *e.g.,* HHFA PHA Low-Rent Housing Manual, Section 102.1, Feb. 21, 1951, "racial policy," which requires that low-rent housing projects "must reflect equitable provisions for eligible families of all races," but "the selection of tenants and assigning of dwelling units are primarily matters for local determination." Housing segregation has been held unconstitutional. See, *e.g., Banks* v. *Housing Authority of San Francisco,* 120 Cal. App. 2d 1 (1953), *cert. den.,* 347 U.S. 974 (1954); *Detroit Housing Commission* v. *Lewis,* 226 F.2d 180 (6th Cir. 1955); *Ming* v. *Horgan,* Sup. Ct. Sacramento County, Action No. 97130, June 23, 1958, 3 R.R.L.R. 693.

[77] Act of April 9, 1866, 14 Stat. 27, as amended; § 18, Act of May 31, 1870, 16 Stat. 144, 42 U.S.C. 1982. It provides: "All citizens of the United States shall have the same right, in every State and Territory, as is enjoyed by white citizens thereof to inherit, purchase, lease, sell, hold, and convey real and personal property."

B. *Federal Statutes Sanctioning Segregation*

A handful of Federal aid statutes permit or require expenditure of the grants to maintain segregation, although they also contain discretionary language which could be construed to authorize withholding of Federal grants from segregated institutions. Statutes specifically sanctioning segregated use are those establishing land-grant colleges, agricultural extension services and school lunches, while those which it has been contended impliedly support segregated institutions are the hospital construction and various aid-to-education laws.

Before discussing their legal effect, we shall examine a few of the statutory provisions sanctioning segregation.

1. *Land-Grant Colleges and Extension Services.* In the same year President Lincoln was drafting his Emancipation Proclamation, he signed the First Morrill Act (1862),[78] setting up the land-grant college system in the United States and donating Federal lands to support them. That act contained no provision dealing with race, but the Second Morrill Act (1890) [79] did. Its "separate but equal" clause now reads: [80]

> No money shall be paid out under sections 321–326 and 328 of this title to any State or Territory for the support or mainte-nance of a college where a distinction of race or color is made in the admission of students, but the establishment and mainte-nance of such colleges separately for white and colored students shall be held to be a compliance with the provisions of said sec-tions if the funds received in such State or Territory are equi-tably divided as hereinafter set forth: . . .

In 1890, the Smith-Lever Act [81] provided for "cooperative agricultural extension work" to benefit persons not attending the colleges aided un-der the Morrill Acts. The paragraph in the Second Morrill Act providing for "separate but equal" treatment was repeated here and is the justifica-tion for continuing separate extension services in the segregated states.[82]

Like the vocational education act, the Morrill Act contains unusual provisions permitting a state to appeal to Congress the withholding of grants by the executive.[83]

2. *School Lunch Program.* The national school lunch program,[84]

---

[78] Act of July 2, 1862, 12 Stat. 503, as amended, 7 U.S.C. 301–08 (1958).

[79] Act of August 30, 1890, ch. 841, 26 Stat. 417, 7 U.S.C. 321–28 (1958).

[80] *Id.* at 7 U.S.C. 323. ". . . the Federal Government has been a silent partner in the creation and perpetuation of separate colleges for Negroes. As to land-grant col-leges particularly, the Federal Government has been heavily involved, not only because of its sponsorship of separate colleges in the second Morrill Act of 1890 . . . but be-cause it has allowed southern legislatures to channel almost all Federal funds for specific programs in such institutions to the separate white colleges. The Federal Government bears a heavy responsibility for the resulting discrimination against past and present generations of Negroes." The United States Commission on Civil Rights, *Equal Protection of the Laws in Public Higher Education* 254–55 (1960).

[81] Act of March 2, 1887, ch. 314, § 1, 24 Stat. 440 as amended, 69 Stat. 671 (1955), 7 U.S.C. 361(a)–(i) (1958).

[82] 7 U.S.C. 361(h) (1958).

[83] 7 U.S.C. 361(g) (1958). See *supra* note 60.

[84] National School Lunch Act, as amended, 42 U.S.C. 1751–60.

administered by the Secretary of Agriculture, provides foods and funds to the states for use in serving nutritious midday meals to children attending school of high school grade or less.

Withholding of Federal funds is authorized by the statute's "separate but equal" clause, if the pre-1954 constitutional standard of equality is not maintained.[85]

3. *No Federal "Control" in Education Statutes.* Practically every statute providing Federal aid to education contains a "no Federal control" section. Typical is this language contained in the Impacted Area Act: [86]

(a) In the administration of this chapter, no department, agency, officer, or employee of the United States shall exercise any direction, supervision, or control over the personnel, curriculum, or program of instruction of any school or school system of any local or State educational agency.

Although it has been contended that this language mandates Federal grants to segregated schools, the contention is unwarranted. By withholding funds from segregated schools, the administrator would not be exercising any "direction, supervision or control over the personnel, curriculum or program of instruction" of the local school district. He would not be hiring or firing local school personnel. He would not be prescribing the subjects to be taught. He would not be telling the teachers or local school officials what to teach or how to teach it.

Within constitutional bounds, a city is free to hire its own school personnel and frame its own curriculum or program of instruction. It cannot, however, operate its admissions and pupil assignment policies so as to segregate children solely on the basis of their race or color and expect to receive funds from the Federal government.[87]

4. *The Hospital Construction Act.* Under the Hospital Survey and Construction Act,[88] popularly known as the Hill-Burton Act, the Federal government may grant funds to the states and municipalities "to assist in the construction of public and other nonprofit hospitals." Such

85 42 U.S.C. 1760(c). And see implementing regulations in Section 210.17(b), 23 C.F.R. 3091, May 9, 1958. The regulation provides: "If a State maintains separate schools for minority and for majority races, no funds made available pursuant to this chapter shall be paid or disbursed to it unless a just and equitable distribution is made within the state, for the benefit of such minority races, of funds paid to it under this chapter." For evidence of unequal distribution to Negro students, see McCauley and Ball, *Southern Schools: Progress and Problems* 150 (1959).

86 20 U.S.C. 242.

87 *Cooper* v. *Aaron*, 358 U.S. 1 (1958). And *cf.* MacDonald, *Federal Aid* 268 (1928): ". . . the expenditure of Federal moneys cannot safely be entrusted to state and local officials without some degree of Federal supervision."

88 42 U.S.C. 291 *et seq.* Originally enacted August 13, 1946, the Hill-Burton Act has provided Federal aid totalling $1.3 billion for 5,200 projects costing $4.4 billion. U.S. Department of Health, Education and Welfare, *Annual Report* 139 (1960). Since 1954, the courts have not ruled squarely on hospital segregation or on the key section of the Hill-Burton Act. *Cf. Johnson* v. *Crawfis*, 128 F. Supp. 230 (E.D. Ark. 1955); *Eaton* v. *Board of Managers* 261 F.2d 521 (4th Cir. 1958), *cert. den.* 358 U.S. 984 (1959).

grants cover from one-third to two-thirds of the cost of construction of general hospitals and other medical facilities.

So that a municipality can receive Federal funds for hospital construction, its state must submit to the Surgeon General, a "state plan" agreeing to certain conditions set out in the Act and the Surgeon General's regulations. Conduit for the city's application is the state, which must attest that the city has agreed to abide by the conditions laid down for receipt of Federal funds.

The key provision [89] requires that the Surgeon General "shall by general regulation prescribe —

> (f) That the State plan *shall* provide for adequate hospital facilities for the people residing in a State, without discrimination on account of race, creed, or color, and *shall* provide for adequate hospital facilities for persons unable to pay therefor. Such regulation *may* require that before approval of any application for a hospital or addition to a hospital is recommended by a State agency, assurance shall be received by the State from the applicant that (1) such hospital or addition to a hospital will be made available to all persons residing in the territorial area of the applicant, without discrimination on account of race, creed, or color, but an exception shall be made in cases where separate hospital facilities are provided for separate population groups, if the plan makes equitable provision of the basis of need for facilities and services of like quality for each such group. . . . [Emphasis added.]

Although it has been contended that this section requires grants for segregated hospitals, it actually provides ample authority for the Surgeon General to require that the State plan and municipal applications filed thereunder contain assurances that the facilities and services of the hospital will be made available without discrimination or segregation.

Careful reading of the Section discloses that *only* the first sentence is mandatory. It provides that the Surgeon General *"shall"* prescribe that the State plan *"shall"* provide for no discrimination because of race, creed or color.[90] The second sentence, beginning with the words "such regulation *may* require . . ." and including within its text the "separate but equal" proviso, is an entirely separate sentence, an entirely divisible thought, purely permissive and wholly discretionary.[91] Moreover, the "exception" which "shall be made" in the latter half of the second sentence applies only if the Surgeon General promulgates the kind of requirement he is *permitted* to make in the entire second sentence.[92]

---

[89] 42 U.S.C. 291(e) (Section 622(f) of Hill-Burton).

[90] "Shall" is generally imperative or mandatory. Black, *Law Dictionary* 1541 (4th ed., 1957).

[91] "May" *id.* at 1131.

[92] See, *e.g., Clement Martin Inc.* v. *Dick Corp.,* 97 F. Supp. 961 (D.C. Pa. 1951), upholding Surgeon General's discretion under Hill-Burton to withhold funds "for violation of his regulations." Such statutory language is permissive. *Arizona* v. *Hobby,* 221 F.2d 498, 94 A.D.C. 170 (1954).

Thus, the Surgeon General is at liberty to disregard the second sentence and follow the Congressional command imposed in the first sentence.

C. *Effect of Pro-Segregation Federal Aid Statutes*

What is the effect of these statutory provisions expressly or impliedly requiring or permitting Federal support of segregated institutions? Are they constitutional? Do they bind the executive? Can the President ignore them in administering the acts?

1. *Congressional Intent to Meet Current Constitutional Standard of Equality.* Congress has not written a "separate, but equal" clause into any Federal law since 1954. All were enacted between 1890 and 1946, when "separate but equal" met the constitutional requirements for equal protection and due process, as interpreted by the United States Supreme Court.[93] Congress evidently intended to require recipients of Federal grant funds to comply with the then constitutional requirements applicable to public facilities.

Since 1954, however, the Supreme Court has ruled that "separate but equal" facilities are "inherently unequal," and violate the Fourteenth and Fifth Amendments to the United States Constitution.[94]

Thus, we may conclude that just as Congress intended to abide by the constitutional requirements before 1954, it intends that these programs be administered in accordance with the current constitutional standard prohibiting governmental action in support of segregation. The executive and the courts may, therefore, construe these clauses in accordance with the Congressional intent to comply with the current constitutional standard of equality.[95]

2. *If Construed as Mandatory or Still Effective, the Segregation Clauses Would Be Unconstitutional.* On the other hand, if the "separate but equal" clauses were to be construed as intended by Congress to be fully effective today or as mandating executive expenditures in support of segregated state or local institutions, they would be clearly unconstitutional and hence void.

But let the United States Supreme Court speak for itself:

> "In view of our decision that the Constitution prohibits the states from maintaining racially segregated public schools, it would be unthinkable that the same Constitution would impose a lesser duty on the Federal Government." [96]

[93] *Plessy* v. *Ferguson,* 163 U.S. 537 (1896).

[94] *Brown* v. *Board of Education,* 347 U.S. 483 (1954); *Bolling* v. *Sharpe,* 347 U.S. 497 (1954).

[95] *United States* v. *Rumely,* 345 U.S. 41 (1953); *Crowell* v. *Benson,* 285 U.S. 22 (1932). And see Justice Frankfurter in *American Communications Association* v. *Douds,* 339 U.S. 382, 417 (1950): "Congress may withhold all sorts of facilities for a better life, but if it affords them it cannot make them available in an obviously arbitrary way or exact surrender of freedoms unrelated to the purpose of the facilities."

[96] *Bolling* v. *Sharpe, supra* note 94 at 500.

"All provisions of federal . . . law requiring or permitting such discrimination must yield to this principle. . . ."[97]

". . . The right of a student not to be segregated on racial grounds in schools so maintained is indeed so fundamental and pervasive that it is embraced in the concept of due process of law."[98]

". . . [I]t is said that no one has doubted the power of Congress to stipulate the sort of education for which money shall be expended. But an appropriation to an educational institution which by its terms is to become available only if the beneficiary enters into a contract to teach doctrines subversive of the Constitution is clearly bad. An affirmance of the authority of Congress so to condition the expenditure of an appropriation would tend to nullify all constitutional limitations upon legislative power."[99]

"This clause is a restraint on Congress as well as on the executive and judicial powers of the National Government; it cannot be so construed as to leave Congress free to make any process it chooses 'due process of law.'"[100]

"It is inconceivable that guaranties embedded in the Constitution of the United States may thus be manipulated out of existence."[101]

"[A] constitutional power cannot be used by way of condition to attain an unconstitutional result."[102]

Thus, it is clear that if Congress had required, explicitly or implicitly, that the Executive Branch expend Federal funds "to attain an unconstitutional result" — the denial of due process and equal protection of the laws to Negroes through the support of segregated institutions — such a Congressional requirement would be unconstitutional and would be declared judicially void at the earliest opportunity.

3. *Executive May Treat Such Statutes as Silent on Segregation Question.* Since the purpose and intent of the "separate but equal" clauses is to support segregation and discrimination, the courts will (and the executive may) strike it out of the legislation.[103] These clauses do not bind the President. He is neither required nor permitted to violate his oath of office by enforcing an unconstitutional provision of the statutes.

He is not required to wait for Congress to repeal or amend the objectionable, void clauses, nor is he required to wait for a court declaration of their invalidity. He may disregard them.[104]

---

97 *Brown* v. *Board of Education* (Implementing), 349 U.S. 294, 298 (1955).

98 *Cooper* v. *Aaron*, 358 U.S. 1, 19 (1958).

99 *United States* v. *Butler*, 297 U.S. 1, 74 (1936).

100 *Den. ex. dem. Murray* v. *Hoboken Land & Improvement Co.* 18 How. (59 U.S.) 272, 276 (1856).

101 *Frost* v. *R.R. Comm. of California*, 271 U.S. 583, 594 (1925).

102 *Western Union Telegraph Co.* v. *Foster*, 247 U.S. 105, 114 (1918).

103 Purpose and intent have always been a proper matter for judicial inquiry. *Guinn* v. *United States*, 238 U.S. 347, 363–364 (1915); *Bush* v. *Orleans Parish School Board*, 188 F. Supp. 916 (E.D. La. 3-judge court, 1960), aff'd 364 U.S. 500 (1960).

104 See precedents and cases cited in footnotes 134–164 and accompanying text. See also cases cited in 30 A.L.R. 390, particularly *Van Horn* v. *State*, 46 Neb. 62, 64 N.W. 365, 383 (1895), where a state court held that even ministerial officers are "not bound to obey an unconstitutional statute."

He may read the objectionable clauses as indicating Congressional intent to follow the Supreme Court's current interpretation of the Constitution and hence authority to withhold funds from segregated institutions, or he may treat the statutes as silent on the question of racial segregation (and withhold funds under other sections of the statutes or his broad Presidential powers).

IV. CONSTITUTIONAL POWERS AND DUTIES OF THE PRESIDENT

Presidential authority to withhold these funds is not dependent on construction of the grant-in-aid laws alone. Such authority may be found, too, in the express and implied constitutional powers of the President.

A. *The Express Powers*

The President's express powers are spelled out in Article II of the Constitution, which vests him with "the executive power"; [105] requires an oath that he will "faithfully execute the office of President" and "preserve, protect and defend the Constitution"; [106] and that "he shall take care that the laws be faithfully executed." [107] These clauses authorize the President to execute both the Constitution and the laws.[108]

1. *To Execute the Constitution.* His oath of office requires the President to execute both the Fifth and Fourteenth amendments to the Constitution. The Fifth Amendment, of course, binds all executive officials, as well as Congress and the courts,[109] although it does not mention any of the three branches. Despite the fact that the Fourteenth Amendment empowers Congress to "enforce" its provisions and does not mention either the Supreme Court or the President, neither the court nor the President is barred from acting against segregation under the Fourteenth Amendment (and the Fifth Amendment).[110]

The discretionary right of the President to withhold funds from segregated institutions is our primary concern, but recent decisions indicate that he has not only a right, but a positive duty not to commit violations of the Fifth Amendment and not to permit violations of the Fourteenth Amendment by providing funds for an illegal activity.[111] "No state legislator or executive or judicial officer can war against the Constitution without violating his undertaking to support it," said the Court.[112] "[I]t

---

[105] § 1.1.
[106] § 1.8.
[107] § 3.
[108] *In re Neagle,* 135 U.S. 1 (1890).
[109] 16 C.J.S. *Constitutional Law* § 554.
[110] For helpful discussion, see Schubert, *The Presidency in the Courts* 347–48, 1957, and Swisher, *The Supreme Court in Modern Role* 160–62, 1958. *Cf.* Hand, *The Bill of Rights,* The Oliver Wendell Holmes Lectures 54–55, 1958.
[111] *Brown* v. *Board of Education,* 349 U.S. 294, 298 (1955); "All provisions of federal, state, or local law requiring or permitting such discrimination must yield. . . ." "Permit" means not only to expressly agree, but "to acquiesce, by failure to prevent . . . the doing of an act." Black, *Law Dictionary* 1298 (4th ed., 1957).
[112] *Cooper* v. *Aaron,* 358 U.S. 1, 18 (1958).

would be unthinkable that the same Constitution would impose a lesser duty on the Federal" President.[113]

The impropriety of Federal participation in activity that state agencies may not constitutionally conduct was also made clear in the restrictive covenant cases.[114] The *Shelley* case [115] established that a state court violates the equal protection clause of the Fourteenth Amendment when it enforces contractual provisions barring the ownership or use of land by specified racial groups. In the *Hurd* case which barred enforcement of such provisions by the Federal courts of the District of Columbia, even though they are not bound by the provisions of the Fourteenth Amendment, the Court said: [116]

> It is not consistent with the public policy of the United States to permit federal courts in the Nation's capital to exercise general equitable powers to compel action denied the state courts where such state action has been held to be violative of the guaranty of the equal protection of the laws.

These same restrictions apply not only to Federal court action enforcing private agreements but also to Federal executive action financing unconstitutional "state action." The Constitution is color-blind,[117] but the President cannot blind himself to constitutional violations. He can not subsidize subversion by supporting segregation with Federal funds.

2. *To Execute the Law.* To sustain the Chief Executive's authority to withhold Federal grants from segregated institutions, further power may be derived from the constitutional requirements that he "shall take care that the laws be faithfully executed." [118] Encompassed within the President's "executive powers" are the spending of public funds and the execution of public contracts, both of which are involved in the administration of Federal grants-in-aid.

a. Expenditure of Public Funds. "No money shall be drawn from the Treasury, but in consequence of appropriations made by law; and a regular statement and account of the receipts and expenditures of all public money shall be published from time to time," says the Constitution.[119] Since only the executive branch can "draw" money from the Treasury and publish an accounting of the funds, this provision

> . . . assumes that expenditure is primarily an executive function, and conversely that the participation of the legislative branch is essentially for the purpose simply of setting bounds to executive discretion, a theory confirmed by early practice under the Constitution.[120]

[113] *Bolling* v. *Sharpe,* 347 U.S. 497, 500 (1954).
[114] *Shelley* v. *Kraemer,* 334 U.S. 1; *Hurd* v. *Hodge,* 334 U.S. 24 (1948).
[115] *Shelley* v. *Kraemer, supra* note 114.
[116] *Hurd* v. *Hodge, supra* note 114 at 35–36.
[117] Justice Harlan coined the phrase in his prophetic dissenting opinion in *Plessy* v. *Ferguson,* 163 U.S. 537, 559 (1896).
[118] U.S. Const. art. II, § 3.
[119] *Id.* at art. I, § 9.7.
[120] Corwin, *The President: Office and Powers* 127–28 (5th ed., 1959).

The executive power to withhold funds, unless specifically earmarked in a constitutional, special act for the benefit of a particular individual, has been upheld by the courts on many occasions.[121] Even when the appropriation was clearly earmarked, Presidents frequently have refused to expend funds.[122]

That Congress itself views its appropriations as "only a ceiling," not a mandate, for executive spending was established in 1950, when it inserted the "reserve power" in the Anti-Deficiency Act,[123] directing Federal administrators "to expend as little as possible out of the funds appropriated." [124] Thus, presidential action to enforce non-discriminatory policies may be justified on purely economy terms: separate facilities are expensive.[125]

    b. Execution of Government Contracts. A Federal grant-in-aid agreement is a contract between the national government and the aid recipient.[126] As such, it falls within the contracting power of the Federal government. Over the years, four broad principles have emerged regarding the Federal contracting power.

First, the United States, even without statutory authorization, has the right to contract and to enforce performance of the contract.[127]

Second, the Federal contracting power lies in the executive branch of the national government.[128]

Third, in executing the contracting powers of the Federal government, the President may impose sweeping terms and conditions on

---

[121] *Campagna* v. *United States,* 26 Ct. Cl. 316 (1891); *Hukill* v. *United States,* 16 Ct. Cl. 562 (1881). And see *Kendall* v. *United States ex rel. Stokes,* 12 Pet. (37 U.S.) 524 (1838).

[122] In 1923, President Harding ordered the War Department to keep expenditures on rivers and harbors within the amount fixed by the Budget Bureau and to ignore an additional appropriation by Congress. The *New York Times,* February 11, 1923. In 1949, President Truman ordered that funds appropriated for building 58 air groups should be expended only to provide for the 48 air groups he had recommended. Powers of the President as Commander-in-Chief, H.R. Doc. No. 443, 84th Cong., 2d Sess. (1956). In 1956, the Defense Department shelved a Congressional appropriation earmarked for construction of 20 superfort bombers. Corwin, *op. cit. supra* note 120 at 134. And see Griffith, *Congress: Its Contemporary Role* 28 (1951).

[123] 31 U.S.C. 665(c) (2).

[124] H.R. Rep. No. 1797, 81st Cong., 2d Sess. (1950).

[125] See, *Hearings on S. 1732 and S. 531 before Senate Committee on Labor and Public Welfare,* 82nd Cong., 2d Sess. 341 (1952); Office of Assistant Secretary of Defense, Manpower and Personnel, *Integration in the Armed Services: A Progress Report* 9 (1955).

[126] *McGehee* v. *Mathis,* 4 Wall. (71 U.S.) 143 (1866).

[127] *Dugan* v. *United States,* 3 Wheat. (16 U.S.) 172 (1818).

[128] *United States* v. *Tingey,* 5 Pet. (30 U.S.) 115 (1831). In this case, the Attorney General had argued that in the performance of the trust enjoined on him by the "take care" clause, the President "not only may, but . . . is bound to avail himself of every appropriate means not forbidden by law"; while the court does not advert to this contention, the "immediate and inevitable result of its holding was the location in the executive department of the power that it ascribed to the United States Government in its corporate capacity." Corwin, *The President: Office and Powers* 148–49 (5th ed., 1959).

would-be beneficiaries of Federal funds.[129] The key case was *Perkins* v. *Lukens Steel Co.*[130] The Public Contracts Act requires those who sell goods to the government to comply with certain requirements concerning labor, and authorizes the Secretary of Labor to interpret the statute in determining wages. Error in the executive determination of the contract stipulation, rather than invalidity of the Congressional enactment, was claimed by the plaintiffs and relied on by the Court of Appeals in granting injunctive relief. In reversing, the Supreme Court held that "the Government enjoys the unrestricted power . . . to fix the terms and conditions upon which it will make needed purchases," and even if the Secretary of Labor had violated Congressional instructions in exercising the complete discretion of the executive branch, she was responsible only to "superior executive and legislative authority." The logical conclusion of the *Lukens* case is that the executive may even include contract provisions which contravene an express Congressional mandate, and no potential contractor can complain.[131] If he doesn't like the President's terms, he need not apply.[132]

Fourth, a Federal grant to a state subject to conditions is a contract, which cannot be violated by any state legislation contrary to the stipulated terms. This point was established in 1866, when the Supreme Court held unconstitutional a state levee tax, imposed in violation of the Federal land-grant agreement.[133] Said the Court:

> It is not doubted that the grant by the United States to the State upon conditions and the acceptance of the grant by the State, constituted a contract. All the elements of a contract met in the transaction — competent parties, proper subject matter, sufficient consideration and consent of minds. This contract was binding upon the State and could not be violated by its legislation without infringement of the Constitution.

[129] This was foreshadowed by the Supreme Court's approval of terms in contracts between state governments and private contractors which it held were unconstitutional when required in private business. *Compare, e.g. Lochner* v. *New York*, 198 U.S. 45 (1905) *with Atkin* v. *Kansas*, 191 U.S. 207 (1903). See also *Heim* v. *McCall*, 239 U.S. 175 (1915).

[130] 310 U.S. 113 (1940).

[131] See Pasley, *The Nondiscrimination Clause in Government Contracts*, 43 Va. L.R. 837, 856 (1957). In other recent cases, the Supreme Court has upheld the broad contracting power of executive officers, even where violations of statutes were alleged, *Larson* v. *Domestic and Foreign Commerce Corp.*, 337 U.S. 682 (1949); *Mine Safety Appliances Co.* v. *Forrestal*, 326 U.S. 371 (1945). In the exercise of contractual powers an officer of the Federal government is not restricted by the requirements of procedural and substantive due process (as he is when exercising governmental or non-contractual powers). *United States* v. *General Petroleum Corp. of Calif.*, 73 F. Supp. 225, (D.C.S.D. Calif. 1947), *aff'd* in *Continental Oil Co.* v. *United States*, 184 F.2d 802 (9th Cir. 1950).

[132] Even when the government is acting in its proprietary capacity, however, it may not discriminate along racial or religious lines. At least Congress may not "enact a regulation providing that no Republican, Jew or Negro shall be appointed to Federal office. . . ." *United Public Workers* v. *Mitchell*, 330 U.S. 75, 100 (1947).

[133] *McGehee* v. *Mathis, supra* note 122.

These contract cases fully sustain the President's power to require inclusion of the non-discrimination clauses in the grant agreements and to withhold Federal funds from those who refuse to abide by the Government's terms.

B. *The "Implied" Powers*

Ample authority exists within the Federal grant-in-aid statutes and his express constitutional powers for the President to require a nondiscrimination agreement from would-be recipients and to withhold grants from segregationists. But, if it be contended that the Constitution does not expressly authorize the President to "make a law" where Congress is silent, to disregard a law which he feels is unconstitutional, or to enforce the "public policy" of the United States, appropriate precedent for his acts may be found in the "implied" powers of the Presidency.

Whether the powers of the President not specified in a statute or the Constitution are termed "implied," "inherent," "residential" or "prerogative" is sterile semantics. Whatever they are called, "they are a part of the panoply of authority of the presidential office . . . ," [134] are derived from a variety of sources, and have been confirmed by the Supreme Court under the nomenclature of "implied" powers.[135]

Just as Congress,[136] and the Supreme Court,[137] have implied powers not spelled out in so many words in the Constitution, so does the President have implicit authority to carry out his constitutional powers.[138]

As Justice Miller said in the famed *Neagle* case,[139] the President's duty to see that the laws are faithfully executed is not limited "to the enforcement of acts of Congress or of treaties of the United States according to their express terms," but includes "the rights, duties and obligations growing out of the Constitution itself, our international relations and all the protection *implied* by the nature of the Government under the Constitution." [Emphasis added.]

1. *Making a Law Where Congress Is Silent.* Executive legislation — orders, proclamations, interpretations — is part of the "supreme law of the land." [140] The President's duty "to take care that the laws be faithfully executed" becomes often a "power to make the laws," says a noted constitutional authority, adding: "Nor was this unforeseen by the Framers." [141]

---

134 Schubert, *The Presidency in the Courts* 353 (1957).

135 *In re Neagle*, 135 U.S. 1, 64 (1890).

136 *McCulloch* v. *Maryland*, 4 Wheat. (17 U.S.) 316 (1819).

137 *Marbury* v. *Madison*, 1 Cranch (5 U.S.) 137 (1803).

138 *In re Neagle, supra* note 135.

139 *Ibid.*

140 Schubert, *The Presidency in the Courts* 311 (1957): "There would seem to be little question of the judicial rule today: executive legislation is law. It can collect money from those who would be liable under a statute; it can cause people to be put in jail; it can cause some people to be shot. Any theory that cannot accommodate these facts has, on this ground alone, outlived its usefulness."

141 Corwin, *The Constitution and What It Means Today* 125 (12th ed., 1958).

In the melodramatic leading case, *In re Neagle*,[142] the Supreme Court held that an executive order of the President was a "law of the United States," and that executive power embraced power not specifically granted in the Constitution or by statute.

Less dramatic, but equally decisive, have been other court decisions upholding presidential orders as a source of law binding on both citizens and courts.[143] Significantly, when acts of Congress have conflicted with the President's exercise of his constitutional powers, the Supreme Court has even gone so far as to declare the acts of Congress unconstitutional.[144]

2. *Disregarding an Unconstitutional Law.* Governmental power in the United States is distributed by the Constitution among three co-equal branches of the Federal government, one of which is the Presidency. Whatever may have been the intention of the framers, the actual operation of the government has shown that powers vested in one branch frequently overlap those vested in another. Not the principle of separation of powers, but the principle of checks by one branch of government on the other has governed our nation.[145]

While Congress controls the executive in a variety of ways,[146] and the courts also have checked the President,[147] he, too, has powers implied from his constitutional status. He is not required to enforce an unconstitutional statutory provision — particularly where the Supreme Court has declared "all provisions of Federal, state and local law" requiring or permitting segregation to be unconstitutional.[148]

Whether or not the President's disregard of an act of Congress which he felt was unconstitutional is "morally justified," [149] the fact is that:

> . . . Presidents have occasionally refused to enforce acts of Congress . . . on the ground that the acts in question were unconstitutional. This was Andrew Johnson's contention in 1867 respect-

142 *In re Neagle, supra* note 135 at 64.

143 *E.g., Albridge* v. *Williams,* 3 How. (44 U.S.) 9 (1845); *United States* v. *Freeman,* 3 How. (44 U.S.) 556 (1845); *United States* v. *Midwest Oil Co.,* 236 U.S. 459 (1915).

144 *E.g., Ex parte Garland,* 4 Wall. (71 U.S.) 333 (1867); *United States* v. *Klein,* 13 Wall. (80 U.S.) 128 (1871); *Armstrong* v. *United States,* 13 Wall. (80 U.S.) 154 (1872).

145 Davis, *Administrative Law Text,* 29–30 (1959). (". . . danger of tyranny or injustice lurks in unchecked power, not in blended power.")

146 In 1942, OPA policies were altered through Congressional influence which brought about a change of administrators. Congressional investigating committees engage in a substantial amount of supervising. Appropriation committees are influential; in their reports are "mingled many shades of suggestions, of precise recommendations, of doubts, of warnings, of commendations and of rebukes." McMahon, *Congressional Oversight of Administration: The Power of the Purse,* 58 Pol. Soc. 161, 380 (1943).

147 In all United States history, the courts have held presidential orders unconstitutional in only 14 cases, Schubert, *op. cit. supra* note 140 at 355. But *cf.* Justice Stone's comment in *United States* v. *Butler,* 297 U.S. 1 (1936) at 87: "Courts are not the only agency of government that must be assumed to have the capacity to govern."

148 *Brown* v. *Board of Education* (Implementing), 349 U.S. 294 (1955).

149 *Compare* Schubert, *op. cit. supra* note 140 at 326; and Corwin, *The Constitution and What It Means Today, op. cit. supra* note 141 at 98, *with* Hart, *The Ordinance-Making Powers of the President of the U.S.* 177 (1925).

ing the Tenure of Office Act; as it was Woodrow Wilson's respecting the Jones Shipping Act of 1920.[150]

3. *Enforcing Public Policy of the United States.* The public policy of the United States is, in the words of the Supreme Court, "manifested in the Constitution, treaties, Federal statutes and applicable legal precedents," [151] as well as "the course of administration and decision." [152] Not only the court, but the President has a right, if not a duty, to execute the public policy of the United States.

Evidencing the public policy of the United States in opposition to discrimination and in support of the President's proposed executive order requiring a non-segregation agreement as a condition for the receipt of Federal grant-in-aid funds are other statutes, treaties and administrative decisions.

Beginning with the Civil Rights Acts of the Civil War [153] and continuing through the Civil Rights Act of 1960,[154] and even the Peace Corps Act of 1961,[155] a consistent thread of hostility to racial discrimination runs through the laws passed by Congress. At least 33 such statutes were on the books a few years ago [156] and one tabulator has pointed out [157] that Congress on at least 23 different occasions in the years 1933–1944 outlawed racial and religious discrimination in legislation for public works projects, the Civilian Conservation Corps, unemployment relief, civil service classification, National Youth Administration, and other acts.

Treaties and executive agreements negotiated by the President have the force of law.[158] They may be enforced by the Chief Executive. But, even if not self-executing, they are expressive of the public policy of the United States, which is a party to at least ten treaties and interna-

[150] Corwin and Koenig, *The Presidency Today* 58 (1958).

[151] *Hurd* v. *Hodge,* 334 U.S. 24 (1948).

[152] License Tax Cases, 5 Wall. (72 U.S.) 462, 469 (1867).

[153] See, *e.g.,* § 20 of the Criminal Code (U.S.C., Title 18, § 52; R.S. § 5510, Mar. 4, 1909. c. 321, § 20; 35 Stat. 1092); for an extensive review and application of the civil rights acts, see *Monroe* v. *Pape,* 81 S. Ct. 473 (Feb. 20, 1961).

[154] P.L. 86-449, 74 Stat. 86. And *cf. Hannah* v. *Larche,* 363 U.S. 420 (1960), upholding constitutionality of Civil Rights Act of 1957, P.L. 85-315, 85th Cong., Sept. 5, 1957, 71 Stat. 634.

[155] P.L. 87-293, 75 Stat. 612 (Sept. 22, 1961).

[156] Acts of Congress which embody our national policy of hostility to racial discrimination include 12 Stat. 805; 13 Stat. 329, 351, 537; 14 Stat. 27, 379, 457; 16 Stat. 3, 67, 140; 18 Stat. 336; 21 Stat. 44; 40 Stat. 1201; 48 Stat. 23; 50 Stat. 320, 357; 52 Stat. 815; 53 Stat. 856, 937, 1148; 54 Stat. 593, 623, 1214; 55 Stat. 363, 405, 491; 56 Stat. 575, 643; 57 Stat. 153; 58 Stat. 536, 874; 59 Stat. 473; 60 Stat. 1030.

[157] 90 Cong. Rec., Part 10, p. A3325 (1944).

[158] *Missouri* v. *Holland,* 252 U.S. 416 (1920); *United States* v. *Curtiss-Wright Export Corp.,* 299 U.S. 304. In the latter case, Justice Sutherland, speaking for the Court, said at 318: "The power . . . to make such international agreements as do not constitute treaties in the constitutional sense . . . none of which is expressly affirmed by the Constitution, nevertheless exist as inherently inseparable from the concept of nationality. This the Court recognized, and in each of the cases cited found the warrant for its conclusions not in the provisions of the Constitution, but in the law of nations."

tional agreements to observe "human rights and fundamental freedoms for all without distinction as to race." [159]

Similarly expressing the public policy of the United States and establishing precedents for executive action to withhold Federal grants from segregated institutions are the actions of a number of Federal executive departments who acted to change their policies after the Supreme Court's 1954 decision. Without any further legislation by Congress, these Federal agencies have barred segregation in interstate travel,[160] in use of Federal land grants,[161] in bank home loans,[162] and in employment on private rural electrification construction projects.[163]

While many of these policies have not been effectively enforced,[164] they not only establish precedents for the right of the Federal Government to require non-discrimination in its own programs and in those to which it contributes financial assistance, but they are also expressive of the current public policy of the United States.

4. *The Court Has Not Limited "Implied" Presidential Power in This Field.* Over the years some court decisions have been interpreted as restricting the "implied" powers of the President, but none would inhibit Presidential authority to require seekers of Federal grants-in-aid to agree to non-segregated use and to withhold funds from recalcitrant recipients.[165] The essential difference between these earlier decisions and a

[159] Treaties and executive agreements to which the United States is a party and which express our policy against racial discrimination include: the Charter of the United Nations, 59 Stat. 1031, 1045–46, 1213; Potsdam Agreement, Aug. 2, 1945; Treaties of Feb. 10, 1947, with Italy, Rumania. Bulgaria and Hungary (93 Cong. Rec. 6307, 6567, 6573, 6578); Resolution 41 of March 7, 1945, at Inter-American Conference on War and Peace at Mexico City which adopted the Act of Chapultapec (Dept. of State Pub. 2497, p. 109); The American Declaration of Human Rights, Resolution 30, Final Act of the Ninth International Conference of American States, Bogota, Colombia, 1948; the Universal Declaration of Human Rights, adopted by the United Nations General Assembly, Dec. 10, 1948.

[160] See, *e.g.,* 49 C.F.R. 180a (Sept. 28, 1961) (I.C.C. regulation barring segregation in any common carrier or terminal facility). And see earlier abandonment of "separate but equal" rule in *N.A.A.C.P.* v. *St. Louis-San Francisco Ry. Co.,* 297 I.C.C. 335, 1 R.R.L.R. 63 (1955); *Keys* v. *Carolina Coach Co.,* 64 I.C.C. 769, 1 R.R.L.R. 272 (1955).

[161] U.S. Department of Interior, Information Service Press Release, May 31, 1961; see also Leadership Conference on Civil Rights, *Proposals for Executive Action to End Federally Supported Segregation and Other Forms of Racial Discrimination,* Aug. 29, 1961, p. 15.

[162] Federal Home Loan Bank Board, *Resolution No. 14656,* June 1, 1961, *New York Times,* Oct. 4, 1961. p. 1.

[163] REA, *Loan Contract Form "L.C.,"* revised Sept. 30, 1953.

[164] See, *e.g.,* the 1948 regulation of the Office of Vocational Rehabilitation and the Office of Education, prohibiting discrimination in Federally assisted vocational programs, 45 C.F.R. 120.18, 401.14(2). President Kennedy's Executive Order 10925, 26 Fed. Reg. 1977 (March 6, 1961), prohibiting discrimination in government employment and on work performed under government contract, was an attempt to put enforcement "teeth" in these Federal policies.

[165] See, *e.g., Little* v. *Barreme.* 2 Cranch (6 U.S.) 170 (1804) (Congress passed embargo act, but President ordered vessel seized in port not covered by Act); *United States* v. *Clarke,* 20 Wall. (187 U.S.) 92 (1874) (private citizen claimed President's proclamation of unconditional amnesty repealed the Confiscation Act of 1862, which Court held Congress had power to enact).

possible future case involving Presidential withholding of grants is that in all such prior cases the President was acting adversely in a field where Congress had the constitutional power to act, while here Congress is barred by the Constitution from enacting a pro-segregation law.[166]

For example, in *Kendall* v. *United States ex rel. Stokes*,[167] Postmaster General Kendall, at President Jackson's instigation, refused to pay money the United States owed Stokes for delivering mail. Congress then passed a special act ordering payment, but when Kendall still refused, Stokes sought and obtained mandamus. Unlike Kendall, the President would have ample discretionary authority under the statutes to withhold funds. The Federal grant-in-aid statutes are general; they are not, as in the *Kendall* case, special acts appropriating funds specifically for a particular individual. Even in the *Kendall* case, the court pointed out that the President and his administrator need not comply with a statutory duty which is "repugnant to any rights secured and protected by the Constitution." [168] There is little doubt that Federal funds to support segregated facilities are clearly "repugnant" to the Constitution.[169]

In the more recent case of *Cole* v. *Young*,[170] the Supreme Court held that a Presidential executive order authorizing the discharge of incumbents in non-sensitive positions without the right of appeal had violated the Veterans Preference Act [171] and was illegal. In a footnote, however, the court pointed out that its decision might be different if President Eisenhower had asserted "his independent power against that of Congress" rather than rely solely on the statute.[172]

Finally, the Steel Seizure case [173] is sometimes cited as restricting Presidential "inherent" or "implied" power, but every thoughtful constitutional authority who has analyzed the various decisions in that 1952 case has come to the conclusion that, if anything, the majority of the justices have confirmed the "inherent" powers of the Presidency.[174]

In an effort to halt a threatened steel strike which he claimed would jeopardize our national defense effort, President Truman had ordered the Secretary of Commerce to seize the steel factories and to operate them. The President based his order on his power as commander-in-chief of the armed forces and the "executive power" of the President. When

166 *Brown* v. *Board of Education* (Implementing), *supra* note 148; *Cooper* v. *Aaron*, 358 U.S. 1 (1958); *Bolling* v. *Sharpe*, 347 U.S. 497 (1954).

167 12 Pet. (37 U.S.) 524 (1838).

168 *Id.* at 610.

169 *Brown* v. *Board of Education* (Implementing), *supra* note 148.

170 351 U.S. 536 (1956).

171 5 U.S.C. 652.

172 *Cole* v. *Young, supra* note 170 at 557 n.20: "When the President expressly confines his action to the limits of statutory authority, the validity of the action must be determined solely by the congressional limitations which the President sought to respect, whatever might be the result were the President ever to assert his independent power against that of Congress."

173 *Youngstown Sheet & Tube Co.* v. *Sawyer*, 343 U.S. 579 (1952).

174 See *e.g.*, Antieau, *Commentaries on the Constitution of the United States* 303–4 (1960); Schubert, *The Presidency in the Courts* 248–251, 284–286, 290–294 (1957); Corwin and Koenig, *The Presidency Today* 41–44 (1958).

the steel companies sought to prevent the seizing of their properties, the Court held that in the absence of Congressional authorization and in view of the fact that Congress had clearly intended not to grant such authority, the Constitutional provisions conferred no such power on the President.[175] The prime reason for the decision was that Congress had weighed seizure and rejected such a solution.[176]

Notwithstanding Justice Black's view "for the Court," it would be highly misleading to cite this case as holding against the President's right to exercise implied constitutional powers.[177] On the contrary, five members of the Court explicitly affirmed their acceptance of the theory of implied presidential powers; two members of the Court reserved the question,[178] and only two held against such a theory, and then only insofar as it would justify the President's action in this particular case.[179] In the words of the concurring opinion of Justice Jackson: [180]

> When the President acts in absence of either a congressional grant or denial of authority, he can only rely upon his own independent powers, but there is a zone of twilight in which he and Congress may have concurrent authority, or in which its distribution is uncertain. Therefore, congressional inertia, indifference or quiescence may sometimes, at least as a practical matter, enable, if not invite, measures on independent presidential responsibility. In this area, any actual test of power is likely to depend on the imperatives of events and contemporary imponderables rather than on abstract theories of law.

All the opinions made it perfectly clear, moreover, that presidential seizure would have been upheld unanimously by the Court *if* the President had enjoyed the support — or even the neutrality — of Congress. As Justice Jackson put the matter: [181]

> When the President acts pursuant to an express or implied authorization of Congress, his authority is at its maximum, for it includes all that he possesses in his own right plus all that Congress can delegate. In these circumstances, and in these only, may he be said (for what it may be worth) to personify the federal sovereignty. If his act is held unconstitutional under these circumstances, it usually means that the Federal Government as an undivided whole lacks power.

In the third category of Presidential-Congressional conflict formulated by Justice Jackson, we see clearly the essential difference between the Steel Seizure case and the proposed Presidential executive order. Said Jackson: [182]

175 *Youngstown Sheet & Tube Co.* v. *Sawyer, supra* note 173.
176 Antieau, *op. cit., supra* note 174 at 303.
177 Schubert, *op. cit., supra* note 174 at 284.
178 Justice Frankfurter, 343 U.S. 579, 597 (1952), and Justice Burton, *id.* at 659.
179 Justice Black, *id.* at 584, 587–8, and Justice Douglas, *id.* at 631, 633.
180 *Id.* at 635–7.
181 *Ibid.*
182 *Ibid.*

When the President takes measures incompatible with the expressed or implied will of Congress, his power is at its lowest ebb, for then he can rely only upon his own constitutional powers minus any *constitutional powers of Congress* over the matter. Courts can sustain exclusive Presidential control in such a case only by *disabling the Congress from acting upon the subject.* [Emphasis added.]

The distinguishing point is that Congress *could* constitutionally provide for seizure of steel plants; it considered the question, but refused to adopt that solution for national emergency strikes. However, Congress could *not* constitutionally require the President to spend Federal funds in support of segregated public schools or other functions encompassed within "state action." By the Fifth Amendment, Congress is disabled "from acting upon the subject." [183]

C. The Court's "Implementation" Decision Did Not Limit Presidential Power

As we have seen, no decision dealing with the powers of the Presidency has limited in any way the President's power to issue the proposed proclamation. Similarly, no case dealing with segregation has retarded presidential power.

Wholly unwarranted are contentions that the Supreme Court's 1955 "implementation" decision,[184] directing the Federal district courts to enter appropriate decrees admitting Negro students "to public schools on a racially non-discriminatory basis with all deliberate speed," has somehow limited Presidential power to act against segregation.

A careful reading of the Court's language fails to disclose a single word that requires the President to continue to supply Federal funds to public school districts without regard to whether or not they are violating the requirements of the Federal Constitution. On the contrary, the Court emphasized at the threshold of its decision that "all provisions of federal, state and local law requiring or permitting" segregation in the public schools must yield to the constitutional standard barring such discrimination.[185]

The expression "with all deliberate speed" was neither meant to delay integration of public schools indefinitely, nor limit the President in his administration of Federal grants-in-aid. The phrase originated in *Vir-*

---

[183] There are, of course, other distinctions between the proposed Presidential executive order and seizure of the steel mills. In the latter case, the President was interfering with vested private property rights; in the former he would be withholding public funds in which there are no vested rights. In the Steel case, the President was opposing Congress without the support of the courts; here he might be in conflict with Congress, but he would be acting in direct support of constitutional decisions and orders of the Supreme Court. In the Steel case, he relied on "executive power" alone; here he would be using the full panoply of Presidential powers, including executive interpretation of the statutes immediately involved, as well as his express and implied powers under the Constitution.

[184] *Brown* v. *Board of Education,* 349 U.S. 294 (1955).

[185] *Id.* at 298.

ginia v. *West Virginia*,[186] an opinion by Justice Holmes in 1912, who wrote:

> . . . a State cannot be expected to move with the celerity of a private business man; it is enough if it proceeds, in the language of the English Chancery, with all deliberate speed.

In the School Segregation cases,[187] as in *Virginia* v. *West Virginia*,[188] the Supreme Court concluded that it was unreasonable to expect immediate action from state officials "where those officials did not control all the state processes necessary to achieve full compliance." [189] In the *Brown* case, however, the Court's orders were directed to local school authorities, where "deliberate" speed was needed, in the words of the Court,[190] to

> . . . consider problems related to administration, arising from the physical condition of the school plant, the school transportation system, personnel, revision of school districts and attendance areas into compact units to achieve a system of determining admission to the public schools on a nonracial basis, and revision of local laws and regulations which may be necessary in solving the foregoing problems. . . .

Since Federal authorities are not charged with "administration" of local schools and have nothing to do with the solution of these local problems, but are charged solely with the duty of determining whether or not Federal grants-in-aid shall be given to local or state institutions which have not taken a single step toward "good faith compliance" with the constitutional requirements, the delays allowed local officials under the Court's ruling do not apply to the Federal administrators of the Federal law.

In its "implementation" decision, the Supreme Court was talking about "courts of equity" and their traditional powers. The President of the United States is not a court of equity.

V. Courts Will Uphold Presidential Action

In effect, we have been looking at what the courts will do if a case of Presidential withholding of grants-in-aid from segregated institutions ever reached them. To see how far the *President can go* in ending segregation, we have viewed how far the *courts have gone*. However, since the powers of the executive are independent of those of the courts, it is necessary to recognize that the frontier of presidential power lies far beyond the point to which the courts have thus far ventured.

---

[186] 222 U.S. 17, 19 (1911). Following a Supreme Court determination that West Virginia owed a sum of money to Virginia, the latter sought an order compelling immediate payment. The motion was denied by a unanimous court.

[187] *Brown* v. *Board of Education, supra* note 184.

[188] *Supra* note 186.

[189] Blaustein and Ferguson, *Desegregation and the Law* 220 (1957).

[190] *Brown* v. *Board of Education, supra* note 184 at 300.

A. *The Court Will Not Review Presidential Withholding of Grants*

It is doubtful that the Supreme Court will ever review on the merits a case involving Presidential withholding of Federal aid. First, since Federal spending legislation ordinarily carries no provision for judicial review,[191] litigants, such as taxpayers,[192] citizens,[193] states,[194] and school districts,[195] have no "standing to sue." Second, the courts will not issue a mandatory injunction against the President,[196] the real party in interest whose executive order would have directed his subordinates to withhold the funds. Third, a suit against the President's administrators would collide with the doctrine of sovereign immunity.[197] The United States cannot be sued without its consent.

B. *The Court Will Uphold Presidential Discretion Under the Statutes*

Assuming that these initial impediments to a suit could be overcome by a provision in the grant-in-aid statutes permitting judicial review of the administrator's action in withholding funds from a segregated institution,[198] such a suit would have to be based on contentions [199] that the Federal grant-in-aid statutes impose a purely ministerial duty on the administrator and that the latter has no discretion, but is mandated under the act "to use the funds for that specific purpose." [200] Clearly, the functions to be exercised here are within the discretionary powers of cabinet members and other administrators.[201] As we have seen, both the

[191] The Hill-Burton Hospital Construction Act, 42 U.S.C. 291j(b), and the Federal Aid to Impacted Areas Education Act, 20 U.S.C. 641(b), provide for "judicial review" of executive withholding of grants. Two other education statutes (see notes 60 and 83) provide for appeal to Congress of the administrator's withholding of funds.

[192] *Frothingham* v. *Mellon,* 262 U.S. 447 (1923). This rule has prevented challenges in the courts of existing Federal aid to segregated institutions.

[193] *Easter* v. *Eisenhower,* 24 U.S. Law Week 3282, *cert. den.* 351 U.S. 908 (1956) (citizen's attempt to compel President to enforce immediate racial desegregation dismissed for lack of jurisdiction).

[194] *Massachusetts* v. *Mellon,* 262 U.S. 447 (1923).

[195] *Dallas* v. *Edgar,* 255 F.2d 455 (5th Cir. 1958).

[196] *Mississippi* v. *Johnson,* 71 U.S. 475 (1866). When an administrative officer acts in the name of the President, it is assumed that the President has authorized him to do so. See 65 Stat. 712 (Act of Oct. 31, 1951), ch. 655, § 10; see also *Porter* v. *Coble,* 246 F. 244, 249 (8th Cir. 1917); *Seltzer* v. *United States,* 98, Ct. Cl. 554, 562 (1943).

[197] See, *e.g., Mine Safety Appliances Co.* v. *Forrestal,* 326 U.S. 371 (1945); *Arizona* v. *Hobby,* 221 F.2d 498 (1954); but *cf. Ex parte Young,* 209 U.S. 123 (1908), involving a state official.

[198] See *supra,* note 191.

[199] An alternative contention might be that the statute relied on by the administrator is unconstitutional, but the party seeking funds under the statute is not likely to raise this argument. In any event, grants-in-aid are constitutional. *Oklahoma* v. *U.S. Civil Service Commission,* 330 U.S. 127 (1947).

[200] *McKay* v. *Central Electric Power Cooperative,* 223 F.2d 623, 625 (C.A.D.C. 1955); *Kendall* v. *United States,* 12 Pet. (37 U.S.) 524 (1838).

[201] *School* v. *Derthick,* 273 F.2d 319 (7th Cir. 1959); *Clement Martin Inc.* v. *Dick Corp.,* 97 F. Supp. 961 (D.C. Pa. 1951); *Arizona* v. *Hobby, supra* note 197.

specific grant-in-aid statutes and the Constitution make clear that the executive branch is not charged with merely ministerial duties in the administration of Federal aid programs.[202]

C. An Injunction Would Be Inequitable

Finally, there is one overriding reason why the courts, even if they had the power to enjoin the President or his administrators, should not (and likely would not) exercise that power in this type of case. Historically, equity courts have refused their discretionary aid, where "the plaintiff is using the right asserted contrary to the public interest." [203] The inevitable effect of such a court order would be to permit a litigant with "unclean hands" [204] to receive Federal funds to maintain unconstitutional and illegal racial segregation.[205]

Issuance of such an injunction would be contrary to the public policy of the United States. In the restrictive covenant cases,[206] the Supreme Court clearly established that the judiciary will not enforce acts which violate public policy or the equal protection of the laws by racial discrimination. "Once the courts put their imprimatur on such a contract, government, speaking through the judicial governmental branch, acts." [207]

It is unlikely that a challenge to the proposed Presidential Proclamation would be tolerated by the Supreme Court which wrote the 1954 School Segregation decisions,[208] which has consistently advanced the frontiers of freedom for non-white citizens unaided by executive leadership, and which decided five civil rights cases during its most recent 1960–61 term, all favorably to the person seeking constitutional relief against racial discrimination.[209]

In upholding Presidential action against segregation, the court will be fulfilling its historic function, as voiced by Justice Black in 1950:

> Under our Constitutional system, courts stand against any winds
> that blow as havens of refuge for those who might otherwise
> suffer because they are helpless, weak, outnumbered, or because
> they are non-conforming victims of prejudice and public excite-

202 See footnotes 46–92 *supra* and accompanying text.

203 *Morton Salt Co.* v. *Suppiger Co.*, 314 U.S. 488, 492 (1942) and see, *e.g.,* Justice Frankfurter in *United States* v. *Bethlehem Steel Corp..* 315 U.S. 289, 312 (1942) (dissent): ". . . the function of the judiciary is not so limited that it must sanction the use of the federal courts as instruments of injustice in disregard of moral and equitable principles which have been part of the law for centuries."

204 *Memphis Keeley Institute* v. *Keeley Co.*, 155 F. 964 (6th Cir. 1907); *Carmen* v. *Fox Film Corp.*, 269 F. 928 (2d Cir. 1920).

205 See, *e.g., Ming* v. *Horgan*, Sup. Ct., Sacramento County, Action No. 97130, June 23, 1958, 3 R.R.L.R. 693.

206 *Shelley* v. *Kraemer*, 334 U.S. 1 (1948); *Hurd* v. *Hodge*, 334 U.S. 24 (1948); *Barrows* v. *Jackson*, 346 U.S. 249 (1953).

207 *Black* v. *Cutter Laboratories*, 351 U.S. 292, 302 (1952) (dissent by Justice Douglas).

208 *Brown* v. *Board of Education*, 347 U.S. 483; *Bolling* v. *Sharpe*, 347 U.S. 497.

209 *Gomillion* v. *Lightfoot*, 364 U.S. 339 (1960); *Boynton* v. *Virginia*, 364 U.S. 454 (1960); *United States* v. *Louisiana*, 364 U.S. 502 (1960); *Monroe* v. *Pape*, 81 S. Ct. 473 (1961); *Burton* v. *Wilmington Parking Authority*, 81 S. Ct. 856 (1961).

ment. . . . No higher duty, no more solemn responsibility rests upon this Court, than that of translating into living law and maintaining this constitutional shield deliberately planned and inscribed for the benefit of every human being subject to our Constitution — of whatever race, creed or persuasion.210

VI. CONCLUSION

President Kennedy can and should issue a new Emancipation Proclamation, requiring all seekers of Federal grants-in-aid to agree to nonsegregated use of the funds and withholding such aid from those who refuse to comply with the anti-bias proviso. Without further legislation by Congress, or waiting for the snail-like movement of adversary litigation in the courts, the President's proclamation would effectively implement the 20th Century constitutional doctrine outlawing state-sanctioned segregation. Presidential power to issue such an executive order lies not only in the Federal grant-in-aid statutes themselves, but in the express and implied Constitutional powers of the nation's Chief Executive. The courts will uphold Presidential action in this field. Such a proclamation would provide irrefutable proof to the world that America practices what it preaches — that "all men are created equal" and that they are "forever free."

The Presidency in the Courts

Glendon A. Schubert, Jr.

. . . The most significant aspect of judicial review of presidential orders is its ineffectiveness. If the courts are the most important bulwark of freedom and liberty in the United States, then we have every right to view with alarm the future security of the republic. And yet, the courts have an indispensable role to perform in ensuring that our government will afford in the future, as it already has ensured in such substantial measure in the past, a maximum of freedom under law, and that balance between the rights of the few and the many, of the individual and society, which has constituted the central problem of all liberal political philosophers. How is this seeming paradox to be explained?

210 *Chambers* v. *Florida,* 309 U.S. 227, 241 (1940).

Reprinted by permission from *The Presidency in the Courts* by Glendon A. Schubert, Jr., pp. 347–357. University of Minnesota Press, Minneapolis. © copyright 1957 by the University of Minnesota.

First and most fundamentally, we should give up the myth that the judiciary either can or should resolve the critical questions of public policy that each generation must face anew. It is both unreasonable and antidemocratic for us to expect the judges to fulfill such a function. This is merely a way of saying that the elected representatives of the people — the President and the Congress — must decide the great questions of constitutional law. Obviously, this places a premium upon the efficacy of political processes, including the enormously expanding job of administering the manifold functions of modern government.

Deciding constitutional questions is a means of making law: law is the formal statement of public policy. If the courts are not to, and normally do not, attempt to second-guess the President on fundamental issues of public policy, what is left for them to do?

Much. There remains, for instance, the obligation of incumbent officials to comply with requirements and limitations imposed by the laws that they themselves, and their predecessors, have made. It is in this sense that "the Rule of Law" assumes its largest significance, and it is here that the courts are peculiarly well adapted to function and act. In truth, there is much evidence to suggest that this is precisely what is happening in the United States today. The day of *Railroad Retirement Bd.* v. *Alton R. R. Co.* is gone, and there are doubtless few who have regrets at its passing; the characteristic case of today is *Peters* v. *Hobby*. For the courts to return to their historic role in Anglo-Saxon polities of enforcing, for citizen and official alike, the requirements of existing law is a large enough task. Our concern, therefore, should be with the extent to which the judiciary have fulfilled this responsibility, rather than with their inevitable failure to discharge the impossible function of substituting their judgment for that of the President in time of crisis. To speak of the federal judiciary alone, it simply is not true that in this sense and at such a time, three hundred heads are better than one.

Measured in terms of such criteria, what is the record of eight generations and eight hundred cases, in which constitutional questions concerning the exercise of presidential power have been raised before the courts?

When the President acts, literally, as Commander in Chief, his constitutional authority is on unimpeachable grounds. He may raise armies and send them where he wills. In addition to regular members of the armed forces, his authority extends (or has extended historically) to militiamen, volunteers, draftees, and conscientious objectors. Although a civilian Court of Military Appeals recently has been created near the apex of the system of military courts, the President continues to function as the highest reviewing authority and the agency of final determination. There are a number of Civil War cases which hold to the contrary, but the preponderance of judicial opinion has upheld and the unquestionable practice has been that the President can declare martial law when in his judgment the exigencies of military necessity make this step imperative; and at such a time and in such places, civilians generally are subject to the jurisdiction of military courts. The vanquished enemy, whether his role was that of professional soldier or politician, may be tried for "unlawful belligerency" or "crimes against humanity" before military commissions authorized by the President alone, or in cooperation with the governments of other states. The civilian residents of territory occupied by the military forces of the United States, as well as the American-citizen entourage of our occupying forces, are subject to the jurisdiction of special military government courts whose constitution lies, again, in the authority and powers of the President. None of these various types of military courts dispensing military justice is subject to the supervision and review of the regular federal judiciary; as to them, the President himself is the Supreme Court.

Alien enemies — a classification which includes, for various purposes, many citizens of the United States, both naturalized and natural-born — are subject to what amounts in practice to almost absolute presidential control, and he may deal with them in ways which unquestionably are contrary to the normal requirements of both permanent statutory law and the Bill of Rights, as these are usually interpreted. The alien enemy may be interned, either in a regular jail with common criminals, or in a special concentration camp specially constructed for thousands like himself. If not incarcerated, he may be placed under surveillance, licensed, restricted in his movement, and required to report periodically like a parolee. His property may be summarily confiscated by the government, and returned to him, if at all, only as an act of grace years after the hostilities have ended. As soon as conditions permit, he may be deported to his country of nationality, although he must, if Congress has granted him such a privilege, be given an opportunity to leave voluntarily for any country of his choice which is willing to admit him. Indeed, the alien who is classified as a "security risk," even though he is not an "alien enemy" in the legal sense, may be interned for what is in effect life imprisonment. The regulatory authority in all these actions is the President; and it is he who in substantial measure makes the laws which determine the obligations of the alien enemy.

The President also legislates to license, prohibit, and otherwise to control the carrying on of commerce with the enemy in time of either civil or international war, whether it be war *de facto* or war *de jure*. Vessels and persons who violate his regulations may be seized; and in the case of property, may be confiscated, while in the case of persons, may be indicted on criminal charges. Where in his judgment this is necessary, the property of any person within the jurisdiction of the United States, enemy or friend, alien or citizen, may be seized for either the temporary or permanent use of the government. In the case of alien friends and citizens, there is an obligation on the part of the government to pay just compensation for this use, but the presidential power of acquisition is untrammeled and the mechanics of payment are, in practice, left up to the discretion and judgment of the President and Congress.

There are no apparent legal limitations upon the power of the President to proclaim the existence of a national emergency. Certainly, the courts will not substitute their judgment of the state of the Union for that of the Chief Executive. He may then claim the right to exercise, throughout the duration of his self-proclaimed emergency, extraordinary powers which would not be considered available for his use in time of "normalcy." Increasingly, Congress has adopted permanent legislation which is automatically invoked and revivified upon a presidential declaration of a national emergency. This state of emergency has no necessary relationship to the existence of war *de jure*. It may be occasioned by domestic crisis, as in the spring of 1933, or it may either precede the outbreak of war *de jure* (as during the period 1939–1941) or extend beyond the end of war *de jure* (as in the case of the continuing extension of the emergency declared by President Truman in December 1950 beyond the date of the ratification of the peace treaty with Japan on April 28, 1952). The whole period of the Civil War was that of a presidentially declared emergency, although there was no war *de jure*. On the other hand, the United States was at war *de jure* throughout the decade extending from December 7, 1941, until April 28, 1952, and there was also the presidentially declared national emergency which includes this same period.

During the period of such a national emergency, the President may exercise such abnormal powers over private property as that of fixing prices for producers, manufacturers, wholesalers, retailers, and consumers; he may allocate raw materials and ration the consumption of finished goods; under his direction, public contracts may be made, modified, and broken, and rights under private contracts may be altered to the extent that they conflict with the requirements of the public contracting power. The President does all these things in the right of his constitutional status and authority as the Commander in Chief, although his constitutional powers are usually reinforced by almost unlimited delegation of statutory powers.

As the Chief of State, his power is, if anything, even more absolute and beyond the scope of challenge in the courts, because in this area, he does not share constitutional power as an equal of the Congress, as he does in the case of the war power of the national government. In the realm of foreign relations, he is either the primary or else the exclusive organ of governmental power. He is, in the words of the Supreme Court, the *sole* organ of the nation. It is he who recognizes, or refuses to recognize, the governments of foreign states. He may make agreements with them which have the same binding force and effect as treaties. He may extend the national *imperium* over new lands which are acquired through discovery, or conquest, or — as in the case of the tidelands — as the result of his own assertion of title. His supplementary regulations may contribute substantially to the national policy governing immigration and admission to the United States. Similarly, he may act to place an embargo upon or to license trade by residents of the United States with foreign countries. Since the power to regulate foreign commerce is vested by the Constitution in the Congress in unequivocal terms, the President's action in this area is usually undertaken on the basis of statutory delegation of authority, but his own independent constitutional power is such that there are no apparent limitations on the power of Congress to transfer to him the power to legislate for the regulation of such foreign commerce. He may also be delegated by statute considerable discretion over the regulation of trade on the part of residents of foreign states with the United States; and his action in this respect has never been successfully challenged in the courts. His decision, in such specific areas of this field as the changing of tariff duties or the licensing of foreign air transportation, may be guided by an administrative fact-finding agency, but based upon other and secret information that reaches him through diplomatic, military, or other non-public channels. For this reason, his judgment in such matters is final.

As the Chief Administrator, his legal authority over the personnel and properties which constitute the executive branch of the government of the United States is limited, as a matter of administrative necessity, by statutory law, regulations of his own making, and the rule-making powers of his subordinates; but only to a very modest extent is he controlled by the power of the courts. His power of removal over his military and civil subordinates has been, throughout most of our history, practically unassailable. This was demonstrated anew in the most recently frictional aspect of this, administrative removals authorized by his own executive order on grounds of disloyalty. His power of administrative direction over his subordinates cannot be challenged by them in the courts, nor has it yet been successfully forestalled before the courts by those outside the government who are indirectly affected by his power to thus control the activities of his subordinates. He may issue regulations, orders, directives, and instructions; he may transfer statutory responsibilities from one official to another; he may change the organizational status and composition of administrative agencies; and his subordinates may present their advice to him — which he of necessity is bound to follow in most instances — and all this without creating justiciable rights of a substantial enough nature for the judiciary to review his judgment.

Furthermore, the courts have since an early period recognized that he must be able to subdelegate his powers, and particularly his statutory powers, if he is to exercise more than a fraction of them, so his authority to act through his subordinates, irrespective of the language used in statutory acts of delegation to him, has been consistently recognized in hundreds of cases. This assumes importance from another point of view in that, when such a subordinate acts for him, in the eyes of the judiciary, it is still in law *the President* who has acted; consequently, the effect of this legal fiction is to expand the scope of executive discretion and judicial non-reviewability into impredictable depths of the administrative hierarchy where these doctrines are inapposite and should be inapplicable. If it is true that he is the Commander in *Chief,* it cannot follow, as the courts have in effect held, that every commander of a military district is in law the Commander in Chief too; if he is the "*Sole* Organ of the Nation," then certainly neither the Secretary of State nor the Attorney

General, nor both of them together, can also be the Sole Organ at the same time; and if he is the *Chief* Administrator, or the "Chief Executive" to use the more common phrase, then neither the director of the Office of Price Stabilization, the Secretary of the Interior, nor a bureau chief in some other agency can also be the Chief Executive. For many purposes, however, they are such in the eyes of the judiciary.

In times past, the President has exercised considerable discretion over the disposition and uses to which the public lands have been put. In the absence of statutory authority, Presidents for more than a century made reservations of the public lands for military purposes, to conserve our natural resources, and for the resettlement of the aboriginal Americans, as well as for such other purposes as lighthouse reservations and bird sanctuaries. This is largely a closed chapter today save for the continuing activities of that recondite specialist, the Indian claims lawyer. Nevertheless, the subject is important to us because of the great liberality with which the courts have characteristically viewed the exercise of presidential authority in this area, creating precedents which are available, and which have been used, to justify an equally broad range of presidential discretion in other areas of substantive activity.

The sources of the President's power are various and in the view of the Supreme Court today it makes little difference whether they are clearly distinguished for purposes of justifying any particular order which is challenged. In quantitative terms, statutes are certainly the most important source, and there are today no apparent limitations upon the power of Congress to make such delegations of authority to the President, either prospectively or retroactively. Whatever the war power is, it is defined by the courts as being largely equivalent to military necessity; and it is constitutionally invested in the President fully as much as in the Congress. At least in some times and with respect to certain subjects, the Supreme Court and other courts have recognized the right of the President to act affirmatively in the public interest, even where there is no apparent authority for his action in either statute or the Constitution. This writer finds it most accurate and most useful to speak of this as the President's implied powers. Whatever they are to be called, they are a part of the panoply of authority of the presidential office. Statutes may occasionally be held unconstitutional where they conflict with or encroach upon the exclusive constitutional authority of the executive, just as presidential orders may occasionally be found unconstitutional where they conflict with valid acts of the Congress within the scope of its own exclusive constitutional authority.

Judicially determined standards of form and procedure for executive legislation are practically nonexistent. There is no necessary form for executive orders or proclamations other than that required by statute and executive order. The President probably should, but does not have to, refer to the source of his authority in his orders and regulations of general effect. He can amend or revoke his own ordinances and those of his predecessors. Statutory and executive law now determines when executive legislation goes into effect. The courts will take judicial notice of his ordinances, and are required by statute to notice the great bulk of them which are printed in the Federal Register. A proclamation or executive order is public law, just as are statutes.

When we turn to the mechanics of the exercise of judicial review, the full extent of the freedom of presidential action from judicial control becomes inescapably apparent. The courts will not review executive discretion: therefore, they will not intervene in presidential decisions of political questions; they must occasionally submit to superior force, or the threat of it, if the President chooses to take direct action to frustrate the judicial process; they cannot compel him to act no matter what the nature or certainty of his obligation may be; they cannot compel him to divulge official information that he chooses to withhold; his formal statement that he has complied with statutory conditions to his action is accepted as binding; and with rare exceptions involving subordinates acting in his name, his findings of "facts" are accepted as conclusive and are not open to judicial re-examination.

It is the duty of the courts to uphold the constitutionality of the President's action, and they must give great weight to his own interpretation and construction of the scope of his own powers. Those who seek to challenge the President's action must assume the burden of proof, and the courts will always assume that the President has complied with the requirements of law. The Chief Executive has not been and apparently cannot be forced to appear personally before any court; he is officially and personally immune from judicial process and prospective judicial control. The courts can neither force him to do anything, nor prevent him from doing anything he may decide to do, although they may, of course, decide (and on rare instances they have decided) that action he had already taken was unconstitutional.

It is also interesting to note the level at which judicial restraint takes place, to the extent that it does. There appears to be an inverse relationship between the status of a court in the hierarchy of courts in the United States (and therefore its own sense of responsibility), and its willingness to subject presidential action to judicial control. The President has been frankly dealt with in several decisions of the Customs Court, as though he were just another misguided administrative officer, bumbling along as one inevitably must who has not enjoyed the advantages of formal legal training; but there is usually a more respectful tone in opinions of the Supreme Court which refer to the Chief Executive. It is also observable that occasionally, in its enthusiasm to give adequate recognition to the President as the embodiment of executive power when the United States is at war, a court will string out all of his available titles in large capitals, giving the impression of being somewhat frustrated at not being able to add: "Defender of the Faith" and "Emperor of the Territories beyond the Seas"!

. . . there have been so very few cases in which presidential orders have been held unconstitutional. Only fourteen cases, throughout our entire national history, were so decided by the United States Supreme Court, the remaining two thirds of the cases have been decided by lower courts, either state or federal. Three of the cases related to President Madison's Embargo Proclamation of August 9, 1809; and another seven — including all these cases that were decided during the decade of the Civil War — related to various orders of President Lincoln suspending the privilege of the writ of habeas corpus for prisoners of the military. This accounts for almost a third of the total of the cases. It is readily apparent that most of these cases relate to the exercise of what were, at the time, extraordinary presidential powers during periods of emergency. It is even more apparent that these cases involve only an infinitesimal fragment of the totality of presidential regulations, orders, and directives during the past century and two thirds; consider that, of the vast outpouring of direct presidential lawmaking during World War II, only *one* case holds adversely to the constitutionality of executive action. The momentous impact of this solitary decision was to permit a few West Virginia bakers to waste flour by reclaiming stale bread from their retail outlets. Finally, only two of these decisions have had the effect of preventing the President from carrying out any important element of his administration's program at the time, and none has appeared to inhibit any subsequent President from exercising the same power at a later time. One of these two exceptions was the *Steel Seizure* case which, supercharged with political implications in a presidential election year, resulted directly and immediately in a disastrous strike which the President successfully had forestalled for over four months. The other was *Cole* v. *Young,* which admittedly portends important limitations on the President's power to authorize the discharge of civil servants without due process of law.

In conclusion then, it may be said that the differential nature of judicial tolerance respecting executive legislation is of considerable practical importance:

1. Emergency ordinances and those of extraterritorial effect are already almost beyond the pale of judicial review; but presidential action of domestic impact and not keyed to emergency powers — an area which is beginning to resemble, to borrow a mathematical concept, a disappearing function — may, under suitable conditions, be subjected to judicial review.

2. It is almost impossible to prevent the President from taking any given action through recourse to judicial process, even though the effect of his action may be to moot what might otherwise have been a justiciable controversy; but there are, subject to limitations already noted, means whereby it is possible to challenge the validity of his action after it has been taken.

3. The courts have been consistently more zealous in denying to the President any power summarily to seize property in time of war or other emergency, except under statutory delegation of authority, than they have been with respect to his summary powers over persons. This can be

explained in various ways, but the fundamental reason probably is that the Anglo-Saxon legal order has always prized rights of property above personal rights. The Supreme Court of the United States is not certain whether the President, when he acts to raise an army, to detain citizens and aliens in protective custody, to declare martial law and to suspend the writ of habeas corpus, to determine standards of loyalty and disloyalty toward the United States, and to try and punish enemy aliens by a summary administrative process for crimes that are defined in no statute, does so under his prerogative powers as Chief of State, his constitutional powers as Commander in Chief, or his executive powers as the constitutional agent of Congress in faithfully executing the laws. All that the Court is sure of is that these powers are inherent in sovereignty and must therefore reside in the political branches of the national government. There has been no such confusion in the courts concerning the President's emergency powers over property. Such powers reside in the Congress; and where the President acts, he acts as the legislative agent of Congress.

4. Finally, inasmuch as subdelegated presidential powers may be further subdelegated and redelegated, it would seem consonant with the premise of executive responsibility in a democratic polity for the courts to recognize an integrated pattern of administrative regulation when it is presented to them, and to hold responsible those who are in a position to command and direct. If this leads to the seeming dead end of presidential immunity from judicial process, all is not necessarily lost. Marbury did not get his commission as justice of the peace for the District of Columbia, but few would say that the adjudication of his rights has left no mark upon the subsequent development of our system of government.

Presidential Succession and Disability:
Policy Analysis for Unique Cases

Aaron Wildavsky

The new constitutional amendment on presidential succession and disability raises in extreme form the problem of recommending policy for unique cases. These special policies have the following outstanding characteristics:

1. The proposed solutions must work every time.
2. There is little historical experience upon which to base generalizations about future probabilities.

Printed by permission of the author.

3. Behavioral science does not contain relevant propositions that could facilitate reasonable prediction of the outcomes of different sets of events under varying conditions.

4. The usual way around this kind of difficulty — the application of rules of thumb, like the incremental method, that depend on repeated adjustments of feedback — is not applicable because

(a) it is so difficult to get the relevant experience, and

(b) there is not enough time. The "error" of "trial and error" must not happen.

These problem characteristics mean that the one certainty is that uniquely favorable solutions cannot be obtained. The existing state of human knowledge means that the problems are insoluble. But there are reasons to believe that no action at all may be worse than any of several alternatives, however unsatisfactory they appear. So how do we proceed? It is possible to clarify the most relevant criteria and to apply them, with some generalizations from political science, to different alternatives. This form of analysis allows us to reject the worst; we can then choose among better although imperfect alternatives.

Application of the relevant criteria to presidential succession will show that the new constitutional amendment represents a reasonable "satisficing" alternative that neither wholly meets nor completely violates the crucial criteria. In the case of presidential disability, however, the constitutional provisions are a parody of what must be avoided: a prolonged struggle over who has the right to be President. The problem simply cannot be solved in advance. We must rely on the presumed virtues of our political elites to work out solutions for problems as they arise.

In our analyses it will be necessary to consider the relationship of Presidents to their important publics within the United States; for the choice of a successor or a person to act as President during periods of disability depends on the probable reactions of the major publics that, in their mutual interaction, make up the larger patterns we call the presidency. In determining whether a successor might come from a particular institution, moreover, we are required to appraise that institution from a presidential perspective. Although existing knowledge is not adequate, we must attempt to specify the causal connections between different successors and their likely behavior in the presidential office. Consideration of reform thus compels us to summarize a substantial part of our knowledge about the presidency.

Great problems of public policy exert an independent force upon the societies that encounter them. Once a problem is recognized, public energies may be mobilized to find solutions and scholarly talents may be directed toward historical inquiries in order to determine how the problem emerged. Yet a great problem of public policy may itself be a source of energy; once its characteristics are determined many new problems arise and numerous old ones become more urgent. Such is the case with the problem of presidential succession and disability. This perennial problem of the American political structure would hardly concern us now with so deep a sense of urgency if it were not for the spectre of nuclear war. Just as the 1964 presidential elections brought out profound anxieties about which candidate would have his finger on the nuclear button, so have we been led to fear that there might be no one around to wiggle the presidential finger at mankind after a nuclear attack.

The tragic death of President Kennedy, and recognition of the possibility that Vice President Johnson might have been shot at the same time, has made us aware of the dangers that might face us if we failed to make adequate provision for presidential succession. That is why we have added the Twenty-fifth Amendment to the Constitution. Two basic questions must still be answered: Who should be next in line if the Vice President is unavailable? How far should the line of succession be lengthened to guard against the possibility of an atomic attack killing all those on call?

In trying to answer these questions, we may ask what history has to tell us. There has never been a need to go beyond the Vice President to fill the presidency, although one or the other office has been vacant for approximately 40 per cent of the time since the beginning of the Republic. The first succession act was passed in 1792 when the Senate was dominated by supporters of, Alexander Hamilton and the House by friends of Secretary of State Thomas Jefferson. The Senate passed a bill putting the President pro tempore of that body next in line, but the House amended it by placing the Secretary of State first in line. A compromise was finally reached by putting the Speaker of the House second in line behind the President pro tempore of the Senate who, if a vacancy occurred during the first two years and seven months of a presidential term, would serve until a special presidential election was held. On November 25, 1885, Vice President Thomas Henricks died, ten days before the first session of the next Congress. A major impetus to change the line of succession was provided by the fact that Cleveland was a Democrat, while the new President pro tempore was a Republican. The Act of 1886 placed succession among Cabinet positions in the following order: the Secretary of State, the Secretary of the Treasury, the Secretary of War, the Attorney General, the Postmaster General, the Secretary of the Navy, and the Secretary of the Interior. After Vice President Truman became President in 1945 there were those who thought that his Secretary of State, Edward R. Stettinius, was not of presidential caliber, and that House Speaker Sam Rayburn would be better. President Truman, who appeared to accept the argument that the Act of 1886 was "undemocratic," waited until the Republicans gained a majority in the House of Representatives and proposed that the succession act be changed to put the Speaker — then Republican Joseph W. Martin — first in line and the President pro tempore of the Senate next.

The Presidential Succession Act passed in 1947 provides a line of succession first through Congress — the Speaker and the President pro tempore — and then through the Cabinet in the order of the 1886 Act with the addition of the Secretaries of Agriculture, Commerce, and Labor. In case a Speaker or President pro tempore was not constitutionally qualified to be President by reason of age or foreign birth, the next qualified person in line would assume the office until a Speaker or President pro tempore who was qualified was elected. The act also said that these officials must resign their existing positions when they act as President. This is essentially the succession plan we have today. Because of the circumstances following Kennedy's death and Johnson's succession — a Speaker in his seventies and a President pro tempore in his eighties — questions have inevitably been raised about the suitability of a plan that would permit them to assume the burdens of the presidency.

What history has to teach us, it appears, is that succession acts have been influenced by somebody's dislike of the idea of a particular person or person of a particular party being next in line to succeed to the presidency. An examination of the problem that avoids considerations of personality or immediate partisan advantage would seem to be in order. Let us begin by developing a set of criteria with which to evaluate the many complicated proposals for dealing with presidential succession. Then we can apply these criteria to the major proposals that have been advanced, with special attention to the victorious alternative embodied in the Twenty-fifth Amendment.

Any method for determining presidential succession must be established with absolute certainty. There must never be any doubt about precisely which person — whether occupying a particular position or chosen in a specified way — is next in line to assume the presidency. Nor must there be any doubt about the new President's term of office or his right to exercise presidential powers. Untold mischief would result if there were two or more claimants for the office or if there was no one with an undisputed right to occupy it. Who, then, could speak for the United States in foreign affairs or rally the nation to meet domestic emergencies? Worse still would be the internal upheaval resulting from the bitter disputes of rival claimants and their supporters. To argue about what the President should do is a normal part of politics in a democracy; to argue over which person should be doing what a President has the right to do is an invitation to civil war.

In addition to being certain, presidential succession should be immediate. Only a few minutes or at most a few hours should elapse between the demise of one President and the accession of another, as was fortunately the case when Johnson succeeded Kennedy. In an atomic era made immensely dangerous by the existence of weapons of huge destructiveness, we simply cannot afford to be without a President. In many ways we would be better off with any one responsible person rather than no one in the presidential office, even if this person was inferior to others who might have been chosen.

One reason for insisting that any plan for succession be certain and immediate is that these features help the new President gain acceptance as the legitimate occupant of the White House. When a political system is called "legitimate" the vast majority of people — especially those active in politics — believe that it is the right system of government. Severe policy conflicts are then less likely to overturn the regime. When the legitimacy of a political system is threatened, as was the case in Weimar Germany and Fourth Republic France, even minor political controversies are dangerous because they raise the question not only of "how much shall each interest receive" but also of "whether this form of government shall survive."

If the person who succeeds to the presidency is to be considered legitimate the plan for determining who he will be should be as stable as possible so that it can gather force from longevity and tradition. Stability is a desirable standard because it gives the greatest assurance that the plan will be known by the largest number of citizens. Taught in the schools and disseminated by the media of information upon suitable occasions the plan can become part of the political lore that every American is expected to know as part of his basic education. Changing the plan every few years could only result in confusion and lack of widespread understanding of the procedures then in operation. It would then be much easier for someone to challenge the existing plan and to suggest that since the procedures had been changed so often there was nothing sacrosanct in abiding by them. The advantage of stability need not imply that the present arrangement be kept, although it does mean that we should try to keep any new plan for as long as possible.

The gravest danger to stability comes from the efforts of those who would tailor a succession act to fit the particular individual they would like to help or hinder in case the need should arise. While it is not feasible to designate a particular individual by name for succession, it is possible to block a current officeholder, in case he is not thought suitable, or to place another current officeholder who is well-liked next in the line of succession. Following such practices would lead to continual changes in the succession act as those who occupied various institutional positions fell in and out of favor. Since no one can guarantee that all of us will always approve of the person designated as the immediate successor, wisdom would appear to require that we make the best, long-range arrangement that we can. The futile hope that we can always get the man we would most prefer has to be weighed against creating instability.

The third criterion for determining presidential succession is continuity. Whoever succeeds to the presidency should serve until the next regularly scheduled election. A man who is in office for only a short period of time, and who must soon give way to another person, can hardly be expected to act with confidence, vigor, and dispatch. At best, he could undertake holding actions because he could not commit the executive branch to any policy that lasted beyond a few months. Weakness, indecision, futility, even challenges of the right of a temporary occupant to act like a President would be the most likely consequences of failing to allow a successor to serve until the end of the established presidential term. It follows, therefore, that any proposal that permits the presidency to be occupied by alternating individuals is to be rejected.

If we are to meet the criteria discussed thus far, the procedures embodied in a succession plan also must be as simple as possible. Simplicity is urged as a criterion because it helps insure certainty, immediacy, and legitimacy. The more complex the plan, the more time is likely to be involved, the more doubt is likely to arise about who is next in line, and the more opportunities are created for something to go wrong. If people are puzzled over what procedures are to be followed, the way is left open for demagogues to claim that the result is not legitimate. If the occupant of the presidency is not determined beforehand, delay and intrigue may be added to confusion. Hence, we should eliminate any proposals concerning succession that involve more than a few simple steps or that involve lengthy deliberations or consultations.

The transfer of power to a new President should be as tranquil as possible. The political life of the country should not be upset by shocks or disruptions in this delicate period, for the death of a President is inevitably traumatic. The nation mourns the loss of the man whose office signifies its unity, virility, and hope. More than we realize, a President provides important guidelines from which we take our bearings in a complicated world. By knowing about him and his customary modes of operation, the world is made somewhat more predictable. Regardless of whether we support his specific policies, his loss creates a void. There is no need, therefore, to add to the disquiet by public contests or controversies, by campaigns or contests that may unleash pent-up emotions.

However admirable a proposal for handling succession might otherwise be, it cannot be acceptable unless it is also consistent with the proper management of presidential disability. Let us suppose that there is no Vice President and the person who is President becomes disabled. A new occupant of the presidency who could serve for the rest of the term or only a few weeks or months until the President recovers is needed. If the person next in line has a very important job, he might be reluctant to resign his position to take over the presidency for a limited period, knowing that he might be unable to regain his former post. Such reluctance, though understandable, would be most dangerous. The successor might be tempted to delay assuming the Presidency until well after the full extent of the disability was evident, thus creating a gap in the effective exercise of presidential responsibility. Or the successor might be tempted to hedge about resigning his previous position, thereby creating dangerous uncertainty about his status and hence his legitimacy and longevity in office. Whoever is next in line, therefore, must be placed so that he can either resume his former position without difficulty or have no profound regrets about risking loosing it.

Any person who succeeds to the presidency should belong to the same political party as the former President. The party system is an essential element of democratic government in the United States and succession proposals should try to strengthen rather than weaken our parties.

That the person who succeeds to the presidency should be a good man, capable of exercising the highest office in the land, is an evident but elusive criterion. It is difficult to say precisely what combination of characteristics is most desirable in a President. Certain qualities — tenacity, firmness, courage — are so personal that it is impossible to tell whether any man will have them when he needs them. Moreover, assessments of attributes like intelligence, knowledge, and skill are clearly related to one's own political preferences. Would a liberal prefer a highly intelligent but extremely conservative man to a moderately intelligent but extremely liberal person? The President's actions depend upon his values and preferences as well as his personal capacities. We can, of course, do our best to appraise the appropriateness of successors who would be drawn from various institutions such as Congress, the Cabinet, or the Supreme Court. We can say, perhaps, that a successor should have some experience in American politics so that he will have been socialized in acceptable modes of political conduct. It would also be desirable for a potential successor to know something about current developments of special presidential responsibility, especially in foreign affairs.

Proposals for handling presidential succession are designed to see that we always have a President who functions with the full powers of the office. There would seem to be little point in adopting proposals at the cost of weakening the presidency or of diluting the quality of the Vice President, who is most likely to take over if something happens to the President. Any plan that would add appreciably to the President's burdens, which are already great, or that would depreciate the worth of the vice presidency, should be turned down. It is difficult, of course, to find any proposal that is costless.

Our ideal presidential succession, then, would be certain, immediate, and widely regarded as legitimate. The succession plan would be simple and stable. It would lead to the choice of good men from the former President's party, who would maintain continuity in office. The President would be able to exercise the full powers of his office, his successor would be ready to take over if a disability occurred, and the strength of the presidency would remain unimpaired.

Proposals for dealing with presidential succession proceed in one of two directions. They either specify that the holders of certain institutional positions, such as Cabinet positions, should succeed to the presidency, or they describe a procedure, such as a special election, through which a successor would be chosen. Let us consider the arguments for and against the occupants of institutional positions providing a line of succession and then consider various other procedures suggested for finding a successor.

One proposal, following the act of 1886, suggests that the Secretary of State, followed by other Cabinet members, should assume the presidency after the Vice President if a vacancy occurs. This plan, supposedly, would keep the presidency moving in the same general direction, especially in the vital field of foreign affairs, because the Secretary of State is assumed to share the President's preferences and usually belongs to the President's political party as well. Moreover, Secretaries of State have often been men of considerable stature who are likely to be qualified for the presidency anyway because of their knowledge and breadth of vision. And the secretary has the additional advantage of being instantaneously ready to assume the presidency.

Perhaps the most serious objection to the Secretary of State is that he is not an elected official and thus might suffer from a lack of legitimacy. In a time of crisis some people might challenge his right to occupy the presidency. Nor is it necessarily the case that the Secretary of State will be a man of stature. The growing importance of foreign policy will lead some Presidents to wish to act as their own policy-maker. They may be wary, therefore, of appointing an individual with an independent national standing or following who might challenge them or make it costly to fire them. Such considerations may have played a part in John F. Kennedy's decision to appoint the little-known and deferential Dean Rusk over the well-known and assertive Adlai Stevenson, who could count on his own support in the Democratic Party. It is not even certain that a Secretary of State would follow the foreign policy of the President he succeeded. Certainly Eisenhower and Dulles differed in their approaches.

The network of associations that envelops Cabinet members, centered around the major interests they serve, gives them a narrower view and pulls them apart from a President who must juggle and balance many concerns at once. Although the proposition that Cabinet members are the President's "natural enemies" may be exaggerated, there is no reason to expect them to agree fully on matters of departmental policy, let alone the broad range of foreign and domestic issues.

In order to avoid some of the difficulties associated with the choice of the Secretary of State and still keep succession within the executive branch, it has been proposed that national conventions nominate, and the voting citizenry elect, two vice presidents. In case two vacancies occurred in the presidential office, the second Vice President would take over. This scheme has the advantage of placing succession in the hands of an elected national official of the same political party who would be kept continuously informed of important developments, who could take over immediately, and whose legitimacy could not be questioned. The major question here is whether this scheme might not create additional difficulties that would be greater than its presumed benefits.

There is, first of all, the problem of getting an outstanding person to accept a position as second Vice President. This official would not have the few formal duties of the first Vice President and he would know that in the course of American history a second Vice President has not been required to assume the presidency. And should a first Vice President look forward to the chance of running for the presidency at some future time, he would know that he had a probable rival right next to him, thus further reducing the incentive for talented and ambitious men to take the job. Debasing the value of the vice presidency in order to meet the more remote contingency that two successors might be required hardly seems advisable.

The introduction of a second Vice President would also lead to what might be called the "politics of polygamy." In polygamous societies, the relationship between the first and second wives is not always noted for light and harmony. Since the President has the discretion to determine what Vice Presidents will or will not do beyond the usual tedium of presiding over the Senate, Vice Presidents such as Richard Nixon and Lyndon Johnson have had to fight to get important assignments. The potentiality of conflict, favoritism, and intrigue would be multiplied with two Vice Presidents looking for work, perhaps by encroaching on the Secretary of State or other highly placed officials. We know that Vice President John Nance Garner was not averse to suggesting means of overturning the "Administration" program to congressional opponents of Franklin Roosevelt's policies. How much greater, then, would be the temptation of mischief with one or even two disgruntled Vice Presidents looking for an outlet for their talents and energies.

Presumably, one Vice President would continue to preside over the Senate and to take on such additional duties as the President saw fit to allot to him. The other Vice President would be assigned as a general presidential assistant. No doubt there is plenty of work around the White House and the President would have no difficulty in finding jobs for any willing hand. But unlike such other high staff assistants as the Director of the Budget and the Chairman of the Council of Economic Advisers, Vice Presidents cannot be fired. Even if the President had originally desired a particular person as second Vice President, the chief executive might change his mind after a year or two and wish to get rid of him. If this Vice President was charged in the Constitution or by statute with specific responsibilities, the President would be in the anomalous position of disagreeing with a high official he could not remove. Moreover, it might be costly to "dump" this Vice President at the next national convention.

It has been customary in recent years for presidential candidates to choose their running mates. One would imagine that this custom might carry over to the choice of a second Vice President. Yet it is conceivable that party leaders, who are prepared to concede the choice of the first Vice President, might find a rationale for a greater voice in the selection of any additional Vice Presidents. While Lyndon Johnson was able to remove Robert Kennedy from consideration for the Democratic vice presidential nomination in 1964, for example, he might have found it more difficult to justify refusing him a consolation prize if there had been more positions to distribute. Johnson — or any President — would thus be faced with the prospect of offending an important party faction or working with a man whom he patently did not want and who possessed sufficient independent strength to make himself troublesome over the next four years.

The problems created by having two Vice Presidents may be avoided by giving the President the right to choose a new Vice President in case there is a vacancy in that office through the death or disability of either the original President or Vice President. There is much to commend this proposal. The successor would certainly be acceptable to the President, would belong to his political party, would be likely to continue his policies, and would be immediately available. There is something inherently plausible in leaving the choice of a successor to the man who has been elected by the voters and whose replacement should perhaps be like him in essential respects. We trust the President with matters of life and death, so the argument goes, why not trust him to pick his possible successor. Indeed, the operation of the national nominating conventions pretty much assures a President the right to choose his first successor — the man he selects as his running mate.

Yet allowing whoever is President to choose his successor is not without its difficulties. Such personal action, without the participation of a customary legitimizing body such as the national convention, might be regarded as an unwarranted exercise of personal power. Even under the Succession Act of 1886 a president would be choosing a Cabinet member — subject to senatorial confirmation — who might incidentally be his successor, rather than a second Vice President whose major function would be precisely to be available in case he was needed to become the next President.

It is not clear whether having the right to name a successor would help or harm a President. He might be helped if a vacancy occurred at a time when he wished to establish the new successor as his heir apparent in a future presidential nomination and election. Other people in his party, however, might not approve. Furthermore, a President might be harmed if he wished to retain freedom of maneuver in his choice for his next running mate or for a candidate for his party's nomination in a future election. The very fact that he designated a new Vice President during his term of office might make it difficult for him to disavow that person in the future. President Lyndon Johnson, for example, apparently decided to hold off naming his choice for the vice presidential nomination in 1964 in order to determine which man might be best in the light of future events such as the identity of the Republican candidates. He would have had trouble doing this if he had been forced to name a successor immediately. Presumably a President who succeeded another because of his death or disability would have to name his successor within two weeks or thirty days after assuming office. Yet it is difficult to believe that any President would wish to undertake this difficult assignment when he was desperately trying to guide himself and the nation through a trying period of transition. Further delay, however, would violate the criterion of immediacy.

The attack on the legitimacy of the plan providing for presidential choice may be mitigated by a somewhat different plan, which calls for acceptance or rejection of the new President's nomination of his Vice President by Congress. While this might solve the problem of legitimacy, this proposal would not meet the wishes of those who feel that the choice of a successor as well as the successor himself should be confined to the executive branch. They would argue that congressmen have different, narrower constituencies than the President, that the President and congressmen have different perspectives, that Congress may be controlled by the opposite party, and that the separation of powers would be violated by giving Congress an important part to play. The President could hardly afford to have a nominee rejected; it would severely damage his prestige. A narrow approval might inflict severe wounds and might question the legitimacy of his choice. Hence the President would have to conduct the widest consultations in order to make certain that his candidate was approved by a substantial if not overwhelming majority. In this case the power to reject, to use the traditional formula for senatorial confirmation, might become the power to select. Consequently, the President might be forced to accept someone he really did not want or pay the price of a long and bitter conflict.

A strong case in favor of having Congress act as the legitimizing authority can also be made. If individual Representatives have rather narrow constituencies, Congress as a collective body spans the nation. Moreover, the increasing urbanization of the United States gives Senators more representative constituencies than in the past. A majority of congressmen, however, might belong to a different political party than the former President and his new successor. This means that bipartisan compromise would be reflected in the choice of a new Vice President so as to assure reasonable cooperation between the legislative and executive branches of government. The separation of powers, as Richard Neustadt has told us, is a form of shared power. Nothing is accomplished by treating the different branches as if they lived in separate worlds when the daily activities of government require their mutual cooperation. While the President might not wish to take the trouble to find an immediate successor and present him to Congress, the chief executive's responsibilities to the nation far outweigh any temporary inconvenience he might suffer in doing so. A man who cannot deal with small political troubles, it might be argued, does not belong in the White House.

Still another variant of the above plan calls for having Congress choose among three to five candidates selected by the President soon after a vacancy arises. But if the President indicated a first preference, even informally, the purpose of the plan would be thwarted, and the President would be faced with the prospect of having his choice publicly rejected. Indeed, there could be no guarantee that Congress would accept any of the President's suggestions or that it would be able to arrive at a decision at all, at least not without extensive hearings and lengthy debates. Aside from the mischief and dissention in Congress that this plan might create, it hardly comports with our ideas of an immediate, simple, and tranquil succession.

In a message to Congress supporting what was to become the existing Succession Act, President Truman declared, "The Speaker of the House of Representatives, who is elected in his own district, is also elected to be the presiding officer of the House by a vote of all the Representatives of all the people of the country. As a result, I believe that the Speaker is the official in the Federal Government whose selection, next to that of the President and Vice President, can be most accurately said to stem from the people themselves." The legitimacy of the Speaker becoming President could not be questioned. More than that, a Speaker is bound to be a product *par excellence* of American political life. Having come up through the ranks over a period of many years, he knows what kinds of behavior are and are not acceptable. He is most unlikely to be an extremist or a person who would threaten our liberties. Conciliation, respect for others, ability to bring men of diverse points of view together for common purposes are his stocks in trade. A Speaker is likely to have a wide-ranging acquaintanceship with other governmental officials and a broad knowledge of the major issues of the day, especially in regard to domestic affairs.

The objections to the Speaker assuming the presidency are numerous. It is said that the Speaker is of lower caliber than other officials such as the Secretary of State, that he is likely to be too old, that he could not be sufficiently well informed, that he has a congressional rather than presidential orientation, and that he might belong to a different party than the late President or Vice President. Far more evidence than has thus far been supplied, however, would be required to demonstrate that the late Sam Rayburn would necessarily have been a worse President than any of the Secretaries of State who served during his long tenure as Speaker, or that Secretary Rusk would make a more vigorous, determined, and forceful President than Speaker McCormack. If a Speaker or potential Speaker does not manifest the toughness, administrative ability, intelligence, and force to run a large and unwieldly body such as the House of Representatives, he is not likely to last, as the deposition of two recent Republican leaders suggests. The political skills and the breadth of knowledge a Speaker develops provide excellent training for the presidency. Age or seniority is not the prime factor in determining who becomes or survives as Speaker. The man is chosen in a contest between different factions in his party for his ability to lead and serve the membership. In this sense the Speaker becomes experienced in a prime task of the presidency — leading, serving, and resolving conflicts among a broad and rather heterogenous collection of interests. True, Speakers are usually somewhat older than Secretaries of State, though this is by no means an invariant rule. Yet an infirm man could hardly carry on as Speaker, so great are the demands on his energy. The long service in government he would have acquired by the time he became Speaker may be considered an asset in terms of experience as well as a liability in terms of age. But, in the era of De Gaulle and Adenauer, disqualification on grounds of age seems out of place.

It may be that Speakers are more oriented toward a congressional view, and to domestic politics, than a Secretary of State. But excessively parochial concerns can hardly dominate a Speaker's thoughts and actions when he must accommodate to some degree a large party in the House as well as the President of the United States. Harry S Truman, the one recent President who came to the White House almost immediately after long congressional experience, although not from the speakership, had one of the best records in foreign affairs of any President in our time. A Speaker is extraordinarily busy and might not have as much time for intensive study as other officials. But it would be foolish to suggest, as have some writers, that the Speaker necessarily would be blatantly uninformed or that the formal separation of powers would provide a serious obstacle to sending information to a person from a rival branch of government. Indeed, it could be argued that a Speaker, with whom the President must cooperate and who has many sanctions at his disposal, is in a much better position to demand information than the much less powerful Vice President is today. Could it be that Secretaries of State are thought to be generally more distinguished than Speakers because their jobs require them to issue lofty pronouncements, while Speakers, like Presidents, are immersed in the muck and mire of partisan politics and domestic strife?

A most serious obstacle in the path of the Speaker is that he might belong to a different political party than the President and might change the party in the White House, contrary to the expressed wishes of the voters. No doubt a Speaker, realizing this and sensitive to his position, would be loathe to alter radically the personnel or the policy direction of the previous President until the voters had made known their approval in an election. He might choose a type of national coalition government in which members of both parties would be represented in the Cabinet. It is also true that the partisan attachments of some Secretaries of State have been ambiguous. In fact, the present Secretary [Dean Rusk] has no base of support in the Democratic party. Nevertheless, a change of party in the presidency should be avoided if possible. The question is whether other plans, which lack this defect, do not contain others of equal or greater importance.

Another obstacle facing the Speaker is that he might be reluctant to resign his eminent position if a case of presidential disability occurred and it appeared that the President might resume his office in a short time. It is difficult to see how proper provision could be made enabling him to resume his seat in Congress once having resigned it, and if this could be managed he might be influenced by the prospect that he will need the support of his colleagues to regain the speakership at a later date. The criterion of compatibility with succession proposals is violated by putting the Speaker next in line unless he is given the vice presidency when a vacancy occurs in that office through the death of a President or Vice President.

There are a host of proposals that leave the decision of a specific successor up to Congress. One calls for the selection of a new Vice President by a majority vote of a joint session of Congress. A second would have the House of Representatives choose the successor, and a third would have the House choose from among a number of individuals nominated by the Senate. A different stipulation is that members of one or both houses should confine their selection to a member of the President's party in Congress. All of these plans share a common defect: they usually propose that part or all of Congress meet soon after a vacancy has occurred. Yet it might be too late if both the President and Vice President are unavailable. To be sure, such plans may provide for an interim President, but instead of violating the criterion of immediacy, they run counter to the criterion of continuity. What could an interim President do while Congress was in the midst of debates on the identity of the successor? If the congressional debates revealed a lack of consensus, the new President would be handicapped from the start, assuming that terrible events had not occurred in the meantime. Should the election be confined to the House, the authority of the Speaker might be undermined by the choice of another person. Confining the choice to members of the President's party is contrary to all congressional precedent. It might be regarded as lacking the legitimacy of full congressional approval, and it would in no way guarantee that the successor would be a follower, rather than an opponent, of the late President. These proposals combine the disadvantages of locating the choice in Congress without the advantages of having an official like the Speaker immediately available for the presidency.

It is apparent that none of the succession proposals give certain promise of meeting all of the relevant criteria. There are five, however, that merit discussion in an imperfect world because they violate the smallest number of criteria. If one is willing to accept the prospect that in the future, Vice Presidents may be of low quality and that they may create continued difficulty for Presidents, the nomination and election of two Vice Presidents may be acceptable. Selection by the President himself may be advocated if one believes that the problem of legitimacy will not be serious, that the President will not have to compromise himself inordinately, that an immediate decision will not prove too taxing for him, and that the nation can afford to wait during the time it takes for him to make up his mind. Nomination by the President and confirmation by both houses of Congress may be appropriate so long as it is thought that the prestige of the President and his possible successor will not be badly damaged, and that the possible lengthy delays in this procedure will not materialize or are not likely to be dangerous if they do. If one believes that succession need not be kept in the executive branch, or that a change of party in the White House ought to be permitted, or that the Speaker would not hesitate about assuming the presidential office in the event of a disability, then succession by the Speaker may be desirable.

Although we have argued that the Secretary of State would not necessarily turn out to be a better man than the Speaker or a presidential nominee, there is little reason to assume that he would probably be worse. The Secretary of State would be likely to meet all our criteria except "legitimacy." Yet how would we know that this would be the case? Perhaps we should cease relying on intuition. We could survey voters and political activists on how they would regard succession by the Secretary of State as opposed to a variety of other possibilities. It might turn out that voters and activists would be willing to accept anyone who is chosen in a manner consistent with the appropriate constitutional provisions and statutes. Yet it might also be the case that certain officials would be widely regarded as more or less legitimate than others.[1]

We can cut into the criteria in another way by dividing the various proposals into two categories: those that promise to solve the direct problem of presidential succession but that may have undesirable side effects, and those that minimize side effects but that may be less than adequate in dealing with succession. If one chose to put the greatest weight on handling the succession itself, then the alternative of two Vice Presidents would emerge as by far the best choice. If one takes the position that other values should not be sacrificed just to deal with a succession problem that has never yet materialized, then allowing the President to choose his own successor would clearly be superior.

Placing the analysis in this light suggests why the Bayh amendment — named after its chief sponsor, the Democratic Senator from Indiana — received such widespread support and easily became the Twenty-fifth Amendment. It provides that vice presidential vacancies shall be filled through nomination by the President, subject to a majority vote in both the Senate and the House. This is a "satisficing" proposal. It sacrifices some immediacy and creates some instant problems for the President in order to secure legitimacy and to minimize his problems with the Vice President in the future. Not every criterion is perfectly satisfied, but neither is any one criterion blatantly violated. No other proposal is evidently better and many are clearly worse. Avoiding the worst is not the same as getting the best, but it has something to be said for it in the context of great uncertainty.

The possibility of an atomic attack that could kill all Cabinet members, many congressmen, and a good part of any institution designated to choose a successor, leads us to consider the desirability of lengthening the line of succession in addition to the question of "who shall be next in line." There are those who say that such an eventuality would be so horrible that they do not wish to think about it. It would be morally impermissible for governmental officials to take this view, however. Their task is to help the living by taking whatever steps they can to promote continuity in government. The most obvious move is to reduce the probability that all top governmental officials will be incapacitated at one time. The President and Vice President can travel separately whenever possible, and there is certainly no reason why the Secretaries of State and Defense and other Cabinet members should be in an airplane at the same time, as happened when President Kennedy was assassinated. Although the likelihood is not great, however, no one can guarantee that an atomic

---

1 In June 1945, a cross-section of citizens was asked to choose among the Secretary of State, the Speaker, and a special meeting of the electoral college. Forty-seven per cent chose the Secretary of State, 20 per cent the Speaker, and 18 per cent the electoral college, with 15 per cent venturing no opinion. Hadley Centril, ed., *Public Opinion 1935–1946* (Princeton, 1951), p. 590.

attack, taking place at a time such as the delivery of the State of the Union message, might not create a vacancy in the presidency with no living successor.

We might meet this problem in part by designating additional members of Congress and men in high executive posts to stand in the line of succession. Further protection might be obtained by including the governors of the fifty states. A permanent order of precedence among governors might be fixed by adopting a wholly arbitrary procedure — taking the states in alphabetical order or in order of their admission to the Union.

To raise the question how a successor to the presidency should be found may imply that some solution is at hand. It is tempting to define problems as things to which there are solutions. Yet there may be problems for which there are no solutions. Let us examine a problem in a related area — presidential disability — for which there appears to be no apparent solution.

Proposals concerned with presidential disability are designed to deal with four kinds of events:

1. The President is so badly incapacitated that he cannot communicate with the Vice President.

2. The President knows he is disabled and tells the Vice President to take over.

3. The President recovers his health and takes back his office.

4. The President really cannot carry out his responsibilities but insists on retaining his office.

History has taught us that Vice Presidents have been reluctant to take great responsibility when a President was out of commission because they feared being accused of usurping power. And at least one President failed to ask a Vice President to take over because the chief executive and his friends feared that it would be difficult for him to get his job back. For a long time, however, the matter did not seem urgent and the obvious remedy was not adopted because congressmen could not agree on any single proposal for handling the entire problem. Different factions coalesced around different plans and it was always possible to show that each plan had some glaring defect. Since Congress would not act, President Eisenhower, aware of public concern over his illnesses, entered into an informal agreement with Vice President Nixon that effectively took care of the first three circumstances outlined above. It was agreed that if the Vice President took over, he succeeded only to the powers and duties but not to the office itself. Therefore, the President, realizing he was disabled, could call upon his Vice President to take over. Or the Vice President, after consulting the Cabinet, could take over if the President was unable to make the announcement. In both cases, the President could take back his job as soon as he felt able to do so simply by announcing that his disability was over. Presidents Kennedy and Johnson have since adopted similar agreements with their potential successors. The fourth instance, however, in which key officials disagree about the President's ability to act as President, remains troublesome.

The possibility that a President might wish to regain office before he is ready must be taken seriously. He might be mentally deranged or he might fear that the acting President was entrenching himself unduly and thus be motivated to take back the office prematurely. Who is to umpire disagreements between the President and Vice President over when the President is ready to go back to work? The Bayh amendment states that this choice would be made by a combination of the Vice President and a majority of the Cabinet whose decision not to let the President back would have to be ratified by a two-thirds majority of both houses of Congress.

On the positive side, the Bayh amendment safeguards the President. By the time the Vice President and a majority of the Cabinet decide that the President is unable to resume his office, and two-thirds of both houses agree, there is very little possibility of a successful plot to deprive the President of his office without due cause. Moreover, the association of the executive and legislative branches of government in this proposal would appear to assure the legitimacy of the action, which would be of the utmost importance when such an unusual act — keeping a duly elected President out of office — was taking place. If one suggests that the scales are being weighted in favor of a President's resuming his office, a proper answer is that he should be denied this right only in the most extraordinary circumstances. Yet there are aspects of this proposal that leave us uneasy.

One could argue that the evils that a dispute over whether the President had a right to his office would bring about would be so great that prevention rather than cure must be our hope. An extended trial procedure in Congress would keep the nation in a state of peril; it would also limit the possibility of emergency action, which is perhaps the greatest good to be obtained by formally dealing with the problem of presidential disability. If an obviously disabled President seeks to hold on to his office while unable to exercise its duties, Congress might be given the power of impeachment to deal with such sins against the Republic. If impeachment is too severe a remedy, especially since a President could no longer hope to resume office, a President who had, in effect, been declared guilty of hiding his disability could serve no useful purpose either for himself or for his country. A disagreement between the President and Vice President would inevitably be serious but the suggested arrangement, far from aggravating the difficulty, merely recognizes it and at least offers a way out.

Another criticism of involving Congress in the matter is that it might alter the traditional distribution of power — whatever that is supposed to be — between the executive and legislative branches. A hostile two-thirds majority of Congress might then get rid of a President without following the rather arduous impeachment procedures prescribed in the Constitution. Since the Vice President and a majority of the Cabinet would have to initiate the procedure before Congress could act, however, it is improbable that all these people would be able to agree on a course adverse to the President. Indeed, a more cogent objection to the plan may be that it requires such widespread agreement as to make it unlikely that any President could be prevented from exercising his office if he was sufficiently determined. Can we, then, devise any plan that would include sufficient safeguards to be acceptable to a President and that would, at the same time, prevent a determined but disabled President from regaining his office?

It is difficult to see how any solution can be found for the problem of a President who is prepared to ruin his country in order to retain his office. So long as the President remains adamant, his Cabinet and Vice President are unlikely to insist that he give up his powers and duties. Anyone who resisted a President's will in such circumstances would find it rather awkward to continue serving him. Congress would find it difficult to act in the midst of these uncertainties; it would have to institute a lengthy investigation, followed by prolonged and perhaps bitter debate, before it arrived at a decision. If Congress was closely divided near the two-thirds mark, as is possible, the resulting uproar, delay, and chaos would be precisely what we wish to avoid. It may be, therefore, that there is no effective remedy in our system for a President who cannot be trusted to protect the nation when its very existence might be threatened,[2] or that such remedies would have to be worked out on the spot.

By this time the fundamental dilemma has become apparent. The structure of problems like presidential succession and presidential disability is much different than that encountered in making most policy recommendations. Ordinarily, we would expect to cumulate experience and adjust our practices accordingly. If our theory was inadequate or required calculations we could not make, we could try various incremental moves and let these small acts generate consequences that we could study while taking further action. If our policy proved to be successful most of the time we would probably be satisfied. But in the case of presidential succession, the stakes are so high that we require a mechanism that will work every time, especially the first time. We might not recover from an experience that tells us that whatever policy we adopt has proven disastrous. No science that I am aware of can claim total predictability for

2 Citizens of the United States do not really know whether their political system contains sufficient safeguards against a President who tries to establish a dictatorship for the excellent reason that no President has ever tried to become a dictator. Indirectly, of course, we can argue in principle that the political system does contain effective safeguards. We can show that political leaders go through a socialization process in which men who do not accept basic democratic procedures are screened out. There is plenty of evidence to suggest that political activists manifest a high degree of commitment to democratic norms. Presidents do not wish to become dictators because they and their leading associates, including military officers, have internalized the desirability of such rules as free elections. As in so many other cases, we have "solved" this problem by never having had to face it at all. Its very appearance in serious form might be a sign of extreme degeneration of the political system for which no remedy might be appropriate.

chains of circumstances that, if not unique, are at least highly irregular.

To end on this note would, however, be too pessimistic. It is true that we cannot have great confidence that the best alternatives will work out exactly as we would like. But we have, perhaps, not used all the resources of political theory at our command. Let us now add an aspect of American political behavior that we have neglected. I refer to the existence of a subculture of political activists whose members manifest a high degree of commitment to democratic processes and an overwhelming determination that free government should continue. Whatever the unforeseen specific events, therefore, we could expect, with a high degree of certainty, that Presidents, Congressmen, Cabinet members, and other members of national political elites would do everything in their power to prevent catastrophe. Whatever their other differences might be, these men are likely to put preservation of the system before other preferences. If the concept of the "public interest" has any meaning at all, members of the nation's highest political elites would work together to protect their nation against the evils stemming from the absence of a President, disagreement over who is President, or questions surrounding the legitimacy of the man who is President.